All-in-One
CCIE™
Study Guide

McGraw-Hill Cisco® Certification Titles

Hutnik and Satterlee, *All-in-One Cisco® CCIE Lab Study Guide*, 0-07-135108-6

Thomas et al., *ICND: Interconnecting Cisco® Network Devices*, 0-07-212522-5

Thomas, Aelmans, and Houniet, *BCSN: Building Cisco® Scalable Networks*, 0-07-212477-6

Thomas, Bass, and Robinson, *BCMSN: Building Cisco® Mutlilayer Switching Networks*, 0-07-212474-1

Thomas, Newcomb, and Mason, *CIT: Cisco® Internetwork Troubleshooting*, 0-07-212483-0

Thomas and Quiggle, *BCRAN: Building Cisco® Remote Access Networks*, 0-07-212480-6

McGraw-Hill Technical Expert Titles

Ammann, *Cisco® Router Internetworking*, 0-07-135627-4

Burton, *Remote Access for Cisco® Networks*, 0-07-135200-7

Caputo, *Cisco® Packetized Voice and Data Integration*, 0-07-134777-1

Fischer, *Configuring Cisco® Routers for ISDN*, 0-07-022073-5

Held, *Cisco® Router Performance Field Guide*, 0-07-212513-6

Held and Hundley, *Cisco® Access Lists Field Guide*, 0-07-212335-4

Held and Hundley, *Cisco® IOS IP Field Guide*, 0-07-212422-9

Held and Hundley, *Cisco® Security Architectures*, 0-07-134708-9

Lewis, *Cisco® Switched Internetworks*, 0-07-134646-5

Lewis, *Cisco® TCP/IP Professional Reference*, Third Edition, 0-07-212557-8

Long, *Cisco® Internetworking and Troubleshooting*, 0-07-135598-7

Nam-Kee, *Configuring Cisco® Routers for Bridging, DLSW+, and Desktop Protocols*, 0-07-135457-3

Parkhurst, *Cisco® Multicast Routing*, 0-07-134647-3

Parkhurst, *Cisco® Router OSPF*, 0-07-048626-3

Rossi, *Cisco® and IP Addressing*, 0-07-134925-1

Rossi, *Cisco® Catalyst LAN Switching*, 0-07-134982-0

Sackett, *Cisco® Router Handbook*, 0-07-058098-7

Slattery and Burton, *Advanced IP Routing in Cisco® Networks*, Second Edition, 0-07-212591-8

ALL-IN-ONE

CCIE™

Study Guide

Second Edition

Roosevelt Giles

McGraw-Hill
New York • San Francisco • Washington, D.C. • Auckland
Bogotá • Caracas • Lisbon • London • Madrid • Mexico City
Milan • Montreal • New Delhi • San Juan • Singapore
Sydney • Tokyo • Toronto

Library of Congress Cataloging-in-Publication Data

Giles, Roosevelt.
   All-in-one CCIE™ study guide / Roosevelt Giles.—2nd ed.
     p. cm.—(McGraw-Hill technical expert series)
   Rev. ed. of: CCIE study guide, 1998.
   ISBN 0-07-135676-2
    I. Giles, Roosevelt. CCIE study guide. II. Title. III. Series.

   QA76.3.G53 1999
   004.6'076—dc21   99-056869
                                          CIP

McGraw-Hill

A Division of The McGraw-Hill Companies

1 2 3 4 5 6 7 8 9 0 DOC/DOC 0 5 4 3 2 1 0

P/N 0-07-135677-0
PART OF ISBN 0-07-135676-2

The executive editor for this book was Steven Elliot, the managing editor was Jennifer Perillo, the associate development editor was Francis Kelly, and the production manager was Clara B. Stanley. It was set in Century Schoolbook by D&G Limited, LLC.

Printed and bound by R. R. Donnelley & Sons Company.

Contents

Acknowledgments

from First Edition

It is difficult to thank all the individuals who have been instrumental in the completion of this project. First, I would like to give honor to God, the creator, without whom nothing I have achieved would be possible.

I would like to thank my wife, Sharon W. Giles, who has been my rock and partner and who has provided unconditional love and support. Sharon, thank you for always being there for the family and me. You bring balance, joy, and love to me always. I place this work with respect and humility at your feet. To my children Nakisha, Bradford, and Justin, thank you for your gift of love and understanding about all the time I spent away from home. You make a father proud. Bradford and Justin, thank you for being patient during this project. I love you all and appreciate the sacrifices you have endured.

I would like to dedicate this book to my mother, Lake Giles, and Father, the late Enourmas Giles, whose love and support has sustained me through all these years. Mother, you and Father made me reach higher than I ever would have; thank you. I would like to thank my sisters Gertrude Good, Shirley Good, Vera Jean Dogan, Dorothy Ngongane, Emily Land, Sandra Mcbeth, Mary Watkins, Ruthie Mae Holland, and Vergie Mae Glenn for all the love, support, and encouragement. A special thanks to my brother, James Giles, who sacrificed himself for us during the lean times. James, thanks for providing the framework of knowledge you taught me about business; I am forever indebted to you. Thank you from the bottom of my heart, and I will always be there when you need me. Mildred Giles, my sister-in-law, is the best, always willing to assist where needed; thanks. My in-laws, Fred and Margaret Watts, without your support and love, I would be nowhere. I don't think that anyone could have in-laws as thoughtful and supporting as you; many thanks.

I would like to thank the village who assisted in shaping me as a individual. First, thanks go to all the students who have attended courses at Information Management Systems, Inc., over the years. Thank you for trusting us in your learning process. We are forever grateful. The Emanuel Chapel Baptist Church membership—thanks for the encouragement. The late Leo and Ila Thomas; Dr. Julia Long, professor of Mathematics at the University of South Carolina, nature has removed the braids; Dr. John Donovan of MIT; and Rick Strasser of Milliken and Company, who saw the positive and gave me a chance. Thanks for the vote of confidence and for being my mentor, Rick. Gus Allen, thanks for the opportunity. Nelson Smith, thanks for the words of encouragement during my tenure in LaGrange. Jessie Johnson, thanks for the promotion, and a special thanks goes to Mr. Roger Milliken, Chairman of the Board of Milliken & Company, who gave me the opportunity to work for one of the best-run companies in the world. Thanks to James Mcbeth and Tony Steward for guiding me through the difficult times in learning my new job at Milliken & Company. Thank you, Becky Sanders and Betty Joe, for helping me hone my typing skills and for being such good friends. Thanks to the late Mr. and Mrs. Emzie Smith, Mrs. Willie Mae Smith, the late Mr. Bennie Smith, Aunt Deara Washington, Frank and Doris Giles, and my late grandmother Beulah Copeland for all the support during my upbringing.

The encouragement and support of friends like Richard and Linda Costa, Dr. Moses and Rita Jones; Dr. Cameron Alexander; John Collier; Marvin Anderson; Alvin and Janice Johnson; James P. Cavanagh; Bill and Sharon Livingston; Curtis Crawford, President of AT&T Micro-Electronics; and Edward Menifee made the time special.

Special thanks to Dave Brambert, who as a friend and business partner, was always willing to encourage and listen. Thanks also for making my writing better with your comments.

Information Management Systems, Inc., Personnel

I am one of the luckiest individuals in the world to have such a dedicated staff of Support and Systems Engineers. I would like to thank the following Systems Engineers for their hard work putting this book together. These individuals deserve special recognition: Curtis Watts and Kenneth Jones who labored very hard and long with this project and were there all the way. Thanks, guys, for keeping the fire alive. Special thanks to Palaniappan Alagan in addition to CCIE for your steadfast devotion: Larry Mobley, J.C Fang, Johnny Bass, Richard Deal, and Patrick Delio. The support staff of Cheryl Johnson, Jackie Derico, Carol Cook, Hanifah McClendon, and Sandra Jones, thanks for putting up with me during this project.

I would like to dedicate this book to my wife, Suh-Jiuan, my son, Yi-Feng, and my daughter, Xin-Hui, for their understanding and caring.

—Jeh-Chuan Fang

I would like to dedicate this book to my beloved parents and sister, Vignes, for all the fond memories.

—Palaniappan Alagan CCIE #1922

I would like to dedicate this book to my father, A.G. Watts, mother, the late Willie Pearl Watts, and the rest of my family who have supported me through all my endeavors. Mom, I will always take you with me, wherever I go. Special thanks go to my Aunt Lonnie Green, who has been a second mother to me and a best friend, and to my partner, Sheryl Jackson, for putting up with me. (Baby, it is all going to be worth it.) To my friends Shelton, Tunji, and Kenny for keeping me motivated. I would like to thank the Rev. R.L. White for his words of inspiration in times of need.

—Curtis Watts

I would like to dedicate this book to my mother, Rosetta M. Jones, for all the love and support that she has given to me; to my brothers for helping me keep it real; to my fraternity, Kappa Alpha Psi Spring '86 Mu Gamma Chapter, for grooming me for life; and to my daughter, Kiesha, and son, Kentrell, who motivate me. I also would like to thank Samella C. Walker for all of her love and support and Rhonda Blassingame for being a true friend.

—Kenneth A. Jones

Vendor Support

Putting together a book of this magnitude requires assistance beyond the author's scope and resources. I would like to thank Imran Qureshi of Cisco for the outstanding support given during this project; Network Associates for the Sniffer Tools used in the frame captures; Laura M. Ellertson of Novell; Prem Kaliappan of Proteon LAN Development Group; and Jay Guillette of Banyan Corporation.

This book would not have come to fruition without the patience and diligence of the staff at McGraw-Hill. I would like to thank Steve Elliot for his unwavering support and guidance during this project. Thanks, Steve, for the encouragement when I felt down and out. Also, special thanks for all the behind-the-scenes support personnel at McGraw-Hill and D&G Limited, LLC. Alan, thank you and the others at D&G—Claude, Kelly, Molly, Denny, and Linda—for a great job.

About the Author

Roosevelt Giles (CCSI, CCNA, CCNP, CNE, MCSE, MCT, and CNX) is president of Information Management Systems (IMS), a technology integration company in Atlanta, Georgia that specializes in providing complete CCIE training and support. Giles is a frequent speaker at COMDEX, ICA, Computer Measurements Group, and NetWorld+ INTEROP, and has authored articles on Internet security, UNIX integration, DLSw, ATM integration, VPNs, and electronic commerce for *Solutions Integrator* magazine.

About the Reviewers

As the leading publisher of technical books for more than 100 years, McGraw-Hill prides itself on bringing you the most authoritative and up-to-date information available. To ensure that our books meet the highest standards of accuracy, we have asked a number of top professionals and technical experts to review the accuracy of the material you are about to read.

We take great pleasure in thanking the following technical reviewers for their insights:

Stephen Hutnik is a Senior Engineer at ATT Global Network Services in Harrison, NY where he is responsible for development, testing, and training for the ATT Global Network Backbone. Stephen is also an adjunct professor of telecommunications at Pace University. He is co-author of the McGraw-Hill bestseller, *All-in-One CCIE Lab Study Guide*.

Michael Satterlee, CCIE, is a technical consultant at ATT Global Network Services in Harrison, NY where he is responsible for the development of new VPN services based on IPSEC and MPLS. He is also co-author of the McGraw-Hill bestseller, *All-in-One CCIE Lab Study Guide*.

We would also like to thank the following reviewers of the first edition who helped us plan the second edition:

Dale Holmes

Jeffrey Jones

Susan Padilla

Lee Christopher Wise

Richard Young

Getting Started

Introduction

Since our last journey, some exciting additions and changes to the Cisco Certification Program have taken place. First and foremost, Cisco has introduced a number of additional certifications, including entry- and intermediate-level programs. The market has responded admirably to these new additions, with Cisco certifications in general being one of the most talked-about and coveted certifications in the history of internetworking.

If you're reading this book, you've already made some important decisions. First, you've decided to work with equipment from Cisco, the world's leading manufacturers of network infrastructure devices. Second, you're so serious about the subject that you've decided to join the ranks of a limited few who have achieved the status of Cisco Certified Professional. That's great! This book was written to help you achieve that goal. Third, you've decided to help yourself with information from many sources.

The book in your hands is not a rehash of information already available from Cisco; it calls on years of experience with Cisco products. It was, however, written with Cisco's educational philosophy in mind. In fact, this book was written in part to put information you need to pass the exams into a larger context so you'll understand and remember the technology for what it is and does. In effect, this book was written to benefit you before, during, and after your CCNA, CCNP, and CCIE Routing and Switching examinations. This book covers the Cisco Routing and Switching CCIE Sylvan exam # 350-001 with bonus questions for Cisco's CCNA exam #640-407, CCNP Foundation Routing and Switching exam #640-409, CIT exam #640-440, and CCIE–SNA/IP exam #350-013. This book does not cover the two-day CCIE Certification Lab. However, the configurations included in each chapter will provide a baseline of understanding required for the two-day hands-on lab.

Certain assumptions were made about you in the preparation of this text. You have a background in networking; otherwise, you wouldn't be preparing to become a Cisco Certified Professional. You understand the Physical layer of networking well and can perform different types of physical connections to a network. Further, you understand LAN environments like Ethernet, Fast Ethernet, Gb Ethernet, FDDI, ATM, and Token Ring and have experience in networking with Windows NT, NetWare, Banyan Vines, RSVP, IGMP, OSPF, IGRP, EIGRP, BGP, ATM LAN Switching, or DECnet. The information here will help you build from that strong foundation.

Let's look briefly at how this information is organized. This chapter has valuable information about Cisco, the company's education programs, CCIE status and how to use it to help you market yourself, how to study for and take the exams, and more. Starting with the Chapter 2, we dive right into the technology, so be prepared. It's not easy, but if you are ready for the journey, you will join an elite class of engineers when you arrive at your destination.

Because the information is highly technical, it is organized by type of technology. Although this book covers a lot of networking technology, it does so in the context of Cisco routing, LAN and Cell switching, and bridging. Each chapter covers a different major area of networking.

Each chapter's introduction briefly covers the major topics within that chapter and brings home the concepts in a manner specific to the needs of a future CCIE. Next, an overview of the specific chapter's technology is given. Then, you'll get into specifics of LAN and WAN routing, bridging, and switching as they each pertain to that chapter's subject.

To help you really understand the technology in a real-world sense, many chapters include configurations, troubleshooting information, and network design worksheets that don't exist anywhere else. All chapters, except this one, include review questions to help hone your skills.

In addition, you'll want to use the configurations on the enclosed CD to further assist you in understanding how Cisco implements these services for real-world networks and certification. Also on the CD, you'll find testing software for FastTrak Express™ to further help you prepare for the exam.

Because a picture is worth a thousand words, this book contains many helpful diagrams. The diagrams help you put the technical details into a larger, real-world perspective. Plus, you'll drill way down into the network with Sniffer traces to find out how everything happens on a Cisco network.

You're beginning a very exciting venture. We'll start the technology discussion in the next chapter. First, let's look at how to become a CCIE, what it means, and what the process covers.

CCIE: An Overview

Make no mistake: The Cisco Certified Internetwork Expert program is all about helping people become experts. It is a very high-level program aimed at making you a Cisco expert. In today's business world, whether you're on the IS staff of a corporation, an ISP, or a network integrator, people are asking more of you. More network use is the norm. More bandwidth is a constant need. More reliability is expected. Companies are putting their most valuable commodity—information—in your hands.

The CCIE program is well named because you will be an expert in the multitude of internetworking technologies in use today. Armed with knowledge gained from this book, on-the-job learning, and from training programs from Cisco Authorized Training Partners, you will provide benefits to your superiors or your customers because you will be able to design, implement, and evolve networks more intelligently and efficiently than your colleagues who perhaps lack the proper training and information.

Besides the recognition that accompanies your CCIE status, other benefits will come your way. CCIEs have the option to jump to second-level Cisco technical support for any technical questions or problems. You can also participate in a special CCIE chat forum and answer questions on a CCO open forum.

When you become a CCIE, *you* are certified, not your company. No matter where you work or live, you retain your certified status as long as you adhere to Cisco requirements.

Cisco does not require you to take Cisco-certified training classes in order to be certified. Theoretically, you could use this book in combination with your existing knowledge to pass the CCIE exams. However, the training courses are highly recommended—in a classroom situation, you have the extra benefit of immediate feedback to questions and comments. Your instructor is already an expert in the technology and can fill in lots of technical gaps for you.

What Background Do I Need to Become a CCIE?

As stated earlier, the CCIE is an advanced certification program. The Cisco entry and intermediate certifications such as *Cisco Certified Network Associate* (CCNA), *Cisco Certified Network Professional* (CCNP), *Cisco Certified Design Associate* (CCDA), and *Cisco Certified Design Professional* (CCDP) can provide you with a Cisco certification career path toward your goal of becoming a CCIE. In order to become a CCIE, Cisco recommends that you complete appropriate course work and obtain significant experience working with internetworks and end-to-end systems before continuing on your journey to certification.

As a rough rule of thumb, Cisco recommends that you have two or more years of internetworking experience. A good understanding of TCP/IP, LAN and WAN protocols, the OSI Reference Model, Internet, security, and client/server architecture is essential. The company also recommends you have experience with packet-level diagnosis as well as real-world experience with Cisco and non-Cisco products. Again, the CCIE certification is to become an expert, not to be introduced to intermediate network subjects.

> **NOTE:**   *It is not a requirement to attend instructor-led training in order to prepare for your Cisco certifications. You may be able to meet your requirements using self-study materials, CCIE study groups, and Web-based training supplemented with remote labs.*

Steps in Becoming a CCIE

When you prepare to become a CCIE, you must choose which of four areas of expertise to pursue (you can pursue all of them, but one at a time). The four areas are CCIE Routing and Switching, CCIE WAN Switching, CCIE SNA/IP Integration, and CCIE ISP Dial. Although it's easy logistically to become CCIE-certified, the demands are great. Only two requirements must be met per CCIE certification: a two-hour CCIE certification test and a two-day CCIE certification laboratory. It is highly recommended that you pursue course work, read this book, obtain on-the-job training, and use remote labs.

Four steps ensure that you are an expert in one of these fields. First, do the course work, obtain real-world experience working with these technologies, supplement your hands-on experience with labs, and use this book. Second, sit for a two-hour qualification test. Third, pass a two-day certification lab. Fourth, in order to keep your certification, you must be recertified every two years. You must first pass the qualification test before you can take the hands-on lab test.

Generally courses are three or five days each. Qualification tests are administered via Sylvan Prometric and are graded on a pass/fail basis. Each test costs $200; if you don't pass the first time, there is no limit (other than your pocketbook) to the number of times you may take the test. These closed-book tests contain 100 questions each. You must score 70 percent or higher to pass. You must score 80 percent or higher to pass the hands-on lab test. The lab tests cost $1,000 each. If you do not pass the first lab test, you must wait 30 days until trying it again.

The lab tests are available at the following Cisco facilities:

- **San Jose, California**
  Tel : 800-829-6387 or 408-526-8063
  Fax : 408-527-8588
  Email: ccie_ucsa@cisco.com

- **Research Triangle Park, North Carolina**
  Tel: 800-829-6387 or 408-527-7177
  Fax: 408-527-8588
  Email: ccie_ucsa@cisco.com

- **Chatswood, NSW, Australia**
  Tel: +61 2 8448 71288
  Fax: +61 2 8448 7375
  Email: ccie_apt@cisco.com

- **Brussels, Belgium**
  Tel: +32 2 704 5000
  Fax: +32 2 704 6000
  Email: ccie_emea@cisco.com

- **Sao Paulo, Brazil**
  Tel: 800-829-6387 or 408-527-7177
  Fax: 408-527-8588
  Email: ccie_ucsa@cisco.com

- **Halifax, Nova Scotia, Canada**
  Tel: 800-829-6387 or 902-492-8811
  Fax: 902-492-3926
  Email: ccie_ucsa@cisco.com

- **Beijing, China**
  Tel: +86 10 6802 3355
  Fax: +86 10 6803 8349
  Email: ccie_apt@cisco.com

- **Bangalore, India**
  Tel: +61 2 8448 7128
  Fax: +61 2 8448 7375
  Email: `ccie_apt@cisco.com`

- **Tokyo, Japan**
  Tel: +81 3 5219 6308
  Fax: +81 3 5219 6026
  Email: `ccie@cisco.co.jp`

- **Capetown, South Africa**
  Tel: +32 2 778 46 70
  Fax: +32 2 778 43 00
  Email: `ccie_emea@cisco.com`

Please contact or visit Cisco's certification home page at `www.cisco.com` for additional facilities because not all CCIE certifications labs are available at these listed facilities.

Cisco believes in the concept of hands-on testing in a somewhat pressured environment to simulate real-world problems such as the ones implemented in normal support of production internetworks. Let's take a look at the course work involved in each certification area.

It's in the Numbers

The Routing and Switching CCIE certification will be discussed first, followed by the CCIE WAN, CCIE ISP, and CCIE SNA/IP Integration. The CCIE Routing and Switching Experts represent the majority of the CCIEs in the world due to the popularity of routers and the number of routing protocols that are deployed. The market is evolving to use Layer 2 and Layer 3 switching with routing—thus the switching slant in CCIE Routing and Switching.

CCIE Routing and Switching Expert

The courses that pertain to you as a CCIE Routing and Switching Expert consist of *Cisco Certified Network Professional* (CCNP) courses such as

- *Advanced Cisco Router Configuration* (ACRC)
- *Cisco LAN Switch Configuration* (CLSC)
- *Configuring, Monitoring, Troubleshooting, and Dial-Up* Services (CMTD)
- *Cisco Internetworking Troubleshooting* (CIT)

Plus

- *Interconnecting Cisco Network Devices* (ICND)
- *Installation and Maintenance of Cisco Routers* (IMCR)
- *Cisco Internetwork Design* (CID)

- *Cisco Data Link Switching Plus* (DLSWP). This course requires that you take SNA Configuration for Multiprotocol Administrators (SNAM) as a prerequisite for Data Link Switching.

The exam required is the CCIE-Routing and Switching Qualification Exam #350-001

I have not included outlines or descriptions for the recommended courses due to emerging changes and updates. A detailed description of these course outline recommendations can be found on Cisco's home page at `http://www.cisco.com` and the Web page of Information Management Systems, Inc. at `http://www.imsinc.com`.

> **NOTE:**   *The ICRC, ACRC, and CLSC courses are being retired in the first quarter of 2000 with the following replacements:*
>
> - Interconnecting Cisco Network Devices *(ICND) (ICRC replacement effective January 2000)*
> - Building Cisco Multilayer Switched Networks *(BCMSN) (ACRC and CLSC replacement effective second quarter 2000)*

The Tests for CCIE Routing and Switching Expert   The qualification test for the CCIE Routing and Switching Expert touches on all areas covered in the courses outlined. The test covers several areas such as

- Cisco device configuration and operations
- IEEE 802.x specifications
- Bridge/router technology
- Internetwork protocols
- LAN switching
- Cisco-specific technology
- Network scenarios
- Local area networks
- Wide area networks
- Performance management
- Internet security
- Cisco multiservice

As with all four areas of CCIE expertise, immediately after your test is completed, you know whether or not you passed. In addition, your score of each section is broken out, giving you a good feedback tool for revisiting weaker areas before taking the lab test.

In the laboratory, you will be given a design to implement from cables, switches, and router modules all the way to logical configuration of the network. After you've completed that task, the proctor will introduce some errors into your hard work. (This will happen in the real world, too!) The proctor will grade you on how well you recognize these errors, isolate problems, document errors, and resolve all error issues.

The Tests for CCIE WAN Switching Expert

The CCIE WAN is the next CCIE certification to discuss. As mentioned earlier, it will be in high demand due to the market's evolution toward voice and data integration. The CCIE WAN represents an excellent upgrade after completion of the CCIE Routing and Switching. One only has to scan the want ads, job sites, and trade publications to see that the WAN certifications will be one of hottest Cisco certifications to possess in the next decade.

CCIE WAN Switching Expert   The courses that pertain to you as a CCIE WAN Switching Expert are

- *WAN Quick Start* (WQS) self-study
- *Installation of Cisco WAN Switches* (ICWS)
- *Multiband Switch and Service Configuration* (MSSC)
- *BPX Switch and Service Configuration* (BSSC)
- Network Operations for BPX/AXIS products
- *MGX ATM Concentrator Configuration* (MACC)
- Multiservice Concentrator 3810 Configuration and Monitoring
- Cisco *StrataView Plus Installation* (SVIO)
- *Project Managing Network Implementation Services* (PMNIS, self-paced study)

The exam required is the CCIE-WAN Sw Qualification Exam #350-007.

Both the CCIE WAN and CCIE ISP Dial Expert certifications are aimed somewhat at service providers, and the tests reflect that fact. In the qualification test for CCIE WAN Switching Expert, you'll be tested on knowledge about WANs, including LAN/WAN media and access control methods, permanent versus switched virtual circuits, error detection and recovery, and how buffers and queues affect load conditions. Transport of video, voice, and data is also covered on the exam. Subjects range from basic WAN technologies to Cisco-specific architectures and products. One section is devoted to service provider technology.

During the lab exam, you'll interconnect nodes, perform trunking and switching, and use StrataView Plus. You'll design and implement a Frame Relay network and an ATM network. You will also be asked to troubleshoot an existing WAN switched network.

CCIE ISP Dial Expert

Many of the courses that pertain to you as a CCIE ISP Dial Expert are found in the CCIE Routing and Switching Expert section. Three other courses are added to that list because this certification is aimed directly at Internet Service Providers. The courses that pertain to you as a CCIE Internet Service Provider (ISP) Expert consist of *Cisco Certified Network Professional* (CCNP*) courses such as

- *Advanced Cisco Router Configuration* (ACRC)*
- *Cisco LAN Switch Configuration* (CLSC)*

- *Configuring, Monitoring, Troubleshooting, and Dial-Up* (CMTD) Services
- *Cisco Internetworking Troubleshooting* (CIT)

plus

- *Introduction to Cisco Router Configuration* (ICRC)
- *Installing and Maintaining Cisco Routers* (IMCR)
- Cisco AS5200 Installation and Configuration (AS5200)
- *Advanced Cisco Router Configuration* (ACRC)
- *Managing Cisco Network Security* (MCNS)
- *Cisco Internetwork Design* (CID)

The Tests for CCIE ISP Dial Expert The qualification test for CCIE ISP Dial Expert covers the following:

- Dial access types (for example, ISDN, T1/E1, and so on)
- Nondial access types (ATM, Frame Relay, SMDS, X.25, and so on)
- Customer premises equipment (modems, ISDN, login types)
- Associated technologies (IP routing and tunneling, MMP, compression)
- Services (virtual private dial network, quality of service, mobile IP)
- Security (authentication, authorization, and accounting)
- Management (administration, troubleshooting)
- Addressing (subnetting, static/dynamic, classless interdomain routing)

The lab test measures your skills in some important areas. For instance, you will be expected to build access lists and firewalls. You also will be expected to know and implement all forms of dial-on-demand routing and prove your knowledge of ISDN, async, T1, Frame Relay, and X.25. In the lab you will configure multiple Cisco routers and set up an environment for Windows networking using WINS and DHCP.

CCIE SNA/IP Integration

The CCIE SNA/IP Integration addresses the needs for SNA professionals to understand in detail IBM SNA Protocols and how they work in a pure SNA environment, while understanding how Cisco SNA products can be used to integrate SNA into a multiprotocol network. CCIEs with SNA experience are highly sought-after individuals to assist the 80–90% of the installed base of SNA networks and integrate them into the multiprotocol world largely driven by TCP/IP. As companies invest in IP networks and applications while continuing to maintain a large complement of SNA applications, there is a tremendous need to bring SNA and IP networks closer together. Cisco offers by far the most impressive product set required to address this evolving market.

The courses that pertain to you as a CCIE SNA/IP Integration Expert consist of *Cisco Certified Network Professional* (CCNP) courses such as

- *Introduction to Cisco Router Configuration* (ICRC)
- *Advanced Cisco Router Configuration* (ACRC)
- *SNA Configuration for Multiprotocol Administrators* (SNAM)
- Cisco *Data Link Switching Plus* (DLWSP)
- *Frame Relay Access Support / Frame Relay Access Device* (FRAS/FRAD)
- *Advanced Peer-to-Peer Networks* (APPN)
- *Channel Interface Processor* (CIP)

Recertification for CCIEs

Cisco requires CCIEs to recertify every 24 months. You must pass one of the written exams and attend a CCIE technical conference. The written tests are available from Sylvan Prometric. The technical conferences are scheduled at Networkers and on weekends so CCIEs with customers need not forsake these customer networks in order to be recertified.

Gaining the Necessary Cisco Training

You realize the need for training of some sort. (Proper training will help you gain the expertise needed to complete your certification goal.) So where do you go, and whom do you talk to about obtaining the proper training? Training comes in many forms and from several sources. For example, you may learn more in an hour of hands-on training than you could ever learn in the classroom (though classroom training or an equivalent is still very important to get the global view of internetworking). In essence, the type of training you choose will depend on your job, goals, and study habits.

As previously mentioned, there are several kinds of training to choose from. The three most common types of training are *on-the-job training* (OJT), Web-based distance learning (also known as *Web-based training*, or WBT), and *instructor-led training*. OJT relies on your ability to learn on your own, whereas classroom time relies on your ability to work with other people. Other types of training include third-party lectures, CBTs, videotapes, audiotapes, self-study manuals, remote labs, instructor-led classes, and of course, the trial-and-error method.

Hands-on Training   *Hands-on training* is just a broader term for OJT. Whenever you think about hands-on training, remember that it involves some type of physical participation by you with the software for which you plan to get certified. OJT is the easiest way to get hands-on training, but it's a little limiting because you don't get to explore the full range of software features and it is difficult to practice on a production network. You can also get directed hands-on training using a number of Internet-based remote preparation labs, third-party aids, and sample configurations at the end of each chapter.

Hands-on training could also be the most time-consuming method of learning new skills. Although this type of training will supply you with the most realistic way of performing a task, you may have to invest years before you have enough information to become certified. However, no matter how much knowledge you obtain from other sources, nothing will replace the knowledge acquired from on-the-job experience. There's something special about going through all of the procedures for installing, configuring, maintaining, and troubleshooting software and hardware yourself that makes the learning experience more complete.

The best place to acquire on-the-job training is on a live system at an existing company or prototyping lab that offers all the software and hardware necessary to design, install, and configure internetworks without disrupting production networks. All you need to do is find a job that's related to your education requirements. Of course, actually getting hired by a company that can offer OJT before you have a certification in hand is a lot harder than it might seem. Unfortunately, most companies require you to have the skills you are trying to learn before they'll hire you. If this is the case, you may have to work out an arrangement with the prospective employer to work as an entry-level person or to work at a reduced rate. At other times, you may be able to work out an arrangement to help out on projects free of charge in return for the hands-on experience. Although this is not putting any money into your pocket, you'll be getting the necessary training that you are looking for. Consider it a payment toward your education.

Instructor-Led Training The fastest way to get the training needed and get up to speed is to enroll in a professional education program. The courses will present you with a lot of information in a relatively short amount of time (three to five days for most classes). The instructor will normally present you with a series of lectures, along with oral or written question and answer periods, lab exercises, and hands-on experience.

Instructor-led courses are available from a variety of different sources. These sources include *Cisco Authorized Training Partners* (CATPs), colleges, universities, and different third-party educational facilities. Each of these different educational facilities provides a myriad of services. The services offered by these institutions range from the very general to the very specific. The lengths of classes also range from just a few hours to four or more years. The cost of the different educational services will range from nothing to thousands of dollars.

Because the educational facilities will vary in class size, materials offered, length, cost, and types of services, you'll need to discuss your educational needs with them.

The best place to obtain the required information for the Cisco certifications would be from a Cisco Authorized Training Partner education center. Cisco provides excellent training for its certifications as well as for its line of products. Although Cisco does offer some training directly, most of the training comes from the Authorized Cisco Training Partners. Cisco requires the partners to teach its courses at a strict quality level. Cisco inspects the centers for proper hardware and software, as well as for the general overall condition of the facility. Each center must use *Certified Cisco Systems Instructors* (CCSI) to teach its courses. The instructors have passed a series of competency exams and have attended special courses designed to ensure they meet the Cisco standards for teaching the course.

Cisco Authorized Training Partners are located worldwide, with the largest concentration in Europe. Some of the partners are quite large, with more than 10 classrooms in one location. Most CATPs are usually smaller. There are also a few partner companies that have education centers in different parts of the country. The centers are all basically the same because Cisco must authorize each one, and each center must meet the Cisco guidelines.

What distinguishes the different partners from each other is the quality of the instructors. Although each instructor is Cisco-certified, they do not all have exactly the same teaching style. Many of the instructors teach only what is in the Cisco course manual. Although this is the base information required for the Cisco certifications, it may not always lend itself to real-world experiences. The extras that the better instructors include usually come from years in the field practicing what they teach. We all have had instructors or professors who really knew the book material that they taught, but if you asked them a question about something that didn't appear in the manual, they did not have a clue. When selecting the center that you want to attend, be sure to ask for references from former students. Talk to these people and get a feel about how the instructor handled the class, subject matter, and questions about related topics not included in the course material. You'll find that most of the instructors will get good reviews.

Cisco has been recognized for a long time by the industry for its proactive approach to training its resellers, users, and systems engineers. You can always count on the course materials written for Cisco software to be current with what's on the market. You can look at Cisco's Web site at `http://www.cisco.com/`. This Web site contains a complete list of courses, current certification requirements, and a listing of Authorized Cisco Training partners.

Self-Study Training   Cisco offers self-study programs, as do other sources. The self-study programs are good for self-starters who have both the time and the discipline to study on their own. By using the self-study programs offered by Cisco and authorized partners, you can save yourself a few dollars. The courses are designed to supply you with the course manuals offered by Cisco and usually include some form of lab training. Most training partners will sell you all the self-study course manuals so you can study them at a convenient time.

The self-study programs are an excellent way to get some form of training, hands-on experience, and knowledge needed to obtain the Cisco certification. The biggest disadvantage of the self-study program is that you don't receive the instructor-student interaction gained in instructor-led courses. If you decide to participate in the self-study program, you'll need to spend the time required to really learn the material.

Other Types of Training
There are times when the standard approaches to training such as OJT or instructor-led training won't fit into your schedule or don't meet some personal need. (You may not study well on your own, for example.) For this reason, alternative forms of education are very popular. The alternative forms of education may include books, audiotapes, videotapes, *Web-based training* (WBT), and *computer-based training* (CBT) programs. These are all excellent sources of information that will help to augment your training process. WBT is really starting to change the way people do everything from learning about internetworking to earning degrees online. This form of learning is available from a number of vendors providing lab supplements for those requiring hands-on equipment with lab exercises to assist not only in the preparation for Cisco's certification exams, but also to provide just-in-time learning for on-the-job project requirements. `Preplab.com` offers such training over the Internet to anyone with a Web browser.

For anyone from the experienced computer technician to the beginner, a bookcase with a wide variety of computer books will be a necessity. This library will prove to be a great asset in your quest for advancement in the computer industry. With a well rounded library, you'll be able to reference the topics and subjects that you may not know very well. You'll find that your library will grow immensely in a short time. Many of the books that you get may have just a few pages on the subject that concerns you right now, but will provide a source of reference on other material in the future.

There are many books written about the Cisco *Internetworking Operating Systems* (IOS) on the shelves of bookstores. As a Cisco expert, you'll need to know about the early versions of Cisco IOS and how they work. You should know the different commands and terminology that were a part of old versions of the IOS. There are many differences in the versions of Cisco IOS. Don't ignore the general networking books. Many of these books have a lot of practical information about how to administer and troubleshoot your Internetwork. Although these books may not provide Cisco-specific information, they will help you gain a better understanding of networks in general. Even if you don't use this information immediately, you'll find it essential later.

Getting the Most from Your Training

As you've seen, many different approaches to training are available to become a Cisco Certified Internetworking Engineer Expert and for general knowledge of the internetworking computer industry. It's normal to feel a bit overwhelmed because of the vast amount of information that you'll receive in preparation for your certification exams. The secret to making this process work and passing the exams will be to find the style, type of training, and study techniques that best stimulate your mind.

To get the most from your training, you should consider some of the following suggestions:

- *Stay focused.*
- *Formulate your goals and develop a plan of action for obtaining them.* Set goals based on your ability, not based on the desires of someone else, such as your employer.
- *Create a good study environment.* Make sure that you have a clean desk or table at which to work. Reduce any distractions by turning off the radio, closing windows, and asking others in the study area to remain quiet. Adding a good indirect light source and sitting in a comfortable chair can help, as well. Make sure that you wear comfortable clothing while you study.
- *Check your actual progress from session to session.* Use this as a gauge for setting new goals for the next session. Set a goal a little higher than what you achieve during an average study session. This will challenge you but will keep the goal within the realm of the achievable.
- *Take the training one topic at a time and work on each topic until you know the subject matter.*
- *Take good notes*—take brief notes during class and fill in information after the discussion/lecture is over.
- *Break the process of studying your manuals and text books down into three steps:*

1. First, quickly read the material in a summary fashion.

2 Second, get a notepad, your sticky notes, and your highlighter. Then reread the manuals making notes and highlighting the important information, as well as the information that's new to you or that you don't understand.

3. Study your notes and marked pages and then research any areas that you do not understand.

- *Use the tests in this book to measure your retention.* Make the first goal of each new session to test the amount of information you retained from the preceding session. The combination of materials provided in your course, plus this book, plus the Cisco manuals and any third-party books, should enable you to retain a minimum of 80 percent of what you learn if you don't go to the Cisco courses. If you don't retain this level of information, then consider slowing down a little and spending a little more time on each topic. If you still can't achieve a high enough retention level and you haven't taken any courses, then consider taking classes at your Cisco Authorized Training Partner.

- *Ask someone to quiz you.* Make sure that they concentrate on one test at a time and that they vary the questions from one session to the next. Ask them to ask the same question in several different ways. This will help you develop a pattern of thinking centered around question *content* rather than around the questions themselves.

- *Always study your weak areas first; then study the areas you feel more confident about.* If you have someone quiz you, make sure that they help you address your weak areas first and the strong areas second.

- *Discuss the test and other study materials with your peers.* Having a group help you with your problem areas not only increases your chances of getting a great answer, it forces you to consider areas that you may not think about normally.

- *Make a game out of it.* Try creating your own set of flash cards. Try modifying existing games to meet your needs or use other traditional game methods. For example, you might want to combine correct answers with the ability to move on a game board.

- *Memorize as many of the facts in this book and in the Cisco manuals as possible.* Recite them to yourself as you perform other network or application-related tasks.

- *Consider the hands-on activities in this book, your student manuals, and the Cisco manuals as the basis for your own exercises.* Create your own case studies based on your weaknesses and the guidelines presented in this book. Make sure that you set a starting point and an ending point. Figuring out how to get from point A to point B is a good way to study. You can even use this in a group setting. Challenge one of your peers to a race. Each of you can set the starting and ending points for the other person. The first person to accomplish their goal wins.

- *Use association to study.* Take the time to associate the items you need to know for the exam with things that you do every day. Some people even create acrostic sayings to learn various elements of the exams. For example, this works especially well when learning the security portions of an operating system, like the different types of access or the attributes you can assign to a file. Of course, it works equally well when memorizing the various menu functions of an application. You can also use mnemonics for association. To learn the names of the seven OSI model layers in order, try taking the first letter from each word of the saying, "All People Seem To Need Data Processing." The initial letters in this saying are the same as in the ordered OSI layers —Application, Presentation, Session, Transport, Network, Data Link, and Physical.

- *Create an outline of the topics you study; then fill in the blanks later.* This forces you to remember what you read and then reinforces it by having you write the information down.

- *Break your study sessions down into short bursts to aid retention and vary your study time from day to day.*

All these training techniques will help you to reach your goal of certification if you apply them. By staying focused on your goals, selecting a training program that's acceptable, and then applying the proper study techniques and refining them to your style, you should find yourself prepared for the exams.

Gathering the Information You Need   The student guides you receive while taking the Cisco courses are your most important asset in taking an exam, especially if you take good notes during class. There are three operative phases here:

1. You must take the Cisco courses to obtain the Cisco view of internetworking (or of any other certification-related task).

2. You must take good notes in class.

3. You must fully participate in the hands-on lab exercises performed in class. I have found that students who attempt to assist their lab partners to understand the technology and hands-on exercises reinforce their understanding of the subject matter.

Unless you perform these steps, there's a good chance that you'll fail at gaining what is required to pass the CCIE written exam. The reason for this failure is simple: while you may have a great understanding of networks in general, you need to know the Cisco way of doing things to pass the exam.

Importance of the Cisco Courses   Your instructor is specially trained to help you understand networking and internetworking from a Cisco and industry perspective. A Cisco certification is a credential that tells the world you know what you're talking about when it comes to Cisco Internetworking and internetworks.

It may seem that prescribing one way of doing things when there are many other equally correct ways of doing them is unnecessarily restrictive and oppressive. However, Cisco can't test everyone's methods of doing a task; yet Cisco must ensure that the methods used by the people Cisco certifies are correct. Any other course would make people ask, "Why should I trust anyone you certify to maintain my network?" As you can see, what may seem restrictive at first is simply a way of making sure that everyone can perform internetworking tasks in a way that works every time. It also ensures that someone certified by Cisco fully tests those techniques in a real-world environment. When people hire you based on your certification, what they are really hiring is someone who knows the Cisco way of performing a task—an extension of Cisco, if you will.

So how does this relate to test taking? Because Cisco must test your ability to maintain a network, and we've seen there's a logical reason for everyone to perform those tasks in the same way, it follows that Cisco will test that one way of doing things. If you walk into the examination room without a knowledge of Cisco's way of performing the task, there's no way for you to answer the questions correctly. (The passing requirements are high enough to void just about any possibility of someone guessing their way through the exam.)

This is the first point you must remember. When you take a certification exam, you are being tested on your knowledge of the industry and Cisco's way of performing a task. This concept is very important for you to grasp. Failure to grasp it could cost you $200 and another two hours of heartache and pain.

By now you're saying, "But Ken over there never went through the courses, and he passed the exams without any problem." You can perform some tasks only one way. When you come across questions that ask about that one way, you'll find that you can answer them even if you haven't gone through the Cisco courses, which is how some people get by without taking the courses. They learn enough about the Cisco methods to pass the exam based on their own knowledge. Of course, these are usually people who have several years' worth of networking and internetworking experience. Unfortunately, unless you're very skilled in networking and internetworking, the cost of approaching the exams from this angle can be devastating. Failure to prepare yourself costs you both time and the money paid for failed exams.

What's Behind the Certification Requirements?

The precise requirements for the CCIE certifications vary by the course of study you plan to follow. You can break these general requirements into four areas: (1) gaining the required knowledge, (2) practicing what you learn, (3) taking your exam, and (4) filling out any required paperwork. It's really that simple.

Let's look at two of those steps: gaining the required knowledge and practicing what you learn. That's what study is all about—getting the knowledge you need to know to do something and then putting that knowledge into practice before you're called upon to do it in real life.

There are two levels of knowledge required in the certification process: practical and Cisco. The practical knowledge is what you need to get your work done every day. For example, installing the IOS system image and adding new network modules are examples of practical knowledge. This is where hands-on training comes into play. Practical knowledge will get you around many of the trickier exam questions.

The Cisco knowledge is what you need to see things from the Cisco perspective. Some people may not see this as very valuable, but it is. In many situations, you can perform a task in more than one way. One way isn't theoretically better than any other, but Cisco wants you to do things its way to enforce a consistent way of handling problems. In some cases, Cisco's way of doing things is also slightly better than any other way of performing the task. You may not even notice the difference immediately; it takes time and experience to learn what Cisco is trying to show you up front.

Of course, Cisco is providing you with this training for a very specific reason. Training of this sort reduces the number of technical support calls Cisco receives. It also makes it a lot

easier for Cisco to help you during a crisis. The technical support person can better antici-
pate the problems that you may encounter if he or she knows what procedure you'll use to
fix an error. (This is a gross oversimplification of the two levels, but it's a good way to look
at them for right now.)

You can gain the knowledge required to pass your certification exams in any number of
ways:

- *Attend classes.* Some people take the Cisco-sponsored classes provided by their
  authorized partners. These classes provide you with the head knowledge about the
  Cisco way of doing things but fall short in the practical experience area.

- *Read the manuals.* A lot of people read the Cisco manuals and then try the things they
  learn on their network. This method certainly provides a lot more practical experience,
  but it usually falls short in teaching the precise Cisco way of learning things. Of course,
  you'll get at least some of the Cisco view going this route because Cisco writes the
  manuals. One potential drawback is that your boss may not look at your practice
  session on a live network favorably.

Ways to Learn about Cisco   Class study provides the best level of Cisco specific knowledge.
You need to enhance it with practical experience to pass your exams. Practical experience
will help you accomplish your everyday tasks, but it won't help you gain a Cisco perspective
on networking. Self-study using the Cisco manuals will provide you with a little of the Cisco
perspective; practicing what you learn will help you gain the practical experience you need.

On-the-job training is another method of learning. Experienced networking people spend
so much time on a network that they learn the things they need to know over time. This
method certainly helps you excel in practical knowledge but almost guarantees that you
won't know the Cisco way of attacking a problem. Gaining only practical knowledge may
get you into a situation in which you'll feel that Cisco marked a question on your exam incorrectly, even though you provided the correct answer. Remember that you must provide
the Cisco view on every test answer.

There's no best way to achieve your goals. You may want to take classes in areas in which
you lack complete understanding. On the other hand, reading the manuals may provide sufficient information in areas in which you have a lot of practical information. This book will
help you study for your exams. Someone with a lot of practical experience will be able to
pass the Cisco exams with what they learn here along with additional material. However,
if you do find that you can't pass the exams in this book, then you may want to invest in
some courses and other forms of education.

The basic requirements for passing the Cisco certification exams are quite simple. You
need to possess a combination of Cisco and practical knowledge in the area tested by your
exam to pass it. Even though it looks simple, gaining the knowledge required may prove
daunting in some situations.

Registering for the Exam

Registering for the exam is one of the easiest parts of the process. All you need to do is to
have a credit card ready and call the testing center. You can register for any test by calling

1-800-204-3926. The person on the other end of the line will ask you a few questions. That's all there is to registering.

If you're a very self-motivated person who tends to rush things, never register for the exam until you feel ready to pass it. Even though there's a limited time in which to take the exam, you won't want to repeat one because you weren't prepared to take it. Make sure that you are ready to take the test before you call to register.

If you tend to procrastinate, you may want to register for your exam immediately after the class is completed. Try setting the date for two weeks from the time your class finishes. This will give you a goal to achieve and enhance your study efforts. Don't let your certificate pass you by—register now for the exam.

Of course, there are a few pieces of information you need to know before you call. You'll need to know the number of the examination you want to take and the location of your nearest test center. If you don't know the location of the nearest test center, the person registering you can provide a list of locations in your area. They can usually provide you with directions to the test center as well.

Make sure that you have several exam dates in mind before you call the test center. Otherwise, you may find that the test center has filled the date you originally wanted, and you might have to rush to find another one.

Tips for Taking the Exams

People do quite a few things during the examination. Many of them are big time wasters. Some people wander between the drinking fountain and their desk. Others seem more interested in staring at the dots on the wall instead of answering questions. Make sure that you use all the time allotted to take the test—don't waste any of it doing other activities. Try to maintain your concentration during the entire exam—don't allow interruptions to rob you of the chance to pass. Of course, time isn't the only thing you need to watch during the exam.

The following hints should help you take the test faster and improve your chances of passing:

- *Look at the time indicator on your screen from time to time but don't waste time staring at it.* Make sure that you pace yourself, allotting enough time for each question you need to answer. You may want to take a quick glance at the time indicator after each question and ignore it the rest of the time.

- *Read the entire question.* Don't skip over small words like *and* or *not* when reading the question. Small words make a real difference—skipping them could cost you the question. People often miss questions not because they didn't know the answer, but because they failed to read the question fully. Make sure that you understand the question before you read the answer choices.

- *Read all the answers provided.* Sometimes, there is more than one correct answer on the screen. You need to pick the *most correct* answer that you find.

- *Remember to put on your Cisco hat before you enter the testing area.* Cisco uses the student manuals as the basis for all the answers in the exam. Even if there is more than one correct way to perform a task, only the Cisco way is the correct answer on the exam. In some cases, you may see more than one correct Cisco answer to a question. Always pick the most complete answer.

- *Go with your first instincts.* Some people get so psyched out before an exam that they actually overthink the answers to questions. Going with the first answer that comes to mind is correct more often than not, especially if you took the time and effort to study. Don't kill your chances to pass the exam by overthinking the answers.

- *Maintain your level of concentration.* Even though the exam center administrator tries to provide the very best testing environment possible, there are always distractions to reduce your concentration level. Concentrate on the test; ignore any outside influences that tend to reduce your level of concentration. You can't perform well on a test on which you aren't concentrating.

- *Make sure that you take care of your comfort needs before the exam.* For example, even if you don't normally need to eat breakfast, you may want to do so on the day of the exam to boost your energy levels. You'll also want to wear comfortable clothing. Wear your glasses or contacts so you can see the screen without squinting.

How well you do during the exam is really a matter of how well you prepare before you go into the test center. For example, your body's energy level always affects your concentration level.

Standard Testing Technique

The standard testing technique uses the same methodology as your instructor used for most of your classes in school. You'll receive an exam with about 100 questions. Cisco creates a unique exam for each person by drawing a specific number of questions at random from the testing base. For example, you might get 10 questions about bridging, another 10 questions about IP addressing, and so forth. Think of this testing method as the Chinese menu approach. You get so many questions from column *A*, so many from column *B*, etc.

It's very important to study everything completely when you take a standard exam. You need an even amount of knowledge about all the testing areas to complete the exam successfully. However, you can do a few things to improve your chances of passing the exam.

- *Talk to other people about their testing experience and the types of questions they saw.* Even though your chances of getting precisely the same questions as any one individual are very small, you can build an overview of all the test questions if you ask enough people. It's important to remember that Cisco constantly updates its test base and that you'll get a random set of questions.

- *Make absolutely certain that your strong areas really are strong.* It is possible to have a weak area and still pass the exam. For example, you might find that you don't know printing very well, yet pass the exam by knowing security perfectly. Of course, having more than one weak area can still be deadly.

- *If you do fail an exam, make sure that you write notes about your weak areas as soon as possible.* Drake, the company that administers the certification tests, won't allow you to record any answers or take any other notes. However, you can take the time to commit these facts to memory and write them down after you leave the test center. It's very important to improve on your weakest areas for the next exam if you want to pass.

What to Do If You Fail

Even if you do fully prepare for an exam, you still may fail it. You cannot take every variable into account to guarantee that you'll pass the exam. You may not realize that you have a weak area that the test asks you about. A cold or flu may strike on the day of the exam. An accident may delay part of your schedule, forcing you to rush to the exam. Any or all of these reasons may prevent you from performing your best on the exam.

How you recover from a failure partially determines how you will react during the next attempt. It may even determine whether you make another attempt to pass the exam. Many people try the exams once, fail, and then give up on their certification. Remember, certification requires a lot of input from you in the form of dedication and hard work. If certification were an easy task, the benefits of certification would be a lot less valuable. Don't give up after one attempt to pass an exam. My father, the late Enormas Giles, always told me don't give up, give out first. Another appropriate quote from an unknown author that I've heard over the years is, "If you throw your heart over the fence, your body will follow."

Nothing is more demoralizing than failing the same test twice. You should do several things after failing an exam to make sure it won't happen again. For example, you can plan to study the areas that gave you the most trouble in the first exam. The following tips will help you pass the exam the second time around. Unlike the other tips in this chapter, these tips usually work for everyone. Make sure that you try them all.

- *Write down the areas where you did well and the areas where you did not.* This will tell you where you need to concentrate your study before you take the next exam. (The test center administrator will provide you with a blank sheet of paper and a pencil you can use for this purpose.)

- *Maintain a positive attitude.* If you convince yourself that you're going to fail, you will. Literally, thousands of other people have gotten their certification; there's no reason that you can't get it with the proper training and study. You need to keep this fact in mind while you study for the retake.

- *Don't overcompensate by studying too much.* Many people make the mistake of punishing themselves for failing by spending hour after hour in front of their desks studying for the next exam. This probably is the worst mistake you can make. Although it's important to study for the next exam and to try to find the weak areas that caused you to fail the first time, studying too much can confuse you and cause you to fail again. Make sure that you don't study more than two hours per day. (You may want to review the study tips in the previous section of this chapter.)

- *Try to remember specific questions with which you may have had trouble.* In fact, you should try to write these down while they're fresh in your memory. Even though it's unlikely that you'll see these questions on the next test, they may help you find weak areas in your study strategy. In some cases, you may even see the same question worded in a different way.

- *Always study for a general exam, not the specific exam you took the first time.* Trying to study for a specific exam is pointless because each exam contains different questions.

Conclusion

You are about to embark on one of the most difficult certifications available in the internetworking industry. Becoming a Cisco Certified Internetworking Engineer puts you into an elite class of highly intelligent and technically proficient internetworking engineers. The CCIE certification, unlike other certifications, uses a two-day hands-on lab to prove that not only do you have an in-depth understanding of the internetworking industry, but also that you can walk the walk and talk the talk. Good luck on your journey.

2

Data Link Layer—MAC Layer Issues

The Data Link Layer media access control protocols are responsible for the delivery of frames from the source station to the destination using 48-bit (6-bytes) MAC address. It is at this layer where the communication between devices really happen. This layer also provides the details for devices such as bridging layer 2 and layer 3 switches and routers for further processing. These devices will be discussed in greater detail in chapter 4.

The Data Link Layer sits one layer above the true peer to peer network. Before it is fully detailed, the concepts of packets (frames) and addressing must be understood. In a transmitting and receiving communication system, if only one cable is available for multiple stations to access, a control mechanism must be in place to allow stations to share the physical cable plant. This is the purpose of the data-link layer, which provides for data encapsulation and network access across different media types. The Data Link portion of ATM will not be addressed in this chapter. Instead it will be discussed in detail in Chapter 14 covering ATM.

Data Link Layer Addressing

All stations active on a LAN are identified by a special address, the *Media Access Control* (MAC) layer address. It is the responsibility of the MAC (the logic that controls the access method) to provide for addressing.

This address is known by many different names: the MAC address, the physical address, the hardware address, or the PROM address. Throughout this text we used the terms MAC or physical for 48-bit MAC addressing. This address is primarily used to physically identify stations on the LAN. It is not a software address, such as an IP or IPX address. It can be called the hardware address, because the address is obtained by the software at initialization time by the *Network Interface Controller* (NIC) or the hardware.

Addressing in either Token Ring, FDDI, Fast Ethernet, Gigabit Ethernet, ATM, or Ethernet is the most basic way in which two stations communicate with each other over a LAN. All data, after the connection is established, is transferred between the source and destination addresses of the two stations.

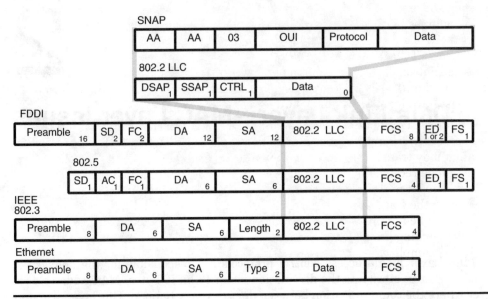

FIGURE 2.1   Ethernet, Token Ring, and FDDI packet

The MAC address is placed by the controller manufacturer into a PROM on the *Network Interface Card* (NIC). Upon start up of the network station software, the network controller software reads its physical address from the PROM and assigns this number to its software. For example, when the Ethernet drivers are loaded into a network station, the drivers read the address from the PROM and use the address in loading software. The drivers use this number as the physical address for all packets transmitted or received by this network station.

Data Link Frames

Figure 2.1 shows the beginning of each type of encapsulation (packet) for Ethernet, Token Ring, and FDDI. In this section, we will examine each address method. The rest of the frame content is fully discussed in each section. Each of the data encapsulation techniques is different, but each of them (Ethernet, Token Ring, and FDDI) use something similar. Under the addressing portion of the Ethernet Specification, each frame transmitted onto a network must have an address associated with it. This associated address enables stations to determine whether they should process a received packet and, if return information is required, to properly set the address of the requesting station. Destination and Source addresses are at this level.

All physical addresses for Ethernet, Fast Ethernet, Gigabit Ethernet, Token Ring, and FDDI are 48 bits long. All MAC addressing for LANs uses the 48-bit address, expressed as 6 bytes for both source and destination devices.

For LAN interfaces, three types of physical addresses exist:

- *Unique station address.* This address is much like a telephone number. One number is assigned per network attachment. When a frame is transmitted onto the network, every station sharing the same LAN segment receives the packet and looks at the destination address field. The network interface card compares this address to its own address. If there is a match, the adapter then passes the frame on to the upper layer software (such as TCP/IP, AppleTalk, IPX, HTTP servers, etc.) for the software to determine the outcome. If there is not a match on the address, the interface card discards the packet. These are known as *unicast packets*. Every station on a LAN segment must have its own unique MAC address.

- *Multicast address*. This special type of address is used to identify a group of network stations. Each network station has this multicast address assigned to it. In this way, a single station may transmit a packet with the destination address set to multicast, and the packet can be received by more than one station. The multicast address is easily determined. One bit is reserved in each of the frame types for multicast/broadcast. When receiving the frame, the NIC determines the state of this bit. If this bit is set to a 1, the frame will be a multicast or broadcast packet. Using a multicast frame is more efficient than sending multiple individual or broadcast frames. The OSPF routing protocol is an example of a protocol that uses multicast addressing. (i.e. MAC Address 01005e00005 and 01005e000006). When a OSPF router needs to send a packet that concerns only other OSPF routers, the router will place the special (reserved) MAC address in the destination MAC address field of the packet so that only routers configured for OSPF will process the packet. All other stations that receive this packet will discard it. With this address, all routers may receive information by one router transmitting it in multicast mode. Source addresses will never be multicast.

- *Broadcast address*. This special form of the multicast address means that the frame is destined for all stations on the network. All stations on the network pick up this frame and automatically send it to the upper layer software. The physical address for broadcast is FF-FF-FF-FF-FF-FF. IBM Token Ring includes C0-00-FF-FF-FF-FF as a broadcast address for Token Ring.

Token Ring has no concept of multicast addresses. The original chip set was built without this capability. Newer chip sets do allow for this, but they must still be backward compatible. To emulate a multicast, Token Ring uses *functional addresses*. To enable this feature, the first two bits of the Token Ring address field are set to 12 (hex C), and bit 0 of byte 2 is set to 0. This indicates a unique functional address. The Token Ring standard also calls for a group functional address, and bit 0 of byte 2 is set to a 1 to enable this.

Only 31 functional addresses are available, and IBM has reserved the ones shown in Figure 2.2. All stations on a Token Ring network are preset to receive and process these special frames. The user-defined ones can be defined by Token Ring implementors. When Token Ring bridges (Source-Route bridges) need to communicate, they formulate their frame and they place the bridge functional address in the destination address field. Every station receives this frame, but only the bridges process the frame.

Another exception from the norm is the Token Ring concept of assigning your own MAC address, the *locally assigned address* (LAA). Although not generally used in Ethernet controllers, Token Ring and FDDI controllers can enable the network administrator to overwrite the PROM address with a private address. To indicate this type of address, bit 1 of byte 0 of a Token Ring frame must be set to a 1 to indicate that it is a locally administered address. Any address that starts out with a 4 in a Token Ring address is a locally administered, unique address.

Function	Functional address (in hex)
Active Monitor	C00000000001
Ring parameter server	C00000000002
Ring error monitor	C00000000008
Configuration report server	C00000000010
NetBIOS	C00000000080
Bridge	C00000000100
LAN network manager	C00000002000
User-defined	C00000008000 through C00040000000

FIGURE 2.2   Token Ring functional addresses

The disadvantage of LAAs is that every address on the LAN must be unique. There are exceptions to this rule, but they are beyond the scope of this book these topics are covered in more detail in the Cisco SNAM Course. For 99.99% of the Token Ring cases, this will hold true. No two MAC addresses should be the same; therefore a central authority usually assigns the addresses. This central authority is usually the LAN administrator's office. In other words, each company that uses LAAs is free to assign its own addresses, but addressing will be managed by one group of people. This can get to be an administrative nightmare. LAAs also allow users to assign their own addresses. This can lead to a security breach. To overcome this, a lot of companies are applying filtering capabilities to their bridges and routers. This enables them to filter a MAC address so that certain addresses are allowed on certain LANs, and other addresses are "filtered" from entering some LANs.

MAC Addressing

As indicated in Figure 2.1, distinct entities are in the addressing portion of any of the MAC layer frames. Pay attention to the address headers of each of the frames. The destination address is 48 bits long and is split up into six eight-bit fields. The first byte is on the leftmost side of the frame and is labeled byte 0. The last byte is on the rightmost side and is labeled byte 5. This is where the similarities between Ethernet, Fast Ethernet, Gigabit Ethernet, Token Ring, and FDDI stop.

The first three bytes of the physical address, whether source or destination address, indicate the vendor *organization unit identification* (OUI). This OUI forms the basis for a unique MAC level address. Originally, Xerox handed out these addresses. Now, assigning the addresses is the responsibility of the IEEE. The purpose of a central authority assigning the addresses is simple—it ensures that there will not be duplicate addresses among network interface cards. Each vendor of a *network interface card* (NIC) must register its use with the IEEE. IEEE will assign the vendor a three-byte address, which is the first three bytes of the physical address. For example, 00-00-0c-00-00-00 is assigned to Cisco; 02-60-8c-00-00-00 is assigned to 3Com Corporation; 08-00-20-00-00-00 is assigned to Sun Microsystems. Having all 0s in the last three bytes only indicates a range. The owner of the first three bytes assigns the last three bytes of the address, which means they are allowed to assign up to 2^{24} addresses (16,777,215) to their NIC cards. Source and destination addresses must be unique.

The destination address for the IEEE 802.3, FDDI, and IEEE 802.5 frame allows for 48 bits of address, of which 46 bits may be used for the actual address. Two of the bits are reserved and known as the *individual / group* (I/G) bit and the *universal / local* (U/L) bit. Thus,

I/G bit = 0 for an individual (unique) address

        = 1 for a group (multicast) address

U/L bit = 0 for universally administered address (IEEE assigned)

        = 1 for locally administered (private networks)

Ethernet reserves only one bit in the destination field for unique/multicast addresses.

The source address will always be a unique address, and the IEEE 802.3 frame reserves only one bit to indicate this; the I/G bit is always a 0. However, the IEEE 802.5 specification allows this bit to be used for the *routing information indicator* (RII) bit, which indicates that the IEEE 802.5 frame contains source-routing information.

FDDI Addressing

The addressing for FDDI is similar to the IEEE 802.5 MAC addressing and are in non-canonical order. The addresses are 48 bits long. In 48-bit addresses, the first two bits of each address are important. In the destination address, bits 0 and 1 of the first byte are the I/G bit and the U/L bit. The I/G bit indicates whether the address is an individual (unique) address or a group (multicast) address. The next bit, U/L, indicates whether the address is universally administered (assigned by the IEEE to a vendor, called the prom address) or a locally administered address. LAAs are generally not used in FDDI, but are available.

Two bits are of particular importance in the source address. The first important bit is the RII bit, which displaces the I/G bit, because all source addresses are individual addresses. This bit indicates whether source-route information is in the field. Source routing generally is not used with FDDI, but the option is there. Bridges that encapsulate frames onto FDDI use source routing if the received packet is originally a source route frame (meaning the bridge forwarded to FDDI from a Token Ring network). The second important source address bit indicates whether the address is universally or locally administered.

Bit Order Transmission

Besides addressing, another important feature must be explained here: *bit order transmission*. Ethernet, Fast Ethernet, Gigabit Ethernet, Token Ring and FDDI do bit order differently, which leads to many incompatibilities between the two architectures.

First, the Ethernet address fields are divided into six bytes. In Figure 2.2a, the frame would be transmitted left to right, but the bits in each of the fields are transmitted right to left. Notice that bit 0 is the rightmost bit, which is called the *least significant bit* of the byte. This bit is transmitted first. The next bit transmitted is the bit to the left of bit 0. After all the bits of the byte are transmitted, the next byte (byte 1) is transmitted. Once again, bit 0 is transmitted first.

Aside from their both being token-passing protocols, Token Ring and FDDI are completely different. As in Ethernet, Fast Ethernet and Gigabit Ethernet, bit 0 is the first bit transmitted on a Token Ring LAN, but for Token Ring, bit 0 is the leftmost bit of the byte. Token

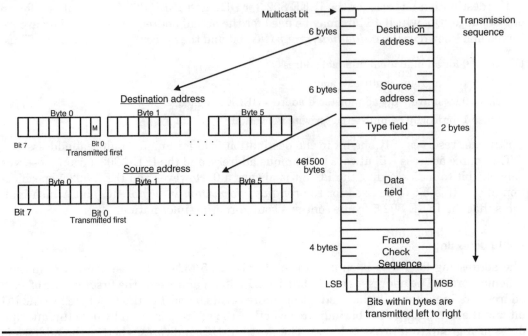

FIGURE 2.2a Ethernet bit order transmission

Ring and FDDI transmissions on the cable are in the same order as they appear. Not that this makes any major difference as to which one is better, but it will make the difference when Ethernet nodes try to communicate with Token Ring devices through a bridge. Communication through a router is not a problem and is the preferred method to allow the two access methods to communicate. Communication through a bridge or layer 2 switch is a different matter.

For addressing, two other bits are important in the address. For Ethernet, bit 0 of byte 0 is on the right side of the first byte of the packet. If this bit is set, the frame is a multicast packet. This bit is the *multicast bit indicator*. IEEE 802.3 (basically, the IEEE version of Ethernet) frames call this the *Individual Group address bit*, which the same as the multicast bit in the Ethernet v2.0 packet. This bit is the first one transmitted on the LAN. Therefore, if the first bit transmitted on an Ethernet or IEEE 802.3 LAN is a 0, then it is a unique address. If the first bit is a 1, then it is a multicast address. For example, for the packet 02-60-8C-00-01-02, the first bit transmitted would be a 0, but for 03-60-8C-01-02-04, the first bit transmitted would be a 1. Therefore, this latter address is a multicast address. If the first byte is odd on an Ethernet frame, it is a multicast frame.

Address Summary

We will now examine the Ethernet Architecture that encompasses Ethernet, Fast Ethernet, and Gigabit Ethernet functionality in detail. MAC addresses physically identify a network attachment on a LAN. There are three types of addresses: unicast, multicast, and broadcast. All the LAN types use 48-bit addresses, and Token Ring is allowed to assign their own. There are two MAC addresses contained in every packet: the source and the destination address. The first three bytes of an address identify the specific vendor of the NIC, and the last three bytes specifically identify the NIC. The last three bytes are allowed to be addressed by the NIC vendor. Token Ring contains the ability to assign its own MAC addresses, which are known as *locally assigned addresses* (LAAs).

Token Ring uses the concept of functional addresses to replace its inability to understand multicast addresses. Token Ring and FDDI both consider the leftmost byte as byte 0. They both state that bit 0 of byte 0 should be the first bit transmitted on the LAN. The problem is that Ethernet has the rightmost bit as bit 0, and Token Ring has the leftmost bit as bit 0. This is a bit reversal of the packet types.

This leads to a complication. Ethernet, Fast Ethernet, and Gigabit Ethernet transmits and receives MAC addresses using *least significant bit* (LSB), and Token Ring transmits and receives them using the *Most Significant Bit* (MSB) in another way. Under these conditions, how would network stations located on different LANs (one on Ethernet and one on Token Ring) communicate with each other? The answer is that they cannot, without the use of a device known as a router, Layer 2 Switch or a bridge. Routers fully understand their specific protocol and what in their packet needs to be translated. Therefore, all routers (and some vendors' bridges) understand how to translate between the two LANs.

Ethernet Architecture

We will now examine the Ethernet Architecture that encompasses Ethernet, Fast Ethernet, and Gigabit Ethernet funcationality in detail. Ethernet is designed around a number of different technologies that are current and in standards process. Today, Ethernet is the most widely used data link layer protocol, connecting millions of devices together supporting a variety of protocols above layer 2.

The standards body known as the *Institute of Electrical and Electronics Engineers* (IEEE) adopted the original Ethernet version and labeled it IEEE 802.3. The IEEE standard is based on the CSMA/CD access protocol. The IEEE version is intended to encompass several wiring types and techniques for signal rates using 10, 100 Mbps, 1000 Gigabits; multiple editions (versions) of this standard exist. See Figure 2.3 for a depiction of the evolution that Ethernet has undergone. The 1985 edition provides the specifications and related parameter values for a 10-Mbps base-band implementation on thick coaxial cable, which has a maximum segment length of 500 m (this specification is also known as 10Base5). The IEEE Standards Board approved the 10Base2 specification for thin coaxial cable in 1986 (10 Mbps baseband at 185 meters). The IEEE 802.3i edition (also known as 10BaseT) was formally adopted in October, 1990. The IEEE 802.3 formerly approved the 100BaseT version of Ethernet in June, 1995. The 1000BaseT version that operates over twisted pair and fiber is under construction.

Ethernet Definition

The Ethernet specification conforms to only the bottom two OSI layers, the Physical and Data Link layers. Ethernet does not pertain to any of the layers above it, but Ethernet can support multiple protocols operating above its MAC layer protocol. For example, *Xerox Network Specifications* (XNS), TCP/IP, NetBIOS over NetBEUI, HTTP, Vines IP, Novell IPX, Apple DDP, and a multitude of other protocols all operate above Ethernet.

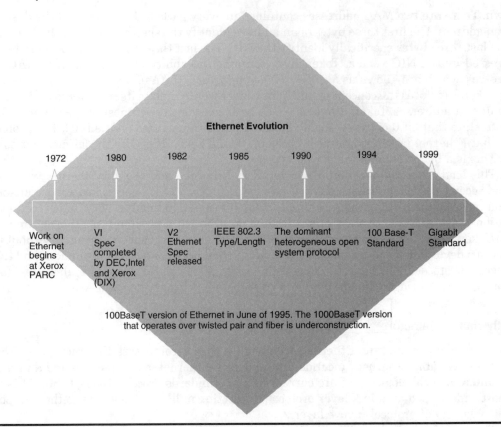

FIGURE 2.3 Ethernet evolution

Ethernet is a multiaccess, packet-switched communications system for carrying digital data among locally distributed computing systems. The shared-communications channel in Ethernet is a passive broadcast medium with no central control point; frame address recognition in each station is used to take frames from the channel. Access to the channel by stations wishing to transmit is coordinated in a distributed fashion by the stations themselves, using a statistical arbitration scheme. Both Ethernet and IEEE 802.3 follow the CSMA/CD access method algorithm. The implementation of the frame format is where the two differ. Therefore, except where noted, the terms IEEE 802.3 and Ethernet are synonymous. The Ethernet specification is the most commonly followed standard. In an Ethernet system, the control mechanism is an access method known as *Carrier Sense Multiple Access with Collision Detection* (CSMA/CD). Ethernet applies the functions of the algorithm of CSMA/CD. Ethernet basically performs three functions:

- Transmitting and receiving formatted data (i.e., frames)
- Decoding the frames and checking for valid addresses before informing upper layer software
- Detecting errors within the data frame on the network

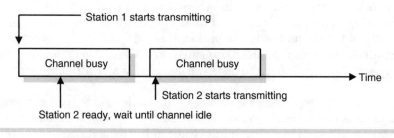

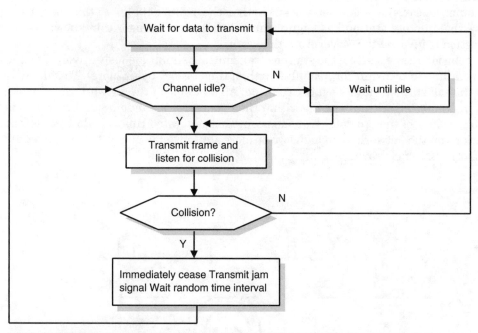

FIGURE 2.4 CSMA/CD operation

Ethernet Transmission

As depicted in Figure 2.4, a station wishing to transmit is said to contend for sole use of the channel. After the cable is acquired, the station uses it to transmit a frame. All other stations on the channel listen for incoming frames or enter into *defer mode* (in which they defer transmission of a frame). Only one station may transmit on the channel at a time.

To contend for sole use of the channel, any station wishing to transmit checks whether the channel is busy (i.e., the station uses its *carrier sense* capability). What the controller is looking for is whether any signals are on the cable. If there are signals on the channel, the channel is said to be busy. If there are no signals on the channel, it is said to be quiet. If the channel has not been busy for a specified amount of time, the station immediately begins to transmit its data. During the transmission, the station listens while transmitting to ensure that no other stations transmit data to the channel while it is transmitting. If no other station transmits during that time and the station transmits all of its data, the transmission is said to have been successful, and the station will return to listening to the channel. A station is permitted to transmit only one packet at a time, and then it must contend with all the other stations for any subsequent transmissions. All stations must wait for 9.6 microseconds (running at 10Mbps) after the last transmission before attempting to transmit.

If any other station transmitted during that time, a collision is said to have occurred. As shown in Figure 2.5, a collision occurs when two or more stations transmit at the same time. Any station transmitting will know a collision has occurred by the structure of the signals on the channel. One example is when the strength of the signal doubles; in this case, a station knows that another station has begun transmitting, and the algorithm known as collision detection is invoked to recover from this error.

When a collision occurs, each of the stations transmitting simultaneously (involved in the collision) continue to transmit for a small length of time (4 to 6 bytes more). This delay is to ensure that all stations have seen the collision. All stations on the network then invoke the *collision backoff* algorithm. The algorithm then generates a random number, which is used as the amount of time to defer transmission. This generated time should be different for all stations on the network. Although two or more stations may generate the same time to backoff, it is extremely rare.

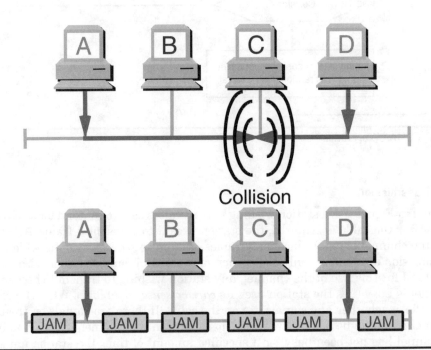

FIGURE 2.5 Ethernet collisions

During the first 10 retransmissions, the delay is doubled. After 10 times, the backoff time remains the same until 16 attempts have been reached. Subsequent collisions force the controller to backoff, with the backoff algorithm generating a larger number of retransmissions with which to backoff (indicating a busy channel). Finally, after 16 attempts (1 for the initial, plus 15 for retransmitting), the controller gives up, and an error message is generated. The reason for allowing only 1,024 stations on a single Ethernet network is that the collision backoff algorithm is optimized for 1,024 nodes when calculating the backoff time. Each controller runs this algorithm by itself. Therefore, all stations should defer transmission for a different amount of time. This should allow no two stations to defer transmission for the same amount of time, and it thereby reduces the possibility of another collision; this is called the *Collision Detect process*.

Ethernet Reception

The receiver function of Ethernet is activated when the controller *sees* the channel become active. When a signal is detected on the channel, the receive circuitry becomes active in a NIC. Figure 2.6 shows the format of an Ethernet II frame.

A receiver processes an incoming packet in the following way (see Figure 2.7): because there is no master clock on an Ethernet network, the first 64 bits of information transmitted on the network constitute the preamble (see Figure 2.6). This bit pattern is used to synchronize all active receiving stations with the message that a station is about to transmit on the network. This preamble is never noticed by the end user.

The next two fields are the address fields discussed at the beginning of this chapter. The next field is the type field. The type field identifies the upper layer protocol. For example, if the field is set to 0x8137, the frame belongs to Novell NetWare. If the type field is set to 0x0800, the frame belongs to the TCP/IP protocol. The type field is a mechanism by which the controller software may determine the ownership of a frame.

The next field is the data field. This may contain upper layer network software information, or it may contain user data. This field in the frame is where the user data is held or enveloped for transmission across the network. The final field is the CRC. This is a 32-bit error detection scheme that the controller uses to determine whether any errors are in the packet. This scheme does not check for things like sequence errors, etc., but it does check to make sure that the packet that is sent is the same as the one that is received.

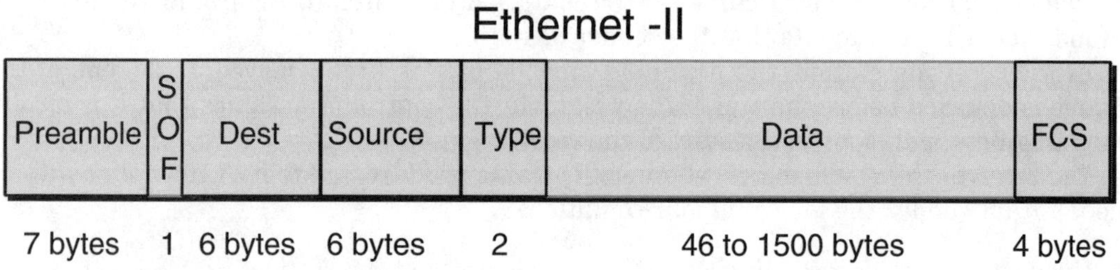

Ethernet -II

Preamble	S O F	Dest	Source	Type	Data	FCS
7 bytes	1	6 bytes	6 bytes	2	46 to 1500 bytes	4 bytes

FIGURE 2.6   Ethernet header

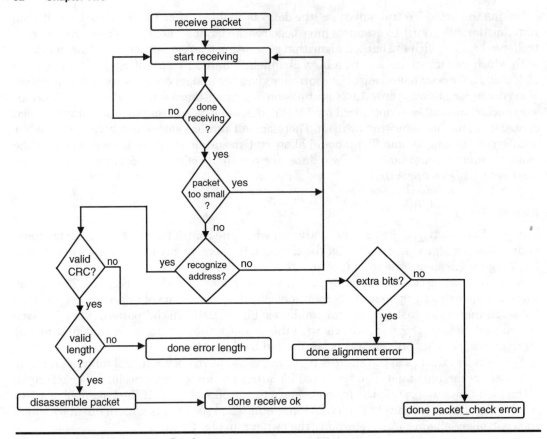

FIGURE 2.7 Ethernet Reception flowchart

Before the frame is transmitted, the sending station performs the CRC error checking algorithm on the frame. This algorithm generates a number, which is placed in the CRC field of the packet. Upon reception, the receiving station also generates a CRC number based on the bits received. This CRC number then is checked with the CRC number in the received frame. If the two do not match, the frame is discarded. If they do match, the frame is sent to the upper layer network software for further processing. Thirty-two bits of CRC provide for 99.999 percent accuracy. If the controller does discard the frame, the Ethernet standard does not mandate that the sender be notified.

At the receiving station, the preamble (first 64 bits) is first removed. If the end of the frame is detected before the end of the preamble, the controller assumes that it is a collision fragment and loops to the start of the receiving process.

The receiver then determines whether the frame is addressed to it. A controller will accept a frame under the following four conditions:

- The destination address matches the specific address of the station.

- The destination address is a broadcast address.

- The destination address is a multicast address.

- The NIC was set in a special mode known as the *promiscuous* mode. Devices such as packet decoders, bridges, and LAN switches operate in this mode.

In the *promiscuous* mode, the controller accepts all frames, no matter what the destination address is, which is how network protocol decoders work. Some Ethernet controllers have been designed to accept the whole frame into their buffers before checking the destination address. This process is inefficient in the sense that if the frame is not addressed to it, the controller has wasted not only a lot of time receiving the frame, but also the buffer space used.

Most controllers check the destination address as they are receiving the frame. If the address is not recognized as its own, the rest of the frame is ignored. If the destination address is recognized, the receiver accepts the rest of the frame into its buffer space. Some simple checks are accomplished on the frame before the upper layer software is notified that it has information. The frame is first checked for a 16-bit boundary. Because all data is transferred as 8-bit bytes, this ensures that the frame has not ended abruptly. If an error occurs, the frame is discarded.

The frame is checked to be of minimum length. At a minimum, the frame has to contain the 6 bytes for each source and destination address, the 2-byte type field, a 46-byte data field, and a 4-byte CRC field, giving the minimum of a 64-byte frame. (You will hear of a minimum packet size of 72 bytes; this occurs when the 8-byte preamble is included in the total length of the packet.) The controller itself strips the preamble from the frame and begins the frame count at the destination address. The length must be greater than or equal to 64 bytes. If the length is less than 64 bytes (usually a fragment of a packet), the packet is once again discarded. The packet is also checked for errors via the CRC.

It is impossible to guarantee that all frames transmitted will be delivered successfully. For example, a frame may be transmitted to a station that has been powered off. The frame incurred no collisions or CRC errors; the receiver was just not there to accept the frame. It is up to the higher layer protocols to ensure proper delivery and to decide what actions to take otherwise.

That is all that the Ethernet algorithm does. It took years of research and development to arrive at these concepts, but the underlying methods are quite simple.

Two similar Ethernet standards exist. Functionally, they work exactly the same, and both types can reside on the same LAN. The IEEE produced a slightly different version of Ethernet, and for the most part, the differences are in the frame format. IEEE 802.3 uses the same CSMA/CD algorithm as Ethernet. As shown in Figure 2.8, the IEEE specifies a seven-byte preamble and a one-byte *Start of Frame* (SFD) delimiter, yielding a total of eight bytes. The bits of the eight bytes are consistent with the bit pattern of the eight-byte preamble of the Ethernet packet. Therefore, this is simply a name change. The IEEE 802.3 packet format does not have a type field. IEEE assumes the use of the IEEE 802.2 protocol, and this protocol emulates the type field with the *Service Access Protocol* (SAP).

The Ethernet frame format does not have a length field. In fact, the length field sits exactly where the type field sits in the Ethernet frame. The length field indicates the exact amount of data bytes in the data field. To correctly determine an Ethernet or IEEE 802.3 packet, the software drivers of the Ethernet controller know that a Type field starts at hex number 0x0600. A number below this indicates a length field. Therefore, if the number is

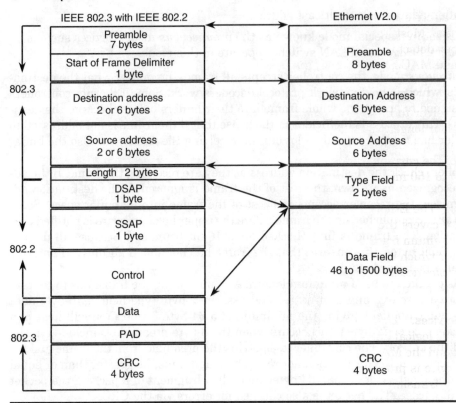

FIGURE 2.8   Ethernet and IEEE 802.3 frame

0x0600 or above in that field, the frame is Ethernet v2.0. Any number below that is an IEEE 802.3 frame format. The highest number for Ethernet frame length is 1518 bytes. Subtracting the 18 bytes of overhead leaves 1500 bytes available for the data field. This equates to 0x5DC in the length field. Therefore, the highest number is the length field is 0x5DC (or 1500 decimal).

Since the adoption of Ethernet by the standards bodies, several differences between Ethernet v1.0 (now obsolete), Ethernet v2.0, and IEEE 802.3 have been noted. The terms Ethernet and IEEE 802.3 are synonymous for the most part. The major similarities and differences are detailed in the following sections.

Electrical Functions.   Ethernet v2.0 and IEEE 802.3 include a *heartbeat* function. To ensure proper operation of the external transceiver, this signal is sent from the transceiver to the Ethernet controller immediately after each transmission. This confirms that the transceiver or MAU collision signaling is working and connected to the station. How does the Ethernet controller know this is a test signal and not a real collision? The signal sent is usually much shorter in duration than it would be if a real collision were detected and the proper collision signal was generated. This is also known as the *signal-quality-error* (SQE) signal. Without this signal, the station is unsure whether the frame was actually sent without a collision or whether a defective MAU failed to properly report a collision. Ethernet v1.0 does not support this function. Most Ethernet controllers do not support this function and misinterpret this signal. They detect the SQE as a collision. Nothing is transmitted or received. On most transceivers and MAUs, a jumper allows this function to be enabled or disabled.

Jabber Function.   IEEE 802.3 has a *jabber* function, which is a self-interrupt capability that allows a transceiver to inhibit transmitting data from reaching the channel if the transmission occurs for longer than the maximum frame size (1518 bytes). The transceiver does not count the number of bytes that it is currently transmitting; it invokes a timer and notes the duration of the current transmission. The transceiver invokes the jabber control function within 20 to 150 ms.

Frame Formats.   The Ethernet v2.0 packet format differs significantly from the 802.3 format. Figure 2.8 covers the differences. Ethernet does not support a length field. (Remember that the minimum frame size for Ethernet is 64 bytes.) The Ethernet-type field is used to determine for which client protocol the frame is intended. This concept is similar to the IEEE 802.2 *service access point* (SAP). Ethernet provides what amounts to LLC Type 1 operation and does not need a control field.

Link Control Services.   The IEEE 802.3 standard is composed of two sublayers: the MAC sublayer and the logical link sublayer. (LLC is explained in Chapter 3.) Ethernet v2.0 combines the link and the MAC functions into a single protocol. Only an unacknowledged connectionless service is provided for Ethernet. (*Connectionless-oriented protocol* means that all packets are transmitted on a best-effort basis. The packets transmitted are not acknowledged by the recipient.) The IEEE 802.3 standard can use the IEEE 802.2 LLC Data Link connection-oriented service. (Connection-oriented service providing for guaranteed delivery of the packet, IEEE 802.2, is further explained in Chapter 3.)

Full-Duplex Ethernet

Full-duplex Ethernet operating at 10 Mbps allows transmission to take place in both directions simultaneously. This allows more data to be transmitted than conventional half duplex Ethernet. Full duplex Ethernet at 10Mbps never really emerge due to its higher speed rival Fast Ethernet full duplex capabilities. The standard provides for several specifications like 10Mbps, 100Mbps and 1Gigabit Ethernet. (With 10GB under consideration) See Figure 2.9 . These will be discussed later.

A station on the Ethernet transmits information, and all others on the network segment listen until that station is done transmitting. Any other station wanting to transmit must wait for the currently transmitting station to finish before it can contend for the cable plant. This is known as *half-duplex operation*. Any station that attempts to transmit at the same time as another station causes a collision. During a collision, each station backs off a certain amount of time in an attempt to throttle back traffic. All collided packets must be retransmitted.

For Ethernet, modern network designers recommend the use of 100BaseT technology with Gigabit Ethernet being recommended for Backbone network operations. With this technology, each workstation has a single wiring cable that attaches it to a single port on a LAN switch. Because only one station attachment is available per LAN switch, two stations

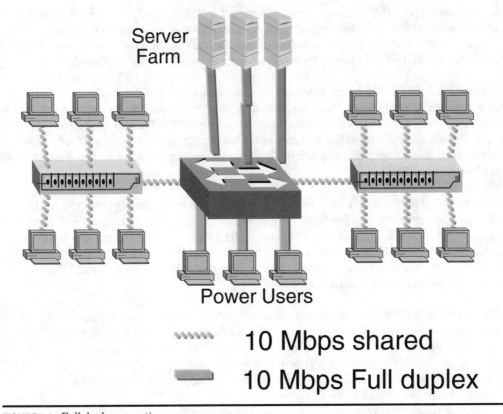

Server Farm

Power Users

10 Mbps shared

10 Mbps Full duplex

FIGURE 2.9   Full-duplex operation

cannot transmit at the same time. Why have the Collision Detect circuitry? It is possible for network interface cards to transmit and receive at the same time, which is the reason behind the standardization of full-duplex Ethernet. This possibility is also one of the driving factors in LAN Switching using micro-segmentation along with Ethernet and Fast Ethernet using full-duplex capabilities.

The key point here is that full duplex only operates under two conditions: one, only one attachment exists to the port on the LAN switch (or between switches—that is, two switches connected to one another for switch extension); two, the network attachment attaches to a switch port and not a concentrator or hub port. This only works when there is a point-to-point relationship between the full-duplex NIC card and its terminating point.

Attempting to connect that network attachment to a simple concentrator or hub port does not allow for full-duplex operation. A concentrator or hub port still shares the medium with every other device attached to that concentrator. Therefore, multiple network attachments exist per segment, or at least it appears that way.

A LAN switch isolates each port and makes it appear that the device attached to that port is the only one. Any data received is then *switched* to another port. The logic in the switch handles all the contention. Therefore, with only one attachment per port, no collisions are possible, and the capability for a network attachment to transmit and receive at the same time is possible by disabling the CD logic and using the wire pairs.

For full-duplex operation to exist, a new controller card must be used. Some vendors claim that existing controller cards may be used, depending on the type of hardware logic on the controller card.

IEEE 802.2 Data Link Service

The IEEE 802.2 protocol provides for a more structured Data Link layer, which provides many services to many different types of standards. Chapter 3 provides an in-depth explanation of the IEEE 802.2 protocol.

The length field is the obvious indicator that a packet is of type IEEE 802.3. If an IEEE 802.3 frame is obtained from the network by an Ethernet controller, the IEEE 802.2 headers usually are included. Therefore, a discussion of IEEE 802.2 is in order here.

This is the preferred Data Link protocol suite of the IEEE and differs tremendously from the Ethernet Version 2.0 specification. IEEE 802.2 is the only Data Link protocol used in IEEE 802.5 Token Ring and FDDI. IEEE 802.2 services are provided for both IEEE 802.3, FDDI, and 802.5 standards. IEEE 802.2 services are not provided for use with Ethernet. The following is just an introduction to the IEEE 802.2 Data Link layer.

A subcommittee of the IEEE 802 committee, the IEEE 802.2 working group, was set up to establish a networking standard for the Data Link module. The working group decided to split the Data Link layer into two distinct sublayers: the *logical link control* (LLC) and the *media access control* (MAC). The IEEE 802 committee had the forethought that many different protocols were going to run on LANs and that the Data Link needed to provide for this.

The IEEE 802.2 working group set up the LLC portion of the Data Link layer. The IEEE 802.2 specification for the Data Link module provides three classes for the delivery of packets: Type 1, which is connectionless, Type 2, which is connection-oriented, and Type 3, which is acknowledge connection-less. LLC Type 3 is not normally used today and will not be addressed.

Their class identifies stations on the network, as in Class I and Class II stations. Class I stations support only Type 1 service, but Class II stations support both Type 1 and Type 2 service. Let's examine an IEEE 802.3 packet with the IEEE 802.2 information (see Figure 2.10). Notice that this packet is different from the Ethernet packet. Besides the obvious length field, the LLC header information (herein called the *LLC data unit*) is what provides the Type 1 service or the Type 2 service. First, an explanation of the terms DSAP and SSAP is needed.

The SAP field basically provides the same functionality as the type field provides in the Ethernet packet. To distinguish between different data exchanges that involve the same station, the term *service access point* (SAP) is used to identify a particular element in a network station involved in a single data exchange.

A SAP involved in sending a particular LLC data unit is known as the *Source Service Access Point* (SSAP), and the SAP involved in receiving an LLC data unit is known as the *Destination Service Access Point* (DSAP). The DSAP address identifies the SAP for which the packet is intended.

The seven DSAP address bits (D) and the user-defined address bit (U) form the address of the SAP for which the packet is intended. The U bit indicates whether the address is defined by the user (a binary 0) or is a group address (a binary 1). IBM has defined 0xFO as the SAP for the NetBIOS protocol, and 0x06 is the SAP for the TCP protocol. The seven SSAP address bits and the user-defined bit identify the address of the SAP that originated the packet. The U bit indicates whether the address is defined by the user (a binary 0) or

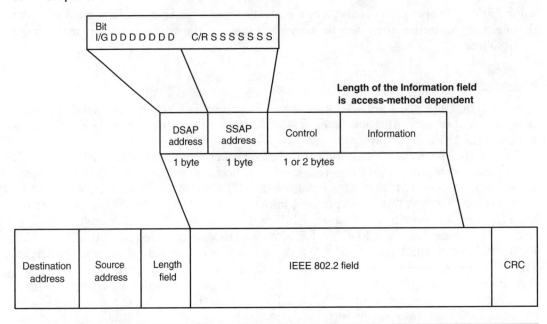

FIGURE 2.10   IEEE 802.3 packet

by the IEEE (a binary 1). Following the DSAP and SSAP is the control field. The control field identifies the type LLC service and is used to maintain the sequence numbers for packet transmission and reception.

The *Subnetwork Access Protocol* (SNAP) allows an Ethernet frame to be encapsulated by an IEEE 802.2 logical protocol data unit (giving it an LPDU or IEEE 802.2 header). SNAP uses the IEEE 802.3 Type 1 service and a DSAP of 0xAA. This setting identifies to the LLC layer that an Ethernet frame is to follow and to treat the following frame accordingly. The control field is set to 03 to indicate Type 1 service. This very simple approach allows the Ethernet drivers out there to reside within the IEEE 802.2 world without anyone having to completely rewrite their code.

Summary of Ethernet Frame Formations and Descriptions

IEEE 802.3 Frame Format

The Ethernet Frame Format as described in the IEEE 802.3 specification defines a 14-byte Data Link header followed by a Logical Link Control header, which is defined by the 802.2 specification (see Figure 2.11).

Destination Address.   The first six bytes of an Ethernet frame make up the *Destination Address*. The Destination Address specifies to which adapter the data frame is being sent. A Destination Address of all ones specifies a Broadcast Message that is read in by all receiving Ethernet adapters. The Destination Address format is identical in all implementations of Ethernet.

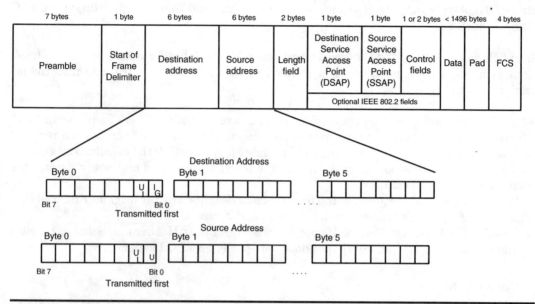

FIGURE 2.11   IEEE 802.3 frame header

Source Address.   The next six bytes of an Ethernet frame make up the *Source Address*. The Source Address specifies from which adapter the message originated. Like the Destination Address, the first three bytes specify the vendor of the card. The Source Address format is identical in all implementations of Ethernet.

Length.   In the IEEE 802.3 Frame Format and the IEEE SNAP Frame Format, bytes 13 and 14 of an Ethernet frame contain the length of the data in the frame, not including the preamble, 32-bit CRC, DLC addresses, or the Length field itself. An Ethernet frame can be no shorter than 64 bytes total length and no longer than 1518 bytes total length.

802.2 LLC Header

Following the Data Link header is the Logical Link Control Header, which is described in the IEEE 802.2 specification. The purpose of the LLC header is to provide a "hole in the ceiling" of the Data Link layer. By specifying into which memory buffer the adapter places the data frame, the LLC header enables the upper layers to find the data, based on destination and source service access point (DSAP and SSAP).

DSAP.   The DSAP is a one-byte field that acts as a pointer to a memory buffer in the receiving station. The DSAP tells the receiving NIC in which buffer to put this information. This functionality is crucial when users are running multiple protocol stacks, etc.

SSAP.   The SSAP is analogous to the DSAP and specifies the source of the sending application. In order to specify that a frame is a SNAP frame, the DSAP and SSAP are set to **AA** hex.

Control Byte.   Following the SAPs is a one-byte control field that specifies the type of LLC frame that this is.

User Data and FCS. Data: 43-1497 Bytes.   Following the 802.2 header are 43 to 1,497 bytes of data, generally consisting of upper layer headers such as TCP/IP or IPX and then the actual user data.

FCS.   The last four bytes that the adapter reads in are the Frame Check Sequence or CRC. When the voltage on the wire returns to 0, the adapter checks the last four bytes it received against a checksum that it generates via a complex polynomial. If the calculated checksum does not match the checksum on the frame, the frame is discarded and never reaches the memory buffers in the station.

The following is a description of the frame format described by the original Ethernet Version II specification, as released by DEC, Intel, and Xerox.

Like the 802.3 spec, the Version II spec defines a Data Link Header consisting of 14 bytes of information, but the Version II spec does not specify an LLC header.

The Data Link Header

The Destination Address.   The first six bytes of an Ethernet frame make up the Destination Address. The Destination Address specifies to which adapter the data frame is being sent. A Destination Address of all ones specifies a Broadcast Message that is read in by all receiving Ethernet adapters. The first three bytes of the Destination Address are assigned by the IEEE to the vendor of the adapter, and are specific to the vendor. The Destination Address format is identical in all implementations of Ethernet.

Source Address.   The next six bytes of an Ethernet frame make up the Source Address. The Source Address specifies from which adapter the message originated. Like the Destination Address, the first three bytes specify the vendor of the card. The Source Address format is identical in all implementations of Ethernet.

Ethertype.   Following the Source Address is a 2-byte field called the Ethertype. The Ethertype is analogous to the SAPs in the 802.3 frame in that it specifies the memory buffer in which to place this frame.

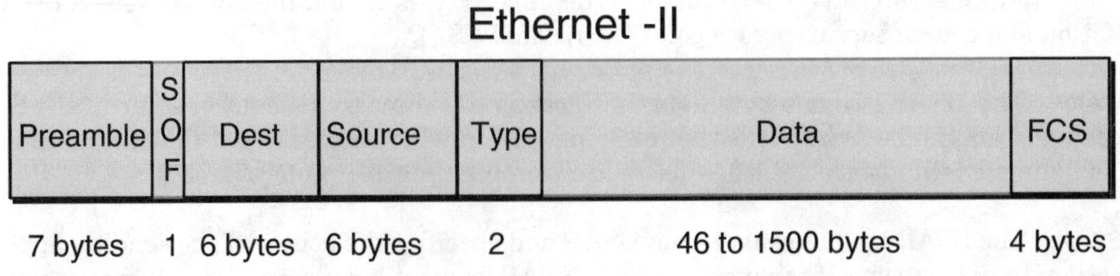

Ethernet -II

Preamble	S O F	Dest	Source	Type	Data	FCS
7 bytes	1	6 bytes	6 bytes	2	46 to 1500 bytes	4 bytes

FIGURE 2.12   Ethernet II frame3 header

An interesting question arises when one considers the 802.3 and Version II frame formats: Both formats specify a 2 byte field following the source address (an Ethertype in Version II, and a Length field in 802.3)—How does a driver know which format it is seeing, if it is configured to support both?

The answer is actually quite simple. All Ethertype have a value greater than 05DC hex, or 1500 decimal. Since the maximum frame size in Ethernet is 1518 bytes, there is no point of overlap between Ethertype and lengths. If the field that follows the Source Address is greater than O5DC hex, the frame is a Version II, otherwise, it is something else (either 802.3, 802.3 SNAP, or Novell Proprietary).

User Data and FCS. Data: 46-1497 Bytes.   Following the Ethertype are 46 to 1,500 bytes of data, generally consisting of upper layer headers such as TCP/IP or IPX and then the actual user data.

FCS: Last 4 Bytes.   The last 4 bytes that the adapter reads in are the Frame Check Sequence or CRC. When the voltage on the wire returns to zero, the adapter checks the last 4 bytes it received against a checksum that it generates via a complex polynomial. If the calculated checksum does not match the checksum on the frame, the frame is discarded and never reaches the memory buffers in the station.

The IEEE 802.3 SNAP Frame Format

Although the original 802.3 specification worked well, the IEEE realized that some upper layer protocols required an Ethertype to work properly. For example, TCP/IP uses the Ethertype to differentiate between ARP packets and normal IP data frames. To provide this backward compatibility with the Version II frame type, the 802.3 SNAP (Subnetwork Access Protocol) format was created (see Figure 2.13). The SNAP Frame Format consists of a normal 802.3 Data Link Header followed by a normal 802.2 LLC Header, and then a 5 byte SNAP field, followed by the normal user data and FCS.

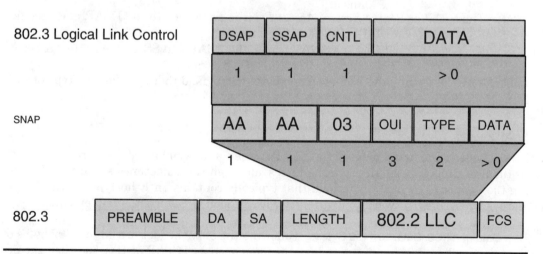

FIGURE 2.13   IEEE 802.3 SNAP frame format

Destination Address. The first six bytes of an Ethernet frame make up the Destination Address. The Destination Address specifies to which adapter the data frame is being sent. A Destination Address of all ones specifies a Broadcast Message that is read in by all receiving Ethernet adapters.

The first three bytes of the Destination Address are assigned by the IEEE to the vendor of the adapter, and are specific to the vendor. The Destination Address format is identical in all implementations of Ethernet.

Source Address. The next six bytes of an Ethernet frame make up the Source Address. The Source Address specifies from which adapter the message originated. Like the Destination Address, the first three bytes specify the vendor of the card. The Source Address format is identical in all implementations of Ethernet.

Length. Bits 13 and 14 of an Ethernet frame contain the length of the data in the frame, not including the preamble, 32 bit CRC, DLC Addresses, or the Length field itself. An Ethernet frame can be no shorter than 64 bytes and no longer than 1518 bytes in total length.

802.2 LLC Header

Following the Data Link Header is the Logical Link Control Header, which is described in the IEEE 802.2 Specification. The purpose of the LLC header is to provide a "hole in the ceiling" of the Data Link Layer. By specifying into which memory buffer the adapter places the data frame, the LLC header allows the upper layers to know where to find the data.

DSAP. The DSAP, or *Destination Service Access Point*, is a 1-byte field that simply acts as a pointer to a memory buffer in the receiving station. It tells the receiving NIC in which buffer to put this information. This functionality is crucial in situations where users are running multiple protocol stacks, etc

SSAP. The SSAP or *Source Service Access Point* is analogous to the DSAP, and specifies the *Service Access Point* (SAP) of the sending process.

In order to specify that this is a SNAP frame, the DSAP and SSAP are set to AA hex.

Control Byte. Following the SAPs is a one-byte control field that specifies the type of LLC frame that this is.

SNAP Header

Vendor Code. The first 3 bytes of the SNAP header is the vendor code, generally the same as the first three bytes of the source address, although it is sometimes set to zero. Following the Vendor Code is a 2-byte field that typically contains an Ethertype for the frame. Here is where the backward compatibility with Version II Ethernet is implemented.

User Data and FCS. Data: 38-1492 Bytes. Following the 802.2 header are 38 to 1,492 bytes of data, generally consisting of upper layer headers such as TCP/IP or IPX and then the actual user data.

FCS: Last 4 Bytes.   The last 4 bytes that the adapter reads in are the *Frame Check Sequence* (CRC). When the voltage on the wire returns to zero, the adapter checks the last 4 bytes it received against a checksum that it generates via a complex polynomial. If the calculated checksum does not match the checksum on the frame, the frame is discarded and never reaches the memory buffers in the station.

802.3 _Raw Novell Proprietary Frame Format

Novell's Proprietary Frame Format was developed based on a preliminary release of the 802.3 specification (see Figure 2.14). After Novell released their proprietary format, the LLC Header was added, making Novell's format incompatible.

Destination Address.   The first six bytes of an Ethernet frame make up the Destination Address. The Destination Address specifies to which adapter the data frame is being sent. A Destination Address of all ones specifies a Broadcast Message that is read in by all receiving Ethernet adapters. The first three bytes of the Destination Address are assigned by the IEEE to the vendor of the adapter, and are specific to the vendor. The Destination Address format is identical in all implementations of Ethernet.

Source Address.   The next six bytes of an Ethernet frame make up the Source Address. The Source Address specifies from which adapter the message originated. Like the Destination Address, the first three bytes specify the vendor of the card. The Source Address format is identical in all implementations of Ethernet.

Length.   Ethernet frame contains the length of the entire data frame, not including the preamble or 32 bit CRC. An Ethernet frame can be no shorter than 64 bytes, and no longer than 1518 bytes.

Data: 46-1497 Bytes.   Following the Data Link header are 46 to 1500 bytes of data. In all Novell frames, the user data begins with an IPX (Novell's network layer protocol) header. The IPX header contains as its first two bytes an optional checksum, with the value FFFF signifying that the checksum is not used. By convention, the checksum is always turned off, and the FFFF that occurs 3 bytes after the end of the source address is how device drivers differentiate Novell frames from 802.3 frames, which look identical until the first byte following the length field.

FCS: Last 4 Bytes.   The last 4 bytes that the adapter reads in are the *Frame Check Sequence* (CRC). When the voltage on the wire returns to zero, the adapter checks the last 4 bytes it

# Octets	6	6	6	2	1	1		4
	Preamble	DA	SA	Length	FF	FF	Data	FCS

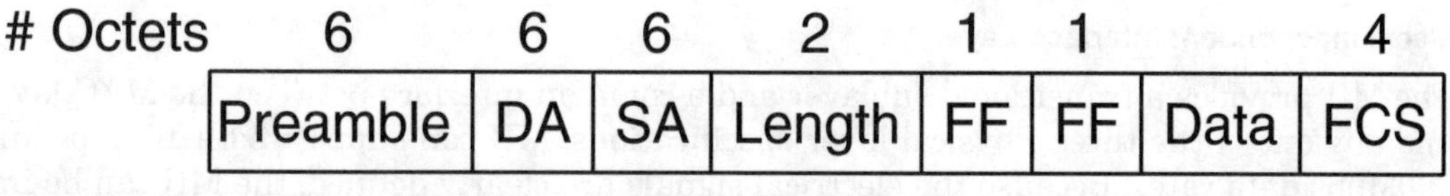

FIGURE 2.14   Novell Ethernet frame

received against a checksum that it generates via a complex polynomial. If the calculated checksum does not match the checksum on the frame, the frame is discarded and never reaches the memory buffers in the station.

Fast Ethernet Architecture

As Internet applications require more and more bandwidth, Ethernet has been scaling to accommodate the insatiable appetite Internet applications have for additional bandwidth. The IEEE committee responded with the approval of the Fast Ethernet standard. Among the high-speed LAN technologies available today, Fast Ethernet, or 100BASE-T, has become the leading choice. Building on the near-universal acceptance of 10BASE-T Ethernet, Fast Ethernet technology provides a smooth, non-disruptive evolution to 100 Mbps performance. This specification provides functionality like that found in the original 10Mbps Ethernet standards with some new features to accommodate high-speed bandwidth to LAN switches, routers, Web servers, and file servers. Fast Ethernet is based on the IEEE 802.3u specification.

Some of the features of Fast Ethernet as compared to Ethernet 10Bps are:

- Same MAC as Ethernet
- Identical frames
- Same CMSA/CD Protocol
- Ethernet>>10BASE-T>>100BASE-T
- 10 times the performance of Ethernet
- Different physical layers

The 100BASE-T standard is comprised of five component specifications. These define the MAC layer, the *Media Independent Interface* (MII) layer, and the three physical layers: 100BASE-TX, 100BASE-T4, and 100BASE-FX. Figure 2.15 shows these components and their interrelationships.

Media Access Control Layer

The MAC layer is based on the same CSMA/CD protocol as 10Mbps Ethernet. The only difference is that MAC runs 10 times faster. Fast Ethernet retains all of the robustness of the traditional Ethernet protocol. Rather than having to learn an entirely new technology, the customer can rely on past experiences working with 10Mbps, retaining a considerable investment in training, management, troubleshooting, and analysis tools.

Media Independent Interface Layer

The MII provides a transitional sublayer and a common interface between the MAC layer and any one of the three Physical layer specifications. MII can support both 10Mbps and 100Mbps data rates. Because the electrical signals are clearly defined, the MII can be implemented in a network device internally or externally.

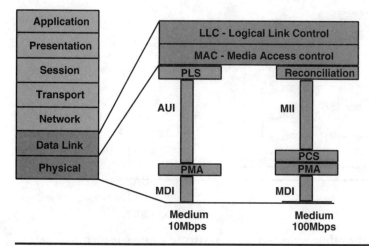

FIGURE 2.15 100Mbps standards model

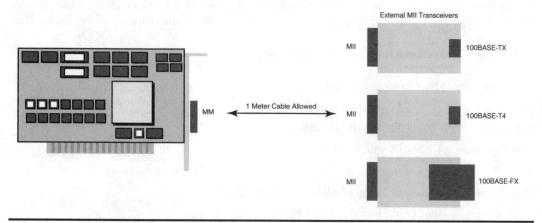

FIGURE 2.16 Media Independent Interface (MII)

The MII can be implemented internally in a network device to connect the MAC layer directly to the Physical layer, which is often the case with network cards. The MII can be implemented externally in a network device via a 40-pin connector. With the MII and the proper transceiver, a repeater can be connected to any STP, UTP, or fiber cable plant installed on the premises—an idea popularized by the AUI connector in 10Mbps Ethernet networks (see Figure 2.16).

100BASE-TX Physical Layer

This physical layer defines the specification for 100BASE-T Ethernet over two pairs of Category 5 UTP (unshielded) or Type 1 STP (shielded) twisted-pair wire (see Figure 2.17). With

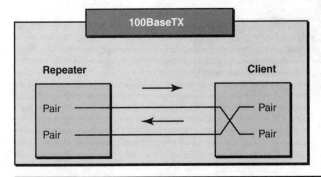

FIGURE 2.17   100BASE-TX

one pair for transmitting and the other for receiving, the wiring scheme is identical to that used for 10BASE-T Ethernet. The UTP connector, an RJ-45, is also identical to the one used for 10BASE-T Ethernet, wired in exactly the same fashion. However, the punch-down blocks in the wiring closet must be Category 5 certified. Where these blocks do not meet the standard, an upgrade is necessary. The STP connector is the same DB-9 used for Token Ring networks.

100BaseTX has the following characteristics:

- Support for 2-pair category 5 wiring
- The same pinout and connectors as 10BaseT
- Optional auto-negotiation (10/100 Mbps)
- Full-duplex capable Physical layer
- 4B/5B, MLT3 signaling scheme
- 125 Mbps on wire/100 Mbps effective data rate
- Maximum copper cable length of 100 meters

100BASE-T4 Physical Layer

This physical layer defines the specification for 100BASE-T Ethernet over four pairs of either Category 3, 4, or 5 UTP wire (see Figure 2.18). With this signaling method, three wire pairs are used for transmit and receive, while the fourth pair listens for collisions. The two additional pairs of bidirectional wires use the four vacant pins on the RJ-45 connector (see Figure 2.18).

100BASE-FX Physical Layer

This physical layer defines the specification for 100BASE-T Ethernet over two strands of 62.5/125-micron fiber cable (see Figure 2.19). One strand is used for transmitting and the

100BASE-T4 Signaling

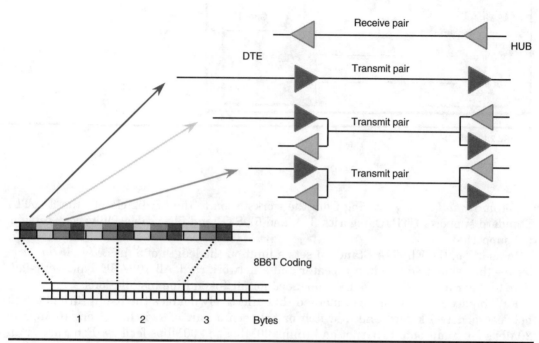

FIGURE 2.18   100BASE-T4

other for receiving. The connectors—ST, MIC, and SC—are the same as those used with other fiber networks. The ST connector is used in 10BASE-F networks; MIC and SC connectors are used in FDDI networks.

100Base FX offers the following features:

- Multimode fiber using SC (preferred), MIC, and ST connectors
- 4B/5B and NRZI signaling scheme
- 125 Mbps on wire/100 Mbps data rate
- Maximum fiber length is 412 meters (half duplex) and 2000 meters (full duplex)

Wiring Standard

Fast Ethernet is designed to run on cable plants that meet the EIA/TIA 568 Commercial Building Telecommunications Wiring Standard. This standard defines the types of cable that may be used, the allowable cable distances, and the manner in which buildings should be wired.

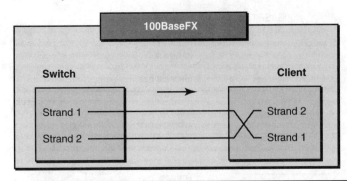

FIGURE 2.19   100BASE-FX

For *horizontal wiring*—wiring from the workstation to the wiring closet—the EIA/TIA Standard supports UTP (Categories 3, 4, and 5), STP, and fiber cables only; coax cable is not supported.

In addition, the EIA/TIA Standard sets a limit on the length of a *twisted-pair link segment*—the cable used to join a repeater and a network card. All 10BASE-T networks adhere to this rule, which also is recommended for all Token Ring installations.

Full duplex is a transmission method that effectively doubles the bandwidth of a link between a network card and a switch or between a pair of switches (from 10Mbps to 20Mbps for traditional Ethernet and from 100Mbps to 200Mbps for Fast Ethernet). Full duplex disables the collision-detection mechanism, so the two devices can transmit and receive concurrently at full wire-speed on each of the transmit and receive paths. A full-duplex segment can use the same Category 5 UTP cable used by both 10BASE-T Ethernet and 100BASE-TX Fast Ethernet. However, 100BASE-T4 wire pairs are not dedicated to sending and receiving data, so full-duplex mode is not supported by this Physical layer signaling method.

Network Diameter

Network diameter—the wire distance between two end stations (two PCs or a PC and a switch, bridge, or router) on the same LAN segment or collision domain—is the primary difference between traditional Ethernet and Fast Ethernet. This physical distance is limited by the maximum round-trip timing delay allowable by the technology and by the type of media being used. Due to its increased speed and adherence to the EIA/TIA 568 wiring rules, the *maximum* diameter of a Fast Ethernet twisted-pair (100BASE-TX or 100BASE-T4) network is 205 meters. By contrast, the *maximum* diameter for an Ethernet twisted-pair (10BASE-T) network is 100 meters.

Repeater Classes

All 10BASE-T repeaters are considered to be functionally identical. Fast Ethernet repeaters, however, are divided into two distinct types: Class I and Class II:

- A Class I repeater has a larger internal delay than a Class II repeater. It is principally used to connect *different* physical media (media conforming to more than one Physical layer specification) to the same collision domain. For example, a Class I repeater could join 100BASE-TX products on two wire pairs with 100BASE-FX products on two strands of fiber. This larger delay is also needed for 100BASE-T4 repeaters and for stackable models. Only one Class I repeater can exist within a single collision domain when maximum cable lengths are used.

- A Class II repeater has a smaller internal delay than a Class I repeater. It typically connects *identical* media to the same collision domain (for example, 100BASE-TX to 100BASE-TX). Two Class II repeaters can exist within a single collision domain when maximum cable lengths are used.

Both Class I and Class II repeaters have multiple *shared ports*—ports on the *same* collision domain.

Ethernet Vendor Addresses

Ethernet hardware addresses are 48 bits, expressed as 12 hexadecimal digits (0−9, plus A−F, capitalized). These 12 hex digits consist of the left six digits that should match the vendor of the Ethernet interface within the station and the right six digits that specify the interface serial number for that interface vendor.

At present, it is not clear how the IEEE assigns Ethernet block addresses: whether in blocks of 2^{24} or 2^{25} or whether multicasts are assigned with that block or separately. A portion of the vendor block address is reportedly assigned serially, with the other portion intentionally assigned randomly. If a global algorithm is used for designating addresses to be physical (in a chipset) versus logical (assigned in software), or globally assigned versus locally assigned addresses, some of the known addresses do not follow the scheme (e.g., AA0003; 02xxxx).

Gigabit Ethernet Architecture

The growing use of Fast Ethernet 100BASE-T connections to Web servers, file servers, LAN Switches and desktops, however, has created a clear need for an even higher-speed network technology at the backbone and server level. Ideally, this technology should also provide a smooth upgrade path, be cost effective and not require retraining (see Figure 2.19a).

The emergence of Gigabit Ethernet will bring more bandwith to internet applications with its Gigabit speed. In short , Gigabit Ethernet employs the same *Carrier Sense Multiple Access with Collision Detection* (CSMA/CD) protocol, same frame format and same frame size as its 10/100 speed predecessors. For the vast majority of network users, this means their existing network investment can be extended to gigabit speeds at reasonable initial cost without the need to re-educate their support staffs and users, and without the need to invest in additional protocol stacks or middleware. The result is low cost of ownership for users.

What is Gigabit Ethernet?

Gigabit Ethernet provides 1 Gbps bandwidth for campus networks with the simplicity of Ethernet at lower cost than other technologies of comparable speed. It offers a natural up-

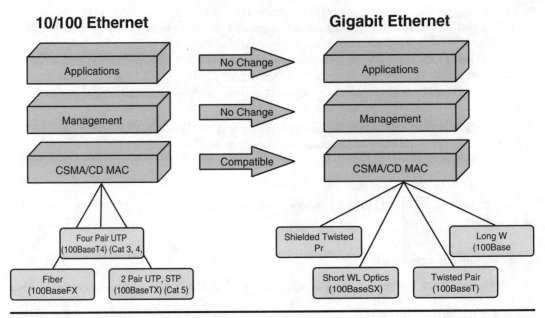

FIGURE 2.19a Gigabit Ethernet

grade path for current Ethernet installations, leveraging existing end stations, management tools and training. Gigabit Ethernet is an extension of the highly successful 10Mbps (10BASE-T) Ethernet and 100Mbps (100BASE-T) Fast Ethernet standards for network connectivity. IEEE has given approval to the Gigabit Ethernet project as the IEEE 802.3z. Gigabit Ethernet is fully compatible with the huge installed base of Ethernet and Fast Ethernet devices. The original Ethernet specification was defined by the frame format and support for *Carrier Sense Multiple Access with Collision Detection* (CSMA/CD) protocol, full duplex, flow control, and management objects as defined by the IEEE 802.3 standard. Gigabit Ethernet employ all of these specifications and more.

Gigabit Ethernet Structure

Gigabit Ethernet specifies technology covering layers 1 and 2 of the OSI model. Gigabit Ethernet implements data link layer functionality by supporting the Ethernet *Media Access Control* (MAC) sublayer. The MAC sublayer transforms data sent by the upper layers of communication, into Ethernet frames and determines how data is scheduled, transmitted, and received. The Gigabit Ethernet MAC is the Ethernet/Fast Ethernet MAC, which ensures backward compatibility between Ethernet/Fast Ethernet and Gigabit Ethernet frames.

Frames are sent or received by the MAC layer through the *Gigabit Media Independent Interface* (GMII) see Figure 2.19b. Because the GMII is designed to enable Gigabit Ethernet MAC devices to hook up in a standard way to any of the physical layers defined by the

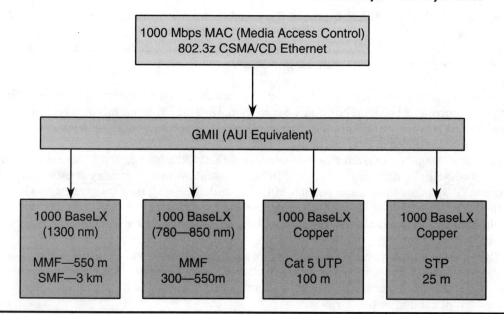

FIGURE 2.19b Cabling support

Table 2.1 **Ethernet Suite of Standards**

Description	Speed Distance	Media
10BASE-T	**10 Mbps 100m**	**Copper**
100BASE-TX	**100Mbps 100m**	**Copper**
100BASE-FX	**100Mbps 2Km**	**Multi-mode Fiber**
1000BASE-LX	**1000 Mbps 5Km** **1000 Mbps 550m**	**Single-mode Fiber** **Multi-mode Fiber**
1000BASE-SX	**1000 Mbps 550m** **1000 Mbps 275m**	**Multi-mode Fiber (50u)** **Multi-mode Fiber** **(62.5 u)**
1000BASE-CX **(not supported by industry products)**	**1000 Mbps 25m**	**Copper**
1000BASE-T	**1000 Mbps 100m**	**Copper**

Gigabit Ethernet standards, the IEEE 802.3ab committee was able to concentrate its effort on designing a physical layer for Gigabit Ethernet over Category 5 copper.

Gigabit Ethernet is a function of technological evolution in response to industry demand. It is an extension of the 10Mbps Ethernet networking standard, 10BASE-T, and the 100Mbps Fast Ethernet standards, 100BASE-TX and 100BASE-FX (Table 2.1). The reasons for the longevity and success of the Ethernet standard are its low cost and ease of implementation.

In June of 1998, the IEEE approved the Gigabit Ethernet standard over fiber (LX and SX) and short-haul copper (CX) as IEEE 802.3z. The fiber implementation was widely supported. With approval of 802.3z, companies could rely on a well-known, standards-based approach to improve traffic flow in congested areas without having to upgrade to a new technology.

Gigabit Ethernet was originally designed as a switched technology, using fiber for uplinks and for connections between buildings. Since then, Gigabit Ethernet has also been used extensively in servers with Gigabit Ethernet network adapters and along backbones to remove traffic bottlenecks in these areas of aggregation.

In June of 1999, the IEEE further standardized IEEE 802.3ab Gigabit Ethernet over copper (1000BASE-T), allowing 1G speeds to be transmitted over Category 5 cable (CAT-5). Since CAT-5 makes up a large portion of the installed cabling base, migrating to Gigabit Ethernet has never been easier. Organizations can now replace network adapters with Gigabit Ethernet and migrate to higher speeds more extensively without having to re-wire the infrastructure.

This is especially important in areas where existing network wiring is difficult to access, such as the utility risers typically located between floors in large office buildings. Without the new standard, future deployment of Gigabit Ethernet might have required costly replacement of cabling in these risers.

However, even with the new standard, existing cabling must meet certain characteristics. Information on how to test existing cabling destined for 1000BASE-T use, including recommended testers and other important considerations, can be found on the Gigabit Ethernet Alliance Web site at hyperlink http://www.Gigabit-ethernet.org/.

It is estimated that only ten percent of existing Category 5 cabling installations will not meet the ANSI/TIA/EIA568-A (1995) standard. These installations would also not support 100BASE-TX Fast Ethernet.

Compatibility and Support

Gigabit Ethernet is fully compatible with the large installed base of Ethernet and Fast Ethernet nodes. It employs all of the same specifications defined by the original Ethernet standard, including:

- CSMA/CD protocol
- Ethernet frame or "packet" format
- Full duplex
- Flow control
- Management objects as defined by the IEEE 802.3 standard

Because it's part of the Ethernet suite of standards, Gigabit Ethernet also supports traffic management techniques that deliver Quality of Service over Ethernet, such as:

- IEEE 802.1p Layer 2 prioritization
- ToS coding bits for Layer 3 prioritization

- Differentiated Services
- *Resource Reservation Protocol* (RSVP)

Gigabit Ethernet can also take advantage of 802.1Q VLAN support, Layer 4 filtering, and Layer 3 switching at Gigabit speeds. In addition, multi-Gigabit speeds can be achieved by trunking several Gigabit switch ports or server adapters together using Link Aggregation-enabled products. Intel server adapters and switches, both Gigabit and Fast Ethernet, support this capability today and will continue to support it in the future with IEEE 802.3ad.

All of these popular Ethernet technologies, which are deployed in a variety of network infrastructure devices, are applicable to Gigabit Ethernet.

Token Ring Architecture

Token Ring is a first and second layer protocol in the *Open Systems Interconnection* (OSI) seven-layer model. Token Ring is a *Local Area Network* (LAN) protocol first developed by IBM (see Figure 2.20). Token Ring is standardized in IEEE 802.5, published in 1985. The protocol deals with the problem of collision, which is defined as a state in which two stations transmit at the same time. To avoid collision, access to the network must be controlled by the use of a permission called token. The token is passed from one station to another according to a set of rules.

The ring consists of ring stations and transmission medium. Data travels sequentially from station to station. Only the station in possession of the token is allowed to transmit data. Each station repeats the data, removes jitter, checks for errors, and copies the data if

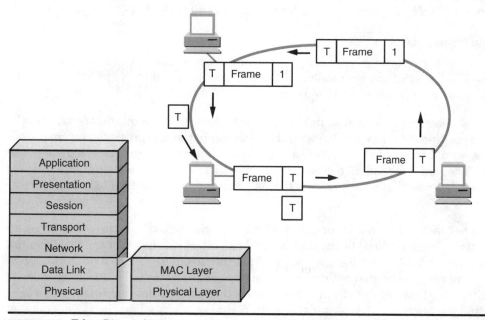

FIGURE 2.20   Token Ring architecture

appropriate. When the data is returned to the sending station, it removes the data from the ring. The Token Ring protocol supports priorities in transmission and is implemented by setting the priority bits in the Token Ring Frame.

The first release of Token Ring was capable of a 4Mbps data transmission rate; the transmission rate was improved later to 16Mbps.

Token Ring Operation

When a station wants to send a frame, it first waits for the token. As soon as it receives the token, the station initiates transmission of the frame, which includes the destination station address at its head. The frame is repeated (received and retransmitted) by each station on the network until it circulates back to the source station, where it is removed. In addition to repeating the frame, the destination station retains a copy of the frame, which is indicated by setting the response bits (Copy Bit plus Address Recognition Bit) at the tail of the frame. A station releases the token in one of two ways depending on the ring rate: with slower rings (4Mbps), the token is released only after the response bits have been received. With higher speed rings (16Mbps), the token is released after transmitting the last bit of the frame (see Figure 2.21).

IEEE 802.5 Details. The current standard for Token Rings, IEEE 802.5-1985, specifies the operation of single-ring networks. However, most implementations of 802.5 have added extensions for multiring networks using source routing of packets at the MAC layer. The MAC header contains one octet of access control, one octet of frame control, 6 octets of source address, 6 octets of destination address, and (for multiring networks) 0−18 octets of *Routing Information Field* (RIF). The MAC trailer contains four octets of FCS, for a total of 18 (10) to 36 (28) octets. One additional octet of frame status is after the FCS.

Token Ring Frame Definitions

Before you can understand exactly how Token Ring operates, you must look at the frame format, because most of the operations on the ring are determined by the settings in the frame or by the type of frame (see Figure 2.22).

***Starting Delimiter* (SD).** This first field of the Token Ring frame indicates the start of the frame. The starting delimiter is filled with the following pattern: represented by ЈКОЈКООО, J and K are nondata symbols and are recognized by the Token Ring card as electrical phase violations. The card will read all 8 bits and note that this is a SD, indicating that a frame is approaching, but not what type it is. This field is static and is always be filled with that pattern.

***Access Control* (AC).** This field contains three bits for priority settings, three bits for reservation settings, one bit called the *monitor bit*, and one bit called the *token bit*. The token bit indicates to the controller whether the arriving frame is a token frame or a data frame. Every token has a priority associated with it, containing values from 0 to 7. These values indicate the priority of the token or data frame. If a station wants to transmit and reads this field as a token, and the priority bits are set higher than its preset priority bits, the station may set the reservation bits to request that the next token be set to its priority.

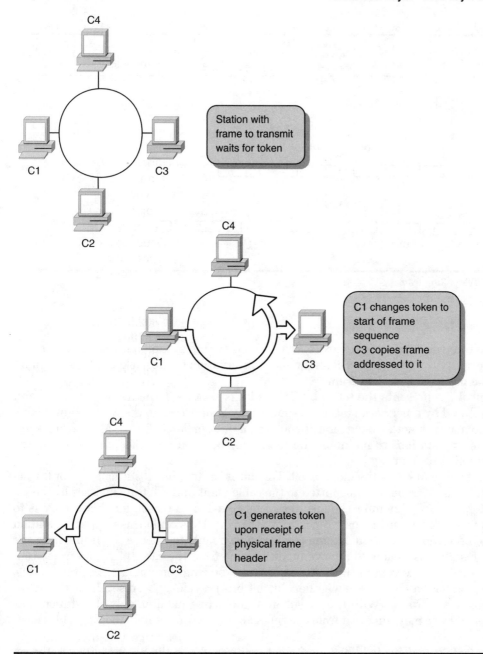

Station with frame to transmit waits for token

C1 changes token to start of frame sequence
C3 copies frame addressed to it

C1 generates token upon receipt of physical frame header

FIGURE 2.21   Token Ring operation

The three bits, RRR, are the reservation bits. These bits are initially set to 0 by any transmitting station. So, when the currently circulating frame is returned to the originating station and a new token is generated, the PPP bits are set to the RRR bits. This is done so that

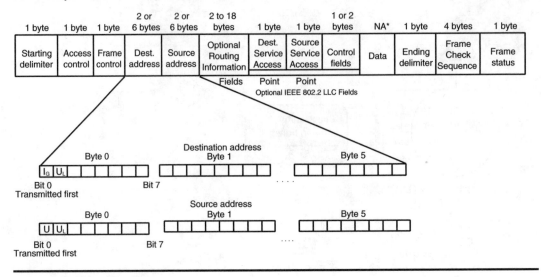

FIGURE 2.22   Token Ring frame

the station can gain access to the next token. If another ring station has reserved an equal or higher priority, the ring station cannot make a reservation in the packet or token; it must wait for the next token or data frame.

The symbol T represents the token bit. If this bit is set to a 0, the frame is a token and may be captured by a network station so that it may gain access to the cable plant. If this bit is set to a 1, it is not a token, and it could be a data or MAC frame. MAC frames are used by the ring stations to maintain the ring. They perform housekeeping chores to ensure the stability of the ring.

The next bit, the M bit, is the monitor bit. This bit is set to 0 by all stations except the active monitor. After a frame is transmitted to the cable plant and the frame passes by the active monitor, the active monitor changes the M bit to a 1. The reason for this change is to disallow a frame to be continuously repeated on the ring. How could this happen? A station may transmit a frame and then become disabled and unable to remove the frame from the cable. If the station is unable to remove its own frame from the cable plant, its frame continuously circulates the ring until timers expire and the ring reinitializes. To prevent this, the active monitor watches to see whether this bit has previously been set. If so, the active monitor aborts the frame. (With the exception of the active monitor, only the station that transmitted a frame may remove it from the ring.) For token frames, only the ED field is next.

Frame Control (**FC**).   This field has the format **FFRRZZZZ**. When the SD field arrives, the receiving controller knows that a frame is arriving, but it does not know what type. This field indicates the type of frame. Only two types of transmission are supported: those of frames containing MAC information (generally used by the servers, discussed at the end of this section) and those containing data.

FC	Description
00	MAC frame
01	Data (LLC data)
11	Reserved

What are the Z bits for? The Z bits further break down this field: if the frame is a MAC frame, the Z bits indicate the type of MAC frame. If the frame is a data frame (LLC frame), the Z bits are ignored. The destination and source address fields are 48 bits (6 bytes) in length. Although the IEEE 802.5 committee does allow for 16-bit address fields, they are not used.

***Destination Address* (DA).**   This field specifies the address of the network station for which the frame is destined.

***Source Address* (SA).**   This field specifies the originator of the frame, which is always a unique address. Because the source address is always unique, the I/G bit takes on a new meaning; it is now called the U bit. The U bit indicates whether source routing is enabled or not. This bit is called the *Routing Information Indicator* (RII).

Information.   This field contains either user data (LLC) or control information (MAC frame information). The information field does exactly what its name implies: it holds information. This information may be data or MAC frame information. The number of bytes in this field is unlimited, unlike the 1,500-byte limit in Ethernet or the 4,472-byte limit for FDDI, although the transmitting station may not transmit longer than it is allowed to hold the token. Given this and the speed of operation (4 or 16Mbps), the maximum frame size for Token Ring is 4,528 for 4 Mbps without a RIF and 4,498 with a maximum RIF of 30 octets and 18,174 octets without a RIF and 18,144 octets with a maximum 30 octet RIF for 16-Mbps operations.

***Frame Check Sequence* (FCS).**   This frame contains the CRC-32 error check performed on the FC, DA, SA, and information fields.

***Ending Delimiter* (ED).**   This field contains special nondata bits and the *intermediate* (I) and *error* (E) bits. The ED has the format JK1JK1IE, which indicates the end of the data or token frame. The J and K are nondata bits, which means that they are special bits that the Token Ring controller recognizes. The only bits that may be changed here are the I and E bits. This E bit is the error bit and may be changed by any station on the network. Every station checks each frame for errors. These errors include FCS errors, illegal frames, or inappropriate nondata symbols. If one is found, this bit is set to a 1. Each station also keeps track of how many times they have set this bit.

The I bit, the intermediate frame bit, indicates whether a frame is the last frame of a multiple-frame sequence or whether more frames are to come. If I=0, this indicates that this frame is the last or maybe the only frame to be transmitted. If I is set to a 1, the receiving station knows that more frames are to follow. This practice originally was set up to allow a network station to transmit more than one frame while holding the token. This bit is not used. Token Ring still allows only one frame to be transmitted by a station, and that station must release the token if the ring speed is 4Mbps.

Frame Status **(FS).**   This frame contains the A and C bits. Because CRC error checking is not accomplished on this field, they are duplicated to ensure their integrity. The r bits are reserved for future use and are automatically set to 0. The A bit represents the address-recognized bit. This bit is initialized to 0 by the transmitting station and is set to a 1 by any station recognizing its address as the destination address or group address (including a broadcast address).

The C bit represents the frame-copied bit. Once again, this bit is initialized to 0 by the transmitting station. This frame is set to a 1 by the station that copies the frame. (The destination station recognized the address as its own.) The frame is copied on the basis of three conditions:

1. The E bit is set to 0.

2. There is no FCS error.

3. The destination address was recognized.

The transmitting station may receive three types of AC fields back:

1. The station does not exist or is not active on the ring (A = 1 and C = 0).

2. The station exists, but the frame was not copied (A = 1 and C = 0).

3. The frame was copied (the A and C bits both equal 1).

Never will the E, A, and C bits be set to a 1 at the same time. For the frame to be copied, the E bit must be set to a 0. Now that you have a complete understanding of the Token Ring frame, you should find it easier to understand exactly how Token Ring transmits, repeats, and copies data on the network. In undergoing each process mentioned, certain bits are changed. A Token Ring controller performs three basic functions: frame transmission, frame reception, and normal repeat mode.

Three basic types of frames traverse a Token Ring network: the token frame, the data packet, and a special management frame called the MAC frame. Let's explain the individual fields (see Figure 2.23).

Token Format

The token is the shortest frame transmitted, 24 bits (see Figure 2.24). The *Most Significant Bit* (MSB) is always transmitted first—unlike Ethernet.

Token Ring.

SD = Starting Delimiter (1 Octet)

AC = Access Control (1 Octet)

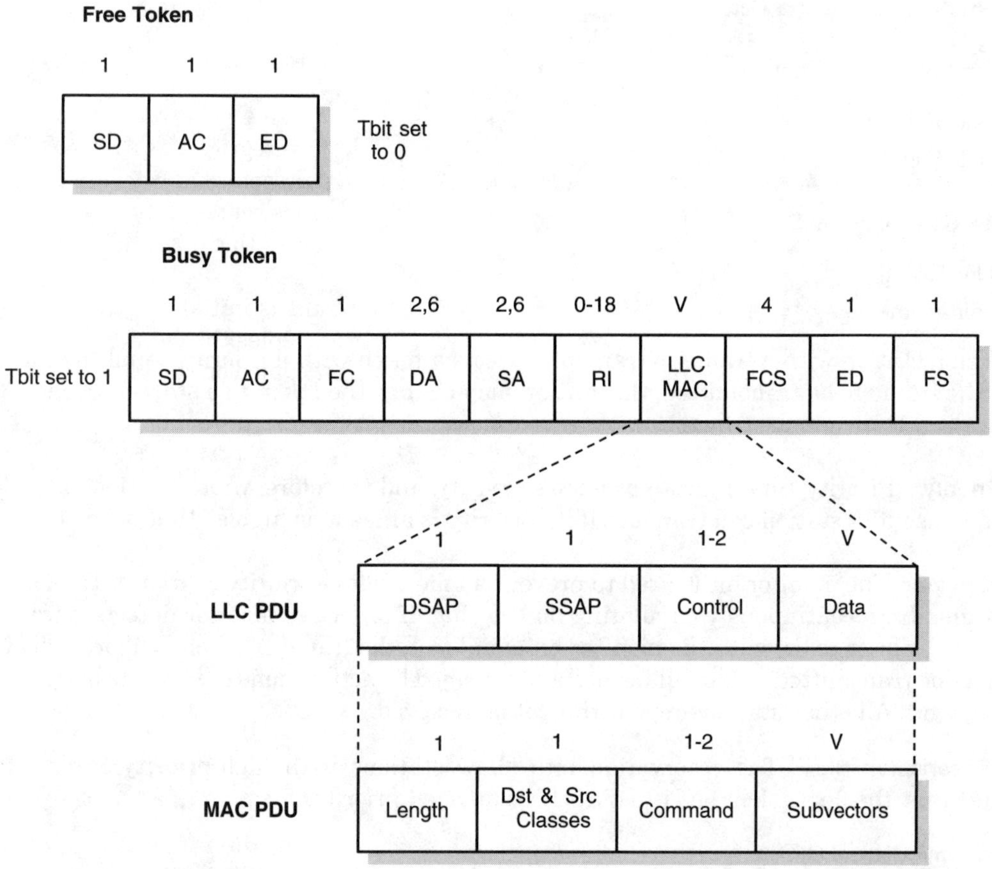

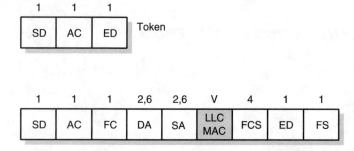

FIGURE 2.23   Token Ring frame header

Token Ring

FIGURE 2.24   Token frame

ED = Ending Delimiter (1 Octet)

Starting Delimiter Format.

J = Code Violation
K = Code Violation

Access Control Format.

T = 0 for Token
T = 1 for Frame

When a station with a frame to transmit detects a token with a priority equal to or less than the frame to be transmitted, the station may change the token to a start-of-frame sequence and transmit the frame.

P = Priority.   Priority Bits indicate a token's priority, and therefore, which stations are allowed to use it. A station can transmit if its priority is at least as high as that of the token.

M = Monitor.   The monitor bit is used to prevent a token whose priority is greater than 0 or any frame from continuously circulating on the ring. If an active monitor detects a frame or a high-priority token with the monitor bit equal to 1, the frame or token is aborted. This bit shall be transmitted as 0 in all frames and tokens. The active monitor inspects and modifies this bit. All other stations repeat this bit as received.

R = Reservation Bits.   The reservation bits allow stations with high-priority frames to request that the next token be issued at the requested priority:

FC = Frame Control (1 Octet)

Ending Delimiter Format.

J = Code Violation
K = Code Violation
I = Intermediate Frame Bit
E = Error Detected Bit

Frame Format.   MSB is always transmitted first—unlike Ethernet.

SD = Starting Delimiter (1 Octet)
J = Code Violation
K = Code Violation
AC = Access Control (1 Octet)
T = 0 for Token
T = 1 for Frame

Token Ring Addressing

Each transmitted frame on a Token Ring network has a Destination Address and Source Address, whose purposes are to identify the receiving and sending stations, respectively. In a multiple-ring environment in which two or more rings are connected by bridges, the destination addresses for frames originating in one ring station, and directed to one or more ring stations on other rings, can be created using a source-routing technique. The route is determined at session connection time when an initiating ring starts the process of collecting routing information to be included in subsequent frames. This method eliminates the need to maintain routing tables at predefined nodes on the ring.

The Token Ring network associates a ring station, or a group of ring stations, with a unique MAC sublayer address, which enables any ring station to attach to the Token Ring network. In the Token Ring environment, address types include the following:

- *Individual Address.* Identifies a specific ring station on the network.

- *Group Address.* Identifies a group of destination ring stations on the network.

- *Null Address.* An address of all 0s, which is not addressed to any ring station.

- *All-Stations Broadcast Address.* The frame is sent to all stations on a given ring or interconnected ring.

- *Functional Address.* Can be a number of functional addresses defined by the IBM Token Ring architecture (see Table 2.2).

    DA = Destination Address (2 or 6 Octets)

    SA = Source Address (2 or 6 Octets)

Group Addresses. A group address is assigned by the station, which sets bit 0 of byte 2 to 1 as shown in Figure 2.25.

TABLE 2.2 **Functional Addresses**

Function	Hex representation bytes 0, 1, 2	Hex representation bytes 3, 4, 5
Active monitor	C00000	000001
Ring parameter server	C00000	000002
Ring error monitor	C00000	000008
Configuration report server	C00000	000010
NetBIOS	C00000	000080
Bridge	C00000	00100
LAN manager	C00000	002000
User-defined	C00000	008000–C00040000000

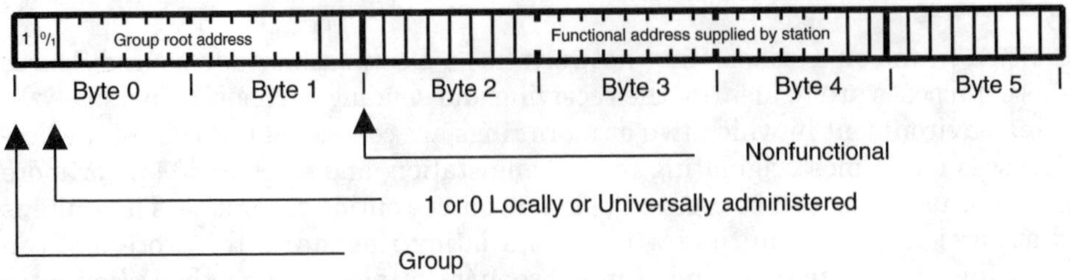

FIGURE 2.25   Group address

The presence of a *Routing Information Field* (RIF) is indicated by the MSB of the source address, called the *Routing Information Indicator* (RII). If the RII equals 0, a RIF is not present. If the RII equals 1, the RIF is present. Although the RII is indicated in the source address, it is not part of a station's MAC layer address. In particular, the MSB of a destination address is the individual/group address indicator. If the MSB is set, it will cause such frames to be interpreted as multicasts. Implementations should be careful to reset the RII to 0 before passing source addresses to other protocol layers that may be confused by their presence.

The RIF consists of a two-octet *Routing Control* (RC) field followed by 0 to 8 two-octet *Route Designator* (RD) fields (see Figure 2.26). The RC for all-routes broadcast frames is formatted as follows:

B—Broadcast Indicators: 3 Bits

The Broadcast Indicators are used to indicate the routing desired for a particular frame. A frame may be routed through a single specified route, through every distinct nonrepeating route in a multiring network, or through a single route determined by a spanning tree algorithm such that the frame appears on every ring exactly once. The values that may be used at this time are (in binary):

000—Nonbroadcast (specific route)

10x—All-routes broadcast (global broadcast)

11x—Single-route broadcast (limited broadcast)

All other values are reserved for future use.

LTH—Length: 5 Bits

The Length bits are used to indicate the length or the RI field, including the RC and RD fields. Only even values between 2 and 30 inclusive are allowed.

D—Direction Bit: 1 Bit

The D bit specifies the order of the RD fields. If D equals 1, the routing-designator fields are specified in reverse order (if d=0 left to right, if d=1 right to left).

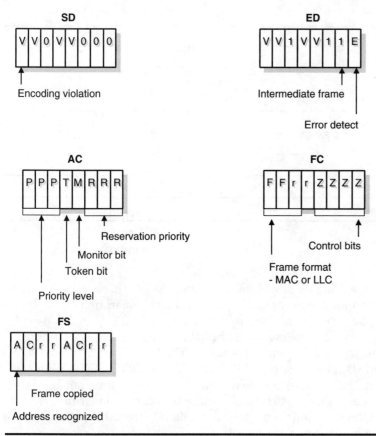

FIGURE 2.26   Token Ring route control field

LF—Largest Frame: 3 Bits

The LF bits specify the maximum MTU supported by all bridges along a specific route. All multiring broadcast frames should be transmitted with a value at least as large as the supported MTU. The values used are LF (binary), MAC MTU, and IP MTU (see Table 2.3).

The receiver should compare the LF received with the MTU. If the LF is greater than or equal to the MTU, then no action is taken; however, if the LF is less than the MTU, the frame is rejected.

Three possible actions are possible if LF < MTU. First is the one required for this specification—reject the frame. Second is to reduce the MTU for all hosts to equal the LF. Third is to keep a separate MTU per communicating host based on the received LFs.

r—Reserved: 4 Bits

These bits are reserved for future use and must be set to 0 by the transmitter and ignored by the receiver.

TABLE 2.3 Largest Frame Bits

Code	Description
000	Up to 516 bytes
001	Up to 1,470 bytes
010	Up to 2,052 bytes
011	Up to 4,472 bytes
100	Up to 8,144 bytes
101	Up to 11,407 bytes
110	Up to 17,800 bytes
111	Initial value of broadcast frames

Token Ring Functions

In Token Ring there is still one cable plant and multiple stations needing access to this cable plant, but only one station may occupy the ring at a time. The operation of the Token Ring access method is completely different from that of the CSMA/CD algorithm used for Ethernet. On a Token Ring network, a formatted 24-bit (three-byte) frame, is continuously transmitted on the ring. This frame is known as the token. The frame contains three eight-bit fields: *starting delimiter* (SD), *access control* (AC), and *ending delimiter* (ED). With a few exceptions, any station that has received this token and has data to transmit may then transmit onto the ring (the cable plant). A station needing to transmit must first capture the token, which takes it off the ring, and then transmit its data to the cable plant. Because no token is on the ring, all other stations must wait.

Using this procedure eliminates the possibility of two stations being able to transmit at the same time. There are no collisions using Token Ring. When the station has received its original transmission, it takes that frame off the ring, builds a new token, and releases it to the network.

Token Ring Initialization

Let's consider a new Token Ring network as an example. Currently, no active stations are on the ring. When power is applied to the Token Ring controller, it begins a five-phase initialization routine. Any one error in this process disables the controller from entering onto the ring. The five-phase initialization procedure is detailed as follows:

- *Phase 0* is a lobe test in which the controller board submits frames to the cable attached to it and waits to see whether it receives frames back. The controller does not insert itself onto the ring (flip the relay in the MAU). The cable is looped back at the MAU, and any frame transmitted is immediately returned in the same format as the transmission.

- In *phase 1*, the controller produces the signal necessary (the phantom voltage) to flip the relay in the MAU to insert itself onto the ring. Flipping the relay causes an interruption on the ring due to electrical noise. This interruption causes an error on the ring in which the token or any transmitting station's data is lost. This error happens when any station inserts itself onto the ring during a transmission. A special station on the ring known as the active monitor recovers the ring from this error and puts a new token on the ring. When this is accomplished, the controller waits for special frames that it knows must be present on the ring. When these frames are found, it knows that the ring is active. If none of these frames are found on the ring, the controller assumes that it is the first station on the ring, inserts the frames, and waits for them to return.

- In *phase 2*, the controller board transmits one or two frames with the source and destination address set to its address. This *duplicate address test* is used to check whether any other controller has its address. If the frame returns with the *address recognized* bit set in the frame, the controller removes itself from the ring.

- In *phase 3*, the controller tries to find its neighbor by waiting for certain control frames to pass by. The controller also identifies itself to its downstream neighbor. In a ring environment, each active station repeats received signals to the next repeater on the ring. With this, a network station identifies who is downstream from it. Likewise, the new station is identified to its upstream neighbor, for it repeats data to it. Keeping track of the downstream neighbor is an important network management facility for Token Ring. As stations are added to and deleted from the ring, any station can report this occurrence to the network management on the ring.

- In *phase 4*, the controller requests its initialization parameters from a station on the network known as the *Ring Parameter Server* (RPS) using functional address c00000000002. The RPS resides on each ring and sends initialization information to new stations attaching to the ring. The RPS ensures that stations on the ring have consistent values for operational parameters. In this request frame to the RPS is registration information from the newly attached station. This information is the individual address of the ring station's *next available upstream neighbor* (NAUN), the product instance ID of the attached product, and the ring station's microcode level. The RPS parameters are the ring number of the attached ring, etc. If no server is present, the initializing controller uses its default parameters.

Providing no errors occurred during this initialization process, the network station is now active on the ring and may transmit and receive data as shown in the following paragraphs. Even after initialization, the controller has the capability to take itself off of the ring if too many errors occur.

Starting the Ring: The Token Claim Process

With a new ring, no token is on the ring, and a new one must be inserted, which is the responsibility of the active monitor. The token claim process is how the ring station elects an active monitor.

When inserting into the ring, if a ring station does not detect the presence of a AMP frame, it will assume the role of the active monitor.

```
MAC:   —-- MAC data —--
MAC:
MAC:   MAC Command: Active Monitor Present
```

```
MAC:    Source: Ring station, Destination: Ring station
MAC:    Subvector type: Physical Drop Number 00000000
MAC:    Subvector type: Upstream Neighbor Address 006097A49E41, SERVER1<20>
MAC:
```

When a ring station detects the loss of the AM, the station enters into the token claim process in which it inserts its master clock. (Only one clock is on a Token Ring, and it transmits special frames called MAC frames to the ring at specified intervals.) Other stations on the ring can be classified as participants or nonparticipants. If they are nonparticipants, they repeat the token claim MAC frame. Other stations participating in this process receive and process the token claim MAC frame.

A participating station with a higher address than the received token claim frame does not repeat that frame. Instead, it inserts its own clock and transmits its own token claim MAC frame. Every other participant invokes this same process. Eventually, the network controller that has the highest address (MAC address) on the ring controls the ring. Each station transmitting their own token claim frames notices the frame with the higher address than theirs, and those stations pull their clock from the ring and repeat the token claim frame that has the higher address. Eventually, the station with the highest address receives three of its own token claim MAC frames back and assumes that it has control. Then it becomes the active monitor, inserts a new token on the ring, and controls the clocking of the ring. The ring is now operational for stations to transmit and receive (see Figure 2.27).

Operation

Basically, a Token Ring controller may be in one of three states: repeat mode, transmit mode, or copy mode. When a Token Ring controller does not contain any data that needs to be transmitted on the network, the controller stays in a mode known as the normal repeat mode. Remember that a ring topology is a closed loop, with each repeater repeating the signals to its downstream neighbor. This arrangement allows the controller to repeat any signals to the next active station on the network.

Normal Repeat Mode

A Token Ring controller normally operates in Repeat mode. When a station does not have any data to transmit, it acts as a repeater on the network, which does not relieve the station from some responsibility. In normal Repeat mode, a station checks the data in the tokens and frames it has received and sets either the error-detected bit, the address-recognized bits (for special types of MAC frames), or the frame-copied bits as appropriate. Remember that every station checks every frame for errors. If any station detects an error in any frame, it sets the error-detected bit as it repeats the frame. If the error bit is set and the frame has not yet traveled to the destination station, the frame is not copied by the destination station.

In normal Repeat mode, a station checks only the data in the tokens and frames it receives and sets the appropriate A, C, and E (address-recognized, frame-copied, and signal error-detected) bits as it repeats the token or frame.

Two key points should be remembered:

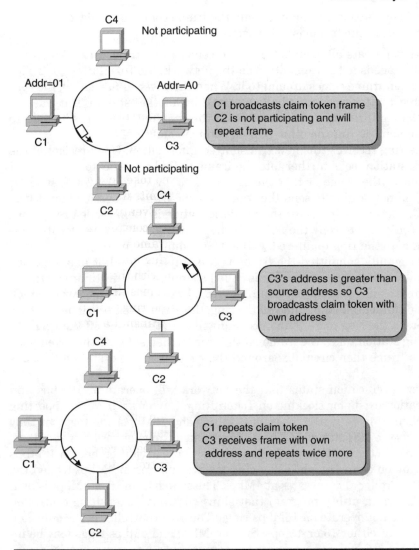

FIGURE 2.27 Neighbor notification

- First, only when a station receives the token may it transmit data onto the ring. Because of this trait, Token Ring is said to be *deterministic*. Two stations can never transmit onto the ring at the same time in the 4Mbps nonearly-release program Token Ring standard. When one station possesses the token, it may hold onto it for only a certain length of time; then it must release the token. Otherwise, other stations might assume that the token is lost and start error-recovery procedures prematurely.

- Second, the destination station copies the frame into its receive buffer as it repeats the frame onto the network. The destination more or less takes a snapshot of the frame as it is being repeated. The destination changes only the frame-copied and address-recognized bits. The rest of the frame is left intact.

This is the mode that repeats all signals from its receiver to its transmitter. When the controller has data that needs to be transmitted on the network, the Token Ring controller must wait until the token frame comes around to it. When the token is presented, the controller makes sure that the token has not been reserved by another station. If it was not reserved, the controller captures the token (takes it off the ring) and transmits its data to the ring. With no token on the ring, no other station can transmit.

Each station on the ring receives this new transmitted information. Upon receipt of the SD field, the network station looks further into the frame to find an indicator saying that the receiving station sent the frame or that the station should receive the frame itself. If the network station did not originally send the frame but the frame is destined for it (the destination address in the frame indicates the network station is the intended recipient), the network station continues to copy the frame. If the frame is not destined for it, it repeats the frame back onto the ring unaltered, without continuing to copy.

The station that originally submitted the frame is the only station that may take the frame off the ring, unless an error occurs. This is called *stripping*. The destination station merely copies the frame as it repeats it back onto the ring. In the case of an error in which the originating station cannot take the frame off the ring, the active monitor will notice that this frame has traversed the ring more than once and will take the frame off the ring.

After the originating station takes the frame off the ring, it then submits the token back to the ring. The token frame then circulates around the ring for the next station that has data to transmit.

While the Ethernet specification states that the network will operate at 10Mbps and 100Mbps, no specification exists for clocking on Token Ring. Currently, IBM is supporting two speeds for its Token Ring networks. These are 4Mbps and 16Mbps, and together they are commonly known as the 16/4 standard. The original Token Ring network ran at 4Mbps. In 1989, IBM began to ship the 16Mbps controllers. Some words of caution here: a 16Mbps station does not operate on a ring in which the stations are running at 4Mbps (called the *ring speed*). The 16/4 controller also operates at 4Mbps. The switch from 16 or 4Mbps is usually software-selectable via a utility program that ships with any Token Ring controller. Four-Mbps controllers do not operate on 16Mbps rings. The 16/4 controller is the only controller that may operate at either 16 or 4Mbps. Sixteen-Mbps and 4Mbps rings may be intermixed (separated by individual rings running the same speeds) through a special device known as a bridge, LAN switch, or a router.

Frame Transmission

When a controller does receive the token, the following procedure is invoked: the controller changes one bit in the access control field (the T bit) from a 0 to a 1, which changes the status of the token. It now is a *data frame*. A Token Ring controller assumes that it has received the token when it receives a starting delimiter followed by an access control field with no code violations (J or K bits) in the priority bits and when the bit that represents the token in the AC field is set to a 0. By changing this one bit, the token has become the header of a data or MAC frame, indicating to all other stations that this frame is now a data or MAC frame and not a token frame.

The controller then checks the token's priority bits. Two possibilities are presented: one, if the priority is equal to or less than the station's priority, the station initiates the transmit data sequence; two, if the priority is higher than the station's priority, the station sets the reservation bits, and the controller waits for another token.

If the single-token method has been chosen, the station must wait for the return of its frame. If the station is finished transmitting the frame and has not yet received the frame back, the station needs to start transmitting idle characters after transmission of a frame. This practice is transmitting a frame shorter than the total ring length. Although you might think you could just add up the total amount of cable and come up with the ring length, this is not true. If a station is not powered on, that particular station is not active on the network. If it is not active on the network, the token or data frame does not travel on the cable that attaches the inactive station to the MAU, which shortens the traveling time of a frame and shortens the ring length. Hence, the ring length is variable.

Returning to the transmission of the frame, if the controller enters the transmit mode, the station finds the SD and AC fields and changes the T bit to a 1. The station then waits for the ED field. Remember, the station does not read the token into a buffer. As the bits of each frame enter the station, each bit is repeated back onto the cable plant. If the station changes any bit in any field, that bit is automatically transmitted (repeated) back onto the cable. A very serious error can occur if the station does not receive the ED field immediately after the AC field and if it has already changed the T bit in the AC field to a 1. In such a case, the controller knows that it has incorrectly interpreted the frame as a token frame and immediately builds an abort frame and transmits it. The station then returns and waits for the next token.

If the controller does find the ED field, it then transmits the rest of its frame. This includes (in order): the destination and source address field, the optional routing information field (discussed in Chapter 4), the information (data) field, the frame check sequence field, the ending delimiter, and the frame status field.

When the transmitted frame returns to the controller, the controller compares the returned source address with its source address. If the two match (regardless of whether or not the early token release option is selected and the token has not been released), the station transmits a token of the appropriate priority followed by idles. When all this is accomplished, the controller returns to the normal repeat mode.

Frame Reception

When the frame reaches its destination station (as determined by the destination address), the destination station copies the frame into its buffer and sets the copy and address-recognized bits (or if an error is detected, the error-detected bit) while replacing the whole frame back on the ring. This process is known as *copying while repeating*. The normal checks are performed on the received frame (such as the CRC check, the minimum length check, and so on).

Early Token Release

The last point to cover with Token Ring is the early-release program. To allow greater use of the bandwidth of the Token Ring architecture, a new algorithm is involved in the early-release program. This algorithm is very simple. A station is allowed to transmit a token even without having received its original frame back. The station releases the token after transmitting the ending delimiter. If the header of the original frame has not been received, it releases the token with the reservation and priority bits set the same as when the controller received the original token enabling it to transmit (see Figure 2.28).

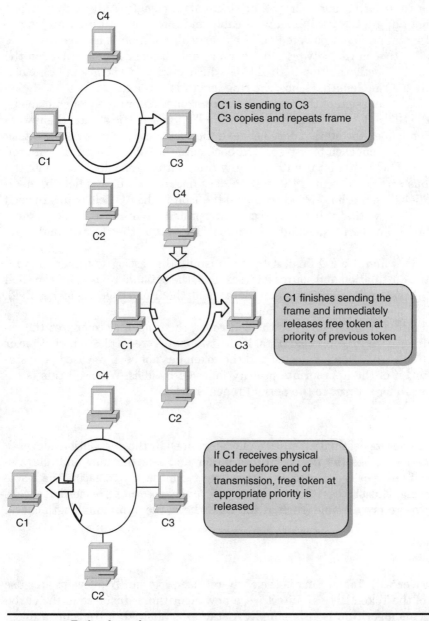

FIGURE 2.28   Early token release

Why implement the early-release program when even with the 24 bits of the token traveling the ring alone (which is the smallest frame that ever travels the ring), it would take a tremendous amount of cable to introduce a sufficiently long delay for the whole token to be transmitted? The primary answer is the efficient use of the available bandwidth. There is no reason to allow stations to remain idle on the network when the possibility exists for more than one controller to transmit on the cable without interference. The early-release program is now an option on 16Mbps Token Ring controller boards.

Fault Isolation and Software Error Reporting

We now introduce some of the common types of errors encountered in a Token ring network. *Soft errors* are intermittent faults that temporarily disrupt normal operation of the LAN. These types of errors, normally tolerated by the error-recovery procedures, include bad CRC checks, timeouts in received or repeated frames, and a ring station's inability to process received frames. The Report Soft Error MAC frame reports the number of errors detected since the last report was made. The information reported in this frame identifies the transmitting ring station's NAUN and includes all the errors and their values. This information is received and processed by the ring error monitor.

Hard errors are more serious. Hard errors are permanent faults, usually in equipment, and they cause a ring to completely stop functioning. A ring station downstream from the hard fault recognizes a hard error at the receive side of its attachment. The ring tries to bypass the error and restores the ring to operational status. Hard errors are generally recognized by the receiver logic. An example of a hard error is the loss of a signal or the inability to recover the token through normal procedures.

During the occurrence of the hard error, the ring tries to recover by initiating the token claim process. When this process does not work, the ring station transmits *beacon* MAC frames set to an all-stations address on its ring only. The transmission of these frames continues until the ring recovers or that ring station has removed itself from the ring.

Inside the beacon frame is the ring station's NAUN and the type of error detected. When the beaconing station's NAUN has copied eight of these frames, that NAUN removes itself from the ring and perform tests on itself and its lobe using the *Lobe Media test* and the *Duplicate Address test* MAC frame. If these tests are successful, the NAUN reattaches to the ring without going through the normal attachment process. If the test fails, the NAUN stays off of the ring.

If the ring still does not recover, the beaconing station assumes that its NAUN has completed its tests. The beaconing station then removes itself from the ring and performs the Lobe Media and Duplicate Address tests. If these tests are successful, the beaconing station reattaches to the ring without going through the normal attachment process. If these tests fail, it does not reattach to the ring. If after all this the ring still fails, the network administrator for the LAN must manually try to find the source of the error.

Lost or duplicate tokens do not present a problem for Token Ring. If the active monitor does not see the token for a specified period of time, it issues a new token. A duplicate token (nonearly-release program) is a little more serious. One algorithm is that when a station sends a frame and the frame returns, the station must check to make sure that the source address is its own. If not, the station aborts its current frame and does not issue a new token. Because it is presumed that both stations perform the same activity, the token eventually is lost.

Token Ring Monitors: Maintaining the Ring

Token Ring has a tremendous quantity of built-in management techniques that constantly monitor the controller and the ring. The most important component of any Token Ring network is the active monitor (see Figure 2.29 and Table 2.4). One station on each ring is assigned the duties of the active monitor, which provides token monitoring among other things. This responsibility may be assigned to any active station on the ring. All other stations on the ring act as standby monitors. One standby monitor becomes the active monitor in the event that the present active monitor fails. These active players in a Token Ring network cannot be detected without the use of a specialized protocol analyzer attached to the ring.

The active monitor resolves certain error conditions that may occur on the ring, such as lost tokens and frames; priority tokens that circle the ring more than once; two active monitors present on the same physical ring; and clocking errors. With the Ethernet specification, a preamble bit pattern is transmitted before each frame is sent to allow all receivers to synchronize their receivers to the incoming signal. Token Ring takes a different approach: the active monitor provides the ring's master clock, which ensures that all other stations on the ring are synchronized.

Table 2.4   Active Monitor Trace announcement

```
MAC:   —- MAC data —-
MAC:
MAC:   MAC Command: Active Monitor Present
MAC:   Source: Ring station, Destination: Ring station
MAC:   Subvector type: Physical Drop Number 97A49E41
MAC:   Subvector type: Upstream Neighbor Address NGC    30341D, This Sniffer
MAC:
```

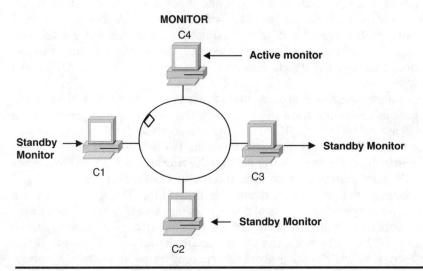

FIGURE 2.29   Active monitor

The active monitor introduces a 24-bit delay to the ring by holding the token for 24-bit times in the buffer and then repeating the bits received. This station is the only one to buffer anything on a Token Ring network. All other stations on the network repeat each bit as it is received, which ensures that all stations can transmit the full token before receiving it back. This is very important, for each station must be able to check the reservation bits to transmit a new token with the appropriate priority.

If you look at the Token Ring frame field formats, you notice a monitor bit in the *access control* (AC) field. This bit is used to detect whether a frame is continually circulating the ring. The possibility can arise for a station to transmit a frame and then be incapable of removing the frame from the ring. (Remember, the only station that may remove a frame from the ring, with the exception of the active monitor, is the station that originated the frame.) The active monitor sets this bit to a 1, and if it sees this frame again with the monitor bit set, the active monitor purges the ring and transmits a new token.

Another function of the active monitor is to detect a lost frame and/or token. The active monitor establishes a predetermined time that it knows is the longest possible time for a token to travel the full path of the ring. (This timer is dynamic, because the physical cable plant may change at any time.) The active monitor starts this timer countdown each time it transmits a starting delimiter. If this timer expires, the active monitor assumes that the token is lost. The active monitor then purges the ring and initiates a new token.

How would the token become lost? In the simplest case, a token may become lost by a user shutting down a PC. In doing this, the MAU loses its phantom voltage, which is needed to keep the relay open for the token to travel the path from the MAU to the individual station. The token is lost because of the relay closing in the MAU. The timer then expires, and the active monitor purges the ring and initiates a new token.

In purging the ring, the active monitor broadcasts a certain type of frame, called the *ring-purge MAC frame*, to all active stations on the network. If the active monitor can receive this frame, it indicates to the active monitor that a frame can travel the ring safely.

Active Monitor Functions.   The role of the active monitor is to ensure normal token operation on the ring. An adapter becomes the active monitor by active participation in the monitor process. The adapter that wins contention becomes the active monitor.

Upon successfully winning contention, the active monitor does the following:

- Provides master clocking for data transmission
- Inserts a 24-bit time latency to guarantee a ring length, which ensures that a token can be circulated properly
- Activates the circulating token removal hardware. The circulating token removal function operates as follows:
  1. When tokens are released on the ring, bit 4 of the AC byte (the MC bit) is transmitted as 0.
  2. When a Token Ring chipset changes the token into a frame, it leaves the MC bit as 0. The chipset indicates a frame by setting only bit 3 of AC (the TI bit) to one.
  3. When a frame or a token of priority greater than 0 passes through the active monitor (which is in repeat mode), the monitor sets the MC bit.

4. The transmitting adapter should strip its frame or token off the ring and release a free token with the MC bit equal to 0. If it does not, the frame or priority token passes into the active monitor for the second time.

5. When a frame or priority token comes into the monitor with its MC bit equal to one, the monitor hardware does not repeat it back onto the ring. The active monitor then increments its token error counter and purges the ring.

- Executes the ring purge process.

- Starts the ring poll process by activating an internal pacing timer and queues an *active monitor present* (AMP) MAC frame for transmission.

- Transmits a free token of priority equal to the token reservation priority in the ring purge MAC frame for transmission.

- Sets the monitor functional address.

- Activates a checking function that confirms that a good token is detected on the ring every 10ms. This timer sets the maximum frame size on the order of 4,048 bytes for a 4Mbps ring and 17,800 bytes on a 16Mbps ring.

- Queues a report new monitor MAC frame for transmission to the network manager.

When an event occurs that requires an action by the active monitor, the active monitor does the following:

- When the active monitor detects a token error (either a circulating frame or priority token) or fails to detect a good token during a 10ms period, the active monitor starts the ring-purge process to recover the ring back to normal token protocols.

- When an internal 7-second timer expires, the active monitor starts the ring-poll process.

Active Monitor Exception Conditions.   The following exception conditions cause the station to deactivate the active monitor function and to take the corresponding action:

- *Receive Ring Purge.*   If the active monitor receives a ring-purge MAC frame from an address not its own, the Token Ring chipset resets the active monitor and queues a report monitor error MAC frame for transmission with an error code subvector indicating that a duplicate monitor has been detected. The Token Ring chipset starts the standby monitor functions.

- *Receive AMP.*   If the active monitor receives an AMP MAC frame that it did not transmit, the Token Ring chipset resets the active monitor function and queues a report monitor error MAC frame with an error code subvector value indicating that a duplicate monitor has been detected. The adapter starts the standby monitor functions.

- *Receive Claim Token.*   The TMS380 Token Ring chipset queues a report monitor error MAC frame for transmission with an error code subvector indicating that a standby monitor detected an error in the active monitor, and the monitor contention process is entered in contention repeat mode. This adapter does not actively participate in the contention process by entering contention repeat mode.

- *Receive Beacon.* If the adapter is inserted, the adapter enters the beacon process in beacon repeat mode. If the adapter is in the insertion process, the OPEN command is terminated with an error.

- *Signal Loss.* The adapter enters the monitor contention process in contention transmit mode.

- *Wire Fault.* If a wire fault condition is detected, the adapter deinserts from the ring and sets the lobe wire fault bit in ring status.

Any station that believes it is the active monitor and receives a ring-purge frame automatically becomes a standby monitor on the ring as shown in Figure 2.30. The standby monitor performs two basic functions on the network: it detects failures of the active monitor, and it detects any disruptions that may occur on the ring.

A standby monitor waits for a predetermined amount of time for the *active monitor present* frame that is sent out from the current active monitor on the ring. If any standby monitor on the ring does not receive this frame within the allotted time limit, it assumes that the active monitor is not present on the ring and tries to become the active monitor by continuously transmitting a claim-token MAC frame:

1. It receives another claim-token MAC frame, and the source address of that frame is higher than its own address.

2. It receives a beacon MAC frame. A beacon MAC frame is transmitted in the case of a major ring failure such as a cable break or a disabled or jabbering station.

3. It receives *a purge* MAC frame. The active monitor sends a purge MAC frame after ring initialization or when another station has won the token-claim process. A new token then is placed on the ring.

One final MAC frame is the *Duplicate Address test* (DAT) MAC frame. This frame is transmitted as part of a Token Ring card's initialization process, phase 3. The station sends this DAT frame with its own address in the destination address field. If the frame returns with the A (address recognized) bit set, the new station knows that its physical address is already being used on the network. The station then notifies the network manager and deinserts itself from the network.

Duplicate Address Test Frame

```
DLC:   --- DLC Header ---
DLC:
DLC:   Frame 49 arrived at   20:10:51.078; frame size is 18 (0012 hex) bytes.
DLC:   FS: Addr recognized indicators: 00, Frame copied indicators: 00
DLC:   AC: Frame priority 0,  Reservation priority 0,  Monitor count 0
DLC:   FC: MAC frame,  PCF attention code: Express buffer
DLC:   Destination = Station 00A0248AD164, C_HOSTTR<20>
DLC:   Source      = Station 00A0248AD164, C_HOSTTR<20>
DLC:
```

The following provides a summary of the functions provided by the servers on a Token Ring. The IBM LAN Network Manager is a PC application that communicates optionally with TME10, IBM's host-based network management product. The LAN Manager allows a network administrator to manage multisegmented IBM Token Ring networks and provides facilities for managing the LAN media and LAN adapters in the network and for managing the bridges that interconnect the networks.

Ring Error Monitor.   The ring-error monitor observes, collects, and analyzes hard-error and soft-error reports sent by ring stations and assists in fault isolation and correction.

Configuration Reports Server.   The configuration report server accepts commands from the LAN Network Manager (a special program obtainable through IBM) to get station information, set station parameters, and remove stations on its ring.

LAN Bridge Server.   The LAN Bridge server keeps statistical information about frames forwarded through a bridge and provides bridge reconfiguration capabilities.

Token Ring Error Codes and Management Capabilities.   Token Ring error-detection capabilities are very extensive and are probably the reason that Token Ring NIC cards are more expensive than Ethernet. These error codes provide extensive management capabilities that assist the network administrator in isolating and detecting problems that Ethernet doesn't address.

Beacon.   The beacon process is used to recover the ring when any attaching ring station has sensed that the ring is inoperable due to a hard error. If necessary, the adapter withdraws itself from the ring (see Figure 2.30).

Hardware Error.   The hardware error process is used to detect when a wire fault, frequency error, or ring signal loss has occurred.

Soft Error Counting.   This process logs and reports an error condition that temporarily degrades system performance but which can be tolerated if error-recovery procedures of higher protocols are used (see Table 2.5).

Ring Error Monitor (REM).   A ring error monitor serves as a collection point of error reports for network management. The REM does not have to be present on each ring. The network management agent in Token Ring-based adapters supports a REM function with the following:

- Adapters within all attached stations count soft errors by the type of soft error that occurred (such as CRC errors, frame copied errors, etc.) and automatically report these errors to the REM (via its functional address).

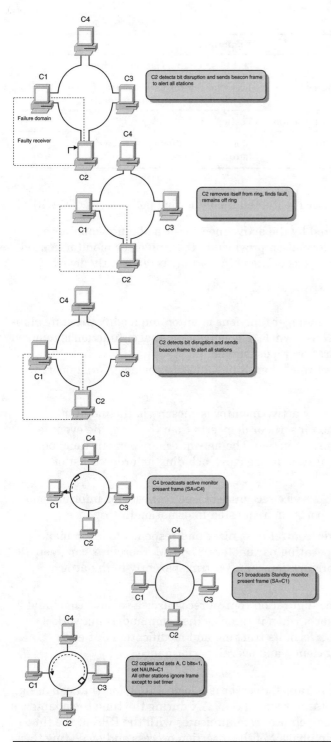

FIGURE 2.30 Beacon process

TABLE 2.5 Soft Errors

Type	Detected by	Action	Examples
1	All stations	None	"Bit hits," multiple active monitors
2	Active monitor	Ring purge	Lost frame or token, circulating frame or priority token
3	All stations	Monitor contention	Lost monitor
4	Station in failure domain	Beaconing	Monitor contention unresolved due to hardware failure

- The adapter that is the active monitor reports failure of the ring poll process to the REM.

- Errors in the active monitor detected by the active monitor or a standby monitor are reported to the REM. When the information provided to the ring error monitor is used, conditions that degrade the performance of the network may be efficiently detected, diagnosed, and corrected.

Network Manager (NM)   The network manager functions monitor and modify the state of individual stations and that of the LAN as a whole. The network manager function is referred to by the IEEE 802.5 as the configuration report server.

The network management agent of the Token Ring Chipset provides NM support with the following functions:

- *Configuration Changes.*   When a new active monitor is chosen via the monitor contention process or when a station inserts or deinserts from the ring, the event is reported to the network management function. The network management function, therefore, can maintain the configuration of the ring, including an ordered list of stations inserted at any moment.

- *Reporting Services.*   The reporting service recognizes three requests for information from the NM and automatically reports the requested information in response.

- *Parameter Control.*   The parameter control recognizes and responds to a command from the NM to modify internal operating parameters. The NM, therefore, can keep all adapters in step with network configuration changes, transparently to the attach product.

- *Reconfiguration Control.*   The reconfiguration control recognizes a remove command from the NM and physically deinserts when it receives the command. A network manager can use this support to perform its tracking and modification duties to maximize the LAN's reliability, efficiency, and overall performance.

Ring Parameter Server (RPS). A ring parameter server is a logical function that can assign operating parameters of individual stations and of the LAN during the time the adapter is inserting into the ring. The Token Ring chipset communicates with the RPS at the time of insertion by requesting parameters in phase 4 of the insertion process and by setting these parameters on a response from the RPS.

Monitor Functions.   An adapter on the ring can be an active monitor or a standby monitor. Only one active monitor is present on any ring; the remaining adapters serve as standby monitors. The active monitor ensures normal token operation on the ring and provides the crystal-controlled master data clocking for data transmission. The standby monitors ensure that the active monitor is functioning properly and is still inserted on the ring.

Ring Purge.   The ring-purge process is used by the active monitor to perform the recovery from a temporary error condition, to release a new token, and to return the ring to a known state.

Ring Poll.   The ring-poll process is initiated periodically by the active monitor to update the UNA in all adapters in the ring and to provide an indication to other stations in the ring that the active monitor is still active.

Standby Monitor Functions.   Any adapter that is not the active monitor but has completed the insertion processes follows the procedures of the standby monitor. The function of the standby monitor is to monitor the events on the ring to determine whether the active monitor is functioning properly.

The standby monitor functions are disabled while the adapter is in the insertion, beacon, or monitor contention processes.

A station activates its standby monitor functions as follows:

- When the adapter completes the ring insertion process and does not get contention in phase 1 of the ring insertion process

- When the adapter receives a ring purge MAC frame while it is in contention repeat mode

- When an inserted active monitor determines that another adapter has assumed the functions of active monitor

As a standby monitor, the station transmits on the ring with the clock derived from the incoming signal. It also deactivates the hardware mechanism for correcting circulating priority tokens and frames.

The following ring conditions are monitored by the standby monitor:

- *Good Token.*   The station verifies that a good token is received at least once every 2.6 seconds. A good token is defined as a token of priority 0 or a token of priority greater than 0 followed by a frame with a priority field greater than 0.

- *Periodic Ring Polls.*   The adapter receive poll timer detects the absence of AMP MAC frames. The receive poll timer is restarted when an AMP MAC frame is received. The absence of AMP MAC frames indicates that no active monitor is in the ring. If the receive poll timer expires after 15 seconds, the Token Ring chipset enters the monitor contention process in the contention transmit mode.

- *Proper Ring Data Frequency.*   The Token Ring chipset uses the hardware *error* process to check the frequency of the data on the ring. If a frequency error is detected by this process, it indicates that there is no active monitor or that the active monitor is not functioning properly. If a frequency error is detected, the Token Ring chipset enters the monitor contention process in contention transmit mode.

Standby Monitor Exception Conditions.   The following exception conditions cause the Token Ring chipset to deactivate the standby monitor functions and to take these actions.

- *Active Monitor Errors.*   If the Token Ring chipset detects an error in the active monitor, the adapter enters the monitor contention process in contention transmit mode.

- *Claim Token Frame.*   If the adapter receives a claim token MAC frame, the adapter enters the monitor contention process.

- *Receive Beacon.*   The receiving station enters the beacon process in beacon repeat mode.

- *Signal Loss.*   If signal loss is detected by the adapter, it enters the monitor contention process in contention transmit mode.

- *Wire Fault.*   If a wire fault condition is detected by the Token Ring Chipset, the adapter deinserts from the ring and sets the lobe wire fault bit in ring status.

Monitor Contention Process.   The monitor contention process involves all the adapters in the ring. The monitor contention process is used to establish a ring station as an active monitor. This process is started when any station on the ring detects that no active monitor is in the ring or that the active monitor is not functioning properly. Other adapters enter the process when a claim token MAC frame is received.

The process starts when a station detects the need for monitor contention and transmits a claim token MAC frame. These stations join the process in an active or passive role by entering contention transmit or contention repeat mode, respectively. The active station with the highest ring station address among those contenders will be established as the active monitor.

The stations that actively participate are as follows:

- Stations detecting the need for contention

- Stations configured to contend by the attached system's OPEN command, which also have not received a claim token MAC frame with a source address higher than their own ring station address, except an adapter that is the active monitor at the time the claim token MAC frame is received.

All other stations on the ring enter contention repeat mode.

Stations that actively participate enter contention transmit mode. These stations repeatedly transmit a claim token MAC frame followed by ring idles to all stations on the local ring without waiting for free tokens. The frame transmission is repeated at 20 millisecond intervals. The claim token MAC frame information field contains the transmitting station's UNA ring station address.

Contention Transmit Mode.   The following describes the conditions required for a station to enter contention transmit mode and to begin the monitor contention process:

- *Good Token Not Received.*   If a standby monitor does not detect a good token within a 2.6-second period

- *Ring Poll Time Out.*   If a standby monitor does not detect an AMP MAC frame within a 15-second period

- *Insertion Timer Time Out.*   If no active monitor is present, no standby monitor is present, or no ring purge MAC frame is detected within 18 seconds of inserting onto the ring, the adapter enters contention transmit mode. When an active monitor is established, the adapter returns to the insertion process.

- *Unsuccessful Purge.*   The active monitor is unable to successfully purge the ring.

- *Frequency Error.*   If a standby monitor detects a frequency error, it enters contention transmit mode.

- *Beacon Transmit Mode.*   A station in beacon transmit mode receives its own beacon frame.

- *Beacon Repeat Mode.*   A station in beacon repeat mode detects a circulating beacon frame.

- *Beacon Escape Timer.*   An adapter in beacon repeat mode detects no beacon frames for 200 milliseconds.

- *Signal Loss.*   A signal loss condition is detected by the adapter.

When the adapter enters contention transmit mode, it starts the monitor contention timer and continually transmits a claim token MAC frame (followed by idles) every 20 milliseconds. Claim token MAC frames are transmitted immediately without waiting for a free token. If the adapter is in beacon repeat mode and receives a claim token MAC frame, it will exit the beacon process.

When a claim token MAC frame is received with a source address higher than the station's own address, the adapter retransmits that frame and, when frame transmission has been completed, enters contention repeat mode. When the adapter receives three successive claim token MAC frames with a source address equal to its own address and a UNA subvector equal to its saved UNA (i.e., receives its own frame), it wins contention. This adapter becomes the new active monitor, exits contention transmit mode, and performs the ring-purge process. It then queues a report new monitor MAC frame for transmission to the network manager.

Contention Repeat Mode.   When an adapter enters contention repeat mode, it starts its monitor contention timer. The monitor contention timer is a one-second timer that serves as a watchdog timer during the contention process to prevent the process from continuing indefinitely if the contention condition cannot be resolved. If this timer expires, the beacon process is entered.

When an adapter receives a claim token MAC frame, the frame is ignored. When an adapter receives a ring purge MAC frame, it resets its monitor contention timer, resumes normal operation, and starts the standby monitor functions.

Adapters Not in Monitor Contention.   An adapter not in contention transmit mode and not in contention repeat mode takes the following action when it receives a claim token MAC frame: if the source address in the received frame is less than this adapter specific address, and the adapter was OPENED with the contender option, the adapter enters contention transmit mode. Otherwise, it enters contention repeat mode. If the source address in the frame is equal to this adapter's specific address, the frame is ignored.

Ring-Purge Process.   The ring-purge process is used to put the ring into a normal condition that enables frames to be transmitted using the token protocol. The ring-purge process is started by the active monitor when one of the following conditions occur:

- A token error condition is detected.
- An adapter becomes the active monitor in the monitor contention process.

Ring-Purge Procedure.   When the active monitor enters the ring-purge process, a ring-purge timer starts, and the active monitor transmits a ring-purge MAC frame. This transmission takes place without waiting for a free token and without releasing a free token upon completion. Following transmission of the ring purge frame, the adapter sends continuous idles (0).

When the active monitor receives the transmission after the frame has circulated the ring, it checks for errors in the transmission. These errors could be code violation errors or frame check sequence (CRC) errors.

If an error is detected, the adapter transmits another ring purge MAC frame until a frame is received error-free or until the ring-purge timer expires.

The ring-purge timer functions as a watchdog timer to limit the time the adapter continues to transmit ring purge MAC frames during the process. This one-second timer is reset when the active monitor has received one ring purge MAC frame that circulated the ring with no errors.

After an error-free frame is received, the adapter transmits a free token of priority equal to the reservation priority in the last ring purge MAC frame that was stripped by the adapter.

Ring-Purge Receiver.   The adapter in contention repeat mode, which receives a ring purge MAC frame, returns to normal operation and starts the standby monitor functions.

If a standby monitor not in contention repeat mode receives a ring purge MAC frame, it resets auto-removal variables and discards the frame.

If an active monitor receives a ring purge MAC frame, it checks the source address of the frame to determine whether it transmitted the frame. The reception of this frame by an active monitor, which did not transmit the frame, is an exception condition of the active monitor.

Exception Conditions.   If the ring-purge timer expires (one second), the adapter enters the monitor contention process in contention transmit mode. If the adapter is in the insertion process when the ring-purge timer expires, the adapter is deinserted, and the OPEN command is terminated with an error.

Ring-Poll Process.   The active monitor sends Ring Poll every seven seconds. This process is used to learn the ring configuration. The Ring Poll routine is as follows: the active monitor sends an AMP frame; each downstream station sends a *Standby Monitor Present* (SMP) frame; each downstream node learns its NAUN. The ring-poll process enables each adapter on the ring to acquire the six-byte specific address of its upstream neighbor station. In this process, each station transmits its specific address (6 bytes) and its physical drop number (4 bytes) to the next downstream station. Each station saves its UNAZ and, if different from the previously saved UNA, queues for the transmission of a report SUA change MAC frame to the network manager.

Ring-Poll Procedure. The active monitor will transmit an AMP MAC frame when its poll timer expires (every seven seconds) or at the end of the ring-purge process. The active monitor also resets an internal flag termed the *Poll Complete Flag*.

The following procedure is applied to every AMP or SMP MAC frame received by the adapter following phase 3 of the insertion process.

If an AMP MAC frame is received by an active monitor and the frame originated from the active monitor, the ARI and FCI bits of the FS field are examined to see whether another station received the frame. If the ARI and FCI bits are all 0, the active monitor is the only station on the ring. The adapter then sets the signal-station bit in the ring status register if not previously set.

If an AMP or SMP MAC frame is received by any adapter, the ARI and FCI bits are examined to see whether another station is in the ring. If these bits are not all 0s, the single station bit in the ring status register (if it was set) is reset.

If an AMP MAC frame is received by a stand-by monitor, it restarts the receive poll timer.

If an AMP MAC frame is received by any station, the adapter resets to 0 an internal status flag called the receive ARI/FCI flag.

If any station receives an AMP or SMP MAC frame and the ARI and FCI bits are not all 0s, the station saves the source address of the frame as the latest poll address. This address is used by the active monitor in a report ring poll failure MAC frame if a failure is detected.

If any station receives an AMP or SMP MAC frame and the ARI and FCI bits are all 0s (no other adapter has copied the frame), the adapter compares the source address of the frame to the UNA previously saved. If the source address does not equal the UNA address, the adapter saves the source address as the adapter's UNA, and a report SUA change MAC frame is queued for transmission to the network manager. Next, the adapter checks the internal receive ARI/FCI flag. If this flag is set to 1, the adapter increments the ARI/FCI error counter and does not queue an SMP MAC frame for transmission. If the flag is 0, it is then set to 1.

> **NOTE:** *When the ARI/FCI error counter is incremented, it indicates that the upstream neighbor station is unable to set the ARI or FCI bits of received frames.*

If the active monitor receives an AMP or SMP MAC frame with the ARI and FCI bits all 0s, it sets the internal poll complete flag, and the process terminates. If a standby monitor receives an AMP or SMP MAC frame with the ARI or FCI bits all 0s, the station starts the poll response timer (20 ms). At the expiration of this timer, the station queues a SMP MAC frame for transmission. This frame propagates the ring poll to the next downstream station.

Beacon Process. When a station detects a failure of token claiming following a hardware error, the station transmits a Beacon frame. When the NAUN receives eight beacon frames, it removes itself from the ring. The NAUN then performs a Lobe Media test and Duplicate Address test. If there's a lobe error, the station remains out of the ring, the ring continues its normal operation, and a token claim process takes place.

The beacon process is started when an adapter inserted in the ring detects that an adapter's monitor contention timer expired in the monitor contention process, indicating that the contention could not be resolved.

When a station beacons, all other stations on the ring enter beacon transmit or beacon repeat mode. In beacon transmit mode, beacon MAC frames are transmitted at 20ms intervals without waiting for a token. Idle 0 bits are transmitted between frames. An adapter not in the beacon process that receives a beacon MAC frame enters beacon repeat mode. An adapter in the insertion process does not enter the beacon process but terminates the OPEN command with an error, indicating that the ring is beaconing.

Beacon Removal Functions.   The beacon removal functions are executed when an adapter detects a sustained hard error. The execution of these functions causes the adapter to deinsert from the ring and executes an internal test. If this test is successful, the adapter reinserts. Otherwise, the adapter is closed and remains off-ring. If the latter occurs, the attached system is notified via ring status that a hard error has removed the adapter from the ring.

Isolating versus Nonisolating Error Counters.   The error counters maintained by the adapter are defined as isolating or nonisolating. Isolating error counters isolate errors to a transmitting adapter, a receiving adapter, and the components (cabling, wiring concentrators) between those two adapters. These errors are counted only by the first detecting adapter. Other adapters also detect these errors but are prevented from counting these errors by the *error detected indicator* (EDI) bit in the ending delimiter of the frame already being set to one by the detecting adapter.

Nonisolating error counters count errors that could have been caused by any other adapter on the ring (the fault cannot be isolated to a specific area of the ring).

Isolating Error Counters.   The following are Isolating error counters:

- *Line Error Counter.* The line error counter is contained in all adapter configurations. It is incremented no more than once per frame whenever a frame is repeated or copied, the EDI is 0 in the incoming frame, or one of the following conditions exists:
  - A code violation exists between the *starting delimiter* (SDEL) and the *ending delimiter* (EDEL) of the frame.
  - A code violation exists in a token.
  - A FCS error exists.

- *Burst Error Counter.* The burst error counter is contained in all adapter configurations and is incremented when the adapter detects the absence of transitions for five half-bit times between SDEL and EDEL. Only one adapter detects the burst five condition because the adapter that detects a burst four condition (four half-bit times without transition) conditions its transmitter to transmit idles if the burst-five condition is detected.

- *ARI / FCI Set Error Counter.* The ARI/FCI set error counter is incremented when an adapter receives more than one AMP or SMP MAC frame with ARI/FCI equal to 0, without first receiving an intervening AMP MAC frame. The counter indicates that the upstream adapter is unable to set its ARI/FCI bits in a frame that it has copied.

Nonisolating Error Counters. The following are the nonisolating error counters:

- *Lost Frame Error Counter.* The lost frame error counter is contained in all adapter configurations and is incremented when an adapter is in transmit (stripping) mode and fails to receive the end of the frame it transmitted.

- *Frame Copied Error Counter.* The frame copied error counter is contained in all configurations and is incremented when an adapter in the receive/repeat mode recognizes a frame address to its specific address but finds the ARI bits not equal to 00 (possible line hit or duplicate address).

- *Receive Congestion Error Counter.* The receive congestion error counter is contained in all adapter configurations and is incremented when an adapter in the repeat mode recognizes a frame addressed to its specific address but has no buffer space available to copy the frame (adapter congestion).

- *Token Error Counter.* This one-byte counter is contained in active monitor adapter configurations and is incremented when the active monitor functions detect an error with the token protocol as follows:

  - A token with priority of non-zero and the monitor count bit equal to one.
  - A frame and the monitor count bit equal to one.
  - No token or frame is received within a 10ms window.
  - The starting delimiter/token sequence has code violation (in an area in which code violations must not exist).

Soft Errors. Soft errors allow the ring recovery protocols to restore normal token protocols but cause performance degradation due to disrupted network operation. Soft errors include line errors, lost frames, lost tokens, lost active monitor, corrupted tokens, circulating priority tokens or frames, delimiter errors, multiple monitors, and list delimiters.

There are four types of soft errors:

- Type 1. These errors require no ring recovery function to be executed.

- Type 2. These errors require the ring-purge process to be executed.

- Type 3. These errors require the monitor contention and ring-purge processes to be executed.

- Type 4. These errors require the beacon, monitor contention, and ring purge functions to be executed.

The detection and recovery of lost frames caused by soft error conditions are not performed by the adapter.

Type 1 Soft Errors. Type 1 errors consist of line errors, the multiple monitor condition, and the ARI/FCI set conditions.

- *Line Errors.* Each adapter checks each frame copied or repeated for a valid FCS or a Manchester code violation. Adapters detecting these errors set the EDI to one in the frame or token's ending delimiter.

- *Multiple Monitors.*   When an active monitor receives a ring purge MAC frame or an AMP MAC frame that it did not transmit, the active monitor queues for transmission a report monitor error MAC frame with an error code indicating the multiple monitor error. It then becomes a standby monitor and enters repeat mode. Note that this action may leave the ring without an active monitor. Another standby monitor enters the monitor contention process in this case.

- *ARI/FCI Set Error.*   Reception of more than one AMP or SMP MAC frame with ARI/FCI equal to 0, without first receiving an intervening AMP MAC frame, causes the adapter to increment the ARI/FCI set error counter and terminate the ring poll process (does not queue the SMP MAC frame).

This process leaves the adapter downstream of a malfunctioning adapter with an incorrect UNA (when the ring poll process terminates), but adapters downstream from the active monitor to the defective adapter have correct UNA.

When an adapter, upon receiving a frame, is unable to set the ARI/FCI bits, the following LAN functions do not operate correctly:

- Higher level protocols may not work correctly because of the inability of the insertion process to detect duplicate addresses.
- A beacon transmitter may identify an incorrect upstream adapter.
- An adapter MAC frame requiring ensured delivery will not be ensured when the destination adapter fails to set the ARI/FCI bits.

Type 2 Soft Error.   Type 2 soft errors consist of the burst-5 error, lost frame, multiple token, corrupted token, lost token, lost delimiter, circulating token, or circulating frame error conditions. These error conditions cause the active monitor to execute its ring-purge function and may cause frames to be lost.

- *Burst-5 error.*   An adapter detects the burst-5 condition when five half-bits of Manchester-coded data are received without a phase change.

A type 2 soft error is detected when the burst error is long enough to remove the token or frame from the ring but not long enough (due to signal loss) to start a hard error recovery.

- *Lost Frames.*   When a transmitting adapter has transmitted the physical trailer, the adapter strips the ring data until EDEL is detected or 4.1 microseconds expires. If the 4.1-millisecond timer expires, the adapter enters repeat mode without generating a token and increments its lost frame error counter.

This error causes the active monitor to detect a lost token and to perform a ring purge to restore normal token protocols.

- *Corrupted Token.*   When an adapter has one or more frames to transmit and receives a token but does not detect an EDEL after the access control field, a corrupted token has been detected. The adapter transmits an abort delimiter (an ADEL/EDEL sequence), queues the frame that was being transmitted for transmission, and does not generate a token.

This error causes the active monitor to detect a lost token and to restore the ring through the ring-purge process.

- *Lost Token.* When the active monitor fails to detect a token or a frame physical header once every 10 milliseconds, the adapter increments the token error counter and restores the ring through the ring purge process.

- *Circulating Frame or Priority Token / Multiple Monitor.* Each time an adapter transmits a frame or a priority token, it sets the monitor bit (AC bit 4) to 0. Each time the active monitor repeats a frame or a priority token, it examines the AC bit 4.

Type 3 Soft Errors. The Type 3 soft error may be caused by the nonexistence of an active monitor and initiates the monitor contention and ring-purge processes. These error conditions or their resultant recovery techniques may cause frames to be lost.

- *Lost Frame.* The standby monitor monitors the ring for good tokens to be received at least once every 2.6 seconds. The standby monitors also monitor to ensure that a ring poll process is executed at least once every 15 seconds. If either of these times expire, the adapter assumes that the ring's active monitor is not functional or not present and enters the monitor contention process in contention transmit mode.

- *Frequency Error.* The standby monitor's detection of a frequency error causes the adapter to enter monitor contention in contention transmit mode. This failure may be resolved by soft error recovery or may cause the hard error recovery function to be executed.

Type 4 Soft Errors. The Type 4 soft error is caused when monitor contention cannot be resolved. This error condition may also require hard error recovery.

This error condition or its resultant recovery may cause frames to be lost.

Hard Errors. These are permanent faults that usually concern hardware (equipment) that stops the ring's normal operation LAN:

- *Streaming Error.* There are two forms of streaming: bit streaming and frame streaming. Bit streaming removes (destroys) tokens and frames by writing over (repeat and transmit both occurring) or replacing (uncontrolled transmit) ring data. Frame streaming consists of the continuous transmission of tokens, abort sequences, or frames. Both streaming types are detected by the adapter's active or standby monitor function and cause monitor contention to be entered.

- *Frequency Error.* A frequency error is a condition in which the ring clock and the crystal clock frequency of the adapter differ by an excessive amount. Detection of this condition causes the adapter to enter the monitor contention process.

- *Signal Loss Error.* A signal loss error occurs as the result of a broken ring, faulty wiring concentrator, transmitter malfunction, or receiver malfunction.

- *Internal Errors.*   Internal errors are detected by the adapter's hardware and/or firmware; they cause the detecting adapter to remove itself from the ring (automatic reconfiguration). When hard errors occur on the ring, reconfiguration of the network is necessary to effect full recovery. Reconfiguration consists of the removal or bypass of the faults station(s) or cabling. Reconfiguration takes two forms: manual reconfiguration and automatic reconfiguration.

  Automatic reconfiguration begins when the adapter executes one of the beacon remove functions or when an internal hardware error is detected by the background diagnostics of the adapter.

  Manual reconfiguration is necessary if the automatic reconfiguration functions have failed to recover the ring's normal token protocol. The fault location can be isolated easily by the beacon process.

Token Ring Architecture Summary

Token Ring is a protocol used at the lower two layers within a network. Token Ring speeds can be either 4 or 16 Mbits/sec. Token Ring uses ring technology in a star configuration. The *media access unit* (MAU) is the device to which participating hosts connect. Cables that connect the interface card to the MAU are called *lobes*.

Token Ring is considered self-healing technology. Because of the relay inside the MAU, a station can be inserted and removed without disrupting operation on the ring. The five-step insertion process was explained in terms of the functions performed at each step. Token Ring uses multiple frames, some of which were presented here: the MAC frame with LLC-PDU data, the MAC frame with MACPDU data, a token frame, and an abort frame. The fields in each frame have specific meanings for the operation of a Token Ring network. The meanings of all fields were supplied for the generic MAC frame. The MAC-PDU components were also presented. A brief list of MAC control frames and their functions were presented.

Some Token Ring concepts and functions were provided such as the active monitor, the standby monitor, the nearest active upstream neighbor, and the beaconing function. Each was explained according to its function. Token Ring addressing was explained. The meanings of a 12-digit hex address, SAP addresses, and link connection addresses were explained. Information was also provided to explain why SAP addresses can have the same number in a network yet not violate addressing structure. See Figure 2.31 for a summation of the Token Ring operation.

Token Ring Protocol Timers.

- *T(Any_Token).*   This timer determines the amount of time the *active monitor* (AM) can wait before it detects a starting delimiter from a token or frame. The timer starts when the AM transmits the first token. The duration of this timer is 10 milliseconds.

- *T(Attach).*   This timer sets the amount of time a station can stay in the ring insertion process. The timer is started at the beginning of phase 1 (monitor check) and times out after 18 seconds if the process is not completed. The timer is canceled when the insertion process completes.

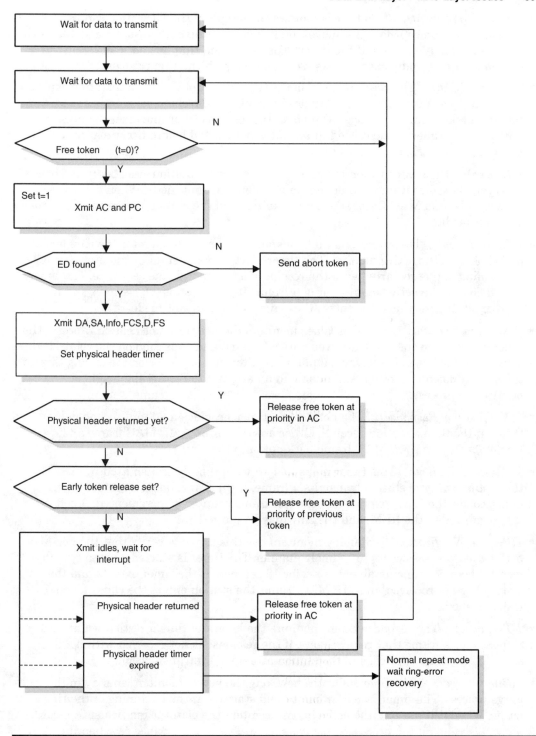

FIGURE 2.31 Token Ring operation summary

- *T(Beacon_Transmit)*. This timer monitors the length of time a station can transmit beacon MAC frames before it removes itself from the ring and performs a self test. The timer is set for 16 seconds. If the timer expires and the ring has not recovered, the station deinserts and runs self tests. The timer stops if the ring recovers.

- *T(Claim_Token)*. The claim token timer is the amount of time that a station can wait for an AM to win the token claiming process while in the claim token repeat mode or the claim token transmit mode. When a station enters either mode, the timer is initiated. The timer is one second. If an AM is not elected before timer expiration, the timer can be canceled.

- *T(Escape)*. The escape timer sets the amount of time a station can stay in the beacon repeat mode before it must enter the claim token transmit mode. When a station receives a beacon MAC frame, the timer expires, and the station enters the claim token transmit mode.

- *T(Good_Token)*. This timer is used by a standby monitor to monitor the ring for problems with the active monitor. The timer starts when a standby monitor begins functioning and is restarted with the receipt of a token or frame sequence. The timer detects loss of the active monitor or of a frame. Its duration is 2.6 seconds, and if it expires, the standby monitor enters the claim token transmit mode.

- *T(Neighbor_Notification)*. This timer monitors the neighbor notification process. The timer starts when the AM transmits an AMP frame and runs for seven seconds. If the active monitor has not received a standby monitor present MAC frame during this time, the AM sends another AMP frame in an attempt to restart the neighbor notification process.

- *T(Notification_Response)*. The notification timer provides a 20-millisecond delay between the time a station receives either an SMP or an AMP MAC frame and transmits its own SMP MAC frame back out onto the ring.

- *T(Physical_Trailer)*. This timer helps to detect improperly transmitted frames. The timer starts when a station transmits a frame. If the frame does not return in 4.1 milliseconds, the timer expires and the lost frame counter is incremented. A soft error is transmitted to the REM, and the ring may be purged.

- *T(Receive_Notification)*. Standby monitors use this timer to verify that the neighbor notification process occurs in a timely manner. The timer is started when a standby monitor becomes functional and is set for 15 seconds. If the timer expires and the station has not received an AMP MAC frame, the station enters the claim token transmit mode.

- *T(Response)*. The response timer monitors the length of time a station waits for a response for a frame that requires one. If the response is not received within 2.5 seconds, the timer expires, and the station attempts a retransmission.

- *T(Ring_Purge)*. This timer indicates how long the active monitor can stay in the ring-purge process. The timer is set for one second starting at the beginning of the ring purge. When it times out, the active monitor enters the claim token transmit mode.

- *T(Soft_Error_Report)*.   The soft error report timer dictates when a station can generate a report soft error MAC frame. This allows the error counter to increment for a specified period of time so that the report contains multiple errors rather than just one. This reduces error reporting traffic on the ring. The timer is set for two seconds when a soft error counter is incremented. Upon expiration, a report soft error MAC frame is transmitted.

- *T(Transmit_Pacing)*.   This timer dictates the length of time a station must wait before retransmission of a beacon or claim token MAC frame. The timer starts when one of these frames is transmitted and times out in 20 milliseconds if the frame was improperly transmitted or not received. Upon timer expiration, the station attempts retransmission.

FDDI Architecture

The FDDI standard is actually of a set of standards as established by the *American National Standards Institute* (ANSI); see Figure 2.32. FDDI is a token-based ring access method that allows stations to access a cable plant that operates at 100 Mbps. FDDI can connect up to 500 dual-attach stations in a 100-km network. FDDI differs from other ring access methods in that it is a timed-token protocol; each ring station is guaranteed network access for a certain time period negotiated between all active stations upon startup and when a new station joins the ring.

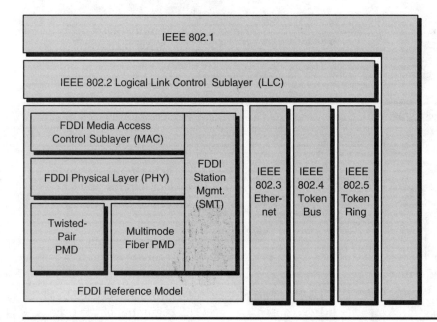

FIGURE 2.32   FDDI architecture

The topology for FDDI is mixed. Logically, FDDI is a ring, but physically it is a point-to-point or a star connection (see Figure 2.33). Without the use of a wiring concentrator, the physical connection is point-to-point. Each network attachment has a physical connection with another attachment. With the use of a concentrator, the physical topology turns into a star configuration, much like Token Ring. The main difference is that Token Ring requires the wiring concentrator; whereas FDDI does not. Network stations in FDDI can be connected directly to each other. FDDI operates at 100 Mbps. FDDI is a ring-based technology similar to Token Ring. However, FDDI differs from Token Ring and can best be understood by examining some of FDDI's characteristics. This section explores FDDI and presents fundamental FDDI operation.

As shown in Figure 2.34, an FDDI dual ring is comprised of two rings (known as the *primary* and the *secondary* ring) that normally operate independently. Data can travel on

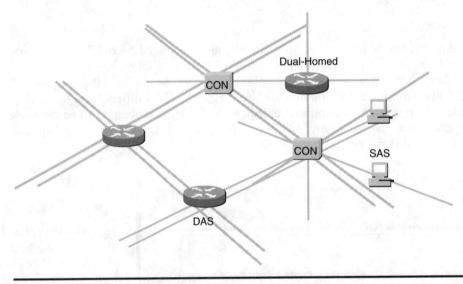

FIGURE 2.33   FDDI topology ring

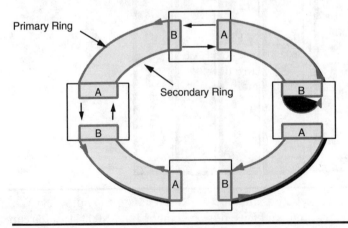

FIGURE 2.34   FDDI dual ring

each ring, in opposite directions. Although data is allowed to travel on both rings, data commonly is transmitted only on the primary ring until a certain fault occurs, in which the two rings may become one ring. When a fault does occur, such as a DAS station powering down or a cable break, and the two rings combine to form one ring, this is known as *wrapping*.

FDDI allows stations to communicate over a dual-ring topology by guaranteeing access to the cable plant at timed intervals, using a token. This may seem similar to the Token Ring architecture, but the operation of FDDI is different than Token Ring. Both are ring architectures, but the algorithms for the access methods are different.

A ring station must wait for the arrival of the token before transmission may begin. Upon arrival of the token, the network station captures the token, which stops the token repeat process (no token is now on the ring, thus guaranteeing that no other station has access to the cable plant). A station transmits a series of frames to the next active stations on the network (data flows in one direction only). Frame transmission continues (meaning multiple frames may be transmitted, not just one) until the token-holding timer expires or until the station has no more frames to transmit. The station then releases the token to the ring.

The downstream neighbor receives these symbols, regenerates them, and repeats them to its downstream neighbor. When the frame returns to the originator, it strips the frame from the ring. The intended destination station does not strip the frame. Only the originator of a frame may take it back off the ring.

Basic FDDI Characteristics

This section lists the highlights of FDDI characteristics and explains their nature of operation with FDDI.

Cable Specifications.   One characteristic of FDDI is that it is intended primarily for operation with multimode fiber cable 62.5/125 pm (62.5-pm core; 125-pm cladding). However, single-mode fiber can be used. Additionally, FDDI protocols can be implemented over shielded twisted-pair cabling, which some refer to as *shielded distributed data interface* (SDDI). Another implementation is FDDI implemented over unshielded twisted-pair cabling; this is sometimes referred to as *copper-stranded distributed data interface* (CDDI).

Ring Speed and Ring Distance.   Another aspect of FDDI is its speed. Its specification is 100 Mbits/sec, which is considerably faster than Token Ring. FDDI specification also calls for a dual-ring implementation. The dual-ring structure defines data transfer in opposite directions. With multimode fiber, any given ring segment can be up to 200 km in length. A total of 500 stations can be connected with a maximum separation of 2 km.

FDDI Data Frame.   An FDDI frame can hold up to 4,500 bytes of data. This data is carried in a frame or packet. Each frame of data has a header including the origin and destination address of each frame.

Maximum Number of Stations.   Any given ring segment may have a maximum number of 500 stations. However, rings can be segmented, and with a two-segment ring, 1,000 stations can be used.

Ring Monitor Functions.   FDDI uses a ring monitor function, but it differs from Token Ring because the monitoring function is distributed. Stations on an FDDI ring do not require a single monitor.

FDDI Layer Components.   Four sublayer components are defined by the ANSI specification and these sublayers are presented by their individual functions.

Physical-Medium-Dependent **(PMD) Sublayer.**   The PMD standard specifies the lower portion of the Physical layer. It describes the necessary requirements for the fiber cable to connect to the *media interface coupler* (MIC). This definition includes optical levels, signal requirements, the connector design for the MIC, and permissible bit error rates. It provides services required to move encoded bit streams from destination to target station. It also determines when a signal is received by the receiver.

Physical-Layer **(PHY) Protocol Sublayer.**   This sublayer is the upper part of the Physical layer. It defines data framing, clocking, and data encoding and decoding specifications. This sublayer transmits data received from the MAC sublayer. It also initializes the medium for data transfer. These two sublayers constitute the *port* on an FDDI interface board. In short, they operate to control and manage the process at the interface level of the connection.

Media Access Control.   The lower sublayer (MAC) of the Data Link layer performs some functions related to data framing. This sublayer also is involved in addressing, data checking, token transmission, and data frames on the ring.

Logical Link Control **(LLC).**   The LLC sublayer of the Data Link uses the 802.2 sublayer. This sublayer is used to enclose data encapsulated with a MAC frame. The ANSI and ISO specification do not specify any further functionality of the LLC sublayer. The Data Link layer components focus on peer operations between two entities. The concentration here is on generation and recognition of addresses. This layer is also responsible for proper delivery of valid data to the layer above it.

Station Management.   The station management function interacts with the FDDI PMD, PHY, and MAC sublayers. The management services receive and collect information from these different sublayers and store them in a *management information base* (MIB). SMT object information reflects a particular FDDI station or FDDI concentrator. Each station is identified in the MIB, and therefore collected information can be associated easily with a specific station. As mentioned previously, SMT uses objects to represent an FDDI station or concentrator. Some examples of SMT object management information are as follows.

- A unique identifier for each FDDI station

- SMT version the station is implementing

- The highest and lowest SMT version that can be supported

- Any special manufacturer data

- Station configuration data

- Number of MACs in the station or the concentrator

- Available paths and their types

- Dual-ring configuration capabilities
- Status report frames queued for transmission
- Current port configuration
- The latest time-stamped event
- Station events reported for configuration changes

FDDI Timers and Frame Formats

FDDI is often compared to Token Ring, and sometimes it is called a faster Token Ring, although this description is not true at all because FDDI is a timed-token protocol. The following text on timers demonstrates the difference.

FDDI Ring Timers   Proper ring operation requires the following:

- Physical connection establishment between two network stations
- Ring initialization (the capability of the ring to continuously, without error, circulate a token)
- Steady-state operation
- Ring maintenance (dynamic ring management capability on the part of the stations on the ring).

To implement the timed-token protocol, a station must use the second, third, and fourth timers. Each of the timers is used to control the scheduling process of transmitting frames. For the most part, they control the length of time during which a station may transmit before the token is released. They also are used to time the total time it takes for the token to travel around the network.

Stations are locally administered; that is, each station has management capabilities built into itself, and these enable the network station to dynamically manage the ring. Various timers in an FDDI network are used to regulate the operation of the ring:

- *Target token rotational timer* (TTRT).   This is a ring latency parameter that sets the delay for the ring. This timer is set only during ring initialization. Special MAC frames are passed between the network stations called *T_Req* frames; these are requests for a token rotation time value. Each station submits a request for how fast it wants the token to rotate. That is, if a station wants to see the token once in X milliseconds, it places a request in for **T_Req = x**. The station requesting the fastest T_Req frames wins, as it satisfies all other stations. The station requesting the lowest time wins because it is assumed that the application running on that station requires the token to circulate at the specified rate. After this process is accomplished, all stations on the ring set the value to the lowest bid.

- *Token rotational timer* (TRT).   This timer measures the time between successive arrivals of the token—that is, how long it takes for the token to return after it has come through. The timer is initialized to the TTRT time. Every station has this timer, and it is locally maintained. If the token arrives within the TRT time, this timer is reset back to the TTRT. If the token does not arrive within the TRT time, the network station increments a late counter and reloads TRT with the value of the TTRT. If this timer expires twice, the network station tries to reinitialize the ring.

- *Token holding timer* (THT). This timer determines the amount of time that a station may hold the token after capturing it. This timer is loaded with the TRT time when a station has captured the token. When the THT is loaded with the time in the TRT, the TRT timer is reloaded with the TTRT to start timing the next token rotation even though this station has the token. When a station is holding the token, the network station may transmit as many frames as it can without letting the THT expire. The station must release the token before the expiration of this timer. The THT is loaded to the time remaining in the TRT every time the token arrives. Therefore, if a station receives a token with 10 ms left in the THT, it may transmit data for 10 ms.

- *Valid transmission timer* (TVX). This timer enables an FDDI ring to recover more quickly from the loss of a token. Normally, when 2 × TTRT time occurs, the ring should reinitialize itself. Because the TTRT max value is 165 ms, in the worst case this could take up to 330 ms. This timer allows for the ring to initialize much more quickly, normally within 2.4 ms. Each station has this timer, which measures the duration between valid frames and is reset upon receipt of a valid frame. This time is calculated from the time it would take to transmit a 4,500-byte frame around a maximum-sized ring, 200 km. This equals 2.5 ms.

The net effect of all the timers is that the token should never take more than two times the TTRT to completely circulate the ring. If the TRT timer should exceed this, the ring will reinitialize, because it is assumed that the ring is no longer operational.

Timers. Each station on an FDDI network is required to maintain certain timers. These timers perform different operations to coordinate data transfer and maintenance on the FDDI network. Table 2.6 lists timers and counters and provides a brief description of their functions.

FDDI Frames. As indicated in Figure 2.35, data to be transmitted on the FDDI ring must be encapsulated in frames, which contain very distinct fields. Unlike Token Ring, there is not a master clock on the FDDI ring. Each station manages its own clock when transmitting frames. Each station's clock is independently generated by its own hardware, and each station's clock has the possibility of being slightly different from the others on the ring. Therefore, for each station to adjust to the transmitting station's clock, FDDI frames use a preamble field at the beginning of each transmitted frame so that receiving stations may synchronize their clocks to the received clock signal of the frame being transmitted.

The SD is a specially formatted field that contains indications of signal phase violations. These phase violations are mistimed signals that normally cause an error. But, the FDDI chipset has been programmed to recognize two special violation flag patterns and to read them as such. The format of the SD field is static, and it contains the violation flags. It is set this way so that the receipt of the SD indicates the presence of a frame approaching.

The frame control (FC) indicates what kind of frame is approaching. For example, it could be a token frame, SMT frame, beacon, claim-token, or LLC (data frame). This field's function is similar to the Token Ring FC field.

TABLE 2.6   FDDI Timers

FDDI Timers	Description
Starting delimiter	This timer reflects maximum circulation delay for the starting delimiter to traverse the ring. This figure includes the maximum delay encountered in the total cable lengths and the latency encountered with attached stations.
Acquisition time	This is the maximum acquisition time for a signal.
Frame transmission time	This is the maximum amount of time required to transmit a maximum-size frame.
MAC frame	This is the maximum number of MAC frames allowed on the network.
Claim Frame	This reflects the time required to transmit a claim frame along with its preamble.
Setup length time	This reflects the amount of time required for set up to transmit after a token is captured.
Insertion time	This is the maximum time required for a station to be physically inserted onto the ring.
Token holding time	This timer governs how long a station can transmit asynchronous frames onto the ring.
Token rotation timer	This timer is used to control ring scheduling for normal operation on the ring. This timer also contributes to detect errors and aids in the recovery of errors encountered on the ring.
Valid transmission timer	Each station uses this timer in the recovery of transient ring errors.

FDDI Frames

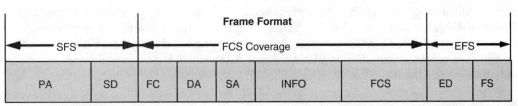

Frame Format

SFS = Preamble (16 or more I symbols)
PA = Starting Delimiter (1 JK symbol pair)
SD = Frame Control (2 symbols) 41-4f SMT;
FC = Frame Control (2 symbols)
DA = Dest. Address (4 or 12 symbols)
SA = Source Address (4 or 12 symbols)

Info = Information (0 or more symbols)
FCS = Frame Check Sequence (8 symbols)
EFS = End of Frame Sequence
ED = Ending Delimiter (1 T symbol)
FS = Frame Status (3 or more R or S symbols)

FIGURE 2.35   FDDI frame

The DA and SA can be set to 16 or 48 bits. This is indicated by the L (length) bits in the FC field. All stations on the ring must be set to 16 or 48. All FDDI implementations use 48-bit addresses. The 16-bit address is not used.

The ED indicates the end of a frame. Like the starting delimiter, it has signal phase violation indicators placed at certain locations in the ED so that the controller recognizes this field as the end of the frame.

The *frame status* (FS) field contains three important bits set by other stations on the ring. They are the *address recognized bit, frame copied bit,* and the *error bit.* The address recognized bit is set by a station for one of two reasons: the station that received the frame recognized its address in a duplicate address SMT frame check, or it recognized its address in a data LLC frame. But, just because a station recognized its address does not mean that it copied the frame; it could have been too busy to copy the frame.

The C bit indicates that a destination station was able to copy the frame. This bit is not set unless the A bit is set. The E bit indicates that some station (not necessarily the destination station) found a signaling error in the frame. If this bit is set, the C bit can never be set, because any frame found in error is not copied. The A bit can be set without the C bit being set.

Connection Establishment

Upon powering up an FDDI controller, certain checks are conducted at the Physical layer to ensure proper connection. The *connection management* (CMT) portion of SMT controls the physical connection process by which stations find out about their neighbors. Even though FDDI is a ring topology, the connection points are really point-to-point. As discussed previously in the Physical layer section, FDDI ports are physically connected in a one-on-one relationship with other attachments.

Determining a good connection is accomplished by stations transmitting and acknowledging defined line state sequences. During this process, network stations exchange information about port types, connection rules, and the quality of the links between them. If the connection type is accepted by each end of the link, and the quality link test passes, the physical connection is considered established. This connection test is accomplished by each point-to-point connection on the FDDI ring. Each station on the ring is considered to have a point-to-point connection with its directly connected neighbor. Each connection between two points accomplishes these checks. After these checks are determined to be good, the ring initializes.

Ring Initialization

Figure 2.36 helps to illustrate that after the station physical attachments have achieved a good physical connection, the ring must be initialized. Because FDDI uses a token for a station to be granted access to the ring, one of the stations must place the token onto the ring. This process is known as the claim process and may be accomplished when:

- A new station attaches to the ring
- There are no other active stations on the ring
- The token gets lost

Any station on the ring can initialize the ring, but there is a bidding process that ensures that only one station initializes the TTRT timers. The station with the lowest TTRT wins the right to initialize the ring.

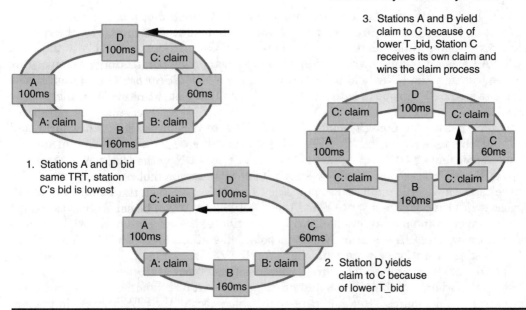

FIGURE 2.36 The claim process

This process starts when the MAC entity in one or more stations enters into the claim state, in which it continually transmits MAC claim frames that contain the station's MAC address and its TTRT bid. When another station on the ring compares a received claim frame with its own bid for TTRT, it may take one of two actions. If the time bid for TTRT in the received frame is shorter, the station quits transmitting its own claim frames and starts repeating the received claim frame. If the time bid for TTRT in the received frame is longer, the station continues transmitting its own claim rather than repeating the received claim frame. The token claim process stops when a station receives its own claim frame back. All other stations on the ring have conceded their right to initialize the ring to that station. The station that won issues a new token to the ring. If two stations bid the same TTRT, the station with the highest address wins.

Neighbor Notification and Duplicate Address Check

When an FDDI controller is initialized or the port on the concentrator is started or restarted, each network station must find out about its NAUN. This process, called the *neighbor notification protocol* (NNP), is similar to the active monitor present and the standby monitor present algorithm used in Token Ring.

This algorithm is invoked when a station first becomes operational on the ring and every 30 seconds thereafter. In this algorithm, a station transmits a management frame, called a *neighborhood information frame* (NIF). Inside the NIF are two fields called the *upstream neighbor address* (UNA) and the *downstream neighbor address* (DNA). Using these frames, a network station not only can find the addresses of the stations on its ring but can check for a duplicate of its own address. The other purpose of the protocol is to verify that the transmit and receive paths are functional. Suppose that three stations are on the ring: X, Y, and Z. Station X transmits the NIF *next station addressing* (NSA) request with the UNA and DNA fields set to unknown. Station X's downstream neighbor, station Y, receives this NIF request, sets the UNA field to X, and transmits a NIF NSA response. Station Y also transmits a NIF NSA request, with UNA set to A, and DNA set to unknown. Station Y now knows that its upstream neighbor is X.

Station Z receives station Y's request, sets the UNA to Y, sets the DNA to unknown, and transmits this as a response NIF NSA. Station Z now knows its UNA is Y. Immediately, station Z transmits a NIF request with UNA set to Y, and DNA set to unknown. Station X receives station Y's response and now knows its downstream neighbor is Y. Station X also receives station Z's NIF request and now knows its UNA is Z. Station X transmits a NIF response with the DNA field set to Y and the UNA field set to Z. Station Y receives station Z's NIF response and now knows its DNA is Z. Station Z receives station X's NIF response and now knows its DNA is station X. At this point, all stations know their UNA and DNA.

During this operation, all stations check for the A bit setting. This setting indicates whether a station recognized its address. Because these types of frames have the DA and SA set to the originator, the A bit should never get set. If it does, another station out there has with the same address. If a duplicate address is detected, the LLC services in the station that recognized the duplicate are disabled. The SMT services are still active. The LLC services are reenabled once the duplicate address problem has been resolved by manual intervention. Now that the ring has been initialized, the first time a new token circulates the ring, it cannot be captured by any station. Instead, each station that receives the token sets its own TTRT to match the TTRT of the winning station. On the second pass of the token, network stations may transmit synchronous traffic. On the third pass of the token, stations may pass asynchronous traffic.

Synchronous and Asynchronous Data Transmission.   Two types of transmission exist on FDDI: *synchronous* and *asynchronous*. Synchronous traffic is reserved bandwidth guaranteed to a network station that holds the token. This service is used primarily for voice and video applications. These types of frames are always transmitted before any asynchronous frame. Its support is optional, and it is generally not used.

Asynchronous traffic is the most common mode of operation available to network stations. It is a service class in which unreserved bandwidth is available to the station that has captured the token. Asynchronous traffic can be classified as restricted and nonrestricted. Nonrestricted asynchronous allocation supports eight priority levels. Asynchronous transmission allows a station to use the FDDI ring using a time-token protocol. This type of transmission allows for dynamic bandwidth allocation. Restricted asynchronous transmission allows for extended transmissions to exist between two or more stations on the FDDI ring and allows ring stations to "hog" the cable for their transmissions. This requires a station to set the token to indicate that the ring is restricted for its use. Restricted asynchronous mode is optionally supported on FDDI.

These two service classes, synchronous and asynchronous, should not be confused with the asynchronous and synchronous services that mainframe (or mini-) computers and their terminals use to communicate.

Normal Operation

After all the verifications and tests have been successfully completed, an FDDI ring may start normal data transmission, or *steady-state* operation. With this network, stations may transmit frames to each other using the rules of the FDDI protocol. The ring remains in steady state until a new claim process is initiated.

Frames are transmitted on a ring using the timed-token protocol. The timed-token protocol is a series of steps that the network station must perform before data transmission is allowed on the ring. A network station wanting to transmit must wait for the arrival of the token. Upon the token's arrival, the network station captures the token, stopping the token repeat process. The TRT timer is loaded into the THT timer, and the TRT is reset to the value contained in TTRT.

A station transmits a series of symbols (data bytes), which when combined form frames, to the next active station on the network. Frame transmission continues until the THT expires or until the station has no more frames to transmit. For example, if a station receives the token and its THT has 10 ms left, the station starts to transmit asynchronous frames, in order of priority, until the THT expires. The station then releases the token to the ring and resets the THT.

Every other active station on the ring receives the transmitted frame and checks it for the destination address. If the destination address of the received frame is not its own, it checks for signal or FCS errors and repeats the frame to its downstream neighbor. If the destination address is its own, it copies the frame into its receive buffer, sets certain control bits in the frame to indicate to the sender that it has copied the frame and that it recognized its address (the A and C bits in the FS field), and repeats the frame to its downstream neighbor.

Any other downstream station that receives this frame checks the frame for errors and repeats the frame. If any station detects an error (usually a signal or framing error), it can set the error bits (E bit in the FS field) in the frame. If the destination station has not copied the frame and detects the error bit set, it may set the address-recognized bit and the E bit and repeat the frame.

This process continues until the frame circles the ring and the station that originally transmitted the frame removes the frame from the ring. This process is known as *stripping*.

Stripping and Scrubbing FDDI.   To minimize delays for data to pass through the controllers, each network station reads and repeats each frame, bit by bit, as it receives the frame. As shown before, the frame contains destination and source MAC addresses to determine what station sent the frame and for which station the frame is intended. Under normal circumstances, the station that transmits a frame is the only one allowed to remove the frame from the ring (through stripping). The source station reads each frame on the network as if to repeat the frame immediately to its downstream neighbor. When a station recognizes its own address in the source address of the frame, it knows that it must strip the frame from the ring. But by the time it recognizes the frame as its own, the frame header and destination address have already been repeated to its downstream neighbor, thus leaving a fragment of the original frame on the ring.

To ensure that the ring does not deteriorate because of this frame fragmentation, each FDDI station can remove these fragments from the ring through SMT. The fragments are either removed by the downstream neighbor or by the operations of each repeat filter in each active station's PHY. This process is called *scrubbing*.

There is no standard definition on how to scrub the ring of unwanted or orphaned frames. The process of scrubbing is enacted to keep the ring from deteriorating due to stray frames. This deterioration can happen when a new station inserts into the ring or leaves the ring. If a station transmitted a frame and leaves the ring before it can strip it, another station must remove this stray frame. To remove the stray frame, a station sends a series of idle frames to the ring. At the same time, the MAC entity of the FDDI controller card strips the ring of frames and tokens, which forces other stations to enter into the claim process. The scrubbing process ensures that any frames on the ring occurred after the ring was scrubbed. It eliminates the possibility of stray frames continually circulating the ring.

FDDI Management

Station management is defined for the MAC Sublayer, PHY Sublayer, and PLD Sublayer. The function of this management is based on maintaining information gathered in a *management information base* (MIB). The flexibility of this management structure supports local or remote stations. The remainder of this section presents the core components of SMT system management service.

Station (SMT) Object Management. The SMT reflects either an FDDI station or FDDI concentrator (see Figure 2.37).

Identification includes the operation that the object performs on the FDDI ring. Station configuration information is ascertainable; this indicates the number of MACs in the concentrator or station, available paths, configuration capabilities for dual rings, and other in-

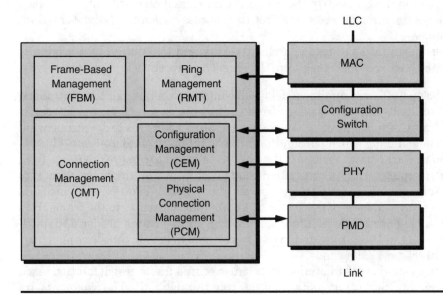

FIGURE 2.37 SMT

formation. Status information, such as port configuration and the port state, is also ascertainable. Also ascertainable are the current state of the primary and secondary stations; time stamps reflecting the latest event; station actions such as disconnect, connect, self-test, and path test; and vendor-specific information. This and other detailed information is manageable via SMT object management.

MAC Object Management.   MAC objects may have multiple instances within a given station. However, the attainable information includes address information of local MAC address attributes; information on operational timers; and configuration information including path, neighbor data, and information reflecting the topology. Frame status information can also be obtained. Counter information for error and nonerror information includes the following:

- Tokens
- Frames not copied
- Error frames
- Transmitted frames
- Received frames
- Expired frames
- Late token

   Vendor-specific information can also be obtained. MAC station actions can be determined. Events generated for the MAC can also be gathered. Other detailed information is also available.

Attachment Object Management.   This type of management includes information of attachment resources and ports. The class of attachment can be determined (such as single, dual, or concentrator). Optical bypass information, and vendor-specific information such as actions and notifications defined by a vendor can be obtained.

Port Object Management.   This management information is focused on port attributes such as configuration, status, operational condition, error counts related to the port, or actions and events. The type of PMD associated with the port can be determined along with connection capabilities. A port's operational state is ascertainable. The line state can be determined: halted, idle, quiet, etc. Other detailed information can also be obtained for the port object.

Path Object Management.   The path object management can derive information about the following:

- Path configuration of available MACs
- Synchronous bandwidth allocation
- Trace status of the ring

- Ring latency

- Lowest valid point for the transmission timer

Other information can also be obtained, such as the vendor-specific information about the MAC managed object.

The MIB level supported at a given installation dictates to a degree the amount and type of data that can be derived about the objects mentioned previously.

FDDI Architecture Summary

FDDI is a ring-based technology with data rate speeds of 100 Mbits/sec. The original specification for this technology was a fiber medium; however, testbed environments have implemented FDDI over unshielded twisted-pair cabling and simple copper-stranded cabling. Ring distances are noted to be a maximum of 200 km in length with a maximum of 500 stations per ring segment no more than 2 km apart.

FDDI layers call for a PMD specification along with a PHY protocol. Additionally, the Data Link layer is also divided into its typical MAC sublayer and the LLC sublayer. In addition to these, the station management layer is positioned vertically from the physical layer through the Data Link layer.

FDDI technology implements timers in each station to maintain normal operations. A list of timers, each performing a specialized function, is provided. FDDI frames are similar to Token Ring frames, but differences do exist. Data that can be moved through an FDDI ring is greater than that of a token ring.

The theory of FDDI frame and token operation was provided. A series of steps showing the functions that occur on the ring was presented. One example is that the ring that puts a frame on itself removes that frame after its destination has copied the contents and received the data. Lists of FDDI frames and their functions were presented. One of these include the beacon frame, which is introduced onto the ring when a serious error occurs such as a break in a cable. The SMT frame is the management frame sent by station management components that control specific operations.

Implementation of FDDI was discussed. An explanation of the differences between dual-attachment stations and single-attachment stations and the role of a concentrator was provided. Explanation of MIC types was provided. Sample topologies were explained and their conceptual implementations were shown. FDDI services were also discussed. These services correlate with the PMD sublayer, the PHY protocol, the MC protocol, and the station management component. FDDI station management and the notion of a station object management were explained. MAC object management, attachment object management, port object management, and path object management were discussed. SMT frame structure and SMT header contents and structure were presented. The SMT information field was presented and its contents explained.

Questions

1. The OSI Physical layer:
   A. Is concerned with the logical topology of networks
   B. Describes transmission media and connectors
   C. Coordinates the rules for transmitting byte
   D. Coordinates the rules for transmitting bits

2. Which are characteristics of a physical ring topology?
   A. Media failure on unidirectional loops causes complete network failure.
   B. Dual loop rings can be very fault tolerant.
   C. Because each device incorporates a repeater, cable faults are easy to locate.
   D. Cable faults are difficult to identify.

3. Which is associated with the Data Link LLC layer?
   A. Route discovery
   B. Media access
   C. Logical topology

4. A method that senses the cable prior to transmission; also detects collisions and initiates retransmission is:
   A. Contention   C. Flow control
   B. Polling   D. CSMA/CD

5. Data at the Data Link layer is called a:
   A. Packet   C. Frame
   B. Datagram   D. Token

6. A message that indicates the reception of a frame is called a(n):
   A. Handshake   C. Reply
   B. Datagram   D. Acknowledgment

7. Which is one benefit of full-duplex dialog?
   A. Both ends can transmit at the same time.
   B. Requires only one channel for both transmission and reception
   C. Requires inexpensive hardware
   D. Permits broad area coverage

8. The transmission capacity of a particular transmission medium is often stated as the
   A. Load factor   C. Bandwidth
   B. Frequency   D. Phase

9. A media connector frequently used for 10Base-T and Fast Ethernet 100 TX with UTP wiring is?
   A. RS-232   C. RG-59
   B. RS-449   D. RJ-45

10. The networking device(s) that extend the maximum distance of a network by connecting separate network segments is called a _____.
    A. Modem   D. Bridge

    B. CodeC   E. LAN Switch
    C. Router

11. The device that connects two or more logically separate networks is a:
    A. Broute.   D. Repeater
    B. Router   E. Layer 3 LAN Switch
    C. Bridge

12. The IEEE 802.2 standard is associated with the_____ layer.
    A. Physical   C. Session
    B. Network   D. Data Link

13. Which IEEE 802.3 standard is referred to as Thin Ethernet?
    A. 1Base5   C. 10BaseF
    B. 10BaseT   D. 10Base2

14. Which is the specification Based upon IBM Token-Ring specification?
    A. IEEE 802.4   C. IEEE 802.7
    B. IEEE 802.6   D. IEEE 802.5

15. Which of the following is a topic addressed by FDDI?
    A. Transmission synchronization   C. Error control
    B. Connection services   D. Media access

16. What is the specification for 10BaseT?
    A. It is a physical star.   C. It is a logical bus.
    B. It is a physical bus.   D. It runs ARCnet over coax cable.

17. How many repeaters may be installed between two segments on a 10BaseT network?
    A. 3   C. 10
    B. 5   D. 4

18. Which of the following statements are true regarding 10Base5 LAN?
    A. The drop cable between the NIC and the bus is made of RG-11 cabling.
    B. The drop cable is made of four-pair AUI cable.
    C. The RG-58 bus is directly attached to the NIC.
    D. Tap markings are located every 2.5 meters.
    E. 10Base5 and 10Base2 networks can be connected by using special adapters.

19. Workstations on a 10Base2 LAN are having problems connecting with the file server. You use a VOM to measure the resistance of the bus and it reads 90 ohms. What could possibly be the problem?
    A. There is a missing terminator.
    B. The bus needs replacing.
    C. A terminator went bad and needs replacing.
    D. The wrong frame type is being used.
    E. The resistance is correct and the problem resides elsewhere.
    F. The network adapters are bad.

20. When two MSAUs are connected together:
    A. Two ports on each MSAU are used for completing the ring.
    B. The Ring In on one MSAU is connected to the Ring Out on the other.
    C. The Ring In ports are interconnected and the Ring Out ports are interconnected.
    D. A CAU is used for the link.

21. The first station powered up on a Token Ring network is called a(n):
    A. Active Monitor   C. File Server
    B. Standby Monitor   D. Beacon

22. Which of the following statements is not true of FDDI networks?
    A. FDDI is based on the structure of two rings rotating in opposite directions.
    B. There is form of FDDI using copper cable.
    C. Speed can reach 100 megabytes per second.
    D. Fiber-optic cable can maintain ground isolation between buildings.

23. What is the LLC 802.2 Protocol ID for the following Protocols?
    A. NetWare   D. TCP/IP
    B. Banyan   E. AppleTalk
    C. OSI

24. Can dual paths exist between two Ethernet segments? If so, what type of bridge would be required?
    A. MAC Layer Bridge   C. Transparent Routing Bridge
    B. Source Routing Bridge   D. Spanning Tree Bridge

25. What is the Interframe gap in microseconds for 10Mbps ethernet?
    A. 11.0   C. 10.5
    B. .965   D. 9.6

26. What is the Interframe gap in microseconds for 100BaseT?
    A. 76   C. 9.6
    B. .960   D. 10.5

27. What is the Interframe gap for Gigabit Ethernet?
    A. 0096
    B. 9.6
    C. 9.60

28. How many nodes/workstations can be attached to a segment supporting the following IEEE standards?
    A. 10Base5   B. 10Base2

29. The first three bytes of the Ethernet packet destination and source address provide you with what type of management information?
    A. User workstation ID   C. Organization Unit ID (OUI)
    B. Management Station   D. Vendor code

30. What is the maximum number of times an Ethernet station will attempt to transmit after a collision?
    A. 17   C. 16
    B. 10   D. 3

31. What is the action that a Token Ring device first undertakes if it detects the absence of tokens or data frames from its upstream neighbor within a specified time period?
    A. Perform a Lobe media test   D. Send ring Purge MAC Frames
    B. Send Beacon MAC frames   E. Send burst error MAC frames
    C. Send line error MAC Frames

32. Which of the following fields within are found in an Ethernet II frame:
    A. Preamble   F. Pad
    B. Start of Frame Delimiter   G. CRC
    C. Destination /Source Address   H. Frame Status
    D. Type   I. Starting Delimiter
    E. Data

33. Token Ring Networks operate at what speeds?
    A. 4Mbps   B. 1Mbps
    C. 16Mbps   D. 100 Mbps

34. The Access Control field in the Token Ring Header is used for what purpose?
    A. Routing Information   C. Frame status checking
    B. MAC layer Addressing   D. Priority, Token, Monitor, etc.

35. What is the function of the active monitor?
- **A.** Station monitor
- **B.** Bridge Monitor
- **C.** Ring Monitor
- **D.** Inject delay into the ring

36. What is a MAC address? Explain.

37. Why must the MAC address to be unique? Explain.

38. Is there a special numbering scheme for MAC addresses? Explain.

39. What is a preamble? Explain.

40. What is a *Start Frame Delimiter* (SFD)? Explain.

41. What does CRC mean? Explain.

42. What is a broadcast address? Explain.

43. What exactly do 10Base5, 10BaseT, 10Base2, and 10Broad36, etc mean? Explain.

44. What does FOIRL mean? Explain.

45. What does SQE mean?

46. What does SQE Test mean? What does heartbeat mean? What are they for? Explain.

47. What does "IPG" mean? Explain.

48. What does "promiscuous mode" mean? Explain.

49. What is a runt? Explain.

50. What causes a runt? Explain.

51. What is jabber? Explain.

52. What causes jabber? Explain.

53. What is a collision? Explain.

54. What causes a collision? Explain.

55. How many collisions are too many? Explain.

56. How do I reduce the number of collisions? Explain.

57. What is a late collision? Explain.

58. What is a jamming signal? Explain.

59. What is a broadcast storm? Explain.

60. How do I recognize a broadcast storm? Explain.

61. How can I prevent a broadcast storm? Explain.

62. What is an Alignment Error? Explain.

63. What is "high" traffic on an Ethernet? 5%? 20%? 90%? Explain.

64. What is a "TDR"? Explain.

65. What does "BERT" mean? Explain.

66. Token Ring uses:
- **A.** Manchester encoding
- **B.** Differential Manchester encoding
- **C.** None of the above

67. Which ring station provides the master clock for the ring?
    - **A.** Standby Monitor station
    - **B.** Active Monitor station
    - **C.** Configuration Ring Server
    - **D.** None of the above

68. Which of the following represents one of the factors that limit the size of a ring?
    - **A.** Delay
    - **B.** Latency
    - **C.** Phase lock loop

69. Identify MAC sub-layer services performed by Token Ring.
    - **A.** Token Management
    - **B.** Frame generation and transmission
    - **C.** Source Routing
    - **D.** Ring Addressing.

70. Identify the Frame Control MAC frames that are processed immediately.
    - **A.** Beacon
    - **B.** Claim Token
    - **C.** Ring Purge
    - **D.** Active Monitor Present
    - **E.** Standby Monitor present
    - **F.** Duplicate Address
    - **G.** Remove Ring Station

71. The Ending delimiter bits consist of:
    - **A.** Non_data J
    - **B.** Non_data K
    - **C.** Data_1
    - **D.** Intermediate Bit
    - **E.** Error Detected bit
    - **F.** None of the above
    - **G.** All of the above

72. Identify the Token format.
    - **A.** SD, DA, SA, ED
    - **B.** SD, FC, ED
    - **C.** SD, AC, FCS
    - **D.** SD, AC,ED

73. The abort sequence is:
    - **A.** SD & FC
    - **B.** FC & ED
    - **C.** SD & AC
    - **D.** SD & ED

74. Identify three Token Ring MAC frames that do not require a free token.
    - **A.** Beacon
    - **B.** Claim Token
    - **C.** Ring Purge
    - **D.** None of the above
    - **E.** All of the above

75. Token Ring's group addressing supports which three types of addresses?
    - **A.** Broadcast
    - **B.** Functional
    - **C.** Group
    - **D.** All of the above

76. The Token Ring, ring delay is called:
    - **A.** Ring latency
    - **B.** Latency
    - **C.** Normal ring delay
    - **D.** Minimum ring latency
    - **E.** None of the above

77. Identify the five steps a station goes through to insert itself into the ring.

78. The NAUN is used for locating the fault domain:
    - **A.** Defective device
    - **B.** Ring Error Monitor
    - **C.** Fault Domain
    - **D.** Hard Error

79. What is the meaning of a Token Ring beacon ? Explain.

80. What are soft errors? Explain.

81. What are hard errors? Explain.

82. Identify four soft errors that do not require ring recovery.

83. Identify 3 isolating errors.

84. Identify 5 non-isolating errors.

85. Token Ring Data Link Layer supports which of the following data frame types?
   A. IEEE 802.5
   B. Token Ring SNAP
   C. IEEE802.2
   D. A & B

86. A virtual ring is used for what purpose? Explain.

87. Identify the frames a ring station must see in order to determine that an Active Monitor is present on the ring.
   A. AMP
   B. SMP
   C. Ring Purge
   D. All of the Above

88. The Active Monitor inserts a ____ bit propagation delay into the ring.
   A. 8
   B. 16
   C. 24
   D. 32

89. What determines whether a Standby Monitor station becomes the active monitor?
   A. No Active monitor present frame
   B. No standby Present frame in 15 sec
   C. No frame detected
   D. Signal Loss
   E. All of the above

90. What frame does the standby monitor send out in order to take part in becoming the Active monitor?
   A. Standby_Token Frame
   B. Release_token Frame
   C. Claim_Token Frame
   D. Active_Token Frame

91. The Ring Purge frame is issued by the following ring station:
   A. Stand by Monitor Station
   B. Ring Error monitor
   C. Active Monitor
   D. None of the above

92. Burst Errors are caused by what?
   A. Signaling Problem
   B. Cabling
   C. Propagation
   D. All of the above

93. Identify the broadcast addresses used in Token Ring.
   A. C000 FFFF FFFF
   B. C000 0000 FFFF
   C. FFFF FFFF FFFF
   D. None of the above

94. 100BaseT is compatible with 10Base-t Ethernet in what aspect?
   A. Frame size
   B. Frame encapsulation
   C. Collisions
   D. Inter-frame gap

95. Ethernet Version 2 was developed by the following vendors:
   A. Digital , IBM, Sun
   B. Digital, Intel, 3COM
   C. Intel, Xerox, Digital
   D. None of the above

96. The IEEE 802.3 specification supports a PAD field for what function?
   A. Addressing
   B. Data padding
   C. Validate CSMA/CD algorithm
   D. Place holder

97. Identify the number of different Ethernet Frame types.
   A. SNAP
   B. Ethernet v2
   C. IEEE 802.3
   D. 802.3_Raw
   E. All of the above

98. What does Cisco call an Ethernet version 2 frame?
- **A.** ARPA
- **B.** Ethernet 2
- **C.** Novell-Ethernet
- **D.** Ethernet Version 2
- **E.** None of the above

99. What does Cisco call a 802.3_ raw frame?
- **A.** Novell-Ether
- **B.** 802.3
- **C.** 802.2
- **D.** All of the above

100. What is the maximum cable length for 10 Base2?
- **A.** 185 meters
- **B.** 200 meters
- **C.** 100 meters
- **D.** 50 meters

101. An Ethernet frame with a DSAP and SSAP value of AA identifies which frame type?
- **A.** SNAP
- **B.** IEEE802.3
- **C.** IEEE 802.2
- **D.** Ethernet

102. What is the Ethernet type value for IP?
- **A.** 0x0600
- **B.** 0x0800
- **C.** 0x0900
- **D.** 0x8136

103. What is the Ethernet type value for IPX?
- **A.** 0x8137
- **B.** 0x0800
- **C.** 0x0600
- **D.** 0x809b

104. The UTP RJ45 pin-out for 10BaseT is:
- **A.** 1to6, 2to5, 3to4, and 7to8
- **B.** 1to1, 2to3, 4to5, and 6to8
- **C.** 1to1 , 2to2, 3to3, and 6to6
- **D.** 2to2, 3to3, 4to4, and 5to5

105. Identify one of the cable specifications does the 100Base-TX support.
- **A.** Four-pair Cat. 3 cable
- **B.** Two-pair Cat. 3 cable
- **C.** Two-pair Cat. 5 cable
- **D.** Four-pair Cat. 5 cable

106. The Ethernet Slot time consists of _____ bits?
- **A.** 512 bits
- **B.** 480 bits
- **C.** 80 bits
- **D.** 48 bits

107. The Ethernet Preamble uses which of the following Manchester encoding pattern?
- **A.** 10101011
- **B.** 10101010
- **C.** 10101110
- **D.** 10110110

108. The Ethernet *Start of Frame Delimiter* (SFD) uses the following Manchester encoding pattern:
- **A.** 10101011
- **B.** 10101010
- **C.** 11111010
- **D.** 10110101

109. How many priority levels are supported in Token Ring?
- **A.** 8
- **B.** 4
- **C.** 10
- **D.** 12
- **E.** 7

110. All nodes or stations on a single Ethernet Cable are considered _____ nodes.
- **A.** adjacent
- **B.** remote
- **C.** non-broadcast
- **D.** router

111. Ethernet Data messages can communicate no less than _____ and no more than _____ bytes of client data.
    A. 25, 16,383   **C.** 46, 1,500
    B. 46, 1,900   **D.** 64, 1,518

112. A Token Ring network can use writing concentrators known as _____ or _____ to create the ring.
    A. *Multi-Section Access Units* (MSAUs), *Central Access Units* (CAUs)
    B. *Multi-Station Access Units* (MSAUs), *Controlled Access Units* (CAUs)
    C. *Multi-Section Access Units* (MSAUs), *Controlled Access Units* (CAUs)
    D. *Multi-Station Access Units* (MSAUs), *Central Access Units* (CAUs)

113. Type 2 Token Ring Cables consist of _____.
    A. four shielded twisted pairs of #22 AWG telephone conductor
    B. two shielded twisted pairs of #22 AWG telephone conductor
    C. four unshielded twisted pairs of #22 AWG telephone conductor
    D. fiber-optic conductors

114. A protocol analyzer can help you perform which of the following tasks?
    A. Monitor network performance   **D.** Plan for growth
    B. Troubleshoot network errors   **E.** All of the above
    C. Optimize the LAN

115. The seven layers of the OSI model include _____.
    A. Application, Presentation, Session, Transport, Network, Data Link, and Physical
    B. Application, Preparation, Session, Transport, Network, Data Link, and Physical
    C. Program, Presentation, Session, Transport, Network, Data Link, and Physical
    D. Program, Preparation, Session, Transport, Network, Data Link, and Physical

116. Both Ethernet and Token Ring networks use what type of switching technique?
    A. Circuit switching   **C.** Packet switching
    B. Message switching   **D.** None of the above

117. Which layer of the OSI model organizes the one and zero bits into "Frames"?
    A. Application   **C.** Data Link
    B. Physical   **D.** Presentation

118. With asynchronous transmission, the data is ____.
    A. sent individually, one character at a time, and is surrounded by a start and stop bit
    B. sent as a block of data, surrounded by a start and stop bit
    C. very susceptible to transmission errors
    D. sent faster than with synchronous transmission, which is why it's used on PCs

119. The function of the Presentation layer is to _____.
    A. transform the data into a mutually agreed upon format
    B. present a stream of bits to the physical layer for transmitting
    C. present the data on the screen for the user to view
    D. all of the above

120. The physical layer is responsible for _____.
    A. grouping bits into frames
    B. determining how ones and zeros are sent via electrical signals across the network
    C. moving the data from one network segment to another
    D. multiplexing signals

121. The function of the Session layer is to _____.
   A. convert the data into a series of one and zero bits that the physical layer can understand
   B. transform the data into a language that both the sending and receiving computers understand
   C. move the data in a reliable manner across the network
   D. maintain the dialog between communicating applications

122. The function of the Transport layer is to _____.
   A. carry the data from one application to another
   B. move data across multiple cable segments
   C. ensure reliable data delivery
   D. none of the above

123. If a Token Ring Beacon process lasts for more than ___ seconds, it is more than likely will not recover on its own.
   A. 26 seconds
   B. 15 seconds
   C. 10 seconds
   D. 7 seconds

124. The Token Ring holding time is what?
   A. 10 ms
   B. 7 ms
   C. 15 ms
   D. A & B

125. During the Token Ring station insertion process, the station issues a lobe test using which destination address?
   A. 00-00-00-00-00-00
   B. c0-00-00-00-00-00
   C. 00-f0-00-00-00-00
   D. None of the above

126. The Token Ring signal travels _____ around the ring.
   A. clockwise
   B. counterclockwise
   C. clocking is provided by the active monitor
   D. none of the above

127. The *Ring Parameter Server* (RPS) provides which of the following services?
   A. Physical drop number
   B. Local Ring number
   C. Access Priority
   D. Soft Error
   E. All of the above

128. The station that discovered the absence or failure of the AM transmits a Claim Token MAC Frame every ___ milliseconds.
   A. 29
   B. 7
   C. 12
   D. 20

129. A station goes into monitor contention mode after 18 seconds when it does not see which of the following frames?
   A. Active Monitor Present MAC frame
   B. Standby Monitor Present MAC frame
   C. Ring Purge MAC frame
   D. All of the above
   E. A & B

130. Select the Abort sequence of fields.
   A. SDEL, EDEL
   B. SDEL, FS
   C. ADEL, AC,EDEL
   D. None of the above

131. Name at least three MAC Frame major vectors in the Token Ring MAC header.
   A. Beacon
   B. Init Ring station
   C. AM Present
   D. Ring Purge
   E. All of the above

132. What is the Token Ring functional address for Active Monitor?
- **A.** C00000000001
- **B.** C00000000002
- **C.** C00000000008
- **D.** C00000000010

133. What is the Token Ring functional address for Ring Parameter Server?
- **A.** C00000000001
- **B.** C00000000002
- **C.** C00000000008
- **D.** C00000000010
- **E.** C00000000080
- **F.** C00000000100

134. What is the Token Ring functional address for Ring Error Monitor?
- **A.** C00000000001
- **B.** C00000000002
- **C.** C00000000008
- **D.** C00000000010
- **E.** C00000000080
- **F.** C00000000100

135. What is the Token Ring functional address for Configuration Report Server?
- **A.** C00000000001
- **B.** C00000000002
- **C.** C00000000008
- **D.** C00000000010
- **E.** C00000000080
- **F.** C00000000100

136. What is the Token Ring functional address for NetBIOS?
- **A.** C00000000001
- **B.** C00000000002
- **C.** C00000000008
- **D.** C00000000010
- **E.** C00000000080
- **F.** C00000000100

137. What is the Token Ring functional address for LAN Bridge?
- **A.** C00000000001
- **B.** C00000000002
- **C.** C00000000008
- **D.** C00000000010
- **E.** C00000000080
- **F.** C00000000100

138. The Highest priority option using Token Ring is:
- **A.** 2
- **B.** 4
- **C.** 8
- **D.** 7

139. The access priority of the token frame is determined by:
- **A.** The values of the last 3 bits of the access control field
- **B.** The values of the first 3 bits of the access control field
- **C.** The bits in the reservation field
- **D.** None of the above

140. The source station in a Token Ring network is responsible for putting data on the ring, but what station is responsible for removing the toke frame?
- **A.** The destination station
- **B.** The next down stream neighbor
- **C.** The source station
- **D.** None of the above

141. Early token release allows the source station to release a free token after transmitting the information frame but before the receipt of transmitted header. What Token Ring speed supports early token release?
- **A.** 4Mbps
- **B.** 10Mbps
- **C.** 16Mbps
- **D.** 100 Mbps

142. In the type field of a Ethernet II frame the value 0x0806 represents:
- **A.** IP
- **B.** ICMP
- **C.** ARP
- **D.** DECnet

143. Cisco encapsulation type, "ARPA," is commonly known as?
    A. Ethernet Type II
    B. IEEE 802.3
    C. Novell 802.3 Raw
    D. SNAP

144. Cisco's encapsulation type, "SAP," is commonly known as:
    A. Ethernet Type II
    B. IEEE 802.3
    C. Novell 802.3 Raw
    D. SNAP

145. Ethernet 10Base5 has a maximum segment length of:
    A. 100 meters
    B. 250 meters
    C. 500 meters
    D. 1000 meters

146. Ethernet 1Base5 has a maximum segment length of:
    A. 100 meters
    B. 250 meters
    C. 500 meters
    D. 1000 meters

147. Which field in the Ethernet frame checks the integrity of the frame?
    A. Preamble
    B. Start of Frame
    C. Frame Check Sequence
    D. Checksum

148. What bit order should be used to carry MAC addresses in the data field of higher layer protocols?
    A. Least-significant-bit first
    B. Most-significant-bit first
    C. Depends on the bit order used by the source system
    D. Depends on the bit order used by the destination system

149. What are the differences between IEEE 802.3 and Ethernet?
    A. There is no difference.
    B. The frame formats are different.
    C. The LLC sublayer can be used in one but not the other.
    D. The routing layer can be used on one but not the other.

150. In the type field of an Ethernet II frame, the value 0x 6004 represents:
    A. IP
    B. DEC LAT
    C. Banyan
    D. XNS
    E. TLS
    F. PPP

151. In the type field of an Ethernet II frame the value 0BAD represents:
    A. IP
    B. DEC LAT
    C. Banyan
    D. AppleTalk

152. MAC address are ___ bits in length.
    A. 32 bits
    B. 48 bits
    C. 64 bits
    D. 72 bits

153. MAC addresses on a router are stored in:
    A. RAM
    B. ROM
    C. Flash
    D. NVRAM

154. Define slave ports in FDDI.
    A. To provide a inexpensive connection to a dual-attachment station.
    B. To do all the hard work required to connect dual-attachment concentrators.
    C. To allow single-attachment stations to be connect to concentrators.
    D. To provide a standby connection from a concentrator.

155. A dual attachment station can support ___ number of ports.

    A. 2   **C.** no limit

    B. 3   **D.** none of the above

156. An FDDI node has two (ports) marked A and B. What is the difference between the two ports?

    A. B port is used as a standby.

    B. An A port is used as a master and B can be used only as a slave.

    C. An A port should normally be connected to a B port on another node.

    D. An A port should normally be connect to an A port on another node.

    E. All of the above

157. Identify a valid FDDI configuration.

    A. There are at least two rings somewhere.

    B. There is at least one concentrator somewhere.

    C. There is at least one tree.

    D. There is at least one master port.

    E. There is at least one slave port.

    F. All of the above.

    G. None of the above.

158. FDDI supports priority by_____.

    A. making the token go faster when needed

    B. slowing down the token when there are no high-priority messages

    C. marking certain bits in tokens

    D. marking certain bits in frames

    E. allowing low-priority traffic only when the token is rotating quickly

159. What is the main difference between the timed token access in FDDI and the token access method used in traditional Token Rings?

    A. The FDDI token has a built-in timer.

    B. The length of an FDDI token and hence its time is kept constant

    C. The difference between successive token rotation times is kept constant in FDDI.

    D. FDDI token rotation of the number of active stations on the ring

160. What happens if a station's token holding timer expires in the middle of a long frame?

    A. The transmission is aborted immediately.

    B. The remaining frame is saved for transmission next time.

    C. This and all other waiting frames are transmitted.

    D. The speed of transmission is increased to ensure timely completion.

    E. This frame is transmitted completely even though this delays the token beyond the target.

161. Define immediate token release in FDDI.

    A. The token is released immediately after its receipt.

    B. The token is released as soon as all transmitted frames are received back at the transmitting station.

    C. The token is released as soon as the last frame is transmitted from the source station without delay.

    D. The token is released as soon as the last frame is acknowledged.

162. What are common uses of void frames?
    A. To void (invalidate) a previous successful transmission
    B. To interrupt the current transmitter
    C. To indicate that the token is corrupted
    D. Just to kill time when necessary
    E. To mark the beginning or end of a transmission sequence

163. How many 1-byte numbers have the same representation in little-endian and big-endian bit order (for example, 1101 1011)?
    A. 1
    B. 8
    C. 16
    D. 512
    E. 1024
    F. 2048

164. What bit order is used for transmitting data bytes in FDDI frames?
    A. Least-significant bit first
    B. Most-significant bit first
    C. Depends on the bit order used by the source adapter
    D. Depends on the bit order used by the destination adapter

165. What bit order is used for transmitting source/destination addresses in FDDI frames?
    A. Least-significant bit first
    B. Most-significant bit first
    C. Depends on the bit order used by the source adapter
    D. Depends on the bit order used by the destination adapter

166. Which of the following apply to all systems with big-endian byte order?
    A. They transmit the most-significant bit first.
    B. They transmit the least-significant bit first.
    C. They transmit the most-significant byte first for all multi-byte quantities.
    D. None of the above

167. The FDDI claim process creates:
    A. To reclaim a token after each rotation
    B. To reset the priority of a token
    C. To reclaim the space used by the token
    D. A New Token for the ring
    E. All of the above

168. What was the original purpose of allowing restricted tokens in FDDI?
    A. To send confidential information
    B. To prevent misbehaving stations from using the token
    C. To allow long dialogs
    D. A & B
    E. None of the above

169. How many bits can a properly functioning elasticity buffer add or delete between two frames?
    A. 0
    B. 1
    C. 4.5
    D. 5
    E. 9
    F. 10
    G. No limit

170. What is the maximum number of bits inside a frame that can be deleted by the elasticity buffer if the clocks are functioning properly?

A. 0
B. 1
C. 4.5
D. 5

E. 9
F. 10
G. No limit

171. Allowing frames longer than 4472 bytes would require the FDDI standard to:

A. Not use crystals
B. Require higher quality crystals
C. Require shorter elasticity buffers
D. None of the above

172. Which of the following applies to an elasticity buffer?

A. It protects two stations from each other.
B. It prevents two frames from accidentally running into each other.
C. It is made of an elastic material.
D. It uses crystals.
E. It is used to buffer store frames.
F. None of the above.

173. Crystals are used in FDDI stations:

A. To provide a local clock
B. To synchronize clocks

C. To predict future bits
D. For good luck

174. A smoother smooths out variations in:

A. Pulse width
B. Pulse height
C. Clock frequency

D. Interframe gaps
E. Frames sizes

175. A smoother must add extra symbols if the Interframe gap is:

A. 16
B. 4

C. 13
D. None of the above

176. A 100/140 -μm step-index fiber has a normalized frequency of 90. What is the approximate number of modes?

A. 90
B. 100
C. 140

D. 4050
E. 8100

177. The dispersion in a fiber is caused by:

A. Too much light coming from the source
B. Reflections caused by loose connectors
C. Microscopic breaks in the fiber
D. None of the above

178. Why was a 1300-nm window chosen over 850 and 1500 nm for FDDI?

A. It provides the lowest attenuation.
B. It provides the lowest dispersion.
C. The devices are lowest cost.
D. All of the above

179. Given the same other physical characteristics, why would you prefer a 62.5/125 fiber over 100/140 fiber?
    A. 62.5/125 has a higher bandwidth.
    B. 62.5/125 has a higher attenuation.
    C. 62.5/125 allows more light to be launched
    D. 62.5/125 has a higher intermodal dispersion.

180. Why should you recommend the use of multimode fibers instead of single-mode fibers in FDDI?
    A. A Multimode fiber can be used for longer distances.
    B. Multimode fiber is cheaper.
    C. Transceivers for multimode fibers are cheaper.
    D. Multimode fiber allows many more modes than a single-mode fiber.

181. Which of the following are valid FDDI configurations?
    A. A 50/125 fiber is used between stations A and B while 62.5/125 fiber is used between stations B and C.
    B. A 50/125 fiber is used to connect station A to a concentrator while 62.5/125 fiber is used to connect station C to the same concentrator.
    C. A 50/125 fiber is used from station A to a patch-panel while 62.5/125 fiber is used from the patch-panel to station B. The two stations are connected via a patch cord.
    D. 30/125 fiber is used from station A to B while 62.5/125 is used from B to A.

182. Why do single-mode links allow longer distances than multimode links in FDDI?
    A. Laser transmitters used in single-mode links are more powerful.
    B. Receivers used in single-mode links are more sensitive.
    C. Single-mode fiber has a lower attenuation.
    D. Single-mode fiber has a lower dispersion.
    E. All of the above

183. Which of the following can you connect directly?
    A. Two stations with Category II transceivers
    B. Two stations with Category I transceivers
    C. One station with a Category I transceiver and another with a Category II transceiver
    D. None of the above

184. The maximum link length allowed by the single-mode fiber PMD is:
    A. 2 km   C. 60 km
    B. 40 km   D. Not specified

185. Optical bypasses are allowed on:
    A. DASs with Category II transceivers
    B. DASs with Category I transceivers
    C. DASs with Category I transceivers but connected to another DAS with a Category II transceiver
    D. DASs with Category II transceivers but connected to another DAS with a Category I transceiver

186. What type connectors are recommended in the FDDI low-cost fiber standard?
    A. Two simplex connectors
    B. Duplex-SC without port-type keying
    C. Duplex-ST without polarity keying
    D. Duplex FDDI MIC with polarity and port-type keying

187. Which Category of UTP would you use for FDDI?
     A. Category 3   C. Category 5
     B. Category 4   D. All of the above

188. Transmitting FDDI signals on UTP requires special coding because:
     A. The new coding prevents electromagnetic radiation at all frequencies.
     B. The new coding lowers the power spectrum to below 30 MHz.
     C. The new coding disperses the power spectrum over a wide frequency band and thus
        reduces the electromagnetic interference.

189. What is SONET?
     A. It is a CCITT standard for networking.
     B. It is an ANSI standard for optical transmission.
     C. It is the scientific optical network funded by the National Science Foundation.
     D. It is a special type of fiber.

190. Which of the following links can you use for FDDI?
     A. STS-1   C. STS-3
     B. STS-3c   D. STM-4

191. What is the maximum length limit for SONET links in FDDI?
     A. 2 km   D. Limited by the total ring latency
     B. 60 km   E. No limit
     C. 200 km

192. What is an SMT announcement?
     A. A message sent by the network manager to announce an emergency such as the
        network shutdown
     B. Unsolicited frames sent by stations for management
     C. A group request to be answered by all stations on the ring
     D. A message used to locate resources in the network

193. What is the purpose of *neighbor information frames* (NIFs)?
     A. To determine the neighboring station
     B. To determine if the neighboring station has changed
     C. To announce the neighboring station's address
     D. All of the above

194. Which SMT frames can be used to find a station's upstream neighbor address?
     A. Neighbor information frame   D. Resource allocation frame
     B. Status information frame   E. Parameter management frame
     C. Echo frame

195. Fiber cables with loose buffering are used outdoors:
     A. Because most of the interbuilding traffic consists of short frames that do not need big
        buffers
     B. To increase the temperature tolerance
     C. To prevent cable strain and to allow free movement
     D. To increase distance

196. To connect two fibers permanently, splicing is preferable to using connectors because:
     A. It is cheaper.   D. Less fiber used
     B. It has less loss.   E. None of the above
     C. It can be done using ordinary pliers.   F. 199

197. Optical time-domain reflectometry is used____.
- **A.** to locate faults
- **B.** to determine a fiber's length
- **C.** to determine a fiber's attenuation
- **D.** to determine connector losses
- **E.** to check the time jitter of the clock

198. When a destination station receives a frame, what happens?
- **A.** Sends data through router
- **B.** Sends back an Acknowledgement on receipt of the data
- **C.** Discards the data
- **D.** Copies the data and marks the Frame Status field and repeats it back out on the ring
- **E.** None of the above

199. FDDI stations that receive data addressed to another station, the station:
- **A.** Checks the MAC Address for its address
- **B.** Deletes the data and send back a ring error
- **C.** Operates in repeater mode by checking for errors and repeating it back onto the ring
- **D.** A & D
- **E.** None of the above

200. Dual attachment stations:
- **A.** Ring wrap in the event of a cable break
- **B.** Master and Slave ports
- **C.** Are always Ring error Monitor
- **D.** Supports Source routing only

201. Single Attached stations connect to a concentrator by:
- **A.** Primary FDDI ring
- **B.** Primary and secondary rings
- **C.** Secondary ring during ring wrap
- **D.** None of the above

202. Identify the FDDI stations that cannot be connected to both the primary and secondary rings:
- **A.** Single MAC/Single Attachment
- **B.** Dual MAC/Dual attachment concentrator
- **C.** Dual MAC/Dual attachment station
- **D.** All of the above

203. What happens if the ring experiences a physical fault while in a wrap state?
- **A.** The one physical network is divided into two distinct rings
- **B.** Report to the Ring Error Monitor
- **C.** Stations enter Beacon state

204. Identify an illegal port connection:
- **A.** Master port connected to Master port
- **B.** Port A connected to B
- **C.** Master port connected to Slave port
- **D.** A & B

205. When a station employing an optical bypass switch is powered off:
- **A.** The node on either side of the station become neighbors.
- **B.** FDDI station wraps.
- **C.** The station uses the second ring.
- **D.** None of the above

206. Define Dual Homing.
  A. *Dual Attachment Station* (DAS) offers a backup connection to the primary ring
  B. Single Attachment station connected to another
  C. DAS sends data on both the primary and secondary rings
  D. A & C

207. Graceful insertion is defined as:
  A. The ability of the concentrator to connect a station without interrupting the ring operation
  B. Avoiding re-initialization
  C. Optical bypass switch that must be used
  D. A & B
  E. None of the above

208. FDDI stations upon reception of a token can:
  A. Transmit one frame prior to releasing the token
  B. Based on the Token holding timer
  C. Once the token is captured, a station can transmit all the data required
  D. None of the above

209. When a station attaches to a concentrator, and a fault occurs, what happens?
  A. Bypasses the connection
  B. Enter beacon state
  C. Ring wrap
  D. None of the above

210. FDDI stations detects physical faults by:
  A. Quiet line state
  B. Beacon station
  C. Ring insertion state
  D. Claim state

211. The B port precedence rule defines:
  A. On a device both the A and B ports , the B port becomes the primary link
  B. B port must be connected to another B port on the ring
  C. A & B
  D. None of the above

212. What happens when a station connected to an FDDI concentrator powers off?
  A. FDDI concentrator automatically bypasses the station
  B. Power the station off
  C. Ring wraps
  D. None of the above

213. What is the cause of a station stuck beaconing?
  A. The station is not transmitting beacons to its downstream neighbor.
  B. The station has failed the self-test.
  C. The station's bypass is stuck.
  D. Its upstream neighbor is not sending beacons.

214. Which of the following apply to the synchronous transmission on FDDI?
  A. They can be made even if the token is late.
  B. They must be periodic.
  C. They have no time limit.
  D. They require more precise clock synchronization.
  E. They require prior reservation.

215. Define an Optical bypass switch.
     A. The incoming optical signal is passed directly to the next station.
     B. It acts like a repeater
     C. MAC layer bridge
     D. All of the above

216. Which station creates the FDDI Token?
     A. Station with the lowest *token rotation time* (TTRT)
     B. First station that attaches to the ring
     C. Station with the lowest token holding time
     D. Each FDDI station creates its own token
     E. None of the above

217. When a FDDI station receives a claim frame from its upstream neighbor containing a lower target token rotation time than its own:
     A. It stops processing its own and repeat the claim frames for its upstream neighbor.
     B. It continues claim token frames and the neighbor will have to wait.
     C. All of the above

218. The FDDI token is created by:
     A. Claim Process   C. Ring insertion time
     B. Beacon frame   D. None of the above

219. FDDI stations must keep track of a (an):
     A. Upstream neighbor   C. Its own station address
     B. Downstream neighbor   D. All of the above

220. A trace is sent:
     A. To upstream neighbor via secondary ring
     B. By claim token process
     C. To the downstream neighbor
     D. None of the above

221. Which of the following are always true for a dual ring of trees configuration?
     A. There is at least one dual-attachment concentrator.
     B. There are at least two single-attachment concentrators.
     C. All nodes have access to both rings.
     D. All nodes are dual-attachment nodes.
     E. All nodes are single-attachment nodes.

222. In order for FDDI stations to communicate to an IEEE 802.3 station the following must happen:
     A. Source Route Bridging
     B. Source Route Translational bridge
     C. Encapsulating bridge
     D. Translational bridge

223. The default state of the Frame status address recognized, frame copied and error indicators are:
     A. reset, reset, reset   C. reset, set, set
     B. set, reset, set   D. set, set, set

224. How does a Translational bridge handle the Ethernet version II type field?
    A. Use SNAP header encapsulation
    B. Delete and replace with an FDDI type field
    C. Delete all together
    D. None of the above

225. Source Routing Transparent bridges set the *frame status* (FS) indicator to:
    A. A is reset and C is Set
    B. E is set and C is Reset
    C. A is Set and C is Reset
    D. A is Set and C is Set

226. FDDI allows a frame size to be set:
    A. True
    B. False

227. FDDI stations that sends frames larger than 1500 bytes to an Ethernet station via a bridge must do the following:
    A. Bridge has to segment frame.
    B. Bridge discards the frame.
    C. The upper layer protocols will not allow this to happen.
    D. A & B

228. FDDI standard was developed by:
    A. IEEE
    B. OSI
    C. ANSI
    D. ITU-T

229. FDDI operates in this type of topology:
    A. Bus
    B. Star
    C. Ring

230. FDDI uses the encapsulation or coding method of:
    A. SONET
    B. 4B/5B
    C. 5B/10B
    D. DS3

231. A token in FDDI is composed of these fields:
    A. Preamble
    B. Starting delimiter
    C. Frame Control
    D. End Delimiter
    E. None of the above

232. FDDI encapsulating bridges:
    A. Allow the Ethernet frame to be placed in the information field
    B. Do not support Source Routing
    C. Allow an FDDI station and Ethernet station to communicate
    D. Bridge perform segmentation

233. What can always be said about a frame whose C indicator is set?
    A. The frame was delivered to the intended application.
    B. The frame was successfully received by the destination station.
    C. The frame was received by the destination without an error.
    D. All of the above.
    E. None of the above.

234. The FDDI frames are limited to 4500 bytes because:
    A. Most frames would not like to stand behind a longer frame.
    B. Longer frames may cause elasticity buffer errors.
    C. Longer frames are unreliable.

    D. Longer frames take longer to transmit.
    E. It is a good round number.
    F. All of the above.

235. Which of the following apply to an FDDI ring with a null-attachment concentrator?
    A. The ring has no stations.
    B. The ring has no other concentrators
    C. The concentrator is broken.
    D. The FDDI has no dual ring.
    E. The FDDI has no trees.
    F. The stations use wireless communication.

236. Master ports in FDDI are used:
    A. To connect stations on the dual ring
    B. To provide an alternate connection from dual-attachment stations
    C. To provide connections between concentrators and some stations
    D. None of the above

237. What is the primary purpose of implementor frames in FDDI?
    A. To implement important *station management* (SMT) functions
    B. For communication among implementors
    C. For uses specific to a particular organization or networking architecture
    D. To help implementors debug their implementations

238. Define the FDDI wrap state.
    A. When both the primary and secondary rings are joined by a dual attachment station
    B. SAS attached to concentrator
    C. Remove fibers from the cable
    D. Master station connected to slave

239. Ring delay is also commonly called:
    A. Minimum ring latency   **C.** Token Rotation Time
    B. Jitter   **D.** None of the above

240. 16Mb Token Ring Early Token Release provide the following:
    A. Multiple Tokens can circulate the ring at the same time
    B. Only one Token can circulate on the ring at one time, but the speed is 16mb versus 4Mb
    C. None of the above

241. Virtual Rings behave as follows to network analyzers:
    A. Physical Ring
    B. Analyzers are not able to capture internal Virtual Rings
    C. This is only useful in DLSw environments
    D. Virtual Rings appear as logical Rings to analyzers
    E. None of the above

242. The following Token Ring address is identified as 400000000002 in non-canonical. What would be the address in canonical?

243. Is the following Ethernet address 08008a121314 identified in non-canonical?

244. The IEEE 802.3-broadcast address 0xFFFFFFFFFFFF is converted to _____ for IEEE 802.5 broadcast networks.
    A. 0xC000000000FF   **C.** 0xC0000000FFF
    B. 0xC000FFFFFFFF   **D.** 0xC0FFFFFFFFF

245. What is the purpose of the Token Ring Active Monitor Bit being set to 1?

```
DLC:   FS: Addr recognized indicators: 11, Frame copied indicators: 11
DLC:   AC: Frame priority 0,  Reservation priority 0,  Monitor count 1
DLC:   FC: LLC frame,  PCF attention code: None
DLC:   Destination = Functional address C00000002000, LAN Manager
DLC:   Source      = Station NGC   30341D, This Sniffer
```

    A. No Active Monitor Present Frame
    B. Active Monitor sets the bit for Ring Management
    C. Active Monitor sets bit to later discard the frame
    D. Available Token
    E. None of the above

246. Identify the largest frame bits for an 8144 byte frame.

    A. 110   **C.** 100
    B. 101   **D.** 110

247. Identify the Token Ring functions that use the functional address of C000FFFFFFFF.

    A. Active Monitor   **D.** Ring Error Monitor
    B. Standby Monitor   **E.** Configuration Server
    C. Token Ring Broadcast   **F.** All of the above

248. The following Frame Trace represent a station that is:

    A. Receiving a frame   **C.** This is a MAC layer management frame.
    B. Sending a frame   **D.** None of the above

```
DLC:   --- DLC Header ---
DLC:
DLC:   Frame 46 arrived at  21:22:44.536; frame size is 19 (0013 hex) bytes.
DLC:   FS: Addr recognized indicators: 00, Frame copied indicators: 00
DLC:   AC: Frame priority 0,  Reservation priority 0,  Monitor count 1
DLC:   FC: LLC frame,  PCF attention code: None
DLC:   Destination = Station 400000000002
DLC:   Source      = Station IBM   E4BD21
DLC:
RI :   --- Routing Indicators ---
RI :
RI :   Routing control = 02
RI :       000. .... = Non-broadcast
RI :       ...0 0010 = RI length is 2
RI :   Routing control = 70
RI :       0... .... = Forward direction
RI :       .111 .... = Largest frame is 41600
RI :       .... 000. = Extended frame is 0
RI :       .... ...0 = Reserved
RI :
LLC:   --- LLC Header ---
LLC:
LLC:   DSAP Address = 00, DSAP IG Bit = 00 (Individual Address)
LLC:   SSAP Address = 04, SSAP CR Bit = 00 (Command)
LLC:   Unnumbered frame: TEST, POLL
LLC:
```

249. The Token Ring address 000524A5FC29 would be ____ in canonical format.

250. The Ethernet Transit OUI is used for:
  A. Ethernet Multicast addressing
  B. Token Ring Functional Addressing
  C. Transporting Ethernet II frames over Token Ring Snap Header
  D. Transporting IEEE 802.3 Ethernet Frames

251. Referring to the show interface token 0 in the previous question, what is the ring number assigned to this interface?
  A. 20
  B. 1
  C. 10
  D. None of the above

252. Identify the NAUN address partner for this Token Ring Interface.
  A. 0000.308C.55c8
  B. 4000.0000.0000
  C. 4000.0000.0002
  D. 0000.308C.af76

```
ATLANTA#sh int contro to 0
TMS380 unit 0: 512 Kb RAM, state 4, idb 0xAF768, ds 0xB1204
  current address: 0000.308C. 55c8, burned in address: 0000.308C.  55c8
  ssb_ptr 0x1040, srb_ptr 0x1140, arb_ptr 0x1240, stb_ptr 0x1400, ipb_ptr 0x1356
  bia_addr 0x8CE, swlev_addr 0x5FC, address_addr 0x902, parm_addr 0x6D8
mac_buff 0x406, ti_ring_speed_ptr 0x8CA, adapter_ram_ptr 0x448
adapter_ram 486, ti_ring_speed 0, memory paragraphs 8
sifsts 0x0000, sifacl 0xE42F, sifadr 0x071C, sifadrx 0x0001
rx internal buf size 40, rx total buffers avail 1016,
rx buffers in use 0, rx frames lost 0,
Last Ring Status: none
Stats: soft: 0/0, hard: 0/0, sig loss: 0/0, throttle: 0/0
tx beacon: 0/0, wire fault 0/0, recovery: 0/0
only station: 0/0, remote removal: 0/0
Bridge: local 10, bnum 1, target 20
max_hops 7, target idb: 0x0, not local
Interface failures: 0
Monitor state: (active)
flags 0xC0, code 0x0, reason 0x0
chip f/w: MDGMF20100, [bridge capable]
SMT versions: 1.01 kernel, 130.00 fastmac
ring mode: F00, internal enables: SRB REM RPS CRS/NetMgr
internal functional: 0800011A, group: 00000000
if_state: 1, ints: 0/0, ghosts: 0/0, bad_states: 0/0
ring: 10, bridge num: 1, target: 20, max hops: 7
last open options: (00001180)
error log reads 0, error log failures 0
too big packets 0, full tx buffer errors 0
input_throttled 0
receive delimiter error 0, receive implicit errors 0
receive explicit error 0, receive dma overrun 0
receive buffer runout 0
Internal controller smt state:
Adapter MAC:      0000.308C. 55c8, Physical drop:     00000000
NAUN Address:     4000.0000.0000, NAUN drop:        00000000
Last source:      4000.0000.0000, Last poll:        0000.308C.  55c8
Last MVID:        0005,         Last attn code:    0005
Txmit priority:   0006,         Auth Class:        7FFF
Monitor Error:    0000,         Interface Errors:  FFFF
Correlator:       0000,         Soft Error Timer:  00C8
```

```
Local Ring:         0000,        Ring Status:         0000
Beacon rcv type: 0000,           Beacon txmit type: 0000
Beacon type:        0000,        Beacon NAUN:         0000.308C.  55c8
Beacon drop:        0000,        Reserved:            0000
Reserved2:          0000
```

253. What is the ring speed of the token ring interface in the following **show** command?

    A. 4Mbytes   **C.** 4464Mbits

    B. 4Mbits   **D.** None of the above

```
SEATTLE#sh int to 0
TokenRing0 is up, line protocol is up
Hardware is TMS380, address is 0000.30bA. a921 (bia 0000.30bA. a921)
Internet address is 192.168.33.1 255.255.255.0
MTU 4464 bytes, BW 4000 Kbit, DLY 2500 usec, rely 255/255, load 1/255
Encapsulation SNAP, loopback not set, keepalive set (10 sec)
ARP type: SNAP, ARP Timeout 4:00:00
Ring speed: 4 Mbps
Single ring node, Source Route Transparent Bridge capable
Source bridging enabled, srn 30 bn 1 trn 20 (ring group)
proxy explorers disabled, spanning explorer enabled, NetBIOS cache disabled
Group Address: 0x00000000, Functional Address: 0x0800011A
Ethernet Transit OUI: 0x0000F8
```

254. The follwoing **show Interface exhibit** represents:

    A. No Keepalive sent   **C.** Administratively down

    B. Cable not connected   **D.** None of the above

```
corp#sh int s 1
Serial1 is down, line protocol is down
Hardware is HD64570
Internet address is 150.100.2.1 255.255.255.0
MTU 1500 bytes, BW 1544 Kbit, DLY 20000 usec, rely 255/255, load 1/255
Encapsulation HDLC, loopback not set, keepalive set (10 sec)
Last input 1:14:34, output 1:17:13, output hang never
Last clearing of "show interface" counters never
Input queue: 0/75/0 (size/max/drops); Total output drops: 0
Output queue: 0/64/0 (size/threshold/drops)
Conversations 0/1 (active/max active)
```

255. What is the interface encapsulation used on the following interface?

    A. IEEE 802.5   **C.** SNAP

    B. IEEE 802.2   **D.** ARPA

```
SEATTLE#Show interface to 0
TokenRing0 is up, line protocol is up
Hardware is TMS380, address is 0000.30bA. a921 (bia 0000.30bA. a921)
Internet address is 192.168.33.1 255.255.255.0
MTU 4464 bytes, BW 4000 Kbit, DLY 2500 usec, rely 255/255, load 1/255
Encapsulation SNAP, loopback not set, keepalive set (10 sec)
ARP type: SNAP, ARP Timeout 4:00:00
Ring speed: 4 Mbps
Single ring node, Source Route Transparent Bridge capable
```

256. When sending a packet from C1 on LAN 1 to C2 on LAN 2 using a Transparent Bridge, what source MAC address will be seen on LAN 2?

    A. The Bridge MAC address on LAN 2   **C.** C2's MAC Address

    B. The Bridge MAC address on LAN 1   **D.** C1 MAC Address

257. What will the destination MAC address be if C1 on LAN 1 sends a frame to LAN2 Station C2 using a layer 2 LAN Switch?
   A. C1 MAC Address
   B. C2 MAC Address
   C. The MAC Address of the Bridge Interface on LAN 2
   D. None of the above

258. What is the Highlighted address in canonical format?
```
DLC: --- DLC Header ---
DLC:
DLC: Frame 119 arrived at 20:11:13.617; frame size is 63 (003F hex) bytes.
DLC: FS: Addr recognized indicators: 00, Frame copied indicators: 00
DLC: AC: Frame priority 0, Reservation priority 0, Monitor count 0
DLC: FC: LLC frame, PCF attention code: None
DLC: Destination = Functional address C00000000080, NetBIOS
DLC: Source = Station 00A0248AD164, C_HOSTTR<20>
DLC:
```

259. Station A attached to ring 100 sends a data frame to station C on the same ring. The frame status bits are as follow: A=1 C=0. What can station A derive from this field regarding station C?
   A. Station C is not active on the ring.
   B. Station C copied the data ok.
   C. Station C was active on the ring but for some reason did not copy the data.
   D. None of the above

260. The Token Ring Frame Status bit address copied bit combinations are as follows:
```
AC=00 (Answer)
AC=01
AC=10(Answer)
AC=11(Answer)
```
   A. None of the above   **B.** All of the above

261. What is the MAC code in Token Ring for Duplicate Address?
   A. 0110   **C.** 0011
   B. 0101   **D.** 0001

262. A Token Ring Addressed starting with 4000.xxx.xxxx represents:
   A. BIA   **D.** A & B
   B. Host based address   **E.** All of the above
   C. Locally administered address (LAA)

263. The Token Bit when set to zero indicates:
   A. Token   **C.** Hard Error
   B. Data Frame   **D.** Monitor Bit

264. Host C1 transmits a frame to host C2. The destination MAC address seen on LAN B?
   A. Host C1   **C.** Host C 2
   B. Bridge Mac Address   **D.** None of the above

265. What is the medium independent interface called in Gigabit Ethernet?
   A. AUI   **C.** GMII
   B. MII   **D.** GMI

266. The data signaling used in gigabit Ethernet is:
- **A.** Serial
- **B.** 4-bit-wide
- **C.** 4b/5b
- **D.** 8-bit-wide, NRZ

267. Gigabit Ethernet is based on the following standard:
- **A.** 802.3u
- **B.** 802.3z
- **C.** 802.3ab
- **D.** 802.3f

268. The Gigabit Ethernet specifications consist of:
- **A.** 1000Base-sx
- **B.** 1000Base-lx
- **C.** 1000Base-cx
- **D.** 1000base-cs

Answers

1. B
2. B, C
3. B
4. D
5. C
6. D
7. A
8. C
9. D
10. D, E
11. B
12. D
13. D
14. D
15. D
16. A, C
17. A
18. A, D, E
19. A, C, D
20. A
21. A
22. B
23. NetWare: E0; Banyan: BC; OSI: FE; TCP/IP: 06; AppleTalk: AA
24. D
25. D
26. B
27. A
28. 10Base5: 100; 10Base2: 20
29. D
30. C
31. B
32. A, B, C, D, E, F, G
33. A, B, D
34. D
35. C
36. It is the unique hexadecimal serial number assigned to each Ethernet network device to identify it on the network. With Ethernet devices (as with most other network types), this address is permanently set at the time of manufacture, though it can usually be changed through software (though this is generally a very bad thing to do).
37. Each card has a unique MAC address, so that it will be able to exclusively grab packets off the wire meant for it. If MAC addresses are not unique, there is no way to distinguish between two stations. Devices on the network watch network traffic and look for their own MAC address in each packet to determine whether they should decode it or not. Special circumstances exist for broadcasting to every device.
38. The MAC addresses are exactly 6 bytes in length, and are usually written in hexadecimal as 12:34:56:78:90:AB (the colons may be omitted, but generally make the address more readable). Each manufacturer of Ethernet devices applies for a certain range of MAC addresses they can use. The first three bytes of the address determine the manufacturer.

RFC-1700 (available via FTP) lists some of the manufacturer-assigned MAC addresses. A more up-to-date listing of vendor MAC address assignments is available on ftp.lcs.mit.edu in pub/map/Ethernet-codes.

39. A seven octet field of alternating one and zero binary bits sent prior to each frame to allow the PLS circuitry to reach its steady state synchronization with received frame timing. (802.3 standard page 24,42).

40. A binary sequence of '10101011' immediately following the preamble and indicating the beginning of a frame. (802.3 standard page 24).

41. Cyclical Redundancy Check—A method of detecting errors in a message by performing a mathematical calculation on the bits in the message and then sending the results of the calculation along with the message. The receiving workstation performs the same calculation on the message data as it receives it and then checks the results against those transmitted at the end of the message. If the results don't match, the receiving end asks the sending end to send again.

42. The unique address that identifies a packet as appropriate to all receiving stations. In 802.3 any address in which the second byte is an odd number. (1,3,...F).

43. These are the IEEE names for the different physical types of Ethernet. The "10" stands for signaling speed: 10MHz. "Base" means Baseband, "broad" means broadband. Initially, the last section as intended to indicate the maximum length of an unreported cable segment in hundreds of meters. This convention was modified with the introduction of 10BaseT, where the T means twisted pair, and 10BaseF where the F means fiber (see the following Q&A for specifics). This actually comes from the IEEE committee number for that media.

44. Fiber Optic Inter Repeater Link. A "IEEE 802 standard" worked out between many vendors some time ago for carrying Ethernet signals across long distances via fiber optic cable. It has since been adapted to other applications besides connecting segments via repeaters (you can get FOIRL cards for PCs). The larger 10BaseF standard have superseded it.

45. SQE is the IEEE term for a collision. (Signal Quality Error)

46. SQE Test (a.k.a. heartbeat) is a means of detecting a transceiver's inability to detect collisions. Without SQE Test, it is not possible to determine if your collision detector is operating properly. SQE Test is implemented by generating a test signal on the collision pair from the transceiver (or its equivalent) following every transmission on the network. It does not generate any signal on the common medium.

    The problem with SQE Test is that it is not part of the Ethernet Version 1.0 specification. Therefore, Version 1.0 equipment may not function with transceiver that generates the SQE Test signal. Additionally, IEEE 802.3 specifications state that IEEE 802.3 compliant repeaters must not be attached to transceivers that generate heartbeat. (This has to do with a jamming signal that prevents redundant collisions from occurring on the network). Therefore, you must usually turn-off SQE Test (heartbeat) between the transceiver and an 802.3 repeater.

47. The InterPacket Gap (more properly referred to as the *Interframe Gap*, or IFG) is an enforced quiet time of 9.6 between transmitted Ethernet frames.

48. Promiscuous mode is a condition where the network interface controller will pass all frames, regardless of destination address, up to the higher level network layers. Normally the network controller will only pass up frames that have that device's destination address. However, when put in promiscuous mode, all frames are passed on up the network stack regardless of destination address. Promiscuous mode is usually used by network monitoring tools and transparent bridges (and, frequently, by network crackers trying to snatch passwords or other data they're normally not able to see, off the wire).

49. A packet that is below the minimum size for a given protocol. With Ethernet, a runt is a frame shorter than the minimum legal length of 60 bytes (at Data Link).

50. Runt packets are most likely the result of a collision, a faulty device on the network, or software gone awry.

51. A blanket term for a device that is behaving improperly in terms of electrical signaling on a network. In Ethernet this is very bad, because Ethernet uses electrical signal levels to determine whether the network is available for transmission. A jabbering device can cause the entire network to halt because all other devices think it is busy.

52. Typically a bad network interface cards in a machine on the network. In bizarre circumstances outside interference might cause it. These are very hard problems to trace with layman tools.

53. A condition where two devices detect that the network is idle and end up trying to send packets at exactly the same time (within 1 round-trip delay). Since only one device can transmit at a time, both devices must back off and attempt to retransmit again.

   The retransmission algorithm requires each device to wait a random amount of time, so the two are very likely to retry at different times, and thus the second one will sense that the network is busy and wait until the packet is finished. If the two devices retry at the same time (or almost the same time. They will collide again, and the process repeats until either the packet finally makes it onto the network without collisions, or 16 consecutive collision occur and the packet is aborted.

54. See above Ethernet is a *Carrier Sense Multiple Access / Collision Detect* (CSMA/CD) system. It is possible to not sense carrier from a previous device and attempt to transmit anyway, or to have two devices attempt to transmit at the same time; in either case a collision results. Ethernet is particularly susceptible to performance loss from such problems when people ignore the "rules" for wiring Ethernet.

55. This depends on your application and protocol. In many cases, collision rates of 50% will not cause a large decrease in perceived throughput. If your network is slowing down and you notice the percentage of collisions is on the high side, you may want try segmenting your network with either a bridge or router to see if performance improves.

56. Disconnect devices from the network. Seriously, you need to cut down on the number of devices on the network segment to affect the collision rate. This is usually accomplished by splitting the segment into two pieces and putting a bridge or router in between them.

57. A late collision occurs when two devices transmit at the same time, but due to cabling errors (most commonly, excessive network segment length or repeaters between devices) neither detects a collision. The reason this happens is because the time to propagate the signal from one end of the network to another is longer than the time put the entire packet on the network, so the two devices that the late collision never see that the other's sending until after it puts the entire packet on the network. The transmitter after the first "slot time" of 64 byte times detects late collisions. They are only detected during transmissions of longer than 64 bytes. Its detection is exactly the same as for a normal collision; it just happens "too late."

   Typical causes of late collisions are segment cable lengths excess of the maximum permitted for the cable type, faulty connectors or improper cabling, excessive numbers of repeaters between network devices, and defective Ethernet transceivers or controllers.

   Another bad thing about late collisions is that they occur for small packets also, but cannot be detected by the transmitter. A network suffering a measurable rate of late collisions (on large packets) is also suffering lost small packets. The higher protocols do not cope well with such losses. Well, they cope, at much reduced speed. A 1% packet loss is enough to reduce the speed of NFS by 90% with the default retransmission timers. A 10X amplification of the problem.

   Finally, Ethernet controllers do not retransmit packets lost to late collisions.

58. When a workstation receives a collision, and it is transmitting, it puts out a jam so all other stations will see the collision also. When a repeater detects a collision on one port, it puts out a jamming signal on all other ports, causing a collision to occur on those lines that are transmitting, and causing any non-transmitting stations to wait to transmit.

59. An overloaded term that describes an overloaded protocol. Basically it describes a condition where devices on the network are generating traffic that by its nature causes the generation of even more traffic. The inevitable result is a huge degradation of performance or complete loss of the network as the devices continue to generate more and more traffic. This can be related to the physical transmission or to very high level protocols.

60. That depends on what level it is occurring. Basically you have to be aware of the potential for it beforehand and be looking for it, because in a true broadcast storm you will probably be unable to access the network. This can change dramatically for a higher level protocol. NFS contention can result in a dramatic drop in Ethernet traffic, yet no one will have access to resources.

61. Avoid protocols that are prone to it. Route when it is practical.

62. A received frame that does not contain an integer number of octets and contains a frame check sequence validation error. A frame in which the number of bits received is not an integer multiple of 8 and has a *Frame Check Sequence* (FCS) error. (802.3 standard, page 41)

63. "High" traffic on an Ethernet constitutes approximately 60%.

64. A Time-Domain Reflectometer is a tool used to detect cable faults. This device operates by sending a brief signal pulse down the cable and looking for its reflection to bounce back. By analyzing the reflected pulse, it is possible to make judgments about the quality of the cable segment. More advanced units can not only detect and identify the nature of the problem, but give a reasonably accurate indication of the problem's location (distance from the point of the test). There is also a device known as an OTDR, which is *Optical Time-Domain Reflectometer* for fiber-optic cables.

65. Bit Error Rate Tester. This equipment is used to analyze the count and types of errors that occur on a cable segment.

66. B

67. B

68. A

69. A, B, C, D

70. A, B, C, D, E, F, G

71. G

72. D

73. D

74. E

75. D

76. D

77. Phase 0: Lobe test; Phase 1: Physical insertion and monitor check; Phase 2: Duplicate address check; Phase 3: Ring poll participation; Phase 4: Request initialization

78. C

79. When a ring station detects a failure of token-claiming following a hard error, it transmits beacon frames. The beacon frame identifies the beaconing station's NAUN and the type of error detected.

80. Soft errors are intermittent faults that temporarily disrupt normal operation of the Token Ring network; soft errors are normally tolerated by error recovery procedures. Soft errors are indicated by architectural inconsistencies (such as cyclic redundancy checks or time-outs) in received or repeated frames and by a ring station's inability to process received frames.

81. Hard errors are faults, usually in equipment, that cause the ring to stop operating within the normal Token Ring architecture protocols. A ring station downstream from the hard fault

recognizes a hard error at the receiver side of its attachment. The ring must be reconfigured to bypass the error. This restores the ring to an operational state, repairs may be required to restore full operation to the ring.

82. Line error; Burst; ARI; FCI
83. Line error; Burst error; AC error
84. Frame copied error; Token error; Frequency error; Lost Frame error; Receiver congestion
85. D
86. Virtual rings are used to allow a source routing bridge to support more than two rings per bridge.
87. D
88. C
89. A, B, C
90. C
91. C
92. D
93. C
94. A, B, C
95. C
96. C
97. E
98. A
99. A
100. A
101. A
102. B
103. A
104. C
105. D
106. A
107. B
108. A
109. A
110. A
111. D
112. B
113. A
114. E
115. A
116. C
117. C
118. A
119. A
120. B
121. D
122. C
123. A
124. A
125. B
126. B

127. E
128. D
129. D
130. A
131. E
132. A
133. B
134. C
135. D
136. E
137. F
138. C
139. B
140. C
141. C
142. C
143. A
144. B
145. C
146. B
147. C
148. B
149. B and C
150. B
151. C
152. B
153. B
154. C
155. C
156. C
157. A
158. E
159. D
160. E
161. C
162. D and E
163. C
164. B
165. C
166. D
167. D
168. C
169. G
170. A
171. B
172. F
173. A
174. D
175. D
176. D
177. D

178. B
179. A
180. C
181. A, B, C
182. E
183. B
184. D
185. B
186. B
187. C
188. B
189. B
190. B
191. E
192. B
193. D
194. A, B, C
195. B, C
196. A, B
197. A, B, C, D
198. D
199. C
200. A
201. A
202. A
203. A
204. A
205. A
206. A
207. A
208. B
209. C
210. A
211. A
212. A
213. D
214. A, E
215. A
216. A
217. A
218. A
219. A
220. A
221. A
222. D
223. A
224. C
225. A
226. B

227. B
228. C
229. C
230. B
231. A, B, C, D
232. A
233. E
234. F
235. D
236. C
237. C
238. A
239. A
240. C
241. A
242. 0200.0000.000040
243. 1000.5148.c828
244. B
245. B and C
246. C
247. A, B, C
248. B
249. 00a0.425a.3f94
250. C
251. C
252. B
253. B
254. B
255. C
256. D
257. B
258. 0050.2451.8b26
259. C
260. A, C, D
261. D
262. C
263. A
264. C
265. C
266. D
267. B
268. A, B, C

Logical Link Control Layer Issues

Introduction

The objective of this chapter is to explain the functions of the IEEE 802.2 protocol known as *Logical Link Control* (LLC). This chapter examines the protocol from an architectural perspective and looks at how Cisco implements LLC in its IOS software to support various upper-layer protocols.

Cisco IOS implements an LLC2 protocol when any of the following features are configured utilizing SNA and NetBIOS over NetBEUI:

- *Data Link Switching* (DLSw)
- *Remote Source Route Bridging* (RSRB)
- *Channel Interface Processor* (CIP)
- *Advance Peer-to-Peer Networking* (APPN)
- *Synchronous Data Link Control* (SDLC) and *Logical Link Control* (LLC2) (SDLLC)

Logical Link Control

Logical Link Control is the standard published by the IEEE 802.2 standards body. The IEEE 802.2 LLC protocol is actually a subset of another protocol. This protocol is *High-Level Data-Link Control* (HDLC), which is a specification presented by the standards body known as the *International Standards Organization* (ISO). It uses the *balanced asynchronous mode* (ABM) of data transfer. The protocol of LLC enables network stations to operate as peers—all stations have equal status on the LAN. LLC is not generally a topic of discussion when dealing with internetworks; however, if your network consists of NetBIOS over NetBEUI and SNA traffic over IEEE 802.x frames, LLC Type 1 and 2 is a integral part of your internetwork.

It is important to understand that IEEE 802 is a data-link protocol, which controls the link between two stations. IEEE 802 has nothing to do with the upper-layer protocols that may run on top of it. As shown in Figure 3.1, the IEEE 802 committee divided the data-link layer into two entities.

Connection-Oriented versus Connectionless Service

Let's examine connection-oriented versus connectionless data transfer. In connection-oriented service, two stations that need to communicate with one another must establish a connection at the data-link layer before any communication can occur. When Station A needs a connection to Station B, Station A will send control frames to Station B to indicate that a connection is wanted. Station B will respond with a control frame to indicate that a session can be established, or it may respond to Station A that it may not have a connection. If a connection can be established, Station A and Station B will exchange a few more control packets that will set up sequence numbers and other control parameters. After this is accomplished, data may flow over the connection. The connection will be strictly maintained with sequence numbers, acknowledgments, retries, and so on.

Connectionless service is just the opposite of connection-oriented service. A connection is not established (at the data-link layer) before data is communicated. Establishing a connection is the responsibility of the particular network protocol (TCP/IP, NetWare IPX, AppleTalk, and so on) before data is transmitted. Some network protocols are also connectionless. With IP, for example, you need TCP to establish a connection. In connectionless service, a frame will be transmitted on the network without regard to a connection at the data-link layer. The upper-layer protocol software takes the responsibility for performing these tasks.

Network protocols that fully implement a connection-oriented transport layer will generally use LLC Type 1 service at the data-link layer.

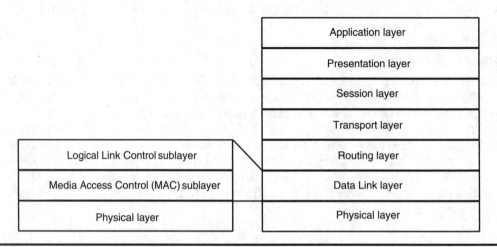

FIGURE 3.1   IEEE and the OSI model

MAC and LLC Layers

The *Media Access Control* (MAC) layer, explained in Chapter 2, provides for peer-to-peer connectivity between two network stations, which reduces the LAN's susceptibility to errors. Because it is a subset of the HDLC architecture, the MAC layer provides a more compatible interface for wide area networks. The LLC layer is independent of the physical access method (Ethernet, Token Ring, FDDI, ATM, Fast Ethernet, 100Base-VG, and Gb Ethernet).

The LLC portion of the data-link layer is protocol-specific, which allows an IEEE 802.2 network more flexibility. LLC is placed between the MAC layer specification of the data-link layer and a network-layer protocol implementation. LLC2 (connection-oriented services) are used to link a local area network to a wide area network and between network stations and SNA hosts. An example is the Microsoft NT Operating System Server program. This network operating system is based on a transport and session-layer protocol called NetBEUI and NetBIOS.

When the IEEE started work on the LLC layer, they knew that providing only a connection-oriented service (Type 2 or LLC2) would limit the capability of this protocol in the LAN arena. Most applications currently operating on a LAN do not need the data integrity and overhead functions provided for with the LLC2 protocol. However, if you are running SNA and NetBIOS Session services over a LAN, LLC2 must be used in some instances.

The IEEE 802.2 committee also provided a connectionless mode of the LLC protocol, as well as a connection-oriented specification. The IEEE 802.2 committee allowed for three types of LLC implementations:

- *LLC Type 1*, known as LLC 1, uses the *unsequenced information* (UI) frame, which sets up communication between two network stations as unacknowledged connectionless service. This is the most popular LLC service in use today, supporting protocols such as TCP/IP, IPX, AppleTalk, DECnet, and so on. See Figure 3.2 for an example of LLC Type 1 service.

- *LLC Type 2*, commonly known as LLC2, uses the conventional (Information Frame) and sets up acknowledged connection-oriented service between two network stations. This is used most commonly in SNA and NetBIOS Session service as shown in Figure 3.3.

- LLC *Type 3*, acknowledged connectionless frames, sets up an acknowledged connectionless service between two network stations as shown in Figure 3.4.

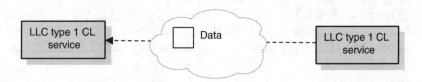

FIGURE 3.2   LLC Type 1 unacknowledged connectionless services

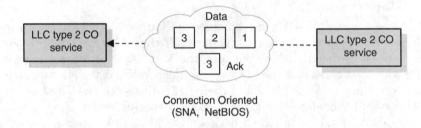

Connection Oriented
(SNA, NetBIOS)

FIGURE 3.3   LLC Type 2 connection-oriented service

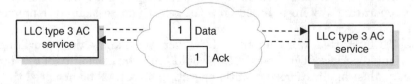

Figure 3.4   Acknowledged connectionless service

LLC Type 2 Operation

LLC2 is the most complicated of the services, so it will be explained first. Connection-oriented services provide the functions necessary to provide reliable data transfer (similar to a transport-layer function). Connection-oriented services allow for error recovery, flow control, and congestion control. LLC2 provides for specific acknowledgments that the connection is established or not. LLC2 provides for flow control, making sure that the data arrives in the order it was sent and that the connection is not overloaded. This type of connection has a tremendous amount of overhead compared to LLC1 connectionless service.

Connection-oriented link methods were originally used with data transfer through serial lines. A little more than 15 years ago, serial lines tended to be noisy. Part of the *High-Level Data-Link Control* (HDLC) protocol provides for the reliability of data. Connection-oriented services are used with some LAN services today. Their most common use is for protocols that do not invoke a transport or network layer. A good example of this type of protocol is NetBEUI/NetBIOS.

Microsoft NT, IBM WARP Server, SCO Advance Server, Sun Solar-net, and others use this type of connection. Most LAN protocols do not use this mode of LLC. Most LAN protocols have network, transport, and session layers built into the protocol and therefore use the connectionless mode of LLC Type 1. Table 3.1 shows the class of service compared to the LLC Type. This table shows that network stations supporting LLC Type 2 services can provide both LLC Type 1 connectionless and LLC Type 2 connection-oriented services. Network stations supporting LLC Type 1 services can provide only LLC Type 1 service.

Frame Formats

An LLC frame is shown in Figure 3.5. The following sections discuss the frame types of IEEE 802.2.

Table 3.1 The Class of Service

LLC Service	LLC Frame Type		
	Unnumbered	Supervisory	Information
Type 1 CL	X		
Type 2 CO	X	X	X
Type 3 AC	X		

CL = Connectionless service

CO = Connection-oriented

AC = Acknowledged connectionless service

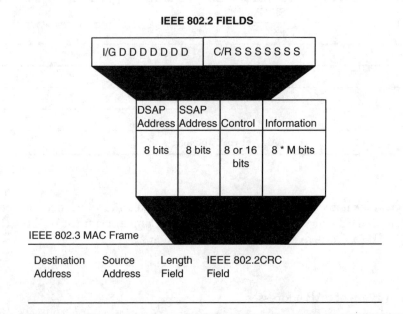

Figure 3.5 LLC frame

Destination Service Access Point (DSAP) identifies one or more service access points (protocols) to which the LLC information should be delivered.

Source Service Access Point (SSAP) identifies the service access point that originated the message.

For LANs implementing LLC, SAPs identify a particular protocol service that resides on a network station. SAPs are used to send or receive a message. For those familiar with the Ethernet Type protocol, an SSAP is analogous to the Type field in the Ethernet II frame. A SAP of 0x06 indicates that the IP protocol owns the packet. A SAP entry of 0xFO indicates NetBIOS over NetBEUI. For a listing of SAPs, refer to Table 3.2. SAPs are used to tell the

TABLE 3.2   IEEE SAP Assignments

SAP ID	Protocol
0x06	TCP/IP
0xE0	Novell IPX
0xF0	NetBIOS
0xFE	OSI CLNS
0x42	IEEE Spanning Tree
0x00	Null SAP
0xF8	Remote Program Load
SAP ID	**Protocol**
0xAA	SNAP
0x80	XNS
0x98	ARP
0xFF	Global SAP
0x7F	ISO 802.2
0xBC	Vines
0xF4	LAN Network Manager

network layer which network process is to accept the packet and which network process submitted the packet. SAPs are registered by the IEEE. Companies must register their protocols with the IEEE to receive a SAP Protocol Identifier.

SAP Addressing

There are four types of SAP addresses:

- Individual address, used by DSAP and SSAP
- Null address, all zeros in the DSAP and or SSAP
- A group address, which is only used by the DSAP
- Global DSAP indicated by all ones in the DSAP field and used to designate a group of all active DSAPs on the network.

Each SAP address consumes exactly one octet. The DSAP address contains seven bits of address (indicated by the D bits and one bit (I/G bit) that identifies the address as an individual SAP or a multicast SAP intended for a group of SAPs). This leftmost bit of the DSAP field is identified by the I/G bit in Figure 3.5. This type of address shows that the packet is intended for a group of SAPs at the destination end of the link. When this bit is set to a 0, the address is an individual address. When this bit is set to a 1, it is a group address.

The SSAP contains seven bits of address, indicated by the S bits and one bit to indicate whether the packet is a command or response packet. If this C/R bit is a 0, it is a command packet; if it is set to a 1, it is a response packet.

Poll and Final (P/F) bits.   These bits are used between two communicating stations (*primary* and *secondary)* to solicit a status response or to indicate a response to that request. A P bit is used by the primary station (the requester), and an F bit is used by the secondary station (the responder). In LLC, any station can transmit a frame with the P bit set or the F bit set. The P/F bit does not reflect a master-slave relationship.

A frame with the F bit set does not indicate the end of a transmission in asynchronous balance mode (ABM), which is the mode used in LLC2. It is used as a housecleaning method between two stations to clear up any ambiguity between those two stations. The F bit also is used to indicate that the frame is an immediate response to a frame in which the P bit is set.

For example, when a station wants to set up a connection with another station, it will submit a frame known as *Set Asynchronous Balance Mode Extended* (SABME). In this frame, the P bit will be set to a 1. The destination station, upon accepting a connection request, will respond with an *Unnumbered Acknowledgment* (UA) frame, and the F bit will be set. A P bit frame is acknowledged immediately. To effect the three preceding functions, three types of frames are transmitted or received in a connection-oriented network.

- *Information frame.*   This frame is used to transfer user data between the two communicating network stations. Included in the information frame may also be an acknowledge receipt of previous data from the originating station.

- *Supervisory frame.*   This frame performs control functions between the two communicating stations. This includes control functions of acknowledgment of frame, the request for the retransmission of a frame, and the request for the control of the flow of frames (rejecting any new data).

- *The unnumbered frame.*   This frame is used for control functions also. In LLC1, it is used to transfer user data. In LLC2, the frame is used for session initialization or session disconnect.

The supervisory frame provides three commands or responses. These commands are *receiver ready* (RR), *reject* (REJ), and *receiver not ready* (RNR). Supervisory frames do not contain any user data and are used to perform numbered supervisory functions.

Receiver ready (RR) is used by the source or destination station to indicate that it is ready to receive data. It is also used to acknowledge any previously received frames indicated by the $N(R)^*$ field. One use for the RR frame comes after a station has already indicated that it cannot receive any more data; by issuing the RNR, the station can send the RR frame to indicate that it can again accept new data. A network station may also use the RR frame to poll a destination station to see whether it is active. When running a protocol over IEEE 802.2 (SNA over Token Ring, for example), these packets will traverse the ring even in the absence of data. As a polling frame, RR ensures that the link is still good. It is usually sent (as a poll) every few seconds. This will consume bandwidth with nondata frames.

> **NOTE:**   *When the Cisco IOS is configured for DLSw, RSRB with Local Acknowledgment, APPN, CIP, and SDLLC, LLC2 RR frames are terminated at the local router in order to prevent the RR traffic from consuming wide area network bandwidth.*

Receiver not ready (RNR) is used by a receiving network station to indicate that it saw the data packet but was too busy to accept it. A network station will send this frame to indicate to the source not to send any more data until a RR is issued.

The *Reject* (REJ) frame is used to indicate a request for a retransmission of frames (more than one), starting with the frame indicated by a sequence number in the field known as N(R). Any frames of N(R)-1 were accepted and are acknowledged. Finally, the unnumbered frame has commands and responses used to extend the number of data-link control functions. These commands are as follows:

- *Set Asynchronous Balance Mode Extended (SABME).*   This frame is used to establish a data-link connection to a destination network station. This frame will establish the link in asynchronous balanced mode. No user data is transferred with this frame. The destination, in response to this packet, will send an *Unnumbered Acknowledge* (UA) frame back to the originator. All sequence counters are set to zero upon receipt of a SABME and receipt of the UA.

- *Disconnect (DISC):* This frame is used to disconnect a session between two communicating stations. No user data is sent with this frame. Upon receipt of the frame, the destination station should acknowledge it with a UA frame.

- *Unnumbered Acknowledge (UA):*   This frame is sent as an acknowledgment to the SABME and DISC commands.

- *Frame Reject Response (FRMR):*   This frame is different from the simple reject frame because the sender of it is rejected. This is a noncorrectable frame.

Sequencing of Data (LLC2)

Most LAN protocols offer some type of sequencing for data delivery. Whether the sequencing is simple or complex (as used with LLC2 and TCP/IP), there will always be some type of sequencing to ensure proper data delivery.

The following text describes a generic method of sequencing—one is that is definitely used with LLC2 operation, but also one that has been around for decades and whose modes and methods have been copied by many different LAN architectures.

Sequencing of transmitted data ensures that when the data is received it will be presented to the receiver of the data in good condition and in the same order in which it was sent. Without sequencing of data, the host's application would receive the data as presented to it by the LAN software and would then process the data (save it to a file, input it into a database, and so on). If the file were saved, the file would not be saved in the way it was sent. In any application, misordering LAN data can have catastrophic effects.

When initiating a connection, part of the handshaking process establishes a data window. For two communicating network stations (for example, A and B), B will establish a window for A and A will establish a window for B. These windows are maintained by state variables. Another name for this is a *counter*. The transmitting station will maintain a send-state variable, V (S). This variable will contain the sequence number of the next frame to be transmitted. A receiving station will maintain a receive-state variable, V(R). This variable will contain the sequence number expected to be the next frame received. V (S) is incremented with each frame transmitted by a network station. This counter is also placed in a sequence field in a transmitted frame.

When a network station receives a frame, it will look for sequence number N (S) in the frame received. If this field matches its V(R), it will increment its V(R) by one and place this number in a frame N(R) of some type of an acknowledgment packet that will be transmitted back to the originator of the frame.

The LLC2 sequence number counters are as follows:

- *V(R) Receive-state variable.* A counter maintained by a network station. This counter indicates the sequence number of the next in-sequence *Information Frame Protocol Data Unit* (IPDU) to be received on a connection. It is maintained in the network station and not the frame.

- *N (S) Sequence number of the frame (called the send sequence number).* Located in the transmitted frame, this field will only be set in information (I) packets (explained in a moment). Prior to sending an I frame, the value of N (S) is set to the value of V (S), the send-state variable. This is located in the frame and not in the network station.

- *V (S) Send-state variable.* This number indicates the next sequence number expected on the connection. It is incremented by one for each successive I-frame transmission. It is maintained in the network station and not the frame.

- *N(R) Receive sequence number.* This is an acknowledgment of a previous frame. It is located in the transmitted frame. All information and supervisory frames will contain this. Prior to sending that type of frame, it is set equal to the value of the receive-state variable V(R) for that connection. N(R) indicates to the receiving station that the station that originated this frame accepts all frames up to the N(R) minus 1.

```
1. Initiate a session setup using SABME
DLC: —- DLC Header —-
DLC:
DLC: Frame 28 arrived at 22:17:18.35460 ; frame size is 60 (003C hex) bytes.
DLC: Destination = Station 006097D8876A, 45<20>
DLC: Source    = Station 006097ECD390, LAP1<03>
DLC: 802.3 length = 3
DLC:
LLC: —- LLC Header —-
LLC:
LLC: DSAP Address = F0, DSAP IG Bit = 00 (Individual Address)
LLC: SSAP Address = F0, SSAP CR Bit = 00 (Command)
LLC: Unnumbered frame: SABME, POLL
LLC:
DLC: Frame padding= 43 bytes
(Station lap1 issued a setup (SABME) request to station 45)

2. Unnumbered frame: UA, FINAL
DLC: —- DLC Header —-
DLC:
DLC: Frame 29 arrived at 22:17:18.35473 ; frame size is 60 (003C hex) bytes.
DLC: Destination = Station 006097ECD390, LAP1<03>
DLC: Source    = Station 006097D8876A, 45<20>
DLC: 802.3 length = 3
DLC:
```

```
LLC: --- LLC Header ---
LLC:
LLC: DSAP Address = F0, DSAP IG Bit = 00 (Individual Address)
LLC: SSAP Address = F0, SSAP CR Bit = 01 (Response)
LLC: Unnumbered frame: UA, FINAL
LLC:
DLC: Frame padding= 43 bytes
Station 45 issues a (UA) in response to the connection setup request (SABME)
```

3. Receiver Ready Polls
Sniffer Network Analyzer data from 17-Feb-98 at 22:16:20, unsaved capture data,
Page 20

```
DLC: --- DLC Header ---
DLC:
DLC: Frame 30 arrived at 22:17:18.35492 ; frame size is 60 (003C hex) bytes.
DLC: Destination = Station 006097D8876A, 45<20>
DLC: Source    = Station 006097ECD390, LAP1<03>
DLC: 802.3 length = 4
DLC:
LLC: --- LLC Header ---
LLC:
LLC: DSAP Address = F0, DSAP IG Bit = 00 (Individual Address)
LLC: SSAP Address = F0, SSAP CR Bit = 00 (Command)
LLC: Supervisory frame: RR, N(R) = 0, POLL
LLC:
DLC: Frame padding= 42 bytes
```

4. Secondary Station respond to Poll with a Final

```
DLC: --- DLC Header ---
DLC:
DLC: Frame 31 arrived at 22:17:18.35502 ; frame size is 60 (003C hex) bytes.
DLC: Destination = Station 006097ECD390, LAP1<03>
DLC: Source = Station 006097D8876A, 45<20>
DLC: 802.3 length = 4
DLC:
LLC: --- LLC Header ---
LLC:
LLC: DSAP Address = F0, DSAP IG Bit = 00 (Individual Address)
LLC: SSAP Address = F0, SSAP CR Bit = 01 (Response)
LLC: Supervisory frame: RR, N(R) = 0, FINAL
LLC:
DLC: Frame padding= 42 bytes
```

5. LLC Poll

```
DLC: --- DLC Header ---
DLC:
DLC: Frame 32 arrived at 22:17:18.35521 ; frame size is 60 (003C hex) bytes.
DLC: Destination = Station 006097D8876A, 45<20>
DLC: Source    = Station 006097ECD390, LAP1<03>
DLC: 802.3 length = 18
DLC:
LLC: --- LLC Header ---
LLC:
LLC: DSAP Address = F0, DSAP IG Bit = 00 (Individual Address)
LLC: SSAP Address = F0, SSAP CR Bit = 00 (Command)
LLC: I frame, N(R) = 0, N (S) = 0, POLL
```

If, during the matching of V(R) to the received sequence number, a mismatch occurred, the station will send a negative acknowledgment packet to the originator, usually after a wait timer expires. In this packet will be the sequence number of its value in V(R). In LLC2, this type of frame is a REJ frame. In other words, the station expected one sequence number but received another. The number it expected will be transmitted back to the sender in hopes of receiving the correct packet and sequence number. Refer to the Sniffer trace above to see N (S) & N(R) in a frame.

When this packet is received by the originating station, it will look at the received sequence number N(R). It will also know that is has already sent this frame, but that something went wrong in the process. If the station can, it will retransmit the old frame.

What is the ordering-for-sequencing numbers? Not all protocols operate the same. For LLC2, the sequence numbering starts at 0 and may go as high as 127 (known as modulo 128). For now, we'll stick with LLC2 sequence numbers, which is modulo 128. This means that sequence numbers may go as high as 127, but then must return (wrap around) to 0. This permits 127 frames to be outstanding (not acknowledged). Modulo 128 does not permit 128 frames to be outstanding because the value of V(R) is the next expected sequence number.

Modulo 128 also guards against wrapping because if a station has 127 outstanding frames (0—126), a sending station may not use 0 again until it has been acknowledged, which is highly unlikely. Most frames will be acknowledged within a few sequence numbers. One important consideration is the actual size of the window. Although having a Modulo of 128 is nice because 127 frames may be transmitted with one acknowledgment, it is also a resource constraint. No transmitted frame may be erased in the sending network station's memory until it has been acknowledged. Therefore, a network station should have enough memory to store that amount of data until it is acknowledged.

The window can be shut down at any time, which will prevent any more frames being received from certain stations. This restriction enables efficient use of resources and eliminates the possibility of one station hogging another station's time. If a window size of seven is opened to another station and six frames are outstanding to a network station, the window will be closed. If an acknowledgment is received for six frames, the window will be opened again for six frames. This is called the *sliding window*. In a Cisco router, the window size for LLC2 is called *LLC2 local-window*.

Timer Functions

Timers are used throughout the LLC2 mode of operation. These timers include the following but not limited to:

- *Acknowledgment timer.* A data-link connection timer that is used to define the time interval for which a network station is expecting to see a response to one or more information frames or in response to one unnumbered frame.
- *P bit timer.* The amount of time that a network station will wait for a response frame regarding a frame sent with the P bit set.
- *Reject timer.* The amount of time that a network station will wait for a response to a REJ frame sent.
- *Busy-state timer.* The amount of time that a network station will wait for a remote network station to exit the busy state.

TABLE 3.3   Some of the Cisco LLC tunable parameters

Cisco IOS Command	LLC Default	Description
Llc2ack-delay-time *milliseconds*	100 msec	Time to wait for a response before sending an acknowledgment
Llc2 ack-max *packet-count*	3 packets	Number of frames to receive before sending an acknowledgment packet
Llc2 idle-time idle periods of time.	10,000	Time between polls during *milliseconds*
Llc2 local-window *packet-count*	7 packets	Number of frames to send before waiting for a response from the receiving station
Llc2 n2 *retry-count*	8 retries	Number of times unacknowledged I frames or polls are sent without receiving a reply before terminating the session
Llc2 t1-time *milliseconds*	1000 msec	Time to wait for a response before resending I frames. This time needs to be large enough to accommodate the round-trip delay.
Llc2 tbusy-time *milliseconds*	9600 msec	The amount of time to wait before polling a station that has sent a RNR. Change the value only to increase the value for stations that have unusually long, busy periods before they clear their status.
Llc2 tpf-time *milliseconds*	1000 msec	The amount of time to wait for a final response before resending the poll frame
Llc2 trej-time *milliseconds*	3200 msec	The amount of time to wait for a correct frame after sending a REJ frame
Llc2 xid-neg-val-time *milliseconds*	0 msec	The amount of time in which the software sends XID frames to other LLC2 stations
Llc2 xid-retry-time *milliseconds*	60,000 msec	The time before software waits for a reply to XID frames prior to dropping the session

Three other parameters that are used in this text are

N2   The maximum number of times that a PDU is sent following the expiration of the P bit timer, the acknowledgment timer, or the reject timer

N1   The maximum number of octets allowed in an I PDU

k   The maximum number of outstanding I PDUs (those that have not been acknowledged)

Table 3.3 shows some of the tunable Cisco LLC parameters.

Connection-Oriented Services of the IEEE 802.2 Protocol

LLC2 has two modes of operation: operational mode and nonoperational mode.

Nonoperational mode is used to indicate that a network station is logically (not physically) disconnected from the physical cable plant. No information is accepted when a network station has entered into this stage. Examples of possible causes for a network station to enter this mode are

- The power is turned on but the receiver is not active.
- The data link has been reset.
- The data-link connection is switched from a local condition to a connected on the data-link (online) condition.

In operational mode, three primary functions are provided:

- *Link establishment.* A source station will send a special frame to a destination indicating that a connection is wanted. This frame is responded to with an acceptance or rejection. When a connection is established, the two network stations provide each other with a series of handshaking protocols to ensure that the other is ready to receive information.
- *Information transfer.* Data from the user's applications is transferred from the originating station to the remote station, and the data is checked for any possible transmission errors. The remote station will send acknowledgments to the transmitting station. During this phase, the two network stations may send control information to each other indicating flow control, missing packets, and so on.
- *Link termination.* The connection between the two stations is disconnected, and no more data is allowed to be transferred between the two stations until the session is reestablished. Usually, the link will remain intact as long as there is data to send between the two stations.

Details of LLC Type 2 Operations

In operational mode, the data link enters into *asynchronous balance mode* (ABM), which means that a connection at the Data Link Layer has been established between two SAPs. Each end of the connection is able to send commands and responses at any time without receiving any type of permission from another station. A master-slave relationship does not exist in this mode. The information exchanged between the two shall be command information (indicating sequence numbers or that a station is busy and cannot accept any more data). ABM is also used for user data transfer.

ABM (LLC2) has four phases of operation:

- Data-link connection phase
- Information Transfer phase
- Data-link resetting phase
- Data-link disconnecting phase

Data-Link Connection Phase. Any network station may enter into this state with the intention of establishing a session with another network station. (Figure 3.6 shows the data link connection phase). It will use the unnumbered frame SABME. When the SABME frame is sent, an acknowledgment timer is set. If the frame is not responded to, it will be re-sent as many as N2 times. If the frame is not responded to in that amount of time, the connection attempt is aborted. This type of frame has the P bit set.

The two responses that may be received back are the UA or the *Disconnect mode* (DM). The DM allows a network station to indicate that a connection is not allowed. If a connection has

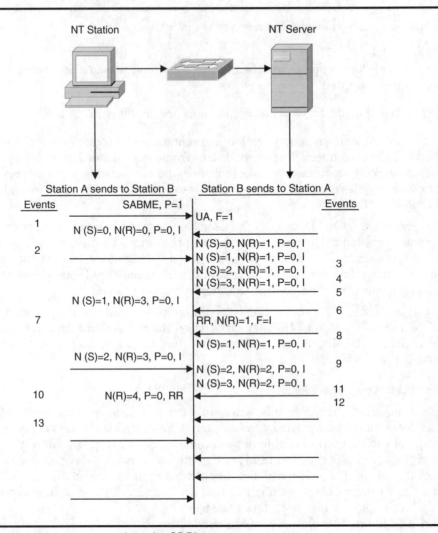

Figure 3.6 Station setting up a connection using LLC2

been set up and a network station received this response from the other end of the connection, the connection would be severed. The F bit will be set in the response packet. With the receipt of the DM frame, the acknowledgment timer is stopped, and that network station will not enter into the information transfer stage. The connection attempt is aborted; this condition is reported to the upper-layer protocols. Upon receiving a UA response frame back, the connection is then established and enters into the information transfer phase.

Information Transfer Phase. When a network station has sent or received a UA response packet, that network station will immediately enter the information transfer phase. The connection will be established, and the frames consist of sending and receiving *information* (I) frames and *supervisory* (S) frames.

If a network station receives a SABME frame while in this phase, it will reset (not disconnect) the connection. A SABME frame is used to return the connection to a known state. All outstanding frames are lost, and sequence numbers are reset to 0. Retransmission of any outstanding frames will occur between the two network stations, and they will be acknowledged at this time.

When a network station has user information that needs to be sent, it will do so with the I frame. In this sequence, numbers need to be put into the packet.

Also, if the transmitting station enters into the busy state, it can still transmit I frames; it just cannot receive any. If the source receives an indication that the destination is busy, it will not send any more I frames until the receipt of a *Receiver Ready* (RR) frame from the remote station. When the transmitting station enters into the *Frame Reject* (FRMR) state, it will not transmit any more information for that particular link. When the sending station transmits this frame, it will start an acknowledgment timer. This is in anticipation of receiving a response packet for its transmission. This is one of the many receive conditions which are discussed next.

Data-Link Disconnection Phase.   While in the information transfer phase, either network station may disconnect the session by transmitting a DISC frame to the other network station. When a station sends this packet, it will start an acknowledgment timer and wait for a response. When it receives a UA or DM response packet, the timer is stopped, and the station enters into the disconnected mode. If this timer expires before receipt of a response packet, the originator will again send the DISC packet and restart the timer. When an upper limit of resends has been reached, that station will enter into disconnected phase but will inform the upper-layer protocols that an error has occurred in attempting to disconnect from the remote station.

When a network station receives a DISC packet, it will respond to it with a UA packet and enter into the data-link disconnected phase. While in the disconnected phase, a network station is able to initiate sessions with other network stations and can respond to session requests. If a station receives a DISC packet, it will respond with a DM packet; and if it receives any other LLC Type 2 command with the P bit set to a 1, it will respond with the F bit set to a 1.

LLC2 Frame Reception   Frame reception for LLC2 has many more functions than the transmitting of a frame. When a network station is not in the busy condition and receives an I frame that contains the sequence number equal to its V(R) variable, it will accept the frame, increment the V(R) by one, and then perform the following:

1. If the receiving station has another I frame to transmit, it will transmit the frame as indicated previously, but will set the N(R) variable in the transmitted packet to its V(R) setting and transmit the packet. LLC2 does not use separate packets to indicate an acknowledgment unless there are no more I frames to be sent.

2. There are no more I frames to be sent. In this case, it will send a *Receive Ready* (RR) frame with N(R) set to its V(R).

3. It may also send a *receive not ready* (RNR) frame back, which indicates that the station is now busy and cannot receive any more data, but acknowledges the packet, indicated by N(R).

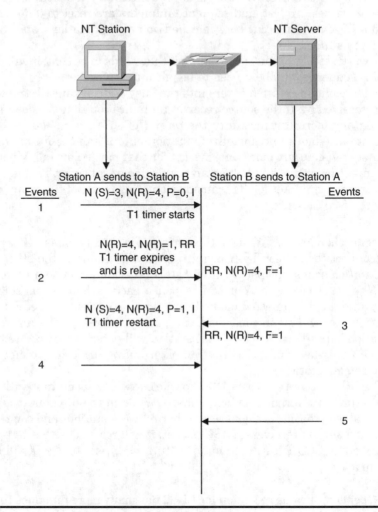

FIGURE 3.7   A LLC Session using NetBIOS over NetBEUI

If any frame is received as an invalid frame (wrong SAPs, and so on), the frame is completely discarded. Figure 3.7 shows the variable states of N(R), N (S), and V(R) and V (S) for a simple transmission between two network stations.

Established Connection

To establish a connection, station A will send a UI frame (a Set Asynchronous Balance Mode) frame with the P bit set. Station B allows the connection to send back a UA with the F bit set.

The connection is now established.

TABLE 3.4 LLC Timers

LLC Timer	NetBIOS	SNA over LLC	Cisco
T2	T2	T2	LLC2 ack-delay-time
N3	Ack	N3	LLC2 ack-max
Ti	Ti	TI	LLC2 idle-time
Window	Window	Modulo 8-127	LLC2 local window
Retries	NetBIOS Retries	N2	LLC2 n2
T1	T1	T1	LLC2 t1-time
N/A	N/A		LLC2 tbusy-time
Poll	N/A	Poll/Final	LLC2 tpf-time
Reject	N/A	Reject	LLC2 trej-time
XID	N/A	XID	LLC2 xid-neg-val-time
XID	N/A	XID	LLC2 xid-retry-time

Transporting SNA or NetBIOS traffic across a WAN is implemented using serial lines to connect remote bridges or routers over *Data Link Switching* (DLSw) or *Remote Source Route Bridging* (RSRB). Usually, serial lines are conditioned to handle the digital traffic, but there may be instances where the serial line is not conditioned and the LLC protocol ensures that data is reliably transferred across these facilities. Table 3.4 highlights LLC timers associated with NetBIOS and SNA.

LLC Type 1 Operation

With the exception of SNA and the multitude of vendors supporting NetBIOS over NetBEUI, Type 1 is the most commonly used class of LLC. LLC Type 1 is used by Novell, TCP/IP, OSI, Banyan, Microsoft NT, IBM, Digital and most other network protocols. No specific subsets exist for the operation of LLC Type 1. Type 1 operation consists of only one mode—information transfer.

Information Transfer

LLC Type 1 operation does not require any prior connection establishment between the source and destination network stations before data is transferred between them. After the SAP information field has been sent, information may be transferred between two network stations.

Two other types of frames, besides information frames, may be transmitted using LLC 1 (XID) operation: The *exchange identification* (XID) and the TEST frames are used in LLC2 to perform the same operations.

XID: The XID frame is used for the following functions:

- An XID frame with a null SAP can be used to retrieve information from a remote network station. This form of the keep-alive packet is used to test the presence of the remote station.

- With the LSAP address set to a group SAP, the XID frame can be used to determine group membership.

- An XID frame can be used to test for duplicate address.

- If the link between the two stations is operating in LLC2 mode, this frame can be used to request receive-window sizes.

- An XID frame can be used to request or identify a service class from a remote station (LLC Type 1 or LLC Type 2 LLC operation).

- An XID frame can be used with Cisco Token Ring Source Routing to find a remote station through source route bridges. This frame is the dynamic explorer frame used by Source Route Bridges.

The primary use of the test frame is for loop-back functions. A network station will transmit a test frame to test a path. The frame will be transmitted on a certain data path with the information field set to a specific entry. The network station will then wait for the frame to be responded to, and the information field in the frame will be checked for errors.

TEST: The TEST command frame is not a requirement in LLC1 operation, but the capability to respond to one is. Although LLC Type 1 operation does not require a response frame to any LLC1 command frame, these two previously mentioned frames do require a response, but are made in unnumbered format (no use of the P or F bits). The most common application used with LLC 1 is called *Sub-network Access Protocol* (SNAP).

Sub-Network Access Protocol (SNAP)   IEEE 802.2 defined two fields known as the *Destination* and *Source Service Access Protocol* (DSAP and SSAP, respectively). For the most part, the SAP fields are reserved for those protocols that implemented the IEEE 802.x protocols. One SAP has been reserved for all non-IEEE standard protocols. Because this is Type 1 operation, the DSAP and SSAP will be set to AA, and the control field (only one byte for Type 1 operation) will be set to 03 to indicate unnumbered information packets. Following this control field will be five bytes collectively called the *protocol discriminator*. This identifies the protocol family to which the packet belongs.

1. The data-link encapsulation headers (destination and source address, and the CRC trailer)

2. The 3-byte 802.2 headers (set to AA, AA, and 03)

3. The 5-byte protocol discriminator immediately following the 802.2 header

4. The data field of the packet

The important field to notice is the protocol discriminator. The first three bytes of this field indicate the vendor (080007 indicates Apple Computer, for example). The next two bytes indicate the type of packet it is (the Ethertype II field).

If the first three bytes of the protocol discriminator are set to 00-00-00, this indicates a generic Ethernet packet not assigned to any particular vendor, and the next two bytes will be the Type field of the Ethernet packet. The use of three bytes of zeroes indicates the use of an Ethernet frame. This is useful when the frame traverses different media types. If that frame is transposed to allow passage on another media type, the field of zeroes indicates that any time the frame is forwarded to the Ethernet media, it will be built as an Ethernet frame and not as an IEEE 802.3 frame. If this field contains an entry other than zeroes, it indicates that the IEEE 802.3 frame (and not the Ethernet frame) should be used when forwarding to an Ethernet LAN. A field of all zeroes simply indicates an encapsulated Ethernet packet. For example, a TCP/IP packet could have this field set to five bytes of 00-00-00-08-00. This signifies an organization ID (protocol discriminator) of 00-00-00 (which states that it is an Ethernet frame), and the Ethertype is a 08-00, which is the Ethertype for IP messages. Following this is the Ethernet data frame.

SNAP allowed for Ethernet vendors to quickly switch their drivers and network protocols over to the IEEE 802.x packet format without rewriting a majority of the code. Using this format allowed the vendors who had drivers written for the Ethernet II frame type to port the network operating code quickly over to the Token Ring and FDDI data-link frame format.

Summary

Today, vendors are switching their code to the LLC frame format. For example, Novell NetWare versions 2.x and 3.11 used a proprietary Ethernet frame. Novell has registered their NetWare operating system with the IEEE, and can now use the SAP address of 0x E0 in their LLC frames. IEEE 802.x frames are now the default for NetWare 3.12, 4.x, and 5.x implementations. They use LLC 1 for their transmission. This means that the DSAP and SSAP are set to E0 and the control field is set to 03 to indicate connectionless or LLC1 communication. Following these fields would be the IPX header starting with the checksum of FFFF.

The choice between connection-oriented networks and connectionless networks centers on the functionality that is needed. The connection-oriented system provides for the integrity of data, but with it comes the extreme burden of overhead. Connectionless systems consume less overhead but are prone to error. Therefore, it does not make a lot of sense to provide for connection-oriented services for a LAN. Error control is usually provided for by the application as well as the upper-layer protocol software of a LAN (the transport layer). Today, with LAN upper-network protocols handling the connection-oriented services, connectionless methods are the most common with LLC Type 1 operation.

The IEEE 802.2 Logical Link Control layer does not require a lot of configuration from the network engineer or implementer. The LLC2 timers outlined in Table 3.4 offer a number of configuration options available for changes using SNA and NetBIOS session service in the Cisco IOS.

Questions

1. Identify the LLC types.
   - **A.** LLC1
   - **B.** LLC2
   - **C.** LLC3
   - **D.** LLC4

2. The LLC1 layer is:
   - **A.** Connection-oriented
   - **B.** Connection-less
   - **C.** Acknowledge connection-less service
   - **D.** All of the above

3. LLC2 layer is:
   - **A.** Connection-less
   - **B.** Connection-oriented
   - **C.** Unacknowledged connection-less service
   - **D.** None of the above

4. Identify the fields in the LLC Sub-header.
   - **A.** DSAP/SSAP
   - **B.** Control
   - **E.** A & B
   - **C.** Information
   - **D.** Type Code

5. LLC supports link multiplexing through the use of:
   - **A.** SAPs
   - **B.** type code
   - **C.** sockets
   - **D.** Protocol ID's

6. When using SNA services over Token Ring, which LLC type is mandatory?
   - **A.** LLC1
   - **B.** LLC2
   - **C.** LLC3
   - **D.** A & B

7. The LLC SAP addresses identify:
   - **A.** MAC layer addresses
   - **B.** Network layer Protocol Addresses
   - **C.** A & B
   - **D.** Protocol addresses

8. LLC makes use of HDLC' s ABM only, not NRM or ARM.
   - **A.** True
   - **B.** False

9. Name some of the differences of LLC Control filed as compared to HDLC.
   - **A.** Uses two additional frames for acknowledges connection-less service
   - **B.** Supports multiplexing by using SAPs
   - **C.** Uses unnumbered information frames to support connection-less service
   - **D.** All of the above

10. Identify commands used in the LLC control field.
    - **A.** N(S) sequence number of frame being sent
    - **B.** N(R) sequence number of last frame received, i.e. next frame expected
    - **C.** P/F bit, to indicate immediate response is requested
    - **D.** SS supervisory frame function bits
    - **E.** MMMMM- unnumbered frame modifier function bits

11. LLC3 uses which of the following control frames for Acknowledgements?
    - **A.** Ack
    - **B.** Sequence number
    - **C.** Two sequence number
    - **D.** Two unnumbered information frames
    - **E.** None of the above

12. LLC type 2 service uses type 1 service to initiate communications.
    A. True   B. False

13. Identify type 2 connection-oriented control field commands.
    A. DISC   E. FRMR
    B. SABME   F. RR
    C. UA   G. RNR
    D. DM   H. REJ

14. Identify LLC Type 1 connection-less control field commands.
    A. Unnumbered information   C. Test
    B. XID   D. RR
    E. RNR

15. Identify Type 3 connection-less control filed commands.
    A. AckConnectionless, seq0   C. A & B
    B. ACK connectionless, seq1   D. None of the above

16. The LLC2 frame control field supports which of the following types of commands?
    A. Unnumbered   D. Test
    B. Information   E. Reject
    C. Supervisor   F. Receiver Ready
    G. All of the above

17. A link station receiving a command frame with the *poll* (P) bit set to 1 must send back what type of response?
    A. Reject   C. Final
    B. Test   D. Sync

18. When using LLC2 with a control field of two bytes, what is the modulo?
    A. 8   C. 256
    B. 128   D. 12

19. When using LLC2 with a control field of one byte, what is the modulo?
    A. 8   C. 256
    B. 128   D. 12

20. When a device sets up a Type II LLC connection, what is the expected sequence of commands prior to the exchange of the first numbered information frame?

21. What is the primary function provided by the *logical link control* (LLC) sub layer?
    A. Error control   C. Congestion control
    B. Flow control   D. Ordered delivery
    E. Protocol discrimination

22. What are the main differences between LLC Type 1 and LLC Type 2?
    A. One is connectionless while the other is connection-oriented.
    B. One provides flow control and the other does not.
    C. One provides error control and the other does not.
    D. One provides protocol discrimination and the other does not.

23. Cisco IOS uses LLC2 when which of the following is configured?

    A. TCP/IP   **C.** DLSw

    B. IPX   **D.** SDLLC

    E. Stun   **F.** All of the above

24. Identify the SAP ID for IP.

    A. E0   **C.** 06

    B. F0   **D.** 09

25. Identify the SAP ID for NetBIOS.

    A. 04   **C.** 0c

    B. 08   **D.** F0

    E. None of the above

26. The supervisor field supports ___ types of commands.

    A. two   **C.** four

    B. three   **D.** eight

27. Identify two SAP IDs used in SNA.

    A. 04   **C.** 0c

    B. 08   **D.** 00

    E. All of the above

28. A station enters ABME after sending or receiving a UA to SABME command.

    A. True   **B.** False

29. What is the Window size called in a Cisco Router?

    A. Window   **C.** LLC2 local-window

    B. LLC window   **D.** Sliding window

    E. None of the above

30. The Window size using LLC2 usually defaults to:

    A. 128   **C.** 8

    B. 7   **D.** 127

Answers

1. A, B, C
2. B
3. B
4. A, B, C, D
5. A
6. B
7. B
8. B
9. D
10. C
11. D
12. A
13. F, G
14. A, B, C
15. C
16. A, B, C
17. C
18. B
19. A
20. The first command is the *Set Asynchronous Balanced Mode Extended* (SABME), which is followed by an *Unnumbered Acknowledgment* (UA). Next the two communicators should notify each other that their *receivers are ready* (RR) and that they are expecting frame number ZERO next. In some implementations, you may see an *exchange of ID information* (XID) preceding the SABME.
21. B, D, E
22. A, B
23. C, D
24. C
25. D
26. B
27. E
28. A
29. C
30. B

4

Bridging Architectures

Bridges operate at layers 1 and 2 relative to the OSI model as shown in Figure 4.1. Bridges work with lower layer protocols such as MAC layer services, and are more complex than repeaters because they function with two layers of protocols. This chapter focuses on what bridges do and how they do it.

A *bridge* is a device that enables devices on different LAN segments to communicate as if they were on the same switch, HUB, or concentrator.

Because bridges operate at the Data Link layer of the OSI Reference Model, they are concerned only with the addresses of network devices and not the actual paths between them. For this reason, high-level protocols, which provide functionality at the Network layer and above in the OSI Reference Model, are totally transparent to bridging—hence, the term *Transparent bridging*.

Several types of bridging methods are used in today's networks: they are as follows:

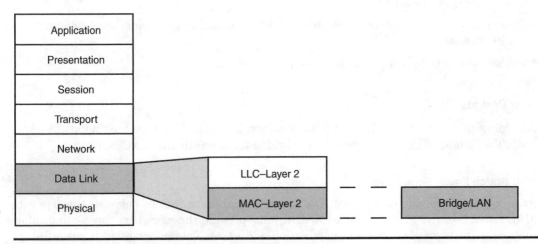

FIGURE 4.1 Data Link layer bridging

- *Transparent bridging* (TB)
- *Source-Route Bridging* (SRB)
- *Source-Route Transparent bridging* (SRT)
- *Source-Route Translational Bridging* (SRTB)
- Encapsulation Bridging
- Other vendor proprietary methods

Bridging Advantages

Isolation from upper layer protocols, such as TCP/IP, IPX, VIP, DECnet, etc., is one of the advantages of bridging. Because bridges function at the layer 2 Data Link layer, they are not concerned with layer 3-protocol information that occurs at the upper layers. This provides lower processing overhead and fast communication of network layer protocol traffic.

Bridges can filter frames based on layer 2 information contained within the MAC layer frame, such as MAC Address, Protocol Type, Byte Offset, etc, which is useful for maintaining effective traffic flow. You can configure a bridge to accept and forward only certain types of frames or only frames that originate from a particular network.

Bridges are advantageous when dividing large networks into manageable segments. The advantages of bridging in large networks can be summed up as follows:

- Bridging lets you isolate specific network areas, giving them less exposure to major network problems.
- Filtering lets you regulate the amount of traffic that is forwarded to specific segments.
- Bridges allow communication between more internetworking devices than would be supported on any single LAN connected to a bridge.
- Bridging eliminates node limitation. Local network traffic is not passed on to all of the other connected networks.
- Bridges extend the connected length of a LAN by allowing the connection of distant workstations.
- Bridges are easy to install and maintain.

How Bridges Work

According to the IEEE 802 LAN standard, all station addresses are specified at the MAC level. The following examples show how a bridge functions at the MAC level.

MAC Bridge Frame Formats

As mentioned, bridges interconnect LANs by relaying data frames between the separate MAC entities of the bridged LANs. MAC frames provide the necessary forwarding information in the form of source and destination addresses. This information is essential for the successful transmission and reception of data.

IEEE 802 supports three types of MAC frames:

- CSMA/CD (802.3)
- Token bus (802.4)
- Token Ring (802.5)

The first bridging method to be discussed is Transparent bridging.

Transparent bridging provides an interconnection of LANs transparent to stations communicating across a bridge. Any station can communicate with any other station in the network as though both stations are on the same LAN. All routing functions are handled entirely within the Transparent bridge based on a path determined by the Spanning Tree Algorithm.

Transparent bridging requires that the bridges dynamically maintain a source address database for each of their LAN connections. Each bridge LAN interface operates in *promiscuous* mode so that every frame on the LAN is received and processed. The source address from each frame is saved in the database. The database then is searched to determine whether the destination address of the frame is located in the database. If so, the frame is forwarded to the appropriate LAN segment. If both the source and destination stations are on the same LAN, the frame is discarded. If, however, the frame destination is not found in the database, the bridge forwards the frame to the all other LAN segments. This decision process is a type of *flooding* (see Figure 4.2).

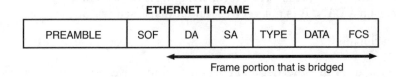

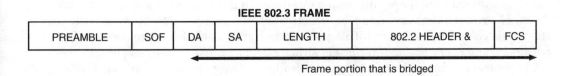

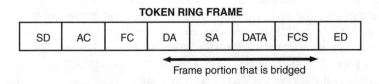

FIGURE 4.2 Bridge frame forwarding MAC addresses

Transparent bridging is used on MAC bridges that interconnect IEEE 802.3 or Ethernet LANs or IEEE 802.5 Token Ring LANs. Bridging is a method of switching packets. In a bridged network, no correspondence is required between addresses and paths; addresses don't imply anything about where hosts are physically attached to the network. Any address can appear at any location. In contrast, routing requires more thoughtful address assignment, corresponding to physical placement. Switching nodes that perform bridging are called *bridges*; those that perform routing are called *routers*; those that can perform both are sometimes called *brouters*. However, today with LAN switching populating the networking landscape, brouters are now called *layer 3 switching*, because LAN switching is a branch of the bridging family tree with Uncle Bridge marrying neighbor Ms. Router whose offspring is called layer 3 switching.

Bridging relies heavily on broadcasting. Because a packet may contain no bridging information other than the destination address, which implies nothing about the path that should be used, the only option may be to send the packet everywhere! This is one of bridging's most severe limitations, because this method of data delivery is very inefficient and can trigger *broadcast storms*. In networks with low-speed links, this method can introduce crippling overhead.

IP and IPX are designed as wide-area networking protocols; they are rarely bridged because of the large networks they typically interconnect. The broadcast overhead of bridging would be prohibitive on such networks. However, the link layer protocol's IP functions, particularly Ethernet and Token Ring, are often bridged. Due to the pseudo-random fashion in which Ethernet and Token Ring addresses are assigned, bridging is usually the only option for switching among multiple networks at this level. Bridging is most commonly used to separate high-traffic areas on a LAN. It is not very useful for dispersed traffic patterns.

Transparent Bridging

Transparent bridging, the type used in Ethernet and documented in IEEE 802.1, is based on the concept of a *spanning tree*. This tree of Ethernet links and bridges spans the entire bridged network. The tree originates at a *root bridge*, which is determined by election, based on bridge priority and either Ethernet addresses or engineer-defined preference. The tree expands outward from there. Any bridge interfaces that would cause loops to form are shut down. If several interfaces could be deactivated, the one with the lowest path cost to the root is chosen for activation. This process continues until the entire network has been traversed, and every bridge interface is either assigned a role in the tree, or deactivated.

Transparent refers to the fact that the bridge silently forwards nonlocal traffic to attached LANs in a way that is transparent to the user. End station applications do not know about the presence of the bridge. The bridge learns about the presence of end stations by listening to traffic passing by. From this listening process, it builds a database of end station addresses attached to its LANs. For each frame it receives, the bridge checks the frame's destination address against the ones in its database. If the destination is on the same LAN, it does not forward the frame. If the destination is on another LAN, it forwards the frame. If the destination address is not present in the database, the bridge forwards the frame to all the LANs connected to the bridge except the LAN from which it originated. All Transparent bridges use the Spanning Tree protocol and algorithm.

The Spanning Tree Algorithm produces and maintains a loop-free topology in a bridged network, which may contain loops in its physical design. In a mesh topology, where more than one bridge is connected between two LANs, data packets can bounce back and forth between two LANs' parallel bridges. This creates a redundancy in data traffic and produces the phenomenon known as looping. Without spanning tree, when looping occurs, you must configure the local and/or remote LAN to remove the physical loop. With spanning tree, a self-configuring algorithm allows a bridge to be added anywhere in the LAN without creating loops. When you add the new bridge, the spanning tree transparently reconfigures all bridges on the LAN into a single loop-free spanning tree.

Spanning tree never has more than one active data route between two end stations, thus eliminating data loops. For each bridge, the algorithm determines which bridge ports to use to forward data and which ones to block to form a loop-free topology. Among its features, spanning tree provides the following:

- *Loop detection.* Detects and eliminates physical data link loops in extended LAN configurations.

- *Automatic backup of data paths.* Deliberately configured from redundant paths, the bridges connecting to the redundant paths enter backup mode automatically. When a primary bridge fails, a backup bridge becomes active.

- *User configurability.* Enables you to tailor your network topology. Sometimes the default settings do not produce the desired network topology. You can adjust the bridge priority, port priority, and path cost parameters to shape the spanning tree to your network topology.

- *Seamless interoperability.* Allows LAN interoperability without configuration limitations caused by diverse communications environments.

- *Bridging of nonrouting protocols.* Provides cost-effective bridging of nonrouting protocols, such as Digital Equipment Corporation's *Local Area Transport* (LAT) terminal protocol.

Transparent bridging has several disadvantages. First, the Spanning Tree protocol must be conservative about activating new links, or loops can develop. Also, all the forwarding tables must be cleared every time the spanning tree reconfigures, which triggers a broadcast storm as the tables are being reconstructed. This process limits the usefulness of Transparent bridging in environments with fluid topologies. Redundant links can sit unused, unless careful attention is given to root bridge selection. In such a network (with loops), some bridges always sit idle anyway. Finally, like all bridging schemes, the unnecessary broadcasting can affect overall performance. Its use is not recommended in conjunction with low-speed serial links.

Transparent bridging gives the engineer a powerful tool to effectively isolate high-traffic areas such as local workgroups. It does this without any host reconfiguration or interaction and without changes to packet format. Transparent bridging has no addressing requirements and can provide a quick fix to certain network performance problems. As usual, careful analysis is needed by the network engineer, with particular attention given to bridge placement.

Again, note that for the IP sub-netting perspective, the entire spanning tree is regarded as a single link. All bridging decisions are based on the 48-bit Ethernet address.

The following describes the Transparent bridge processes.

Receive Process. A bridge receives network traffic on both ports and stores received frames in its frame buffer memory. *All* frames are stored, regardless of the destination MAC address or the filtering status of the bridge. The receiver process handles frame reception and storage for both ports. The bridge usually passes received frames to the learning process and then to the forwarding and transmitting processes for ultimate disposal.

Learning Process. Bridges *learn* based on the source MAC address and *forward* based on destination MAC addresses. Learning and forwarding, along with a third process called *filtering* and an additional refinement known as the *Spanning Tree Algorithm* (STA) comprise the basic functionality of all bridges.

The bridge's automatic examination and recording of network station locations is known as the learning process. Normally, the bridge scans the MAC source address field of each frame that it receives and adds an entry to its address database when it encounters an unknown source address. If an entry for the source address already exists, the bridge updates it to reflect new information. Each address database entry contains information indicating that the source address is on one side of the bridge or the other; with this information, the bridge can make forwarding decisions. The bridge's basic criterion for forwarding is whether the path to the frame's destination passes through the bridge.

What happens when client A.1 transmits a packet destined for client A.2? The bridge, which is listening in promiscuous mode, examines its internal address and determines that client A.2 is attached to port e2. It then forwards the packet on to only port e2. (See Figure 4.3.)

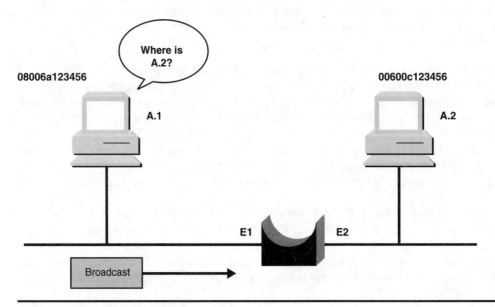

FIGURE 4.3 Transparent bridging learning process

Forwarding Process.   The forwarding process determines whether to discard a frame or forward it to the other network. If it can find an address database entry with a MAC address that matches the frame's destination MAC address, the bridge uses the contents of the disposition field for that entry to determine whether or not to forward the frame. Normally, if the bridge cannot find a corresponding address database entry (i.e., the destination is unknown), it forwards the frame.

Transmit Process.   Frames that pass all forwarding criteria—whether created statically or automatically by the learning process—are submitted to the transmit process, which handles frame transmission on both ports. If too many frames are queued for transmission on a port, the bridge discards the frame at this point. If not, the transmitter sends the frame out onto the network, assuming the proper network connection is made.

Aging Process.   This process examines all address database entries that have been dynamically added to the table by the bridge's learning process. As the bridge receives frames from each station, it creates new address database entries, initializes their age fields, and marks the entries as active. If an incoming frame's source address matches one in the address database, the bridge reinitializes the entry's age field and marks the entry as active.

Spanning Tree Algorithm

Learning, filtering, and forwarding rely on the existence of a single path between any two devices on the network. In simple topologies, it is relatively easy to guarantee the existence of one, and only one, path between two devices. But, as the number of connections increases or the internetwork becomes more complex, the probability of inadvertently creating multiple paths or *active loops* between devices increases dramatically. Active loops can be a severe problem for bridge-based networks—one that can lead to unnecessary and indefinite duplication of packets. This redundant traffic can quickly degrade overall network performance.

The problem of active loops in a bridged network has been recognized and addressed by a networking standards committee of IEEE. That organization has selected a standard approach for dealing with active loops arising in bridge-connected internetworks, and their solution is known as the *Spanning Tree Algorithm*. STA has now become a basic part of bridge functionality.

The STA developed by Digital Equipment Corporation and later revised by the IEEE 802 committee and implemented as IEEE 802.1d, is a means by which bridges can eliminate loops in the network topology. DEC's spanning tree and IEEE 802.1d are not compatible with each other. A bridging loop occurs when packets can get from an arbitrary point A on the network to an arbitrary point B on the network through more than one path. For an example of a simple bridging loop, imagine a network with two stations, client A and client B, and two bridges, bridge 1 and bridge 2. For the sake of clarity, we will also divide the network into two halves, the top half and the bottom half. Client A is connected to the top half of the network, and client C is connected to the bottom half of the network. Both bridge 1 and bridge 2 connect the top and bottom halves of the network (see Figure 4.4). This is a bridging loop because packets coming from client A to client C can pass through either bridge 1 or bridge 2.

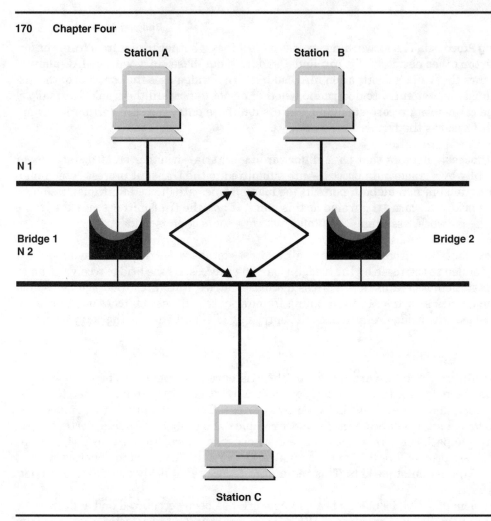

Station A   Station B

N 1

Bridge 1
N 2   Bridge 2

Station C

FIGURE 4.4   Spanning Tree using two bridges

We could leave it up to the network administrator to make sure that bridging loops never occur, but this solution is hardly desirable. Even if the administrator is willing to invest the time and effort to make sure that such things didn't happen, human error is working against us. With the Spanning Tree algorithm, the administrator needn't worry about whether loops are out there; the bridges take care of the problem. A spanning tree is any unique device-to-device path in the network. The STA constructs a spanning tree through a series of bridge-to-bridge negotiations. These negotiations determine which path the active loop will leave enabled for transmissions, and which path(s) will remain at least temporarily disabled. As a result of these negotiations, one port on each bridge in the tree is placed in a forwarding state. Other ports may be placed in a blocking state. This process ensures a single path between any two devices on the network; for example, there are no active loops.

Although the STA solves many problems, it can also create one for wide-area networks. If active loops are in the long-distance part of the network, the STA disables one or more lines to eliminate them. However, even though a line is disabled, the physical connection remains intact. Because long-distance lines are most often leased, network managers who choose bridging as a basis for wide-area internetworking may find themselves paying for long-distance lines that cannot be used because they have been disabled by the STA.

Because the topology is now loop-free, we can broadcast across the entire network without too much worry, and any Ethernet broadcasts are flooded in this manner. All other packets are flooded throughout the network, like broadcasts, until information that is more definite is determined about their destination. Each bridge finds such information by monitoring source addresses of packets and matching them with the interfaces on which it was received. This process tells each bridge which of its interfaces leads to the source host. The bridge recalls this when it needs to bridge a packet sent to that address. Over time, the bridges build complete tables for forwarding packets along the tree without extraneous transmissions.

Topological change messages consist of only four bytes. They include a protocol identifier field, which contains the value 0; a version field, which contains the value 0; and a message type field, which contains the value 128.

Spanning trees prevent problems resulting from the interconnection of multiple networks by means of parallel transmission paths. In various bridging circumstances, it is possible to have multiple transmission routes between computers on different networks. If multiple transmission routes exist, unless there is an efficient method for specifying only one route, it is possible to have an endless duplication and expansion of routing errors that saturates the network with useless transmissions, quickly disabling the network. Spanning trees are the method used to specify one, and only one, transmission route.

How STB Works

During startup, all participating bridges in the network exchange Hello *Bridge Protocol Data Units* (BPDUs) (see Figure 4.5). These provide configuration information about each bridge. BPDUs include information such as the bridge ID, root ID, and root path cost. This information helps the bridges to determine unanimously which bridge is the *root bridge* and which bridges are the designated bridges for LANs to which they are connected.

Of the information exchanged in the Hello messages, the following parameters are the most important for computing the spanning tree:

- *Root bridge ID*. The bridge ID of the root bridge, the designated bridge for all the LANs to which it is connected.

- *Root path cost*. The sum of the designated path costs to the root via this bridge's root port. This information is transmitted by both the root bridge and the designated bridges to update all bridges on path information if the topology changes.

- *Bridge ID*. A unique ID used by the spanning tree algorithm to determine the spanning tree. Each bridge in the network is assigned a unique bridge identifier.

- *Port ID*. The ID of the port from which the current Hello BPDU messages was transmitted.

With this information available, the spanning tree begins to determine its shape and direction and then creates a logical path configuration as follows:

1. A root bridge for the network is selected by comparing the bridge IDs of each bridge in the network. The bridge with the lowest ID value (i.e., highest priority) wins.

2. The Spanning Tree Algorithm then selects a designated bridge for each LAN. If more than one bridge is connected to the same LAN, the bridge with the smallest path cost to the root is selected as the designated bridge. In the case of duplicate path costs, the bridge with the lowest bridge ID is selected as the designated bridge.

3. The nondesignated bridges on the LANs put each port that has not been selected as a root port into a *blocked* state. In the *blocked* state, a bridge still listens to Hello BPDUs so that it can act on any changes made in the network (e.g., if a designated bridge fails) and change its state from blocked to forwarding (forwarding data).

```
DLC:    --- DLC Header ---
DLC:    Frame 6 arrived at  10:06:50.953; frame size is 52 (0034 hex) bytes.
DLC:    FS: Addr recognized indicators: 11, Frame copied indicators: 11
DLC:    AC: Frame priority 0,  Reservation priority 0,  Monitor count 0
DLC:    FC: LLC frame,  PCF attention code: None
DLC:    Destination = Functional address C00000000100, All Bridges
DLC:    Source      = Station 000030DCCF5C
LLC:    --- LLC Header ---
LLC:
LLC:    DSAP Address = 42, DSAP IG Bit = 00 (Individual Address)
LLC:    SSAP Address = 42, SSAP CR Bit = 00 (Command)
LLC:    Unnumbered frame: UI
LLC:
BPDU: --- Bridge Protocol Data Unit Header ---
BPDU:
BPDU: Protocol Identifier = 0000
BPDU: Protocol Version    = 00
BPDU:
BPDU: BPDU Type = 00 (Configuration)
BPDU:
BPDU: BPDU Flags = 00
BPDU:   0... .... = Not Topology Change Acknowledgment
BPDU:   .... ...0 = Not Topology Change
BPDU:   .000 000. = Unused
BPDU:
BPDU: Root Identifier   = 8000.00000C3BE106
BPDU:   Priority        = 8000
BPDU:   MAC Address      = 00000C3BE106
BPDU:
BPDU: Root Path Cost    = 128
BPDU:
BPDU: Sending Bridge Id = 8000.00000C3BF33A.0015
BPDU:   Priority        = 8000
BPDU:   MAC Address      = 00000C3BF33A
BPDU:   Port            = 0015
BPDU:   Message Age          = 2.000 seconds
BPDU:   Information Lifetime = 10.000 seconds
BPDU:   Root Hello Time      = 2.000 seconds
BPDU:   Forward Delay        = 4.000 seconds
BPDU:
```

FIGURE 4.5   Bridge Protocol Data Units (BPDU)

Through this process, the Spanning Tree Algorithm reduces a bridged LAN network of arbitrary topology into a single spanning tree. With the spanning tree, no more than one active data path exists between any two end stations, thus eliminating data loops.

This new configuration is bounded by a time factor. If a designated bridge fails or is physically removed, other bridges on the LAN detect the situation when they do not receive Hello BPDUs within the time period set by the bridge maximum age time. This event triggers a new configuration process in which another bridge is selected as the designated bridge. A new configuration is also created if the root bridge fails.

Shaping the Spanning Tree

When the spanning tree uses its default settings, the Spanning Tree Algorithm generally provides acceptable results. The algorithm may, however, sometimes produce a spanning tree with poor network performance. In this case, you can adjust the bridge priority, port priority, and path cost to shape the spanning tree to meet your network performance expectations.

In an example with three LANs networked together using three bridges, each bridge is using default bridge priority settings for its spanning tree configuration. In this case, the bridge with the lowest physical address is chosen as the root bridge because the bridge priority of each bridge is the same. In this example, this is bridge 2. The newly configured spanning tree stays intact due to the repeated transmissions of Hello BPDUs from the root bridge at a preset interval (bridge Hello time). Through this process, designated bridges are updated with all configuration information. The designated bridges then regenerate the information from the Hello BPDUs and distribute that information to the LANs for which they are designated bridges.

The spanning tree algorithm designates the port connecting bridge 1 to bridge 3 (port e2) as a backup port and blocks this port from forwarding frames that would cause a loop condition. The spanning tree created by the algorithm using the default values connects bridge 1 to bridge 2 and then bridge 2 to bridge 3. The root bridge is bridge 2.

This spanning tree results in poor network performance because the workstations on LAN C can get to the file server on LAN A only indirectly through bridge 2 rather than by using the direct connection between bridge 1 and bridge 3.

Normally, this network uses the port between bridge 2 and bridge 3 infrequently. Therefore, you can improve network performance by making bridge 1 the root bridge of the spanning tree. You can do this by configuring bridge 1 with the highest priority of 1,000. The spanning tree that results from this modification connects bridge 1 to bridge 3 and bridge 1 to bridge 2. The root bridge is now bridge 1. The connection between bridge 2 and bridge 3 is now blocked and serves as a backup data path.

The Spanning Tree Algorithm generates Bridge Protocol Data Units during configurable intervals. The BPDUs consist of configuration and topology change messages. Figures 4.6A, 4.6B, and 4.7 highlight DEC's and IEEE 802.1d Spanning Tree Protocol's BPDU's header formats and descriptions.

The fields of the BPDU Transparent bridge configuration message are as follows

- *Protocol identifier*. This field contains the value 0 that identifies the Spanning Tree Algorithm and Protocol.

- *Version*. 0 value specified by standard.

```
SUMMARY   Delta T      Destination   Source       Summary
M    1      DEC_lv1_Bridges 00E01E5DD4AD      DLC Ethertype=8038, size=60 bytes
                                    Ethertype=8038 (DEC bridge mgmt)


DLC:  --- DLC Header ---
DLC:
DLC:  Frame 1 arrived at  15:16:09.21141 ; frame size is 60 (003C hex) bytes.
DLC:  Destination = Multicast 09002B010001, DEC_lv1_Bridges
DLC:  Source      = Station 00E01E5DD4AD
DLC:  Ethertype  = 8038 (DEC bridge mgmt)
DLC:
???:  --- DEC bridge mgmt Ethertype data ---
???:  No protocol interpreter is installed for this Ethertype.
???:  [46 bytes of data
DLC:  --- DLC Header ---
DLC:
DLC: Frame 2 arrived at 15:16:10.21109; frame size is 60 (003C hex) bytes.
DLC:  Destination = Multicast 09002B010001, DEC_lv1_Bridges
DLC:  Source      = Station 00E01E5DD4AD
DLC:  Ethertype  = 8038 (DEC bridge mgmt)
???:  --- DEC bridge mgmt Ethertype data ---
???:  No protocol interpreter is installed for this Ethertype.
???:  [46 bytes of data]
```

FIGURE 4.6A   DEC's spanning tree BPDU

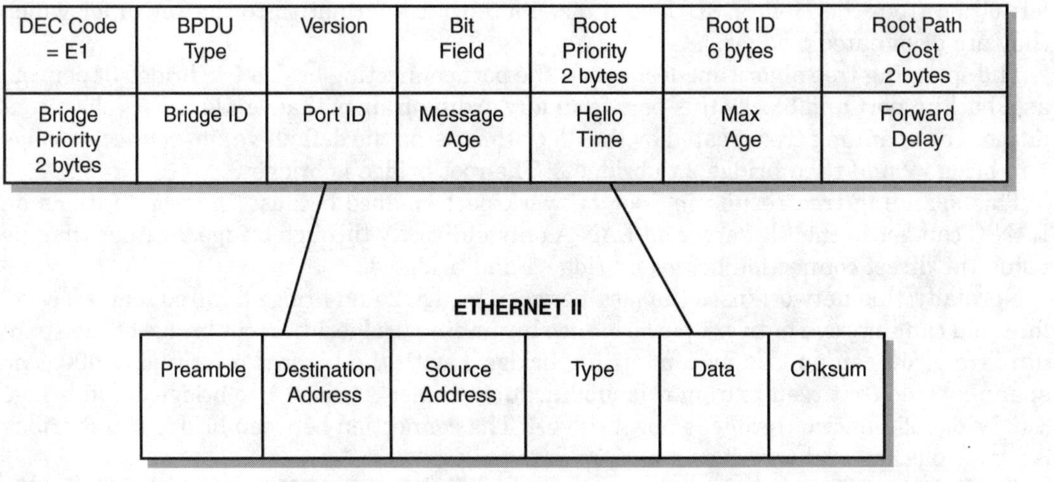

DEC Code = E1	BPDU Type	Version	Bit Field	Root Priority 2 bytes	Root ID 6 bytes	Root Path Cost 2 bytes
Bridge Priority 2 bytes	Bridge ID	Port ID	Message Age	Hello Time	Max Age	Forward Delay

ETHERNET II

Preamble	Destination Address	Source Address	Type	Data	Chksum

FIGURE 4.6B   DEC's spanning tree

- *Message type.* 0 value.

- *Flag.* A 1-byte field, of which only the first two bits are used. The *topology change* (TC) bit signals a topology change. The *topology change acknowledgment* (TCA) bit is set to acknowledge the receipt of a configuration message with the TC bit set.

- *Root ID.* Identifies the root bridge by listing its 2-byte priority followed by its 6-byte ID.

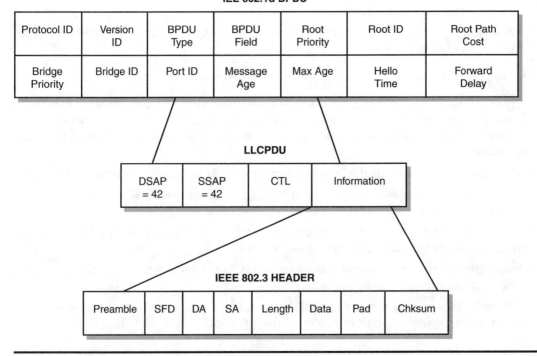

FIGURE 4.7   IEEE 802.1d bridge protocol data unit

- *Root path cost*. Contains the cost of the path from the bridge sending the configuration message to the root bridge. The root path cost can be adjusted.
- *Bridge ID*. Identifies the priority and ID of the bridge sending the message.
- *Port ID*. Identifies the port from which the configuration message was sent. This field enables loops created by multiple attached bridges to be detected and dealt with.
- *Message age*. Specifies the amount of time since the root sent the configuration message on which the current configuration message is based.
- *Maximum age*. Two bytes that indicate when the current configuration message should be deleted.
- *Hello time*. Provides the time period between root bridge configuration messages.
- *Forward delay*. Provides the length of time that bridges should wait before transitioning to a new state after a topology change. If a bridge transitions too soon, not all network links may be ready to change their state, and loops can result.

Transparent bridges are typically simple to install and offer many advantages.

1. Because the bridge is solely responsible for the forwarding of packets, no changes are required to the end-station software. The extended network appears to the end stations on one large LAN.

2. Network changes are easily made because new locations are learned as end-station packets pass through the LAN.

3. The Spanning Tree Algorithm automatically reconfigures new paths between LANs if the primary path goes down.

On the other hand, costs are associated with Transparent bridging:

1. Transparent bridges do not allow parallel or multiple paths. (Although some vendors allow parallel paths between LANs for load balancing and multiple paths between adjacent LANs, they use proprietary methods that are not compatible from one vendor to the next.)

2. The backup paths are idle during normal operation, thus wasting network bandwidth.

3. There is no provision for load balancing in the case of congested paths or bridges. Alternate paths are only used if there is a link failure.

4. Transparent bridges have difficulty passing traffic between or through LANs, which support different maximum frame sizes.

5. Some controllers cannot tolerate the delay of LANs extended with Transparent bridges, thus causing timing conflicts.

6. Network management is more difficult because the Transparent bridge views all network components as part of one large flat network.

Cisco Transparent Bridging Features

Cisco's transparent bridging software implementation has the following features:

- Complies with the IEEE 802.1D standard.

- Provides the capability to logically segment a transparently bridged network into virtual LANs.

- Provides two spanning-tree protocols—an older bridge protocol data unit compatible with Digital and other LAN bridges for backward compatibility and the IEEE standard bridge protocol data unit format. In addition to features standard with these spanning-tree protocols, Cisco's proprietary software provides for multiple domains for spanning trees. The spanning-tree parameters are configurable.

- Allows frame filtering based on MAC address, protocol type, or the vendor code. Additionally, the bridging software can be configured to selectively filter local area transport multicast service announcements.

- Provides deterministic load distribution while maintaining a loop-free spanning tree.

- Provides the capability to bridge over *Asynchronous Transfer Mode* (ATM), *dial-on-demand routing* (DDR), *Fiber Distributed Data Interface* (FDDI), Frame Relay, multiprotocol *Link Access Procedure Balanced* (LAPB), *Switched Multimegabit Data Service* (SMDS), and X.25 networks.

- Provides concurrent routing and bridging, which is the capability to bridge a given protocol on some interfaces in a router and concurrently route that protocol on other interfaces in the same router.

- Provides fast-switched transparent bridging for Frame Relay encapsulated serial and *High-Speed Serial Interfaces* (HSSIs), according to the format specified in RFC 1490.

- Provides fast-switched Transparent bridging for the ATM interface on the Cisco 7000, according to the format specified in RFC 1483.

- Provides for compression of LAT frames to reduce LAT traffic through the network.

- Provides bridging and routing of virtual LANs (VLANs)

Cisco access servers and routers can be configured to serve as both multiprotocol routers and MAC-level bridges, bridging any traffic that cannot otherwise be routed. For example, a router for the IP can also bridge Digital's LAT protocol or NetBIOS traffic. Cisco routers also support remote bridging over synchronous serial lines. As with frames received on all other media types, dynamic learning and configurable filtering applies to frames received on serial lines. Transit bridging of Ethernet frames across FDDI media is also supported. The term *transit* refers to the fact that the source or destination of the frame cannot be on the FDDI media itself. FDDI, therefore, can act as a highly efficient backbone for the interconnection of many bridged networks. The configuration of FDDI transit bridging is identical to the configuration of transparent bridging on all other media types.

Source-Route Bridging (SRB)

The Source-Routing scheme operates at the LLC sublayer of the Data Link layer, as shown in Figure 4.8, but takes a different approach to determine the path. Source-Routing bridges are not considered transparent because they rely on the end stations for determining the route the packet should take through the network. A process called *Route Discovery* is used to find the optimal path for the communications session. Through this process, the route is discovered using broadcast packets (discovery packets) sent between the source and destination end stations.

Source-Route bridging is a means of determining the path used to transfer data from one workstation to another. Workstations that use Source-Routing participate in route discovery and specify the route used for each transmitted packet. Source-Route bridges merely carry out the routing instructions placed into each data packet when the packet is assembled by the sending workstation—hence the name *Source-Routing*. Although it includes the term *routing*, Source-Routing is a part of bridging technology at layer 2, not layer 3 routing using network addresses such as IP 32-bit Classes A, B, and C. Source-Route bridging is important because it is a bridge-routing method used on Token Ring networks installed in a large number of major networks throughout the world. Source-Route bridging also offers very good throughput when designed properly.

SRB is popular in Token Ring environments and is documented in IEEE 802.5. Source-Route bridging technology is a combination of bridging and routing functions. A Source-Route bridge can make routing decisions based upon the contents of the MAC frame header. Keeping the routing function at the MAC, or level 2, layer allows the higher layer protocols to execute their tasks more efficiently and allows the LAN to be expanded without the knowledge of the higher layer protocols.

Unlike Transparent bridging, SRB puts most of the smarts in the hosts and uses simple bridges. SRB bridges recognize a *routing information field* (RIF) in packet headers, essentially a list of bridges that a packet should traverse to reach its destination. Each bridge/

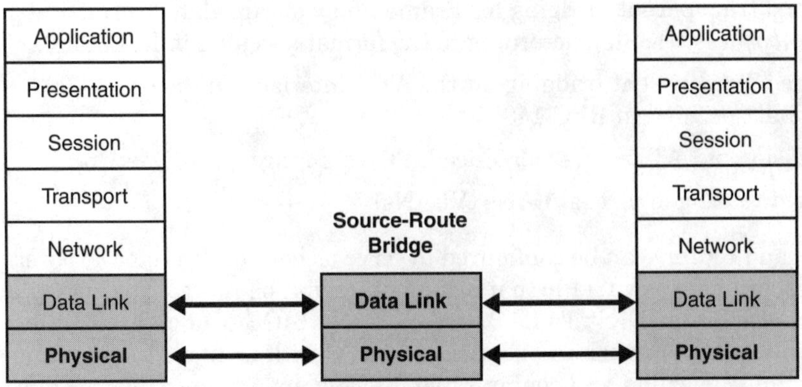

FIGURE 4.8   Source-Route bridging network

interface pair is represented by a *Route Designator* (RD), the 2-byte number used in the RIF. An *All Rings Broadcast* (ARB) is forwarded through every path in the network. Bridges add their RDs to the end of an ARB's RIF field and use this information to prevent loops (by never crossing the same RD twice). When the ARB arrives at the destination (and several copies may arrive) from the source, the RIF contains an RD path through the bridges. Flipping the RIF's *Direction Bit* (D) turns the RIF into a path from destination to source.

Source-Route bridging has its problems. It is even more broadcast intensive than Transparent bridging, because each host must broadcast to find paths, as opposed to each bridge having to broadcast. Source-Route bridging requires support in host software for managing RIF fields. To take advantage of a redundant network, a host must remember multiple RIF paths for each remote host with which it communicates and must have some method of retiring paths that appear to be failing. Because few SRB host implementations do this, SRB networks are notorious for requiring workstation reboots after a bridge failure.

On the other hand, if you want to bridge a Token Ring network, SRB is just about your only choice. Like Transparent bridging, SRB does allow the savvy engineer to quickly improve network performance when high-traffic areas can be segmented behind bridges.

How Source-Routing Works

To understand how Source-Routing works, you must first have a basic understanding of the following:

- Architecture of Token Ring frames
- Source-Routing bridge operation
- How Source-Route determination process works

Token Ring Frame Structure.   As the basic unit of transmission on a Token Ring network, the frame is made up of several fields. These fields, each consisting of one or more bytes, define such things as addressing, error checking, and the priority level of the frame.

Figure 4.9 shows the components of a simple 802.5/802.2 Token Ring frame—one that does not include Source-Routing fields. This structure can hold sufficient information to get a frame from one station to another station on the same ring. However, this frame has no fields to hold information about the route between stations on different rings. In order for a frame to hold the necessary information for travel between stations on different rings, the frame must be modified. A frame with routing information is shown in Figure 4.10.

Figure 4.10 highlights the three most important areas of the frame for Source-Routing:

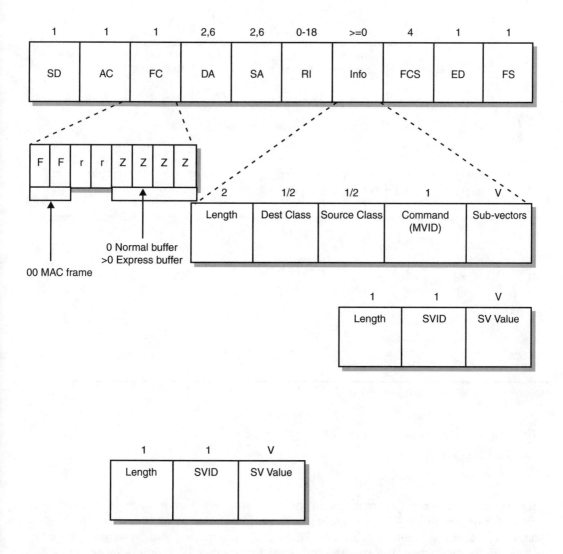

FIGURE 4.9 Token Ring MAC frame

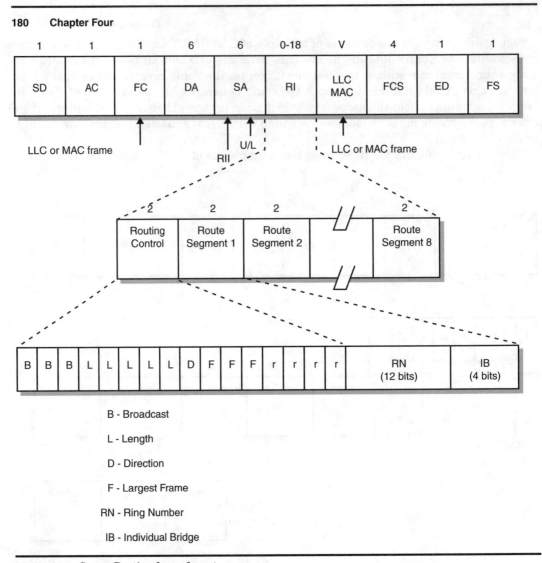

FIGURE 4.10   Source-Routing frame format

- The first *bit* of the Source Address field
- The Routing Control field
- The Route Designator fields

The Source Address Field. The binary 0 in the first bit of the Source Address field indicates that the frame contains no Source-Routing information. When a station includes routing information in a frame, it sets this bit to 1. This signals a receiving station to account for the routing information when it parses the contents of the frame. When a bridge detects a 1 in the first bit of the Source Address field, the bridge examines the frame's Routing Information field to see whether it should pass the frame to the bridge's adjoining ring (see Figure 4.11).

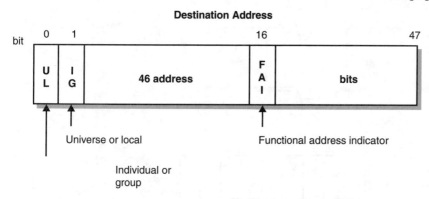

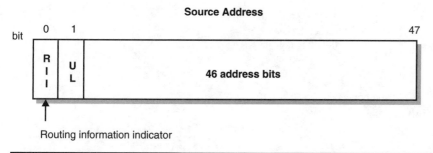

FIGURE 4.11 Address fields

Token Ring Routing Control Field. The Routing Control Field consists of the following:

- *Broadcast indicator.* Indicates whether the frame is to be sent along a specified path to all the segments in a network or to all the segments so that only one copy of the frame appears on each segment in the network (see Figure 4.12).

- *Non-broadcast (000).* The route designator contains a specific route for the frame.

- *All-routes broadcast (100).* The frame is transmitted along every route in the network to the destination. All-route explorer frames exist if the RT bits are set to 10x where x is a *don't care* bit. These frames are generated and routed along every nonrepeating route in the network (from source to destination). This routing results in as many frames arriving at the destination end station as there are different routes from the source end station. This routing type can be used as a response to receiving a route discovery frame sent along the spanning tree to the present originating station for all the routes available. The forwarding bridges add routing designators to the frame (see Figure 4.13).

- *Spanning tree explorer frame.* This frame exists if the RT bits are set to 11x where x is a *don't care* bit. Only spanning tree bridges relay the frame from one network to another. This means that the frame appears only once on every ring in the network and therefore only once at the destination end station. A station initiating the route

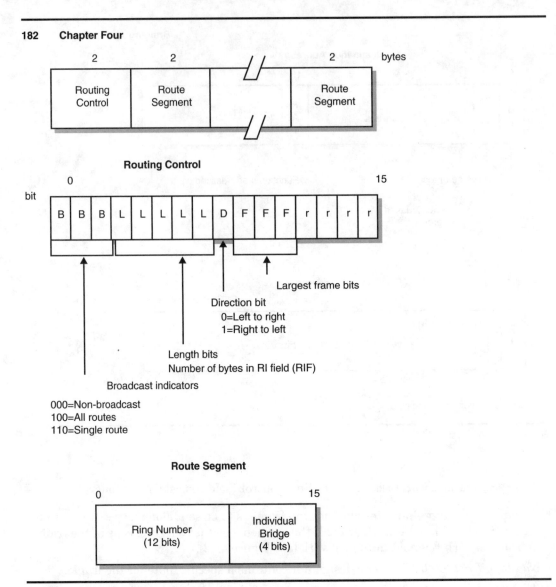

FIGURE 4.12 Routing Information field

discovery process may use this frame type. The bridge adds routing designator fields to the frame. It also can be used for frames sent to stations using a group address (see Figure 4.14).

- *Single-route broadcast (110)*. Only certain designated bridges relay the frame from one segment to another so that only one copy appears on each segment. Specifically routed frames exist if the first RT bit is set to 0. When this is the case, the Route Designator fields containing specific routing information guide the frame through the network to the destination address. During the route discovery phase, this type of frame is used as a response to the ARE frame. The user data is always carried in SRF frame format.

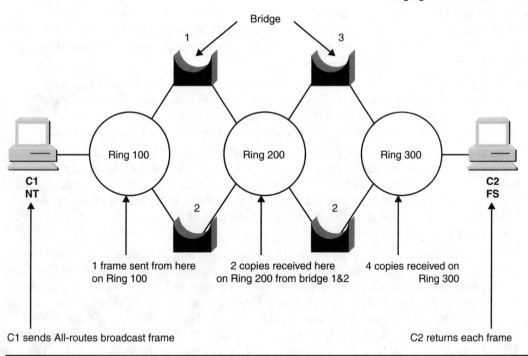

FIGURE 4.13   All-routes broadcast frame

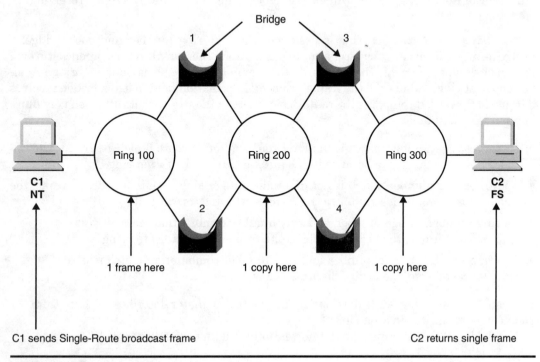

FIGURE 4.14   Spanning explorer

- *Length Bit.* The length bit indicator specifies the RIF's length in bytes. For all-routes or single-route broadcasts, this field is 2 bytes long and is used by bridges to add routing descriptors. Nonbroadcast frames have a predetermined fixed length because they already contain predetermined routing information.

- *Direction Bit.* Enables the bridge to correctly interpret the route designators. The indicator informs the bridge whether the routing information should be read right-to-left or left-to-right, allowing the list of ring numbers and bridge numbers in the RIF to appear in the same order for frames traveling in either direction along the route.

- *Largest Frame Bits.* Indicates the largest size information field that can be transmitted between two communicating stations on a specific route. A station originating a broadcast frame sets the largest frame bits value indicating the largest size frame that can travel any path. Bridges that relay a broadcast frame examine this field. If the indicated size is greater than the capacity of that part of the route, the bridge reduces the largest frame indicator.

The route designator field using the IEEE definition can hold from 2 to 14 Route Designators, allowing it to traverse up to 14 rings across 13 bridges in a given direction from source to destination. (Real-world implementations differ due to compatibility with IBM, for IBM only allows 2 to 8 Route Designators, allowing frames to traverse up to 8 rings across 7 bridges in a given direction.) This is one reason that DLSw allows Source-Routing networks to span larger than 8 rings and 7 bridges, because the Route Designator is terminated in the routers *virtual* ring. Because the information in the Routing Control field gives the current length of the Routing Information field, the number of Route Designators can vary without being parsed incorrectly by receiving stations.

Route Designator Field.   Each ring is assigned a unique ring number and each bridge, a bridge number. Together, they form a route designator. When an all-routes broadcast frame is transmitted, each bridge that forwards the frame to another ring adds its bridge number and that ring's number to the frame's routing information field. When a bridge receives a frame to forward, it compares the route designators in the RIF with its attached ring number and bridge number:

- If a target ring number match is in an all-route or single-route broadcast frame, the bridge discards the frame because it has already circled the target ring.

- If a target ring number match is not in an all-route or single-route broadcast frame, the bridge adds its route designator to the frame's RIF and forwards it.

- If a ring number, bridge number, and ring number combination match is in a nonbroadcast frame, the bridge forwards the frame to the indicated ring.

- If no ring number, bridge number, and ring number combination match is in a nonbroadcast frame, the bridge discards the frame.

When the frame reaches its destination, the route designator describes the path from the source ring to the destination ring.

The field contains administrative information including the following:

- The frame type (single-route broadcast, all-routes broadcast, or specifically routed)
- The length of the entire Routing Information field (the Routing Control field plus the Route Designator fields)
- The direction the Route Designator fields should be read by the bridge (forward or backward)
- The largest size the information field can be as it is sent along the route

Source-Routing Bridge Operation.   The basic function of a Source-Routing bridge is to provide connections between stations on different rings. When the bridge is started, several parameters are configured, including the bridge number, ring numbers, and the broadcast selection mode. Each bridge in a Source-Routing environment must be assigned a bridge number using a hexadecimal number (0–9, A–F). This number does not have to be unique unless bridges are used in parallel (attached to the same two rings). This bridge number is contained in the bridge portion of the Route Designators.

During bridge configuration, each ring, or segment, connected to a Source-Routing bridge is assigned a unique hexadecimal number (001-FFF). All bridges connected to the same ring must be configured to use the same ring number for that ring. When the Route Designator fields are used, this unique ring number is placed in the ring portion of each Route Designator. The ring numbering feature of the bridge allows all stations on a ring to know the number of the ring to which they are connected.

The source station defines the entire route in the transmitted frame in a Source-Routing configuration. Both end stations and bridges participate in the route discovery and forwarding process. The following steps describe this process:

1. A source station sends out a frame and finds that the frame's destination is not on its own (local) segment or ring.
2. The source station builds a route discovery broadcast frame and transmits it onto the local segment.
3. All bridges on the local segment capture the route discovery frame and send it over their connected networks.

   As the route discovery frame continues its search for the destination end station, each bridge that forwards it adds its own bridge number and segment number to the *Routing Information Field* (RIF) in the frame. As the frame continues to pass through the bridged network, the RIF compiles a list of bridge and segment number pairs describing the path to the destination. When the broadcast frame finally reaches its destination, it contains the exact sequence of addresses from source to destination.

4. When the destination end station receives the frame, it generates a response frame including the route path for communication. Frames that wander to other parts of the bridged network (accumulating irrelevant routing information in the meantime) never reach the destination end station and are ignored by other end stations.
5. The originating station receives the learned route path. It then can transmit information across this established path.

Source-Routing Frames. Bridges interconnect LANs by relaying MAC frames between the MAC layers of the bridged LANs. MAC frames provide the necessary information in the form of source and destination addresses. In Source-Routing, the data frame forwarding decision is based on routing information within the frame. The source station that originates the frame designates the route that the frame travels by embedding a description of the route in the RIF of the transmitted frame. A closer look at the various types of source-routing bridge frames helps to further explain how bridges obtain and transmit routing information (see Figure 4.15).

Because Source-Routing MAC frames contain routing information necessary for data communication over multiring environments, their formats differ slightly from the typical Token Ring MAC frames. The presence of a 1 in the *Routing Information Indicator* (RII) within the source address field indicates that a RIF containing routing information follows the source address (see Figure 4.16 and Table 4.1).

Ways to Configure a Source-Routing Bridge Configuration. A Cisco router configured for Source-Route bridging can be configured manually as a single-route broadcast bridge or as an all-routes broadcast bridge. The bridge also can be allowed to configure itself automatically to all-routes or single-route mode by negotiating with other bridges on the network.

A Source-Routing bridge set up as a single-route broadcast bridge forwards the following frames:

- All-routes broadcast (SNA)
- Single-route broadcast (NetBIOS)
- Specifically routed

A Source-Routing bridge set up as an all-routes broadcast bridge forwards the following frames:

- All-routes broadcast
- Specifically routed

A bridge set up this way is also described as "single-route broadcast forwarding inactive" because it does not forward single-route broadcasts. Two features of bridges prevent all-routes route determination frames from traveling endlessly around the network. The first is that a bridge does not forward a frame to its other ring if the Route Designator fields indicate that the frame has already been on the bridge's other ring. The second feature is the Hop Count Limit, which restricts the number of bridges an all-routes broadcast frame may cross.

The default setting for IBM's Token Ring bridges are 7, and the range is 1–7. When either an all-routes broadcast or a single-route broadcast frame has crossed seven IBM bridges and reaches the eighth, it is discarded.

Source-Route Determination. A ring station that requires the resources of a file server or peer on a connected ring must first find a route to that station. When a route is known, the two stations use it to exchange all frames. Ring stations may use either an all-routes or single-route broadcast frame to determine the route to another station.

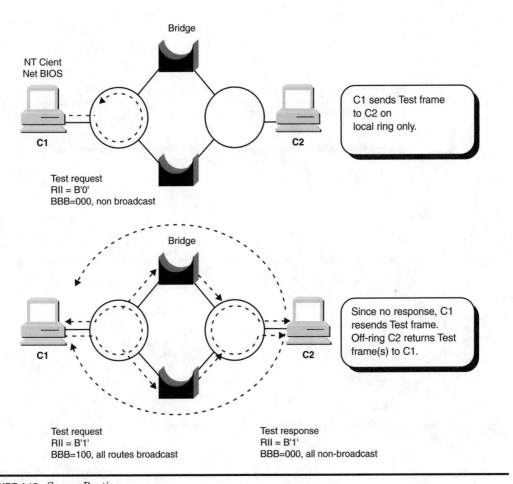

Bridge

NT Cient
Net BIOS

C1

C2

> C1 sends Test frame
> to C2 on
> local ring only.

Test request
RII = B'0'
BBB=000, non broadcast

Bridge

C1

C2

> Since no response, C1
> resends Test frame.
> Off-ring C2 returns Test
> frame(s) to C1.

Test request
RII = B'1'
BBB=100, all routes broadcast

Test response
RII = B'1'
BBB=000, all non-broadcast

FIGURE 4.15 Source-Routing

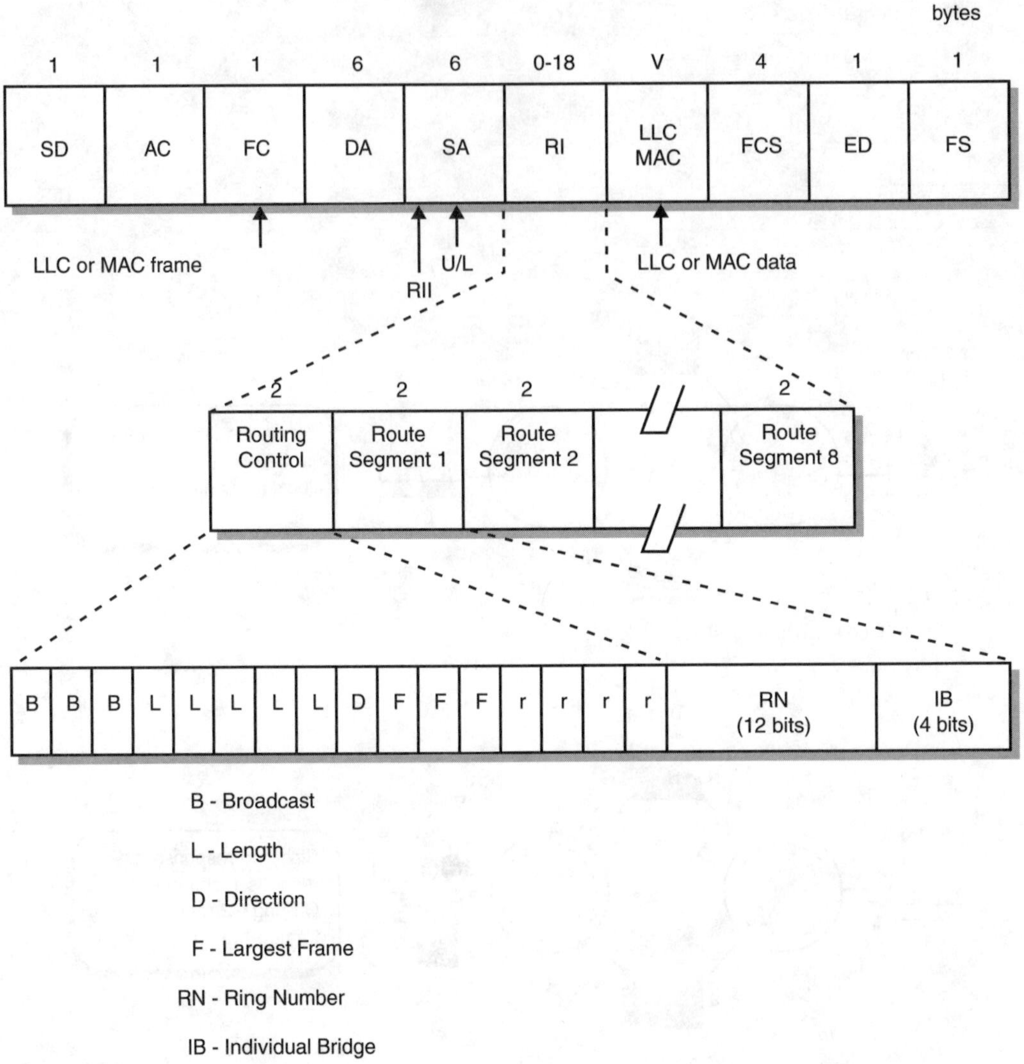

FIGURE 4.16 Source-Routing frame format

This selection is dependent on the type of applications used, such as NetBIOS and SNA.

Figure 4.17 illustrates how *NetWare Client* (NWC) finds a route to *NetWare Server* (NWS) using an all-routes broadcast frame. NWC places a frame on Ring 1 that contains the node address of NWS as its Destination Address and is labeled as an all-routes broadcast in the Routing Control field. This frame is copied by all of the Source-Routing bridges onto their adjacent rings (unless the frame is marked in the Route Designator fields as having been on the adjacent ring already).

Because two paths are available to Ring 400 from Ring 100, two copies of the frame appear on Ring 400. (Two copies also appear on Ring 300.) As each bridge copies the frame onto its adjoining ring, it adds Route Designators to indicate the following:

TABLE 4.1 **Source-Routing Frame Format**

	Routing Control Field				LAN 1		LAN 2		LAN 3	
Step	**Broadcast**	**Length**	**Direction**	**Large-Frame**	**Ring #**	**Bridge**	**Ring #**	**Bridge**	**Ring #**	**Bridge**
1	100	00010	0	111	—	—	—	—	—	—
2	100	00110	0	011	100	1	200	null	—	—
3	100	01000	0	010	100	1	200	2	300	null
4	000	01000	1	010	100	1	200	2	300	null
5	000	01000	1	010	100	1	200	2	300	null
6	000	01000	1	010	100	1	200	2	300	null

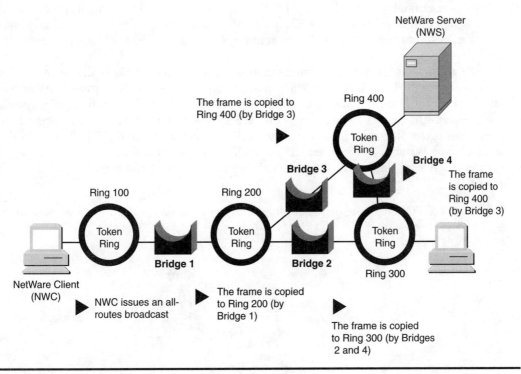

FIGURE 4.17 Route determination (© Novell Inc.)

- The ring number from which the frame is copied
- The number of the bridge passing the frame
- The ring number to which the frame is copied

When NWS receives the all-routes broadcast frames, it realizes that a station is trying to determine its location on the network. NWS can respond to each of these frames either with a single-route or all-routes broadcast frame. Or, NWS can reverse the order of the routes that the bridges have placed in the Route Designator fields of NWC's all-routes broadcast frames and return specifically routed frames addressed to NWC.

After receiving the response, NWC can choose the shorter of the two routes (in this case, the route through bridge 3) for all subsequent communication with NWS.

In contrast with this example, if NWC were to use a single-route broadcast frame to locate NWS, only those bridges configured to pass single-route broadcasts will copy the frame to their adjacent rings.

This combination of options is flexible enough to allow either the source station or the destination station to determination the best route. Which options are used in a network is an implementation issue, decided by each vendor whose software is used on the network stations (or by the user if the software is configurable).

Source-Routing Route Selection Process. If you need to read network analyzer traces to examine what is happening on a network, you must understand not only the principles of Source-Routing, but the underlying method each station uses as it communicates with other stations. The following example examines a small part of the Source-Routing frame at the binary level.

Figure 4.18 shows the broadcast frame sent by NWC during the first three stages of the route determination process.

When NWC originates the route determination frame (broadcast), it indicates in the first bit of the Source Address field that the frame contains routing information. This signals the bridge that the frame should be examined and possibly passed on to the adjoining ring.

NWC inserts the unique node address of NWS in the frame's Destination Address field. Higher level protocols such as NetBIOS or *NetWare Core Protocol* (NCP) can obtain this unique address through a search for the name NWS on the network.

Figure 4.19 shows the specific numbers placed in the RIF at the three stages shown in Figure 4.18.

Stage 1. As NWC issues the frame, it places the Destination and Source Addresses in the MAC header.

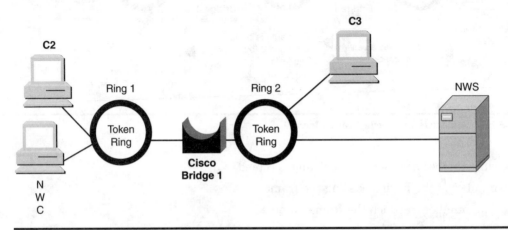

FIGURE 4.18 Step one—Source-Routing route

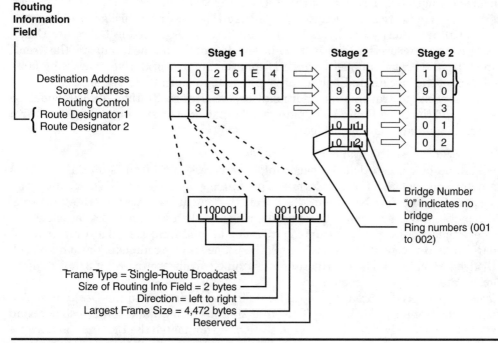

Routing Information Field

Destination Address
Source Address
Routing Control
{ Route Designator 1
{ Route Designator 2

FIGURE 4.19 Number placement in the RIF (© Novell Inc.)

The first byte (C2) of the two-byte Routing Control portion of the RIF contains the following:

- The binary 110 at the beginning of the byte signifies a single-route broadcast.
- The remaining binary 00010 (or decimal 2) indicates that the RIF is two bytes long.

The second byte (30) contains the following information:

- The binary 0 at the beginning of the byte indicates that the RIFs (which do not exist yet) should be read from left to right.
- Binary 011 designates the largest frame size (excluding headers) that NWC can transmit and is reduced by any bridge that cannot handle the current given size.
- The remaining binary 0000 is blank and is reserved for future use.

The Destination Address and the Source Address remain the same throughout the first three stages. Note, however, that the hard-coded Source Address of the adapter in NWC is actually 1000 5A38 106A.

When NWC changes the first bit of the Source Address set from 0 to 1 to designate a Source-Routing frame (before sending the frame), the equivalent hexadecimal Source Address becomes 9000 5A38 106A.

Stage 2. As the bridge prepares to pass the frame to Ring 2, it modifies parts of the RIF.

The bridge changes the first byte of the Routing Control Field from C2 to C6. The last five bits change to indicate a new length of 6 for the RIF, because the bridge is adding four bytes to the RIF (previously two bytes long). These four bytes, added in the Route Designator fields, can be interpreted directly in their hexadecimal form: the number of the "from" ring (Ring 001), the bridge number (Bridge 1), and the number of the "to" ring (Ring 002). The final digit of the last Route Designator is always 0, to indicate no bridge.

If the frame were to traverse an additional bridge (Bridge 2), that final 0 would be changed to 2, and the third Route Designator would read 0030 (assuming a Ring 003), with the last digit again indicating no bridge.

Stage 3. NWS receives the frame exactly as it left the bridge.

To understand how all stations on each ring have access to all frames on the ring, it is important to note that the route determination frame originated by NWC travels completely around Ring 1 before NWC removes it from the ring. If NWS were on the same ring, it would copy the frame as it moved around the ring and then issue a direct response.

In this example, however, as the frame is traveling around Ring 1, Bridge 1 copies it. After Bridge 1 puts this copied frame on Ring 2, the frame travels completely around Ring 2 before Bridge 1 removes it. During the time this frame travels around Ring 2, NWS copies it and formulates a response (see Figure 4.20).

NWS responds to NWC's broadcast because its unique address is in the Destination Address field of the frame's MAC header. The other stations (NWC2 and NWC3) do not send response frames back to NWC because these stations do not match the Destination Address of the frame.

Figure 4.21 shows the specific numbers in the Routing Information field at the three stages shown in Figure 4.20.

Stage 4. As NWS issues the response frame, it includes six bytes in the RIF. The first byte (06) contains the following information:

- The binary 000 at the beginning of the byte signifies a specifically routed frame.

- The remaining binary 00110 (or decimal six) indicates that the RIF is six bytes long.

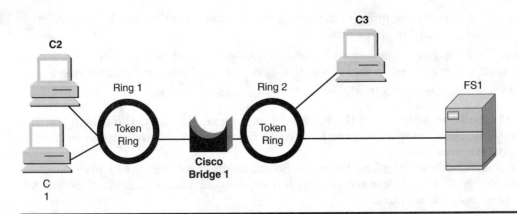

FIGURE 4.20   Final step in the Source-Routing route determination

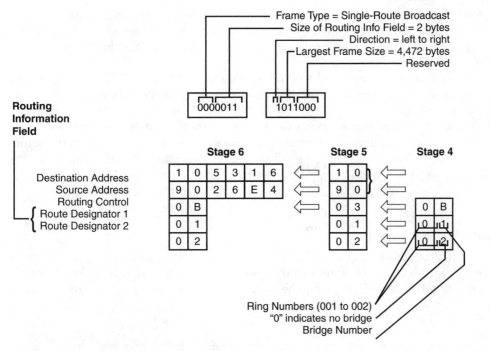

Frame Type = Single-Route Broadcast
Size of Routing Info Field = 2 bytes
Direction = left to right
Largest Frame Size = 4,472 bytes
Reserved

0000011   1011000

Routing Information Field

Destination Address
Source Address
Routing Control
Route Designator 1
Route Designator 2

Stage 6   Stage 5   Stage 4

Ring Numbers (001 to 002)
"0" indicates no bridge
Bridge Number

FIGURE 4.21   Specific number in the RIF (© Novell Inc.)

The second byte (B0) contains the following information:

- The binary 1 at the beginning of the byte indicates that the Route Designator fields should be read backwards (this feature allows all bridges to read the same Route Designator fields for frame travel in either direction).
- The next part, binary 011, designates the largest frame size (excluding headers) that can be transmitted between NWC and NWS.
- The remaining binary 0000 is blank and is reserved for future use.

The Destination Address now reflects the hard-coded unique adapter address of NWC (1000 5A38 106A). The Source Address contains the unique adapter address of NWS (1000 2866 E04A), slightly modified to *9000 2866 e04a* to reflect the setting of the first bit of the Source Address field from 0 to 1, to indicate a Source-Routing frame.

Stage 5.   Because this frame is a specifically routed frame, the bridge does not change any of the information in the frame.

The RIF contains the routing information that directs the bridge to pass the frame from Ring 2 to Ring 1.

Stage 6.   NWC receives the frame exactly as it left the bridge (and NWS). NWC and NWS continue to use this route until the route between them is altered.

When route determination is complete, each station on a network maintains a table of the routes to other stations with which it communicates. Figure 4.22 shows how three workstations (C1, C2, and C3) maintain a table of individual routes to NWS, the file server with which they have a current session.

Conversely, NWS1 maintains a table of the routes to C1, C2, and C3. The same idea applies for peer-to-peer communication. For example, C1 and C3 could each keep track of the route to the other stations.

As you can see from the step-by-step examples, a thorough understanding of the route determination process requires knowledge of the pieces of Source-Routing information in Token Ring frames. Now that you have a better understanding of how Source-Routing works, we can look at a few examples of how to apply that knowledge in managing broadcast traffic overhead, balancing the network load, and implementing parallel bridges.

Source-Route Traffic Overhead

The major difference between an all-routes broadcast frame and a single-route broadcast frame is in the number of frames that appear on the destination ring. An all-routes frame appears on the destination ring the same number of times as there are routes to that ring.

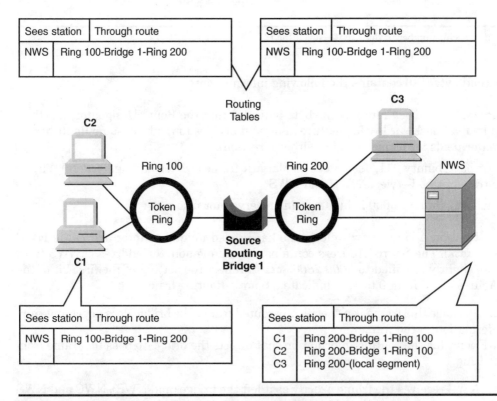

Sees station	Through route
NWS	Ring 100-Bridge 1-Ring 200

Sees station	Through route
NWS	Ring 100-Bridge 1-Ring 200

Routing Tables

Sees station	Through route
NWS	Ring 100-Bridge 1-Ring 200

Sees station	Through route
C1	Ring 200-Bridge 1-Ring 100
C2	Ring 200-Bridge 1-Ring 100
C3	Ring 200-(local segment)

FIGURE 4.22 Routing tables are kept at each communicating station

In contrast, a single-route frame appears on the destination ring as many times as there are single-route broadcast routes to that ring. That is, if all the bridges on the network were set up as single-route bridges, a single-route broadcast from C1 would appear two times on Ring 400.

However, if only bridges 1, 2, and 3 were set up as single-route bridges, only one copy of a single-route broadcast from C1 would appear on Ring 400. Because the intent of having a single route over the network is to reduce traffic, creating more than one "single route" would defeat the purpose. It is important, therefore, to effectively place each bridge and to know its broadcast mode.

Using single-route broadcast frames and single-route bridges can clearly reduce the amount of traffic caused by the route determination process. By placing single-route bridges strategically in the network, you can create preferred routes for route determination, freeing from most broadcast traffic those rings whose operation is most sensitive to additional traffic.

Parallel Bridges and Load Balancing

Source-Routing makes it possible to connect two or more bridges to the same two rings. This configuration, called *parallel bridging*, not only guards against the failure of a single bridge, but it can also help balance the network load.

This section contains two examples of parallel bridging during route determination. In both examples, two bridges are used in parallel: bridge 1 is a single-route broadcast bridge, and bridge 2 is an all-routes broadcast bridge. The first example shows how they work with a single-route broadcast; the second shows an all-routes broadcast.

Figures 4.23 and 4.24 show the operation of parallel bridges during a single-route broadcast. In Figure 4.23, C1 sends a single-route broadcast to locate NWS1 on the network.

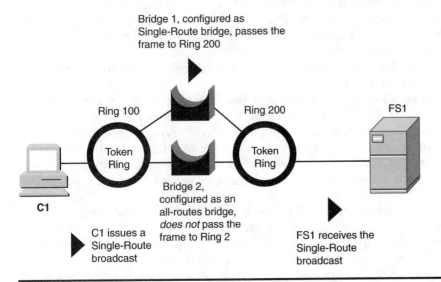

FIGURE 4.23   A single-route broadcast over parallel bridges

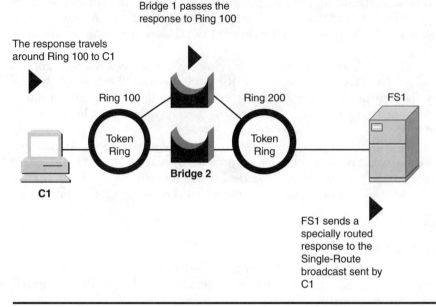

FIGURE 4.24   A response to a single-route broadcast over parallel bridges

Because only the single-route bridge forwards the single-route broadcast from Ring 100 to Ring 200, NWS1 receives just one copy of the broadcast frame.

In the second part of the example, NWS1 responds to the single-route broadcast with a specifically routed frame (see Figure 4.24.) The frame is sent back across the same bridge that was used by the original broadcast frame. This technique keeps the number of broadcasts and responses to a minimum, which reduces the load on the network.

C1 chooses the route of the first response frame that it receives from NWS1. (In this case, only one response was sent.) C1 sends subsequent frames as specifically routed frames, which contain the routing information (ring numbers and bridge numbers) needed to route these frames to NWS1. After NWS1 receives the first specifically routed frame from C1, it also uses the route selected by C1.

Figure 4.25 shows an all-routes broadcast over parallel bridges. C1 sends an all-routes broadcast frame in search of NWS1. Both bridges copy the frame to Ring 200.

Remember that an all-routes broadcast route determination frame appears on the destination ring the same number of times as there are routes to that ring. Although an all-routes broadcast creates more network traffic than single-route broadcast frames, all-routes broadcast frames have a unique advantage because they balance the load on the network.

Figure 4.26 shows a response to an all-routes broadcast over parallel bridges. C1 and NWS1 have the option of selecting which bridge they use to communicate with each other. If bridge 1 is heavily loaded with traffic when C1 issues the all-routes frame, C1 and NWS1 can route subsequent frames over bridge 2 for better performance.

In the route determination process, nodes can use either single-route broadcasts or all-routes broadcasts. Single-route broadcasts reduce the amount of traffic overhead caused by route determination packets and allow you to create preferred routes on the network. All-

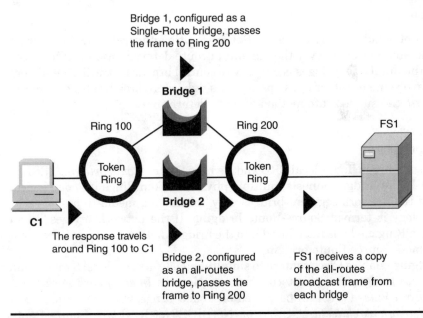

FIGURE 4.25   A response to an all-routes broadcast over parallel bridges

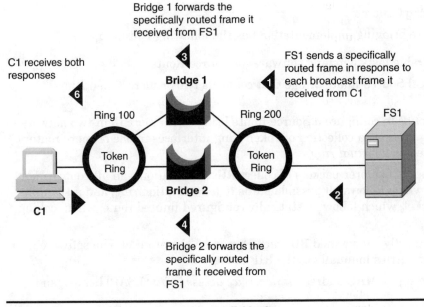

FIGURE 4.26   An all-routes broadcast over parallel bridges

routes broadcasts create more traffic overhead, but they also allow for load balancing. Ultimately, Source-Routing gives you the flexibility to customize networks to the needs of your environment, whether the priority is performance, reliability, or ease of management.

Route Determination

The number of copies of broadcast frames used in Source-Routing illustrates the importance of maintaining some kind of control over the amount of route determination traffic on the network. Reducing the number of bridges is one way to control broadcast traffic, but a more flexible way is to have some of the bridges operate in single-route broadcast mode and to have workstations use the single-route method of route determination.

Cisco Source-Route Bridging

Cisco IOS bridging software includes local SRB and *Remote Source-Route bridging* (RSRB) capability. A Source-Route bridge connects multiple physical Token Rings into one logical network segment. If the network segment bridges only Token Ring media to provide connectivity, the technology is termed Source-Route bridging. If the network bridges Token Ring and if non-Token Ring media is introduced into the bridged network segment, the technology is termed remote Source-Route bridging.

Source-Route bridging enables Cisco routers to simultaneously act as a level 3 router and a level 2 Source-Route bridge. Thus, protocols such as Novell's *Internetwork Packet Exchange* (IPX) or *Banyan Vines* (VIP) can be routed on Token Rings, while other protocols such as *Systems Network Architecture* (SNA) or NetBIOS/NetBEUI are Source-Route bridged.

Source-Route Bridging Features

Cisco's Source-Route bridging implementation has the following features:

- Provides configurable fast-switching software for Source-Route bridging.
- Provides for a local Source-Route bridge that connects two or more Token Ring networks.
- Provides *ring groups* to configure a Source-Route bridge with more than two network interfaces. A ring group is a collection of Token Ring interfaces in one or more routers collectively treated as a *virtual ring*.
- Provides two types of explorer packets to collect RIF information—an all-routes explorer packet, which follows all possible paths to a destination ring, and a spanning-tree explorer packet, which follows a statically configured limited route, when looking for paths.
- Provides a dynamically determined RIF cache based on the protocol. The software also allows you to add entries manually to the RIF cache.
- Provides for filtering by MAC address, *link service access point* (LSAP) header, and protocol type.
- Provides for filtering of NetBIOS frames either by station name or by a packet byte offset.
- Provides for translation into transparently bridged frames to allow Source-Route stations to communicate with nonSource-Route stations (typically on Ethernet).

- Provides support for the SRB *Management Information Base* (MIB) variables as described in the IETF draft "Bridge MIB" document.

- Provides support for the Token Ring MIB variables

Remote Source-Route Bridging

In contrast to SRB, which involves bridging between Token Ring media only, RSRB involves multiple routers separated by non-Token Ring network segments.
   Cisco's RSRB software implementation includes the following features:

- Provides for multiple routers separated by non-Token Ring segments. Three options are available:

  - Encapsulate the Token Ring traffic inside IP datagrams passed over a *Transmission Control Protocol* (TCP) connection between two routers.
  - Use *Fast-Sequenced Transport* (FST) to transport RSRB packets to their peers without TCP or *User Datagram Protocol* (UDP) header or processor overhead.
  - Use MAC-layer encapsulations over a single serial line, Ethernet, Token Ring, or FDDI ring connected between two routers attached to Token Ring networks.

- Provides for configurable limits to the size of the TCP back-up queue.

   The virtual ring can extend across any non-Token Ring media supported by RSRB, such as serial, Ethernet, FDDI, and WANs. The type of media you select determines the way you set up RSRB.

   NOTE: *If you bridge across Token Ring media, I recommended that you do not use RSRB. Use SRB instead.*

DLSw+

DLSw+ is Cisco's implementation of DLSw, an SNA-over-IP routing standard that helps to integrate SNA and LAN internetworks by encapsulating nonroutable SNA and NetBIOS protocols within routable IP. DLSw is a means of transporting SNA and NetBIOS traffic over an IP network. DLSw is an alternative to SRB and addresses the following limitations of SRB:
   Source-Routing bridges offer a number of important advantages:

- Optimal paths between end stations are used.

- Parallel and redundant paths can be used (on a per session basis), so there are no idle links wasting link bandwidth.

- Network troubleshooting is enhanced because the route each packet took is contained in the routing information field.

- Because there is only one location containing the bridge and LAN number that must be compared for the forwarding decision, the hardware is simpler.

- Traffic between and through LANs supporting different maximum frame sizes is easily supported.

- IBM controller timing is set properly for extended LANs.

Disadvantages include the following:

- An increase in LAN overhead occurs if many stations are in route-discovery mode at the same time. The amount of overhead is directly related to the number of paths between stations. The overhead would be most evident on remote bridges in which the link speed is many times slower than the LAN.

- Temporary congestion on a route during route discovery may cause the originating station to fail to pick the best route.

- The route does not dynamically change if a link should go down or be congested during a session. A new discovery sequence must be initiated. Most existing Source-Routing software does not support automatic rediscovery of a new route.

SRB Summary

The main differences between Transparent bridging and Source-Route bridging is how the bridge determines whether or not to forward the packet and the structure of the packets. These differences make the two bridging schemes incompatible.

Source-Route Transparent

Although both Transparent and Source-Route bridging methods work well in their respective environments, they are not particularly well-suited to work in each other's environments. In addition, because these bridging schemes are not compatible, they do not interoperate in a mixed environment. Source-Route bridges cannot operate in a transparent environment simply because the packets do not contain routing information. Without routing information, a Source-Route bridge has no way to recognize that the packet should be forwarded. Bridges function differently in Token Ring and Ethernet networks. Aside from the differences in bit-ordering, packet size, and acknowledgment bits, bridging methods are another obstacle. Ethernet bridges use Transparent bridging in which the bridges determine the route of the traffic through the network. Token Ring networks use Transparent bridging in some instances but generally depend on Source-Routing as the primary bridging method.

The SRT Solution

Source-Route Transparent (SRT) bridging, an IEEE extension to the 802.1D Transparent bridging standard, resolves a large part of the incompatibility in bridging Token Ring and Ethernet. SRT saves you the cost of installing multiple bridges and separate links to support the two types of traffic by adding a parallel bridging architecture (rather than an alternative) to the Transparent bridging standard (see Figure 4.27).

The problems using bridges in a Source-Routing environment are subtler, because Transparent bridges *can* pass Source-Routing packets. The major issue is that the routing information is ignored; thus the advantages offered by Source-Routing are not used, and packet size information is not passed to the end stations.

The packet size issue is a particular problem in extended networks in which both 4/16 Mbps Token Rings can be included in the path. Transparent bridges cannot indicate the correct packet size to the end stations.

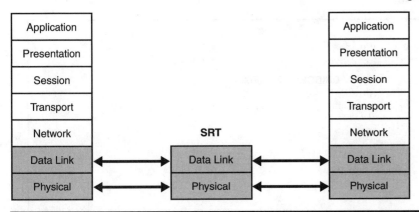

FIGURE 4.27 SRT bridge

The real problems exist in environments in which Source-Routing and transparent environments are combined. In extended networks in which support for both Source-Routing and nonSource-Routing LAN operating systems is present, duplicate bridges are often needed to carry the traffic.

In the mixed environment, both types of bridges are present. The Transparent bridge spanning tree calculation does not recognize the SR bridges, and thus loops may exist in the network. If Source-Routing networks are on both sides of a transparent link, problems may be encountered, because the proper ring and bridge numbers are not present in packets passed over the link.

To address the issues of coexistence and interoperability, the IEEE 802 standards organization has endorsed the *Source-Routing Transparent Standard*.

Bridges function differently in Token Ring and Ethernet networks. Aside from the differences in bit ordering, packet size, and acknowledgment bits, bridging methods are another obstacle. Ethernet bridges use Transparent bridging in which the bridges determine the route of the traffic through the network. Token Ring networks use Transparent bridging in some instances but generally depend on Source-Route bridging as the primary bridging method especially in SNA and NetBIOS environments.

SRT Bridging

A SRT bridge combines both bridging schemes on a single platform, allowing both Source-Routing and transparent data to be passed. An SRT bridge Source-Routes frames that are received with routing information, as determined by the routing information bit, and transparently send packets received without routing information.

As Figure 4.28 shows, there are essentially two bridge logical paths for packets depending on their type. All the packets on the network are looked at (filtered) to determine whether the routing information bit is set. If not, the packet takes the transparent (MA) path. The address database is checked for a match (as in the Transparent bridge) to determine whether it should be forwarded or not. The packet address is then learned and the

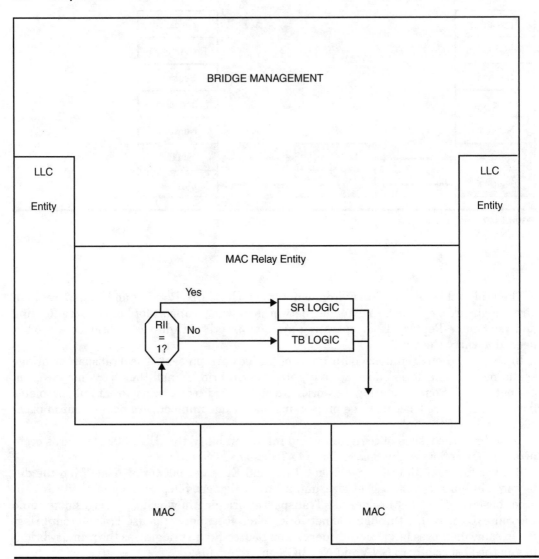

FIGURE 4.28   SRT bridge operation logic

table is updated to reflect the packet. Because loops are not allowed in Transparent bridging applications, the transparent portion of the bridge still determines the spanning tree
paths with other SRT bridges on the extended network.

If the routing information bit is set, the packet takes the Source-Routing (LLC) path. In
the SRT Standard, four methods are presented to determine the best path between source
and destination end stations. These methods are referred to as *Route Discovery Protocols*. The
proposed SRT Standard defines three packets that can be used for route discovery:

- The *All-Route Explorer* (ARE) frame traverses all routes between end stations and is equivalent to the all-routes discovery packet.

- The *Specifically Routed Frame* (SRF) has no routing information but performs the function of the single-route broadcast packet.

- *Spanning Tree Explorer* (STE)

About SRT

An SRT bridge is a MAC bridge that performs Source-Routing when it receives source-routing frames with routing information and performs Transparent bridging when it receives frames without routing information. In SRT, all the bridges between Ethernet and Token Rings are transparent. The bridges operate at the MAC sublayer of the Data Link layer and are invisible to the end stations.

The SRT bridge distinguishes between the two types of frames by checking the value in the RII field of the frame. An RII value of 1 indicates that the frame is carrying routing information while a value of 0 indicates that it is not. With this distinction, the SRT Bridge forwards Transparent bridging frames without any conversions to the outgoing media (including Token Ring). Source-Routing frames are restricted to the Source-Routing bridging domain.

The Spanning Tree protocol and algorithm form a single tree involving all the networks connected by SRT bridges. The SRT-bridged network offers a larger domain of Transparent bridging with a subdomain of Source-Routing. Thus, transparent frames are capable of reaching to the farthest side of SRT and TB-bridged LANs, but Source-Routed frames are limited to only SRT and SRB-bridged LANs. In the SRT bridging model, Source-Routing and Transparent bridging ports use the same spanning tree. In the SRT bridged domain, end stations are responsible for deciding which bridging method to choose—Source-Routing or Transparent bridging.

The major advantage of SRT bridging is that a single SRT bridge provides the advantages of both Source-Routing and Transparent bridging and eliminates the need for multiple platforms. Other advantages include the following:

- Enhanced route discovery and more robust optimal route selection process

- Less route discovery overhead, because both source and destination end stations can discover the route simultaneously

- The capability to save back-up paths for dynamic route change if a link should fail

- Platform for eventual true Transparent to Source-Routing compatibility

Source-Route Transparent Bridging Features

Cisco routers support Transparent bridging on Token Ring interfaces that support SRT bridging. Both Transparent and SRT bridging are supported on all Token Ring interface cards that can be configured for either 4/16Mbps transmission speeds. As with all other media types, all the features that use *bridge-group* commands can be used on Token Ring interfaces. As with other interface types, the bridge group can be configured to run either the IEEE or Digital spanning-tree protocols. When configured for the IEEE spanning-tree protocol, the bridge cooperates with other SRT bridges and constructs a loop-free topology across the entire extended LAN.

You can run the Digital spanning-tree protocol over Token Ring as well. Use it when you have other non-IEEE bridges on other media and do not have any SRT bridges on Token Ring. In this configuration, all the Token Ring Transparent bridges must be Cisco routers. This is because the Digital spanning-tree protocol has not been standardized on Token Ring.

As specified by the SRT bridging specification, only packets without a *routing information field* (RIF) (RII = 0 in the SA field) are transparently bridged. Packets with a RIF (RII = 1) are passed to the Source-Route bridging module for handling. An SRT-capable Token Ring interface can have both Source-Route bridging and Transparent bridging enabled at the same time. However, with SRT bridging, frames that did not have a RIF when they were produced by their generating host never gain a RIF, and frames that did have a RIF when they were produced never lose that RIF.

> **NOTE:** *Because bridges running only SRT bridging never add or remove RIFs from frames, they do not integrate Source-Route bridging with Transparent bridging. A host connected to a Source-Route bridge that expects RIFs can never communicate with a device across a bridge that does not understand RIFs. SRT bridging cannot tie in existing Source-Route bridges to a Transparent bridged network. If you want to tie them in, you must use* Source-Route Translational Bridging (SR/TLB) *instead (see Figure 4.29).*

Bridging between Token Ring and other media requires certain packet transformations. In all cases, the MAC addresses are bit-swapped because the bit ordering on Token Ring is different from that on other media. In addition, Token Ring supports one packet format, LLC, while Ethernet supports two formats (LLC and Ethernet). The transformation of LLC frames between media is simple. A length field is either created (when the frame is transmitted to non-Token Ring) or removed (when the frame is transmitted to Token Ring). When an Ethernet format frame is transmitted to Token Ring, the frame is translated into an LLC-1 SNAP packet. The *destination service access point* (DSAP) value is AA, the *source service access point* (SSAP) value is AA, with the *organizational unique identifier* (OUI) value is 0000F8. Likewise, when a packet in LLC-1 format is bridged onto Ethernet media, the packet is translated into Ethernet format.

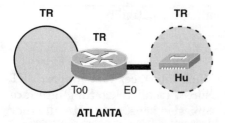

ATLANTA

FIGURE 4.29   SR/TLB configuration

CAUTION: *Bridging between dissimilar media presents several problems that can prevent communication from occurring. These problems include bit order translation (or using MAC addresses as data),* maximum transmission unit *(MTU) differences, frame status differences, and multicast address usage. Some or all of these problems might be present in a multimedia bridged LAN. Because of differences in the way end nodes implement Token Ring, these problems are most prevalent when bridging between Token Ring and Ethernet or between Ethernet and FDDI LANs.*

Problems currently occur with the following protocols when bridged between Token Ring and other media: Novell IPX, DECnet Phase IV, AppleTalk, Banyan VINES, XNS, and IP. Further, problems can occur with the Novell IPX and XNS protocols when bridged between FDDI and other media. We recommend that these protocols be routed when possible.

Translational and Encapsulation Bridging

Cisco supports all bridging standards, including Translational and Encapsulation bridging.

- Translational bridging—bridging between LAN media with dissimilar MAC sublayer protocols
- Encapsulation bridging—bridging that carries Ethernet frames from one router to another across dissimilar media, like serial and FDDI lines

Translational Bridging

Translational bridging enables you to bridge between dissimilar LANs, commonly Ethernet and Token Ring, or Ethernet and FDDI. In the case of Ethernet/Token Ring bridging, translational bridging only allows connectivity for nonroutable protocols like LAT, Maintenance Operations Protocol, and NetBIOS.

The translation for bridging between Ethernet/Token Ring and Ethernet/ FDDI requires bit order reversal because the internal representation of MAC addresses is different on Ethernet, Token Ring, and FDDI. Ethernet is little Indian (it transmits least order bit first) and Token Ring and FDDI are big Indian (they transmit high order bit first). For example, address `0000.0cxx.xxxx` on Ethernet would appear as `0000.30yy.yyyy` on Token Ring because every byte needs to be bit-swapped. Both Ethernet and Token Ring use the first transmitted bit of a frame's destination address to determine whether the frame is unicast or multicast. With no address conversion, a unicast frame (a frame that has only one destination) on one network may appear as a multicast address (an address for more than one station) on another network.

Remember that Ethernet/Token Ring bridging is only possible with nonroutable protocols. Sometimes, MAC addresses are carried in the data portion of a frame. For example, ARP places the hardware address in the data portion of the link-layer frame. It is simple to convert source and destination addresses in the header, but conversion of hardware addresses that may appear in the data portion is more difficult. When performing Source-Route Transparent or Source-Route Translational bridging between Ethernet and Token Ring, Cisco does not search for instances of hardware addresses in the data portion. So, only nonroutable protocols work with Ethernet/Token Ring bridging.

Translational bridging between Ethernet/FDDI carries the issue of bit reversal a little further since few protocols work across the FDDI/ Ethernet barrier. One reason for this is the concept of a canonical address above the MAC layer—any address above the Mac layer on FDDI should be ordered canonically according to Ethernet order. This is how IP is done on FDDI, and it's why Cisco can bridge it when going from Ethernet to FDDI. Unfortunately, other protocols don't necessarily do this.

These protocols can be translationally bridged between Ethernet and FDDI:

- IP
- OSI
- DECnet
- Nonroutable Protocols such as NetBIOS, MOP, LAT

Encapsulation Bridging

Encapsulation bridging encloses the Ethernet frame into the FDDI frame, allowing it to be moved from one Ethernet network to the other across the FDDI backbone. After the packet has arrived at the Destination Bridge, it is de-encapsulated before being forwarded to the host on the destination Ethernet. There is not a standard method for encapsulating frames so that each vendor's implementation is propriety. This also means that interoperability between vendors is a problem. Cisco supports encapsulation bridging on FDDI interfaces along with TLB. Encapsulation bridging gives you a good solution for LAT connectivity issues in DEC environments.

Translation from Token Ring Frames to Ethernet

The process flow for the translation of a Token Ring frame to Ethernet is as follows:

1. When a Token Ring frame arrives at the Translation bridge, the Access Control, Frame Control, and Routing Information fields are removed.
2. A new field called Frame Length is added.
3. The Destination Address and Source Address fields are converted to canonical format.
4. The Routing Information Present bit of the Source Address field is cleared.
5. The LLC802.2 fields and the Data field remain untouched.
6. The newly modified frame, which is now an 802.3 Ethernet frame, is delivered to the bridge module for transmission on the Ethernet segment of the network.

Translation from Ethernet Frames to Token Ring

The process flow for the translation of an Ethernet frame to Token Ring is described as follows:

1. When an Ethernet frame arrives at the Translation bridge, the Frame Length field is removed.
2. The Access Control, Frame Control, and Routing Information fields are added.

The Translation bridge sets only two bytes of the Routing Information field. They are passed to the virtual bridge, which adds four bytes of route designator information.

3. The Destination Address field and the Source Address field are converted to noncanonical format.

   If the destination address is unknown, a spanning tree explorer frame is created and passed to the virtual bridge for transmission.

   If the destination is known, the RIF is set to nonbroadcast, and the entire routing information is contained in the frame.

4. The Routing Information Present bit of the Source Address field is set.

5. The LLC802.2 fields and the Data field remain untouched.

6. The newly modified frame, which is now the 802.5 Token Ring frame, is delivered to the bridge module for transmission on the proper Token Ring segment of the network.

If there are multiple Token Ring segments, explorer frames are sent to all of them. Specific routed frames are sent on the ring indicated by the Routing Information field.

Questions

1. Transparent Bridging operates at the _____ Layer.
   - A. Physical
   - B. Data Link
   - C. Network
   - D. Session

2. Transparent Bridging uses _____ Media Access Control Addresses for forwarding decisions?
   - A. Destination
   - B. Source
   - C. Multicast
   - D. Broadcast

3. MAC Addresses used in transparent bridging are ____ bits in length.
   - A. 48
   - B. 32
   - C. 16
   - D. 64

4. Identify the major functions of a Transparent Bridge.
   - A. Loop detection and avoidance
   - B. Forwarding
   - C. Learning MAC addresses
   - D. Filtering
   - E. All of the above

5. When a transparent bridge receives a frame, it compares the Frame's destination address with addresses in the forwarding table. What will happen if there is no match?
   - A. The frame will be dropped.
   - B. The frame will be flooded.
   - C. The frame will be broadcast out all interfaces.
   - D. The frame's destination address will be added to the forwarding table and then the frame will be flooded.

6. With respect to the Spanning Tree algorithm, a Bridge ID Comprises a:
   - A. Bridge priority and serial number
   - B. Bridge priority and port priority
   - C. Bridge priority and interface number
   - D. Bridge priority and bridge MAC address

7. When bridge priorities are equal, which of the following serves as a tiebreaker for determining the root bridge?
   - A. The bridge with the lowest MAC address
   - B. The bridge with the highest MAC address
   - C. The bridge with the lowest port priority
   - D. The bridge with the highest port priority

8. With respect to the Spanning tree algorithm, a bridge that forwards traffic on behalf of a LAN is said to be the:
   - A. Root bridge
   - B. Chosen bridge
   - C. Direct bridge
   - D. Designated bridge

9. Transparent bridges are not transparent to end stations.
   - A. True
   - B. False

10. End node devices behave the same with Transparent bridges and Multi-port Repeaters.
   - A. True
   - B. False

11. The Bridge Identifier, which determines the bridge that becomes the Root Bridge in the spanning Tree Protocol, consist of:
    - **A.** Bridge's MAX Age
    - **B.** Bridge's Priority
    - **C.** Bridge's MAC address
    - **D.** Bridges Port Number
    - **E.** B & C
    - **F.** None of the above

12. Define the parameter that determines the length of time a node can remain dormant before it is deleted from bridges forwarding table.
    - **A.** Max Age
    - **B.** Agetime
    - **C.** Hellotime
    - **D.** Holdtime

13. In the Spanning Tree Protocol, the default priority for IEEE Spanning Tree is _____.
    - **A.** 10
    - **B.** 100
    - **C.** 128
    - **D.** 32768

14. Identify the Routing Control Broadcast Bit combinations.
    - **A.** 110
    - **B.** 101
    - **C.** 100
    - **D.** 000
    - **E.** 001
    - **F.** None of the above

15. In the Spanning Tree Protocol, which port state indicates that the port is either a Designated Port or a Root Port?
    - **A.** Blocking State
    - **B.** Listening State
    - **C.** Learning State
    - **D.** Forwarding State

16. Cisco supports transparent bridging over the following media types?
    - **A.** ATM
    - **B.** DDR
    - **C.** SMDS
    - **D.** X.25
    - **E.** LAPB
    - **F.** Frame Relay
    - **G.** All of the above

17. A bridge that connects dissimilar media is:
    - **A.** Transparent bridge
    - **B.** Source-route bridge
    - **C.** Source-route transparent bridge
    - **D.** Translational bridge
    - **E.** Encapsulation bridge

18. Identify the configuration parameters Cisco supports using Spanning-Tree.
    - **A.** Bridge Priority
    - **B.** Interface Priority
    - **C.** Path Cost
    - **D.** Bridge Protocol Data Unit Interval
    - **E.** Spanning Tree disable on the interface

19. The following fields are not present in the RIF field in Source Routing?
    - **A.** Largest Frame
    - **B.** Length
    - **C.** Direction
    - **D.** Explorer Type
    - **E.** Reserved
    - **F.** Frame Status

20. The default bridge priority for DEC Spanning Tree is _____.
  A. 32768   **C.** 128
  B. 65535   **D.** 512

21. The path cost parameter is assign using ____/data rate of the attached interface.
  A. 1000   **D.** 512
  B. 500   **E.** None of the above
  C. 128

22. The Cisco Bridge Hello time ranges from ____ seconds?
  A. 1–10   **C.** 5–10
  B. 5–20   **D.** 30–40

23. The bridge forward delay ranges in seconds?
  A. 10–200 seconds   **C.** 20–30 seconds
  B. 1–10 seconds   **D.** None of the above

24. Transparent bridging base its routing decision based on _____.
  A. A RIF field   **C.** All Routes Explorer (ARE)
  B. MAC addresses   **D.** Spanning Tree Explorer (STE)

25. Which of the following is responsible for determining the path that a SRB frame will use in order to reach a destination?
  A. Source Route Bridge   **D.** Repeater
  B. Destination Station   **E.** Source Routing LAN Switch
  C. Source Station

26. Which of the following comprise the RIF in an SRB Frame?
  A. Routing management and routing designators
  B. Routing management and routing path
  C. Routing management and routing hops
  D. Routing management and routing designators
  E. Routing control and routing designator
  F. Routing control and routing hops

27. How many types of SRB explorer frames are there?
  A. 1   **D.** 4
  B. 2   **E.** 5
  C. 3

28. Which of the following is not true?
  A. VLANS can be used to create layer 3 broadcast domains.
  B. VLANS can be used to create layer 2 broadcast domains.
  C. VLANS are only used in support of IP.
  D. VLANS using layer 2 allows routing.
  E. All of the above are correct

29. Which byte and Bit in the source address field is used to designate Source Routing?
  A. 0,0   **D.** 3,1
  B. 1,1   **E.** 4,1
  C. 2,0

30. Source Route Bridging based its routing decision on _____.
- **A.** A RIF field
- **B.** A Mac address
- **C.** All Routes Explorer (ARE)
- **D.** Spanning Tree Explorer (STE)

31. The Routing Control Field identifies the following fields:
- **A.** Frame Size
- **B.** Direction
- **C.** Length
- **D.** Type Explorer
- **E.** Reserved
- **F.** All of the above

32. Identify the Routing Control Broadcast combinations.
- **A.** Non-broadcast
- **B.** All routes Broadcast
- **C.** Single Routes broadcast, all routes return
- **D.** Single Routes broadcast, single routes return
- **E.** All of the above

33. Identify the largest frame sizes typically used in Token Ring networks?
- **A.** 516
- **B.** 1470
- **C.** 2052
- **D.** 4472
- **E.** 8144
- **F.** 11407
- **G.** 17800
- **H.** ABC
- **I.** CDE
- **J.** All of the above

34. The Source Routing Route Designators Ring Number and Bridge numbers combined are __ bits in length.
- **A.** 10
- **B.** 12
- **C.** 14
- **D.** 16
- **E.** 24

35. If the direction bit in the Routing Control Field is 0 it means?
- **A.** The RIF direction is left to right.
- **B.** The RIF direction is right to left.
- **C.** A & B
- **D.** None of the above

36. If the direction bit in the Routing Control field is 1 it means?
- **A.** The RIF direction is left to right.
- **B.** The RIF direction is right to left.
- **C.** Local Ring
- **D.** A & B

37. Cisco supports Ring 0 and bridge 0?
- **A.** True
- **B.** False

38. The LAN Network Manager uses SAP ID.
- **A.** F4
- **B.** 04
- **C.** C0
- **D.** FE
- **E.** F5

39. Which LAN switch that examines only MAC addresses for forwarding decision operates at what layer ?
- **A.** Layer 1
- **B.** Layer 3
- **C.** Layer 2
- **D.** Layer 4
- **E.** All of the above

40. Source Routing is supported over the following:
A. Token Ring
B. FDDI
C. Ethernet
D. Arcnet
E. None of the above

41. Source Route Bridges has a hop count limit of____ that supports IBM source routing.
A. 16 Bridges
B. 7 Bridges
C. 10 Bridges
D. 13 Bridges
E. None of the above

42. Define the need for a Virtual Ring Number.

43. The Token Ring Chip set assumes that bridges support only __ rings per Source Route Bridge.
A. 2
B. 4
C. 3
D. 8
E. A & B

44. How can you overcome the limitation of a two port bridge in using Cisco IOS source-route bridging configuration?
A. Use another Source Route Bridge
B. Migrate to Ethernet
C. Create a Virtual Ring
D. Assign multiple ring numbers per token ring segment

45. When you connect a local ring to a remote ring over a WAN what bridging methods are supported using Cisco IOS software?
A. Remote Source Route Bridging
B. Half Bridges
C. DLSw
D. Transparent bridging
E. B & C

46. Cisco's Remote Source Route bridging uses the following encapsulations.
A. TCP
B. IP only
C. Direct
D. Standard
E. None of the above

47. What Cisco IOS command can be used to reduce the number of explorer packets entering the network?
A. Filters
B. NetBIOS Name Caching
C. Source Bridge Proxy Explorer
D. DLSw
E. All of the above
F. A & B only

48. List the configuration required for a two port source route bridge using manual spanning tree.

49. What bridging type use a combination of RIF and MAC addresses to bridge frames?
A. Source Routing
B. Transparent Bridging
C. Source Route Transparent
D. Source Route Translational
E. Encapsulation Bridging

50. Explain Multi-Ring Support command.

51. Token Ring Networks use the Data Link Sublayer LLC for communications while Ethernet uses the entire Data Link layer using a Type field. What options is provided by the Cisco IOS to support Token Ring and Ethernet?
    A. Token Ring LLC2 to Ethernet Type II (0x80d5)
    B. Token Ring LLC2 to Ethernet 802.3 LLC2 (Standard)
    C. Cisco
    D. Standard
    E. 90 Option
    F. All of the above

52. What is the name of the IBM Network Management product used to manage Source Routing networks only?
    A. SNMP
    B. Optivity
    C. IBM LAN Network Manager
    D. Cisco Works

53. Cisco supports what type of filtering using Token Ring.
    A. Protocol type
    B. Token Ring Vendor
    C. Source address
    D. Destination Address
    E. All of the above

54. Source routing is not required on the following Networks.
    A. Single ring networks
    B. Ethernet networks
    C. FDDI
    D. ATM

55. Source routing uses _____ routing tables?
    A. centralized
    B. distributed
    C. hybrid
    D. none of the above

56. Source route bridges can be configured with the same Bridge number if?
    A. The bridges are not in parallel.
    B. Same ring numbers are being used.
    C. Cisco and IBM bridges not on the same network.
    D. Router separates Ring segments.
    E. None of the above

57. Source route transparent bridging allows Ethernet stations to communicate with token ring stations if the following guidelines are followed?
    A. MTU must be the same
    B. No RIF Allowed
    C. Address conversion
    D. MTU Segmentation
    E. None of the above

58. Cisco Multi-Ring works with which of the following protocols?
    A. AppleTalk
    B. IP
    C. IPX
    D. Vines
    E. NetBIOS

59. Source Route Translational Bridging allows Ethernet stations and Token Ring stations to communicate with RIFs coming from the token ring station segment only if the following options are addressed?
    A. The Bridge segments the larger token ring frames to Ethernet
    B. Address Conversion

    C. MTU

    D. Cache RIF in the router

    E. Configure a ring around the Ethernet segment

60. The Source Route Transparent specification is based on the following standard?

    A. IEEE802.1   **C.** IEEE802.2

    B. IEEE802.1d   **D.** IEEE802.3u

61. Identify two Spanning Tree Protocols specifications.

    A. IBM Spanning Tree   **C.** DEC's

    B. IEEE 802.1d Spanning Tree   **D.** All of the above

62. What happens when the root spanning Tree Bridge is disabled?

    A. A Backup Spanning tree becomes root

    B. Any end node with the highest MAC address

    C. The bridge with the lowest bridge ID

    D. Lowest cost path

63. The Spanning tree protocol sends out hello frames called _____.

    A. Bridge Protocol Data Units   **C.** Bridge Update hellos

    B. Bridge Hello's   **D.** None of the above

64. The DEC and IEEE 802.1d spanning tree protocols can interoperate together.

    A. True   **B.** False

65. The Spanning Tree BPDU SAP ID is _____.

    A. 23   **C.** F5

    B. 42   **D.** 09

66. The routers pictured below are configured for translational bridging. Which of the clients attached to the FDDI ring can communicate? When C1 is accessing the SQL Database from C3 the session times out? What is the possible cause?

    A. Change the ring speed from 100 to 16 Mb

    B. Increase the number of buffers allocated in the router

    C. Check the MTU on Station C3

    D. Check if station C3 generates a RIF to station C1

    E. None of the above

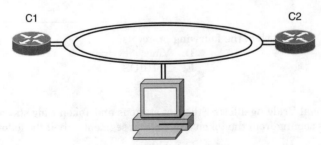

67. Identify the bits used for the largest frame size of 41,600?
- **A.** 000
- **B.** 100
- **C.** 011
- **D.** 111
- **E.** None of the above

68. Ethernet transmit using the least-significant bit first while Token Ring transmits using the most-significant bit first?
- **A.** True
- **B.** False

69. What is the action that a Token Ring device first undertakes if it detects the absence of tokens or data frames from its upstream neighbor within a specified time period?
- **A.** Perform a Lobe media test
- **B.** Send Beacon MAC frames
- **C.** Send line error MAC Frames
- **D.** Send ring Purge MAC Frames
- **E.** Send burst error MAC frames

70. 16Mb Token Ring Early Token Release provide the following ?
- **A.** Multiple Tokens can circulate the ring at the same time.
- **B.** Only one Token can circulate on the ring at one time, but the speed is 16mb versus 4Mb.
- **C.** Only one Token can circulate the ring but multiple data frames are allowed.
- **D.** None of the above

71. Virtual Rings behave as follows to network analyzers:
- **A.** As Physical Ring
- **B.** Analyzers are not able to capture internal Virtual Rings
- **C.** This is only useful in DLSw environments
- **D.** Virtual Rings appear as logical Rings to analyzers
- **E.** None of the above

72. Identify the following RIF Field : All Routes Explorer, Length of 6 bytes, Direction 0, Largest frame 2052
- **A.** 8620
- **B.** 8630
- **C.** c720
- **D.** 0620
- **E.** None of the above

73. Identify the bits used in the Explorer type field for a single Route explorer.
- **A.** 000
- **B.** 001
- **C.** 100
- **D.** 110
- **E.** None of the above

74. Identify the bit pattern used in the Explorer type field for All Routes Explorer.
- **A.** 000
- **B.** 100
- **C.** 111
- **D.** 010
- **E.** 110

75. Identify the bits for the largest frame size of 65,535.
- **A.** 011
- **B.** 111
- **C.** 100
- **D.** 110

76. What is the function of the largest frame size bits used for in Source Routing?
    A. To handle MTU issues between bridges
    B. To handle Source Routing to Translational bridging MTU's between Ethernet and Token Ring
    C. All of the above

77. The Routing Control Field of 8830 represents the following:
    A. Single Route Explorer
    B. Single Route Explorer, 8 byte length, Direction left to right, 4472 largest frame size
    C. All Routes Explorer, 8 bytes length , Direction left to right, 2052 largest frame size
    D. All of the Above
    E. None of the above

78. The following Ethernet address 08008a121314 is identified in non-canonical as?
    A. 1000.5148.c828   C. 1000.4851.28c8
    B. 1000.5184.8c28   D. None of the above

79. The following Ethernet address 02609087faa8 in non-canonical would be?

80. The following Token Ring address is identified as 400000000002 in non-canonical. What would be the address in canonical?

81. The Routing Control Field 8A30 represents the following?

82. The Routing Control Field 8C30 represents the following?

83. The Routing Control Field 0830 represents the following?

84. The Routing Control Field 0630 represents the following?

85. The Routing Designator field 0052.2201.0ff0 represents?
    A. Ring 5, Bridge2, Ring 220 Bridge 1 Ring 255 Bridge 0
    B. Ring 50 Bridge 2, Ring 22 Bridge 01, Ring 15 Bridge 15 Ring 0
    C. Ring 52 Bridge 1, Ring 22 Bridge 1 Ring 255 Bridge 0
    D. None of the above

86. *Boundary Access Node* (BAN) allows source routing frames to be encapsulated in?
    A. X.25   D. TCP/IP
    B. IP   E. Frame Relay
    C. UDP/IP

87. Cisco Translational bridging uses ___ frames?
    A. Spanning Tree Explorer C. Single Routes
    B. All Routes   D. None of the above

88. Identify issues that arise in Transparent to Source Route Bridging?
    A. Speed   D. MAC Address Formats
    B. Frame MTU   E. A & D only
    C. Frame Format   F. All of the above

89. What is the default frame size required for Translational Bridging?
    A. 516   C. 4472
    B. 2052   D. 1470

90. Source Route Bridging allows an End station to:
    A. Maintain routing tables
    B. Perform the function of a bridge
    C. Determine the path /route to the destination device
    D. None of the above

91. What Cisco bridging feature most likely would be used, if a token ring device needs to communicate with an Ethernet device across a WAN? The Token ring device uses RIF?
    A. Transparent Bridging   E. DLSw
    B. Source Routing   F. RSRB
    C. Source Route Translational   G. None of the above
    D. Source Route Transparent

92. What is the Spanning Tree Root ID in the trace below?

```
DLC:   ---- DLC Header ----
DLC:
DLC:   Frame 1 arrived at  19:59:15.806; frame size is 52 (0034 hex) bytes.
DLC:   FS: Addr recognized indicators: 00, Frame copied indicators: 00
DLC:   AC: Frame priority 0,  Reservation priority 0,  Monitor count 0
DLC:   FC: LLC frame,  PCF attention code: None
DLC:   Destination = Functional address C00000000100, All Bridges
DLC:   Source      = Station 00609087FA28
DLC:
LLC:   ---- LLC Header ----
LLC:
LLC:   DSAP Address = 42, DSAP IG Bit = 00 (Individual Address)
LLC:   SSAP Address = 42, SSAP CR Bit = 00 (Command)
LLC:   Unnumbered frame: UI
LLC:
BPDU:  ---- Bridge Protocol Data Unit Header ----
BPDU:
BPDU:  Protocol Identifier = 0000
BPDU:  Protocol Version    = 00
BPDU:
BPDU:  BPDU Type = 00 (Configuration)
BPDU:
BPDU:  BPDU Flags = 00
BPDU:   0... .... = Not Topology Change Acknowledgment
BPDU:   .... ...0 = Not Topology Change
BPDU:   .000 000. = Unused
BPDU:
BPDU:  Root Identifier   = 8000.02609087FAA8
BPDU:    Priority        = 8000
BPDU:    MAC Address      = 02609087FAA8
BPDU:
BPDU:  Root Path Cost    = 0
BPDU:
BPDU:  Sending Bridge Id = 8000.02609087FAA8.12C1
BPDU:    Priority        = 8000
BPDU:    MAC Address      = 02609087FAA8
BPDU:    Port            = 12C1
BPDU:  Message Age          = 0.000 seconds
BPDU:  Information Lifetime = 10.000 seconds
```

```
BPDU:   Root Hello Time      = 2.000 seconds
BPDU:   Forward Delay        = 4.000 seconds
```

93. What is the primary benefit of the Time to Live field in the IP header?
    A. Only used with OSPF
    B. To reduce the impact of routing loops
    C. The number of hops before being discarded
    D. Life is good
    E. So that packets will not propagate through the network indefinitely

94. What type of MAC frame is identified below?
```
DLC:  --- DLC Header ---
DLC:
DLC:  Frame 15 arrived at  09:54:50.830; frame size is 18 (0012 hex) bytes.
DLC:  FS: Addr recognized indicators: 00, Frame copied indicators: 00
DLC:  AC: Frame priority 0,  Reservation priority 0,  Monitor count 0
DLC:  FC: MAC frame,  PCF attention code: Express buffer
DLC:  Destination = Station 00A0248AD43A
DLC:  Source      = Station 00A0248AD43A
DLC:
MAC:  --- MAC data ---
MAC:
MAC:  MAC Command: ?
MAC:  Source: Ring station, Destination: Ring station
MAC:
```
    A. Active Monitor   D. Hard Error frame
    B. Ring Error Monitor   E. Soft Error frame
    C. Duplicate Address Test frame

95. The initial route control field is ____ bytes in length during the initial route discovery?
    A. 4   C. 6
    B. 2   D. 8

96. Cisco Translational Bridge software is supported on which of the interfaces listed?
    A. Serial   E. FDDI
    B. Ethernet   F. SMDS
    C. Token Ring   G. Native SRB on FDDI
    D. Frame Relay   H. All of the above

97. Network bandwidth utilization, without spanning tree enabled using transparent bridging could have the following effects on traffic based on the following?
    A. Frame sent to a known station upon initialization
    B. Frame sent to an unknown station
    C. Frame sent as a broadcast to FFFFFFFFFFFF
    D. Frame sent to a multicast address
    E. None of the above

98. A Token Ring Station will send the following type of frame for a local or off ring test?
    A. Test   D. UA
    B. XID   E. None of the above
    C. SABME

99. Identify the largest frame size in bytes in the trace below?

```
RI :    —- Routing Indicators —-
RI :    Routing control = C2
 RI :           110. .... = Single-route broadcast, all-routes broadcast return
RI :           ...0 0010 = RI length is 2
RI :    Routing control = 7
RI :           0... .... = Forward direction
RI :           .111 .... = Largest frame is what is your answer?
```

    A. 4472   **C.** 65535

    B. 1500   **D.** Not a valid frame size

100. What is the size of the RIF in the trace below?

```
RI :    —- Routing Indicators —-
RI :    Routing control = CA
RI :           110. .... = Single-route broadcast, all-routes broadcast return
RI :           ...0 1010 = RI length is ?
RI :    Routing control = 30
RI :           0... .... = Forward direction
RI :           .011 .... = Largest frame is 4399
RI :           .... 000. = Extended frame is 0
RI :           .... ...0 = Reserved
RI :    Ring number 009 via bridge C
RI :    Ring number 008 via bridge 9
RI :    Ring number 005 via bridge 4
RI :    Ring number 002
RI :
```

    A. 2   **D.** 10

    B. 8   **E.** 14

    C. 12

101. What is the size of the RIF in the trace below?

```
RI :    —- Routing Indicators —-
RI :    Routing control = CE
RI :           110. .... = Single-route broadcast, all-routes broadcast return
RI :           ...0 1110 = RI length is ?
RI :    Routing control = 30RI :        0... .... = Forward directionRI :
.011 .... = Largest frame is 4399
RI :           .... 000. = Extended frame is 0
RI :           .... ...0 = Reserved
RI :    Ring number 001 via bridge 5
RI :    Ring number 006 via bridge A
RI :    Ring number 007 via bridge B
RI :    Ring number 008 via bridge 9
RI :    Ring number 005 via bridge 4
RI :    Ring number 002
```

    A. 8   **D.** 14

    B. 10   **E.** 16

    C. 12   **F.** None of the above

102. With Remote Source Route Bridging, the IP WAN cloud consists of ____Virtual Ring?

    A. 2

    B. 1

    C. WAN link doesn't require a ring number

    D. Ring number required only for DLSw

    E. None of the above

103. Both Translational and Transparent bridges use the same _____?
- **A.** Forwarding Table
- **B.** MAC Address
- **C.** Port Circuit ID
- **D.** Spanning Tree

104. The Length of the Token Ring Route Control field (length field) in bits?
- **A.** 2
- **B.** 4
- **C.** 5
- **D.** 8

105. The IEEE802.5 specifies a maximum of ___ bridges and ___ rings?
- **A.** 7, 8
- **B.** 13,14
- **C.** 8, 9
- **D.** 10,12

106. Source Route Transparent bridges removes and insert RIF routing information?
- **A.** True
- **B.** False

107. Bridge Priority supplies the most significant ____ bits of the bridge ID.
- **A.** 8
- **B.** 16
- **C.** 32
- **D.** 48

108. The Bridge Priority along with the MAC address supplies ____ bits Bridge ID to the Router.
- **A.** 32
- **B.** 48
- **C.** 64
- **D.** 128

109. The Port Priority of an Interface plays a role in Root Bridge election?
- **A.** True
- **B.** False

110. Source Routing functional addresses always conform to the following rules?
- **A.** Byte 0 = 0xC0
- **B.** Byte 1 = 0x00
- **C.** Byte 0 = 0xFF
- **D.** The first half of Byte 2 = 0x to 0x7
- **E.** Byte 1 = 0xFF
- **F.** None of the above

111. The DEC bridge Protocol Data Unit ID?
- **A.** 6003
- **B.** 6004
- **C.** 8038
- **D.** 8137

112. The following will cause loops with redundant bridges?
- **A.** Dual Paths between LAN Segments
- **B.** Same ring number
- **C.** Spanning Tree not enabled
- **D.** Transparent Bridging
- **E.** None of the above

113. Identify the devices used to link LAN Segments.
- **A.** Repeater
- **B.** Muxiplexer
- **C.** Bridge
- **D.** LAN Switch
- **E.** Router
- **F.** Gateway

114. When using source Routing, the Initial Bridge will add ___ bytes to the length of the RIF ?
- **A.** 2
- **B.** 4
- **C.** 6
- **D.** 1

115. In Source Route Bridging, who is responsible for setting the RIF Field in the source MAC address individual/group bit?
    A. Bridge
    B. Destination Station by setting the Direction to 1
    C. Router
    D. Source Station

116. In what scenario would a bridge translate a MAC Address?
    A. Ethernet v1 to IEEE 802.3
    B. SNAP to IEEE 802.5
    C. Ethernet to Token Ring using Translational Bridging
    D. Source Route Transparent
    E. DLSw/Ethernet to Token Ring
    F. All of the above
    G. None of the above

117. What is the length of the RIF in bytes regarding the trace below?
    A. 10   C. 15
    B. 8   D. 12

```
RI :   ––– Routing Indicators –––
RI :
RI :   Routing control = CC
RI :          110. .... = Single-route broadcast, all-routes broadcast return
RI :          ...0 1100 =
RI :   Routing control = 10
RI :          0... .... = Forward direction
RI :          .001 .... = Largest frame is 1470
RI :          .... 000. = Extended frame is 0
RI :          .... ...0 = Reserved
RI :   Ring number 121 via bridge 2
RI :   Ring number 127 via bridge 2
RI :   Ring number 122 via bridge 2
RI :   Ring number 0C8 via bridge 2
RI :   Ring number 12A
RI :
```

118. A virtual ring must be configured when using the following bridge options?
    A. Transparent
    B. Source Routing
    C. Translational Bridging
    D. Transparent with Spanning Tree
    E. More than 2 physical rings per bridge

119. Transparent bridge's forwarding table contains which of the following?
    A. RIF   D. Spanning Tree ID
    B. MAC Address   E. None of the above
    C. Port ID

120. From a Source Routing perspective, the entire transparent bridge domain, using Translational bridging appear as a?
    A. Physical Ring   C. Transparent Bridge Domain
    B. Virtual Ring   D. None of the above

121. With Translational Bridging on the source routing module, what happens if the destination address is not in the RIF and forwarding table of the transparent module?
    A. Flood the frame on transparent segment only
    B. Flood it out all Source Routing ports only
    C. Flood it out all transparent and source routing ports
    D. Only flood if Spanning tree is enable

122. Frames received from a source routing segment destined for a transparent Ethernet segment with a MTU size of 2052 bytes will do the following?
    A. Segment
    B. Discard
    C. Forward due to the largest frame size bits in the RIF limiting the frame size to 1500
    D. It depends on the application.

123. The Token Ring address 000524A5FC29 would be ____ in canonical format.

124. The Ethernet Address 00e0.1e5d.d526 (bia 00e0.1e5d.d526) canonical would be _____ in Token Ring non-canonical.

125. What is the purpose of the `dlsw bridge-group 1` command in the DLSw configuration?
```
A. dlsw local-peer peer-id 1.1.1.2
dlsw remote-peer 0 TCP 1.1.1.1
dlsw bridge-group 1
!
interface Ethernet0
 no ip address
 bridge-group 1
! hostname ORLANDO
!
!
no ip domain-lookup
dlsw local-peer peer-id 1.1.1.2
dlsw remote-peer 0 tcp 1.1.1.1
dlsw bridge-group 1
!
interface Ethernet0
 no ip address
 bridge-group 1
!
interface Serial0
 ip address 1.1.1.2 255.255.255.0
 bandwidth 56
clockrate 56000
!
bridge 1 protocol IEEE
!line con 0
 exec-timeout 0 0
line aux 0
line vty 0 4
end
```

126. The Ethernet Address 00e0.1e5d.d4ad in canonical format would be ____ using Token Ring Non-Canonical format.

127. The Ethernet Transit OUI is used for:
   A. Ethernet Multicast addressing
   B. Token Ring Functional Addressing
   C. Used to transport Ethernet II frames over Token Ring Snap Header
   D. Used to transport IEEE 802.3 Ethernet Frames

128. Examine the `show interface Token 0` below for the bandwidth advertised:
```
ATLANTA#sh int to 0
TokenRing0 is up, line protocol is up
  Hardware is TMS380, address is 0000.308c.55c8 (bia 0000.308c.55c8)
  Internet address is 192.168.31.1/24
  MTU 4464 bytes, BW 4000 Kbit, DLY 2500 usec, rely 255/255, load 1/255
  Encapsulation SNAP, loopback not set, keepalive set (10 sec)
  ARP type: SNAP, ARP Timeout 04:00:00
  Ring speed: 4 Mbps
  Single ring node, Source Route Transparent Bridge capable
  Source bridging enabled, srn 10 bn 1 trn 20 (ring group)
    proxy explorers disabled, spanning explorer enabled, NetBIOS cache disabled
  Group Address: 0x00000000, Functional Address: 0x0800011A
  Ethernet Transit OUI: 0x000000
  Last input 00:00:02, output 00:00:02, output hang never
  Last clearing of "show interface" counters never
```

129. Referring to the `show interface token 0` in question 185, what is the ring number assigned to this interface?
   A. 20   **C.** 10
   B. 1   **D.** None of the above

130. The Token Ring address bia 0000.308c.55c8 would be _____ in Ethernet.

131. When sending a packet from C1 on LAN 1 to C2 on LAN 2 using a Multi-port Repeater, what MAC address will be seen on LAN 2?
   A. The Multi-Port Repeater address on LAN 2
   B. The Multi-Port address on LAN 1
   C. C2's MAC Address
   D. C1 MAC Address

132. When sending a packet from C1 on LAN 1 to C2 on LAN 2 using a Transparent Bridge, what MAC address will be seen on LAN 2?
   A. The Bridge MAC address on LAN 2
   B. The Bridge MAC address on LAN 1
   C. C2's MAC Address
   D. C1 MAC Address

133. What will the destination MAC address be if C1 on LAN 1 sends a frame to LAN2 Station C2 using a layer 2 LAN Switch?
   A. C1 MAC Address
   B. C2 MAC Address
   C. The MAC Address of the Bridge Interface on LAN 2
   D. None of the above

134. How many Source Route Brides are included in the RIF below?
    RIF=0630.0053.00b0
    A. 2   D. 4
    B. 3   E. None of the above
    C. 1

135. Line 3 in the Show output below represents a frame that is to be forwarded to ?
    A. Ethernet Device
    B. Source Route Translational Bridge segment
    C. Token Ring
    D. Virtual Ring
    E. None of the above

```
Router#sho bridge

Total of 300 station blocks, 297 free
Codes: P - permanent, S - self

Bridge Group 1:

       Address         Action    Interface      Age    RX count    TX count
1.  0260.8cad.28ab    forward    Ethernet0      0         52          16
2.  0005.2451.8b26    forward    TokenRing0     0         17          15
3.  0006.e925.f942    forward    RingGroup100   0          4           0
```

136. Station A attached to ring 100 sends a data frame to station C on the same ring. The frame status bits are as follow: A=1 C=0. What can station A derive from this field regarding station C?
    A. Station C is not active on the ring.
    B. Station C copied the data ok.
    C. Station C was active on the ring but for some reason did not copy the data.
    D. None of the above

137. The Token Ring Routing Information Field is _____ in length?
    A. fixed   C. Set by LAN Network Manager
    B. variable   D. None of the Above

138. Identify the IOS command for configuring a virtual ring.
    A. Source-bridge group group-number
    B. Source-bridge ring-group group-number
    C. Source-bridge ring-group ring number
    D. None of the above

139. Token Ring Source Routing Ring Segments are assigned _____ in hex.
    A. 002-fff   C. 110-ff0
    B. 001-fff   D. 001-ff0

140. All Source route bridges connected to the same ring must use?
    A. Different ring number
    B. Different bridge number
    C. Same ring number and different bridge number if bridges are in parallel
    D. Ring Parameter Server will assigned bridge and ring numbers
    E. None of the above

141. Identify the Token Ring server that allows stations on the ring to receive their ring number.
    A. Configuration Server   **C.** Ring Parameter Server
    B. NetBIOS Server   **D.** None of the above

142. What is the function of the Cisco IOS Source-bridge COS enable command?
    A. Activate the Priority bits in the token ring header
    B. Prioritize RIF Field
    C. Priority for PU4 to PU4 devices using FID4 headers
    D. None of the above

143. The Remote Source Route Bridging Port numbers are?
    A. 1997, 1989, 1988, 1987   **C.** 1981, 1982, 1983, 1984
    B. 1996, 1987, 1988, 1989   **D.** 2067, 2065, 1981, 1982

144. The Cisco default bridge priority for Digital Spanning Tree Protocol is?
    A. 32768   **C.** 65,536
    B. 128   **D.** 512

145. Cisco *Remote Source Route Bridging* (RSRB) supports the following encapsulations?
    A. TCP   **D.** Direct
    B. FST   **E.** All of the above
    C. UDP

146. What is the default Cisco IOS Bridge Hello-Time in seconds?
    A. 5   **C.** 1
    B. 7   **D.** 17

147. Identify the Cisco IOS command that enable Integrated Routing and Bridging.
    A. Bridge IRB   **C.** IRB Bridge enable
    B. Bridge IRB enable   **D.** None of the above

148. Source Route Transparent Bridging is based on which of the IEEE standards listed?
    A. IEEE 802.1c Appendix C   **C.** IEEE 802.1d Appendix A
    B. IEEE 802.1d Appendix C   **D.** IEEE 802.1d Appendix D

149. Identify the states a given port can transition to using transparent bridging?
    A. Disable   **E.** Forwarding
    B. Blocking   **F.** None
    C. Listening   **G.** A, B, and C only
    D. Learning   **H.** A through E

150. What is meant by the term Transit Bridge used in FDDI?

151. In Cisco Transparent Bridging, can an interface be a member or more than one transparent bridge group?
    A. Yes   **B.** No

152. The default aging-time for Cisco IOS bridging table?
    A. 5 hours
    B. 30 minutes
    C. 4 hours
    D. No limit based on amount of system memory

153. Identify the following commands from the Source route translational statements. (check)
    Source-bridge transparent 20 14 1 4
    A. What is the virtual ring id?20
    B. Source Route Bridge Number?14
    C. Pseudo Ring Number ?1
    D. Transparent Bridge Group?4

154. The Cisco Default IOS Bridge Forward Time Delay in Seconds?
    A. 10
    B. 40
    C. 30
    D. 15

155. The Cisco Transparent Bridge configuration adopts which of the following from the Root Bridge regardless of configuration?
    A. Forward Time
    B. Max Age
    C. Hello Time
    D. Bridge Priority
    E. None of the above

156. Which of the following protocols provide for connection oriented service?
    A. UDP
    B. LLC2
    C. TCP
    D. NSP
    E. SPX
    F. SPP
    G. IPX
    H. DDP

157. The Cisco IOS Circuit-group is supported on the following WAN encapsulations?
    A. X.25
    B. PPP
    C. Frame Relay
    D. HDLC

158. When a NetBIOS client send a Name Query Frame seeking a Server the Frame is sent as a Single Route Explorer. What type of explorer is returned via the NetBIOS Name Recognized frame?
    A. Direct
    B. SRE
    C. All Routes Explorer
    D. Spanning Tree
    E. None of the above

159. The Cisco IOS default path cost for FDDI is?
    A. 10
    B. 28
    C. 100
    D. 647
    E. None of the above

160. IEEE 802.10 VLAN specification is based on using the following MAC layer Protocol
    A. Ethernet II
    B. Token Ring 16Mb
    C. IEEE 802.3
    D. 802.4 Token Passing
    E. FDDI
    F. ATM

161. Identify the commands used to initiate an All Routes Explorer Broadcast in Source Routing.
  A. XID   C. SABME
  B. Test   D. UA

162. The NetBIOS command Name-Recognized returns to the source station as what type broadcast?
  A. Single Route Broadcast   C. Routed-non-broadcast
  B. All routes Broadcast   D. None of the above

163. The Largest frame size uses the following bit pattern during a Source Routing Initial broadcast?
  A. 111   C. 110
  B. 101   D. 001

164. The Topology change notification protocol used in Transparent Bridging is used for what purpose?
  A. Update the Bridge filtering database
  B. Update the bridge MAC address Table
  C. Flooding the Network segments connected to the bridge
  D. None of the above

165. Novell *Get Nearest Server* (GNS) using source routing generates which of the following broadcast types?
  A. SRE   D. A & B
  B. ARE   E. A & C
  C. Non-routing

166. The Default priority for DEC Spanning Tree is?
  A. 128   C. 100
  B. 60   D. 48

167. The Priority range for DEC Spanning Tree is?
  A. 0–255   C. 0–254
  B. 0–128   D. 1–255

168. The Priority range for IEEE Spanning Tree is?
  A. 0–64000   C. 0–128
  B. 0–32768   D. 0–255

169. DEC's spanning tree is calculated using?

170. IEEE spanning tree is calculated using?

171. The Transparent Bridge Group number must be between?
  A. 1–64   C. 1–63
  B. 1–32   D. 1–48

172. What is the bridge number for this token ring interface?
  A. 2   D. 1
  B. 10   E. 500
  C. 100

```
TokenRing0 is up, line protocol is up
  Hardware is TMS380, address is 0008.deec.eb68 (bia 0008.deec.eb68)
  Internet address is 2.0.0.1 255.0.0.0
  MTU 4464 bytes, BW 4000 Kbit, DLY 2500 usec, rely 255/255, load 1/255
  Encapsulation SNAP, loopback not set, keepalive set (10 sec)
  ARP type: SNAP, ARP Timeout 4:00:00
  Ring speed: 4 Mbps
  Single ring node, Source Route Transparent Bridge capable
  Source bridging enabled, srn 500 bn 1 trn 100 (ring group)
    proxy explorers disabled, spanning explorer enabled, NetBIOS cache disabled
  Group Address: 0x00000000, Functional Address: 0x0800011A
  Ethernet Transit OUI: 0x0000F8
```

173. Host C1 transmits a frame to host C2. The destination MAC address seen on LAN B is?

    A. Host C1

    B. Bridge Mac Address

    C. Host C 2

    D. None of the above

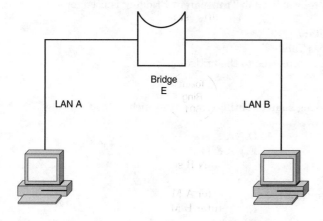

174. What will be the source MAC address on LAN B when a frame is sent from host C1 to C2?

    A. Host C1

    B. Host C2

    C. The Multi-port repeaters address on LAN B

    D. Not enough information to tell

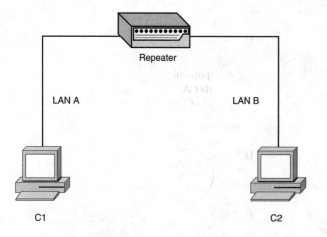

175. What is the Destination MAC address seen on LAN B when a frame is sent from Host C1 to Host C2 through the router using TCP/IP Protocol?

    A. Router LAN A MAC Address   **C.** Host C2

    B. Router LAN B MAC Address   **D.** None of the above

176. What will be the source MAC address on LAN A when a frame sent from C2 to C1 using a Router?

    A. MAC address of C2   **D.** Broadcast address

    B. MAC address of Router B   **E.** Multi-cast address

    C. MAC address Router A

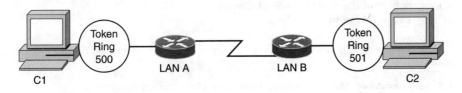

177. What will be the Destination MAC Address seen on LAN B sent from Host C1 using TCP/IP and Routing?

    A. Host C1   **C.** Router A MAC Address

    B. Host C2   **D.** Router B MAC Address

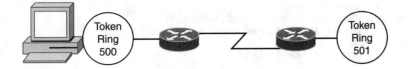

178. The serial link is configured for Frame Relay in the cloud. If an error occurs during C1 transmission to C2, which device in the network is responsible for retransmitting?

    A. Host C1   **D.** Router A

    B. Host C2   **E.** None of the above

    C. Frame Relay Service Provider

179. The serial link is configured for X.25 in the cloud. If an error occurs during C2 transmission to C1, which device in the network is responsible for retransmitting?

A. Host C1
B. Host C2
C. X.25 Service Provider

D. Router A
E. None of the above

180. The serial link is configured for Cisco's HDLC in the cloud. If an error occurs during C1 transmission to C2, which device in the network is responsible for retransmitting?

A. Host C1
B. Host C2
C. HDLC

D. Router A
E. None of the above

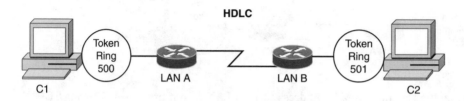

181. Bridges and switches share which of the following?

A. Each LAN segment is a collision domain.
B. All devices are part of the same broadcast domain.
C. Forwarding is based on network addresses.

182. What Spanning tree protocol is configured from the show spanning command below?

```
ATLANTA#sh spanning

Bridge Group 1 is executing the ___ compatible Spanning Tree protocol
  Bridge Identifier has priority 128, address 00e0.1e5d.d380
  Configured hello time 1, max age 15, forward delay 30
  Current root has priority 128, address 00e0.1e5d.39d7
  Root port is 2 (Ethernet0), cost of root path is 84
  Topology change flag not set, detected flag not set
  Times:   hold 1, topology change 30, notification 30
           hello 1, max age 15, forward delay 30, aging 300
  Timers: hello 0, topology change 0, notification 0

  Port 2 (Ethernet0) of bridge group 1 is forwarding
    Port path cost 10, Port priority 128
    Designated root has priority 128, address 00e0.1e5d.39d7
    Designated bridge has priority 128, address 00e0.1e5d.d4ad
    Designated port is 2, path cost 74
    Timers: message age 3, forward delay 0, hold 0
```

A. IEEE
B. IBM Spanning

C. DEC
D. None of the above

183. Which direction is the RIF in the command below?

```
ATLANTA#sh rif
Codes: * interface, - static, + remote

Dst HW Addr      Src HW Addr    How    Idle (min)   Routing Information Field
0004.acf3.0766 N/A              BG1        10       0890.0011.00A1.0030
0000.30fc.860a N/A              To0        *        -
```

    A. Left to right
    B. Right to left
    C. Cannot tell/not enough information

184. What type of frame is being sent from this RSRB client in the trace below?
    A. Explorer   **C.** Status Frame
    B. Name Claim   **D.** None of the above

185. What is the virtual ring ID in Decimal ?
    A. 120   **C.** 64
    B. 100   **D.** 200

```
DLC:  --- DLC Header ---
DLC:
DLC:  Frame 6 arrived at  17:22:49.3360; frame size is 248 (00F8 hex) bytes.
DLC:  Destination = DTE
DLC:  Source = DCE
DLC:
ROUTER: --- Cisco Router/Bridge ---
ROUTER:
ROUTER: Header = 0F000800
ROUTER:
IP:   --- IP Header ---
IP:
IP:   Version = 4, header length = 20 bytes
IP:   Type of service = 00
IP:         000. .... = routine
IP:         ...0 .... = normal delay
IP:         .... 0... = normal throughput
IP:         .... .0.. = normal reliability
IP:   Total length   = 244 bytes
IP:   Identification = 4882
IP:   Flags          = 0X
IP:         .0.. .... = may fragment
IP:         ..0. .... = last fragment
IP:   Fragment offset = 0 bytes
IP:   Time to live   = 255 seconds/hops
IP:   Protocol       = 6 (TCP)
IP:   Header checksum = A2F0 (correct)
IP:   Source address      = [2.0.0.1]
IP:   Destination address = [3.0.0.1]
IP:   No options
TCP:  --- TCP header ---
TCP:
TCP:  Source port         = 11000
TCP:  Destination port    = 1996 (CiscoTR-rsrb)
TCP:  Sequence number     = 2825383563
TCP:  Acknowledgment number = 2846029973
TCP:  Data offset         = 20 bytes
TCP:  Flags               = 18
TCP:         ..0. .... = (No urgent pointer)
```

```
TCP:                    ...1 .... = Acknowledgment
TCP:                    .... 1... = Push
TCP:                    .... .0.. = (No reset)
TCP:                    .... ..0. = (No SYN)
TCP:                    .... ...0 = (No FIN)
TCP: Window             = 9144
TCP: Checksum           = 9457 (correct)
TCP: No TCP options
TCP: [204 byte(s) of data]
TCP:
Cisco: —- Cisco Token Ring Encapsulation —-
Cisco: Version = 3
Cisco: Operation = 2 (Explorer)
Cisco: Target ring number = 000
Cisco: Virtual ring number/group = 064
Cisco: Offset = 18
Cisco: Length = 188
Cisco: Parameter = F9280014
TRING: —- Token Ring Header —-
TRING:
TRING: Physical Control Field :
TRING: Access Control = 10
TRING:      000. .... = Priority Bits
TRING:      ...1 .... = Token Bit
TRING:      .... 0... = Monitor Bit
TRING:      .... .000 = Reservation Bits
TRING: AC: Frame priority 0,  Reservation priority 0,  Monitor count 0
TRING: Frame Control = 40
TRING:      01.. .... = Frame Type (LLC)
TRING:      ..00 .... = Reserved
TRING:      .... 0000 = Reserved
TRING: FC: LLC frame,  PCF attention code: None
TRING: Destination = Functional address C00000000080
TRING: Source      = Station 006097A49E41, SERVER1<20>

RI :  —- Routing Indicators —-
RI :
RI : Routing control = C8
RI :      110. .... = Single-route broadcast, all-routes broadcast return
RI :      ...0 1000 = RI length is 8
RI : Routing control = 30
RI :      0... .... = Forward direction
RI :      .011 .... = Largest frame is 4399
RI :      .... 000. = Extended frame is 0
RI :      .... ...0 = Reserved
RI : Ring number 1F4 via bridge 1
RI : Ring number 064 via bridge 0
RI : Ring number 000
RI :
LLC: —- LLC Header —-
LLC:
LLC: DSAP Address = F0, DSAP IG Bit = 00 (Individual Address)
LLC: SSAP Address = F0, SSAP CR Bit = 00 (Command)
LLC: Unnumbered frame: UI
LLC:
NETB: —- NETBIOS Datagram —-
NETB:
NETB: Header length = 44, Data length = 119
NETB: Delimiter = EFFF (NETBIOS)
NETB: Command = 08
```

```
NETB: Data1 = 00
NETB: Data2 = 0000
NETB: Transmit correlator = 0000
NETB: Response correlator = 0000
NETB: Receiver's name = WORKGROUP<1D> <Master Browser backup>
NETB: Sender's name   = SERVER1<20> <Server service>
SMB: --- SMB Transaction Command ---
SMB: Function = 25 (Transaction)
SMB: Tree id     (TID) = 0000
SMB: Process id   (PID) = 0000
SMB: Word count = 17
SMB: Transaction name = "\MAILSLOT\BROWSE"
SMB: Total size of mail data = 33
SMB: Additional information = 0000
SMB:    .... .... .... ..0. = Response expected
SMB:    .... .... .... ...0 = Do not disconnect TID
SMB: Time to wait for completion: 1000 msec
SMB: Op code = 1 (Write mail slot)
SMB: Priority of transaction = 0
SMB: Class = 2 (Unreliable)
SMB: [33 byte(s) of mail data]
```

Answers

1. B
2. A
3. A
4. E
5. B, C
6. D
7. A
8. A
9. B
10. A
11. E
12. A
13. D
14. D
15. D
16. G
17. D
18. A, B, C, D, E
19. E, F
20. C
21. A
22. A
23. A
24. B
25. C
26. E
27. C
28. A
29. A
30. A
31. F
32. E
33. D
34. D
35. A
36. B
37. B
38. A, E
39. D
40. A, B
41. B
42. A Virtual Ring Number is used when two or more physical rings need to communicate to each other. The Token Ring chip set only specifies two rings per Source Route Bridge thus limiting expandability.
43. A
44. C
45. A, C, D
46. A, B, C

47. E
48. Define a bridge group, define spanning tree
49. D
50. Multi-ring is used to route Network Layer packets across a Source Route Bridge Network by inserting a RIF
51. F
52. C
53. E
54. A, B, D
55. B
56. A
57. A, B, C
58. A, B, C, D
59. B, C, D, E
60. B
61. B, C
62. A
63. A
64. B
65. B
66. C, D
67. A, B, C, D
68. A
69. B
70. C
71. A
72. A
73. D
74. B
75. B
76. C
77. E
78. A
79. 4006.09d1.5415
80. 0200.0000.000040
81. ARE, 10 byte Length, Direction left to right, 4472 largest frame size
82. ARE, 12-byte length, Direction left to right, largest frame 4472
83. Direct, 8-byte length, Direction left to right, largest frame 4472
84. Direct, 6-byte length, Direction left to right, largest frame 4472
85. A
86. E
87. A
88. F
89. D
90. C
91. C, E
92. 8000.02609087FAA8
93. E
94. C

95. B
96. H
97. A
98. A, B
99. C
100. D
101. D
102. B
103. A
104. C
105. B
106. B
107. B
108. C
109. A
110. A, B, D
111. C
112. A, C
113. A, C, D, E
114. B
115. D
116. C, D, E
117. D
118. C
119. B, C
120. B
121. C
122. B
123. 00a0.425a.3f94
124. 0007.787b.ab64
125. It bridges the Ethernet interface to the DLSw virtual ring.
126. 0007.787a.2bb5
127. C
128. 4000K bits
129. C
130. 0000.0c31.aa13
131. D
132. D
133. B
134. C
135. B, D
136. C
137. B
138. B
139. B
140. C
141. C
142. C
143. B

144. B
145. A, D
146. C
147. A
148. B
149. H
150. The sending and receiving station cannot be on the FDDI ring.
151. B
152. C
153. A = 20; B = 14; C = 1; D = 4
154. C
155. A, B, C
156. B, C, D
157. D
158. C
159. A
160. E
161. A, B
162. B
163. A
164. A
165. A, B
166. A
167. A
168. A
169. 100000/data rate
170. 10000/data rate
171. C
172. D
173. C
174. B
175. C
176. C
177. B
178. A
179. C
180. A
181. A, C
182. C
183. B
184. A
185. B

NetBIOS Architecture

NetBIOS is an *application programming interface* (API) that provides a method for an application running on one network node to communicate with an application running on another network node. Sytek Corporation developed NetBIOS as a proprietary protocol, and since that time, NetBIOS has become the protocol for linking applications over multivendor network operating systems such as IBM WARP Server, Microsoft NT, SCO Open Server, Sun Solarnet, DEC PathWorks, and others. The first products to use NetBIOS were the original IBM PC Network Adapter and the IBM PC LAN program. NetBIOS is not a true standard, such as TCP/IP or OSI, despite the fact that many people refer to it as such, because no national or international standards organization defines NetBIOS. Many vendors support NetBIOS and provide interoperability between their implementations. NetBIOS is a *de facto* standard first introduced by IBM as PC Network program. The NetBIOS protocol stack is shown in Figure 5.1.

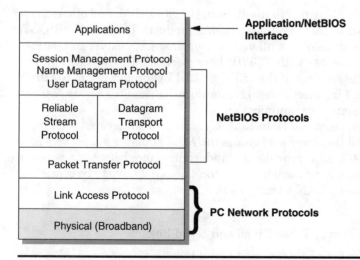

FIGURE 5.1 NetBIOS protocol stack

As part of that network, NetBIOS was designed for use only on a LAN. It is not a routable protocol and is typically bridged or switched using *Remote Source Route Bridging* (RSRB) and/or *Data Link Switching* (DLSw). NetBIOS relies on broadcast frames for most of its functions. Although this may not present a problem in LAN environments, these broadcasts can be costly in internetwork environments by causing congestion, as well as increased costs for WAN links.

NetBIOS uses LLC type 1 (LLC1) and LLC type 2 (LLC2) services:

- LLC1 provides connectionless data transfer. It requires name conflict resolution, station status-gathering flows, and circuit and connection setup flows.

- LLC2 provides a connection-oriented data transfer that uses I-frame traffic sent on established LLC2 connections.

NetBIOS Names

NetBIOS names are the key to communication between NetBIOS stations. A NetBIOS station must know its name to communicate with other NetBIOS stations. NetBIOS names have 16 ASCII characters, the last byte (the 16th byte) reserved by IBM.

Two types of NetBIOS names exist:

- *Individual* names represent a single NetBIOS client or server and should be unique within the NetBIOS network.

- *Group* names represent a group of NetBIOS stations (an NT Server domain, for example). These names should not be the same as any individual NetBIOS names in the network.

A single NetBIOS station can have multiple individual or group names. The NetBIOS application generates names based on the name or names the network administrator configures.

Several vendors, such as Novell, Banyan, Microsoft, Sun, HP, SCO, IBM, and others, have implemented NetBIOS emulators in their LAN networking products. Because NetBIOS is a program interface instead of a protocol, not all vendor implementations are compatible. Efforts to standardize NetBIOS for use with TCP/IP have been made. Current implementations of NetBIOS require the services of the IEEE 802.2 LLC protocol. The NetBIOS datagram service uses LLC Type 1 (connectionless) communication, and the session service uses LLC Type 2 (connection-oriented) communication.

The IEEE 802 standards implement the Data Link layer as two sublayers. The upper sublayer is the LLC sublayer, and the lower sublayer is the MAC sublayer supporting Ethernet, Token Ring, FDDI, and ATM. LLC provides a standard interface between a network layer and the MAC sublayer so that a network layer protocol does not have to be concerned with which MAC sublayer protocol a LAN adapter uses.

CISCO supports the following:

- Source-Route bridging NetBIOS over Token Rings and serial links
- Transparent bridging NetBIOS over Ethernet and serial links

- Data link switching NetBIOS over serial links, Ethernet, and Token Rings
- Remote Source Route Bridging (RSRB)

NetBIOS Services

NetBIOS offers several services that applications can use to request application services across the network. NetBIOS APIs enable applications to use interrupt capabilities to access the four services provided, such as:

- General Services
- Naming Service
- Session Services
- Datagram Services

NetBIOS General Service Commands

NetBIOS general service commands provide various types of services for NetBIOS applications. The general service commands are shown in Table 5.1.

Naming Services

When IBM first introduced NetBIOS, one of its most innovative features was its naming services, which manages network names. When application software refers to network adapters, NetBIOS enables it to use a network name of its own (or of the remote software's)

TABLE 5.1 NetBIOS General Service Commands

Command	NetBIOS General Command Descriptions
Reset	A process should issue a reset command to deallocate its resources and return them to the NetBIOS pool for subsequent use by other applications
Status	This command reports the status of the local and remote LAN adapter. The Status command reports some of the following:
	NetBIOS version
	Adapter up time
	Number of soft errors
	Traffic statistics
	Burned-in MAC address
Cancel	This command is used to cancel a pending command
Alert	This command is used by applications that want to be notified of soft error conditions at the adapter level, which last over a certain period of time
Unlink	This command is used for backward compatibility

TABLE 5.2   NetBIOS Name Service Commands

NetBIOS Name Service	Name Service Command Description
Add Name	This command allows NetBIOS to add a unique name to the local NetBIOS Name table.
Add Group	This command allows NetBIOS to add a unique Group to the local NetBIOS Name table.
Delete Name	Applications use this command to delete both unique names and group names.
Find Name	This command is used to find a NetBIOS name on the network. NetBIOS broadcasts a query and returns whether the name is a unique name or group name.

choosing, which can be simple, logical, and mnemonic. Each PC application that runs over a LAN has a NetBIOS name. Applications use NetBIOS names to start and end sessions. You can configure a single station with multiple applications, each of which has a unique NetBIOS name. Each PC that supports an application also has a NetBIOS station name that you assign or that NetBIOS derives by that station's internal means.

NetBIOS names can contain up to 16 alphanumeric characters. The combination of characters must be unique within the entire network. Most applications extend this convenience to their users so that they can use simple, logical, and mnemonic names as well. Neither users nor application programs need to keep track of cryptic hexadecimal numbers or other forms of network addresses. You can configure a Cisco Source-Routing bridge so that it can cache NetBIOS names based on the length specified by the administrator. This feature is useful in application environments that use the first 15 characters of the NetBIOS name to identify the station, and the last character to identify the application. Name services occur in several phases, such as name registration, name discovery, and name deletion. Table 5.2 describes the NetBIOS name service commands.

Name Registration.   Before anyone can use a network name, someone has to register that name. When an application program registers a name, it identifies itself and its name to the network adapter. Before granting the registration, the adapter makes sure that the name is a valid name and that using this name will not cause a conflict with other names on the network.

Two NetBIOS commands provide name registration services. Each tells the adapter to register a network name, but they differ in the type of name they identify. Add Name registers a unique name—only one application at a time can use a unique name. As part of the registration process, the adapter must be sure that no other application is already trying to use the name. Add Group Name registers a group name—many applications on a network can use the same group name at the same time. In many cases, data sent to a group name arrives at all the applications using that name. For group name registration, an adapter need only make sure that no application is using the name as a unique name.

All NetBIOS stations advertise their names when they become active. A station is considered to be registered when it can successfully advertise its own name without any other station sending back a response claiming it has the same name. The registration process for a station name to register itself is as follows:

1. A NetBIOS station sends *Add Name Query* or *Add Group Name Query* frames for each name it wants to use (see Figure 5.2). These frames contain each station's assigned name. Different vendors' NetBIOS stations repeat these commands typically between 5 to 11 times to increase the chances that all other stations hear them.

2. If another station already has the same name, that NetBIOS station issues an *Add Name Response* command to indicate that the name is already in use. The station issuing the query must stop trying to use that name.

3. When a partitioned Source-Route bridge network reconnects, two stations may have the same name. When a NetBIOS station detects this (for example, if it receives two or more *Name-Recognized* responses to a *Name Query* request), it issues a *Name in Conflict* broadcast frame.

4. Upon receiving a *Name in Conflict* frame, the user is presented with an error message that does not allow the station to join the network.

NetBIOS Name Discovery.   The second phase of naming services is name discovery, which identifies the specific network adapter at which a name exists. Both of these programs can use network names to identify each other, but the adapter software on the sending computer must actually locate the network adapter of the receiving program. The sending adapter must discover the network address of the receiving adapter. Most of the time, name discovery takes place without the knowledge of application programs. When an application establishes a session or transfers a datagram, the application uses only names. The adapter software must translate these names to network addresses. The adapter software, therefore, most often uses name discovery.

Some implementations of NetBIOS provide a Find Name command so that application software can access the name discovery service directly. After an application discovers a name, however, there is not much it can do with the information.

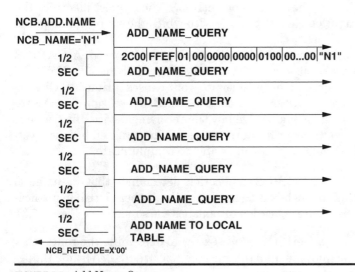

FIGURE 5.2   Add Name Query

NetBIOS Name Deletion.   Name deletion is the opposite of name registration; this command cancels any association between the name and the application, and it allows other applications to use the name. An application must delete a name before the name can be moved to another computer, even if the second computer is using a copy of the same application. Although users may think of these two applications as being the same program, NetBIOS views them as two separate applications. NetBIOS provides the Delete Name command for deleting a name. Applications use this command to delete both unique names and group names.

See Listing 5.1 in CH05CODE on the CD for an example of the NetBIOS Add Name query trace.

What Is a NetBIOS Session?

For its session service, NetBIOS establishes and maintains a connection between two NetBIOS names. Two NetBIOS names communicate using special NetBIOS commands. A NetBIOS name is 1 to 16 characters (16 bytes) in length and is used to identify a network device or a function within a network device. NetBIOS names are configured by the user and are optional. If the user does not configure a name for a NetBIOS device, NetBIOS creates a name by preceding the device's universally administered address (6 bytes) with 0s (10 bytes).

More than one NetBIOS device may be configured with the same NetBIOS name. NetBIOS implementers should guard against configuring duplicate unique names.

> **NOTE:**   *When using Microsoft NT NetBIOS over TCP/IP, you can define a scope that allows duplicate NetBIOS names to reside on the same LAN segment. Microsoft's implementation appends the scope ID number to the name to make the name unique.*

When a NetBIOS device enters a network, it advertises its NetBIOS name in an attempt to claim the name. If a unique name is being used by another device on the network, the name claim is rejected, and NetBIOS must retry later. A NetBIOS session is established when an application program requests the services of NetBIOS. The request identifies the source NetBIOS name and a destination NetBIOS name with which the source name wants to communicate.

Table 5.3 lists the NetBIOS session commands. Each session is numbered. A NetBIOS name can maintain multiple, concurrent sessions with other NetBIOS names. NetBIOS maintains a session as long as it is needed, or until some event causes a timeout. One aspect of session maintenance is error-detection and control. NetBIOS session frames are numbered so that each packet must be acknowledged by the receiving device. If a frame is not acknowledged within the receive timeout limit, the session is terminated because NetBIOS assumes that the destination device is no longer able to communicate.

Establishing NetBIOS Sessions.   After a NetBIOS application determines that its name is unique on the network, the application establishes a session with another NetBIOS application. The following steps describe how the application establishes the session (see Figure 5.3):

1. The originating station sends out a NetBIOS *Name Query* to determine the route to the destination application. The query is a *Spanning Tree Explorer* (STE) frame that invites a specific remote application to respond.

TABLE 5.3 NetBIOS Session Commands

NetBIOS Session Commands	NetBIOS Session Command Description
Call	This command attempts to open a session with another name.
Listen	This command allows you to accept a session call.
Send	This command sends data to the session partner as defined in the LSN NCB field.
Chain Send	This command is like the send command except that you can point to two data buffers that get sent as a single message.
Send Ack	This command is like the Send command except that no data acknowledgment is required at the NetBIOS level.
Chain Send No-Ack	This command is like the Chain send except that no data acknowledgment is required at the NetBIOS level.
Receive	This command receives data from a session partner that sends data using any of the session send commands.
Receive Any	This command is like the Receive command except that data can be received from any partner in session with the specified name.
Hang Up	This command closes an open session identified by the LSN field in the NCB.
Session Status	This command obtains information about all the sessions with a local name or for all local names.

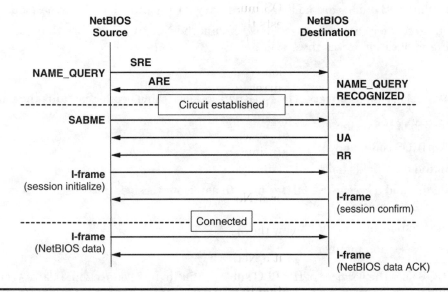

FIGURE 5.3 NetBIOS Session Establishment

2. As the *Name Query* STE frame propagates along its spanning tree route, the frame accumulates RIF data, which traces its unique path through the loop-free topology of the network.

   - If you do not have a Source-Routed spanning tree configured on your network, the STE propagates along all available routes to the destination application. Multiple copies of the *Name Query* STE frame may arrive at the destination station.

   - If your network has a spanning tree topology, only one copy of the *Name Query* STE frame arrives at the destination remote station.

3. The NetBIOS interface on the destination station recognizes the name of one of its own applications in the query frame. The NetBIOS interface responds by broadcasting a *name-recognized All-Routes Explorer* (ARE) frame.

4. As the *name-recognized* ARE frame propagates toward the calling station along multiple paths, each frame accumulates RIF information that traces its unique path through the network. The originating Source-Routing interface receives multiple copies of the *name-recognized* frame.

5. Depending on the number of parallel paths from the destination application back to the calling application, one or more copies of the *name-recognized* ARE response frame arrive at the originating station. The originating station accepts only the first *name-recognized* frame it receives, assuming that this frame contains the RIF for the shortest path to the destination station. The calling station uses this RIF for any subsequent frames sent to the destination station. All subsequent frames associated with the impending session are *specifically routed frames* (SRFs).

6. Based on the information gained from the *name-recognized* frame accepted by the originating application, the NetBIOS interface establishes a session directly between the originating and destination application. After the session between applications is open, NetBIOS names are no longer necessary for the duration of that session.

7. When no further session transactions remain, the NetBIOS interface that serves the calling application closes the session.

NetBIOS Session Frame Format.   The NetBIOS session frame header contains the following:

- The length of the frame
- The NetBIOS command
- Command data fields (optional)
- A transmit and a receive correlator used to associate received responses with transmitted requests
- The destination session number
- The source session number

NetBIOS uses the services of the LLC sublayer for its link connection. The LLC sublayer encapsulates the session frame into an LLC frame, whose header contains a *destination service access point* (DSAP) and a *source service access point* (SSAP). LLC uses SAPs to identify higher level protocols that use LLC, such as NetBIOS.

Between the NetBIOS SAPs at any two nodes is only one link station connection. That link station is used to support all NetBIOS sessions between the two nodes. Consequently, a link station may support multiple sessions. The control field indicates the type of LLC frame. Because NetBIOS session service is connection-oriented, the frame type is always an Information frame, which is a numbered frame.

NetBIOS Datagram Services

When a NetBIOS station wants to send information that does not require a response from the destination application, the local station transmits a NetBIOS *datagram* frame. Datagrams resemble mailed letters in the manner that sessions resemble phone calls. When an application sends data in a datagram, it gives the data to the adapter software and tells the adapter to whom it should be sent. The application need not bother with preliminary commands to establish a session. Datagrams have two significant disadvantages compared with session-data transfer. First, datagrams support only a limited amount of data. Although an application can send as much data as possible with a single Chain Send command, datagrams limit the application to 512 bytes at a time. Second, datagrams are not reliable. NetBIOS gives a sender no assurance that data sent by a datagram is ever delivered to the recipient.

An application can use datagrams in three ways: it can send data to a single remote application; it can send data to a group of applications; or it can send data to all NetBIOS applications. These methods are discussed in the following sections. Table 5.4 lists the NetBIOS Datagram commands.

Point-to-Point Data Transfer.   The simplest way an application can use datagrams is to send data to another application. Because this type of transfer involves one sender and one recipient, it is called a *point-to-point transfer*. (Session-data transfer is also a form of point-to-point transfer.) To prepare for receiving a point-to-point datagram, an application issues

TABLE 5.4   **NetBIOS Datagram Commands**

NetBIOS Datagram Command	NetBIOS Datagram Command Descriptions
Send Datagram	This command is used to send a datagram message to any unique name or group name on the network.
Send Broadcast Datagram	This command sends a datagram to every station on the network that has an outstanding Receive Broadcast Datagram.
Receive Datagram	This command receives a datagram from any name on the network that issues a send datagram to the local name table.
Receive Broadcast Datagram	This command receives a datagram from any name that issues a Send Broadcast Datagram. If the receive buffer is not large enough, you are notified, but the overflow data is lost.

a Receive Datagram command, and the sending application executes a Send Datagram command. If an application sends a datagram to a remote name that has not issued an appropriate Receive Datagram command, the data is lost, and the sender is not notified.

Group-Data Transfer.   Applications use the same NetBIOS commands for group-data transfer that they use for point-to-point transfer: Receive Datagram and Send Datagram. For group transfer, however, the recipient's name is a group name instead of a unique name. Many applications on many different adapters can all issue Receive Datagram commands for the same group name. Then when someone sends a datagram to that name, all of these applications can receive a copy of the data.

Broadcast-Data Transfer.   Applications also use datagrams for broadcast-data transfer. NetBIOS provides two commands just for broadcast transfer: Receive Broadcast Datagram and Send Broadcast Datagram. These commands behave like the regular datagram commands except that they do not require a specified destination name for the datagram. For broadcast traffic, the implied destination is every adapter on the network. However, not everybody receives a broadcast datagram; only those applications that have issued Receive Broadcast Datagram commands can do so.

NetBIOS Interface.   The interface is accessed through interrupt 5ch—this interrupt is called with ES:BX pointing to a 64-byte data structure, which is known as the *Network Control Block* (NCB). The NCB contains the required data, such as names, command codes, pointers to buffers, etc. The NCB must be unaltered until the command is completed, so it cannot be used for other commands, although a command is still executed. However, after a command has completed, the NCB can be altered and reused for another command.

NetBIOS Network Control Block.   The NCB is the most important function NetBIOS requires to perform within the network. An NCB is required for every single command. The NCB is passed as a data structure to NetBIOS; therefore you do not see the following header fields in the NetBIOS Header.

A NCB is always 64 bytes in length and has the following structure:

- *Command.* This is a command code listing the command you require.
- *Return code.* This field returns the completion code for a synchronous command or the initiation code for an asynchronous command.
- *Local session.* This field specifies the session number for a command. A session number is returned every time a session is opened.
- *Name number.* This field specifies the unique number for the name being used. Every time a name is added, a unique number is returned. This field must be set to the number of the name you want to use. The easiest way to do this is have a separate NCB for every name you use, and after you have added the name, this field is set, so it can be left untouched for every other command on that particular name.

- *Buffer address*. This field specifies the address of the buffer for transmit/receive commands. It is in `segment:offset` form, with byte 4 being the least significant byte of the offset and byte 7 the most significant byte of the segment.

- *Buffer length*. This field specifies the length of the buffer, with byte 8 being the least significant byte.

- *Call name*. The call name is the name on a local or remote station that you want to contact in send commands or the name from which received data has come.

- *Name*. The local name is a name on the local station—it is only required when adding or deleting a name, because after a name has been added, a unique number is assigned, which is used for all subsequent commands.

- *Receive timeout* (RTO). This field is the timeout for receive commands, measured in 500ms.

- *Send timeout* (STO). This field is the timeout for send commands, measured in 500ms.

- *POST address*. This field is the address of the POST routine, for asynchronous commands, which is called when the command has completed. If it is set to `0000:0000`, no routine is called when an asynchronous command has completed. This field is ignored for synchronous commands. It has the same byte order as the buffer address field.

- *LAN_A_Number*. If more than one network adapter is in a station, this specifies which one to use.

- *Command complete*. This field is the completion code for asynchronous commands. It is set to `FFh` while the command is still being executed and changed once it has completed.

- *Reserved*. This byte must be present and not be unchanged. The network software uses these for workspace.

Tables 5.5 through 5.13 list the NetBIOS frames and their functions.

When NetBIOS is discussed, the protocol most likely used or talked about is NetBEUI. NetBIOS is not limited to using NetBEUI protocol. In fact, NetBIOS runs over a range of protocols from a variety of vendors using standard and proprietary protocols. NetBEUI is a protocol stack available from a number of vendors offering Network Operating Systems for file and print services. NetBEUI is an acronym for NetBIOS Extended User Interface. A NetBEUI protocol stack was first introduced by IBM in 1985. The objective for NetBEUI was to provide a small and efficient stack optimized to run on a departmental LAN. With the advent of Client Server computing, users needed to link their networks over wide area links using bridges and routers to mainframes, midrange systems, and file servers. These design criteria assumed NetBEUI would be used locally, although more scaleable protocols would be used to connect over the WAN.

In this context, we refer to Microsoft's implementation of NetBEUI. IBM's implementation offers similar services in scope because the two operating systems can interoperate using *NetBIOS Extended User Interface* (NetBEUI). Microsoft's NetBEUI is the precursor to the *NetBEUI Frame* (NBF) protocol included with Windows NT, which has become very popular. NBF provides compatibility with existing LAN Manager and MS-Net installations and with IBM WARP Server installations. On Windows NT, the NetBIOS interface is supported under MS-DOS, 16-bit Windows, Win32 subsystem, and IBM OS/2 WARP environments.

TABLE 5.5   NetBIOS Frames

Frame Name	Code	Function
ADD_GROUP_NAME_QUERY	X `00`	Check for duplicate group name on network
ADD_NAME_QUERY	X `01`	Check for duplicate name on network
ADD_NAME_RESPONSE	X `0D`	Negative response: add name is duplicated
DATA_ACK	X `14`	DATA_ONLY_LAST acknowledgment
DATA_FIRST_MIDDLE	X `15`	Session data message—first or middle frame
DATAGRAM	X `08`	Application program-generated datagram
DATAGRAM_BROADCAST	X `09`	Application program-generated broadcast datagram
DATA_ONLY_LAST	X `16`	Session data message—only or last frame
NAME_IN_CONFLICT	X `02`	Duplicate names detected
NAME_QUERY	X `0A`	Request to locate a name on the network
NAME_RECOGNIZED	X `0E`	Name Recognized: NAME_QUERY response
NO_RECEIVE	X `1A`	No receive command to hold received data
RECEIVE_CONTINUE	X `1C`	Indicates receive pending
RECEIVE_OUTSTANDING	X `1B`	Retransmit last data-receive command up
SESSION_ALIVE	X `1F`	Verify session is still active
SESSION_CONFIRM	X `17`	SESSION_INITIALIZE acknowledgment
SESSION_END	X `18`	Session termination
SESSION_INITIALIZE	X `19`	A session has been set up
STATUS_QUERY	X `03`	Request remote node status
STATUS_RESPONSE	X `0F`	Remote node status information, STATUS_QUERY response
TERMINATE_TRACE	X `07`	Terminate traces at remote nodes
TERMINATE_TRACE	X `13`	Terminate traces at local and remote nodes

TABLE 5.6   NETBIOS Name Management Frames

Frame Name	Code	Function
ADD_GROUP_NAME_QUERY	X `00`	Check for duplicate group name on network
ADD_NAME_QUERY	X `01`	Check for duplicate name on network
ADD_NAME_RESPONSE	X `0D`	Negative response: add name is duplicate
NAME_IN_CONFLICT	X `02`	Duplicate names detected

TABLE 5.7   NETBIOS Session Establishment and Termination Frames

Frame Name	Code	Function
NAME_QUERY	X '0A'	Request to locate a name on the network
NAME_RECOGNIZED	X '0E'	Name Recognized: NAME_QUERY response
SESSION_ALIVE	X '1F'	Verify session is still active
SESSION_CONFIRM	X '17'	SESSION_INITIALIZE acknowledgment
SESSION_END	X '18'	Session termination
SESSION_INITIALIZE	X '19'	A session has been set up

TABLE 5.8   NETBIOS Data Transfer Frames

Frame Name	Code	Function
DATA_ACK	X '14'	DATA_ONLY_LAST acknowledgment
DATA_FIRST_MIDDLE	X '15'	Session data message—first or middle frame
DATAGRAM	X '08'	Application program-generated datagram
DATAGRAM_BROADCAST	X '09'	Application program-generated broadcast datagram
DATA_ONLY_LAST	X '16'	Session data message—only or last frame
NO_RECEIVE	X '1A'	No receive command to hold received data
RECEIVE_CONTINUE	X '1C'	Indicates receive pending
RECEIVE_OUTSTANDING	X '1B'	Retransmit last data-receive command up

TABLE 5.9   NETBIOS Frames

Frame Name	Code	Function
STATUS_QUERY	X '03'	Request remote node status
STATUS_RESPONSE	X '0F'	Remote node status information, STATUS_QUERY response
TERMINATE_TRACE	X '07'	Terminate traces at remote nodes
TERMINATE_TRACE	X '13'	Terminate traces at local and remote nodes

The NetBEUI protocol contains the following headers:

- *Length*. The length of the NetBIOS header.
- *NetBIOS Indicator*. Indicates that subsequent data is destined for NetBIOS.
- *Command*. Identifies the function of the frame and its format.
- *Command Data*. Data specific to a particular type of frame.
- *Transmit Correlator*. Correlates a value returned in a response with a previous message.

TABLE 5.10   NetBIOS UI Frames to Functional Address, Single-Route Broadcast

Frame Name	Code	Function
ADD_GROUP_NAME_QUERY	x `00`	Check for duplicate group name on network
ADD_NAME_QUERY	x `01`	Check for duplicate name on network
DATAGRAM	x `08`	Application program-generated datagram
DATAGRAM_BROADCAST	x `09`	Application program-generated broadcast datagram
NAME_IN_CONFLICT	x `02`	Duplicate names detected
NAME_QUERY	x `0A`	Request to locate a name on the network
STATUS_QUERY	x `03`	Request remote node status
TERMINATE_TRACE	x `07`	Terminate traces at remote nodes
TERMINATE_TRACE	x `13`	Terminate traces at local and remote nodes

TABLE 5.11   NetBIOS UI Frames to Specific Address, No Broadcast

Frame Name	Code	Function
ADD_NAME_RESPONSE	x `0D`	Negative response: add name is duplicate
STATUS_RESPONSE	x `0F`	Remote node status information, STATUS_QUERY response

TABLE 5.12   NetBIOS UI Frames to Specific Address, General Broadcast

Frame Name	Code	Function
NAME_RECOGNIZED	x `0E`	Name Recognized: NAME_QUERY response

TABLE 5.13   NetBIOS I Frames to Specific Address, No Broadcast

Frame Name	Code	Function
DATA_ACK	x `14`	DATA_ONLY_LAST acknowledgment
DATA_FIRST_MIDDLE	x `15`	Session data message—first or middle frame
DATA_ONLY_LAST	x `16`	Session data message—only or last frame
NO_RECEIVE	x `1A`	No receive command to hold received data
RECEIVE_OUTSTANDING	x `1B`	Retransmit last data-receive command up
SESSION_CONFIRM	x `17`	SESSION_INITIALIZE acknowledgment
SESSION_END	x `18`	Session termination
SESSION_INITIALIZE	x `19`	A session has been set up
RECEIVE_CONTINUE	x `1C`	Indicates receive pending
SESSION_ALIVE	x `1F`	Verify session is still active

- *Response Correlator*. Correlates a value to be returned in a response (in the transmit correlator field) with this message.
- *Destination ID*. Identifies the message destination. This can be either a name or a session number assigned when a NetBIOS session in established.
- *Source ID*. Identifies the message source. This can be either a name or a session number assigned when the NetBIOS session was established.
- *User Data*. The information passed to NetBIOS by the user.

> **NOTE:** *Microsoft calls its implementation* NetBEUI NetBIOS Frame *(NBF).*

The NBF protocol, like NetBEUI, provides for connectionless and connection-oriented traffic. Connectionless communications can be either unreliable or reliable. NBF and Net-BEUI provide only *unreliable connectionless*, not reliable connectionless communications.

NBF communicates via the NDIS interface at the LLC sublayer. A connection at the LLC sublayer is called a *link*, which is uniquely defined by the adapter's address and the DSAP. A SAP can be thought of as the address of a port to a layer as defined by the OSI model. Because NBF is a NetBIOS implementation, it uses the NetBIOS SAP (0xF0). Although the 802.2 protocol governs the overall flow of data, the primitives are responsible for passing the data from one layer to the next. The primitives are passed through the SAPs between layers.

NBF and Sessions

Each process within Windows NT that uses NetBIOS can communicate with up to 254 different computers. The implementation of NetBIOS under Windows NT requires the application to do a few more things that have traditionally been done on other platforms, but the capacity for doing up to 254 sessions from within each process is well worth the price. Prior implementations of NetBIOS had the 254-session limit for the entire computer, including the workstation and server components. Note that the 254-session limit does not apply to the default workstation or server components.

NetBEUI and the OSI Model

The NetBEUI interface lies at the top of the Transport layer, and the NDIS interface lies at the bottom of the LLC sublayer. The DLC layer of the OSI model provides a virtual communication link for sending error-free packets over a physical medium. To separate the physical components, the IEEE has split the DLC into the MAC and LLC sublayers. The MAC sublayer is responsible for delivering error-free data between two stations. This sublayer is implemented by the NIC driver. On Microsoft NT, this driver communicates with the LLC sublayer through the device driver. All network topology and hardware dependencies are contained within the MAC sublayer.

Connectionless Traffic

For connectionless traffic that requires a response from remote stations, NetBEUI sends out a certain number of frames depending on the command. The total number is a function of the *netbiosretries* parameter. The time between sending each frame is determined by the *netbiostimeout* parameter. The default value for *netbiosretries* is 2. The default value for *netbiostimeout* is 1/2 second.

Three types of NetBIOS commands generate connectionless traffic: name claim and resolution, datagrams, and miscellaneous commands like `Adapter.Status`. These are sent out as *Unnumbered Information* (UI) frames at the LLC sublayer. The miscellaneous commands are not used.

As an example of how vendors use the *netbiosretries* and *netbiostimeout* parameters, let's review what occurs when names are registered. Various NetBIOS Application Services register (via NetBEUI) unique names for the *computername, messengername,* and any messenger alias names. Group names are registered for the *domain* and *othdomains*. The NetBIOS `Add.Name` command is used for unique names. The NetBIOS `Add.GroupName` command is used for group names. When the `Add.Name` or `Add.GroupName` command is issued, NetBEUI sends out `netbiosretries+1` `ADD_NAME_QUERY` or `ADD_GROUP_NAME_QUERY` frames at a time interval of *netbiostimeout* to the destination address of `03 00 00 00 00 01` hex on Ethernet or `C0 00 00 00 00 80` hex on Token Ring LANs. Sending the ADD_NAME_QUERY frame out *netbiosretries* + 1 times allows stations on the LAN time to inform the sending station whether the name has already been registered as a unique name on another station.

The destination address of `03 00 00 00 00 01` hex is a multicast address, which is a more efficient way to send undirected broadcasts than sending out undirected broadcasts to `FF FF FF FF FF FF` hex, because only stations registered to receive frames from the multicast address need to process them. NetBEUI uses the functional address of `C0 00 00 00 00 80` hex on Token Ring LANs. A functional address works in much the same way as the Ethernet multicast address to differentiate which machines listen for NetBEUI's packet.

To process a *net use* command, a workstation service sends a NetBIOS Call command to NetBEUI. NetBEUI then sends a NAME_QUERY frame, which requests the station with the name to respond with a NAME_RECOGNIZED frame. For example, a user may want to use the DATA resources on the 4508 and make it appear as the local G drive by typing the command `NET USE F:\\4508\root`. NetBEUI sends a NAME_QUERY frame requesting the location of 4508. NetBEUI then sends out (*netBioSretries*+1)*2 NAME_QUERY frames before it reports that 4508 cannot be found.

Connection-Oriented Traffic

The net use command is an example of connection-oriented communication using LLC2 at the Data Link layer. When a net use is performed, NetBEUI has to first locate the server using UI frames and then initialize the link. This process is handled by the redirector sending NetBEUI the CALL NetBIOS command. NetBEUI then starts a long sequence of events. When the server is found, a session is set up with LLC2 frames following the standard 802.2 protocol. The workstation sends a SABME; the server station returns a UA frame. Then both sides send an RR frame notifying each other that they are ready to receive I frames whose sequence number is currently 0. Link-oriented frames achieve reliable transfer by numbering the I frames. This process allows the receiving station to determine whether the frames were lost and in what order they were received.

Two sets of parameters guide the performance of NetBEUI for connection-oriented traffic at the LLC level. The first set is for control of the adaptive sliding window. These include the *adaptrate, maxin, maxout,* and *windowerrors* parameters. The second set is for control of the link timers. These include the *T1, T2,* and *Ti* timers.

Adaptive Sliding Window Protocol

NetBEUI uses an adaptive sliding window algorithm to improve performance while reducing network congestion and providing flow control. A sliding window algorithm allows a sender to transmit multiple LLC frames before an acknowledgment.

Link Timers

NetBEUI uses the three timers $T1$, $T2$, and Ti to help regulate network traffic. The three timers are commonly referred to as the response timer (T1), the acknowledgment timer (T2), and the inactivity timer (Ti). The response timer is used to determine how long the sender should wait before it assumes the I frame is lost. In some vendor's implementations, the value for each link's T1 parameter is determined by the speed of the link. Because the transmit speed does not take into account WAN environments in which multiple hops can occur, the value of T1 can still be set in the registry file found on some NetBEUI implementations or the Registry using NT and Windows 98. If it is, all links use this value.

After T1 milliseconds, NetBEUI retransmits an I frame that has not been ACKed and doubles the value for T1. NetBEUI retransmits the I frame *dlcretries* times and continues to double the T1 value until the T1 value is 16 times the original value. If the I frame is not ACKed within this time, the link is dropped. Given the default values for T1 and *dlcretries* in LAN Manager 2.0 ($T1 = 500$ *ms, dlcretries = 5*), a link is dropped if an ACK is not received for the send frame within 23.5 seconds (i.e.: `1/2+1+2+4+8+8=23.5`). NetBEUI always maintains the default time of 1/2 second. Where the return traffic does not allow the receiver to send an I frame within the legitimate time period, the acknowledgment timer fires, and the ACK is sent. The value for this timer is set by the T2 variable.

The default value for T2 is 200ms. If the sender has to wait until the T2 timer fires to receive a response, the link is under utilized while the sender waits for the ACK. This rare situation could occur over slow links. If the timer is too low, it fires off and sends unnecessary ACKs, generating excess traffic. NetBEUI is optimized so that the last frame the sender wants to send is sent with the POLL bit turned on. This process forces the receiver to immediately send an ACK.

The inactivity timer, Ti, is used to detect whether the link has gone down. The default value for Ti is three seconds. If Ti milliseconds go by without activity on the link, NetBEUI sends an I frame containing a NetBIOS SESSION_ALIVE frame. This frame is then ACKed, and the link is maintained. Keep in mind that $T2<=T1<=Ti$. On slow links, you should increase the Ti timer to 60,000 to generate fewer SESSION_ALIVE frames.

Two likely causes of links being dropped are either frames coming in out of sequence or the receiver not sending an ACK before the $T1*dlcretries$ time is up. Frames should not arrive out of sequence over a LAN, but they could arrive out of sequence if packets are sent over a bridge, switch, or router.

NetBIOS Session Timers

Under normal traffic conditions, no reason to change timer values exists. However, these parameters may need to be altered on slower links or links over multiple hops. Timers are used at two levels, the link level and the NetBIOS session level. The T1, T2, Ti, and *dlcretries* parameters for managing link timeouts already have been discussed.

To establish a NetBIOS session (which is what occurs when you use a resource on NT server via the net use command), the side that acts as the server to a request must be listening for a call. In NetBIOS, this is done by the LISTEN command. The NetBIOS server application issues the LISTEN command, filling in the NetBIOS Control Block (NCB) with information on what name it responds to when a CALL command is executed by a remote station, as well as timer thresholds that inform the underlying protocol stack how long it waits before it assumes something is wrong when the send and receive commands are issued to transfer data. The two timeout intervals are the *Receive Time Out* (RTO) and *Send Time Out* (STO).

NetBEUI on Multisegmented LANs

The most common method to interconnect LAN segments is via bridges, switches, or routers. Because bridges and layer 2 switches access only services up to the MAC level of the OSI model, they are protocol-independent. Routers use addresses found in the Network layer of the OSI model, and thus are protocol-dependent. Internetworked Token Ring LANs characteristically use Source Routing. Because NetBEUI does not implement the Network layer, routing is not supported. However, NetBEUI does implement Source Routing over Token Ring because this occurs at the MAC sublayer.

Cisco NetBIOS Support

The Cisco IOS supports NetBIOS when end-node devices running NetBIOS must communicate with other devices over the network using Cisco routers. This communication is accomplished via a number of options provided in the Cisco IOS software. Because NetBIOS is a non-routable protocol, it must be bridged to allow network connectivity between devices not located on the same LAN segment. Cisco IOS supports a number of bridging options to link NetBIOS devices across an internetwork. These options consist of but are not limited to the following:

- Source-Route bridging
- Transparent bridging
- Source-Route Translational bridging
- Source-Route Transparent bridging
- Integrated bridging and routing
- Remote Source-Route Bridging (RSRB)
- Data Link Switching (DLSw)

Source Routing and Transparent bridging of NetBIOS frames is the most common due in part to the popularity of Ethernet, IBM WARP Server, Microsoft NT, and Token Ring in large SNA environments. The Cisco IOS bridging functions enable you to configure filters for source and destination NetBIOS names. You can set filters to instruct the router to block or pass NetBIOS frames that contain the specified names. The bridge filters facilitate controlling broadcasts of NetBIOS frames from one LAN segment to another and can be used to restrict communication between users on different networks. Cisco offers several options to reducing NetBIOS traffic:

- NetBIOS name cache
- NetBIOS broadcast throttling
- NetBIOS datagram broadcast handling
- NetBIOS broadcast damping

NetBIOS Name Caching

NetBIOS name caching allows the Cisco router to maintain a local cache of NetBIOS names so that it can reduce the amount of NetBIOS traffic sent across the network. Name caching works by allowing the router to detect when a NetBIOS station sends multiple Name Query frames to the same destination NetBIOS name. The cache includes the NetBIOS Station name and MAC address. The name cache allows the router to send broadcast requests from clients to find servers and from servers in reply to their clients directly to their destinations. It does this rather than sending the broadcast across the entire bridged network.

As NetBIOS stations initialize and start forwarding queries, the router caches the NetBIOS name in the NAME_QUERY and NAME_RECOGNIZED broadcast frames along with the station MAC address, RIF, and the physical port from which the broadcast was received. Because the router has the NetBIOS name as well as the route to the station, it can respond locally to broadcasts and eliminate the overhead of propagating broadcast frames throughout the network.

NetBIOS name caching can be enabled on each interface by using the following Cisco IOS interface configuration commands:

```
Source-bridge proxy-explorer netbios enable-name-cache
Source-bridge proxy-netbios-only
```

The source-bridge proxy-explorer command is a prerequisite for NetBIOS name caching. NetBIOS names are cached in several ways:

- Static entries are those that you enter at the NetBIOS command line.

- Dynamic entries are those that the router learns through Name-Query and Name-Recognized processing. A timer removes dynamic entries that have not been referenced within a configurable amount of time. The router does not save dynamic entries, and they are not available after you restart the router.

- Data link switching uses local and remote caches, in addition to Ring Lists for directing NetBIOS explorer packets to the Rings required. This option will be further dicussed in Chapter 13, "Data Link Switching (DLSw)."

NetBIOS Broadcast Throttling

NetBIOS applications broadcast by issuing multiple successive copies of broadcast frames into the network. For example, some NetBIOS implementations send from 5 to 11 successive copies of a NAME_QUERY frame, with a pause of a half-second between each repeated transmission. Some applications enable you to tune this behavior, but tuning NetBIOS broadcasts is difficult to maintain if the number of NetBIOS workstations in your network is high.

When NetBIOS name caching is enabled, the router forwards the first of the many received broadcasts from a NetBIOS station and drops the duplicate broadcasts frames. The duplicate broadcasts, which originated from the same station, continue to be dropped until the dead timer expires. Two Cisco IOS global configuration commands control relevant timers:

```
netbios name-cache query-timeout seconds
netbios name-cache timeout minutes
```

The default is 6 seconds.

```
netbios name-cache recognized-timeout seconds
```

The default is 1 second.

NetBIOS Broadcast Damping

The router remembers the actual physical port from which a NetBIOS station's route was cached. As a result, the router can remember where a cached station resides relative to the router. If the router receives a broadcast frame addressed to a cached NetBIOS name and if the router knows that the route to that station exists off of the same interface, the router does not need to forward the broadcast to find the target station. Instead, the router drops the broadcast and prevents unnecessary broadcast traffic from traversing the network.

NetBIOS Datagram Broadcast Handling

The router also checks the NetBIOS name cache when it receives NetBIOS datagram broadcasts (addressed to unique names), which enables the router to handle NetBIOS datagram broadcasts locally in a way similar to NAME_QUERY and NAME_RECOGNIZED broadcast handling. The difference is that datagram broadcasts are generally one-way flows with no corresponding reply. If datagram broadcasts represent a small percentage of overall broadcast traffic, you can disable datagram handling and avoid expending additional router overhead for relatively minor effect. This decision can be made only with an understanding of your broadcast traffic patterns.

Three types of NetBIOS names are kept in the name cache:

- *Individual* is a NetBIOS individual name.
- *Group* is a NetBIOS group name.
- *Unknown* means the router does not yet have information about the name, indicating that a search for the name is not complete.

Broadcast Reduction

To increase the bandwidth available on your network, Cisco routers configured for Source-Route bridging can convert broadcast frames (*add name query*, *add group name query*, *name-recognized query* response, and certain datagram frames) to *specifically routed explorers* (SREs). This process is called *netbios name caching*. NetBIOS name caching can be enabled on Cisco routers supporting Remote Source-Route bridging and local Source-Route bridging with the following IOS command:

```
Netbios enable-name-cache
```

If you are using Source Routing, use source-bridge proxy explorer in conjunction with NetBIOS Name Caching. This option allows SREs and NetBIOS names to be cached to reduce broadcast radiation across the network.

NetBIOS Cache Aging

The router ages name cache entries to ensure those cached routes remain consistent with the current network topology. If the name cache table lookup mechanism does not access a cache entry within the interval set by the administrator, the cache entry is aged, and the router deletes the entry from the table. Cisco allows you to adjust the aging time for the name/RIF cache using the `netbios-name-cache timeout` *minutes*, which is a Source-Routing bridge global configuration command. You can also adjust the NetBIOS name cache name length for the number of characters to cache in the NetBIOS table.

Cisco provides a NetBIOS option that enables the router to drop frames when the router detects multiple NetBIOS Add.Name, Add_Query frames generated from the same station. The command used to configure this option is `netbios name-cache query-timeout` *seconds*. The Cisco IOS command for FIND_NAME and NAME_RECOGNIZED is `netbios name-cache recognized-timeout` *seconds.*

Statically Configured NetBIOS Names

You can add static NetBIOS names and associated RIF entries into the router for those servers and stations static with heavy communications among multiple network users. These entries are independent of the name and RIF entries learned dynamically in the name cache. The static RIF must reflect a valid learned route. The Cisco IOS command for building static entries for a particular interface is `netbios name-cache` *mac-address netbios-name interface-name*. The Cisco IOS command for building static entries for a remote device is as follows:

```
Netbios name-cache mac-address netbios-name ring-group group-number.
```

Questions

1. What is NetBIOS?
   A. Network Basic Input/Out System   C. Network Basic Interface System
   B. Network Broadcast input/output System   D. None of the above

2. Cisco supports which of the following NetBIOS Protocols?
   A. NetBIOS Extended user interface (NetBEUI)
   B. Server Message Block (SMB)
   C. Add Name Query
   D. All of the above

3. NetBIOS over NetBEUI is a _____ Protocol.
   A. Layer 2   D. Layer 4
   B. Layer 3   E. Layer 7
   C. Layer 5

4. NetBIOS over NetBEUI uses which of the following protocol services?
   A. Connection-oriented   C. Acknowledge connection-less service
   B. Connection-less   D. All of the above

5. Identify the NetBIOS commands used by clients to initiate station registration.
   A. Add Name Query   C. Find name
   B. Add Group   D. All of the above

6. NetBIOS uses Broadcasts for which of the following operations?
   A. Registering a name   D. Session maintenance
   B. Registering a group   E. None of the above
   C. Finding a name

7. What is the NetBIOS name size in Bytes?
   A. 10   C. 16
   B. 15   D. 12

8. A NetBIOS name must be unique only:
   A. Between routers   C. Single LAN segments
   B. Between switches   D. Between bridges

9. The LAN_A_Num in the NetBIOS header is used to identify what?
   A. The number of NIC adapters in a end station
   B. The number of NetBIOS sessions
   C. The number of NetBIOS connections
   D. The number of NetBIOS commands supported

10. The Send and Receive Time Out options in the NetBIOS Control Block (NCB) are:
    A. 500ms   C. 150ms
    B. 200ms   D. None of the above

11. The NetBIOS Add Name query is used to do what?
   A. Find a service on the network   **D.** Register a name on the NetBIOS network
   B. Locate a Window 95 Client   **E.** A & D
   C. Add overhead to the router   **F.** None of the above

12. Routers can route NetBIOS over NetBEUI frames using which of the following?
   A. IP Only   **D.** APPN
   B. DLSw   **E.** EIGRP
   C. RSRB

13. Cisco routers can filter NetBIOS traffic using which of the following?
   A. MAC Address   **C.** Wildcards
   B. NetBIOS Name

14. Cisco Routers support NetBIOS Name Caching using:
   A. Token Ring   **D.** Serial
   B. FDDI   **E.** HSSI
   C. Ethernet

15. Cisco Routers support Static NetBIOS Name Tables.
   A. True   **B.** False

16. NetBIOS was developed by whom?
   A. IBM   **D.** Novell
   B. Sytek   **E.** Digital Equipment Corporation (DEC)
   C. Microsoft

17. NetBIOS supports which of the following Services to Applications and Protocols?
   A. Data Gram Service   **C.** Session Service
   B. Name Service   **D.** Route discovery

18. What does the NetBIOS `Name in conflict` command define?
   A. Duplicate Name detected   **C.** Negative response to add name
   B. Duplicate NetBIOS Address   **D.** Duplicate ring number discovered

19. NetBIOS over Token Ring uses what type of Source Routing Broadcasts?
   A. All Routes Broadcast   **C.** Spanning tree
   B. Single Routes Broadcast   **D.** None of the above

20. The NetBIOS Datagram service uses LLC ____ communication?
   A. LLC3   **C.** LLC1
   B. LLC2   **D.** None of the above

21. The NetBIOS session service uses LLC ____ communication?
   A. LLC1   **C.** LLC3
   B. LLC2

22. NetBIOS over IPX uses which packet type?
   A. 451   **C.** 4
   B. 20   **D.** 6

23. NetBIOS Datagram Service uses which UDP Port Number?
  A. 138
  B. 137
  C. 139
  D. 121

24. NetBIOS Session Service uses which TCP port number?
  A. 139
  B. 69
  C. 111
  D. 53

25. NetBIOS Name Service uses which TCP Port Number?
  A. 137
  B. 141
  C. 161
  D. 121

26. What is the NetBIOS ADD GROUP Query command used for?
  A. To register a group
  B. To find a group
  C. To name a group
  D. None of the above

27. NetBIOS over TCP/IP is defined in which RFC?
  A. RFC 1795
  B. RFC 1001/1002
  C. RFC 1276
  D. RFC 1700

28. What is the size of the Destination and Source MAC addresses in NetBEUI?
  A. 16 Bytes
  B. 8 Bytes
  C. 6 Bytes
  D. None of the above

29. What is the LLC Protocol Data Unit SAP ID for NetBIOS over NetBEUI?
  A. F0
  B. E0
  C. 06
  D. BC

30. Which of the following commands define the dead time interval for NetBIOS?
  A. netbios name-cache query-timeout *seconds*
  B. netbios name-cache seconds
  C. netbios name-cache seconds query-timeout
  D. none of the above

31. What is NetBIOS over NetBEUI name resolution?
  A. A server configured as a DNS Server
  B. /etc/Hosts
  C. Broadcast for registration and resolution
  D. Local cache of local names

32. Identify the command to enable NetBIOS name caching.
  A. netbios cache-enable
  B. netbios enable-name-cache
  C. netbios name-cache-enable
  D. netbios enable-cache

33. Identify the NetBIOS command used to limit the number of characters validated by the cache.
  A. netbios name-cache name-len length
  B. netbios name-cache length
  C. netbios name-len length

34. What is the purpose of the NetBIOS `name-cache query-timeout` command?

35. What is the purpose of the NetBIOS `name-cache recognized-timeout` command?

36. What is the NetBIOS functional address for Token Ring ?
    A. c00000000080
    B. c00000000100
    C. c00000000200
    D. c00000000400

37. What is the NetBIOS address over Ethernet?
    A. 030000000001
    B. 300000000010
    C. 030000000010
    D. 030000000100

38. The NetBIOS `name query` command is sent using which explorer type?
    A. All Routes Explorer
    B. Single Route Explorer
    C. Direct
    D. None of the above

39. The NetBIOS `name recognize` command is sent from the server to the client using which explorer type?
    A. All Routes Explorer
    B. Single Route Explorer
    C. Direct

40. You can customize NetBIOS broadcast reduction capabilities using which caching mechanisms?
    A. NetBIOS name caching
    B. Cache Aging
    C. NetBIOS broadcast damping
    D. RIF Caching
    E. All of the above

41. NetBIOS sends a local ring test command to discover if a device is on its local ring in source routing.
    A. True
    B. False

Answers

1. A
2. D
3. C
4. A and B
5. A
6. A, B, and C
7. C
8. B, C, and D
9. A
10. A
11. D
12. A, B, C
13. A and B
14. A, B, and C
15. A
16. A and B
17. D
18. A
19. B
20. C
21. B
22. B
23. A
24. A
25. A
26. A
27. B
28. C
29. A
30. A
31. C
32. B
33. A
34. this command is used to drop any repeat or duplicate (add name query, add group query, status_query)
35. This command is used to drop any repeat find_name or name_recognized frame.
36. A
37. A
38. B
39. A
40. E
41. A

Working with AppleTalk

AppleTalk is a networking architecture developed by Apple Computer, Inc., as shown in Figure 6.1. The architecture was developed to interconnect Apple's network devices, such as workstations, servers, and printers. The protocols fit the framework of the seven-layer *Open System Interconnection* (OSI) reference model.

Cisco Systems AppleTalk Routing

Cisco's AppleTalk implementation supports the following protocols:

- *AppleTalk Address Resolution Protocol* (AARP)
- *Routing Table Maintenance Protocol* (RTMP)
- *Name-Binding Protocol* (NBP)
- *AppleTalk Echo Protocol* (AEP)
- *AppleTalk Transaction Protocol* (ATP)
- *Zone Information Protocol* (ZIP)

At the Physical layer, Apple supports the standard wiring plans used with technologies such as Ethernet, Token Ring, FDDI, and ATM. AppleTalk networks running these technologies must adhere to the physical limitations imposed by the standards body that developed these specifications. AppleTalk offers the following features to network applications:

- Data link-layer independence
- Capability to run on a variety of cabling and data-link network types
- Multiple Transport Technologies (i.e., LocalTalk, EtherTalk, TokenTalk, FDDITalk, etc.)
- Internetwork routing
- Capability to build large or geographically dispersed networks

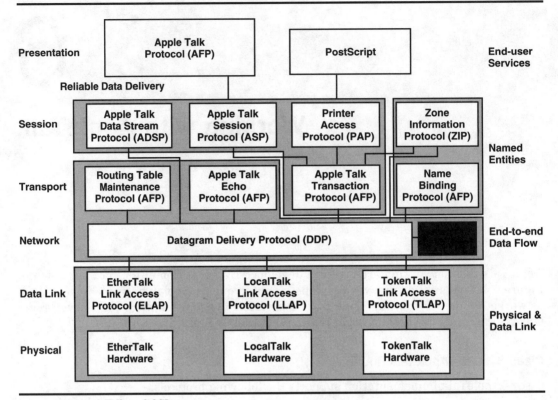

FIGURE 6.1   AppleTalk and OSI

- Naming service
- Easy identification of network resources
- Broad session-layer support
- Reliable data transfer for file and print services over the network
- AppleTalk tunneling via AURP

Data Link and Physical Layers

The Data Link and Physical layers provide for connectivity. The hardware media and the device drivers comprise the Physical layer.

The physical hardware provides nodes on a network with a shared data transmission medium called a *link*. The Data Link layer includes a protocol that specifies the physical aspects of the data link and the link-access protocol, which handles the logistics of sending the data packet over the transport medium. AppleTalk is designed to be data-link independent, allowing for the use of various types of hardware and their link-access protocols.

Link-Access Protocols

AppleTalk supports various network (or link) types and allows the user to select and switch among the types of networks to be used based on how the user's machine is configured; that is, if the machine has the proper hardware and software installed for a link type, the user can select that link. AppleTalk includes the link-access protocols for LocalTalk, EtherTalk, TokenTalk, ATM, and FDDITalk. To achieve link independence, AppleTalk relies on the *Link-Access Protocol* (LAP) Manager, which is a set of operating-system utilities, not an AppleTalk protocol. The LAP Manager is similar to Novell's *Open Datalink Interface* (ODI) and Microsoft's NDIS Link Layer device drivers. The main function of the LAP Manager is to act as a switching mechanism that connects the AppleTalk link-access protocol for the link type that the user selects to both the higher level AppleTalk protocols and the lower level hardware device driver for that data link.

Data Links

The data link protocols, which lie between the Physical layer and the end-to-end data flow protocols, handle the delivery of information between nodes on a local area network. The AppleTalk protocol architecture currently includes the following Data Link layer protocols:

- *LocalTalk Link Access Protocol* (LLAP)
- *AppleTalk Address Resolution Protocol* (AARP)
- *EtherTalk Link Access Protocol* (ELAP)
- *FDDITalk Link Access Protocol* (FLAP)
- *TokenTalk Link Access Protocol* (TLAP)

AppleTalk Address Resolution Protocol (AARP)

AARP is used by Macintoshes when they boot to dynamically learn their AppleTalk addresses; AARP ensures that each Macintosh has its own unique address. After a Macintosh boots successfully, it stores that address in its memory and attempts to use the same address the next time it boots. To achieve link-layer independence, AppleTalk packets are addressed to an AppleTalk Phase 2 address, which consists of a 16-bit network number and an 8-bit Node ID. In addition, when transmitting a packet, this module maps an AppleTalk node address onto a hardware address understood by the hardware being used (e.g., Ethernet, Token Ring, etc.).

AARP is also used for AppleTalk node to MAC address translation on Ethernet, Token Ring, and FDDI link layer networks. The AARP resides between the link access protocol and the LAP Manager.

AARP performs three basic functions:

- Determines the unique protocol address of an AppleTalk node for a given protocol set (such as the AppleTalk protocols)
- Maps between two address sets
- Filters packets within a given protocol set

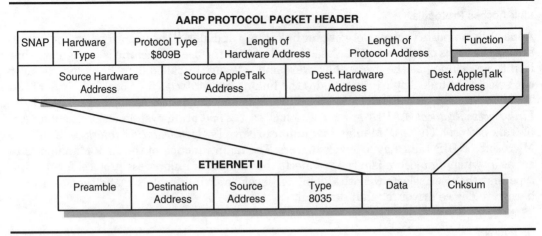

FIGURE 6.2 AARP stack

Within a node, AARP maintains an *Address Mapping Table* (AMT) for a given node to MAC address pair. In the case of EtherTalk, the AMT contains a list of AppleTalk protocol addresses and their corresponding Ethernet hardware addresses. AARP maps between any two sets of addresses.

A node's protocol address is unique from that of any other node attached to the network. Given an address for a node's protocol, AARP returns a corresponding hardware address for that node (or an error, if no node has such a protocol address). AARP verifies the protocol destination node address of all packets received by a given node and ensures that the destination address is either a broadcast address or the receiving node's protocol address. AARP helps dispatch the packet to the correct hardware address, and for incoming packets, makes sure that the corresponding protocol address is correct for that physical node.

AppleTalk AARP Addressing

The address-handling process consists of assigning new addresses and actually mapping a protocol address to a hardware address. The AARP format is shown in Figure 6.2.

Assigning New Addresses.   When a node is initialized, AARP assigns a unique protocol address for each protocol set running on the node. AARP can make this assignment, or the client can assign the address and then inform AARP.

The AARP approach takes three steps:

1. AARP assigns a tentative random address not already in the AMT.

2. AARP broadcasts probe packets to determine whether any other node is using the address.

3. If it is not in use, the tentative address becomes permanent, and AARP returns it to the client.

Otherwise, a receiving node notifies the probing node that the address is in use by returning a response packet. The probing node tries a new address and repeats this process until it can return a valid address to its client.

Mapping Addresses.   The process of actually mapping a protocol address to a hardware address begins with a request from an AARP client. Upon receiving a request, AARP scans the AMT to see whether the mapping is already there. If so, it returns the mapping information to the client. Otherwise, AARP initiates the following procedure:

1. AARP broadcasts a request packet that includes the protocol address for which mapping is required and the protocol set for mapping.
2. If a receiving node can match the protocol type to its protocol address, AARP returns a reply packet with the mapping information.
3. AARP enters this information in its AMT and passes it on to the client.

If the request packet does not result in a reply, AARP retransmits the packet a given number of times, after which it concludes that the node does not exist. AARP then returns an error message to the client.

AppleTalk implements dynamic address assignment. With this process, AppleTalk does not require that you specify all fields of an AppleTalk address when configuring a router. If another preconfigured AppleTalk router appears on the network, it can be called on to supply the required network number for the new router. The preconfigured router, known as a seed router, sends out the address information to all other routers on its connected network. The seed router is the one that comes up first and verifies the configuration of the other routers. If the configuration is valid, the other routers start functioning. The seed router comes up even if there are no other routers on the network. Routers that are not seed routers must first communicate with a seed router before they can function.

With dynamic addressing, a nonextended network device's node number is negotiated between AppleTalk hosts on the network (it may also be assigned by the network manager). AppleTalk automatically assigns node numbers, or when a user-defined address is in use, it randomly selects an initial value.

The node first tries the node number that was its most recent address. If that value is not available, the node then searches for the next available address. If it reaches up to 254 without finding an available node number, it keeps returning to 1 until it finds a free address. For nonseed routers, interfaces with AppleTalk enabled participate only in local routing until that interface's network number is determined. If 0 was specified for a network number, that interface does not forward any packets until it receives a valid network number. Upon receiving a routing table update, the router is informed of the network number for the interface receiving the packet with the update. Every table update contains the network number of the network on which the packet was sent. Through this exchange, the router determines the network number of the receiving interface.

AppleTalk Extended Networks and Address Resolution.   Nodes in an extended AppleTalk network always communicate by network number and node number. When a router is not used, dynamic address resolution occurs by assigning a random network number within a network range as well as by assigning a node number. Multiple zone names can be assigned to extended networks as well as network ranges. In this case, a node can access anything in any of the zones on the same cable as the node itself. A node can exist in only one zone and one network.

By adding a router to the network, a node starts up by using its newly obtained address for a short time. The node then requests a list of valid network numbers from the routers. These Apple nodes then select an unassigned address to obtain the actual AppleTalk address.

Maintaining the Address Mapping Table.   An AMT contains the known set of corresponding hardware and protocol addresses. To keep an AMT current, AARP performs three maintenance operations:

- Updating the table with new addresses
- Removing unused addresses
- Aging table entries

When AARP establishes a new mapping, it updates the table to reflect the new address. Should the table become full, AARP removes unused addresses via a least-recently-used algorithm.

When a node shuts down and a new node takes its address, the remaining nodes can have invalid addresses in their AMTs, or they may send replies to the wrong hardware address. To prevent invalid entries, AARP can use a timer with each entry. Within the timer value, the reception of a packet within a given time period causes an entry update or confirmation. If the timer expires before AARP receives a packet for an entry, AARP removes the entry from the AMT.

As another approach to avoid invalid entries, AARP can age-on-probe, removing an entry from the AMT upon receipt of a probe packet for the entry's protocol address. Although unnecessary removal can occur when a new node probes for an address already in use, age-on-probe guarantees that the AMT always contains the current mapping information.

Network Layer

The network layer specifies the network routing of data packets between nodes and the communication between networks (see Figure 6.3). AppleTalk's network layer protocol is the *Datagram Delivery Protocol* (DDP). DDP provides connectionless, socket-to-socket delivery of AppleTalk packets across an AppleTalk network. DDP routes AppleTalk packets from a source socket within one AppleTalk node to a destination socket within another node. The AppleTalk data encapsulated within a DDP packet is a datagram. DDP transfers data as discrete packets and does not ensure that all packets sent are received at the destination or are in the correct order. Higher level protocols that use DDP services provide for this kind of reliability.

DDP defines Internet/internetwork addressing schemes, while relying on the network hardware for the definition of node addressing. The network range assigned during network set up is the basis of DDP's internetwork addressing. Each network segment on an AppleTalk phase 2 network must be assigned a unique range of network addresses. This num-

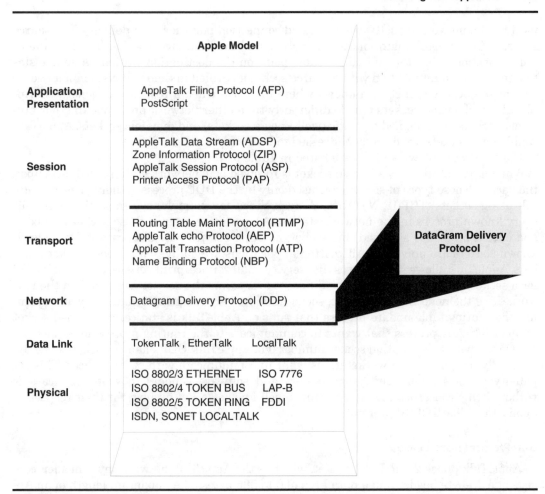

Apple Model

| Application Presentation | AppleTalk Filing Protocol (AFP) PostScript |

| Session | AppleTalk Data Stream (ADSP) Zone Information Protocol (ZIP) AppleTalk Session Protocol (ASP) Printer Access Protocol (PAP) |

| Transport | Routing Table Maint Protocol (RTMP) AppleTalk echo Protocol (AEP) AppleTalt Transaction Protocol (ATP) Name Binding Protocol (NBP) |

| Network | Datagram Delivery Protocol (DDP) |

| Data Link | TokenTalk , EtherTalk   LocalTalk |

| Physical | ISO 8802/3 ETHERNET   ISO 7776 ISO 8802/4 TOKEN BUS   LAP-B ISO 8802/5 TOKEN RING   FDDI ISDN, SONET LOCALTALK |

DataGram Delivery Protocol

FIGURE 6.3 AppleTalk DDP.

ber is used by routers to forward packets to their final destination. The AppleTalk Layer 3 Network address comes in the form of socket numbers. Because Apple's network operating system is multitasking and other non-Apple systems are multiuser and multitasking, socket numbers provide a means of addressing each process so that each process can be distinguished by DDP. As a process communicates across the network, it requests that a socket number be assigned. Any packets that DDP receives addressed to that socket are passed on to the upper layer process.

To communicate with another device, a network workstation needs an addressable endpoint to connect to. The initiator of the communication transfer must indicate the final destination for this data. The socket number tells network station software to deliver the incoming packet to a specific process or application in the network station. The only purpose of the socket numbers are as addressable endpoints in any network station.

All communications between a source and destination station on the network are achieved using a socket. Source and destination *sockets* are not physical devices but are used by the networking software as an end connection point for data delivery. The source socket is from the originator of the connection, and the destination socket indicates the final connection point (the end addressable point on the destination station). A source station initiates communication with a source socket identified in the DDP header of a packet so that the destination station knows where to attach when a response is generated. AppleTalk implements sockets a little differently than other network protocols. In other protocols, sockets are assigned as static (well-known sockets) and dynamic sockets. AppleTalk well-known sockets are directly addressed to DDP only.

The DDP well-known sockets are listed in Table 6.1.

When a packet that has a known socket is received by a network station, DDP acts upon the packet. These types of sockets are used only by the DDP process. Other types of protocols using sockets (TCP/IP, NetWare, Banyan Vines, for example) assign static sockets for every known process in the network station. A committee assigns these socket numbers, and once a process is assigned this socket, no other service may duplicate it. Those well-known sockets are universal. All written applications are addressed to these socket numbers. AppleTalk allows its processes (file service, mail service, print service, etc.) to ask DDP for a socket number, which could be different every time the service is started on the network. Like the node ID assignment, socket numbers are assigned dynamically. For example, the routing table update process that runs on AppleTalk is statically assigned socket number 0/h. Any process that wants to communicate to the routing process must identify the packet with a destination socket number 0/h. AppleTalk DDP enables sockets to be dynamically assigned when workstations want to communicate with other devices. This capability enables application programmers and software vendors to write applications without being concerned about acquiring a well-known socket number for their respective applications like TCP/IP protocols.

DDP Protocol Packet Layout

In AppleTalk phase 2, the DDP packet, which is the AppleTalk network-layer header, consists of a 13-byte header and a data area of 0 to 586 bytes. The maximum length of an AppleTalk packet, therefore (including the DDP header but not including any data link headers), is 599 bytes. Figures 6.3 and 6.4 show a description of the DDP packet header:

TABLE 6.1   AppleTalk DDP Sockets

Apple DDP Socket Number	Description
00h	Invalid
FFh	Invalid
01h	RTMP socket
02h	Names information socket
04h	Echoer socket
06h	*Zone information socket* (ZIP)
80h-FEh	Dynamically assigned

- *Hop Count.* This 6-bit field controls packet lifetime. When a packet is forwarded from the router, the sending node sets this field to 0. Each intermediate router on the path to the destination network increases this field by 1. If a router receives a DDP packet with a hop count of 15, the router does not forward the packet to another router. If the destination node is not locally attached to this router, the packet is discarded. This field prevents packets from circulating indefinitely.

- *Datagram Length.* This 10-bit field contains the length of the DDP packet and is set to 0.

- *Destination Network Number.* This 16-bit field contains the network number of the destination node.

- *Source Network Number.* This 16-bit field contains the network number of the source node.

- *Destination Node ID.* This 8-bit field contains the node ID of the destination node.

- *Source Node ID.* This 8-bit field contains the node ID of the source node.

- *Destination Socket Number.* This 8-bit field contains the socket number in the destination node that receives the packet. A destination Internet socket address is formed by this field and the destination network number field, and the destination node ID field.

```
LLC:    -- LLC Header --
LLC:
LLC:    DSAP Address = AA, DSAP IG Bit = 00 (Individual Address)
LLC:    SSAP Address = AA, SSAP CR Bit = 00 (Command)
LLC:    Unnumbered frame: UI
LLC:
SNAP: -- SNAP Header --
SNAP:
SNAP: Vendor ID = Apple
SNAP: Type = 809B (AppleTalk)
SNAP:
DDP:-- DDP header --
DDP:
DDP:    Hop count          = 0
DDP:    Length             = 25
DDP:    Checksum           = 0000
DDP:    Destination Network Number = 0
DDP:    Destination Node          = 255
DDP:    Destination Socket        = 6 (Zone)
DDP:    Source Network Number     = 1474
DDP:    Source Node               = 1
DDP:    Source Socket             = 6 (Zone)
DDP:    DDP protocol type = 6 (Zone)
DDP:
ZIP:-- ZIP header --
ZIP:
ZIP:    ZIP command     = 5 (GetNetInfo)
ZIP:    Zone            = "ZoneD"
ZIP:[Normal end of "ZIP header".]
```

FIGURE 6.4 AppleTalk DDP header trace

- *Source Socket Number.*   This 8-bit field contains the socket number in the source node that originated the packet. A source Internet socket address is formed by this field and the source network number and source node ID fields.

- *DDP Type.*   DDP is used by other AppleTalk protocols to transmit information. This 1-byte field contains a hexadecimal value which identifies the protocol client that originated the packet.

- *DATA.*   This field can contain up to 586 bytes of packet data.

What Is an AppleTalk Network Number?

AppleTalk uses an addressing scheme to uniquely identify each device on an AppleTalk network. This AppleTalk addressing scheme consists of a network number, node number, and socket number. Think of this addressing scheme as an address on an envelope. The network number is equivalent to the street name; the node number is equivalent to the street number; and the socket is equivalent to a suite within the building. When an AppleTalk router is used to combine two different AppleTalk network segments, each segment is assigned its own unique network number by the router. The Macintoshes and peripherals are responsible for assigning themselves a valid node and socket number. Users are rarely interested in the socket number so an AppleTalk address is usually written as a net and node ID pair.

AppleTalk network devices are identified by a unique 24-bit Internet address that consists of a 16-bit network number and an 8-bit AppleTalk node identifier. In AppleTalk phase 2, each network device has a unique range of network numbers. Each network number in the range specified can be associated with 253 available node IDs. Thus, the number of active devices that a network can support is equal to the number of network numbers multiplied by 253.

AppleTalk phase 2 introduced the capability to support routed and nonrouted nodes.

AppleTalk Phase 1 Architecture

AppleTalk phase 1 provided support for one 16-bit network. The network supported only 254 nodes per segment, which consisted of 127 end nodes and 127 servers, and each node was dynamically assigned the AppleTalk DDP `network.node` address using a 16-bit network number and an 8-bit node number pair. Phase 1 supports only one AppleTalk zone. Zones will be discussed later.

AppleTalk Phase 2 Architecture

AppleTalk phase 2 removed the single network limitation to a LAN segment and replaced it with a network cable-range. This modification allows network architects to implement multiple networks per LAN segment, supporting 253 nodes per network number, not per LAN segment as was the case with phase 1 AppleTalk. With phase 2, network numbers are still dynamically assigned using the 24-bit `network.node` pair from DDP address space. The number of zones has been increased from 1 to 255, making segmentation by service more definable to the corporate environment.

Integrating AppleTalk Phase 1 and 2

Two major problems with the phase 1 specification were lack of support for Token Ring and that it worked only with Xerox's version of Ethernet rather than the IEEE 802.3 standard implementation. Phase 2 solves both of these problems, supporting 802.3 Ethernet and 4- and 16-Mbit/sec 802.5 Token Ring networks.

In a phase 1 network, the Ethernet backbone could have only one zone. Phase 2 solves this problem by introducing the idea of multiple Ethernet zones and removing the one-to-one relationship between the LAN backbone and the zone name. Phase 2 networks can assign as many as 255 zone names to one LAN segment and its devices. Multiple zone names give network managers the flexibility to place file, communications, database, mail, and other servers and devices on the high-speed backbone, but users see only the devices they need in their local network. With phase 2, the LAN and Local Talk zone names are maintained in the AppleTalk routers on the backbone. Each router contains a *Zone Information Table*. This table is used by the routers to maintain the integrity of the network. Each router's Zone Information Table contains all known networks that it can reach.

Probably the most significant advantage of phase 2 is its extended addressing format. In both phase 1 and phase 2, each node has an 8-bit node number and a 16-bit network number that combine to make the network node's address. When an AppleTalk device is started, it uses AARP to generate and broadcast a node number between 1 and 254. This number is used for its node address. If another node on the same network is using that number, that node replies that the number is already in use. The requesting Macintosh then generates and broadcasts another number until it does not hear a response from the network. At this point, it assumes that the number is unique and uses that number for its node address.

Phase 1 placed strict limits on the 16-bit network number. All devices on a phase 1 network had to have the same network number. In effect, the node address was the network address, so the Internet could have only 254 nodes. Phase 2 increased this number by establishing network ranges with the 16-bit network number. A network range is a contiguous range of numbers that the network administrator gives to Macintoshes on the network.

Phase I networks allowed only a single network number per LAN or WAN. Phase II allows multiple network numbers per network signal. This range of network numbers is referred to as a cable range.

> *NOTE:* *On a LAN, LocalTalk couldn't take advantage of phase 1, much less phase 2, addressing because of its inherent cabling limitations—Local Talk supports only 32 devices per network. By comparison, Ethernet FDDI, ATM, and Token Ring are not held to these limits.*

Table 6.2 provides a comparison of AppleTalk phase 2 and phase 1 capabilities.

Transport Layer

The Transport layer isolates some of the physical and functional aspects of a packet network from the upper three layers (see Figure 6.1). This layer provides for end-to-end accountability, ensuring that all packets of data sent across the network are received and are in the correct order. This process is *reliable delivery of data* and provides a means of identifying packet loss and supplying a retransmission mechanism. The Transport layer also provides connection and session management services.

TABLE 6.2   Comparison of Appletalk phase 2 and phase 1 capabilities

Function	AppleTalk Phase 1	AppleTalk Phase 2
Maximum number of nodes	254 (node addresses 0 and 255 are reserved)	253
Number of networks per cable system	1	65,279
Number of zones/network	1	255 extended, 1 non-extended
Maximum number of end nodes	127	Not applicable
Maximum number of servers	127	Not applicable

AppleTalk implements the following protocols at the Transport layer, and these protocols are implemented in the Cisco IOS software:

- *Name-Binding Protocol* (NBP)
- *AppleTalk Transaction Protocol* (ATP)
- *AppleTalk Echo Protocol* (AEP)
- *Routing Table Maintenance Protocol* (RTMP)

AppleTalk routers can use the RTMP, which is a Transport layer protocol to keep other AppleTalk configured routers informed of network reachability information measured in hops. This is accomplished by each router sending an RTMP broadcast every 10 seconds and informing all other routers on the internetwork of its network number and the network start and end ranges. Within the RTMP broadcasts are the number of hops required to reach a given network. Therefore, when a router joins a network, it sends a *Zone Information Protocol* (ZIP) broadcast, a component of RTMP, to alert other routers of its existence. RTMP's aging plays a vital role in maintaining the integrity of a network. Aging is the process whereby routers purge their tables of networks that they have not heard from lately. When a router receives an RTMP packet from another router, the Zone Information Table maintains a *good* entry for this network. When a network goes down, the router for that network fails to send RTMP broadcasts. All existing routers flag the silent network as *suspect*. After 90 seconds without hearing from the suspect router, the router flags the suspect router *bad* and deletes its network name and number from its table. Traffic is no longer routed to or from this zone. Figure 6.5 shows the RTMP packet format.

Routing Table Maintenance Protocol

RTMP builds and maintains the routing tables used by Internet routers to forward AppleTalk packets through the Internet as depicted in Table 6.3 and Figure 6.6.

When a router is activated on a network, it generates an initial table that contains descriptive information about each of its ports, including the port number, AppleTalk network number range of the network attached to the port, and the node address of the router where

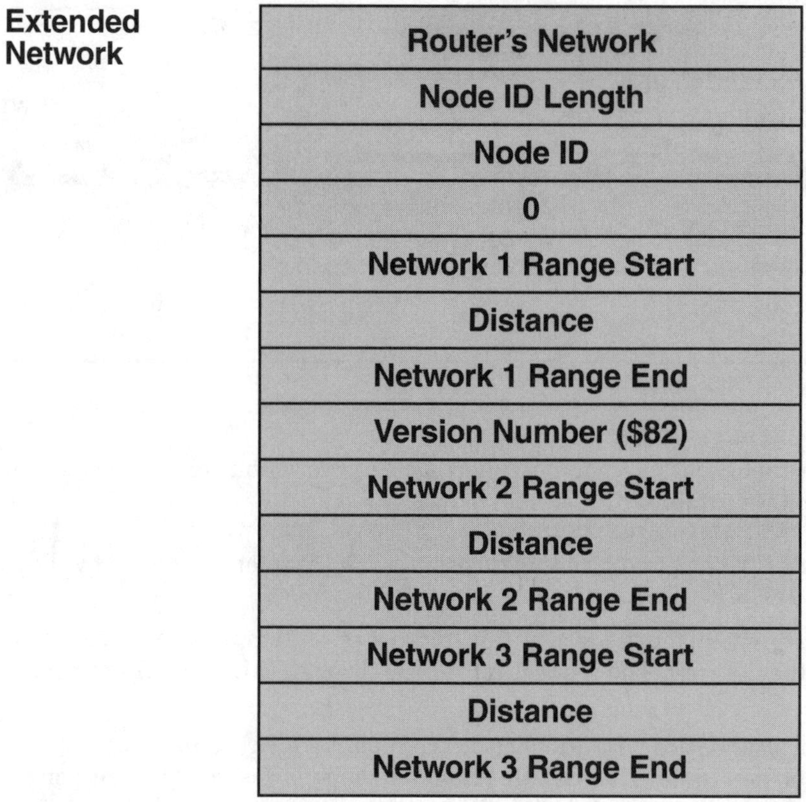

Extended Network

Router's Network
Node ID Length
Node ID
0
Network 1 Range Start
Distance
Network 1 Range End
Version Number ($82)
Network 2 Range Start
Distance
Network 2 Range End
Network 3 Range Start
Distance
Network 3 Range End

FIGURE 6.5 RTMP header format

TABLE 6.3 RTMP routing table

Network Range	Distance	Port	Next Intermediate Router	Status
100	0	1	0	Good
300–400	0	2	0	Good
500	0 at least 1 hop away	2	300.1	Good

the network is attached. The table also identifies router ports not connected to AppleTalk networks.

After the initial table is built, the router receives RTMP data packets from all other routers accessible to it. The receiving router uses the information in the packet to update its own routing table with entries indicating the shortest path to reachable networks in the Internet.

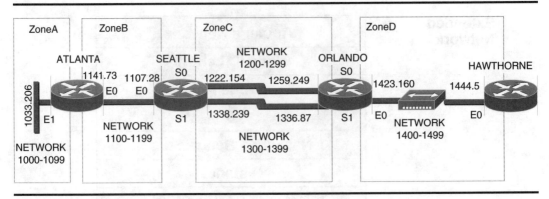

FIGURE 6.6 AppleTalk Phase II network

The routing table contains one entry for each network that can be reached from the router. Each entry contains:

- *Network Range.* This network number exists on the Internet as defined by the network administrator.
- *Distance.* The request must traverse this number of routers in its path between two systems on the network. The request must pass through this number of physical router devices.
- *Port.* The physical device port attached to the router, which corresponds to the network number. If the hop count is 0, then this number range is assigned to that port. If the hop count is larger than 0, this port indicates the one from which the network number was learned. Likewise, this entry indicates the port to which the router forwards the packet directly.
- *Next Intermediate Router.* The next router allows requests that cannot be handled by the local router to be forwarded to a designated router to get a path to the final destination. If the network number is directly attached to the router, the table does not have an entry for this option.

AppleTalk, like other protocols such as TCP/IP, XNS, DECnet, and OSI, must allow its routing tables to be maintained throughout the network. This process of letting other routers in the network exchange data in their routing tables for periodic updates is paramount in letting users access resources unavailable to them on their network cable range. This routing table update allows routers to find the shortest path to a destination and to know when a new router comes on line or when a route is no longer available. The distance to a network is measured in hops. The number of hops is equal to the number of routers a packet passes through on its way to the destination network. A router can access networks up to 15 hops away.

> **NOTE:** *The hop count from a router port to a locally connected network is 0.*

The AppleTalk RTMP aging table changes each time a routing update is transmitted by a router. AppleTalk is one of the few routing protocols that use a hop count of 0. Any network number associated with a hop count of 0 is considered to be the local network number. Each entry in a router table must be updated periodically to ensure that the path to a destination is still available. Otherwise, a route stays in the table and may not be valid. To delete older entries, a timer is started upon receipt of each routing update.

RTMP broadcasts a routing table every 10 seconds. Entries in the table are aged to keep the routing information current. The validity of entries is checked every 20 seconds. If an RTMP update has not been received for a network within that time, the entry is flagged as suspect. If a suspect entry is not confirmed as valid within 20 seconds, the entry is flagged as bad. If a bad entry is not confirmed as valid within 90 seconds, the entry is removed from the table. To quickly inform routers that a path to a network is no longer valid, RTMP uses a technique called notify neighbor. When RTMP flags an entry as bad in a routing table, it notifies neighboring routers of this fact in the next RTMP data packet sent, by setting the hop count for the bad entry to 31. Each router receiving the RTMP data packet checks to see whether the router the packet was sent from is the next router on the path to the network. If the router that sent the RTMP data packet is the next router in the path, the receiving router also flags its routing table entry for the network as bad. If the router is not the next router in the path, the receiving router ignores the notification because it has an alternate route to the network.

RTMP uses another technique called *split horizon* to reduce the amount of routing table information broadcast in the Internet. The split horizon technique is based on the concept that when a router receives information about a network on a port, it does not need to forward that information back out of the same port. Consequently, RTMP does not send a routing table entry out of the same port on which it was received. RTMP removes these entries from the RTMP data packet before transmitting the packet. This technique reduces the size of the routing tables broadcast from each port and prevents routing loops.

> **NOTE:** *To solve problems associated with excessive RTMP traffic on local and wide area networks, Apple has developed and implemented a new routing protocol,* Apple Update Routing Protocol *(AURP), which is similar to link state protocols in that updates to the network occur only when changes have been made to the network. This practice reduces the overall maintenance protocol overhead associated with the routing table updates.*

AppleTalk Update-Based Routing Protocol

The *AppleTalk Update Routing Protocol* (AURP) is an AppleTalk standard routing protocol used as an enhancement for AppleTalk Phase II networks. This feature enables two isolated AppleTalk networks to be connected over a TCP/IP network. AURP provides update-based routing and reliable delivery of routing information. To reduce the amount of bandwidth, update-based routing sends updates to peer routers only when network routing information changes, rather than sending periodic broadcasts of the routing table (see Figure 6.7).

Like RTMP, AURP provides distance-vector, split-horizon routing. AURP has a maximum hop count of 15; a tunnel counts as one hop. Apple's plan to grow AppleTalk to serve the new wide area world is embodied in a new set of phase 2-compatible routing enhancements. AURP is intended to serve the networking and interconnect needs of the full spectrum of users, from small workgroups to enterprise-wide networks. AURP was developed as a complement to, and not a replacement for, RTMP. The main difference between the two routing protocols, AURP and RTMP, is that there is little or no routing traffic over the AURP link if the Internet is stable.

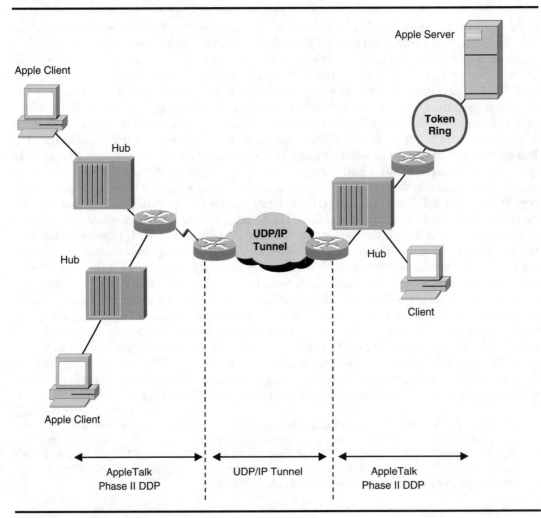

FIGURE 6.7   AURP example

AURP features include the following:

- Tunneling (encapsulating AppleTalk) in TCP/IP and other foreign (non-AppleTalk) networks
- Uses currently in place infrastructure to provide wide area connectivity
- Basic system security through device- and network-hiding
- Easily tailored to meet enterprise security standards
- Hop-count reduction
- Allows creation of larger Internets
- Update-based (changes only) routing information
- Reduces WAN traffic

- Point-to-point tunneling provides connectivity over serial lines and X.25
- Minimizes traffic and improves efficiency
- Remapping of remote network numbers
- Automatically resolves network-numbering conflicts
- Internet networks number clustering
- Minimizes LAN routing traffic and route information storage
- Improved use of alternate paths through hop-count weighting and backup paths
- More efficient use of network resources

AURP is used by external routers to exchange routing information over TCP/IP tunnels. The external router interacts with AppleTalk's existing DDP and other upper layer protocols to exchange routing information across the network using AURP as the tunnel. To forward data across the tunnel, the exterior router must assign a domain identifier to the local AppleTalk network. The domain identifier contains three fields:

- *Length*. A single octet containing the length of the identifier
- *Authority*. The authority that administrates the identifier of the domain
- *Identifier*. Domain identifier

On a stable network, AppleTalk routers using RTMP broadcast the same information to each other every 10 seconds. Because most networks are stable after initial setup, these frequent broadcasts unnecessarily consume bandwidth that could be used to transport more user data. This is particularly noticeable on slow WAN links. Unlike RTMP, AppleTalk routers using the AURP protocol exchange routing information every 30 seconds by default.

Routing information exchanged with AURP must be communicated reliably. Because only changes are communicated among AURP routers, the possibility of lost information is increased. Therefore, AURP is a transport protocol that provides reliable delivery. AURP requires the receiving router to acknowledge the receipt of the updates.

Name Binding Protocol

Name Binding Protocol (NBP) is an AppleTalk distributed name service, which means that each network station acts as a name server. The NBP process provides four types and levels of services:

- *Name registration*. Registers its name for name to address mapping
- *Name deletion*. Deletes the name to address mapping to terminate operation
- *Name lookup*. Responds to a name registration
- *Name confirmation*. Confirms name mapping

The AppleTalk NBP protocol, when started on a network station, registers the name and associated socket number in the names table. When this process removes itself from the network station, it also asks NBP to remove its name and socket number from the name table. NBP then places the *Network Visible Entity* (NVE) in the name directory. Name

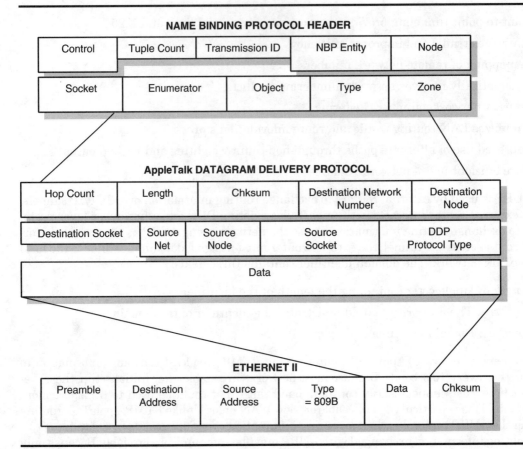

FIGURE 6.8 NBP stack

lookup occurs when a request for a name-to-internet address binding is required, and name confirmation occurs to check the validity of the current binding. The NBP stack is shown in Figure 6.8).

Name Binding Protocol Header Descriptions

- *Function.* This 4-bit field is used to identify the type of NBP message contained within the NBP packet: the values are Broadcast Request, Lookup Request, Lookup Reply, and Forward Request.

- *Tuple Count.* Number of address mapping in the packet. Broadcast Request, Forward Request, and Lookup packet carry one tuple. The tuple counts for these packets are always equal to one.

- *NBP ID.* This 8-bit field allows a node to have multiple lookup requests.

- *NBP tuple.* The NBP tuple addresses the name-address pairs. The tuple consists of the entity's Internet socket address.

- *Node ID*. This field contains the AppleTalk node ID of the named entity.
- *Socket Number*. This field contains the AppleTalk socket address of the named entity.
- *Enumerator*. This field differentiates between various aliases assigned to the same entity.
- *Object Field Length*. This field is the network visible entity length of the object.
- *Object*. This field contains 1 to 32 characters that identify the NVE.
- *Type Field Length*. This field contains the length of the type portion.
- *Type*. This field contains 1 to 32 characters that identify the type of NVE.
- *Zone Field Length*. This field contains the length of the zone portion of the name.
- *Zone*. This field contains the zone portion of the NVE name.

***Name Binding Protocol* (NBP).**   The router uses this Transport layer protocol when mapping entity names to protocol addresses for named entities on the Internet. These network names are associated with the type of service provided by the entity. Printing, file sharing, and mail service are examples of service types. All NBP Broadcast Requests received by a router are transformed into one or more NBP lookup packets. The router forwards lookup packets as normal DDP data packets. The router does not have an entity name.

AppleTalk refers to the individual sockets in a node as *network-visible entities*. These entities provide services and can be accessed using DDP. An example of an entity would be an electronic mailbox on a mail server. AppleTalk entities can have one or more logical names, each of which is represented by a character string. The NBP maps the logical name of an entity to an Internet socket address. The use of names simplifies the identification of resources in the AppleTalk network and allows the underlying address of an entity to change dynamically without affecting end users.

Entity names take the form `object: type@zone`, where each of the object, type, and zone fields can be a string of up to 32 characters. The colon (:) and at-sign (@) characters are required delimiters. The name `Printer1: Laser@engineering`, for example could describe a laser printer resource available to the engineering department.

Special characters can be used within entity names. The equal sign (=) can be used in place of an object or type field string to signify all possible values (for example, `=Laser@Engineering`). A single tilde (~) can be used as a wildcard character representing 0 or more characters anywhere within the object or type fields (for example, `Print~:Laser@Engineering`). An asterisk (*) can be used in a zone field to signify the default zone (the requester's zone).

All AppleTalk entity names are case insensitive. Consequently, the name `brad:Mailbox@Home` is equivalent to the name `BRAD:MAILBOX@HOME`.

Each AppleTalk node maintains a names directory that maps all entity names in the node to their Internet socket addresses. The NBP implementation in each node is responsible for registering names in the directory, searching for names, and deleting names from the directory. Names are registered in the directory each time the node is started. NBP is used by nodes to learn the addresses of resources in other nodes. The NBP process in a node transmits an NBP Broadcast Request packet to an Internet router to request information about resources in specified zones. The router forwards the packet to other routers on the paths to networks associated with the specified zones when the request reaches a router directly connected to a destination network; the router broadcasts the request on the network. Replies are returned through the Internet to the requesting node. AppleTalk routers limit the broadcasting of name searches to those networks that contain nodes, which are members of the zone specified in the search request.

AppleTalk Echo Protocol. The *AppleTalk Echo Protocol* (AEP) is used to test whether a node can be reached through the network. AEP uses DDP to transmit an Echo Request packet to a node on the network. If the node is reachable, it responds with an Echo Reply packet. The AEP function in the sending node checks the reply packet to verify that it is identical to the packet sent to the destination node. AppleTalk requires that all routers implement AEP.

This protocol is used when a network workstation has found the designation station it wants to talk to and submits an echo packet (DDP socket number 4) to test the path. When the reply comes, it notes the time and submits the packet to establish a connection to that station. A value of 4 identifies it as an AEP packet, and AEP then examines the first byte of the packet's data portion. A value of 1 identifies the packet as an echo request packet (sent out from your endpoint), and a value of 2 identifies the packet as an echo reply packet (returned to your endpoint from the remote node). If the packet is an echo request packet, AEP changes this first byte to a value of 2 (an echo reply packet) before calling DDP to send the packet back to the socket from which it originated. This protocol can be used to establish timers for packet time-outs and can assist in the tuning of the protocols as related to the *AppleTalk Transaction Protocol* (ATP), the *AppleTalk Session Protocol* (ASP), and other upper layer protocols.

You can use the AEP, a client of DDP, to measure the performance of an AppleTalk network or to test for the presence of a given node. Knowing the approximate speed at which an AppleTalk network delivers packets is helpful in understanding the behavior of an application that uses higher level AppleTalk protocols. AEP is implemented in each node as a DDP client process referred to as the AEP Echoer. When the endpoint associated with this socket receives a packet, AEP examines the packet's DDP type.

AppleTalk Transaction Protocol (ATP). ATP is a transaction-based protocol that ensures that data flows reliably between network nodes. A transaction is a single packet request that results in a multipacket response; both the request and the response carry data. The request/response framework of transactions provides a mechanism for detecting errors and for retransmitting data. ATP uses the services of DDP to deliver data and, in turn, provides a transport service on which session protocols, like ASP and PAP, are built. If used directly, ATP provides reliable but independent data transfers, sometimes called *reliable datagrams*. The ATP ensures reliable delivery of AppleTalk packets sent from a source socket to a destination socket. ATP is based on a model in which a process in one node requests services from a process in another node. The process in the responding node then reports back on the outcome of the request. The interaction between the two nodes is called a transaction.

ATP transactions consist of one workstation initiating the communications transaction by asking or giving a command—in this case issuing a request for the contents of a subdirectory. The ATP transaction request is numbered to provide a link between request and response. The ATP also informs the responding devices of how many packets (up to a maximum of eight) it can hold in memory for the answer. The series of response packets is sent until the requester's memory space is full or the answer request is complete. In this case, with a window size of 8, packets are not big enough to hold the entire answer; the requester can immediately initiate a new transport request to receive the remaining portion of the answer. ATP is useful if your application sends small amounts of data and can tolerate a minor degree of performance degradation.

Session Layer Protocols.   The Session layer serves as an interface into the Transport layer, which is below it. The Session layer allows for *session establishment,* the process of setting up a connection over which a dialog between two applications or processes can occur. Some of the functions that the Session layer provides for are flow control, establishment of synchronization points for checks and recovery for file transfer, full-duplex and half-duplex dialogs between processes, and aborts and restarts.

The AppleTalk protocols implemented at the Session layer are ADSP, ASP, and ZIP. Cisco implements only *Zone Information Protocol* (ZIP) at this layer.

- *AppleTalk Data Stream Protocol* (ADSP) provides its own stream-based Transport layer services that allow for full-duplex dialogs.

- *AppleTalk Session Protocol* (ASP) uses the transaction-based services of ATP to transport workstation commands to servers.

- *Zone Information Protocol* (ZIP) provides applications and processes with access to zone names. Each node on a network belongs to a zone.

One physical address is available for every network station on the Internet. Network layer addresses are provided so that the network layer is able to route the data over the network if needed. Socket numbers are needed so that when data arrives at the final destination, the data is forwarded by DDP to the appropriate software process. Many addresses are used throughout the AppleTalk network. To eliminate the need for users to remember all the network addresses, node addresses, sockets, and so forth of the network and Data Link layers, a naming scheme has been devised. Also, because network addresses may change frequently (dynamic node IDs, etc.), all services (file, print, mail, etc.) on a network are assigned user-definable (string) names. These string names may not change frequently, so AppleTalk uses a name process to identify network stations on a network. This process enables network users to remember names and not numeric addresses and enables network stations to acquire different network addresses while retaining a static name.

Names on an AppleTalk network are usually assigned by the network administrator. Anyone needing access to these services usually cannot change the names being used. Names are used to request a service to be processed. This includes attaching to a file server or sending a print job to a network-attached printer. All of these processes on the network are assigned numbers so that the network stations may communicate with each other. Network stations do not communicate with each other using the symbolic character ASCII names we type into the network station. Symbolic names are for users only on the AppleTalk network. When network stations communicate with one another, they still use the full network address of the network station and not the user-defined name of the network station.

What Is an AppleTalk Zone?

The Macintosh uses a mechanism called the Chooser for selecting network resources on an AppleTalk network. Rather than using the AppleTalk network number, Apple decided to introduce the concept of a zone to make the Chooser more user friendly in locating shared resources.

Zone Information Protocol

The ZIP protocol occupies the Session layer of the AppleTalk protocol stack. The ZIP maps network numbers and zone names. A zone is a logical grouping of network stations no matter where these network stations are located on the internetwork. Because it is central to Internet communications, it is handled by network devices responsible for Internet activity. Network stations grouped into a zone have many different network addresses. The grouping of zones is called the AppleTalk Internet. Each network number requires at least one zone name. Network station placement in a zone is fairly liberal. Network stations may participate in one zone or many zones. Zones may cross networks (across a router or routers). These zones may be spread through many different network numbers.

To assist users in locating resources within an Internet, AppleTalk supports the concept of zones. Multiple networks can be within a zone and, in some cases, multiple zones are assigned to a network segment. An AppleTalk router is responsible for assigning zone information to the AppleTalk networks to which it is attached. The ZIP maps zone names to networks in the Internet. The protocol is primarily used by routers, which maintain zone information for the networks. With AppleTalk phase 2, nodes within the same network can belong to different zones. Each zone is identified by a zone name (a string of up to 32 ASCII characters) that uniquely identifies the zone within the Internet.

The following are Zone Information Protocol header descriptions as shown in Figure 6.9:

- *ZIP Command.* Describes the type of ZIP message: Request or Reply
- *Network Count.* The number of networks contained in this request
- *Zone Name Length.* Number of bytes in the zone name
- *Zone Name.* Zone name for which information is being requested
- *ZIP Function.* Describes the message purpose for GetNetlnfo reply
- *Flags.* Used to alert nodes of specific conditions. Bit 7 is used to alert nodes that the zone name contained in the GetNetlnfo request is invalid; bit 6 is used to alert nodes that the underlying data link does not support multicasting and that broadcasting should be used in its place; and bit 5 indicates that this network's zone list contains only one name.
- *Network Number Range Start.* The start low end of the network number range for the configured network
- *Network Number Range End.* The end high end of the network number range for the configured network
- *Zone Name Length.* Length of the zone name that was sent as part of the request
- *Zone Name.* Determines whether the zone name is still valid
- *Multicast Address Length.* Number of bytes in the multicast address for this network

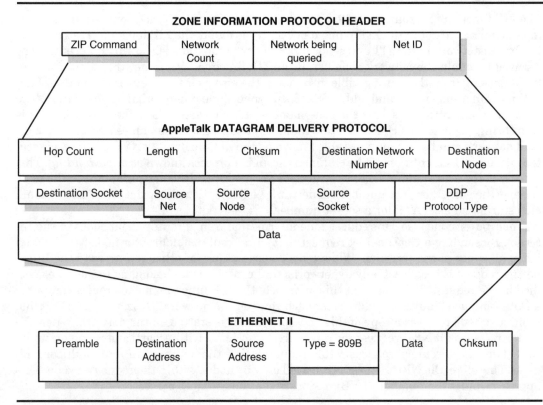

FIGURE 6.9   Zone Information Protocol

- *Multicast Address.* The zone multicast address used to communicate with other nodes in this zone on this network

- *Default Zone Name Length.* Number of bytes in the default zone name for this network

- *Default Zone Name.* The default zone name for this network

AppleTalk Routers maintain a zone list for each network attached to a router port. The zone list contains the default zone for the network and any additional zone names defined by a network administrator when configuring the port. A zone list can contain up to 255 zones names, including the default zone name.

When a node is started, it chooses the zone to which it will belong. If the node was previously started on the network, it will have saved the last zone name used. A node can choose a new zone name; however, by issuing the ZIP request, GetLocalZones. This request accesses the zone list maintained by the router and allows the node to choose a new zone from the list. Until a node explicitly chooses to belong to a zone, it will belong to the default zone for the network. Additionally, if a node is restarted, and the zone it was associated with is no longer within the zone list, the node is assigned to the default zone for the network.

In addition to local zone lists, routers also maintain a copy of the Internet zone list in a *Zone Information Table* (ZIT). The table contains one entry for each network on the Internet, which includes the network number range of the network and its associated zone list.

The ZIP function in a router monitors the routing table to identify new entries in the routing table that are not in the ZIT. When a new entry is found, the ZIP function creates an entry for the network in the ZIT and sends a ZIP query to the router from which the entry was received to obtain the network zone list. If the ZIP function determines that a network entry is missing from the routing table, it removes the entry for that network from the ZIT.

You claim a zone name and add NVEs to this zone. Zone names originate in routers. The network administrator assigns the zone name and broadcasts this to the network. This is what brings logic to this chaos. Routers maintain a listing of zone names and their associated network numbers through a table known as the ZIT. Before any NVE can be accessed, the address of that entity must be obtained through a process known as *name binding*. This process maps a network name to its Internet socket address (the network number, the node ID, and the socket, or port number). A network visible entity (file, print, database, E-mail, etc.) starts and asks ATP for a socket number.

A nonrouter node also can request zone information from a router about zones in the Internet. By sending a GetZoneList request to its local router, a nonrouter node can obtain a list of all zones in the Internet. When a node is searching for other resources in the Internet, its request is broadcast only to networks that contain nodes belonging to the zone specified in the request. To implement this approach, the ZIP function in each router computes a Data Link level multicast address for each zone on the network. By issuing a GetNetInfo request, a node receives a copy of this address when it is started on the network. When the router receives an NBP request for a resource associated with a particular zone on its local network, the router broadcasts this request using the appropriate zone multicast address. Therefore, the NBP request is received only by nodes within the requested zone. This approach limits the number of NBP requests that nodes must process.

AppleTalk Session Protocol

The Primary function of the ASP protocol is to provide services to the Apple Filing protocol that assist users in accessing AppleShare file servers for resources. The Apple Session protocol allows workstations to establish sessions with a server with an assigned session reference number, similar to NetBIOS session ID numbers. Communications between workstation and server occur using this session identifier.

Printer Access Protocol (PAP)

The *Printer Access Protocol* (PAP) is an asymmetrical connection-oriented transactionless protocol that enables communication between client and server endpoints, allowing multiple connections at both ends. PAP uses ATP packets to transport the data once a connection is open to the server. PAP is the protocol that ImageWriter and LaserWriter printers in the AppleTalk environment use for direct printing—when a workstation sends a print job directly to a printer connected to the network instead of using a print spooler. Open Transport PAP provides a single protocol implementation for all AppleTalk printers, which is integrated into the AppleTalk protocol stack.

The ADSP is a connection-oriented transactionless protocol that supports sessions over which applications can exchange full-duplex streams of data. In addition to ensuring reliable delivery of data, ADSP provides a peer-to-peer connection; that is, both ends of the connection can exert equal control over the exchange of data. ADSP also provides an application that can send expedited attention messages that pass control information between two communicating applications without disrupting the main data flow. ADSP appears to its clients to maintain an open pipeline between the two entities at either end. Either entity can write a stream of bytes to the pipeline or read data bytes from the pipeline. However, because ADSP, like all other higher level AppleTalk protocols, is a client of DDP, the data is actually sent as packets. This allows ADSP to correct transmission errors in a way that would not be possible for a true data stream connection. Thus, ADSP retains many of the advantages of a transaction-based protocol while providing to its clients a connection-oriented full-duplex data stream. ADSP also includes features that let you authenticate the identity of the party at the other end of the connection and send encrypted data, which is then decrypted at the other end.

Presentation Layer Protocols

The Presentation layer assumes that an end-to-end path or connection already exists across the network between the two communicating parties, and this layer is concerned with the representation of data values for transfer, or the *transfer syntax*. In the OSI model, the *AppleTalk Filing Protocol* (AFP) spans the presentation and application layers. AFP provides an interface between an application and a file server. It uses the services of ASP, which, in turn, is a client of ATP. AFP allows a workstation on an AppleTalk network to access files on an AFP file server, such as an AppleShare file server. When the user opens a session with an AppleShare file server over an intranet, it appears to any application using File Manager routines and running on the workstation as though the files are located on a disk drive connected to the workstation.

AppleTalk Filing Protocol

Two of the upper layer AppleTalk protocols, ASP and AFP are critical to the hypothetical file access request (see Figure 6.10). ASP creates a session to permit file access requests to be recognized and serviced and then disconnects the network link between the requester and server when the service is no longer required. At this level, a connection between two sockets on the two end nodes acts much like a single process on a single machine.

AFP is a presentation-layer protocol that specifies how Macintosh workstations access files located on remote file servers. AFP decodes the file access request, checking the access rights and availability of the file requested and formulating the reply to the requests (either a window into the file or an access denial). Because such activity requires ongoing dialog, it must be managed through a session protocol in which ongoing communication is provided and maintained. A translator program inside the AppleShare client software converts native Macintosh file system calls into AFT calls. As long as applications use the Macintosh's native filing interface, the user remains unaware of whether files are located on the workstation's local disk or on a server computer's disk. This is Apple's method of controlling server, volume, directory, file, and desktop calls between a client and server on an AppleTalk network.

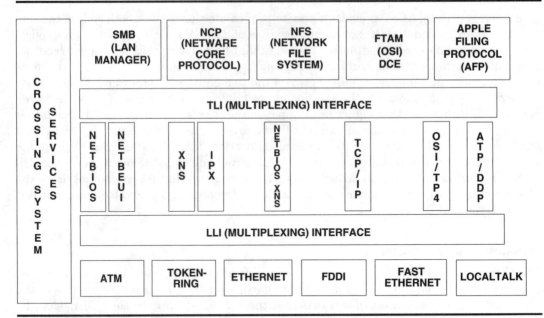

FIGURE 6.10   Apple Filing Protocol (AFP)

Cisco Enhancements to Standard AppleTalk Services

The Cisco AppleTalk implementation includes the following enhancements to standard AppleTalk support:

- Support for AppleTalk Enhanced Internet Gateway Protocol (Enhanced IGRP). AppleTalk Enhanced IGRP provides the following features:
  - Automatic redistribution. By default, AppleTalk RTMP routes are automatically redistributed into Enhanced IGRP, and AppleTalk Enhanced IGRP routes are automatically redistributed into RTMP. You can turn off redistribution and AppleTalk Enhanced IGRP and AppleTalk RTMP on the device or on individual interfaces.
  - Configuration of routing protocols on individual interfaces. You can configure interfaces configured for AppleTalk to use either RTMP, Enhanced IGRP, or both routing protocols. If two neighboring routers are configured to use RTMP and Enhanced IGRP, the Enhanced IGRP routing information supersedes the RTMP information. However, both routers continue to send RTMP routing updates. This feature enables you to control the excessive bandwidth usage of RTMP on WAN links. Because a WAN link is a point-to-point link (that is, no other devices are on the link), there is no need to run RTMP to perform end-node router discovery. Using Enhanced IGRP on WAN links enables you to save bandwidth and, in the case of *Packet-Switched Data Networks* (PSDN), traffic charges.
  - Support for EtherTalk 1.2 and EtherTalk 2.0 without the need for translation or transition routers
  - Support for Ethernet-emulated LANs

- Support for VLANs
- Support for WAN protocols, including SMDS, Frame Relay, X.25, and HDLC
- Configurable protocol constants (including the control of the aging of entries in the routing table and control of the AARP interval and number of retransmissions)
- No software limits on the number of zones or routes. However, per AppleTalk specification, you can have only a maximum of 255 zones per segment.
- MacTCP support via a MacIP server
- Support of IPTalk, which provides *Internet Protocol* (IP) encapsulation of AppleTalk, IPTalk, and the Columbia AppleTalk Package (CAP)
- Access control for filtering network traffic by network number, ZIP filtering, by NBP entity names, filtering routing table updates, and filtering GetZoneList (GZL) responses
- Integrated node name support to simplify AppleTalk network management
- Interactive access to AEP and NBP provided by the `test AppleTalk` command
- Configured (seed) and discovered interface configuration
- Support for the AppleTalk Responder, which is used by network monitoring packages such as *Inter Poll*
- SNMP over AppleTalk
- Encapsulation (tunneling) of AppleTalk RTMP packets over an IP backbone
- Support for AppleTalk static routes
- SMRP over AppleTalk

Security

AppleTalk, like many network protocols, makes no provisions for network security. The design of the AppleTalk protocol architecture requires that security measures be implemented at higher application levels. Cisco supports AppleTalk distribution lists, allowing control of routing updates on a per-interface basis. This security feature is similar to those that Cisco provides for other protocols.

Cisco offers a very comprehensive list of features designed to enhance the internetworking of AppleTalk. These features allow users to increase the scalability and security of their networks without having to make significant changes to end node devices. These features together allow MACs to continue their low cost of network ownership. Reference the Cisco Network Protocol Command Reference guide for a very comprehensive list of available options to optimize your AppleTalk network.

Questions

1. Identify the layer AppleTalk Print protocol resides in.
   A. Data Link
   B. Network
   C. Session
   D. Transport
   E. Application

2. AppleTalk DDP performs what two functions?
   A. Retransmission of packets
   B. Reception of packets
   C. Transmission of packets
   D. All of the above

3. What Ethernet frame type does AppleTalk support?
   A. Ethernet-II
   B. IEEE 802.3
   C. SNAP
   D. 802.4
   E. 802.5

4. With respect to the AppleTalk protocol suite, which is a topic addressed by ATP?
   A. Segment development
   B. Session administration
   C. Route discovery
   D. Transmission synchronization
   E. Reliable Datagrams

5. The network portion of an AppleTalk address is comprised of __.
   A. 4 bits
   B. 8 bits
   C. 16 bits
   D. 24 bits
   E. 32 bits

6. Which of the following is a characteristic of an AppleTalk phase 2 network?
   A. Each network is defined by a range of network numbers.
   B. Each node in the network is always manually assigned a network number.
   C. Each network supports up to 2048 zones.
   D. Each network supports up to 254 nodes per network number.
   E. A and D

7. When will a router send a ZIP request to learn the zones associated with a remote AppleTalk network?
   A. Only after learning about the remote network via NBP and validating that the network does not already exist in the routing table.
   B. Only after learning about the remote network via NBP and validating that the network does already exist in the routing table.
   C. Only after learning about the remote network via RTMP and validating that the network does not already exist in the routing table.
   D. Only after learning about the remote network via RTMP and validating that the network does already exist in the routing table.

8. Multiple seed routers can reside on the same network, however:
   A. They must all be configured with the same network ranges only.
   B. They must be configured with the same default zone name only.
   C. They must be configured with the same default zone name and zone list only.
   D. They must be configured with the same network ranges, default zone name, and zone list.

9. Each AppleTalk network must have at least one seed router.
   A. True   B. False

10. The AppleTalk aging algorithm uses a validity timer that expires every _____.
    A. 10 seconds   D. 40 seconds
    B. 20 seconds   E. 60 seconds
    C. 30 seconds

11. Define an AppleTalk Zone.

12. LocalTalk is a _____ based network.
    A. CSMA/CA   C. Both A & B
    B. CSMA/CD   D. None of the above

13. AppleTalk RTMP is a layer _____ protocol?
    A. 2   C. 3
    B. 4   D. 5

14. AppleTalk phase 2 removes the single network limitation to a LAN segment and replaces it with a _____.
    A. Network ID of 64   D. Single segment cable-range
    B. Network cable-range   E. None of the above
    C. Single segment

15. The *Name Binding Protocol* (NBP) provides a means of translating between _____.
    A. Socket Address & Entity Names   C. Zone Names & Entity Names
    B. Socket Address & Zone Names   D. None of the above

16. AppleTalk uses *Routing Table Maintenance Protocol* (RTMP) protocol with a hop count of _____.
    A. 16   C. 12
    B. 15   D. 4

17. AppleTalk ATP provides?
    A. Datagram delivery
    B. Reliable delivery
    C. Reliable delivery between sockets
    D. All of the above

18. If an AppleTalk network is configured with more than one network number, this network is defined as a____.
    A. Phase 1 Network   C. B only
    B. Phase II Network   D. All of the above

19. An AppleTalk Phase I network can support up ___ nodes per cable segment.
    A. 254   C. 127
    B. 126   D. 128

20. An AppleTalk Phase II network can support up to ___ nodes per cable segment.
    A. 253   **D.** 1518
    B. 254   **E.** 126
    C. 128

21. Identify the AppleTalk ethernet multicast address.
    A. 0x090007 ffffff   **C.** 0x090080 ffffff
    B. 0x090008 fffffe   **D.** None of the above

22. Identify an AppleTalk Token Ring Multicast address.
    A. 0xc00040 000000   **C.** 0xd00030 000000
    B. 0xc00030 000000   **D.** All of the above

23. The AppleTalk network address consists of a __ byte network number and a ___byte node ID.
    A. 2, 1   **C.** 8,4
    B. 4, 2   **D.** 4,6

24. A LocalTalk network has a limit of ___ active nodes over a span of 300 meters.
    A. 32   **C.** 16
    B. 48   **D.** 10

25. AppleTalk Ethernet and Token Ring uses Multicast addressing for the following protocols?
    A. DDP   **C.** RTMP
    B. ATP   **D.** AARP

26. The name Binding Protocol has ___ stages in AppleTalk?
    A. 6   **D.** 5
    B. 3   **E.** None of the above
    C. 4

27. AARP perform ___ functions.
    A. 2   **C.** 4
    B. 3   **D.** 6

28. AppleTalk Phase II increased the number of zones to _____.
    A. 253   **C.** 254
    B. 255   **D.** 128

29. AppleTalk networks with a hop count of 0 is considered _____.
    A. Non-existence   **C.** Remote network via router
    B. Local network   **D.** None of the above

30. AppleTalk nodes are divided into which two classes?
    A. User Node ID   **C.** Router Node IDs
    B. Server Node Ids   **D.** None of the Above

31. What AppleTalk Phase-II Nodes are identified in the range of 1–127?
    A. User   **C.** Router
    B. Server   **D.** Switch

32. What AppleTalk phase-II Node are identified in the range of 128–254?
   A. User
   B. Server
   C. Router
   D. None of the above

33. The AppleTalk *Name Binding Protocol* (NBP) entity name consists of which three fields?
   A. Object, type, and zone
   B. Object, zone, name
   C. Object, name, entity
   D. None of the above

34. ZIP stands for _____.
   A. Zone Information Protocol
   B. Zone Internet Protocol
   C. Zone Identity Protocol
   D. None of the above

35. There can be ___ Zone name(s) per cable-range in AppleTalk phase-II.
   A. only 2
   B. only 1
   C. multiple
   D. 2 (if zone 0 is not used)

36. What is the size of the AppleTalk DDP Node ID in bytes?
   A. 2
   B. 3
   C. 6
   D. 1

37. AppleTalk RTMP Sends routing updates every __ seconds.
   A. 10
   B. 15
   C. 60
   D. 30

38. AppleTalk Routing Table Maintenance Protocol is based on ____ routing.
   A. Link State
   B. Distance Vector
   C. Hybrid
   D. All of the above

39. What Cisco IOS command is used to configure a zone name?
   A. `Appletalk zonename`
   B. `Appletalk zone zone-name`
   C. `Appletalk zone-name zone`
   D. None of the above

40. How many zones are supported on an AppleTalk Phase 1 Network?
   A. 1 per segment
   B. 5 per segment
   C. 6 per segment
   D. 3 per segment

41. What IOS command is used to assisgn an Appletalk address to an interface?
   A. `Appletalk address network.node`
   B. `Appletalk address node.network`
   C. `Appletalk network.node address`

42. Cisco supports ____routes using AppleTalk.
   A. dynamic
   B. static
   C. none of the above

43. What Cisco IOS command will configure an interface for AppleTalk discovery mode?
   A. `AppleTalk Address 0-0`
   B. `AppleTalk Discovery`
   C. `AppleTalk address Net.ID`
   D. All of the above

44. AppleTalk can be tunneled into IP.
- **A.** True
- **B.** False

45. AppleTalk Routing Protocol can be tunneled into _____.
- **A.** E-IGRP
- **B.** GRE
- **C.** AURP
- **D.** A, B & C
- **E.** A & C
- **F.** None of the above

46. AppleTalk AURP sends routing updates every __ seconds.
- **A.** 10
- **B.** 15
- **C.** 60
- **D.** 30
- **E.** when changes occur only

47. What is the IOS command for AURP last-heard from timer?
- **A.** `Appletalk aurp tickle-time seconds`
- **B.** `Appletalk aurp time-tickle seconds`
- **C.** `Appletalk aurp seconds tickle-time`
- **D.** None of the above

48. The Cisco AppleTalk Access-list range is between____.
- **A.** 600–699
- **B.** 300–399
- **C.** 500–599
- **D.** none of the above

49. Identify the command for configuring a GRE tunnel.
- **A.** `Tunnel gre mode ip`
- **B.** `Tunnel mode gre ip`
- **C.** `Tunnel gre ip mode`

50. The AppleTalk PAP protocols provides for the following:
- **A.** Manages AppleTalk Routers
- **B.** Manages Printers
- **C.** Manages Printers and Servers
- **D.** Print Servers and Clients

51. The *AppleTalk Address Resolution Protocol* (AARP) uses which type code?
- **A.** 00000080F3h
- **B.** 000000A0F3h
- **C.** 0000A00003h
- **D.** None of the above

52. The DDP Socket Identifiers for Statically assigned sockets range from __to __.
- **A.** 01, 7F
- **B.** 01, 4f
- **C.** 01, FF
- **D.** 01h, 0fh

53. Identify the AppleTalk DDP sockets range for dynamically assigned socket numbers.
- **A.** 80, FE
- **B.** 80, FF
- **C.** 81, FE
- **D.** None of the above

54. Which AppleTalk Type Field is used for identifying RTMP Response or DATA?
- **A.** $01
- **B.** $03
- **C.** $02
- **D.** $F0

55. Which AppleTalk type field is used for identifying ZIP protocol?
- **A.** $06
- **B.** $07
- **C.** $04
- **D.** $01

56. Identify the Network ID reserved for node startup and address acquisition.
   A. FF00h-FFFEh
   C. FF00h-FFE0h
   B. FF00h-FFFFh
   D. None of the above

57. The Reserved Node Address __ indicates unknown.
   A. $0
   C. $FF
   B. $FE
   D. $A

58. AppleTalk networks require DDP address assignments to all but the following?
   A. Routers
   C. Servers
   B. Clients
   D. Web servers

59. The AppleTalk RTMP routing tables contains the _____.
   A. distance to the network
   B. state
   C. address of the next router to reach the destination
   D. port for sending packets
   E. all of the above

60. Identify the functions perform by a Seed Router.
   A. Provide Node ID's for Clients
   B. Provide Network and Node ID for Appletalk devices
   C. Provide Network address assignments for clients
   D. None of the above

61. It is recommended that all seed routers must _____.
   A. have the same information
   B. have the same number of clients
   C. have no more than 2 seed routers per segment
   D. none of the above

62. Identify the command to turn off appletalk checksum.
   A. `Appletalk nochecksum`
   C. `Appletalk no-checksum disable`
   B. `No appletalk checksum`
   D. None of the above

63. The AppleTalk zone name is __ characters in length.
   A. 16
   C. 20
   B. 15
   D. 32

64. The Cisco Router Zone Information Table contains _____.
   A. Networks known
   C. A only
   B. Zone names associated with the network
   D. A & B

65. Identify the field in the AppleTalk DDP Header.
   A. checksun
   H. destination node
   B. hop count
   I. destination socket
   C. ddp length
   J. protocol type
   D. source network
   K. DDP type
   E. source node
   L. Transport ID
   F. source socket
   M. TTL
   G. destination network

66. Identify the Cisco IOS command used for displaying objects that the router has learned.
- **A.** `Show appletalk name`
- **B.** `Show appletalk nbp`
- **C.** `Show appletalk nbp name`
- **D.** `Show appletalk name nbp`

67. Which IOS command will show AppleTalk network addresses?
- **A.** `Show appletalk network.node`
- **B.** `Show appletalk interface`
- **C.** `Show appletalk node`
- **D.** None of the above

68. Identify the IOS command used to show the *zone information table* (ZIT).
- **A.** `Show appletalk zone`
- **B.** `Show apple zone`
- **C.** `Show appletalk zone`
- **D.** `Show zip table`

69. Identify the AppleTalk command used to disable gleaning.
- **A.** `No appletalk glean`
- **B.** `No appletalk glean-packets`
- **C.** `No appletalk glean-packet`
- **D.** `Disable appletalk glean-packets`

70. Chooser shows no zones; what are some probable causes?
- **A.** It disconnects from the network
- **B.** No router exists on the network
- **C.** The network is down between Router and MAC Client
- **D.** All of the above

71. Cisco supports Split Horizon on AppleTalk for the following protocols?
- **A.** Phase I
- **B.** Phase-II
- **C.** AURP
- **D.** E-IGRP
- **E.** IGRP

72. The AppleTalk AURP is based on the following RFC:
- **A.** RFC 1504
- **B.** RFC 1577
- **C.** RFC 1200
- **D.** RFC 1700

73. AURP uses the following Protocols?
- **A.** TCP/IP
- **B.** UDP/IP
- **C.** SPX/IPX
- **D.** SPP/IP
- **E.** Not enough information

74. The AURP is a _____ layer protocol.
- **A.** Transport
- **B.** Session
- **C.** Network
- **D.** Data Link
- **E.** None of the above

75. The Apple DDP header is not included in the ____ packet.
- **A.** ATP
- **B.** AURP
- **C.** ASP
- **D.** PAP

76. Cisco Supports all but the following Interfaces on its Routers.
- **A.** Ethernet
- **B.** Token Ring
- **C.** FDDI
- **D.** ATM
- **E.** HSSI
- **F.** Localtalk

77. The Cisco IOS command for setting the time out of the AppleTalk ARP table?.
   A. `Appletalk arp-timeout interval`
   B. `Appletalk interval arp-timeout`
   C. `Appletalk arp interval`
   D. `Appletalk time-out interval`

78. Cisco IOS sends zip queries every ___ seconds.
   A. 30
   B. 10
   C. 20
   D. not applicable

79. The first zone assigned becomes the ____ for the cable-range.
   A. only zone for the network segment
   B. default zone
   C. none of the above

80. Identify the command to enable E-IGRP for AppleTalk in global configuration mode.
   A. `Appletalk routing protocol eigrp`
   B. `Appletalk routing eigrp routing-number`
   C. `Appletalk protocol eigrp`
   D. None of the above

81. Cisco supports the following routing protocols for AppleTalk:
   A. RTMP
   B. E-IGRP
   C. AURP
   D. IGRP
   E. All of the above

82. Identify the types of packets that can be filtered.
   A. Data packet
   B. Zip Reply
   C. Routing tables
   D. GetZoneList
   E. All of the above

83. An AppleTalk Router configured for RTMP routing protocol will change the status of a route if it is not revalidated within ____ seconds.
   A. 10
   B. 20
   C. 30
   D. 40

84. Identify the command to disable RTMP routes into E-IGRP and E-IGRP routes into RTMP.
   A. `Appletalk route-redistribution disable`
   B. `No appletalk route-redistribution`
   C. `Disable appletalk route-redistribution`
   D. None of the above

85. It is not recommended to leave the Apple Chooser open with no activity. Why?
   A. Because a getzonelist query goes to a router to populate the zone list
   B. Because Name binding protocol requests are constantly being sent out
   C. Because you can not access the network with the chooser open
   D. None of the above

86. How does a device operating in an AppleTalk environment resolve its layer three address to a layer two address?
   A. It uses an ARP request sent out as a broadcast and the owner of the address responds.
   B. The layer two address is the node portion of the layer three address.

C. It uses DNS to resolve the addresses.
D. It uses WINS to resolve the addresses.

87. What is the default routing protocol used for AppleTalk in a Cisco router when the following
command is issued (AppleTalk routing)?
    A. IGRP   **C.** AURP
    B. EIGRP   **D.** RTMP

88. Which of the following does not support routing AppleTalk in a Cisco router?
    A. IGRP   **C.** AURP
    B. EIGRP   **D.** RTMP

89. How does a node acquire its address?
    A. By using a bootp request to a tftp server
    B. By using DHCP
    C. Through the network portion from a seed router on the local network and randomly
selecting the node number
    D. The network portion is randomly selected from a pre-configured range and the node por-
tion is feed from a seed node server.

90. Zone information is propagated by what type of protocol?
    A. RTMP   **C.** NBP
    B. ZIP   **D.** RIP

91. When a user selects a zone and a service from chooser, who responds?
    A. The router from a table kept in its' buffer
    B. The router that owns the zone
    C. Every device of that type in the zone
    D. Devices in the default zone

92. Which of the following are not required to configure AppleTalk on a Cisco router?
    A. Select AppleTalk routing protocol
    B. Assign network number or range to an interface
    C. Select the type of interface encapsulation
    D. Assign the interface into a zone

93. What does the ISO interface command `appletalk protocol eigrp` do on an interface?
    A. Enables EIGRP as the routing protocol to be used for AppleTalk on that interface
    B. Redistributes IP routes into AppleTalk
    C. Replaces the need for the `appletalk zone` command
    D. EIGRP does not support AppleTalk.

94. What is the command to assign a AppleTalk phase II network address 100 to 150 to an
interface
    A. `Appletalk phase-ii-network 100-150`
    B. `Appletalk network-range 100-150`
    C. `Appletalk cable-range 100-150`
    D. `Appletalk network 100`

95. AppleTalk Transaction Protocol is _____.
- **A.** Connection Oriented
- **B.** Connectionless
- **C.** Acknowledge connection-less
- **D.** None of the above

96. In a SNAP frame the value 0x809B represents_____.
- **A.** IPX
- **B.** AppleTalk DDP
- **C.** DECnet
- **D.** None of the above

97. Identify the AppleTalk layer 3 protocols?
- **A.** DDP
- **B.** RTMP
- **C.** AARP
- **D.** ATP
- **E.** ASP
- **F.** PAP

98. AppleTalk determines the best route based on _____.
- **A.** cost
- **B.** hops
- **C.** ticks/hops
- **D.** bandwidth

99. Cisco routers set the AppleTalk distance metric to __ for a bad entry.
- **A.** 10
- **B.** 21
- **C.** 31
- **D.** 42

100. A Cisco router configured for AppleTalk routing will remove a route from the routing table after ___ seconds.
- **A.** 20
- **B.** 30
- **C.** 40
- **D.** 50
- **E.** 60
- **F.** 80

101. AppleTalk DDP packet can be ___ bytes in length.
- **A.** 200
- **B.** 100
- **C.** 512
- **D.** 600

102. The AppleTalk Socket size is ___bits in length.
- **A.** 8
- **B.** 16
- **C.** 32
- **D.** 12

103. The AppleTalk socket ID 4 is used to identify which echo application?
- **A.** Zone
- **B.** NBP
- **C.** Ping
- **D.** PAP

104. What is the range for extended AppleTalk access lists?
- **A.** 700–799
- **B.** 800–899
- **C.** 900–999
- **D.** There is no range for extended AppleTalk access lists.

105. What is the access list statement for AppleTalk to permit everything?
- **A.** `Access-list` *number* `permit any`
- **B.** `Access-list` *number* `permit all`
- **C.** `Access-list` *number* `permit other-access`
- **D.** `Access-list` *number* `permit -1`

106. What is the purpose of the following commands?

```
Access-list 601 deny within cable-range 100-110
Access-list 601 permit within cable-range 111-120

Interface ethernet 0
Appletalk cable-range 100-120
Appletalk zone yomomma
Appletalk access-group 601

Interface ethernet 1
Appletalk cable-range 200-220
Appletalk zone fred
```

    A. Invalid access list

    B. Will permit traffic from 111–120 network numbers

    C. Will permit traffic from 100–110 network numbers

    D. Access list not applied to correct interface, won't do anything

107. What is the AppleTalk zone for Ethernet 0?

```
Ethernet0 is up, line protocol is up  AppleTalk cable range is 1100-1199
AppleTalk address is 1141.73, Valid
  AppleTalk zone is "ZoneB"
  AppleTalk port configuration verified by 1107.28
  AppleTalk address gleaning is disabled
  AppleTalk route cache is enabled
```

    A. 1141.73   **C.** Gleaning

    B. ZoneB   **D.** None of the above

108. Identify the AppleTalk address:

```
Ethernet0 is up, line protocol is up  AppleTalk cable range is 1100-1199
AppleTalk address is 1141.73, Valid
  AppleTalk zone is "ZoneB"
  AppleTalk port configuration verified by 1107.28
  AppleTalk address gleaning is disabled
  AppleTalk route cache is enabled
```

    A. 1107.28   **C.** 1100–1199

    B. 1141.73   **D.** None of the above

109. What is address gleaning in the preceding?

```
Ethernet0 is up, line protocol is up
  AppleTalk cable range is 1400-1499
  AppleTalk address is 1444.5, Valid
  AppleTalk zone is "ZoneD"
  AppleTalk port configuration verified by 1423.160
  AppleTalk address gleaning is disabled
  AppleTalk route cache is enabled
```

    A. Used in Fast switching

    B. Can be used to reduce Apple ARP requests

    C. Route Cache

    D. Default zone name explorer

```
Codes: R - RTMP derived, E - EIGRP derived, C - connected, A - AURP
       S - static  P - proxy
5 routes in internet
```

```
The first zone listed for each entry is its default (primary) zone.

R Net 1200-1299 [1/G] via 1423.160, 1 sec, Ethernet0, zone ZoneC
R Net 1300-1399 [1/G] via 1423.160, 1 sec, Ethernet0, zone ZoneC
C Net 1400-1499 directly connected, Ethernet0, zone ZoneD
```

110. In the AppleTalk route statement what is the meaning of G in [1/G]?
  A. This is a Gateway.   **C.** This route is gone.
  B. This route is good.   **D.** None of the above

111. In the AppleTalk route statement what is the meaning of 1 in [1/G]?
  A. Tick count   **C.** Hop count
  B. Administrative distance   **D.** First route learned

Answers

1. E
2. B and C
3. C
4. D, E
5. C
6. A
7. C
8. D
9. B
10. E
11. An AppleTalk Zone is an arbitrary grouping of Macintosh systems into some organizational structure without necessary any regard to physical network location.
12. A
13. B
14. B
15. A
16. B
17. C
18. B
19. A
20. A
21. A
22. A
23. A
24. A
25. D
26. C
27. B
28. B
29. B
30. B
31. A
32. B
33. A
34. A
35. C
36. D
37. A
38. B
39. B
40. A
41. A
42. A, B
43. A, B
44. A
45. D
46. D
47. A

48. A
49. B
50. D
51. A
52. A
53. A
54. A
55. A
56. C
57. A
58. B, C, D
59. E
60. C
61. A
62. A
63. C
64. D
65. A, B, C, D, E, F, G, H, I, K
66. B
67. B
68. C
69. B
70. D
71. D
72. A
73. B
74. A
75. B
76. F
77. A
78. B
79. A
80. B
81. A, B, C
82. E
83. A
84. B
85. A
86. A
87. D
88. A
89. C
90. B
91. C
92. C
93. A
94. C
95. A
96. B
97. A, C

98. B
99. C
100. E
101. D
102. A
103. C
104. D
105. C
106. B
107. B
108. B
109. B
110. B
111. C

Working with Novell NetWare

Novell NetWare is a popular Network operating system, and this popularity has increased the need for connecting and scaling NetWare networks across an Enterprise Internet. Novell has responded to this requirement with the introduction of key networking technologies such as NDS, Native TCP/IP Support, and NLSP. Our focus in this chapter concentrates on NetWare protocols surrounding IPX, NLSP SAP, RIP, and SPX with Cisco enhancements for scaling NetWare networks as shown in Figure 7.1.

Novell Directory Services™ (NDS), based on the international X.500 standard, makes organizing, categorizing, and naming resources possible in an easy-to-access and manage network. Its hierarchical, object-oriented name structure resembles an upside-down tree with a root or trunk at the top and branches extending below.

The object-oriented nature of NDS provides for some very powerful management capabilities. NDS has container and leaf objects. Container objects are like buckets with certain characteristics or attributes. Containers hold leaf objects that automatically inherit all of the characteristics of the container object.

The container objects in NDS are called *Organizational Units* (OUs). If an OU for Finance is created with access to the accounting database but not the payroll records, every user object in the Finance OU automatically inherits the same access privileges and restrictions. Although each object can be managed separately, hierarchical object inheritance makes it possible to modify an entire organization by making simple changes at the top of the tree. Every object on the tree can be uniquely identified by the combination of its name and location. For example, two identical printers with the same name are uniquely identified in NDS because one is in Marketing and the other in Engineering.

Building the Directory Framework

One of the many reasons NDS is more powerful than other directory services is its capability to extend the schema or to create and define new objects (i. e., applications, PBXs, fax servers) with a customizable list of properties or attributes that define objects (see Figure 7.2). For example, a user object's attributes can include more than 100 properties such as

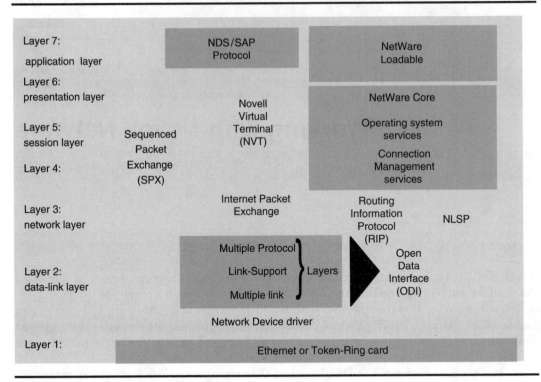

FIGURE 7.1   NetWare architecture

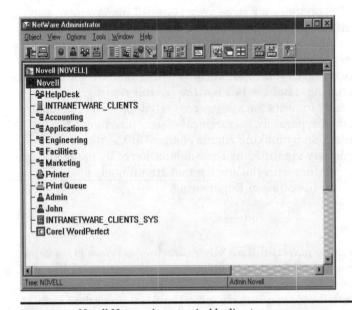

FIGURE 7.2   Novell Netware's customizable directory

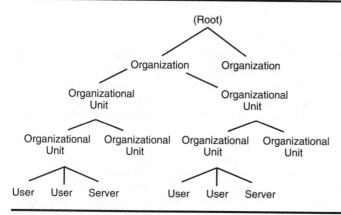

FIGURE 7.3 Directory logical structure

name, phone number, login name, and password. You can extend the user object schema by adding properties such as salary, assigned projects, hire date, and even a scanned photograph or video.

Directory Logical Structure

NDS defines three types of container objects: Country, Organization, and Organizational Unit objects. If Country objects are used, they must appear immediately below the root. Organization objects are immediately below Country objects or below the root if Country objects are not used. Every directory must contain at least one Organization object. Organizational Unit objects can be used to provide further structuring below an Organization object. Multiple levels of Organizational Unit objects can be used to any desired depth. NDS also defines specific types of leaf objects, which are described in Figure 7.3.

Media Access Control Protocols (MAC)

MAC Layer protocols operate at the OSI Data Link layer. Their primary task is to transport frames from one node to another on a network segment. Several MAC protocols have been defined, many of which can be used with NetWare. Three of the most common MAC protocols currently in use are IEEE 802.5 (Token Ring), IEEE 802.3 (Ethernet), and FDDI.

MAC protocols define the addressing that identifies each node on a network segment. Node addressing is implemented within the hardware of each network interface board. In the case of Ethernet, Token Ring, and FDDI boards, these physical addresses are assigned at the factory. The IEEE administers physical addresses to ensure that no two manufacturers use the same one. MAC protocols also provide bit-level error checking in the form of a *cyclic redundancy check* (CRC). The CRC is appended at the end of every transmitted packet, also called the MAC trailer. The CRC ensures that every received packet is free of corruption. To get a packet to its destination node, MAC protocols place the node addresses and other information in a MAC header at the front of every outgoing packet and place the CRC in the MAC trailer.

MAC Header

The MAC header contains source node and destination node address fields. These fields contain the physical addresses that indicate where the frame originated and where it is going. Each interface adapter attached to the network checks the Destination Address field in the MAC header of every frame it receives. If the frame finds its own address in this field, or if the packet is a broadcast packet (intended for all nodes), the board copies the packet. The frame then is passed to a higher layer process such as IPX- or NetWare IP for further examination and processing.

> *NOTE: The destination and source MAC addresses are the same as those in the Destination and Source Node fields in the IPX header. The MAC header and trailer encapsulate each frame with the node addresses, the upper layer protocol, the CRC, the message length, and additional information specific to the network medium. This information is specified in a format conforming to a particular frame type.*

Data Link Frames and Frame Types

A frame is the data link layer data unit used for communication between two nodes on a network. The frame's MAC header contains information that specifies the sending and receiving nodes, the upper layer protocol to which the frame is passed, and—for source-routed Token Ring networks—the exact forwarding path the packet follows to its destination. NetWare supports several frame types, such as Ethernet_II, IEEE 802.3, SNAP, etc., for interoperability with many different network protocols on various network media.

In a mixed network, how NetWare deals with the different Data Link packet formats imposed by other communication protocols is especially important.

The original Ethernet specification was developed by Xerox Corporation and then refined with the help of DEC and Intel. The refined frame specification is known as Ethernet version 2, or Ethernet II. As more and more companies embraced Ethernet technology, the IEEE 802.3 standards committee eventually stepped in to create a formal Ethernet specification.

About this same time, Novell was developing Ethernet LAN drivers based on the then unfinished 802.3 standard. The Ethernet 802.3 frame Novell used to encapsulate IPX packets is slightly different from the Ethernet II frame, as shown in Figure 7.4. In the two-byte Type field, Ethernet II frames contain a protocol ID number. Novell substituted a two-byte Length field instead. IEEE subsequently decided to add 802.2 headers to the 802.3 specification to provide the PID and type information in the frame, thus creating a third Ethernet frame type called Ethernet 802.2.

> *NOTE: Novell 802.3_raw is not IEEE802.3 Ethernet, which has caused a lot of communication problems in the naming and format of the frames.*

Two Token Ring frame types are supported as shown in Figure 7.6.

FDDI SNAP

In FDDI *Subnetwork Access Protocol* (SNAP) packets, the DSAP and SSAP values illustrated in Figure 7.5 indicate SNAP encapsulation. The Protocol Identification value indicates that the frame contains an IPX packet. The presence of the Route fields indicates the use of Source-Route bridging.

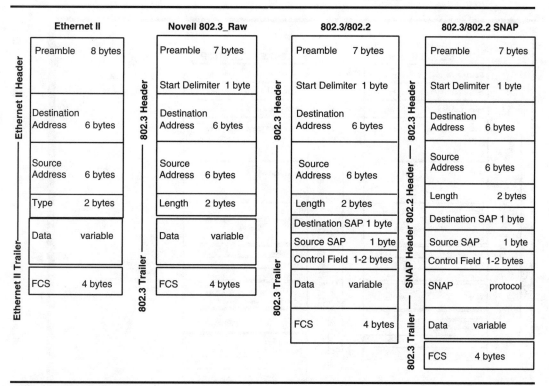

FIGURE 7.4 Ethernet packets

Frame Control	1	
Destination Address	6	
Source Address	6	
Route Control Broadcast/Length	1	
Route Control Direction	1	
Route Designator 1	2	
... ...	2	
Route Designator n	2	
DSAP	1	0xAA
SSAP	1	0xAA
Control	1	0x03
Protocol Identification	5	0x0000008137

FIGURE 7.5   FDDI SNAP

802.2 frames are used with IPX and OSI protocols and include the frame types listed in Table 7.1.

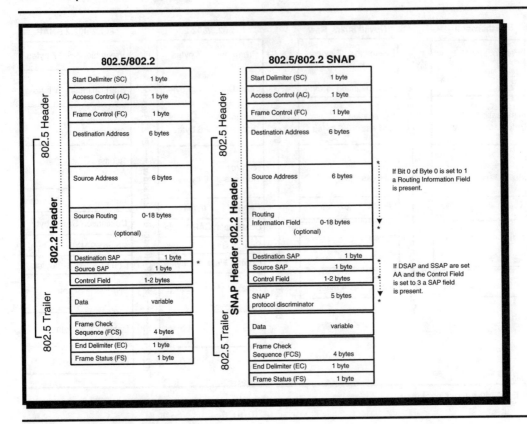

FIGURE 7.6 Token Ring frames

TABLE 7.1 Novell Frame Types

Novell Supported Frame Types	Cisco's Implementation of Novell Frame Types
Ethernet-II	ARPA
802.2	SAP or ISO1
Ethernet 802.3_raw	Novell-ether
Ethernet_snap	snap
Token-Ring	SAP
Token_Ring_SNAP	SNAP
Fddi_raw	Novell-fddi
Fddi_802.2	SAP
Fddi_Snap	SNAP

NOTE: *Before the release of Version 3.12, NetWare workstations and drivers were configured with ETHERNET_802.3 as the default frame type. The default frame type for NetWare 3.12 and 4.x and later releases is 802.2.*

You can configure multiple frame types on the same Cisco router, interface, server, or workstation. However, for two nodes on a network to communicate, they must have in common at least one frame type. If one node accepts only ETHERNET_II frames and the other accepts only ETHERNET_802.2 frames, the nodes cannot communicate directly, although they share the same physical network. For the nodes to communicate, they must pass through the router. Also, using more than one frame type on a node does not increase packet throughput but helps in accessing servers with different frame encapsulations.

NOTE: Using multiple frame types causes Service Advertising and Routing Information Protocol packets to be broadcast using both frame types. Network bandwidth is decreased due to the increased number of SAPs and RIPs.

You can mix frame types and network protocols on the same network. For example, IP can use ETHERNET_II while IPX uses ETHERNET_802.2.

IPX is the network-layer routing protocol used in the NetWare environment. The primary tasks of IPX are addressing, routing, and switching information packets from one location to another on a network.

Originally, protocol stacks were linked directly to the LAN adapter or device. Because the driver could not be separated from the protocol stack, the user was limited to one protocol stack per LAN adapter. The Novell 802.3_RAW frame type has been primarily used to support IPX; this has worked well for single driver and single protocol installations. However, many users now want to support multiple protocols and frame types on the same wire.

Novell is promoting *Open Data-Link Interface* (ODI) technology that provides this support as well as other advantages such as reduced system administration and management and increased performance and connectivity. Because Novell 802.3_Raw was not intended to be used as a frame type by itself and does not lend itself to this new architecture, a migration away from 802.3 Raw to the 802.2 header is necessary. IEEE has also specified that 802.3 should be used with the 802.2 header (see Figure 7.4).

NetWare Internet Packet Exchange (IPX)

Internet Packet Exchange (IPX) defines the internetwork and intranode addressing as follows: network numbers form the basis of the IPX internetwork-addressing scheme for sending packets between network segments. Every network segment of an internetwork is assigned a unique network address by which routers forward packets to their final destination network. A network number in the NetWare environment consists of eight hexadecimal characters. Socket numbers are the basis for an IPX intranode address—that is, the address of individual entities within a node. Socket numbers enable a process (for example, RIP or SAP) to distinguish itself to IPX. To communicate on the network, the process must request a socket number. Any packets IPX receives addressed to that socket are passed on to the process within the node.

IPX Addressing

An IPX address specifies the location of a particular entity in a network or internetwork. Addresses enable two entities not directly connected to communicate. Each entity, such as a host, server, communication device, or printer, in a network or Internet must have a unique identifier or address. The IPX header is shown in Figure 7.7

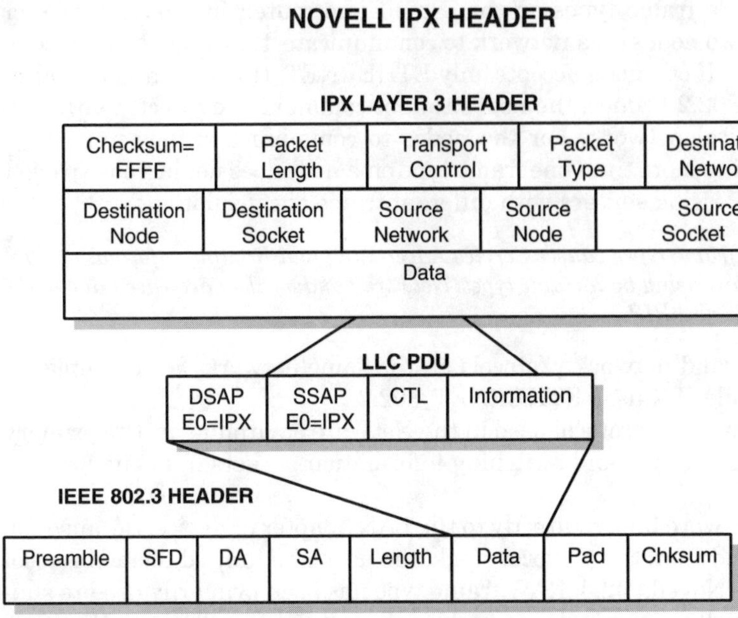

NOVELL IPX HEADER

IPX LAYER 3 HEADER

Checksum= FFFF	Packet Length	Transport Control	Packet Type	Destination Network
Destination Node	Destination Socket	Source Network	Source Node	Source Socket
Data				

LLC PDU

DSAP E0=IPX	SSAP E0=IPX	CTL	Information

IEEE 802.3 HEADER

Preamble	SFD	DA	SA	Length	Data	Pad	Chksum

FIGURE 7.7 IPX header

```
DLC:  -- DLC Header --
DLC:
DLC:  Frame 1 arrived at   09:44:41.16543 ; frame size is 84 (0054 hex) bytes.
DLC:  Destination = BROADCAST FFFFFFFFFFFF, Broadcast
DLC:  Source       = Station 00E01E5DD4AD
DLC:  802.3 length = 70
DLC:
IPX:  -- IPX Header --
IPX:
IPX:  Checksum = 0xFFFF
IPX:  Length = 70
IPX:  Transport control = 00
IPX:          0000 .... = Reserved
IPX:          .... 0000 = Hop count
IPX:  Packet type = 0 (Novell)
IPX:
IPX:  Dest   network.node = A.FFFFFFFFFFFF, socket = 34238 (0x85BE)
IPX:  Source network.node = A.00E01E5DD4AD, socket = 34238 (0x85BE)
IPX:
IPX:  [40 bytes of IPX data]
IPX:
```

FIGURE 7.8 IPX trace

Host Number

There is a unique hardware address required by each node on the network. An example of a hardware address is a 48-bit Ethernet, Token Ring, or FDDI node address. Proper node addressing ensures that the network efficiently delivers and receives packets. Each IPX interface uses its right-justified hardware node address as its 48-bit host number. WAN interfaces use the first MAC address of the router or the node address referenced in the IPX routing command. The hexadecimal address FF-FF-FF-FF-FF-FF is the broadcast address.

Network Number

A unique network address is required by each IPX network, the network number is a 32-bit hexadecimal number. You must configure the router with the IPX network number for each IPX network interface. The combined network number and host number creates an 80-bit IPX address.

Socket Number

The socket number is the location within the protocol that binds the packet to an application service. In general, IPX networks can be separated into two physical elements: local and remote networks.

Checksum

This field is normally set to 0xFFFF indicating that no checksum was performed. The sending station performs the checksum algorithm on the packet and puts the result of the checksum in this field. The receiving station performs a checksum on the IPX portion of the packet and generates a checksum. If the two match, the packet is good. If the two do not match, that packet contains an error and will be discarded. This field is configurable in NetWare 4.x and intraNetWare. The default is no checksum.

Length

This field is used to indicate the total length of an IPX packet, including the IPX header checksum and data fields. The minimum length allowed is 30 bytes (the size of the IPX header fields), and its maximum total is 576 (indicating a maximum of 546 bytes for the data fields). For communications on a LAN, the total may be as high as the transmission medium allows: 1,500 bytes for Ethernet; 1,496 for IEEE 802.3 (including IEEE 802.2 headers); and 4,472 for 4-Mbps Token Ring. Under Novell's packet burst mode available in NetWare 4.x and higher, large packets may be transferred between two stations residing on different LANs.

Transport Control

This field is used by IPX routers and sets a hop count limit of 15 (with 16 being infinity). This field also is used by routers that support SAP reporting and other file servers to indicate how far away a server (providing certain services) is from the recipient of the packet.

When a packet is transmitted onto the network, the sending station sets this field to 0. As the packet traverses each router (if needed) on its way to the destination, each router increments this by 1. The router that sets it to 16 discards the packet.

Packet Type

This field indicates the type of service offered or required by the packet. The following values are defined:

- 0   Unknown packet type (do not use)
- 1   Routing information packet
- 2   Echo packet (not currently supported)
- 3   Error packet (not currently supported)
- 4   Packet exchange packet (normal IPX packet, also used by SAP)
- 5   Sequenced packet (SPX and SPX II)
- 17   NetWare Core Protocol standard packet
- 20   IPX NetBIOS broadcast

Destination Network

This field contains the network number of the network to which the destination node belongs. Networks within an internetwork are assigned unique 4-byte network numbers by a network administrator. When this field is 0, the destination node is assumed to reside on the same network as the source node. It is used by IPX in routers and workstations to deliver the packet to the local network or to use routers to deliver the packet to another network on the internet. (The destination network number is not on the same LAN as the transmitter).

Destination Host Node

This field contains the Data Link layer physical address of the destination node. A node on an Ethernet, Token Ring, and FDDI network requires all six bytes to specify its address. If a physical network needs less than six bytes to specify a node address, the address occupies the least significant portion of the field, and the most significant bytes are set to 0.

Destination Socket

This field contains the socket address of the packet's destination process. Sockets route packets to different processes within a single node. Each service that runs on a file server is assigned a socket number. The following socket numbers are reserved by the IPX protocol suite:

- 2h   Echo protocol socket (currently not used)
- 3h   Error handler packet

In addition, Novell has defined and reserved the following sockets for use by intraNetWare:

- 0×451   NetWare Core Protocol
- 0×452   NetWare Service Advertising Protocol
- 0×453   NetWare Routing Protocol
- 0×456   NetWare Diagnostics Protocol

Novell provides a list of well-known socket numbers to software developers. Novell's well-known sockets start at 0x8000, and dynamic sockets begin at 0x4000 -0x7FFF.

Source Network

The IPX source network contains the network number of the network to which the source node belongs. This field may contain a value of 0, which means that the physical network to which the source node is connected is unknown. All packets with a 0 in this field, which pass through a IPX router, have this field set to their source network number. Thus, when a packet is received from a node on a different network, the source network field is always set properly. Packets whose source and destination nodes are on the same network may contain a 0 in this field.

Source Node

This field contains the physical address of the source node. If a physical network needs less than six bytes to specify a node address, the address should occupy the least significant portion of the field. The most significant bytes should occupy the Source Node field.

Source Socket

This field contains the socket address of the process that transmits the packet. In a client server dialogue, the server node usually listens on a specific socket for connection requests. In such a case, all that matters is that the server sends its replies to the source socket contained in the connection request packet. As in the case of destination sockets, these numbers can be static or dynamic. Source socket numbers follow the same conventions as those for destination sockets. The source socket field is usually set to the number in the dynamic range (user definable range).

Novell IPX Routing

The routing function of IPX enables packets to be forwarded locally or to different networks using a router. Routing enables networks to become segmented and more manageable. Two types of routers are available on a Novell network. First, Novell implements a routing function in the operating system that allows for two types of NetWare-supplied routers: internal and external. The internal router operates in a server that is usually performing some other tasks as well as the routing function. These tasks may be file and print services, or a gateway service to SNA. The external router is a workstation (for example, a personal computer) containing multiple network interface cards. This workstation's sole function is to route packets.

The *Novell multiprotocol router* (MPR) is standard with Novell's intraNetWare Server software. The MPR is a low-end routing program that runs in a PC. The difference between this router and previous versions of NetWare external routers is that the MPR not only runs the NetWare protocols but also runs other protocols such as TCP/IP, AppleTalk, DLSw, Frame Relay, OSPF, IP RIP, and NLSP.

Distance-Vector Algorithms

IPX/RIP is a distance-vector protocol. In distance-vector algorithms, a router maintains a table that contains only the distance to the target network and the direction or vector a packet must travel to reach the destination network. The vector usually takes the form of the address of a router through which a packet must traverse to reach its ultimate destination. With distance-vector algorithms, the best-cost routes can be computed when the only information exchanged by routers is a list of reachable networks along with their distances. Each router can calculate a route and its associated distance to each network by choosing the neighbor with the shortest path available.

In an internetwork using distance-vector routing, routers periodically determine whether the internetwork configuration has changed. They also periodically broadcast packets to their immediate neighbors; these packets contain all information they currently have about the internetwork's topology.

After receiving an update, distance-vector routers consolidate the information and pass summarized data along to other routers, servers, and end devices. Through this periodic checking and broadcasting, which is performed at regular intervals regardless of whether the internetwork has changed, all routers are kept updated with correct internetwork addresses. Because RIP is a distance-vector protocol, routers configured for NetWare RIP work in the same way: performing periodic checking and information exchange while updating their routing tables with new information. RIP is one of a number of well-known distance-vector routing protocols.

Cisco IOS IPX Routing Table

Routers need to know about other available routers and all other active networks on their internets, and the routing information protocol (IPX-RIP) process is the method for exchanging this information. Upon receipt of a packet, the router extracts the destination network number from the IPX header and compares it to a table, an example of which is shown in Figure 7.9. The IPX router keeps a complete listing of the networks in a *routing table*. The entries in the routing table let the router determine the path along which to forward a packet.

Network numbers are 32 bits in length. Among other things, Novell's IPX protocol changes the XNS RIP implementation slightly to add a timer. This is known as *ticks* and provides the ability of a distance-vector algorithm with true cost attributes, not just a hop count. Ticks are the amount of time required to reach that path. Most IPX routing implementations do not perform tick counts.

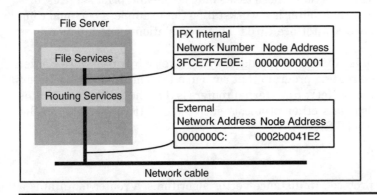

FIGURE 7.9 IPX internal network number

RIP support provides end stations and routers with the information required to dynamically establish the best route to each network.

A route indicates the path an entity's packet follows to reach another entity. IPX uses the RIP protocol to maintain the routes in its routing tables. Valid entries remain in the routing tables for three multiples of the RIP interval. (The default value of 60 seconds allows a valid entry to remain in the table for 180 seconds.) During this time, if a route entry is not refreshed by RIP updates, the route is marked with an infinite hop count (16). Any packet locally addressed to the router, including broadcast packets, are passed to the appropriate internal module for processing. Examples of this are SAP packets and RIP packets.

Broadcast messages sent to an unimplemented socket do not elicit error replies. If the packet size is greater than the output size of the next hop network, the router discards the packet and returns an error message.

The first entry of the router table, the network number, contains the network numbers that are in place on the Internet. A router exchanges its routing table with other routers on the network. The actual entries in the table that are exchanged with other routers are network number, hops, and ticks. A router receives these updates (routing tables) from other routers on the Internet. From this received information, a router builds its own table and picture of the Internet.

The next entry is the number of the tick counts. This number indicates an estimated time necessary to deliver a packet to a destination on that network. This time is based on the segment type. A tick is about 1/18 second. This number is derived from an IBM personal computer clock being ticked at 18 times a second. In actuality, 18.21 ticks occur in a personal computer clock for every second that elapses. Cisco routers support Novell's tick-based routing for IPX networks. Tick-based routing uses a lowest network delay metric, measured in ticks (1/18 of a second increments) to determine the best path from source to destination. The next entry shows the number of routers that must be traversed to reach this network. Any time that a packet must traverse a router to reach a destination, the process of traversing the routers is known as a *hop*. Therefore, if a packet must cross over three routers to reach the final network, the network is three hops away. The term hops is also called a *metric*. Three hops are the same as a 3-metric count. The cost metric used by IPX RIP is first ticks and then hops. When multiple least-cost routes of equal tick delay exist between IPX networks, the best path is the one with the lowest hop count. If both values are still equal, IPX randomly selects one best path. A Cisco router can be configured to make routing decisions using Novell IPX RIP, Novell NLSP, and Cisco IPX EIGRP routing protocol as shown in Figure 7.10.

For locally attached segments with more than one Mbps transmission speed (Ethernet and Token Ring), the NIC driver assumes a tick of 1. For serial network segments (X.25,

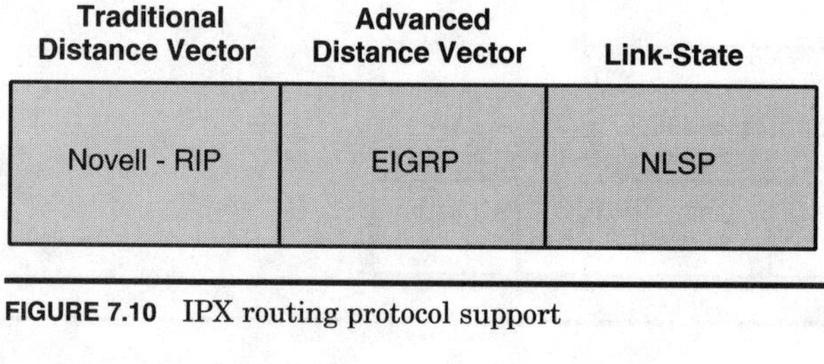

Traditional Distance Vector	Advanced Distance Vector	Link-State
Novell - RIP	EIGRP	NLSP

FIGURE 7.10 IPX routing protocol support

synchronous line of T1 and 64 KBPS, and asynchronous), the driver periodically polls to determine the time delay. For a T1 circuit, the tick counter is usually 6 to 7 ticks per segment. Any changes in this time are communicated to the router and propagated to other routers on the network. These numbers in the tables are cumulative—as each router broadcasts its routing table, this number is not reset. It is the sum of all the paths' tick counts to reach a destination network.

The MAC Address entry field records the host/node number from which the network can be reached. This field indicates the port from which the router received this reachability information. A Novell file server can support up to 16 network interface cards or NICs. It is the same as a physical port number in a stand-alone router (not a personal computer or file server acting as a router). The Intermediate Address entry contains the physical node address of the router that can forward packets to each segment. If the network is directly attached, the entry is empty. If the network to be reached requires the use of another router, this entry contains the physical address of the next router to which to send the packet. This physical address is extracted from RIP updates (a router broadcasting its table) sent by those routers. The RIP packet format is shown in Figure 7.11.

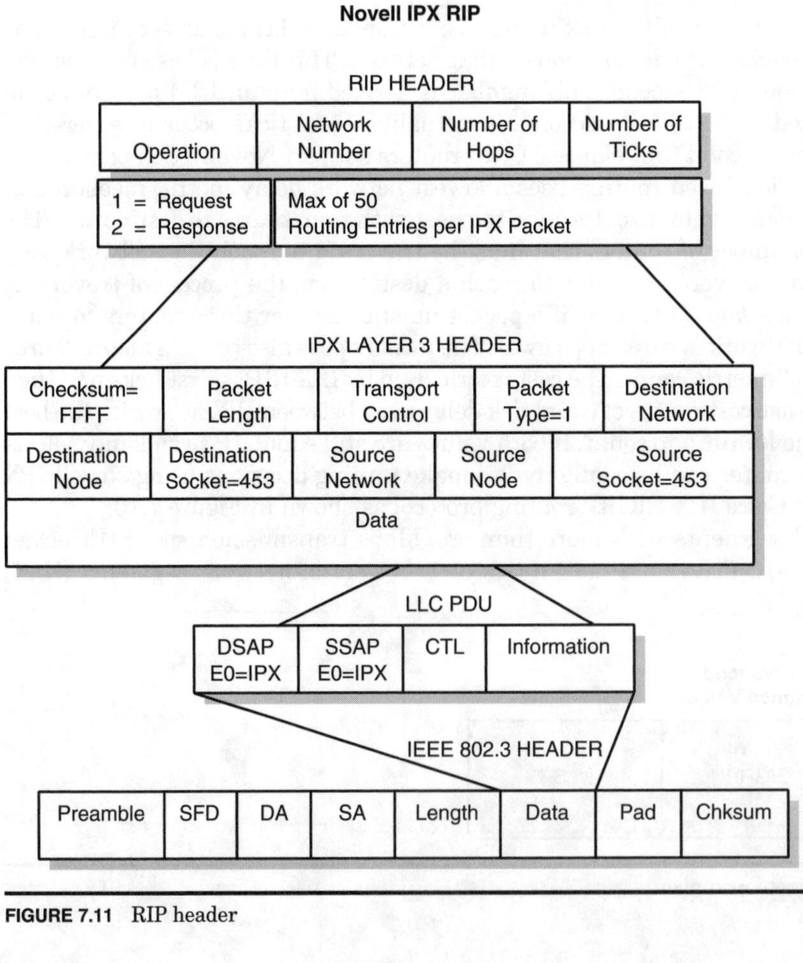

Novell IPX RIP

FIGURE 7.11   RIP header

Client and Router Interaction

Sending Node's Responsibility. When a node wants to send information to another node with the same network number, the sending node can address and send packets directly to the destination node. However, if the two nodes have different network numbers, the sending node must find a router on its own segment that can forward packets to the destination node's network segment. To find this router, a workstation broadcasts a RIP packet requesting the fastest route to the destination node's network number. The router residing on the sending node's segment with the shortest path to the desired segment responds to the RIP request.

When the sending node knows the router's node address, it is prepared to send packets to the destination node. The sending node addresses these packets in the following way:

1. Places the destination node's internetwork address (network, node, and socket number) in the destination address field of the IPX header.
2. Places its own internetwork address in the source address field of the IPX header. (All other fields in the IPX header must be filled out as well.)
3. Places the node address of the router (the one that responded to the RIP request if the sending node is a workstation) in the destination address field of the MAC header.
4. Places its own node address in the source address field of the MAC header and sends the packet.

Router's Responsibility. When a router receives an IPX packet, its IPX handling process should do the following:

1. Check the IPX header Transport Control field (hop count). If this field is equal to or greater than 16, the packet should be discarded.
2. Check the IPX header Packet Type field. If the Packet Type is 20, the router acts according to what the NetBIOS propagation level has set.
3. Check the IPX header Destination Address field (network, node, and socket) to determine how to route the packet. If the packet is addressed to the router, it should be handled internally by the appropriate socket process; otherwise further routing is required.

When forwarding packets, the router can take one of two possible actions. If the packet is destined for a network number that the router is directly connected to, the router performs the following steps:

1. Places the destination node address from the IPX header in the destination address field of the MAC header.
2. Places its own node address in the source address field of the MAC header.
3. Increments the Transport Control field of the IPX header (hop count) and transmits the packet onto the destination node's segment.

Note that each frame type bound to a router's interface is treated as a separate, logical segment—each segment having its own distinct network address. This information is stored in the router's RIP table, and the router forwards the packets just the same as to a physical segment.

If, however, the router is not directly connected to the segment on which the final destination node resides, it will send the packet to the next router in the path to the destination node:

1. The router places the node address of the next router in the destination address field of the MAC header.

2. The router places its own node address in the source address of the MAC header.

3. The router increments the Transport Control field in the IPX header (hop count) and sends the pack to the next router.

Note that in the two cases just described, under normal conditions the only modification that the router makes to the IPX header when routing a packet is incrementing the Transport Control field (hop count). All other fields are left as initially set by the sending node. Of course, if the router is generating one of its own packets, it needs to fill in the entire IPX header and perform the functions of a sending node.

IPX RIP Interval

Cisco allows the IPX RIP update interval to be configured on any interface, which allows users to control or reduce traffic on heavily used low-speed WAN lines. All router interfaces on the same IPX network segment must use the same RIP interval.

Configurable RIP Timers

The Cisco IOS `ipx update-time` command extends the standard 60-second IPX periodic RIP broadcast interval in user-defined increments of 10 seconds on a per-interface basis. Periodic RIP broadcasts can be eliminated by setting configurable RIP timers to 0, propagating only RIP updates triggered by changes in the internetwork topology of the interface. Configurable RIP timers reduce IPX RIP overhead and enhance bandwidth availability. When changing the RIP update timer, all routers and servers should have the same update interval for stability. NCP uses an inefficient one-to-one request/response ratio when transferring packets. Novell realized this was inefficient and developed the Burst Mode protocol.

Multiple Routes

Cisco IOS supports several equal cost, parallel paths to a given destination instead of only one. This feature provides a more stable IPX configuration. Previously, if multiple best routes existed to a target network, RIP kept only one. If the route is lost, the router sends out unreachable network RIP broadcasts. When the next RIP packet arrives from the alternate route, the router learns the new route and sends another RIP packet announcing that to the world.

IPX and Split Horizon

In actuality, routing tables are broadcast out all active ports of a router. Most RIP-type routers use Split Horizon. Split Horizon instructs the router not to broadcast a learned route back through a port from which it received the learned information. Split Horizon, as defined by the IPX specification, does not allow a router to propagate any RIP or SAP broadcasts learned from a particular interface out that same interface. Because Frame Relay and

SMDS services support single line interfaces, Split Horizon prevents the propagation of complete RIP and SAP information in nonfully meshed topologies. The Configurable Split Horizon feature allows disabling of IPX Split Horizon, permitting a complete view of IPX internetworks (routes and services) to be disseminated over nonfully meshed Frame Relay and SMDS topologies.

IPX Static Routing

Cisco IPX static routing allows manual definition of IPX routes between source and destination networks. Static routing allows configuration of the *next hop network* (interface) and the *next hop host* (router) toward a destination network. With static routing, all RIP and SAP broadcasts can be eliminated, reducing IPX overhead. Static routing is most valuable over wide area links in which bandwidth is a premium. Broadcast mechanisms such as IPX, RIP, and SAP can cause the continuous establishment of dial-on-demand connections, preventing user-defined expiration time limits from being reached.

Novell Burst Mode Architecture

In early 1992, *NetWare Core Protocol* (NCP) (both client and server software) was modified to allow a requester to transmit a single request for up to a 64K segment of data. NetWare v3.11 and earlier versions required an NLM to enable this protocol on the server. Later versions implemented Burst Mode protocol into the server's operating system.

Let's sum up what Burst Mode is, and then we can continue into the specifics. Transactions between a workstation and its file server really consist of reading and writing information between the two.

A workstation reads a file from the file server or writes information back to the file server. Instead of sending one packet and waiting for a reply, why not group a set of packets together and send them all at one time? For example, a workstation requests that a read be performed from a file on the file server. The file server knows that the read is 64K long. Instead of sending one packet at a time to the workstation, the file server gets the 64K, puts the bytes into a set of packets, and then transmits the packets in the form of groups to the workstation. The Burst Mode protocol allows a workstation to send or accept a burst of packets containing an aggregate of up to 64K of data on file reads and writes before requiring an acknowledgment. As each group is received by the workstation, the workstation acknowledges to the file server that it received the specified group, and then the file server sends the next group. Burst Mode allows a set of packets to be sent all at the same time, the server or workstation acknowledges that group, and the next group can be sent.

The actual amount of data sent and received in a burst is determined by the maximum packet size multiplied by the number of Burst Mode buffers allocated on the client or the server. When a Burst Mode connection is established between a client and server, the workstation shell automatically uses Burst Mode for file reads and writes (see Figures 7.12 and 7.13).

The introduction of this protocol did not require any application using NetWare to be modified; this application-transparency is one of the advantages of Burst Mode. This service can be used by any NetWare interface application. The application does not need to

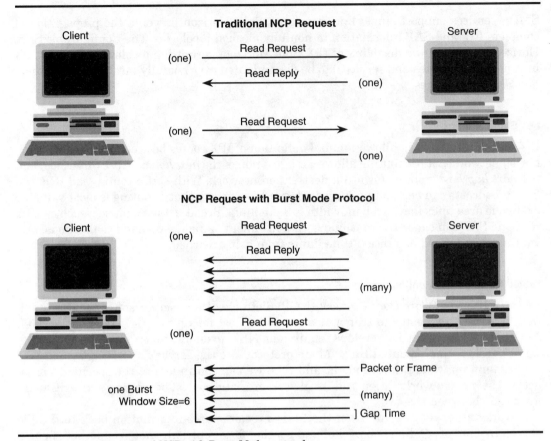

FIGURE 7.12   Traditional and NCP with Burst Mode protocol

be aware of the protocol to take advantage of it. NetWare 3.12 and above have this capability built into the server (VLMs client).

Table 7.2 describes the flags available in the Burst Mode packet header.

Novell Burst Mode Sequence Number

All replies in response to a single request are members of a burst set. Each packet in the set contains the same burst sequence number. When a client and server set up the burst connection, this sequence number is 0 and increments with each successive burst sent.

- *ACK sequence number.*   The ACK sequence number is the burst sequence number the node expects to receive next; it determines whether the last burst transmitted was successfully received. All packets of a burst set have the same burst sequence and ACK sequence number until the last packet of the burst set. The last packet contains an ACK sequence number equal to the current burst sequence number plus one. This number indicates the next burst sequence expected.

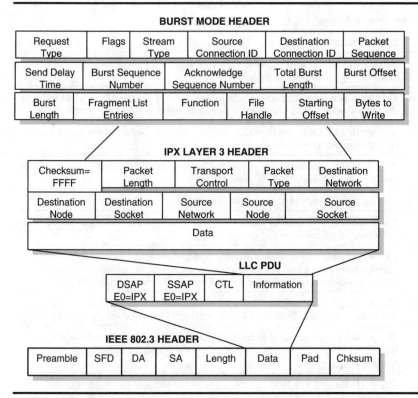

FIGURE 7.13 Novell Burst Mode header

- *Total Burst Length.*   The Total Burst Length field defines the length of the entire burst transaction (in actual data bytes). This number is the sum of all burst sets.

- *Burst Offset.*   The Burst Offset field defines where in the burst this packet's data will fit. If the offset is 0, this is the first packet of the burst transaction.

- *Burst Length.*   The Burst Length field specifies the total length of the burst being transmitted (in bytes).

- *Fragment List Entries.*   The Fragment List Entries field defines the number of elements missing from the burst transaction. The missing fragment list follows this number, if applicable. The value 0 indicates that no fragments are missing.

- *Function.*   The Function field defines whether the current burst transaction is a read or write.

NLSP: A Link-State Routing Protocol

The NetWare Link Services protocol is a link-state routing protocol. This type of protocol derives its name from the fact that link-state routers track the status of other routers and links. Link-state protocols adapt more quickly to network topology changes than do

TABLE 7.2   Burst Mode Packet Header Flags

Flag	Description
SYS	Setting this bit indicates that the burst is a system packet and does not have any burst data associated with it.
SAK	This bit function is not currently implemented but eventually is set to indicate that the sender would like the receiver to transmit its missing fragment list.
EOB	Setting this bit indicates that this packet contains the last of the burst data that the sender transmits.
BSY	This field is not currently implemented but eventually notifies a requester that the server is busy and that it should wait.
ABT	Setting this bit indicates to the client that the session is no longer valid.
Stream Type	The stream type is used by the server, and the only current value is 0x02, which indicates "Big send burst."
Source Connection ID	The source connection ID is a random number generally formed from the current time of day and provides a unique identifier for a burst connection. This number is generated by the sender and cannot contain the value 0.
Destination Connection ID	The destination connection ID is a random number similar to the source connection ID, but it is defined by the receiver. The value cannot be zero.
Packet Sequence Number	The packet sequence number tracks the current burst transaction and is incremented by 1 for every new packet a node transmits in each service transaction.
Send Delay Time	The Send Delay Time field identifies the delay times between each of the sender's packet transmissions and is specified in units of approximately 100 microseconds.

distance-vector protocols. Thus, they are better than distance-vector protocols for managing internetworking on large, complex internetworks.

NLSP significantly reduces the communication overhead required for routing. NLSP can significantly improve network performance because it frees resources to be used for transferring data packets rather than routing information. NLSP is particularly efficient for wide area network routing, in which available communication bandwidth is limited.

NLSP is designed to be functional only with routers. NLSP does not require workstations to report their status to a router, and a workstation does not know that the network is working with the NLSP or IPX RIP protocol.

NLSP allows for large NetWare internetworks to be designed and implemented and is not constrained by the limitations of the IPX RIP protocol. In addition to the elimination of RIP/SAP broadcasts, NLSP provides load balancing across equally weighted segments. NLSP updates and converges the network three to four times faster than RIP. Faster convergence increases the reliability and efficiency of your network. It is designed as a hierarchical topology. In doing this, NLSP divides a NetWare internetwork into three items:

- Local network segments within an area
- Areas: a collection of routers within the internetwork
- Domains: a part of the routing hierarchy

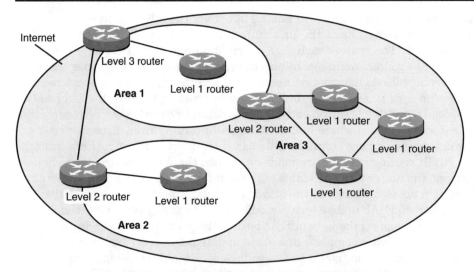

Level 1 --- Involves the interaction of routers within the *same area*
Level 2 --- Involves routing between Level 1 areas forming a *routing domain*
Level 3 --- Involves routing between routing domains to create a *global internetwork*

FIGURE 7.14 The three levels of routing provided by NLSP.

To accommodate this, NLSP provides for three levels of routing (see Figure 7.14):

- Level 1 routers, which route data within an area
- Level 2 routers, which route data between areas
- Level 3 routers, which route data between domains

A level 2 router also assumes the role of the level 1 router. Likewise, a level 3 router assumes the role of both a level 2 and level 1 router. Many local network numbers are within an area, and many areas can be within a domain.

Dividing the internetwork up like this has many advantages. For example, the level 1 routers must store link information about every link in its area. However, it does not store link information about links in other areas. To route data to another area, it has to know about its nearest level 2 router. For data packets destined for another area, a level 1 router hands the packet off to the level 2 router for further forwarding. Likewise, level 2 routers exchange only level 2 (area) information between them. They do not exchange level 1 information between them. Similarly, level 3 routers exchange only domain information between them.

NLSP is known as a *link state protocol*. Link state protocols were developed to address the demands and complications of large internetworks. As shown in previous sections on the RIP protocol, information about networks travels slowly, and every router is dependent on every other router for correct information. If any router makes a mistake in the computation of its routing table, this mistake is propagated throughout the Internet. The RIP protocol is also based on point-to-point links with other routers; it is a two-way conversation.

NLSP is called a link state protocol because the router maintains the status of every link in its area. Link state protocols scale better than distance vector protocols and adapt easily to topology changes (i.e., losing a link and having to update the other routers). In general, upon initialization, a router running the link state protocol forms adjacencies with other routers on the network. The routers exchange information about their directly connected links. Furthermore, the routers exchange information about the other adjacencies that they know about. The router floods information about itself and its adjacent neighbors to every router in an area (an area is a subset of routers in an internetwork). After the information is obtained, a special algorithm is run on each router to determine the best route to any other network on the internet. This is where link state algorithms differ from distance vectors.

Each router determines its own routing table based on information it gathers from the network. With NLSP, routing updates are made only when there is a change. If no changes occur on a network, the router remains stable with the information in its table. If the router receives information about a change in the status of a link, it performs the operation and rebuilds its table. RIP and SAP update on a periodic basis—typically every 60 seconds, even when there is not a change on the network. At best, if there are no changes in the NLSP topology, NLSP requires that a complete link-state update occur every two hours.

NLSP does not depend on a hop count to determine entries in the routing table like IPX-RIP. Each link is assigned a cost, represented by a positive integer number. This is a 16-bit number ranging from 1 to 65,535. These costs are very important. They are used in the decision algorithm to determine the best path to a destination. The costs are assigned when the router is configured. The summation of costs to a destination network determines the best path to the final network. The lower the cost, the better the path. Higher speed paths are assigned a lower cost, and lower speed paths have higher costs. NLSP is based on an algorithm known as the Dijkstra algorithm (after Edsger W. Dijkstra, who devised the algorithm used in the forwarding method).

Link-State Databases

NLSP forms a series of databases. Information about link states of each router in each area is exchanged between routers using the *link state packet* (LSP).

The adjacency database keeps track of the router's immediate neighbors (those on directly connected networks) and the information about its own links (directly attached segments). The routers exchange simple "hello" messages. These messages help maintain this database. Routers send hello messages to find other routers on directly attached segments. Sending these hello packets allows for routers on the same network to discover the identity of other level 1 routers on the same network. The router also listens for hello messages from other routers to build the adjacent database. Any changes in the state of the hello messages are reflected in this database. The adjacency database is a subset of the link-state database. Routers transfer information about their links to other routers known in the adjacency database.

When a router or a link of a router is initialized, the network numbers configured on its ports are put into the *link-state database*. Using information in the LSP, each router in an area that receives this information is able to build its own map of that area; this map is the link-state database (see Figure 7.15). The information stored in this map records the area's routers and servers, the links that connect them, and other information. It contains information about all the other routers and their links in the area. The link-state database does not contain any end nodes. Every router in an area should contain the same information in its link-state database, as does its neighbor. NLSP provides for this synchronization.

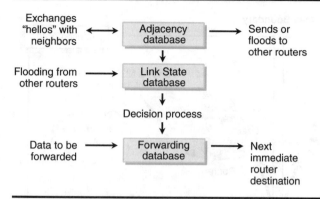

FIGURE 7.15 NLSP databases

Flooding is the means by which the link-state databases in all routers synchronize. Each router sends information from its adjacency database to each of its neighbors.

This information is sent via the LSP packet. When a new LSP arrives at a router, two events happen. First, that LSP is retransmitted on all links of that router except those on which the LSP was received. Second, the LSP is merged into the router's link-state database. The database is nothing more than a collection of LSP packets obtained from the router's own adjacency database and received from other routers through the flooding procedure. When a link state changes, each router detecting this event floods an LSP indicating that change. The receiving routers mark that link as being down. At this point, they are not yet removed. Another method of determining that a link state has changed is the router's own timer for an LSP. As each entry is made in the table, a countdown timer is applied. If a new LSP arrives to update that entry, the timer resets. If no LSP arrives to update that entry, the timer expires; that entry is purged, and the router floods an LSP to the area to indicate this.

The final database is the *forwarding* database or table, where a network number entry and its associated cost are kept. A forwarding table maps a network number into the next hop, which is the same as the routing table in RIP networks (see Figure 7.16). The decision process builds or rebuilds the forwarding table. The decision process is based on Dijkstra's algorithm. This algorithm determines the shortest path to every other network in an area. The algorithm is very complex and requires extreme resources to compute the forwarding table. Routers of received packets use this table to determine the next hop for the received packet.

One of the benefits for using this algorithm is that a change in one area does not invoke Dijkstra's algorithm in another area. Only in the area in which the link-state change occurs is the Dijkstra's algorithm invoked. This outcome requires all routers to flood information throughout the area to synchronize link-state databases in all the routers there. Other areas are not affected and merely receive the computed changes through level 2 routers. In a stable environment, this update should not occur often, and when it does, it takes less than two seconds for an area to reconverge.

Novell's NLSP protocol can coexist with networks currently using RIP and SAP protocols. Therefore, a router running the NLSP protocol can process and broadcast RIP packets that it may receive. An NLSP router can respond to RIP requests and responses on a network.

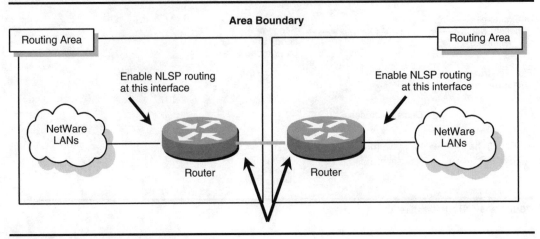

FIGURE 7.16 Creating routing areas

NLSP Addressing

All NLSP packet types can be sent by a router/server as either a broadcast or a multicast packet. If NLSP packets are sent by multicast transmission, all NLSP routers on the directly connected segment recognize the multicast address. The following destination MAC addresses are used in the data-link header:

```
IEEE 802.3 0x09001BFFFFFF
IEEE 802.5 0xC00010000000 (non-canonical)
FDDI       0xC00010000000 (non-canonical)
```

Devices on NLSP segments must be able to receive multicast packets, while devices on RIP-IPX/SAP segments must be able to receive broadcast packets.

NLSP still uses the 32-bit network number as it pertains to IPX, which maintains the packet format compatibility for the vast installations of NetWare. However, the 32-bit address is used differently than before; the concept of masking has been introduced. The 32-bit network number is now split, to allow for an area ID and a local network number to be assigned.

A typical 32-bit address could resemble the following:

```
4444d088
```

What is different is that a 32-bit mask must be applied to this network number. The mask for this address could be as follows:

```
FFFFFF00
```

Applying this type of mask yields an area address and a local network address. In this case, the network address is **4444d0**. The last two digits represent the local network address. A mask shows how much of the network number should be used for the area and how much of the address should be used for the local network number. The preceding mask allows 254 local network numbers to be assigned to an area. (All 0s or all 1s are not allowed in a network number.) The router maintains a listing of network IDs and area IDs in its routing table.

Packets received with a destination area ID that matches the router's area ID can be routed through L1 (level 1) routers. When a packet is received that contains a destination area ID different from the routers, the router must find a level 2 router to which to route the packet. The level 1 router hands the packet off to the level 2 router without any network database lookup. The receiving level 2 router routes the packet to the appropriate router containing that area ID, and then the packet is routed to its local network ID using L1 services.

Assigning your own network numbers is still allowed. However, Novell is requesting that NetWare installations register their networks with the Novell network registry. Although registration is not required, the purpose of this program is to ensure that no two sites have the same network number range assignment. The largest requirement for this program is when two NetWare networks migrate into one. This can happen during a business merger or when two or more businesses would like to communicate with one another. Sites having similar network numbers cause a disruption on the network. Multiple domains may be used in the case when two companies are merging their NetWare networks together. No hard and fast rule exists, but Novell's recommendation is a maximum of 400 networks to an area.

NLSP Advantages

Link-state protocols offer many advantages over distance-vector protocols. Besides the obvious advantages of using MAC multicast addresses for updates and of the lower CPU utilization because updates are made only during a change, using the NLSP protocol offers many other advantages. NLSP maintains the original IPX packet format for workstations and servers. NLSP does not affect the normal client/server operation of NetWare. Workstations and servers are not aware that they are operating under the NLSP protocol. Workstations and servers do not register themselves with the routers. Only the routers perform new functions, and they talk to themselves only for building and updating routing tables.

Unlike the RIP protocol, which stores the next hop address for a forwarded packet, NLSP maintains an entire map of the network. This map allows it to make a much more intelligent decision about which path may be the best. Each router determines its own entries in the routing table and is not dependent on other routers' tables to build its tables. Best paths are calculated based on a cost number assigned to a router's link (physical port) when the router is configured and initialized. After the initial exchange of information between neighbor routers, they only communicate with other routers if a link-state change occurs in their area. This is unlike the RIP protocol, which periodically transmits its routing table, whether a change occurs or not. Furthermore, NLSP uses a special multicast MAC address when initializing or updating. This is important, because only those stations assigned the same MAC multicast address process the received packet. All other stations discard it. The RIP/SAP protocol uses broadcast addresses. NLSP must do a complete topology update every two hours even when there are no changes at all.

NLSP not only works on routing tables, it also works with SAP broadcasts. The same rules apply to the SAP protocol. NLSP advertises only a service change when there is one. Otherwise, the SAP protocol does not broadcast its table periodically. NLSP also allows for more than seven services to be advertised within one update. Where all this has significance is over WAN links. These links are generally lower speed serial circuits. Conserving bandwidth on these links is very beneficial, especially when the WAN link is X.25 or Frame Relay, in which a business gets charged based on the amount of usage.

NLSP also uses IPX header compression when used across a WAN link. Compression is the technique of taking a packet header and compressing the contents. NLSP and IPX use a modified compression technique that originated with the Van Jacobson protocol. IPX compression is specified in RFC 1533: *Compressing IPX Headers of WAN Media.* This technique can allow for up to 30 bytes (the IPX header length) to be compressed into one byte in the best case or seven bytes in the worst-case scenario. Furthermore, the IPX compression protocol can also compress NCP request and reply headers of 37 bytes to two bytes in the best case and eight bytes in the worst case. The best- and worst-case scenarios depend on whether the packet is using the CRC checksum and whether the data length can be determined at the MAC level.

NLSP supports load splitting. If there are parallel paths (two or more) to a destination and the costs of these paths are the same, NLSP splits the traffic load over these parallel paths. This is an option, and you can tell NLSP how many parallel paths may be used for load splitting or that load splitting should not be used.

NLSP is better suited for scaling up to larger internetworks. Using RIP, the diameter of the network is limited to 15 routers. A packet cannot traverse more than 15 routers before being discarded. NLSP supports network diameters of up to 127 routers.

Finally, one of the biggest advantages of NLSP is cost assignment. Each link of a router is assigned a cost. Although IPX RIP allowed for this as well, assigning a cost higher than one to any link effectively reduces the network diameter.

For example, imagine a simple network topology, consisting of three routers linked together through WAN links in a triangular configuration (see Figure 7.17). Router A to B has a WAN link speed of T1 (1.544 Mbps). Router B and Router C are linked together using a T1. Router C to A has a WAN link speed of 56Kbps. Assuming a RIP cost of 1 for each

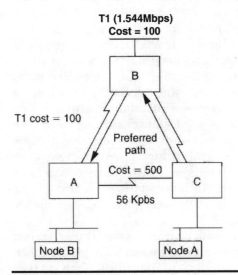

FIGURE 7.17 NLSP cost

link, a network station attached to Router C that is conversing with a network station on Router A automatically takes the 56Kbps link, because it is the shorter cost (or hop count).

NLSP assigns costs to every link, but not based on a simple 1-to-16 value design. Using the same network design as before, the Router C to Router A link could be assigned a cost of 500, while the two T1 links could be assigned a cost of 100 each. NLSP then automatically takes the two-T1-link route without affecting the overall diameter of the network.

Level 1 LSP

The NLSP level 1 link-state packet is shown in Figure 7.18 and includes the following fields:

- *Protocol ID.* 0x83, identifies the NLSP routing layer.
- *Length Indicator.* The number of bytes in the fixed portion of the header (up to and including the Router Type field).
- *Minor Version.* 1 or 2 (if the router supports aggregated routes).

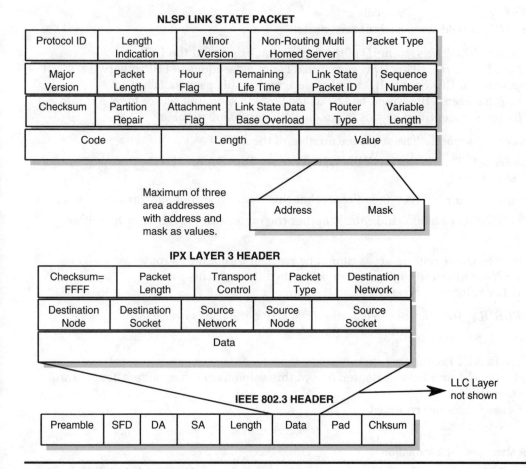

FIGURE 7.18 Level 1 link-state packet

- *Reserved.*   0, ignored on receipt.

- *Non-routing multihomed server* (1 bit).   When this field contains 1, the system has more than one network interface but does not forward traffic from one network segment to another.

- *Res* (2 bits).   0, ignored on receipt.

- *Packet Type* (5 bits).   18.

- *Major Version.*   1.

- *Reserved.*   0, ignored on receipt.

- *Packet Length.*   The entire length of this packet, in bytes, including the fixed portion of the NLSP header.

- *Hour Flag.*   1 bit. When this field is set to one, the Remaining Lifetime field represents the number of hours before this LSP is considered to expire.

- *Remaining Lifetime.*   The number of seconds before this LSP is considered to expire.

- *LSP ID.*   A field composed of three parts:

  - *Source ID.*   The system ID of the router that originated the LSP.
  - *Pseudonode ID.*   This ID is zero if this is not a pseudonode LSP; otherwise, it is a unique (for this Source ID) number designating this pseudonode.
  - *LSP Number.*   If a would-be LSP is too large to send, the source breaks it into fragments identified by this monotonically increasing number.

- *Sequence Number.*   The sequence number of the LSP.

- *Checksum.*   The checksum of the LSP contents from Source ID (the first part of LSP ID) to the end.

- *Partition Repair* (1 bit).   0, indicates that this router does not support partition repair.

- *Attached Flag* (4 bits).   Indicates whether the router can provide a path to other routing areas.

  - 0 = No. Other routing areas cannot be reached through this router.
  - 1 = Yes. Other routing areas can be reached through this router.
  - Other values are reserved.

- *LSPDBOL.*   (one bit) Set to one when the LSP database is overloaded.

- *Router Type.*   (two bits):

  - 1 = Level 1 Router operation.
  - 3 = Level 1 and Level 2 Router. Accept this value from other routers, for forward compatibility.
  - Other values are reserved.

NLSP Management Information

Figure 7.19 shows the NLSP link-state packet management information, which contains the following fields:

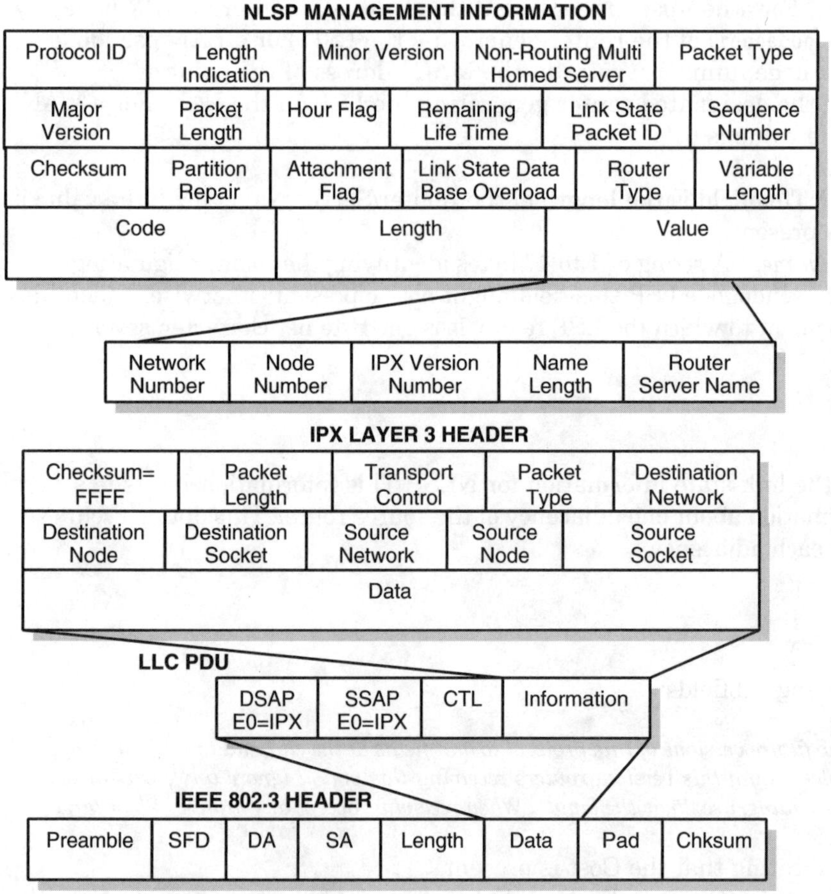

NLSP MANAGEMENT INFORMATION

Protocol ID	Length Indication	Minor Version	Non-Routing Multi Homed Server	Packet Type
Major Version	Packet Length	Hour Flag	Remaining Life Time	Link State Packet ID	Sequence Number
Checksum	Partition Repair	Attachment Flag	Link State Data Base Overload	Router Type	Variable Length
Code		Length		Value	

Network Number	Node Number	IPX Version Number	Name Length	Router Server Name

IPX LAYER 3 HEADER

Checksum= FFFF	Packet Length	Transport Control	Packet Type	Destination Network
Destination Node	Destination Socket	Source Network	Source Node	Source Socket
Data				

LLC PDU

DSAP E0=IPX	SSAP E0=IPX	CTL	Information

IEEE 802.3 HEADER

Preamble	SFD	DA	SA	Length	Data	Pad	Chksum

FIGURE 7.19 NLSP link-state packet

- *Variable Length fields.*   A series of optional fields, each of which has the following three-part code/length/value option form:

  Code = 0×C1

  Length = 12 to 60, or more

  Value = the following five subfields:

  > **NOTE:**   *To allow future versions of this protocol to add fields at the end and remain compatible with routers implementing this version, routers receiving this option ignore any fields after those listed here.*

  - *Network Number.*   The internal IPX network number of the router generating the LSP. For a LAN pseudonode or a numbered WAN pseudonode, it is the IPX network number of the network segment that the pseudonode represents. For an unnumbered WAN pseudonode, the value is 0.

- *Node Number.*   For a non-pseudonode LSP, this field is the internal IPX node number (0x000000000001) of the router generating the LSP. For a LAN pseudonode, this field is the node number (typically, the MAC address of the point of attachment) of the designated router generating the LSP on the LAN. For a WAN pseudonode, the value is 0.
- *IPX Version Number.* 1.
- *Name Length.*   This field is the length of the Router/Server Name field; the value is 0 if no name is present.
- *Router/Server Name.*   A string of 1 to 47 bytes identifying the router originating the LSP. If this is a pseudonode LSP, this field might not be present; otherwise, it identifies the network segment to which the LSP refers. It is one byte per character, seven-bit ASCII.

Link-State Information

Figure 7.20 shows the link-state information for NLSP. This information refers to several subfields with information about one adjacency of the source router. This option occurs several times, once for each adjacency.

- Code = 0×C2
- Length = 25 or more
- Value = The following subfields:

> **NOTE:**   *To allow future versions of this protocol to add fields at the end and to remain compatible with routers implementing this version; routers receiving this option ignore any fields after those listed here. When sending, use 25 as the length. When receiving, accept any number 25 or larger.*

- S1 (1 bit): 0, indicating that the Cost is present.
- *Internal/External* (1 bit).   0, indicating that the cost is an internal metric. Note that a Level 1 LSP is rejected if the bit is not set to 0.

> **NOTE:**   *With hierarchical routing, costs internal to one's own routing area are not usually comparable with those outside it. An internal route is chosen over an external one, if there is a choice. The I/E bit provides information to the decision process that enables the choice to be made.*

- *Cost* (6 bits).   This field is the cost of a link to the listed neighbor; an unsigned positive integer.
- *Reserved* (3 bytes).   0, ignored on receipt.
- *Neighbor ID.*   For a nonpseudonode neighbor, this field is the neighboring router's system ID plus one byte of 0; for a pseudonode neighbor, the first six bytes are the designated router's system ID, and the seventh byte is the unique nonzero pseudonode ID value assigned by the designated router.
- *MTU Size.*   This field indicates the maximum number of bytes that can be transmitted on this link by the originating router, including the IPX header but not including the data-link headers. It is 0 for a pseudonode LSP.
- *Delay.*   This field is the time, in microseconds, that it takes to transmit one byte of data (excluding protocol headers) to a destination if the media is free of other traffic. It is 0 for a pseudonode LSP.

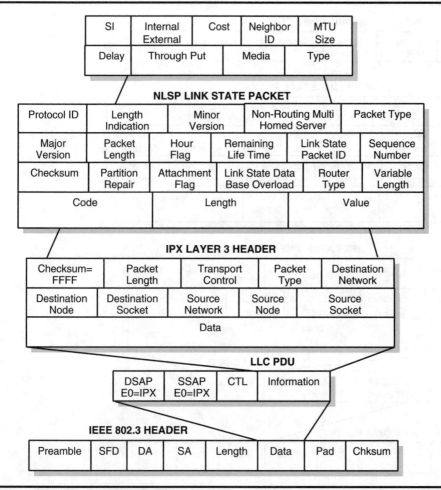

FIGURE 7.20 Link-state information

- *Throughput.* The amount of data, in bits, that can flow through the media and be received at the other side in one second, if there is no other traffic using the interface. It is zero for a pseudonode LSP.
- *Media Type.* This field is a code identifying the type of circuit; the most significant bit is one for WAN media, 0 for others.

Services Information

Figure 7.21 shows the services information for NLSP. The *Services Information* describes services that advertise themselves by the SAP protocol.

- Code = 0×C3
- Length = 16 to 62
- Value = The following subfields:

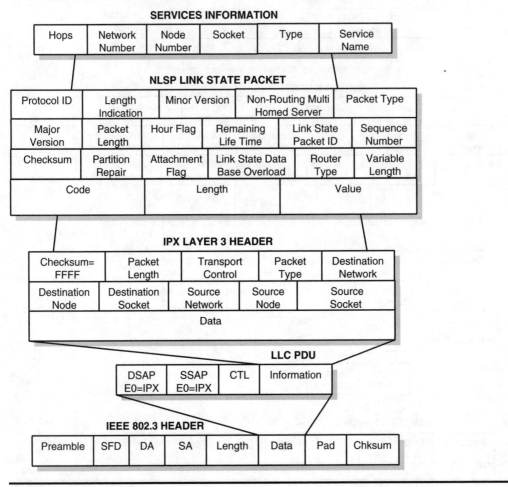

FIGURE 7.21   Level 1 LSP

- *Hops.*   This field is the number of hops to reach the service.
- *Network Number, Node Number, Socket.*   The IPX address at which the service is available.
- *Type.*   This field indicates the type of service offered for a partial list of defined types.
- *Service Name.*   This field shows the name of the service; its length is determined implicitly by the length of this option—the name is not null-terminated.
- *External Routes.*   Describes routes obtained by the source router through non-NLSP protocols; for example, RIP.

- Code = 0×C4
- Value = The following subfields:

  - *Hops.*   The number of hops reported by the non-NLSP protocol.
  - *Network Number.*   The IPX network number to which this entry refers.

- *Ticks.* The RIP Delay (that is, the number of RIP timer ticks) from the source router to the network number, as reported by the non-NLSP protocol.

- External Routes   Number of Bytes

  Hops   1
  Network Number Node Number   4
  Ticks   2

- *Protocol ID.* 0x83, identifies the NLSP routing layer.

- *Length Indicator.* This field indicates the number of bytes in the fixed portion of the header (up to and including the NLSP Link State Packet/Router Type field).

- *Hour Flag* (1 bit). When this field is set to 1, the Remaining Lifetime field represents the number of hours before this LSP is considered to expire.

- *Remaining Lifetime.* The number of seconds before this LSP is considered to expire.

- *LSP ID.* A field composed of three parts:

  - *Source ID.* The system ID of the router that originated the LSP.
  - *Pseudonode ID.* This field is 0 if this is a non-pseudonode LSP; otherwise, it is a unique (for this Source ID) number designating this pseudonode.
  - *LSP Number.* If a would-be LSP is too large to send, the source breaks it into fragments identified by this monotonically increasing number.

- *Sequence Number.* This field is the sequence number of the LSP.

- *Checksum.* This field is the checksum of the LSP contents from Source ID (the first part of LSP ID) to the end.

- *P* (one bit). 0, indicates that this router does not support partition repair.

- *Attached Flag* (4 bits). This field indicates whether the router can provide a path to other routing areas.

  - 0 = No, other routing areas cannot be reached through this router.
  - 1 = Yes, other routing areas can be reached through this router.
  - Other values are reserved.

- *LSPDBOL* (1 bit). This field is set to one when the LSP database is overloaded.

- *Router Type* (2 bits).

  - 1 = Level 1 Router operation.
  - 3 = Level 1 and Level 2 Router. Accept this value from other routers, for forward compatibility.
  - Other values are reserved.

- *Variable Length fields.* A series of optional fields, each of which has a three-part code/length/value Option form.

External Routes Header

Figure 7.22 shows the external routes header of the NSLP link-state packet and contains the following fields:

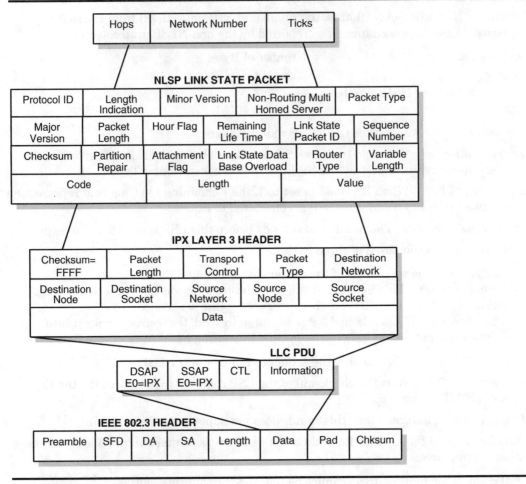

FIGURE 7.22   External router header

- *Protocol ID.*   0x83, identifies the NLSP routing layer.
- *Length Indicator.*   The number of bytes in the fixed portion of the header (up to and including the Router Type field).
- *Minor Version.*   1 or 2 (if the router supports aggregated routes).
- *Reserved.*   0, ignored on receipt.
- *Non-routing Multi-homed Server* (1 bit).   When this field contains 1, the system has more than one network interface but does not forward traffic from one network segment to another.
- *Res* (2 bits).   0, ignored on receipt.
- *Packet Type* (5 bits).   18.
- *Major Version.*   1.
- *Reserved.*   0, ignored on receipt.

- *Packet Length.* The entire length of this packet, in bytes, including the fixed portion of the NLSP header.

- *Hour Flag* (1 bit). When this field is set to 1, the Remaining Lifetime field represents the number of hours before this LSP is considered to expire.

- *Remaining Lifetime.* The number of seconds before this LSP is considered to expire. If the Hour Flag field is set to 1, this field represents the number of hours before this LSP is considered to expire.

- *LSP ID.* A field composed of three parts:

  - *Source ID.* The system ID of the router that originated the LSP.
  - *Pseudonode ID.* Is 0 if this is a non-pseudonode LSP; otherwise, it is a unique (for this Source ID) number designating this pseudonode.
  - *LSP Number.* If an LSP is too large to send, the source breaks it into fragments identified by this monotonically increasing number.

- *Sequence Number.* This field is the sequence number of the LSP.

- *Checksum.* This field is the checksum of the LSP contents from Source ID (the first part of LSP ID) to the end.

- *P* (one bit). 0—Indicates that this router does not support partition repair.

- *Attachment Flag* (4 bits). This field indicates whether the router can provide a path to other routing areas.

  - 0 = "No," other routing areas cannot be reached through this router.
  - 1 = "Yes," other routing areas can be reached through this router.
  - Other values are reserved.

- *LSPDBOL* (1 bit). This field is set to 1 when the LSP database is overloaded.

- *Router Type* (2 bits).

  - 1 = "Level 1 Router" operation.
  - 3 = "Level 1 and Level 2 Router;" accept this value from other routers for forward compatibility.
  - Other values are reserved.

- *Variable Length fields.* A series of optional fields, each of which has the following three-part code/length/value Option form:

  Code = 0xC2
  Length = 25 or more
  Value = the following subfields:

  - S1 (1 bit): 0, indicating that the cost is present. The link information for this NLSP is contained in several subfields with information about one adjacency of the source router. This option occurs several times, in general, once for each adjacency.

  NOTE: *To allow future versions of this protocol to add fields at the end and remain compatible with routers implementing this version, routers receiving this option ignore any fields after those listed. When sending, use 25 as the Length. When receiving, accept any number 25 or larger.*

- *Internal/External* (1 bit).   0, indicating that the Cost is an internal metric. Note that a Level 1 LSP is rejected if the bit is not set to 0.

NOTE: *With hierarchical routing, costs internal to one's own routing area are not usually comparable with those outside it. An internal route is chosen over an external one, if there is a choice. The I/E bit provides information that allows the choice to be made.*

- *Cost* (6 bits).   The cost of a link to the listed neighbor; an unsigned positive integer.
- *Reserved* (3 bytes).   0, ignored on receipt.
- *Neighbor ID.*   For a nonpseudonode neighbor, this field is the neighboring router's system ID plus one byte of 0; for a pseudonode neighbor, the first six bytes are the designated router's system ID, and the seventh byte is the unique nonzero pseudonode ID value assigned to this pseudonode by the designated router.
- *MTU Size.*   The maximum number of bytes that can be transmitted on this link by the originating router, including the IPX header but not including the data-link headers. It is 0 for a pseudonode LSP.
- *Delay.*   The time, in microseconds, that it takes to transmit one byte of data (excluding protocol headers) to a destination, if the media is free of other traffic. It is 0 for a pseudonode LSP.
- *Throughput.*   The amount of data, in bits, that can flow through the media and be received at the other side in one second, if there is no other traffic using the interface. It is 0 for a pseudonode LSP.
- *Media Type.*   A code identifying the type of circuit; the most significant bit is 1 for WAN media, 0 for others.
- *External Routes.*   Describes routes obtained by the source router through non-NLSP protocols.

- Code = 0xC4
- Value = The following subfields:

  - *Hops.*   The number of hops reported by the non-NLSP protocol.
  - *Network Number.*   The IPX network number to which this entry refers.
  - *Ticks.*   The RIP Delay (that is, the number of RIP timer ticks) from the source router to network number, as reported by the non-NLSP protocol.

IPX Level 1 Hello Packet

Figure 7.23 shows the IPX LAN Level 1 Hello Packet, which contains the following fields:

- *Protocol ID.*   0x83, identifies the NLSP routing layer.
- *Length indicator.*   The number of bytes in the fixed portion of the header (up to and including the LAN ID field).
- *Minor Version.*   1 or 2 (if the router supports aggregated routes).
- *Reserved* (3 bits) .   0, ignored on receipt.
- *Packet Type* (5 bits) .   15.
- *Major Version.*   1.

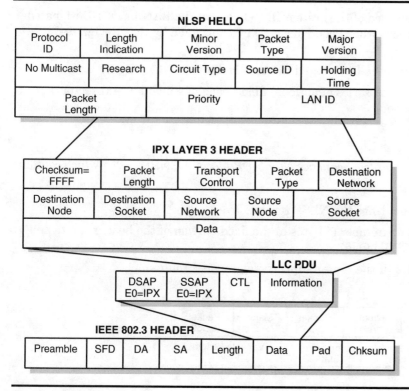

NLSP HELLO

Protocol ID	Length Indication	Minor Version	Packet Type	Major Version
No Multicast	Research	Circuit Type	Source ID	Holding Time
Packet Length		Priority		LAN ID

IPX LAYER 3 HEADER

Checksum= FFFF	Packet Length	Transport Control	Packet Type	Destination Network
Destination Node	Destination Socket	Source Network	Source Node	Source Socket
Data				

LLC PDU

DSAP E0=IPX	SSAP E0=IPX	CTL	Information

IEEE 802.3 HEADER

Preamble	SFD	DA	SA	Length	Data	Pad	Chksum

FIGURE 7.23 LAN Level 1 Hello packet

- *Reserved* (3 bits). 0, ignored on receipt.
- *No Multicast* (1 bit). When set to 1, this field indicates that the sender of the packet cannot receive traffic addressed to a multicast address; future packets on this LAN (which would otherwise be transmitted multicast) must be sent to the broadcast address.
- *Res* (2 bits). 0, ignored on receipt.
- *Circuit Type* (2 bits):
  - 0 = Reserved value, ignore entire packet.
  - 1 = Level 1 routing only.
  - 2 = Level 2 routing only (sender uses this link for Level 2 routing only).
  - 3 = Both Level 1 and Level 2 (sender is a Level 2 router and uses this link for Level 1 and Level 2 traffic).
- *Source ID*. The system ID of the sending router.
- *Holding Time*. The Holding Timer, in seconds, to be used for the sending router.
- *Packet Length*. The entire length of this packet, in bytes, including the NLSP header.
- *R* (1 bit). 0, ignored on receipt.
- *Priority* (7 bits). The priority for being the LAN Level 1 Designated Router; higher numbers have higher priority; an unsigned integer.

- *LAN ID.*   A field composed of the system ID (6 bytes) of the LAN Level 1 Designated Router, followed by a low-order Pseudonode ID byte assigned by that Designated Router.

    This field is copied from the Designated Router's Hello.

- *Variable Length fields.*   A series of optional fields, each of which has a three-part code/length/value option.

CSNP Header

Figure 7.24 shows the *Complete Sequence Number Protocol* (CSNP) header, which contains the following fields:

- *Protocol ID.*   0x83, identifies the NLSP routing layer.
- *Length Indicator.*   The number of bytes in the fixed portion of the header (up to and including the End LSP ID field).
- *Minor Version.*   1 or 2 (if the router supports aggregated routes).

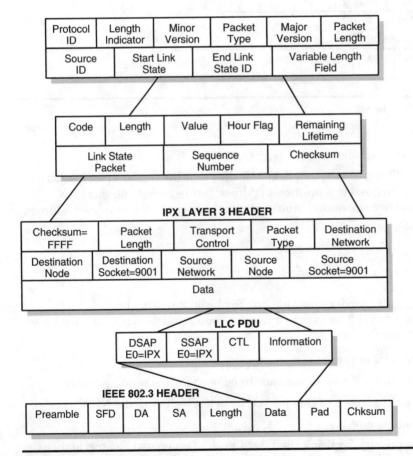

FIGURE 7.24   Level 1 CSNP header

- *Reserved* (3 bits).   0, ignored on receipt.
- *Packet Type* (5 bits).   24.
- *Major Version*.   1.
- *Reserved*.   0, ignored on receipt.
- *Packet Length*.   The entire length of this packet, in bytes, including the fixed portion of the NLSP header.
- *Source ID*.   The six-byte system ID of the sending router, followed by one byte of 0.
- *Start LSP ID, End LSP ID*.   The first and last LSP in the range covered by this CSNP. Each is a field composed of three parts:
  - *Source ID*.   The systemID of the router that originated the LSP being reported.
  - *Pseudonode ID*.   Zero if this is a nonpseudonode LSP; otherwise, it is unique (for this Source ID number designating this pseudonode).
  - *LSP Number*.   If a would be LSP is too large to send, the source breaks it into fragments identified by this monotonically increasing number.
- *Variable Length fields*.   A series of optional fields, each of which has a three-part code/length/value option form.

Service Advertising Protocol

SAP is a distributed database used to find NetWare services such as file servers. The service advertisement protocol allows a service to register its name on the network. A SAP request then asks for the translation of that name to a socket on a particular node of a network. A user might send out a SAP request for all file servers. The request is broadcast to all nodes on the network (and possibly other networks).

The use of SAP has dramatically changed with the advent of *NetWare Directory Services* (NDS). If a NetWare network is using SAP and NDS, the services of SAP are reduced to enabling a workstation to find its nearest NDS. NetWare clients and servers initiate communication with each other with NDS and naming. Naming entities in a network provide an easier way for users to access services on the network. For the workstation to find a server's name, log in to the network, or to use printing or E-mail services, it must be able to locate a server and the services running on that server. Routers are intricately involved in this process and keep tables of server names, their full Internet address, the services they provide, and how far away they are. This process is known as the *service advertising protocol* (SAP).

Services are uniquely identified by a two-byte numeric type and a name of up to 48 characters. Each service provider advertises its services, such as type, name, and address. The router accumulates this information and sends it to other routers. The IPX SAP interval permits users to configure the interval between SAP updates on any interface. This allows users to reduce traffic on heavily used low-speed WAN lines and dial circuits. All router interfaces on a given network must use the same SAP interval.

The SAP makes the process of adding and removing servers and their services on the internetwork dynamic. When file servers are initialized, they broadcast their available services using the SAP protocol (see Figure 7.25). When the file servers are brought down, they broadcast that their services will no longer be available using the SAP process. Routers, in

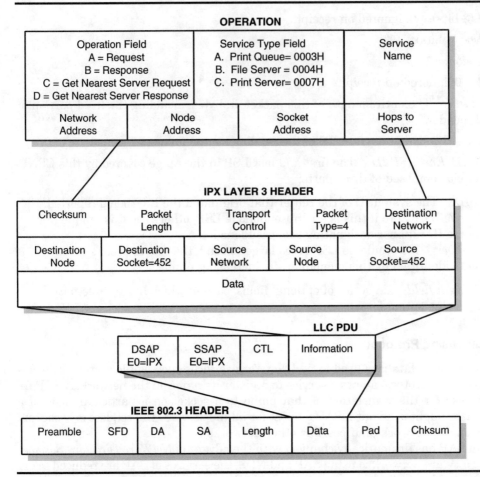

OPERATION

Operation Field A = Request B = Response C = Get Nearest Server Request D = Get Nearest Server Response		Service Type Field A. Print Queue= 0003H B. File Server = 0004H C. Print Server= 0007H		Service Name
Network Address	Node Address	Socket Address		Hops to Server

IPX LAYER 3 HEADER

Checksum	Packet Length	Transport Control	Packet Type=4	Destination Network
Destination Node	Destination Socket=452	Source Network	Source Node	Source Socket=452
Data				

LLC PDU

DSAP E0=IPX	SSAP E0=IPX	CTL	Information

IEEE 802.3 HEADER

Preamble	SFD	DA	SA	Length	Data	Pad	Chksum

FIGURE 7.25   NetWare SAP header

turn, delete this information from their tables. The SAP process allows workstations on the network to find a service and to connect to that service. This process is transparent to the user. All the user wants to know is where a server is in order to connect to it. With SAP, this task is easily accomplished. With the introduction of NetWare 4.x, SAPs are no longer the required method of locating services over the Internet.

The propagation of this information is very similar to the way routing tables are updated using the RIP protocol.

SAP Header Format and Fields

A SAP packet is provided in two formats, one format for requests and one format for responses. The type of packet is indicated by the value in the operation field. SAP response packets contain information on up to seven servers. Should a SAP response require information for more than seven servers, multiple SAP response packets must be sent.

The SAP headers consist of the following:

- *Operation.* This field indicates the type of operation. The operation is either a SAP Request or a SAP Response. Two types of SAP requests are possible, a Nearest Service Query and a General Service Query. A router broadcasts unsolicited response packets once every update interval.

- *Server Type.* This field indicates the type of service required or provided. The server type is indicated by the following values:

0×0003	Print queue
0×0004	File server
0×0005	Job server
0×0007	Print server
0×0009	Archive server
0×000A	Job queue
0×0021	NAS SNA gateway
0×002D	Time Synchronization VAP (old but still in use)
0×002E	Dynamic SAP
0×0047	Advertising print server
0×004B	Btrieve VAP 5.0 (old but still in use)
0×004C	SQL VA
0×007A	TES-NetWare VMS (old but still in use)
0×0098	NetWare Access server
0×009A	Named Pipes server (old but still in use)
0×009E	Portable NetWare-UNIX (old but still in use)
0×0107	NetWare 386 (old but still in use)
0×0111	Test server
0×0166	NetWare management

- *Server Name.* This field, which is 48 bytes in length, contains the name of the server that is unique on the internetwork.

- *Network Address.* This field contains the 32-bit network address to which the server of router is known.

- *Socket Address.* This field contains the socket number for request and responses sent to and from the server.

- *Hops.* This field contains the number of routers between the source client and destination server.

> **NOTE:** *Be aware that NetWare 3.x and 4.x servers are 1 hop away from the physical network due to the internal network number assigned to the server.*

Cisco Static SAP Tables

Cisco static SAP tables provide nodes with access to a limited subset of NetWare services, increasing security by limiting service visibility. Static SAP tables also improve bandwidth use by alleviating the need for periodic SAP broadcasts.

Cisco Configurable SAP Timers

A Cisco router can control the interval between SAP advertisements sent over LAN or WAN interfaces. Transmission of unsolicited SAP advertisements across point-to-point links can be restricted to improve bandwidth use and to decrease delay over the WAN link. The frequency of SAP advertisement transmissions can be configured on an interface-by-interface basis. SAP advertisement transmissions can be set to 0 to completely disable SAP advertisements. Instantaneous SAP updates are triggered by changes in server configuration or offered services. At the remote router, a SAP table cache is built, and SAP advertisements are sent every 60 seconds over LAN interfaces.

IPX SAP Interval

The Cisco IPX-output-SAP-delay interval permits users to configure the interval between SAP updates on an interface, which allows users to reduce traffic on heavily used low-speed WAN lines and dial-on-demand links. All router interfaces on a given network must use the same SAP interval. Cisco IOS supports output SAP filters that allow administrators to control which SAP services are included in SAP updates sent from the router. The Cisco IOS command `ipx router-sap-filter` allows SAP updates received by an interface to be filtered. Another feature available for controlling SAP updates is IPX SAP static entries. This option allows the router not to announce a static SAP entry unless a route is available. The IPX SAP-incremental IOS command allows updates only when a change occurs in the network.

SPX Architecture

SPX is a transport protocol in the ISO seven-layer model. It is a guaranteed delivery protocol with packet-oriented data transmission and delivery. The SPX packet header has fields for managing sequencing, acknowledgments, and transmission window size. SPX is packet-oriented, and the numbers in these fields are relative to packets rather than to bytes. SPX always uses a transmission window size of one packet, regardless of the window size reported by the connection partner. Under normal server operations, SPX is rarely used. Applications such as R-console and P-console are users of SPX.

Large Packets

The original XNS specification defined a network packet size as 576 bytes in length, allowing 512 bytes of data and 64 bytes of header. IPX does not enforce this packet size, although it does require that all physical networks which transmit IPX packets must be able to transmit packets of this size. IPX provides very little assistance in determining whether a larger packet can be used, although all IPX routers will, if possible, route larger packets. However, if a network segment cannot transmit a larger packet, the packet is dropped with no notification to the originating endpoint.

Several IPX-based services use larger than 576-byte packets by using a simple algorithm for determining the packet size. If both endpoints share the same physical wire and if the media supports larger packets, then the largest media packet size is used. Other IPX services attempt to determine the end-to-end large packet size by sending a large packet and having it echoed back. If the large packet is echoed back successfully, then the application uses the larger packet size. This echo procedure requires a recovery mechanism in case the network dynamically reconfigures, and the larger packets are no longer viable over the new route.

SPX is constrained by these features of IPX and as such does not support larger packets without the application making some determination outside of the SPX environment.

SPX Packet Format

SPX packet structure consists of a packet header followed by optional data. The SPX header contains addressing, sequencing, and acknowledgment information.

SPX Header Description

Figure 7.26 shows the SPX header definition and contains the following fields:

- *Connection Control.* This field contains four single-bit flags used by SPX and SPX II to control the bidirectional flow of data across a connection.

  Value   Description

  0×01 Reserved by SPX II for extended header

  0×02 Undefined, must be 0

  0×04 SPX II negotiate size request/response, must be 0 for SPX

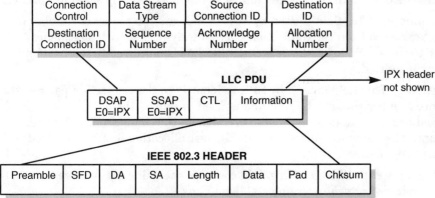

FIGURE 7.26 SPX header definition

Value   Description

0×08   SPX II type packet, must be 0 for SPX

0×10   Set by an SPX client to indicate end of message.

0×20   Reserved for attention indication (not supported by SPX)

0×40   Set to request that the receiving partner acknowledge that this packet has been received. Acknowledgment requests and responses are handled by SPX.

0×80   Set to indicate a packet is a system packet. System packets are internal SPX packets, are not delivered to the application, and do not consume sequence numbers.

- *Datastream Type.* This field is a 1-byte flag that indicates the type of data found in the packet. For SPX, the following types are defined:

0x00-0x7F	Defined by the client
0x80-0xFD	Reserved
0xFE	End of connection notification
0xFF	End of connection acknowledge

- *Source Connection ID.* This field contains a connection identification number assigned by SPX at the packet's source and was generated during connection establishment.

- *Destination Connection ID.* This field contains a connection identification number assigned by SPX at the packet's destination that was generated during connection establishment. On a connection request this field is set to 0xffff. Connection ID numbers are used to demultiplex incoming packets from multiple connections arriving on the same socket. All currently active connections and all recent connections on a given machine are guaranteed to have unique connection ID numbers.

- *Sequence Number.* This field keeps a count of packets exchanged in one direction on the connection. Each side of the connection keeps its own count. SPX acknowledgment packets have this field set to the sequence number of the most recently sent data packet.

- *Acknowledge Number.* This field is used by SPX to indicate the sequence number of the next packet expected from the connection partner. Any packet with a sequence number less than the specified acknowledge number has been correctly received and need not be retransmitted.

- *Allocation Number.* This field is used by SPX to identify to the connection partner the largest sequence number that can be sent and is used to control the number of unacknowledged packets outstanding in one direction on the connection. SPX sends packets only until the sequence number equals the last allocation number received from the connection partner.

- *Negotiation Size* (only with SPXII). This field contains the value of the largest packet size that can be received or sent over an established link.

SPX Acknowledgment Packets

SPX is a guaranteed delivery service and requires that the connection endpoints verify that each packet has been received. The SPX ACK is an SPX header with the SYS bit set in Connection Control and the Acknowledge Number set to acknowledge the packet(s) received (all packets up to but not including the acknowledge number have been received) the allocation number is set to open/adjust the transmission window.

SPX Connection Management Packets

For SPX to establish and maintain a connection between two endpoints, a specific connection request packet exchange must take place. SPX does not support an orderly connection termination but supports two different types of termination. One type requires a packet exchange between the endpoints, but the second type does not. The primary connection management packets are Connection Request, Connection Request ACK, Informed Disconnect, and Informed Disconnect ACK.

Connection Management

SPX is a connection-oriented guaranteed delivery service and tracks state information about the endpoints using the connection.

Session Termination

One endpoint of an SPX session can terminate the connection in two ways: Unilateral Abort or Informed Disconnect.

SPX Watchdog Algorithm

The watchdog routine is a passive element in SPX. Watchdog packets are sent only if a period of time with no traffic on the session occurs.

There are two timeout values associated with the watchdog. The first, VERIFY_TIMEOUT (default is 3 seconds) is how long SPX waits after a data transmit before sending a watchdog packet. Any packet sent resets this timer to 0. The second timeout value, ABORT_TIMEOUT (default 30 seconds) is how long SPX waits after receiving a packet from its connection partner before the connection is aborted. Any packet that arrives for a session resets the watchdog timer for that session, including system packets and user data packets (i.e., incoming data, an incoming ACK for transmitted data, or an incoming ACK to a watchdog packet that would reset the timer).

A watchdog request packet consists of an SPX header with the SYS and the ACK bits set. The receiver responds to this packet with a watchdog acknowledgment packet. The Sequence, ACK, and Alloc fields contain the current values. If the watchdog algorithm has sent repeated watchdog request packets (default 10, every 3 seconds) for 30 seconds and has not received a response from the connection partner, SPX assumes that the partner is unreachable and performs a Unilateral Abort to terminate the connection.

Session Watchdog during Connection Establishment

SPX considers a connection to exist once an endpoint has both connection IDs. This connection happens after the receipt of a Connection Request at the passive endpoint or after the receipt of a Connection ACK at the active endpoint. When this exchange has taken place, the connection is established, and the watchdog timers begin running. Cisco IOS supports an SPX idle timer that sets the elapsed time in seconds after spooling of keepalive packets occur following data transfer termination.

Windowing Algorithm

Although the SPX header has fields for managing the transmission window, SPX does not currently use these fields fully. SPX uses a transmission window of one, requests an ACK for each data packet sent, and does not send the next data packet until the ACK packet has arrived.

Managing Sequence and Acknowledge Numbers

The sequence number is an ever-increasing (except when wrapping past 0) number that identifies the order of the data being sent and received. The acknowledge number is also an ever-increasing number identifying all the data packets that have been successfully received. The acknowledge number also indicates the sequence number of the next packet expected by the receiving endpoint. The first data packet sent has a Sequence Number of 0, and the ACK sent in response to that data packet has the Acknowledge Number set to one.

An easy way to manage these two values (actually two sets of values, the numbers for sending and the numbers expected when receiving) exist. When sending a data packet, increment Sequence Number after placing the data packet on the "to be sent" queue, or if no queuing mechanism is used, increment the Sequence Number upon return from the send function. When generating an ACK, set Acknowledge Number in the ACK packet to the received data packet's Sequence Number plus one.

Acknowledgments

A normal SPX acknowledgment is defined as an SPX header with the SYS bit set in Connection Control, the Sequence Number set to the current transmission sequence number, and the Acknowledge Number set to the next packet expected by the receiver. An acknowledgment can be piggy-backed on a data packet with Acknowledge Number set to the next packet expected by the receiver (ACKs can be piggy-backed on any packet, data, system, or watchdog).

Extensive Error-Recovery Mechanisms

When standard SPX detects an error it does not know how to handle, it aborts the session. However, SFT III has introduced the need for better SPX error handling, to correctly handle an SFT III switch over.

Data Packet Timeout

During normal operation, if the connection partner fails to acknowledge a packet, the sender must retry the packet RETRY_COUNT/2 times, each time increasing the round trip time value by 50 percent, up to MAX_RETRY_DELAY (default is 5 seconds). If the packet still has not been acknowledged, the sender must attempt to locate a new route to the connection partner. If a new route is located, reset the retry count and retransmit. If no new route is found, continue to retransmit until all retries are exhausted, and if unsuccessful, the connection is aborted with a Unilateral Abort.

After a successful retransmission on the new route, resume normal operation.

The algorithm is using half the RETRY_COUNT to give preference to the possibility of route failure over endpoint failure or network congestion. By retrying less before attempting to relocate a new route, the protocol recovers faster on very dynamic networks. This is better than just reducing the RETRY_COUNT to a smaller number, because it still provides more retries and longer delays between retries on congested networks.

Window Size

It is the responsibility of the receiver at each endpoint to calculate the window size for packets received by that endpoint. The receiver then communicates this number to the transmitter via the allocation number field in the SPX II header by adding the calculated window size to the current sequence number. The receiver is free to change the window size during the session with the stipulation that the receiver can never reduce an already granted window. The transmitter is allowed to send packets while the sequence number is less than or equal to the allocation number.

SPX currently ignores the reported allocation window size and uses a window of one.

The reason that the advertised window size cannot be reduced has to do with the processing of the allocation and sequence numbers. The transmitter is allowed to send packets until the sequence number is equal to the allocation number. If the receiver tried to reduce the allocation number after the transmitter had already sent a packet with that sequence number, the transmitter would perceive that the window had grown to nearly 64K packets. The only way for the receiver to reduce the window size is to allow the acknowledgement number to grow without increasing the allocation number.

Congestion Control Algorithm

SPX has a very simple congestion control algorithm: don't send traffic until the ACK for the previous packet has arrived. Thus, if the previous packet is delayed or dropped due to congestion, SPX does not flood the net with packets.

NetWare Core Protocol

The *NetWare Core Protocol* (NCP) is the means by which NetWare clients transmit requests to servers to perform tasks such as read and write files, create queue jobs, log in, and log out.

Procedures exists to be followed by a NetWare file server to respond to workstation requests. An NCP service protocol exists for every service that a workstation may request from a file server:

- Directory Maintenance
- File Maintenance
- Data Access Synchronization

- Print
- Network Management
- Software Protection
- Bindery Maintenance
- Accounting
- Queue Management

An NCP packet is encapsulated in the data portion of an IPX packet. NCP creates and manages a virtual connection with a server. An NCP user requires an acknowledgment for every packet transmitted. With a one-to-one request/reply ratio, normal NCP transactions are not as efficient as SPX, and the sliding window protocol that SPX uses.

NCP uses two different packet formats for requests and replies. The NCP request header contains the fields shown in Figure 7.27.

NCP Header Descriptions

- *Request Type.*   This field indicates the type of NCP request sent from the client to the server. The following values apply to this field:

1111(hex)   Create a service connection

2222   Service request

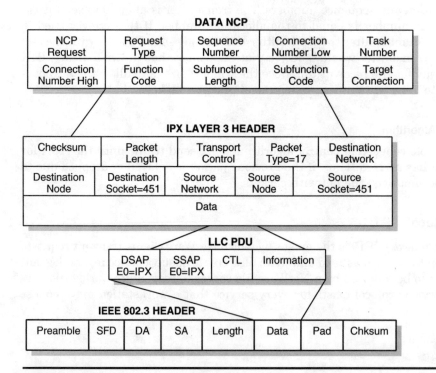

FIGURE 7.27 NCP packet

3333	Service reply
5555	Destroy service connection
7777	Burst Mode request/reply transfer
9999	Previous request still being processed

When a client wants to connect to a server, it issues a Create Service Connection NCP request and specifies type **1111** in the Request Type field. When a station wants to detach from a server, it issues a Destroy Service Connection request, specifying type **5555** in the Request Type field. Client requests use **2222** in the Request Type field to specify a general service request. This may be a request for a file, a query of the bindery, a submission of a queue job, and so on. When using the Burst Mode protocol for file reads and writes, the client uses **7777** in the Type field.

- *Sequence Number.*   Use the sequence number to track the sequence of the communication between the server and client. Clients place the last sequence number plus 1 in this field.

- *Connection Number Low.*   The Connection Number Low field contains the service connection number assigned to the client upon logging into the server.

- *Task Number.*   The task number indicates which client task is making the request. The server tracks these tasks and automatically deallocates resources when a task ends. Task number 0 signals to the server that all tasks have ceased execution and that resources may be deallocated.

- *Connection Number High.*   The Connection Number High field is used only on the 1,000-user version of NetWare. On all other versions of NetWare, the value in this field is set at **0x00**.

- *Completion Code.*   The completion code indicates whether the client's request was successful. A 0 in the Completion Code field indicates that the request was successful. Any other value in this field indicates that an error occurred while the server was processing the client's request.

- *Connection Status Flags.*   NetWare clients must check the Connection Status Flags field in all incoming NCP replies from a server. If **DOWN** is typed at the console prompt to bring the server down, the fourth bit in this byte is set to 1.

NCP Function Codes

During client and server interaction, NCP messages must contain an NCP function code identifying the service being requested or replied to. For example, if a workstation requests to open a file, it transmits an NCP message type **2222** (request) with a function code of **76**. This function code is defined by Novell as Open File. Upon receipt of an NCP message containing the type **2222** and the function code **76**, the server knows the client is requesting to open a file. The file name and access level requested appear later in the NCP packet.

NetBIOS over IPX

The Novell NetBIOS emulator requires special support from bridges and routers. This support allows the NetBIOS naming functions to operate across routers. NetBIOS Novell's specification for NetBIOS over IPX is fully supported by the Cisco IOS IPX implementation (see Figure 7.28). Figure 7.29 shows the Novell NetBIOS packet. The IPX implementation features a NetBIOS static routing mechanism that selectively converts IPX NetBIOS

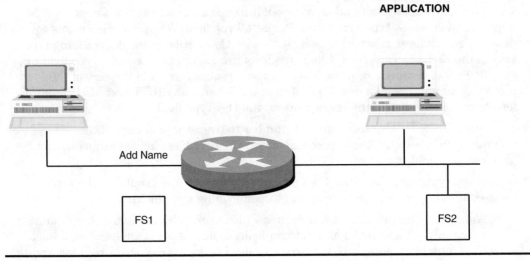

FIGURE 7.28   NetBIOS over IPX

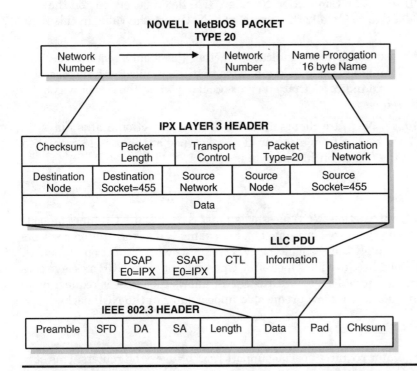

FIGURE 7.29   NetBIOS packet

Type 20 broadcast packets to NetBIOS directed broadcasts. This capability minimizes the amount of broadcast traffic produced by the normal NetBIOS All-Networks broadcast mechanism. Furthermore, this feature allows a more precise logical partitioning of an IPX NetBIOS internetwork, enhancing security. Each static route specifies a NetBIOS resource name and a destination network.

IPXWAN

IPXWAN allows you to exchange configuration information from router to router over WAN networks. This exchange of information occurs prior to exchanging standard IPX routing information and traffic over the WAN. IPX currently supports IPXWAN over the *Point-to-Point Protocol* (PPP). For simplified configuration and maximum interoperability, Cisco routers support IPXWAN Version 1.0 (RFC 1362), which allows the routers to interoperate with other vendors supporting IPXWAN over PPP and Frame Relay connections (see Figure 7.30). Figure 7.31 shows the IPXWAN Hello packet. The IPXWAN specification defines how different routers supporting IPX interoperate over wide area links. IPXWAN defines a router-to-router negotiation process, which allows routers to dynamically determine delay (in ticks) for wide area links, to assign the appropriate IPX network number for that link, and to negotiate the routing protocol to be used. IPXWAN over Frame Relay (RFC 1294) and PPP encapsulates IPX packets using the standardized Frame Relay and PPP encapsulation methods.

Connection Establishment

Before any communications take place between a client and its associated file server, a connection must be established between the two. Table 7.3 shows how this is accomplished. The numbers under the *Call* heading are shown in the sequence of events. The shell uses a combination of the processes of NCP, RIP, and SAP to establish a connection to a file server. The shell can use two methods to connect to a file server: 1) the shell program and 2) the preferred server shell.

The Shell Program

When IPXODI.com and NETx.com (IPX is loaded first) are loaded, the workstation automatically attaches to the first server that responds to it. This provides for fast log-in service

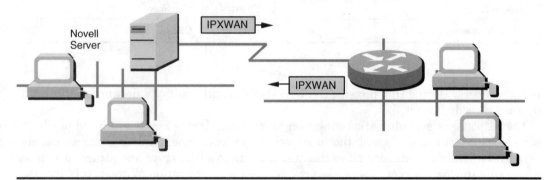

FIGURE 7.30 Novell IPXWAN

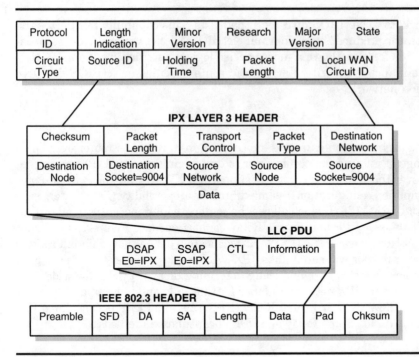

FIGURE 7.31   IPXWAN Hello packet

TABLE 7.3   Initial Connection Sequence of the NetWare Shell

Call	Source	Destination	Protocol
1. Get Nearest Server	Client	Broadcast	SAP
2. Give Nearest Server	Router	Client	SAP
3. Get Local Target	Client	Broadcast	RIP
4. Give Local Target	Router	Client	RIP
5. Create Connection	Client	File Server	NCP
6. Request Processed and Connection Number Assigned	File Server	Client	NCP
7. Propose Packet Size	Client	File Server	NCP
8. Return Maximum Packet Size	File Server	Client	NCP

to the network. During this process, the workstation can identify its network number, if it does not already have it.

The response is an automatic connection to a virtual drive seen as **F:** on the user's PC screen. This connection gives the user access to two other utilities: **LOGIN.exe** and **ATTACH.exe**. These applications allow the user to log in to a file server and attach to another server (not the login server). **Login.exe** provides user authentication. Without this, the user has just connected to the network but has yet to log into any server. The user may then use

TABLE 7.4 LOGIN.exe Sequence

1. Query Bindery for Preferred Shell	Client	File Server X	NCP
2. Address of Preferred Server	File Server X	Client	NCP
3. Get Local Target	Client	Broadcast	RIP
4. Give Local Target	File Server X Router	Client	RIP
5. Create Connection	Client	File Server V	NCP
6. Request Processed and Connection Number Assigned	File Server Y	Client	NCP
7. Propose Packet Size	Client	File Server Y	NCP
8. Return Maximum Packet Size	File Server Y	Client	NCP
9. Destroy Service Connection	Client	File Server X	NCP

the ATTACH commands to reach a desired network server. Table 7.4 shows this sequence of events.

To accomplish this, the shell must find the file server's address and the nearest route to that server. To find the server's address, the shell invokes one of the services of SAP, which is called the Get Nearest Server Request. All routers on the local network (the network to which the workstation is attached) should respond with the SAP information. The contents of this information are the nearest server's name, its full internetwork address, and the number of hops required to reach the server (how many routers are between the shell and its requested server).

After the shell receives this information, it tries to find the best route to a server. The shell invokes the routing services of IPX for this request. This process is known as the Get Local Target request. When the response packet is received, IPX compares the network number returned (this network number was obtained through the Get Nearest Server request) in this request with its own network number. If the two numbers match, IPX informs the shell that the server is located on this local network and to send requests directly to the server on the local network. However, if the network numbers do not match, IPX submits a broadcast routing information request to the network through the RIP request packet. The routers located on the local network respond with the known routes to this server. IPX finds the shortest route, discards all others, and returns the address of that router to the shell. The shell then uses the address and submits a Create Connection Request packet to the router (for a connection to the server, not to the router). These requests are illustrated in Table 7.5.

The IPX header contains the actual addresses of the file server with which it wants to communicate. The packet then is transmitted on the network and accepted by the router. The router looks at the final destination address (destination network number) and routes the packet to that network.

Preferred Server Shell. There is a new shell known as the *preferred server shell,* which contains new features that enable the user to tell the shell to which server it wants to connect. This either may be at the command line or located in a file called **net.cfg**. The first eight steps are still the same. The ninth step causes a lookup in the nearest server's database

TABLE 7.5 Novell NETX Sequence

	Destination	Layer	Summary
1	Broadcast	sap	Query Nearest File Server
2	Brad	sap	Resp Nearest;
3	Broadcast	rip	Req network=**00 00 11 62**
4	Brad	rip	Resp network=**00 00 11 62; 1**
5	FS	ncp	Req Create Service
6	Brad	ncp	Rply Create Service Connection
7	FS	ncp	Req Get File Server Info
8	Brad	ncp	Rply Get File Server Info
9	Brad	sap	Rsp Nearest; Server=**FS3**
10	FS	ncp	Req Negotiate Buffer
11	Brad	ncp	Rply Negotiate Buffer
12	FS	ncp	Req
13	Brad	ncp	Rply Logout
14	FS	ncp	Req Get File Server Date and Time
15	Brad	ncp	Rply Get File Server Date and Time

table to acquire the preferred server's address. Steps 11 and 12 might not be used if the preferred server is on the same local network (not separated by a router). The shell skips this and submits a connection request directly to the server.

One other difference between the old shell and the new shell is the process of Get Nearest Server responses. Previous shells accept the first response they receive and discard all other responses. The problem that arose with this is that a server responds even if it has no free connections available for the shell. Shells then cannot establish a connection to that server. The preferred server shell accepts the first response, but it saves up to the next four responses it receives in case a connection cannot be made to the first response. If the first server response cannot be connected to, the shell uses the next response and tries to establish a connection to that server.

Logging in to a Server. Anytime after the initial connection is made, users may log in to a file server. The utility LOGIN transmits the user's name and password to the file server for validation. LOGIN can also create a connection to a file server, if prompted to on the command line. Please note that steps 3 and 4 are not needed if the file server is located on the same local network. During this connection process, the shell and the file server exchange a few packets. (This is commonly called handshaking.) The workstation requests of a file server that a connection number be assigned to the shell and that the two need to negotiate a maximum packet size that each can accept. A workstation may attach to eight different servers at one time, no matter where the servers are located on the NetWare internet.

Questions

1. The SPX protocol is always used in the transmission of data between the client and server.
   A. True   B. False

2. The IPX protocol is connection-oriented.
   A. True   B. False

3. IPX can be tunneled in TCP/IP.
   A. True   B. False

4. If the answer to the previous question is true, what protocol does Cisco support that allows NetWare to be tunneled?

5. What Ethernet frame type does Novell support?
   A. Ethernet_II   C. Ethernet 802.2
   B. Ethernet 802.3   D. Ethernet 802.4

6. You receive the following message at your file server console: 'WARNING! ROUTER CONFIGURATION ERROR! Router claims to be 10 should be A". What is the cause of the problem?
   A. A file server internal IPX Network Number has been designated as 10 and should be A.
   B. The network adapter on the offending file server has been given a Network Number 10 where A should have been selected.
   C. The wrong frame type was selected when the MLID driver was loaded on the file server.
   D. A workstation network adapter is "chattering".

7. Which are reasons why a file server may not show that it is sending SAPs?
   A. Volumes SYS: is not mounted.
   B. IPX is not bound to the card device driver.
   C. The wrong frame type is being used.
   D. TRACK ON has not been loaded.

8. IPX and NETX have been loaded at a workstation. Which protocols can be accessed simultaneously?
   A. IPX and GOSIP   D. AppleTalk and TCP/IP
   B. IPX and TCP/IP   E. None of the above
   C. IPX and AppleTalk

9. Which is true about the Multiple Link Interface Drivers?
   A. It transfers data bits in the form of electrical impulses across the transmission medium.
   B. It is the interface between a network board and the upper-layer protocol stacks.
   C. It is a datagram Network layer protocol.
   D. It is Novell's name for a network interface board driver.

10. Which is a method associated with IPX RIP routing?
    A. Link-state   C. Division and combination
    B. Distance vector   D. OS redirector

11. To facilitate the communication of IPX packets, Novell supports the following protocols for address to MAC resolution.
    A. ARP
    B. IPX-ARP
    C. AARP
    D. None of the above. Novell's protocols do not require address resolution protocols.

12. Which of the following protocols facilitates the sharing of network information in an IPX network?
    A. RIP
    B. RTMP
    C. NLSP
    D. ARP
    E. NDS
    F. OSPF
    G. SAP

13. An IPX network address is:
    A. An 8-digit hexadecimal value
    B. An 8-digit decimal value
    C. A 12-digit hexadecimal value
    D. A 12-digit decimal value

14. An IPX internal network number does what?
    A. Uniquely identifies a cable segment
    B. Uniquely identifies multiple capable segments
    C. Defines a logical network within a server
    D. Defines a logical service within a server

15. What is the command to enable IPX routing?
    A. `Novell routing`
    B. `Ipx routing`
    C. `Ipx routing (node)`
    D. `Ipx node (routing)`

16. The number of IPX interfaces that can be configured on a single Ethernet segment is determined by:
    A. The maximum transfer unit size
    B. The maximum size of the routing table
    C. The number of frame types that Novell IPX supports
    D. The number of network protocols configured on that circuit
    E. Media types

17. Identify the Novell Frame types Cisco supports at the Data Link layer.
    A. Ethernet Ver 2.0
    B. IEEE 802.3
    C. SNAP
    D. 802.3_ Raw
    E. All of the above

18. Which of the following Ethernet Data Link frame encapsulation protocols are proprietary to Novell?
    A. IEEE 802.2
    B. SNAP
    C. 802.3_raw
    D. None of the above

19. What is Novell's IPX Network address length in bytes?
   A. 10   **C.** 8
   B. 4   **D.** 12

20. The Host field in the IPX header identifies what layer in the OSI Model?
   A. Network layer   **C.** Data Link
   B. Transport   **D.** Physical

21. Identify the well-known *Service Advertising Protocol* (SAP) ID for a file server.
   A. 4   **C.** 15
   B. 6   **D.** A

22. Novell IPX Network Address is expressed in?
   A. Decimal   **C.** Octal
   B. Hexadecimal   **D.** ASCII

23. Split horizon cannot be disable for the following protocols?
   A. E-IGRP   **C.** RIP
   B. GRE   **D.** SAP

24. What metric is used in IPX to *Routing Information Protocol* (RIP) in choosing the best path?
   A. Hop Count   **D.** Router ID
   B. Tick Count   **E.** Hop and Tick Count
   C. Cost   **F.** None of the above

25. The maximum number of hops supported for routing IPX using E-IGRP is?
   A. 16   **C.** 254
   B. 255   **D.** 128

26. What is the Ethernet Version 2 type code for IPX?
   A. 0x8135   **C.** 0x0800
   B. 0x8137   **D.** 0x809b

27. What is the SAP ID for IPX using an IEEE 802.3 frame?
   A. e0   **C.** A0
   B. 0BAD   **D.** C0

28. Novell identifies its IEEE 802.3 frame type as _____.
   A. IEEE 802.3   **C.** 802.2
   B. 802.3   **D.** All of the above

29. Cisco refers to Novell 802.3_Raw-frame type as _____.
   A. Novell-Ether   **C.** SNAP
   B. Novell-802.3   **D.** A & B

30. How many Services can be advertised in one SAP update?
   A. 10   **D.** 40
   B. 7   **E.** None of the above
   C. 20

31. NetWare 4.x and 5.x can support how many Networks?
A. 16   C. 2
B. 4   D. 8

32. Novell IPX RIP sends out Routing updates every __ seconds.
A. 30   C. 15
B. 60   D. 45

33. Novell IPX SAPs are sent out every ___seconds.
A. 45   C. 10
B. 30   D. 60

34. Novell Files servers send out Watch dog packets every _____.
A. 60 Seconds   C. 30 Seconds
B. 5 Minutes   D. 10 Minutes

35. What packet type does Cisco routers use in order to filter NetBIOS over IPX?
A. Type 20   C. Type 40
B. Type 451   D. None of the Above

36. SPX uses sequence number and acknowledgments. Which protocol in the TCP/IP suite would relate to it?
A. UDP   D. BootP
B. ARP   E. TCP
C. RARP

37. Name the three logical parts of the IPX header.
A. Network, Host and Socket   C. Network, Socket
B. Network, Subnetwork, Socket   D. A & B

38. Novell IPX NLSP uses which of the following routing algorithms?
A. Link State   C. Distance Vector
B. Hybrid   D. COST

39. What is the default packet size for IPX networks using Ethernet and Routers?
A. 1500   D. 128
B. 512   E. 576
C. 265

40. What does Cisco call Novell's use of the following Frame types?
A. Ethernet   D. IEEE 802.3
B. 802.3_Raw   E. FDDI
C. SNAP   F. ATM

41. How many areas using NLSP can be implemented in Cisco IOS?
A. 1   C. 20
B. 104   D. 32

42. The IPX standard access-list numbers are?
A. 800–899   C. 200–299
B. 900–999   D. 100–199

43. The IPX Extended Access-list numbers are _____.
A. 900–999
B. 300–399
C. 700–799
D. none of the above

44. SAP filters Access-list numbers are _____.
A. 1000–1099
B. 500–599
C. 300–399
D. 200–299

45. NLSP Route aggregation Access-Lists are _____.
A. 1200–1299
B. 1300–1399
C. 2000–2099
D. 1400–1499

46. What is the payload used by IPX when using a router without *Large Internet Packet* (LIP)?
A. 576
B. 1500
C. 512
D. 1518

47. Which is the Socket number for NCP?
A. 451
B. 452
C. 455
D. 457

48. Which of the following can a Novell Ethernet IPX Source host address contain?
A. C0-00-00-00-00-00
B. ff-ff-ff-ff-ff-ff
C. c0-00-00-00-00-ff
D. None of the above

49. In IPX RIP the TICK field is equal to _____.
A. 1/18th of a second
B. 60 seconds
C. 1/110th
D. 1 second

50. What is the RIP default inter packet delay sent out all interfaces?
A. 55ms
B. 60ms
C. 70ms
D. 80ms

51. What is the SAP default inter packet delay sent out all interfaces?
A. 55ms
B. 60ms
C. 70ms
D. 80ms

52. What command is used to set the IPX tick delay?
A. `IPX delay Ticks`
B. `IPX Ticks Delay`
C. `IPX Ticks Count`
D. None of the above

53. What command is used for disabling the sending of replies to IPX GNS queries?
A. `IPX-GNS-reply-disable`
B. `IPX-GNS Off`
C. `IPX-GNS disable`
D. None of the above

54. What command is used for forwarding packets to a specific server?
A. `IPX-Helper address`
B. `IPX-Forward address`
C. `IPX-Destination address`

55. What is the command for setting an internal network number for NLSP and IPXWAN?
A. `IPX-network Number`
B. `IPX-Internal Network`
C. `IPX-Address Number`

56. What is the maximum number of hops for IPX RIP?
A. 32   C. 15
B. 15   D. 8

57. NLSP send out Routing updates _____.
A. every 30 minutes
B. every 15 minutes
C. when a change is detected

58. Large Internet Packet and Packet Burst are:
A. Part of the Cisco IOS software
B. Loaded on the server as an NLM
C. EXE files that must be run at the workstation
D. Part of the NetWare operating system

59. Novell 3.x servers using Ethernet frame type default is _____.
A. Ethernet_II   C. 802.2
B. IEEE 802.3   D. 802.3_raw

60. Novell 4.x servers using Ethernet frame type default to _____.
A. Ethernet_II   C. 802.2
B. IEEE 802.3   D. 802.3

61. The acronym ACL is short for _____.
A. Access Common List   C. Access Control List
B. All Control Lines   D. None of the above

62. Burst mode allows the client to issue a single read or write request for blocks of data up to _____ in size without intermediate acknowledgement of individual packets.
A. 16K   C. 64K
B. 32K   D. 128K

63. The Novell SAP Restore allows you to filter SAP's from a _____.
A. Cisco Router   C. Access List
B. Novell Server   D. None of the above

64. The IPX best route for a WAN link is based in part on the following:
A. Hops
B. Ticks
C. Hops & Ticks
D. Tick count based on the link supported by the router

65. What is the maximum number of bits make up an IPX address (network and node)?
A. 32   C. 80
B. 48   D. 128

66. Which is not a valid frame format for an Ethernet interface supporting IPX?
   A. Ethernet_II
   B. Ethernet_802.3
   C. Ethernet_SNAP
   D. Ethernet_RIF

67. To configure the Novell Ethernet_II frame format on a Cisco router's Ethernet interface, you must use which encapsulation command?
   A. `Encapsulation arpa`
   B. `Encapsulation sap`
   C. `Encapsulation novell-ether`
   D. `Encapsulation snap`

68. To configure the Novell Ethernet_802.3 frame format on a Cisco router's Ethernet interface, you must use which encapsulation command?
   A. `Encapsulation arpa`
   B. `Encapsulation sap`
   C. `Encapsulation novell-ether`
   D. `Encapsulation snap`

69. To configure the Novell Ethernet_802.2 frame format on a Cisco router's Ethernet interface, you must use which encapsulation command?
   A. `Encapsulation arpa`
   B. `Encapsulation sap`
   C. `Encapsulation novell-ether`
   D. `Encapsulation snap`

70. In a Novell network, how does a client find the nearest server?
   A. Through a ARP request
   B. Through a SAP request
   C. Through a GNS request
   D. They must be statically configured into the client

71. Which routing protocol does not support IPX in Cisco routers?
   A. IGRP
   B. IPX-RIP
   C. EIGRP
   D. NLSP

72. Identify the default routing protocol for IPX in the Cisco routers.
   A. IGRP
   B. IPX-RIP
   C. EIGRP
   D. NLSP

73. Of the following steps, which one is not part of configuring IPX on a Cisco router?
   A. IPX network 1f2c encapsulation novell-ether
   B. IPX routing
   C. IPX maximum-paths 2
   D. IPX hold-time 60

74. What is the default update interval for IPX-RIP?
   A. 10 seconds
   B. 30 seconds
   C. 60 seconds
   D. 90 seconds

75. How are Novell services advertised?
   A. Via RIP update packets
   B. Via SAP packets
   C. Via NBP packets
   D. Via NDS

76. What metric does IPX-RIP use?
   A. Ticks, with hop count as a tie breaker
   B. Hop count, with ticks as a tie breaker
   C. Cost
   D. Hop count

77. How does a device operating in an IPX environment resolve its layer three address to a layer two address?
  A. It uses an ARP request sent out as a broadcast and the owner of the address responds.
  B. The layer two address is the node portion of the layer three address.
  C. It uses DNS to resolve the addresses.
  D. It uses WINS to resolve the addresses.

78. The checksum field in an IPX packet is always set to _____.
  A. FFFF
  B. 1110
  C. FFFE

79. In an IPX packet the Packet Type field value of 17 represents _____.
  A. SPX
  B. IPX
  C. NCP

80. A Novell RIP frame can contain a maximum of how many entries?
  A. 25   **C.** 50
  B. 30   **D.** 60

81. In a Service advertisement protocol packet the service type field value 07 represents _____.
  A. NCP   **C.** Printer server
  B. File server   **D.** Application Server

82. SPX operates at what layer?
  A. Data Link layer   **C.** Transport layer
  B. Network layer   **D.** Session layer

83. SPX provides what type of connection?
  A. Connectionless Connection
  B. Connection Oriented Connection
  C. Connectionless with Acknowledgement
  D. None of the above

84. File access, print access, name management is accomplished by _____.
  A. RPC   **C.** NLM
  B. NCP   **D.** NDS

85. To connect multiple vendors router across a WAN requires which of the following protocols?
  A. RIP
  B. NLSP
  C. IPXWAN

Novell Show Commands

```
Ethernet0 is up, line protocol is up  IPX address is B.0000.0c3a.966a, NOVELL-ETHER
[up]  Delay of this IPX network, in ticks is 1 throughput 0 link delay 0  IPXWAN
processing not enabled on this interface.  IPX SAP update interval is 1 minute(s)
  IPX type 20 propagation packet forwarding is disabled
  Incoming access list is not set
```

```
   Outgoing access list is not set
   IPX helper access list is not set
   SAP GNS processing enabled, delay 0 ms, output filter list is not set
   SAP Input filter list is not set
   SAP Output filter list is not set
   SAP Router filter list is not set
   Input filter list is not set
   Output filter list is not set
   Router filter list is not set
   Netbios Input host access list is not set
   Netbios Input bytes access list is not set
   Netbios Output host access list is not set
   Netbios Output bytes access list is not set
   Updates each 60 seconds, aging multiples RIP: 3 SAP: 3
   SAP interpacket delay is 55 ms, maximum size is 480 bytes
   RIP interpacket delay is 55 ms, maximum size is 432 bytes
    IPX accounting is disabled
   IPX fast switching is configured (enabled)
   RIP packets received 0, RIP packets sent 0
   SAP packets received 0, SAP packets sent 1
Ethernet1 is up, line protocol is up
   IPX address is A.0000.0c3a.966b, NOVELL-ETHER [up]
   Delay of this IPX network, in ticks is 1 throughput 0 link delay 0
   IPXWAN processing not enabled on this interface.
   IPX SAP update interval is 1 minute(s)
   IPX type 20 propagation packet forwarding is disabled
   Incoming access list is not set
   Outgoing access list is not set
   IPX helper access list is not set
   SAP GNS processing enabled, delay 0 ms, output filter list is not set
   SAP Input filter list is not set
   SAP Output filter list is not set
   SAP Router filter list is not set
   Input filter list is not set
   Output filter list is not set
   Router filter list is not set
   Netbios Input host access list is not set
   Netbios Input bytes access list is not set
   Netbios Output host access list is not set
    Netbios Output bytes access list is not set
   Updates each 60 seconds, aging multiples RIP: 3 SAP: 3
   SAP interpacket delay is 55 ms, maximum size is 480 bytes
   RIP interpacket delay is 55 ms, maximum size is 432 bytes
   IPX accounting is disabled
   IPX fast switching is configured (enabled)
   RIP packets received 0, RIP packets sent 0
   SAP packets received 0, SAP packets sent 1
```

86. What is the IPX encapsulation on interface E0?

  A. IPXWAN   **C.** NOVELL-ETHER

  B. IPX SAP   **D.** Nebios

87. How often is RIP sending out updates?

  A. 55ms   **C.** 60 seconds

  B. Link change   **D.** 3 seconds

88. What is the IPX address of an interface?

    A. A.0000.0c3a.966b   **C.** No IPX address

    B. 20   **D.** None of the above

```
Codes: C - Connected primary network,    c - Connected secondary network
       S - Static, F - Floating static, L - Local (internal), W - IPXWAN
       R - RIP, E - EIGRP, N - NLSP, X - External, A - Aggregate
       s - seconds, u - uses

6 Total IPX routes. Up to 1 parallel paths and 16 hops allowed.

No default route known.

C             A (NOVELL-ETHER),   Et1
C             B (NOVELL-ETHER),   Et0
R             C [02/01] via       B.00e0.1e42.b2ae,   57s, Et0
R             D [02/01] via       B.00e0.1e42.b2ae,   57s, Et0
R             E [08/02] via       B.00e0.1e42.b2ae,   57s, Et0
R             FF [08/02] via      B.00e0.1e42.b2ae,   57s, Et0
```

89. Identify the tick count for the route learned for network E.

    A. 08   **C.** E

    B. 02   **D.** B.00e0.1e42.b2ae

90. Identify the hop count for the route learned for network E.

    A. 08   **C.** E

    B. 02   **D.** B.00e0.1e42.b2ae

91. What is the interface the routes are learned from?

    A. Interface E1   **C.** No learned routes

    B. Interface E0   **D.** None of the above

92. What encapsulation is set on interface E0 for IPX?

```
ipx routing 0000.0c09.7979
!
interface Ethernet0
 ip address 5.0.0.2 255.0.0.0
 ipx network E
!
line con 0
 password cisco
 login
line aux 0
line vty 0 4
 password cisco
 login
!
end
```

    A. Arpa   **C.** Snap

    B. Novell-Ether   **D.** No encapsulation set

Answers

1. B
2. B
3. A
4. GRE
5. A, B, C
6. B
7. B, C
8. B
9. B
10. A, B
11. D
12. A, C, E, G
13. A
14. C
15. B, C
16. C
17. E
18. C
19. B
20. C
21. A
22. B
23. A, C, D
24. E
25. C
26. G
27. A
28. C
29. A
30. B
31. A
32. B
33. E
34. B
35. A
36. E
37. A
38. A
39. B
40. A = AXPA; B = Novell-Ether; C, E, F = SNAP; D = SAP
41. A
42. A
43. A
44. A
45. A
46. A
47. A
48. B
49. A

50. A
51. A
52. A
53. A
54. A
55. B
56. B
57. C
58. B
59. D
60. C
61. C
62. D
63. B
64. D
65. C
66. D
67. A
68. C
69. B
70. C
71. A
72. B
73. D
74. C
75. B, D
76. B
77. B
78. A
79. C
80. C
81. C
82. C
83. B
84. B, D
85. C
86. C
87. C
88. A
89. A
90. B
91. B
92. B

TCP/IP Architecture Overview

Internet Protocol (IP)

Internet protocol is designed to interconnect packet-switched communication networks to form an internet through which to pass data. IP is responsible for transmitting blocks of datagrams received from its upper layer protocols. IP does not establish a session with the destination before transmitting its data; therefore classifying it as a connectionless service. IP provides best-effort or connectionless delivery service between a source and destination.

The *Department of Defense* (DoD) Four-Layer model was developed in the 1970s for the DARPA Internetwork Project that eventually grew into the Internet (see Figure 8.1). The

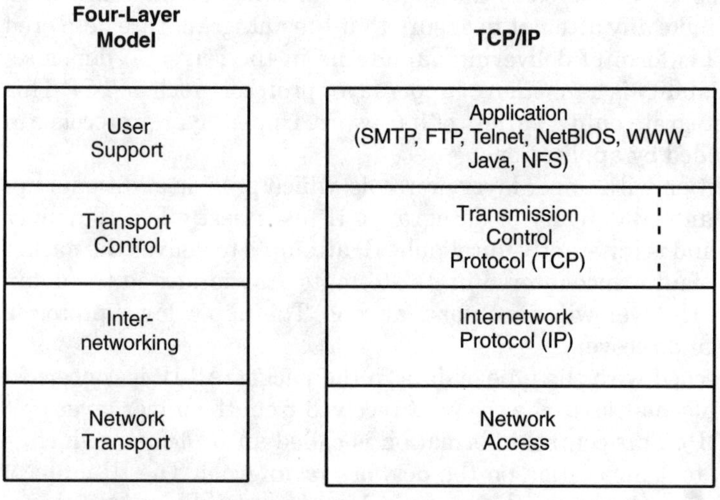

Four-Layer Model	TCP/IP
User Support	Application (SMTP, FTP, Telnet, NetBIOS, WWW Java, NFS)
Transport Control	Transmission Control Protocol (TCP)
Inter-networking	Internetwork Protocol (IP)
Network Transport	Network Access

FIGURE 8.1   Department of Defense Four-Layer model

core Internet protocols adhere to this model, although the OSI Seven-Layer model is justly preferred for new designs.

The four layers in the DoD model, from bottom to top, are as follows:

- The *Network Access layer* is responsible for delivering data over the particular hardware media in use. Different protocols are selected from this layer, depending on the type of physical network.

- The *Internet layer* is responsible for delivering data across a series of different physical networks that interconnect a source and destination machine. Routing protocols are most closely associated with this layer, as is the IP protocol, the Internet's fundamental protocol.

- The *Transport layer* handles connection rendezvous, flow control, retransmission of lost data, and other generic data flow management. The mutually exclusive TCP and UDP protocols are this layer's most important members.

- The *Application layer* contains protocols that implement user-level functions, such as mail delivery, NetBIOS, FTP, Telnet, WWW, SNMP, and remote login.

The IP protocol provides four main functions:

- Basic unit for transfer
- Protocol addressing
- Routing of datagrams or packets
- Fragmentation of datagrams

IP provides a connectionless, best-effort delivery service. When datagrams are transmitted from the source to the destination, it is possible that the datagrams could arrive at the destination in a different sequence from that in which they were sent. The IP layer does not ensure that the datagrams are delivered to the application in the destination host in the correct order. Nor does it make any attempt to ensure that the datagrams are delivered reliably to the destination. This form of delivering datagrams in the correct order is *sequencing*. Sequencing and reliability is a function of upper layer protocols such as TCP. This makes IP more versatile to integrate onto a variety of hardware. Upper layer protocols can add levels of reliability as needed by applications.

IP is mostly used in conjunction with upper layer protocols, which provide additional upper layer functions like guaranteed delivery of datagrams. IP uses best effort to deliver datagrams to the destination and is inherently unreliable. IP attempts to deliver the packet and does not make up for the faults encountered in its attempts. Any failure in the delivery of the datagram, and the IP layer will not inform anyone. The upper layer protocols must provide error discovery and recovery.

The IP protocol is not concerned with the type of data in the packet. All IP is concerned about is applying its control information to the segment received from the upper layer protocol (presumably TCP or UDP). This control information is called an *IP header*, which is used to deliver the datagram to some station on the network or internet. The IP protocol does provide some means of control on how the hosts and routers should process transmitted or received packets or when an error should be generated and when an IP packet should be discarded. The IP datagram format contains an IP header and the IP data from upper layer protocols (see Figure 8.2). The IP header is designed to accommodate the features of the IP layers.

IP Datagrams

An IP datagram is the unit of data exchanged between IP modules. In addition to data, a datagram includes a header with fields that provide the information used by IP routers.

Let's take a look at control information added to the packet (IP header) to understand the functionality of IP. In Figure 8.3, the IP header is encapsulated in an Ethernet frame, which shows the position of the IP header in the packet.

- *Version.*   This field specifies the IP protocol version and is used to verify that the sender, receiver, and gateways in-between agree on the format of the datagram. The current version is 4 (IPv4). This field is four bits long. IP software is required to check the version field to ensure that the IP header format is the one it expects. If the software can process only Version 4 datagrams, it rejects datagrams with a different value in the Version field.

- *IHL.*   This field specifies the length of the header (all fields but the IP data field). This field is also 4 bits long and is measured in 32-bit words, which is required because the IP header contains a variable-length options field. All other fields have a fixed length. If necessary, the options field is padded to accommodate a multiple of 32-bit words. The shortest IP header is 20 bytes. In this case, this field contains a 5 (20 bytes = 160 bits; 160 bits/32 bits = 5).

- *Type of Service.*   Specifies how the datagram should be handled and informs the network of the *Quality of Service* (QoS) desired. The Type of Service field can be further divided into an 8-bit field as shown in Figure 8.4.

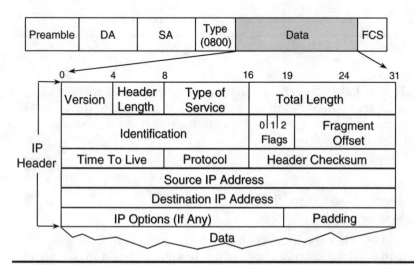

FIGURE 8.2   IP datagram format

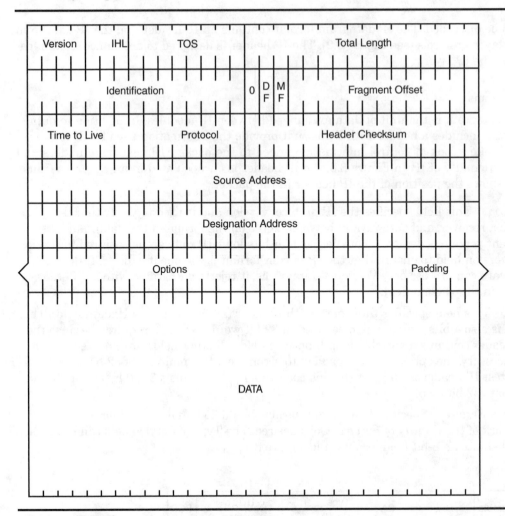

FIGURE 8.3 IP Header

- *Precedence.* This field may have an entry of 0 (normal precedence) to 7 (network control), which allows the transmitting station's application to indicate to the IP layer the priority of sending the datagram. This entry is combined with *Delay*, *Throughput*, and *Reliability* bits. These bits indicate which route to take.

The Type of Service identifiers are as follows:

- *Delay* bit.   Requests low delay when set to a 1
- *Throughput* bit.   Requests high throughput
- *Reliability* bit.   Requests high reliability

- *Total Length.* This field specifies the length of the IP header and data in bytes. Because this field is a 16 bits long, the data area of the IP datagram is a maximum of 65,535 bytes.

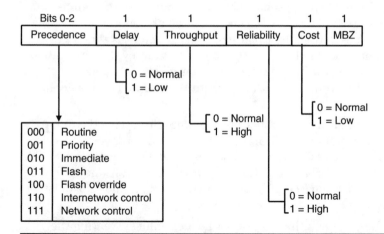

FIGURE 8.4 Type of Service field for IP packets

- *Identification, flags, Fragment Offset.* Because packets transmitting from one network may be too large to transmit on another network, a TCP/IP router must be able to fragment the larger packet into smaller packets. For example, the IP layer has the functionality to transmit a packet from a FDDI network that supports a maximum size of 4472 bytes to an Ethernet network that supports a maximum packet size of 1518.

These fields indicate how to fragment a forwarded datagram that is too large for the attached network. They control the fragmentation and reassembly of datagrams. The Identification field contains a unique integer that identifies the datagram. Its primary purpose is to allow the destination to collect all fragments from a datagram. As a fragment arrives, the destination uses the identification field along with the source address to identify the datagram to which the fragment belongs. The host usually generates a unique value for identification by incrementing a global counter each time it creates a datagram. The host assigns the new counter value to the datagram's identification field. Any gateway that fragments the datagram copies the identification field into every fragment.

The *FLAGS* field controls fragmentation. It specifies whether the datagram may be fragmented (it is called the *do not fragment* bit because setting this bit to 1 specifies that the datagram should not be fragmented). The low-order *FLAGS* bit specifies whether this is the last fragment (i.e. the fragment with the highest offset) and is referred to as the *more fragment* field. The FRAGMENT OFFSET specifies the offset of this fragment in the original datagram, measured in units of 8 octets, starting at offset 0. To reassemble the datagram, the destination must obtain all fragments starting with offset 0 through the fragment with the highest offset. Fragments do not necessarily arrive in order, and there is no communication between the destination that receives fragments and the router that fragmented the datagram. If one or more fragments are lost, the entire datagram must be discarded.

- *Time to Live* (TTL).   The TTL field specifies how long in seconds the datagram is allowed to remain in the network. TTL should be decremented at each router by one. When the TTL field becomes 0, the TTL timer expires. The intent is that TTL expiration causes a datagram to be discarded by the router, but not by the destination host. Hosts acting as routers by forwarding datagrams must follow the same rules as native routers. TTL should not be confused with hop count but should be considered a countdown field.

- *Protocol*.   This field is used to indicate the upper layer protocol to receive the data. The Protocol field is used for multiplexing/demultiplexing of data to upper layer protocols. For example, when IP sees a value of 6, it knows that the IP header encapsulates TCP data and delivers the data to the TCP module. If IP sees a value of 17, it knows that this must be delivered to the UDP module. If IP sees a value of 89, it knows it must be delivered to OSPF.

- *Header Checksum*.   This field ensures the integrity of header values. Treating the header as a sequence of 16-bit integers (in network byte order), adding them together forms the IP checksum, which uses 1s complement arithmetic and then takes the 1s complement result. This result is recomputed at each router because the TTL field is decremented at the router, and this results in the modification of the IP header.

- *Source and Destination Address*.   The *Source* and *Destination Address* fields contain the 32-bit addresses of the source and destination nodes. These addresses are sent in every IP datagram because the IP network is a connectionless network, and each IP datagram must include the sender and destination IP addresses. The routers use the destination IP address value to perform the routing for each IP datagram.

- *Options*.   The Options field indicates the security of a datagram, source routing information, and timestamp information. This field may or may not be present in a datagram; therefore, IP datagrams vary in length. The three classes of options are as follows:

  - *Security*, which specifies security level and distribution restrictions
  - *Timestamps*, which is a 32-bit value measured in milliseconds since midnight universal time or any other value if the high-order bit is set to 1
  - *Special Routing*, which specifies host-discovered paths to other hosts or a specific path for the datagram to take.

  The IP options must be handled by all IP nodes and optionally appear in IP datagrams near the IP header. Depending on the environment, the security option may be required in all datagrams.

- *Padding*.   Padding is the last field in the IP header that represents octets containing 0, which may be needed to ensure that the Internet header extends to an exact multiple of 32 bits (recall that the header length field is specified in units of 32-bit words).

IP Addresses

One of the most important design decisions of an Internet engineer is the assignment of IP addresses, 32-bit numbers that identify Internet hosts. These numbers are placed in the IP packet header and are used to route packets to their destination. Several things should be kept in mind about IP address assignment:

- *Prefix-based addressing.* A basic concept of IP addressing is that initial prefixes of the IP address can be used for generalized routing decisions. For example, the first 16 bits of an address might identify a company; the first 20 bits identify the company's Atlanta office; the first 26 bits identify a particular network in that office; and the entire 32 bits identify a particular host on that network. Prefix-based addressing has its origins in IP Address classes and has evolved into Subnetting and CIDR.

- *Per-interface assignment.* IP addresses are assigned on a per-interface basis, so a host might possess several IP addresses if it has several interfaces. For example, a host with Ethernet and serial interfaces would have an IP address for each. This is an important consequence of prefix-based addressing. An IP address doesn't really refer to a *host*, it refers to an *interface port*.

- *Multiple addresses.* If a host is known by multiple addresses, every service on this host can be referred to by multiple names. Addressing this host requires picking one of these. Because the packet is addressed to the interface and not the host, path information is introduced into the address. The exact ramifications of this effect depend heavily on the network design. In particular, careless design can result in a host becoming reachable by one address but not by another. The simplest solution to this problem is to select the host's most reliable interface and to advertise its IP address as the host's primary IP address.

Address Classes

In the original Internet routing scheme developed in the 1970s, sites were assigned addresses from one of these *classes*: A, B and C. The address classes differ in size and number. Class A addresses are the largest, but few of them exist. Class Cs are the smallest, but they are numerous. Classes D and E also are defined but are used in protocols such as OSPF, RIPv2, and E-IGRP for multicast operation. Therefore, Classes D and E are not used in normal operation. To say that class-based IP addressing is still used would be true only in the loosest sense. Many addressing designs are still class-based, but an increasing number can be explained using only the more general concept of *Classless Inter-Domain Routing* (CIDR), which is backwards compatible with address classes.

The position of the first bit set to 0 (whether it is the first, second, third, or fourth bit) in the first octet of an IP address indicates the network class (A, B, C, or D). If no bit is set to 0, it is a Class E network. You specify IP addresses in dotted decimal notation. To express an IP address in dotted decimal notation, you convert each 8-bit octet of the IP address to a decimal number and separate the numbers by decimal points.

Internet routing used to work like this: a router receiving an IP packet extracted its destination address, which was classified (literally) by examining its first one to four bits. When the address's class had been determined, it was broken down into network and host bits. Routers ignored the host bits and only needed to match the network bits to find a route to the network. When a packet reached its target network, its host field was examined for final delivery.

Summary of IP Address Classes

Class A—0nnnnnnn hhhhhhhh hhhhhhhh hhhhhhhh

- First bit 0; 7 network bits; 24 host bits
- Initial byte: 0—127
- 126 Class As exist (0 and 127 are reserved)
- 16,777,214 hosts on each Class A

Class B—10nnnnnn nnnnnnnn hhhhhhhh hhhhhhhh

- First two bits 10; 14 network bits; 16 host bits
- Initial byte: 128–191
- 16,384 Class Bs exist
- 65,532 hosts on each Class B

Class C—110nnnnn nnnnnnnn nnnnnnnn hhhhhhhh

- First three bits 110; 21 network bits; 8 host bits
- Initial byte: 192–223
- 2,097,152 Class Cs exist
- 254 hosts on each Class C

Class D—1110mmmm mmmmmmmm mmmmmmmm mmmmmmmm

- First four bits 1110; 28 multicast address bits
- Initial byte: 224–247
- Class Ds are multicast addresses

Class E—1111rrrr rrrrrrrr rrrrrrrr rrrrrrrr

- First four bits 1111; 28 reserved address bits
- Initial byte: 248–255
- Reserved for experimental use

Classless InterDomain Routing (CIDR)

Faced with the exhaustion of Class B address space and the explosion of routing table growth triggered by a flood of new class Cs, IETF began implementing *Classless Interdomain Routing* (CIDR) in the early 1990s. CIDR is documented in RFC 1518 and RFC 1519. The primary requirement for CIDR is the use of routing protocols that support it, such as RIP Version 2, OSPF Version 2, and BGP Version 4.

CIDR can be thought of as "subnetting on steroids." The subnetting mask, previously a magic number set in a computer's boot sequence, becomes an integral part of routing tables and protocols. A route is no longer an IP address, broken down into network and host bits according to its class. A route is now a combination of address and mask. Not only can we break networks into *subnets*, but we can combine networks into supernets, so long as they have a common network prefix. CIDR defines address assignment and aggregation strategies designed to minimize the size of top-level Internet routing tables.

Subnetting

Subnetting, documented in RFC 950, originally referred to the subdivision of a class-based network into subnetworks but now refers more generally to the subdivision of a CIDR block into smaller CIDR blocks. Subnetting allows single-routing entries to refer either to the larger block or to its individual constituents. This permits a single, general routing entry to be used through most of the Internet, more specific routes being required only for routers in the subnetted block.

A *subnet mask* is a 32-bit number that determines how an IP address is split into network and host portions on a bitwise basis. For example, `255.255.0.0` is a standard Class B subnet mask, because the first two bytes are all 1s (network), and the last two bytes are all 0s (host). In a subnetted network, the network portion is extended. For example, a subnet mask of `255.255.255.0` would subnet a Class B address space using its third byte. Using this scheme, the first two bytes of an IP address would identify the class B network; the next byte would identify the subnet within that network; and the final byte would select an individual host. Because subnet masks are used on a bit-by-bit basis, masks like `255.255.240.0` (4 bits of subnet; 12 bits of host) are perfectly normal.

In a traditional subnetted network, several restrictions apply, which have been lifted by CIDR. However, if older, non-CIDR routing protocols (such as RIP Version 1) are in use, these restrictions must still be observed.

- *Identical subnet masks.* Because non-CIDR routing updates do not include subnet masks, a router must assume that the subnet mask it has been configured with is valid for all subnets. Therefore, a single mask must be used for all subnets with a network. Different masks can be used for different networks.

  Based on this assumption, a router can exchange subnet routes with other routers within the network. Because the subnet masks are identical across the network, the routers interpret these routes in the same manner. However, routers not attached to the subnetted network can't interpret these subnet routes, because they lack the subnet mask. Therefore, subnet routes are not relayed to routers on other networks.

- *Contiguous subnets.* A subnetted network can't be split into isolated portions. All the subnets must be contiguous, because routing information can't be passed to nonmembers. Within a network, all subnets must be able to reach all other subnets without passing traffic through other networks.

Variable Length Subnet Masks (VLSM)

VLSM, conceptually a stepping stone from subnetting to CIDR, lifted the restrictions of subnetting by relaying subnet information through routing protocols. This idea leads us directly to CIDR.

Listing 8.1 in CH08CODE on the CD lists the host/subnet quantities.

IP Addressing and Subnetting Exercises

Complete the following steps to design an IP network:

1. Make it easy; start with the smaller number.

   If the number of networks required is less than the number of hosts per network, start your design using the number of required networks; otherwise, start with the number of hosts per network.

   Designing an IP network requires that you identify the number of networks and the number of hosts on each network. Step 1 says to look at both numbers and choose the smaller one. So, if you had a requirement of 50 networks and 700 hosts per network, you should start with the 50. You solve for the number of bits that you need to allow for 50 networks.

   EXAMPLE: For example, you are given the 10.0.0.0 network, and you need 4,000 networks and 1,000 hosts per network. Step 1 says to use which number?

   ANSWER: Use the 1,000 hosts per network.

2. Find the number of bits needed to satisfy the requirement.

   EXAMPLE: Solve the equation $2^N-2\geq$ *the required number.* Our example requires 1,000 hosts per network. How do we solve for N?

   ANSWER: We can start with 1 and work our way up:

   2^1=2; 2^2=4; 2^3=8; 2^4=16; 2^5=32; 2^6=64; 2^7=128; 2^8=256; 2^9=512; 2^{10}=1,024; etc.

   The second step says to solve for the equation $2^N-2\geq1,000$. You may not know how to solve this equation at first glance. However, you can start out with 2 to the first power. We know that this equals 2. From this point, we just add one to the power (N) and double the result. Using this method, it should take about 30 seconds to find that 2 to the tenth power solves our equation. Our subnet mask uses 10 bits for hosts, which is very important for tracking the part for which you are solving.

3. Determine the number of bits left over for the second requirement. An IP address has 32 bits total.

   EXAMPLE: How many bits are used, by default, for Classes A, B, and C?

   ANSWER: 8, 16, and 24

   EXAMPLE: In our example, we have a class A. We start with 32 bits and use up 8 for network. That leaves us with 24 bits. Of the 24 bits, we need 10 for each host per network. What will this leave us with for the number of networks?

   ANSWER: 14

   Step 3 says to find the number of bits left over. We know that a natural subnet mask for a class A is 8 bits. From step 2, we also know that we need 10 bits for the host. So, we take the total number of bits in an IP address (32) and subtract 18. This leaves us with 14 bits left over for networks.

4. Are there enough bits left over? We said that 14 bits are left over. The requirement is for 4,000 networks.

EXAMPLE: Lets solve $2^{14}-2$.

ANSWER: We already have $2^{10}=1{,}024$. Lets continue: $2^{11}=2{,}048$; $2^{12}=4{,}096$; $2^{13}=8{,}192$; $2^{14}=16{,}384$

Now we need to solve for the part that we left alone in step 1. Step 4 asks the question: Are there enough bits left over? Again we need to solve the equation $2^{N}-2$. This time, we know that 14 network bits exist. We can use the result for 10 (1,024) and continue until we hit 14. Solving the equation, we find that 14 bits are enough to provide for 4,000 networks.

5. Detemine the subnet mask. The number of bits for subnetting is equal to the number of network bits by default (8 in our example) and the number of bits for networks (14). The total for the example is 22.

EXAMPLE: Take the 22 bits and convert to dotted decimal notation.

```
11111111-11111111-11111100-00000000
```

```
255 · 255 · 252 · 0
```

We now need to determine the subnet mask. The natural subnet mask for a Class A network is 8 bits for networks. Our solution says that we need 14 more bits for subneting. Writing the subnet mask in dotted decimal notation, we have `255.255.252.0`.

6. Find the first network number. You need to satisfy the requirement that the subnet bits are not all 0. The subnet bits are the 14 bits used for networks that are not part of the default.

The first network occurs when the least significant bit of the subnet bits is set to 1. This means that bits 9 through 21 are 0, and bit 22 is 1.

Many solutions to finding the networks are available to use. The approach used here is to keep things simple. We are going to use the least significant network bit. We are going to turn this bit on (set to 1).

```
Second Octet
Bit       9      10      11      12      13      14      15      16
         128     64      32      16      8       4       2       1
          0       0       0       0       0       0       0       0 = 0
Third Octet
Bit      17      18      19      20      21      22      23      24
         128     64      32      16      8       4       2       1
          0       0       0       0       0       1     host    host = 4
```

The first network is 10.0.4.0

This slide shows that the least significant bit is 22. If we convert this back to a decimal, we see that the value is 4. We are going to use this value in the next step.

7. Find additional networks. Take the network number from step 6 (4) and increment by that amount:

- Net 1 = `10.0.4.0`
- Net 2 = `10.0.8.0`
- Net 3 = `10.0.12.0`
- Net 4 = `10.0.16.0`

Step 7 says to find the rest of your networks, use the value of step 6 and increment by that amount. This process gives you all of the wire numbers throughout your IP network. Note that the broadcast address is one less than the next network number. For example, the broadcast for the network 10.0.4.0 is 10.0.7.255. The available host addresses are between these two values: 10.0.4.1 to 10.0.7.254.

The following eight easy steps enable you to find the network, hosts, and broadcast addresses of a subnet when you are given the IP addresses and the subnet mask.

1. Define the interesting octect. Which is the interesting octet for the following:

   ▪ 10.70.241.100
   ▪ 255.255.240.0

ANSWER: 3rd octet

Which is the interesting octet for the following:

   ▪ 192.17.23.189
   ▪ 255.255.255.248

ANSWER: 4th octet

The *interesting octet* is the octet from which with visual observation you cannot determine the network number or the broadcast number. We can also define the interesting octet to be the octet with a subnet mask other than 0 or 255. If we look at the first example shown (10.70.241.100), we can tell that the first octet has a network number of 10. The broadcast for the first octet also is 10. Because we can use a visual inspection to arrive at these results, the first octet is not interesting. Similarly, octet 2 has a network and broadcast number of 70. Moving ahead to the fourth octet, we can see that the network number is 0, and the broadcast address is 255 because these are all hosts bits. The third octet leaves us with some questions. We cannot determine what the network number or broadcast number is just by visual inspection because some of the bits are host bits, but others are network bits.

2. Write the interesting octect in binary. Write 241 in binary:

128	64	32	16	8	4	2	1
1	1	1	1	0	0	0	1

Write 189 in binary:

128	64	32	16	8	4	2	1
1	0	1	1	1	1	0	1

Step 2 says to take the IP address of the interesting octet only and convert it to binary. We now see the bit pattern for the interesting octet.

3. Write the interesting octet's subnet mask in binary. Write 240 in binary:

128	64	32	16	8	4	2	1	
1	1	1	1	0	0	0	1 = 241
1	1	1	1	0	0	0	0 = 240

Write 248 in binary

128	64	32	16	8	4	2	1	
1	0	1	1	1	1	0	1	= 189
1	1	1	1	1	0	0	0	= 248

Step 3 says that we need to write the subnet mask in binary. Keep in mind that the subnet mask only has one transition from 1 to 0. All of the bits on the left are 1s, or network bits, and all of the bits on the right are 0s, or host bits.

4. Draw a line between the 1s and 0s in the subnet mask:

128	64	32	16	8	4	2	1	
1	1	1	1	0	0	0	1	= 241
1	1	1	1	0	0	0	0	= 240
	Network			Host				
128	64	32	16	8	4	2	1	
1	0	1	1	1	1	0	1	= 189
1	1	1	1	1	0	0	0	= 248
	Network			Host				

Step 4 says to draw a line between the transition point in the subnet mask. Be careful not to look at the 1s-to-0s transition in the IP address bit pattern. Usually several transitions occur from 1 to 0 in the address. This line is now the dividing point between the network bits and the hosts bits.

5. EXAMPLE 1: Do a logical AND to find the network number.

128	64	32	16	8	4	2	1	
1	1	1	1	0	0	0	1	= 241
1	1	1	1	0	0	0	0	= 240
	Network			Host				

RESULT:

1	1	1	1	0	0	0	0	= 240

Step 5 says that in order to find the network number, we need to do a logical AND on the subnet mask and the IP address. A logical AND can be determined using three methods. The first method says that if both numbers are 1, the result is 1. The second method says to use the number 1 like a pipe that allows the preceding number to flow down. The 0 is a closed value that does not allow the preceding number to flow, and all answers are 0. The third method is to multiply the two numbers.

EXAMPLE 2: Do a logical AND to find the network number.

128	64	32	16	8	4	2	1	
1	0	1	1	1	1	0	1	= 189
1	1	1	1	1	0	0	0	= 248
		Network			Host			

RESULT:

1	0	1	1	1	0	0	0	= 184

6. Convert the resultant binary number back to decimal, and the result is the network or wire number.

EXAMPLE 1: Network Number is 10.70.240.0

EXAMPLE 2: Network Number is 192.17.23.184

Congratulations! You have already found the network number. Now you just need to plug the result back into the interesting octet of the IP address. Then, we are going to solve for the broadcast address.

7. Find the Broadcast; put all 1s in the host bits (keep the same network number) and convert back to decimal.

EXAMPLE 1: Broadcast address is

1   1   1   1   1   1   1   1 = 255

Broadcast = 10.70.255.255

EXAMPLE 2: Broadcast address is

1   0   1   1   1   1   1   1 = 191

Broadcast = 192.17.23.191

All that we need to do to find the broadcast address is change the host's bits to 1s. Remember to keep the network bits the same. Also as in the preceding step, we just take the result and plug it back into the interesting octet of the IP address. Note that in example 1, the fourth octet was not interesting because they are all host bits. The network number is 0, and the broadcast number is 255. This is why the fourth octet changes with the result for the network and broadcast numbers.

8. Valid network addresses are between the network number and the broadcast number.

EXAMPLE 1:

- Network Address   10.70.240.0
- Broadcast Address   10.70.255.255
- Valid Host: 10.70.240.1 to 10.70.255.254

EXAMPLE 2:

- Network Address: 192.17.23.184
- Broadcast Address: 192.17.23.191
- Valid Host: 192.17.23.185 to 192.17.23.190

Step number 8 says that all the addresses between the network address and broadcast address are the possible host addresses for that subnet. So, what type of address is 10.70.240.5? What about 10.70.241.0 and 10.70.250.255? Looking at the first address, it is easy to see that it is a host address. However, sometimes seeing a 0 and a 255 in the fourth octet may lead us to say automatically it is a network address or a broadcast address. The real question is, "Are these addresses between the network and broadcast addresses?" The answer is yes, so these are just host addresses on the 10.70.240.0 subnet. It is advisable not to use these addresses (addresses that end in 0 or 255) in your network because most people would confuse them with network and broadcast addresses.

ARP Architecture

ARP is used to resolve a Layer 3 address to a Layer 2 Macc address. It works by broadcasting a packet to all hosts attached to an LAN. The packet contains the IP address with which the sender is interested in communicating. Most hosts ignore the packet. The target machine, recognizing that the IP address in the packet matches its own, returns an answer. Hosts typically keep a cache of ARP responses, based on the assumption that IP-to-hardware address mapping rarely changes.

ARP is transparent to bridging but not to routers. Bridges propagate ARP broadcasts like any other Ethernet broadcast and transparently bridge the replies. A router does not propagate ARP broadcasts, because the router is a network level 3 device, and Ethernet, Token Ring, FDDI, and ATM are data-link protocols.

ARP: Frame Encapsulation

Figure 8.5 details how an ARP packet is encapsulated in an Ethernet packet as it travels from one machine to another on the physical network. Note that ARP is not an IP protocol in the sense that the ARP datagrams do not have IP headers. ARP does not use the services of IP because ARP messages do not leave the logical network and never need to be routed. ARP requests must be sent as *broadcasts*. An ARP request cannot be sent directly to the correct host. After all, the whole reason for sending an ARP request is that the source host does not know the destination host Ethernet address.

An Ethernet address of all 1s is used (`FF.FF.FF.FF.FF.FF`) as the broadcast address. By convention, every machine on Ethernet is required to pay attention to packets with this as a destination address. Every host listens to the broadcast ARP requests. When a machine sees an ARP request for itself, it is required to respond.

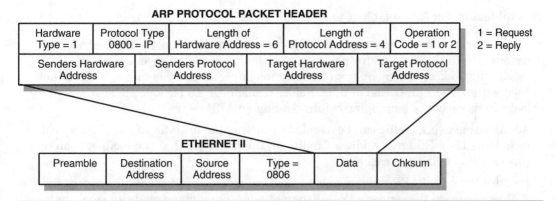

FIGURE 8.5 ARP protocol packet header

The Ethernet type field is used to identify the type of ARP packet carried in the data field:

- ARP type = 0x0806

ARP: Header Format

ARP packets do not have a fixed-format header. To allow ARP to work with many different types of network technologies, the early header fields contain values that specify the lengths of succeeding fields. Therefore, ARP can be used with technologies that implement arbitrary physical addresses and arbitrary protocol addresses (see Figure 8.5).

- *Hardware Type.*   This field indicates the type of hardware used at the network level. For Ethernet, this value is 1.
- *Protocol Type.*   This field indicates the protocol used at the network level.
- *Hardware Address Length.*   This field indicates the length of the hardware address in bytes. For Ethernet, this value is 6.
- *Protocol Address Space.*   This field indicates the length of the protocol address in bytes. For TCP/IP protocols, this value is 4.
- *Operation Code.*   This field describes the function of this packet: ARP request or ARP response.
- *Senders Hardware Address.*   This field is the hardware address of the sending station.
- *Senders Protocol Address.*   This field is the Internet address of the sending station.
- *Target Hardware Address.*   When making an ARP request, this field is the destination hardware address. The response carries both the destination machine's hardware and Internet address.
- *Target Protocol Address.*   When making an ARP request, this field is the destination Internet address. The response carries both the destination machine's hardware and Internet address.

ARP Features

Several features of ARP enable it to operate very efficiently:

- To reduce communication costs, hosts that use ARP maintain a cache of recently acquired IP-to-Ethernet address mapping so that they do not have to use ARP repeatedly. To keep the cache from growing too large, an entry is removed if it is not used within a certain period of time. Before transmitting a packet, the host always looks in its cache for a mapping before sending an ARP request.
- Additional network traffic can be avoided by having the initiator of an ARP request include its IP-to-Ethernet address binding in the packet so that the recipient can add this mapping to its own cache.

  Because the initial ARP request is broadcast, all machines on the local network receive it, they can learn the sender's IP-to-Ethernet address mapping, and can store that mapping in their own cache.

- A new host can appear on the network, or the operating system of an old host can reboot. All devices quickly learn the IP-to-Ethernet address binding of the new machine when it broadcasts its first ARP request. The new machine's mapping is placed in the cache before all other devices on the network.

The following process is used when a PING command is initiated to a remote host:

1. The ARP cache is checked; if no mapping exists, then send an ARP request that is not on the same network.
2. An ARP request for the IP address of the default gateway is broadcast on the local network.
3. The default gateway initiates an ARP response listing its hardware address.
4. The source host sends an ICMP echo request to the MAC address of the default gateway to be transmitted to the destination host.

Proxy ARP

Proxy ARP can assist machines on a subnet to reach remote subnets without having either routing or default gateways configured. Proxy ARP is a technique that can be used by routers to handle traffic between hosts that don't expect to use a router. Probably the most common case of its use would be the gradual subnetting of a larger network. Those hosts not yet converted to the new system expect to transmit directly to hosts now placed behind a router.

A router using Proxy ARP recognizes ARP requests for hosts on the "other side" of the router that can't reply for themselves. The router answers for those addresses with an ARP reply that matches the remote IP address with the router's Ethernet address.

Reverse ARP

Reverse ARP is a fairly simple bootstrapping protocol that allows a workstation to broadcast using its Ethernet address and expects a server to reply, telling it its IP address. A machine's Internet address is usually kept on its secondary storage where the operating system can find it at start up. How does a diskless workstation determine its Internet address? The diskless machine must resort to using physical addressing to broadcast a request to a server on the local network. The diskless machine uniquely identifies itself to the server by using its physical address (Ethernet address). We make the assumption that the server has secondary storage that contains a database of Internet addresses. The requesting machine waits until it receives responses from one or more servers. After the machine learns its Internet address, it can communicate across the Internet.

Diskless machines use the *Reverse Address Resolution Protocol* (RARP) to request a server to supply its Internet address. This protocol is adapted from the ARP protocol and uses the same message format. Like an ARP message, a RARP message is sent from one machine to another encapsulated in the data portion of an Ethernet frame.

DHCP Protocol Architecture

DHCP is a protocol that assists in solving the IP addressing assignment used with TCP/IP. DHCP, through the use of a client/server paradigm, allows clients that are DHCP aware to discover a DHCP server and to have that server assign an IP address without operator intervention. From the client's point of view, DHCP is an extension of the BOOTP mechanism. This behavior allows existing BOOTP clients to interoperate with DHCP servers without requiring any change to the clients' initialization software as depicted in Figure 8.6.

DHCP Scopes

You must configure a range of addresses for every IP subnet in which clients request a DHCP assigned address; each range of addresses is called a DHCP *scope*. A DHCP server can support multiple scopes, and does not need to be connected to the same network as the client. If the DHCP server is on a different IP subnet from the client, you need to use DHCP relay to forward DHCP requests to your DHCP server.

DHCP Relay

DHCP relay typically runs on a router; DHCP relay support is also available on Windows NT server. You can turn on DHCP relay on a Cisco router by configuring `ip helper-address` with the address of the DHCP server on each interface that has DHCP clients. The `ip helper-address` command forwards many other IP broadcasts, including DNS, *Trivial File Transfer Protocol* (TFTP), and NetBIOS name service packets.

Figure 8.7 gives the format of a DHCP message, and Table 8.1 describes each of the fields in the DHCP message. The numbers in parentheses indicate the size of each field in octets. The names for the fields given in the figure are used to refer to the fields in DHCP messages.

Two primary differences exist between DHCP and BOOTP. First, DHCP defines mechanisms through which clients can be assigned a network address for a finite lease, allowing for serial reassignment of network addresses to different clients. Second, DHCP provides

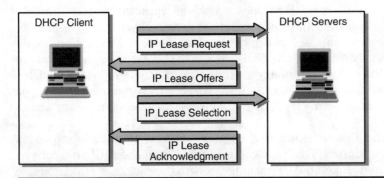

FIGURE 8.6   DHCP address assignment

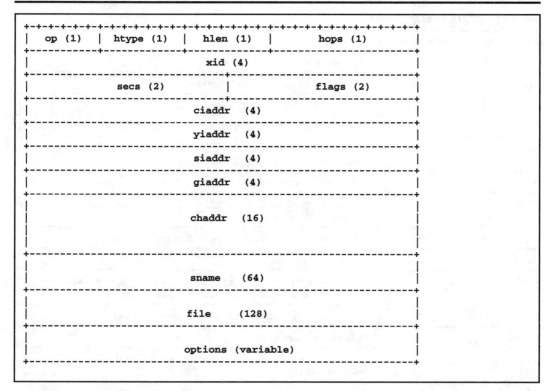

```
+-+-+-+-+-+-+-+-+-+-+-+-+-+-+-+-+-+-+-+-+-+-+-+-+-+-+-+-+-+-+
|   op  (1)  |  htype (1)  |   hlen (1)  |        hops (1)         |
+------------+-------------+-------------+------------------------+
|                         xid (4)                                 |
+---------------------------+-------------------------------------+
|           secs (2)        |           flags (2)                 |
+---------------------------+-------------------------------------+
|                       ciaddr   (4)                              |
+-----------------------------------------------------------------+
|                       yiaddr   (4)                              |
+-----------------------------------------------------------------+
|                       siaddr   (4)                              |
+-----------------------------------------------------------------+
|                       giaddr   (4)                              |
+-----------------------------------------------------------------+
|                                                                 |
|                     chaddr   (16)                               |
|                                                                 |
+-----------------------------------------------------------------+
|                                                                 |
|                     sname    (64)                               |
+-----------------------------------------------------------------+
|                                                                 |
|                     file     (128)                              |
+-----------------------------------------------------------------+
|                     options (variable)                          |
+-----------------------------------------------------------------+
```

FIGURE 8.7 Format of a BOOTP message

the mechanism for a client to acquire all of the IP configuration parameters that it needs to operate.

DHCP introduces a small change in terminology intended to clarify the meaning of one of the fields. What was the vendor extensions field in BOOTP has been renamed the options field in DHCP. Similarly, the tagged data items that were used inside the BOOTP vendor extensions field are now termed *options*.

DHCP defines a client identifier option used to pass an explicit client identifier to a DHCP server. The *client identifier* is an opaque key, not to be interpreted by the server; for example, the client identifier may contain a hardware address, identical to the contents of the chaddr field, or it may contain another type of identifier, such as a DNS name. The client identifier chosen by a DHCP client *must* be unique to that client within the subnet to which the client is attached. If the client uses a client identifier in one message, it *must* use that same identifier in all subsequent messages, to ensure that all servers correctly identify the client.

DHCP clarifies the interpretation of the Server IP Address (siaddr) field as the address of the server to use in the next step of the client's bootstrap process. A DHCP server may return its own address in the Server IP Address (siaddr) field, if the server is prepared to supply the next bootstrap service (e.g., delivery of an operating system's executable image). A DHCP server always returns its own address in the server identifier option.

TABLE 8.1 **BOOTP Message Format**

Field Name	Length in Bytes	Description
op	1	Opcode; 1 = boot request, 2 = boot reply
htype	1	Hardware address type; (see options used by ARP)
hlen	1	Hardware address length; 6 for 10 Mbps Ethernet
hops	1	The client always sets this field to 0, and this field is used by routers
xid	4	Transaction ID. A random number assigned by the client; this is used by the client to match a reply with a specific request.
secs	2	Number of seconds since client started the boot process
flags	2	Flags; the most significant bit of the field in the broadcast bit. All other bits must be set to 0.
ciaddr	4	Client IP address. Filled in by client using DHCPREQUEST
yiaddr	4	Your client IP address
siaddr	4	Server IP address of next server to use in bootstrap; returned in DHCPOFFER, DHCPACK, and DHCPNAK by server
giaddr	4	Relay agent IP address, used in booting via a router
chaddr	16	Client hardware address
sname	64	Server host name. The client may fill this field in if it knows the name of its server (optional)
file	128	Boot file name. a null-terminated string
vend	64	Vendor-specific information

The options field is now variable length. A DHCP client must be prepared to receive DHCP messages with an options field of at least length 312 octets. This requirement implies that a DHCP client must be prepared to receive a message of up to 576 octets, the minimum IP datagram size an IP host must be prepared to accept. DHCP clients may negotiate the use of larger DHCP messages through the *maximum DHCP message size* option. The options field may be further extended into the file and sname fields.

The TCP/IP software should accept and forward to the IP layer of any IP packets delivered to the client's hardware address before the IP address is configured; DHCP servers and BOOTP relay agents may not be able to deliver DHCP messages to clients that cannot accept hardware unicast datagrams before the TCP/IP software is configured.

Configuration Parameters

The first service provided by DHCP is storage of network parameters for network clients. The model of DHCP persistent storage is that the DHCP service stores a key-value entry for each client, in which the key is some unique identifier (for example, an IP subnet number and a unique identifier within the subnet), and the value contains the configuration parameters for the client.

For example, the key might be the pair, (IP-subnet-number, hardware-address). Note that the hardware-address should be the type of hardware used to accommodate possible duplication of hardware addresses resulting from bit-ordering problems in a mixed-media, bridged network. This pair allows for serial or concurrent reuse of a hardware address on different subnets and for hardware addresses that may not be globally unique. Alternately, the key may be the pair, (IP-subnet-number, hostname), allowing the server to assign parameters intelligently to a DHCP client that has been moved to a different subnet or has changed hardware addresses (perhaps because the network interface failed and was replaced). The protocol defines that the key is (IP-subnet-number, hardware-address) unless the client explicitly supplies an identifier using the client identifier option. A client can query the DHCP service to retrieve its configuration parameters. The client interface to the configuration parameters repository consists of protocol messages to request configuration parameters and responses from the server carrying the configuration parameters.

Network Address Allocation

The second service provided by DHCP is the allocation of temporary or permanent network addresses to clients. The basic mechanism for the dynamic allocation of network addresses is simple: a client requests the use of an address for some period of time. The allocation mechanism (the collection of DHCP servers) guarantees not to reallocate that address within the requested time and attempts to return the same network address each time the client requests an address. The period over which a network address is allocated to a client is referred to as a *lease*. The client may extend its lease with subsequent requests. The client may issue a message to release the address back to the server when the client no longer needs the address. The client may ask for a permanent assignment by asking for an infinite lease. Even when assigning permanent addresses, a server may choose to give out lengthy, but finite, leases to allow detection of the fact that the client has been retired.

In some environments, reassigning network addresses becomes necessary due to the exhaustion of available addresses. In such environments, the allocation mechanism reuses addresses with expired leases. The server should use whatever information is available in the configuration information repository to choose an address to reuse. For example, the server may choose the least recently assigned address. As a consistency check, the allocating server *should* probe the reused address before allocating the address (e.g., with an ICMP echo request), and the client *should* probe the newly received address (e.g., with ARP).

Client-Server Protocol

DHCP uses the BOOTP message format defined in RFC 951 and given in Figure 8.7. The *op* field of each DHCP message sent from a client to a server which contains BOOTREQUEST. BOOTREPLY is used in the *op* field of each DHCP message sent from a server to a client. The first four octets of the options field of the DHCP message contain the decimal values 99, 130, 83, and 99, respectively (this is the same magic cookie as is defined in RFC 1497). The remainder of the options field consists of a list of tagged parameters called *options*.

Several options have been defined so far. One particular option—the DHCP message type option—must be included in every DHCP message. This option defines the type of the

DHCP message. Additional options may be allowed, required, or not allowed, depending on the DHCP message type.

DHCP messages that include a DHCP message type option are referenced by the type of the message. For example, a DHCP message with `DHCP message type` option type 1 is referenced as a DHCPDISCOVER message.

Client-Server Interaction—Allocating a Network Address.

The following summary of the protocol exchanges between clients and servers refers to the DHCP messages. If the client already knows its address, some steps may be omitted. See Table 8.2 and Figures 8.8–8.11 for the various DHCP message headers enclosed in Ethernet Data Link layer frames.

1. The client broadcasts a DHCPDISCOVER message on its local physical subnet. The DHCPDISCOVER message may include options that suggest values for the network address and lease duration. BOOTP relay agents may pass the message on to DHCP servers not on the same physical subnet.

2. Each server may respond with a DHCPOFFER message that includes an available network address in the Your IP Address (yiaddr) field and other configuration parameters in DHCP options. Servers need not reserve the offered network address, although the protocol works more efficiently if the server avoids allocating the offered network address to another client. When allocating a new address, servers should check that the offered network address is not already in use; for example, the server may probe the offered address with an ICMP Echo Request. The server transmits the DHCPOFFER message to the client, using the BOOTP relay agent if necessary.

3. The client receives one or more DHCPOFFER messages from one or more servers. The client may choose to wait for multiple responses. The client chooses one server from which to request configuration parameters, based on the configuration parameters

TABLE 8.2 DHCP Messages

Message	Use
DHCPDISCOVER	Client broadcast to locate available servers
DHCPOFFER	Server to client in response to DHCPDISCOVER with offer of configuration parameters
DHCPREQUEST	Client message to servers either requesting offered parameters from one server and implicitly declining offers from all others; confirming correctness of previously allocated address after, e.g., system reboot; or extending the lease on a particular network address.
DHCPACK	Server to client with configuration parameters, including committed network address
DHCPNAK	Server to client indicating client's notion of network address is incorrect (e.g., client has moved to new subnet) or client's lease as expired
DHCPDECLINE	Client to server indicating network address is already in use
DHCPRELEASE	Client to server relinquishing network address and cancelling remaining lease
DHCPINFORM	Client to server, asking only for local configuration parameters; client already has externally configured network address.

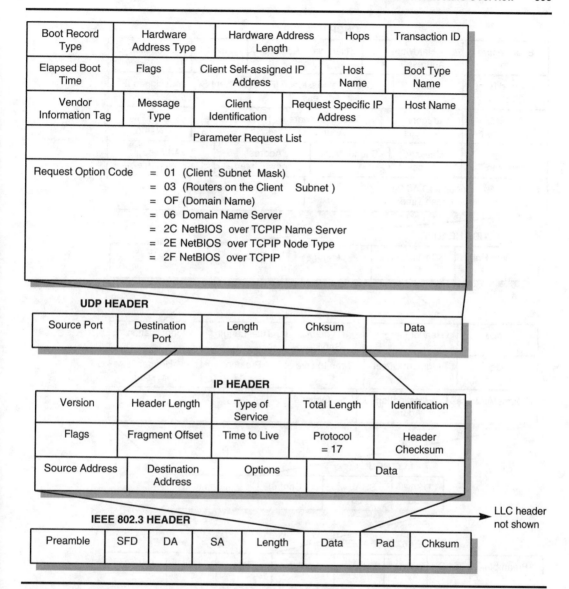

Boot Record Type	Hardware Address Type	Hardware Address Length		Hops	Transaction ID

Elapsed Boot Time	Flags	Client Self-assigned IP Address		Host Name	Boot Type Name

Vendor Information Tag	Message Type	Client Identification	Request Specific IP Address	Host Name

Parameter Request List

Request Option Code   = 01 (Client Subnet Mask)
                    = 03 (Routers on the Client   Subnet)
                    = OF (Domain Name)
                    = 06 Domain Name Server
                    = 2C NetBIOS over TCPIP Name Server
                    = 2E NetBIOS over TCPIP Node Type
                    = 2F NetBIOS over TCPIP

UDP HEADER

Source Port	Destination Port	Length	Chksum	Data

IP HEADER

Version	Header Length	Type of Service	Total Length	Identification
Flags	Fragment Offset	Time to Live	Protocol = 17	Header Checksum
Source Address	Destination Address	Options	Data	

IEEE 802.3 HEADER   LLC header not shown

Preamble	SFD	DA	SA	Length	Data	Pad	Chksum

FIGURE 8.8   DHCP Request header

offered in the DHCPOFFER messages. The client broadcasts a DHCPREQUEST message that *must* include the server identifier option to indicate which server it has selected and that *may* include other options specifying desired configuration values. The `requested IP address` option *must* be set to the value of `Your IP Address (yiaddr)` in the DHCPOFFER message from the server. This DHCPREQUEST message is broadcast and relayed through DHCP/BOOTP relay agents. To help ensure that any BOOTP relay agents forward the DHCPREQUEST message to the same set of DHCP servers that received the original DHCPDISCOVER message, the DHCPREQUEST

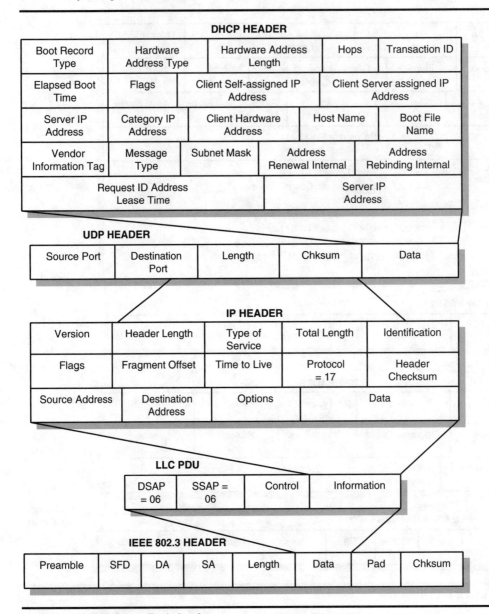

FIGURE 8.9 DHCP Server Reply header

message *must* use the same value in the DHCP message header's *secs* field and be sent to the same IP broadcast address as the original DHCPDISCOVER message. The client times out and retransmits the DHCPDISCOVER message if the client receives no DHCPOFFER messages.

4. The servers receive the DHCPREQUEST broadcast from the client. Those servers not selected by the DHCPREQUEST message use the message as notification that the client has declined that server's offer. The server selected in the DHCPREQUEST

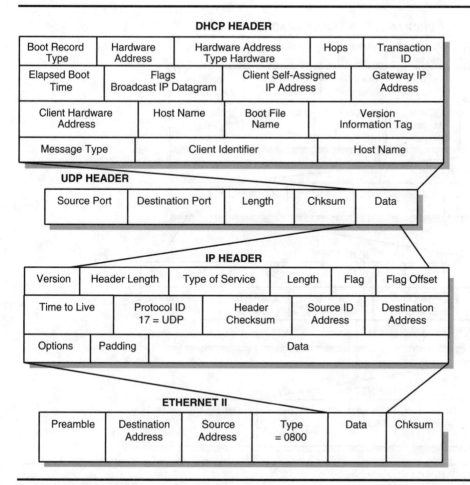

FIGURE 8.10   DHCP Discover Packet header

message commits the binding for the client to persistent storage and responds with a DHCPACK message containing the configuration parameters for the requesting client. The combination of client identifier or chaddr and assigned network address constitute a unique identifier for the client's lease and are used by both the client and server to identify a lease referred in any DHCP messages. Any configuration parameters in the DHCPACK message should not conflict with those in the earlier DHCPOFFER message to which the client is responding. The server should not check the offered network address at this point. The *Your IP Address (yiaddr)* field in the DHCPACK message is filled in with the selected network address. If the selected server is unable to satisfy the DHCPREQUEST message (e.g., the requested network address has been allocated), the server should respond with a DHCPNAK message. A server may choose to mark addresses offered to clients in DHCPOFFER messages as unavailable. The server should mark an address offered to a client in a DHCPOFFER message as available if the server does not receive a DHCPREQUEST message from that client.

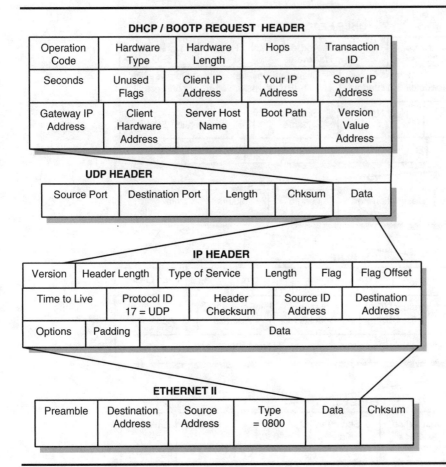

FIGURE 8.11 DHCP BOOTP Request header

5. The client receives the DHCPACK message with configuration parameters. The client should perform a final check on the parameters (e.g., ARP for allocated network address) and note the duration of the lease specified in the DHCPACK message. At this point, the client is configured. If the client detects that the address is already in use (e.g., through the use of ARP), the client *must* send a DHCPDECLINE message to the server and restart the configuration process. The client should wait a minimum of 10 seconds before restarting the configuration process to avoid excessive network traffic in case of looping.

If the client receives a DHCPNAK message, the client restarts the configuration process.

The client times out and retransmits the DHCPREQUEST message if the client receives neither a DHCPACK or a DHCPNAK message. The client retransmits the DHCPREQUEST according to the retransmission algorithm. The client should choose to retransmit the DHCPREQUEST enough times to give adequate probability of contacting the server without causing the client (and the user of that client) to wait overly long before giving up. For example, a client retransmitting might retransmit the DHCPREQUEST message four times, for a total delay of 60 seconds, before restarting the initialization procedure. If the client receives neither a DHCPACK or a DHCPNAK message after using the retransmission algorithm, the client reverts to INIT state and restarts the initialization process. The client should notify the user that the initialization process has failed and is restarting.

6. The client may choose to relinquish its lease on a network address by sending a DHCPRELEASE message to the server. The client identifies the lease to be released with its client identifier, or chaddr and network address in the DHCPRELEASE message. If the client used a client identifier when it obtained the lease, it must use the same client identifier in the DHCPRELEASE message.

Client-Server Interaction—Reusing a Previously Allocated Network Address. If a client remembers and wants to reuse a previously allocated network address, a client may choose to omit some of the steps described in the previous section.

1. The client broadcasts a DHCPREQUEST message on its local subnet. The message includes the client's network address in the `requested IP address` option. As the client has not received its network address, it *must not* fill in the `client IP Address (ciaddr)` field. BOOTP relay agents pass the message on to DHCP servers not on the same subnet. If the client used a client identifier to obtain its address, the client *must* use the same client identifier in the DHCPREQUEST message.

2. Servers with knowledge of the client's configuration parameters respond with a DHCPACK message to the client. Servers should not check that the client's network address is already in use; the client may respond to ICMP Echo Request messages at this point.

If the client's request is invalid (e.g., the client has moved to a new subnet), servers should respond with a DHCPNAK message to the client. Servers should not respond if their information is not guaranteed to be accurate. For example, a server that identifies a request for an expired binding owned by another server should not respond with a DHCPNAK unless the servers are using an explicit mechanism to maintain coherency among the servers. If `Relay IP Address (giaddr)` is 0x0 in the DHCPREQUEST message, the client is on the same subnet as the server. The server *must* broadcast the DHCPNAK message to the `0xffffffff` broadcast address because the client may not have a correct network address or subnet mask, and the client may not be answering ARP requests. Otherwise, the server *must* send the DHCPNAK message to the IP address of the BOOTP relay agent, as recorded in `Relay IP Address (giaddr)`. The relay agent, in turn, forwards the message directly to the client's hardware address so that the DHCPNAK can be delivered even if the client has moved to a new network.

1. The client receives the DHCPACK message with configuration parameters. The client performs a final check on the parameters and notes the duration of the lease specified in the DHCPACK message. The specific lease is implicitly identified by the client identifier or chaddr and the network address. At this point, the client is configured.

If the client detects that the IP address in the DHCPACK message is already in use, the client *must* send a DHCPDECLINE message to the server and restart the configuration process by requesting a new network address. This action corresponds to the client moving to the initialization state in the DHCP state diagram.

If the client receives a DHCPNAK message, it cannot reuse its remembered network address. It must instead request a new address by restarting the configuration process. This action also corresponds to the client moving to the INIT state in the DHCP state diagram.

The client times out and retransmits the DHCPREQUEST message if the client receives neither a DHCPACK nor a DHCPNAK message. The client retransmits the DHCPREQUEST according to the retransmission algorithm. The client should choose to retransmit the DHCPREQUEST enough times to give adequate probability of contacting the server without causing the client (and the user of that client) to wait overly long before giving up; for example, a client retransmitting may retransmit the DHCPREQUEST message four times, for a total delay of 60 seconds, before restarting the initialization procedure. If the client receives neither a DHCPACK or a DHCPNAK message after using the retransmission algorithm, the client *may* choose to use the previously allocated network address and configuration parameters for the remainder of the unexpired lease. This corresponds to moving to a BOUND state in the client state transition diagram.

2. The client may choose to relinquish its lease on a network address by sending a DHCPRELEASE message to the server. The client identifies the lease to be released with its client identifier, or chaddr and network address in the DHCPRELEASE message.

    NOTE: *In this case, in which the client retains its network address locally, the client does not normally relinquish its lease during a graceful shutdown. Only when the client explicitly needs to relinquish its lease, e.g., the client is about to be moved to a different subnet, does the client send a DHCPRELEASE message.*

Interpretation and Representation of Time Values.   A client acquires a lease for a network address for a period of time (which may be infinite). Throughout the protocol, times are to be represented in units of seconds. The time value of `0xffffffff` is reserved to represent infinity.

As clients and servers may not have synchronized clocks, times are represented in DHCP messages as relative times, to be interpreted with respect to the client's local clock. Representing relative times in units of seconds in an unsigned 32-bit word gives a range of relative times from 0 to approximately 100 years, which is sufficient for the relative times to be measured using DHCP.

The algorithm for lease duration interpretation given in the previous paragraph assumes that client and server clocks are stable relative to each other. If a drift is between the two clocks, the server may consider the lease expired before the client does. To compensate, the server may return a shorter lease duration to the client than the server commits to its local database of client information.

Constructing and Sending DHCP Messages

DHCP clients and servers both construct DHCP messages by filling in fields in the fixed format section of the message and appending tagged data items in the variable length option area. The options area includes first a four-octet *magic cookie*, followed by the options. The last option must always be the *end* option.

DHCP uses UDP as its transport protocol. DHCP messages from a client to a server are sent to the DHCP server port (67), and DHCP messages from a server to a client are sent to the DHCP client port (68). A server with multiple network address (e.g., a multihomed host) *may* use any of its network addresses in outgoing DHCP messages.

The server identifier field is used to identify a DHCP server in a DHCP message and as a destination address from clients to servers. A server with multiple network addresses must be prepared to accept any of its network addresses as identifying that server in a DHCP message. To accommodate potentially incomplete network connectivity, a server *must* choose an address as a server identifier that, to the best of the server's knowledge, is reachable from the client. For example, if the DHCP server and the DHCP client are connected to the same subnet (i.e., the `Relay IP Address (giaddr)` field in the message from the client is 0), the server should select the IP address the server is using for communication on that subnet as the server identifier. If the server is using multiple IP addresses on that subnet, any such address may be used. If the server has received a message through a DHCP relay agent, the server should choose an address from the interface from which the message was recieved as the server identifier (unless the server has other, better information on which to make its choice). DHCP clients must use the IP address provided in the server identifier option for any unicast requests to the DHCP server.

DHCP messages broadcast by a client prior to that client obtaining its IP address must have the source address field in the IP header set to 0.

If the `Relay IP Address (giaddr)` field in a DHCP message from a client is not 0, the server sends any return messages to the DHCP server port on the BOOTP relay agent whose address appears in `Relay IP Address (giaddr)`. If the `Relay IP Address (giaddr)` field is 0 and the `Client IP Address (ciaddr)` field is not 0, the server unicasts DHCPOFFER and DHCPACK messages to the address in `Client IP Address (ciaddr)`. If `Relay IP Address (giaddr)` is 0, `Client IP Address (ciaddr)` is 0, and the broadcast bit is set, the server broadcasts DHCPOFFER and DHCPACK messages to `0xffffffff`. If the broadcast bit is not set, `Relay IP Address (giaddr)` is 0, and `Client IP Address (ciaddr)` is 0, the server unicasts DHCPOFFER and DHCPACK messages to the client's hardware address and `Your IP Address (yiaddr)` address. In all cases, when `Relay IP Address (giaddr)` is 0, the server broadcasts any DHCPNAK messages to `0xffffffff`.

If the options in a DHCP message extend into the sname and file fields, the overload option must appear in the options field, with value 1, 2, or 3. If the option overload option is present in the options field, the options in the options field must be terminated by an end option and may contain one or more pad options to fill the options field. The options in the sname and file fields (if in use as indicated by the *options overload* option) must begin with the first octet of the field, must be terminated by an end option, and must be followed by pad options to fill the remainder of the field. Any individual option in the options, sname, and file fields must be entirely contained in that field. The options in the options field must be interpreted first so that any option overload options may be interpreted. The file field must be interpreted next (if the option overload option indicates that the file field contains DHCP options), followed by the sname field.

The values to be passed in an option tag may be too long to fit in the 255 octets available to a single option. Options may appear only once, unless otherwise specified in the options document. The client concatenates the values of multiple instances of the same option into a single parameter list for configuration.

DHCP clients are responsible for all message retransmission. The client must adopt a retransmission strategy that incorporates a randomized exponential backoff algorithm to determine the delay between retransmissions. The delay between retransmissions should be chosen to allow sufficient time for replies from the server to be delivered based on the characteristics of the internetwork between the client and the server. For example, in a 10M/sec Ethernet internetwork, the delay before the first retransmission should be four seconds randomized by the value of a uniform random number chosen from the range -1 to $+1$. Clients with clocks that provide resolution granularity of less than one second may choose a noninteger randomization value. The delay before the next retransmission should be eight seconds randomized by the value of a uniform number chosen from the range -1 to $+1$. The retransmission delay should be doubled with subsequent retransmissions up to a maximum of 64 seconds. The client *may* provide an indication of retransmission attempts to the user as an indication of the progress of the configuration process.

The xid field is used by the client to match incoming DHCP messages with pending requests. A DHCP client must choose xids in such a way as to minimize the chance of using an xid identical to one used by another client. For example, a client may choose a different, random initial xid each time the client is rebooted and subsequently use sequential xids until the next reboot. Selecting a new xid for each retransmission is an implementation decision. A client may choose to reuse the same xid or to select a new xid for each retransmitted message. Normally, DHCP servers and BOOTP relay agents attempt to deliver DHCPOFFER, DHCPACK, and DHCPNAK messages directly to the client using unicast delivery. The IP destination address (in the IP header) is set to the DHCP `Your IP Address (yiaddr)` address, and the link-layer destination address is set to the DHCP chaddr address. Unfortunately, some client implementations are unable to receive such unicast IP datagrams until the implementation has been configured with a valid IP address (leading to a deadlock in which the client's IP address cannot be delivered until the client has been configured with an IP address).

A client that cannot receive unicast IP datagrams until its protocol software has been configured with an IP address should set the BROADCAST bit in the flags field to 1 in any DHCPDISCOVER or DHCPREQUEST messages that client sends. The BROADCAST bit provides a hint to the DHCP server and BOOTP relay agent to broadcast any messages to the client on the client's subnet. A client that can receive unicast IP datagrams before its protocol software has been configured should clear the BROADCAST bit to 0.

A server or relay agent sending or relaying a DHCP message directly to a DHCP client (i.e., not to a relay agent specified in the `Relay IP Address (giaddr)` field) should examine the BROADCAST bit in the flags field. If this bit is set to 1, the DHCP message should be sent as an IP broadcast using an IP broadcast address (preferably `0xffffffff`) as the IP destination address and the link-layer broadcast address as the link-layer destination address. If the BROADCAST bit is cleared to 0, the message should be sent as an IP unicast to the

IP address specified in the `Your IP Address (yiaddr)` field and the link-layer address specified in the chaddr field. If unicasting is not possible, the message *may* be sent as an IP broadcast using an IP broadcast address (preferably `0xffffffff`) as the IP destination address and the link-layer broadcast address as the link-layer destination address.

DHCP Server Controls

DHCP servers are not required to respond to every DHCPDISCOVER and DHCPRE-QUEST message they receive. For example, a network administrator, to retain stringent control over the clients attached to the network, may choose to configure DHCP servers to respond only to clients that have been previously registered through some external mechanism. The DHCP specification describes only the interactions between clients and servers when the clients and servers choose to interact; it is beyond the scope of the DHCP specification to describe all of the administrative controls that system administrators may want to use. Specific DHCP server implementations may incorporate any controls or policies desired by a network administrator.

In some environments, a DHCP server has to consider the values of the vendor class options included in DHCPDISCOVER or DHCPREQUEST messages when determining the correct parameters for a particular client.

A DHCP server needs to use some unique identifier to associate a client with its lease. The client *may* choose to explicitly provide the identifier through the client identifier option. If the client supplies a client identifier, the client *must* use the same client identifier in all subsequent messages, and the server *must* use that identifier to identify the client. If the client does not provide a client identifier option, the server *must* use the contents of the chaddr field to identify the client. It is crucial for a DHCP client to use an identifier unique within the subnet to which the client is attached in the client identifier option. Use of chaddr as the client's unique identifier may cause unexpected results, as that identifier may be associated with a hardware interface that could be moved to a new client. Some sites may choose to use a manufacturer's serial number as the client identifier, to avoid unexpected changes in a client's network address due to the transfer of hardware interfaces among computers. Sites also may choose to use a DNS name as the client identifier, causing address leases to be associated with the DNS name rather than a specific hardware box.

DHCP clients are free to use any strategy in selecting a DHCP server among those from which the client receives a DHCPOFFER message. The client implementation of DHCP *should* provide a mechanism for the user to select directly the vendor class identifier values.

DHCP Server Behavior

A DHCP server processes incoming DHCP messages from a client based on the current state of the binding for that client. A DHCP server can receive the following messages from a client:

- DHCPDISCOVER
- DHCPREQUEST
- DHCPDECLINE

- DHCPRELEASE
- DHCPINFORM

DHCPDISCOVER Message. When a server receives a DHCPDISCOVER message from a client, the server chooses a network address for the requesting client. If no address is available, the server may choose to report the problem to the system administrator. If an address is available, the new address *should* be chosen as follows:

- The client's current address as recorded in the client's current binding, ELSE
- The client's previous address as recorded in the client's (now expired or released) binding, if that address is in the server's pool of available addresses and not already allocated, ELSE
- The address requested in the Requested IP Address option, if that address is valid and not already allocated, ELSE
- A new address allocated from the server's pool of available addresses; the address is selected based on the subnet from which the message was received (if **Relay IP Address (giaddr)** is 0) or on the address of the relay agent that forwarded the message (**Relay IP Address (giaddr)** when not 0).

A server *may*, for administrative reasons, assign an address other than the one requested or may refuse to allocate an address to a particular client even though free addresses are available.

Note that in some network architectures (e.g., internets with more than one IP subnet assigned to a physical network segment), the DHCP client should be assigned an address from a different subnet than the address recorded in **Relay IP Address (giaddr)**. Thus, DHCP does not require that the client be assigned as address from the subnet in **Relay IP Address (giaddr)**. A server is free to choose some other subnet, and it is beyond the scope of the DHCP specification to describe ways in which the assigned IP address may be chosen. Although not required for correct operation of DHCP, the server *should not* reuse the selected network address before the client responds to the server's DHCPOFFER message. The server may choose to record the address as offered to the client.

The server must also choose an expiration time for the lease, as follows:

- IF the client has not requested a specific lease in the DHCPDISCOVER message and IF the client already has an assigned network address, the server returns the lease expiration time previously assigned to that address (note that the client must explicitly request a specific lease to extend the expiration time on a previously assigned address), ELSE
- IF the client has not requested a specific lease in the DHCPDISCOVER message and IF the client does not have an assigned network address, the server assigns a locally configured default lease time, ELSE
- IF the client has requested a specific lease in the DHCPDISCOVER message (regardless of whether the client has an assigned network address), the server may

choose either to return the requested lease (if the lease is acceptable to local policy) or to select another lease.

Table 8.3 lists the DHCP server message formats, and Table 8.4 lists the DHCP server options.

When the network address and lease have been determined, the server constructs a DHCPOFFER message with the offered configuration parameters. It is important for all DHCP servers to return the same parameters (with the possible exception of a newly allocated network address) to ensure predictable client behavior regardless of which server the client selects. The configuration parameters *must* be selected by applying the following rules

TABLE 8.3 DHCP Server Message Formats

Field	Length in Bytes	DHCPOFFER	DCHCPACK	DHCPNAK
op	1	BOOTREPLY	BOOTREPLY	BOOTREPLY
htyp	1	hardware type	hardware type	hardware type
hlen	1	hardware address length	hardware address length	hardware address length
hops	1	0	0	0
XID	4	*xid* from client DHCPDISCOVER message	*xid* from client DHCPDISCOVER message	*xid* from client DHCPDISCOVER message
secs	2	0	0	0
ciaddr	2	0	ciaddr from DHCPREQUEST or 0	*ciaddr* from DHCPREQUEST or 0
yiaddr	4	IP address offered t client	IP address assigned to client	0
siaddr	4	IP address of next bootstrap serer	IP address of next bootstrap server	0
flags	4	if request *diaddr* is not0 then *flags* from client message else 0	SHOULD NOT	SHOULD
giaddr	4	0	0	0
Chaddr	16	*chaddr* from client DHCPDISCOVER message	*chaddr* from client DHCPREQUEST message	*chaddr* from DHCPREQUEST message
sname	64	Server host name or options	Server host name or options	(unused)
file	128	Client boot file name or options	Client boot file name or options	(unused)
options	312	options	options	

TABLE 8.4 DHCP Server Options

Options	DHCPOFFER	CHCPACK	DHCPNAK
Request IP address	MUST NOT	MUST NOT	MUST NOT
IP address lease time	MUST	MUST	MUST NOT
Use file/sname fields	MAY	MAY	MUST NOT
DHCP message type	DHCPOFFER	DHCPACK	DHCPNAK
Parameter request list	MUST NOT	MUST NOT	MUST NOT
Message	SHOULD	SHOULD	SHOULD
Client identifier	MUST NOT	MUST NOT	MUST NOT
Class identifier	MUST NOT	MUST NOT	MUST NOT
Server identifier	MUST	MAY	MAY
Maximum message size	MUST NOT	MUST NOT	MUST NOT
All others	MAY	MAY	MUST NOT

in the order given. The network administrator is responsible for configuring multiple DHCP servers to ensure uniform responses from those servers. The server *must* return to the client:

- The client's network address, as determined by the rules given earlier in this section
- The expiration time for the client's lease, as determined by the rules given earlier in this section
- Parameters requested by the client, according to the following rules:
  - IF the server has been explicitly configured with a default value for the parameter, the server *must* include that value in an appropriate option in the option field, ELSE
  - IF the server recognizes the parameter as a parameter defined in the Host Requirements, the server *must* include the default value for that parameter as given in the Host Requirements in an appropriate option in the option field, ELSE
  - The server *must not* return a value for that parameter.
  - The server *must* supply as many of the requested parameters as possible and *must* omit any parameters it cannot provide.
- Any parameters from the existing binding that differ from the Host Requirements defaults.
- Any parameters specific to this client (as identified by the contents of chaddr or client identifier in the DHCPDISCOVER or DHCPREQUEST message), e.g., as configured by the network administrator.
- Any parameters specific to this client's class (as identified by the contents of the vendor class identifier option in the DHCPDISCOVER or DHCPREQUEST message), e.g., as

configured by the network administrator; the parameters *must* be identified by an exact match between the client's vendor class identifiers and the client's classes identified in the server

- Parameters with nondefault values on the client's subnet

The server may choose to return the vendor class identifier used to determine the parameters in the DHCPOFFER message to assist the client in selecting which DHCPOFFER to accept. The server inserts the **xid** field from the DHCPDISCOVER message into the **xid** field of the DHCPOFFER message and sends the DHCPOFFER message to the requesting client.

DHCPREQUEST Message. A DHCPREQUEST message may come from a client responding to a DHCPOFFER message from a server, from a client verifying a previously allocated IP address or from a client extending the lease on a network address. If the DHCPREQUEST message contains a server identifier option, the message is in response to a DHCPOFFER message. Otherwise, the message is a request to verify or extend an existing lease. If the client uses a client identifier in a DHCPREQUEST message, it must use that same client identifier in all subsequent messages. If the client included a list of requested parameters in a DHCPDISCOVER message, it must include that list in all subsequent messages.

Any configuration parameters in the DHCPACK message *should not* conflict with those in the earlier DHCPOFFER message to which the client is responding. The client *should* use the parameters in the DHCPACK message for configuration.

Clients send a DHCPREQUEST message generated during SELECTING state: Client inserts the address of the selected server in **server identifier**; client IP Address (ciaddr) must be 0; requested IP address must be filled in with the **Your IP Address (yiaddr)** value from the chosen DHCPOFFER.

Note that the client may choose to collect several DHCPOFFER messages and select the best offer. The client indicates its selection by identifying the offering server in the DHCPREQUEST message. If the client receives no acceptable offers, the client may choose to try another DHCPDISCOVER message. Therefore, the servers may not receive a specific DHCPREQUEST from which they can decide whether or not the client has accepted the offer. Because the servers have not committed any network address assignments on the basis of a DHCPOFFER, servers are free to reuse offered network addresses in response to subsequent requests. As an implementation detail, servers should not reuse offered addresses and may use an implementation-specific timeout mechanism to decide when to reuse an offered address.

Clients sent a DHCPREQUEST generated during INIT-REBOOT state: The server identifier field must not be filled in, the requested IP address option must be filled in with client's notion of its previously assigned address. Client IP Address (ciaddr) must be set to 0. The client is seeking to verify a previously allocated, cached configuration. The server should send a DHCPNAK message to the client if the requested IP address is incorrect or is on the wrong network.

Determining whether a client in the INIT-REBOOT state is on the correct network is done by examining the contents of **Relay IP Address (giaddr)**, the requested IP address option, and a database lookup. If the DHCP server detects that the client is on the wrong net—i.e., the result of applying the local subnet mask or remote subnet mask (if `Relay IP Address (giaddr)` is not 0) to the requested IP address' option value doesn't match reality—the server should send a DHCPNAK message to the client.

If the network is correct, then the DHCP server should check whether the client's notion of its IP address is correct. If not, the server should send a DHCPNAK message to the client. If the DHCP server has no record of this client, then it must remain silent and may output a warning to the network administrator. This behavior is necessary for peaceful coexistence of non-communicating DHCP servers on the same wire.

If `Relay IP Address (giaddr)` is 0x0 in the DHCPREQUEST message, the client is on the same subnet as the server. The server must broadcast the DHCPNAK message to the `0xffffffff` broadcast address because the client may not have a correct network address or subnet mask, and the client may not be answering ARP requests.

If `Relay IP Address (giaddr)` is set in the DHCPREQUEST message, the client is on a different subnet. The server must set the broadcast bit in the DHCPNAK so that the relay agent broadcasts the DHCPNAK to the client, because the client may not have a correct network address or subnet mask, and the client may not be answering ARP requests.

Clients send a DHCPREQUEST generated during RENEWING state: The server identifier must not be filled in; the `requested IP address` option must not be filled in; and the `Client IP Address (ciaddr)` must be filled in with client's IP address. In this situation, the client is completely configured and is trying to extend its lease. This message is unicast, so no relay agents are involved in its transmission. Because `Relay IP Address (giaddr)` is therefore not filled in, the DHCP server trusts the value in `Client IP Address (ciaddr)` and uses it when replying to the client.

A client may choose to renew or extend its lease prior to T1. The server may choose not to extend the lease (as a policy decision by the network administrator) but should return a DHCPACK message regardless.

Clients send a DHCPREQUEST generated during REBINDING state: The server identifier must not be filled in; the `requested IP address` option must not be filled in; and the `Client IP Address (ciaddr)` must be filled in with the client's IP address. In this situation, the client is completely configured and is trying to extend its lease. This message must be broadcast to the `0xffffffff` IP broadcast address. The DHCP server should check `Client IP Address (ciaddr)` for correctness before replying to the DHCPREQUEST.

The DHCPREQUEST from a REBINDING client is intended to accommodate sites with multiple DHCP servers and a mechanism for maintaining consistency among leases managed by multiple servers. A DHCP server may extend a client's lease only if it has local administrative authority to do so.

DHCPDECLINE message.   If the server receives a DHCPDECLINE message, the client has discovered through some other means that the suggested network address is already in use. The server must mark the network address as not available and should notify the local system administrator of a possible configuration problem.

DHCPRELEASE message.   Upon receipt of a DHCPRELEASE message, the server marks the network address as not allocated. The server should retain a record of the client's initialization parameters for possible reuse in response to subsequent requests from the client.

DHCPINFORM message. The server responds to a DHCPINFORM message by sending a DHCPACK message directly to the address given in the `Client IP Address (ciaddr)` field of the DHCPINFORM message. The server must not send a lease expiration time to the client and should not fill in `Your IP Address (yiaddr)`.

DHCP Client Behavior

Figure 8.12 is a state-transition diagram for a DHCP client. A client can receive the following messages from a server: DHCPOFFER, DHCPACK, and DHCPNAK.

A client sends the DHCPINFORM and waits for DHCPACK messages. After the client has selected its parameters, the client has completed the configuration process. Table 8.5 lists the options in a DHCP client message.

Initialization and Allocation of Network Address. The client begins in INIT state and forms a DHCPDISCOVER message. The client should wait a random time between 1 and 10 seconds to desynchronize the use of DHCP at startup. The client sets `Client IP Address (ciaddr)` to `0x00000000`. The client may request specific parameters by including the `parameter request list` option. The client may suggest a network address and/or lease time by including the

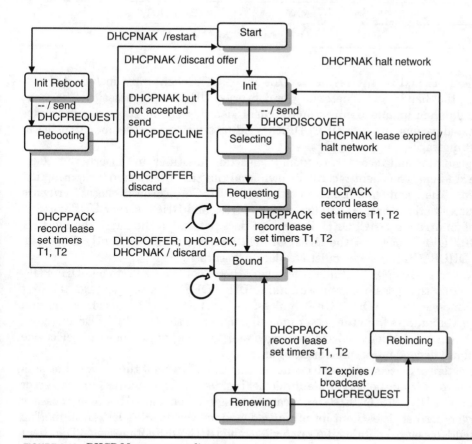

FIGURE 8.12 DHCP Message state diagram

TABLE 8.5   DHCP Options by Client

Options	DHCPDISCOVER	DHCPREQUEST	DHCPDECLINE, DHCPRELEASE
Request IP address	MAY	MUST NOT	MUST NOT
IP address lease time	MAY	MAY	MUST NOT
Use file/sname fields	MAY	MAY	MAY
DHCP message type	DHCPDISCOVER	DHCPREQUEST	DHCPDECLINE, DHCPRELEASE
Client identifier	MAY	MAY	MAY
Class identifier	SHOULD	SHOULD	MUST NOT
Server identifier	MUST NOT	MUST after DHCPDISCOVER, MUST NOT when renewing	MUST
Parameter request list	MAY	MAY	MUST NOT
Maximum message size	MAY	MAY	MUST NOT
Message	SHOULD NOT	SHOULD NOT	SHOULD
Site-specific	MAY	MAY	MUST NOT
All others	MUST NOT	MUST NOT	MUST NOT

`requested IP address` and `IP address lease time` options. The client must include its hardware address in the chaddr field, if necessary for delivery of DHCP reply messages. The client may include a different unique identifier in the client identifier option. If the client includes a list of requested parameters in a DHCPDISCOVER message, it must include that list in all subsequent messages.

The client generates and records a random transaction identifier and inserts that identifier into the xid field. The client records its own local time for later use in computing the lease expiration. The client then broadcasts the DHCPDISCOVER on the local hardware broadcast address to the `0xffffffff` IP broadcast address and DHCP server UDP port.

If the xid of an arriving DHCPOFFER message does not match the xid of the most recent DHCPDISCOVER message, the DHCPOFFER message must be silently discarded. Any arriving DHCPACK messages must be silently discarded.

The client collects DHCPOFFER messages over a period of time, selects one DHCPOFFER message from the (possibly many) incoming DHCPOFFER messages (e.g., the first DHCPOFFER message or the DHCPOFFER message from the previously used server), and extracts the server address from the server identifier option in the DHCPOFFER message. The time over which the client collects messages and the mechanism used to select one DHCPOFFER are dependent of implementation.

If the parameters are acceptable, the client records the address of the server that supplied the parameters from the server identifier field and sends that address in the server identifier field of a DHCPREQUEST broadcast message. When the DHCPACK message from the server arrives, the client is initialized and moves to a BOUND state. The DHCPREQUEST message contains the same xid as the DHCPOFFER message. The client records the lease expiration time as the sum of the time at which the original request was sent and the duration of the lease from the DHCPACK message. The client should perform a check on the suggested address to ensure that the address is not already in use. For example, if the client is on a network that supports ARP, the client may issue an ARP request for the suggested request. When broadcasting an ARP request for the suggested address, the client must fill in its own hardware address as the sender's hardware address and 0 as the sender's IP address to avoid confusing ARP caches in other hosts on the same subnet. If the network address appears to be in use, the client must send a DHCPDECLINE message to the server. The client should broadcast an ARP reply to announce the client's new IP address and to clear any outdated ARP cache entries in hosts on the client's subnet.

Initialization with Known Network Address.   The client begins in the INIT-REBOOT state and sends a DHCPREQUEST message. The client msut insert its known network address as a `requested IP address` option in the DHCPREQUEST message. The client may request specific configuration parameters by including the `parameter request list` option. The client generates and records a random transaction identifier and inserts that identifier into the xid field. The client records its own local time for later use in computing the lease expiration. The client must not include a server identifier in the DHCPREQUEST message. The client then broadcasts the DHCPREQUEST on the local hardware broadcast address to the DHCP server UDP port.

When a DHCPACK message with an xid field matching that in the client's DHCPRE-QUEST message arrives from any server, the client is initialized and moves to a BOUND state. The client records the lease expiration time as the sum of the time at which the DHCPREQUEST message was sent and the duration of the lease from the DHCPACK message.

Initialization with an Externally Assigned Network Address.   The client sends a DHCPINFORM message. The client may request specific configuration parameters by including the parameter request list option. The client generates and records a random transaction identifier and inserts that identifier into the xid field. The client places its own network address in the `Client IP Address (ciaddr)` field. The client should not request lease-time parameters.

The client then unicasts the DHCPINFORM to the DHCP server if it knows the server's address; otherwise, it broadcasts the message to the limited (all 1s) broadcast address. DHCPINFORM messages must be directed to the DHCP server UDP port.

When a DHCPACK message with an xid field matching that in the client's DHCPIN-FORM message arrives from any server, the client is initialized.

If the client does not receive a DHCPACK within a reasonable period of time (60 seconds or four tries if using timeout), it should display a message informing the user of the problem and then should begin network processing using suitable defaults.

Use of Broadcast and Unicast.   The DHCP client broadcasts DHCPDISCOVER, DHCPREQUEST, and DHCPINFORM messages, unless the client knows the address of a DHCP server. The client unicasts DHCPRELEASE messages to the server. Because the client is declining the use of the IP address supplied by the server, the client broadcasts DHCPDECLINE messages. When the DHCP client knows the address of a DHCP server, in either INIT or REBOOTING state, the client may use that address in the DHCPDISCOVER or DHCPREQUEST rather than the IP broadcast address. The client may also use unicast to send DHCPINFORM messages to a known DHCP server. If the client receives no response to DHCP messages sent to the IP address of a known DHCP server, the DHCP client reverts to using the IP broadcast address.

Reacquisition and Expiration.   The client maintains two times, T1 and T2, that specify the times at which the client tries to extend its lease on its network address. T1 is the time at which the client enters the RENEWING state and attempts to contact the server that originally issued the client's network address. T2 is the time at which the client enters the RE-BINDING state and attempts to contact any server. T1 must be earlier than T2, which, in turn, must be earlier than the time at which the client's lease expires.

To avoid the need for synchronized clocks, T1 and T2 are expressed in options as relative times. At time T1 the client moves to RENEWING state and sends (via unicast) a DHCPRE-QUEST message to the server to extend its lease. The client sets the `Client IP Address (ciaddr)` field in the DHCPREQUEST to its current network address. The client records the local time at which the DHCPREQUEST message is sent for computation of the lease expiration time. The client must not include a server identifier in the DHCPREQUEST message.

Any DHCPACK messages that arrive with an xid that does not match the xid of the client's DHCPREQUEST message are silently discarded. When the client receives a DHC-PACK from the server, the client computes the lease expiration time as the sum of the time at which the client sent the DHCPREQUEST message and the duration of the lease in the DHCPACK message. The client has successfully reacquired its network address, returns to BOUND state, and may continue network processing. If no DHCPACK arrives before time T2, the client moves to REBINDING state and sends (via broadcast) a DHCPREQUEST message to extend its lease. The client sets the `Client IP Address (ciaddr)` field in the DHCPREQUEST to its current network address. The client must not include a server identifier in the DHCPREQUEST message. Times T1 and T2 are configurable by the server through options. T1 defaults to (0.5 * duration_of_lease). T2 defaults to (0.875 * duration_of_lease). Times T1 and T2 should be chosen with some random fuzz around a fixed value, to avoid synchronization of client reacquisition.

A client may choose to renew or extend its lease prior to T1. The server may choose to extend the client's lease according to policy set by the network administrator. The server should return T1 and T2, and their values should be adjusted from their original values to take account of the time remaining on the lease.

In both RENEWING and REBINDING states, if the client receives no response to its DHCPREQUEST message, the client should wait one-half of the remaining time until T2 (in RENEWING state) and one-half of the remaining lease time (in REBINDING state), down to a minimum of 60 seconds, before retransmitting the DHCPREQUEST message.

If the lease expires before the client receives a DHCPACK, the client moves to INIT state, must immediately stop any other network processing and requests network initialization parameters as if the client were uninitialized. If the client then receives a DHCPACK allocating that client's previous network address, the client should continue network processing. If the client is given a new network address, it must not continue using the previous network address and should notify the local users of the problem.

DHCPRELEASE.   If the client no longer requires the use of its assigned network address (e.g., the client is gracefully shut down), the client sends a DHCPRELEASE message to the server. Note that the correct operation of DHCP does not depend on the transmission of DHCPRELEASE messages.

Applications and Benefits

Managing DNS

Organizations currently manage DNS by editing text files. The syntax of these files, known as zone files, is cumbersome and prone to errors, except to those few individuals who have become DNS experts. The Domain Name Manager eliminates the need to edit zone files. Instead, all DNS entries are checked for proper syntax and duplicate IP addresses, and PTR records for the "reverse lookup" are automatically generated. The Domain Name Manager includes a back-end server and a graphical front end called the Domain Name Manager browser. The Domain Name Manager client/server architecture and the easy-to-learn graphical user interface allow the management of DNS to be distributed to many network administrators.

The Cisco DHCP server automatically updates the Domain Name Manager with the IP addresses and domain names of each new node on the network. The Domain Name Manager then relays this information to all DNS servers on the network. Thus, the Domain Name Manager replaces the existing primary DNS server of an organization and becomes the source of DNS information for the entire network.

DHCP in a Switched Network

Cisco's DHCP server allows organizations to use DHCP in a large, switched network. The depletion of IP addresses on the Internet has forced organizations to use *classless interdomain routing* (CIDR) blocks or groups of Class C network numbers to build physical networks with more than 256 nodes. This set up has created problems for network administrators who want to use DHCP in a large, switched network with more than 256 nodes.

Existing DHCP servers, including the Microsoft DHCP server shipping with Windows NT, do not support the creation of address pools with multiple logical IP networks or subnets on a single, physical network. This secondary address problem is attributed to a router with primary addresses and multiple secondary addresses on the same interface. Cisco's DHCP server supports address pools that can contain multiple logical networks or subnets on the same physical network.

Enhanced TCP/IP Servers for Windows NT and UNIX

The Cisco DNS/DHCP Manager, unlike Microsoft's service offerings for Windows NT, has a complete range of TCP/IP services for building and maintaining a TCP/IP network. Each of these services is easily configured using the Cisco Service Manager, a graphical configuration tool.

No Duplicate IP Addresses

The Domain Name Manager browser automatically tracks IP addresses allocated in the network. When adding new nodes to DNS, the Domain Name Manager browser searches for the next available IP address and assigns it to the new node.

Improved Security and Reliability.   Many TCP/IP services, such as the World Wide Web, NFS, rlogin, and FTP, use information in DNS to verify that incoming connections are from a legitimate computer. If both an A record and a PTR record are registered for an incoming client, the server assumes that a responsible network administrator has assigned this name and address.

When adding a new node to the DNS, the Cisco Domain Name Manager automatically adds the PTR record, a step commonly neglected in managing a DNS server. Also known as reverse mapping, the PTR record is the mapping between an IP address and a DNS name.

TCP/IP Networks Easier to Configure

Network nodes, particularly PCs, use the DHCP to dynamically get configuration information from a DHCP server, including IP address, domain name, default router, and subnet mask. DHCP allows managers to add new nodes to a network without statically defining IP addresses for every node. Table 8.6 lists the features and benefits of DNS/DHCP.

Internet Control Message Protocol (ICMP)

ICMP is a required companion to the *Internet Protocol* (IP) and must be included in every IP implementation. ICMP's basic function is to provide feedback about problems that occur in the communication's environment.

In a connectionless environment, each host or router operates independently in the routing and delivery of datagrams. This system works well if all machines are operating prop-

TABLE 8.6   Features and Benefits of DNS/DHCP

Features	Benefits
Graphical DNS Management Tool	Manages DNS more easily
Lookup of Next Available IP Address	Eliminates duplicate IP addresses
Automatically Add PTR Records	Prevents service failures from incomplete information
Username/Password Authentication for Domain Name Manager	Controls who can modify DNS information
DNM Client/Server Architecture	Multiple administrators can manage DNS remotely
Dynamic Update of DNS	Synchronizes DNS and DHCP
Address Pools with Logical Subnets	Enables use of DHCP in a switched network
Server Support of BOOTP	Uses one server to manage BOOTP and DHCP
TFTP Server	Configures network devices over network
NTP Server	Synchronizes time on all machines
Syslog Server	Logs errors in a central location
Cisco Service Manager	Graphical tool that easily configures TCP/IP services
Windows NT Support	Eliminates need for UNIX server

erly. Unfortunately, this is not always the case. The Internet can fail to deliver datagrams in the following situations:

- When the Time-to-Live counter expires
- When the routers become so congested that they cannot process any more traffic
- When communication lines and processors fail
- When the destination machine is disconnected from the network

IP is not designed to be absolutely reliable. The purpose of ICMP is to provide feedback about problems in the communication environment, not to make IP reliable. The higher lever protocols that use IP must implement their own reliability procedures if reliable communication is required. Datagrams carrying ICMP messages are routed exactly like datagrams carrying information for users. No additional reliability is provided for these error messages. As a result, error messages themselves may be lost or discarded. To avoid the infinite regress of messages about messages, no ICMP messages are sent about ICMP messages. Thus, ICMP messages are not generated for errors that result from the loss or discarding of datagrams carrying ICMP messages.

ICMP Encapsulation

Although ICMP is, in effect, at the same level as IP, it is a user of IP. Each ICMP message travels across the Internet in the data portion of an IP datagram.

An ICMP message is constructed and then passed on to IP. IP encapsulates the message with an IP header and then transmits it over the physical network to the destination host or router. The reason IP is used to deliver the ICMP messages is that the messages may need to travel across several different physical networks to reach their final destination. Therefore, they cannot be delivered by the physical network transport alone.

The ultimate destination of the ICMP message is not a user process on the destination machine but the Internet software on that machine. The IP software module on the destination machine handles the problem itself without passing the message to the application's program whose datagram generated the problem.

ICMP Header Format

Although each ICMP message has its own format, the general format of an ICMP message is shown in Figure 8.13.

Echo Request (Type 8) or Echo Reply Message (Type 0)

These messages provide a mechanism for testing if communication is possible between two machines. The recipient of an echo message is obligated to return the message in an Echo Reply message. The most common ICMP messages when used for diagnostic purposes are type 0 and type 8. These messages are generated by the utility program widely known as *ping*. Ping sends ICMP type 8 datagrams to a node and expects an ICMP type 0 reply, returning the data sent in the request. The identifier and sequence numbers are used to identify these datagrams uniquely. If data is sent in the optional data field, it must be returned

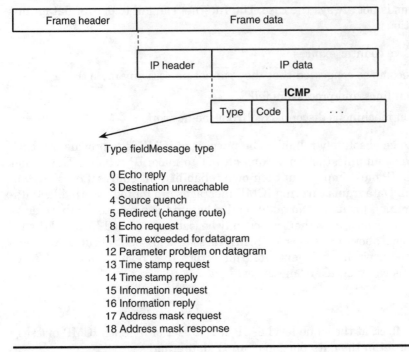

Type fieldMessage type

0 Echo reply
3 Destination unreachable
4 Source quench
5 Redirect (change route)
8 Echo request
11 Time exceeded for datagram
12 Parameter problem on datagram
13 Time stamp request
14 Time stamp reply
15 Information request
16 Information reply
17 Address mask request
18 Address mask response

FIGURE 8.13   ICMP message format

in the reply. Varying data sizes on a ping are used to test for data transmission problems. Figure 8.14 shows how an ICMP Echo Reply/Request is inserted into an IP packet and then into an Ethernet Frame.

IP Fields

- *Addresses*:   The address of the source in an echo message is the destination of the echo reply message. To form an echo reply message, the source and destination addresses are reversed; the type code is changed to 0; and the checksum is recomputed.

- *Type*:   8 for echo message; 0 for echo reply message.

- *Code*:   0

- *Checksum*:   The checksum is the 16-bit 1s' complement of the 1s complement sum of the ICMP message starting with the ICMP Type. For computing the checksum, the checksum field should be 0. If the total length is odd, the received data is padded with one octet of 0s for computing the checksum. This checksum may be replaced in the future.

- *Identifier*:   If code = 0, an identifier to aid in matching echos and replies may be 0.

- *Sequence Number*:   If code = 0, a sequence number to aid in matching echos and replies may be 0.

- *Description*:   The data received in the echo message must be returned in the echo reply message.

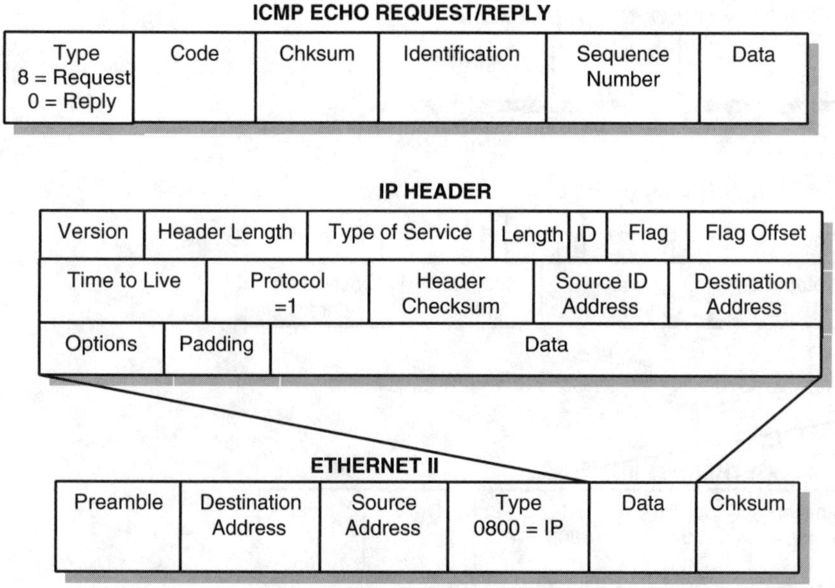

ICMP ECHO REQUEST/REPLY

Type 8 = Request 0 = Reply	Code	Chksum	Identification	Sequence Number	Data

IP HEADER

Version	Header Length	Type of Service	Length	ID	Flag	Flag Offset
Time to Live	Protocol =1	Header Checksum	Source ID Address	Destination Address		
Options	Padding	Data				

ETHERNET II

Preamble	Destination Address	Source Address	Type 0800 = IP	Data	Chksum

FIGURE 8.14   Echo Request and Echo Reply

The identifier and sequence number may be used by the echo sender to aid in matching the replies with the echo requests. For example, the identifier may be used like a port in TCP or UDP to identify a session, and the sequence number may be incremented on each echo request sent. The echoer returns these same values in the echo reply.

Code 0 may be received from a router or a host.

Ping is the command that implements the ICMP echo functions. It is a useful confidence test if you can successfully ping IP equipment. Most network connections identified with an IP address should reply to ping. The time to reply is usually given in milliseconds, although the resolution may be limited to units of 10 or 20 ms. In some implementations, ping gives access to the other features of the datagram header such as record route, MTU, timestamp, loose source routing, and strict source routing. Ping can be used to gather statistics about network operation and to test the integrity and composition of a path to a remote node. Sending different size datagrams to see whether any limitation exists in the intervening network hardware is possible. Ping normally reports on the response to each of its requests. Setting ping to operate continuously can be very useful for debugging a node that is failing to connect, as it provides a regular identified datagram that can be trapped on a protocol analyzer.

Destination Unreachable Message

This message covers a number of contingencies:

- A router returns this message if it does not know how to reach the destination network.

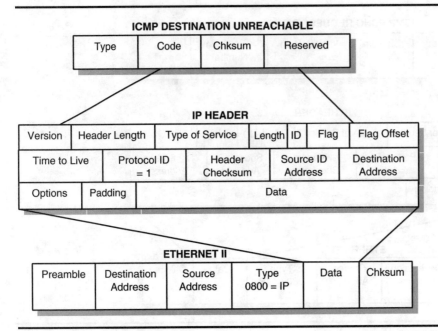

FIGURE 8.15 Destination Unreachable message

- If the user protocol or some high-level service access point is not active, the destination host may send a **Destination Unreachable** message to the source host. Figure 8.15 shows the format of an ICMP **Destination Unreachable** message and how it fits in an IP packet.

- If the datagram specifies an unstable source route, a **Destination Unreachable** message is returned.

- If a router must fragment a datagram, but the DON'T FRAGMENT Flag is set, a message is returned, and the datagram is discarded.

If, according to the information in the router's routing tables, the network specified in the internet destination field of a datagram is unreachable (e.g., the distance to the network is infinity), the router may send a destination unreachable message to the internet source host of the datagram. In addition, in some networks, the gateway may be able to determine whether the internet destination host is unreachable. Gateways in these networks may send destination unreachable messages to the source host when the destination host is unreachable. If, in the destination host, the IP module cannot deliver the datagram because the indicated protocol module or process port is not active, the destination host may send a destination unreachable message to the source host. Another case is when a datagram must be fragmented to be forwarded by a gateway yet the DON'T FRAGMENT flag is on. In this case, the router must discard the datagram and may return a destination unreachable message. Codes 0, 1, 4, and 5 may be received from a router. Codes 2 and 3 may be received from a host:

```
3 Code
0 = net unreachable;
1 = host unreachable;
2 = protocol unreachable;
3 = port unreachable;
4 = fragmentation needed and DF set;
5 = source route failed.
6 = target network unknown
7 = target host unknown
```

Source Quench Message

This message type provides a basic form of flow control. When datagrams arrive too quickly for a router or host to process, they must be discarded. The machine discarding the datagrams sends an ICMP source quench message to request that the original source slow down its rate of sending datagrams.

Usually machines send one source quench message for every datagram that must be discarded. Some implementations attempt to avoid having routers discard datagrams by having the router send quench requests as soon as their queues start to become long.

No ICMP message type can be used to reverse the effect of a source quench. The recipient of a source quench lowers the rate at which it sends datagrams until it stops receiving source quench messages. It then gradually increases its transmission rate as long as it does not receive any more source quench requests.

ICMP Fields

- *Destination Address*:   The source network and address of the original datagram's data

- *Type*:   4

- *Code*:   0

- *Checksum*:   The checksum is the 16-bit 1s' complement of the 1's complement sum of the ICMP message starting with the ICMP Type. For computing the checksum, this field should be 0.

- *Description*:   A gateway may discard internet datagrams if it does not have the buffer space needed to queue the datagrams for output to the next network on the route to the destination network. If a gateway discards a datagram, it may send a source quench message to the internet source host of the datagram. A destination host may also send a source quench message if datagrams arrive too fast to be processed. The source quench message is a request to the host to cut back the rate at which it is sending traffic to the internet destination. The gateway may send a source quench message for every message that it discards. On receipt of a source quench message, the source host should cut back the rate at which it is sending traffic to the specified destination until it no longer receives source quench messages from the gateway.

The source host then gradually can increase the rate at which it sends traffic to the destination until it again receives source quench messages. The gateway or host may send the source quench message when it approaches its capacity limit rather than waiting until the capacity is exceeded. Therefore, the datagram that triggered the source quench message may be delivered. Code 0 may be received from a gateway or a host.

Redirect Message

Routers exchange routing information periodically to reflect network changes and to keep their routing tables up to date. Thus, a router usually has access to better and more current routes that hosts.

When a router detects that a host is using a nonoptimal route, the router sends an ICMP Redirect Message to the host. The router also forwards the original datagram on to its destination network. Figure 8.16 shows the format of an ICMP redirect message and how it fits into an IP datagram.

Routers send only ICMP Redirect requests to hosts on directly connected networks and not to other routers. Therefore, Redirect Messages are not used to propagate and update routing information among routers.

IP Fields

- *Destination Address*:   The source network and address of the original datagram's data.

ICMP Fields

- *Type*:   5
- *Code*:
    - 0 = Redirect datagrams for the Network
    - 1 = Redirect datagrams for the Host

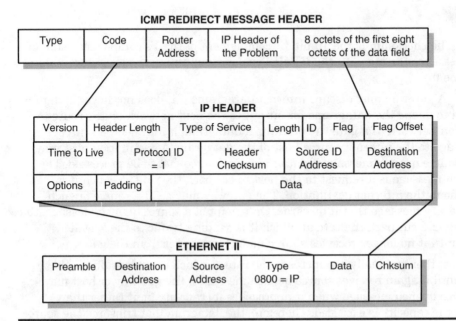

FIGURE 8.16   Redirect Message

- 2 = Redirect datagrams for the Type of Service and Network
- 3 = Redirect datagrams for the Type of Service and Host

- *Checksum*: The checksum is the 16-bit 1s' complement of the 1's complement sum of the ICMP message starting with the ICMP Type. For computing the checksum, the checksum field should be 0.

- *Routers Internet Address*: Address of the gateway to which traffic for the network specified in the internet destination network field of the original datagram's data should be sent.

- *Description*: The route sends a redirect message to a host in the following situation: a router, R1, receives an internet datagram from a host on a network to which the router is attached. The router checks its routing table and obtains the address of the next router, R2, on the route to the datagram's internet destination network, X. If R2 and the host identified by the internet source address of the datagram are on the same network, a redirect message is sent to the host. The redirect message advises the host to send its traffic for network X directly to router R2 as this is a shorter path to the destination. The router forwards the original datagram's data to its internet destination.

  For datagrams with the IP source route options and the gateway address in the destination address field, a redirect message is not sent even if there is a better route to the ultimate destination than the next address in the source route.

  Codes 0, 1, 2, and 3 may be received from a router.

Time Exceeded Message

A router returns a Time Exceeded Message if it is forced to discard a datagram because the time-to-live field is 0.

If the gateway processing a datagram finds the time-to-live field is 0, it must discard the datagram. The gateway also may notify the source host via the time exceeded message. If a host reassembling a fragmented datagram cannot complete the reassembly due to missing fragments within its time limit, it discards the datagram, and it may send a time exceeded message. If fragment 0 is not available, no time exceeded need be sent. Code 0 may be received from a gateway. Code 1 may be received from a host.

IP Fields

- Destination Address: The source network and address from the original datagram's data.

ICMP Fields

- *Type*: 11
- *Code*:

  - 0 = time to live exceeded in transit
  - 1 = fragment reassembly time exceeded

- *Checksum*:   The checksum is the 16-bit 1s' complement of the 1's complement sum of the ICMP message starting with the ICMP Type. For computing the checksum, the checksum field should be 0.

- Description: If the router processing a datagram finds the time to live field is 0, it must discard the datagram. The router also may notify the source host via the time exceeded message. If a host reassembling a fragmented datagram cannot complete the reassembly due to missing fragments within its time limit, it discards the datagram, and it may send a time exceeded message. If fragment 0 is not available, no time exceeded need be sent. Code 0 may be received from a gateway. Code 1 may be received from a host.

Parameter Problem Message

If a router or host processing a datagram finds a problem with the header parameters so that it cannot complete processing the datagram, it must discard the datagram. The router or host also may notify the source host via the Parameter Problem message. Figure 8.17 shows the format of the ICMP Parameter Problem message.

The parameter field contains a pointer to the octet in the original header where the error was detected.

IP Fields

- *Destination Address*:   The source network and address from the original datagram's data.

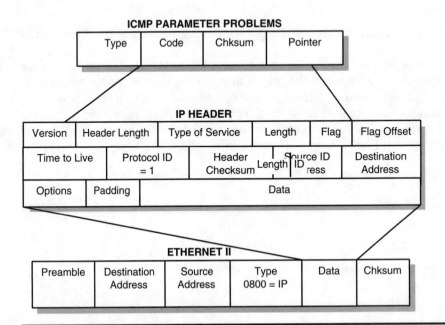

FIGURE 8.17 Parameter Problem message

ICMP Fields

- *Type*: 12
- *Code*:

  - 0 = pointer indicates the error.

- *Checksum*:   The checksum is the 16-bit 1s' complement of the 1's complement sum of the ICMP message starting with the ICMP Type. For computing the checksum, the checksum field should be 0.

- *Description*:   If the router or host processing a datagram finds a problem with the header parameters so that it cannot complete processing the datagram, it must discard the datagram. One potential source of such a problem is with incorrect arguments in an option. The gateway or host also may notify the source host via the parameter problem message. This message is sent only if the error caused the datagram to be discarded. The pointer identifies the octet of the original datagram's header in which the error was detected (it may be in the middle of an option). For example, 1 indicates something is wrong with the Type of Service, and (if there are options present) 20 indicates something is wrong with the type code of the first option. Code 0 may be received from a gateway or a host.

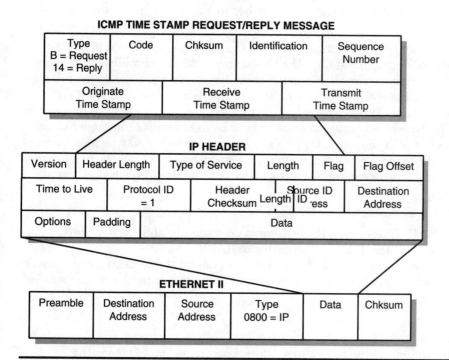

FIGURE 8.18 Timestamp Request or Timestamp Reply Message

Timestamp Request or Timestamp Reply Message

These messages provide a mechanism for sampling the delay characteristics of the network. The sender of a Timestamp message includes an identifier in the parameters field and places the time that the message was sent in the information field. The receiver appends a receive timestamp and transmit timestamp and return the message as a timestamp reply.

Hosts use the Timestamp fields to compute estimates of the delay time between them and to synchronize their clocks(see Figure 8.18).

IP Fields

- *Addresses*:   The address of the source in a timestamp message is the destination of the timestamp reply message. To form a timestamp reply message, the source and destination addresses are reversed; the type code changed to 14; and the checksum recomputed.

ICMP Fields

- *Type*:   13 for timestamp message; 14 for timestamp reply message.

- *Checksum*:   The checksum is the 16-bit 1s' complement of the 1's complement sum of the ICMP message starting with the ICMP Type. For computing the checksum, the checksum field should be 0.

- *Identifier*:   If code = 0, an identifier to aid in matching timestamp and replies.

- *Sequence Number*:   If code = 0, a sequence number to aid in matching timestamp and replies.

- *Description*:   The data received (a timestamp) in the message is returned in the reply together with an additional timestamp. The timestamp is 32 bits of milliseconds since midnight UT. The Originate Timestamp is the time the sender last touched the message before sending it; the Receive Timestamp is the time the echoer first touched it on receipt; and the Transmit Timestamp is the time the echoer last touched the message on sending it. The identifier and sequence number may be used by the echo sender to aid in matching the replies with the requests. For example, the identifier may be used like a port in TCP or UDP to identify a session, and the sequence number may be incremented on each request sent. The destination returns these same values in the reply.

Information Request or Information Reply Message

Machines use the ICMP Information Request message to obtain an Internet address for a network to which they attach. It is an alternative to RARP.

The sender sends the message with the network portion of the IP destination address set to 0 and waits for a reply. The reply arrives with the network portion of the sender's IP filled in.

IP Fields

- *Addresses*:   The address of the source in a information request message is the destination of the information reply message. To form a information reply message, the source and destination addresses are reversed; the type code changed to 16; and the checksum recomputed.

ICMP Fields

- *Type*:   15 for information request message; 16 for information reply message

- *Checksum*:   The checksum is the 16-bit 1s' complement of the 1's complement sum of the ICMP message starting with the ICMP Type. For computing the checksum, the checksum field should be 0.

- *Identifier*:   If code = 0, an identifier to aid in matching request and replies.

- *Sequence Number*:   If code = 0, a sequence number to aid in matching request and replies.

- *Description*:   This message may be sent with the source network in the IP header source and destination address fields set to 0 (which means "this" network). The replying IP module should send the reply with the addresses fully specified. This message is a way for a host to find out the number of the network it is on. The identifier and sequence number may be used by the echo sender to aid in matching the replies with the requests. For example, the identifier may be used like a port in TCP or UDP to identify a session, and the sequence number may be incremented on each request sent. The destination returns these same values in the reply.

Address Mask Request or Address Mask Reply Message

The function can be used in conjunction with subnet addressing to allow a node to discover the subnet mask of the network to which it is connected. The node can either send the request to a known address, probably a router, or broadcast the request to the network. The reply is directed back, if the node knows its address, or broadcast if not. To use subnet addressing, machines need to know which bits of the Internet address correspond to their physical network and which bits correspond to other physical networks. To learn its subnet mask, a machine can send an Address Mask Request message to a router and receive an Address Mask Reply. Figure 8.19 shows the format of the ICMP Address mask request/reply message.

TCP Protocol Overview

The *Transmission Control Protocol* (TCP), makes up for IP's deficiencies by providing reliable, stream-oriented connections that hide most of IP's shortcomings. The protocol suite gets its name because most TCP/IP protocols are based on TCP, which is in turn based on IP. TCP and IP are the twin pillars of TCP/IP. Figure 8.20 depicts the format of the TCP header.

TCP adds a great deal of functionality to the IP service over which it is layered:

- *Streams*.   TCP data is organized as a stream of bytes, much like a file. The datagram nature of the network is concealed. A mechanism (*Urgent Pointer*) exists to let out-of-band data be specially flagged.

- *Reliable delivery*.   Sequence numbers are used to coordinate which data has been transmitted and received. TCP arranges for retransmission if it determines that data has been lost.

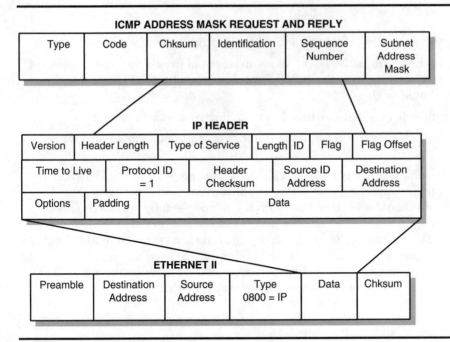

FIGURE 8.19   Address Mask Request or Address Mask Reply Message

- *Network adaptation.*   TCP dynamically learns the delay characteristics of a network and adjusts its operation to maximize throughput without overloading the network.

- *Flow control.*   TCP manages data buffers and coordinates traffic so its buffers never overflow. Fast senders are stopped periodically to keep up with slower receivers.

Full-Duplex Operation

No matter what the particular application, TCP almost always operates full-duplex. The algorithms described operate in both directions, in an almost completely independent manner. It's sometimes useful to think of a TCP session as two independent byte streams, traveling in opposite directions. No TCP mechanism exists to associate data in the forward and reverse byte streams. Only during connection start and close sequences can TCP exhibit asymmetric behavior (i.e., data transfer in the forward direction but not in the reverse, or vice versa).

Sequence Numbers

TCP uses a 32-bit *sequence number* that counts bytes in the data stream. Each TCP packet contains the starting sequence number of the data in that packet, and the sequence number (called the *acknowledgment number*) of the last byte received from the remote peer. With this information, a sliding-window protocol is implemented. Forward and reverse sequence numbers are completely independent, and each TCP peer must track both its own sequence numbering and the numbering being used by the remote peer.

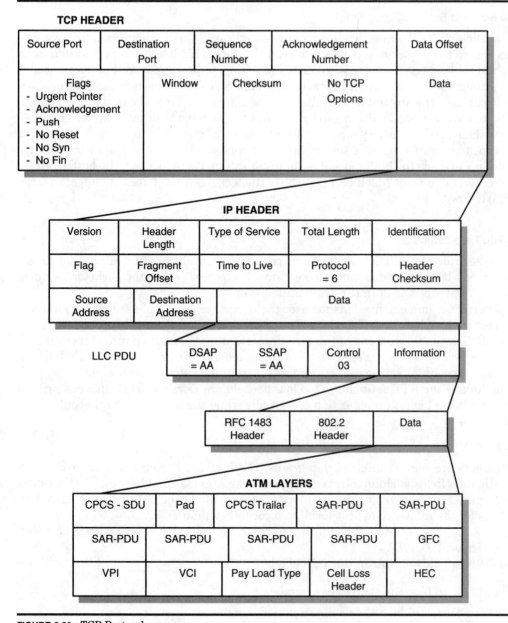

FIGURE 8.20 TCP Protocol

TCP uses a number of control flags to manage the connection. Some of these flags pertain to a single packet, such as the URG flag indicating valid data in the Urgent Pointer field, but two flags (SYN and FIN) require reliable delivery as they mark the beginning and end of the data stream. To ensure reliable delivery of these two flags, they are assigned spots in the sequence number space. Each flag occupies a single byte.

Window Size and Buffering

Each endpoint of a TCP connection has a buffer for storing data that is transmitted over the network before the application is ready to read the data. This lets network transfers take place while applications are busy with other processing, improving overall performance.

To avoid overflowing the buffer, TCP sets a Window Size field in each packet it transmits. This field contains the amount of data that may be transmitted into the buffer. If this number falls to 0, the remote TCP can send no more data. It must wait until buffer space becomes available, and it receives a packet announcing a nonzero window size.

Sometimes, the buffer space is too small. This happens when the network's bandwidth-delay product exceeds the buffer size. The simplest solution is to increase the buffer, but for extreme cases, the protocol itself becomes the bottleneck (because it doesn't support a large enough Window Size).

Round-Trip Time Estimation

When a host transmits a TCP packet to its peer, it must wait a period of time for an acknowledgment. If the reply does not come within the expected period, the packet is assumed to have been lost, and the data is retransmitted.

All modern TCP implementations monitor the normal exchange of data packets and develop an estimate of how long is too long. This process is called *Round-Trip Time* (RTT) estimation. RTT estimates are one of the most important performance parameters in a TCP exchange, especially when you consider that on an indefinitely large transfer, *all* TCP implementations eventually drop packets and retransmit them, no matter how good the quality of the link. If the RTT estimate is too low, packets are retransmitted unnecessarily; if the estimate is too high, the connection can sit idle while the host waits to timeout.

Header Format

TCP segments are sent as internet datagrams. The Internet Protocol header carries several information fields, including the source and destination host addresses. A TCP header follows the internet header, supplying information specific to the TCP protocol. This division allows for the existence of host level protocols other than TCP.

Figures 8.21a shows the TCP header format and Figure 8.21b shows a trace of a NetBIOS service over TCP/IP.

The following fields appear in the TCP header:

- *Source Port:*   16 bits; the source port number.

- *Destination Port*:   16 bits; the destination port number.

- *Sequence Number*:   32 bits; the sequence number of the first data octet in this segment (except when SYN is present). If SYN is present, the sequence number is the initial sequence number (ISN) and the first data octet is ISN+1.

- *Acknowledgment Number*:   32 bits; if the ACK control bit is set, this field contains the value of the next sequence number the sender of the segment is expecting to receive. After a connection is established, this is always sent.

Source Port			Destination Port	
Sequence Number				
Acknowledgment number				
Data Offset	Reserved	U A P R S F R C S S Y I G K H T N N	Window	
Checksum			Urgent Pointer	
Options Padding				
TCP data				

FIGURE 8.21a   TCP Header Format

- *Data Offset*:   4 bits; the number of 32-bit words in the TCP Header. This field indicates where the data begins. The TCP header (even one including options) is an integral number of 32-bits.

- *Reserved*:   6 bits; reserved for future use. Must be 0.

- *Control Bits*:   6 bits (from left to right):
  - URG   Urgent Pointer field significant
  - ACK   Acknowledgment field significant
  - PSH   Push Function
  - RST   Reset the connection
  - SYN   Synchronize sequence numbers
  - FIN   No more data from sender

- *Window*:   16 bits; the number of data octets beginning with the one indicated in the acknowledgment field, which the sender of this segment is willing to accept.

- *Checksum*:   16 bits; the checksum field is the 16-bit 1s' complement of the 1s' complement sum of all 16-bit words in the header and text. If a segment contains an odd number of header and text octets to be checksummed, the last octet is padded on the right with 0s to form a 16-bit word for checksum purposes. The pad is not transmitted as part of the segment. While computing the checksum, the checksum field itself is replaced with 0s.

  The checksum also covers a 96-bit pseudoheader conceptually prefixed to the TCP header. This pseudoheader contains the Source Address, the Destination Address, the Protocol, and TCP length. This gives the TCP protection against misrouted segments. This information is carried in the Internet Protocol and is transferred across the TCP/Network interface in the arguments or results of calls by the TCP on the IP.

```
DLC:    --- DLC Header ---
DLC:    Frame 1 arrived at  13:48:13.17684 ; frame size is 60 (003C hex) bytes.
DLC:    Destination = Station 00A024A5401D
DLC:    Source      = Station 3Com  F425DA
DLC:    Ethertype   = 0800 (IP)
IP:     --- IP Header ---
IP:     Version = 4, header length = 20 bytes
IP:     Type of service = 00
IP:            000. .... = routine
IP:            ...0 .... = normal delay
IP:            .... 0... = normal throughput
IP:            .... .0.. = normal reliability
IP:     Total length    = 44 bytes
IP:     Identification  = 44410
IP:     Flags           = 4X
IP:            .1.. .... = don't fragment
IP:            ..0. .... = last fragment
IP:     Fragment offset = 0 bytes
IP:     Time to live    = 128 seconds/hops
IP:     Protocol        = 6 (TCP)
IP:     Header checksum = E79A (correct)
IP:     Source address      = [155.229.22.245]
IP:     Destination address = [155.229.22.247]
IP:     No options
TCP:    -- TCP header --
TCP:    Source port          = 2974
TCP:    Destination port     = 139 (NetBIOS-ssn)
TCP:    Sequence number      = 695530828
TCP:    Acknowledgment number   = 61723330
TCP:    Data offset          = 20 bytes
TCP:    Flags                = 18
TCP:                ..0. .... = (No urgent pointer)
TCP:                ...1 .... = Acknowledgment
TCP:                .... 1... = Push
TCP:                .... .0.. = (No reset)
TCP:                .... ..0. = (No SYN)
TCP:                .... ...0 = (No FIN)
TCP:    Window               = 7648
TCP:    Checksum             = A5D7 (correct)
TCP:    No TCP options
TCP:    [4 byte(s) of data]
```

FIGURE 8.21b   Trace of NetBIOS service over TCP/IP

The TCP Length is the TCP header length plus the data length in octets (this is not an explicitly transmitted quantity but is computed), and it does not count the 12 octets of the pseudoheader.

- *Urgent Pointer*:   16 bits; this field communicates the current value of the urgent pointer as a positive offset from the sequence number in this segment. The urgent pointer points to the sequence number of the octet following the urgent data. This field is interpreted only in segments with the URG control bit set.

- *Options*:   variable; options may occupy space at the end of the TCP header and are a multiple of 8 bits in length. All options are included in the checksum. An option may begin on any octet boundary. Two cases exist for the format of an option:

- Case 1:　A single octet of option-kind.
- Case 2:　An octet of option-kind, an octet of option-length, and the actual option-data octets.

The option-length counts the two octets of option-kind and option-length as well as the option-data octets. A TCP must implement all options. Currently defined options include (kind indicated in octal):

Kind	Length	Meaning
0	—	End of option list
1	—	No-Operation
2	4	Maximum Segment Size

The following option code indicates the end of the option list, which might not coincide with the end of the TCP header according to the Data Offset field. This code is used at the end of all options, not the end of each option, and need be used only if the end of the options would not otherwise coincide with the end of the TCP header:

```
00000000
Kind=0
```

This following option code, indicating no operation, may be used between options, for example, to align the beginning of a subsequent option on a word boundary. There is no guarantee that senders will use this option, so receivers must be prepared to process options even if they do not begin on a word boundary:

```
+--------+
|00000001|
+--------+
Kind=1
```

- *Maximum Segment Size Option Data*:　16 bits; if this option is present, it communicates the maximum receive segment size at the TCP which sends this segment. This field must be sent only in the initial connection request (i.e., in segments with the SYN control bit set). If this option is not used, any segment size is allowed.

```
|00000010|00000100|   max seg size   |
Kind=2    Length=4
```

- *Padding*:　variable; the TCP header padding is used to ensure that the TCP header ends and that data begins on a 32-bit boundary. The padding is composed of 0s.

Sequence Numbers

A fundamental notion in the design is that every octet of data sent over a TCP connection has a sequence number. Because every octet is sequenced, each of them can be acknowledged. The acknowledgment mechanism used is cumulative so that an acknowledgment of sequence number X indicates that all octets up to but not including X have been received. This mechanism allows for straight-forward duplicate detection in the presence of retransmission. In the numbering of octets within a segment, the first data octet immediately following the header is the lowest numbered, and the following octets are numbered consecutively.

Remember that the actual sequence number space is finite, although very large. This space ranges from 0 to $2**32-1$. Since the space is finite, all arithmetic dealing with sequence numbers must be performed Modulo $2**32$. This unsigned arithmetic preserves the relationship of sequence numbers as they cycle from $2**32-1$ to 0 again. Some subtleties exist in computer modulo arithmetic, so great care should be taken in programming the comparison of such values. The symbol =< means less than or equal (Modulo $2**32$).

The typical kinds of sequence number comparisons that the TCP must perform include:

- Determining that an acknowledgment refers to some sequence number sent but not yet acknowledged.

- Determining that all sequence numbers occupied by a segment have been acknowledged (e.g., to remove the segment from a retransmission queue).

- Determining that an incoming segment contains sequence numbers that are expected (i.e., that the segment overlaps the receive window).

We have taken advantage of the numbering scheme to protect certain control information as well. This protection is achieved by implicitly including some control flags in the sequence space so that they can be retransmitted and acknowledged without confusion (i.e., one and only one copy of the control is acted upon). Control information is not physically carried in the segment data space. Consequently, we must adopt rules for implicitly assigning sequence numbers to control. The SYN and FIN are the only controls requiring this protection, and these controls are used only at connection opening and closing. For sequence number purposes, the SYN is considered to occur before the first actual data octet of the segment in which it occurs, although the FIN is considered to occur after the last actual data octet in a segment in which it occurs. The segment length (SEG.LEN) includes both data and sequence space occupying controls. When a SYN is present, SEG.SEQ is the sequence number of the SYN.

Initial Sequence Number Selection

A send sequence number and a receive sequence number exist for each connection. The *initial send sequence* number (ISS) is chosen by the data sending TCP, and the *initial receive sequence* number (IRS) is learned during the connection establishing procedure.

For a connection to be established or initialized, the two TCPs must synchronize on each other's initial sequence numbers, which is done in an exchange of connection-establishing segments carrying a control bit called SYN (for synchronize) and the initial sequence numbers. As a shorthand, segments carrying the SYN bit are also called SYNs. Hence, the solution requires a suitable mechanism for picking an initial sequence number and a slightly involved handshake to exchange the ISN's. The synchronization requires each side to send its own initial sequence number and to receive a confirmation from the other side. Each side also must receive the other side's initial sequence number and send a confirming acknowledgment:

1. A→B   SYN my sequence number is X

2. A←B   ACK your sequence number is X

3. A←B SYN my sequence number is Y

4. A→B ACK your sequence number is Y

Because steps 2 and 3 can be combined in a single message, this is called the three-way (or three-message) handshake. A three-way handshake is necessary because sequence numbers are not tied to a global clock in the network, and TCPs may have different mechanisms for picking the ISNs. The receiver of the first SYN has no way of knowing whether the segment was an old delayed one or not, unless it remembers the last sequence number used on the connection (which is not always possible), and so it must ask the sender to verify this SYN.

Establishing a Connection

The *three-way handshake* is used to establish a connection. This procedure normally is initiated by one TCP and responded to by another TCP in Figure 8.22. The procedure also works if two TCP simultaneously initiate the procedure. When simultaneous attempts occur, each TCP receives a SYN segment that carries no acknowledgment after it has sent a SYN. Of course, the arrival of an old duplicate SYN segment can potentially make it appear to the recipient that a simultaneous connection initiation is in progress.

Several examples of connection initiation follow. Although these examples do not show connection synchronization using data-carrying segments, this is perfectly legitimate, so long as the receiving TCP doesn't deliver the data to the user until it is clear that the data is valid (i.e., the data must be buffered at the receiver until the connection reaches the ESTABLISHED state). The three-way handshake reduces the possibility of false connections. It is the implementation of a trade-off between memory and messages to provide information for this checking.

The principle reason for the three-way handshake is to prevent old duplicate connection initiations from causing confusion. To deal with this, a special control message, reset, has been devised. If the receiving TCP is in a nonsynchronized state (i.e., SYN-SENT,

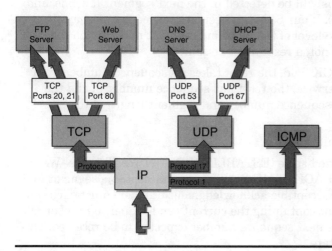

FIGURE 8.22 TCP/IP application

SYN-RECEIVED), it returns to LISTEN on receiving an acceptable reset. If the TCP is in one of the synchronized states (ESTABLISHED, FIN-WAIT-1, FIN-WAIT-2, CLOSE-WAIT, CLOSING, LAST-ACK, TIME-WAIT), it aborts the connection and informs its user.

A variety of other cases are possible, all of which are accounted for by the following rules for RST generation and processing.

Reset Generation.   As a general rule, reset (RST) must be sent whenever a segment arrives that apparently is not intended for the current connection. A reset must not be sent if it is not clear that this is the case.

Three groups of states exist:

- If the connection does not exist (CLOSED), a reset is sent in response to any incoming segment except another reset. In particular, SYNs addressed to a nonexistent connection are rejected by this means.

  If the incoming segment has an ACK field, the reset takes its sequence number from the ACK field of the segment; otherwise, the reset has sequence number 0, and the ACK field is set to the sum of the sequence number and segment length of the incoming segment. The connection remains in the CLOSED state.

- If the connection is in any nonsynchronized state (LISTEN, SYN-SENT, SYN-RECEIVED), and the incoming segment acknowledges something not yet sent (the segment carries an unacceptable ACK), or if an incoming segment has a security level or compartment that does not exactly match the level and compartment requested for the connection, a reset is sent.

  If our SYN has not been acknowledged and if the precedence level of the incoming segment is higher than the precedence level requested, either raise the local precedence level (if allowed by the user and the system) or send a reset. Or, if the precedence level of the incoming segment is lower than the precedence level requested, continue as if the precedence matched exactly (if the remote TCP cannot raise the precedence level to match ours, this will be detected in the next segment it sends, and the connection then is terminated). If our SYN has been acknowledged (perhaps in this incoming segment), the precedence level of the incoming segment must match the local precedence level exactly; if it does not, a reset must be sent.

  If the incoming segment has an ACK field, the reset takes its sequence number from the ACK field of the segment; otherwise, the reset has sequence number 0, and the ACK field is set to the sum of the sequence number and segment length of the incoming segment.

  The connection remains in the same state.

- If the connection is in a synchronized state (ESTABLISHED, FIN-WAIT-1, FIN-WAIT-2, CLOSE-WAIT, CLOSING, LAST-ACK, TIME-WAIT), any unacceptable segment (out of window sequence number or unacceptible acknowledgment number) must elicit only an empty acknowledgment segment containing the current send-sequence number and an acknowledgment indicating the next sequence number expected to be received. The connection remains in the same state.

If an incoming segment has a security level, compartment, or precedence that does not exactly match the level, compartment, and precedence requested for the connection, a reset is sent, and the connection goes to the CLOSED state. The reset takes its sequence number from the ACK field of the incoming segment.

Reset Processing.   In all states except SYN-SENT, all reset (RST) segments are validated by checking their SEQ-fields. A reset is valid if its sequence number is in the window. In the SYN-SENT state (a RST received in response to an initial SYN), the RST is acceptable if the ACK field acknowledges the SYN.

The receiver of a RST first validates it and then changes state. If the receiver was in the LISTEN state, it ignores the RST. If the receiver was in SYN-RECEIVED state and had previously been in the LISTEN state, the receiver returns to the LISTEN state; otherwise, the receiver aborts the connection and goes to the CLOSED state. If the receiver was in any other state, it aborts the connection, advises the user, and goes to the CLOSED state.

Closing a Connection.   CLOSE is an operation meaning, "I have no more data to send." The notion of closing a full-duplex connection is subject to ambiguous interpretation, because it may not be obvious how to treat the receiving side of the connection. The user who CLOSEs may continue to RECEIVE until told that the other side has CLOSED also. Thus, a program could initiate several SENDs followed by a CLOSE and continue to RECEIVE until signaled that a RECEIVE failed because the other side has CLOSED. We assume that the TCP signals a user, even if no RECEIVEs are outstanding, that the other side has closed, so the user can terminate his side gracefully. A TCP reliably delivers all buffers SENT before the connection was CLOSED so that a user who expects no data in return need only wait to hear that the connection was CLOSED successfully to know that all his data was received at the destination TCP. Users must keep reading connections they close for sending until the TCP says no more data. Three cases are possible:

- The user initiates by telling the TCP to CLOSE the connection.
- The remote TCP initiates by sending a FIN control signal.
- Both users CLOSE simultaneously.

Precedence and Security.   The intent is that connection be allowed only between ports operating with exactly the same security and compartment values and at the higher of the precedence level requested by the two ports. The precedence and security parameters used in TCP are exactly those defined in the IP. Throughout this TCP specification, the term security/compartment is intended to indicate the security parameters used in IP including security, compartment, user group, and handling restriction.

A connection attempt with mismatched security/compartment values, or a lower precedence value, must be rejected by sending a reset. Rejecting a connection due to too low a precedence only occurs after an acknowledgment of the SYN has been received. The security parameters may be used even in a nonsecure environment (the values would indicate unclassified data); thus, hosts in nonsecure environments must be prepared to receive the security parameters, although they need not send them.

The Communication of Urgent Information

The objective of the TCP urgent mechanism is to allow the sending user to stimulate the receiving user to accept some urgent data and to permit the receiving TCP to indicate to the receiving user when all the currently known urgent data has been received by the user. This mechanism permits a point in the data stream to be designated as the end of urgent information. When this point is in advance of the receive sequence number (RCV.NXT) at the receiving TCP, that TCP must tell the user to go into urgent mode; when the receive sequence number catches up to the urgent pointer, the TCP must tell user to go into normal mode. If the urgent pointer is updated while the user is in urgent mode, the update is invisible to the user.

The method uses an urgent field that is carried in all segments transmitted. The URG control flag indicates that the urgent field is meaningful and must be added to the segment sequence number to yield the urgent pointer. The absence of this flag indicates that no urgent data is outstanding.

To send an urgent indication, the user must also send at least one data octet. If the sending user also indicates a push, timely delivery of the urgent information to the destination process is enhanced.

Managing the Window

The window sent in each segment indicates the range of sequence numbers the sender of the window (the data receiver) is currently prepared to accept. There is an assumption that this is related to the currently available data buffer space available for this connection. Indicating a large window encourages transmissions. If more data arrives than can be accepted, the data is discarded, which results in excessive retransmissions, adding unnecessarily to the load on the network and the TCPs. Indicating a small window may restrict the transmission of data to the point of introducing a round-trip delay between each new segment transmitted.

The mechanisms provided allow a TCP to advertise a large window and to subsequently advertise a much smaller window without having accepted that much data. This *shrinking the window* is strongly discouraged. The robustness principle dictates that TCPs do not shrink the window themselves, but they are prepared for such behavior on the part of other TCPs.

The sending TCP must be prepared to accept from the user and send at least one octet of new data even if the send window is 0. The sending TCP must regularly retransmit to the receiving TCP even when the window is 0. Two minutes is recommended for the retransmission interval when the window is 0. This retransmission is essential to guarantee that when either TCP has a 0 window the reopening of the window is reported reliably to the other.

When the receiving TCP has a 0 window and a segment arrives, it must still send an acknowledgment showing its next expected sequence number and current window (0).

The sending TCP packages the data to be transmitted into segments that fit the current window and may repackage segments on the retransmission queue. Such repackaging is not required but may be helpful.

In a connection with a one-way data flow, the window information is carried in acknowledgment segments that all have the same sequence number so there will be no way to reorder them if they arrive out of order. This problem is not serious, but it allows the window information to be on occasion temporarily based on old reports from the data receiver. A refinement to avoid this problem is to act on the window information from segments that carry the highest acknowledgment number (segments with acknowledgment numbers equal to or greater than the highest number previously received).

The window management procedure has significant influence on the communication performance.

User Datagram Protocol (UDP)

The *User Datagram Protocol* (UDP) is defined in RFC 768. This protocol makes available a datagram mode of packet-switched computer communication in the environment of an interconnected set of computer networks. UDP is used by applications that need only a connectionless, best effort transport service. UDP assumes that the IP is used as the underlying protocol. UDP provides a procedure for application programs to send messages to other programs with a minimum of protocol mechanism. UDP is transaction oriented, and delivery and duplicate protection are not guaranteed. The major uses for this protocol are to support the following application-level protocols: *Domain Name Service* (DNS), *Trivial File Transfer Protocol* (TFTP), NetBIOS Name and Datagram Service and *Simple Network Management Protocol* (SNMP).

Because UDP uses the services of IP, it provides the same connectionless delivery service as the IP. UDP does not flow control the rate of information exchange between machines; UDP does not use acknowledgements to guarantee the arrival of messages; and UDP does not order incoming messages. UDP provides a way to send a message with a high probability of arrival, but without a specific guarantee. This service is termed *unreliable* because the receipt of a message is not acknowledged by the destination host.

Figures 8.23 and 8.24 illustrate what is contained within a UDP packet.

To use UDP, the application must supply the IP address and port number of the destination application. A port is an abstraction to give transport protocols like UDP and TCP the capability of handling communications between multiple hosts. Ports enable a communication to be uniquely identified by a positive integer.

UDP and the ISO Model

UDP provides one additional capability beyond those provided by IP. Although IP allows communication between two hosts across the Internet, UDP creates a mechanism to distinguish among multiple destinations within a given host, which allows multiple application programs executing on a given host to send and receive datagrams independently. Think of the ultimate destination within a machine as a collection of destination points, or ports. Each port is identified by a positive integer. The protocol software in each destination machine queues the packets arriving for a particular port until an application process extracts them.

To communicate with another machine, the source station must know the Internet address of the destination machine, and the port number of the destination process within that machine. The source station also supplies one of its own port numbers to which replies may be sent. Depending on the application, the destination machine may, or may not, send a reply.

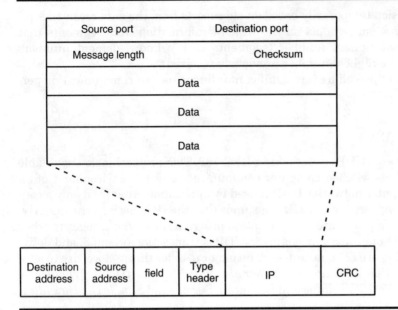

FIGURE 8.23 UDP packet

Source Port	Dest. Port	Length	Checksum	Data . . . .

| Number of Bits | 16 | 16 | 16 | 16 |

User Datagram Protocol
    No windowing or acknowledgments
    Faster than TCP
Assumes upper layer protocolos provide reliability
    Network File System (NFS)
    Domain Name Service (DNS) lookups
    Trivial File Transfer Protocol (TFTP) file transfers
    Simple Network Management Protocol (SNMP)
Message Format:
    Source/Destination Ports
    - The UDP port numbers that identify the application programs at the ends of the connection
    Length = The number of octets including the UDP header and user data
    Checksum = Optional; the 16 Bit checksum is used to verify data integrity

FIGURE 8.24 UDP and OSI model

UDP Header Encapsulation

The complete UDP message, including the header and data, is encapsulated in an IP datagram as it travels across the Internet. The Ethernet layer is responsible for transferring data between two hosts or routers on the same physical network. The IP layer is responsible for transferring data across routers between hosts on the Internet.

- *Source Port*: This field is optional. When used, it indicates the port of the sending process, as well as the port to which a reply should be addressed. If the transmitting host does not supply a source port, this field should have a value of 0.

- *Destination Port*: This field is used to demultiplex datagrams among the processes in the destination machine.

- *Length*: This field is the combined length of the UDP header and data, expressed in octets.

- *Checksum*: The UDP checksum is optional. A value of 0 indicates that the checksum has not been computed. Because IP does not compute a checksum on the data portion of the datagram (the IP checksum is based only on the IP header), the UDP checksum provides the only means to determine whether the data has arrived without errors.

Header and Checksum.   The UDP checksum is calculated from the fields used to create a pseudoheader. This pseudoheader is composed of fields that are part of the actual IP and UDP headers.

The pseudoheader contains the source address, destination address, and protocol fields from the IP header. It also contains the UDP length and the UDP data fields. The data field is padded with a 0 octet (if necessary) to ensure the object is an exact multiple of 2 octets. (There must be an exact number of octets in the pseudoheader. For example, if the data field contains 13 octets, it must be padded with one extra octet of 0s to make it even.)

This checksum gives protection against misrouted datagrams. We know that a datagram has reached the proper location if it is delivered to the correct destination machine on the Internet and to the proper port within that machine. The UDP header specifies only the destination port number but does not specify the destination Internet address. The destination Internet address can be obtained only from the IP header. Thus, to verify datagram arrival, the checksum must span fields in both the IP and the UDP headers.

To verify the checksum, the receiving machine must extract the required fields from the IP header, assemble them into the pseudoheader format, and compute the checksum. If the checksums agree, the datagram has reached the correct port on the destination machine.

NetBIOS over TCP/IP

This section covers NetBIOS over TCP/IP. We cover NetBIOS over TCP/IP here due to its dependence on IP, TCP, and UDP protocols.

The NetBIOS service has become the dominant mechanism for personal computer networking. NetBIOS provides a vendor-independent interface for the Intel and non-Intel systems supporting NetBIOS and the Server Message Block protocols. NetBIOS over TCP/IP implementations are prevalent throughout the industry with vendors such as Microsoft NT, SCO Advance Server, IBM Warp Server, Sun SolarNet Digitial Pathworks, etc. All support NetBIOS over TCP/IP (see Figure 8.25).

Interface to Application Programs

NetBIOS on personal computers includes a set of services and an exact program interface to those services. NetBIOS on other computer systems may present the NetBIOS services

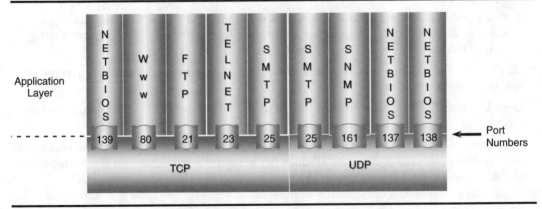

FIGURE 8.25   NetBIOS over TCP/IP protocol stacks

to programs using other interfaces. Except on personal computers, no clear standard for a NetBIOS software interface has emerged.

Name Service.   NetBIOS resources are referenced by name. Lower level address information is not available to NetBIOS applications. An application, representing a resource, registers one or more names that it wants to use as shown in Figure 8.26.

The name space is flat and uses 16 alphanumeric characters. Names may not start with an asterisk (*). Registration is a bid for use of a name. The bid may be for *exclusive* (unique) or *shared* (group) ownership. Each application contends with the other applications in real time. Implicit permission is granted to a station when it receives no objections. That is, a bid is made, and the application waits for a period of time. If no objections are received, the station assumes that it has permission.

A unique name should be held by only one station at a time. However, duplicates (*name conflicts*) may arise due to errors. All instances of a group name are equivalent. An application referencing a name generally does not know (or care) whether the name is registered as a unique name or a group name.

An explicit name-deletion function is specified so that applications may remove a name. Implicit name deletion occurs when a station ceases operation. In the case of personal computers, implicit name deletion is a frequent occurrence.

The Name Service primitives are as follows:

- *Add Name*:   The requesting application wants exclusive use of the name.

- *Add Group Name*:   The requesting application is willing to share use of the name with other applications.

- *Delete Name*:   The application no longer requires use of the name. Note that typical use of NetBIOS is among independently operated personal computers. A common way to stop using a PC is to turn the PC off; in this case, the graceful give-back mechanism, provided by the Delete Name function, is not used. Because this behavior occurs frequently, the network service must provide support.

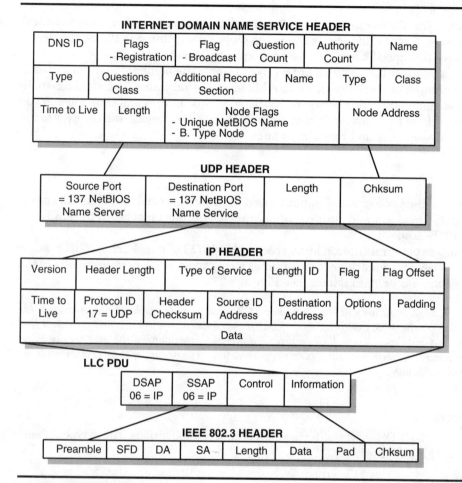

FIGURE 8.26 NetBIOS Name Service

Session Service.   A session is a reliable message exchange, conducted between a pair of Net-BIOS applications. Sessions are full-duplex, sequenced, and reliable. Data is organized into messages. Each message may range in size from 0 to 131,071 bytes. No expedited or urgent data capabilities are present. Multiple sessions may exist between any pair of calling and called names. The parties to a connection have access to the calling and called names.

The NetBIOS specification does not define how a connection request to a shared (group) name resolves into a session. The usual assumption is that a session may be established with any one owner of the called group name. An important service provided to NetBIOS applications is the detection of sessions failure. The loss of a session is reported to an application via all of the outstanding service requests for that session. For example, if the application has only a NetBIOS receive primitive pending and the session terminates, the pending receive aborts with a termination indication.

Datagram Service.   The Datagram service is an unreliable, nonsequenced, connectionless service. Datagrams are sent under cover of a name properly registered to the sender. Datagrams may be sent to a specific name or may be explicitly broadcast.

Datagrams sent to an exclusive name are received by only the holder of that name. Datagrams sent to a group name are multicast to all holders of that name. The sending application program cannot distinguish between group and unique names and thus must act as if all nonbroadcast datagrams are multicast. As with the session service, the receiver of the datagram is told the sending and receiving names.

NetBIOS Scope

A *NetBIOS Scope* is the population of computers across which a registered NetBIOS name is known. NetBIOS broadcast and multicast datagram operations must reach the entire extent of the NetBIOS scope.

An internet may support multiple, nonintersecting NetBIOS scopes. Each NetBIOS scope has a *scope identifier*. This identifier is a character string meeting the requirements of the domain name system for domain names (see Figure 8.27).

> **NOTE:**   *Each implementation of NetBIOS-over-TCP must provide mechanisms to manage the scope identifier(s) to be used. Control of scope identifiers implies a requirement for additional NetBIOS interface capabilities. These may be provided through extensions of the user service interface or other means (such as node configuration parameters.) The nature of these extensions is not part of this specification.*

NetBIOS End-Nodes

End-nodes support NetBIOS service interfaces and contain applications. Three types of end-nodes are part of this standard:

- Broadcast (B) nodes
- Point-to-point (P) nodes
- Mixed mode (M) nodes

An IP address may be associated with only one instance of one of the preceding types.

Without having preloaded name-to-address tables, NetBIOS participants are faced with the task of dynamically resolving references to one another. This can be accomplished with broadcast or mediated point-to-point communications.

B nodes use local network broadcasting to effect a rendezvous with one or more recipients. P and M nodes use the *NetBIOS Name Server* (NBNS) and the *NetBIOS Datagram Distribution* Server (NBDD) for this same purpose. End-nodes may be combined in various topologies. No matter how combined, the operation of the B, P, and M nodes is not altered.

> **NOTE:**   *The administration of a NetBIOS scope should avoid using both M and B nodes within the same scope. A NetBIOS scope should contain only B nodes or only P and M nodes.*

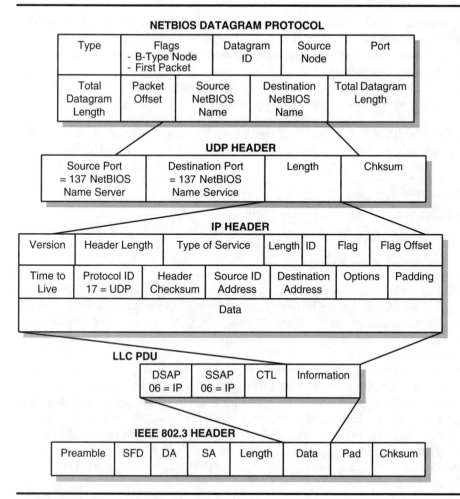

FIGURE 8.27   NetBIOS Datagram protocol

Broadcast (B) Nodes.   Broadcast (or B) nodes communicate using a mix of UDP datagrams (both broadcast and directed) and TCP connections. B nodes may freely interoperate with one another within a broadcast area. A broadcast area is a single MAC-bridged B-LAN.

Point-to-Point (P) Nodes.   Point-to-point (or P) nodes communicate using only directed UDP datagrams and TCP sessions. P nodes neither generate nor listen for broadcast UDP packets. P nodes do, however, offer NetBIOS level broadcast and multicast services using capabilities provided by the NBNS and NBDD.

P nodes rely on NetBIOS name and datagram distribution servers. These servers may be local or remote; P nodes operate the same in either case.

Mixed Mode (M) Nodes.   Mixed mode nodes (or M) nodes are P nodes with certain B-node characteristics. M nodes use broadcast and unicast. Broadcast is used to improve response time based on the assumption that most resources reside on the local broadcast medium rather than somewhere in an internet.

M nodes rely upon NBNS and NBDD servers. However, M nodes may continue limited operation should these servers be temporarily unavailable.

H Nodes.   H nodes, which are still under construction and are an enhancement to M nodes, use P nodes first for unicast and B nodes to register and resolve names on the network.

NetBIOS Support Servers

Two types of support servers are part of this standard:

- NetBIOS name server nodes
- Netbios datagram distribution nodes

NBNS and NBDD nodes are invisible to NetBIOS applications and are part of the underlying NetBIOS mechanism. NetBIOS name and datagram distribution servers are the focus of name and datagram activity for P and M nodes. Both the name (NBNS) and datagram distribution (NBDD) servers are permitted to shift part of their operation to the P or M end-node requesting a service.

Because the assignment of responsibility is dynamic, and because P and M nodes must be prepared to operate should the NetBIOS server delegate control to the maximum extent, the system naturally accommodates improvements in NetBIOS server function. For example, as Internet Group Multicasting becomes more widespread, new NBDD implementations may elect to assume full responsibility for NetBIOS datagram distribution.

Interoperability between different implementations is ensured by imposing requirements on end-node implementations. They must be able to accept the full range of legal responses from the NBNS or NBDD.

NetBIOS Name Server (NBNS) Nodes

The NBNS is designed to allow considerable flexibility with its degree of responsibility for the accuracy and management of NetBIOS names. On one hand, the NBNS may elect not to accept full responsibility, leaving the NBNS essentially a bulletin board on which name/address information is freely posted (and removed) by P and M nodes without validation by the NBNS. Alternatively, the NBNS may elect to completely manage and validate names. The degree of responsibility that the NBNS assumes is asserted by the NBNS each time a name is claimed through a simple mechanism. Should the NBNS not assert full control, the NBNS returns enough information to the requesting node so that the node may challenge any possible holder of the name.

This capability to shift responsibility for NetBIOS name management between the NBNS and the P and M nodes allows a network administrator (or vendor) to make a tradeoff between NBNS simplicity, security, and delay characteristics. A single NBNS may be implemented as a distributed entity, such as the DNS.

Relationship of NetBIOS Support Servers and B Nodes

NetBIOS servers do not listen to broadcast traffic on any broadcast area to which they may be attached. Nor are the NetBIOS support servers even aware of B-node activities or names claimed or used by B nodes. It may be possible to extend both the NBNS and NBDD so that they participate in B-node activities and act as a bridge to P and M nodes. However, such extensions are beyond the scope of this specification.

Topologies

B, P, M, NBNS, and NBDD nodes may be combined in various ways to form useful NetBIOS environments. This section describes some of these combinations.

Three classes of operation are possible:

- Class 0.   B nodes only
- Class 1.   P nodes only
- Class 2.   P and M nodes together

In the cases that follow, any P node may be replaced by an M node. The effects of such replacement are mentioned in conjunction with each example.

Local.   A NetBIOS scope is operating locally when all entities are within the same broadcast area.

B Nodes Only.   Local operation with only B nodes is the most basic mode of operation. Name registration and discovery procedures use broadcast mechanisms. The NetBIOS scope is limited by the extent of the broadcast area. This configuration does not require NetBIOS support servers.

P Nodes Only.   This configuration typically is used when the network administrator desires to eliminate NetBIOS as a source of broadcast activity. This configuration operates the same as if it were in an internet and is cited here only due to its convenience as a means to reduce the use of broadcast.

Replacement of one or more of the P nodes with M nodes does not affect the operation of the other P and M nodes. P and M nodes can interact with one another. Because M nodes use broadcast, overall broadcast activity increases.

Mixed B and P Nodes.   B and P nodes do not interact with one another. Replacement of P nodes with M nodes allows Bs and Ms to interact.

> **NOTE:**   *B and M nodes may be intermixed only on a local broadcast area. B and M nodes should not be intermixed in an internet environment.*

P Nodes Only.   P nodes may be scattered at various locations in an internetwork. They require both an NBNS and an NBDD for NetBIOS name and datagram support, respectively.

The NetBIOS scope is determined by the NetBIOS scope identifier (domain name) used by the various P (and M) nodes. An internet may contain numerous NetBIOS scopes.

Any P node may be replaced by an M node with no loss of functionality to any node. However, broadcast activity is increased in the broadcast area to which the M node is attached.

Mixed M and P Nodes. M and P nodes may be mixed. When locating NetBIOS names, M nodes tend to find names held by other M nodes on the same common broadcast area in preference to names held by P nodes or M nodes elsewhere in the network.

> *NOTE: B and M nodes should not be intermixed in an internet environment. Doing so allows undetected NetBIOS name conflicts to arise and cause unpredictable behavior.*

Retransmission of Requests

UDP is an unreliable delivery mechanism in which packets can be lost, received out of transmit sequence, duplicated, and subject to delayed delivery. Because the NetBIOS protocols make heavy use of UDP, they have compensated for its unreliability with extra mechanisms.

Each NetBIOS packet contains all the necessary information to process the packet. None of the protocols use multiple UDP packets to convey a single request or response. If more information is required than will fit in a single UDP packet, for example, and a P-type node wants all the owners of a group name from a NetBIOS server, a TCP connection is used. Consequently, the NetBIOS protocols do not fail because of out-of-sequence delivery of UDP packets.

To overcome the loss of a request or response packet, each request operation retransmits the request if a response is not received within a specified time limit.

Protocol operations sensitive to successive response packets, such as name-conflict detection, are protected from duplicated packets because they ignore successive packets with the same NetBIOS information. Because no state on the responder's node is associated with a request, the responder just sends the appropriate response whenever a request packet arrives. Consequently, duplicate or delayed request packets have no impact.

For all requests, if a response packet is delayed too long, another request packet is transmitted. A second response packet being sent in response to the second request packet is equivalent to a duplicate packet. Therefore, the protocols ignore the second packet received. If the delivery of a response is delayed until after the request operation has been completed, successfully or not, the response packet is ignored.

Requests without Responses: Demands

Some request types do not have matching responses. These requests are known as *demands*, because the receiving node is expected to obey. However, because demands are unconfirmed, they are used in situations where, at most, limited damage would occur if the demand packet should be lost.

Transaction ID

Because multiple simultaneous transactions may be in progress between a pair of entities, a transaction ID is used.

The originator of a transaction selects an ID unique to the originator. The transaction ID is reflected back and forth in each interaction within the transaction. The transaction partners must match responses and requests by comparison of the transaction ID and the IP address of the transaction partner. If no matching request can be found, the response must be discarded.

A new transaction ID should be used for each transaction. A simple 16-bit transaction counter ought to be an adequate ID generator. It is probably not necessary to search the space of outstanding transaction IDs to filter duplicates: it is extremely unlikely that any transaction has a lifetime that is more than a small fraction of the typical counter cycle period. Use of the IP addresses in conjunction with the transaction ID further reduces the possibility of damage should transaction IDs be prematurely reused.

TCP and UDP Foundations

This version of the NetBIOS-over-TCP protocols uses UDP for many interactions. In the future, this RFC may be extended to permit such interactions to occur over TCP connections (perhaps to increase efficiency when multiple interactions occur within a short time or when NetBIOS datagram traffic reveals that an application is using NetBIOS datagrams to support connection-oriented service.)

Representation of NetBIOS Names

NetBIOS names as seen across the client interface to NetBIOS are exactly 16 bytes long. Within the NetBIOS-over-TCP protocols, a longer representation is used. Two levels of encoding exist. The first level maps a NetBIOS name into a domain system name. The second level maps the domain system name into the compressed representation required for interaction with the domain name system.

Except in one packet, the second level representation is the only NetBIOS name representation used in NetBIOS-over-TCP packet formats. The exception is the RDATA field of a NODE STATUS RESPONSE packet.

First Level Encoding

The first level representation consists of two parts: NetBIOS name and NetBIOS scope identifier.

The 16-byte NetBIOS name is mapped into a 32-byte wide field using a reversible, half-ASCII, biased encoding. Each half-octet of the NetBIOS name is encoded into one byte of the-32 byte field. The first half octet is encoded into the first byte; the second half-octet is encoded into the second byte, etc.

Each 4-bit, half-octet of the NetBIOS name is treated as an 8-bit, right-adjusted, 0-filled binary number. This number is added to the value of the ASCII character 'A' (hexidecimal 41). The resulting 8-bit number is stored in the appropriate byte. This encoding results in a NetBIOS name being represented as a sequence of 32 ASCII, uppercase characters from the set {A,B,C...N,O,P}.

The NetBIOS scope identifier is a valid domain name (without a leading dot). An ASCII dot (2E hexidecimal) and the scope identifier are appended to the encoded form of the NetBIOS name, the result forming a valid domain name. For example, the NetBIOS name "The NetBIOS name" in the NetBIOS scope "SCOPE.ID.COM" would be represented at level one by the ASCII character string:

```
FEGHGFCAEOGFHEECEJEPFDCAHEGBGNGF.SCOPE.ID.COM
```

Second Level Encoding

The first-level encoding must be reduced to second level encoding.

NetBIOS Name Service

Before a name may be used, the name must be registered by a node. Once acquired, the name must be defended against inconsistent registration by other nodes. Before building a NetBIOS session or sending a NetBIOS datagram, one or more holders of the name must be located.

The NetBIOS name service is the collection of procedures through which nodes acquire, defend, and locate the holders of NetBIOS names. The name service procedures are different depending on whether the end-node is of type B, P, or M.

Name Registration (Claim)

Each NetBIOS node can own more than one name. Names are acquired dynamically through the registration (name claim) procedures. Every node has a permanent unique name. This name, like any other name, must be explicitly registered by all end-node types.

A name can be unique (exclusive) or group (nonexclusive). A unique name may be owned by a single node; a group name may be owned by any number of nodes. A name ceases to exist when it is not owned by at least one node. No intrinsic quality of a name determines its characteristics; these are established at the time of registration.

Each node maintains state information for each name it has registered. This information includes the following:

- Whether the name is a group or unique name
- Whether the name is in conflict
- Whether the name is in the process of being deleted

B nodes perform name registration by broadcasting claim requests, soliciting a defense from any node already holding the name. P nodes perform name registration through the agency of the NBNS. M nodes register names through an initial broadcast, like B nodes, (in the absence of an objection, by following the same procedures as a P node). The broadcast action may terminate the attempt but is not sufficient to confirm the registration.

Name Query (Discovery)

Name query (also known as *resolution* or *discovery*) is the procedure by which the IP address(es) associated with a NetBIOS name are discovered.

During session establishment, calling and called names must be specified. The calling name must exist on the node that posts the CALL. The called name must exist on a node that has previously posted a LISTEN. Either name may be a unique or group name.

When a directed datagram is sent, a source and destination name must be specified. If the destination name is a group name, a datagram is sent to all the members of that group.

Different end-node types perform name resolution using different techniques but using the same packet formats:

- B nodes solicit name information by broadcasting a request.
- P nodes ask the NBNS.
- M nodes broadcast a request. If that request does not provide the desired information, an inquiry is sent to the NBNS.

Name Release

NetBIOS names may be released explicitly or silently by an end-node. Silent release typically occurs when an end-node fails or is turned off. Most of the mechanisms described are present to detect silent name release.

Explicit Release

B nodes explicitly release a name by broadcasting a notice. P nodes send a notification to their NBNS. M nodes broadcast a notice and inform their supporting NBNS.

NetBIOS Session Service

The NetBIOS session service begins after one or more IP addresses have been found for the target name. These addresses may have been acquired using the NetBIOS name-query transactions or by other means, such as a local name table or cache.

NetBIOS session service transactions, packets, and protocols are identical for all end-node types. They involve only directed (point-to-point) communications. Figure 8.28 shows the server Block message format.

Overview of NetBIOS Session Service

Session service has three phases:

- *Session establishment*:   During this phase, the IP address and TCP port of the called name is determined, and a TCP connection is established with the remote party.
- *Steady state*:   During this phase, NetBIOS data messages are exchanged over the session. Keep-alive packets may also be exchanged if the participating nodes are so configured.
- *Session close*:   A session is closed when either a party (in the session) closes the session or when one of the parties has gone down.

Session Establishment Phase Overview

An end-node begins establishment of a session to another node by somehow acquiring (perhaps using the name query transactions or a local cache) the IP address of the node or nodes purported to own the destination name.

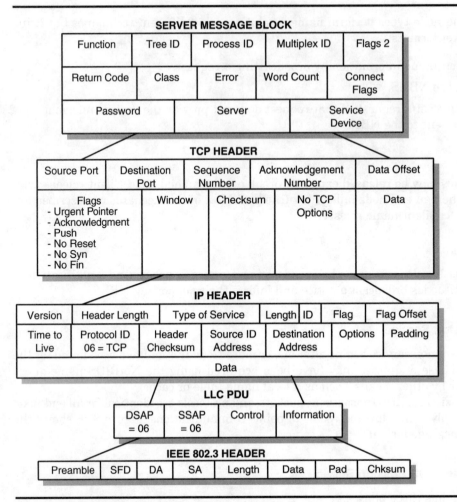

FIGURE 8.28 NetBIOS over TCP/IP NetBIOS session service

Every end-node awaits incoming NetBIOS session requests by listening for TCP calls to a well-known service port, SSN_SRVC_TCP_PORT. Each incoming TCP connection represents the start of a separate NetBIOS lession initiation attempt. The NetBIOS session server, not the ultimate application, accepts the incoming TCP connection(s).

When the TCP connection is open, the calling node sends a session service request packet containing the following information:

- Calling IP address
- Calling NetBIOS name
- Called IP address
- Called NetBIOS name

When the session service request packet arrives at the NetBIOS server, one of the the following situations does not exist: a NetBIOS LISTEN compatible with the incoming call exists, and adequate resources are available to permit session establishment to proceed; a NetBIOS LISTEN compatible with the incoming call exists, but inadequate resources are available to permit the establishment of a session; the called name does, in fact, exist on the called node, but a pending NetBIOS LISTEN compatible with the incoming call does not exist; or the called name does not exist on the called node.

In all but the first case, a rejection response is sent back over the TCP connection to the caller. The TCP connection then is closed, and the session phase terminates. Any retry is the responsibility of the caller. For retries in the case of a group name, the caller may use the next member of the group rather than immediate retrying the instant address. In the case of a unique name, the caller may attempt an immediately retry using the same target IP address unless the called name did not exist on the called node. In that one case, the NetBIOS name should be resolved.

If a compatible LISTEN exists, and there are adequate resources, the session server may transform the existing TCP connection into the NetBIOS data session. Alternatively, the session server may redirect, or retarget the caller to another TCP port (and IP address).

NetBIOS Datagram Service

Every NetBIOS datagram has a named destination and source. To transmit a NetBIOS datagram, the datagram service must perform a name query operation to learn the IP address and the attributes of the destination NetBIOS name. (This information may be cached to avoid the overhead of name queries on subsequent NetBIOS datagrams.) NetBIOS datagrams are carried within UDP packets. If a NetBIOS datagram is larger than a single UDP packet, it may be fragmented into several UDP packets.

End-nodes may receive NetBIOS datagrams addressed to names not held by the receiving node. Such datagrams should be discarded. If the name is unique, a DATAGRAM ERROR packet is sent to the source of that NetBIOS datagram.

NetBIOS Datagrams by B Nodes

For NetBIOS datagrams with a named destination (i.e. nonbroadcast), a B node performs a name discovery for the destination name before sending the datagram. (Name discovery may be bypassed if information from a previous discovery is held in a cache.) If the name type returned by name discovery is *unique*, the datagram is unicast to the sole owner of the name. If the name type is *group*, the datagram is broadcast to the entire broadcast area using the destination IP address BROADCAST_ADDRESS.

A receiving node always filters datagrams based on the destination name. If the destination name is not owned by the node or if no RECEIVE DATAGRAM user operations are pending for the name, the datagram is discarded. For datagrams with a unique name destination, if the name is not owned by the node, the receiving node sends a DATAGRAM ERROR packet. The error packet originates from the DGM_SRVC_UDP_PORT and is addressed to the SOURCE_IP and SOURCE_PORT from the bad datagram. The receiving node quietly discards datagrams with a group name destination if the name is not owned by the node.

Because broadcast NetBIOS datagrams do not have a named destination, the B node sends the DATAGRAM SERVICE packet(s) to the entire broadcast area using the destination IP address BROADCAST_ADDRESS. For the receiving nodes to distinguish this datagram as a broadcast NetBIOS datagram, the NetBIOS name used as the destinaton name is * (hexadecimal 2A) followed by 15 bytes of hexidecimal 00. The NetBIOS scope identifier is appended to the name before it is converted into second level encoding. For example, if the scope identifier is NETBIOS.SCOPE, the first level encoded name would be:

```
CKAAAAAAAAAAAAAAAAAAAAAAAAAAAAAA.NETBIOS.SCOPE
```

For each node in the broadcast area that receives the NetBIOS broadcast datagram, if any RECEIVE BROADCAST DATAGRAM user operations are pending, the data from the NetBIOS datagram is replicated and delivered to each. If no such operations are pending, the node silently discards the datagram.

NetBIOS Datagrams by P and M Nodes

P and M nodes do not use IP broadcast to distribute NetBIOS datagrams. Like B nodes, P and M nodes must perform a name discovery or use cached information to learn whether a destination name is a group or a unique name.

Datagrams to unique names are unicast directly to the destination by P and M nodes, exactly as they are by B nodes. Datagrams to group names and NetBIOS broadcast datagrams are unicast to the NBDD. The NBDD relays the datagrams to each of the nodes specified by the destination name.

An NBDD may not be capable of sending a NetBIOS datagram to a particular NetBIOS name, including the broadcast NetBIOS name (*) defined previously. A query mechanism is available to the end-node to determine whether a NBDD can relay a datagram to a given name. Before a datagram or its fragments are sent to the NBDD, the P or M node may send a DATAGRAM QUERY REQUEST packet to the NBDD with the DESTINATION_NAME from the DATAGRAM SERVICE packet(s). The NBDD responds with a DATAGRAM POSITIVE QUERY RESPONSE if it relays datagrams to the specified destination name. After a positive response, the end-node unicasts the datagram to the NBDD. If the NBDD cannot relay a datagram to the destination name specified in the query, a DATAGRAM NEGATIVE QUERY RESPONSE packet is returned. If the NBDD cannot distribute a datagram, the end-node has the option of getting the name's owner list from the NBNS and sending the datagram directly to each of the owners.

An NBDD must be able to respond to DATAGRAM QUERY REQUEST packets. The response may always be positive. However, the usage or implementation of the query mechanism by a P or M node is optional. An implementation may always unicast the NetBIOS datagram to the NBDD without asking whether it will be relayed. Except for the datagram query facility described previously, an NBDD provides no feedback to indicate whether it forwarded a datagram.

Cisco's TCP/IP Options

Cisco routers can route NetBIOS frames encapsulated within IP datagrams to provide efficient routing of NetBIOS information across an IP-based internetwork. The router's Net-

BIOS over IP support is based on RFC 1001 and RFC 1002 broadcast node (B). This allows the router to rebroadcast NetBIOS packets beyond a local subnet to ensure unique Net-BIOS name registration and to provide immediate visibility of new NetBIOS resources as they become available on the network.

The router also provides a number of enhancements that improve the efficiency of routing NetBIOS over IP—NetBIOS Name Caching, NetBIOS Broadcast Access List, and Net-BIOS Local Acknowledgment.

In addition to IP and TCP, the Cisco TCP/IP implementation supports ARP, RARP, ICMP, Proxy ARP (in which the router acts as an ARP server on behalf of another device), Echo, Discard, and Probe (an address resolution protocol developed by Hewlett-Packard Company and used on IEEE 802.3 networks). Cisco routers also can be configured to use the DNS when host name-to-address mappings are needed.

IP hosts need to know how to reach a router, which they can do in several ways:

- Adding a static route in the host pointing to a router
- Running RIP or some other IGP on the host
- Running the *ICMP Router Discovery Protocol* (IRDP) in the host
- Running Proxy ARP on the router

Cisco routers support all of these methods.

Cisco provides many TCP/IP value-added features that enhance applications' availability and reduce the total cost of internetwork ownership. The most important of these features are described in the following section.

Access Restrictions

Most networks have reasonably straightforward access requirements. To address these issues, Cisco implements access lists, a scheme that prevents certain packets from entering or leaving particular networks.

An access list is a sequential list of instructions to either permit or deny access through a router interface based on an IP address or other criteria. For example, an access list can be created to deny access to a particular resource from all computers on one network segment but to permit access from all other segments. Another access list could be used to permit TCP connections from any host on a local segment to any host in the Internet but to deny all connections from the Internet into the local net except for electronic mail connections to a particular designated mail host. Access lists are extremely flexible, powerful security measures and are available not only for IP, but for many other protocols supported by Cisco routers.

Other access restrictions are provided by the Department of Defense-specified security extensions to IP. Cisco supports both the Basic and the Extended security options as described in RFC 1108 of the *IP Security Option* (IPSO). Support of both access lists and the IPSO makes Cisco a good choice for networks in which security is an issue.

Multivendor Tunneling

Cisco's TCP/IP implementation includes several schemes that allow foreign protocols to be tunneled through an IP network. Tunneling allows network administrators to extend the size of AppleTalk and Novell IPX networks beyond the size that their native protocols can handle. This allows Cisco's implementation of IP to be used to scale AppleTalk and Novell IPX networks beyond 15 hops.

IP Multicast Support

The applications that use the TCP/IP protocol suite continue to evolve. The next set of applications will include those that use video and audio information. Cisco is actively involved with the *Internet Engineering Task Force* (IETF) in defining standards that will enable network administrators to add audio and video applications to their existing networks. IP multicasting (the ability to send IP datagrams to multiple nodes in a logical group) is an important building block for applications such as video. Video teleconferencing, for example, requires the capability to send video information to multiple teleconference sites. If one IP multicast datagram containing video information can be sent to multiple teleconference sites, network bandwidth is saved, and time synchronization is closer to optimal.

Routing Protocol Update Suppression

In some cases, suppressing information about certain networks may be useful. Cisco routers provide an extensive set of configuration options that allow an administrator to tailor the exchange of routing information within a particular routing protocol. Both incoming and outgoing information can be controlled using a set of commands designed for this purpose. For example, networks can be excluded from routing advertisements; routing updates can be prevented from reaching certain networks; and other similar actions can be taken.

Administrative Distance

In large networks, some routers and routing protocols are more reliable sources of routing information than others. Cisco IP routing software permits the reliability of information sources to be quantified by the network administrator with the administrative distance metric. When administrative distance is specified, the router can select between sources of routing information based on the reliability of the source. For example, if a router uses both IGRP and RIP, one might set the administrative distances to reflect greater confidence in the IGRP information. The router then would use IGRP information when available. If the source of IGRP information failed, the router automatically would use RIP information as a backup until the IGRP source became available again.

Routing Protocol Redistribution

Translation between two environments using different routing protocols requires that routes generated by one protocol be redistributed into the second routing protocol environment. Route redistribution gives a company the capability to run different routing protocols in workgroups or areas in which each is particularly effective. By not restricting customers to using only a single routing protocol, Cisco's route redistribution feature minimizes cost while maximizing technical advantage through diversity.

Cisco permits routing protocol redistribution between any of its supported routing protocols. Static route information can also be redistributed. Further, defaults can be assigned so that one routing protocol can use the same metric for all redistributed routes—thereby simplifying the routing redistribution mechanism.

Serverless Network Support

Cisco pioneered the mechanisms that allow network administrators to build serverless networks. Helper addresses, RARP, and BOOTP allow network administrators to place servers far away from the workstations that depend on them—thereby easing network design constraints.

Network Monitoring and Debugging

With today's complex, diverse network topologies, a router's capability to aid the monitoring and debugging process is critical. As the junction point for multiple segments, a router sees more of the complete network than most other devices. Many problems can be detected and/or solved using information that routinely passes through the router.

The Cisco IP routing implementation provides commands that display the following:

- The current state of the routing table, including the routing protocol that derived the route, the reliability of the source, the next IP address to send to, the router interface to use, whether the network is subnetted, whether the network in question is directly connected, and any routing metrics
- The current state of the active routing protocol process, including its update interval, metric weights (if applicable), active networks for which the routing process is functioning, and routing information sources
- The active accounting database, including the number of packets and bytes exchanged between particular sources and destinations
- The contents of the IP cache, including the destination IP address, the interface through which that destination is reached, the encapsulation method used, and the hardware address found at that destination
- IP-related interface parameters, including whether the interface and interface physical layer hardware are up, whether certain protocols (such as ICMP and Proxy ARP) are enabled, and the current security level
- IP-related protocol statistics, including the number of packets and number of errors received and sent by the following protocols: IP, TCP, UDP, EGP, BGP, IGRP, Enhanced IGRP, OSPF, IS-IS, ARP, DHCP, TN3270, and Probe
- Logging of all BGP, EGP, ICMP, IGRP, Enhanced IGRP, OSPF, IS-IS, RIP, TCP, and UDP transactions
- The number of intermediate hops taken as a packet traverses the network
- Reachability information between nodes

Summary

Cisco has added features to its IP implementation that optimize the performance of Cisco routers in larger, enterprise-wide internetworks.

Listing 8.6 in CH08CODE on the CD shows a sample session set up using NetBIOS over TCP/IP.

Questions

1. TCP is an acronym for _____.
   - **A.** Terminal Control Program
   - **B.** Transmission Control Protocol
   - **C.** Technical Connection Protocol
   - **D.** Transfer Control Point

2. IP is an acronym for _____.
   - **A.** Interface Program
   - **B.** Internal Protocol
   - **C.** Independent Path
   - **D.** Internet Protocol

3. TCP/IP was first implemented using the _____ operating system.
   - **A.** DOS
   - **B.** BSD UNIX
   - **C.** MVS
   - **D.** OS/2

4. IP is a _____ protocol.
   - **A.** Connection-oriented
   - **B.** Connectionless
   - **C.** Application-level
   - **D.** Media-Access Control

5. _____ provides a reliable delivery service.
   - **A.** IP
   - **B.** UDP
   - **C.** TCP
   - **D.** DLC

6. IP is implemented in _____ that connect networks and relay traffic between networks.
   - **A.** Repeaters
   - **B.** Bridges
   - **C.** Routers
   - **D.** Modems
   - **E.** Layer 3 Switches

7. The _____ protocol resolves higher level IP addresses to hardware physical addresses?
   - **A.** *Reverse Address Resolution Protocol* (RARP)
   - **B.** *Routing Information Protocol* (RIP)
   - **C.** *Address Resolution Protocol* (ARP)
   - **D.** *User Datagram Protocol* (UDP)

8. The *Simple Network Management Protocol* (SNMP) uses _____ protocol to deliver network management information.
   - **A.** *Management Information Base* (MIB)
   - **B.** *User Datagram Protocol* (UDP)
   - **C.** *Open Shortest Path First* (OSPF)
   - **D.** Transmission Control Protocol

9. Each IP version 4 datagram includes a _____ source and destination address.
   - **A.** 4-bit
   - **B.** 8-bit
   - **C.** 16-bit
   - **D.** 32-bit

10. _____ is a form of broadcasting in which a data packet is sent to a subset of all possible hosts on a network.
    - **A.** Multicasting
    - **B.** Subnetting
    - **C.** Partitioning
    - **D.** Masking

11. Each router in an internet maintains _____ that describe how other networks can be reached.
- **A.** class tables
- **B.** relational databases
- **C.** routing tables
- **D.** statistics

12. Datagrams are _____ if they cannot be delivered using IP in a reasonable period of time.
- **A.** retransmitted
- **B.** copied
- **C.** logged
- **D.** discarded
- **E.** forwarded
- **F.** don't care

13. During initial TCP session establishment, TCP uses a _____ between two end systems.
- **A.** 3-way handshake
- **B.** routing protocol
- **C.** 2-way handshake
- **D.** datagram service
- **E.** Token-Ring protocol

14. A _____ is used to connect an application to TCP/UDP in the transport layer.
- **A.** socket
- **B.** primitive
- **C.** port number
- **D.** logical unit

15. Identify the fields used in the TCP handshaking process.
- **A.** Urgent bit
- **B.** Final
- **C.** Sync
- **D.** Ack
- **E.** Push
- **F.** Reset

16. The _____ field is carried in the IP header and specifies the number of routing hops allowed before a datagram is discarded.
- **A.** TTL
- **B.** Window
- **C.** Checksum
- **D.** Protocol

17. The _____ field is used to tell the receiver how much data the sender will receive in the next transmission.
- **A.** TTL
- **B.** Window
- **C.** Fragment offset
- **D.** Options

18. Some fields in an IP header are used to control _____—the splitting of datagrams into smaller units.
- **A.** routing
- **B.** fragmentation
- **C.** encapsulation
- **D.** padding

19. The _____ and _____ identify the pair of sending and receiving programs.
- **A.** Code bits, data offset
- **B.** Sequence number, acknowledgement
- **C.** Checksum, urgent pointer
- **D.** Source, destination ports

20. The _____ fields in the TCP header is used to ensure that data is not lost.
- **A.** Urgent pointer
- **B.** Sequence number
- **C.** Window

21. _____in the TCP header is used for various control functions.
   A. Control bits
   B. Reserved bits
   C. Port numbers
   D. Sequence numbers

22. IP datagrams are _____in length.
   A. fixed   C. variable
   B. long   D. short

23. Which of the following is associated with the SMTP application layer service?
   A. Error control   C. Message services
   B. Connection identifier   D. Bit synchronization

24. The amount of time required to reach the destination network is called a _____.
   A. Lag   C. Hop
   B. Delay   D. Tick

25. The primary objective of the Network layer is to:
   A. Move information between multiple independent networks
   B. Deliver data to all devices attached to a single network
   C. Hide the intricacies of the network structure from upper-layer processes
   D. Organize the Physical layer bits into frames

26. Given the IP address 192.36.4.0, which of the following subnet masks would be proper for implementing sub-networks with 14 hosts on each subnet?
   A. 255.255.224.0   D. 255.255.255.240
   B. 255.255.248.0   E. 255.255.255.248
   C. 255.255.255.192

27. Which of the following is a secondary function of IP?
   A. Routing datagrams through the network
   B. Packet lifetime control
   C. Advertising known networks
   D. Discovering the MAC address associated with an IP address

28. Which of the following is an interior gateway protocol?
   A. RIP   E. IGRP
   B. EGP   F. E-IGRP
   C. PPP   G. IS-IS
   D. BGP

29. A destination address of 0.0.0.0 in an IP routing table signifies:
   A. Any manager can manage that router.
   B. All routes are unreachable.
   C. All routes are reachable.
   D. A default route

30. Which of the following protocols can be used to retrieve and load a Cisco IOS image file?

   A. RARP
   B. Telnet
   C. FTP
   D. TFTP
   E. BootP

31. RARP is used to obtain:

   A. A DLCI number
   B. An IP address
   C. A MAC address
   D. An AppleTalk address

32. Which of the following protocols provides terminal access through an IP network?

   A. UDP
   B. RARP
   C. Telnet
   D. FTP
   E. TFTP
   F. BootP

33. Which of the following is not categorized as an SNMP operation?

   A. Get
   B. Put
   C. Set
   D. Trap

34. A device that can send an SNMP trap message is an SNMP:

   A. Client
   B. Manager
   C. Mediator
   D. Agent

35. You are designing a network and have been assigned the address 201.14.6.0. You want to have six subnets and must be able to support 12 hosts. Which subnet masks meet your requirements?

   A. 255.255.255.240
   B. 255.255.255.128
   C. 255.255.255.224
   D. 255.255.255.248

36. You have been assigned a Class A address and intend to have eight subnets on your network. Which subnet mask would you use to maximize the number of hosts of each subnet?

   A. 255.255.255.0
   B. 255.0.0.0
   C. 255.240.0.0
   D. 255.255.240.0

37. Write the appropriate address class next to each IP address.

   A. 131.107.2.89   _____
   B. 3.3.57.0   _____
   C. 200.200.5.2   _____
   D. 191.107.2.10   _____

38. Which address class(es) will allow you to have more than 1000 hosts per network?

   A. Class A
   B. Class B
   C. Class C
   D. Class D
   E. All of the above

39. What is a domain name?

   A. The Microsoft implementation of a NetBIOS name server
   B. A test file in the same format as the 4.3 BSD UNIX file
   C. A hierarchical name that is implemented using a *Domain Name Server* (DNS)
   D. A flat name that is implemented using a *Domain Name Server* (DNS)

40. Which utility in TCP/IP communications is used to check connectivity between the Network Interface layer and the Internet layer?
    A. ARP
    B. NETSTAT
    C. PING
    D. NBTSTAT

41. What are two popular ways to troubleshoot a TCP/IP problem from a router?
    A. PING
    B. NETSTAT /a
    C. Establish a session
    D. Trace Route

42. What is the Protocol Identifier for RIP?
    A. Protocol number 17, Port Number 520
    B. Protocol number 6, Port number 520
    C. Protocol number 1, Port number 530
    D. None of the above

43. What is the Protocol Identifier for ARP?
    A. 20
    B. 16
    C. 8
    D. None of the above
    E. ARP doesn't use IP.

44. What is the NetBIOS Well know Port Number for Session Service?
    A. 138
    B. 137
    C. 139
    D. 135

45. Which command is used to add the classfull IP address 172.16.134.1 to an interface?
    A. `IP ADDRESS 172.16.134.1`
    B. `IP ADDRESS 172.16.134.1 255.255.0.0`
    C. `IP ADDRESS 172.16.134.1 255.255.255.0 SECONDARY`
    D. `IP-ADDRESS 172.16.134.1 255.255.255.0`

46. Which command is used to add a second IP address, of 192.168.14.1, to an interface?
    A. `IP ADDRESS 192.168.14.1`
    B. `IP ADDRESS 192.168.14.1 255.255.255.0`
    C. `IP ADDRESS 192.168.14.1 255.255.255.0 SECONDARY`
    D. Can't add a second IP address to an interface

47. Which command is used to add a third IP address, of 192.168.224.1, to a interface?
    A. `IP ADDRESS 192.168.224.1`
    B. `IP ADDRESS 192.168.224.1 255.255.255.0 TIRSHIARY`
    C. `IP ADDRESS 192.168.224.1 255.255.255.0 SECONDARY`
    D. Can't add a third IP address to an interface

48. With the display of 136.240.15.124/24, what does the /24 mean?
    A. There are 24 hosts per subnet.
    B. The mask is 255.255.255.0.
    C. The mask is invalid.
    D. The mask is 255.255.224.0.

49. What is the subnet address for the following host address and mask combination of 192.168.201.211 255.255.255.224?
   A. 192.168.201.0
   B. 192.168.201.192
   C. 192.168.201.128
   D. You can't subnet a class C address.

50. What is the subnet address for the following host address and mask combination of 172.16.224.211 255.255.224.0?
   A. 172.16.0.0
   B. 172.16.192.0
   C. This is an invalid address/mask combination.
   D. 172.16.224.0

51. What is the subnet and directed broadcast addresses for the following host address and mask combination of 127.166.224.5 255.255.252.0?
   A. Subnet of 127.166.224.0 and broadcast of 127.166.227.255
   B. Subnet of 127.166.192.0 and broadcast of 127.166.227.255
   C. Subnet of 127.166.224.0 and broadcast of 127.166.224.255
   D. 127.x.x.x is not available for hosts addresses.

52. What mask is required to subnet a class C address into at least 6 subnets, with at least 25 hosts per subnet?
   A. 255.255.255.224
   B. 255.255.255.248
   C. 255.255.255.252
   D. You can't subnet a class C address.

53. A class B address of 172.24.138.138 has a mask of 255.255.252.0. What is the subnet address and the directed broadcast address?
   A. Subnet of 172.24.138.0 and broadcast of 172.24.138.255
   B. Subnet of 172.24.136.0 and broadcast of 172.24.139.255
   C. Subnet of 172.24.136.0 and broadcast of 172.24.136.255
   D. Subnet of 172.24.138.0 and broadcast of 172.24.139.255

54. A class B address with a mask of 255.255.252.0 will give how many subnets and how many hosts per subnet?
   A. 62 subnets, with 1022 hosts each
   B. 64 subnets, with 1022 hosts each
   C. 62 subnets, with 1024 hosts each
   D. 1022 subnets, with 62 hosts each

55. Which of the following is not a function of TCP?
   A. Uses sequence and acknowledge numbers
   B. Uses window sizes for flow control
   C. Uses application layer for reliability

56. Which of the following is not part of the UDP header?
   A. Source Port   **C.** Urgent Pointer
   B. Length   **D.** Checksum

57. Which of the following is not part of the IP header?

    A. Source IP Address   **C.** Protocol

    B. Destination IP Address   **D.** Source Port

58. Which of the following is not a message from ICMP?

    A. Echo Reply   **D.** Stack overflow

    B. Destination Unreachable   **E.** Interface resets

    C. Buffer Full   **F.** Timestamp Reply

59. With three routers in the path between a client and a server, which router will return the destination unreachable message to the client if the server is down?

    A. The router closest to the client

    B. The router closest to the server

    C. The router between the other two routers

    D. None of the above

60. What is the purpose of RARP?

    A. Resolves the MAC to IP from a RARP server

    B. Resolves the IP to MAC from a RARP server

    C. There is no such thing as a RARP.

    D. RARP is another name for DHCP.

61. You have a device with the IP address of 10.232.165.12 with the mask of 255.255.255.248. The router has an address of 10.232.165.18. Is there a problem?

    A. No, there is no problem.

    B. Yes, the router should have an address of 10.232.165.1.

    C. Yes, the device is in subnet 10.232.165.8 and the router is in 10.232.165.16.

    D. Yes, the device is in subnet 10.232.165.0 and the router is in 10.232.165.16.

62 A class C with a mask of 255.255.255.248 will give how many subnets and how many hosts per subnet?

    A. 30 subnets, with 6 hosts each

    B. 32 subnets, with 6 hosts each

    C. 30 subnets, with 8 hosts each

    D. You can't subnet a class C.

63. How does a device operating in an IP environment resolve a destination layer three address to a layer two address?

    A. It uses an ARP request sent out as a broadcast and the owner of the address responds.

    B. The layer two address is the node portion of the layer three address.

    C. It uses DNS to resolve the addresses.

    D. It uses WINS to resolve the addresses.

64. You have a device with the IP address of 192.168.36.224/25, what is the subnet and directed broadcast for this device?

    A. Subnet of 192.168.26.0, broadcast of 192.168.36 255

    B. Subnet of 192.168.26.0, broadcast of 192.168.36 191

    C. Subnet of 192.168.26.192, broadcast of 192.168.36.255

    D. 192.168.36.224/25 is not a valid address/mask combination.

65. What is the range for Standard IP access list?

    A. 0–99

    B. 1–99

    C. 100–199

    D. 1–199

66. What is the command to apply IP access list 101 to an interface?

    A. `IP access-group 101`

    B. `IP access-list 101`

    C. `Access-list 101`

    D. `Access-group 101`

67. When applying an access list to an interface, what is the default for examining packets?

    A. Incoming IP packets

    B. Outgoing IP packets

    C. Both directions

    D. None of the above

68. What does the following access list command do? Access-list 1 permit 172.16.36.0 0.0.0.255

    A. Permits traffic originating from the 172.16.36.0 subnet

    B. Permits traffic distended for the 172.16.36.0 subnet

    C. Permits traffic to and from the 172.16.36.0 subnet

    D. This is an invalid statement.

69. What is the purpose of the following commands?

```
Access-list 1 deny 172.16.36.236 0.0.0.0
Access-list 1 permit 172.16.36.0 0.0.0.255
Access-list 1 deny any

Interface ethernet 0
Ip address 172.16.36.1 255.255.255.0
Ip access-group 1 in
```

    A. Blocks all traffic destined for the host 172.16.36.236, but allows all other traffic

    B. Blocks all traffic destined for the host 172.16.36.236, and only allows traffic for others on the 172.16.36.0 subnet

    C. Blocks all traffic originating from the host 172.16.36.236, but allows all other traffic

    D. Blocks all traffic originating from the host 172.16.36.236, and only allows traffic from others on the 172.16.36.0 subnet

70. Where and in which direction would you put a standard access list to block a device from accessing a specific subnet?

    A. As an inbound access list on the router interface servicing the devices subnet

    B. As an outbound access list on the router servicing the devices subnet, but on it's WAN interface

    C. As an outbound access list on the router interface servicing the subnet not to be accessed

    D. As an inbound access list on a core backbone router

71. What is the purpose of the following configuration commands?

```
Access-list 1 deny 136.146.27.236 0.0.0.0
Interface ethernet 0
Ip address 136.146.27.1 255.255.255.0
Ipx network 1f3c
Ip access-group 1 in
```

    A. Keeps traffic originating from 136.146.27.236 from being transmitting into ethernet 0

    B. Keeps traffic distended for 136.146.27.236 from being transmitted into ethernet 0

    C. Keeps all traffic originating from the ethernet from transmitting into ethernet 0

    D. Keeps all ip traffic originating from the ethernet from transmitting into ethernet 0

72. Is the following access list valid? Access-list 1 deny 136.146.27.236 0.0.0.0
   A. Yes, it's fine.
   B. No, there is an implied deny any at the end.
   C. None of the above

73. Which application service is an example of a connection oriented service?
   A. TFTP and FTP   C. TFTP and SNMP
   B. TELNET and FTP   D. None of the above

74. A station sending out an ARP request receives back a ARP response as a _____.
   A. Multicast address   C. Unicast address
   B. Broadcast address   D. None of the above

75. Which field in the IP header is used to give precedence and priority to different types of IP traffic flowing through the network.
   A. Version   D. Protocol
   B. Time to Live (TTL)   E. Flag
   C. Type of Service

76. Suppose the destination station is on a different LAN segment and a different subnet. The IP-to-hardware mapping is resolved using what function?
   A. ARP   D. BootP
   B. Proxy ARP   E. DHCP
   C. RARP

77. The TCP message unit format is called a _____.
   A. packet   C. segment
   B. frame   D. bit

78. The IP message unit format is called a _____.
   A. packet   C. segment
   B. frame   D. bit

79. What version of TCP/IP is currently used throughout the Internet?
   A. Version 4   C. Version 8
   B. Version 6   D. Version 3

80. TCP port number 23 represents _____.
   A. Telnet   C. SNMP
   B. FTP   D. WWW

81. In the type field of a Ethernet II frame the value 0x0806 represents _____.
   A. IP   C. ARP
   B. ICMP   D. RARP

82. A class A address is represented by how many bits in the network portion of the address?
   A. 8 bits   C. 24 bits
   B. 16 bits   D. None of the above

83. In this address 144.254.100.10 which portion makes up the network number?
    A. 144.0.0.0   C. 144.254.100.0
    B. 144.254.0.0   D. All of the above

84. Ping is a function of the following protocol?
    A. ARP   D. RARP
    B. Bootp   E. ICMP
    C. DHCP

85. Sequencing and acknowledgements of IP packets are a part of which header?
    A. Network layer header
    B. Transport layer connection-oriented header
    C. Transport layer connection-less header
    D. Session layer header
    E. Application layer Header

86. A TCP destination port number of 21 represents?
    A. Telnet   C. TFTP
    B. FTP   D. SMTP

87. A TCP destination port number of 25 represents?
    A. Telnet   C. TFTP
    B. Ftp   D. SMTP

88. An IP address is how many bytes in length?
    A. 8   C. 24
    B. 4   D. 16

89. The TCP/IP protocol uses the ____ to verify whether a segment was sent without any errors?
    A. Checksum Field   D. Sequence Number
    B. Window   E. Urgent pointer
    C. Acknowledgment   F. Frame check sequence (FCS)

90. A _____is defined using the internet address of a host and a port number.
    A. socket   C. sliding window
    B. well-known port   D. All of the above

91. UDP supports multiple processes within an end node called?
    A. Demultiplexing   C. Urgent Pointer
    B. Multiplexing   D. A & B

92. RIP Poison Reverse is a technique where a router advertises a route over the same network interface that supplied the route, but the route is sent with a metric of ___.
    A. 15   D. 64
    B. 16   E. None of the above
    C. 32

93. A Router sends this type of ICMP message to a source station if it cannot accept data at this time:
    A. Source-Quence   C. Host unreachable
    B. Time Exceeded   D. Redirect

94. A Router sends this type of ICMP message to a source station if it must fragment a packet?
     A. Redirect   **D.** Host should segment
     B. Destination unreachable   **E.** Fragmentation required
     C. Host unreachable

95. The Internet address 192.6.115.130 is considered a class ___ address
     A. A   **D.** D
     B. B   **E.** E
     C. C

96. The IP ___ field header determines if a packet may or may not be fragmented.
     A. Flag   **D.** MTU
     B. Time to live   **E.** Flag offset
     C. Type of service

97. A router sends which ICMP message if the Time to Live field is zero?
     A. Redirect   **D.** Time Exceeded
     B. Fragmentation Required   **E.** None of the Above
     C. Parameter Problems

98. You use this mask to indicate that the entire second octet of a Class A address will be used to specify subnets:
     A. 255.0.0.0   **D.** 255.224.255.0
     B. 255.255.255.0   **E.** 255.255.0.0
     C. 255.255.255.255

99. TCP Header compression is useful for what type of networks?
     A. Small packets   **C.** Ethernet Networks only
     B. FTP File transfers   **D.** UDP Only packets

100. What is the Ethernet type field for ARP Request and Reply?
     A. 0x0806   **C.** 0x0800
     B. 0x8035   **D.** 0x8137

101. Identify the Type of Service field options.
     A. Delay   **D.** Cost
     B. Throughput   **E.** All of the above
     C. Reliability

102. A router will return this ICMP message if it doesn't know how to reach a given destination network?
     A. Host unreachable   **C.** Time exceeded
     B. Destination unreachable   **D.** Information rely

103. A class D IP address range from?
     A. 224.0.0.1 to 239.255.255.255
     B. 224.0.0.0 to 239.255.255.255
     C. 224.0.0.2 to 238.255.255.255
     D. 223.0.0.0 to 239.255.255.255

104. A Class D IP address of 243.0.0.1 would map into the Multicast Ethernet address of _____.
   A. 02608c123456   **C.** 01:5e:00:00:00:01
   B. 01:00:5e:00:00:01   **D.** Invalid Class D Address

105. FTP uses which of the following port numbers?
   A. 20   **C.** 69
   B. 21   **D.** 111

106. SNMP message uses which port number?
   A. 161   **C.** 137
   B. 138   **D.** 54

107. Identify the illegal subnet mask.
   A. 255.255.255.254   **C.** 255.255.255.128
   B. 255.255.255.0   **D.** 255.255.255.192

108. Convert the 8 bit binary number to decimal—10110101.
   A. 145   **C.** 191
   B. 139   **D.** 181

109. Identify the illegal subnet mask for a Class C network.
   A. 255.255.255.0   **C.** 255.255.255.224
   B. 255.255.255.194   **D.** 255.255.255.192

110. How many bits are available for subnetting in a Class B address.
   A. 16   **C.** 6
   B. 8   **D.** 14

111. Find the subnet for the IP address 192.9.200.43 subnet mask—255.255.255.248.
   A. 192.9.200.0   **C.** 192.9.200.32
   B. 192.9.200.8   **D.** 192.9.200.40

112. Find the first valid host address for the Class A address 10.0.0.0 with a subnet 255.255.0.0.
   A. 10.1.0.1   **C.** 10.0.0.1
   B. 10.1.1.1   **D.** 10.0.1.1

113. Find the first valid host address for the Class C address 192.9.200.0 with a subnet that will provide 14 host per network and 14 networks.
   A. 192.9.200.16   **C.** 192.9.200.1
   B. 192.9.200.31   **D.** 192.9.200.17

114. What is the broadcast address for the network 192.9.200.48 subnet mask 255.255.255.248?
   A. 192.9.200.63   **C.** 192.9.200.255
   B. 192.9.200.55   **D.** 192.9.200.127

115. What is the broadcast address for the network 172.16.192.0 subnet mask 255.255.255.0?
   A. 172.16.255.255   **C.** 172.16.192.255
   B. 172.16.223.255   **D.** 172.16.199.255

116. Find the valid host addresses for the first subnet with a Class C address of 192.9.200.0 and a subnet mask of 255.255.255.224.
  A. 192.9.200.17-31
  B. 192.9.200.33-62
  C. 192.9.200.65-127
  D. 192.9.200.49-53

117. What kind of address is 10.3.3.1 subnet mask 255.255.0.0?
  A. A broadcast address
  B. A subnet number
  C. A valid host address
  D. Invalid

118. What kind of address is 10.255.3.3 subnet mask 255.255.0.0?
  A. A broadcast address
  B. A subnet number
  C. A valid host address
  D. Invalid

119. What kind of address is 172.16.47.255 subnet mask 255.255.248.0?
  A. A broadcast address
  B. A subnet number
  C. A valid host address
  D. Invalid

120. What kind of address is 10.252.3.255 subnet mask 255.255.0.0?
  A. A broadcast address
  B. A subnet number
  C. A valid host address
  D. Invalid

121. What kind of address is 192.9.200.127 subnet mask 255.255.255.224?
  A. A broadcast address
  B. A subnet number
  C. A valid host address
  D. Invalid

122. If you are using VLSM what is the best subnet mask to use for point to point links?
  A. It depends on the Class address.
  B. 255.255.255.254
  C. 255.255.255.253
  D. 255.255.255.252

123. Which routing protocols support VLSM?
  A. OSPF, EIGRP, BGP
  B. RIP, OSPF, EIGRP
  C. BGP, IGRP, EIGRP
  D. OSPF, ODR,NLSP, EIGRP

124. You are given 172.16.1.32 /27. You have 2 networks connected over a PPP serial link with 6 hosts on each network. Which of the following will provide a solution (6 address in each subnet and 2 host addresses on the PPP link)?
  A. 172.16.1.32 /30, 172.16.1.40 /29, 172.16.1.48 /29
  B. 172.16.1.32 /29, 172.16.1.36 /30, 172.16.1.40 /29
  C. 172.16.1.32 /30. 172.16.1.36 /29, 172.16.1.48 /29
  D. 172.16.1.32 /30, 172.16.1.40 /28, 172.16.1.48 /29

125. You are given 10.1.1.128 /25, you have 3 networks connected to each other using PPP serial links. You have 14 hosts at each site. What are the subnet mask that you will need to use?
  A. /27 at each site and /30 for each PPP link
  B. /28 at each site and /30 for each PPP link
  C. /29 at each site and /30 for each PPP link
  D. /26 at each site and /30 for each PPP link

126. Which is the best way to summarize the following addresses: 192.9.17.22, 192.9.30.203, 192.9.17.232, 192.9.21.9?

    A. 192.9.0.0–255.255.0.0

    B. 192.9.16.0–255.255.240.0

    C. 192.9.8.0–255.255.248.0

    D. 192.9.64.0–255.255.224.0

You will use the following TCP Show commands to answer the questions which follow.

```
Ethernet0 ip address 192.168.21.1 255.255.255.0
 no ip split-horizon
!
interface Ethernet1
 ip address 192.168.29.1 255.255.255.0
 no ip split-horizon
!
interface Serial0
 ip address 192.168.22.1 255.255.255.0
 ip access-group 100 in
 no ip split-horizon
!
router rip
 redistribute igrp 200
 network 192.168.21.0
 network 192.168.22.0
!
router igrp 200
 redistribute rip
 network 192.168.29.0
!
no ip classless
access-list 100 deny    tcp any any eq telnet
access-list 100 permit ip any any
access-list 100 permit icmp any any
!
line con 0
line aux 0
line vty 0 4
 password cisco
 login
end
```

127. The access list in this configuration will:

    A. Discard all telnet session from exiting out of interface S0

    B. Deny all telnet session from entering interface S0

    C. Discard all telnet session on all interfaces

    D. None of the above

128. What type of access list is this?

    A. IPX sap filtering   **C.** IP extended access list

    B. IP standard access list   **D.** IP enhance access list

129. What interface is the access list applied to?

    A. Interface E1   **C.** Interface S0

    B. Interface E0   **D.** Interface S1

130. Why is the command `access-list 100 permit ip any any` needed?
  A. To allow telnet session from other locations
  B. Use as a catch all, after telnet has been denied
  C. Permit IP routing
  D. None of the above

131. Why in the command `ip access-group 100 in` must you supply the keyword?
  A. Because outgoing is default
  B. It denies every telnet packet from entering in any port.
  C. If it is not specified, you will receive invalid configuration.
  D. None of the above

```
ATLANTA#telnet 192.168.26.1
Trying 192.168.26.1 ... Open


Password required, but none set

[Connection to 192.168.26.1 closed by foreign host]
```

132. What can you do to allow a telnet session to host 192.168.26.1?
  A. Ping the host first.
  B. Assign a vty password on the host telnet ports.
  C. Reload the host.
  D. None of the above

```
SEATTLE#ping 192.168.29.1Type escape sequence to abort.Sending 5, 100-byte ICMP
Echoes to 192.168.29.1, timeout is 2 seconds:.!!!!Success rate is 100 percent
(5/5), round-trip min/avg/max = 32/35/36 ms
```

133. What is the meaning of .!!!!?
  A. Destination host could not be reached.
  B. The first ping out of 5 timed out because of an ARP.
  C. The destination host could not be reached.
  D. None of the above

134. Identify which protocols that support ARP functions.
  A. CLNS, AppleTalk, IPX   **D.** IP only
  B. SNA, NetBIOS/NetBEUI   **E.** None of the above
  C. IP, AppleTalk, Vines IP

The TCP/IP trace below will be used to for the following questions.

135. What type of connection is being established in the following trace?
  A. ICMP   **C.** TCP 3-way handshake
  B. IP DNS request   **D.** TCP 2 way handshake

```
DLC:  —- DLC Header —-
DLC:
DLC:  Frame 1 arrived at   11:52:06.5391; frame size is 48 (0030 hex) bytes.
DLC:  Destination = DCE
DLC:  Source = DTE
DLC:
```

```
ROUTER: —- Cisco Router/Bridge —-
ROUTER:
ROUTER: Header = 0F000800
ROUTER:
IP:     —- IP Header —-
IP:
IP:     Version = 4, header length = 20 bytes
IP:     Type of service = 00
IP:         000. .... = routine
IP:         ...0 .... = normal delay
IP:         .... 0... = normal throughput
IP:         .... .0.. = normal reliability
IP:     Total length    = 44 bytes
IP:     Identification  = 0
IP:     Flags           = 0X
IP:         .0.. .... = may fragment
IP:         ..0. .... = last fragment
IP:     Fragment offset = 0 bytes
IP:     Time to live    = 255 seconds/hops
IP:     Protocol        = 6 (TCP)
IP:     Header checksum = A0A8 (correct)
IP:     Source address      = [137.144.4.2]
IP:     Destination address = [137.144.4.1]
IP:     No options
TCP:    —- TCP header —-
TCP:    Source port         = 11005
TCP:    Destination port    = 179 (BGP)
TCP:    Initial sequence number = 736698698
TCP:    Data offset         = 24 bytes
TCP:    Flags               = 02
TCP:                ..0. .... = (No urgent pointer)
TCP:                ...0 .... = (No acknowledgment)
TCP:                .... 0... = (No push)
TCP:                .... .0.. = (No reset)
TCP:                .... ..1. = SYN
TCP:                .... ...0 = (No FIN)
TCP:    Window              = 16384
TCP:    Checksum            = C41F (correct)
TCP:
TCP:    Options follow
TCP:    Maximum segment size    = 1460
TCP:
- - - - - - - - - - - - - - - Frame 2 - - - - - - - - - - - - - - - -

DLC:    —- DLC Header —-
DLC:
DLC:    Frame 2 arrived at   11:52:06.5391; frame size is 48 (0030 hex) bytes.
DLC:    Destination = DTE
DLC:    Source = DCE
DLC:
ROUTER: —- Cisco Router/Bridge —-
ROUTER:
ROUTER: Header = 0F000800
ROUTER:
IP:     —- IP Header —-
IP:
IP:     Version = 4, header length = 20 bytes
IP:     Type of service = 00
IP:         000. .... = routine
IP:         ...0 .... = normal delay
IP:         .... 0... = normal throughput
```

```
IP:          .... .0.. = normal reliability
IP:    Total length    = 44 bytes
IP:    Identification  = 0
IP:    Flags           = 0X
IP:          .0.. .... = may fragment
IP:          ..0. .... = last fragment
IP:    Fragment offset = 0 bytes
IP:    Time to live    = 255 seconds/hops
IP:    Protocol        = 6 (TCP)
IP:    Header checksum = A0A8 (correct)
IP:    Source address      = [137.144.4.1]
IP:    Destination address = [137.144.4.2]
IP:    No options
IP:
TCP:   ---- TCP header ----
TCP:
TCP:   Source port             = 179 (BGP)
TCP:   Destination port        = 11005
TCP:   Initial sequence number = 257022771
TCP:   Acknowledgment number   = 736698699
TCP:   Data offset             = 24 bytes
TCP:   Flags                   = 12
TCP:               ..0. .... = (No urgent pointer)
TCP:               ...1 .... = Acknowledgment
TCP:               .... 0... = (No push)
TCP:               .... .0.. = (No reset)
TCP:               .... ..1. = SYN
TCP:               .... ...0 = (No FIN)
TCP:   Window                  = 16384
TCP:   Checksum                = D989 (correct)
TCP:
TCP:   Options follow
TCP:   Maximum segment size    = 1460
TCP:
- - - - - - - - - - - - - - - Frame 3 - - - - - - - - - - - - - - - - - -


DLC:   ---- DLC Header ----
DLC:
DLC:   Frame 3 arrived at  11:52:06.5391; frame size is 44 (002C hex) bytes.
DLC:   Destination = DCE
DLC:   Source = DTE
DLC:
ROUTER: ---- Cisco Router/Bridge ----
ROUTER:
ROUTER: Header = 0F000800
ROUTER:
IP:    ---- IP Header ----
IP:
IP:    Version = 4, header length = 20 bytes
IP:    Type of service = 00
IP:          000. .... = routine
IP:          ...0 .... = normal delay
IP:          .... 0... = normal throughput
IP:          .... .0.. = normal reliability
IP:    Total length    = 40 bytes
IP:    Identification  = 1
IP:    Flags           = 0X
IP:          .0.. .... = may fragment
IP:          ..0. .... = last fragment
IP:    Fragment offset = 0 bytes
IP:    Time to live    = 255 seconds/hops
```

```
IP:     Protocol       = 6 (TCP)
IP:     Header checksum = A0AB (correct)
IP:     Source address     = [137.144.4.2]
IP:     Destination address = [137.144.4.1]
IP:     No options
IP:
TCP:    —- TCP header —-
TCP:
TCP:    Source port          = 11005
TCP:    Destination port     = 179 (BGP)
TCP:    Sequence number      = 736698699
TCP:    Acknowledgment number  = 257022772
TCP:    Data offset          = 20 bytes
TCP:    Flags              = 10
TCP:               ..0. .... = (No urgent pointer)
TCP:               ...1 .... = Acknowledgment
TCP:               .... 0... = (No push)
TCP:               .... .0.. = (No reset)
TCP:               .... ..0. = (No SYN)
TCP:               .... ...0 = (No FIN)
TCP:    Window             = 16384
TCP:    Checksum           = F146 (correct)
TCP:    No TCP options
TCP:
- - - - - - - - - - - - - - - Frame 4 - - - - - - - - - - - - - - - -


DLC:    —- DLC Header —-
DLC:
DLC:    Frame 4 arrived at   11:52:06.5391; frame size is 73 (0049 hex) bytes.
DLC:    Destination = DCE
DLC:    Source = DTE
DLC:
ROUTER: —- Cisco Router/Bridge —-
ROUTER:
ROUTER: Header = 0F000800
ROUTER:
IP:     —- IP Header —-
IP:
IP:     Version = 4, header length = 20 bytes
IP:     Type of service = C0
IP:           110. .... = internetwork control
IP:           ...0 .... = normal delay
IP:           .... 0... = normal throughput
IP:           .... .0.. = normal reliability
IP:     Total length    = 69 bytes
IP:     Identification  = 2
IP:     Flags           = 0X
IP:           .0.. .... = may fragment
IP:           ..0. .... = last fragment
IP:     Fragment offset = 0 bytes
IP:     Time to live    = 1 seconds/hops
IP:     Protocol        = 6 (TCP)
IP:     Header checksum = 9DCE (correct)
IP:     Source address     = [137.144.4.2]
IP:     Destination address = [137.144.4.1]
IP:     No options
IP:
TCP:    —- TCP header —-
TCP:
TCP:    Source port          = 11005
TCP:    Destination port     = 179 (BGP)
```

```
TCP:    Sequence number            = 736698699
TCP:    Acknowledgment number      = 257022772
TCP:    Data offset                = 20 bytes
TCP:    Flags                      = 18
TCP:                   ..0. .... = (No urgent pointer)
TCP:                   ...1 .... = Acknowledgment
TCP:                   .... 1... = Push
TCP:                   .... .0.. = (No reset)
TCP:                   .... ..0. = (No SYN)
TCP:                   .... ...0 = (No FIN)
TCP:    Window                     = 16384
TCP:    Checksum                   = 6056 (correct)
TCP:    No TCP options
TCP:    [29 byte(s) of data]
TCP:
```

Answers

1. B
2. D
3. B
4. B
5. C
6. C, E
7. C
8. B
9. D
10. A
11. C
12. D
13. A
14. D
15. C
16. A
17. B
18. B
19. D
20. B, C
21. A
22. C
23. C
24. B
25. A, C
26. D
27. B
28. A, E, F, G
29. D
30. D
31. B
32. C
33. B
34. D
35. A
36. C
37.
IP Address	Address Class
131.107.2.89	B
3.3.57.0	A
200.200.5.2	C
191.107.2.10	B
38. A, B
39. C
40. C
41. A, D
42. A
43. E
44. C
45. B
46. C

47. C
48. B
49. B
50. D
51. D
52. A
53. B
54. B
55. C
56. C
57. D
58. C, D, E
59. B
60. A
61. C
62. A
63. A
64. D
65. B
66. A
67. B
68. A
69. D
70. C
71. A
72. B
73. B
74. C
75. C
76. B
77. C
78. A
79. A
80. A
81. C
82. A
83. B
84. E
85. B
86. B
87. D
88. B
89. A, C
90. A
91. A
92. B
93. A
94. E
95. C
96. A
97. D

98.	E
99.	A, B
100.	A
101.	E
102.	B
103.	B
104.	D
105.	A, B
106.	A
107.	A
108.	D
109.	B
110.	D
111.	D
112.	C
113.	D
114.	B
115.	C
116.	B
117.	C
118.	D
119.	A
120.	C
121.	A
122.	B
123.	A
124.	A
125.	B
126.	B
127.	B
128.	C
129.	C
130.	B
131.	A
132.	B
133.	B
134.	C
135.	C

Routing Information Protocol (RIP)

The key to understanding how Cisco routers work is understanding the routing protocols that serve as a foundation in today's networks. The *Routing Information Protocol* (RIP) is a method of routing with great longevity. Although other routing protocols and methodologies of routing have gained favor in the market, RIP is still widely used.

RIP gauges network efficiency by the number of stops on the data path. Each device is counted as a *hop*; the fewer the hops, the more efficient the path. In a way, this assumes democracy on the network, and it is a very effective routing protocol if bandwidth is equal in different parts of the network. However, one can imagine that if a particular network segment represents a bottleneck or has low bandwidth, some of the efficiency of RIP is lost.

Routers that use RIP build a table of devices on the network. This table is the basis for routing decisions. At any given time, any router knows about any other router on the network, and thus the router has all the information it needs to make decisions about routing paths.

In this chapter, you will learn about the distance-vector algorithm and how it relates to RIP's functionality. We will discuss how RIP builds a routing table and how this information is updated throughout a network. Also covered is the actual RIP routing table format.

RIP has inherent stability features, which you learn about in this chapter. RIP-specific information on hop-count limits, hold-downs, split horizons, and poison reverse updates is included.

We also discuss the future of RIP. What are the limitations of RIP? How does RIP 2 compare to RIP 1? Will RIP survive into the next millennium?

RIP is a distance-vector protocol that enables IP routers in the same autonomous system to exchange routing information by means of periodic RIP updates. IP routers use the information in the RIP updates to keep their internal routing tables current. For RIP 1, the *best* path to a destination is the shortest path (the path with the fewest hops). RIP computes distance as a metric, usually the number of hops (or routers) from the origin network to the target network.

RIP Limitations

RIP has the following limitations. These limitations apply to both RIPv1 and RIPv2.

- Limits an *Autonomous System* (AS) diameter to 15 hops.
- Can result in suboptimal routing because the hop count cannot adequately describe variations in a path's characteristics.
- Finds new routes slowly when the network changes. This search consumes considerable bandwidth, and, in extreme cases, exhibits a slow convergence behavior referred to as a count to infinity.

RIP has become a de facto standard for the exchange of routing information among gateways, routers, and hosts. RIP is implemented for this purpose by most commercial vendors of IP routers, and operating system vendors included RIP with their TCP/IP implementations.

This protocol is more useful as a interior routing protocol in local network environments. In the current Internet, we could not scale the Internet using RIP as a single routing protocol for the whole network. Rather, the network is organized as a collection of *autonomous systems*. An autonomous system generally is administered by a single entity, or at least has some reasonable degree of technical and administrative control. With each autonomous system is a routing protocol, or protocols, that exports routes out to other autonomous systems. The routing protocol used within an autonomous system is referred to as an *interior gateway protocol* (IGP). A separate protocol is used to interface among the autonomous systems. The earliest such protocol, still used in the Internet, is *exterior gateway protocol* (EGP), but this exterior protocol has been replaced by *Border Gateway Routing Protocol* (BGP). Such protocols are now usually referred to as inter-AS routing protocols. RIP was designed to work with moderate-size networks using reasonably homogeneous technology.

RIP is intended for use within the IP-based Internet. The Internet is organized into a number of networks connected by routers. The networks may be either point-to-point links or more complex networks. Routing is the method by which the host or gateway decides where to send the datagram. It may be able to send the datagram directly to the destination, if that destination is on one of the networks directly connected to the host or gateway. However, the interesting case is when the destination is not directly reachable. In this case, the host or gateway attempts to send the datagram to a gateway nearer the destination. The goal of a routing protocol is very simple. It is to supply the information needed to find the shortest path between source and destination networks.

This protocol does not solve every possible routing problem. As mentioned, RIP is primarily intended for use as an IGP, in reasonably homogeneous networks of moderate size. In addition, the protocol is limited to networks whose longest path involves 15 hops.

RIP advertises only network addresses and distances (number of hops). It uses a hop count to compute the route cost, but it uses a maximum value of 16 to indicate that a network is unreachable. RIP requires information on all networks within the autonomous system. RIP exchanges information only with neighbors. Devices that participate in RIP operations are either active or passive devices. Active devices (usually gateways) advertise and receive routes to other devices; passive devices (usually host computers) do not advertise routes but receive messages and update their routing tables.

The hop count is a metric for the cost of the route. Other metrics can be used, such as delay, security, and bandwidth, but most implementations use a simple hop count. RIP uses UDP port 520 to send and receive RIP messages. Each device that uses RIP must have a routing table. The table contains an entry for each destination serviced by the device. Each entry in the table must contain at least the following information:

- Destination IP address
- A metric between 1 and 15 (16 is unusable) of the cost (number of hops) to reach the destination
- IP address of the next gateway in the path to the destination
- Indicators to determine whether the route has changed recently

Let's examine what happens when a datagram is sent from source to destination. If the source and destination are in the same autonomous system, it is advertised by IGP. If the destination is in another autonomous system, however, the datagram should be transferred to that autonomous system. The datagram will be delivered by that system's IGP routers.

A more practical way is having many routers, each connected to a few autonomous systems. Suppose that a datagram is sent from one autonomous system to another. The router of the first autonomous system transfers the datagram to that autonomous system (if it can) or transfers the datagram to another router that knows how to reach the destination. Eventually, the datagram reaches a router with a connection to that autonomous system, and the datagram is transferred correctly.

This way requires each router to hold a database of all the possible destinations. Each entry in the database should hold the next router to which datagrams should be sent. This way could work very well. Alas, the network cannot be kept still. New routers can be installed; old routers can crash; and crashed routers can come up. Therefore, our connection through a router is not guaranteed. Even if the router doesn't crash, a new router may be installed, providing better path.

We have to define what we mean by saying that one line is better than the other. A connection can be measured in many ways: by the dollar cost, the number of hops in the way, the error rate, latency, etc. We assume that a connection is measured by the number of hops in its path. This assumption is in no way obligatory; any system administrator can define a measure of his own. We treat measure as costs; the lower the number associated with the connection, the better. RIP treats any number higher than 15 as infinity (16). This method of calculating the cost is called *metric*.

After a router is installed, or started, it should send messages to all of its neighbors. This is necessary to update their tables.

The RIP algorithm sends update messages every 30 seconds. Every update message contains a list of the networks the routers know to reach and their metrics. If the metric in an update message is lower than the metric in the router's table, the router updates the metric and the next hop fields in its table. If, for some destination, an update comes from the next hop, indicating a different metric, the metric in the table should be changed. This change is necessary because if the metric changes in the next hop, we must change the metric in our router as well, which guarantees correct performance. However, this performance is not good enough.

Split Horizon

The occurrence of loops between two routers may be greatly reduced by the use of Split Horizon. The problem of the mutual deception can be overcome by being careful about where routing information is sent. Split Horizon is a technique in which a router does not propagate a route over the same interface that supplied the route. A router does not advertise network reachability to a neighbor from which the route was learned.

Triggered Updates

Split Horizon with *poison reverse* is a technique in which a router propagates a route over the same interface that supplied the route, but the route is identified as unreachable by providing a hop count of 16. A router claims a network as unreachable to a neighbor from which the route was learned. In a static sense, advertising reverse routes with a metric of 16 does not provide any additional information. However, advertising reverse routes improves dynamic behavior when many routers share a single broadcast network. When the topology changes, mentioning routes that should not go through a router as well as those that should can speed up convergence which happens because erroneous routes do not have to be eliminated by waiting for a time-out. Generally, poison reverse is an option that may be enabled or disabled by the network administrator. The major disadvantage of poison reverse is that it increases the size of the routing update messages as well as the size of the routers' routing tables. The network manager may be willing to accept a slower convergence to reduce the overhead of the routing table update messages.

Split Horizon with poisoned reverse breaks any loop of two routers. However, loops of three or more routers can still occur. This loop breaks only when infinity will be reached. Triggered updates are an attempt to speed up this convergence. To imply triggered updates, we add a rule that whenever a router changes the metric of a route, it is required to send update messages almost immediately. The triggered update messages are sent even if it is not time for the regular update message. The ones that updated their tables send their own update messages. Some of the neighbors' neighbors update their tables and send their own update messages. The update messages propagate back, until they reach a portion of the network that uses another route to connect to the target.

Route States

A route learned through RIP may go through a series of stages as it attempts to remain active in the routing table. A typical implementation would have the stages as depicted in Figure 9.1.

UP

A route is considered UP if it is reachable with a finite (15 or less) metric. The route remains UP for six times the value of the user configurable update interval. This value is known as the *route timer*. The route timer is reset each time a new update for the route is received. If the route timer expires, the route enters the GARBAGE-COLLECTION state.

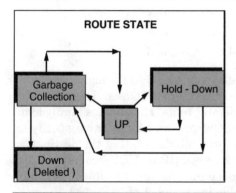

FIGURE 9.1 RIP routing state

GARBAGE Collection

When the timer for a route that has to be UP expires, the route changes to the GARBAGE COLLECTION state. The route may remain in this state for a length of time equal to four times the value of the update interval. This value is known as the Garbage Collection timer. If no updates are received before the Garbage Collection timer expires, the route is deleted from the routing table. If a neighboring router advertises the route with a finite metric, the route returns to an UP state with the new metric and a new next hop router.

Hold-Down

A route in an UP state changes to a hold-down state if the router receives a RIP update for the route with an infinite metric (16 hops) from the router that originally reported the route. The route may remain in this state for a period of time equal to four times the value of the update interval. This value is known as the hold-down timer. Hold-down forces a router to ignore information about a network for the specified length of time following the receipt of a message that claims the network to be unreachable. If the hold-down timer expires, the route enters the GARBAGE-COLLECTION state.

   If a RIP update message containing a finite entry for the hold-down route is received from the original router before the hold-down timer expires, the route can go back to an UP state. The purpose of the hold-down state is to allow time for all other routers in the autonomous system to receive the news that the route is down and not have the router in hold-down state mistakenly accept an out-of-date message.

1. The router receives a RIP update message with an infinite metric from the neighbor that was the original source of the route.

2. The route timer expires before the router receives a RIP update for the route.

3. An update with a finite metric is received from the original router supplying the route before the hold-down timer expires.

4. The hold-down timer expires before the router receives a RIP update message from the original source of the route containing a finite metric.

5. The router receives a RIP update with a finite metric before the GARBAGE-COLLECTION timer expires.

6. The GARBAGE-COLLECTION timer expires, and the route is deleted.

The RIP Header portion of the datagram from the address family field through metric may appear up to 25 times. The IP address is the usual 4-octet Internet address, in network order. The special address 0.0.0.0 is used to describe a default route. The address family identifier for IP is 2. The metric field must contain a value between 1 and 15 inclusive, specifying the current metric for the destination, or the value 16, which indicates that the destination is not reachable. The maximum datagram size is 512 octets. (IP or UDP headers are not counted.) Every datagram contains a command, a version number, and possible arguments.

Listed here is a summary of the commands available in version 1 of RIP:

- **request**   A request for the responding system to send all or part of its routing table

- **response**   A message containing all or part of the sender's routing table. This message may be sent in response to a request or poll, or it may be an update message generated by the sender.

- **traceon**   Obsolete; messages containing this command are to be ignored.

- **traceoff**   Obsolete; messages containing this command are to be ignored.

- **reserved**   This value is used by Sun Microsystems for its own purposes. If new commands are added in any succeeding version, they should begin with 6. Messages containing this command may safely be ignored by implementations that do not choose to respond to it.

For request and response, the rest of the datagram contains a list of destinations, with information about each. Each entry in this list contains a destination network or host, and the metric for it. The packet format is intended to allow RIP to carry routing information for several different protocols. Thus, each entry has an address family identifier to indicate what type of address is specified in that entry. The address family identifier for IP is 2. None of the RIP implementations available to the author implement any other type of address. However, to allow for future development, implementations are required to skip entries that specify address families not supported by the implementation. (The size of these entries is the same as the size of an entry specifying an IP address.) Processing of the message continues normally after any unsupported entries are skipped. The IP address is the usual Internet address, stored as 4 octets in network order. The maximum datagram size is 512 octets, which includes only the portions of the datagram described. This size does not count the IP or UDP headers. The commands that involve network information allow information to be split across several datagrams. No special provisions are needed for continuations, because correct results occur if the datagrams are processed individually.

RIPv1 Commands

RIP is built using connectionless UDP. Each router that uses RIP transmits and accepts datagrams on UDP port number 520. The complete RIP update message, including header and data, is encapsulated as the data portion of a UDP packet. The complete UDP message, including the header and data (containing the RIP data), is encapsulated in an IP header datagram. The Data Link layer is responsible for transferring data between two hosts or routers on the same physical network using link layer topologies such as Ethernet, Token Ring, FDDI, and ATM.

This field is used to specify the purpose of the datagram. The command is generally either a RIP Request (1) or a RIP Response (2). Other commands exist, but they are obsolete and thus no longer used. The router broadcasts unsolicited response packets every UpdateTime. Figure 9.2 illustrates the IP RIP header and its fields.

- *Version.*   This field contains the protocol version number. It verifies that the packet is processed correctly by the receiving router.

- *Address Family Identifier.*   The RIP packet format is intended to carry routing information for several different protocols. Each entry has an address family identifier to indicate the type of address for that entry. The address family identifier for IP is 2.

- *IP Address.*   This field contains the IP address stored as four octets in network order. It may contain a host address, a network number, a subnet number, or 0 to indicate a default route. The RIP packet format does not distinguish among these various types of addresses.

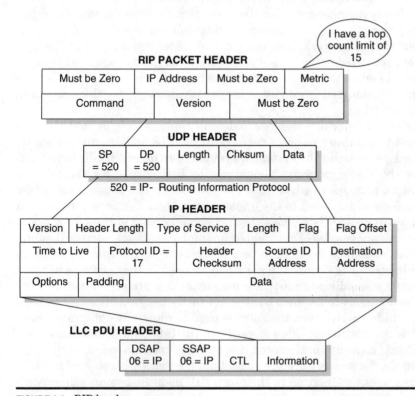

FIGURE 9.2   RIP header

- *Must Be Zero.*   These fields are actually part of the address field but are not used because IP addressing consumes only four octets. As a result, these unused octets are padded with 0s. Note that RIP can carry network addresses up to 12 octets in length.

- *Hop Count.*   This field specifies the current metric for the specified network address. It contains a value of 16 if the network is unreachable.

Addressing Considerations

The RIP packet formats do not distinguish among various types of addresses. Fields labeled "address" can contain any of the following:

- host address
- subnet number
- network number
- 0, indicating a default route

When routing a datagram, its destination address must first be checked against the list of host addresses. Then it must be checked to see whether it matches any known subnet or network number. Finally, if none of these match, the default route is used.

Border gateways send only a single entry for the network as a whole to hosts in other networks; a border gateway sends different information to different neighbors. For neighbors connected to the subnetted network, a border gateway generates a list of all subnets to which it is directly connected, using the subnet number. For neighbors connected to other networks, it makes a single entry for the network as a whole, showing the metric associated with that network. (This metric normally is the smallest metric for the subnets to which the gateway is attached.)

The special address 0.0.0.0 is used to describe a default route. A default route is used when it is not convenient to list every possible network in the RIP updates and when one or more closely connected gateways in the system are prepared to handle traffic to the networks not listed explicitly. These gateways should create RIP entries for the address 0.0.0.0, just as if it were a network to which they are connected. The decision as to how gateways create entries for 0.0.0.0 is left to the implementor. Most commonly, the system administrator is given a way to specify which gateways should create entries for 0.0.0.0. However, other mechanisms are possible. For example, an implementor may decide that any gateway that speaks EGP should be declared to be a default gateway. It may be useful to allow the network administrator to choose the metric to be used in these entries. If more than one default gateway exists, the administrator may express a preference for one over the other. The entries for 0.0.0.0 are handled by RIP in exactly the same manner as if an actual network had this address. However, the entry is used to route any datagram whose destination address does not match any other network in the table. Implementations are not required to support this convention. However, it is strongly recommended.

Implementations that do not support 0.0.0.0 must ignore entries with this address. In such cases, they must not pass the entry on in their own RIP updates. System administrators should take care to make sure that routes to 0.0.0.0 do not propagate further than is intended. Generally, each autonomous system has its own preferred default gateway. Thus, routes involving o.o.o.o should generally not leave the boundary of an autonomous system.

RIP Timers

Two timers are associated with each route: a time-out timer and a garbage-collection timer. The time-out timer is set each time a route is initialized or updated. If 180 seconds elapse before an update is received or if the update contains a distance metric of 16, the route is considered obsolete. The route is not removed, however, until the garbage-collection timer has also expired. This timer is set for another 60 seconds, and after it expires, the route is removed from the routing table. The route continues to be included in all update messages until the garbage collection timer expires. If there are no updates after 240 seconds, the router removes all routing table entries for such routes.

Another timer is used to send updates (called *responses in RIP*) to neighboring machines. Every 30 seconds, these messages are broadcast by active gateways. They contain pairs of values; one value of the pair is an IP address, and the other is the hop count to that address from the source of the message. The original versions of RIP broadcast their entire routing table every 30 seconds, regardless of whether the table has changed—a rather obvious deficiency that has been corrected in RIPv2.

Every 30 seconds, the output process is instructed to generate a complete response to every neighboring router. Two timers are associated with each route, a time-out timer and a garbage-collection timer. Upon expiration of the time-out, the route is no longer valid. However, it is retained in the table for a short time, so that neighbors can be notified that the route has been dropped. Upon expiration of the garbage-collection timer, the route is finally removed from the table.

The time-out is initialized when a route is established and any time an update message is received for the route. If 180 seconds elapse from the last time the time-out was initialized, the route is considered to have expired, and the deletion process that we are about to describe is started for it.

Deletions can occur for one of two reasons: 1) the time-out expires or 2) the metric is set to 16 because of an update received from the current gateway. In either case, the following events happen:

- The garbage-collection timer is set for 120 seconds.

- The metric for the route is set to 16 (infinity). This causes the route to be removed from service.

- A flag is set noting that this entry has been changed, and the output process is signaled to trigger a response.

Until the garbage-collection timer expires, the route is included in all updates sent by this host, with a metric of 16 (infinity). When the garbage-collection timer expires, the route is deleted from the tables.

Should a new route to this network be established while the garbage-collection timer is running, the new route replaces the one about to be deleted. In this case, the garbage-collection timer must be cleared.

Routes to subnets are meaningless outside the network and must be omitted if the destination is not on the same subnetted network. They should be replaced with a single route to the network of which the subnets are a part. Similarly, routes to hosts must be eliminated if they are subsumed by a network route.

If the route passes these tests, the destination and metric are put into the entry in the output datagram. Routes must be included in the datagram even if their metrics are infinite. If the gateway for the route is on the network for which the datagram is being prepared, the metric in the entry is set to 16, or the entire entry is omitted. Omitting the entry is simple split horizon. Including an entry with metric 16 is split horizon with poisoned reverse.

RIP Header Format and Fields

RIP messages consist of a fixed length header followed by a list of networks that may be reached via the transmitting router. The portion of the datagram from the Address Family Identifier field to the Hop Count of Entry field may appear up to 25 times. This allows each RIP update message to carry 25 addresses that will consume 5000 octets. (See Listing 9.1 in CH09CODE.DOC for the RIP Routing Update.) The maximum RIP datagram size is 512 octets excluding the IP and UDP headers. A router may need more than one datagram to transmit its entire routing table to a neighbor based on the scale of the network. Special provisions for continuations are not necessary because all is processed correctly even if the datagrams are processed individually.

RIP Summary

Of Internet interior routing protocols, RIP is probably the most widely used. It is a distance-vector protocol based on a 1970s Xerox design. Ported to TCP/IP when LANs first appeared in the early 80s, RIP has changed little in the past decade and suffers from several limitations, some of which have been overcome with RIP-2, which is discussed later. See Table 9.1 for a summary of RIP.

- *Width restriction.* RIP uses a 4-bit metric to count router hops to a destination. A RIP network can be no wider than 15 hops (16 is infinity). If hop counts are elevated on slower or less reliable links, this can quickly become a problem.

TABLE 9.1 RIP Summary

Parameter	RIP Default Value
Infinity	16 (fixed)
Update time	30 sec.
Invalid time	180 sec.
Flush time	120 sec.
Hold-down	Not used

- *No direct subnet support.*   RIP was deployed prior to subnetting and has no direct support for it. It can be used in subnetted environments, subject to restrictions. VLSM cannot be used in RIP networks.

- *Bandwidth consumptive.*   Every 30 seconds or so, a RIP router broadcasts lists of networks and subnets that it can reach. Depending on the lengths of these lists, which depend on the size of the network, bandwidth usage can become prohibitive on slow links.

- *Difficult diagnosis.*   Like any distance-vector protocol, RIP can be difficult to debug, because the routing algorithm is distributed over many different routers. Most reported RIP problems probably can be traced to poor understanding, incorrect configuration, and inadequate diagnosis.

- *Weak security.*   RIP itself has no security features, but some developers have produced RIP implementations that only accept updates from configured hosts, for example. Various security attacks can be imagined.

However, RIP has several benefits. In widespread use, RIP is the only interior gateway protocol that can be counted on to really run everywhere. Configuring a RIP system requires little effort, beyond setting path costs. Finally, RIP uses an algorithm that does not impose serious computation or storage requirements on hosts or routers.

Routing Information Protocol Version 2

RIP 2 is an extension of RIP, as defined in the previous sections. Its purpose is to expand the amount of useful information in the RIP packets and to add security elements.

The current RIP protocol does not consider autonomous systems and IGP/EGP interactions, subnetting, and authentication because implementations of these postdate RIP. The lack of subnet masks is a serious problem for routers because they need a subnet mask to know how to determine a route. If a RIP route is a network route (all nonnetwork bits are 0), the subnet mask equals the network mask. However, if some of the nonnetwork bits are set, the router cannot determine the subnet mask. Worse still, the router cannot determine whether the RIP route is a subnet or host route. Currently, some routers choose the subnet mask of the interface over which the route was learned and determine the route type from that. Figure 9.3 shows the RIP 2 packet header.

The justifications of maintaining old RIP in a world of newer and stronger routing protocols are mainly its vast distribution and its small overhead requirements in CPU, configuration, and management time. In addition, RIP is very easy to implement, especially in relation to the newer IGPs. Under the assumption that RIP will remain in service for some more years, some people thought it was reasonable to increase RIP's usefulness, especially since the gain looked far greater than the expense of the change.

Recently, RIP version 2 became the standard version of RIP, and the original RIP is now historic. The main disadvantages of RIP version 1 are the minimal amount of information included in every packet, the large amount of unused space in the header of each packet, and the ignorance from implementations and topics that postdated it—namely, autonomous systems and basically EGP interactions, subnetting, and authentication.

The trace on the following page shows the format of a RIP2 datagram.

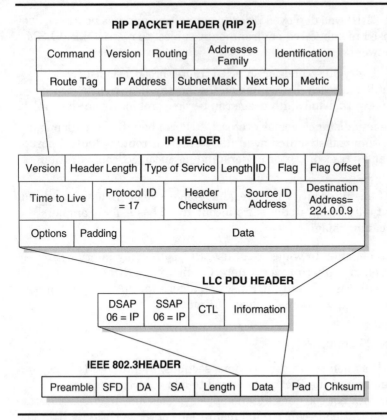

FIGURE 9.3 RIP 2 packet header

```
RIP:   --- RIP Header ---
RIP:
RIP:   Command = 2 (Response)
RIP:   Version = 2
RIP:   Unused  = 0
RIP:
RIP:   Routing data frame 1
RIP:       Address family identifier = 2 (IP)
RIP:       Route Tag                 = 0
RIP:       IP Address   = [192.168.25.0]
RIP:       Subnet Mask  = [255.255.255.0]
RIP:       Next Hop     = [0.0.0.0]
RIP:       Metric       = 1
```

The first four octets of a RIP message contain the RIP header. The remainder of the message is composed of 1–25 route entries (20 octets each).

The Command, *Address Family Identifier* (AFI), IP Address, and Metric fields all have the same meanings as in RIP 1. The Version field specifies version number 2 for RIP datagrams that use authentication or that carry information in any of the newly defined fields. In RIP 2, an optional authentication mechanism exists. When in use, this option abuses an entire RIP entry and leaves space to at most 24 RIP entries in the remainder of the packet.

The most widespread authentication type is simple password—type 2. The Routing domain field enables some routing domains to *interwork* upon the same physical infrastructure, while logically ignoring each other. This field provides the capability to implement various kinds of policies. A default routing domain is assigned the value 0.

Route Tag

The *Route Tag* (RT) field is an attribute assigned to a route that must be preserved and readvertised with a route. The intended use of the route tag is to provide a method of separating internal RIP routes (routes for networks within the RIP routing domain) from external RIP routes, which may have been imported from an EGP or another IGP. Routers supporting protocols other than RIP should be configurable to allow the route tag to be configured for routes imported from different sources. For example, routes imported from EGP or BGP should be able to have their route tag set to an arbitrary value, or at least to the number of the autonomous system from which the routes were learned. Other uses of the route tag are valid, as long as all routers in the RIP domain use it consistently.

Subnet Mask

The Subnet Mask field contains the subnet mask applied to the IP address to yield the no network/subnet portion of the address. If this field is 0, no subnet mask is included for this entry.

Next Hop

Next Hop is the immediate next hop IP address to which packets to the destination specified by this route entry should be forwarded. The purpose of the Next Hop field is to eliminate packets being routed through extra hops in the system. This field is particularly useful when RIP is not being run on all of the routers on a network. Multicasting is an optional feature in RIP 2 using IP address 224.0.0.9. This feature reduces unnecessary load on those hosts not listening to RIP 2. The IP multicast address is used for periodic broadcasts. To maintain backwards compatility, the use of the multicast address is configurable.

Specifying a value of 0.0.0.0 in this field indicates that routing should be via the originator of the RIP advertisement. An address specified as a next hop must be directly reachable on the logical subnet over which the advertisement is made. The purpose of the Next Hop field is to eliminate packets being routed through extra hops in the system. It is particularly useful when RIP is not being run on all of the routers on a network. Note that Next Hop is an "advisory" field. That is, if the provided information is ignored, a possibly suboptimal, but absolutely valid, route may be taken. If the received Next Hop is not directly reachable, it should be treated as 0.0.0.0.

RIP 2 is totally backwards compatible with RIP 1. Its applications support fine tuning to be RIP 1 emulation, RIP 1 compatible, or fully RIP 2.

The protocol depends upon *counting to infinity* to resolve certain unusual situations.

Queries

If a RIP 2 router receives a RIP 1 request, it should respond with a RIP 1 Response. If the router is configured to send only RIP 2 messages, it would not respond to a RIP 1 Request.

Authentication

The following algorithm should be used to authenticate a RIP message. If the router is not configured to authenticate RIP 2 messages, RIP 1 and unauthenticated RIP 2 messages are accepted; if the router is configured to authenticate RIP-2 messages, RIP-1 messages and RIP-2 messages that pass authentication testing shall be accepted; unauthenticated and failed authentication RIP 2 messages shall be discarded. For maximum security, RIP 1 messages should be ignored when authentication is in use. Because an authentication entry is marked with an Address Family Identifier of `0xFFFF`, a RIP 1 system ignores this entry because it would belong to an address family other than IP. Therefore, use of authentication does not prevent RIP 1 systems from seeing RIP 2 messages.

Larger Infinity

One item that people have requested is increasing infinity. The primary reason that this cannot be done is that it would violate backwards compatibility. A larger infinity would obviously confuse older versions of RIP. At best, they would ignore the route as they would ignore a metric of 16. A proposal to make the metric a single octet and to reuse the high three octets also has been put forward, but this proposal would break any implementations that treat the metric as a 4-octet entity.

Security Considerations

The basic RIP protocol is not a secure protocol. To bring RIP 2 in line with more modern routing protocols, an extensible authentication mechanism has been incorporated into the protocol enhancements.

When Should I Choose RIPv1 over RIPv2?

You can configure each interface on your router to use RIPv1, RIPv2, or both. Follow these guidelines in choosing a routing configuration:

- Choose RIPv1 if you want routing advertisements to be aggregated on the network class boundary; otherwise, choose RIPv2.
- Configure all the router interfaces on the *same* physical IP network to run either RIPv1 or RIPv2, but not both.
- Configure your router to run both RIPv1 and RIPv2 if some routers on the same physical network must use RIPv1 and if others must use RIPv2. Setting the *Both* option allows your router to *interoperate* with the RIPv1 routers and the RIPv2 routers at the same time.

TCP/IP RIP Routing Protocol
Design Checklist

Date: ___/___/___

Customer: _____   Designer: _____

Type of Network: _____

Host Operating System _____

Host Support Routed: Y / N

Gated: Y / N

Client OS: OS/2 _____   Win95 _____   Win 3.1 _____   Router: _____

         NT _____   Apple OS _____   UNIX _____

Client TCP/IP Software: _____

Support Multiple Gateway: Y / N

Client Support: DHCP   Y / N

Bootp: Y / N

Network ID: _____   Subnet Mask: _____

Split Horizon: Y / N

Poison Reverse: Y / N

Max Hops (limited to 15): _____

Triggered Update: Y / N

Update Time Configurable: Y / N

Update Interval: Y / N

Networks that should be advertised: _____

Support Default Router: Y / N

Static Router: Y / N

RIP Router Redistribution to Another Protocol: Y / N

_____   OSPF

_____   I-IS-IS

_____   IGRP

_____   E-IGRP

Advertise RIP Default Route: _____

Serial Unnumbered: Y / N

Exterior Routing Protocol used: _____

A/S #:   _____

Hop Count (limited to 15):   _____

CIDR Support: Y / N

Support for Discontinued Subnets: _____

Questions

1. What metric does IP RIP use?
   A. Hop count
   B. Tick count then Hop count
   C. Bandwidth, Load, Reliability, delay and MTU
   D. Cost

2. RIP has an default administrative distance of:
   A. 1
   B. 110
   C. 120
   D. 90
   E. 100

3. IP RIP sends out its routing table updates every:
   A. 30 seconds
   B. 60 seconds
   C. 90 seconds
   D. link state change

4. IP RIP uses ____ to distribute routing information.
   A. anycasts
   B. multicast
   C. broadcast
   D. direct

5. IP RIP is which type of routing protocol?
   A. Distance Vector
   B. Link State
   C. Hybrid
   D. None of the above

6. The maximum hop count for IP RIP is:
   A. 5
   B. 10
   C. 15
   D. 20

7. Hop count and what other metrics are used by RIP?
   A. Administrative cost
   B Delay
   C. Bandwidth
   D. None of the above

8. IP RIP is a _____ routing protocol.
   A. classless
   B. classful
   C. integrated
   D. autonomous

9. IP RIP was originally implemented on which operating system?
   A. Novell NetWare
   B. Digital VMS
   C. Cisco IOS
   D. Berkeley UNIX

10. IP RIP can effectively make use of parallel paths.
    A. True
    B. False

11. Which of the following is valid network statement for the purpose of adding Network 131.127.13.128 with a subnet mask of 255.255.255.252 into IP RIP's advertisements?
    A. Network 131.127.13.128 255.255.255.252
    B. Network 131.127.13.128
    C. Network 131.127.0.0
    D. Network 151.127.0.0 255.255.255.252

12. RIP version II provides which of the following enhancements?
    A. Multicast updates   **C.** Variable length subnet mask support
    B. MD5 Authentication   **D.** All of the above

13. It is possible to have ____ updates in a single IP RIP packet.
    A. 1   **C.** 25
    B. 7   **D.** 50

14. RIP-2 uses multicast address _____.
    A. 224.0.0.6   **C.** 224.0.0.9
    B. 224.0.0.5   **D.** 224.0.0.10

15. Identify the command for configuring RIP.
    A. `router rip`
    B. `router rip network`
    C. `none of the above`

16. Which is a Cisco router's default mode of operation concerning RIP and RIP2?
    A. Does not support both concurrently
    B. Accepts RIP and RIP2 updates, but only sends RIP updates
    C. Accepts and send both RIP and RIP2 updates
    D. Accepts RIP and RIP2 updates, but only sends RIP2 updates

17. RIP routing information not received within ____ seconds is removed from the routing table.
    A. 60   **C.** 90
    B. 180   **D.** None of the above

18. Which of the following are characteristics of IP RIP ?
    A. Link state, Hop count and routing table broadcast every 30 seconds
    B. Distance vector, Hop count and routing table broadcast every 30 seconds
    C. Distance vector, Hop count and routing table broadcast every 90 seconds
    D. Link state, Hop count and routing table broadcast every 30 seconds

19. If information about RIP networks if not received within ___ seconds the metric associated with the network is raised to infinity.
    A. 60   **C.** 30
    B. 90   **D.** 45

20. Identify the files in the RIP Header.
    A. Command   **D.** IP address
    B. Version   **E.** Metric
    C. Address family Identify   **F.** All of the above

21. Define the fields in the RIP-2 header.
    A. Command   **H.** Route Tag
    B. Version   **I.** P Address
    C. Must be zero   **J.** SubNet Address
    D. 0xFFFF   **K.** Next Hop
    E. Authentication Type   **L.** Metric
    F. Authentication Password   **M.** All of the above
    G. Address family

22. Identify the MAC address used for RIP-2 link layer frames.
    A. 01-00-5e-00-00-09   C. 01-00-05-00-00-09
    B. 01-00-4e-00-00-09   D. 01-00-5e-00-00-06

23. A RIP-1 route will be completely removed from the routing table if no update is received after ___ seconds.
    A. 120   C. 240
    B. 270   D. 180

24. A RIP directly connected network has a metric of _____.
    A. 1   C. 0
    B. 2   D. Not applicable

25. RIP treats network _____ as a default route?
    A. 1.0.0.0   C. 0.0.0.1
    B. 0.0.0.0   D. None of the above

26. Cisco's implementation of RIP-2 supports which of the following?
    A. Plain text   C. L2tp
    B. MD5 authentication   D. PPTP

27. What is the command syntax for sending RIP-1 and RIP-2 updates?
    A. `IP rip send version 1`   C. `IP rip send version 1 2`
    B. `IP rip send version 2`   D. All of the above

Rip Show Commands

```
hostname ATLANTA
!
!
no ip domain-lookup
!
interface Ethernet0
 ip address 192.168.21.1 255.255.255.0
!
interface Ethernet1
 ip address 192.168.29.1 255.255.255.0
!
interface Serial0
 ip address 192.168.22.1 255.255.255.0
!
interface Serial1
 no ip address
 shutdown
!
router rip
 redistribute igrp 200
 network 192.168.21.0
 network 192.168.22.0
!
router igrp 200
 redistribute rip
 network 192.168.29.0
!
```

```
no ip classless
!
!
line con 0
line aux 0
line vty 0 4
 login
!
end
```

28. Which interface or interfaces will propagate RIP updates?
   A. E0 and S0
   B. All interfaces
   C. E0, E1 and S0
   D. S1

29. Which interface will not propagate any routing updates?
   A. E0 and S0
   B. All interfaces
   C. E0, E1 and S0
   D. S1

30. What command is used to turn on IGRP?
   A. `redistribute rip`
   B. `router rip`
   C. `no ipclassless`
   D. `router igrp 200`

31. What is the meaning of the number 200 in router IGRP 200?
   A. Router group number
   B. Autonomous system number
   C. Border area number
   D. Router number

32. If interface E1 will not pass RIP updates, explain why.
   A. E1 on Cisco router does not support RIP.
   B. The network statement for the network E1 is in is not configured with router RIP.
   C. Inter E1 has an IP address assigned to it.
   D. None of the above

33. What is the purpose of redistribute IGRP 200?
   A. To propagate IGRP updates over interfaces configure for RIP
   B. To discard all IGRP updates
   C. To flood IGRP updates out of all interfaces
   D. None of the above

34. If you type the command **show interface**, what will be the status of interface S1?
   A. Serial is up, line is protocol down
   B. Serial is up, line is protocol up
   C. Administratively down
   D. Interface S0 shutdown

35. What command was used to display the following information?
```
Codes: C - connected, S - static, I - IGRP, R - RIP, M - mobile, B - BGP
       D - EIGRP, EX - EIGRP external, O - OSPF, IA - OSPF inter area
       N1 - OSPF NSSA external type 1, N2 - OSPF NSSA external type 2
       E1 - OSPF external type 1, E2 - OSPF external type 2, E - EGP
       i - IS-IS, L1 - IS-IS level-1, L2 - IS-IS level-2, * - candidate default
       U - per-user static route, o - ODR

Gateway of last resort is not set
```

```
R      192.168.25.0/24 [120/1] via 192.168.22.2, 00:00:08, Serial0
R      192.168.26.0/24 [120/2] via 192.168.22.2, 00:00:08, Serial0
R      192.168.27.0/24 [120/2] via 192.168.22.2, 00:00:08, Serial0
C      192.168.29.0/24 is directly connected, Ethernet1
C      192.168.21.0/24 is directly connected, Ethernet0
C      192.168.22.0/24 is directly connected, Serial0
R      192.168.23.0/24 [120/1] via 192.168.22.2, 00:00:08, Serial0
```

A. display router RIP   **C.** display IP RIP
B. show IP route   **D.** show route table

36. The dynamic route was learned by which routing protocol?
    A. Directly connected   **C.** IGRP
    B. Static   **D.** RIP

37. All the routing updates were learned via which interface?
    A. Ethernet 1   **C.** Serial 0
    B. Ethernet 0   **D.** No interfaces

38. Which number determines the hop count?
    A. R   192.168.25.0/24 [120/1] via 192.168.22.2, 00:00:08,
    B. R   192.168.25.0/24 [120/1] via 192.168.22.2, 00:00:08,
    C. R   192.168.25.0/24 [120/1] via 192.168.22.2, 00:00:08,
    D. R   192.168.25.0/24 [120/1] via 192.168.22.2, 00:00:08,

39. Which number determines the subnet mask?
    A. R   192.168.25.0/24 [120/1] via 192.168.22.2, 00:00:08,
    B. R   192.168.25.0/24 [120/1] via 192.168.22.2, 00:00:08,
    C. R   192.168.25.0/24 [120/1] via 192.168.22.2, 00:00:08,
    D. R   192.168.25.0/24 [120/1] via 192.168.22.2, 00:00:08,

40. Which number determines the network learned?
    A. R   192.168.25.0/24 [120/1] via 192.168.22.2, 00:00:08,
    B. R   192.168.25.0/24 [120/1] via 192.168.22.2, 00:00:08,
    C. R   192.168.25.0/24 [120/1] via 192.168.22.2, 00:00:08,
    D. R   192.168.25.0/24 [120/1] via 192.168.22.2, 00:00:08,

Answers

1. A
2. C
3. A
4. C
5. A
6. C
7. D
8. B
9. D
10. A
11. C
12. D
13. C
14. C
15. A
16. B
17. B
18. B
19. B
20. F
21. M
22. A
23. C
24. C
25. B
26. A, B
27. C
28. A
29. D
30. D
31. B
32. B
33. A
34. C
35. B
36. D
37. C
38. D
39. B
40. A

10

Interior Gateway Routing Protocol and Enhanced IGRP

The *Interior Gateway Routing Protocol* (IGRP) was developed in the mid-1980s by Cisco Systems, Inc. Cisco's principal goal in creating IGRP was to provide a robust protocol for routing within an *autonomous system* (AS) having arbitrarily complex topology and consisting of media with diverse bandwidth and delay characteristics. An AS is a collection of networks under common administration that share a common routing strategy. Autonomous systems typically are assigned a unique 16-bit number by the *Defense Data Network* (DDN) *Network Information Center* (NIC). In the mid-1980s, the most popular intra-AS routing protocol was RIP. Although RIP was quite useful for routing within small-to moderate-sized, relatively homogeneous internetworks, its limits were being pushed by network growth. In particular, RIP's small hop-count limit (15) restricted the size of internetworks, and its single metric (hop count) did not allow for much routing flexibility in complex environments. The popularity of Cisco routers and the robustness of IGRP have encouraged many organizations with large internetworks to replace RIP with IGRP.

Cisco's initial IGRP implementation worked only in IP networks. Cisco developed Enhanced IGRP in the early 1990s to improve the operating efficiency of IGRP and to support protocols other than IP.

IGRP

IGRP is a *distance-vector interior-gateway protocol* (IGP). Distance-vector routing protocols call for each router to send all or a portion of its routing table in a routing update message at regular intervals to each of its neighboring routers. As routing information proliferates through the network, routers can calculate distances to all nodes within the internetwork. Distance-vector routing protocols are often contrasted with link-state routing protocols, which send local connection information to all nodes in the internetwork. *Open Shortest Path First* (OSPF) and *Intermediate System-to-Intermediate System* (IS-IS) are two popular link-state routing algorithms. IGRP uses a combination (vector) of metrics. Internetwork delay, bandwidth, reliability, MTU, and load are all factored into the routing decision. Network administrators can set the weighting factors for each of these metrics. IGRP uses either the administrator-set or the default weightings to automatically calculate optimal routes.

IGRP provides a wide range for its metrics. For example, reliability and load can take on any value between 1 and 255; bandwidth can take on values reflecting speeds from 1,200 bps to 10MB per second; and delay can take on any value from 1 to 2 to the 24th power. Wide metric ranges allow satisfactory metric setting in internetworks with widely varying performance characteristics. Most importantly, the metric components are combined in a user-definable algorithm. As a result, network administrators can influence route selection in an intuitive fashion.

To provide additional flexibility, IGRP permits multipath routing. Dual equal-bandwidth lines may run a single stream of traffic in round-robin fashion, with automatic switchover to the second line if one line goes down. Also, multiple paths can be used even if the metrics for the paths are different. For example, if one path is three times better than another because its metric is three times lower, the better path is used three times as often. Only routes with metrics within a certain range of the best route are used as multiple paths.

Stability Features

IGRP provides a number of features designed to enhance its stability. These include *hold-downs*, *split horizons*, and *poison reverse updates*.

Hold-Downs.   Hold-downs are used to prevent regular update messages from inappropriately reinstating a route that may have gone bad. When a router goes down, neighboring routers detect this via the lack of regularly scheduled update messages. These routers then calculate new routes and send routing update messages to inform their neighbors of the route change. This activity begins a wave of triggered updates that filter through the network.

These triggered updates do not instantly arrive at every network device. Therefore, a device that has yet to be informed of a network failure may send a regular update message (indicating that a route that has just gone down is still good) to a device that has just been notified of the network failure. In this case, the latter device would now contain (and potentially advertise) incorrect routing information. Hold-downs tell routers to hold down any changes that may affect routes for some period of time. The hold-down period is usually calculated to be just greater than the period of time necessary to update the entire network with a routing change.

Split Horizons.   Split horizons derive from the fact that it is never useful to send information about a route back in the direction from which it came.

Router 1 (R1) initially advertises that it has a route to Network A. Router 2 (R2) has no reason to include this route in its update back to R1, as R1 is closer to Network A. The split-horizon rule says that R2 should strike this route from any updates it sends to R1. The split-horizon rule helps prevent routing loops. Suppose that R1's interface to Network A goes down. Without split horizons, R2 continues to inform R1 that it can get to Network A (through R1). If R1 does not have sufficient intelligence, it may actually pick up R2's route as an alternative to its failed direct connection, causing a routing loop. Although hold-downs should prevent this, split horizons are implemented in IGRP because they provide extra algorithm stability.

Poison Reverse Updates.   Whereas split horizons should prevent routing loops between adjacent routers, poison reverse updates are intended to defeat larger routing loops. Increases in routing metrics generally indicate routing loops. Poison reverse updates then are sent to remove and place the route in hold-down. In Cisco's implementation of IGRP, poison reverse updates are sent if a route metric has increased by a factor of 1.1 or greater.

Timers

IGRP maintains a number of timers and variables containing time intervals, including an update timer, an invalid timer, a hold-time period, and a flush timer. The update timer specifies how frequently routing update messages should be sent. The IGRP default for this variable is 90 seconds. The invalid timer specifies how long a router should wait, in the absence of routing update messages about a specific route, before declaring that route invalid. The IGRP default for this variable is three times the update period. The hold-time variable specifies the hold-down period. The IGRP default for this variable is three times the update timer period plus 10 seconds. Finally, the flush timer indicates how much time should pass before a route should be flushed from the routing table. The IGRP default is seven times the routing update period.

IGRP Header Format Description

Figure 10.1 shows the IGRP header format. The following list describes the fields contained within the IGRP header:

- Version.   The version number is currently 1. Packets having other version numbers are ignored.

- *Operation Code*.   The opcode is either `update` or `request`. This field indicates the type of message. The format of the two message types is given later in this chapter.

- *Edition*.   This field is a serial number incremented when a change occurs in the routing table (when the pseudo-code says to trigger a routing update). The edition number allows gateways to avoid processing updates containing information that they already have seen. (This is not currently implemented. The edition number is generated correctly, but it is ignored on input. Because packets can be dropped, the edition number probably is not sufficient to avoid duplicate processing. All of the packets associated with the edition have to be processed.)

- *Autonomous System*.   This field contains the autonomous system number. In Cisco's implementation, a router can participate in more than one autonomous system. Each such system runs its own IGRP protocol. Conceptually, each autonomous system has separate routing tables. Routes that arrive via IGRP from one autonomous system are sent in updates for only that AS. This field allows the gateway to select which set of routing tables to use for processing this message. If the gateway receives an IGRP message for an AS for which it is not configured, it is ignored. In fact, Cisco's implementation allows information to be "leaked" from one AS to another. However, I regard that as an administrative tool and not part of the protocol.

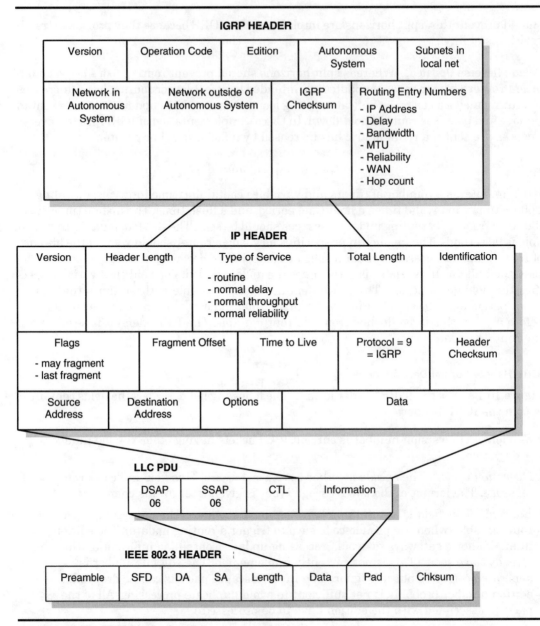

FIGURE 10.1 The IGRP header format

- *Networks in Autonomous System,* number of system, and *Networks outside of Autonomous System.*   These fields indicate the number of entries in each of the three sections of update messages. There is no other demarcation between the sections. The first interior entries are taken to be interior, the next system entries as being system, and the final number of exterior as exterior.

- *IGRP Checksum.* This field is an IP checksum, computed using the same checksum algorithm as a UDP checksum. The checksum is computed on the IGRP header and any routing information that follows it. The checksum field is set to 0 when computing the checksum. The checksum does not include the IP header, nor any virtual header as in UDP and TCP.

Enhanced IGRP

With Software Release 9.21, Cisco introduced an enhanced version of IGRP that combines the advantages of link-state protocols with the advantages of distance-vector protocols. Enhanced IGRP incorporates the *Diffusing Update Algorithm* (DUAL) developed at SRI International by Dr. J.J. Garcia-Luna-Aceves. Enhanced IGRP includes the following features:

- *Fast convergence.* Enhanced IGRP uses DUAL to achieve convergence quickly. A router running Enhanced IGRP stores all of its neighbors' routing tables so that it can quickly adapt to alternate routes. If no appropriate route exists, Enhanced IGRP queries its neighbors to discover an alternate route. These queries propagate until an alternate route is found.

- *Variable length subnet masks.* Enhanced IGRP includes full support for variable length subnet masks. Subnet routes are automatically summarized on a network number boundary. In addition, Enhance IGRP can be configured to summarize on any bit boundary at any interface.

- *Partial, bounded updates.* Enhanced IGRP does not make periodic updates. Instead, it sends partial updates only when the metric for a route changes. Propagation of partial updates is bounded automatically so that only those routers that need the information are updated. As a result of these two capabilities, Enhanced IGRP consumes significantly less bandwidth than IGRP.

- *Multiple network-layer support.* Enhanced IGRP includes support for AppleTalk, IP, and Novell NetWare. The AppleTalk implementation redistributes routes learned from the *Routing Table Maintenance Protocol* (RTMP). The Novell implementation redistributes routes learned from Novell RIP or *Service Advertisement Protocol* (SAP).

Enhanced IGRP features four new technologies:

- *Neighbor discovery/recovery.* This technology is used by routers to dynamically learn about other routers on their directly attached networks. Routers must also discover when their neighbors become unreachable or inoperative. This process is achieved with low overhead by periodically sending small multicast Hello packets every 5 seconds for high speed *Now Broadcast Multiaccess* (NBMA) networks. There is an exception to the 5 second interval on low-speed NBMA media types. The default Hello interval is 60 seconds. As long as a router receives Hello packets from a neighboring router, it assumes that the neighbor is functioning, and they can exchange routing information.

- *Reliable Transport Protocol* (RTP). This technology is responsible for guaranteed, ordered delivery of Enhanced IGRP packets to all neighbors. RTP supports intermixed transmission of multicast or unicast packets. For efficiency, only certain Enhanced IGRP packets are transmitted reliably. For example, on a multiaccess network with multicast capabilities, such as Ethernet, it is not necessary to send Hello packets reliably to all neighbors individually. For that reason, Enhanced IGRP sends a single multicast Hello packet containing an indicator that informs the receivers that the packet need not be acknowledged. Other types of packets, such as updates, indicate in the packet that acknowledgment is required. RTP has a provision for sending multicast packets quickly when unacknowledged packets are pending, which helps ensure that convergence time remains low in the presence of varying speed links.

- *DUAL finite state machine.*   This technology embodies the decision process for all route computations and tracks all routes advertised by all neighbors. DUAL uses distance information to select efficient, loop-free paths and to select routes for insertion in a routing table based on feasible successors. A *feasible successor* is a neighboring router used for packet forwarding that is a least-cost path to a destination guaranteed not to be part of a routing loop. When a neighbor changes a metric or when a topology change occurs, DUAL tests for feasible successors. If one is found, DUAL uses it to avoid recomputing the route unnecessarily. When no feasible successors are available, but neighbors are advertising the destination, a recomputation (also known as a *diffusing computation*) must occur to determine a new successor. Although recomputation is not processor intensive, it does affect convergence time, so it is advantageous to avoid unnecessary recomputations.

- *Protocol-dependent modules.*   This technology is responsible for network-layer protocol-specific requirements. For example, the *IP-Enhanced IGRP module* is responsible for sending and receiving Enhanced IGRP packets encapsulated in IP. IP Enhanced IGRP is also responsible for parsing Enhanced IGRP packets and informing DUAL of the new information received. IP Enhanced IGRP asks DUAL to make routing decisions, the results of which are stored in the IP routing table. IP Enhanced IGRP is responsible for redistributing routes learned by other IP routing protocols.

Figure 10.2 shows the Enhanced IGRP Hello packet header.
The consistent and superior performance of Enhanced IGRP relies on several new features:

- Packet types
- Neighbor tables
- Topology tables
- Route states
- Route tagging

Packet Types

Enhanced IGRP uses the following packet types:

- *Hello* and *acknowledgment.*   Hello packets are multicast for neighbor discovery/recovery and do not require acknowledgment. An acknowledgment packet is a Hello

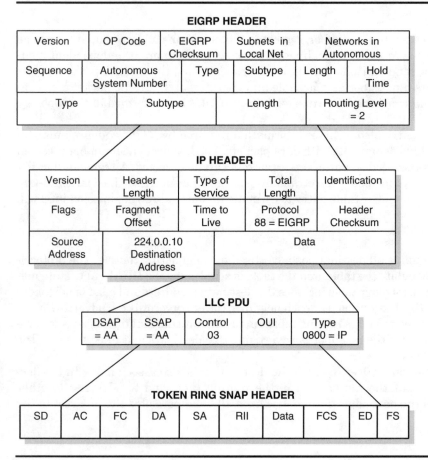

FIGURE 10.2 Cisco's EIGRP routing Hello packet header

packet with no data. Acknowledgment packets contain a nonzero acknowledgment number, and they are always sent using a unicast address.

- *Update.*   Update packets are used to convey reachability of destinations. When a new neighbor is discovered, unicast update packets are sent, so the neighbor can build up its topology table. In other cases, such as a link-cost change, updates are multicast. Updates are always transmitted reliably.

- *Query and reply.*   Query and reply packets are sent when a destination has no feasible successors. Query packets are always multicast. Reply packets are sent in response to query packets to indicate to the originator that the originator does not need to recompute the route because there are feasible successors. Reply packets are unicast to the originator of the query. Both query and reply packets are transmitted reliably.

- *Request.*   Request packets are used to get specific information from one or more neighbors. They are used in route-server applications and can be multicast or unicast. Request packets are transmitted unreliably.

Neighbor Tables

When a router discovers a new neighbor, it records the neighbor's address and interface as an entry in the *neighbor table*. One neighbor table exists for each protocol-dependent module. When a neighbor sends a Hello packet, it advertises a hold time, which is the amount of time a router treats a neighbor as reachable and operational. If a Hello packet is not received within the hold time, the hold time expires, and DUAL is informed of the topology change.

The neighbor table entry also includes information required by RTP. Sequence numbers are used to match acknowledgments with data packets. The last sequence number received from the neighbor is recorded so out-of-order packets can be detected. A transmission list is used to queue packets for possible retransmission on a per-neighbor basis. Round-trip timers are kept in the neighbor table entry to estimate an optimal retransmission interval.

Topology Tables

The *topology table* contains all destinations advertised by neighboring routers. The protocol-dependent modules populate the table, and the table is acted on by the DUAL finite state machine. Each entry in the topology table includes the destination address and a list of neighbors that have advertised the destination. For each neighbor, the entry records the advertised metric, which the neighbor stores in its routing table. An important rule that distance-vector protocols must follow is that if the neighbor is advertising this destination, it must be using the route to forward packets.

The metric that the router uses to reach the destination is also associated with the destination. The metric that the router uses in the routing table and to advertise to other routers is the sum of the best advertised metric from all neighbors plus the link cost to the best neighbor.

Route States

A topology table entry for a destination can be in one of two states, active or passive. A destination is in the passive state when the router is not performing a recomputation or in the active state when the router is performing a recomputation. If feasible successors are always available, a destination never has to go into the active state; thereby avoiding a recomputation.

A recomputation occurs when a destination has no feasible successors. The router initiates the recomputation by sending a query packet to each of its neighboring routers. The neighboring router can send a reply packet, indicating that it has a feasible successor for the destination, or it can send a query packet, indicating that it is participating in the recomputation. While a destination is in the active state, a router cannot change the destination's routing table information. When the router has received a reply from each neighboring router, the topology table entry for the destination returns to the passive state, and the router can select a successor.

Route Tagging

Enhanced IGRP supports internal and external routes. Internal routes originate within an Enhanced IGRP AS. Therefore, a directly attached network configured to run Enhanced IGRP is considered an internal route and is propagated with this information throughout the Enhanced IGRP AS. External routes are learned by another routing protocol or reside in the routing table as static routes. These routes are tagged individually with the identity of their origin. External routes are tagged with the following information:

- Router ID of the Enhanced IGRP router that redistributed the route
- AS number of the destination
- Configurable administrator tag
- ID of the external protocol
- Metric from the external protocol
- Bit flags for default routing

Route tagging allows the network administrator to customize routing and maintain flexible policy controls. Route tagging is particularly useful in transit autonomous systems in which Enhanced IGRP typically interacts with an interdomain routing protocol that implements more global policies, resulting in very scaleable, policy-based routing.

Compatibility with IGRP

Enhanced IGRP provides compatibility and seamless interoperation with IGRP routers. An automatic redistribution mechanism allows IGRP routes to be imported into Enhanced IGRP and Enhanced IGRP routes to be imported into IGRP, so it is possible to add Enhanced IGRP gradually into an existing IGRP network. Because the metrics for both protocols are directly translatable, they are as easily comparable as if they were routes that originated in their own autonomous systems. In addition, Enhanced IGRP treats IGRP routes as external routes and provides a way for the network administrator to customize them.

EIGRP provides support for non-IP based networks such as AppleTalk and Novell IPX. The ability to support these non-scalable desktop protocols allows implementers to increase the size and scope of these networks without workstation or server intervention.

EIGRP Support for IPX

EIGRP support for Novell provides the following:

- Increase hop count diameter to 224 hops from 15
- Supports incremental RIP and SAP updates
- RIP and SAP updates are only sent when changes occur rather than at 60 second intervals.
- EIGRP uses bandwidth and delay to determine best route rather than IPX hop and tick count.

EIGRP Support for AppleTalk

EIGRP provides the following features for AppleTalk:

- Event driven updates versus 10 second
- EIGRP routes are preferred over Apple's *Routing Table Maintenance Protocol* (RTMP)

> **NOTE:**   *EIGRP in an AppleTalk environment requires a clientless design, because AppleTalk clients receive RTMP routing information from a local device.*

**Cisco IGRP Design
Worksheet**

Router Name: _____

# of Interfaces: _____

AS #: _____

# of Networks: _____

IP Address: _____

Subnet Mask: _____

Route Summarization Required: Y / N

Variable Length Subnet? Y / N   Tunnel Multiple Protocols?   Y / N
    if yes, use EIGRP   if yes, check protocols

                                    ____   IP

                                    ____   IPX

                                    ____   AppleTalk

Redistribution Required: Y / N

If yes select Protocol OSPF_____, RIP_____, BGP_____

Default Metric (Mandatory)

Passive Interface Required: Y / N   (used if routing information should not be
propagated from this interface.)

Administrative Distance: Y / N Setting:_____

Questions

1. IGRP is designed for use:
   - **A.** Between areas
   - **B.** Within areas
   - **C.** Between autonomous systems
   - **D.** Within an autonomous systems

2. IGRP is which of the following types of routing protocols?
   - **A.** Open
   - **B.** Distance-vector
   - **C.** Link state
   - **D.** Classless

3. IGRP uses which of the following to advertise changes in network status?
   - **A.** Flash updates
   - **B.** Link state updates
   - **C.** Periodic updates
   - **D.** Flooded updates

4. Which of these methods is not used by IGRP?
   - **A.** Split horizons
   - **B.** Poison reverse
   - **C.** Holddown timers
   - **D.** Backwards pressure

5. Which of the following is not one of the metrics used by IGRP?
   - **A.** Hop count
   - **B.** Delay
   - **C.** Load
   - **D.** Bandwidth

6. Which of the following is not used as part of an IGRP configuration?
   - **A.** Network address
   - **B.** Subnet mask
   - **C.** Autonomous system
   - **D.** Interface bandwidth

7. IGRP can provide routing services for the following routing protocols:
   - **A.** IP
   - **B.** IPX
   - **C.** AppleTalk
   - **D.** All of the above

8. IGRP updates are:
   - **A.** Periodic
   - **B.** Incremental
   - **C.** Neither
   - **D.** A combination of both

9. IGRP takes into account which of the following parameters?
   - **A.** Load
   - **B.** Cost
   - **C.** Remote subnet mask
   - **D.** All of the above

10. How many alternate unequal paths to a given network can IGRP keep within its routing table?
    - **A.** 4
    - **B.** 7
    - **C.** 8
    - **D.** 12

11. Characteristics of IGRP are:
    - **A.** Link state, Hop count and routing table broadcast every 30 seconds
    - **B.** Distance vector, Composite metric and routing table broadcast every 90 seconds
    - **C.** Distance vector, ticks and routing table broadcast every 90 seconds
    - **D.** Link state, cost and routing table broadcast every 90 seconds

12. The command `redistribute eigrp` accomplishes:
    A. Making EIGRP-learned routes available to another routing protocol
    B. Making routes learned by another protocol available to EIGRP
    C. Re-initializing EIGRP's network database
    D. Enabling EIGRP on an additional interface

13. The "E" in E-IGRP stands for:
    A. "Enhanced"   C. "Enriched"
    B. "Extended"   D. "External"

14. E-IGRP advertises changes in network topology via:
    A. Flooded updates   C. Link state updates
    B. Unbounded updates   D. Partially bounded updates

15. When EIGRP has established that a particular route is the one along which traffic will be forwarded, that route is then considered in be in a (n) _____ state.
    A. active   C. dormant
    B. passive   D. preferred

16. EIGRP uses which of the following algorithms for convergence?
    A. DUAL   C. Singular Path
    B. Dijsktra's   D. Perlman's

17. EIGRP is a _____ routing protocol.
    A. classless   C. dependent
    B. classful   D. autonomous

18. EIGRP is most concerned with:
    A. Speed   C. Time to live
    B. Service cost   D. Signaling type

19. Each IP EIGRP router process on a router must have a unique:
    A. Process ID   C. Network ID
    B. Router ID   D. Autonomous System ID

20. Each IPX EIGRP router process on a router must have a unique:
    A. Process ID   C. Network ID
    B. Router ID   D. Autonomous System ID

21. Each AppleTalk EIGRP router must have a unique:
    A. Process ID   C. Network ID
    B. Router ID   D. Autonomous System ID

22. EIGRP keeps track of which of these parameters within its database?
    A. Designated router   C. Actual Distance
    B. Advertised distance   D. Preferred Neighbor

23. Which of these routing protocols does not use LSAs to advertise network reachability?
    A. OSPF   C. EIGRP
    B. NLSP   D. None of the above

24. EIGRP keeps entries in its database for which of the following:
    A. All routers within an area
    B. All routers within an autonomous system
    C. All directly connected neighbor routers
    D. All of the above

25. EIGRP forwards packets to the _____ for destination network.
    A. Successor
    B. Feasible successor
    C. Lead router
    D. Trailing router

26. EIGRP can be used to increase the amount of usable bandwidth on serial links in an IPX environment.
    A. True
    B. False

27. EIGRP is less bandwidth intensive than:
    A. IS-IS
    B. OSPF
    C. RIP-2
    D. RIP

28. A Hybrid routing protocol is:
    A. A distance vector routing protocol with advanced features
    B. A link state routing protocol with advanced features
    C. An advanced way for routers to determine which device will provide the best route
    D. A combining of the best features of distance vector and link state protocols

29. EIGRP fits into which of the following classes of routing protocols:
    A. Distance vector
    B. Link state
    C. Hybrid
    D. None of the above

30. Which of the following is not a metric used by IGRP and EIGRP?
    A. Media type
    B. Load
    C. Delay
    D. MTU

31. IGRP sends a routing update how often?
    A. 30 seconds
    B. 60 seconds
    C. 90 seconds
    D. 120 seconds

32. Identify the command used to disable hold-down.
    A. `No metric holddown`
    B. `Disable holddown`
    C. `No holddown`

33. IGRP advertises which types of routes?
    A. Exterior
    B. Interior
    C. System
    D. All of the above

34. Define the function of interior routes.
    A. Routes between subnets
    B. Routes between areas
    C. Routes between Autonomous Systems
    D. None of the above

35. Define the function of System Routes.
  A. Routes to networks within an autonomous system
  B. Routes to networks within an area
  C. Static Routes to networks within an autonomous system
  D. None of the above

36. IGRP declares a route inaccessible if it does not receive an update within __ update period's __ seconds?
  A. 4, 300
  B. 3, 270
  C. 1, 60
  D. 3, 128

37. Identify three tasks necessary to configure IGRP.
  A. Disable Hold down
  B. IGRP Routing process
  C. Control Distribution of Traffic
  D. Adjust IGRP Metric Weights

38. What is the default number of hops for IGRP?
  A. 16
  B. 32
  C. 33
  D. 128
  E. 100

39. What is the maximum hop count supported using IGRP?
  A. 255
  B. 128
  C. 512
  D. 32
  E. 16

40. What is the syntax for configuring E-IGRP?
  A. `router eigrp`
  B. `router eigrp (process id)`
  C. `router eigrp (AS number)`
  D. None of the above

41. Explain the log-neighbor-changes IOS command.

42. What is the default administrative distance for E-IGRP?
  A. 90
  B. 100
  C. 110
  D. 120

43. What is the default administrative distance for IGRP?
  A. 60
  B. 90
  C. 100
  D. 110

44. IGRP supports up to __ paths for a destination network?
  A. 4
  B. 2
  C. 1
  D. 8

45. Explain the IGRP variance multiplier.

46. Identify the command to enable IGRP.
  A. `router igrp process number`
  B. `router igrp`
  C. `router igrp netid`
  D. `router igrp autonomous system number`

47. Identify Enhanced IGRP routes.
  A. Internal
  B. External
  C. Summary
  D. Border
  E. None of the above

48. Identify the command that can be used to change the default metric values for IGRP and EIGRP.
  A. metric weights
  B. metric bandwidth
  C. metric cost

49. If EIGRP is added to an existing IGRP network with a different autonomous system number, how can redistribution occur?
  A. Manually
  B. Manually using the redistribute command
  C. Automatic distribution
  D. None of the above

50. Define the term route feedback.

51. Explain the following command: `Passive-interface serial 0`

52. Using EIGRP with Novell IPX allows the Novell network diameter to extend _____.
  A. 128 hops
  B. 224 hops
  C. 32 hops
  D. No change

53. The formula for converting RTMP metrics to AppleTalk Enhanced IGRP metrics is hop count multiplied by:
  A. 252524800
  B. 252528481
  C. 9600
  D. 560000
  E. None of the above

54. EIGRP uses which multicast address for routing table hellos?
  A. 224.0.0.5
  B. 224.0.0.6
  C. 224.0.0.10
  D. 224.0.0.9

55. Identify the maximum number of routes in a 1500 byte packet.
  A. 50
  B. 32
  C. 64
  D. 107
  E. 104

56. IGRP variance is set to ___ by default.
  A. 2
  B. 6
  C. 8
  D. 1

57. IGRP variance using fast or autonomous switching should be set to ___.
  A. 1
  B. 3
  C. 5
  D. 8

58. IGRP process switched over the WAN, variance should be set to __.
  A. 1   **C.** 2
  B. 3   **D.** 4

59. IGRP has a _____ timer that helps in preventing routing loops.
  A. trigger update timer   **D.** All of the above
  B. hold-down timer   **E.** None of the above
  C. periodic update time

60. What is IGRP flush timer in seconds?
  A. 90 seconds   **C.** 280 seconds
  B. 270 seconds   **D.** 630 seconds

61. What is IGRP invalid timer in seconds?
  A. 120 seconds   **C.** 270 seconds
  B. 630 seconds   **D.** 180 seconds

62. EIGRP summarizes at the network boundary by _____.
  A. default   **C.** Hello update
  B. manual intervention   **D.** None of the above

63. IGRP uses a ___ bit metric for finding the best route.
  A. 16   **C.** 32
  B. 24   **D.** 64

64. IGRP uses by default a combination of ___ and ___ as a routing metric.
  A. Delay and bandwidth   **D.** Bandwidth and delay
  B. Loading and bandwidth   **E.** None of the above
  C. Hops and delay

65. The IGRP hold-down timer is _____ seconds.
  A. 280   **C.** 128
  B. 270   **D.** 90

66. Enhanced IGRP uses a ___ bit metric based on the IGRP metric.
  A. 32   **C.** 16
  B. 24   **D.** 64

67. Identify the Enhanced IGRP protocol engine.
  A. DUAL   **C.** Reliable transport
  B. Neighbor Discovery   **D.** All of the above

68. EIGRP networks can converge faster with the _____ timer disabled.
  A. hold-down timer   **C.** trigger update
  B. hello   **D.** None of the above

69. Identify the message types defined by EIGRP.
  A. Hello   **D.** Reply
  B. Update   **E.** Request
  C. Query   **F.** All of the above

70. EIGRP hello packets are ____ to all routers in the network?
  A. unicast
  B. multicast
  C. broadcast
  D. anycast

71. Identify the protocol ID used in IP for EIGRP?
  A. 89
  B. 17
  C. 1
  D. 88

IGRP Show Commands

```
Codes: C - connected, S - static, I - IGRP, R - RIP, M - mobile, B - BGP        D
- EIGRP, EX - EIGRP external, O - OSPF, IA - OSPF inter area        N1 - OSPF NSSA
external type 1, N2 - OSPF NSSA external type 2        E1 - OSPF external type 1,
E2 - OSPF external type 2, E - EGP
        i - IS-IS, L1 - IS-IS level-1, L2 - IS-IS level-2, * - candidate default
        U - per-user static route, o - ODR

Gateway of last resort is not set

D EX 192.168.11.0/24 [170/2195456] via 192.168.15.1, 00:01:17, Ethernet0
D EX 192.168.12.0/24 [170/2246656] via 192.168.15.1, 00:01:17, Ethernet0
D      192.168.13.0/24 [90/2195456] via 192.168.15.1, 01:44:53, Ethernet0
D      192.168.14.0/24 [90/2195456] via 192.168.15.1, 01:44:53, Ethernet0
C      192.168.15.0/24 is directly connected, Ethernet0
C      192.168.16.0/24 is directly connected, Ethernet1
```

72. What is the administrative distance of EIGRP?
  A. /24
  B. 90
  C. 100
  D. 120

73. The dynamic routes were learned by which routing protocol?
  A. EIGRP
  B. Static
  C. IGRP
  D. RIP

74. All the routing updates were learned via which interface?
  A. Ethernet 1
  B. Ethernet 0
  C. Serial 0
  D. No interfaces

75. In the line "D   192.168.13.0/24 [90/2195456] via 192.168.15.1, 01:44:53," what does the number 2195456 refer to?
  A. EIGRP metric
  B. Identification code
  C. Administrative distance
  D. Hop count

76. E-IGRP hello on a multi-access network are sent out every____ seconds.
  A. 60
  B. 30
  C. 10
  D. 5

77. E-IGRP hello on a non-broadcast mulitaccess network are sent out every _____.
  A. 20 seconds
  B. 30 seconds
  C. 60 seconds
  D. 120 seconds

78. E-IGRP provides primary and backup routes in its topology table. How many routes per destination is supported?

    A. 2   **C.** 6

    B. 4   **D.** 8

79. E-IGRP holdtime is set at _____ times the hello interval.

    A. 2   **C.** 6

    B. 3   **D.** 10

80. E-IGRP holdtime on WAN links is:

    A. 30 seconds   **C.** 60 seconds

    B. 45 seconds   **D.** 180 seconds

Answers

1. D
2. B
3. A, C
4. D
5. A
6. B
7. A
8. A
9. A
10. A
11. B
12. A
13. A
14. D
15. B
16. A
17. A
18. A
19. D
20. D
21. D
22. B
23. C
24. C
25. A
26. A
27. D
28. D
29. C
30. A
31. C
32. A
33. D
34. A
35. A
36. B
37. B, C, D
38. E
39. A
40. C
41. It is used to monitor the stability of routing protocol and to detect errors.
42. A
43. C
44. A
45. The variance multiplier allows for the balancing of traffic across all feasible paths, and take advantage of new paths if one should fail.
46. D
47. A, B, C
48. A

49. B
50. Route feedback occurs when distributing one routing protocol routes learned back to the router in which they were learned.
51. The `passive interface` command disables the sending of routing updates out of serial interface 0.
52. B
53. A
54. C
55. E
56. D
57. A
58. C
59. B
60. D
61. C
62. A
63. B
64. D
65. A
66. A
67. D
68. A
69. F
70. B
71. D
72. B
73. A
74. B
75. A
76. D
77. C
78. C
79. B
80. D

11

Open Shortest Path First

Open Shortest Path First (OSPF) is a link-state, non-proprietary routing protocol used by the Internet community. OSPF is classified as an *Interior Gateway Protocol* (IGP), which means that it distributes routing information between routers belonging to a single autonomous system.

OSPF allows for enhanced features, such as route summarization, variable-length subnet masks, and authentication of routing updates. Each OSPF router maintains an identical database describing the autonomous system's topology. From this database, a routing table is calculated by constructing a shortest-path tree. OSPF recalculates routes quickly in the face of topological changes, using a minimum of routing protocol traffic. Separate routes can be calculated for each IP type of service.

OSPF allows sets of networks to be grouped together. Such a grouping is called an *area*, and its topology is hidden from the rest of the autonomous system. This information hiding enables a significant reduction in routing traffic. An area is a generalization of an IP subnetted network. All OSPF routing protocol exchanges can be authenticated, which means that only trusted routers can participate in the autonomous system's routing.

The Shortest-Path Tree

When no OSPF areas are configured, each router in the autonomous system has an identical link-state database, leading to an identical graphical representation. A router generates its routing table from this graph by calculating a tree of shortest paths with the router itself as the root. Obviously, the shortest-path tree depends on the router doing the calculation.

The tree gives the entire path to any destination network or host. However, only the next hop to the destination is used in the forwarding process. Note also that the best route to any router also has been calculated. For the processing of external data, the next hop and distance to any router advertising external routes is noted.

Link-state routers exchange information about the state of their network connections or links. Using this information, each router can construct the topology of the internetwork and derive routing information.

OSPF converges on common routing information faster than RIP does because OSPF link-state information is flooded instantaneously rather than processed on each hop. The faster convergence prevents loss of connectivity and temporary routing loops. Therefore, its metric does not have to be limited to 15. An OSPF metric can be as large as 65,535. With a larger metric, you can build a larger internetwork. You also can assign a wide range of costs for different types of networks, based on characteristics such as bandwidth.

Finally, OSPF generates less traffic. Unlike RIP, which requires periodic updates, OSPF routers update their link-state information only when the link state changes, or every 30 minutes, as opposed to 30 seconds for RIP. Consequently, more bandwidth is available for data traffic.

OSPF Topology

OSPF areas are connected in a hierarchical manner. The OSPF *Autonomous System* (AS) can be partitioned into different areas. All OSPF areas are connected to the backbone area. The backbone area is represented in Figure 11.1 by Area 0.

Routers that attach an area to the backbone are called *area border routers*. An area border router has at least one interface in a nonbackbone area and one interface in the backbone area.

OSPF routers can exchange information with other autonomous systems or domains running different routing protocols, such as EIGRP, IGRP, or RIP. The exchanges between rout-

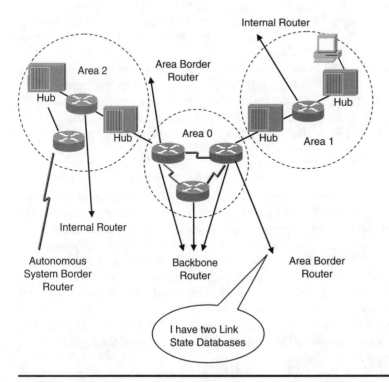

FIGURE 11.1 OSPF areas

ing protocols are performed by the gateway at the border of the OSPF domain. This gateway is an autonomous system boundary router, or ASBR. To learn routing information from other domains or autonomous systems, an ASBR must be running a different routing process along with OSPF. The *Autonomous System Border Router* (ASBR) then disseminates that information throughout the OSPF domain.

Area Partitioning

When an OSPF domain grows, the probability of link-state changes increases, because the domain includes more routers and networks. Consequently, each link-state change causes route recomputation on all routers, and burdens the CPU. In addition, each route computation is more time-consuming because more destination networks exist. When the OSPF domain becomes too large, you may want to partition it into multiple areas. Partitioning reduces the burden on the CPU. Cisco recommends that you limit the size of an area to include fewer than 200 routers. However, under certain conditions, you can enable the route aggregation feature to increase this limitation.

Partitioning the OSPF domain into areas provides several advantages. It permits administrative separation of different geographical or organizational groups, such as engineering and marketing. Creating areas enables you to limit the sharing of routing information between areas. This makes a particular area more secure. Creating areas reduces the number of *Link State Advertisements* (LSAs) per area and enables you to isolate an area with frequent topological changes.

OSPF Router Classes

OSPF supports a number of different router classifications based on how OSPF areas are designed. OSPF supports four types of routers: Internal Router, Area Border Router, Backbone Router, and Autonomous System Boundary Router. A description of each router class follows. (Also see Figure 11.1 for each OSPF router's position in the network.)

Internal Router. A router with all directly connected networks belonging to the same area. These routers run a single copy of the basic routing algorithm.

Area Border Routers. ABRs share information that advertises destinations through the backbone area into the nonbackbone area. ABRs also share information that advertises destinations through the nonbackbone area into the backbone area. ABRs have network connection in more than one area.

Backbone Routers. A router with an interface to the backbone area, including all routers that interface to more than one area (i.e., area border routers). However, backbone routers do not have to be area border routers. Routers with all interfaces connecting to the backbone area are supported.

Autonomous System Boundary Routers. Routing information from other autonomous systems and exterior gateway protocols can be combined and disseminated through ASBRs. Because ASBRs provide an interface to other autonomous systems and routing protocols, ASBRs have access to routing information learned from routers outside the OSPF domain.

OSPF Network Support

OSPF is flexible because it can support point-to-point, broadcast, point-to-multipoint, and nonbroadcast networks.

Point-to-point networks, as shown in Figure 11.2, are serial lines that connect a pair of routers, for example, a 56-Kbps line that connects a remote site to a main campus. This implementation results in more efficient routes because only one route is available.

Broadcast networks, as shown in Figure 11.3, can support more than two attached routers and can broadcast a single physical message to all the attached routers. Ethernet and Token Ring are examples of broadcast networks. Networks supporting many (more than two) attached routers can address (*broadcast*) a single physical message to all of the attached routers. Neighboring routers are discovered dynamically on these nets using OSPF's Hello protocol. The Hello protocol takes advantage of the broadcast capability. The OSPF protocol makes further use of multicast capabilities, if they exist. Each pair of routers on a broadcast network is assumed to be able to communicate directly.

Nonbroadcast networks can connect more than two routers or hosts but have no broadcast capability. However, you must specify OSPF neighbors because this network does not broadcast data. Also, the configuration does not have to be fully symmetric; you do not have to configure all the neighbors for all routers. As long as at least one router has the complete list of neighbors in the network, the configuration works. This capability minimizes the chance of malfunction caused by misconfiguration. However, due to the lack of broadcast capability, some configuration information may be necessary to aid in the discovery of neighbors. On nonbroadcast networks, OSPF protocol packets normally multicast and need to be sent to each neighboring router, via a unicast. An X.25 *Public Data Network* (PDN) is an example of a *Nonbroadcast Multiple Access* (NBMA) network as shown in Figure 11.4.

Atlanta   Seattle

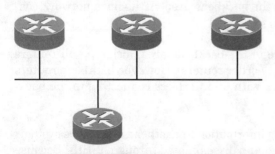

FIGURE 11.2 Point-to-Point network

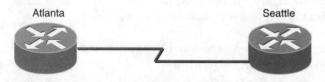

FIGURE 11.3 Broadcast network

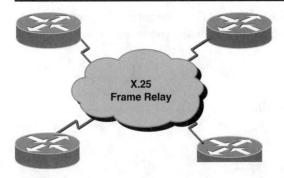

FIGURE 11.4 Nonbroadcast network

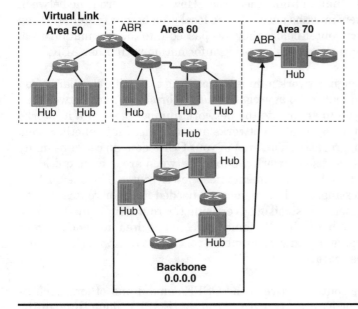

FIGURE 11.5 OSPF virtual and transit areas

Virtual Links

A virtual link enables you to extend a backbone area by joining two partitioned areas and to isolate an area with frequent topological changes.

Networks and routers in an OSPF backbone area must be interconnected. However, when the OSPF domain is divided into areas, the backbone area can become partitioned. The partitioned parts of the backbone area can be reconnected with a virtual link.

A virtual link is a path through the transit area, or nonbackbone area. The ABRs at each end of the virtual link treat the path between the two as a point-to-point link. When that virtual point-to-point link is used, the partitioned area is reconnected to the Backbone area, as shown in Figure 11.5.

The use of a virtual link is complicated and error-prone. Consequently, Cisco recommends that you make every effort to keep the backbone area physically connected. The virtual link should be used only when necessary.

Hierarchical Routing

OSPF supports three types of hierarchical routing:

- Intra-area routing
- Inter-area routing
- External link advertisement

Intra-Area Routing and Inter-Area Routing.   Routing within an area, or intra-area, can occur without knowledge of routing information from other areas. However, with routing between areas, or inter-area routing, packets must be passed to the local area border router and then to the destination's area boundary router before they are passed into the destination area.

Inter-area routing requires sharing an area's routing information with other ABRs.

Route Aggregation.   When you assign network numbers according to specific standards, you can enable the route aggregation feature to aggregate route information sent between areas. Route aggregation enables you to aggregate the network number of several networks into one network number when the aggregated networks are advertised into another area. You might want to enable route aggregation if an area in your OSPF domain contains many networks. This enables ABR to advertise network numbers between areas more quickly.

Routers that receive the aggregated advertisements need fewer routes. This means that faster routing lookups, less processing, and less memory is needed than for routes that do not receive aggregated advertisements. Instead of advertising the routes individually, route aggregation combines network numbers with the same prefix in one area into one network number. For example, you can aggregate network numbers `20.4.0.0`, `20.5.0.0`, `20.6.0.0`, and `20.7.0.0` into the network number `20.0.0.0`.

External Link Advertisement.   The routing between the OSPF domain and others, such as *Interior Gateway Protocol* (IGP) or *Exterior Gateway Protocol* (EGP), is done through the ASBRs. This process is called *external link advertisement*. The ASBRs are located on the border of the OSPF domain. To disseminate the external destinations, they flood external advertisements throughout the OSPF domain.

Two types of external link advertisements, type 1 and type 2, are possible. The meaning of the external link advertisement metric depends on the type.

- *Type 1.*   Metric is the sum of the internal and external metrics.
- *Type 2.*   Metric does not add internal metrics.

Stub Areas

OSPF supports the use of stub areas as shown in Figure 11.6. When only one ABR exists for an area, all destinations outside the area go through that router. In this case, you may want to configure the area as a stub area. A stub area does not allow its ABRs to advertise

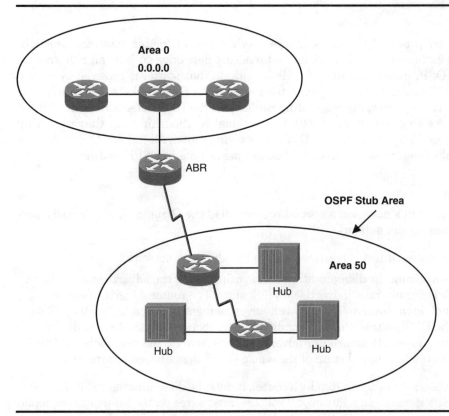

FIGURE 11.6 Stub area

external routes, including routes to other areas as well as routes external to the OSPF domain. Instead, ABRs advertise a single default route. By not generating advertisements for individual destinations, a stub area saves memory, CPU, and bandwidth resources on all OSPF routers.

The stub area does not allow its ABRs to pass on external link-state advertisements to other areas. Consequently, ASBRs cannot be placed inside a stub area. An ASBR within a stub area circulates external link advertisements only within the area. Therefore, all OSPF routers outside the stub area do not learn about external destinations.

OSPF Concepts

This section describes the OSPF concepts that provide IP routing:

- Neighbors
- Designated Router
- Adjacency
- Flooding
- Dijkstra algorithm

Neighbors

OSPF neighbors are peer OSPF routers on a network. An OSPF router discovers its neighbors through the exchange of Hello packets. In broadcast networks, such as an Ethernet local network, the OSPF router multicasts a Hello packet. That packet is received by all the router's neighbors. To indicate that it is alive, the router sends Hello packets to its configured neighbors. In the Hello packet, the originating router lists the ID of neighbors from which it has heard. The receiving router assumes a bidirectional relationship with the originating router if the received Hello contains the ID of the receiving router. All links in OSPF must be bidirectional. Links that are not bidirectional do not participate in OSPF routing.

Designated Router

Among OSPF routers in a network, a special router called the *Designated Router* (DR) performs two functions on the network:

- It generates the network link advertisement on behalf of the network.
- It acts as the coordinator for disseminating and synchronizing the advertisements. Each node in the OSPF domain must advertise its link state. The router advertisement is originated by individual routers. The network advertisement is generated by the DR on the network. The DR lists the IDs of its qualifying neighbors on that network. By linking the network advertisements and router advertisements from all the neighbors, an OSPF router constructs the topological state of the whole OSPF domain (see Figure 11.7).

When an advertisement is originated by a router, it must be disseminated to all the OSPF routers in the OSPF domain. In addition, all routers must agree on the internetwork topology. If the routers do not agree, OSPF routing breaks down, and a loss of connectivity or routing loops can occur. The dissemination and synchronization of link-state advertisements among OSPF routers is achieved through the use of adjacencies. The DR is the central point of all adjacent relationships on the network.

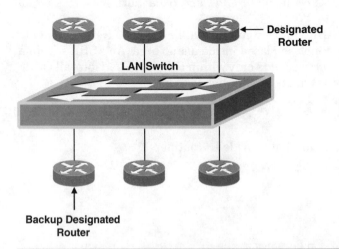

FIGURE 11.7   OSPF Designated Router and backup Designated Router

The DR for a network is selected from among all bidirectional neighbors, through a selection process. When no DR exists, the neighbors select the DR according to the priority value conveyed in the Hello packets. The router with the highest priority value becomes the DR. After a DR is selected, it continues to act as the DR until the network goes down.

The election process chooses the backup DR. Both the DR and the backup DR maintain an adjacency relationship with their neighbors. However, the backup DR is not responsible for generating network advertisements for the network, except when the DR goes down. Because the backup DR maintains adjacency relationships with its neighbors, it does not have to reestablish adjacencies. Consequently, the transition from one DR to another is faster with a backup DR than without a backup DR.

Adjacency

For OSPF to work properly, all OSPF routers must be in agreement on the link state, or topology, of the OSPF domain. OSPF achieves that agreement by requiring a router to be constantly in synchronization with some subset of its neighbors. The router then is said to be adjacent to those neighbors.

To ensure synchronization among routers, not all routers must be in synchronization with all their neighbors. For example, if Atlanta is in synchronization with Boston, and Boston is in synchronization with Charlotte, then Atlanta is in synchronization with Charlotte. Therefore, Atlanta needs to be adjacent only to Boston and not to Charlotte. In practice, OSPF simplifies the synchronization by requiring the adjacency between only the DR, the backup DR, and their neighbors on a broadcast network. If the router is not a DR or a backup DR, it forms an adjacency only with the DR and backup DR. Because adjacent neighbors must agree on the link state of the OSPF domain, they exchange their link-state databases with each other to synchronize their databases at the beginning. After their link-state databases are exchanged and become identical to each other, the adjacent neighbors are said to be full. Only after both neighbors on an adjacency become full is the adjacency considered completely formed. In addition to link-state database synchronization, the adjacency serves as the path for disseminating a newly originated link-state advertisement throughout the OSPF domain.

Flooding

The process of disseminating a link-state advertisement is called *flooding*. When a new advertisement is flooded throughout the OSPF domain, it is disseminated along adjacencies. Because all routers are interconnected by adjacencies, they have a chance to receive the new advertisement. All routers must synchronize their link-state databases, so that flooding will be reliable. OSPF achieves reliability through positive ACK and retransmission.

The flooding algorithm can detect duplicate advertisements and install the correct one. For example, a router that goes down and comes back up might encounter an advertisement that it originated. To prevent ambiguity, OSPF uses a sequence number and an age to decide which version of the advertisement is the correct one.

Dijkstra Algorithm

When the complete link-state information becomes available, the OSPF router can compute the reachable network destinations and routes to them. The router must recompute the routing table when a new network or router link-state advertisement is received. To compute the routes from link-state information, OSPF uses the Dijkstra algorithm, a method to compute the shortest path to destinations in a topology.

The summary and external link advertisements do not represent topological link states. Instead, they are advertisements of reachable destinations by the originating routers, similar to RIP. Therefore, a change in the summary or external link-state advertisements does not require that the Dijkstra algorithm be used to compute the route. These destinations are computed by an update of the individual routing entries in the route table, according to the change conveyed by the new advertisement.

Routing Protocol Packets

The OSPF protocol runs directly over IP, using IP protocol 89. OSPF does not provide any explicit fragmentation/reassembly support. When fragmentation is necessary, IP fragmentation/reassembly is used. OSPF packets have been designed so that large packets can generally be split into several smaller packets. This practice is recommended; however, IP fragmentation should be avoided when possible.

OSPF's Hello protocol uses Hello packets to discover and maintain neighbor relationships. The Database Description and Link State Request packets are used in the forming of adjacencies. OSPF's reliable update mechanism is implemented by the Link State Update and Link State Acknowledgment packets. Figure 11.8 shows the OSPF router link-state advertisement types.

Each Link State Update packet carries a set of new link-state advertisements one hop further away from their point of origin. A single Link State Update packet may contain the link-state advertisements of several routers. Each advertisement is tagged with the ID of the originating router and a checksum of its link-state contents. The five different types of OSPF link-state advertisements are shown in Figures 11.9–11.13 and listed in Table 11.1.

OSPF routing packets (with the exception of Hellos) are sent over only adjacencies. Therefore, all OSPF protocol packets travel a single IP hop, except those sent over virtual adjacencies. The IP source address of an OSPF protocol packet is one end of a router adjacency, and the IP destination address is either the other end of the adjacency or an IP multicast address.

Figures 11.14–11.16 shows the OSPF router link-state advertisement types by OSPF router classification.

OSPF Message Header

OSPF supports a number of functions that must occur in order to send and receive an OSFP packet. These nodes first must build an OSPF message header included in all OSPF packets sent or received between routers (see Figure 11.17).

The message header consists of the following fields:

- *Version #.*   This field contains the OSPF version number.
- *Type.*   The OSPF packet types are as follow:

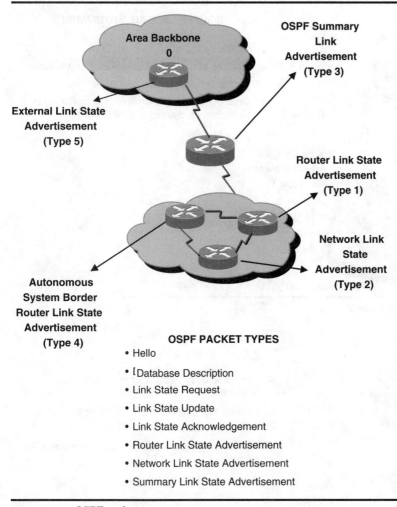

OSPF Summary Link Advertisement (Type 3)

Area Backbone 0

External Link State Advertisement (Type 5)

Router Link State Advertisement (Type 1)

Network Link State Advertisement (Type 2)

Autonomous System Border Router Link State Advertisement (Type 4)

OSPF PACKET TYPES

- Hello
- [Database Description
- Link State Request
- Link State Update
- Link State Acknowledgement
- Router Link State Advertisement
- Network Link State Advertisement
- Summary Link State Advertisement

FIGURE 11.8   OSPF packet types

Type	Description
1	Hello
2	Database Description
3	Link State Request

Type	Description
4	Link State Update
5	Link State Acknowledgment

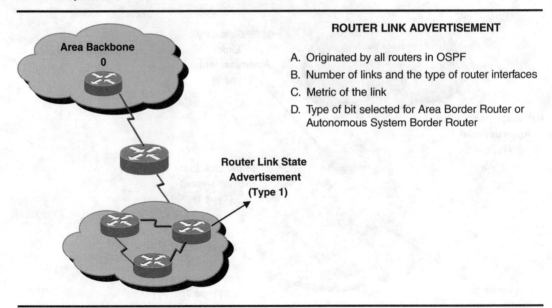

FIGURE 11.9   Router link advertisement

ROUTER LINK ADVERTISEMENT

A. Originated by all routers in OSPF
B. Number of links and the type of router interfaces
C. Metric of the link
D. Type of bit selected for Area Border Router or Autonomous System Border Router

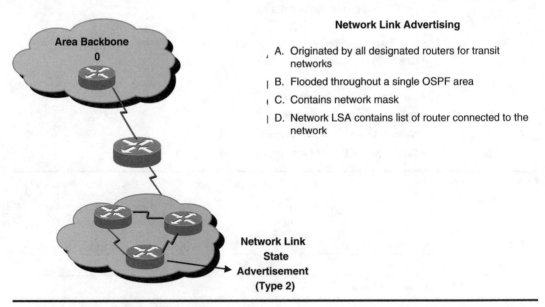

FIGURE 11.10   Network link advertisement

Network Link Advertising

A. Originated by all designated routers for transit networks
B. Flooded throughout a single OSPF area
C. Contains network mask
D. Network LSA contains list of router connected to the network

- *Packet length.* This field indicates the length of the OSPF protocol packet in bytes. This length includes the standard OSPF header.
- *Router ID.* This field indicates the Router ID of the packet's source.

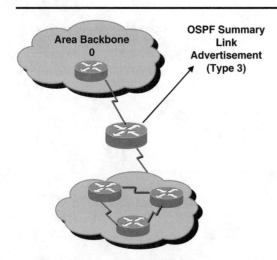

OSPF Summary Link Advertisement (Type 3)

Summary Link State Advertisement

A. Originated by Area Border Router

B. Summary for route to destination from one area to another

C. Mask can be network subnet

D. Metric

FIGURE 11.11   Summary link advertisement

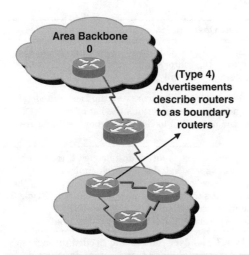

(Type 4) Advertisements describe routers to as boundary routers

Summary Link State Advertisement

A. Router links into each area

B. Network links if it is the DR

C. Summary network for route summarization

D. Summary - ASBR into other areas

FIGURE 11.12   Autonomous System Border router link-state advertisement

- *Area ID.* This field is a 32-bit number identifying the area to which this packet belongs. All OSPF packets are associated with a single area. Most travel a single hop. Packets traveling over a virtual link are labeled with the backbone Area ID of 0.0.0.0.

- *Checksum.* This field is the standard IP checksum of the entire contents of the packet, starting with the OSPF packet header but excluding the 64-bit authentication field. This checksum is calculated as the 16-bit 1's complement of the 1's complement sum of all the 16-bit words in the packet, excepting the authentication field. If the packet's length is

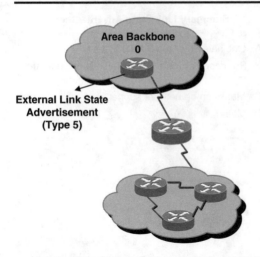

External Link State Advertisement

A. Originated by AS boundary router
B. Flooded into the autonomy system
C. Default route for AS

FIGURE 11.13   External link-state advertisement

TABLE 11.1   OSPF Router Link-State Advertisement Types

Link-State Type	Advertisement Name	Advertisement Description
1	Router links advertisement	Originated by all routers. This advertisement describes the collected states of the router's interfaces to an area. Flooded throughout a single area only.
2	Network links advertisement	Originated for multiaccess networks by the Designated Router. This advertisement contains the list of routers connected to the network. Flooded throughout a single area only.
3 and 4	Summary link advertisement	Originated by area border routers and flooded throughout the advertisement's associated area. Each summary link advertisement describes a route to a destination outside the area, yet still inside the AS (i.e., an inter-area route). Type 3 advertisements describe routes to networks. Type 4 advertisements describe routes to AS boundary routers.
5	AS external link advertisement	Originated by AS boundary routers and flooded throughout the AS. Each AS external link advertisement describes a route to a destination in another autonomous system. Default routes for the AS also can be described by AS external link advertisements.

not an integral number of 16-bit words, the packet is padded with a byte of 0 before checksumming. The checksum is considered to be part of the packet authentication procedure; for some authentication types the checksum calculation is omitted.

- *Authentication Type.*   This field identifies the authentication procedure to be used for the packet.

- *Authentication.*   This is a 64-bit field for use by the authentication scheme.

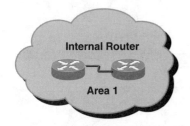

**Internal Router
Type of Link-State Advertisements**

A. Router Link-State Advertisement (Type 1) (sent to each router attached)

B. Network links advertisement (Type 2) (list of routers connected to the transit network if acting as DR)

FIGURE 11.14   Internal router type of link-state advertisement

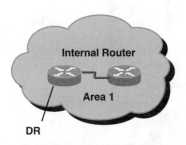

**Designated Router Type of
Link-State Advertisement**

A. Router Link State (Type 1)

B. Network Link State (Type 2)

C. Summary Network (Type 3)

D. Summary as BR (Type 4)

E. External Link State (Type 5)

FIGURE 11.15   Designated Router type of link-state advertisement

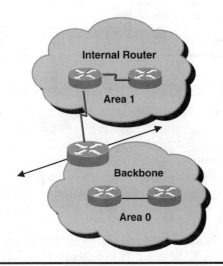

**Area Border Router Type of Link–
State Advertisement**

A. Router links into each area

B. Network links if it is the DR

C. Summary network for route summarization

D. Summary - ASBR into other areas

FIGURE 11.16   Area border router type of link-state advertisement

The Hello Protocol

The Hello protocol is responsible for establishing and maintaining neighbor relationships. It ensures that communication between neighbors is bidirectional. Hello packets are sent periodically out to all router interfaces. Bidirectional communication is indicated when the

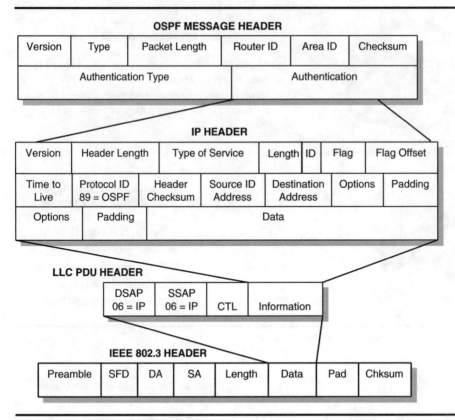

OSPF MESSAGE HEADER

Version	Type	Packet Length	Router ID	Area ID	Checksum

Authentication Type			Authentication		

IP HEADER

Version	Header Length	Type of Service	Length	ID	Flag	Flag Offset

Time to Live	Protocol ID 89 = OSPF	Header Checksum	Source ID Address	Destination Address	Options	Padding

Options	Padding	Data

LLC PDU HEADER

DSAP 06 = IP	SSAP 06 = IP	CTL	Information

IEEE 802.3 HEADER

Preamble	SFD	DA	SA	Length	Data	Pad	Chksum

FIGURE 11.17 OSPF message header

router sees itself listed in the neighbor's Hello packet. On multiaccess networks, the Hello protocol elects a DR for the network. Among other things, the DR controls what adjacencies are formed over the network.

The Hello protocol works differently on broadcast networks, as compared to nonbroadcast networks. On broadcast networks, each router advertises itself by periodically multicasting Hello packets. This broadcasting allows neighbors to be discovered dynamically. These Hello packets contain the router's view of the DR's identity and the list of routers whose Hello packets have been seen recently.

On nonbroadcast networks, some configuration information is necessary for the operation of the Hello protocol. Each router that may become a DR has a list of all other routers attached to the network. A router with DR potential sends Hello packets to all other potential DRs when its interface to the nonbroadcast network first becomes operational. This is an attempt to find the DR for the network. If the router is elected DR, the router begins sending Hello packets to all other routers attached to the network.

After a neighbor has been discovered, bidirectional communication has been ensured, and (if on a multiaccess network) a DR has been elected, a decision is made regarding whether an adjacency should be formed with the neighbor. An attempt is always made to establish adjacencies over point-to-point networks and virtual links. The first step in bringing up an adjacency is to synchronize the neighbors' topological databases.

Hello packets are OSPF packet type 1. These packets are sent periodically on all interfaces (including virtual links) to establish and maintain neighbor relationships. In addition, Hello packets are multicast on those physical networks with a multicast or broadcast capability, enabling dynamic discovery of neighboring routers.

The OSPF Hello header contains the following fields (see Figure 11.18):

- *Network mask.* This field is the network mask associated with this interface. For example, if the interface is for a class B network whose third byte is used for subnetting, the network mask is 0xffffff00.

- *Hello Interval.* The number of seconds between this router's Hello packets.

- *Options.* This field is for the optional capabilities supported by the router.

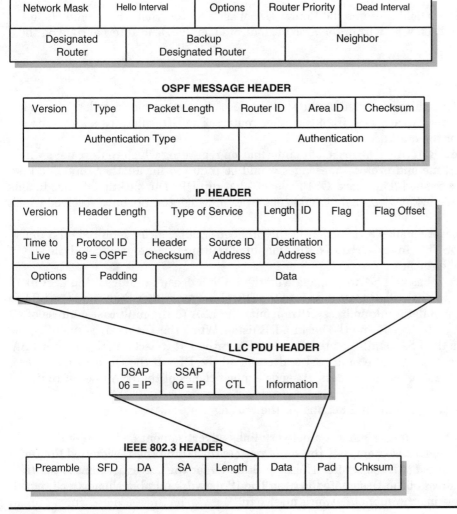

OSPF HELLO HEADER

Network Mask	Hello Interval	Options	Router Priority	Dead Interval
Designated Router	Backup Designated Router		Neighbor	

OSPF MESSAGE HEADER

Version	Type	Packet Length	Router ID	Area ID	Checksum
Authentication Type			Authentication		

IP HEADER

Version	Header Length	Type of Service	Length	ID	Flag	Flag Offset
Time to Live	Protocol ID 89 = OSPF	Header Checksum	Source ID Address	Destination Address		
Options	Padding	Data				

LLC PDU HEADER

DSAP 06 = IP	SSAP 06 = IP	CTL	Information

IEEE 802.3 HEADER

Preamble	SFD	DA	SA	Length	Data	Pad	Chksum

FIGURE 11.18 OSPF Hello header

- *Router Priority.*   This field is for this router's priority and is used in (Backup) Designated Router election. If set to 0, the router is ineligible to become (Backup) Designated Router.

- *Dead Interval.*   This field indicates the number of seconds before declaring a silent router down.

- *Designated Router.*   This field indicates the identity of the Designated Router for this network, according to the sending router. The Designated Router is identified here by its IP interface address on the network. This field is set to 0.0.0.0 if no Designated Router exists.

- *Backup Designated Router.*   This field indicates the identity of the Backup Designated Router for this network, according to the sending router. The Backup Designated Router is identified here by its IP interface address on the network. If this field is set to 0.0.0.0, no Backup Designated Router exists.

- *Neighbor.*   This field contains the Router IDs of each router from whom valid Hello packets have been seen within the amount indicated as the Dead Interval time on the network.

Designated Router

In OSPF, the DR, which is elected by the Hello protocol, is responsible for collecting explicit acknowledgments for each LSA from the other routers. The DR generates a link-state advertisement for the multiaccess network.

Because the DR in OSPF keeps a lot of information regarding which routers have which LSAs, a lot of time and protocol messages would be required for another router to take over if the DR crashed. Therefore, OSPF elects a backup DR. The backup DR also listens to all the explicit acknowledgments and keeps track of which routers have received which LSAs.

The DR concept enables a reduction in the number of adjacencies required on a multiaccess network. This, in turn, reduces the amount of routing protocol traffic and the size of the topological database.

When router R has an LSA to propagate on the LAN, R doesn't multicast the LSA to all the other routers. Instead, R transmits it to the DR. However, rather than send the LSA to the DR's personal data-link address, R transmits the LSA to the multicast address of all DRs, to which both the DR and the backup DR listen. When the DR receives the LSA, the DR multicasts the LSA to all the other routers. Then the DR collects ACKs for that LSA, which are transmitted to the multicast address of all the DRs. If the DR does not receive an ACK from a subset of the routers, it sends explicit copies of the LSA to each router in that subset.

The DR performs two main functions for the routing protocol:

- The Designated Router originates a network links advertisement on behalf of the network. This advertisement lists the set of routers (including the Designated Router) currently attached to the network. The Link State ID for this advertisement is the IP interface address of the Designated Router. The IP network number then can be obtained by using the subnet/network mask.

- The Designated Router becomes adjacent to all other routers on the network. Because the link-state databases are synchronized across adjacencies (through adjacency bring-up and then the flooding procedure), the Designated Router plays a central part in the synchronization process.

The Backup Designated Router does not generate a network links advertisement for the network. (If it did, the transition to a new DR would be even faster. However, this is a trade-off between database size and speed of convergence when the DR disappears.) In some steps of the flooding procedure, the Backup DR plays a passive role, letting the DR do more of the work. This reduces the amount of local routing traffic.

When the DR and the backup DR are elected, OSPF makes every effort to keep them, even if another router subsequently comes up with a higher priority or ID. The reason behind the election algorithm's complexity is the desire for an orderly transition from backup DR to DR, when the current DR fails. This orderly transition is ensured through the introduction of *hysteresis*: no new backup DR router can be chosen until the old backup accepts its new DR responsibilities.

Database Description Packets

Database Description packets are identified by using OSPF packet Type 2. These packets are exchanged when an adjacency is being initialized. They describe the contents of the link-state database. Multiple packets may be used to describe the database. For this purpose, a poll-response procedure is used. One of the routers is designated to be the master; the other is designated as the slave. The master sends Database Description packets (polls) that are acknowledged by Database Description packets sent by the slave (responses). The responses are linked to the polls via the packets' DD sequence number as shown in Figure 11.19. Figure 11.20 displays the Database Description packet.

The format of the Database Description packet is very similar to both the Link State Request and Link State Acknowledgment packets. The main part of all three is a list of items, each item describing apiece of the link-state database:

- *Options.* This field indicates the optional capabilities supported by the router.
- *Init. Bit.* When this field is set to 1, this packet is the first in the sequence of Database Description packets.
- *More Bit.* When the More bit is set to 1, it indicates that more Database Description packets are to follow.
- *Master Bit.* When the Master/Slave bit is set to 1, it indicates that the router is the master during the Database Exchange process. Otherwise, the router is the slave.
- *Database Sequence Number.* This field is used to sequence the collection of Database Description packets. The initial value (indicated by the Init bit being set) should be unique. The DD sequence number then increments until the complete database description has been sent.

The rest of the packet consists of a (possibly partial) list of the link-state database's pieces. Each LSA in the database is described by its LSA header.

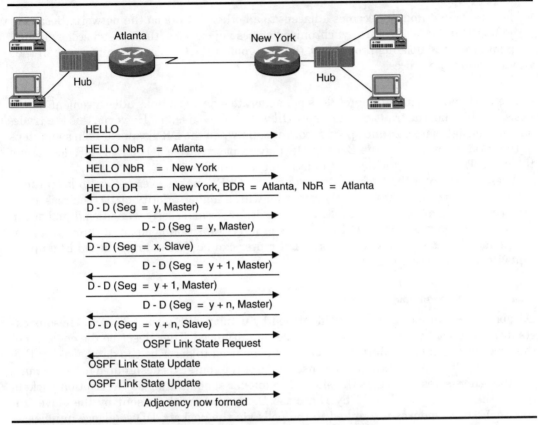

FIGURE 11.19   OSPF initial database synchronization for forming adjacencies

Link State Request Packets

Link State Request packets are OSPF packet Type 3. After exchanging Database Description packets with a neighboring router, a router may find that parts of its link-state database are out-of-date. The Link State Request packet is used to request the pieces of the neighbor's database that are more up-to-date. Multiple Link State Request packets may need to be used.

A router that sends a Link State Request packet has in mind the precise *instance* of the database pieces it is requesting. Each instance is defined by its LS sequence number, LS checksum, and LS age, although these fields are not specified in the Link State Request Packet itself. The router may receive even more recent instances in response.

Link State Update Packets

Link State Update packets are OSPF packet Type 4 (see Figure 11.21). These packets implement the flooding of LSAs. Each Link State Update packet carries a collection of LSAs one hop further from their origin. Several LSAs may be included in a single packet. Link State Update packets are multicast on those physical networks that support multicast/broadcast. To make the flooding procedure reliable, flooded LSAs are acknowledged

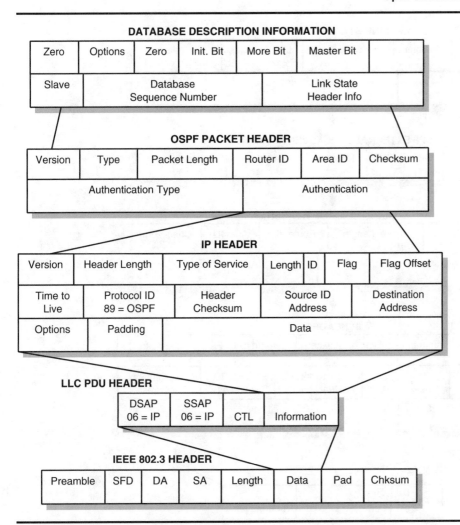

DATABASE DESCRIPTION INFORMATION

Zero	Options	Zero	Init. Bit	More Bit	Master Bit	

Slave	Database Sequence Number		Link State Header Info	

OSPF PACKET HEADER

Version	Type	Packet Length	Router ID	Area ID	Checksum

Authentication Type	Authentication

IP HEADER

Version	Header Length	Type of Service	Length	ID	Flag	Flag Offset

Time to Live	Protocol ID 89 = OSPF	Header Checksum	Source ID Address	Destination Address

Options	Padding	Data

LLC PDU HEADER

DSAP 06 = IP	SSAP 06 = IP	CTL	Information

IEEE 802.3 HEADER

Preamble	SFD	DA	SA	Length	Data	Pad	Chksum

FIGURE 11.20 Database Description packet

in Link State Acknowledgment packets. If retransmission of certain LSAs is necessary, the retransmitted LSAs always are carried by unicast Link State Update packets.

All LSAs begin with a common 20-byte header. This header contains enough information to uniquely identify the LSA (Link State type, Link State ID, and Advertising Router). Multiple instances of the LSA may exist in the routing domain at the same time; therefore, it is necessary to determine which instance is more recent. This is accomplished by examining the LS age, LS sequence number, and LS checksum fields that also are contained in the LSA header:

- *Link State Age.*   This field is the time in seconds since the LSA was originated.

- *Options.*   The optional capabilities supported by the described portion of the routing domain.

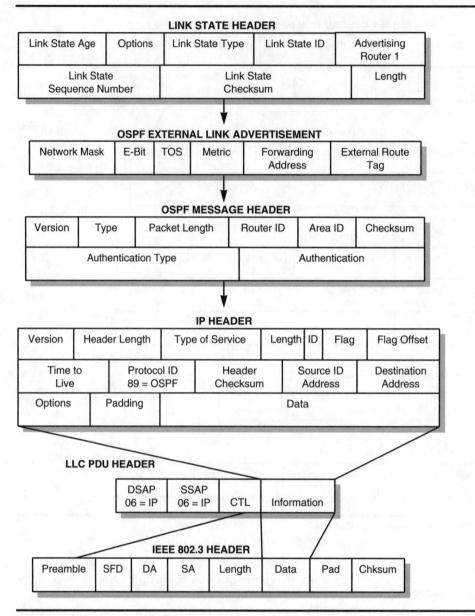

FIGURE 11.21   Link State Update packet

- *Link State Type.*   Each LSA type has a separate advertisement format. The LSA types defined here are as follows:

LS Type	Description
1	Router—LSAs
2	Network—LSAs

3	Summary—LSAs (IP network)
4	Summary—LSAs (ASBR)
5	AS-external—LSAs

- *Link State ID.*   This field identifies the portion of the Internet environment being described by the LSA. The contents of this field depend on the LSA's LS type. For example, in network LSAs, the Link State ID is set to the IP interface address of the network's Designated Router (from which the network's IP address can be derived).

- *Advertising Router.*   This field is the Router ID of the router that originated the LSA. For example, in network LSAs, this field is equal to the Router ID of the network's Designated Router.

- *Link State Sequence Number.*   This field detects old or duplicate LSAs. Successive instances of an LSA are given successive LS sequence numbers.

- *Link State Checksum.*   The Fletcher checksum of the complete contents of the LSA, including the LSA header but excluding the LS age field.

- *Length.*   This field is the length in bytes of the LSA. This includes the 20-byte LSA header.

Router Link State Advertisements

Router LSAs are Type 1 LSAs (see Figure 11.22). Each router in an area originates a router LSA. The LSA describes the state and cost of the router's links (i.e., interfaces) to the area. All of the router's links to the area must be described in a single router LSA.

In router LSAs, the Link State ID field is set to the router's OSPF Router ID. Router LSAs are flooded throughout a single area only.

- *bit V.*   When set, the router is an endpoint of one or more fully adjacent virtual links having the described area as Transit area (V is for virtual link endpoint).

- *bit E.*   When set, the router is an AS boundary router (E is for external).

- *bit B.*   When set, the router is an area border router (B is for border).

- *Number of links.*   The number of router links described in this LSA. This must be the total collection of router links (i.e., interfaces) to the area.

- *Type.*   A quick description of the router link; one of the following. Note that host routes are classified as links to stub networks with network a mask of `0xffffffff`.

Type	Description
1	Point-to-point connection to another router
2	Connection to a transit network
3	Connection to a stub network
4	Virtual link

- *Link ID.*   This field identifies the object to which this router link connects. Value depends on the link's type. When connecting to an object that also originates an LSA

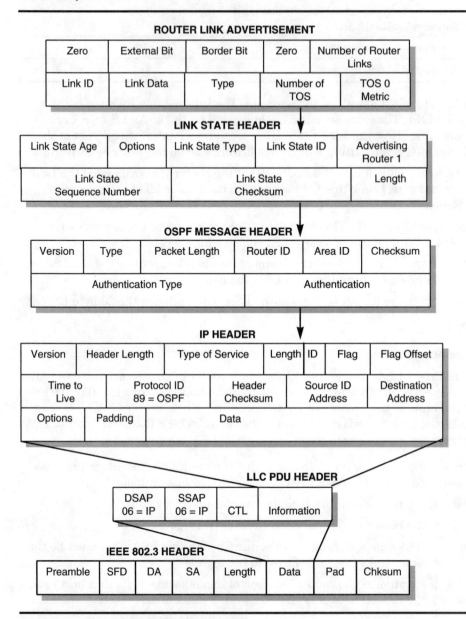

FIGURE 11.22 Router Link State Advertisement

(i.e., another router or a transit network), the Link ID is equal to the neighboring LSA's Link State ID. This provides the key for looking up the neighboring LSA in the link-state database during the routing table calculation.

Type	Link ID
1	Neighboring router's Router ID
2	IP address of Designated Router

3	IP network/subnet number
4	Neighboring router's Router ID

- *Link Data.* Value again depends on the link's type field. For connections to stub networks, Link Data specifies the network's IP address mask. This latter piece of information is needed during the routing table build process, when calculating the IP address of the next hop.

- *# TOS.* This field is the number of different TOS metrics given for this link, not counting the required link metric. For example, if no additional TOS metrics are given, this field is set to 0.

- *Metric.* This field is the cost of using this router link. Additional TOS-specific information may also be included, for backward compatibility with previous versions of the OSPF specification.

- *TOS IP.* This field indicates the type of service to which this metric refers.

- *TOS metric.* This field contains TOS-specific metric information.

Network LSAs

Network LSAs are Type 2 LSAs. A network LSA is originated for each broadcast and NBMA network in the area that supports two or more routers. The network LSA is originated by the network's Designated Router. The LSA describes all routers attached to the network, including the Designated Router itself. The LSA's Link State ID field lists the IP interface address of the Designated Router.

- *Network Mask.* This field indicates the IP address mask for the network. For example, a class A network would have the mask 0xff000000.

- *Attached Router.* The Router IDs of each of the routers attached to the network. Actually, only those routers fully adjacent to the Designated Router are listed. The Designated Router includes itself in this list. The number of routers included can be deduced from the LSA header's length field.

Summary LSAs

Summary LSAs are Type 3 and 4 LSAs (see Figure 11.23). These LSAs are originated by area border routers. Summary LSAs describe inter-area destinations.

Type 3 summary LSAs are used when the destination is an IP network. In this case, the LSA's Link State ID field is an IP network number (if necessary, the Link State ID can also have one or more of the network's *host* bits set). When the destination is an AS boundary router, a Type 4 summary LSA is used, and the Link State ID field is the AS boundary router's OSPF Router ID. (Other than the difference in the Link State ID field, the format of Type 3 and 4 summary LSAs is identical).

For stub areas, Type 3 summary LSAs also can be used to describe a (per-area) default route. Default summary routes are used in stub areas instead of flooding a complete set of external routes. When describing a default summary route, the summary LSA's Link State ID is always set to Default Destination (0.0.0.0), and the Network Mask is set to 0.0.0.0.

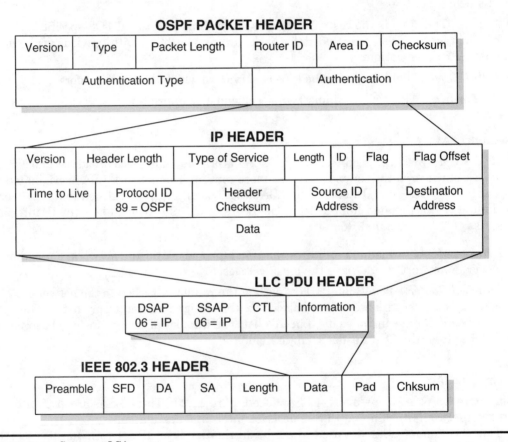

FIGURE 11.23 Summary LSA

- *Network Mask.*   For Type 3 summary LSAs, this field indicates the destination network's IP address mask. For example, when advertising the location of a class A network, the value 0xff000000 would be used. This field is not meaningful and must be 0 for Type 4 summary LSAs.

- *Metric.*   This field indicates the cost of this route. Expressed in the same units as the interface costs in the router LSAs.

Additional TOS-specific information may also be included, for backward compatibility with previous versions of the OSPF specification.

Autonomous System External LSAs

AS external LSAs are Type 5 LSAs. These LSAs are originated by AS boundary routers and describe destinations external to the AS. AS external LSAs usually describe a particular external destination. For these LSAs, the Link State ID field specifies an IP network number (if necessary, the Link State ID can also have one or more of the network's *host* bits set). AS external LSAs are also used to describe a default route. Default routes are used when no specific route exists to the destination. When describing a default route, the Link State ID is always set to Default Destination (0.0.0.0), and the Network Mask is set to 0.0.0.0.

- *Network Mask.*   This field indicates the IP address mask for the advertised destination. For example, when advertising a class A network, the mask 0xff000000 would be used.

- *bit E.*   This field indicates the type of external metric. If bit E is set, the metric specified is a Type 2 external metric, which means the metric is considered larger than any link-state path. If bit E is 0, the specified metric is a Type 1 external metric, which means that it is expressed in the same units as the link-state metric (i.e., the same units as interface cost).

- *Metric.*   This field indicates the cost of this route. Interpretation depends on the external type indication (bit E).

- *Forwarding address.*   Data traffic for the advertised destination is forwarded to this address. If the forwarding address is set to 0.0.0.0, data traffic is forwarded instead to the LSA's originator (i.e., the responsible AS boundary router).

- *External Route Tag.*   This is a 32-bit field attached to each external route. This is not used by the OSPF protocol. This tag may be used to communicate information between AS boundary routers; the precise nature of such information is outside the scope of this specification. Additional TOS-specific information may also be included, for backward compatibility with previous versions of the OSPF specification.

OSPF Routing Protocol Design Worksheet

Designer: _____

Customer: _____

Need Variable Length Subnets? Y / N   Discontinue Subnets? Y / N

# of areas: _____   Area 0 Mandatory: _____   Area Numbers: _____

Transit Area: Yes / No   Stub Area: Yes / No

Authentication Type: None   Yes / No   Simple   Yes / No

Link Cost: Types of Links:
   Serial 56K: _____   Ethernet: _____
   Serial T1/E1: _____   FDDI: _____
   Ethernet 10M: _____   Token Ring: _____
   Token Ring 16M: _____
   FDDI 100 MB: _____
   ATM: _____

Fast Ethernet 100M: _____

Cost Formula:
   Designated Router: _____   Backup Designated Router: _____
                                   (Use Fastest Router)

Type of Service Option: _____

Link State Advertising Timer: _____
(Default 30 min.)

Hello Timer: _____

Virtual Links? Y / N   External Links? Y / N

Process ID Number: _____   Exterior Protocol: _____
                                   EGP: _____

Wildcard-Mask: _____   BGP: _____

IP Address: _____

Subnet Mask: _____

Secondary Addresses: _____

IP Unnumbered (Apply to Serial Link) _____

Route Summarization: Y / N

LoopBack Interface: Y / N

List of OSPF neighbors:
   IP address of Neighbor _____   Designated Router Capable: Yes / No

OSPF network ranges:
   Network Number: _____   Network Mask: _____

List of Virtual Links:
   Virtual Link ID: _____   Virtual Neighbor ID: _____   Transit Area ID: _____

Reference Note: See RFC 1583 OSPF.

Questions

1. Identify the Protocol ID used to identify OSPF.

2. Identify the Router types used in OSPF.
   A. Area Border Router
   B. AS Boundary Router
   C. Backbone Routers
   D. Internal Router
   E. All of the above

3. OSPF is a:
   A. Link State Routing protocol based on path cost
   B. Distance vector protocol based on hop count
   C. Hybrid routing protocol
   D. None of the above

4. Cisco's implementation of OSPF supports:
   A. Variable length subnet masks
   B. Cost
   C. Multiple type of service routing
   D. Authentication using MD5
   E. IPSec
   F. All of the above

5. Dijkstra's algorithm is used to:
   A. Determine which routes are added to the IP routing table
   B. Build the link state database
   C. Build the shortest path first (SPF) tree
   D. Provide neighbor routing information

6. Which of the following statements are true concerning OSPF Routing?
   A. Link state updates are not permitted after an adjacency is formed
   B. Hello packets maintain an adjacency
   C. Link state information can be exchanged after an adjacency is formed
   D. None of the above

7. OSPF identifies routers with a unique:
   A. Link state ID
   B. IP address
   C. OSPF Router ID
   D. AS number

8. To form an adjacency, which parameters must be set identically among routers on the same physical network?
   A. Router ID
   B. Subnet Mask
   C. Area Number
   D. Dead Interval Timer
   E. Hello Interval Timer

9. OSPF supports which media for broadcast networks?
   A. Token Ring
   B. FDDI
   C. Ethernet
   D. Fast Ethernet
   E. Gigabit Ethernet
   F. All of the above

10. What are the disadvantages of using OSPF?
    A. Routing updates every 30 seconds
    B. Large amount of memory and processing power are needed
    C. Long convergence times
    D. All areas must be connected to Area 0
    E. Bandwidth used during the initial link state flood
    F. Difficult to implement

11. OSPF is a member of which of the following routing protocols?
    A. Exterior Routing Protocols
    B. Interior Routing Protocol
    C. Hybrid Routing Protocol
    D. None of the above

12. OSPF routing table update frequency is _____.
    A. 15 seconds
    B. 30 minutes
    C. 45 seconds
    D. 60 minutes

13. What is the network diameter in hops with OSPF?
    A. 65k
    B. 60
    C. 16

14. The IP address used for the designated router is:
    A. 224.0.0.4
    B. 224.0.0.6
    C. 127.0.0.1
    D. 224.0.0.5

15. The IP address used for the backup designated router is:
    A. 224.0.0.5
    B. 224.0.0.7
    C. 224.0.0.9
    D. 224.0.0.6

16. The designated router in OSPF is chosen by the:
    A. Hello Protocol
    B. First Router configured on the network
    C. MAC Address
    D. None of the above

17. When is a backup designated router promoted to DR?
    A. DR failed
    B. Backup DR failed
    C. First router enabled on the network
    D. A & B
    E. None of the above

18. The design of a properly configured OSPF network requires a Backbone Area number ____.
    A. 0
    B. 2
    C. 4
    D. 5
    E. None of the above

19. Which of the following types of networks are supported by OSPF?
    A. Point to Point
    B. Non-Broadcast
    C. Broadcast
    D. Point to Multipoint
    E. All of the above

20. Identify three link state advertisements.
    A. Router Link Advertisement   E. External Link Advertisement
    B. Network Links Advertisement   F. All of the above
    C. Summary Links Advertisement   G. A, B, C, and E
    D. AS Boundary Router Summary Link Adv

21. In order to do effective route summarization, IP address network numbers must _____.
    A. reside in the same class of address
    B. be contiguous
    C. virtual links cannot be supported
    D. None of the above

22. How many areas 0s should there be in an OSPF network design?
    A. 1   C. 3
    B. 2   D. 4

23. Which of the following is used to bridge a discontinuous backbone area?
    A. Link State   C. Virtual Link
    B. Virtual Bridge   D. Area Link

24. OSPF advertises routing information via _____.
    A. Multicasts   C. Anycast
    B. Broadcasts   D. a combination of the two

25. There is one designated router per:
    A. Workgroup   C. Ethernet Segment
    B. Area   D. Autonomous System

26. OSPF sends packets to address 224.0.0.5 to communicate with:
    A. All Routers   C. Shortest Path First Routers
    B. Stub Routers   D. Slave Routers

27. OSPF sends packets to address 224.0.0.6 to communicate with:
    A. Designated Routers   C. Shortest Path First Routers
    B. Stub Routers   D. Slave Routers

28. Which of the following is termed a stub area?
    A. An area with no externally learned routes
    B. A small area
    C. An area that has been cut off from the backbone area
    D. An area with only one router
    E. None of the above

29. OSPF is a _____ routing protocol.
    A. classless   C. integrated
    B. classful   D. autonomous

30. Which of the following may cause two OSPF routers not to communicate?
    A. Both configured in area 0
    B. Neither configured in area 0
    C. Both configured for stub area
    D. Only one configured for stub area

31. OSPF updates progress through a network via which means:
    A. Flooding
    B. Step-by-step progress
    C. All routes receiving updates simultaneously
    D. Flash updates

32. Identify a feature of OSPF.
    A. Authentication
    B. Automatic redistribution into EIGRP
    C. Automatic interface configuration
    D. Unacknowledged updates

33. OSPF routers form adjacencies with which of the following routers?
    A. Designated router   C. Next hop router
    B. EIGRP router   D. Peer router

34. A router ID is:
    A. the administrative name given to the router
    B. the OSPF process number defined on the router
    C. the lowest IP address defined on the router
    D. the loopback interface or the highest IP address defined on the router
    E. none of the above

35. How may a loopback address be related with OSPF?
    A. Updates are sent out the loopback interface
    B. The loopback interface is the interface with which the OSPF pros is associated
    C. The loopback interface keeps OSPF from going down
    D. The loopback interface provides the OSPF router ID

36. In the absence of network changes, OSPF sends out updates:
    A. Every 30 seconds   C. Every 60 minutes
    B. Every 30 minutes   D. Never

37. The command redistribute RIP under the OSPF process causes which of the following to happen?
    A. Routing information to be given to RIP
    B. Routing information to be received from RIP
    C. RIP to send out routing updates immediately
    D. Nothing

38. The default metric used by OSPF is:
    A. Type-1   C. Type-3
    B. Type-2   D. Type-4

39. A type-2 metric takes into account:
- **A.** The cost of getting from the ASBR to the destination network
- **B.** The cost of getting from the current router to the ASBR
- **C.** The cost of getting from the current router to the ASBR and from the ASBR to the destination network
- **D.** None of the above

40. An OPSF router with which of the following is elected as the designated router?
- **A.** Highest priority
- **B.** Lowest priority
- **C.** Highest router ID
- **D.** Lowest router ID

41. An OSPF process number can be denoted in which of the following formats?
- **A.** Decimal
- **B.** Hexadecimal
- **C.** Octal
- **D.** Dotted decimal

42. OSPF keeps entries in its database for which of the following?
- **A.** All routers within an area
- **B.** All routers within an autonomous system
- **C.** All directly connected neighbor routers
- **D.** All of the above

43. When an OSPF router with a higher priority than the current designated router joins a network:
- **A.** It becomes a neighbor router.
- **B.** It forms an adjacency with all its neighbor routers.
- **C.** It is elected as the designated router.
- **D.** It causes the OSPF network to cease functioning correctly.

44. When using the default administrative distances, which of the following routing protocols will take precedence?
- **A.** IGRP
- **B.** OSPF
- **C.** EIGRP
- **D.** RIP

45. When redistributing routing information from OSPF into IGRP, the basis for IGRP's routing decisions is:
- **A.** The administrative distance of OSPF
- **B.** Whether or not the redistribution is being done on the designated router
- **C.** Which route has been known longer by IGRP
- **D.** None of the above

46. The default priority for an OSPF router is:
- **A.** 1
- **B.** 32
- **C.** 64
- **D.** 128

47. Cisco defines the default cost for an OSPF interface as:
- **A.** 103 / (Bandwidth of the interface in bits per second)
- **B.** 100M / (Bandwidth of the interface in bits per second)
- **C.** 1010 / (Bandwidth of the interface in bits per second)
- **D.** There is no default value.

48. Which of the following terms are associated with OSPF?
    A. LSP   C. LSA
    B. DUAL   D. All of the above

49. OSPF is _____ in nature.
    A. flat   C. hierarchical
    B. hub and spoke   D. none of the above

50. The OSPF router ID is related to which of the following?
    A. Highest IP address   D. Designated router
    B. Source IP address   E. All of the above
    C. Area number

51. The sum of which interface value determines OSPF optimal path selection?
    A. Cost   C. Delay
    B. Bandwidth   D. All of the above

52. OSPF supports IP subnetting using which of the following?
    A. VLSM   D. Network number and mask pair
    B. Discontinuous subnets   E. All of the above
    C. Supernets/subnet prefixes

53. Cisco OSPF implementation supports only Type of Service ___.
    A. 0   C. 2
    B. 1   D. 3

54. Identify the OSPF protocol that is responsible for establishing and maintaining neighbor relationships.
    A. LSA   C. Router ID
    B. Hello   D. NLA

55. Identify options carried in the Hello Packet.
    A. Network mask   D. Hello interval
    B. Router priority   E. All of the above
    C. List of neighbors

56. The OSPF Router dead interval is ___ seconds by default.
    A. 20   C. 30
    B. 40   D. 60

57. One of the steps in converting from a RIP network to OSPF network is to add:
    A. Backbone Routers running RIP
    B. Backbone Routers running OSPF
    C. ASBR Routers running both OSPF and RIP
    D. A & B
    E. None of the above

58. An OSPF router can be prevented from becoming a designated router by changing the router priority to:

A. 10   **D.** 15

B. 0   **E.** None of the above

C. 5

59. A backup designated router is elected for what reason?

A. OSPF DR and BDR both are used for sending updates simultaneously

B. It is used in case the DR fails.

C. A BDR is not required in OSPF.

D. None of the above

60. The OSPF link state advertisement contains:

A. Status of the link   **D.** Subnet mask

B. Metric of the link   **E.** A, B and C

C. IP network number assigned to the link   **F.** All of the above

61. Identify items contained within the hello packet.

A. Router Priority   **D.** Choice for DR

B. Hello interval   **E.** All of the above

C. List of routers

62. OSPF neighbor adjacency is established if any of the following hold.

A. Router is DR   **C.** Network is point-to-point

B. Router is BDR   **D.** All of the above

63. The OSPF link state sequence number is __ bits.

A. 16   **C.** 64

B. 32   **D.** 8

64. An Area Border Router generates how many different link state advertisements?

A. 2   **C.** 4

B. 3   **D.** 5

65. OSPF summary Network links advertise a route to a specific IP network using:

A. Metric   **C.** Network mask

B. Network Number   **D.** All of the above

66. Each ABR in an AS must belong to the OSPF if:

A. Area attached to the virtual link

B. Backbone area 0.0.0.0

C. Area is not the backbone

D. None of the above

67. Identify the levels in which OSPF routing can take place.

A. Import from another routing protocol

B. Routing between areas

C. Routing within an area

D. All of the above

68. The OSPF shortest path tree is calculated after:
  A. Full adjacency   **C.** Complete topology of the network
  B. Least cost metric   **D.** All of the above

69. Define the functions of the Autonomous System Boundary Router.
  A. Exchange routing information with routers outside of the OSPF domain
  B. Exchange information between routers within the same areas
  C. Exchange information between routers within different areas.
  D. None of the above

70. Identify OSPF packet types.
  A. Hello   **E.** Link state update
  B. Data base description   **F.** All of the above
  C. Link state request   **G.** A & B
  D. Link state ack

71. Define an OSPF Internal Router.
  A. An OSPF internal router is a router with all interfaces connected to networks in the same OSPF Area.
  B. An OSPF internal router is a router with all interfaces connected to networks in different OSPF Areas.
  C. An OSPF internal router is a router with all interfaces connected to networks in Area 0.
  D. Not enough information.

72. Define an Area Border Router.
  A. OSPF Area Border Router is a router with an Interface in multiple OSPF areas and maintains a separate link state database for each area.
  B. OSPF Area Border Router is a router with an Interface in multiple OSPF areas and maintains a single link state database.
  C. OSPF Area Border Router is a router with all Interface in the same OSPF area.

OSPF Show Commands

```
hostname ATLANTA
no ip domain-lookup
!
interface Ethernet0
 ip address 192.168.1.1 255.255.255.0
!
interface Ethernet1
 ip address 192.168.4.1 255.255.255.0
!
router ospf 100
 network 192.168.1.0 0.0.0.255 area 1
 network 192.168.4.0 0.0.0.255 area 4
 area 1 virtual-link 192.168.2.1
!
no ip classless
!
!
line con 0
line aux 0
```

```
line vty 0 4
 login
 !
 end
```

73. OSPF routing updates will be sent out of which interfaces?
- **A.** E0
- **B.** E0 and E1
- **C.** S0
- **D.** All of the above

74. What is the process ID for the OSPF router?
- **A.** 192.168.4.0 0.0.0.255
- **B.** 100
- **C.** 4
- **D.** 8

75. Interface E0 is connected to the backbone area by:
- **A.** Backbone
- **B.** Area 1
- **C.** Area 4
- **D.** None of the above

76. What area is interface E1 connected to?
- **A.** Area 1
- **B.** Area 2
- **C.** Area 4
- **D.** None of the above

77. The router ID for the router will be:
- **A.** 192.168.1.1
- **B.** 192.168.4.1
- **C.** 100
- **D.** None of the above

78. What type of router is this?
- **A.** Internal Router
- **B.** Area Boarder Router
- **C.** Backbone Router
- **D.** None of the above

79. How is this router connected to area 0?
- **A.** Via area 0
- **B.** Via area 1
- **C.** Via area 4
- **D.** None of the above

```
ATLANTA#sh ip route
Codes: C - connected, S - static, I - IGRP, R - RIP, M - mobile, B - BGP
       D - EIGRP, EX - EIGRP external, O - OSPF, IA - OSPF inter area
       N1 - OSPF NSSA external type 1, N2 - OSPF NSSA external type 2
       E1 - OSPF external type 1, E2 - OSPF external type 2, E - EGP
       i - IS-IS, L1 - IS-IS level-1, L2 - IS-IS level-2, * - candidate default
       U - per-user static route, o - ODR

Gateway of last resort is not set

C    192.168.1.0/24 is directly connected, Ethernet0
O    192.168.2.0/24 [110/1795] via 192.168.1.2, 00:16:53, Ethernet0
O IA 192.168.3.0/24 [110/1805] via 192.168.1.2, 00:13:54, Ethernet0
C    192.168.4.0/24 is directly connected, Ethernet1
```

80. Which network was not learned via an OSPF routing update?
- **A.** 192.168.1.0
- **B.** 192.168.2.0
- **C.** 192.168.3.0
- **D.** 192.168.4.0

81. What does the O mean in the routing table?

    A. Route learned by OSI   **C.** Route learned by RIP

    B. Route learned by OSPF   **D.** None of the above

82. What does the /24 represent in the routing table?

    A. Number of host on the network

    B. Number of hops to get to the network

    C. The Subnet mask of that network

    D. The administrative distance

83. The administrative distance for network 192.168.3.0 is:

    A. 24   **C.** 1805

    B. 110   **D.** All of the above

```
ATLANTA#sh ip ospf 100
 Routing Process "ospf 100" with ID 192.168.4.1
 Supports only single TOS(TOS0) routes
 It is an area border router
 Summary Link update interval is 00:30:00 and the update due in 00:01:56
 SPF schedule delay 5 secs, Hold time between two SPFs 10 secs
 Number of DCbitless external LSA 0
 Number of DoNotAge external LSA 0
 Number of areas in this router is 3. 3 normal 0 stub 0 nssa
     Area BACKBONE(0)
     Number of interfaces in this area is 1
     Area has no authentication
     SPF algorithm executed 16 times
     Area ranges are
     Link State Update Interval is 00:30:00 and due in 00:10:50
     Link State Age Interval is 00:20:00 and due in 00:10:49
     Number of DCbitless LSA 4
     Number of indication LSA 0
     Number of DoNotAge LSA 0
     Area 1
     Number of interfaces in this area is 1
     Area has no authentication
     SPF algorithm executed 13 times
     Area ranges are
      Link State Update Interval is 00:30:00 and due in 00:10:49
     Link State Age Interval is 00:20:00 and due in 00:10:48
     Number of DCbitless LSA 3
     Number of indication LSA 0
     Number of DoNotAge LSA 0
     Area 4
     Number of interfaces in this area is 1
     Area has no authentication
     SPF algorithm executed 6 times
     Area ranges are
     Link State Update Interval is 00:30:00 and due in 00:10:49
     Link State Age Interval is 00:20:00 and due in 00:10:49
     Number of DCbitless LSA 1
     Number of indication LSA 1
     Number of DoNotAge LSA 0
```

84. How many areas is this router connected to?

    A. 1   **C.** 3

    B. 2   **D.** 4

85. Which area has had the least number of changes?
- **A.** Area 0
- **B.** Area 1
- **C.** Area 4

86. OSPF default update interval is:
- **A.** 30 seconds
- **B.** 30 minutes
- **C.** 60 minutes
- **D.** None of the above

87. What is the minimum amount of time that a router must wait before it can send out a second LSA?
- **A.** 5 seconds
- **B.** 10 seconds
- **C.** 1 minute
- **D.** 5 minutes
- **E.** 30 minutes

```
ATLANTA# sh ip ospf database

        OSPF Router with ID (192.168.4.1) (Process ID 100)


        Router Link States (Area 0)

Link ID          ADV Router       Age      Seq#         Checksum Link count
192.168.2.1      192.168.2.1      415      0x8000001B 0xD1B0   3
192.168.3.1      192.168.3.1      415      0x8000000F 0xA570   2
192.168.4.1      192.168.4.1      1067     0x8000000F 0x24AB   1

        Summary Net Link States (Area 0)

Link ID          ADV Router       Age      Seq#         Checksum
192.168.1.0      192.168.2.1      415      0x80000002 0xF08A
192.168.1.0      192.168.4.1      1060     0x80000009 0xF25F
192.168.3.0      192.168.3.1      416      0x80000006 0xCBA8
192.168.4.0      192.168.4.1      1696     0x80000001 0xE175
```

88. The link count of a router represents:
- **A.** Number of hope to the network
- **B.** Number of networks within a given area
- **C.** Number of interfaces within a given area

89. Sequence numbers help keep track of:
- **A.** Number of data packets sent
- **B.** Duplicate LSAs
- **C.** Number of times the designated router receives an update
- **D.** None of the above

```
ATLANTA#sh ip ospf int
Ethernet0 is up, line protocol is up
  Internet Address 192.168.1.1/24, Area 1
  Process ID 100, Router ID 192.168.4.1, Network Type BROADCAST, Cost: 10
  Transmit Delay is 1 sec, State DR, Priority 1
  Designated Router (ID) 192.168.4.1, Interface address 192.168.1.1
  Backup Designated router (ID) 192.168.2.1, Interface address 192.168.1.2
  Timer intervals configured, Hello 10, Dead 40, Wait 40, Retransmit 5
    Hello due in 00:00:00
```

```
Neighbor Count is 1, Adjacent neighbor count is 1
   Adjacent with neighbor 192.168.2.1  (Backup Designated Router)
Suppress hello for 0 neighbor(s)
```

90. What type of OSPF network is E0 connected to?
    A. Point-to-point
    B. Non-broadcast
    C. Broadcast

91. The outgoing interface cost of OSPF is:
    A. 10   C. 30
    B. 20   D. 40

92. Which of the following best describes the benefits of OSPF?
    A. Allows the use of a more robust addressing scheme
    B. Allows for a larger more scaleable network
    C. Reduces convergence time
    D. Allows supernetting
    E. All of the above

93. The main difference between OSPF and RIP is:
    A. Both are IGPs, but RIP has a quicker convergence time.
    B. RIP is a distance vector protocol whereas OSPF is a link state protocol.
    C. There is no difference between the two.
    D. OSPF has a lower hop count limit than RIP.
    E. RIP works better in large networks.

94. Which statement best describes an *Area Border Router* (ABR)?
    A. A router on a countries border
    B. A router with interfaces in two OSPF autonomous systems
    C. A router on the access layer of a network
    D. A router with interfaces in two OSPF Areas
    E. A router on the end of an Ethernet segment

95. What is the main difference between OSPF External Type 1 and External Type 2 Routes?
    A. External type 1 has a lower cost than External type 2.
    B. External type 2 has a lower cost than External type 1.
    C. External type 2 identifies one cost and External Type 1 identifies internal and external costs.
    D. There is no difference.
    E. There is no such thing as an External Type 2 route.

96. Which of the following statements is correct?
    A. Area 0 can not be configured as a stub area.
    B. Totally stubby area is an IEEE standard and can be used on all makes of routers.
    C. An internal router will have routes to other autonomous systems in its' routing table by default.
    D. LSA type 7 is used exclusively between *Area Border Routers* (ABR).
    E. None of the above

97. Which statement is true for OSPF?
  A. Bandwidth, Delay, load, Reliability and MTU Size are used to calculate routes.
  B. OSPF is a Cisco specific routing protocol.
  C. OSPF can use MD5 Authentication in its routing updates.
  D. OSPF has distance vector properties.
  E. OSPF uses 10 000 000 /bandwidth.

98. Which of the following are used in an OSPF Multicast?
  A. 224.255.255.255   **D.** 224.0.0.6
  B. 255.255.255.255   **E.** 224.0.0.255
  C. 224.0.0.5

99. In an OSPF network where can route summarization take place?
  A. ABR   **D.** Backbone router
  B. Stub router   **E.** ASBR
  C. Internal router

100. Where would you use a Virtual Link in an OSPF network?
  A. To connect Areas together when there is no Area 0
  B. To connect routers that are not running OSPF to an OSPF network
  C. To connect an Area to Area 0 through a transit Area
  D. To connect dialup routers to an OSPF network
  E. None of the above

101. What is the maximum number of hops allowed in an OSPF area?
  A. 5   **D.** 15
  B. 7   **E.** None of the above
  C. 14

102. What would the OSPF metric be on a router with a 10 mb/s interface?
  A. 10   **D.** 1785
  B. 100   **E.** 6
  C. 128

103. Where is LSA 7 used?
  A. Router link entry   **D.** Autonomous system external link entry
  B. Network link entry   **E.** Not so stubby area
  C. Summary link entry

104. What is the maximum amount of equal cost routes allowed in OSPF?
  A. 2   **D.** 8
  B. 4   **E.** 10
  C. 6

105. On a Cisco router what is the default administrative distance of OSPF?
  A. 130   **D.** 90
  B. 110   **E.** 5
  C. 100

106. On a broadcast network which OSPF router with multicast all updates to other OSPF routers on the same segment?
     A. ABR
     B. ASBR
     C. Backbone Router
     D. BDR
     E. DR

107. Which of the following routed protocols can be used with OSPF?
     A. IPX
     B. Banyan Vines
     C. AppleTalk
     D. IP
     E. DECnet

108. What IOS command is used to define a stub area?

109. What is a network called that does not have connectivity directly to the backbone area?
     A. Virtual Link
     B. Area Router
     C. Internal Router
     D. AS Router
     E. None of the above

110. If an OSPF interface with the largest IP address becomes inoperative what happens to the router ID?
     A. Nothing
     B. Recalculate a new router ID
     C. Must be recalculated on another Routers interface
     D. None of the above

Answers

1. A
2. E
3. A
4. A, B, D
5. C
6. B, C
7. C
8. B, C, E
9. F
10. B, D, E
11. B
12. B
13. A
14. B
15. D
16. A
17. A
18. A
19. E
20. G
21. B
22. A
23. C
24. A
25. C
26. A
27. A
28. A
29. A
30. D
31. A
32. A
33. A
34. D
35. D
36. B
37. B
38. B
39. B
40. A
41. A, D
42. D
43. A
44. C
45. D
46. A
47. B
48. C

49. C
50. A
51. A
52. A
53. A
54. B
55. A, B, D
56. B
57. C
58. B
59. B
60. F
61. A, B, D
62. D
63. B
64. C
65. D
66. B
67. D
68. D
69. A
70. F
71. A
72. A
73. B
74. B
75. B
76. C
77. B
78. B
79. B
80. A, D
81. B
82. C
83. B
84. C
85. C
86. B
87. A
88. C
89. B
90. C
91. A
92. E
93. B
94. D
95. C
96. A
97. C

98. C, D
99. A, E
100. C
101. E
102. A
103. E
104. C
105. B
106. E
107. D
108. Area area-ID stub [no-summary]
109. E
110. B

12

Border Gateway Protocol

The *Border Gateway Protocol* (BGP) is an interautonomous system routing protocol whose primary function is to exchange network reachability information with other BGP systems. This network reachability information includes information on the list of autonomous systems that it traverses. This information is sufficient to construct a graph of AS connectivity from which routing loops may be pruned and some policy decisions at the AS level may be enforced.

BGP is an exterior gateway routing protocol used to exchange network reachability information among autonomous systems. An AS is essentially a collection of routers and endnodes that operate under a single administrative organization. Within each AS, routers and endnodes share routing information using an interior gateway protocol. The interior gateway protocol may be RIP, IGRP, EIGRP, or OSPF.

BGP was introduced to facilitate the loop-free exchange of routing information between autonomous systems. Based on *Classless Inter-Domain Routing* (CIDR), BGP has evolved to support the aggregation and reduction of routing information.

CIDR eliminates the concept of address classes and provides a method for summarizing different routes into single routes. This significantly reduces the amount of routing information that BGP routers must store and exchange.

In essence, CIDR is a strategy designed to address the following problems:

- Exhaustion of Class B address space
- Routing table growth

BGP-4 provides a new set of mechanisms for supporting classless interdomain routing. These mechanisms include support for advertising an IP prefix and eliminate the concept of network class within BGP (CIDR). BGP-4 also introduces mechanisms that allow aggregation of routes, including aggregation of autonomous systems paths. To characterize the set of policy decisions that can be enforced using BGP, one must focus on the rule that a BGP speaker advertises only the routes it uses to its peers (other BGP speakers with which it communicates) in neighboring autonomous systems. This rule reflects the hop-by-hop routing paradigm generally used throughout the current Internet. Note that some policies cannot be supported by the hop-by-hop routing paradigm and thus require techniques such as source routing to enforce.

For example, BGP does not enable one AS to send traffic to a neighboring AS intending that the traffic take a different route from that taken by traffic originating in the BGP. This eliminates the need to implement explicit update fragmentation, retransmission, acknowledgement, and sequencing. Any authentication scheme used by the transport protocol may be used in addition to BGP's own authentication mechanisms. The error-notification mechanism used in BGP assumes that the transport protocol supports a graceful close (i.e., that all outstanding data will be delivered before the connection is closed).

BGP uses TCP version 4 as its transport protocol. TCP meets BGP's transport requirements and is present in all commercial routers and hosts running TCP/IP. BGP uses TCP port 179 for establishing its connections. When the connection starts, BGP peers exchange complete copies of their routing tables, which can be quite large. However, only changes (deltas) then are exchanged, which makes long-running BGP sessions more efficient than shorter ones.

BGP has a number of significant advantages over Exterior Gateway Protocol. First, it can operate with networks that have looped topologies, using algorithms that prune the loops out. Second, BGP does not have the *count to infinity* problem found in many route-discovery protocols because it advertises all autonomous systems (transit machines) on the path to a destination address. Third, as a result of this full advertising, a node that receives more than one possible path (in advertisements) to a destination can, without ambiguity, choose the best path. In addition, BGP does not care what type of intraautonomous route-discovery protocol is used, or whether multiple interautonomous protocols are used.

Two systems form a transport protocol connection between one another. They exchange messages to open and confirm the connection parameters (see Figures 12.1 and 12.7). The initial data flow is the entire BGP routing table. Incremental updates are sent as the routing tables change. BGP does not require periodic refresh of the entire BGP routing table. Therefore, a BGP speaker must retain the current version of the entire BGP routing tables of all of its peers for the duration of the connection. KEEPALIVE messages are sent periodically to ensure that the connection remains "alive." Notification messages are sent in response to errors or special conditions. If a connection encounters an error condition, a notification message is sent, and the connection is closed.

The hosts executing the Border Gateway Protocol need not be routers. If a particular AS has multiple BGP speakers and is providing transit service for other autonomous systems, care must be taken to ensure a consistent view of routing within the AS.

A consistent view of the interior routes of the AS is provided by the interior routing protocol. A consistent view of the routes exterior to the AS can be provided by having all BGP speakers within the AS maintain direct BGP connections with each other. Using a common set of policies, the BGP speakers arrive at an agreement as to which border routers will serve as exit/entry points for particular destinations outside the AS. This information is communicated to the autonomous system's internal routers, possibly via the interior routing protocol. Care must be taken to ensure that the interior routers have all been updated with transit information before the BGP speakers announce to other autonomous systems that transit service is being provided.

Connections between BGP speakers of different autonomous systems are referred to as *external* links. BGP connections between BGP speakers within the same AS are referred to as *internal* links. Similarly, a peer in a different AS is referred to as an external peer, while a peer in the same AS may be described as an internal peer.

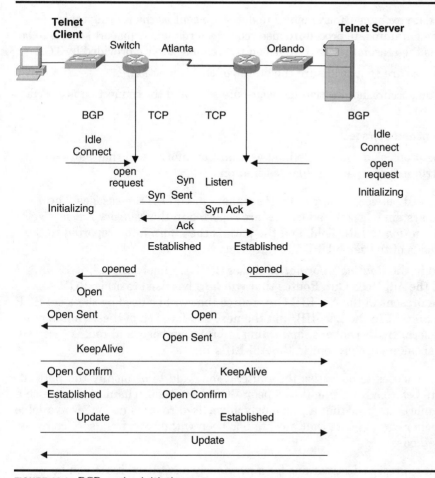

FIGURE 12.1 BGP session initiation

How BGP Works

BGP uses the following steps to activate a session between two routers:

1. Two routers desiring to exchange BGP information form a TCP transport connection. A transport connection is established so that BGP can assume reliable communication with its peer. BGP uses TCP Port 179 to establish its connections.

2. After the transport connection is established, the neighboring routers exchange messages to open and confirm the BGP session parameters. These session parameters include the BGP protocol version number, autonomous system numbers, protocol message timeout values, and message authentication information.

3. After the BGP session is opened, routers initially exchange their entire BGP routing table with their peer. The routing information for each entry includes a list of the autonomous systems that traffic must transit to reach the target network.

4. After the initial data exchange, incremental updates are sent as the routing tables change. An incremental update procedure also requires a reliable transport service to be successful. This is the reason that BGP relies on the reliable service provided by TCP.

5. KeepAlive messages are sent to ensure the status of the connection.

6. If an error condition occurs, notification messages are sent, and the connection is closed.

Routes: Advertisement and Storage

For purposes of this protocol, a route is defined as a unit of information that pairs a destination with the attributes of a path to that destination.

- Routes are advertised between a pair of BGP speakers in UPDATE messages. The destination is the system whose IP addresses are reported in the *Network Layer Reachability Information* (NLRI) field, and the path is the information reported in the path attributes fields of the same UPDATE message.

- Routes are stored in the *Routing Information Bases* (RIBs): namely, the Adj-RIBs-In, the Loc-RIB, and the Adj-RIBs-Out. Routes that will be advertised to other BGP speakers must be present in the Adj-RIB-Out; routes that will be used by the local BGP speaker must be present in the Loc-RIB, and the next hop for each of these routes must be present in the local BGP speaker's forwarding information base; and routes received from other BGP speakers are present in the Adj-RIBs-In.

If a BGP speaker chooses to advertise the route, it may add to or modify the path attributes of the route before advertising it to a peer. BGP provides mechanisms by which a BGP speaker can inform its peer that a previously advertised route is no longer available for use. A BGP speaker can indicate that a route has been withdrawn from service by using one of three methods:

- The IP prefix that expresses destinations for a previously advertised route can be advertised in the Withdrawn Routes field in the UPDATE message, thus marking the associated route as being no longer available for use.

- A replacement route with the same Network Layer Reachability Information can be advertised.

- The BGP speaker connection can be closed, which implicitly removes from service all routes that the pair of speakers had advertised to each other.

Routing Information Bases

The RIB within a BGP speaker consists of three distinct parts:

- *Adj-RIBs-In.*   The Adj-RIBs-In store routing information that has been learned from inbound UPDATE messages. Their contents represent routes available as an input to the decision process.

- *Loc-RIB.*   The Loc-RIB contains the local routing information that the BGP speaker has selected by applying its local policies to the routing information contained in its Adj-RIBs-In.

- *Adj-RIBs-Out*. The Adj-RIBs-Out store the information that the local BGP speaker has selected for advertisement to its peers. The routing information stored in the Adj-RIBs-Out will be carried in the local BGP speaker's UPDATE messages and advertised to its peers.

In summary, the Adj-RIBs-In contain unprocessed routing information advertised to the local BGP speaker by its peers; the Loc-RIB contains the routes that have been selected by the local BGP speaker's decision process; and the Adj-RIBs-Out organize the routes for advertisement to specific peers by means of the local speaker's UPDATE messages. Although the conceptual model distinguishes between Adj-RIBs-In, Loc-RIB, and Adj-RIBs-Out, this neither implies nor requires that an implementation must maintain three separate copies of the routing information.

Operational Features

Topologies Supported. The BGP protocol is a true interautonomous system routing protocol. As such, it does not place any restrictions on the interconnection of autonomous systems. The information exchanged by BGP speakers allows the creation of an Internet topology free of routing loops.

IGPs Supported. The BGP protocol does not place any restrictions on the IGP used within an autonomous system. Also, BGP does not require that all autonomous systems run the same IGP.

BGP Peers. The BGP protocol views the Internet as a set of interconnected autonomous systems. The BGP speakers from each autonomous system exchange routing information. If Autonomous System 300 has multiple connections to other autonomous systems, it may also have multiple BGP speakers. An autonomous system may have an unlimited number of BGP speakers.

Routers that communicate directly with each other using the BGP protocol are known as *BGP peers*. BGP peers may be located in the same or different autonomous systems. BGP communication between peers in different autonomous systems is called External BGP. Communication between peers contained in the same autonomous system is called Internal BGP.

External BGP. External BGP peers belong to different autonomous systems. External BGP usually shares a common network; however, Cisco permits more than one hop with the "ebgp multi-hop" command.

Internal BGP. Internal BGP peers belong to the same autonomous system. However, they are not required to share a common network. The BGP transport connection may be made across the autonomous system. All BGP speakers representing the same autonomous system must present a consistent view of the autonomous system to neighboring autonomous systems. This means that all BGP speakers within an autonomous system are required to share the same routing information. The BGP speakers within an autonomous system communicate with each other using the BGP protocol to guarantee that all BGP speakers have consistent information. A set of policy constraints is applied to all BGP speakers to provide a consistent view to neighboring autonomous systems.

BGP Message Header Format

Each message has a fixed-size header. There may or may not be a data portion following the header, depending on the message type. The layout of these fields is shown in Figure 12.2.

- *Marker*.   This 16-octet field contains a value that the receiver of the message can predict. If the Type of the message is OPEN, or if the OPEN message carries no Authentication Information (as an Optional Parameter), the Marker must be all 1s. Otherwise, the value of the marker can be predicted by some computation specified as part of the authentication mechanism used. The Marker can be used to detect loss of synchronization between a pair of BGP peers and to authenticate incoming BGP messages.

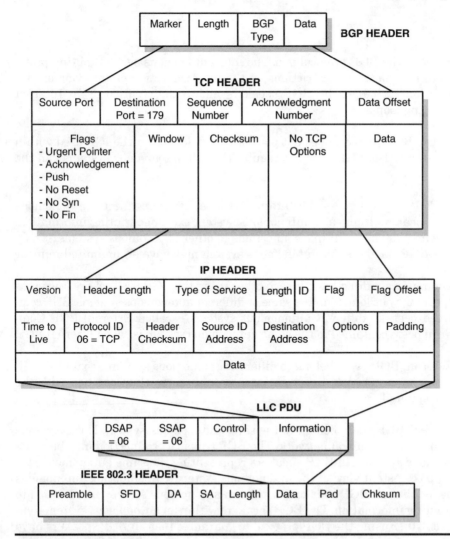

FIGURE 12.2   BGP header

- *Length.* This two-octet unsigned integer indicates the total length of the message, including the header, in octets. Thus, it allows one to locate in the Transport level stream the Marker field of the next message. The value of the Length field must always be at least 19 and no greater than 4,096 and may be further constrained, depending on the message type. No padding of extra data after the message is allowed, so the Length field must have the smallest value required given the rest of the message.

- *Type.* This one-octet unsigned integer indicates the type code of the message. The following type codes are defined:

  - 1—OPEN
  - 2—UPDATE
  - 3—NOTIFICATION
  - 4—KEEPALIVE

OPEN Message Format

After a transport protocol connection is established, the first message sent by each side is an OPEN message. If the OPEN message is acceptable, a KEEPALIVE message confirming the OPEN is sent back. When the OPEN is confirmed, UPDATE, KEEPALIVE, and NOTIFICATION messages may be exchanged (see Figures 12.3 and 12.4).

In addition to the fixed-size BGP header, the OPEN message contains the following fields:

- *Version.* This 1-octet unsigned integer indicates the protocol version number of the message. The current BGP version number is 4.

- *Autonomous System.* This two-octet unsigned integer indicates the Autonomous System number of the sender.

- *Hold Time.* This two-octet unsigned integer indicates the number of seconds that the sender proposes for the value of the Hold Timer. Upon receipt of an OPEN message, a BGP speaker must calculate the value of the Hold Timer by using the smaller of its configured Hold Time and the Hold Time received in the OPEN message. The Hold Time MUST be either 0 or at least three seconds. An implementation may reject connections on the basis of the Hold Time. The calculated value indicates the maximum number of seconds that may elapse between the receipt of successive KEEPALIVE and/or UPDATE messages by the sender.

- *BGP Identifier.* This four-octet unsigned integer indicates the BGP Identifier of the sender. A given BGP speaker sets the value of its BGP Identifier to an IP address assigned to that BGP speaker. The value of the BGP Identifier is determined on startup and is the same for every local interface and every BGP peer.

- *Parameter Length.* This one-octet unsigned integer indicates the total length of the Optional Parameters field in octets. If the value of this field is 0, no Optional Parameters are present.

- *Optional Parameters.* This field may contain a list of optional parameters, in which each parameter is encoded as `<Parameter Type, Parameter Length, Parameter Value>`.

- *Parameter Type.* This one-octet field unambiguously identifies individual parameters.

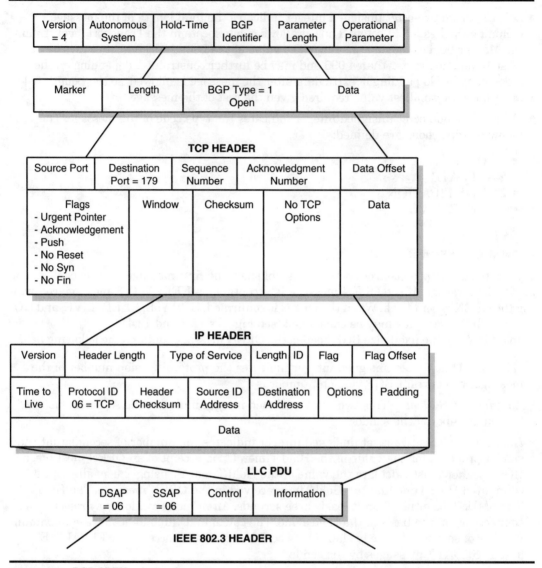

FIGURE 12.3   BGP OPEN message format

- *Parameter Length.*   This one-octet field contains the length of the Parameter Value field in octets.

- *Parameter Value.*   This variable-length field is interpreted according to the value of the Parameter Type field.

UPDATE Message Format

UPDATE messages are used to transfer routing information between BGP peers. The information in the Update packet can be used to construct a graph describing the relation-

```
BGP:   --- BGP Message ---
BGP:   16 byte Marker  (all 1's)
BGP:   Length        = 52
BGP:   BGP type      = 2 (Update)
BGP:   Unfeasible Routes Length   = 0
BGP:      No Withdrawn Routes in this Update
BGP:   Path Attribute Length    = 25 bytes
BGP:   Attribute Flags = 4X
BGP:           0... .... = Well-known
BGP:           .1.. .... = Transitive
BGP:           ..0. .... = Complete
BGP:           ...0 .... = 1 byte Length
BGP:   Attribute type code    = 1 (Origin)
BGP:   Attribute Data Length   = 1
BGP:   Origin type           = 2 (Incomplete)
BGP:   Attribute Flags = 4X
BGP:           0... .... = Well-known
BGP:           .1.. .... = Transitive
BGP:           ..0. .... = Complete
BGP:           ...0 .... = 1 byte Length
BGP:   Attribute type code    = 2 (AS Path)
BGP:   Attribute Data Length   = 4
BGP:   AS Identifier        = 513
BGP:   AS Identifier        = 100
BGP:   Attribute Flags = 4X
BGP:           0... .... = Well-known
BGP:           .1.. .... = Transitive
BGP:           ..0. .... = Complete
BGP:           ...0 .... = 1 byte Length
BGP:   Attribute type code    = 3 (Next Hop)
BGP:   Attribute Data Length   = 4
BGP:   Next Hop             = [192.168.5.1]
BGP:   Attribute Flags = 8X
BGP:           1... .... = Optional
BGP:           .0.. .... = Non-transitive
BGP:           ..0. .... = Complete
BGP:           ...0 .... = 1 byte Length
BGP:   Attribute type code     = 4 (Multi Exit Disc)
BGP:   Attribute Data Length   = 4
BGP:   Multi Exit Disc Attribute = 1795
BGP:
BGP:   Network Layer Reachability Information:
BGP:    IP Prefix Length = 24 bits, IP subnet mask [255.255.255.0]
BGP:       IP address [192.168.3.0]
```

FIGURE 12.4 BGP message headers

ships of the various autonomous systems. By applying rules to be discussed, routing information loops and some other anomalies may be detected and removed from inter-AS routing (see Figure 12.5).

An UPDATE message is used to advertise a single feasible route to a peer or to withdraw multiple unfeasible routes from service. An UPDATE message may simultaneously advertise a feasible route and withdraw multiple unfeasible routes from service. The UPDATE message always includes the fixed-size BGP header and can include the other fields as shown in Table 12.1.

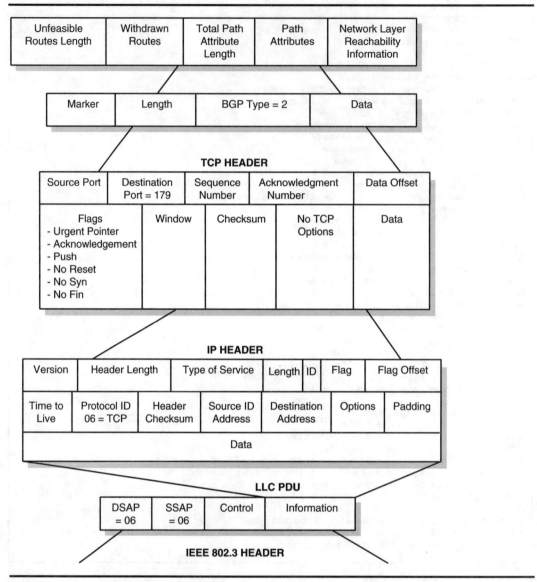

FIGURE 12.5 BGP UPDATE message

- *Unfeasible Routes Length.*   This two-octet unsigned integer indicates the total length of the Withdrawn Routes field in octets. Its value must allow the length of the Network Layer Reachability Information field to be determined. A value of 0 indicates that no routes are being withdrawn from service and that the Withdrawn Routes field is not present in this UPDATE message.

- *Withdrawn Routes.*   This variable length field contains a list of IP address prefixes for the routes being withdrawn from service. Each IP address prefix is encoded as a two-tuple of the form `<length, prefix>`:

TABLE 12.1 BGP Update Message Fields

Field	Length
Unfeasible Routes Length	2 octets
Withdrawn Routes	variable
Total Path Attribute Length	2 octets
Path Attributes	variable
Network Layer Reachability Information	variable

- *Length.* The Length field indicates the length in bits of the IP address prefix. A length of 0 indicates a prefix that matches all IP addresses (with a prefix of 0 octets).
- *Prefix.* The Prefix field contains IP address prefixes followed by enough trailing bits to make the end of the field fall on an octet boundary. Note that the value of trailing bits is irrelevant.

- *Total Path Attribute Length.* This two-octet unsigned integer indicates the total length of the Path Attributes field in octets. Its value must allow the length of the Network Layer Reachability field to be determined.

A value of 0 indicates that no Network Layer Reachability Information field is present in this UPDATE message.

- *Path Attributes.* A variable-length sequence of path attributes is present in every UPDATE. Each path attribute is a triple `<attribute type, attribute length, attribute value>` of variable length. Attribute Type is a two-octet field that consists of the Attribute Flags octet followed by the Attribute Type Code octet.

The high-order bit (bit 0) of the Attribute Flags octet is the Optional bit. It defines whether the attribute is optional (if set to 1) or well-known (if set to 0).

The second high-order bit (bit 1) of the Attribute Flags octet is the Transitive bit. It defines whether an optional attribute is transitive (if set to 1) or nontransitive (if set to 0). For well-known attributes, the Transitive bit must be set to 1.

The third high-order bit (bit 2) of the Attribute Flags octet is the Partial bit. It defines whether the information contained in the optional transitive attribute is partial (if set to 1) or complete (if set to 0). For well-known attributes and for optional nontransitive attributes, the Partial bit must be set to 0.

The fourth high-order bit (bit 3) of the Attribute Flags octet is the Extended Length bit. It defines whether the Attribute Length is one octet (if set to 0) or two octets (if set to 1). Extended Length may be used only if the length of the attribute value is greater than 255 octets.

The lower order four bits of the Attribute Flags octet are unused. They must be 0 (and must be ignored when received).

The Attribute Type Code octet contains the Attribute Type Code.

If the Extended Length bit of the Attribute Flags octet is set to 0, the third octet of the Path Attribute contains the length of the attribute data in octets. If the Extended Length bit of the Attribute Flags octet is set to 1, the third and fourth octets of the path attribute contain the length of the attribute data in octets.

The remaining octets of the Path Attribute represent the attribute value and are interpreted according to the Attribute Flags and the Attribute Type Code. The supported Attribute Type Codes, their attribute values, and uses are the following:

- *ORIGIN* (Type Code 1).   ORIGIN is a well-known mandatory attribute that defines the origin of the path information. The data octet can assume the following values:

Value	Meaning
0	IGP—Network Layer Reachability Information is interior to the originating AS
1	EGP—Network Layer Reachability Information learned via EGP
2	INCOMPLETE—Network Layer Reachability Information learned by some other means

- *AS_PATH* (Type Code 2).   AS_PATH is a well-known mandatory attribute composed of a sequence of AS path segments. Each AS path segment is represented by a triple `<path segment type, path segment  length, path segment value>`.

The path segment type is a one-octet long field with the following values defined:

Value	Segment Type
1	AS_SET: unordered set of autonomous systems a route in the UPDATE message has traversed
2	AS_SEQUENCE: ordered set of autonomous systems a route in the UPDATE message has traversed

The path segment length is a one-octet long field containing the number of autonomous systems in the path segment value field. The path segment value field contains one or more AS numbers, each encoded as a two-octet field.

- *NEXT_HOP* (Type Code 3).   This is a well-known mandatory attribute that defines the IP address of the border router that should be used as the next hop to the destinations listed in the Network Layer Reachability field of the UPDATE message.
- *MULTI_EXIT_DISC* (Type Code 4).   This is an optional nontransitive attribute that is a four-octet nonnegative integer. The value of this attribute may be used by a BGP speaker's decision process to discriminate among multiple exit points to a neighboring autonomous system.
- *LOCAL_PREF* (Type Code 5).   LOCAL_PREF is a well-known discretionary attribute that is a four-octet nonnegative integer. It is used by a BGP speaker to inform other BGP speakers in its own autonomous system of the originating speaker's degree of preference for an advertised route.

- *ATOMIC_AGGREGATE* (Type Code 6).   ATOMIC_AGGREGATE is a well-known discretionary attribute of length 0. It is used by a BGP speaker to inform other BGP speakers that the local system selected a less specific route.
- *AGGREGATOR* (Type Code 7).   AGGREGATOR is an optional transitive attribute of length 6. The attribute contains the last AS number that formed the aggregate route (encoded as 2 octets), followed by the IP address of the BGP speaker that formed the aggregate route (encoded as 4 octets).

- *Network Layer Reachability Information.*   This variable-length field contains a list of IP address prefixes. The length in octets of the Network Layer Reachability Information is not encoded explicitly but can be calculated as follows:

```
UPDATE message Length 2 23 2 Total Path Attributes Length 2 Unfeasible
Routes Length
```

where UPDATE message Length is the value encoded in the fixed-size BGP header; Total Path Attribute Length and Unfeasible Routes Length are the values encoded in the variable part of the UPDATE message; and 23 is a combined length of the fixed-size BGP header, the Total Path Attribute Length field, and the Unfeasible Routes Length field.

Reachability information is encoded as one or more two-tuples of the form `<length, prefix>`, whose fields are described here:

- *Length.*   The Length field indicates the length in bits of the IP address prefix. A length of 0 indicates a prefix that matches all IP addresses (with prefix, itself, of 0 octets).
- *Prefix.*   The Prefix field contains IP address prefixes followed by enough trailing bits to make the end of the field fall on an octet boundary. Note that the value of the trailing bits is irrelevant. The minimum length of the UPDATE message is 23 octets— 19 octets for the fixed header + 2 octets for the Unfeasible Routes Length + 2 octets for the Total Path Attribute Length (the value of Unfeasible Routes Length is 0, and the value of Total Path Attribute Length is 0). An UPDATE message can advertise at most one route, which may be described by several path attributes. All path attributes contained in a given UPDATE messages apply to the destinations carried in the Network Layer Reachability Information field of the UPDATE message.

    An UPDATE message can list multiple routes to be withdrawn from service. Each such route is identified by its destination (expressed as an IP prefix), which unambiguously identifies the route in the context of the BGP speaker—BGP speaker connection to which it has been previously been advertised. An UPDATE message may advertise only routes to be withdrawn from service, in which case it will not include path attributes or Network Layer Reachability Information. Conversely, it may advertise only a feasible route, in which case the Withdrawn Routes field need not be present.

KEEPALIVE Message Format

BGP does not use any transport protocol-based KEEPALIVE mechanism to determine whether peers are reachable. Instead, KEEPALIVE messages are exchanged between peers often enough as not to cause the Hold Timer to expire. A reasonable maximum time between KEEPALIVE messages would be one third of the Hold Time interval. KEEPALIVE messages must not be sent more frequently than one per second. An implementation may adjust the rate at which it sends KEEPALIVE messages as a function of the Hold Time interval. If the negotiated Hold Time interval is 0, periodic KEEPALIVE messages must not be sent.

KEEPALIVE messages consist of only the message header and have a length of 19 octets (see Figure 12.6).

```
IP:     Version = 4, header length = 20 bytes
IP:     Type of service = C0
IP:          110. .... = internetwork control
IP:          ...0 .... = normal delay
IP:          .... 0... = normal throughput
IP:          .... .0.. = normal reliability
IP:     Total length   = 59 bytes
IP:     Identification = 2
IP:     Flags          = 0X
IP:          .0.. .... = may fragment
IP:          ..0. .... = last fragment
IP:     Fragment offset = 0 bytes
IP:     Time to live   = 1 seconds/hops
IP:     Protocol       = 6 (TCP)
IP:     Header checksum = 9DD8 (correct)
IP:     Source address      = [137.144.4.1]
IP:     Destination address = [137.144.4.2]
TCP:    --- TCP header ---
TCP:    Source port              = 179 (BGP)
TCP:    Destination port         = 11005
TCP:    Sequence number          = 257022801
TCP:    Acknowledgment number    = 736698747
TCP:    Data offset              = 20 bytes
TCP:    Flags                    = 18
TCP:          ..0. .... = (No urgent pointer)
TCP:          ...1 .... = Acknowledgment
TCP:          .... 1... = Push
TCP:          .... .0.. = (No reset)
TCP:          .... ..0. = (No SYN)
TCP:          .... ...0 = (No FIN)
TCP:    Window                   = 16336
TCP:    Checksum                 = ECFB (correct)
TCP:    [19 byte(s) of data]
BGP:    -- BGP Message --
BGP:    16 byte Marker  (all 1's)
BGP:    Length       = 19
BGP:    BGP type     = 4 (KeepAlive)
BGP:
```

FIGURE 12.6   BGP KEEPALIVE message

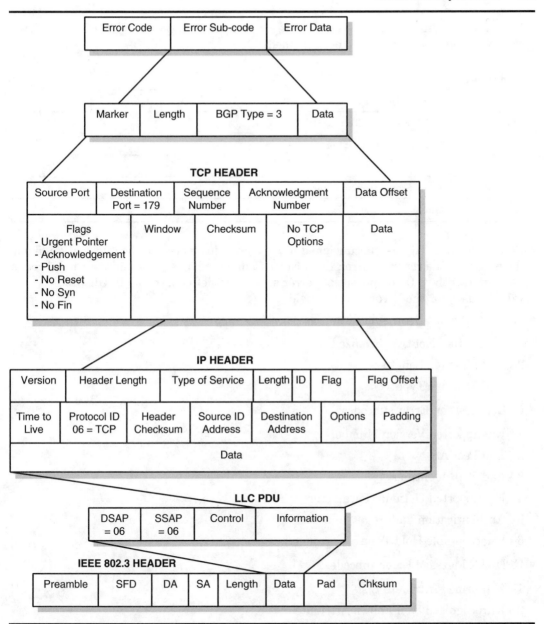

FIGURE 12.7 BGP Notification message

NOTIFICATION Message Format

A NOTIFICATION message is sent when an error condition is detected (see Figure 12.7). The BGP connection is closed immediately after sending it. In addition to the fixed-size BGP header, the NOTIFICATION message contains the following fields:

- *Error Code.* This one-octet unsigned integer indicates the type of NOTIFICATION. The following error codes have been defined:

Error Code	Symbolic Name
1	Message Header Error
2	OPEN Message Error
3	UPDATE Message Error
4	Hold Timer Expired
5	Finite State Machine Error
6	Cease

- *Error subcode.* This 1-octet unsigned integer provides more specific information about the nature of the reported error. Each Error Code may have one or more error subcodes associated with it. If no appropriate error subcode is defined, then a 0 (Unspecific) value is used for the Error Subcode field.

- Message Header Error subcodes:

  1—Connection Not Synchronized

  2—Bad Message Length

  3—Bad Message Type

- OPEN Message Error subcodes:

  1—Unsupported Version Number

  2—Bad Peer AS

  3—Bad BGP Identifier

  4—Unsupported Optional Parameter

  5—Authentication Failure

  6—Unacceptable Hold Time

- UPDATE Message Error subcodes:

  1—Malformed Attribute List

  2—Unrecognized Well-known Attribute

  3—Missing Well-known Attribute

  4—Attribute Flags Error

  5—Attribute Length Error

  6—Invalid ORIGIN Attribute

  7—AS Routing Loop

  8—Invalid NEXT_HOP Attribute

  9—Optional Attribute Error

10—Invalid Network Field

11—Malformed AS_PATH

- *Data.* This variable-length field is used to diagnose the reason for the NOTIFICATION. The contents of the Data field depend upon the error code and error subcode. Note that the length of the Data field can be determined from the message Length field by the following formula:

```
Message Length = 21 + Data Length
```

The minimum length of the NOTIFICATION message is 21 octets (including message header).

Path Attributes. This section discusses the path attributes of the UPDATE message. Path attributes fall into four categories:

- 1. well-known mandatory
- 2. well-known discretionary
- 3. optional transitive
- 4. optional nontransitive

Well-known attributes must be recognized by all BGP implementations. Some of these attributes are mandatory and must be included in every UPDATE message. Others are discretionary and may or may not be sent in a particular UPDATE message. All well-known attributes must be passed along (after proper updating, if necessary) to other BGP peers. In addition to well-known attributes, each path may contain one or more optional attributes. It is not required or expected that all BGP implementations support all optional attributes. The handling of an unrecognized optional attribute is determined by the setting of the transitive bit in the attribute flags octet. Paths with unrecognized transitive optional attributes should be accepted. If a path with an unrecognized transitive optional attribute is accepted and passed along to other BGP peers, the unrecognized transitive optional attribute of that path must be passed along with the path to other BGP peers with the partial bit in the Attribute Flags octet set to 1.

If a path with a recognized transitive optional attribute is accepted and passed along to other BGP peers, and the partial bit in the Attribute Flags octet is set to 1 by some previous AS, it is not set back to 0 by the current AS. Unrecognized nontransitive optional attributes must be quietly ignored and not passed along to other BGP peers. New transitive optional attributes may be attached to the path by the originator or by any other AS in the path. If they are not attached by the originator, the partial bit in the Attribute Flags octet is set to 1. The rules for attaching new nontransitive optional attributes will depend on the nature of the specific attribute.

The description of the MULTI_EXIT_DISC attribute gives an example. All optional attributes (both transitive and nontransitive) may be updated (if appropriate) by autonomous systems in the path. The sender of an UPDATE message should order path attributes within the UPDATE message in ascending order of attribute type. The receiver of an UPDATE message must be prepared to handle path attributes within the UPDATE message that are out of order. The same attribute cannot appear more than once within the Path Attributes field of a particular UPDATE message.

ORIGIN. ORIGIN is a well-known mandatory attribute. The ORIGIN attribute shall be generated by the autonomous system that originates the associated routing information. It shall be included in the UPDATE messages of all BGP speakers that choose to propagate this information to other BGP speakers.

AS_PATH. AS_PATH is a well-known mandatory attribute. This attribute identifies the autonomous systems through which routing information carried in this UPDATE message has passed. The components of this list can be AS_SETs or AS_SEQUENCEs.

When a BGP speaker propagates a route that it has learned from another BGP speaker's UPDATE message, it shall modify the route's AS_PATH attribute based on the location of the BGP speaker to which the route will be sent:

1. When a given BGP speaker advertises the route to another BGP speaker located in its own autonomous system, the advertising speaker does not modify the AS_PATH attribute associated with the route.

2. When a given BGP speaker advertises the route to a BGP speaker located in a neighboring autonomous system, the advertising speaker updates the AS_PATH attribute as follows:

   - If the first path segment of the AS_PATH is of type AS_SEQUENCE, the local system prepends its own AS number as the last element of the sequence (put it in the leftmost position).
   - If the first path segment of the AS_PATH is of type AS_SET, the local system prepends a new path segment of type AS_SEQUENCE to the AS_PATH, including its own AS number in that segment.

When a BGP speaker originates a route, the following happens:

- The originating speaker includes its own AS number in the AS_PATH attribute of all UPDATE messages sent to BGP speakers located in neighboring autonomous systems. (In this case, the AS number of the originating speaker's autonomous system is the only entry in the AS_PATH attribute).

- The originating speaker includes an empty AS_PATH attribute in all UPDATE messages sent to BGP speakers located in its own autonomous system. (An empty AS_PATH attribute is one whose length field contains the value 0).

NEXT_HOP. The NEXT_HOP path attribute defines the IP address of the border router that should be used as the next hop to the destinations listed in the UPDATE message. If a border router belongs to the same AS as its peer, the peer is an internal border router. Otherwise, it is an external border router. A BGP speaker can advertise any internal border router as the next hop provided that the interface associated with the IP address of this border router (as specified in the NEXT_HOP path attribute) shares a common subnet with both the local and remote BGP speakers. A BGP speaker can advertise any external border router as the next hop, provided that the IP address of this border router was learned from one of the BGP speaker's peers and the interface associated with the IP address of this border router (as specified in the NEXT_HOP path attribute) shares a common subnet with the local and remote BGP speakers. A BGP speaker needs to be able to support disabling advertisement of external border routers. A BGP speaker must never advertise an address of a peer to that peer as a NEXT_HOP, for a route that the speaker is originating. A BGP speaker must never install a route with itself as the next hop.

When a BGP speaker advertises the route to a BGP speaker located in its own autonomous system, the advertising speaker shall not modify the NEXT_HOP attribute associated with the route. When a BGP speaker receives the route via an internal link, it may forward packets to the NEXT_HOP address if the address contained in the attribute is on a common subnet with the local and remote BGP speakers.

MULTI_EXIT_DISC. The MULTI_EXIT_DISC attribute may be used on external (inter-AS) links to discriminate among multiple exit or entry points to the same neighboring AS. The value of the MULTI_EXIT_DISC attribute is a four-octet unsigned number called a metric. All other factors being equal, the exit or entry point with lower metric should be preferred. If received over external links, the MULTI_EXIT_DISC attribute may be propagated over internal links to other BGP speakers within the same AS. The MULTI_EXIT_DISC attribute is never propagated to other BGP speakers in neighboring autonomous systems.

LOCAL_PREF. LOCAL_PREF is a well-known discretionary attribute included in all UPDATE messages, which a given BGP speaker sends to the other BGP speakers located in its own autonomous system. A BGP speaker calculates the degree of preference for each external route and includes the degree of preference when advertising a route to its internal peers. A BGP speaker uses the degree of preference learned via LOCAL_PREF in its decision process. A BGP speaker does not include this attribute in UPDATE messages that it sends to BGP speakers located in a neighboring autonomous system. If it is contained in an UPDATE message received from a BGP speaker not located in the same autonomous system as the receiving speaker, this attribute is ignored by the receiving speaker.

ATOMIC_AGGREGATE. ATOMIC_AGGREGATE is a well-known discretionary attribute. When presented with a set of overlapping routes from one of its peers, if a BGP speaker selects the less specific route without selecting the more specific one, the local system attaches the ATOMIC_AGGREGATE attribute to the route when propagating it to other BGP speakers (if that attribute is not already present in the received less specific route). A BGP speaker that receives a route with the ATOMIC_AGGREGATE attribute does not remove the attribute from the route when propagating it to other speakers. A BGP speaker that receives a route with the ATOMIC_AGGREGATE attribute does not make any NLRI of that route more specific when advertising this route to other BGP speakers. A BGP speaker that receives a route with the ATOMIC_AGGREGATE attribute needs to be aware of the fact that the actual path to destinations, as specified in the NLRI of the route, while having the loop-free property, may traverse autonomous systems not listed in the AS_PATH attribute.

AGGREGATOR. AGGREGATOR is an optional transitive attribute that may be included in updates formed by aggregation. A BGP speaker that performs route aggregation may add the AGGREGATOR attribute, which contains its own AS number and IP address.

BGP Error Handling

This section describes actions to be taken when errors are detected while processing BGP messages. When any of the conditions described here are detected, a NOTIFICATION message with the indicated error code, error subcode, and Data fields is sent, and the BGP connection is closed. If no error subcode is specified, then a 0 must be used. The phrase "the BGP connection is closed" means that all resources for that BGP connection have been deallocated. Routing table entries associated with the remote peer are marked as invalid. The fact that the routes have become invalid is passed to other BGP peers before the routes are deleted from the system. Unless specified explicitly, the Data field of the NOTIFICATION message is sent to indicate an error is empty.

Connection Collision Detection

If a pair of BGP speakers try simultaneously to establish a TCP connection to each other, two parallel connections between this pair of speakers might be formed. This situation is *connection collision*. Clearly, one of these connections must be closed.

Based on the value of the BGP identifier, a convention is established for detecting which BGP connection is to be preserved when a collision does occur. The convention is to compare the BGP identifiers of the peers involved in the collision and to retain only the connection initiated by the BGP speaker with the higher valued BGP identifier. Upon receipt of an OPEN message, the local system must examine all of its connections in the OpenConfirm state. A BGP speaker may also examine connections in an OpenSent state if it knows the BGP identifier of the peer through outside of the protocol. If among these connections there is a connection to a remote BGP speaker whose BGP identifier equals the one in the OPEN message, the local system performs the following collision resolution procedure:

1. The BGP identifier of the local system is compared to the BGP identifier of the remote system (as specified in the OPEN message).

2. If the value of the local BGP identifier is less than the remote one, the local system closes the BGP connection that already exists (the one already in the OpenConfirm state) and accepts the BGP connection initiated by the remote system.

3. Otherwise, the local system closes newly created BGP connection (the one associated with the newly received OPEN message) and continues to use the existing one (the one already in the OpenConfirm state).

Comparing BGP identifiers is done by treating them as 4-octet long unsigned integers. A connection collision with an existing BGP connection in established states causes unconditional closing of the newly created connection. Note that a connection collision cannot be detected with connections in Idle, Connect, or Active states. Closing the BGP connection (resulting from the collision resolution procedure) is accomplished by sending the NOTIFICATION message with the Error Code Cease.

BGP Version Negotiation

BGP speakers may negotiate the version of the protocol by making multiple attempts to open a BGP connection, starting with the highest version number each supports. If an open attempt fails with an Error Code OPEN Message Error and an Error Subcode Unsupported

Version Number, the BGP speaker has available the version number it tried, the version number its peer tried, the version number passed by its peer in the NOTIFICATION message, and the version numbers that it supports. If the two peers support one or more common versions, this will allow them to rapidly determine the highest common version. To support BGP version negotiation, future versions of BGP must retain the format of the OPEN and NOTIFICATION messages.

BGP Finite State Machine

This section specifies BGP operation in terms of a *Finite State Machine* (FSM). Following is a brief summary and overview of BGP operations by state as determined by this FSM.
    Initially BGP is in the Idle state.

Idle State.   In this state, BGP refuses all incoming BGP connections. No resources are allocated to the peer. In response to the Start event (initiated by either system or operator), the local system initializes all BGP resources, starts the ConnectRetry timer, initiates a transport connection to other BGP peers while listening for connection that may be initiated by the remote BGP peer, and changes its state to Connect. The exact value of the ConnectRetry timer is a local matter but should be sufficiently large to allow TCP initialization.
    If a BGP speaker detects an error, it shuts down the connection and changes its state to Idle. Getting out of the Idle state requires generation of the Start event. If such an event is generated automatically, persistent BGP errors may result in persistent flapping of the speaker. To avoid such a condition, Start events should not be generated immediately for a peer that was previously transitioned to Idle due to an error. The time between consecutive generation of Start events, if such events are generated automatically, should exponentially increase. The value of the initial timer is 60 seconds. The time is doubled for each consecutive retry. Any other event received in the Idle state is ignored.

Connect State.   In this state, BGP is waiting for the transport protocol connection to be completed.
    If the transport protocol connection succeeds, the local system clears the ConnectRetry timer, completes initialization, sends an OPEN message to its peer, and changes its state to OpenSent.
    If the transport protocol connect fails (e.g., retransmission timeout), the local system restarts the ConnectRetry timer, continues to listen for a connection that may be initiated by the remote BGP peer, and changes its state to an Active state.
    In response to the ConnectRetry timer expired event, the local system restarts the ConnectRetry timer, initiates a transport connection to other BGP peers, continues to listen for a connection that may be initiated by the remote BGP peer, and stays in the Connect state. Start events are ignored in the Active state.
    In response to any other event (initiated by either system or operator), the local system releases all BGP resources associated with this connection and changes its state to Idle.

Active State.   In this state, BGP is trying to acquire a peer by initiating a transport protocol connection. If the transport protocol connection succeeds, the local system clears the ConnectRetry timer, completes initialization, sends an OPEN message to its peer, sets its Hold Timer to a large value, and changes its state to OpenSent.

In response to the ConnectRetry timer expired event, the local system restarts the ConnectRetry timer, initiates a transport connection to other BGP peers, continues to listen for a connection that may be initiated by the remote BGP peer, and changes its state to Connect.

If the local system detects that a remote peer is trying to establish a BGP connection to it, and the IP address of the remote peer is not an expected one, the local system restarts the ConnectRetry timer, rejects the attempted connection, continues to listen for a connection that may be initiated by the remote BGP peer, and stays in the Active state. Start events are ignored in the Active state.

In response to any other event (initiated by either system or operator), the local system releases all BGP resources associated with this connection and changes its state to Idle.

OpenSent State. In this state, BGP waits for an OPEN message from its peer. When an OPEN message is received, all fields are checked for correctness. If the BGP message header checking or open message checking detects an error or a connection collision, the local system sends a NOTIFICATION message and changes its state to Idle.

If no errors are in the OPEN message, BGP sends a KEEPALIVE message and sets a KeepAlive timer. The Hold timer, which originally was set to a large value, is replaced with the negotiated Hold Time value.

If the negotiated Hold Time value is 0, the Hold Time timer and KeepAlive timers are not started. If the value of the autonomous system field is the same as the local autonomous system number, the connection is an internal connection; otherwise, it is external. Finally, the state is changed to OpenConfirm.

If a disconnect notification is received from the underlying transport protocol, the local system closes the BGP connection, restarts the ConnectRetry timer while continuing to listen for a connection that may be initiated by the remote BGP peer, and goes into the Active state. If the Hold Timer expires, the local system sends a NOTIFICATION message with the error code `Hold Timer Expired` and changes its state to Idle.

In response to the Stop event (initiated by either system or operator) the local system sends a NOTIFICATION message with the Cease error code and changes its state to Idle. Start events are ignored in the OpenSent state.

In response to any other event, the local system sends a NOTIFICATION message with the error code `Finite State Machine Error` and changes its state to Idle.

Whenever BGP changes its state from OpenSent to Idle, it closes the BGP (and transport-level) connection and releases all resources associated with that connection.

OpenConfirm State. In this state, BGP waits for a KEEPALIVE or NOTIFICATION message. If the local system receives a KEEPALIVE message, it changes its state to Established.

If the Hold Timer expires before a KEEPALIVE message is received, the local system sends a NOTIFICATION message with error code `Hold Timer Expired` and changes its state to Idle.

If the local system receives a NOTIFICATION message, it changes its state to Idle.

If the KeepAlive timer expires, the local system sends a KEEPALIVE message and restarts its KeepAlive timer.

If a disconnect notification is received from the underlying transport protocol, the local system changes its state to Idle.

In response to the Stop event (initiated by either system or operator) the local system sends a NOTIFICATION message with the `Cease` error code and changes its state to Idle.

Start event is ignored in the OpenConfirm state.

In response to any other event, the local system sends a NOTIFICATION message with the error code `Finite State Machine Error` and changes its state to Idle. Whenever BGP changes its state from OpenConfirm to Idle, it closes the BGP (and transport-level) connection and releases all resources associated with that connection.

Established State.   In the Established state, BGP can exchange UPDATE, NOTIFICATION, and KEEPALIVE messages with its peer.

If the local system receives an UPDATE or KEEPALIVE message, it restarts its Hold Timer if the negotiated Hold Time value is nonzero.

If the local system receives a NOTIFICATION message, it changes its state to Idle. If the local system receives an UPDATE message and the UPDATE message error-handling procedure detects an error, the local system sends a NOTIFICATION message and changes its state to Idle.

If a disconnect notification is received from the underlying transport protocol, the local system changes its state to Idle. If the Hold Timer expires, the local system sends a NOTIFICATION message with the error code `Hold Timer Expired` and changes its state to Idle.

If the KeepAlive timer expires, the local system sends a KEEPALIVE message and restarts its KeepAlive timer.

Each time the local system sends a KEEPALIVE or UPDATE message, it restarts its KeepAlive timer, unless the negotiated Hold Time value is 0.

In response to the Stop event (initiated by either system or operator), the local system sends a NOTIFICATION message with the `Cease` error code and changes its state to Idle.

Start event is ignored in the Established state.

In response to any other event, the local system sends a NOTIFICATION message with the error code `Finite State Machine Error` and changes its state to Idle.

Whenever BGP changes its state from Established to Idle, it closes the BGP (and transport-level) connection, releases all resources associated with that connection, and deletes all routes derived from that connection.

Decision Process

The Decision Process selects routes for subsequent advertisement by applying the policies in the local *Policy Information Base* (PIB) to the routes stored in its Adj-RIB-In. The output of the Decision Process is the set of routes that will be advertised to all peers; the selected routes will be stored in the local speaker's Adj-RIB-Out.

The selection process is formalized by defining a function that takes the attribute of a given route as an argument and returns a nonnegative integer denoting the degree of preference for the route. The function that calculates the degree of preference for a given route shall not use as its inputs any of the following: the existence of other routes, the nonexistence of other routes, or the path attributes of other routes. Route selection, then, consists of individual application of the degree of preference function to each feasible route, followed by the choice of the one with the highest degree of preference.

The Decision Process operates on routes contained in each Adj-RIB-In and is responsible for the following:

- Selection of routes to be advertised to BGP speakers located in the local speaker's autonomous system
- Selection of routes to be advertised to BGP speakers located in neighboring autonomous systems
- Route aggregation and route information reduction

The Decision Process takes place in three distinct phases, each triggered by a different event:

1. Phase 1 is responsible for calculating the degree of preference for each route received from a BGP speaker located in a neighboring autonomous system and for advertising to the other BGP speakers in the local autonomous system the routes that have the highest degree of preference for each distinct destination.

2. Phase 2 is invoked on completion of phase 1. It is responsible for choosing the best route out of all those available for each distinct destination and for installing each chosen route into the appropriate Loc-RIB.

3. Phase 3 is invoked after the Loc-RIB has been modified. It is responsible for disseminating routes in the Loc-RIB to each peer located in a neighboring autonomous system, according to the policies contained in the PIB. Route aggregation and information reduction optionally can be performed within this phase.

Breaking Ties (Phase 2)

In its Adj-RIBs-In, a BGP speaker may have several routes to the same destination that have the same degree of preference. The local speaker can select only one of these routes for inclusion in the associated Loc-RIB. The local speaker considers all equally preferable routes, both those received from BGP speakers located in neighboring autonomous systems and those received from other BGP speakers located in the local speaker's autonomous system.

The following tie-breaking procedure assumes that for each candidate route all the BGP speakers within an autonomous system can ascertain the cost of a path (interior distance) to the address depicted by the NEXT_HOP attribute of the route. Ties shall be broken according to the following algorithm:

1. If the local system is configured to take into account MULTI_EXIT_DISC and the candidate routes differ in their MULTI_EXIT_DISC attribute, select the route that has the lowest value of the MULTI_EXIT_DISC attribute.

2. Otherwise, select the route that has the lowest cost (interior distance) to the entity depicted by the NEXT_HOP attribute of the route. If several routes have with the same cost, the tie-breaking is broken as follows:

   - If at least one of the candidate routes was advertised by the BGP speaker in a neighboring autonomous system, select the route that was advertised by the BGP speaker in a neighboring autonomous system whose BGP identifier has the lowest value among all other BGP speakers in neighboring autonomous systems.

- Otherwise, select the route that was advertised by the BGP speaker whose BGP identifier has the lowest value.

Phase 3: Route Dissemination

The Phase 3 decision function is invoked on completion of Phase 2 or when any of the following events occur:

1. When routes in a Loc-RIB to local destinations have changed
2. When locally generated routes learned by means outside of BGP have changed
3. When a new BGP speaker—BGP speaker connection has been established

The Phase 3 function is a separate process that completes when it has no further work to do. The Phase 3 Routing Decision function shall be blocked from running while the Phase 2 decision function is in process. All routes in the Loc-RIB shall be processed into a corresponding entry in the associated Adj-RIBs-Out. Route aggregation and information reduction techniques optionally may be applied.

For the benefit of future support of inter-AS multicast capabilities, a BGP speaker that participates in inter-AS multicast routing advertises a route it receives from one of its external peers and if it installs that route in its Loc-RIB, the BGP speaker advertises it back to the peer from which the route was received. For a BGP speaker that does not participate in inter-AS multicast routing such an advertisement is optional. When doing such an advertisement, the NEXT_HOP attribute should be set to the address of the peer. An implementation may also optimize such an advertisement by truncating information in the AS_PATH attribute to include only its own AS number and that of the peer that advertised the route (such truncation requires the ORIGIN attribute to be set to INCOMPLETE). In addition, an implementation is not required to pass optional or discretionary path attributes with such an advertisement.

Overlapping Routes

A BGP speaker may transmit routes with overlapping NLRI to another BGP speaker. NLRI overlap occurs when a set of destinations are identified in nonmatching multiple routes. Because BGP encodes NLRI using IP prefixes, overlap will always exhibit subset relationships. A route describing a smaller set of destinations (a longer prefix) is said to be more specific than a route describing a larger set of destinations (a shorted prefix); similarly, a route describing a larger set of destinations (a shorter prefix) is said to be less specific than a route describing a smaller set of destinations (a longer prefix).

The precedence relationship effectively decomposes less-specific routes into two parts:

- A set of destinations described only by the less specific route
- A set of destinations described by the overlap of the less specific and the more specific route

When overlapping routes are present in the same Adj-RIB-In, the more specific route takes precedence, in order from more specific to least specific.

The set of destinations described by the overlap represents a portion of the less specific route that is feasible but is not currently in use. If a more specific route is later withdrawn, the set of destinations described by the overlap will still be reachable using the less specific route.

If a BGP speaker receives overlapping routes, the Decision Process takes into account the semantics of the overlapping routes. In particular, if a BGP speaker accepts the less-specific route while rejecting the more specific route from the same peer, the destinations represented by the overlap may not forward along the autonomous systems listed in the AS_PATH attribute of that route. Therefore, a BGP speaker has the following choices:

1. Install both the less and the more specific routes

2. Install the more specific route only

3. Install the nonoverlapping part of the less specific route only (that implies deaggregation)

4. Aggregate the two routes and install the aggregated route

5. Install the less specific route only

6. Install neither route

If a BGP speaker chooses number 5, it should add ATOMIC_AGGREGATE attribute to the route. A route that carries ATOMIC_AGGREGATE attribute cannot be deaggregated. That is, the NLRI of this route cannot be made more specific. Forwarding along such a route does not guarantee that IP packets will actually traverse only autonomous systems listed in the AS_PATH attribute of the route. If a BGP speaker chooses the number, it must not advertise the more general route without the more specific route.

Update-Send Process

The Update-Send process is responsible for advertising UPDATE messages to all peers. For example, it distributes the routes chosen by the Decision Process to other BGP speakers that may be located in either the same autonomous system or a neighboring autonomous system. Rules for information exchange between BGP speakers located in different autonomous systems are rules for information exchange between BGP speakers located in the same autonomous system. Distribution of routing information between a set of BGP speakers, all of which are located in the same autonomous system, is referred to as internal distribution.

Internal Updates

The internal update process is concerned with the distribution of routing information to BGP speakers located in the local speaker's autonomous system.

When a BGP speaker receives an UPDATE message from another BGP speaker located in its own autonomous system, the receiving BGP speaker does not redistribute the routing information contained in that UPDATE message to other BGP speakers located in its own autonomous system.

When a BGP speaker receives a new route from a BGP speaker in a neighboring autonomous system, it advertises that route to all other BGP speakers in its autonomous system by means of an UPDATE message if any of the following conditions occur:

1. The degree of preference assigned to the newly received route by the local BGP speaker is higher than the degree of preference that the local speaker has assigned to other routes that have been received from BGP speakers in neighboring autonomous systems.

2. No other routes have been received from BGP speakers in neighboring autonomous systems.

3. The newly received route is selected as a result of breaking a tie between several routes that have the highest degree of preference and the same destination.

When a BGP speaker receives an UPDATE message with a nonempty WITHDRAWN ROUTES field, it removes from its Adj-RIB-In all routes whose destinations were carried in this field (as IP prefixes). The speaker takes the following additional steps:

1. If the corresponding feasible route had not been previously advertised, no further action is necessary.

2. If the corresponding feasible route had been previously advertised, one of the following occurs:

   ▪ If a new route is selected for advertisement that has the same NLRI as the unfeasible routes, the local BGP speaker advertises the replacement route

   ▪ If a replacement route is not available for advertisement, the BGP speaker includes the destinations of the unfeasible route (in the form of IP prefixes) in the WITHDRAWN ROUTES field of an UPDATE message and sends this message to each peer to whom it had previously advertised the corresponding feasible route.

All feasible routes advertised are placed in the appropriate Adj-RIBs-Out, and all unfeasible routes advertised are removed from the Adj-RIBs-Out.

Breaking Ties (Internal Updates)

If a local BGP speaker has connections to several BGP speakers in neighboring autonomous systems, multiple Adj-RIBs-In are associated with these peers. These Adj-RIBs-In might contain several equally preferable routes to the same destination, all of which were advertised by BGP speakers located in neighboring autonomous systems. The local BGP speaker selects one of these routes according to the following rules:

▪ If the candidate routes differ only in their NEXT_HOP and MULTI_EXIT_DISC attributes and if the local system is configured to take into account the MULTI_EXIT_DISC attribute, select the route with the lowest value of the MULTI_EXIT_DISC attribute.

▪ If the local system can ascertain the cost of a path to the entity depicted by the NEXT_HOP attribute of the candidate route, select the route with the lowest cost.

▪ In all other cases, select the route advertised by the BGP speaker whose BGP identifier has the lowest value.

External Updates

The external update process is concerned with the distribution of routing information to BGP speakers located in neighboring autonomous systems. As part of the Phase 3 route-selection process, the BGP speaker has updated its Adj-RIBs-Out and its forwarding table. All newly installed routes and all newly unfeasible routes for which there is no replacement route are advertised to BGP speakers located in neighboring autonomous systems by means of an UPDATE message. Any routes in the Loc-RIB marked as unfeasible are removed. Changes to the reachable destinations within its own autonomous system are advertised in an UPDATE message.

Controlling Routing Traffic Overhead. The BGP protocol constrains the amount of routing traffic (that is, UPDATE messages) to limit the link bandwidth needed to advertise UPDATE messages and the processing power needed by the decision process to digest the information contained in the UPDATE messages.

Frequency of Route Advertisement. The parameter `MinRouteAdvertisementInterval` determines the minimum amount of time that must elapse between the advertisement of routes to a particular destination from a single BGP speaker. This rate-limiting procedure applies on a per-destination basis, although the value of `MinRouteAdvertisementInterval` is set on a per BGP peer basis. Two UPDATE messages sent from a single BGP speaker, which advertise feasible routes to some common set of destinations received from BGP speakers in neighboring autonomous systems, must be separated by at least `MinRouteAdvertisement Interval`. Clearly, this can be achieved precisely only by keeping a separate timer for each common set of destinations.

This would be unwarranted overhead. Any technique ensuring the interval between two UPDATE messages, which advertise feasible routes to common destinations, sent from a single BGP speaker is at least `MinRouteAdvertisementInterval` and ensures that a constant upper bound on the interval is acceptable. Because fast convergence is needed within an autonomous system, this procedure does not apply for routes received from other BGP speakers in the same autonomous system. To avoid long-lived black holes, the procedure does not apply to the explicit withdrawal of unfeasible routes, whose destinations (expressed as IP prefixes) are listed in the Withdrawn Routes field of an UPDATE message.

This procedure does not limit the rate of route selection but only the rate of route advertisement. If new routes are selected multiple times while awaiting the expiration of `MinRouteAdvertisementInterval`, the last route selected is advertised at the end of `MinRouteAdvertisementInterval`.

Originating BGP Routes

A BGP speaker may originate BGP routes by injecting routing information acquired by some other means (e.g., via an IGP) into BGP. A BGP speaker that originates BGP routes assigns the degree of preference to these routes by passing them through the Decision Process. These routes may also be distributed to other BGP speakers within the local AS as part of the internal update process. The decision to distribute non-BGP acquired routes within an AS via BGP or not depends on the environment within the AS (e.g., type of IGP) and should be controlled via configuration.

Listing 12.1 in CH12CODE on the CD highlights a BGP sample network and Network General Sniffer captures.

Questions

1. BGP dynamically learns new networks from:
   A. BGP advertising routers
   B. Distance vector routing advertising routers
   C. Link state advertising routers
   D. None of the above

2. BGP routers are associated together via:
   A. TCP connections
   B. Autonomous system numbers
   C. Area numbers
   D. Group Ids

3. What is BGP? Explain.

4. What does CIDR stand for? Explain.

5. BGP runs over the following_____ protocol using port number ___.
   A. TCP, 139
   B. UDP, 179
   C. TCP, 179
   D. IP, Protocol ID 89
   E. None of the above

6. What is a BGP Border Gateway speaker?
   A. Router running the BGP protocol exchanging reachability information with other BGP speakers
   B. First BGP router on the network
   C. Area Boarder BGP router
   D. None of the above

7. During path switching, using either per-packet or per destination using load balancing, what is the maximum number of paths supported using BGP?
   A. 6
   B. 8
   C. 4
   D. None of the above

8. Identify several features of BGP-4.
   A. Route aggregation
   B. AS aggregation
   C. AS numbers must match
   D. All of the above

9. What is the maximum BGP-4 message size in octets?
   A. 512
   B. 1128
   C. 4096
   D. 128

10. The Smallest message that may be sent consists of a BGP header without a data portion, or ___ octets.
    A. 19
    B. 16
    C. 8
    D. 32

11. The minimum length of the UPDATE message is ___ octets.
    A. 23
    B. 42
    C. 38
    D. 16

12. The Cisco BGP route selection process has ___ phases.
   A. 2   **C.** 10
   B. 1   **D.** 5

13. Define BGP Route selection Process phase 2.
   A. Phase 1 calculates the best route based on hop count.
   B. It prefers the path with largest weight.
   C. Phase 1 advertises routes based on administrative distance.
   D. All of the above

14. The final BGP Route selection tie-breaking algorithm is?
   A. The route coming from the router with the lowest router ID value
   B. The route that has the lowest cost
   C. The route with the lowest cost and bandwidth
   D. Both A and B
   E. None of the above

15. Identify the message types supported by BGP.
   A. KEEPALIVE   **D.** KEEPALIVE
   B. UPDATE   **E.** All of the above
   C. NOTIFICATION   **F.** None of the above

16. The command to enable BGP routing is?
   A. `network network-number [mask network mask]`
   B. `route-map route-map-name`
   C. `router bgp autonomous-system`
   D. `router as-number bgp`

17. What is the command to redistribute network 0.0.0.0 into BGP?
   A. `IP route 0.0.0.0`   **C.** `IP default route`
   B. `default-originate`   **D.** None of the above

18. BGP transit policies is based on distribution of routing information using which three values?
   A. IP Address   **D.** Hello
   B. AS_PATH attribute   **E.** Link updates
   C. COMMUNITIES

19. BGP network weight is defined as:
   A. Administrative distance   **D.** All of the above
   B. Best path selection   **E.** A & B
   C. Closest AS router

20. Define the BGP term Stub Autonomous System.

21. Define the BGP term Transit Traffic.

22. Define the BGP term Multi-homed Non-transit Autonomous System.

23. Autonomous systems are identified by:
   A. Autonomous Systems Number   **C.** Router Priority
   B. Router ID   **D.** All of the above

24. BGP selects routes based on:
- **A.** Weight
- **B.** Preference
- **C.** AS_path length
- **D.** All of the above

25. BGP sends out a keepalive ___ to ensure the status of the link.
- **A.** once per session
- **B.** one half the hold time
- **C.** one third the hold time
- **D.** never

26. Routers that communicate directly to each other using BGP are known as:
- **A.** Peers
- **B.** Neighbor
- **C.** Link associate
- **D.** None of the above

27. Identify the path attributes of selecting a route in BGP.
- **A.** ORGIN
- **B.** AS-PATH
- **C.** NEXT-HOP
- **D.** AGGREGATOR
- **E.** ATOMIC-AGGREGATE
- **F.** LOCAL-PREF
- **G.** MULTI-EXIT-DISC
- **H.** All of the above

28. Define the purpose of route maps.

29. Identify three community attributes.
- **A.** Public
- **B.** No-export
- **C.** No-advertise
- **D.** Internet
- **E.** Private

30. The administrative distance for BGP External routes is:
- **A.** 19
- **B.** 20
- **C.** 30
- **D.** 100

31. The administrative distance for BGP Internal routes is:
- **A.** 100
- **B.** 30
- **C.** 200
- **D.** 120

32. The administrative distance for BGP local routes is:
- **A.** 150
- **B.** 200
- **C.** 275
- **D.** 300

33. Identify the command that can be used for filtering the sending and receiving of routing updates.
- **A.** `Prefix Filters`
- **B.** `AS-path Filtering`
- **C.** `Route Map Filtering`
- **D.** `Community Filtering`
- **E.** All of the above
- **F.** None of the above

34. Define route flap dampening.

35. CIDR is also known by the name_____.
- **A.** VLSM
- **B.** Subnetting
- **C.** Supernetting
- **D.** None of the above

36. Which of the following statements is true?
  A. BGP is always a superior routing protocol when connecting to an ISP.
  B. Static routes should always be used when connecting to an ISP.
  C. Neither static routes nor BGP should be used when connecting to an ISP.
  D. BGP should be used when implementing policy for ISP connections.
  E. Static routes should be used when policy is not needed when connecting to an ISP.

37. Which is more true than the others ? BGP dynamically learns new networks from _____.
  A. other BGP neighbor routers
  B. other link state routing protocols with route redistribution
  C. other distance vector routing protocols with route redistribution
  D. via static routes and route redistribution
  E. All of the above

38. BGP neighbors talk to each other via which methodology?
  A. TCP connections
  B. Area numbers
  C. Group identification numbers
  D. Autonomous System numbers

39. Which of the following is true about CIDR?
  A. It is an IP based mechanism to summarize routing information for distance vector protocols.
  B. It has been replaced by VLSM by ISP's implementation of routing.
  C. VLSM reduces route flapping more so than CIDR.
  D. CIDR allows a block of C-Class network numbers to be summarized into one entry in the routing table.

40. What is a BGP Speaker?
  A. The master router in a BGP connection
  B. The BGP router with the highest ID
  C. A BGP router between internal areas
  D. A BGP router sharing reachability information with other BGP routers

41. What is a BGP announcement?
  A. Reachability information sent by a BGP router
  B. Hello messages sent to sync BGP peers
  C. Message sent by a BGP router to internal routing protocols
  D. None of the above

42. BGP transit policies are based on distribution of routing using which three values?
  A. IP address, AS_PATH attribute, Hop count
  B. IP address, AS_PATH attribute, Communities
  C. AS_PATH attribute, Communities, Internal versus External neighbor status
  D. AS_PATH attribute, Internal versus External neighbor status, Hop count

43. Which of the following is not true about BGP?
  A. The network weight is defined as the best path selected.
  B. Speakers within an Autonomous System must establish a peer relationship with each other.
  C. Transit Autonomous Systems allow multiple connections to other Autonomous Systems.
  D. Stub areas allow multiple entry points into the stub.

44. Which is not true about BGP?
   A. Selects routes based on policy and perference
   B. Allows for multiple connections to more than one autonomous system
   C. Requires all routers in an autonomous system to run BGP
   D. Uses the AS-PATH attribute to eliminate routing loops

45. Which of the following is not used in the path attributes in selecting a route?
   A. Origin
   B. AS-Path value
   C. Next hop
   D. Local preference
   E. The internal routing protocol running
   F. Multi-exit discriminator

46. Which of the following is a community attribute?
   A. No-export
   B. No-advertise
   C. Test
   D. No-IGP allowed

47. Which of the following is true about BGP?
   A. BGP routers that share routing information are known as border routers.
   B. Routing is based on a distance vector approach to choosing destination paths for a packet.
   C. Whenever a change occurs, BGP routers share only the change itself; the only time BGP routers share their whole table is when their connection is re-established with a neighbor.
   D. BGP routers automatically announce all internal network numbers that are part of their autonomous system.

48. Which of the following is true about the BGP neighbor connection process?
   A. BGP peers will automatically discover each other, like OSPF.
   B. All BGP peers must be physically connected to each other.
   C. The Cisco Router command `show IP bgp status` displays the current connection status between BGP peers.
   D. BGP speakers within an AS must be fully meshed logically or synchronization must be turned off.

49. What is true about using loopback interface for a router configured with BGP?
   A. Reduces overhead on the TCP connection
   B. Provides greater reliability for peer connections
   C. Only physical interfaces can be used for BGP peer connections
   D. Can be used to Tunnel IP BGP connections to peers
   E. None of the above

50. What is true about two BGP peers?
   A. They must be directly connected.
   B. The Cisco router command `neighbor ebgp-multihop` allows connectivity between internal and external BGP peers not directly connected.
   C. The Cisco router command `update-source loopback` is the only command required to connect two external BGP peers.
   D. For two directly connected external BGP peers, the only Cisco router command needed to bring up the TCP connection is `neighbor neighbor's-IP-address remote-as neighbor's-autonomous-system`.

51. Which of the following is true about BGP and synchronization?
    A. A BGP router will broadcast all routes defined by "network" statements specified in the BGP routing configuration for a Cisco router to other BGP peers in all instances.
    B. BGP can only share routing information with a peer once its own autonomous system has converged.
    C. A BGP router will share routing information with a peer once an internal routing protocol has also learned that information.
    D. It is a good practice to turn off synchronization for BGP and its internal autonomous system.
    E. The command to turn synchronization off is `synchronization off` which is specified under the `router bgp` configuration section.

52. Which of the following is false concerning route maps and BGP?
    A. Route maps are used to control or modify routing information.
    B. Route maps are used to define what is redistributed between routing domains.
    C. In the `route-map map-tag permit|deny sequence-number` command, the *sequence-number* determines the order of which route-maps should be executed, the lowered numbered ones being executed first.
    D. The `match` sub-command is used to specify what criteria to look at for the route-map condition.
    E. The `set` sub-command is used to enable BGP neighbors.

53. BGP provides three ways for an AS to advertise the networks that it originates. Which of the following is not one of them?
    A. Redistribution of external BGP routes
    B. Redistributing Static Routes
    C. Redistributing Dynamic Routes
    D. Using the network Command

54. The AS_path attribute is a one factor that BGP uses in the decision-making process in choosing a route. Which of the following is false about the AS_path attribute and its uses?
    A. When an update passes through an AS, BGP prepends its AS number to the update.
    B. The AS_path attribute is the list of AS numbers that an update has traversed in order to reach a destination.
    C. The AS_path cannot be used to implement policy decisions.
    D. An AS-SET is a mathematical set of all the ASs that have been traversed.

55. There are three ways to set the weight for updates coming in from a Router. Which of the following is not one of them?
    A. Using the weight option in the redistribution command
    B. Using an access list to set the weight attribute
    C. Using a route map to set the weight attribute
    D. Using the neighbor weight command to set the weight attribute

56. The community attribute provides a way of grouping destinations to which routing decisions can be applied. What is used to set this attribute?
    A. Access lists
    B. Route maps
    C. Network statements
    D. Community lists
    E. MED statements

57. BGP uses a certain order for the following criteria to select a path for a destination:
    1. If the path specifies a next hop that is inaccessible, drop the update.
    2. Prefer the path with the largest weight.
    3. Prefer the path with the largest local preference.
    4. Prefer the path that was originated by BGP running on this router.
    5. Prefer the route that has the shortest AS_path.
    6. Prefer the path with the lowest origin type (IGP versus EGP versus Incomplete)
    7. Prefer the path with the lowest MED attribute.
    8. Prefer the external path over the internal path.
    9. Prefer the path through the closest IGP neighbor.
    10. Prefer the path with the lowest IP address, as specified by the BGP router ID.

    Which of the following is the correct order?
    A. 1,2,3,4,5,6,7,8,9,10
    B. 2,3,4,5,6,7,9,10,8,1
    C. 5,6,7,8,1,2,3,4,9,10
    D. 5,6,7,8,2,3,4,9,10,1

58. Which of the following is not a mechanism to control the flow of BGP updates?
    A. BGP Filtering and Peer Groups
    B. CIDR and Summary Addressing
    C. Confederations
    D. Static Routes

59. What is the maximum number of entries supporting the "network mask" portion of the BGP network command?
    A. 100
    B. 50
    C. 200
    D. 150
    E. None of the above

60. What are some negatives surrounding clearning BGP sessions?
    A. Poor Routing
    B. Unstable routing updates
    C. Cache invalidation
    D. None of the above

61. The BGP community attribute provide the following:
    A. A means of grouping related destinations into communities
    B. Apply routing decisions based on communities
    C. Less overhead for speaker BGP routers
    D. None of the above

62. Identify one of the well know communities.
    A. Add AS
    B. Extranet
    C. No-export
    D. None of the above

63. A destination in BGP can only belong to how many communities?
    A. 1
    B. 4
    C. 6
    D. More than 1
    E. None of the above

64. By default all destinations belong to which community?
- **A.** No-advertise
- **B.** Advertise
- **C.** Internet
- **D.** Export
- **E.** No-export
- **F.** There are no defaults, the community must be configured

65. BGP requires that all IBGP speakers be:
- **A.** Fast switched
- **B.** Partial mesh
- **C.** Full mesh
- **D.** All of the above

66. A route reflector and its peer client form a:
- **A.** AS system
- **B.** Cluster
- **C.** Peer
- **D.** Neighbors

67. What happens when a route reflector receives an advertised route?
- **A.** Routes are advertised to all clients.
- **B.** Client routes do not receive advertisement of routes.
- **C.** Routes from IGP speakers are advertised to clients and non clients.
- **D.** All of the above

68. What is the default local preference value?
- **A.** 30
- **B.** 60
- **C.** 100
- **D.** 200
- **E.** 300
- **F.** None of the above

69. When a route flaps, what is the penalty assigned by the router configured for route dampening?
- **A.** 200
- **B.** 180
- **C.** 520
- **D.** 1000

70. BGP uses the following security authentication:
- **A.** SHA-1
- **B.** MD4
- **C.** MD5
- **D.** RC2

71. Given the following BGP packet trace, what type of BGP packet is this?
- **A.** Packet type not showed
- **B.** Keepalive
- **C.** Update
- **D.** Not enough information

```
BGP:   --- BGP Message ---
BGP:
BGP:   16 byte Marker   (all 1's)
BGP:   Length          = 52
BGP:   BGP type        = 2 (Update)
BGP:
BGP:   Unfeasible Routes Length    = 0
BGP:      No Withdrawn Routes in this Update
BGP:   Path Attribute Length     = 25 bytes
BGP:   Attribute Flags = 4X
BGP:         0... .... = Well-known
BGP:         .1.. .... = Transitive
```

```
BGP:            ..0. .... = Complete
BGP:            ...0 .... = 1 byte Length
BGP:    Attribute type code     = 1 (Origin)
BGP:    Attribute Data Length   = 1
BGP:    Origin type             = 0 (IGP)
BGP:    Attribute Flags = 4X
BGP:            0... .... = Well-known
BGP:            .1.. .... = Transitive
BGP:            ..0. .... = Complete
BGP:            ...0 .... = 1 byte Length
BGP:    Attribute type code     = 2 (AS Path)
BGP:    Attribute Data Length   = 4
BGP:    AS Identifier           = 513
BGP:    AS Identifier           = 100
BGP:    Attribute Flags = 4X
BGP:            0... .... = Well-known
BGP:            .1.. .... = Transitive
BGP:            ..0. .... = Complete
BGP:            ...0 .... = 1 byte Length
BGP:    Attribute type code     = 3 (Next Hop)
BGP:    Attribute Data Length   = 4
BGP:    Next Hop                = [137.144.4.2]
BGP:    Attribute Flags = 8X
BGP:            1... .... = Optional
BGP:            .0.. .... = Non-transitive
BGP:            ..0. .... = Complete
BGP:            ...0 .... = 1 byte Length
BGP:    Attribute type code     = 4 (Multi Exit Disc)
BGP:    Attribute Data Length   = 4
BGP:    Multi Exit Disc Attribute = 46251776
BGP:
BGP:    Network Layer Reachability Information:
BGP:     IP Prefix Length = 24 bits, IP subnet mask [255.255.255.0]
BGP:        IP address [137.144.6.0]
BGP:
```

Answers

1. A
2. B
3. BGP stands for Border Gateway Protocol and is the de-facto standard for routing between Autonomous Systems in the Internet. All communications between Internet Service Providers (ISP) is handled via BGP4, which supports CIDR.
4. CIDR stands for Classless Inter-Domain Routing and is documented in RFC1517/1518/1519/1520. CIDR is an effective method to stem the tide of IP address allocation as well as routing table overflow. Without CIDR having been implemented in 1994 & 1995, the Internet would not be functioning today.

   Basically, CIDR eliminates the concept of class A, B, and C networks and replaces this with a generalized "IP prefix". CIDR can be used to perform route aggregation in which a single route can cover the address space of several "old-style" network numbers and thus replace a lot of old routes.

   This lessens the local administrative burden of updating external routing, saves routing table space in all backbone routers and reduces route flapping (rapid changes in routes), and thus CPU load, in all backbone routers. CIDR will also allow delegation of pieces of what used to be called "network numbers" to customers, and therefore make it possible to utilize the available address space more efficiently.
5. C
6. A
7. A
8. D
9. C
10. A
11. A
12. C
13. B
14. A
15. E
16. C
17. B
18. A, B, C
19. B
20. Stub AS allows only one entry and exist point into the autonomous system.
21. Transit Traffic is any traffic with an origin and destination that does not belong to the AS.
22. The Multi-homed Non-transit Autonomous System allows for multiple connections to more than one Autonomous System, but does not allow traffic with an origin and destination that does not belong to the AS to pass through.
23. A
24. D
25. C
26. A
27. H
28. BGP route maps are used to control to and modify routing information and to define the conditions by which routes are redistributed between routing domains.
29. B, C, D
30. B
31. C

32. B
33. E
34. Route flap dampening is used to minimize the instability caused by flapping.
35. C
36. D
37. E
38. A
39. D
40. D
41. A
42. B
43. D
44. C
45. E
46. A, B
47. C
48. D
49. B
50. D
51. C
52. E
53. A
54. C
55. B
56. B
57. A
58. D
59. C
60. C
61. A, B, C
62. C
63. D
64. C
65. C
66. B
67. A
68. C
69. D
70. C
71. C

Data Link Switching (DLSw)

This chapter reviews the architecture of *data link switching* (DLSw) and highlights the operation and features found within the DLSw RFC 2166, RFC 1795, version 2.0, and Cisco DLSw+ functions.

Objective of DLSw

The heterogeneous networks that companies have built require that a method of integration be agreed on between communication equipment vendors, particularly those vendors who provide SNA connectivity. Although more IP devices are in use, the IBM connectivity market represents the majority of large commercial customers. Each of the vendors in this market has created its own method of providing SNA connectivity. Many of them operate quite effectively and efficiently. Unfortunately, these methods do not work together, which has resulted in many connectivity problems for companies after they have invested in an assortment of equipment from different vendors. Although these vendors have a certain vested interest in keeping their customers closely tied, they still do not want their customers upset or concerned that they are being sold a totally closed system with which the customer will not be able to operate. As a result, DLSw was created to provide a standardized method of connectivity.

Transport of SNA over TCP/IP

The achievement of a common method of transporting SNA data across an IP network was the driving force for the creation of DLSw (see Figure 13.1). This process had to allow for participation of all interested vendors. To this end, IBM provided an informational RFC describing a method of transporting SNA across an arbitrarily sized IP network. The IETF incorporated this information as RFC 1434 in March, 1993. IBM made the technology available to the public in an effort to get it accepted as the standard method for SNA transport across an IP network. IBM later created a *related interest group* (RIG)

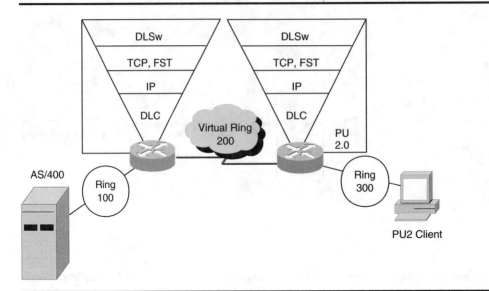

FIGURE 13.1   DLSw overview

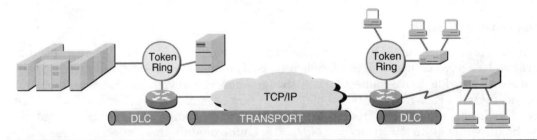

FIGURE 13.2   DLSw sample design

within the APPN Implementers Workshop in a further effort to standardize a methodology for SNA transport.

Overview of DLSw

Data Link Switching was developed to provide support for SNA and NetBIOS in multiprotocol routers as shown in Figure 13.2. Because SNA and NetBIOS sessions over NetBEUI use connection-oriented protocols, the Data Link Control procedure that they use on the LAN is IEEE 802.2 LLC Type 2. The IEEE 802.2 LLC Type 2 was designed with the assumption that the network transit delay would be predictable (i.e., a local LAN). Therefore, the LLC Type 2 elements of procedure use a fixed timer for detecting lost frames. When remote bridging is used over wide area links (especially at lower speeds), the network delay is larger, and it can vary greatly based upon congestion. When the delay exceeds the timeout value, LLC Type 2 attempts to retransmit. If the frame is not actually lost, only delayed, it is possible for the LLC Type 2 procedures to become confused. As a result, the link eventually may be taken down if the delay exceeds the T1 timer $\times$ N2 retry count.

NetBIOS makes extensive use of datagram services that use connectionless LLC Type 1 service, such as Broadcast Control of Explorer Packets and Source-Route Bridging Hop Count Limits.

The principal difference between Data Link Switching and bridging is that connection-oriented data DLSw terminates the Data Link Control, whereas bridging does not. Data Link Switching defines a reliable means of transporting SNA and NetBIOS traffic in a multiprotocol router network using TCP/IP encapsulation. Data Link Switching is an alternative to Cisco's *Remote Source-Route Bridging* (RSRB) and, therefore, solves many inherent problems associated with RSRB. Those problems include the following:

- SRB hop count limit (seven bridges and eight rings)
- Broadcast storms in the network due to SRB explorers
- Unnecessary traffic (LLC2 acknowledgments) across the WAN
- Susceptible to timeout
- Lack of data flow control
- No dynamic rerouting during failure
- Multivendor interoperability
- DLC time-outs
- DLC Acknowledgments over the WAN
- Flow and congestion control
- Broadcast control of search packets

A Data Link Switch that transmits the *Link Protocol Data Unit* (LPDU) received in a *Switch-to-Switch Protocol* (SSP) message to a local DLC will perform retries in a manner appropriate for the local DLC. This may involve running a reply timer and maintaining a poll retry count. The length of the timer and the number of retries is an implementation choice based on user configuration parameters and the DLC type.

Data Link Switching uses LAN addressing to set up connections between SNA systems. SDLC attached devices are defined with MAC and SAP addresses to enable them to communicate with LAN attached devices in the Cisco IOS software. For NetBIOS systems, Data Link Switching uses the NetBIOS name to forward datagrams and to set up connections for NetBIOS sessions. For LLC Type 2 connection establishment, SNA systems send TEST (or in some cases, XID) frames to the null (0x00) SAP. NetBIOS systems have an address-resolution procedure, based upon the Name Query and Name Recognized frames. This procedure is used to establish an end-to-end circuit.

Because Data Link Switching may be implemented in multiprotocol routers, there may be situations in which both bridging and switching are enabled. SNA frames can be identified by their link SAP. Typical SAP values for SNA are 0x04, 0x08, and 0x0c. NetBIOS always uses a link SAP value of 0xF0.

Transport Connection

Data Link Switches can be in used in pairs or by themselves. A paired DLSw multiplexes data links over a reliable transport using a *Switch-to-Switch Protocol* (SSP). Before Data Link Switching can occur between two routers, they must establish two TCP connections between them. Cisco requires only one TCP session if both routers are Cisco. Each Data Link Switch maintains a list of DLSw capable routers and their status (active/inactive). After the TCP connection is established, SSP messages are exchanged to establish the capabilities of the two Data Link Switches. When the exchange is complete, DLSw uses SSP control messages to establish end-to-end circuits over the transport connection. Within the transport connection, DLSw SSP messages are exchanged.

Two or more Data Link Switches may be attached to the same LAN, consisting of a number of Token Ring segments interconnected by Source-Routing bridges. In this case, a TCP connection is not defined between bridges attached to the same LAN. End systems, therefore, can select one of the possible Data Link Switches in a similar manner to the selection of a bridge path through a Source-Routed bridged network. The virtual ring segment in each Data Link Switch attached to a common LAN must be configured with the same ring number. This configuration prevents LAN frames sent by one Data Link Switch from being propagated through to other Data Link Switches.

The communication between DLSw devices is prefixed with one of two data headers. These headers are an *information header* and a *control header*. The control header is used for all communication except for information and independent flow control messages.

Table 13.1 shows the format of the control header. This header is 72 bytes long and provides addressing for the data link and circuit IDs. Table 13.2 shows the format of the information header. This header, which is 16 bytes long, is used to identify the logical connection being used for a particular communication. Because the first 16 bytes of these headers are the same, the parsing of the headers is made easier.

The first 16 bytes of control and information message headers contain identical fields. A brief description of the fields in an SSP message are given in the following list.

- The Version Number field (offset 0) is set to `0x31` (ASCII '1'), indicating a decimal value of 49. This is used to indicate DLSw version 1.

- The Header Length field (offset 1) is `0x48` for control messages, indicating a decimal value of 72 bytes, and `0x10` for information and Independent Flow Control messages, indicating a decimal value of 16 bytes.

- The Message Length field (offset 2) defines the number of bytes within the data field following the header.

- The Flow Control Byte field (offset 15)

- The Header Number field (offset 17) is `0x01`, indicating a value of 1.

- The Circuit Priority field (offset 22).

- The Frame Direction field (offset 38) is set to `0x01` for frames sent from the origin DLSw to the target DLSw and is set to `0x02` for frames sent from the target DLSw to the origin DLSw.

TABLE 13.1 DLSw Control Header

(Even Byte)		(Odd Byte)	
(00)	Version Number	(01) Header Length (= 72)	
(02)	Message Length		
(04)	Remote Data Link Correlator		
(08)	Remote DLC Port ID		
(12)	Reserved Field		
(14)	Message Type	|(15) Flow Control Byte	
(16)	Protocol ID	|(17) Header Number	
(18)	Reserved		
(20)	Largest Frame Size	| (21) SSP Flags	
(22)	Circuit Priority	| (23) Message Type	
(24)	Target MAC Address (non-canonical format)		
(30)	Origin MAC Address (non-canonical format)		
(36)	Origin Link SAP	| (37) Target Link SAP	
(38)	Frame Direction	| (39) Reserved	
(40)	Reserved		
(42)	DLC Header Length		
(44)	Origin DLC Port ID		
(48)	Origin Data Link Correlator		
(52)	Origin Transport ID		
(56)	Target DLC Port ID		
(60)	Target Data Link Correlator		
(64)	Target Transport ID		
(68)	Reserved Field		
(70)	Reserved Field		
	(Even Byte)	(Odd Byte)	

TABLE 13.2 Information Header (16 Bytes)

(00)	Version Number	(01)	Header Length (= 16)
(02)	Message Length		
(04)	Remote Data Link Correlator		
(08)	Remote DLC Port ID		
(12)	Reserved Field		
(14)	Message Type	(15)	Flow Control Byte

- The Remote Data Link Correlator and Remote DLC Port ID are set equal to the Target Data Link Correlator and Target DLC Port ID if the Frame Direction field is set to `0x01` and are set equal to the Origin Data Link Correlator and Origin DLC Port ID if the Direction Field is set to `0x02`.

- The Protocol ID field is set to `0x42`, indicating a decimal value of 66.

- The DLC Header Length is set to 0 for SNA and is set to `0x23` for NetBIOS datagrams, indicating a length of 35 bytes. This includes the *Access Control* (AC) field, the *Frame Control* (FC) field, *Destination MAC Address* (DA), the Source MAC Address (SA), the *Routing Information* (RI) field (padded to 18 bytes), the *Destination link SAP* (DSAP), the *Source link SAP* (SSAP), and the LLC control field (UI).

The SSP Flags field contains additional information related to the SSP message. The flags are defined as follows (bit 7 being the most significant bit and bit 0 the least significant bit of the octet):

Bit(s) 76543210	Name	Meaning
x	SSPex	1 = explorer message (CANUREACH and ICANREACH)

Reserved fields are set to 0 upon transmission and should be ignored upon receipt.

Address Parameters

A data link is defined as a logical association between the two end stations using Data Link Switching. It is identified by a Data Link ID (14 bytes) consisting of the pair of attachment addresses associated with each end system. Each attachment address is represented by the concatenation of the MAC address (6 bytes) and the LLC address (1 byte). Each attachment address is classified as either Target in the context of the Destination MAC/SAP addresses of an explorer frame sent in the first frame used to establish a Data Link ID.

The following is the Data Link ID 14-byte control message (offset 24 decimal).

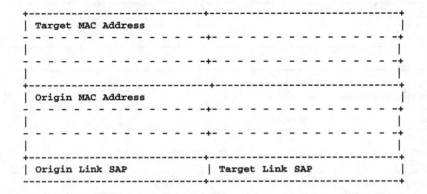

An end-to-end circuit is identified by a pair of Circuit IDs. A circuit ID is a 64-bit number that identifies the DLC circuit within a single DLSw. It consists of a DLC Port ID (4 bytes)

and a Data Link Correlator (4 bytes). The Circuit ID must be unique in a single DLSw and is assigned locally. The pair of Circuit IDs along with the Data Link IDs, uniquely identify a single end-to-end circuit. Each DLSw must keep a table of these Circuit ID pairs, one for the local end of the circuit and the other for the remote end of the circuit. To identify which Data Link Switch originated the establishment of a circuit, the terms, *Origin DLSw* and *Target DLSw*, are used in this chapter. The following is the Circuit ID (8 bytes).

```
+-----------------------------------+-----------------------------------+
| DLC Port ID                       |                                   |
+- - - - - - - - - - - - - - - -+- - - - - - - - - - - - - - -+
|                                   |                                   |
+-----------------------------------+-----------------------------------+
| Data Link Correlator              |                                   |
+- - - - - - - - - - - - - - - -+- - - - - - - - - - - - - - -+
|                                   |                                   |
+-----------------------------------+--------------------------- -----+
```

The Origin Transport ID and the Target Transport ID fields in the message header are used to identify the individual TCP/IP port on a Data Link Switch. The values have only local significance. However, each Data Link Switch is required to reflect the values contained in these two fields, along with the associated values for DLC Port ID and the Data Link Correlator, when returning a message to the other Data Link Switch.

DLSw Operations

The following steps provide a overview of how DLSw connections are established using the *Switch-to-Switch Protocol* (SSP):

1. An end-station sends a connection establishment request over the network. The link control software in the router passes the request to the SSP software.
2. The SSP software checks its cache of MAC/SAP addresses of devices known to be on the local LAN and remote LAN via remote peer. (This information can be statically entered using Cisco IOS configuration commands, or it can be dynamically learned by monitoring traffic on the LAN via caching and static MAC addressing.)
3. If the destination MAC/SAP address is not known to be local, the SSP in the datalink switch attempts to establish a connection to its remote peer router.
4. The local Data Link switch checks its local and remote cache of known remote end-stations.
5. If the cache is empty or the destination address is not found, the local Data Link switch establishes DLSw connections over a pair of TCP connections to each of its peer Data Link switches and issues a special SSP message called CANUREACH.
6. Each remote Data Link switch searches its cache for the destination end-station. If the search is successful, the remote Data Link switch responds with an SSP message called ICANREACH. (The local Data Link switch maintains a cache of local and remote devices' ICANREACH responses for use in responding to future requests. This prevents unnecessary broadcasts of CANUREACH messages.)

7. When the local Data Link switch has discovered where the destination end-station is located, it establishes a circuit connection between the pair of LLC2 end-stations (or stations that appear to be LLC2 devices, as discussed in "Supporting Non-LLC2 Data Links"). The remote Data Link switch issues an LLC2 connection establishment control frame. When the destination station responds affirmatively, the circuit is established, and the data can be tunneled between the two end-stations.

Figures 13.3 and 13.4 show the use of the addressing parameters during the establishment of an end-to-end connection. The CANUREACH, ICANREACH, and REACH_ACK message types all carry the Data Link ID, consisting of the MAC and Link SAP addresses

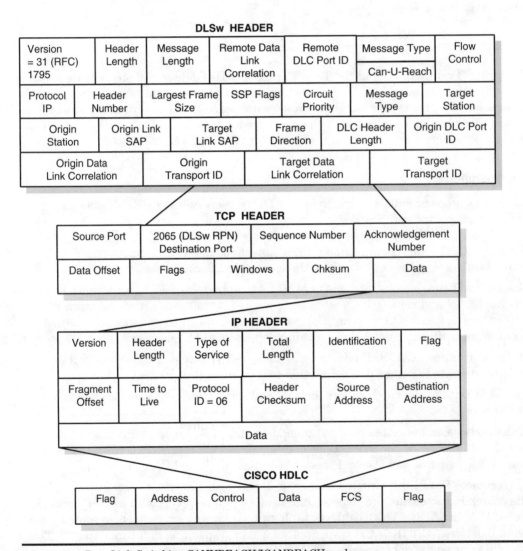

FIGURE 13.3 Data Link Switching CANUREACH/ICANREACH explorer

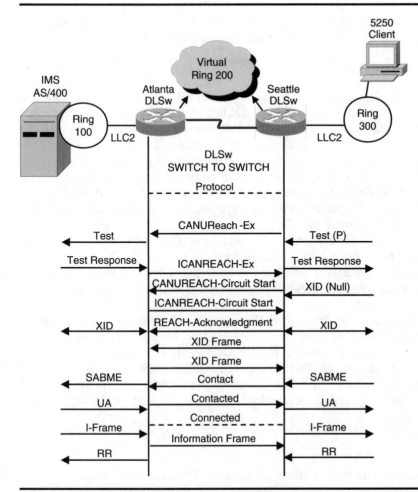

FIGURE 13.4   DLSw LLC2 connection establishment

associated with the two end stations. The CANUREACH and ICANREACH messages are qualified by the SSPex flag into CANUREACH_ex, ICANREACH_ex (explorer messages), CANUREACH_cs, and ICANREACH_cs (circuit start). The CANUREACH_ex is used to find a remote MAC and Link SAP address without establishing an SSP circuit. Upon receipt of a CANUREACH_cs message, the target DLSw starts a Data Link for each port; thereby obtaining a Data Link Correlator. If the target station can be reached, an ICANREACH_cs message is returned to the origin DLSw containing the Target Circuit ID parameter. Upon receipt, the origin DLSw starts a Data Link and returns the Origin Circuit ID to the target DLSw within the REACH_ACK message.

The pair of Circuit ID parameters is included in the message format along with the Data Link ID parameter. When the connection has been established, the INFOFRAME messages are exchanged with the shorter header. This header contains only the Circuit ID associated with the remote DLSw. The Remote Data Link Correlator and the Remote DLC Port ID are set equal to the Data Link Correlator and the DLC Port ID associated with the origin or target Data Link Switch, dependent upon the direction of the packet.

Correlators

The local use and contents of the Data Link Correlator, Port ID, and Transport ID fields in SSP messages is an implementation choice. These fields have local significance only.

The Transport ID fields are learned from the first SSP message exchanged with a DLSw partner (the Capabilities exchange). This field should not be varied by DLSw after the capabilities exchange and must be reflected to the partner DLSw in every SSP control message.

The Target Data Link Correlator, Target Port ID, and Target Transport ID must remain the same after the Target DLSw has sent the ICANREACH_cs for a given circuit. The Origin DLSw must store the values specified in the ICANREACH_cs and use these on all subsequent SSP messages for this circuit.

The Origin DLSw must allow these fields to vary until the ICANREACH_cs is received. Each SSP message issued for a circuit must reflect the values specified by the Target DLSw in the last SSP message for this circuit received by the Origin DLSw. Binary 0 should be used if no such message has yet been received for a given circuit (apart from the Target Transport ID).

The Origin Data Link Correlator, Origin Port ID, and Origin Transport ID must remain the same after the Origin DLSw has issued the REACH_ACK for a given circuit. The Target DLSw must store the values specified in the REACH_ACK and use these on all subsequent SSP messages for this circuit. The Target DLSw must allow these fields to vary until the REACH_ACK is received. Each SSP message issued for a circuit must reflect the values specified by the Origin DLSw in the last SSP message for this circuit received by the Target DLSw.

Message Types

Table 13.3 lists the protocol data units exchanged between Data Link Switches.

DLSw State Machine

Table 13.4 describes the states for a single circuit through the Data Link Switch. State information is kept for each connection. The initial state for a connection is DISCONNECTED. The steady state is either CIRCUIT_ESTABLISHED or CONNECTED. In the former state, an end-to-end circuit has been established allowing the support of Type 1 LLC between the end systems. The latter state exists when an end-to-end connection has been established for the support of Type 2 LLC services between the end systems.

For SNA, LLC Type 2 connection establishment is via the use of IEEE 802.2 Test or XID frames. SNA devices send these frames to the null SAP to determine the source-route information in support of bridging. (Most SNA LLC2 devices that have a single PU per MAC address use a default of 0×04.) Typically the SAP would be used to determine whether the test frames should be sent to DLSw in the router. If both bridging and DLSw are enabled, this allows the product to ensure that SNA frames are not both bridged and switched. This allows multiple PUs to share connections between two given MAC addresses (each PU-to-PU session uses one LLC2 connection).

TABLE 13.3   Message Types

Command	Description	Type	Flags/Notes
CANUREACH_ex	Can U Reach Station-explorer	0×03	SSPex
CANUREACH_cs	Can U Reach Station-circuit	start	0×03
ICANREACH_ex	I Can Reach Station-explorer	0×04	SSPex
ICANREACH_cs	I Can Reach Station-circuit	start	0×04
REACH_ACK	Reach Acknowledgment	0×05	
DGRMFRAME	Datagram Frame	0×06	
XIDFRAME	XID Frame	0×07	
CONTACT	Contact Remote Station	0×08	
CONTACTED	Remote Station Contacted	0×09	
RESTART_DL	Restart Data Link	0×10	
DL_RESTARTED	Data Link Restarted	0×11	
ENTER_BUSY	Enter Busy	0×0C	
EXIT_BUSY	Exit Busy	0×0D	
INFOFRAME	Information (I) Frame	0×0A	
HALT_DL	Halt Data Link	0×0E	
DL_HALTED	Data Link Halted	0×0F	
NETBIOS_NQ_ex	NETBIOS Name Query-explorer	0×12	SSPex
NETBIOS_NQ_cs	NETBIOS Name Query-circuit	setup	0×12
NETBIOS_NR_ex	NETBIOS Name Recognized-explorer	0×13	SSPex
NETBIOS_NR_cs	NETBIOS Name Recog-circuit	setup	0×13
DATAFRAME	Data Frame	0×14	
HALT_DL_NOACK	Halt Data Link with no Ack	0×19	
NETBIOS_ANQ	NETBIOS Add Name Query	0×1A	
NETBIOS_ANR	NETBIOS Add Name Response	0×1B	
KEEPALIVE	Transport Keepalive Message	0×1D	
CAP_EXCHANGE	Capabilities Exchange	0×20	
IFCM	Independent Flow Control Message	0×21	
TEST_CIRCUIT_REQ	Test Circuit Request	0×7A	
TEST_CIRCUIT_RSP	Test Circuit Response	0×7B	

NOTE: *Although typically SNA uses a DSAP and SSAP of 0×04, it allows for other SAPs to be configured and supports unequal SAPs.*

TABLE 13.4 **State for Main Circuit FSM**

State Name	Description
CIRCUIT_ESTABLISHED	The end-to-end circuit has been established. At this time, LLC Type 1 services are available from end-to-end.
CIRCUIT_PENDING	The target DLSw is awaiting a REACH_ACK response to an ICANREACH_cs message.
CIRCUIT_RESTART	The DLSw that originated the reset is awaiting the restart of the data link and the DL_RESTARTED response to a RESTART_DL message.
CIRCUIT_START	The origin DLSw is awaiting a ICANREACH_cs in response to a CANUREACH_cs message.
CONNECTED	The end-to-end connection has been established; thereby allowing LLC Type 2 services from end-to-end in addition to LLC Type 1 services.
CONNECT_PENDING	The origin DLSw is awaiting the CONTACTED response to a CONTACT message.
CONTACT_PENDING	The target DLSw is awaiting the DLC_CONTACTED confirmation to a DLC_CONTACT signal (i.e., DLC is waiting for a UA response to an SABME command).
DISCONNECTED	The initial state with no circuit or connection established, the DLSw is awaiting either a CANUREACH_cs or an ICANREACH_cs.
DISCONNECT_PENDING	The DLSw that originated the disconnect is awaiting the DL_HALTED response to a HALT_DL message.
HALT_PENDING	The remote DLSw is awaiting the DLC_DL_HALTED indication following the DLC_HALT_DL request (i.e., DLC is waiting for a UA response to a DISC command), due to receiving a HALT_DL message.
HALT_PENDING_NOACK	The remote DLSw is awaiting the DLC_DL_HALTED indication following the DLC_HALT_DL request (i.e., DLC is waiting for a UA response to a DISC command), due to receiving a HALT_DL_NOACK message.
RESTART_PENDING	The remote DLSw is awaiting the DLC_DL_HALTED indication following the DLC_HALT_DL request (i.e., DLC is waiting for a UA response to a DISC command) and the restart of the data link.
RESOLVE_PENDING	The target DLSw is awaiting the DLC_DL_STARTED indication following the DLC_START_DL request (i.e., DLC is waiting for a Test response as a result of sending a Test command).

For NetBIOS, LLC Type 2 connection establishment is via the Name Query and Name Recognized frames. These frames are used for both address resolution and source-route determination.

The Switch-to-Switch protocol is formally defined through the state machines described in this chapter. A separate state machine instance is used for each end-to-end circuit maintained by the Data Link Switch.

The DISCONNECTED state is the initial state for a new circuit. One end station starts the connection via an XID or SABME command (i.e., DLC_XID or DLC_CONTACTED). Upon receipt, the Data Link Switches exchange a set of CANUREACH_cs, ICANREACH_cs and REACH_ACK messages. Upon completion of this three-legged exchange, both Data

Link Switches are in the CIRCUIT_ESTABLISHED state. Three pending states also exist during this exchange. The CIRCUIT_START state is entered by the origin Data Link Switch after it has sent the CANUREACH_cs message. The RESOLVE_PENDING state is entered by the target Data link Switch awaiting a test response to a test command. Lastly, the CIRCUIT_PENDING state is entered by the target DLSw awaiting the REACH_ACK reply to an ICANREACH_cs message.

The CIRCUIT_ESTABLISHED state allows for the exchange of LLC Type 1 frames, such as the XID exchanges between SNA stations that occur prior to the establishment of a connection. Also, datagram traffic (i.e., UI frames) may be sent and received between the end stations. These exchanges use the XIDFRAME and DGRMFRAME messages sent between the Data Link Switches.

In the CIRCUIT_ESTABLISHED state, the receipt of a SABME command (i.e., DLC_CONTACTED) causes the origin DLSw to issue a CONTACT message, to send an RNR supervisory frame (i.e., DLC_ENTER_BUSY) to the origin station, and to enter the CONNECT_PENDING state awaiting a CONTACTED message. The target DLSw, upon the receipt of a CONTACT message, issues a SABME command (i.e., DLC_CONTACT) and enters the Contact Pending state. When the UA response is received (i.e., DLC_CONTACTED), the target DLSw sends a CONTACTED message and enters the CONNECTED state. When received, the origin DLSw enters the CONNECTED state and sends an RR supervisory frame (i.e., DLC_EXIT_BUSY).

The CONNECTED state is the steady state for normal data flow after a connection has been established. Information frames (i.e., INFOFRAME messages) are sent back and forth between the end points of the connection. This is the path that should be optimized for performance.

The connection is terminated upon the receipt of a DISC frame or under some other error condition detected by DLC (i.e., DLC_ERROR). Figure 13.5 depicts the circuit termination. Upon receipt of this indication, the DLSw halts the local data link, sends a HALT_DL message to the remote DLSw, and enters the DISCONNECT_PENDING State. When the HALT_DL frame is received by the other DLSw, the local DLC is halted for this data link; a DL_HALTED message is returned; and the DISCONNECTED state is entered. Receipt of this DL_HALTED message causes the other DLSw to also enter the DISCONNECTED state.

The CIRCUIT_RESTART state is entered if one of the Data Link Switches receives a SABME command (i.e., DLC_RESET) after data transfer while in the CONNECTED state (see Figure 13.6). This causes a DM command to be returned to the origin station and a RESTART_DL message to be sent to the remote Data Link Switch. This causes the remote data link to be halted and then restarted. The remote DLSw then sends a DL_RESTARTED message back to the first DLSw. The receipt of the DL_RESTARTED message causes the first DLSw to issue a new CONTACT message, assuming that the local DLC has been contacted (i.e., the origin station has resent the SABME command). This is eventually responded to by a CONTACTED message. Following this exchange, both Data Link Switches will return to the CONNECTED state. If the local DLC has not been contacted, the receipt of a DL_RESTARTED command causes the Data Link Switch to enter the CIRCUIT_ESTABLISHED state awaiting the receipt of a SABME command (i.e., DLC_CONTACTED signal).

The HALT_PENDING, HALT_PENDING_NOACK, and RESTART_PENDING states correspond to the cases when the Data Link Switch is awaiting responses from the local station

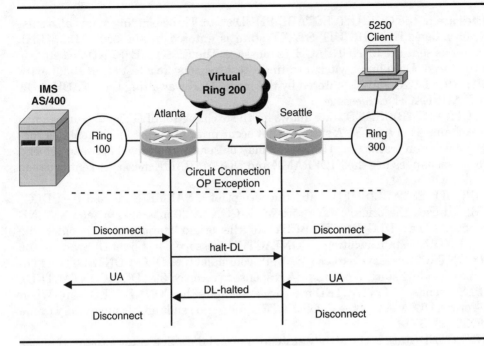

FIGURE 13.5 Circuit termination

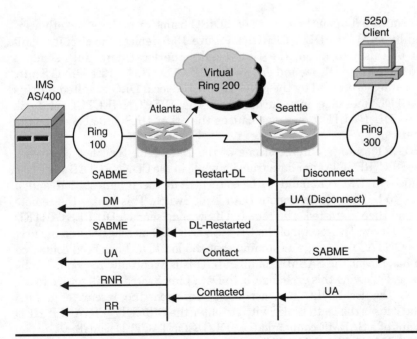

FIGURE 13.6 DLSw circuit restart session activation

on the adjacent LAN (e.g., a UA response to a DISC command). Also in the RESTART_
PENDING state, the Data Link Switch attempts to restart the data link prior to sending
a DL_RESTARTED message. For some implementations, the start of a data link involves
the exchange of a test command/response on the adjacent LAN (i.e., DLC_START_DL).

Explorer Traffic

The CANUREACH_ex, ICANREACH_ex, NETBIOS_NQ_ex, and NETBIOS_NR_ex SSP
messages explore the topology of the DLSw cloud and the networks attached to it. These
explorer frames are used to determine the DLSw peers through which a MAC or NetBIOS
name can be accessed. This information may be cached to reduce explorer traffic in the
DLSw cloud.

If DLSw is aware from cached information that a given MAC address or NetBIOS name
is accessible through a given peer DLSw router, it should direct all circuit setup attempts
to that partner. If the circuit setup fails, or no such data is available in the MAC or name
cache database, the DLSw may fallback to issuing the setup attempt to all DLSw peers on
the assumption that the cached data is now out of date.

DLSw implementations may use a local MAC cache to enable responses to
CANUREACH_ex requests to be issued without the need for test frame exchange (or equivalent) until the CANUREACH_cs is received. Again, the fallback mechanism for determining when such local cache data is out-of-date is implementation defined. The use of either
cache is an optional feature in DLSw but is implemented by Cisco IOS.

For the purposes of correlator exchange, explorer messages form a separate circuit. Both
DLSw partners must reflect the last received correlator values as specified. However, correlators learned on explorer messages need not be carried over to a subsequent circuit setup
attempt. In particular, the Origin DLSw may elect to use the same values for the Origin
Data Link Correlator and Origin Port ID when it issues a CANUREACH_cs after receiving an ICANREACH_ex or NETBIOS_NR_ex. However, the Target DLSw must not assume
that the CANUREACH_cs specifies any of the Target Data Link Correlator or Target Port
ID that were exchanged on the explorer messages. Received SSP messages that require a
valid Remote Circuit ID but cannot be associated with an existing circuit should be rejected
with a HALT_DL_NOACK message. This is done to prevent a situation in which one DLSw
peer has a circuit defined while the other peer does not. The exception would be a
HALT_DL_NOACK message with an invalid Remote Circuit ID. The HALT_DL_NOACK
message is typically used in error situations in which a response is not appropriate.

The SSP messages requiring a valid Remote Circuit ID are all messages except the
following: CANUREACH_ex, CANUREACH_cs, ICANREACH_ex, ICANREACH_cs,
NETBIOS_NQ_cs, NETBIOS_NR_cs, DATAFRAME, NETBIOS_ANQ, NETBIOS_ANR,
KEEPALIVE, and CAP_EXCHANGE.

Largest Frame Size Field

The Largest Frame Size field in the SSP Control header is used to carry the LF Size bits
across the DLSw connection. This field should be used to ensure that the two endstations always negotiate a frame size to be used on a circuit that does not require the

Origin and Target DLSw peer to resegment frames. This field is valid on CANUREACH_ex, CANUREACH_cs, ICANREACH_ex, ICANREACH_cs, NETBIOS_NQ_ex, and NETBIOS_NR_ex messages only. The contents of this field should be ignored on all other frames. Every DLSw forwarding a SSP frame to its DLSw peer must ensure that the contents of this frame reflect the minimum capability of the route to its local end-station or any limit imposed by the DLSw Circuit, or origin in the context of the Source MAC/SAP addresses. All MAC addresses are expressed in noncanonical (Token Ring) format.

Capabilities Exchange Formats/Protocol

The Data Link Switching Capabilities Exchange is a special DLSw Switch-to-Switch control message that describes the capabilities of the sending data link switch. This control message is sent after the switch-to-switch connection is established and during run time if certain operational parameters have changed and need to be communicated to the partner switch.

The actual contents of the Capabilities Exchange are in the data field following the SSP message header.

The SSP Message header has the fields shown in Table 13.5 set for the Capabilities Exchange.

Figure 13.7 shows the Cisco Capability Exchange IOS commands, and Figure 13.8 shows the Sniffer Trace. Figure 13.8 shows the DLSw protocol header.

Control Vector ID Range

Control Vector identifiers (i.e., Type) in the range of 0×80 through $0\times CF$ are reserved for use by the Data Link Switching standard.

Control Vector identifiers (i.e., Type) in the range of $0\times D0$ through $0\times FD$ are used for vendor-specific purposes.

Currently defined vectors are shown in Table 13.6.

TABLE 13.5   SSP Message Header

Offset	Field	Value
0×00	Version Number	0×31
0×01	Header Length	0×48 (decimal 72)
0×02	Message Length	same as LL in GDS Variable
0×14	Message Type	0×20 (CAP_EXCHANGE)
0×16	Protocol Id	0×42
0×17	Header Number	0×01
0×23	Message Type	0×20 (CAP_EXCHANGE)
0×38	Direction	0×01 for CapEx request
		0×02 for CapEx response

```
DLSW Show commands


Atlanta#show dlsw capability
DLSw: Capabilities for peer 150.150.1.1(2065)
   vendor id (OUI)          : '00C' (cisco)
   version number          : 1
   release number          : 0
   init pacing window      : 20
   unsupported saps        : none
   num of tcp sessions     : 1
   loop prevent support    : no
   icanreach mac-exclusive : no
   icanreach netbios-excl. : no
   reachable mac addresses : none
   reachable netbios names : none
   cisco version number    : 1
   peer group number       : 0
   border peer capable     : no
   peer cost               : 3
   biu-segment configured  : no
   local-ack configured    : yes
   priority configured     : no
   version string          :
Cisco Internetwork Operating System Software
IOS (tm) 3000 Software (IGS-J-L), Version 11.0(17), RELEASE SOFTWARE (fc1)
Copyright (c) 1986-1997 by cisco Systems, Inc.
Compiled Thu 04-Sep-97 13:54 by richv
```

FIGURE 13.7 Cisco Capability Exchange IOS Commands

FIGURE 13.8 DLSw protocol header and capabilities exchange request

```
DLSw:   --- Data Link Switching Protocol ---
DLSw:
DLSw:
DLSw:   Version = 31 (RFC 1795)
DLSw:   Header length = 72 bytes
DLSw:   Message length = 283 bytes
DLSw:   Remote data link correlator = 5020183
DLSw:   Remote DLC port ID = DC051401
DLSw:   Message type = 20 (Capabilities exchange)
DLSw:   Flow control = 43
DLSw:      0... .... = FCI (No indicator)
DLSw:      .1.. .... = FCA (Ack)
DLSw:      .... .011 = FCO (Reset window operator)
DLSw:   Protocol ID = 42
DLSw:   Header number = 1
DLSw:   Circuit priority = 0 (Unspecified)
DLSw:   Message type = 00
DLSw:   Target = Station 010100040101
DLSw:   Origin = Station 01010003000B
DLSw:   Origin link SAP = 53
DLSw:   Target link SAP = 65
DLSw:   Frame direction = 1 (Origin DLSw to target)
DLSw:   DLC header length = 0 bytes
DLSw:   Origin DLC port ID = 4000800
```

(Continues)

FIGURE 13.8   Continued

```
DLSw:   Origin data link correlator = 300
DLSw:   Origin transport ID = 500D243
DLSw:   Target DLC port ID = 6973636F
DLSw:   Target data link correlator = 20496E74
DLSw:   Target transport ID = 65726E65
DLSw:
DLSw:   --- Capabilities Exchange Request --
DLSw:
DLSw:   Length = 283 bytes
DLSw:   GDS ID = 1520 (Request)
DLSw:   Subfield length = 5 bytes
DLSw:   Control vector type = 81 (Vendor ID)
DLSw:   OUI = 00000C
DLSw:   Subfield length = 4 bytes
DLSw:   Control vector type = 82 (DLSw version)
DLSw:   DLSw version number = 1
DLSw:   DLSw release number = 0
DLSw:   Subfield length = 4 bytes
DLSw:   Control vector type = 83 (Initial pacing window)
DLSw:   Pacing window size = 20
DLSw:   Subfield length = 18 bytes
DLSw:   Control vector type = 86 (Supported SAP list)
DLSw:   SAP control byte # 1 = FF (SAPs 00 thru 0E enabled)
DLSw:   SAP control byte # 2 = FF (SAPs 10 thru 1E enabled)
DLSw:   SAP control byte # 3 = FF (SAPs 20 thru 2E enabled)
DLSw:   SAP control byte # 4 = FF (SAPs 30 thru 3E enabled)
DLSw:   SAP control byte # 5 = FF (SAPs 40 thru 4E enabled)
DLSw:   SAP control byte # 6 = FF (SAPs 50 thru 5E enabled)
DLSw:   SAP control byte # 7 = FF (SAPs 60 thru 6E enabled)
DLSw:   SAP control byte # 8 = FF (SAPs 70 thru 7E enabled)
DLSw:   SAP control byte # 9 = FF (SAPs 80 thru 8E enabled)
DLSw:   SAP control byte #10 = FF (SAPs 90 thru 9E enabled)
DLSw:   SAP control byte #11 = FF (SAPs A0 thru AE enabled)
DLSw:   SAP control byte #12 = FF (SAPs B0 thru BE enabled)
DLSw:   SAP control byte #13 = FF (SAPs C0 thru CE enabled)
DLSw:   SAP control byte #14 = FF (SAPs D0 thru DE enabled)
DLSw:   SAP control byte #15 = FF (SAPs E0 thru EE enabled)
DLSw:   SAP control byte #16 = FF (SAPs F0 thru FE enabled)
DLSw:   Subfield length = 208 bytes
DLSw:   Control vector type = 84 (Version string)
DLSw:   Software version = "Cisco Internetwork Operating System Software .IOS
(tm) 3000 Soft"
DLSw:   Subfield length = 3 bytes
DLSw:   Control vector type = 87 (TCP connections)
DLSw:   TCP connections for duration of DLSw connection = 1
DLSw:   Subfield length = 3 bytes
DLSw:   Control vector type = 85 (MAC address exclusivity)
DLSw:   MAC address exclusivity = 0 (No)
DLSw:   Subfield length = 3 bytes
DLSw:   Control vector type = 88 (NetBIOS name exclusivity)
DLSw:   NetBIOS names exclusivity = 0 (No)
DLSw:   Subfield length = 5 bytes
DLSw:   Control vector type = 8B (Vendor context)
DLSw:   OUI = 00000C
DLSw:   Subfield length = 4 bytes
DLSw:   Control vector type = D5 (Cisco version) ——— Cisco DLSw+ feature
DLSw:   Cisco version = 1
```

```
DLSw:   Subfield length = 3 bytes
DLSw:   Control vector type = D0 (Local ack) ────────┐
DLSw:   Local ack = 1 (Configured)                   │
DLSw:   Subfield length = 3 bytes                     │
DLSw:   Control vector type = D1 (Priority) ──────────┤
DLSw:   Priority = 0 (Not configured)                 │
DLSw:   Subfield length = 4 bytes                     │
DLSw:   Control vector type = D2 (Peer group) ────────┤──── Cisco DLSw+ features
DLSw:   Peer group = 0                                │
DLSw:   Subfield length = 3 bytes                     │
DLSw:   Control vector type = D3 (Border peer) ───────┤
DLSw:   Border peer = 0 (Not configured)              │
DLSw:   Subfield length = 3 bytes                     │
DLSw:   Control vector type = D4 (Cost) ──────────────┘
DLSw:   Cost = 3
DLSw:   Subfield length = 3 bytes
DLSw:   Control vector type = D7 (Vendor specific)
DLSw:   Value = 01
DLSw:   Subfield length = 3 bytes
DLSw:   Control vector type = D8 (Vendor specific)
DLSw:   Value = 00
DLSw:
```

TABLE 13.6 Control Vector Types

Vector Description	Hex Value
Vendor ID Control Vector	0×81
DLSw Version Control Vector	0×82
Initial Pacing Window Control Vector	0×83
Version String Control Vector	0×84
MAC Address Exclusivity Control Vector	0×85
Supported SAP List Control Vector	0×86
TCP Connections Control Vector	0×87
NetBIOS Name Exclusivity Control Vector	0×88
MAC Address List Control Vector	0×89
NetBIOS Name List Control Vector	0×8A
Vendor Context Control Vector	0×8B
Reserved for future use	0×8C–0×CF
Vendor Specific	0×D0–0×FD

Control Vector Order and Continuity

Because their contents can greatly affect the parsing of the Capabilities Exchange GDS Variable, the required control vectors must occur first and appear in the following order: Vendor ID, DLSw Version Number, Initial Pacing Window, and Supported SAP List. The remainder of the Control Vectors can occur in any order. Control Vectors that can be repeated within the same message (e.g., MAC Address List Control Vector and NetBIOS Name List Control Vector) are not necessarily adjacent. It is advisable, but not required, to have the Exclusivity Control Vector occur prior to either of the other two vectors so that the use of the individual MAC addresses or NetBIOS names will be known prior to parsing them.

Both the Vendor Context and Vendor Specific control vectors can be repeated. If multiple instances of the Vendor Context control vector exist, the specified context remains in effect for all Vendor Specific control vectors until the next Vendor Context control vector is encountered in the Capabilities Exchange.

Initial Capabilities Exchange

Capabilities Exchange is always the first SSP message sent on a new SSP connection between two DLSw routers. This initial Capabilities Exchange is used to identify the DLSw version that each switch is running and other required information, plus details of any optional extensions that the switches can support (see Figure 13.8). When two Cisco routers detect each other during a capability exchange, the Cisco DLSw+ features are made available for further configuration. If a DLSw router receives an initial capabilities message that is incorrectly formatted or contains invalid or unsupported data that prevents correct interoperation with the partner DLSw, it should issue a Capabilities Exchange negative response.

If a DLSw router receives a negative response to its initial capabilities message, it should take down its TCP connections with the offended partner.

Run-Time Capabilities Exchange

Capabilities Exchange always occurs when the SSP connection is started between two DLSw routers. Capabilities Exchange can also occur at run-time, typically when a configuration change is made.

Support for run-time Capabilities Exchange is optional. If a node does not support receiving/using Run-Time Capabilities Exchange and receives one, it should discard it quietly (not send back a negative response). If a node supports receipt of run-time capabilities, it should send a positive or negative response as appropriate. The receiver of a negative response to a run-time capabilities message is not required to take down its TCP connections with the offended partner. Run-time Capabilities Exchange can consist of one or more of the following control vectors:

- MAC Address Exclusivity CV
- NetBIOS Name Exclusivity CV
- MAC Address List CV
- NetBIOS Name List CV
- Supported SAP List CV
- Vendor Context CV
- Vendor Specific CVs

A run-time capabilities exchange is a replacement operation. As such, all pertinent MAC addresses and NetBIOS names must be specified in the run-time exchange. In addition, run-time changes in capabilities do not affect existing link-station circuits. Cisco supports the Run-Time Capability Exchange Operation.

Capabilities Exchange Filtering Responsibilities

Recipients of the SAP, MAC, and NetBIOS lists are not required to actually use them to filter traffic, etc., either initially or at run-time.

DLSw Capabilities Exchange Structured Subfields

The Capabilities Exchange Subfields are listed in Table 13.7 and are described in the following sections:

Vendor ID (0x81) Control Vector

The Vendor ID control vector identifies the manufacturer's IEEE assigned *Organizationally Unique Identifier* (OUI) of the Data Link Switch sending the DLSw Capabilities Exchange. The OUI is sent in noncanonical (Token Ring) format. This control vector is required and must be the first control vector.

TABLE 13.7   Capability Exchange Subfields

Required ID	Allowed Startup	Length	Repeatable*	Runtime	Order	Content
0×81	Y	0×05	N	N	1	Vendor ID
0×82	Y	0×04	N	N	2	DLSw Version
0×83	Y	0×04	N	N	3	Initial Pacing Window
0×84	N	$\geqq$0×02	N	N	5+	Version String
0×85	N	0×03	N	Y	5+	MAC Address Exclusivity
0×86	Y	0×12	N	Y	4	Supported SAP List
0×87	N	0×03	N	N	5+	TCP Connections
0×88	N	0×03	N	Y	5+	NetBIOS Name Exclusivity
0×89	N	0×0E	Y	Y	5+	MAC Address List
0×8A	N	$\leqq$0×13	Y	Y	5+	NetBIOS Name List
0×8B	N	0×05	Y	Y	5+	Vendor Context
0×D0	N	varies	Y	Y	5+	Vendor Specific

Offset	Length	Value	Contents
0	1	0×05	Length of the Vendor ID structured subfield
1	1	0×81	Key = 0×81, which identifies this as the Vendor ID structured subfield
2–4	3		The 3-byte OUI for the vendor (noncanonical format)

DLSw Version (0x82) Control Vector

The DLSw Version control vector identifies the particular version of the DLSw standard supported by the sending Data Link Switch. This control vector is required and must follow the Vendor ID Control Vector.

Offset	Length	Value	Contents
0	1	0×04	Length of the Version String structured subfield
1	1	0×82	Key = 0×82, which identifies this as the DLSw Version structured subfield
2	1		The hexadecimal value representing the DLSw standard Version number of the sending Data Link Switch.
		0×01	(indicates version 1—closed pages)
3	1		The hexadecimal value representing the DLSw standard Release number of the sending Data Link Switch.
		0×00	(indicates release 0)

Initial Pacing Window (0x83) Control Vector

The Initial Pacing Window control vector specifies the initial value of the receive pacing window size for the sending Data Link Switch. This control vector is required and must follow the DLSw Version Control Vector.

Offset	Length	Value	Contents
0	1	0×04	Length of the Initial Pacing Window structured subfield
1	1	0×83	Key = 0×83 that identifies this as the Initial Pacing Window structured subfield
2–3	2		The pacing window size, specified in byte normal form.

NOTE: *The pacing window size must be nonzero.*

Version String (0x84) Control Vector

The Version String control vector identifies the particular version number of the sending Data Link Switch. The format of the actual version string is vendor-defined. This control vector is optional.

Offset	Length	Value	Contents
0	1	0×n	Length of the Version String structured subfield
1	1	0×84	Key = 0×84, which identifies this as the Version String structured subfield
2–n	n–2		The ASCII string that identifies the software version for the sending DLSw.

MAC Address Exclusivity (0x85) Control Vector

The MAC Address Exclusivity control vector identifies how the MAC Address List control vector data is to be interpreted. Specifically, this control vector identifies whether the MAC addresses in the MAC Address List control vectors are the only ones accessible via the sending Data Link Switch.

If a MAC Address List control vector is specified and the MAC Address Exclusivity control vector is missing, the MAC addresses are not assumed to be the only ones accessible via this switch.

A node may specify that it supports no local MAC addresses by including in its capabilities the MAC Address List Exclusivity CV (with byte 2 = 0×01) and not including any instances of the MAC Address List CV.

Offset	Length	Value	Contents
0	1	0×03	Length of the Exclusivity structured subfield
1	1	0×85	Key = 0×85 that identifies this as the MAC address Exclusivity structured subfield
2	1		An indicator of the relationship of the MAC addresses to the sending Data Link Switch.

Offset	Length	Value	Contents
		0×00	The MAC addresses specified in this Capabilities Exchange can be accessed via this switch but are not the exclusive set (i.e., other entities are accessible in addition to the ones specified)
		0×01	The MAC addresses specified in this Capabilities Exchange are the only ones accessible via this switch.

SAP List Support (0x86) Control Vector

The SAP List Support control vector identifies support for Logical Link Control SAPs (DSAPs and SSAPs) by the sending Data Link Switch.

This is used by the DLSw that sent the SAP List Support control vector to indicate which SAPs can be used to support SNA and optionally NetBIOS traffic. This may be used by the DLSw router that receives the SAP list to filter explorer traffic (TEST, XID, or NetBIOS UI frames) from the DLSw state machine. For SNA, a DLSw should set bits for all SAP values (SSAP or DSAP) that may be used for SNA traffic. For NetBIOS support, the bit for SAP 0×F0 should be set.

Each bit in the SAP control vector data field represents a SAP as defined here. This vector is required and must follow the Initial Pacing Window Control Vector.

Offset	Length	Value	Contents
0	1	0×12	Length of the Supported SAP List structured subfield
1	1	0×86	Key = 0×86, which identifies this as the Supported SAP List structured subfield
2–17	16		The 16-byte bit vector describing all even numbered SAPs enabled.
			Each Bit within the 16-byte bit vector will indicate whether an even numbered SAP is enabled (b'1') or disabled (b'0').
			Each Byte within the 16-byte bit vector will be numbered from 0–F. (Most significant byte first).
			Byte 0 1 2 3 . . . F XX XX XX XX . . . XX
			The bits in each byte indicate whether an even numbered SAP is enabled (b'1') or disabled (b'0'). (Most significant bit first)
			Bits 7 6 5 4 . . . 0 SAP 0 2 4 6 . . . E
			By combining the byte label with the enabled bits, all supported SAPs can be determined.
			In the following diagram, 'n' would equal 0 through F depending on which byte was being interpreted.
			Bit ordering is shown here with bit 7 being the most significant bit and bit 0 the least significant bit.

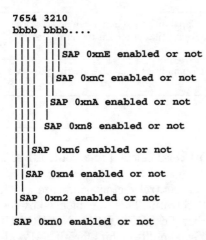

```
7654 3210
bbbb bbbb....
|||| ||||
|||| |||SAP 0xnE enabled or not
|||| |||
|||| ||SAP 0xnC enabled or not
|||| ||
|||| |SAP 0xnA enabled or not
|||| |
|||| SAP 0xn8 enabled or not
||||
|||SAP 0xn6 enabled or not
|||
||SAP 0xn4 enabled or not
||
|SAP 0xn2 enabled or not
|
SAP 0xn0 enabled or not
```

An example of using all User Definable SAPs of 0×04 to 0×EC for SNA Data Link Switching and SAP 0×F0 for NetBIOS Data Link Switching is shown in Table 13.8.

TABLE 13.8 SAP IDs

Offset	SAPs	Binary	Hex
0	4,8,C	0010 1010	0×2A
1	10,14,18,1C	1010 1010	0×AA
2	20,24,28,2C	1010 1010	0×AA
3	30,34,38,3C	1010 1010	0×AA
4	40,44,48,4C	1010 1010	0×AA
5	50,54,58,5C	1010 1010	0×AA
6	60,64,68,6C	1010 1010	0×AA
7	70,74,78,7C	1010 1010	0×AA
8	80,84,88,8C	1010 1010	0×AA
9	90,94,98,9C	1010 1010	0×AA
A	A0,A4,A8,AC	1010 1010	0×AA
B	B0,B4,B8,BC	1010 1010	0×AA
C	C0,C4,C8,CC	1010 1010	0×AA
D	D0,D4,D8,DC	1010 1010	0×AA
E	E0,E4,E8,EC	1010 1010	0×AA
F	F0	1000 0000	0×80

TCP Connections (0x87) Control Vector

The TCP Connections control vector indicates the support of an alternate number of TCP Connections for the Data Link Switching traffic. The base implementation of Data Link Switching supports two TCP Connections, one for each direction of data traffic.

This control vector is optional. If it is omitted in a DLSw Capabilities Exchange, two TCP Connections are assumed. It is further assumed that if a Data Link Switch can support one TCP Connection, it can support two TCP Connections. If TCP Connections CV values agree and the number of connections is one, the DLSw with the higher IP address must tear down the TCP Connections on its local port 2065.

The format of the TCP Connections Control Vector is as follows:

Offset	Length	Value	Contents
0	1	0×03	Length of the TCP Connections structured subfield
1	1	0×87	Key = 0×87, which identifies this as the TCP Connections structured subfield
2	1		An indicator of the support for an alternate number of TCP Connections by the sending Data Link Switch.

Offset	Length	Value	Contents
		0×01	The number of TCP Connections may be brought down to one after Capabilities Exchange is completed.
		0×02	The number of TCP Connections remains at two for the duration of the DLSw connection.

NetBIOS Name Exclusivity (0x88) Control Vector

The NetBIOS Name Exclusivity control vector identifies how the NetBIOS Name List control vector data is to be interpreted. Specifically, this control vector identifies whether the NetBIOS Names in the NetBIOS Name List control vectors are the only ones accessible via the sending Data Link Switch.

If a NetBIOS Name List control vector is specified and if the NetBIOS Name Exclusivity control vector is missing, the NetBIOS Names are not assumed to be the only ones accessible via this switch.

A node may specify that it supports no local NetBIOS names by including in its capabilities the NetBIOS Name List Exclusivity CV (with byte 2 = 0×01) and not including any instances of the NetBIOS Name List CV.

Offset	Length	Value	Contents
0	1	0×03	Length of the exclusivity structured subfield
1	1	0×88	Key = 0×88, which identifies this as the NetBIOS Name Exclusivity structured subfield
2	1		An indicator of the relationship of the NetBIOS Names to the sending Data Link Switch.
		0×00	The NetBIOS Names specified in this Capabilities Exchange can be accessed via this switch but are not the exlusive set (i.e., other entities are accessible in addition to the ones specified)
		0×01	The NetBIOS Names specified in this Capabilities Exchange are the only ones accessible via this switch.

MAC Address List (0x89) Control Vector

The MAC Address List control vector identifies one or more MAC addresses accessible through the sending Data Link Switch. This control vector specifies a single MAC address value and MAC address mask value to identify the MAC address or range of MAC addresses. MAC addresses and masks are in noncanonical (Token Ring) format in this control vector. This control vector is optional and can be repeated if necessary.

NetBIOS Name List (0x8A) Control Vector

The NetBIOS Name List control vector identifies one or more NetBIOS names accessible through the sending Data Link Switch.

NetBIOS group names can exist across several LANs/networks. As such, NetBIOS group names received in a NetBIOS Name List Control vector cannot be treated the same as Net-BIOS individual names. The Individual/Group Flag allows Data Link Switches to distinguish between the two.

This control vector is optional and can be repeated if necessary.

Offset	Length	Value	Contents
0	1	0×n	Length of the NetBIOS Name List structured subfield (maximum = 0×13)
1	1	0×8A	Key = 0×8A, which identifies this as the NetBIOS Name List structured subfield
2	1		Individual/Group Flag 0×00—Individual NetBIOS Name
		0×01	Group NetBIOS Name
	3-n	n-3	The NetBIOS name with possible embedded '?' and terminating '*'

Vendor Context (0x8B) Control Vector

The Vendor Context control vector identifies the manufacturer's IEEE assigned *Organizationally Unique Identifier* (OUI) of the Data Link Switch sending the DLSw Capabilities Exchange. The OUI is sent in noncanonical (Token-Ring) format.

This control vector is optional and is used to provide the context for any Vendor Specific control vectors that follow in the Capabilities Exchange. If there are multiple instances of the Vendor Context control vector, the specified context remains in effect for all Vendor Specific control vectors until the next Vendor Context control vector is encountered.

Offset	Length	Value	Contents
0	1	0×05	Length of the Vendor Context structured subfield
1	1	0×8B	Key = 0×8B, which identifies this as the Vendor Context structured subfield
2-4	3		The 3-byte OUI for the vendor (non-canonical format)

Capabilities Exchange Responses

Two kinds of DLSw Capabilities Exchange Responses are possible: positive and negative. A positive response is returned to the sending Data Link Switch if no errors are encountered in the DLSw. A negative response is returned to a Capabilities Exchange Request if at least one error is encountered.

A positive DLSw Capabilities Exchange Response, as shown in Figure 13.9, has the following overall format:

```
+----+----+
| LL | ID |
+----+----+
```

```
DLSw:   --- Data Link Switching Protocol ---
DLSw:
DLSw:   Version = 31 (RFC 1795)
DLSw:   Header length = 72 bytes
DLSw:   Message length = 4 bytes
DLSw:   Remote data link correlator = 5020183
DLSw:   Remote DLC port ID = DC051401
DLSw:   Message type = 20 (Capabilities exchange)
DLSw:   Flow control = 47
DLSw:       0... .... = FCI (No indicator)
DLSw:       .1.. .... = FCA (Ack)
DLSw:       .... .111 = FCO (? window operator)
DLSw:   Protocol ID = 42
DLSw:   Header number = 1
DLSw:   Circuit priority = 0 (Unspecified)
DLSw:   Message type = 00
DLSw:   Target = Station 010100040101
DLSw:   Origin = Station 01020003000B
DLSw:   Origin link SAP = 53
DLSw:   Target link SAP = 65
DLSw:   Frame direction = 2 (Target DLSw to origin)
DLSw:   DLC header length = 0 bytes
DLSw:   Origin DLC port ID = 4000800
DLSw:   Origin data link correlator = 300
DLSw:   Origin transport ID = 500D243
DLSw:   Target DLC port ID = 6973636F
DLSw:   Target data link correlator = 20496E74
DLSw:   Target transport ID = 65726E65
DLSw:   -- Capabilities Exchange Response ---
DLSw:
DLSw:   Length = 4 bytes
DLSw:   GDS ID = 1521 (Positive response)
DLSw:
```

FIGURE 13.9   Capabilities Exchange Response

0–1	Length, in binary, of the DLSw Capabilities Exchange Response GDS Variable. The value of LL in this case is 0×0004.
2–3	GDS Id: 0×1521

A negative DLSw Capabilities Exchange Response has the following overall format:

```
+----+----+---------+-00000---+
| LL | ID | Offset  | Reason  |
+-00-+----+---------+---------+
```

0–1	Length, in binary, of the DLSw Capabilities Exchange Response GDS Variable. The value of LL is the sum of the length of all fields in the GDS Variable (i.e., length of LL + length of ID + length of Offsets/Reasons).
2–3	GDS Id: 0×1522

4–5	Offset into the DLSw Capabilities Exchange Request of the error. Offset should always point to the start of the GDS Variable or a specific control vector.

6–7	Reason code that uniquely identifies the error. Specific values for the reason code are as follow:	
	0×0001	Invalid GDS length for a DLSw Capabilities Exchange Request. (The value of Offset is ignored.)
	0×0002	Invalid GDS ID for a DLSw Capabilities Exchange Request. (The value of Offset is ignored.)
	0×0003	Vendor ID control vector is missing. (The value of Offset is ignored.)
	0×0004	DLSw Version control vector is missing. (The value of Offset is ignored.)
	0×0005	Initial Pacing Window control vector is missing. (The value of Offset is ignored.)
	0×0006	Length of control vectors doesn't correlate to the length of the GDS variable
	0×0007	Invalid control vector ID
	0×0008	Length of control vector is invalid
	0×0009	Invalid control vector data value
	0×000A	Duplicate control vector (for nonrepeating control vectors)
	0×000B	Out-of-sequence control vector (for repeating control vector)
	0×000C	DLSw Supported SAP List control vector is missing.

Flow and Congestion Control

Subarea SNA, APPN, and TCP have flow control on a session basis. This flow control method is based on the idea of a *send window,* which specifies the number of transmits that can be issued without requiring an acknowledgment of the transmission.

High Performance Routing (HPR) supports APPN flow control but also can use ABR flow control. This flow control method uses a window that adapts to the throughput being realized on both sides of the connection. Although this is an advanced flow control algorithm, the impact on throughput across a DLSw connection is minimal. The SNA architectures also provide flow control at the link layer. Because the SNA protocols are all based on a session at a higher level, the flow control mechanism is based on a flow control at a higher level. IP, on the other hand, does not recognize the same type of flow control because frames at this level are all datagrams. As such, there is no basis for flow control or recovery.

DLSw supports a flow control procedure between nodes. This allows for backward flow control to be applied so that the transport between DLSw nodes is not overrun with data. The DLSw standard specifies flow control on a per-circuit basis and calls for two independent, unidirectional circuit flow-control mechanisms. Flow control is handled by a windowing mechanism that can dynamically adapt to buffer availability, TCP transmit queue depth, and end-station flow-control mechanisms. Windows can be incremented, decremented, halved, or reset to 0. The granted units (the number of units that the sender has permission to send) are incremented with a flow-control indication from the receiver (similar to classic SNA session-level pacing). Flow-control indicators can be one of the following types:

- *Repeat*. Increment granted units by the current window size.

- *Increment*. Increment the window size by 1 and increment granted units by the new window size.

- *Decrement*. Decrement window size by 1 and increment granted units by the new window size.

- *Reset*. Decrease window to 0 and set granted units to 0 to stop all transmission in one direction until an increment flow-control indicator is sent.

- *Half*. Cut the current window size in half and increment granted units by the new window size.

Flow-control indicators and flow-control acknowledgments can be piggybacked on information frames or can be sent as independent flow-control messages, but reset indicators are always sent as independent messages. The flow and congestion control method described in RFC 1795 is not complete. It makes assumptions about the network topology and provides limited flow control. Because the method has not been implemented nor has it been modeled for operational characteristics, the effects of the described method are unknown. It is also unknown if a congested state actually can be exited or if the flow control mechanism is sufficiently effective. Because the receiver grants the sender approval for a specific window, the tools are sufficiently robust for use. The receiver is the station with a buffer problem, allowing it to determine when flow control is required is a reasonable choice. In addition, because flow control indicators can flow on information frames, it is reasonable to expect that flow will be controlled and that deadlocks will not be a serious problem. At the same time, analysis of this type of process is extremely complex. A method that works under normal conditions may assume quite different characteristics when congestion actually occurs.

Figure 13.10 shows how DLSW establishes a connection. Figure 13.11 depicts the DLSw capabilities exchange.

The trace in Figure 13.12 involves an IBM AS/400 connected to a Cisco router with Microsoft NT Server running SNA Gateway software. The trace highlights the DLSw setup messages between routers and SNA connectivity from the NT Server to the AS/400. Remember from our discussion in DLSw theory that the objective of DLSw is for SNA and NetBIOS to appear transparent to each other's peers as though they were directly connected using LAN media or serial communications. While examining the trace, look for the DLSw message types, flow control indicators, Token Ring Source-Route Bridging information, Type LLC, SAP IDs, and SNA session setup messages from the SNA Session Activation. Figure 13.13 shows the connection establishment.

Cisco DLSw Implementations

Cisco supports the *Internet Engineering Task Force* (IETF) *Request for Comments* (RFC) 1795, DLSw Version 1 and Version 2.0, and RFC 2166, Data Link Switching.

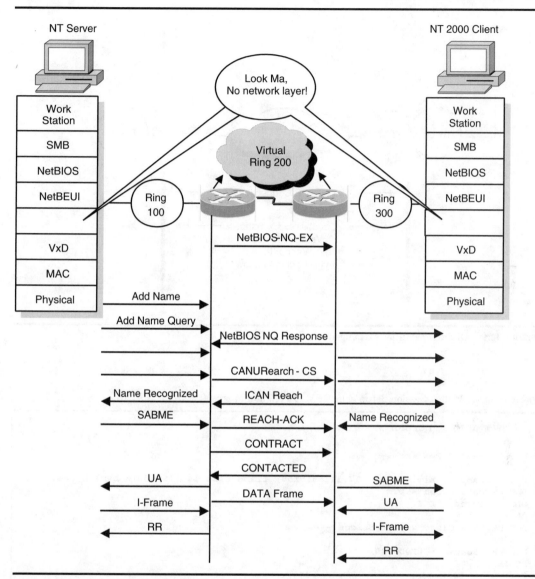

FIGURE 13.10   DLSw NetBIOS/NetBEUI connection establishment

Standard Data Link Switching

Cisco DLSw implementation is compliant with RFC 1795 and RFC 2166, ensuring an industry-standard approach for reliable and efficient transport of SNA and NetBIOS traffic across a multiprotocol internetwork.

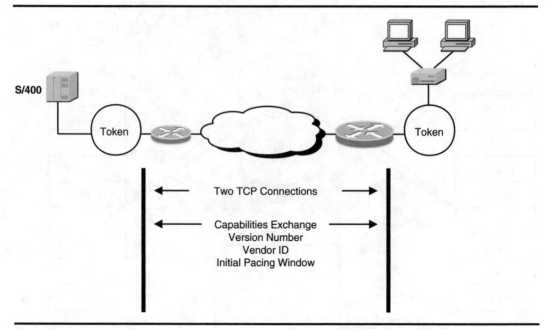

FIGURE 13.11   DLSw capabilities exchanged

Figure 13.12   IBM SNA Session Setup using IBM AS/400 and Microsoft SNA for NT

```
DLSw canureach explorer

DLC:   --- DLC Header ---
DLC:
DLC:   Frame 74 arrived at  17:11:53.0150; frame size is 116 (0074 hex) bytes.
DLC:   Destination = DTE
DLC:   Source = DCE
DLC:
ROUTER: --- Cisco Router/Bridge ---
ROUTER:
ROUTER: Header = 0F000800
ROUTER:
IP:    --- IP Header ---
IP:
IP:    Version = 4, header length = 20 bytes
IP:    Type of service = 00
IP:         000. .... = routine
IP:         ...0 .... = normal delay
IP:         .... 0... = normal throughput
IP:         .... .0.. = normal reliability
IP:    Total length  = 112 bytes
IP:    Identification = 4
IP:    Flags         = 0X
IP:         .0.. .... = may fragment
IP:         ..0. .... = last fragment
IP:    Fragment offset = 0 bytes
```

Figure 13.12 Continued

```
IP:    Time to live     = 255 seconds/hops
IP:    Protocol         = 6 (TCP)
IP:    Header checksum  = 8B55 (correct)
IP:    Source address      = [150.150.2.1]
IP:    Destination address = [150.150.1.1]
IP:    No options
IP:
TCP:   --- TCP header ---
TCP:
TCP:   Source port              = 11007
TCP:   Destination port         = 2065 (DLSw-rpn)
TCP:   Sequence number          = 2939809944
TCP:   Acknowledgment number    = 2940297586
TCP:   Data offset              = 20 bytes
TCP:   Flags                    = 18
TCP:                   ..0. .... = (No urgent pointer)
TCP:                   ...1 .... = Acknowledgment
TCP:                   .... 1... = Push
TCP:                   .... .0.. = (No reset)
TCP:                   .... ..0. = (No SYN)
TCP:                   .... ...0 = (No FIN)
TCP:   Window                   = 20480
TCP:   Checksum                 = 07C2 (correct)
TCP:   No TCP options
TCP:   [72 byte(s) of data]
TCP:

DLSw:  --- Data Link Switching Protocol ---
DLSw:
DLSw:  Version = 31 (RFC 1795)
DLSw:  Header length = 72 bytes
DLSw:  Message length = 0 bytes
DLSw:  Remote data link correlator = 0
DLSw:  Remote DLC port ID = 0
DLSw:  Message type = 03 (Can U reach station)
DLSw:  Flow control = 00
DLSw:     0... .... = FCI (No indicator)
DLSw:     .0.. .... = FCA (No ack)
DLSw:     .... .000 = FCO (Repeat window operator)
DLSw:  Protocol ID = 42
DLSw:  Header number = 1
DLSw:  Largest frame size = A0
DLSw:          1... .... = Don't fail circuit if size smaller
DLSw:          ..10 0... = Largest frame bit base
DLSw:          .... .000 = Largest frame bit extended
DLSw:  SSP flags = 8X
DLSw:  1... .... = Explorer
DLSw:  Circuit priority = 0 (Unspecified)
DLSw:  Message type = 03
DLSw:  Target = Station 400000000002
DLSw:  Origin = Station IBM    E4BD21
DLSw:  Origin link SAP = 04
DLSw:  Target link SAP = 00
DLSw:  Frame direction = 1 (Origin DLSw to target)
DLSw:  DLC header length = 0 bytes
DLSw:  Origin DLC port ID = B54F4
```

(Continues)

Figure 13.12   Continued

```
DLSw:   Origin data link correlator = F
DLSw:   Origin transport ID = 1
DLSw:   Target DLC port ID = B000100
DLSw:   Target data link correlator = 1
DLSw:   Target transport ID = 1060000
DLSw:
```

ICANREACH EXPLORER

```
DLC:    --- DLC Header ---
DLC:
DLC:    Frame 76 arrived at  17:11:53.0404; frame size is 116 (0074 hex) bytes.
DLC:    Destination = DCE
DLC:    Source = DTE
DLC:
ROUTER: --- Cisco Router/Bridge ---
ROUTER:
ROUTER: Header = 0F000800
ROUTER:
IP:     --- IP Header ---
IP:
IP:     Version = 4, header length = 20 bytes
IP:     Type of service = 00
IP:           000. .... = routine
IP:           ...0 .... = normal delay
IP:           .... 0... = normal throughput
IP:           .... .0.. = normal reliability
IP:     Total length  = 112 bytes
IP:     Identification = 4
IP:     Flags         = 0X
IP:           .0.. .... = may fragment
IP:           ..0. .... = last fragment
IP:     Fragment offset = 0 bytes
IP:     Time to live  = 255 seconds/hops
IP:     Protocol      = 6 (TCP)
IP:     Header checksum = 8B55 (correct)
IP:     Source address      = [150.150.1.1]
IP:     Destination address = [150.150.2.1]
IP:     No options
IP:
TCP:    --- TCP header ---
TCP:
TCP:    Source port         = 2065 (DLSw-rpn)
TCP:    Destination port    = 11007
TCP:    Sequence number     = 2940297586
TCP:    Acknowledgment number = 2939810016
TCP:    Data offset         = 20 bytes
TCP:    Flags               = 18
TCP:            ..0. .... = (No urgent pointer)
TCP:            ...1 .... = Acknowledgment
TCP:            .... 1... = Push
TCP:            .... .0.. = (No reset)
TCP:            .... ..0. = (No SYN)
TCP:            .... ...0 = (No FIN)
TCP:    Window              = 19978
TCP:    Checksum            = B1D9 (correct)
```

Figure 13.12 Continued

```
TCP:   No TCP options
TCP:   [72 byte(s) of data]
TCP:

DLSw:   --- Data Link Switching Protocol ---
DLSw:
DLSw:   Version = 31 (RFC 1795)
DLSw:   Header length = 72 bytes
DLSw:   Message length = 0 bytes
DLSw:   Remote data link correlator = 0
DLSw:   Remote DLC port ID = B54F4
DLSw:   Message type = 04 (I can reach station)
DLSw:   Flow control = 00
DLSw:       0... .... = FCI (No indicator)
DLSw:       .0.. .... = FCA (No ack)
DLSw:       .... .000 = FCO (Repeat window operator)
DLSw:   Protocol ID = 42
DLSw:   Header number = 1
DLSw:   Largest frame size = 30
DLSw:               0... .... = Fail circuit if size smaller
DLSw:               ..11 0... = Largest frame bit base
DLSw:               .... .000 = Largest frame bit extended
DLSw:   SSP flags = 8X
DLSw:   1... .... = Explorer
DLSw:   Circuit priority = 0 (Unspecified)
DLSw:   Message type = 04
DLSw:   Target = Station 400000000002
DLSw:   Origin = Station IBM    E4BD21
DLSw:   Origin link SAP = 04
DLSw:   Target link SAP = 00
DLSw:   Frame direction = 2 (Target DLSw to origin)
DLSw:   DLC header length = 0 bytes
DLSw:   Origin DLC port ID = B54F4
DLSw:   Origin data link correlator = 1F400
DLSw:   Origin transport ID = 1
DLSw:   Target DLC port ID = B54F4
DLSw:   Target data link correlator = FF010000
DLSw:   Target transport ID = 1
```

CANUREACH CIRCUIT START

```
DLC:   --- DLC Header ---
DLC:
DLC:   Frame 78 arrived at  17:11:53.0819; frame size is 116 (0074 hex) bytes.
DLC:   Destination = DTE
DLC:   Source = DCE
DLC:
ROUTER: --- Cisco Router/Bridge ---
ROUTER:
ROUTER: Header = 0F000800
ROUTER:
IP:    --- IP Header ---
IP:
IP:    Version = 4, header length = 20 bytes
IP:    Type of service = 00
```

(Continues)

Figure 13.12   Continued

```
IP:            000. .... = routine
IP:            ...0 .... = normal delay
IP:            .... 0... = normal throughput
IP:            .... .0.. = normal reliability
IP:    Total length    = 112 bytes
IP:    Identification  = 6
IP:    Flags           = 0X
IP:            .0.. .... = may fragment
IP:            ..0. .... = last fragment
IP:    Fragment offset = 0 bytes
IP:    Time to live    = 255 seconds/hops
IP:    Protocol        = 6 (TCP)
IP:    Header checksum = 8B53 (correct)
IP:    Source address      = [150.150.2.1]
IP:    Destination address = [150.150.1.1]
IP:    No options
IP:
TCP:   --- TCP header ---
TCP:
TCP:   Source port            = 11007
TCP:   Destination port       = 2065 (DLSw-rpn)
TCP:   Sequence number        = 2939810016
TCP:   Acknowledgment number  = 2940297658
TCP:   Data offset            = 20 bytes
TCP:   Flags                  = 18
TCP:                  ..0. .... = (No urgent pointer)
TCP:                  ...1 .... = Acknowledgment
TCP:                  .... 1... = Push
TCP:                  .... .0.. = (No reset)
TCP:                  .... ..0. = (No SYN)
TCP:                  .... ...0 = (No FIN)
TCP:   Window                 = 20408
TCP:   Checksum               = C7DA (correct)
TCP:   No TCP options
TCP:   [72 byte(s) of data]
TCP:

DLSw:  --- Data Link Switching Protocol ---
DLSw:
DLSw:  Version = 31 (RFC 1795)
DLSw:  Header length = 72 bytes
DLSw:  Message length = 0 bytes
DLSw:  Remote data link correlator = 0
DLSw:  Remote DLC port ID = 0
DLSw:  Message type = 03 (Can U reach station)
DLSw:  Flow control = 00
DLSw:     0... .... = FCI (No indicator)
DLSw:     .0.. .... = FCA (No ack)
DLSw:     .... .000 = FCO (Repeat window operator)
DLSw:  Protocol ID = 42
DLSw:  Header number = 1
DLSw:  Largest frame size = 30
DLSw:             0... .... = Fail circuit if size smaller
DLSw:             ..11 0... = Largest frame bit base
DLSw:             .... .000 = Largest frame bit extended
DLSw:  SSP flags = 0X
DLSw:  0... .... = Circuit start
```

Figure 13.12 Continued

```
DLSw:   Circuit priority = 0 (Unspecified)
DLSw:   Message type = 11
DLSw:   Target = Station 400000000002
DLSw:   Origin = Station IBM    E4BD21
DLSw:   Origin link SAP = 04
DLSw:   Target link SAP = 04
DLSw:   Frame direction = 1 (Origin DLSw to target)
DLSw:   DLC header length = 0 bytes
DLSw:   Origin DLC port ID = B54F4
DLSw:   Origin data link correlator = 168A54
DLSw:   Origin transport ID = 12F700
DLSw:   Target DLC port ID = 0
DLSw:   Target data link correlator = 0
DLSw:   Target transport ID = 0
DLSw:
```

ICANREACH CIRCUIT START

```
DLC:    --- DLC Header ---
DLC:
DLC:    Frame 80 arrived at   17:11:53.1029; frame size is 116 (0074 hex) bytes.
DLC:    Destination = DCE
DLC:    Source = DTE
DLC:
ROUTER: --- Cisco Router/Bridge ---
ROUTER:
ROUTER: Header = 0F000800
ROUTER:
IP:     --- IP Header ---
IP:
IP:     Version = 4, header length = 20 bytes
IP:     Type of service = 00
IP:           000. .... = routine
IP:           ...0 .... = normal delay
IP:           .... 0... = normal throughput
IP:           .... .0.. = normal reliability
IP:     Total length    = 112 bytes
IP:     Identification  = 6
IP:     Flags           = 0X
IP:           .0.. .... = may fragment
IP:           ..0. .... = last fragment
IP:     Fragment offset = 0 bytes
IP:     Time to live    = 255 seconds/hops
IP:     Protocol        = 6 (TCP)
IP:     Header checksum = 8B53 (correct)
IP:     Source address      = [150.150.1.1]
IP:     Destination address = [150.150.2.1]
IP:     No options
IP:
TCP:    --- TCP header ---
TCP:
TCP:    Source port            = 2065 (DLSw-rpn)
TCP:    Destination port       = 11007
TCP:    Sequence number        = 2940297658
```

(Continues)

Figure 13.12 Continued

```
TCP:   Acknowledgment number    = 2939810088
TCP:   Data offset              = 20 bytes
TCP:   Flags                    = 18
TCP:                   ..0. .... = (No urgent pointer)
TCP:                   ...1 .... = Acknowledgment
TCP:                   .... 1... = Push
TCP:                   .... .0.. = (No reset)
TCP:                   .... ..0. = (No SYN)
TCP:                   .... ...0 = (No FIN)
TCP:   Window                   = 19906
TCP:   Checksum                 = 0883 (correct)
TCP:   No TCP options
TCP:   [72 byte(s) of data]
TCP:



DLSw:  --- Data Link Switching Protocol ---
DLSw:
DLSw:  Version = 31 (RFC 1795)
DLSw:  Header length = 72 bytes
DLSw:  Message length = 0 bytes
DLSw:  Remote data link correlator = 168A54
DLSw:  Remote DLC port ID = B54F4
DLSw:  Message type = 04 (I can reach station)
DLSw:  Flow control = 80
DLSw:      1... .... = FCI (Indicator)
DLSw:      .0.. .... = FCA (No ack)
DLSw:      .... .000 = FCO (Repeat window operator)
DLSw:  Protocol ID = 42
DLSw:  Header number = 1
DLSw:  Largest frame size = 30
DLSw:          0... .... = Fail circuit if size smaller
DLSw:          ..11 0... = Largest frame bit base
DLSw:          .... .000 = Largest frame bit extended
DLSw:  SSP flags = 0X
DLSw:  0... .... = Circuit start
DLSw:  Circuit priority = 2 (Medium)
DLSw:  Message type = FF
DLSw:  Target = Station 400000000002
DLSw:  Origin = Station IBM    E4BD21
DLSw:  Origin link SAP = 04
DLSw:  Target link SAP = 04
DLSw:  Frame direction = 2 (Target DLSw to origin)
DLSw:  DLC header length = 0 bytes
DLSw:  Origin DLC port ID = B54F4
DLSw:  Origin data link correlator = 168A54
DLSw:  Origin transport ID = 12F700
DLSw:  Target DLC port ID = B54F4
DLSw:  Target data link correlator = 1642B8
DLSw:  Target transport ID = 12F700
DLSw:

REACHACK

DLC:   --- DLC Header ---
DLC:
DLC:   Frame 82 arrived at  17:11:53.1581; frame size is 188 (00BC hex) bytes.
```

Figure 13.12 Continued

```
DLC:   Destination = DTE
DLC:   Source = DCE
DLC:
ROUTER: --- Cisco Router/Bridge ---
ROUTER:
ROUTER: Header = 0F000800
ROUTER:
IP:    --- IP Header ---
IP:
IP:    Version = 4, header length = 20 bytes
IP:    Type of service = 00
IP:          000. .... = routine
IP:          ...0 .... = normal delay
IP:          .... 0... = normal throughput
IP:          .... .0.. = normal reliability
IP:    Total length    = 184 bytes
IP:    Identification  = 8
IP:    Flags           = 0X
IP:          .0.. .... = may fragment
IP:          ..0. .... = last fragment
IP:    Fragment offset = 0 bytes
IP:    Time to live    = 255 seconds/hops
IP:    Protocol        = 6 (TCP)
IP:    Header checksum = 8B09 (correct)
IP:    Source address      = [150.150.2.1]
IP:    Destination address = [150.150.1.1]
IP:    No options
IP:
TCP:   --- TCP header ---
TCP:
TCP:   Source port            = 11007
TCP:   Destination port       = 2065 (DLSw-rpn)
TCP:   Sequence number        = 2939810088
TCP:   Acknowledgment number  = 2940297730
TCP:   Data offset            = 20 bytes
TCP:   Flags                  = 18
TCP:          ..0. .... = (No urgent pointer)
TCP:          ...1 .... = Acknowledgment
TCP:          .... 1... = Push
TCP:          .... .0.. = (No reset)
TCP:          .... ..0. = (No SYN)
TCP:          .... ...0 = (No FIN)
TCP:   Window                 = 20336
TCP:   Checksum               = ED9E (correct)
TCP:   No TCP options
TCP:   [144 byte(s) of data]
TCP:

DLSw:  --- Data Link Switching Protocol ---
DLSw:
DLSw:  Version = 31 (RFC 1795)
DLSw:  Header length = 72 bytes
DLSw:  Message length = 0 bytes
DLSw:  Remote data link correlator = 1642B8
DLSw:  Remote DLC port ID = B54F4
```

(Continues)

Figure 13.12   Continued

```
DLSw:   Message type = 05 (Reach acknowledgement)
DLSw:   Flow control = 80
DLSw:      1... .... = FCI (Indicator)
DLSw:      .0.. .... = FCA (No ack)
DLSw:      .... .000 = FCO (Repeat window operator)
DLSw:   Protocol ID = 42
DLSw:   Header number = 1
DLSw:   Circuit priority = 7 (?)
DLSw:   Message type = DC
DLSw:   Target = Station 400000000002
DLSw:   Origin = Station IBM    E4BD21
DLSw:   Origin link SAP = 04
DLSw:   Target link SAP = 04
DLSw:   Frame direction = 1 (Origin DLSw to target)
DLSw:   DLC header length = 0 bytes
DLSw:   Origin DLC port ID = B54F4
DLSw:   Origin data link correlator = 168A54
DLSw:   Origin transport ID = 12F700
DLSw:   Target DLC port ID = B54F4
DLSw:   Target data link correlator = 1642B8
DLSw:   Target transport ID = 12F700
DLSw:
DLSw:   --- Data Link Switching Protocol ---
DLSw:
DLSw:   Version = 31 (RFC 1795)
DLSw:   Header length = 72 bytes
DLSw:   Message length = 0 bytes
DLSw:   Remote data link correlator = 1642B8
DLSw:   Remote DLC port ID = B54F4
DLSw:   Message type = 07 (XID frame)
DLSw:   Flow control = 40
DLSw:      0... .... = FCI (No indicator)
DLSw:      .1.. .... = FCA (Ack)
DLSw:      .... .000 = FCO (Repeat window operator)
DLSw:   Protocol ID = 42
DLSw:   Header number = 1
DLSw:   Circuit priority = 2 (Medium)
DLSw:   Message type = FF
DLSw:   Target = Station 400000000002
DLSw:   Origin = Station IBM    E4BD21
DLSw:   Origin link SAP = 04
DLSw:   Target link SAP = 04
DLSw:   Frame direction = 1 (Origin DLSw to target)
DLSw:   DLC header length = 0 bytes
DLSw:   Origin DLC port ID = B54F4
DLSw:   Origin data link correlator = 168A54
DLSw:   Origin transport ID = 12F700
DLSw:   Target DLC port ID = B54F4
DLSw:   Target data link correlator = 1642B8
DLSw:   Target transport ID = 12F700
DLSw:

DLC:    --- DLC Header ---
DLC:
DLC:    Frame 86 arrived at   17:11:54.7528; frame size is 116 (0074 hex) bytes.
DLC:    Destination = DCE
DLC:    Source = DTE
DLC:
```

Figure 13.12 Continued

```
ROUTER: --- Cisco Router/Bridge ---
ROUTER:
ROUTER: Header = 0F000800
ROUTER:
IP:    --- IP Header ---
IP:
IP:    Version = 4, header length = 20 bytes
IP:    Type of service = 00
IP:          000. .... = routine
IP:          ...0 .... = normal delay
IP:          .... 0... = normal throughput
IP:          .... .0.. = normal reliability
IP:    Total length    = 112 bytes
IP:    Identification  = 8
IP:    Flags           = 0X
IP:          .0.. .... = may fragment
IP:          ..0. .... = last fragment
IP:    Fragment offset = 0 bytes
IP:    Time to live    = 255 seconds/hops
IP:    Protocol        = 6 (TCP)
IP:    Header checksum = 8B51 (correct)
IP:    Source address      = [150.150.1.1]
IP:    Destination address = [150.150.2.1]
IP:    No options
IP:
TCP:   --- TCP header ---
TCP:
TCP:   Source port            = 2065 (DLSw-rpn)
TCP:   Destination port       = 11007
TCP:   Sequence number        = 2940297730
TCP:   Acknowledgment number  = 2939810232
TCP:   Data offset            = 20 bytes
TCP:   Flags                  = 18
TCP:            ..0. .... = (No urgent pointer)
TCP:            ...1 .... = Acknowledgment
TCP:            .... 1... = Push
TCP:            .... .0.. = (No reset)
TCP:            .... ..0. = (No SYN)
TCP:            .... ...0 = (No FIN)
TCP:   Window                 = 19762
TCP:   Checksum               = 0546 (correct)
TCP:   No TCP options
TCP:   [72 byte(s) of data]

DLSw:  --- Data Link Switching Protocol ---
DLSw:
DLSw:  Version = 31 (RFC 1795)
DLSw:  Header length = 72 bytes
DLSw:  Message length = 0 bytes
DLSw:  Remote data link correlator = 168A54
DLSw:  Remote DLC port ID = B54F4
DLSw:  Message type = 07 (XID frame)
DLSw:  Flow control = 40
DLSw:       0... .... = FCI (No indicator)
DLSw:       .1.. .... = FCA (Ack)
```

(Continues)

Figure 13.12 Continued

```
DLSw:       .... .000 = FCO (Repeat window operator)
DLSw:   Protocol ID = 42
DLSw:   Header number = 1
DLSw:   Circuit priority = 5 (?)
DLSw:   Message type = 16
DLSw:   Target = Station 400000000002
DLSw:   Origin = Station IBM    E4BD21
DLSw:   Origin link SAP = 04
DLSw:   Target link SAP = 04
DLSw:   Frame direction = 2 (Target DLSw to origin)
DLSw:   DLC header length = 0 bytes
DLSw:   Origin DLC port ID = B54F4
DLSw:   Origin data link correlator = 168A54
DLSw:   Origin transport ID = 12F700
DLSw:   Target DLC port ID = B54F4
DLSw:   Target data link correlator = 1642B8
DLSw:   Target transport ID = 12F700
DLSw:
```

AS/400 And Microsoft NT session startup

```
DLSw:   Message type = 07 (XID frame)
DLC:    --- DLC Header ---
DLC:
DLC:    Frame 88 arrived at  17:11:54.7854; frame size is 216 (00D8 hex) bytes.
DLC:    Destination = DTE
DLC:    Source = DCE
DLC:
ROUTER: --- Cisco Router/Bridge ---
ROUTER:
ROUTER: Header = 0F000800
ROUTER:
IP:     --- IP Header ---
IP:
IP:     Version = 4, header length = 20 bytes
IP:     Type of service = 00
IP:          000. .... = routine
IP:          ...0 .... = normal delay
IP:          .... 0... = normal throughput
IP:          .... .0.. = normal reliability
IP:     Total length  = 212 bytes
IP:     Identification = 10
IP:     Flags         = 0X
IP:          .0.. .... = may fragment
IP:          ..0. .... = last fragment
IP:     Fragment offset = 0 bytes
IP:     Time to live  = 255 seconds/hops
IP:     Protocol      = 6 (TCP)
IP:     Header checksum = 8AEB (correct)
IP:     Source address    = [150.150.2.1]
IP:     Destination address = [150.150.1.1]
IP:     No options
IP:
TCP:    --- TCP header ---
TCP:
TCP:    Source port          = 11007
TCP:    Destination port     = 2065 (DLSw-rpn)
TCP:    Sequence number      = 2939810232
```

Figure 13.12 Continued

```
TCP:   Acknowledgment number      = 2940297802
TCP:   Data offset                = 20 bytes
TCP:   Flags                      = 18
TCP:                   ..0. .... = (No urgent pointer)
TCP:                   ...1 .... = Acknowledgment
TCP:                   .... 1... = Push
TCP:                   .... .0.. = (No reset)
TCP:                   .... ..0. = (No SYN)
TCP:                   .... ...0 = (No FIN)
TCP:   Window                     = 20264
TCP:   Checksum                   = 4E54 (correct)
TCP:   No TCP options
TCP:   [172 byte(s) of data]
TCP:

DLSw:  --- Data Link Switching Protocol ---
DLSw:
DLSw:  Version = 31 (RFC 1795)
DLSw:  Header length = 72 bytes
DLSw:  Message length = 100 bytes
DLSw:  Remote data link correlator = 1642B8
DLSw:  Remote DLC port ID = B54F4
DLSw:  Message type = 07 (XID frame)
DLSw:  Flow control = 00
DLSw:       0... .... = FCI (No indicator)
DLSw:       .0.. .... = FCA (No ack)
DLSw:       .... .000 = FCO (Repeat window operator)
DLSw:  Protocol ID = 42
DLSw:  Header number = 1
DLSw:  Circuit priority = 0 (Unspecified)
DLSw:  Message type = 11
DLSw:  Target = Station 400000000002 (AS/400)
DLSw:  Origin = Station IBM    E4BD21
DLSw:  Origin link SAP = 04
DLSw:  Target link SAP = 04
DLSw:  Frame direction = 1 (Origin DLSw to target)
DLSw:  DLC header length = 0 bytes
DLSw:  Origin DLC port ID = B54F4
DLSw:  Origin data link correlator = 168A54
DLSw:  Origin transport ID = 12F700
DLSw:  Target DLC port ID = B54F4
DLSw:  Target data link correlator = 1642B8
DLSw:  Target transport ID = 12F700
DLSw:

DLSW:
SNA:   --- XID (Exchange Information) ---
SNA:
SNA:   XID format = 3, type = 2
SNA:   Length of I-field = 100
SNA:   Node ID = Block number 05D, ID number FFFFF
SNA:   Node characteristics = B0
SNA:               1... .... = INIT-SELF cannot be sent
SNA:               .0.. .... = BIND may be sent without prior INIT-SELF
SNA:               ..1. .... = Node does not generate BIND PIU segments
```

(Continues)

Figure 13.12   Continued

```
SNA:                  ...1 .... = Node cannot receive BIND PIU segments
SNA:   Node characteristics (continued) = 88
SNA:                  1... .... = ACTPU for an SSCP-PU session not requested
SNA:                    .0.. .... = Sender is not a network node
SNA:                    ..0. .... = CP services are not requested or
provided
SNA:                    ...0 .... = CP-CP sessions are not supported on
this TG
SNA:                    .... 10.. = Exchange state: Pre-negotiation
exchange
SNA:                    .... ..0. = Nonactivation exchange by 2nd station
not supported
SNA:                    .... ...0 = Sender cannot process CP names in XID3s
SNA:   BIND pacing support over TG = 10
SNA:                  0... .... = Adaptive BIND pacing as a BIND sender not
supported
SNA:                    .0.. .... = Adaptive BIND pacing as a BIND receiver not
supported
SNA:                    ..0. .... = Sender requests the TG is operative
SNA:      1 .... = Does support ACTPU with PU capabilities control vector
SNA:                    .... 0... = Sending node is not an APPN peripheral
border node
SNA:                    .... ..00 = Adaptive BIND pacing supports indep/dep LUs
(nonnegotiable)
SNA:   Node characteristics = 00
SNA:                  0... .... = Parallel TGs are not supported
SNA:                    .0.. .... = DLUR XID sender has no preference on receipt of
ACTPU
SNA:                    ..0. .... = DLUS-served LU registration is not supported
SNA:   Transmission group number = 0X00
SNA:   DLC type = 1 (SDLC)
SNA:   Length of DLC dependent section = 11 bytes
SNA:   Link station flags = 70
SNA:                    .1.. .... = Sender can be an ABM combined station
SNA:                    ..11 .... = Sender as primary/secondary is negotiable
SNA:                    .... 0... = Sender not engaged in connection using short-hold mode
SNA:                    .... .0.. = Short hold mode not supported
SNA:                    .... ..00 = Two-way alternating transmit-receive
SNA:   ABM link station flags = 00
SNA:                  0... .... = XID sender does not initiate a nonactivation XID
exchange
SNA:   Maximum receivable I-field length = 1929 bytes
SNA:   SDLC profile = SNA link station
SNA:   SDLC initialization mode options = 00
SNA:                    ..0. .... = SIM and RIM not supported
SNA:   Maximum number of outstanding I-frames = 2
SNA:   Control Vector = 10 (Product Set ID),  Length = 55
SNA:      Network Product ID = "......021000..MS SNA
SERVER..0000000......0000000000000"
SNA:   Control Vector = 0E (Network Name),  Length = 12
SNA:      Network name type = '4' (CP)
SNA:      Network name = "APPN.TOKEN2"
SNA:

DLC:   --- DLC Header ---
DLC:
DLC:   Frame 89 arrived at   17:11:54.8364; frame size is 186 (00BA hex) bytes.
DLC:   Destination = DCE
DLC:   Source = DTE
```

Figure 13.12 Continued

```
DLC:
ROUTER: --- Cisco Router/Bridge ---
ROUTER:
ROUTER: Header = 0F000800
ROUTER:
IP:     --- IP Header ---
IP:
IP:     Version = 4, header length = 20 bytes
IP:     Type of service = 00
IP:          000. .... = routine
IP:          ...0 .... = normal delay
IP:          .... 0... = normal throughput
IP:          .... .0.. = normal reliability
IP:     Total length   = 182 bytes
IP:     Identification = 9
IP:     Flags          = 0X
IP:          .0.. .... = may fragment
IP:          ..0. .... = last fragment
IP:     Fragment offset = 0 bytes
IP:     Time to live   = 255 seconds/hops
IP:     Protocol       = 6 (TCP)
IP:     Header checksum = 8B0A (correct)
IP:     Source address      = [150.150.1.1]
IP:     Destination address = [150.150.2.1]
IP:     No options
IP:
TCP:    --- TCP header ---
TCP:
TCP:    Source port           = 2065 (DLSw-rpn)
TCP:    Destination port      = 11007
TCP:    Sequence number       = 2940297802
TCP:    Acknowledgment number = 2939810232
TCP:    Data offset           = 20 bytes
TCP:    Flags                 = 18
TCP:                ..0. .... = (No urgent pointer)
TCP:                ...1 .... = Acknowledgment
TCP:                .... 1... = Push
TCP:                .... .0.. = (No reset)
TCP:                .... ..0. = (No SYN)
TCP:                .... ...0 = (No FIN)
TCP:    Window                = 19762
TCP:    Checksum              = CA84 (correct)
TCP:    No TCP options
TCP:    [142 byte(s) of data]
TCP:

DLSw:   --- Data Link Switching Protocol ---
DLSw:
DLSw:   Version = 31 (RFC 1795)
DLSw:   Header length = 72 bytes
DLSw:   Message length = 70 bytes
DLSw:   Remote data link correlator = 168A54
DLSw:   Remote DLC port ID = B54F4
DLSw:   Message type = 07 (XID frame)
DLSw:   Flow control = 00
DLSw:        0... .... = FCI (No indicator)
```

(Continues)

Figure 13.12 Continued

```
DLSw:       .0.. .... = FCA (No ack)
DLSw:       .... .000 = FCO (Repeat window operator)
DLSw:    Protocol ID = 42
DLSw:    Header number = 1
DLSw:    Circuit priority = 5 (?)
DLSw:    Message type = 16
DLSw:    Target = Station 400000000002
DLSw:    Origin = Station IBM    E4BD21
DLSw:    Origin link SAP = 04
DLSw:    Target link SAP = 04
DLSw:    Frame direction = 2 (Target DLSw to origin)
DLSw:    DLC header length = 0 bytes
DLSw:    Origin DLC port ID = B54F4
DLSw:    Origin data link correlator = 168A54
DLSw:    Origin transport ID = 12F700
DLSw:    Target DLC port ID = B54F4
DLSw:    Target data link correlator = 1642B8
DLSw:    Target transport ID = 12F700

DLSw:
SNA:    --- XID (Exchange Information) ---
SNA:
SNA:    XID format = 3, type = 2
SNA:    Length of I-field = 70
SNA:    Node ID = Block number 056, ID number 1086A
SNA:    Node characteristics = 00
SNA:             0... .... = INIT-SELF may be sent
SNA:             .0.. .... = BIND may be sent without prior INIT-SELF
SNA:             ..0. .... = Node can generate BIND PIU segments
SNA:             ...0 .... = Node can receive BIND PIU segments
SNA:    Node characteristics (continued) = 0A
SNA:                       0... .... = ACTPU for an SSCP-PU session requested
SNA:                       .0.. .... = Sender is not a network node
SNA:                       ..0. .... = CP services are not requested or
provided
SNA:                       ...0 .... = CP-CP sessions are not supported on
this TG
SNA:             .... 10.. = Exchange state: Pre-negotiation exchange
SNA:             .... ..1. = Nonactivation exchange by 2nd station supported
SNA:             .... ...0 = Sender cannot process CP names in XID3s
SNA:    BIND pacing support over TG = 00
SNA:                       0... .... = Adaptive BIND pacing as a BIND sender not
supported
SNA:                       .0.. .... = Adaptive BIND pacing as a BIND receiver not
supported
SNA:                       ..0. .... = Sender requests the TG is operative
SNA:                       ...0 .... = Does not support ACTPU with PU capabilities
control vector
SNA:                       .... 0... = Sending node is not an APPN peripheral
border node
SNA:                       .... ..00 = Adaptive BIND pacing supports indep/dep LUs
(nonnegotiable)
SNA:    Node characteristics = 00
SNA:             0... .... = Parallel TGs are not supported
SNA:             .0.. .... = DLUR XID sender has no preference on receipt of
ACTPU
SNA:             ..0. .... = DLUS-served LU registration is not supported
SNA:    Transmission group number = 0X15
```

Figure 13.12   Continued

```
SNA:   DLC type = 1 (SDLC)
SNA:   Length of DLC dependent section = 11 bytes
SNA:   Link station flags = 70
SNA:              .1.. .... = Sender can be an ABM combined station
SNA:              ..11 .... = Sender as primary/secondary is negotiable
SNA:              .... 0... = Sender not engaged in connection using short-hold mode
SNA:              .... .0.. = Short hold mode not supported
SNA:              .... ..00 = Two-way alternating transmit-receive
SNA:   ABM link station flags = 00
SNA:              0... .... = XID sender does not initiate a nonactivation XID
exchange
SNA:   Maximum receivable I-field length = 1994 bytes
SNA:   SDLC profile = SNA link station
SNA:   SDLC initialization mode options = 00
SNA:                      ..0. .... = SIM and RIM not supported
SNA:   Maximum number of outstanding I-frames = 7
SNA:   Control Vector = 0E (Network Name),  Length = 14
SNA:     Network name type = '4' (CP)
SNA:     Network name = "APPN.S101086A"
SNA:   Control Vector = 10 (Product Set ID),  Length = 23
SNA:     Network Product ID = "1......9401P0310001086A"
SNA:
```

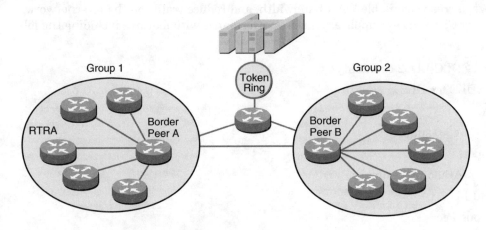

- Peer connections established as needed
- Peer connections taken down when not in use
- After 5 minutes of inactivity

FIGURE 13.13   DLSw LLC2 connection establishment

Switch-to-Switch Protocol (DLSw SSP) with features including the following:

- *Data Link Control* (DLC) termination for LLC2 and SDLC
- TCP/IP transport

- End-to-end flow control
- Source-Route bridging
- Explorer broadcast reduction
- NetBIOS name caching
- Peer groups
- Local, remote, and border peer chaching
- UDP unicast support
- On-demand peers
- Ring list
- Load balancing
- Dial-on-demand
- Border peers
- IP and Link layer encapsulations
- APPN support

These features ensure session availability and reliability, expand Source-Route bridge network size, increase available WAN bandwidth, and reduce traffic on the internetwork.

Additionally, Cisco DLSw+ application adds performance with features including the following:

- Integrated SDLC-LLC2 capability
- Reverse SDLC for DLSw
- Ethernet
- BNN (RFC 1490) support
- BAN support
- Duplicate MAC address support
- PU2.0 and PU 2.1
- Promiscuous Peers

A DLSw+ traffic prioritization technique is also provided for efficient data transfer using DLSw+ TCP port numbers.

Cisco DLSw implementation supports standardized methods for the following features:

- Availability by storing alternative paths to a destination so that if a link is lost, an alternative path can be used immediately without dropping the user's session
- Any-to-any connectivity in very large networks using name caching and other methods to reduce the need for broadcasting discovery frames
- Simplified configuration reducing the number of routers that need to be configured
- Load balancing by using all available paths

- Supporting other transport methods, such as using only HDLC between directly connected DLSw+ routers (which avoids the extra overhead of TCP/IP) and Fast Sequence Transport (IP) to further reduce overhead

- SDLLC Support for Token Ring and Ethernet

- End-to-end flow control

- RIF termination for Source-Route bridging

- Explorer broadcast reduction

- MAC and NetBIOS name caching

- Port/ring list for controlling Explorer traffic

- Peer groups

- Border peers

- Priority

- Backup peers

- Peer on Demand

DLSw is supported on most Cisco routers to provide high session reliability and to extend multivendor interoperability for SNA and NetBIOS transport over a multiprotocol internetwork. Additionally, DLSw specifies TCP/IP as the standard transport mechanism for SNA and NetBIOS traffic across an internetwork. Cisco's TCP/IP transport feature is a robust method for carrying SNA and NetBIOS traffic across a multiprotocol internetwork and allows SNA and NetBIOS to share a wide area backbone connection with multiprotocol LAN traffic such as IPX, AppleTalk, Vines, DECnet, etc. Cisco's DLSw implementation offers several encapsulation features such as Direct Layer 2 Encapsulation, *Fast Sequenced Transport* (FST) in IP only, and TCP, which the DLSw standard implements. Data packets from a Token Ring or Ethernet network are carried in LLC2 frames to an attached Cisco DLSw node where the data is translated from LLC2 into TCP/IP datagrams. The data then is routed over the multiprotocol backbone to a remote Cisco DLSw node using standard IP routing technologies such as IGRP, EIGRP, OSPF, RIP, RIP Version 2, or static routes. When the TCP/IP datagram reaches the remote Cisco DLSw node, it is translated back into LLC2 frame and is Source-Route bridged or transparently bridged to the destination.

TCP/IP provides dynamic routing that increases network availability by automatically rerouting traffic around a failed link. Using TCP as the transport mechanism across the backbone ensures reliable transport supporting local acknowledgement. Cisco routers cache out-of-order packets, alleviating the need to retransmit multiple packets if part of the transmission is received. This maintains the response times required by many applications and reduces the burden on bandwidth and CPUs if a packet retransmission is needed.

In today's integrated multiprotocol internetworks, connectivity between SNA devices and the popularity of Microsoft NT Server and IBM Warp Server running NetBIOS over NetBEUI is being extended across more diverse topologies. This introduces new network delays and increases the possibility of LLC2 session timeouts. Additionally, the large amount of data acknowledgment and "keep alive" traffic crossing the backbone significantly diminishes the wide area network's usable bandwidth.

Data Link Switching terminates the Data Link Control (LLC2 or SDLC) session at the router and provides Local Acknowledgment for LLC2 and SDLC traffic. Logical Link Control Type 2 (LLC2) is a connection-oriented protocol that operates at the Data Link layer, providing sequencing of MAC layer frames, error correction, and flow control between endstations. SNA and NetBIOS sessions generate large amounts of nondata transfer messages for controller synchronization and pre- and postdata transfer acknowledgment. Each message requires a response in a predefined amount of time. If a response is not received, the message is retransmitted.

Cisco DLC Termination maintains SNA sessions and lowers overhead traffic across the backbone by enabling the local router to terminate LLC2 sessions and to issue data acknowledgment frames, such as Receiver Ready, Receiver Not Ready, and Reject. DLC Termination reduces wide area network overhead and the possibility of session timeouts by eliminating acknowledgment frames from the backbone; only SNA and NetBIOS data traffic are passed over the backbone. Additionally, all timers are terminated locally, eliminating session timeouts.

Cisco DLSw routers also maintain full DLC protocol state information, effectively preventing unnecessary DLC state information from traversing across the backbone. Additionally, the router dynamically learns about each MAC address, reducing the amount of required router configuration. Furthermore, because the router maintains a record of the status of each MAC session, the router can properly inform each workstation of any network failure.

Cisco DLSw implementation provides flow control, which efficiently and reliably manages the DLSw data stream and safeguards it against data loss. These mechanisms ensure that only manageable amounts of data are transferred across the interface between the LLC2 and the TCP/IP protocols. Cisco DLSw implementation supports RFC 1795's Version 2.0 and RFC 2166 variable window size of information, which adjusts based on whether previous traffic reached its destination or whether congestion is encountered.

Cisco DLSw also overcomes the seven-hop count limit inherent in Source-Route bridging. Through this feature, end-to-end paths of unlimited hops can be established via DLSw routers connected to an IP backbone. Up to six hops are supported on either side of the DLSw backbone, which can be an unlimited number of hops and appear to be a Source-Route bridge network with a hop count of one. For example, with RIF Termination, when a LLC2 packet is received, the local DLSw router terminates the *routing information field* (RIF) and translates the packet into a TCP/IP datagram. The packet then is routed over the backbone to a DLSw router attached to the destination's Source-Route bridge network. When the packet is received by the remote DLSw router, it is translated back into a LLC2 packet with its hop count set at 1. The packet then is Source-Route bridged to the destination using route information stored in the DLSw router.

Cisco fully supports the DLSw specification for Explorer Broadcast Reduction that uses special control packets to reduce explorer traffic across the network backbone. These packets, referred to as CANUREACH and ICANREACH, dynamically discover endstations and then direct subsequent Source-Route bridge traffic to the DLSw router closest to the destination endstation. This function reduces the global broadcast messages sent when new sessions are established.

When a DLSw router receives an explorer packet, it sends a CANUREACH packet to all known remote DLSw peer routers in the network. The remote peer routers, in turn, translate these packets into local explorer packets and send them out over their attached LANs. If the destination endstation is found, the endstation sends an explorer response packet to the router that sent the local explorer packet. All DLSw routers that can reach the destination send an ICANREACH packet to the originating DLSw router. The originating router uses the first packet received to route traffic to the destination.

By supporting Source-Route Bridge Explorer Broadcast Reduction, Cisco reduces broadcasts by limiting the number of CANUREACH messages. A Cisco router allows only a single CANUREACH packet to be sent for a particular destination address, eliminating unnecessary bandwidth consumption. Any additional requests for the same MAC address are queued at the router. When the address and nearest DLSw router information have been cached, subsequent requests generated by other endstations on the network use the cache to forward packets. Cisco DLSw builds a local and remote cache for station reachability.

MAC and NetBIOS Name Caching significantly reduce another source of broadcast overhead in a Source-Route bridge environment. DLSw specifies NetBIOS Name Caching as the method used for reducing broadcasts of NetBIOS FIND NAME packets. NetBIOS Name Caching uses packets similar to the CANUREACH and ICANREACH packets used in Explorer Broadcast Reduction to dynamically discover endstations. It then directs new NetBIOS traffic to specific routers using the same method described in Explorer Broadcast Reduction. This improves network efficiency and reduces global broadcast messages sent when new sessions are established.

Cisco DLSw+ Enhancements

Cisco provides features to enhance DLSw performance, flexibility, and connectivity. Cisco's DLSw+ is fully compliant with RFC 1795 and RFC 2166. These features include the following:

- Fully distributed Promiscuous Peers
- SDLLC support
- Reverse SDLLC support
- Peer groups
- Border peers
- Ring list
- Routed SNA over Frame Relay (RFC 1490) support
- *Boundary Access Node* (BAN) support
- *Boundary Network Node* (BNN) support
- DLSw prioritization

Cisco fully distributed DLSw implementation scales to support large networks and increase network availability. Multiple Data Link switches can be implemented on a single router, providing a cost-effective and manageable solution in IBM data center environments.

Cisco's Promiscuous Peers feature enables RFC 1434/1795/2166 and Version 2.0 -compliant DLSw peers, routers, and/or devices with similar DLSw capabilities to receive and respond to broadcast frames forwarded by a configured peer. This mechanism increases DLSw service connectivity by allowing DLSw peers in an IP network to learn the locations of previously unknown peers.

Cisco support for SDLC conversion functionality is an extension of its DLSw+ features and is a critical component for the integration of SNA and multiprotocol LAN networks. Through this feature, SDLC sessions are terminated by a local Cisco router, which also converts the SDLC frames to LLC2 format, maps the SDLC addresses to Token Ring addresses, and arranges for transport to the destination host. Local termination of the SDLC sessions also allows the polling and acknowledgment activity normally conducted between the *front-end processor* (FEP) and the SDLC devices to be conducted between the local internetworking device and the SDLC devices, reducing overhead traffic across the wide area network. Cisco DLSw implementation also decreases overhead and reduces traffic on the network via local termination of SDLC sessions at the DLSw router in software. SDLC termination provides local polling and acknowledgment to SDLC devices (PU Type 2.0 and PU 2.1) from the DLSw router, thereby eliminating the need for traditional SDLC polling from the FEP across the wide area links.

SDLLC conversion seamlessly merges the low-speed SDLC traffic of an SNA network with the high-speed multiprotocol traffic capabilities of LANs onto one strategic, readily extensible and manageable backbone. This increases SNA network efficiency and productivity while providing a higher level of internetwork efficiency. Through a Cisco router, remote networks can be interconnected via WAN media operating over a range of services to form a highly reliable, high-performance, and extensible enterprise network.

Cisco DLSw implementation allows LLC2 conversion to be implemented either in a single DLSw router local switch or DLSw peer switch implementation that involves two DLSw nodes and a TCP/IP connection over a wide area network. This allows the router to be configured to meet exact network configuration and transport requirements. A single router implementation can be used in environments that do not need to send DLSw traffic over a WAN. Each SDLC interface also can be configured to support a number of SDLC and performance-tuning parameters, *Non-Return to Zero / Non-Return to Zero Inverted* (NRZ/NRZI), half–full duplex, and maximum frame size. This allows the interface to be tailored to meet exact requirements, ensuring maximized operation.

In LAN-attached device environments, routers function as a remote LAN gateway. Local termination is used in SDLC-attached environments, providing enhanced response times and session availability. SDLC support allows a single line into the FEP to support multiple downstream SNA devices. Downstream devices on different media and routers can share a line into the FEP.

Cisco fully supports RFC 1490 Multiprotocol Interconnect over Frame Relay and the Frame Relay Forum FRF.3 Multiprotocol Encapsulation Implementation Agreement. These allow direct communications from a Cisco router to an IBM communications controller via a Frame Relay network, eliminating the need for additional routers. They also allow communications from a downstream Frame Relay SNA device directly to a Cisco router for connection to an APPN network. Additionally, native SNA also can be used between two Cisco routers.

Cisco support of *Boundary Access Node* (BAN) eases the configuration of SNA devices into a multiprotocol LAN environment while ensuring the performance and reliability critical to SNA applications. Dual host attachment to mainframes with the same MAC address also is supported to provide the additional redundancy required by SNA environments. BAN also reduces administrative costs by easing network configuration.

Port/Ring Lists

Ring lists enable you to create broadcast domains in a DLSw+ network (see Figure 13.14). Using port or ring lists, you can control where broadcasts are forwarded. You can distinguish among different Token Ring ports and serial ports using port lists, but all Ethernet ports are treated as a single entity (Ethernet bridge group).

Peer Group Concept

Perhaps the most significant optimization feature found in DLSw+ is a feature known as *peer groups*. Peer groups are designed to address the broadcast replication that occurs in a fully meshed network. When any-to-any communication is required (for example, for Net-BIOS or *Advanced Peer-to-Peer Networking* [APPN] environments), RSRB or standard DLSw implementations require peer connections between every pair of routers. This setup is not only difficult to configure, but it results in branch access routers having to replicate search requests for each peer connection. Having peer connections between every pair of

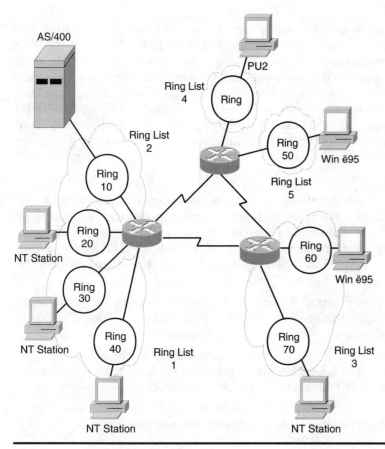

FIGURE 13.14   Cisco DLSw+ ring list

routers wastes bandwidth and router cycles. A better concept is to group routers into clusters and designate a focal router to be responsible for broadcast replication.

With DLSw+, a cluster of routers in a region or a division of a company can be combined into a peer group. Within a peer group, one or more of the routers is designated to be the *border peer*. Instead of all routers peering to one another, each router within a group peers to the border peer; border peers establish peer connections with each. When a DLSw+ router receives a TEST frame or NetBIOS NAME-QUERY, it sends a single explorer frame to its border peer. The border peer forwards the explorer on behalf of the peer group member. This setup eliminates duplicate explorers on the access links and minimizes the processing required in access routers.

When the correct destination router is found, an end-to-end peer connection (TCP or IP) is established to carry end-system traffic. This connection remains active as long as end-system traffic is on it, and it is dynamically torn down when not in use, permitting casual, any-to-any communication without the burden of specifying peer connections in advance. It also allows any-to-any routing in large internetworks in which persistent TCP connections between every pair of routers is not possible.

Prioritization

Prioritization is a feature implemented in multiprocotol router software which ensures that time-critical protocols do not time-out when a temporary peak in the traffic load on the WAN link occurs. This feature usually is needed most for *legacy* protocols (such as SDLC), which were designed to work on dedicated, single-protocol links in which the delays are known and predictable. When a router combines many protocols onto a single WAN link (to reduce communication costs), the delay between networks depends on the WAN loading (due to the other protocols). Because some protocols cannot tolerate delays, (at best, there may be re-transmissions needlessly further loading the WAN link, and at worst, users may be unceremoniously disconnected), a method is needed to give them priority over other protocols.

Five methods are common:

- *Custom Queuing*, in which each protocol is assigned a percentage of the total WAN bandwidth so that regardless of the total WAN traffic load, a predetermined amount of bandwidth is available for the time-critical protocol. When a protocol does not need all of its reserved bandwidth, other protocols can use it. A problem is that if a time-critical protocol temporarily needs more than its assigned priority (and the other protocols also need all of theirs), the time-critical protocol may still time-out.

- *Priority Queuing*, in which each protocol is assigned a relative priority. The most time-critical protocol gets the highest priority. A problem is that if the time-critical protocol needs all of the bandwidth, the other protocols get no bandwidth.

- *Weighted Fair Queuing*, which classifies Web traffic into conversations and applies priority weights to the traffic to determine how much bandwidth each conversation gets. Example: Frame Relay, TCP/IP, and UDP/IP port numbers.

- *First In First Out Queuing*, which provides the simplest of all the queuing options in the Cisco IOS. FIFO is effective only if links encounter minimal congestion.

- *DLCI Prioritization*, which places different types of traffic on separate DLCI with different CIR for every traffic class.

Of these methods, bandwidth reservation is best for most applications, as long as the amount of bandwidth reserved for each protocol is the minimum required to provide acceptable service.

Summary

DLSw was created as a standard method of allowing SNA and NetBIOS data to be transported across a nonnative network. An IP transport network is the foundation of the backbone between DLSw nodes. This type of network architecture is created for several reasons. Among these are the inexpensive cost of TCP/IP components. This segment of the networking arena has experienced so much growth that these components have become commodities. The development of client/server products built on inexpensive platforms that often use TCP/IP as their native transport has increased the development of IP-based networks.

Cisco has met and exceeded the requirements of the DLSw standard in RFC1795 and offers the most comprehensive features in DLSw. These features allow DLSw networks designed around Cisco IOS to scale to very large networks with minimal configuration.

REFERENCE: *Cisco offers an excellent DLSw Design and Configuration guide located at the following url:*

```
http://www.cisco.com/warp/partner/synchronicd/cc/cisco/mkt/iworks/protocol/dlsw/
toc_rg.htm
```

- Cisco *SNA Configuration for Multi-Protocol Administrators* (SNAM) Course
- Cisco *Data Link Switching* (DLSw) Course
- RFC 1795
- RFC 2166

Questions

The questions in this chapter were derived from the DLSw chapter and Cisco's Multiprotocol for *SNA Administrators* (SNAM) course.

1. Multi-link transmission groups are:
   A. One link between subarea nodes
   B. Allows lines to be added or deleted as needed
   C. Can be used between PU4 and PU2.0 devices
   D. None of the above

2. Which SNA component initiates a request for an LU to LU session?

3. Which SNA component initiates a request to terminate an LU to LU session?

4. List the SNA command(s) in the order that establishes an LU to LU session when the action is initiated from a non-host node.

5. List the SNA command(s) in the order that establishes an LU to LU session when the action is initiated from a host node.

6. List the SNA command(s) in the order that terminate an LU to LU session when the action is initiated by a non-host node.

7. List the SNA command(s) in the order that terminate an LU to LU session when the action is initiated by a host node.

8. Describe how FM data traffic mode is enabled for an LU to LU session.

9. Describe how FM data traffic mode is disabled for an LU to LU session.

10. Define an LU to LU session.

11. Explain APPN Node type Low Entry Node.

12. Explain APPN Network Node.

13. Explain APPN End Nodes.

14. Which SNA components must agree to the initiation of an LU to LU session?

15. Explain how bracketing is initiated.

16. How is a bracket terminated?

17. Which LU session partner is allowed to start and end a bracket?

18. How is the BID command used in Bracket protocol?

19. How is the *Ready-to Receive* (RTR) command used in Bracket protocol?

20. The roles of the session partners (sender or receiver) are changed by the _____ indicator for Half Duplex Flip Flop.

21. The *Local Form Session ID* (LSFID) is assigned for the duration of the LU-LU session?
    A. True   **B.** False

22. APPN is know as:
    A. First Generation SNA   **C.** Both
    B. Second Generation SNA

23. A session is initiated that will use Half Duplex Contention protocol. One LU is specified as the first one to send.
    A. True   **B.** False

24. Which indicators are used to put both communicating LUs in a contention status?

25. For Half Duplex Contention, who wins the right to send first when both LUs try to send at the same time?

For questions 26-30, Match the following lettered commands with their numbered descriptions by writing corresponding letters next to each numbered question. **NOTE: Not all lettered commands need to be used.**
    A. Assign Network Addresses
    B. ACTIVATE LINK
    C. *Exchange Identification* (XID)
    D. SET CONTROL VECTOR
    E. CONNECT OUT
    F. FREE NETWORK ADDRESS
    G. ACTIVATE LOGICAL UNIT
    H. *Start Data Traffic* (SDT)
    I. BIND
    J. ACTIVATE CONNECT IN
    K. ABANDON CONNECTION

26. When it is issued by the host, this command contains the phone number and line number which the host wishes to call.

27. It is used by nodes to exchange identification or ID.

28. Using this command, SSCP sends control block information to NCP for the PU contacted after the dialed connection is made.

29. SSCP uses this command to tell NCP the network addresses for each LU on the switched line.

30. It causes a specified line in the Communications Controller Node to go on hook.

31. A Cisco Router can provide functions similar to which of the following PUs using DownStream PUs?
    A. PU4   **C.** PU2
    B. PU5   **D.** PU1

32. List the two major functions of NCP.
    A. Boundary functions for PU2 devices
    B. Physical Unit Control Point services
    C. Basic Link unit services
    D. None of the above

33. Data flow from a primary NAU to a secondary NAU is called outbound data flow.
    A. True   **B.** False

34. Identify the SNA layers included in the Boundary Function.
    A. Path Control   **C.** Connection Point Management
    B. Data Link Control   **D.** All of the above

35. Virtual Routes must be defined in both directions using explicit routes.
    A. True   **B.** False

36. Identify the SNA layers included in the Intermediate Network Function.
    A. Data Link   **C.** Session Layer
    B. Layer 3 Path Control   **D.** Presentation Layer

37. Identify the SNA layers included in the PU.

38. Which SNA layer(s) manages the flow across the S/370 channel and across telecommunication data links?

39. Which SNA layer(s) modifies the PIU format and length?
    A. Layer 3 Path Control   **C.** Transmission Control Layer
    B. Data Link Layer   **D.** None of the above

40. Which SNA layer(s) gets involved in pacing?
    A. Path Control   **C.** Session Layer Control
    B. Data Flow Control   **D.** All of the above

41. An SSCP-to-LU session defines?
    A. LU activation   **C.** Session start
    B. LU deactivation   **D.** None of the above

42. Which SNA layer(s) monitors session initiation and termination requests?

43. Define LPARS.

44. Identify the full name next to each acronym.
    A. BF-
    B. PN-

45. SDLC is connection oriented.
    A. True   **B.** False

46. The _____ is the unit of SDLC transmission.
    A. bit   C. message
    B. byte   D. frame

47. Identify the order in which the following fields appear in the SDLC unit of transmission.
    A. Information Field   D. Control Field
    B. Flag Field   E. Address Field
    C. FCS Field

48. In current SNA systems, a PU5 is considered the primary station on a data link.
    A. True   B. False

49. In current SNA systems, a PU2.0 is considered a secondary station on a data link.
    A. True   B. False

50. The primary station has control of the data link layer; it issues commands, and any secondary station that is polled must respond.
    A. True   B. False

51. Describe how SDLC recognizes a transmission error.

52. A secondary station sends to a primary station only when it is polled by the primary station.
    A. True   B. False

53. How does a secondary station notify the primary station that it has nothing more to send?

54. Name the three types of SDLC frames.
    A. Supervisor   C. Unnumbered frames
    B. Information   D. All of the above

55. Assume that the primary station sends the SNRM command to the secondary station and then receives an UA response. Next the primary station sends B,RR-P(0). What does the secondary send back, if anything?

56. The secondary station sends the following information frames to the primary station. The third frame is rejected because of a transmission error. Which frames, if any, are re-transmitted?
    1. B,I(0)F(1)
    2. B,I(1)F(1)
    3. B,I(2)F(1)
    4. B,I(3)F(1)
    5. B,I(4)F(1)
    6. B,I(5)F(1)
    7. B,I(6)F(1)

57. The primary station sends B,RR-P(0) to the secondary station and the response is B,ROL-F. What mode is the secondary station in?

58. The secondary station responded with B,CMDR-F. This means that the primary station had sent an _____ command.

For question 59, assume that the commands/responses on a communication link appeared as follows:

```
B,RR-P(1)Æ
C,RR-P(4)Æ    ←B,I(1)-F(0)
←B,I(2)-F(0)
←C,I(4)-F(0)
```

59. The type of communication facility being used is:
   A. Point-to-point duplex
   B. Multipoint duplex
   C. Multipoint half-duplex
   D. Point-to-point half-duplex

For question 60, assume that the commands/responses on a communication link appeared as follows:

```
←B,RR-F(4)
```

   1. B,I(4)-P(1) →
   2. B,I(5)-P(1) →
   3. B,I(6)-P(1) →
   4. B,I(7)-P(1) →
   5. B,I(0)-P(1) →
   6. B,I(1)-P(1) →
   7. B,I(2)-P(1) →
   8. B,I(3)-P(1) →
   9. B,I(4)-P(1) →

60. Which one of the following statements is true?
   A. Sequence is correct as shown.
   B. Primary station must request confirmation after frame 7 (Ns=2) is sent.
   C. Primary station must request confirmation after frame 9 (Ns=4) is sent.
   D. Primary station must request confirmation after frame 4 (Ns=7) is sent.

For question 61, assume the commands/responses on a communication link appear as follows.

```
  1.  B,I(5)-P(2) Æ
←2.  B,I(2)-F(5)
  3.  C,I(7)-P(3) Æ
←4.  C,RR-F(8)
B,RR-P(3) Æ
```

61. Which one of the following statements is true?
   A. Command sequence is correct as shown.
   B. Ns count is incorrect in 3.
   C. Nr count is incorrect in 4.
   D. Station B is indicating an error.

62. Which SDLC command can a station send to indicate that it is in a busy condition?

63. An SNA Transport communications system consists of:
   A. End users, Connection Point Manager, and Transmission Subsystem
   B. Path Control, Data Link Control, and SDLC
   C. Application Layer, Function Management Layer, Transmission Subsystem Layer
   D. Logical unit, physical unit, and SSCP

64. Which one of the following components manages as SNA system?
   A. SSCP
   B. NCP
   C. Host telecommunication access method
   D. Function Management

65. What is the SNA unit of information passed between the Host Node and the Communications Controller Node?
   A. *Path Information Unit* (PIU)
   B. *Basic Link Unit* (BLU)
   C. *Basic Information* (BIU)
   D. Frame

66. What is the SNA unit of information passed between a Subarea Node and a Physical Unit 2.0 Node?
   A. *Path Information Unit* (PIU)
   B. *Basic Link Unit* (BLU)
   C. *Basic Information Unit* (BIU)
   D. Frame

67. What is the unit of information passed between Function Management and Connection Point Management?
   A. *Path Information Unit* (PIU)
   B. Request/Response Header and Transmission Header
   C. *Basic Information Unit* (BIU)
   D. *Request / Response Unit* (RU)

68. Which of the following is not a session within an SNA system?
   A. LU to LU
   B. PU to PU
   C. SSCP to PU
   D. SCP to LU

69. What are the *Network Addressable Units* (NAUs) in an SNA system?
   A. Application Layer, Function Management Layer, and Transmission Subsystem Layer
   B. Host Node, Communications Controller Nodes, and remote nodes
   C. Host access method, Network Control Program, and access methods in remote nodes
   D. Physical units, logical units, and system services control point

70. An LU in the Host Node requests a session with an LU in a Cluster Controller Node. Select the correct sequence of sessions to accomplish the LU-LU session.
   A. SSCP-PU(CUCN), LU(host)-PU(CCN), LU(host)-LU(CCN)
   B. SSCP-PU(CUCN), SSCP-PU(CCN), LU (host)-LU(CCN)
   C. SSCP-PU(CUCN), PU(CUCN), PU(CUCN)-LU(CCN), LU(host)-LU(CCN)
   D. SSCP-PU(CUCN), PU(CUCN)-PU(CCN), PU(CUCN)-LU(CCN), LU(host)-LU(CCN)

71. What establishes a session between two LUs?
   A. An SDT command from the remote LU
   B. An SDT command from the host LU
   C. A BIND command from the remote LU
   D. A BIND command from the host LU

72. Which component creates the Request/Response Header?
    A. Function Management
    B. Path Control
    C. Data Link Control
    D. Connection Point Manager

73. Which Component creates the Transmission Header?
    A. Function Management
    B. Path Control
    C. Data Link Control
    D. Connection Point Manager

74. Which one of the following is not found in a *Request/Response Unit* (RU)?
    A. Response information
    B. Header information
    C. Request sequence number
    D. SNA commands

75. How are responses matched to requests?
    A. By sequence numbers
    B. There can be only one outstanding response when responses are specified.
    C. By the origin and destination fields of the PIU
    D. By the order in which requests are sent

76. Which one of the following is not assigned sequence numbers?
    A. Normal requests (Primary To Secondary. And Secondary. To Primary. flow)
    B. Requests that do not specify responses
    C. Expedited requests (Primary. to Secondary. and Secondary. to Primary. flow)
    D. All requests that contain SNA commands.

77. Sequence numbers are assigned to responses by:
    A. The receiving LU
    B. The sending LU
    C. The receiving Connection Point manager
    D. The sending Connection Point manager

78. Which node(s) is/are assigned a subarea number?
    A. Host Node and Communications Controller Nodes
    B. Communications Controller Nodes only
    C. Cluster Controller Nodes and Terminal Nodes
    D. All SNA nodes

79. Full duplex protocol means that:
    A. Independent requests may flow both directions simultaneously.
    B. Requests and responses may flow simultaneously.
    C. Normal and expedited requests may flow in opposite direction to each other simultaneously.
    D. Responses are not specified for any requests.

80. Half duplex protocol means that:
   A. Responses cannot be in the data path at the same time as requests.
   B. Requests on the normal flow may flow only one direction at a time.
   C. Normal and expedited requests must flow in the same direction.
   D. Responses must be specified for every request.

81. Which control modes(s) can expedited requests use?
   A. All of the following modes
   B. Only immediate request mode
   C. Only delayed request mode
   D. Only immediate control mode

82. Which control mode(s) can normal requests use?
   A. All of the following modes
   B. Only immediate request mode
   C. Only delayed request mode
   D. Only immediate control mode

83. Which NAU may initiate a change in flow direction when two LUs are using the Half Duplex Flip Flop protocol?
   A. Only the receiving LU
   B. Only the sending LU
   C. Both LUs
   D. SSCP

84. How is the direction of flow changed in a session using Half Duplex Flip Flop protocol?
   A. By the change direction command
   B. By the change direction indicator in the RU
   C. By the change direction indicator in the RH
   D. By the change direction indicator in the TH

85. A session is established to use Half Duplex Contention protocol. Which LU may send first?
   A. Defined at session initiation
   B. Only the primary LU
   C. Only the secondary LU
   D. Either LU

86. A bracket is identified by:
   A. The *Begin Bracket* (BB) and *End Bracket* (EB) indicators in the RH
   B. The BB and EB indicators in the TH
   C. The BB and EB indicators in the RU
   D. The BB and EB commands

87. Bracket protocol is specified at session initiation. Each LU is defined as either first speaker or bidder _____.
   A. at network definition
   B. by the BID command
   C. at session initiation
   D. according to which LU sends first

88. The last chain of a bracket is being sent. Which request of this chain will signal the end of the bracket?
   A. The first request of the chain
   B. The last request of the chain
   C. Anyone of the requests in the chain
   D. All of the requests will signal

89. Concerning chains, which one of the following is not true?
   A. There may be a single element (request) in a chain.
   B. There are two or more elements (requests) in every chain.
   C. Normal requests are sent as elements of a chain.
   D. Expedited requests are sent as elements of a chain.

90. Which SNA command is sent by the receiving LU, requesting the sending LU to stop sending temporarily?
   A. QC
   B. QEC
   C. RELQ
   D. *Logical Unit Status* (LUSTAT)

91. Which one of the SNA commands terminate a session?
   A. UNBIND   C. CLEAR
   B. SHUTDOWN   D. All of the above

92. A session is to be established between a host LU and remote LU that is to be connected via a switched data link. Which SNA command causes the Communications Controller Node to dial the remote station?
   A. BIND   C. ACTIVATE LINK
   B. ACTIVATE LOGICAL UNIT   D. CONNNECT OUT

93. A remote LU wishes to connect to a host LU via a switched data link. The remote station is to perform the dial operation to make the data link connection between the remote station and the Communications Controller Node. Which SNA command prepares the Communications Controller Node to receive the call?
   A. ACTIVATE CONNECT IN
   B. ACTIVATE LINK
   C. REQUEST CONTACT
   D. ASSIGN NETWORK ADDRESS

94. Which NAU may initiate a connection request for an LU-LU session?
   A. The primary LU only
   B. The secondary LU only
   C. The primary or secondary LU
   D. SSCP

95. Which NAU may initiate the action to terminate an LU to LU session?
   A. The primary LU only
   B. The secondary LU only
   C. The primary or secondary LU
   D. SSCP

96. Which response mode(s) may be specified for an expedited request?

97. The Host Node generates a PIU. What is the size of the OAF and the DAF?

98. Which SNA layer performs user processing?

99. Which SNA layer is responsible for data flow control and device dependencies?

100. Which SNA sublayer assigns sequence numbers to requests?

101. Name the technique that can be employed to control the rate of flow between PU4 nodes.

102. Name the three type of chains.
    A. Definite Response   D. Response
    B. Exception Response   E. None of the above
    C. No Response

103. Name the NAU that controls the resources local to its associated node.

104. Which SNA sublayer manages telecommunication data links?

105. Name the SDLC unit of transmission across a telecommunication data link.

106. Name the SNA command that discards all normal requests and their responses in both directions within a session.

107. Identify IBM Application subsystems.
    A. IMS   D. TSO
    B. CICS   E. All of the above
    C. RJE

108. Define VTAM and its function in the SNA Network.

109. VTAM performs the following functions:
    A. Central control point for controlling the network
    B. Acts as a pass-through for end to end LU sessions
    C. Perform end user session initiation requests for application
    D. Controls network resources
    E. All of the above

110. The Network Control Program resides in the Host.
    A. True   B. False

111. Identify the functions perform by NCP.
    A. Polling of communications controllers
    B. Provide Boundary functions to PU2 devices
    C. Collects disgnostic and message traffic information
    D. Buffers and formats data between PU2s and PU5s
    E. None of the above
    F. All of the above

112. The source program for NCP is referred to as resource definition?
    A. True   **B.** False

113. Identify the three types of *Network Addressable Units* (NAUs)?
    A. Logical Unit   **D.** NCP
    B. Physical Unit   **E.** APPN
    C. SSCP   **F.** Control Point

114. Define *Systems Services Control Point* (SSCP).

115. An SNA PU5 supports:
    A. Subarea functions   **D.** Boundary Functions
    B. SSCP   **E.** All of the above
    C. Support full network addressing

116. An SNA PU4 supports:
    A. Subarea functions   **C.** A only
    B. Supports full network addressing   **D.** D. A&B

117. A Physical UNIT 2 (PU2) can read and process FID4 headers.
    A. True   **B.** False

118. A PU2 relies on PU4 and PU5 to translate between full and local addressing.
    A. True   **B.** False

119. Define a Logical Unit.

120. There are __ types of Logical Units.
    A. 1   **D.** 7
    B. 4   **E.** 8
    C. 2   **F.** 6

121. Logical Unit 6.2 is only used in Peer to Peer networks.
    A. True   **B.** False

122. Logical Unit 3 is used for 5250 emulation.
    A. True   **B.** False

123. Logical Unit 7 is used for 3270 emulation.
    A. True   **B.** False

124. There are ___ type of sessions.
    A. 2   **C.** 4
    B. 6   **D.** 8

125. In response to question 124, identify the types of sessions.
    A. SSCP-to-SSCP   **C.** SSCP-to-LU
    B. SSCP-to-PU   **D.** LU-to-LU

126. An SNA Domain consist of the following:

A. SSCP	**D.** PU2
B. NCP	**E.** Links
C. PU5	**F.** All of the above

127. Each subarea within SNA is assigned a unique number defined in the VTAM or NCP resource definition.

A. True   **B.** False

128. A Basic Link Unit consists of:

A. Channel	**E.** X.25
B. SDLC	**F.** B & C
C. Token Ring, Ethernet, ATM, FDDI	**G.** All of the above
D. LLC	

129. The Basic information unit is made up of the following:

A. RH	**C.** PIU
B. RU	**D.** All of the above

130. Identify the sequence of a Request Unit flow through the layers.

1. RU	**4.** BIU
2. BLU	**5.** TH
3. PIU	**6.** RH

131. A *Format Identifier Header* (FID2) is used between ____devices.

A. PU4	**C.** PU3
B. PU2	**D.** PU5

132. Identify three fields in the FID2 Header.

133. Identify three fields in the FID4 Header.

134. Segmentation is not supported on the following PUs:

A. PU5	**D.** PU1
B. PU4	**E.** None of the above
C. PU2	

135. Identify the codes found in the first byte or first three bytes of the *Request Unit* (RU).

A. Bind	**D.** SDT
B. ACTPU	**E.** A & D
C. ACTLU	**F.** All of the above

136. Identify the fields that are not part of the FID2 header.

A. Virtual Route	**D.** Transmission Groups
B. Orgin and destination addresses	**E.** Segmentation
C. Explicit Routes	

137. The FID 2 header is __ bytes in length.

A. 4	**C.** 6
B. 32	**D.** 12

138. The FID 4 header is __ bytes in length.
   A. 32
   B. 26
   C. 6
   D. 8

139. The SNA data size option is called:
   A. MTU
   B. MAXDATA
   C. Payload
   D. None of the above

140. The *Start Data Traffic* (SDT) is sent by the primary LU to the secondary LU to enable sending and receiving of data.
   A. True
   B. False

141. The VTAM network resources are found in a partitioned data set named SYS1.VTAMLST.
   A. SYS1.VTAMLST
   B. SYS1.1VTAMLST
   C. SYS1.PARMLIB
   D. None of the above

142. Identify three definition statements used with NCP.
   A. BUILD
   B. HOST
   C. PATH
   D. SYSCNTRL
   E. All of the above

143. The IDBLK and IDNUM are found in the _____ section of VTAM.
   A. CDRM
   B. SWNET
   C. LOCAL
   D. CTCA

144. The LOCADDR=n specifies the:

145. Define CDRM.

146. What SNA Service manages an SNA Domain?
   A. NCP
   B. SSCP
   C. VTAM
   D. MSF

147. Define Subarea.

148. The IDNUM is __ hexadecimal digits.
   A. 3
   B. 6
   C. 8
   D. 5

149. The IDBLK is __ hexadecimal digits.
   A. 8
   B. 1
   C. 2
   D. 3

150. Define Explicit Routes.

151. Define Virtual Routes.

152. Define Transmission Groups.

153. Explicit Routes are only defined as:
  A. Bi-directional
  B. One direction
  C. Forward direction from a sub-area node
  D. Forward and backward direction
  E. None of the above

154. Identify several functions supported by Transmissions groups.
  A. Delay   D. Explicit Routes
  B. Security   E. Virtual Routes
  C. User defined   F. None of the above

155. LU 6.2 is known by this name as well:
  A. Peer-to-Peer
  B. LU 6.2
  C. Advance Program-to-Program Communications
  D. None of the above

156. Why is bracketing used in SNA?

157. Cisco 2600 and 4000 series routers use which default SDLC encoding scheme?
  A. NRZI   D. DDCMP
  B. NRZ   E. None of the above
  C. SDLC

158. A migration data host is:
  A. A VTAM host   C. Used only with the CIP card
  B. A PU4 Host   D. All of the above

159. What is the service called that allows user to access resources in another SNA Domain?
  A. Multi-Systems Networking   C. VTAM Domain
  B. Transmission Groups   D. Cross Domain Resource Manager

160. How many instances of SSCP per domain are allowed in SNA?
  A. 2   C. 3
  B. 1   D. 4

161. When a PU2 is connected to a PU5 host it provides all but the following:
  A. Rpacing   C. SSCP-SSCP Sessions
  B. Boundary functions   D. Transmission groups

162. SNA is based on what subarea networking model?
  A. Hierarchical Model
  B. Client Server
  C. Terminal to host
  D. None of the above

163. APPN is an extension of sub-area SNA with the ability to support Peer-to-peer networking.
  A. True   B. False

164. APPN *High performance Routing* (HPR) is:
   A. Connection-Less
   B. Connection Oriented at the Transport Layer and Connection Less at the link layer
   C. Connection-Less at the Transport Layer and Connection-oriented at the Link layer
   D. Connection-Oriented

165. *Intermediate Session Routing* (ISR) is:
   A. Connection-Less
   B. Connection Oriented
   C. Acknowledge connection-less
   D. All of the above

166. Define Physical Unit 2.1.

167. LU 6.2 encompasses the following SNA layers:
   A. Path Control
   B. Data Flow Control
   C. Presentation Services
   D. Data Link Control
   E. Transmission Control

168. NetBIOS circuit establishment uses the following:
   A. CANUREACH_EX
   B. ICANUREACH_EX
   C. CANUREACH_CS
   D. ICANUREACH_CS

169. DLSw sends a RR packet at each:
   A. Idle Period
   B. When connecting to a remote peer
   C. When the TCP queue is full
   D. All of the above

170. The DLSw idle time default is:
   A. 5 seconds
   B. 10 seconds
   C. 16 seconds
   D. 30 seconds

171. APPN End Nodes consist of:
   A. PU5
   B. AS/400
   C. VTAM
   D. Microsoft SNA Server
   E. All of the above

172. Hierarchical SNA is based on _____routing while APPN is ____ routing.
   A. Dynamic, Static
   B. Static, Dynamic
   C. Distance Vector, Link State
   D. All of the above

173. ____ is also know as a Physical Unit Control Point.
   A. SSCP
   B. NCP
   C. VTAM
   D. TCAM
   E. BTAM

174. A Cisco Router can be a _____Node in APPN.
   A. Network
   B. CNN
   C. LEN
   D. EN

175. What is the purpose of the `DLSw icannotreach-block-time` command?

176. APPN routing is session oriented using a session identifier called:
- **A.** Session ID
- **B.** Node ID
- **C.** *Local Form Session Identifier* (LSFID)
- **D.** None of the above

177. Identify services defined by Control Point.
- **A.** Session
- **B.** Directory
- **C.** Configuration
- **D.** Routing
- **E.** Management Topology

178. What is the purpose of the DLSw explorer-wait-time command?

179. The input hold queue is used for the following:
- **A.** Hold input frames of serial interfaces
- **B.** Hold input frames of LAN interfaces
- **C.** Implement Priority queuing
- **D.** Drop frames

180. Define Dependent LU Requester.

181. Define Composite Network Node.

182. Which device in an APPN network is a Composite Network Node?
- **A.** PU 2
- **B.** PU 4
- **C.** PU 4 and 5
- **D.** PU5

183. A Cisco Router can function as a:
- **A.** DLU Requester
- **B.** DLU Server
- **C.** A & B
- **D.** None of the above

184. What type of DLSw frame is contained within the TCP header?
- **A.** CANUREACH
- **B.** ICANREACH
- **C.** CONNECT
- **D.** Remote Connection
- **E.** Capability Exchange

```
TCP:    —-- TCP header —--
TCP:
TCP:    Source port              = 11007
TCP:    Destination port         = 2065 (DLSw-rpn)
TCP:    Sequence number          = 2939811363
TCP:    Acknowledgment number    = 2940299311
TCP:    Data offset              = 20 bytes
TCP:    Flags                    = 19
TCP:                    ..0..... = (No urgent pointer)
TCP:                    ...1.... = Acknowledgment
TCP:                    .... 1... = Push
TCP:                    .....0.. = (No reset)
TCP:                    ......0. = (No SYN)
TCP:                    .......1 = FIN
TCP:    Window                   = 20468
TCP:    Checksum                 = 3FCA (DLSw:   Header number = 1
DLSw:   Circuit priority = 1 (Low)
DLSw:   Message type = CC
DLSw:   Target = Station 000496966402
```

```
DLSw:   Origin = Station 0003000B5365
DLSw:   Origin link SAP = 72
DLSw:   Target link SAP = 69
DLSw:   Frame direction = 1 (Origin DLSw to target)
DLSw:   DLC header length = 0 bytes
DLSw:   Origin DLC port ID = 8000000
DLSw:   Origin data link correlator = 5000500
DLSw:   Origin transport ID = D1436973
DLSw:   Target DLC port ID = 636F2049
DLSw:   Target data link correlator = 6E746572
DLSw:   Target transport ID = 6E657477
DLSw:
DLSw:   --- Capabilities Exchange Request ---
DLSw:
DLSw:   Length = 282 bytes
DLSw:   GDS ID = 1520 (Request)
DLSw:   Subfield length = 5 bytes
DLSw:   Control vector type = 81 (Vendor ID)
DLSw:   OUI = 00000C
DLSw:   Subfield length = 4 bytes
DLSw:   Control vector type = 82 (DLSw version)
DLSw:   DLSw version number = 1
DLSw:   DLSw release number = 0
DLSw:   Subfield length = 4 bytes
DLSw:   Control vector type = 83 (Initial pacing window)
DLSw:   Pacing window size = 20
DLSw:   Subfield length = 18 bytes
DLSw:   Control vector type = 86 (Supported SAP list)
DLSw:   SAP control byte # 1 = FF (SAPs 00 thru 0E enabled)
DLSw:   SAP control byte # 2 = FF (SAPs 10 thru 1E enabled)
DLSw:   SAP control byte # 3 = FF (SAPs 20 thru 2E enabled)
DLSw:   SAP control byte # 4 = FF (SAPs 30 thru 3E enabled)
DLSw:   SAP control byte # 5 = FF (SAPs 40 thru 4E enabled)
DLSw:   SAP control byte # 6 = FF (SAPs 50 thru 5E enabled)
DLSw:   SAP control byte # 7 = FF (SAPs 60 thru 6E enabled)
DLSw:   SAP control byte # 8 = FF (SAPs 70 thru 7E enabled)
DLSw:   SAP control byte # 9 = FF (SAPs 80 thru 8E enabled)
DLSw:   SAP control byte #10 = FF (SAPs 90 thru 9E enabled)
DLSw:   SAP control byte #11 = FF (SAPs A0 thru AE enabled)
DLSw:   SAP control byte #12 = FF (SAPs B0 thru BE enabled)
DLSw:   SAP control byte #13 = FF (SAPs C0 thru CE enabled)
DLSw:   SAP control byte #14 = FF (SAPs D0 thru DE enabled)
DLSw:   SAP control byte #15 = FF (SAPs E0 thru EE enabled)
DLSw:   SAP control byte #16 = FF (SAPs F0 thru FE enabled)
DLSw:   Subfield length = 207 bytes
DLSw:   Control vector type = 84 (Version string)
DLSw:   Software version = "Cisco Internetwork Operating System Software.IOS (tm)
3000 Soft"
DLSw:   Subfield length = 3 bytes
DLSw:   Control vector type = 87 (TCP connections)
DLSw:   TCP connections for duration of DLSw connection = 1
DLSw:   Subfield length = 3 bytes
DLSw:   Control vector type = 85 (MAC address exclusivity)
DLSw:   MAC address exclusivity = 0 (No)
DLSw:   Subfield length = 3 bytes
DLSw:   Control vector type = 88 (NetBIOS name exclusivity)
DLSw:   NetBIOS names exclusivity = 0 (No)
DLSw:   Subfield length = 5 bytes
DLSw:   Control vector type = 8B (Vendor context)
DLSw:   OUI = 00000C
DLSw:   Subfield length = 4 bytes
```

```
DLSw:   Control vector type = D5 (Cisco version)
DLSw:   Cisco version = 1
DLSw:   Subfield length = 3 bytes
DLSw:   Control vector type = D0 (Local ack)
DLSw:   Local ack = 1 (Configured)
DLSw:   Subfield length = 3 bytes
DLSw:   Control vector type = D1 (Priority)
DLSw:   Priority = 0 (Not configured)
DLSw:   Subfield length = 4 bytes
DLSw:   Control vector type = D2 (Peer group)
DLSw:   Peer group = 0
DLSw:   Subfield length = 3 bytes
DLSw:   Control vector type = D3 (Border peer)
DLSw:   Border peer = 0 (Not configured)
DLSw:   Subfield length = 3 bytes
DLSw:   Control vector type = D4 (Cost)
DLSw:   Cost = 3
DLSw:   Subfield length = 3 bytes
DLSw:   Control vector type = D7 (Vendor specific)
DLSw:   Value = 01
DLSw:   Subfield length = 3 bytes
DLSw:   Control vector type = D8 (Vendor specific)
DLSw:   Value = 00
```

185. Explain the difference between HPR and ISR Routing in APPN.

186. Cisco supports APPN over:
    A. DLSw
    B. RSRB
    C. EIGRP
    D. OSPF

187. When a resource is found in APPN the receiving node sends back the following command:
    A. ICANREACH
    B. REACHACK
    C. LOCATEACK
    D. Locate Found

188. What is the direction of the frame in the Sniffer trace in question 191?
    A. From Destination to origin
    B. From origin to target
    C. Not enough information
    D. DLSw control frame used for status checking

189. Define Dynamic definition of dependent LUs.

190. Using Cisco's Downstream PU functionality, routers can perform the same PU2.0 Cluster controller functions as:
    A. Novell's SAA gateway
    B. IBM 3174 controller
    C. Microsoft SNA gateway
    D. All of the above

191. Cisco's Downstream Physical Unit allows the router to appear to as PU5 to downstream:
    A. PU4
    B. PU5
    C. PU2
    D. PU1

192. When using FST encapsulation with DLSw, how many bytes are saved by not using the TCP header?
    A. 10
    B. 20
    C. 5
    D. 24

193. Downstream PU definitions reduce the VTAM definitions on the host and shift them to the:
    A. Controller
    B. Router
    C. SNA Gateway
    D. Downstream Controller

194. Downstream PU reduces the overall WAN bandwidth required due to less polling and receiver ready terminations.
    A. True
    B. False

195. Describe Dedicated LU routing.

196. Describe Pooled LU routing.

197. Identify the type of Channel connections used with the Channel Interface Processor card.
    A. A. Bus and Tag
    B. ESCON
    C. Serial
    D. Frame relay

198. ESCON operates at a speed of ___mbytes per second.
    A. 4.5
    B. 10
    C. 16
    D. 17

199. Bus and Tag operates at a speed of___mbytes per second.
    A. 4
    B. 2.5
    C. 5
    D. 4.5

200. Identify the IBM communication controllers that the CIP card and IOS software can replace in some instances.
    A. 3174 controller
    B. 3172 LAN controller
    C. 3745 Front End Processor
    D. IBM S/390
    E. None of the above

201. The CIP card uses __ slot in a Cisco 7000 series Router.
    A. 2
    B. 1
    C. 3
    D. 4

202. The TN3270 server function allows the CIP to offload _____ of the TCP/IP processing from the mainframe.
    A. 50%
    B. 75%
    C. Only UDP/IP Packets
    D. ARP request and replies
    E. IP routing
    F. 100%

203. The CIP card allows users to take advantage of Cisco's SNA services such as:
    A. APPN
    B. TN3270 Server
    C. IP Offload
    D. DLSw
    E. SDLLC
    F. DLUR
    G. All of the above

204. What is the DLSw command for sending a NetBIOS explorer to a remote peer router?

A. `CANUREACH_ex`

B. `NB_NQ_ex`

C. `ICANREACH_ex`

D. `NB_NR_ex`

E. `NB_RR_ex`

F. `NB_RNR_ex`

205. Multiple *logical partition* (LPAR) connections to the mainframe using *ESCON Multiple Image Facility* (EMIF).

A. True

B. False

206. CIP appears as an _____ when transmitting SNA across a channel.

A. *External Communications Adapter* (XCA)

B. Switched major node

C. PU4

D. PU5

E. None of the above

207. CiscoWorks Blue consists of the following products:

A. Internetwork performance monitor

B. Maps

C. Internetwork Status Monitor

D. Host Netview

E. All of the above

208. HPR supports the following components:

A. DLUR

B. DLUS

C. VNODE

D. RTP

E. ANR

209. Cisco Multipath Channel is a streamlined channel protocol for *Advanced Peer-to-Peer Networking* (APPN).

A. SNA

B. APPN

C. SDLLC

D. DLSw

210. When using CMPC, the CIP opens ___communication subchannels for each adjacent SNA device, with one subchannel dedicated to reading and the other dedicated to writing.

A. 2

B. 1

C. 4

D. 6

211. APPN Rapid Transport Protocol (RTP) can be compared to:

A. UDP

B. TCP

C. SPX

D. SPP

E. None of the above

212. *Automatic Network Routing* (ANR) provides fast intermediate node routing and is similar to?

A. UDP

B. IPX

C. IP

D. CLNS

E. None of the above

213. The DLSw local-peer peer-id command is only configured on the following peer types?

A. Remote only

B. Local only

C. Both local and remote

D. Used only with Data Link encapsulation

214. He CIP IP Data gram mode doesn't support which of the following?

    A. TCP/IP offload   **C.** SNA support

    B. Telnet Server   **D.** None of the above

215. The following trace represents what type of DLSw command?

    A. `ICANREACH`   **C.** `CANUREACH_ex`

    B. `REACH ACK`   **D.** None of the above

```
DLSw:   --- Data Link Switching Protocol ---
DLSw:
DLSw:   Version = 31 (RFC 1795)
DLSw:   Header length = 72 bytes
DLSw:   Message length = 0 bytes
DLSw:   Remote data link correlator = 0
DLSw:   Remote DLC port ID = 0
DLSw:   Message type = 03 (Can U reach station)
DLSw:   Flow control = 00
DLSw:       0....... = FCI (No indicator)
DLSw:       .0...... = FCA (No ack)
DLSw:       .....000 = FCO (Repeat window operator)
DLSw:   Protocol ID = 42
DLSw:   Header number = 1
DLSw:   Largest frame size = A0
DLSw:           1....... = Don't fail circuit if size smaller
DLSw:           ..10 0... = Largest frame bit base
DLSw:           .....000 = Largest frame bit extended
DLSw:   SSP flags = 8X
DLSw:   1....... = Explorer
DLSw:   Circuit priority = 0 (Unspecified)
DLSw:   Message type = 03
DLSw:   Target = Station 400000000002
DLSw:   Origin = Station IBM    E4BD21
DLSw:   Origin link SAP = 04
DLSw:   Target link SAP = 00
DLSw:   Frame direction = 1 (Origin DLSw to target)
DLSw:   DLC header length = 0 bytes
DLSw:   Origin DLC port ID = B54F4
DLSw:   Origin data link correlator = 164E3A4
DLSw:   Origin transport ID = 1
DLSw:   Target DLC port ID = B000100
DLSw:   Target data link correlator = FF010000
DLSw:   Target transport ID = 1896960A
DLSw:
```

216. Cisco's MPC implementation supports one read channel and one write subchannel per adjacent SNA PU.

    A. True   **B.** False

217. What multi-path channel is used for communication in the Cisco IOS Release 11.3?

    A. VTAM to VTAM

    B. VTAM to APPN/Intermediate Session Routing

    C. VTAM to APPN High Performance Routing

    D. All of the above

218. The DLSw target MAC address in question 222 represents:
   A. Burned in MAC Address
   B. Locally Administered
   C. DLSw Assigned
   D. Target stations real MAC address

219. A single CIP can support _____ SNA PUs.
   A. 18000
   B. 6000
   C. 8000
   D. 5000

220. Define NPSI.

221. In the TCP/IP Profile on the mainframe, the Home statement contains a(n):
   A. LPAR
   B. Control Unit Number
   C. IP Address
   D. IODEVICE

222. Using the Claw statement identify the following fields:
   Ex. Claw 151E 00 192.6.115.130 HOSTB C7000 TCPIP TCPIP
   A. ESCON switch port #
   B. Device address
   C. Control unit logical address
   D. Channel logical address-partition number
   E. None of the above

Link the options on the claw statement with the description.

223. The Broadcast statement should be coded on the CIP configuration statement if Dynamic routing protocols are being used.
   A. True
   B. False

224. Cisco supports ____output queueing.
   A. 1
   B. 4
   C. 6
   D. 8

225. Define Priority Queuing.

226. Define *First in, First Out* (FIFO) Queuing.

227. Define Custom Queueing.

228. Define Weighted Fair Queuing.

229. When you define the priority keyword on the DLSw statement, what happens?
   A. DLSw prioritizes traffic by SNA over all other traffic
   B. DLSw identifies port numbers (2065,1981,1982,1983)
   C. DLSw opens four TCP connections
   D. None of the above

230. The queuing of traffic only occurs when the total number of outbound packets exceeds the capacity of the:
   A. Outbound interface
   B. TCP queue
   C. HDLC queue
   D. None of the above

231. The DLSw TCP port _____ defaults to high Priority.
- **A.** 2067
- **B.** 1996
- **C.** 1983
- **D.** 2065

232. The DLSw TCP port____ defaults to medium Priority.
- **A.** 1982
- **B.** 1995
- **C.** 2065
- **D.** 1981

233. The DLSw TCP port___ defaults to normal Priority.
- **A.** 1994
- **B.** 1993
- **C.** 1981
- **D.** 1982

234. The DLSw TCP port____ defaults to low priority.
- **A.** 1987
- **B.** 1988
- **C.** 1989
- **D.** 1983

235. The DLSw port 1983 carries what type of traffic?
- **A.** CANUREACH_ex
- **B.** Name_query_ex
- **C.** Datagram broadcast
- **D.** ICANREACH_ex
- **E.** All of the above

236. In order to Prioritize traffic for a particular LLC 2 session, what options must be specified?
- **A.** Source MAC Address
- **B.** Destination MAC Address
- **C.** Destination Service Access Point
- **D.** Source Service Access Point
- **E.** TCP Port Number
- **F.** Interface Type

237. Custom Queuing supports ___ queues.
- **A.** 10
- **B.** 15
- **C.** 16
- **D.** 32

238. RSRB SDLLC doesn't provide support for the following devices:
- **A.** PU2.1
- **B.** PU2.0
- **C.** PU5
- **D.** PU4

239. Remote Source Route Bridging and DLSw can use the same virtual ring number.
- **A.** True
- **B.** False

240. Cisco supports the following DLSw standards:
- **A.** DLSw version 2.0
- **B.** DLSw RFC 1495
- **C.** DLSw RFC 1795
- **D.** DLSw RFC 2166

241. Cisco supports SDLLC over the following interfaces:
- **A.** Ethernet
- **B.** Token Ring
- **C.** FDDI
- **D.** HSSI

242. In order to increase performance using SDLLC media translation, what options are available?
- **A.** LLC2 I frame size
- **B.** LLC2 ti timer
- **C.** LLC2 T2 timer
- **D.** All of the above

243. Define the purpose of the *exchange identification* (XID).

244. The Serial link connecting to the router over DLSW appears to the Front end Processor as a:
   A. SDLC device
   B. Token Ring LLC Controller
   C. SDLC definition in VTAM
   D. A & B
   E. None of the above

245. SDLLC supports the following encapsulations:
   A. IP
   B. TCP
   C. Direct
   D. Ethernet
   E. Token Ring
   F. All of the above

246. Define SDLC Stun.

247. Stun operates over the following encapsulations:
   A. HDLC
   B. Token Ring
   C. FDDI
   D. TCP
   E. IP
   F. Direct

248. Explain the Stun Route Statement.

249. Explain the Stun Group command.

250. DLSw support for SDLC is limited to the following SNA devices:
   A. PU1
   B. PU2
   C. PU4
   D. PU5

251. Identify the different Stun tunnels.
   A. Basic
   B. SDLC
   C. SDLC-TG
   D. e
   E. All of the above

252. The Stun Route Address allows the SDLC address to be:
   A. Allow the SDLC address to be modified
   B. Pass all SDLC addresses
   C. Examine for the remote peer

253. Define SDLC Stun Tunnel.

254. DLSw maintains ___ queues.
   A. 4
   B. 2
   C. 1
   D. 6

255. DLSw can use cost as a means of choosing the preferred peer router.
   A. True
   B. False

256. A link configured for Stun can run the following protocols:
   A. IPX
   B. AppleTalk
   C. SNA Only
   D. HDLC
   E. Frame Relay

257. Define *Normal Response Mode* (NRM).

258. Define Asynchronous Response Mode.

259. Define *Asynchronous Balance Mode* (ABM).

260. What is the advantage of using the loopback interface when defining a peer?

261. What is the maximum number of loop back interfaces that can be defined?
- **A.** 100
- **B.** 128
- **C.** 32
- **D.** Unlimited

262. How can a Front End processor support multiple cluster controllers with the same SDLC address?
- **A.** Use Multiple Stun Protocol groups
- **B.** Run a separate line for each controller
- **C.** Cisco doesn't support this option
- **D.** None of the above

263. Supporting Stun with Local Acknowledgement allows the Router at the Control site to appear as a:
- **A.** Front End Processor
- **B.** PU2 Device
- **C.** LU 6.2
- **D.** A & B

264. Identify two SDLC timers.
- **A.** SDLC n1
- **B.** SDLC n2
- **C.** SDLC t1
- **D.** SDLC Slow Poll
- **E.** All of the above

265. Identify several Data Link LLC commands used on the Token Ring side of the SDLC link for station activation.
- **A.** SABME
- **B.** UA
- **C.** RR
- **D.** RNR
- **E.** All of the above

266. What are the Data Link SDLC commands used on the Serial side of the SDLC link for station activation?
- **A.** Contact
- **B.** Poll/Final
- **C.** UA
- **D.** SNRM
- **E.** None of the above

267. The *Native Client Interface Architecture* (NCIA) allows SNA to be terminated in the _____.
- **A.** Router
- **B.** PU5 Host
- **C.** End Station
- **D.** Front end processor

268. Cisco supports the RFC____ for SNA over Frame Relay.
- **A.** 1795
- **B.** 1625
- **C.** 1490
- **D.** 1725

269. SNA over Frame Relay congestion control scheme depends on the congestion notification bits and the ____.
A. RPACING
B. Session Pacing
C. LLC2 Window
D. None of the above

270. Cisco Frame Relay Access supports the following:
A. PU1
B. PU5
C. PU2.0
D. PU2.1

271. Cisco Frame Relay Access support is supported with the following:
A. APPN
B. DLSw
C. Remote Source Route Bridging
D. All of the above

272. Explain SNA *Boundary Access Node* (BAN).

273. Data Link Switching is based on what RFC Standards?
A. RFC 1495
B. RFC 2166
C. RFC 1005
D. RFC 1795
E. A & B

274. DLSw provides for multi-vendor inter-operability.
A. True
B. False

275. Cisco uses ____ TCP sessions when using DLSw with Cisco routers.
A. 2
B. 1
C. 4
D. A & B

276. What Port Number is used for reading using DLSw?
A. 1983
B. 1981
C. 111
D. 2065

277. What TCP Port Numbers is used for Writing using DLSw?
A. 2065
B. 1983
C. 1986
D. 2067

278. The SSP protocol is called:
A. Simple Server Protocol
B. Switch to Switch Protocol
C. A & B
D. None of the above

279. DLSw supports the following protocols:
A. IPX
B. TCP/IP
C. SNA
D. NetBIOS over NetBEUI
E. NetBIOS over TCP/IP
F. All of the above

280. What are Ring Lists used for?

281. LSw peers cannot use different Virtual Ring numbers.
A. True
B. False

282. DLSw terminates routing Information in the:
A. Virtual Ring
B. Destination router
C. Local Ring
D. None of the above

283. Cisco supports the following encapsulations using DLSw:
A. Data Link
B. Fast Sequence Transport
C. TCP
D. All of the above

284. FST Encapsulation allows for:
A. Sequencing and delivery
B. Multi-path routing
C. Connection oriented services
D. None of the above

285. The *APPN Implementers Workshop* (AIW) DLSW standard supports:
A. Port List
B. Peer Groups
C. Border Peers
D. Direct Encapsulation
E. Ring List
F. None of the above

286. The capability exchange is used for:
A. Determine the number of TCP sessions to support
B. Vendor's ID
C. Any static MAC or Name table
D. Type of Protocols using SAP Ids
E. All of the above
F. None of the above

287. Cisco DLSw implementation supports the following Physical UNIT types:
A. PU1
B. PU 2.0
C. PU 2.1
D. PU 4
E. B & C
F. All of the above

288. Cisco's DLSw+ enhancement can only be used between Cisco Routers.
A. True
B. False

289. The DLSw Standard calls for TCP Encapsulation with Local Acknowledgements:
A. TCP/IP Encapsulation with Local Ack
B. TCP/IP Encapsulation without local Ack
C. IP Encapsulation only
D. Frame Relay encapsulation
E. All of the above

290. The Switch-to-Switch protocol performs some of the following functions:
A. Establish, restart, and take down circuits between local and remote peers
B. Mapping between SDLLC and SSP messages
C. Circumvent broadcast messaging
D. All of the above

291. DLSw allows you to extend a Source Routing Bridge hop count another ___ hops.
A. 6
B. 7
C. 1
D. none

292. What is the default Window size between Cisco Routers using DLSw?
   A. 20   C. 10
   B. 32   D. unknown

293. Define the Information Frame Header.

294. Identify the Switch-to-Switch Message types.

295. Identify the fields in the capability exchange header.

296. Define Peer groups and their use in Cisco's implementation of DLSw+.

297. Identify the advantage of using DLSw in promiscuous mode.
   A. Reduce Remote Peer Definitions at the host router
   B. Source Routing Explorer reduction
   C. RIF Termination
   D. None of the above

298. What is the Cisco DLSw Vendor ID in the capability exchange frame?
   A. 00000c   C. 0a0a00
   B. 00000a   D. 00000d

299. DLSw cache entries become stale after __ minutes if no connection is established.
   A. 15   C. 13
   B. 20   D. 21

300. Identify the DLSw Flow Control indicators.
   A. Repeat   E. Halve
   B. Increment   F. All of the above
   C. Decrement   G. A, B, & D
   D. Reset

301. What is the ring list valid range?
   A. 1–255   C. 1–64
   B. 1–128   D. 128–255

302. Explain the difference between Ring List and Ports List.

303. Explain the DLSw ICANNOTREACH SAPs command.

304. What is the disadvantage of running DLSw and RSRB in the same Router?

305. What information is exchanged in the Supported SAP list?

306. *Data Link Switching* (DLSw) is a forwarding mechanism for the IBM *Systems Network Architecture* (SNA) and IBM *Network Basic Input Output Systems* (NetBIOS) Protocol.
   A. True   B. False

307. Data Link Switching addresses the following bridging problems:
   A. DLC Time-outs
   B. DLC Acknowledgement over the WAN
   C. Flow and Congestion Control
   D. Broadcast Control of Search Packets
   E. Source-Route Bridging Hop count Limits
   F. All of the above
   G. A & B

308. NetBIOS cannot use LLC1 Link Layer services.
   A. True
   B. False

309. Identify the NetBIOS address resolution procedure.
   A. Name Query
   B. Name Recognized Frames
   C. Find name
   D. A & B
   E. A & C
   F. All of the above

310. SNA systems send ___ or ____ frames to the Null (0x00) SAP.
   A. Test, XID
   B. Test, SABME
   C. XID, RR
   D. A & B
   E. None of the above

311. SNA frames can be identified by the following link SAP ID values:
   A. 0x04
   B. 0x08
   C. 0x0c
   D. All of the above

312. The CANUREACH, ICANREACH, and REACH_ACK message types all carry the Data Link ID consisting of the following:
   A. MAC Address
   B. Link SAP IDs
   C. Curcuit IDs
   D. A & B
   E. All of the above

313. CANUREACH_ex is used to find a remote MAC and Link SAP Address.
   A. True
   B. False

314. Identify the DLSw Correlators that provide local significance only.
   A. Port _ID
   B. Transport ID
   C. SAP ID
   D. All of the above
   E. A & B
   F. A & C

315. Identify the fields that carry the largest frame size option.
   A. CANUREACH_ex
   B. ICANREACH_ex
   C. ICANREACH_CS
   D. CAUREACH_cs
   E. NetBIOS_ex
   F. NetBIOS_cs
   G. NetBIOS_NR-ex
   H. A, B, C, E, F, & G
   I. B, E G, E, & F
   J. A, B, C, D, E, F, & G

316. Define the five priority options available using the Circuit Priority byte.

317. Which protocol used with DLSw allows for Unequal SAP support?
  A. SNA
  B. NetBIOS
  C. IP
  D. IPX

318. ___ command received by either Data Link Switch will cause the two Data Link Switches to leave the CONNECTED state and attempt to restart the connection.
  A. RR
  B. SNRME
  C. SABME
  D. RNR

319. An ICANREACH_cs received after the transition to CONNECTED state indicates that more than one CANUREACH_cs was sent at circuit establishment time and the target station was found by more than ___ Data Link Switch partner(s).
  A. 2
  B. 1
  C. 4
  D. 8

320. The DLSw local cache allows for the following type frames to be reduced on the network:
  A. Receiver Ready
  B. Spanning Tree BPDU
  C. Explorers
  D. A & B
  E. All of the above

321. DLSw+ ensures that duplicate MAC addresses are found, using a cache for up to ___ DSLw peers or interface ports.
  A. 2
  B. 4
  C. 6
  D. 8

322. NetBIOS NAME_QUERY and NAME_RECOGNIZED frames exchange NetBIOS session numbers between the end stations.
  A. True
  B. False

323. The vendor ID control vector identifies the manufacturers:
  A. SAP ID
  B. OUI
  C. Circuit ID
  D. All of the above

324. The OUI is sent in non-canonical Token Ring format.
  A. True
  B. False

325. What is the DLSw duplicate-path-bias command used for?

326. What are the two types of flows which are covered by the flow control mechanism:
  A. Connection oriented
  B. ConnectionLess
  C. Unacknowledge connectionless
  D. Acknowledge connectionless

327. DLSw only works with the following interfaces:
  A. ATM
  B. Token Ring
  C. Ethernet
  D. FDDI

328. The DLSw `explorerq-dept` command:
  A. Limits the number of explorers
  B. Limits the number of explorers in the queue
  C. Applies only to FST encapsulation
  D. All of the above

329. Explain the DLSW ICANNOTREACH sap IOS Command.

330. If the TCP queue length reaches the high water mark, what LLC control commands are sent in response?
   A. RR   C. Test
   B. RNR   D. XID

331. What is the IOS command for enabling DLSw on an Ethernet interface?

332. What is the ISO command for enabing SDLC on an interface?

333. The default cache age for NetBIOS Names is:
   A. 300 seconds   C. 60 seconds
   B. 120 seconds   D. 180 seconds

334. Explain the IOS (Show DLSw capabilities command).

335. Explain the IOS (Show DLSw circuits command).

336. Explain the IOS (Show DLSw peers command).

337. Explain the IOS (Show DLSw reachability).

338. The default DLSw default pacing window is:
   A. 20   C. 42
   B. 35   D. 50

339. Before any communications can take place over DLSw, the following must take place:
   A. Establish ciruits
   B. Establish Peer Connections with local and Remote peers
   C. Router Exchange Capabilities
   D. Establish operational parameters
   E. All of the above

340. What types of traffic impose a limit on the size of a Wide Area Network using DLSw?
   A. Explorer Traffic   C. Number of NetBIOS applications
   B. Number of TCP sessions   D. Number of SNA PU 2.0 applications

341. In order to reduce NetBIOS and SNA Explorers, DLSw must be configured for Proxy Explorer and NetBIOS Name Caching.
   A. True   B. False

342. What is the number following the TCP remote peer called?
   A. Port Number   C. Ring List
   B. SAP ID   D. None of the above

343. DLSw always transfers data in:
   A. Canonical format
   B. Non-Cononical format
   C. All of the above

344. SDLC devices (PU 2.0) using DLSw must specify the following:
- **A.** IDBLK
- **B.** IDNUM
- **C.** MAC Address
- **D.** IP Address

Answers

1. B
2. Logical Unit
3. The primary or secondary LU
4. INIT-SELF,CINIT,BIND,SESSST, SDT
5. INIT-SELF,CINIT,BIND,SESSST, SDT
6. TERM-SELF, CTERM, CLEAR, UNBIND, SESSEND
7. TERM-SELF, CTERM, CLEAR, UNBIND, SESSEND
8. The SDT command is initiated by the host LU after the LU to LU session is established. This enables all nodes that support this session to allow FM data traffic.
9. A CLEAR command initiated by the host node disables FM data traffic mode.
10. It is a dynamically constructed data path on which two LUs communicate. It may be a logical half or full duplex path that consists of physical units, programming, and control blocks. An LU to LU session also includes the rules or protocol to which the two session partners will adhere when communicating, to avoid confusion. The BIND command carries the protocol.
11. LEN nodes implements a PU 2.1 appearance to the host to allow dynamic LU allocation, but does not support the directory services of APPN.
12. The Network Nodes provides all the services of an End Node but includes routing topology, and full directory services.
13. End Nodes is a full APPN node because it supports many of the APPN features and fully participates in APPN networks.
14. SSCP and the two LUs
15. The Begin Bracket indicator is set by the sending LU in the Request Header of the first message.
16. An LU sets the *End Bracket* (EB) indicator in the RH of the first request of a chain or the only request of a chain.
17. Either LU may start or end a bracket, unless a BIND parameter limits issuance.
18. This command is used by the Bidder to request permission from the First Speaker to begin a bracket.
19. This command is issued by the First Speaker, and indicates that the bidder is now allowed to initiate a bracket.
20. *Change Direction* (CD)
21. A
22. B
23. A
24. The last in chain indicator returns both LUs to the contention status.
25. Defined at BIND time.
26. E
27. C
28. D
29. A
30. K
31. B
32. A, B
33. A
34. D
35. A
36. A, B
37. Data Flow control using session; Function Management

38. Layer 2 Data Link Control
39. A
40. D
41. A, B
42. Connections Point Manager
43. Logical partitions
44. BN = Boundary Network Function performed by sub-area nodes such as PU4 and PU5
    PN= Peripheral Node Supports FID2 header formats and is always secondary
45. A
46. D
47. B, E, D, A, C, B
48. A
49. A
50. A
51. The SDLC frame uses the Frame Check Sequence placed by the sending station for recovery by the receiving station
52. A
53. By setting the final bit to on.
54. D
55. B,RR-F0 B no data to send
56. Frames numbered 3, 4, 5, 6, 7 must be retransmitted.
57. Normal Disconnect Mode
58. invalid
59. B
60. B
61. D
62. *Receiver Not Ready* (RNR)
63. B
64. A
65. A
66. B
67. D
68. B
69. D
70. C
71. D
72. D
73. B
74. C
75. A
76. C
77. A
78. A
79. A
80. B
81. D
82. A
83. B
84. C

85. D
86. A
87. C
88. A
89. B
90. B
91. B
92. D
93. A
94. C
95. C
96. Immediate Response Mode
97. 2 Bytes
98. Application/Transaction
99. Functional management Layer (FMH1-10)
100. Connection Point Manager
101. Rpacing in path control layer and session level pacing Data Flow Control layer
102. A, B, C
103. Physical Unit
104. Data Link Layer
105. Data Link Frame
106. Clear
107. E
108. VTAM is the focal point of all SNA network functions. All devices in a SNA network must be defined in VTAM. The Main task is to mediate, or act as a go-between for all network requests.
109. E
110. B
111. F
112. A
113. A, B, F
114. SSCP is the manager of an SNA Domain.
115. E
116. D
117. B
118. A
119. A
120. D
121. B
122. B
123. B
124. C
125. A, B, C
126. F
127. A
128. G
129. A, B
130. 1, 6, 4, 5, 3, 2
131. A, B, D

132. Any three of the following are correct: Mapping field; Origin Address field; Destination Address field; Expedited flow indicator; Sequence number field
133. Any three of the following are correct: TG_Sweep; VR pacing indicator; Network Priority; Initial explicit route number; Virtual Route Number; Transmission Priority field; Transmisson Group Sequence number; Destination subarea address; Source subarea address; Virtual route reset window indicator; Mapping Filed; Expedited flow indicator
134. E
135. F
136. A, C, D
137. C
138. B
139. B
140. A
141. A
142. E
143. B
144. LU local address at the physical unit
145. Cross Domain Resource Manager is responsible for handling cross-domain logons. CDRM is an NAU type and has its own element address.
146. B
147. A subarea node in SNA used format Identification 4 frames and provides boundary network functions to PU2 type NAUs.
148. D
149. D
150. Explicit Routes provide the underlying forward and reverse routes underlying Virtual Routes.
151. SNA Virtual Routes is a bidirectional route with a forward and a reverse direction. Virtual routes are used for mapping PIUs across the network between subarea network devices.
152. Transmission Groups appear as a single logical link to the rest of the network. Transmission Groups are used to mapped to explicit routes and explicit routes are mapped to virtual routes.
153. D
154. D, E
155. C
156. IBM LU2 and LU3 devices use a bracket protocol to prevent unsolicited data from interrupting a task that is currently in progress.
157. B
158. A
159. D
160. B
161. A, C, D
162. A
163. A
164. B
165. B
166. PU2.1 is known as a independent LU in APPN that can provide peer-to-peer services without the need for SSCP. It can also be a Dependent LU supporting PU2.0 functions.
167. B, C, E
168. C, D
169. A

170. B
171. E
172. B
173. B
174. A
175. This command represents the time that the router will mark a resource unreachable after failing to find it.
176. C
177. A, B, C, D
178. It represents the number of seconds that Cisco DLSw+ will wait after sending an explorer to choose the best path to a peer router.
179. B
180. DLUR is an interface to the DLUS for dependent LU session setup function. This allows Non APPN devices to operate using APPN.
181. CNN is a PU4 and PU5 combined in APPN.
182. C
183. A
184. E
185. HPR is APPN version 2 while ISR is Version 1. HPR allows for session rerouting around failed links while ISR doesn't support such functions.
186. A
187. D
188. B
189. This options allows SNA devices to define and activate LUs automatically upon power up.
190. D
191. B
192. B
193. B, D
194. A
195. Dedicated LU routing allows a downstream LU to be defined to an upstream LU. This assures that a LU will be available
196. Pooled LUs allow an Upstream LU to be used among multiple Downstream LUs but not simultaneously.
197. A, B
198. D
199. D
200. A, B, C
201. B
202. F
203. G
204. B
205. A
206. A
207. A, B, C
208. D, E
209. B
210. A
211. B, C, D
212. B, C, D
213. C
214. A

215. C
216. A
217. E
218. B, D
219. B
220. *NCP Packet Switched Interface* (NPSI) allows the NCP to connect to other SNA devices over X.25 networks. It supports both SNA and non-SNA devices. For non-SNA (asynchronous and Binary Synchronous Communications Protocol) devices, it supports conversion to SNA.
221. C
222. A, B, C, D
223. A
224. B
225. Priority queuing allows administrators to define packet filters that provide the ability to base priorities traffic on the queue number. The Queue with the highest number will be in service before all other queues. Priority Queuing uses four queues with priority values of high, medium, normal and low. If there is data present in the High Priority queue, all other queues will be starved until the High Priority Queue is empty.
226. This is Cisco's simplest form of queueing used in the IOS software. The basic principal is information placed on the queue will be serviced in the order received.
227. Custom Queuing allows Network administrators to reserve a portion of the bandwidth of an interface for each traffic class type. This Queuing options allows for flexibility in assigning various types of traffic the amount of bandwidth needed to sustain good performance without unnecessary upper layer protocol timeouts. Custom Queuing works by first defining the number of bytes that the IOS service prior to serving the next queue.
228. Weighted Fair Queuing defines traffic into two categories: Applications that require significant amounts of bandwidth and those requiring less. The objective is to provide bandwidth when required by the to types of applications.
229. B, C
230. A
231. D
232. D
233. D
234. D
235. E
236. A, B, C, D
237. C
238. A, C
239. A
240. A, B, C, D
241. A, B
242. A
243. XID is a VTAM configuration option used to identify the secondary station.
244. B
245. F
246. Serial Tunneling (Stun provides support for connecting PU4's and PU2's over a IP based network.) The Routers using TCP encapsulation, terminates the timers between the routers.
247. A, D, E, F
248. The Stun Route statement is used for routing static SNA over an IP based network. This is because SNA is a static network without dynamic routing.
249. The Stun group command ties the interface to the Stun Tunnel.
250. A, B, C, D

251.   A, B, C
252.   C
253.   SDLC Stun provides for routing based on SDLC address and supports TCP local acknowledgment.
254.   B
255.   A
256.   C
257.   One side is primary
258.   Either side can be primary
259.   Both sides are primary at the same time.
260.   It is important to use the most reliable interface in the router in order for the tunnel to stay operational. The loop back interface is a software only interface that is always operational.
261.   D
262.   A
263.   B
264.   E
265.   E
266.   A, B, C, D
267.   C
268.   C
269.   C
270.   C, D
271.   B, C
272.   BAN provides bridging over IEEE 802.5 Token Ring.
273.   A, B, D
274.   A
275.   D
276.   D
277.   D
278.   B
279.   B, C, D
280.   Direct Broadcast traffic to a specific Ring
281.   B
282.   A
283.   D
284.   B
285.   F
286.   E
287.   B, C, D
288.   B
289.   A
290.   D
291.   A
292.   A
293.   Version Number; Header Length; Remote Data Link Correlator; Remote DLC Port ID; Message Type; Flow Control
294.   CANUREACH; ICANREACH; REACH_ACK; CONTACT
295.   Vendor ID; DLSw Version; Initial pacing Window; Version String; MAC Address Exclusivity; Supported SAP List; TCP Connection; NetBIOS Name Exclusivity; MAC address List; NetBIOS Name List; Vendor context; Reserved; Vendor defined

296. Peer Groups are used to reduce the broadcast generated by SNA and NetBIOS applications that occur in a fully meshed network. This feature is a Cisco enhancement to their implementation of DLSw. Peer Groups and is very effective in controlling Broadcast explorer radiation.

297. A

298. A

299. A

300. F

301. A

302. Both options provide the same features limiting explorer traffic to selected rings

303. This option is used to limit explorer by the protocols that can be reached via this peer.

304. Both are separate processses and use lots of System resources

305. A list of Protocols supported by each peer

306. A

307. F

308. B

309. F

310. A

311. D

312. E

313. A

314. E

315. J

316. Unsupported; Low Priority; Medium Priority; High Priority; Highest Priority

317. A

318. C

319. C

320. C

321. B

322. A

323. B

324. A

325. This command determines how DLSw handles duplicate paths to a remote node using the same MAC Address.

326. A, B

327. B, C, D

328. B

329. The ICANNOTREACH command causes the originating router to send a control vector to its peer during capability exchange and not to send a canureach message type for a DSAP that is not available from the destination

330. B

331. Dlsw bridge-group (group-number)

332. sdlc dlsw (sdlc-address)

333. A

334. Used to show the capabilities used by each router during SSP setup. Capabilities include but not limited to SAPs, NetBIOS Names, MAC Addresses, DLSw Version, Vendor ID, Number of TCP sessions supported

335. This command is used to determine end to end session information.

336. Determine the status of remote peers defined

337. Examines the DLSw cache for SNA and NetBIOS end nodes.

338. A
339. E
340. A
341. B
342. C
343. B
344. B

14

ATM Architecture

Overview

This chapter introduces ATM and associated technologies. We will examine the technologies, architecture, implementation, configuration, and legacy integration.

Asynchronous transfer mode (ATM) was developed as a high-speed networking technique for public networks capable of supporting many classes of traffic. ATM can support a wide array of traffic types such as voice, video, image, and various data traffic over a single physical connection.

ATM is a packet-switching technique that uses short fixed-length packets called *cells*. Fixed length cells simplify the design of an ATM switch that allows high switching speeds. The selection of a short fixed-length cell reduces the delay and, most significantly, the jitter (variance of delay) for delay-sensitive services such as voice and video. These short cell lengths allow the switches to know exactly where to parse the header and forward the cell on to its destination. With shared media networks using variable length frames and conventional broadcast, the bridge or router doesn't know how many bytes are in each frame, thus introducing latency. (I guess that's why it's called variable length.)

Using ATM, information to be sent is segmented into fixed length cells, transported to, and reassembled at the destination. Because the length is fixed, the information can be transported in a predictable manner. This predictability accommodates different traffic types on the same network. The cell is divided into two main sections, the header and the payload. The payload (48 bytes) is the portion that carries the actual information—either voice, data, or video. The five-byte header is the addressing mechanism.

Figure 14.1 is a layered architecture allowing multiple services like voice, data, and video to be mixed over the same network. Three lower layers have been defined to implement the features of ATM. The Adaptation layer ensures the appropriate service characteristics and divides all classes of data into the 48-byte payload that makes up the ATM cell. The ATM layer takes the data to be sent and adds the five-byte header information that ensures the cell is sent on the right connection.

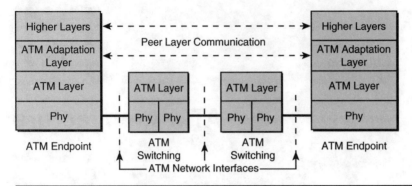

Figure 14.1 ATM network

The Physical layer defines the electrical characteristics and network interfaces. This layer "puts the bits on the wire." ATM is not tied to a specific type of physical transport. The Physical layer used in ATM provides services similar to those provided by Ethernet, token ring, and FDDI networks.

ATM has several key benefits:

- *One Network.*   ATM provides a single network for all traffic types—voice, data, video. ATM allows for the integration of networks, improving efficiency and manageability.

- *ATM enables new applications.*   Due to its high speed and the integration of traffic types, ATM enables the creation and expansion of new applications (such as multimedia) to the desktop.

- *Compatibility.*   Because ATM is not based on a specific type of physical transport, it is compatible with currently deployed physical networks. ATM can be transported over twisted pair, co-ax, and fiber optic media.

- *Incremental migration.*   Efforts within the standards organizations and the ATM Forum continue to assure that embedded networks can gain the benefits of ATM— incrementally upgrading portions of the network based on new application requirements and business needs.

- *Simplified network management.*   ATM is evolving into a standard technology for local, campus/backbone, public, and private wide area services. This uniformity is intended to simplify network management by using the same technology for all levels of the network.

- *Long architectural lifetime.*   The information systems and telecommunications industries are focusing on and standardizing ATM, which has been designed from the onset to be scaleable and flexible in the following areas:
  - Geographic distance
  - Number of users
  - Access and trunk bandwidths (As of today, the speeds range from megabits to gigabits)

This flexibility and scaleability ensures that ATM will be around for a very long time.

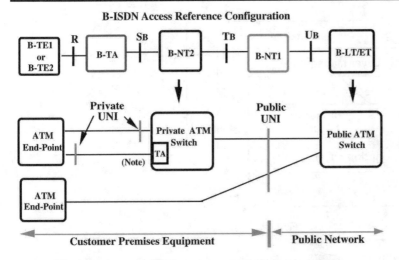

Figure 14.2   User-Network Interfaces configuration

User-Network Interface Configuration

The Public UNI is modeled after the B-ISDN *User-Network Interface* (UNI) standard defined in the *International Telecommunications Union* (ITU) Recommendations and ANSI Standards (see Figure 14.2). Public UNI embraces the physical characteristics corresponding to both U_B and T_B reference points. The Public UNI specifies the criteria for connecting Customer Premises Equipment (for example, ATM end-points, and private ATM switches) to a public service provider's ATM switch.

The Private UNI is an interface optimized for local campus or on-premise applications. It provides an alternative Physical layer interface for short distance links with reduced operation and management complexity. The Private UNI specifies criteria for connecting user's equipment (for example, workstations, servers, routers) to a private (on-premise) ATM switch.

User-Network Interface Protocol Architecture

The B-ISDN protocol reference model defined in ITU-T Recommendation I.121 is shown in Figure 14.3.

The reference model is divided into multiple planes as follows:

- *U-plane.* The User plane provides for the transfer of user application information. It contains the Physical layer, ATM layer, and multiple ATM Adaptation layers required for different service users (for example, CBR service, VBR service).

- *C-plane.* The Control plane protocols deal with call establishment, release, and other connection control functions necessary for providing switched services. The C-plane

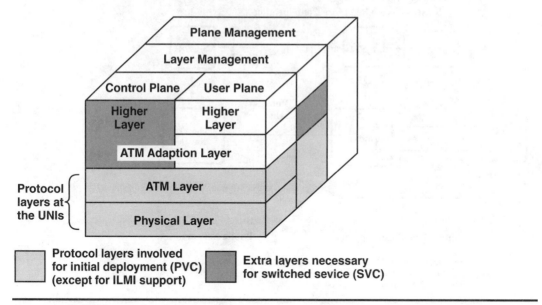

Figure 14.3   B-ISDN protocol model

structure shares the Physical and ATM layers with the U-plane, as shown in Figure 14.3. This plane includes the *ATM adaptation layer* (AAL) procedures and higher layer signaling protocols.

- *M-plane.* The Management plane provides management functions and the capability to exchange information between the U-plane and C-plane. The M-plane contains two sections: Layer Management and Plane Management. The Layer Management performs layer-specific management functions, whereas the Plane Management performs management and coordination functions related to the complete system.

Just as the OSI layered protocol model describes communication between two computers over a network, the ATM protocol model describes how two end systems communicate via ATM switches. The front and right sides of the B-ISDN protocol cube yields the two-dimensional layered model shown in Figure 14.3, which shows the functions of the four B-ISDN/ATM layers along with the sublayer structure of the AAL and *Physical* (PHY) layer, as defined in ITU-T Recommendation 1.321. Starting from the bottom, the physical layer has two sublayers: *Transmission Convergence* (TC) and *Physical Medium Dependent* (PMD). The PMD sublayer interfaces with the actual physical medium and passes the recovered bit stream to the TC sublayer. The TC sublayer extracts and inserts ATM cells within the *Plesiochronous* or *Synchronous* (PDH or SDH) *Time-Division Multiplexed* (TDM) frame and passes these to and from the ATM layer, respectively.

The ATM layer performs multiplexing, switching, and control actions based upon information in the ATM cell header and passes cells to, and accept cells from, the *ATM Adaptation Layer* (AAL). The AAL has two sublayers: *Segmentation and Reassembly* (SAR) and *Convergence Sublayer* (CS). The CS is further divided into the *Common Part*

(CP) and *Service-Specific* (SS) components. The AAL passes *Protocol Data Units* (PDUs) to and accepts PDUs from higher layers. PDUs may be of variable length, or may be of fixed length different from the ATM cell length.

Physical Layer

Let's examine the layers of the B-ISDN/ATM model starting at layer 1 and progressing up the protocol stack. The physical layer provides for transmission of ATM cells over a physical medium connecting ATM devices. The Physical layer is divided into two sublayers: the *Physical Medium Dependent* (PMD) sublayer and the *Transmission Convergence* (TC) sublayer.

The next step is to get the cells onto a physical transport medium such as fiber optics, UTP, or coaxial cable for local and wide-area network connections. This step happens at the physical layer, which is divided into two sublayers, the *Physical Medium Dependent* (PMD) and *Transmission Convergence* (TC) sublayers.

The PMD sublayer is concerned with bit transfer between two network nodes. It deals with wave shapes, timing recovery, line coding, and electro-optic conversions for fiber-based links.

The *Transmission Convergence* (TC) sublayer generates and receives transmission frames and is responsible for all overhead associated with the transmission frame. The TC sublayer packages cells inside the transmission frame. As it does this, it calculates the *header error control* information (HEC byte of the ATM cell header) and inserts it into the HEC position. Similarly, before handing a recovered cell to the ATM layer, the TC sublayer checks the header against the received HEC and discards the cell if the first four bytes are not error-free. The TC sublayer also provides bit scrambling before the ATM cells are inserted into a *Synchronous Optical Network* (SONET) frame. Only the 48 bytes of the information field are scrambled. Scrambling is used to prevent data in the information field from producing a pattern identical to the SONET framing pattern.

Many different physical layers are in use for data communications, but only a couple of rational choices are available for network services: SONET or DS3.

SONET has been defined as the bearer for BISDN using ATM as the Layer 2 protocol. The first physical layer for ATM was defined around Transmit AXI 4B/5B for fiber using the FDDI Physical Media Dependent Interface operating at 100MB.

SONET Physical Layer Architecture

The SONET transmission convergence sublayer for ATM is usually based on either an STS-3c, STS-12c, or STS-48c structure. The STS-3c 155.520 Mb/s format defines a continuous *synchronous payload envelope* (SPE) that cannot be demultiplexed into three STS-1 signals as the STS-3 format can. (The STS-3c is not unique to ATM; it is used for mapping FDDI into SONET, for example.) ATM cells are mapped into the SPE as 53-byte blocks in a horizontal format (unlike *virtual tributaries* [VTs] used to carry DS1s, which are mapped in a vertical format). Like any other SONET signal, the SPE floats inside the SONET frame structure with the H1 and H2 overhead bytes pointing to the start of the SPE. In the path overhead, the H4 byte points to the start of the first ATM cell following the H4 byte. The 622 Mb/s STS-12c is similar, but the H4 byte is not used for cell delineation. Instead, cell boundaries are established by checking the validity of an assumed HEC byte against the previous four bytes. The process is continued until agreement is found. The STS-48c operates at 2.488.32 Mbps and is specified in the ANSI T1.105-1995 and SDH VC-4-16c as specified in recommendation G.707. Frame formats are used to transport ATM cells.

The SONET STS3c frame, for example, contains 2,430 bytes arranged in 270 nine-byte columns. The payload field, columns 11-270, contains 2,340 bytes. This is not an integer number of 53-byte ATM cells, so cells are allowed to cross SPE boundaries. An STS-3c SPE can carry a little more than 44 ATM cells.

DS3 Physical Layer

Mapping cells into a DS3 signal is slightly more difficult because of the distributed frame structure of DS3. Unlike SONET, which places the framing and all the overhead in one place and then leaves a wide open field for traffic, the basic DS3 frame format intersperses frame, control, and overhead bits throughout the frame. Eighty-four information bits are always followed by one of these other bits. Furthermore, the available information field between overhead bits, 84 bits, is not an even number of bytes (but it is 21 nibbles). When ATM cells are mapped into the DS3, there is no relation between the DS3 frame and the ATM frame. The DS3 TC sublayer first creates a frame structure. (The TC sublayer used is identical to that previously chosen for carrying SMDS payloads in DS3 signals.)

Because the TC frame is to have no relation to the DS3 frame, a framing pattern is necessary to find the start of the ATM cells; this is the purpose of the A1A2 bytes. The DS3 signal provides little in the way of operations and maintenance capability in the overhead bits. Therefore, in addition to the ATM cell, bytes were included for this capability, such as the M, G, B, and F bytes. As soon as this was decided, it became necessary to add bytes to indicate which particular subframe was being addressed so one could tell the overhead bytes apart. This is the purpose of the P bytes. The Z bytes are left for growth.

This frame has a nominal period of 125 microseconds and contains 690.5 or 691 bytes, depending on trailer length. In the same 125 microsecond period, a DS3 frame provides about 690.78 bytes of information field capacity. The TC frame is mapped into a DS3 frame using a 13-nibble trailer; the second a 14-nibble trailer. The third cycle provides a stiff opportunity to maintain the nominal 125 microsecond frame rate. The C1 byte indicates the position in the cycle of a frame, whether it is a stuff opportunity position, and whether the trailer length is 13 or 14 nibbles. The TC frame is mapped into the DS3 signal on nibble boundaries, but with no relation between TC frame and DS3 frame. Scrambling is not used when ATM cells are transported by a DS3 physical layer.

Rate Decoupling

In any information transport system, the amount of traffic to be transferred may be less than the available capacity. In TDM situations, this is not a problem; a time slot is simply left empty. In ATM systems, this is a bit more of a problem because cells are packed one after another inside the SONET SPE with no gaps. The system assumes that after one cell has been delineated, they continue to come in 53-byte intervals. If a brief lull occurs in traffic, an arbitrary gap cannot be left until traffic resumes. Instead, unassigned cells are inserted to make such voids exact multiples of 53 bytes long. When traffic resumes, it follows

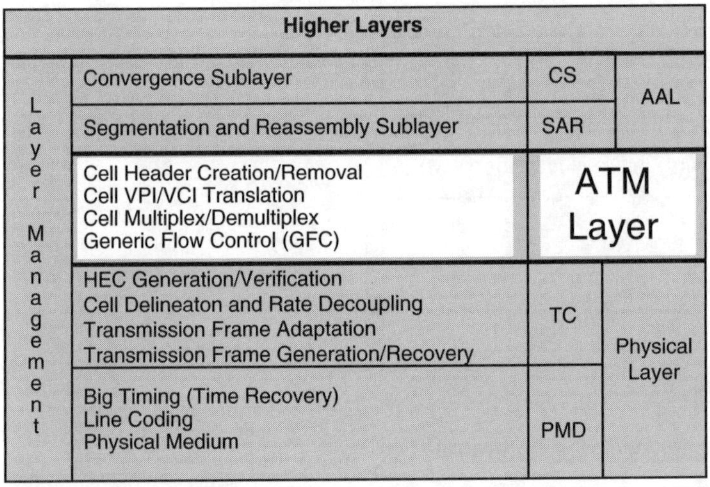

Higher Layers			
L a y e r M a n a g e m e n t	Convergence Sublayer	CS	AAL
	Segmentation and Reassembly Sublayer	SAR	
	Cell Header Creation/Removal Cell VPI/VCI Translation Cell Multiplex/Demultiplex Generic Flow Control (GFC)	ATM Layer	
	HEC Generation/Verification Cell Delineaton and Rate Decoupling Transmission Frame Adaptation Transmission Frame Generation/Recovery	TC	Physical Layer
	Big Timing (Time Recovery) Line Coding Physical Medium	PMD	

Figure 14.4 Physical layer

the end of the last unassigned cell inserted, which may entail a slight delay. Unassigned cells are identified by an address (VPI/VCI) field of all zeros.

Unassigned cells will also be used to provide rate conversion between network and user interface speed. For example, the service provider may deliver cells over an OC-3 link to a customer, but provide a DS3 physical user interface. Network equipment would discard unassigned cells to reduce the rate from 155 to 45 Mb/s and insert them as required to build it back up. In either case, the DS3 signal might still contain unassigned cells inserted by the user if the actual traffic rate were less than DS3.

Figure 14.4 shows the ATM layer providing four basic functions. It multiplexes and de-multiplexes cells of different connections. Multiplexing refers to the process of taking several different data streams and consolidating them into a fast-flow data stream. At the other end of the communication path, demultiplexing reverses the process and directs the data back to its appropriate data stream and toward its ultimate destination. Standard bodies choose a constant-length ATM cell to simplify the design of electronics in ATM switches and multiplexers. Hardware processing of variable-length packets is more complex than processing fixed-length packets. Indeed, many packet-switching devices allocate hardware buffers for each packet equal to the size of the maximum packet to simplify the hardware design. These connections are identified by their *virtual channel identifier* (VCI) and *virtual path identifier* (VPI) values. The ATM layer also translates VCI or VPI values at the switches or cross connections, if required. It's also responsible for extracting/inserting the header before or after the cell is delivered to or from the ATM adaptation layer. The primary unit of operation in ATM is the fixed-length 53-byte cell.

The ATM Cell Header

The ATM standard defines a fixed-size cell with a length of 53 octets (or bytes) made up of a five-octet header and a 48-octet payload, as shown in Figure 14.5. The bits in the cells are transmitted over the transmission path from left to right in a continuous stream.

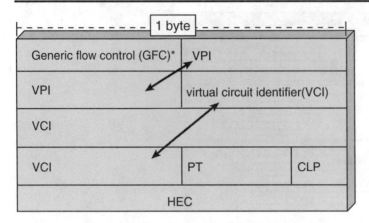

* At the NNI the GFC field becomes part of the VPI field

Figure 14.5 ATM cell header

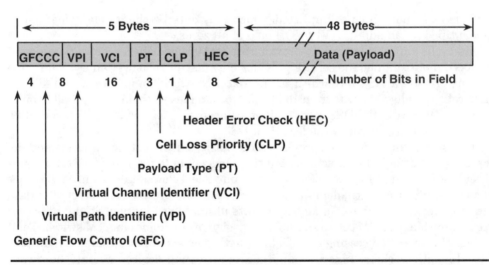

Figure 14.6 ATM cell format at *User Network Interface* (UNI)

All information is switched and multiplexed in an ATM network using these fixed-length cells. Figures 14.6 and 14.7 identify the ATM UNI and NNI headers. The cell header identifies the destination, cell type, and priority. The *virtual path identifier* (VPI) field is used to identify virtual paths consisting of eight bits across the UNI and 12 bits across the NNI. The field isn't defined by either the CCITT or ATM forums. The *virtual channel identifier* (VCI) field is 16 bits long. ATM switches assign a value to the VPI and VCI fields when end devices request a connection to an end system.

The VPI and VCI are locally significant only within a single ATM interface. Each switch translates the VPI/VCI values from input port to output port along the path of an end-to-

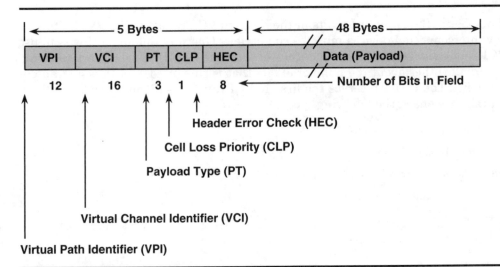

Figure 14.7 ATM cell format at *Network Node Interface* (NNI)

end connection. Therefore, the VPI/VCI values differ on the input and output ports of the same switch, which is part of an end-to-end connection. The sequence of VPI/VCI mappings in the switches along the path makes up the end-to-end connection.

We will now define each of the fields that make up the ATM cell header.

Generic Flow Control (GFC)

The first four bits of the first byte contain a *generic flow control field* (GFC). This field is used to control the flow of traffic across the *user-network interface* (UNI) and thus into the network. Exact mechanisms for flow control are still under construction, and no explicit definition for use of this field exists at this time. (This field is used only at the UNI; for NNI-NNI use (between network nodes), these four bits provide additional network address capacity.) ATM switches require more VPIs than UNIs. The format of the ATM cell at the *Network-Node Interface* (NNI) eliminates the GFC field and instead uses the four bits to increase the VPI field to 12 bits as compared to eight bits at the *User-Network Interface* (UNI).

Virtual Path Identifier (VPI)/Virtual Channel Identifier (VCI)

The next 24 bits; the last half of bytes one, two, and three; and the first half of byte four make up the ATM cell address. This three-byte field is divided into two subfields. The first byte contains the *virtual path identifier* (VPI) and the second and third byte contains the *virtual channel identifier* (VCI).

The number of bits allocated in the ATM cell header to the VPI limits each physical UNI to no more than 256 virtual paths and each physical NNI to no more than $2^{12} = 4096$ virtual paths. Each virtual path can support no more than 65,536 virtual channels on the UNI or the NNI. Although the UNI and NNI cell formats specify 8 and 12 bits respectively for the VPI and 16 bits for the VCI on both interfaces, systems typically support a smaller number of the lower-order bits in the VPI and VCI. Ranges of VPI/VCI bits supported by interconnected devices must be compatible. One way to handle this is to use the ATM Forum's *Integrated Local Management Interface* (ILMI), which allows each system to query the other about the number of bits that is supported, and thus guarantees interoperability. The ITU-T reserves the first 16 VCI values (0–15) on every VPI to indicate that cells are one of the following types:

- Idle/unassigned
- Reserved for physical layer
- VP-level *Operations Administration and Maintenance* (OAM)
- Signaling or metasignaling channel

The ATM Forum assigns the next 16 VCI values (16–31) on every VPI to indicate that cells are one of the following types:

- Integrated local management
- *Private Network-Network Interface* (PNNI) routing channel

The *Payload Type* (PT) indicates whether the cell contains

- User data
- VCC-level OAM information
- *Explicit Forward Congestion Indication* (EFCI)
- AAL information
- Resource management information

Payload Type (PT)

The next three bits of the payload type indicate the type of information carried by the cell. ATM cells are used to carry different types of user information that may require different handling by the network or terminating equipment. Cells also are used to transfer operations and maintenance messages across the network between users or between the user and service provider. Codes within this three-bit field indicate the type of message in the payload. At this time, values 0–3 are reserved for identifying various types of user data; 4 and 5 indicate management information; 6 and 7 are reserved for future definition.

Cell Loss Priority (CLP)

The last bit of byte four, CLP, indicates the *cell loss priority* and is set by the user. This bit indicates the eligibility of the cell for discard by the network under congested conditions. If the bit is set to one, the cell may be discarded by the network depending on traffic conditions. Lower-priority cells may be discarded before higher-priority cells by the *Usage Parameter Control* (UPC) at the ingress to the ATM network if cells violate the predetermined user contract, or if network congestion is experienced.

Header Error Control (HEC)

The final byte, the HEC, is the *header error control* field. HEC is an error-correcting code, calculated across the previous four bytes of the header, designed to detect multiple header errors and correct single bit errors. It primarily provides protection against misdelivery of cells due to address errors. Note the HEC does not provide any indication of the quality of data in the payload or information field.

ATM Cell Information Field

Following the HEC is the 48-byte cell information field containing the user data. Inserting user data into the information field is accomplished by the *ATM adaptation layer* (AAL). Note that depending on the type of adaptation process, not all 48 bytes are user information. Up to four bytes may be used by the adaptation process itself. The *ATM Adaptation Layer* (AAL) converts ATM cell streams into formats that a broad range of different applications can use.

AAL Service Attributes Classified

ITU-T Recommendation 1.362 defines the basic principles and classification of AAL functions. The attributes of the service class are the timing relationship required between the source and destination, whether the bit rate is constant or variable, and whether the connection mode is connection-oriented or connectionless. The service class is a separate concept from the ATM layer's service category and *quality of service* (QoS). The service class (or bearer capability), service category, and QoS class (or optionally, explicit parameters) can all be signaled separately in a SVC call setup message. Following is a summary of the four currently defined AAL service classes, labeled A through D:

- *Class A.*   *Constant Bit Rate* (CBR) service with end-to-end timing, connection-oriented
- *Class B.*   *Variable Bit Rate* (VBR) service with end-to-end timing, connection-oriented
- *Class C.*   VBR service with no timing required, connection-oriented
- *Class D.*   VBR service with no timing required, connectionless

AAL Protocol Structure Defined

The B-ISDN protocol model adapts the services provided by the ATM layer to those required by the higher layers through the AAL. Figure 14.8 depicts the structure and logical interfaces of the AAL. An AAL *Service Access Point* (SAP) provides services to higher layers by passing primitives (for example, request, indicate, response, and confirm) concerning the *AAL Protocol Data Units* (AAL-PDUs).

Standards further subdivide the AAL into the *Convergence Sublayer* (CS) and the *Segmentation and Reassembly* (SAR) sublayer. The CS is further subdivided into *Service-Specific* (SS) and *Common Part* (CP) components. The SSCS may be null, which means it does nothing. The CPCS must always be implemented along with the SAR sublayer. These layers pass primitives regarding their respective PDUs among themselves, resulting in the passing of SAR-PDU primitives (which is the ATM cell payload) to and from the ATM layer via the ATM-SAP.

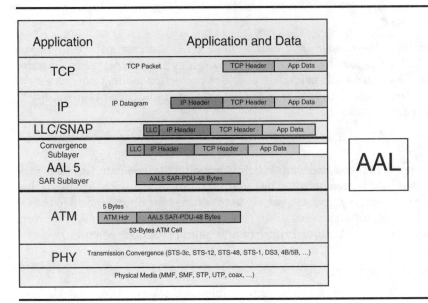

Figure 14.8   The structure and logical interfaces of the AAL

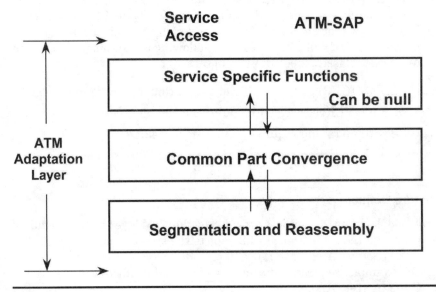

Figure 14.9   AAL layers

The layered AAL protocol model is rather abstract, so let's look at it from another point of view down at the PDU level. Figure 14.10 depicts the ATM layer at the bottom and moves up to the AAL SAR sublayer and up through the AAL CS sublayers to the higher-layer protocol. This model follows the general layered methodology first defined in the OSI reference model. The PDU at each layer has a header, and optionally a trailer, that conveys information for use at the particular sublayer. Starting at the bottom of the figure, the ATM layer

- 1 octet header and 47 octets of payload

- Sequence number (SN) consists of 1-bit CSI and a 3-bit SN to detect deletion or misinserted cells

- Sequence number protection (SNP) consist of a 3-bit CRC with even parity for correcting SN errors

SAR PDU Header

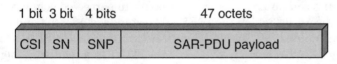

Figure 14.10   The AAL protocol model at the PDU level

passes cell payloads from cells with valid headers up to the AAL SAR sublayer for a particular VCC. The SAR sublayer interprets the header (and optional trailer) for SAR-PDUs constructed from the cell payloads. The SAR-PDU and cell payload boundaries need not be aligned. If the SAR layer successfully reassembles an entire AAL CPCS-PDU, it passes it up to the CPCS layer, which has its own header and optional trailer. The CPCS layer extracts the AAL SDU. If the AAL-SSCS layer is null, the AAL-SDU is passed directly to the AAL user across the AAL SAP.

If the SSCS sublayer is non-null, the CPCS sublayer passes its payload up to the SSCS sublayer. The SSCS sublayer finally extracts the AAL-SDU using its header and optional trailer. In some AAL definitions, the SSCS layer may derive multiple AAL *Interface Data Unit* (IDUs) from a single SSCS-PDU to the higher-layer protocol. If the SSCS is null, the IDU is exactly the same as the CPCS payload. The process of receiving AAL-IDUs from the higher-layer protocol and processing them down through the AAL convergence sublayer and segmentation is the reverse of the previous process.

The IDU provides the all-important interface to the AAL that makes the cell level accessible to voice, video, and packet data applications, as shown in later chapters. The IDU, for example, is the API in the Windows operating system for packet-layer transmission. In the case of AAL1 emulating a TDM circuit, the IDU is a sequence of bits. The following sections summarize the CPCS and SAR sublayer for each of the currently standardized CP AALs:

- AAL1—constant bit rate traffic
- AAL3/4—variable bit rate traffic
- AAL5—lightweight variable bit rate traffic

ATM Adaptation Layer

The ATM adaptation layer is arguably the single most important layer of the ATM communications process. This AAL gives ATM the versatility to carry many different types of service from continuous processes like voice to the highly bursty messages generated by LANS, all within the same format. Interestingly enough, the AAL is not a network process, but is performed by the network terminating equipment on the user side of the UNI. The

AAL is what frees the network from worrying about many different classes of traffic and enables it to concern itself only with routing cells from one point to another based on the information contained in the header (see Figure 14.11).

The ITU-T initially defined AAL1 through AAL4 to directly map AAL service classes A through D. The history of AAL development for VBR services changed this simple concept. Initially, AAL3 was targeted for connection-oriented services, whereas AAL4 would support connectionless services. However, as the experts defined the details, they realized that AAL3 and AAL4 were common enough in structure and function to be combined into one, called AAL3/4. AAL5 was conceived by the computer industry in response to perceived complexity and implementation difficulties in AAL3/4, which the IEEE 802.6 standard adopted and applied to SMDS. Initially, AAL5 was named the *Simple Efficient Adaptation Layer* (SEAL) for this reason. AAL5 was adopted by the ATM Forum, ANSI, and the ITU-T in a relatively short time compared to the usual standards process and has become the predominant AAL of choice in a great deal of data communications equipment. AAL5 is employed for the transport of signaling messages and frame relay. AAL1 was defined by the ITU-T and further clarified in the ANSI T1.630 and ATM Forum circuit emulation standards for CBR applications. The standards bodies have not yet competed AAL2, intended to support variable bit-rate voice and video.

We will now examine each of the AAL types in more detail and, with the architectures, how they are implemented.

AAL1: Constant Bit Rate (CBR) Services.   This AAL handles isochronous traffic like DS0s and DS3s, allowing an ATM network to emulate voice or DS services. This process is fairly well defined and includes mechanisms for recovering source timing of the data.

The AAL1 header is shown in Figure 14.12.

The AAL1 protocol specifies the means to

- Transfer service data units received from a source at a constant source bit rate and deliver them at the same bit rate to the destination

- Optionally transfer timing information between source and destination

Class:	A	B	C	D
Examples	Voice/ Video	Packet Video	Data IP, X.25	Data SMDS
Connection Mode	Connection - Oriented			Connec- tionless
Bit Rate	Constant	Variable		
ATM Adaptation Layer	AAL 1	AAL 2	AAL 3/4 AAL 5	AAL 3/4

Figure 14.11 The AAL allows the network to focus on routing cells.

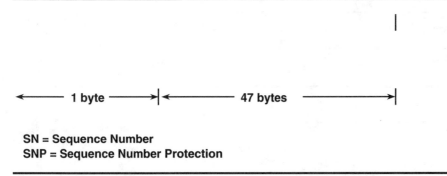

←——— 1 byte ———→|←——— 47 bytes ———————→|

SN = Sequence Number
SNP = Sequence Number Protection

Figure 14.12   AAL1 header

- Optionally transfer structure information between source and destination
- Optionally perform *Forward Error Correction* (FEC) on the transferred data
- Optionally indicate the status of lost or erroneous information

The AAL1 SAR sublayer provides the following services:

- Map between the 47-octet CS-PDU and the 48-octet SAR-PDU using a one-octet SAR-PDU header
- Indicate the existence of CS function using a bit in the SAR-PDU header
- Generate sequence numbering for SAR-PDUs at the source and validate received sequence numbers at the destination before passing them to the CS sublayer
- Perform error detection and correction on the *Sequence Number* (SN) field

The AAL1 CS defines various functions needed for the transport of *Time Division Multiplexing* (TDM) circuits, video signals, voiceband signals, and high-quality audio signals. The AAL1 CS protocol provide a menu that these higher-layer applications use to provide required service features (for example, timing recovery), deliver end-to-end performance (for example, loss and delay), and account for anticipated network impairments (for example, cell loss and delay variation).

AAL 2: Variable Bit Rate (VBR) Timing Sensitive Services.   This AAL is presently undefined but reserved for data and data services requiring transfer of timing between the end point. Packet video is the most often cited service requiring this AAL. (See Figure 14.13.) Although video may seem like a continuous service better served by a Type 1 AAL, video compression algorithms tend to generate bursty messages of very irregular lengths. This AAL is intended to interface such video codecs directly into ATM services in their native bursty mode, eliminating complex buffers and rate smoothing circuits now used to produce DS0 or DS1 interfaces.

AAL3/4.   AAL3 and AAL4 are combined into a single CP, AAL3/4, in support of VBR traffic, both connection-oriented and connectionless. Figure 14.14 depicts the SAR and CS sublayers for AAL3/4. Starting from the bottom of the figure, the 48-octet payload of a sequence of cells on the same *Virtual Channel Connection* (VCC) (that is, cells having the same *Virtual*

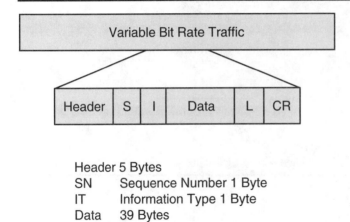

Header 5 Bytes
SN   Sequence Number 1 Byte
IT   Information Type 1 Byte
Data   39 Bytes
LI   Length Indicator 1 Byte
CRC   Cyclic Redundancy Check 1

Figure 14.13   AAL2 header

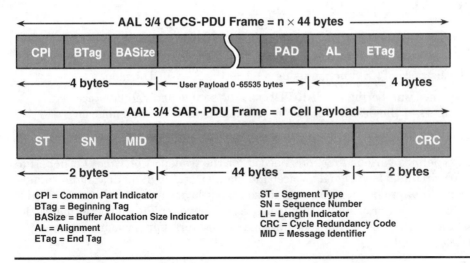

Figure 14.14   AAL 3/4

Path Identifier [VPI] and *Virtual Channel Identifier* [VCI] values) are passed up to the AAL3/4 SAR sublayer. The AAL3/4 SAR-PDU encoding and protocol function and format are nearly identical to the Layer 2 PDU defined in the IEEE 802.6 *Distributed Queue Dual Bus* (DQDB) standard. A two-bit *Segment Type* (ST) field indicates whether the SAR-PDU is a *Beginning of Message* (BOM), a *Continuation of Message* (COM), or an *End of Message* (EOM). The protocol also defines a *Single Segment Message* (SSM). The two-bit SN is incremented by the sender and checked by the receiver. Numbering and checking begins when an ST or BOM is received. The 10-bit *Multiplex Identification* (MID) field allows as many as

1,024 different CPCS-PDUs to be multiplexed over a single ATM VCC, allowing multiple logical connections to be multiplexed over a single VCC. This is important when a carrier charges per VCC, which motivates users to do their own multiplexing to minimize cost. The SAR-PDU trailer has two fields: a six-bit *Length Indicator* (LI) that specifies how many of the octets in the SAR-PDU contain CPCS-PDU data, and a *Cyclic Redundancy Check* (CRC).

When all SAR-PDUs are received in sequence and with correct CRC values, the reassembled packet is passed up to the CPCS layer. The *Common Part Indicator* (CPI) indicates the number of counting units (bits or octets) for the *Buffer Allocation Size* (BASize) field. The sender inserts the same value for the two-octet *Beginning Tag* (BTag) and *Ending Tag* (ETag) so the receiver can match them as an additional error check. The two-octet BASize indicates to the receiver how much buffer space should be reserved to reassemble the CPCS-PDU. A variable-length padding field (PAD) of between 0 and 3 octets is inserted into the CPCS-PDU, an integral multiple of 32 bits to make end-system processing simpler.

The trailer has three fields, as shown in Figure 14.14. The one-octet *Alignment* field (AL) makes the trailer a full 32 bits to simplify the receiver design. The length field encodes the length of the CPCS-PDU field so the pad portion may be subtracted before the payload is delivered to the CPCS user. In message mode, AAL3/4 accepts one AAL-IDU at a time and optionally sends multiple AAL-IDUs in a single SSCS-PDU. In streaming mode, the higher-layer protocol may send multiple AAL-IDUs separated in time; the SSCS may deliver these in multiple AAL-IDUs, or reassemble the pieces and deliver only one AAL-IDU. The principal advantages of AAL3/4 are multiplexing of multiple logical connections over a single ATM VCC, additional error checking fields, and the indication of message length in the first cell that can be used for efficient buffer allocation in intermediate switches.

AAL 5: Simple and Efficient Adaptations Layer (SEAL)

If AAL1, AAL2, and AAL3/4 seem complicated, you can now appreciate the motivation for developing SEAL. The ATM Forum assigned the next available number to this lightweight protocol, which made it AAL5. The SEAL format is a well-defined AAL that offers improved efficiency over AAL3/4. It serves the same purpose, but by assuming that current higher layer processes will provide error recovery, simplifies the SAR portion of the adaptation layer to pack all 48 bytes of the cell information field with data. From this point of view, the SEAL AAL5 makes ATM look like high-speed frame relay. The SEAL AAL5 also assumes that only one message is crossing the UNI at a time. That is, multiple end users at one location cannot interleave messages on the same VC, but must queue them for sequential transmission.

Figure 14.15 depicts the SAR and CPCS layers for AAL5. The relative simplicity of AAL5 should be readily apparent by comparing this figure with Figure 14.14. Starting from the ATM cell stream on a single VCC at the bottom of the figure, note that the only overhead the SAR sublayer uses is the payload type field in the last cell of a sequence of cells corresponding to a single PDU (that is, packet). A nonzero value of the AAL_Indicate field identifies the last cell of the sequence of cells, indicating that reassembly should begin.

This was intended to make the reassembly design simpler and make more efficient use of the ATM bandwidth than AAL3/4, which was the root of the name for the original AAL5 proposal. The CPCS payload may be any integer number of octets in the range of 1 to 2¹⁶-1 (that is, 65,535). The PAD is of a variable length chosen such that the entire CPCS-PDU is

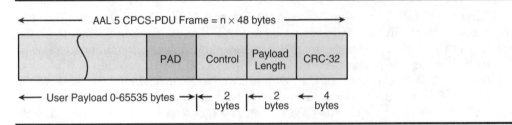

Figure 14.15 AAL5 header

an exact multiple of 48 so it can be directly segmented into cell payloads. The *User-to-User* (UU) information is conveyed between AAL users transparently. The only current function of the CPI is to align the trailer to a 64-bit boundary, with other functions being the subject of further study. The length field identifies the length of the CPCS-PDU payload so the PAD can be removed. Because 16 bits are allocated to the length field, the maximum payload length is 2^{16} -1 65,535 octets. The CRC-32 detects errors in the CPCS-PDU. The CRC-32 is the same one used in IEEE 802.3, IEEE 802.5, FDDI, and Fiber Channel.

Control Plane Overview

The control plane handles all virtual connection related functions; most importantly, the switched virtual circuit capability. The control plane also performs the critical functions of addressing and routing. The higher-layer, service-specific AAL portions of the signaling protocol are now well standardized.

The control plane provides the means to support the following types of connections on behalf of the user plane:

- *Switched Virtual Connections* (SVCs)

- *Semipermanent Virtual Connections* (SPVCs)

SVCs and SPVCs can be either point-to-point or point-to-multipoint *Virtual Path Connections* (VPCs) or VCCs. A VPC or VCC of a particular service category provides a specified QoS for specified traffic parameters in an ATM-layer traffic contract. SVCs allow users or applications to set up connections on demand, such as using services like LAN Emulation and Multiprotocol instead of ATM.

The specifications for the *Service-Specific Connection-Oriented Protocol* (SSCOP) provide a guaranteed, reliable packet delivery service to all signaling protocols, as indicated in the figure. First, we will cover the signaling protocols at the *User-to-Network Interface* (UNI). The ATM Forum has produced three versions of UNI signaling protocols numbered 3.0, 3.1, and 4.0. ITU-T Recommendation Q.2931 specifies B-ISDN signaling on the ATM UNI. The ITU-T's formal name for the ATM UNI signaling protocol is the *Digital Subscriber Signaling System 2* (DSS2), a natural evolution from the DSS1 name employed for ISDN UNI signaling.

The *Network-Node Interface* (NNI) signaling protocols are used between switches and between networks. B-ISDN adapts the *ISDN User Part* (ISUP) at the NNI in a manner similar to narrowband ISDN, resulting in a protocol called B-ISUP. The ATM Forum's adaptation of BISUP at the NNI for a *Broadband Intercarrier Interface* (B-ICI) has two versions, 2.0 and 2.1, aligned with UNI 3.1. The ATM Forum defined an *Interim Inter-switch Signaling Protocol* (IISP) as a simple, multivendor interoperable NNI protocol. Finally, the ATM Forum's PNNI protocol defines not only signaling at the NNI, but a scaleable, hierarchical topology distribution and routing protocol.

To date, the following SSCS protocols have been developed specifically for the user plane:

- SSCOP
- *Frame relay SSCS* (FR-SSCS)

Although SSCOP was originally developed for signaling, some proprietary user plane higher-layer implementations use it to provide an assured data transfer service in the user plane, such as ATM over satellite networks. More SSCS protocols likely be defined in the future as standards work on the B-ISDN protocol suite progresses.

The management plane covers the layer management and plane management functions. Layer management interfaces with the Physical and ATM layers, AAL, and higher layers. Plane management is responsible for coordination across layers and planes in support of the user and control planes through layer management facilities. This ensures that everything works properly. Layer management will be discussed first, followed by plane management.

Layer Management

This two-dimensional view results from cutting the B-ISDN cube open from the back and then folding it out flat. Standards for these management interfaces are being defined by the ITU-T and the ATM Forum for telecommunications equipment using the *Common Management Information Protocol* (CMIP). Some higher-layer User plane and Control plane functions are defined by the IETF and the ATM Forum using the *Simple Network Management Protocol* (SNMP). Note that standards for the Physical, ATM, and Common Part AALs are identical for both the Control and User plane.

Layer management has the responsibility for monitoring the User and Control planes for faults, generating alarms, and taking corrective actions, as well as monitoring for compliance with the performance stated in the traffic contract. The operation and maintenance information functions found within specific layers are handled by layer management. These functions include fault management, performance management, and configuration management. The standards for physical-layer management utilize overhead fields within the physical bit stream and are well defined in wide area networks. The standards for ATM-layer fault and performance management are now well defined. Standardization for management for the AAL and higher layers exists mainly in the definition of object-oriented *Management Information Bases* (MIBs). Standards-based *Network Management Systems* (NMSs) can then utilize the objects within these MIBs to determine status, detect failures, and automatically configure the managed network element.

Management Plane

Plane management has no defined structure, but instead performs management functions and coordination across all layers and planes in the entire system. The *Telecommunication Management Network* (TMN) architecture developed by the ITU-T for managing all types of telecommunications networks is being extended to perform the B-ISDN plane management role.

Signaling and Routing in the Control Plane

The B-ISDN Control plane performs a pivotal role in the switched virtual connection service. First, we summarize the signaling protocol stacks, showing their relationship to basic telephony and ISDN. SVC signaling protocols operate in an analogous manner to using a telephone. However, in ATM there are many more parameters, such as different logical channel and physical network level addresses, quality of service categories, and traffic parameters. Specifically formatted fields, called *Information Elements* (IEs), convey these user requests within B-ISDN signaling messages. We summarize the definition and use of signaling messages to help you understand the basic functions available to the signaling user. Remember that in many applications employing ATM, a computer program, and not a human being, issues the B-ISDN signaling messages, as is frequently the case in the telephone network.

We then summarize the signaling AAL, specifically the Service-Specific Coordination Function and Service-Specific Connection-Oriented Protocol that provide reliable data transport for the signaling messages. Next, we discuss the UNI signaling protocols by introducing the key signaling messages and their information elements. Simple examples of point-to-point and point-to-multipoint signaling procedures illustrate how users and networks employ the messages to establish and release connections. The treatment addresses the simplest network-network protocol first—the ATM Forum's Interswitch Signaling Protocol—before moving on to a more complex protocol: the ATM Forum's *Private Network-Network Interface* (PNNI). The sophisticated PNNI protocol combines concepts from B-ISDN signaling, local area networks, and Internet routing to automatically provide guaranteed quality and routing in networks that can scale to global proportions.

The B-ISDN control plane handles all virtual connection related functions, most importantly *Switched Virtual Circuits* (SVCs). The control plane also performs the critical functions of addressing and routing. The higher-layer and service-specific AAL portions of the signaling protocol are now well standardized.

Use of Signaling Protocols

ATM switches are connected together in networks, which in turn may interconnect with other networks. These networks uses various types of signaling. Usually, a private switched network is connected to one or more public switched networks. ATM switches are connection-oriented devices that utilize signaling protocols to establish connections. Users interface to switches and communicate the connection request information via a *User-Network Interface* (UNI) signaling protocol. Between switches, an interswitch protocol may be used. Networks are interconnected via a more complex *Network-Network Interface* (NNI) signaling protocol. Signaling functions also may be emulated by network management protocols that make individual ATM cross-connects, often at a very slow rate. Some higher-layer protocols require that ATM devices set up large numbers of connections. For example, in LAN Emulation, an SVC is set up to each link-layer LAN address. Although each user would typically set up only a few connections to various servers, the aggregate call rate will scale roughly with the number of LAN users. The basic ATM signaling architecture responds to this challenge by distributing intelligence to each device, thus maximizing scaleability of B-ISDN networks by eliminating any centralized control.

The specifications for the *Signaling AAL* (SAAL) were developed by the ITU-T and subsequently adopted by the ATM Forum, ETSI, and ANSI. ITU-T Recommendation Q.2931 (previously called Q.93B) specifies the B-ISDN signaling on the ATM UNI. The two don't interoperate, so beware of equipment vendors peddling support for the older, preliminary Q.93B standard. Q.2931 was derived from both the Q.931 UNI signaling protocol specified for N-ISDN and the Q.933 UNI signaling protocol for frame relay. The formal name for the ATM UNI signaling protocol is the *Digital Subscriber Signaling System 2* (DSS2), the next step after the DSSL signaling used for ISDN. ITU-T Recommendation Q.2130 (previously called Q.SAAL.2) specifies the *Service-Specific Coordination Function* (SSCF) for the UNI. ITU-T Recommendation Q.2110 (previously called Q.SAAL.1) specifies SSCOP. The *ISDN User Part* (ISUP) is being adapted to broadband in a manner similar to the way the UNI protocol was used in defining the parameters of broadband NNI signaling; the result is called B-ISUP. The B-ISUP protocol operates over the *Message Transfer Protocol 3* (MTP3), identical to that used in *Signaling System 7* (SS7) for out-of-band N-ISDN and voice signaling. This will allow B-ISDN network signaling the flexibility to operate over existing signaling networks or directly over new ATM networks. The series of ITU-T Recommendations Q.2761 through Q.2764 specify the B-ISUP protocol. ITU-T Recommendation Q.2140 specifies the SSCF at the NNI. The NNI signaling uses the same SSCOP protocol as the UNI.

Control Plane Addressing and Routing Defined

Two capabilities are critical to a switched network: addressing and routing. *Addressing* occurs at the ATM *Virtual Path Identifier/Virtual Channel Interface* (VPI/VCI) level and at the logical network level. Because the VPI/VCI is unique only to a physical interface, there is a need to have a higher-level address unique within each network. Ideally, the address should be unique across all networks in order to provide universal connectivity. After each entity involved in switching virtual connections has a unique address, another even more onerous problem exists: finding a route from the calling party to the called party. *Routing* solves this problem by using either static, manual configuration, or dynamic, automatic discovery.

ATM Layer Addressing. The signaling protocol automatically assigns the VPI/VCI values to ATM addresses and physical ATM UNI or NNI ports according to a set of rules. SVCs may be either point-to-point or point-to-multipoint. Each physical ATM UNI port must have at least one unique ATM address in order to support SVCs. An ATM UNI port may have more than one ATM address. Also, in some cases, the same ATM address may be assigned to more than one UNI port within a network. This case is called an anycast address, where the network routes SVCs to the anycast port that is closest to the source. Anycast enables a user to request an ATM connection to a group of ATM nodes.

Recall that a *Virtual Channel Connection* (VCC) or *Virtual Path Connection* (VPC) is defined in only one direction; that is, it is simplex. A point-to-point duplex SVC or a *Permanent Virtual Connection* (PVC) is actually implemented as a pair of simplex VCCs or VPCs:

a forward connection from the calling party to the called party, and a backward or return connection from the called party. Applications may request different forward and backward traffic parameters, for example, as would be used in a video broadcast or in the transfer of a large file or database backup.

ATM Signaling and Addressing.   Currently two types of ATM Control Plane (SVC) addressing plans identify an ATM UNI address: a data-oriented *Network Service Access Point* (NSAP) format defined by the International Standards Organization and the telephony-oriented ITU-T E.164 standard.

An ATM address may be a native E.164 number up to 15 digits in length, or a 20-octet ATM Endsystem Address based on the ISO NSAP encoding format. This format is highlighted in Figure 14.16. Use of the standard ATM addresses for private and public networks is specified in this section. Procedures to register addresses across UNI ATM signaling protocols vary by the type of ATM link. ATM UNI signaling is used between an ATM end-system and an ATM switch across an ATM UNI; ATM NNI signaling is used across NNI links. UNI signaling requests are carried across the UNI in a well known default connection: VPI=0, VCI=5. The UNI 3.1 specification is based upon Q.2931, a public network signaling protocol developed by the International Telecommunications Union-Telecommunications, which in turn was based upon the Q.931 signaling protocol used with *Narrowband ISDN* (N-ISDN). The ATM signaling pro-

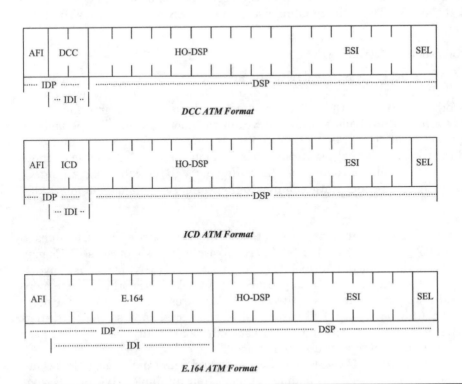

Figure 14.16   ATM addressing

tocols run on top of a *Service-Specific Convergence Protocol* (SSCOP), defined by the ITU-T Recommendations Q.2100, Q.2110, and Q.2130.

Private Networks

For the purposes of switched virtual connections established by the procedures of this specification, an ATM endsystem address identifies one or more ATM endpoints. The format of an ATM address for endpoints in private ATM networks is modeled after the format of an OSI Network Service Access Point, as specified in ISO 8348 and ITU-T X.213; specifically, using the same structure, abstract semantics, abstract syntax, and preferred binary encoding. The structure of the low-order part (ESI and SEL) of the *Domain Specific Part* (DSP) is as specified in ISO 10589. Three *Initial Domain Identifier* (IDI) formats are specified in this specification.

In ATM networks, there are two types of ATM addresses: individual and group. An ATM individual address identifies a single ATM end system, whereas an ATM group address identifies one or more ATM end systems.

The ability of an endpoint to originate a call to any other endpoint shall be independent of the structure of the ATM address of the called system. All private networks shall be able to accept the initial call setup messages containing ATM addresses with any of the IDI formats that are listed in this chapter and progress the corresponding call towards the destination endpoint, if it is reachable. Selection of one of the IDI formats to be used for the addresses of endpoints attached to any particular private ATM network is beyond the scope of this specification.

The *Initial Domain Part* (IDP) uniquely specifies an administration authority with the responsibility for allocating and assigning values of the *Domain Specific Part* (DSP). The IDP consists of two fields, the *Authority and Format Identifier* (AFI) and *Initial Domain Identifier* (IDI). The AFI identifies the authority allocating the Data Country Code, International Code Designator, or E.164 number, the format of the IDI, and the syntax of the remainder of the address. The length of this field is one octet as shown in Table 14.1.

Data Country Code

The Data Country Code specifies the country in which an address is registered. The codes are given in ISO 3166. The length of this field is two octets. The digits of the Data Country Code are encoded in *Binary Code Decimal* (BCD) syntax. The codes are left-justified and padded on the right with the hexadecimal value "F" to fill the two octets.

Table 14.1   **IDP codes**

	AFI		Format
Hexadecimal	**Bits**		**Format**
0x39	0 0 1 1	1 0 0 1	DCC ATM Format
0x47	0 1 0 0	0 1 1 1	ICD ATM Format
0x45	0 1 0 0	0 1 0 1	E.164 ATM Format

International Code Designator (ICD)

The *International Code Designator* (ICD) identifies an authority that administers a coding scheme. The body responsible for the coding scheme identified by the ICD provides an Administrative authority that is responsible for the allocation of identifiers within this coding scheme to organizations. The registration authority for the International Code Designator is maintained by the British Standards Institute. The length of this field is two octets. The digits of the ICD are encoded in *Binary Coded Decimal* (BCD) syntax. The codes are left-justified and padded on the right with the hexadecimal value "F" to fill the two octets.

E.164

E.164 specifies Integrated Services Digital Network numbers. These numbers include telephone numbers. The international format of these numbers is used, meaning the numbers can be up to 15 digits long. The length of this field is eight octets. The digits of the E.164 number are encoded in *Binary Coded Decimal* (BCD) syntax. The E.164 address is padded with as many leading semi-octets 0000 as needed to obtain the maximum length of 15 digits. A single semi-octet 1111 is then added at the end to obtain an integral number of octets.

Domain Specific Part (DSP)

The Domain Specific Part is subdivided into the *High Order DSP* (HO-DSP) and Low-Order part, which consists of the *End System Identifier* (ESI) and *Selector* (SEL).

High Order Domain Specific Part (HO-DSP)

The coding of this field is specified by the authority or the coding scheme identified by the IDP. The authority determines how identifiers will be assigned and interpreted within that domain. The authority can create further subdomains. That is, the authority may define some number of subfields of the HO-DSP and use these to identify a lower authority, which in turn defines the balance of the HO-DSP. Sub-fields of the HO-DSP to the left are always more significant than fields to the right. The contents of this field not only describes the hierarchy of addressing authority, but also conveys topological significance. That is, the HO-DSP should be constructed in such a way that routing through interconnected ATM subnetworks is facilitated.

End System Identifier (ESI)

The *end system identifier* (ESI) must be unique within a particular value of the IDP and HO-DSP. In addition, to ensure the ability of an end system to autoconfigure its address, this end system identifier can be a globally unique identifier specified by an IEEE MAC address. The length of this field is 48 bits.

Selector (Sel)

The *selector* (Sel) is not used for ATM routing, but may be used by endsystems. The length of this field is one octet.

NSAP-Based Address Format

An important contribution of the ATM Forum UNI 3.0 and 3.1 specifications was the adoption of an address structure based upon the ISO NSAP syntax. UNI 4.0 continued to use this addressing structure and clarified several points. The ITU-T initially adopted the use of telephone number-like E. 164 addresses as the addressing structure for public ATM (B-ISDN) networks to internetwork with legacy telephone and narrowband ISDN networks. Because E.164 addresses are available only to carriers, preventing the assignment of addresses to the private business sector, the ATM Forum chose NSAP-based addresses, which provide unique ATM addresses for *both* private and public networks. The ITU-T is now also standardizing use of NSAP-based formats.

International (for example, British Standards Institute) and national (for example, ANSI) standards bodies assign the *Initial Domain Part* (IDP) to various organizations such as carriers, companies and governments, usually for only a nominal fee. The remainder of the 20-octet address is called the *Domain-Specific Part* (DSP).

The network provider supplies the IDP part obtained from an administrative body:

PAD   Country Code (CC)   Nationally Significant Number (NSN)

as well as part of the DSP. The remaining octets are assigned by the end user. The end-user part contains at least seven octets. The NSAP standards define a structure that is much more rigid than the one adopted by the ATM Forum; this is why we note that the Forum's address structure is NSAP-based. The reason the forum chose a more flexible format was to achieve better scaleability through hierarchical assignment of the IDP part of the address. This topic is covered further in the section on PNNI later in this chapter.

The ITU-T-specified E.164 address format is the same format used for international telephone numbers; it begins with a country code (for example, 01 for North America, 44 for the UK, and so on), followed by a number defined within that country. This plan has served voice telecommunications well, but it was developed during a time when there was only one major monopoly phone company per country. With the proliferation of fax machines, cellular phones, and multiple phones per residence, the E.164 numbering plan has too few digits, necessitating renumbering of area codes and even individual numbers.

Unfortunately, this need to change addresses to continue growth in the telephony sector occurs on an increasingly frequent basis in response to growing demand. Recent standards work to evolve the E.164 plan to assign a country code to specific carriers is an attempt to address the emerging global competitive nature of networking. The ATM Forum is specifying further details regarding the use of NSAPbased addresses by ATM service providers.

Signaling AAL

SAAL provides a layer two reliable data transfer service to the layer three B-ISDN signaling protocol. The SAAL contain a common part and a service-specific part. The *Common Part AAL* (CP-AAL) is AAL5. The SSCS portion of the SAAL is composed of the following two protocols:

The SSCF provides the following services to the SAAL user:

- Independence from the underlying layers
- Unacknowledged data transfer mode

- Ensured data transfer mode
- Transparent relay of information
- Establishment of connections for assured data transfer mode

The SSCF provides these capabilities primarily by mapping between a simple-state machine for the user and the more complex-state machine employed by the SSCOP protocol. The SSCOP is a peer-to-peer protocol that performs the following functions:

- Guaranteed sequence integrity, or ordered delivery
- Error-correction via error detection and retransmission
- Receiver-based flow control of the transmitter
- Error reporting to layer management
- Keep-alive messaging when other data is not being transferred
- Local retrieval of unacknowledged or enqueued messages
- Capability to establish, disconnect, and synchronize an SSCOP connection
- Transfer of user data in either unassured or assured mode
- Protocol-level error detection
- Status reporting between peer entities

SSCOP is a fairly complicated protocol, but it is specified in the same level of detail as a more successful protocol such as HDLC. The unassured mode is a simple unacknowledged datagram protocol similar to the *User Datagram Protocol* (UDP). SSCOP *Protocol Data Units* (PDUs) also employ a 24-bit sequence number that allows for very high sustained rates to be achieved in a window-flow-controlled protocol.

The signaling SSCF and SSCOP protocols and the CP-AAL are all managed as separate layers by corresponding layer management functions. Layer management sets parameters in the individual layer protocols such as timers and monitors their state and performance. For example, the state of SSCOP can be used to determine the state of the underlying physical link or virtual path connecting two ATM devices. Plane management coordinates across the layer management functions to provide the overall end-to-end signaling capability.

User-Network Interface Signaling

Signaling ATM Adaptation Layer

The SAAL resides between the ATM layer and Q.2931. The purpose of the SAAL is to provide reliable transport of Q.2931 messages between peer Q.2931 entities (for example, ATM Switch and host) over the ATM layer. The SAAL is composed of two sublayers, a common part and a service specific part. The service specific part is further subdivided into a *Service-Specific Coordination Function* (SSCF) and a *Service-Specific Connection-Oriented Protocol* (SSCOP). The SAAL for supporting signaling shall use the protocol structure. The Common Part AAL protocol provides unassured information transfer and a mechanism for detecting corruption of SDUs. AAL Type 5 Common Part protocol shall be used to support signaling. The *Service-Specific Connection-Oriented Protocol* (SSCOP) resides in the *Service-Specific Convergence Sublayer* (SSCS) of the SAAL. SSCOP is used to transfer variable length *Service Data Units* (SDUs) between users of SSCOP. SSCOP provides for the recovery of lost or corrupted SDUs.

An SSCF maps the service of SSCOP to the needs of the SSCF user. Different SSCFs may be defined to support the needs of different AAL users. The SSCF used to support Q.2931 at the UNI is specified in Q.2130.

Signaling Virtual Channel

The signaling virtual channel shall be that identified by VPI=0, VCI=5. A default ATM layer service category and default traffic contract are defined in this specification to be, respectively, the service category and values of traffic contract parameters for the signaling VCC that apply absent any configuration or subscription option. The specification of standard defaults means that degradation of signaling performance due to cell loss can be avoided without requiring configuration or use of optional ILMI procedures.

Signaling Setup Description

ATM signaling shares many characteristics with basic telephony—extensions that add capabilities to specify bandwidth, quality, end system attributes, different connection topologies, and address formats. Keep in mind that a B-ISDN signaling user will most likely be a computer program and not a human being. First, we introduce some of the basic messages and concepts involved in point-to-point and point-to-multipoint SVC connections.

Signaling Messages and Information Elements

The ITU-T's Q.2931 UNI signaling protocol standard and the ATM Forum UNI specification version 4.0 use the following message types for point-to-point and point-to-multipoint connections:

For point-to-point connection control:

- Two-call establishment messages
  - CALL PROCEEDING
  - CONNECT ACKNOWLEDGE
  - SETUP
- Two-call clearing messages
  - RELEASE
  - RELEASE COMPLETE
- Two status messages
  - STATUS ENQUIRY
  - STATUS (Response)

For point-to-multipoint connection control:

- ADD PARTY
- ADD PARTY ACKNOWLEDGE
- ADD PARTY REJECT

- DROP PARTY
- DROP PARTY ACKNOWLEDGE
- LEAF SETUP REQUEST
- LEAF SETUP FAILURE

Each signaling message has a number of *Information Elements* (IEs), some of which are *Mandatory* (M) and others of which are *Optional* (O). All messages related to a particular call attempt contain a common mandatory information element, the call reference, that is unique at the signaling interface.

The key mandatory information elements used in the UNI signaling protocol are

- ATM user cell rate requested
- Called party number
- Connection identifier (assigned VPI/VCI value)
- Bearer capability
- *Quality of service* (QoS) class requested

Signaling Procedures

Signaling procedures specify the sequence of messages that must be exchanged, the rules for verifying consistency of the parameters, and actions to be taken in order to establish and release ATM-layer connections. A significant portion of the specification is involved with handling error cases, invalid messages, inconsistent parameters, and a number of other unlikely situations. These are all important functions because the signaling protocol must be highly reliable in order to support user applications. Because the standards bodies based the Q.2931 protocol upon the ISDN Q.931 and frame relay Q.933 protocols, the prospects for interoperability are good.

ATM Connection Setup

ATM connections are established as either *permanent virtual circuits* (PVCs) or *switched virtual circuits* (SVCs). As their name implies, PVCs are always present, whereas SVCs must be established each time a connection is set up. To set up a connection, a signaling circuit is used first. A signaling circuit is a predefined circuit (with VPI=0 and VCI=5) that is used to transfer signaling messages, which are in turn used for making and releasing calls or connections. If a connection request is successful, a new set of VPI and VCI values are allocated on which the parties that set up the call can send and receive data. Six message types are used to establish virtual circuits, each message occupying one or more cells and containing the message type, length, and parameters. Table 14.2 lists these message types.

The sequence for establishing and releasing a call is as follows:

1. The host sends a SETUP message on the signaling VPI=0/VCI=5 using UNI Signaling Q.2931 SVC. (See Figure 14.17.)

TABLE 14.2   **ATM SETUP Commands**

Message	Significance if sent by host	Significance if sent by the network
SETUP	Requests that a call be established	Indicates an incoming call
CALL PROCEEDING	Acknowledges the incoming call	Indicates the call request will be attempted
CONNECT	Indicates acceptance of the call	Indicates the call was accepted
CONNECT ACK	Acknowledges acceptance of the call	Acknowledges making the call
RELEASE	Requests that the call be terminated	Terminates the call
RELEASE ACK	Acknowledges releasing the call	Acknowledges releasing the call

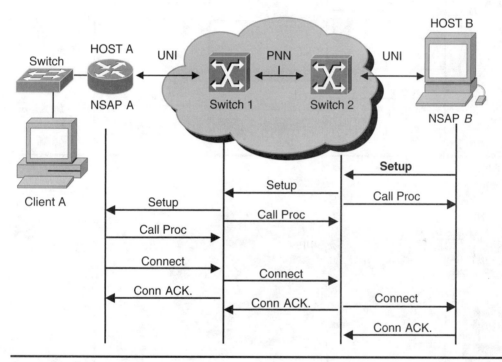

Figure 14.17   Setup

2. The network responds by sending a CALL PROCEEDING message to acknowledge receiving the request. (See Figure 14.18.)

3. Along the route to the destination, each switch receiving the SETUP message acknowledges it by sending the CALL PROCEEDING message.

4. When the SETUP message reaches its final destination, the receiving host responds by sending the CONNECT message to accept the call. (See Figure 14.19.)

5. The network sends a CONNECT ACK message to acknowledge receiving the CONNECT message.

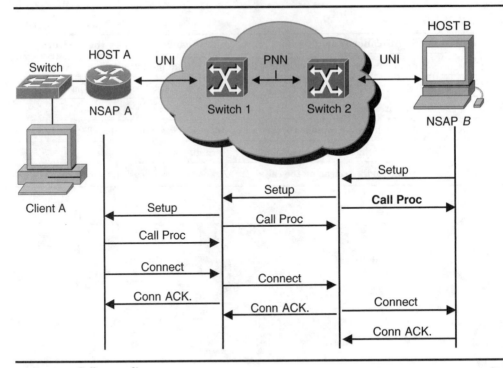

Figure 14.18 Call proceeding

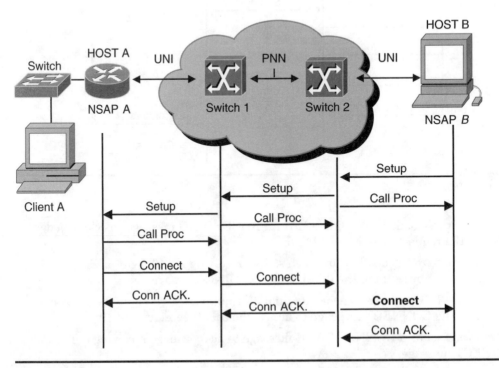

Figure 14.19 Connect

6. Along the route back to the sender, each switch that receives the CONNECT message acknowledges it by sending CONNECT ACK. (See Figure 14.20.)

7. To terminate the call, a host (either the caller or the receiver) sends a RELEASE message, causing the message to propagate to the other end of the connection, and then releasing the circuit. Again, the message is acknowledged at each switch along the way.

Sending Data to Multiple Receivers

In ATM networks, users can set up point-to-multipoint calls with one sender and multiple receivers. A point to multipoint VC allows an endpoint called the "root" node to exchange data with a set of remote endpoints called leaves. To set up a point-to-multipoint call, a connection to one of the destinations is set up in the usual way. After the connection is established, users can send the ADD PARTY message to attach a second destination to the VC returned by the previous call. To add receivers, users can then send additional ADD PARTY messages. This process is similar to a user dialing multiple parties to set up a telephone conference call. One difference is that an ATM P/MP call doesn't allow data to be sent by parties towards the root (or the originator of the call). This is because the ATM Forum Standard UNI 3.1 restricts data flow on point-to-multipoint VCs from the root to the leaves only.

The reference configuration and conventions are the same as in the point-to-point connection establishment example. Either party may initiate the release process, just as either party may hang up first in a telephone call. In this example, the calling party is the one

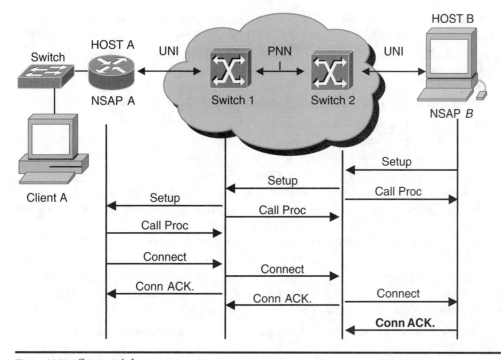

Figure 14.20 Connect Ack

who initiates the disconnect process by sending the RELEASE message. The network then propagates the RELEASE message across the network to the other party, Host B. The other party acknowledges the RELEASE request by returning a RELEASE COMPLETE message, which is then propagated back across the network to the calling-party RELEASE originator. This two-way handshake completes the call release process.

Multiplexing Different ATM Connections

This function multiplexes ATM connections with different QoS requirements. ATM connections may have either a specified or unspecified QoS class. The QoS class is the same for all cells belonging to the same connection and remains unchanged for the duration of the connection.

The primary role of Traffic Control and Congestion Control parameters and procedures is to protect the network and the user in order to achieve network performance objectives. An additional role is to optimize the use of network resources. The uncertainties of broadband traffic patterns and the complexity of Traffic Control and Congestion Control suggest a step-wise approach for defining traffic parameters and network Traffic Control and Congestion Control mechanisms.

Generic Functions

To meet these objectives, the following functions form a framework for managing and controlling traffic and congestion in ATM networks and may be used in appropriate combinations.

- Network Resource Management *(NRM).* Provisioning may be used to allocate network resources in order to separate traffic flows according to service characteristics.

- Connection Admission Control *(CAC).* The set of actions taken by the network during the call setup phase (or during call renegotiations phase) in order to determine whether a virtual channel/virtual path connection request can be accepted or should be rejected (or whether a request for re-allocation can be accommodated). Routing is part of CAC actions.

- *Feedback controls.* The set of actions taken by the network and by the users to regulate the traffic submitted on ATM connections according to the state of Network Elements.

- Usage Parameter Control *(UPC).* The set of actions taken by the network to monitor and control traffic, in terms of traffic offered and validity of the ATM connection, at the user access. Its main purpose is to protect network resources from malicious as well as unintentional misbehavior, which can affect the QoS of other already established connections by detecting violations of negotiated parameters and taking appropriate actions.

- *Priority Control.* The user may generate different priority traffic flows by using the Cell Loss Priority bit. A Network Element may selectively discard cells with low priority if necessary to protect the Network Performance for cells with high priority.

- *Traffic Shaping.* Traffic-shaping mechanisms may be used to achieve a desired modification of the traffic characteristics.

All of these functions can make use of information that passes across the UNI. As a general requirement, it is desirable that a high level of consistency be achieved between the above traffic control capabilities.

QoS, Network Performance, and Cell Loss Priority

The ATM layer QoS is defined by a set of parameters such as delay and delay variation, cell loss ratio, and so on.

A user requests one ATM Layer QoS class for each direction of an ATM layer connection. For each direction, a user requests a specific ATM layer QoS from the QoS classes provided by a network. These requested QoS classes are a part of the Traffic Contract. The network commits to meet the requested QoS.

A requested QoS class may be the "Unspecified QoS class" or may be one of the "Specified QoS classes." A specified QoS class may contain at most two cell loss ratio objectives. If a specified QoS class does contain two cell loss ratio objectives, one objective is for the CLP=0 cells and the other objective is for the CLP=1 cells of the ATM connection.

Network Performance objectives at the ATM Layer Service Access Point are intended to capture the network's ability to meet the requested ATM Layer quality of service. The role of the upper layers, including the ATM Adaptation layer, is to translate this ATM layer QoS to any specific application requested QoS.

ATM Quality of Service

ATM provides great flexibility for applications to set QoS requirements. Video conferencing might require a high QoS, whereas data may allow a lower setting. A very granular set of parameters exists by which to specify what QoS is required. An application can specify the amount of bandwidth, the maximum delay, and the maximum cell-loss rate. There are about twenty different parameters, all related to time guarantees. Some of the most important QoS parameters are listed.

Peak Cell Rate (PCR)

PCR is the maximum rate (in cells per second) at which the sender wants to send the cells.

Sustained Cell Rate (SCR)

SCR is the expected or required cell rate averaged over a long interval.

Minimum Cell Rate (MCR)

MCR is the minimum number of cells per second that the user considers acceptable. If the carrier cannot guarantee this much bandwidth, it must reject the connection.

Cell Delay Variation (CDV or Jitter)

CDV or Jitter is how uniformly the ATM cells are delivered. ATM layer functions may alter the traffic characteristics by introducing cell delay variation. When cells from two or more

ATM connections are *multiplexed* (MUX), cells of a given connection may be delayed when cells of another connection are being inserted at the output of the multiplexer. (Multiplexing at the transport layer refers to placing several transport connections onto one virtual circuit.)

Cell Delay Variation Tolerance (CDVT)

CDVT is the amount of variation present in cell transmission times. CDVT is specified independently for peak cell rate and sustained cell rate. For a perfect source operating at PCR, every cell will appear exactly 1/PCR after the previous cell. However, for a real source operating at PCR, some variation in cell transmission time will occur. CDVT controls the amount of variation acceptable using a leaky bucket algorithm, described later in this section.

Cell Loss Ratio (CLR)

CLR is the fraction of the transmitted cells that are not delivered or are delivered so late as to be useless (for example, for real-time traffic).

Cell Transfer Delay (CTD)

CTD is the average transit time from source to destination.

Cell Error Ratio (CER)

CER is the fraction of cells that are delivered with one or more bits wrong.

For example, using more bandwidth increases the cell loss, the delay, and the delay variation incurred, therefore decreasing the QoS for cells of all connections that share those resources.

The ATM Forum has specified a service category called *available bit rate* (ABR) for more efficiently and fairly managing excess bandwidth capacity. ABR is designed for applications that do not have rigorous cell transfer delay tolerances but do have low cell-loss requirements, such as distributed computing applications. ABR applications, which compete fairly for excess capacity through flow control algorithms, specify minimum throughput requirements. Examples of ABR applications include existing UBR applications (news and weather pictures, LAN interconnection, telecommuting, file transfer, and electronic mail) that require more predictable behavior. Additional examples are defense applications and banking applications with critical data transfer requirements.

ATM Service Categories

Four service categories are specified by the ATM Forum:

Constant bit rate (CBR)

Variable bit rate (VBR)

Available bit rate (ABR)

Unspecified bit rate (UBR)

Constant Bit Rate (CBR).   CBR guarantees that the entire network, including each intervening switch from origin to destination, provides an agreed-upon quantity of bandwidth at all times. From the standpoint of a carrier, CBR is expensive to provide because the guaranteed bandwidth must be reserved for that customer even if the customer isn't using it. The carrier can't let another customer use that bandwidth in the switch because the purpose of CBR is to provide an absolute guarantee, which also assures that no cells will be lost.

A quality-of-service contract, like any other contract, has two sides. An application using CBR will ask for a certain quantity of bandwidth, such as two megabits per second. The UNI, in turn, has to guarantee that it won't send more than the agreed-upon amount of data. If it exceeds that limit, the switch may dump the extra bits. Making sure that no cells are lost depends on the UNI fulfilling its side of the contract. If it does not, the switch can simply dump packets that exceed the terms of the contract. For this reason, the ATM end node must do traffic shaping, or flow control, to ensure that nothing is lost.

Variable Bit Rate.   Another form of QoS is *variable bit rate* (VBR). It may be used in cases where an adapter would like two megabits per second, but can live with an average of only one megabit per second. It could negotiate for two megabits for a certain number of seconds in each minute, as a peak, with no cells lost. The switch guarantees an average, over time, of one megabit per second, with two megabits provided when available. VBR also can guarantee an average peak bandwidth per period in addition to the flat average. VBR can be used efficiently for voice traffic, taking advantage of silence suppression. During pauses in a normal conversation, other data can be sent on the vacant bandwidth. For example, a video conferencing application, with the audio over a speaker, could use VBR with silence suppression. Because VBR gives an average bandwidth, software and algorithms can be sent when the peak bandwidth is available. This works when the average is adequate to transfer the voice traffic in compressed, silence-suppressed form. When less flexibility exists, CBR may be necessary, but it usually isn't required for video on demand, video conferencing, and so on. Those can typically be done with VBR.

Available Bit Rate (ABR).   ABR is the newest and least expensive of the three already covered. ABR is the most complex QoS, but is the cheapest service to buy from a carrier. ABR employs a feedback loop between the end system and switch. ABR lets an end system say that it would like, for example, two megabits, but will take whatever it can get. The switch says that it can provide two megabits initially, but the elaborate protocol in ABR allows the switch to lower that bandwidth. Packets from the switch tell the end system that its bandwidth is being reduced and the card can agree to source a reduced amount of data. Later on, the switch might reduce bandwidth again and later increase it. A constant feedback loop guarantees that each side knows the status of the other.

ABR is very popular because it resembles a LAN: Although in theory it has a certain amount of bandwidth available, in practice, data is transferred at a much lower rate. Sometimes it will be fast, and sometimes it will be slow. ABR makes sense because QoS applications are rare today. Users like the idea of QoS, but might initially still be using Ethernet, which acts like ABR. Therefore, when users use ATM cards, their applications will often use ABR.

Unspecified Bit Rate (UBR).   UBR has no bandwidth guarantee. The other forms of QoS all require the end system to know that if it doesn't exceed a certain limit, the switch will not drop packets. UBR provides no contract whatsoever. An end system just gets whatever bandwidth is available at the time. Cells being sent out onto the net may all be dropped, or they could all be sent. UBR is of course the cheapest because the carrier makes absolutely no guarantees at all. It's similar to being on standby. UBR is useful because it's like *User Datagram Protocol* (UDP) today on TCP/IP. UDP provides no guarantee. There may be no bandwidth available, and no way to determine if a packet reaches its destination.

Variable bit rate has two variants or subclasses: real-time VBR and non-real-time VBR.

Each service category has several attributes or parameters associated with it. Some are traffic parameters, which describe the inherent characteristics of a connection's traffic source. Others are called *quality-of-service* (QoS) parameters, which define performance attributes required by an application. In the ATM Forum's Version 4.0 traffic management specification, some QoS parameters are negotiable via signaling, whereas others are non-negotiable.

Constant bit-rate (CBR) service is the highest priority service category, designed for isochronous traffic that must meet strict throughput and delay requirements. A bit stream originating at a source must be able to be reconstructed from cells at the destination within the constraints of the CBR connection attribute values to ensure that the required quality of the received bit stream is attained.

Examples of CBR traffic are telephone voice, interactive video, video (television) and audio (radio) distribution, and emulation of digital circuits, such as T1 and DS3.

Applications whose information transfer is bursty can utilize one of two *variable bit-rate* (VBR) options: real-time VBR as defined in UNI 3.1, or non-real-time VBR as defined in the ATM Forum Version 4.0 traffic management specification. For example, a voice connection that utilizes functions such as voice compression and silence suppression can be implemented using real-time VBR instead of CBR to save bandwidth while continuing to meet delay constraints. Examples of non-real-time VBR applications are airline reservations, banking transactions, process monitoring, and frame relay interworking.

Traffic that requires no service guarantees can utilize the *unspecified bit-rate* (UBR) service category. Examples of applications that can use "background" bandwidth allocated to UBR traffic are image information such as news and weather pictures, LAN interconnection, telecommuting, file transfer, and electronic mail.

In Version 4.0 of the traffic management specification, a user can specify two attributes for a UBR connection: peak cell rate and cell delay variation tolerance. Network vendors may optionally choose to subject UBR traffic to connection admission controls and usage parameter controls. UBR is a good way to utilize excess bandwidth for applications that will occasionally have cells discarded without serious consequence, such as TCP/IP-based applications that are able to recover packets using routine re-transmission protocols.

ATM Traffic Management

Networks must be designed to maximize the utilization of resources so the best possible cost-to-performance ratio is attained while meeting user service expectations. ATM standards and implementation agreements specify many capabilities for meeting these goals, whereas other capabilities are left to vendors and network providers to implement using proprietary technology.

Traffic management is based on the service category and associated *quality of service* (QoS) that a user or group of users requires on a connection. The service contract for a connection is determined according to whether the connection is permanent or switched.

Permanent Virtual Connections (PVCs)

For *permanent virtual connections* (virtual path or virtual channel), the service contract is defined at the user end-points and along the route that has been selected for the connection using the provisioning capabilities of the network vendor.

Switched Virtual Connections (SVCs)

Switched virtual connections enable the network to allocate bandwidth on demand. End users make their service request to the network using functions provided by the end system for accessing the ATM *user-to-network interface* (UNI). After the UNI switched virtual connection request is made, the network must determine if the connection request can be accepted and then route the connection appropriately.

Connection Admission Control

To determine whether a permanent or switched virtual connection will be accepted or rejected, *connection admission control* (CAC) functions are executed by the network. They determine whether sufficient link (trunk) and switch resources exist to support the requested traffic contract without affecting the quality of service of existing connections. If the connection is accepted, traffic parameters for the connection are given to the traffic shaping and policing function in each switch (called *usage parameter control* [UPC]), and the connection is completed. These do not occur if the connection is denied. Cisco CAC algorithms are consistent with the traffic conformance requirements specified in UNI 3.0 and UNI 3.1 and will support the UNI 4.0 conformance requirements as these standards become available.

Routing

Routing methodologies, executed during the call setup process, are key to meeting *quality-of-service* (QoS) and availability requirements of users. This process involves signaling between the switches over a *network-to-network interface* (NNI)—sometimes called node-to-node interface. Two principal routing methodologies are used in ATM networks: hop-by-hop routing and source routing. Hop-by-hop routing is the method used in the Interim Interswitch Signaling Protocol (IISP). Source routing is a more sophisticated capability that determines routes based on network state.

VBR/ABR Bandwidth

Controlling the cost/performance efficiency of the network requires accurate assignment of VBR/ABR bandwidth. This accuracy depends upon the accuracy with which the assignment algorithms represent the actual traffic on VBR/ABR connections.

Cell Loss Priority

Cell loss priority (CLP) enables the end user and the network to mark data that can be discarded first in the event of congestion. Users can use CLP to distinguish between control data and information data. Networks use CLP to differentiate between committed data and excess data.

The ATM cell header contains a CLP bit that allows cells to be marked as high (CLP=1) or low (CLP=0) priority.

Traffic Shaping

When traffic does not conform to the terms of a traffic contract, the traffic can be routed through a shaping function to bring it into conformance with the contract. For example, real-time VBR traffic whose peak rate bursts are higher than the contracted peak cell rate can be modified to extend the duration of the burst by spreading the cells in time—as long as the burst tolerance and other parameters associated with the contract remain valid.

Traffic Policing

Network switches must protect (police) network resources from malicious or unintentional misbehavior by monitoring incoming (ingress) traffic for conformance to the connection traffic contract.

The ATM Forum specifies traffic monitoring and control for traffic at the UNI, which is called *usage parameter control* (UPC). Monitoring and traffic control at the NNI is called *network parameter control* (NPC). The term UPC is used generically for both UPC and NPC.

Cisco provides usage parameter control (compatible with the ATM Forum's definitions for traffic policing) at UNIs and NNIs for virtual path and virtual channel connections. UPC and NPC functions can be disabled at a UNI or NNI.

The Cisco Lightstream 1010 supports dual leaky buckets so policing can be executed on one or two connection flows: the CLP=0 or CLP=0 + 1 (aggregate) flows, or both.

Congestion Control

Congestion control allows the management of traffic when many users contend for finite network resources. The ATM CBR and VBR service categories have been designed to avoid network congestion conditions when implemented with robust connection admission controls and usage parameter controls. ABR and UBR service categories have been defined to take advantage of the excess capacity beyond that required for CBR and VBR connections.

ABR Traffic

Rate-based ABR defines a closed-loop feedback system in which traffic source and destination use congestion state information provided by the network to alter ingress traffic to match available network resources and thus minimize cell loss.

The simplest ABR option is called *explicit forward congestion indication* (EFCI) marking, which is currently supported by Cisco ATM Switches.

Another option, called explicit rate marking, is superior to the EFCI method. Explicit rate marking is a mechanism by which the network continuously informs the source of the maximum rate it can use.

ABR flow control can be made even more effective with *virtual source* (VS) and *virtual destination* (VD) components placed in the network, functioning the same way as the end sources and destinations. This ABR option is called VS/VD control.

UBR Traffic

UBR is sometimes referred to as a best-effort service. As in frame relay, congestion control is provided on an end-to-end basis by the end user. Flow control is available on most data protocols—for example, TCP/IP. Studies show that UBR services enhanced with early packet discard or partial packet discard capabilities provide excellent network efficiency—better than ABR with closed-loop control based on EFCI marking. This proven solution requires no enhancements to existing end devices. When coupled with intelligent buffer management features, it provides excellent network efficiency, fairness, and reliability.

Network-Node Interface Signaling

This section covers the Network-Network Interface. These two meanings of the same acronym identify its dual purpose: use between nodes in a single network, and interconnection between different networks. The treatment in this section begins in the private network domain and then moves to the public network domain and covers the following major NNI signaling protocols:

- ATM Forum IISP (Also known as PNNI phase 0)
- ATM Forum PNNI

ATM Forum Interim Interswitch Signaling Protocol (IISP)

To build a multivendor ATM SVC network, IISP is the simplest way to get started. However, as your networking needs mature and the ATM network grows, the design should move to a dynamic routing protocol using PNNI phase 1. The ATM Forum recognized the need to produce a standard for a minimum level of interoperability for multivendor private ATM networks. The Forum announced that the IISP standard would fill the void until the complete PNNI specification could be finished. IISP basically extended the UNI 3.0/3.1 protocol to a simple network context.

The IISP Specification is based on the UNI 3.1 signaling protocol (with optional support of the UNI 3.0 protocol through bilateral configuration arrangements), with minor changes intended to minimize the additional development effort, yet allow the inter-switch connectivity in private networks in a multivendor environment. Consequently, at a specific link, one switching system plays the role of the user side, and the other plays the role of the network side, as defined in the UNI 3.1 Specification. The roles are assigned manually so one end of the link terminates at a "user interface card" of one switching system and the other end terminates at a "switch interface card" of the other switching system. No restrictions exist regarding the roles that a switching system can play at different links (that is, a switching system can play one role at one link, and another role at another link). Moreover, a transit switching system can play one role at the incoming side of a call and the same role or another role at the outgoing side of the same call.

The UNI 3.1 Specification differentiates between the origination side (at the calling party) and the destination side (at the called party) of a call. For the IISP links, such differentiation is not necessary. However, to maintain synergy with the UNI 3.1 Specification, the different sections are preserved with the understanding that they apply according to the direction in which the call is traveling; that is, from the user side to the network side versus from the network side to the user side.

The use of SVCs across IISP links is supported much as those at the UNI 3.1 links are. Call collisions on an IISP link (due to assignment of identical VPI/VCI by two switching systems to calls occurring simultaneously) are eliminated by allowing only the "network side" to assign VPI/VCI values. The use of PVCs across IISP links is supported much as those at the UNI 3.1 links are. Call collisions on an IISP link (due to assignment of identical VPI/VCI by two switching systems to calls occurring simultaneously) are eliminated by allowing only the "network side" to assign VPI/VCI values.

IISP added several conventions to the UNI 3.0/3.1 UNI signaling specifications. The IISP physical layer, ATM layer, and traffic management specifications are identical to the UNI 3.0/3.1 specification. IISP uses the UNI cell format, there is no *Integrated Local Management Interface* (ILMI), and IISP makes policing optional. IISP specifies a limited set of VCIs ranging from 32 to 255 on VPI 0 to ensure interoperability. A key addition of IISP to UNI signaling is identification of each side of a trunk as either the user or the network side. IISP defines a simple hop-by-hop routing based upon matching the longest address prefix in a statically configured routing table. Such manual configuration limits the scaleability of IISP networks. Also, the switches must clear an SVC call in response to link failures. Support for other features is optional, such as routing over parallel links between nodes, connection admission control for guaranteeing quality of service, and alternative routing. Furthermore, manual configuration of hop-by-hop routing tables may introduce routing loops, a potential problem the IISP specification identifies.

PNNI Routing Protocol

The abbreviation PNNI stands for either *Private Network-Node Interface* or *Private Network-to-Network Interface*, reflecting its two possible uses.

PNNI Phase I is a switch-to-switch routing protocol that is used to route SVC requests with QoS through an ATM Network. PNNI is based on link-state protocols (for example, OSPF) with extensions that enable switches to advertise their own capabilities (such as capacity, delay, and so on). PNNI supports a hierarchical system in which topology information from one group of nodes (called peer groups) is aggregated (compressed and summarized) and presented as a single node in the next higher-level peer group. This keeps the complexity and volume of information exchanged down while giving peer group nodes at least partial reachability data.

The PNNI software provides the routing protocols required for an ATM switch to operate in an ATM network. The protocol specifies a mechanism for updating routing information at each ATM switch. It also specifies mechanisms for specifying a source-route for a call, leaving vendors free to implement their own algorithms for computing the routes from the routing information database.

PNNI Architecture

The PNNI protocol specifies two separate, but interrelated, protocols and functions to achieve the goal of controlling the user cell stream between nodes and networks. The PNNI protocol operates on dedicated links or may be tunneled over virtual path Identifier 0 Virtual Channel Identifier 18.

A topology distribution protocol defines the methods and messages for distributing topology information between switches and clusters of switches. Information exchanged by this protocol is used to compute optimized paths throughout the network. A hierarchy mechanism enables this protocol to scale well for large ATM networks. A key feature of the PNNI hierarchy mechanism is its ability to automatically configure itself in networks in which the address structure reflects the topology. The PNNI signaling protocol uses message flows to establish point-to-point and point-to-multipoint SVCs across an ATM network. The PNNI signaling protocol is based on the ATM Forum UNI signaling standard, augmented with mechanisms to support source routing and the ability to crank back to earlier nodes in order to route around an intermediate node that blocks a call request. The PNNI specification also defines SVC-based *Semipermanent Virtual Paths and Channel Connections* (SPVPC and SPVCC). Phase 1 of the ATM Forum's PNNI specification has the following characteristics:

- Supports all UNI 3.1 and some UNI 4.0 capabilities
- Supports hierarchical routing, enabling scaling to very large networks
- Supports QoS-based routing
- Supports multiple routing metrics and attributes
- Uses source-routed connection setup
- Operates in the presence of partitioned areas (PNNI Phase II)
- Provides dynamic routing, responsive to changes in resource availability
- Uses separate routing protocols within and between peer groups (PNNI Phase II)
- Interoperates with external routing domains, not necessarily using PNNI
- Supports both physical links and tunneling over VPCs as NNIs
- Supports SPVPC/SPVCCs
- Supports anycast

PNNI Introduction

In a PNNI network, routing is based on the first 19 bytes of the 20-byte ATM address. The 20th byte, the selector, is used inside the end system to distinguish between different higher-layer protocols and applications. Each switching system, or "node," in the network has a unique (20-byte check) *node identifier* (node ID). The node ID of a switch is based on the switch's ATM address; therefore, it is automatically generated by the implementation (no configuration required).

In PNNI, nodes are grouped into clusters called peer groups. This is analogous to the OSPF concepts of an area. The peer group is identified by a 14 byte *peer group identifier* (peer group ID) and therefore all nodes in the same peer group must have the same peer group ID. In virtually all circumstances, the peer group ID is derived from the switch's ATM address and is generated automatically. All nodes in a peer group (and by implication the end systems attached to those nodes) must be assigned addresses with a common prefix that is unique to that peer group. By looking at the address prefix, the administrator or routing protocol can determine the location of a node. The most logical choice for the peer group ID is the unique common address prefix shared by nodes in the given peer group.

The only missing piece of information is the length of this address prefix, which is called the level indicator or simply level in PNNI. A default value for the level may be used if this matches the address assignment scheme, or one may be configured. PNNI allows levels of 0 through 104. This tight coupling between peer group IDs and addressing is not a requirement of PNNI or the implementation. An administrator may choose to configure the peer group ID if that is more convenient.

Network Addressing Philosophy

The ATM Forum chose the Internet routing protocol as its addressing and routing model over the older, manually maintained telephone network hierarchy—mainly because private network customers insist upon a high degree of automatic configuration. An undesirable side effect of hierarchical addressing, however, is the generally low utilization of the total available address space. This sparse filling of the address space occurs because an organization must leave room for growth, or perhaps the fact that the network design dictates peer relationships between groups of devices with widely different population sizes. The ATM Forum's choice of the 20-octet NSAP address format for PNNI meets these requirements well because there is never likely to be a network that approaches PNNI's theoretical limit of 2,160 (approximately 1,048) nodes. In practice, however, the real number of useable addresses is much less.

The PNNI addressing plan provides an unprecedented level of hierarchy, supporting up to 105 levels. PNNI exploits the flexibility of such a huge address space with the objective of providing an extremely scaleable network in the specification of routing its protocols. In contrast to other network routing protocols developed before it, the PNNI specification begins with global scaleability as an underlying requirement instead of an afterthought as it now confronts IP in its transition from version 4 to version 6.

PNNI Protocol Between Switches

Two separate PNNI protocols operate between ATM switching systems connected by either physical or virtual PNNI links: signaling and routing. The signaling protocol sets up the ATM connection along the path determined by the routing protocol. The routing protocol utilizes two types of addresses—topology and end user—in a hierarchical manner. Through the exchange of information over PNNI links, every node learns about a hierarchically summarized version of the entire network. The distribution of reachability information along with associated metrics, such as administrative cost to reach a particular address prefix over a PNNI link, is similar to that of the OSPF protocol in TCP/IP networks.

Given that the source node has a summarized, hierarchical view of the entire network and the associated administrative and quality metrics of the candidate paths to the destination, PNNI places the burden of determining the route on the source. The information about the source-to-destination path is computed at the source node and placed in a *Designated Transit List* (DTL) in the signaling message originated by the source. Intermediate nodes in the path expand the DTL in their domain and crank back to find alternative paths if the call is blocked within their domain. Hence, PNNI DTLs are similar to token ring networks, which employ source routing. Also note that source routing prevents loops; therefore, a standard route determination protocol isn't necessary, simplifying interoperability.

Although PNNI builds upon experience gained from older protocols, its complexity exceeds that of any routing protocol conceived to date. As subsequent discussions illustrate, the complexity of PNNI stems from requirements for scaleability, support for QoS-based routing, and the additional complexities of connection-oriented service, which are not considered in the legacy connectionless protocols of the past.

PNNI Routing Hierarchy and Topology Aggregation

PNNI employs the concept of embedding topological information in hierarchical addressing to summarize routing information. This summarization of address prefixes constrains processing and memory space requirements to grow at lower rates than the number of nodes in the network. At each level of the hierarchy, the PNNI routing protocol defines a uniform network model composed of logical nodes and logical links. PNNI proceeds upwards in the hierarchy recursively; that is, the same functions are used again at each successive level. The PNNI model defines

- Neighbor discovery via a Hello protocol
- Link status determination via a Hello protocol
- Topology database synchronization procedures
- Peer-group determination and peer group-leader election
- Reliable *PNNI Topology State Element* (PTSE) flooding
- Bootstrapping of the PNNI hierarchy from the lowest level upwards

PNNI Hello Protocol.   Switches continuously execute the Hello protocol on all enabled PNNI links. The periodic exchange of Hello packets with neighboring nodes accomplishes several things:

- Hellos received from the neighbor provide an indication that the PNNI entity in the neighbor is (still) active.
- The node sending a Hello includes its peer group ID. Through the exchange of Hellos, two neighbor nodes can determine if they are in the same peer group. If so, they execute the remaining protocols.
- The node's node ID and an identifier for the port (automatically generated by the implementation) are sent in all Hellos. Furthermore, after the node ID and port

identifier for the neighbor node are known, they are also echoed back to the neighbor in outgoing Hellos. Thus, after a Hello has been received with both remote and local node and port ID information, the local node knows that the exchange has been successful, and it also has sufficient information to start using this link in the remainder of the PNNI protocol.

Database Synchronization.   When the Hello protocol has declared the link as functional, the adjacent switches exchange a summary of their database contents. This mechanism is similar to the OSPF database synchronization procedures. The synchronization is governed by a master and slave relationship of switches. Nodes exchange database summary packets that contain header information of all *PNNI Topology State Elements* (PTSEs) in a node database. After such an exchange, differences in the topological databases are updated. When completed, both nodes have consistent topological databases.

PNNI Topology Description and Distribution.   *PNNI Topology State Packets* (PTSP) containing one or more PTSEs are used to disseminate information in the ATM network. PTSPs contain reachability, link, and node status information necessary for PNNI to calculate QoS paths in an ATM network.

Supported Metrics and Attributes.   As a topology state routing protocol, PNNI advertises detailed information about the status of the links and nodes. The status of the topological entities (links and nodes) is described via metrics and attributes. Metrics are combined along a path. The simplest example of a metric is the administrative weight. The administrative weight of a path is the sum of the weights of links and nodes along the path.

Attributes are treated by PNNI in a different way. If an attribute value for a parameter violates the QoS constraint, PNNI excludes that topological entity from consideration while making a path selection.

Supported metrics and attributes include the following:

- Administrative Weight *(AW).*   Indicates the relative preference of a link or node assigned by the private network operator
- Available Cell Rate *(AvCR).*   Reflects the amount of equivalent bandwidth that is available on the link or node
- Maximum Cell Transfer Delay *(MaxCTD).*   The (1-a) quantile of the elapsed time for transmission of cells across a link or node. This includes processing and queueing delays plus propagation delay.
- Cell Loss Ratio *(CLR).*   The ratio of the number of lost cells to the total number of cells transmitted across the link or node
- Peak-to-Peak Cell Delay Variation *(CDV).*   The (1-a) quantile of the cell transfer delay minus the fixed delay experienced by all cells crossing the link or node
- Maximum Cell Rate *(MaxCR).*   The maximum capacity usable by connections belonging to the specific service category

PNNI is a very complex routing protocol that will allow ATM to scale to very large networks. This protocol is outside the scope of this book. The ATM Forum PNNI Phase 1 specification provides an excellent reference on the protocol and implementation considerations.

References

For more information, consult the following reference works:

- ATM Forum, ATM *User Network Interface* (UNI) Specification, Version 3.0
- ATM Forum, ATM *User Network Interface* (UNI) Specification, Version 3.1
- ATM Forum, ATM *User Network Interface* (UNI) Specification, Version 4.0
- ATM Forum, ATM *Interim Interswitch Signaling Protocol Specification* (IISP)
- ATM Forum, *Private Network-Network Interface Specification, Version 1.0* (PNNI 1.0)

Classical IP over ATM, RFC 1577

Because *Internet Protocol* (IP) is so prevalent, the ATM Forum defined a special module called "Classical IP Over ATM," which is an *Address Resolution Protocol* (ARP) module (defined in RFC 1577). See Figures 14.21 and 14.22. In the Classical model, the conventional IP subnet architecture is preserved. ATM adapters are treated as a network interface to the IP protocol stack. ATM networks under this model are divided into *logical IP Subnets* (LIS) in which all members have the same IP network/subnetwork address and netmask. Each member is connected to the ATM network directly and should be able to communicate with

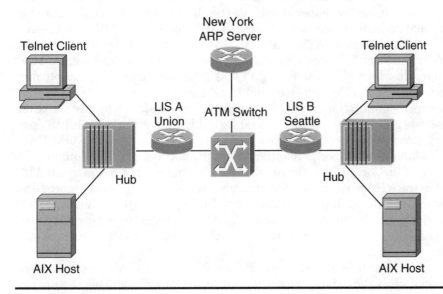

Figure 14.21 ARP server

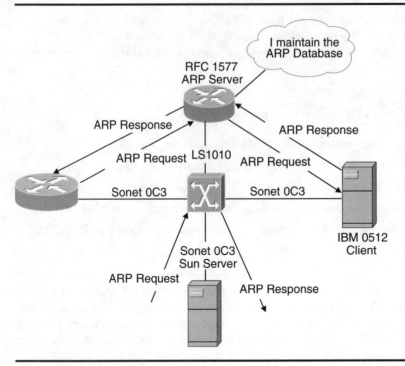

Figure 14.22 RFC 1577 ARP server

other members in the same LIS directly via ATM (that is, a full mesh of VCs is established among members of the LIS). Each member should also be able to map between IP addresses and ATM NSAP-format addresses using an ATM-based ARP and Inverse ARP service—ATMARP and InATMARP. One or more ATMARP/InATMARP servers may be used to provide address resolution in a unicast ATM environment for all members in the LIS. Figure 14.22 illustrates the manner in which ATMARP and InATMARP servers function in order to map back and forth between NSAP ATM addresses and IP addresses.

With IP Subnetwork Configuration in the LIS scenario, each separate administrative entity configures its hosts and routers within a closed logical IP subnetwork. Each LIS operates and communicates independently of other LISs on the same ATM network. Hosts connected to ATM communicate directly to other hosts within the same LIS. Communication to hosts outside of the local LIS is provided via an IP router. This router is an ATM endpoint attached to the ATM network that is configured as a member of one or more LISs. This configuration may result in a number of disjointed LISs operating over the same ATM network. Hosts in different IP subnets communicate via an intermediate IP router even though it may be possible to open a direct virtual circuit between the two IP members over the ATM network.

Packet Format Implementations support IEEE 802.2 LLC/SNAP encapsulation. LLC/SNAP encapsulation is the default packet format for IP datagrams. This section recognizes that other encapsulation methods may be used; however, in the absence of other knowledge or agreement, LLC/SNAP encapsulation is the default. The default MTU size for IP members operating over the ATM network is 9,180 octets. The LLC/SNAP header is eight octets; therefore, the default ATM AAL5 protocol data unit size is 9,188 octets. In classical IP subnets, values other than the default can be used if and only if all members in the LIS have been configured to use the non-default value. Address resolution within an ATM logical IP subnet makes use of the ATM Address Resolution Protocol (ATMARP) and the *Inverse ATM Address Resolution Protocol* (InATMARP). ATMARP is the same protocol as the ARP protocol with extensions needed to support ARP in a unicast server ATM environment. InATMARP is the same protocol as the original InARP protocol except it is applied to ATM networks. Use of these protocols differs depending on whether PVCs or SVCs are used.

Permanent Virtual Connections. An IP station must have a mechanism (for example, manual configuration) for determining what PVCs it has and, in particular, which PVCs are being used with LLC/SNAP encapsulation. All IP members supporting PVCs are required to use the *Inverse ATM Address Resolution Protocol* (InATMARP) on those VCs using LLC/SNAP encapsulation. In a strict PVC environment, the receiver infers the relevant VC from the VC on which the InATMARP request (InARP_REQUEST) or response (InARP_REPLY) was received. When the ATM source or target address is unknown, the corresponding ATM address length in the InATMARP packet must be set to zero (0) indicating a null length; otherwise, the appropriate address field should be filled in and the corresponding length set appropriately. When the requesting station receives the InARP reply, it may complete the ATMARP table entry and use the provided address information. It is the responsibility of each IP station supporting PVCs to re-validate ATMARP table entries as part of the aging process.

Switched Virtual Connections. SVCs require support for ATMARP in the non-broadcast, non-multicast environment that ATM networks currently provide. To meet this need, a single ATMARP server must be located within the LIS. This server must have authoritative responsibility for resolving the ATMARP requests of all IP members within the LIS. The server itself does not actively establish connections. It depends on the clients in the LIS to initiate the ATMARP registration procedure. An individual client connects to the ATMARP server using a point-to-point VC. The server, upon the completion of an ATM call/connection of a new VC specifying LLC/SNAP encapsulation, will transmit an InATMARP request to determine the IP address of the client. The InATMARP reply from the client contains the information necessary for the ATMARP server to build its ATMARP table cache.

This information is used to generate replies to the ATMARP requests it receives. The ATMARP server mechanism requires that each client be administratively configured with the ATM address of the ATMARP server. One and only one ATMARP server can be operational per logical IP subnet. It is recommended that the ATMARP server also be an IP station. This station must be administratively configured to operate and recognize itself as the ATMARP server for a *Logical IP Subnet* (LIS). The ATMARP server must be configured with an IP address for each logical IP subnet it is serving to support InATMARP requests.

The ATMARP server accepts ATM calls and connections from other ATM end points. At call setup and if the VC supports LLC/SNAP encapsulation, the ATMARP server will transmit to the originating ATM station an InATMARP request (InARP_REQUEST) for each logical IP subnet the server is configured to serve. After receiving an InATMARP reply (InARP_REPLY), the server will examine the IP address and the ATM address. The server adds (or updates) the ATM address, IP address map entry, and time stamp into its ATMARP table. If the InATMARP IP address duplicates a table entry IP address, the InATMARP ATM address does not match the table entry ATM address, and there is an open VC associated with that table entry, the InATMARP information is discarded and no modifications are made to the table. ATMARP table entries persist until aged or invalidated. VC call tear down does not remove ATMARP table entries. The ATMARP server, upon receiving an ATMARP request (ARP_REQUEST), will generate the corresponding ATMARP reply (ARP_REPLY) if it has an entry in its ATMARP table. Otherwise, it will generate a negative ATMARP reply (ARP_NAK).

The ARP_NAK response is an extension to the ARMARP protocol and is used to improve the robustness of the ATMARP server mechanism. With ARP_NAK, a client can determine the difference between a catastrophic server failure and an ATMARP table lookup failure. The ARP_NAK packet format is the same as the received ARP_REQUEST packet format with the operation code set to ARP_NAK; that is, the ARP_REQUEST packet data is merely copied for transmission with the ARP_REQUEST operation code reset to ARP_NAK.

Updating the ATMARP Table Information Timeout: The Short Form.   When the server receives an ATMARP request over a VC, where the source IP and ATM address match the association already in the ATMARP table and the ATM address matches that associated with the VC, the server may update the timeout on the source ATMARP table entry. In other words, if the client is sending ATMARP requests to the server over the same VC that it used to register its ATMARP entry, the server should examine the ATMARP requests and note that the client is still "alive" by updating the timeout on the client's ATMARP table entry.

Adding Robustness to the Address Resolution Mechanism Using ATMARP.   When the server receives an ARP_REQUEST over a VC, it examines the source information. If no IP address is associated with the VC over which the ATMARP request was received and if the source IP address is not associated with any other connection, the server will add the ATM address, IP address entry, and time stamp into its ATMARP table and associate the entry with this VC.

ATMARP Client Operational Requirements.   The ATMARP client is responsible for contacting the ATMARP server to register its own ATMARP information and to gain and refresh its own ATMARP entry/information about other IP members. This means that ATMARP clients must be configured with the ATM address of the ATMARP server. ATMARP clients must do the following:

1. Initiate the VC connection to the ATMARP server for transmitting and receiving ATMARP and InATMARP packets.

2. Respond to ARP_REQUEST and InARP_REQUEST packets received on any VC appropriately.

3. Generate and transmit ARP_REQUEST packets to the ATMARP server and to process ARP_REPLY and ARP_NAK packets from the server appropriately. ARP_REPLY packets should be used to build/refresh its own client ATMARP table entries.

4. Generate and transmit InARP_REQUEST packets as needed and to process InARP_REPLY packets appropriately. InARP_REPLY packets should be used to build/refresh its own client ATMARP table entries.

5. Provide an ATMARP table aging function to remove its own old client ATMARP tables entries after a convenient period of time.

NOTE: *If the client does not maintain an open VC to the server, the client must refresh its ATMARP information with the server at least once every 20 minutes. This is done by opening a VC to the server and exchanging the initial InATMARP packets.*

ATMARP and InATMARP Packet Format

Internet addresses are assigned independently of ATM addresses. Each host implementation must know its own IP and ATM address(es) and must respond to address resolution requests appropriately. IP members also must use ATMARP and InATMARP to resolve IP addresses to ATM addresses when needed.

The ATMARP and InATMARP protocols use the same hardware type, protocol type, and operation code data formats as the ARP and InARP protocols. The location of these fields within the ATMARP packet are in the same byte position as those in ARP and InARP packets. A unique hardware type value has been assigned for ATMARP. In addition, ATMARP makes use of an additional operation code for ARP_NAK. The remainder of the ATMARP/InATMARP packet format is different from the ARP/InARP packet format.

The ATMARP and InATMARP protocols have several fields that have the following format and values (see Listing 14.1).

Listing 14.1

```
16 bits Hardware type.
16 bits Protocol type.
8 bits type and length of source ATM number (q).
8 bits type and length of source ATM subaddress (r).
16 bits operation code (request, reply, or NAK).
8 bits length of source protocol address (s).
8 bits type and length of target ATM number (x).
8 bits type and length of target ATM subaddress (y).
8 bits length of target protocol address (z).
Source ATM number.
Source ATM subaddress.
Source protocol address.
Target ATM number.
Target ATM subaddress.
Target protocol address.
Assigned to ATM Forum address family and is 19 decimal (0x0013).
The operation type value (decimal):
ARP_REQUEST=1.
ARP_REPLY=2.
InARP_REQUEST=8.
InARP_REPLY=9.
ARP_NAK=10.
Length in octets of the source protocol address. For IP ar$spln is 4.
Length in octets of the target protocol address. For IP ar$tpln is 4.
Source ATM number (E.164 or ATM Forum NSAPA).
Source ATM subaddress (ATM Forum NSAPA).
Source protocol address.
Target ATM number (E.164 or ATM Forum NSAPA).
Target ATM subaddress (ATM Forum NSAPA).
Target protocol address.
```

RFC 1577 Client Connection Setup

1. Logical IP Subnet Client A and B establish a connection to the ARP server New York using the configured ATM addresses of New York.

2. ARP server (New York) will detect a connection from LIS A and B.

3. ARP server (New York) will issue an InARP request to client A and request the following:

   a. Nodes layer three's IP address
   b. ATM address of client A

4. ARP Server (New York) will store the IP and ATM address mapping in its ARP cache. (This sounds like IP to MAC address.)

5. Client A want to establish a session with client B.

6. Client A issues an ATM ARP request for client B ATM address to the ATM ARP server (New York).

7. ARP server (New York) will respond with an ATM ARP reply with client B's ATM address. If ARP server (New York) doesn't have an entry for client B in its table, an ATM NAK will be returned at this point.

8. Client A will now establish a connection using UNI Signaling Q.2931 with A using B's ATM address.

LAN Emulation Overview

Asynchronous Transfer Mode (ATM) networks differ from traditional, or "legacy" networks in many ways. One significant difference in the local area is that legacy LANs and their associated protocols were developed with the assumption that broadcast to all hosts attached to the LAN was easy (see Figure 14.23). This was generally true because all the hosts shared some communications medium such as a length of coaxial cable or a shared media concentrator.

ATM networks, in contrast, are connection-oriented. So, even if a continual piece of cable is used between all the hosts on a LAN, the connection to each host from another host is logically separate from all other connections. Although this approach has many benefits (for example, increased security, better possibilities for sharing of bandwidth, and so on), it does have some drawbacks. One drawback is that the broadcast abilities of the legacy Shared Media LANs have to be emulated to enable existing protocol stacks to appear transparent to connection-oriented ATM.

The connections defined by the ATM Forum UNI specification 3.0/3.1 include both point-to-point and point-to-multipoint type connections. Point-to-multipoint connections can be set up to connect a single point to all the other hosts on the emulated LAN (ELAN) to emulate the broadcast capability of the traditional shared medium. Point-to-multipoint connections can also be set up to connect a single point to selected hosts, which is also known as "multicast." Legacy LANs also support the idea of multicast traffic, but typically they broadcast the traffic and let the destinations that were not addressed filter out the traffic. ATM networks transport multicast traffic in a more efficient fashion, because the traffic will only be transmitted to the intended hosts.

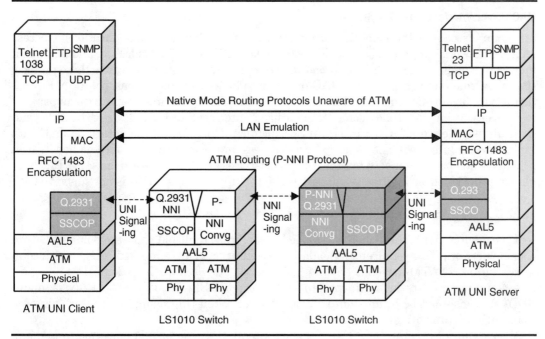

Figure 14.23 LAN Emulation protocol

If a LAN Emulation service is provided for an ATM network, end systems (for example, workstations, servers, LAN switches, bridges, and so on) can connect to the ATM network while the software applications interact as if they are attached to a traditional LAN. This service also supports the interconnection of ATM networks with traditional LANs by means of today's bridging methods. This allows interoperability between software applications residing on ATM-attached end systems and on traditional LAN end systems. To emulate a LAN-like service, different types of emulation can be defined, ranging from emulating the MAC service (for example, that of IEEE 802.x LANs) up to emulating the services of network and transport layers. This specification defines a MAC service emulation, including encapsulation of MAC frames (user data frames). This approach to LAN Emulation provides support for the maximum number of existing applications.

LAN-Specific Characteristics to Be Emulated

Connectionless Services

LAN stations today are able to send data without previously establishing connections. LAN emulation provides the appearance of such a connectionless service to the participating end systems so existing applications are unchanged. The LAN Emulation service supports the use of multicast MAC addresses (for example, broadcast, group, or functional MAC addresses). The need for a multicast service for LAN emulation comes from classical LANs where end stations share the same media.

MAC Driver Interfaces in ATM Stations

The main objective of the LAN Emulation service is to enable existing applications to access an ATM network via protocol stacks like APPN, NetBIOS, IP, IPX, AppleTalk, and so on as if they were running over traditional broadcast shared media networks. Because these protocol stacks are communicating with a MAC driver in today's implementations, the LAN Emulation service has to offer the same MAC driver service primitives, thus keeping the upper protocol layers unchanged. Today, some "standardized" interfaces for MAC device drivers do exist (for example, Network Driver Interface Specification, Open Data-Link Interface, and Data Link Provider Interface). They specify how to access a MAC driver. Each of them has its own primitives and parameter sets, but the essential services and functions are the same. LAN emulation provides these interfaces and services to the upper layers. FDDI is not supported.

Emulated LANs

In some environments there might be a need to configure multiple, separate domains within a single network. This requirement leads to the definition of an "emulated LAN," which comprises a group of ATM-attached devices. This group of devices would be logically analogous to a group of LAN stations attached to an Ethernet/IEEE 802.3 or 802.5 LAN segment. FDDI stations must be bridged into an Ethernet or token ring using existing bridging options such as translational bridging.

Several *emulated LANs* (ELANs) could be configured within an ATM network, and membership in an emulated LAN is independent of where an end system is physically connected. An end system could belong to multiple emulated LANs. Because multiple emulated LANs over a single ATM network are logically independent, a broadcast frame originating from

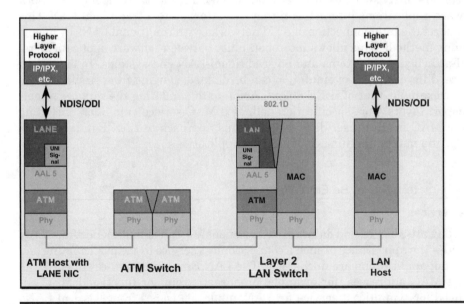

Figure 14.24 LANE protocol architecture

a member of a particular emulated LAN is distributed only to the members of that emulated LAN.

LANE Architectural Overview

LAN Emulation enables the implementation of emulated shared media LANs over an ATM network. An emulated LAN provides communication of user data frames among all its users, similar to a physical LAN. One or more emulated LANs could run on the same ATM network. However, each of the emulated LANs is independent of the others and users cannot communicate directly across emulated LAN boundaries without the use of a router.

Each emulated LAN is one of two types: Ethernet II/IEEE 802.3 or IEEE 802.5 token ring. Each emulated LAN is composed of a set of LAN Emulation Services such as LE clients or LECs, *LE Configuration servers* (LECS), an *LE server* (LES), and a *Broadcast and Unknown server* (BUS). Each LE client is part of an ATM end station. It represents a set of users, identified by their MAC address. The LE service may be part of an end station or a LAN switch; it may be centralized or distributed over a number of stations.

Communication among LE clients and between LE clients and the LE server is performed over ATM *virtual channel connections* (VCCs). Each LE client must communicate with the LE service over control and data VCCs. Emulated LANs operate in any of the following environments: *switched virtual circuit* (SVC), *permanent virtual circuit* (PVC), or mixed SVC/PVC. In a PVC-only LAN, no call setup and close-down procedures exist; instead, layer management is used to set up and clear connections. In this PVC environment, the layer management is responsible for both setting up and clearing connections and has full responsibility for ensuring that the emulated LAN functions correctly.

Architectural Perspective

The architecture of a communication system emphasizes the logical divisions of the system and how they fit together. This section incorporates the following types of architectural views:

- The (internal) layer interfaces that specify the interaction between the LAN emulation entity and the other entities within the end-station
- The user-to-network interface that specifies the interaction between an LE client and the LE server over the ATM network

Layer Interfaces

In this architectural model, the layers interact by way of well-defined service interfaces, providing services. In general, the interface requirements are as follows (see Figure 14.25):

1. The interface between the LAN Emulation layer and the Higher layers includes facilities for transmitting and receiving user data frames.
2. The interfaces between the LAN Emulation layer and the *ATM adaptation Layer* (AAL) include facilities for transmitting and receiving AAL-5 frames. AAL-5 utilizes lower layers, including the ATM and Physical layers. Interface service access points are identified by SAP-IDs (that have a one-to-one mapping to VCCs).

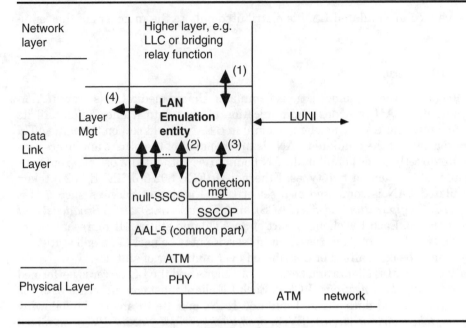

Figure 14.25   The layered architecture of LAN emulation

3. The interface between the LAN Emulation entity and the Connection management entity includes facilities to request the setup or release of virtual connections. This entity handles both SVCs and PVCs.

4. The interface between the LAN Emulation entity and the Layer Management entity includes facilities to initialize and control the LAN Emulation entity and to return status information.

LAN Emulation User to Network Interface (LUNI)

In this architectural model, the LE clients and the LE service interact by way of a well-defined interface using Protocol Data Units and implementing protocols as specified later in this chapter. In general, the interface requirements are as follows (see Figure 14.26):

- Initialization:
  - Learning and obtaining the ATM address(es) of the LE services that are available on a particular ATM network
  - Joining or leaving a particular emulated LAN specified by the ATM Address of the LE service
  - Declaring whether this LE client wants to receive address resolution requests for all the frames with unregistered destinations
- Registration: Informing the LE service of the following:
  - The list of individual MAC addresses that the LE client represents

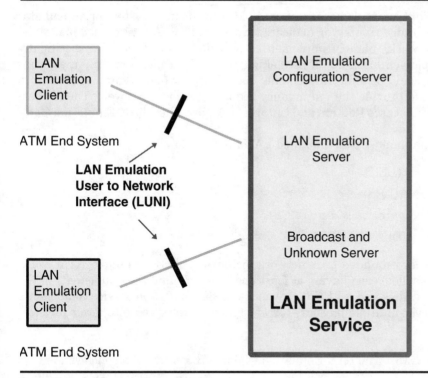

Figure 14.26 Implementation perspective

- The list of Source Route descriptors (that is, segment/bridge pairs) that the LE client represents for source route bridging

- Address resolution: Obtaining the ATM address representing the LE client with a particular MAC address (unicast, broadcast or segment/bridge pair)

  - Data transfer: Moving the data from the source to the destination by encapsulation of the LE-SDU (Service Data Unit) in an AAL-5 frame and transmission by the LE client

Users connect to the LAN emulation service via LE clients. LE clients are typically implemented in ATM end stations, either as part of the software driver (between the operating system and the ATM hardware) or on a special processor that is part of the ATM adapter (the ATM-specific hardware).

LAN Emulation is expected to be used in either of two configurations:

- Intermediate systems (for example, bridges, LAN switches, or routers). These devices enable the communication among "legacy" LANs over ATM backbone networks.

- End stations (for example, hosts or PCs). These devices enable the communication between ATM end stations and end stations on "legacy" LAN or among ATM end stations.

The LE service might be implemented in an ATM intermediate system or an end station (for example, a bridge, router, or dedicated work station). Alternatively, it may be "part of the ATM network," namely, implemented in switches or other ATM-specific devices. A possible implementation might be a single (centralized) LE service. An alternative implementation could be a distributed one, for example, where a number of servers operate in parallel and provide the redundancy required for error-recovery. The LE service can be co-located on Cisco Routers and Catalyst LANSwitches, LAN Emulation Components.

The components that make up an emulated LAN are as follows:

- *LAN Emulation client* (LEC)
- *LAN Emulation server* (LES)
- *LAN Emulation Configuration server* (LECS)
- *Broadcast and Unknown server* (BUS)

The components of an Emulated LAN network include clients (for example, ATM workstations and ATM switches) each having at least one LE client and the components of the LE service (an LES, a BUS, and a LECS). Any of the LAN Emulation service components may be distributed over multiple physical LANs or may be collapsed into fewer physical LANs, even a single one.

LAN Emulation Client (LEC).   The LAN Emulation Client is the entity in an end system that performs data forwarding, address resolution, and other control functions. This provides a MAC-level emulated Ethernet/IEEE 802.3 or IEEE 802.5 service interface to higher level software and implements the LUNI interface when communicating with other entities within the Emulated LAN. A LEC can be a router, LAN switch, Windows 98/Windows 2000 client with ATM card and drivers, Novell file server, UNIX host, and so on.

LAN Emulation Server (LES).   The LES implements the control coordination function for the Emulated LAN. The LE server provides a facility for registering and resolving MAC addresses or route descriptors to ATM addresses. Clients may register the LAN destinations they represent with the LE server. A client also queries the LE server when the client wishes to resolve a MAC address or route descriptor to an ATM address. The LE server will either respond directly to the client or forward the query to other clients so they may respond.

Broadcast and Unknown Server (BUS).   The Broadcast and Unknown server handles data sent by an LE client to the broadcast MAC address, all multicast traffic, and initial unicast frames, which are sent by a LAN Emulation Client before the data direct target ATM address has been resolved (before a data direct VCC has been established).

NOTE: All broadcast, multicast, and unknown traffic to and from an LE client passes through the BUS server. Distributed and redundant implementations of the BUS are explicitly permitted with this architecture. Cisco supports redundant LANE services using the Simple Server Redundancy Protocol *(SSRP) Protocol and LANE 2.0. The multicast server function provided in the BUS is required as part of LAN Emulation to provide the connectionless data delivery charac-*

teristics of a shared network to LAN Emulation clients. The main task is to distribute data with multicast MAC addresses (for example, group, broadcast, and functional addresses); to deliver initial Unicast data, where the MAC address hasn't been resolved to a direct ATM connection; and to distribute data with explorer source routing information.

The multicast function provided in the BUS may be implemented by an underlying ATM multicast service. A LEC sends data frames to the BUS that serializes the frames and re-transmits them to a group of attached LECs. Serialization is required to prevent AAL5 frames from different sources from being inter-leaved. In an SVC environment, the BUS needs to participate in the LE Address Resolution Protocol (LE_ARP) to enable a LEC to locate the BUS. The BUS handles ATM connections and manages its distribution group. This BUS must always exist in the Emulated LAN and all LECs must join its distribution group via multicast forward VCC.

LE Configuration Server (LECS). The LECS implements the assignment of individual LE clients to different emulated LANs. Based upon its own policies, configuration database, and information provided by clients, it assigns any client that requests configuration information to a particular emulated LAN service by giving the client the LES's ATM address. This method supports the capability to assign a client to an emulated LAN based on either the physical location (ATM address) or the identity of a LAN destination that it is representing. It is optional for the LEC to obtain information from the LECS using the configuration protocol. The LECS allows the LEC to automatically configure. Cisco provide the ability for LANE clients to be restricted to a given ELAN, allowing membership to be based on a security policy.

Connections

A LAN Emulation client has separate VCCs for control traffic such as LE_ARP requests and for data traffic to transfer encapsulated IEEE 802.3 or IEEE 802.5 frames. Each VCC carries traffic for only one Emulated LAN. The VCCs form a mesh of connections between the LECs and other LAN Emulation entities such as the LECS, LES, and the BUS.

Control Connections. A control VCC connects the LEC to the LECS. Control VCCs also connects the LEC to the LES and carry LE_ARP traffic and control frames. The control VCCs never carry data frames. Control VCCs are set up as part of the LEC initialization phase and are shown in Figures 14.27 and 14.28.

Configuration Direct VCC. This bidirectional VCC may be set up by the LEC as part of the LECS connect phase and is used to obtain configuration information, including the address of the LES. The LEC may still maintain this VCC while participating in the emulated LAN. It may continue to keep it open for further queries to the LE configuration service while participating in the Emulated LAN. The configuration direct VCC may be used to inquire about an LE client other than the one to which the configuration direct VCC is attached (see Figure 14.29).

Control Direct VCC. The LEC sets up a bidirectional point-to-point VCC to the LES for sending control traffic. This is set up by the LEC as part of the initialization phase. Because the

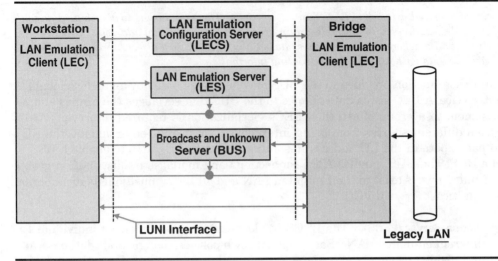

Figure 14.27   Basic LAN Emulation client connections across LUNI

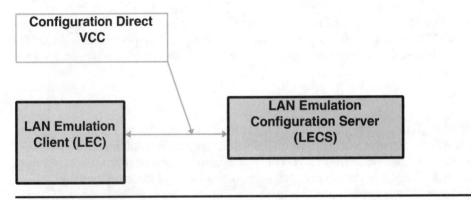

Figure 14.28   LAN Emulation client to *LAN Emulation Configuration Server* (LECS) control connection

LES has the option to use the return path to send control data to the LEC, this requires the LEC to accept control traffic from this VCC. The LEC and LES must maintain this VCC while participating in the Emulated LAN.

Control Distribute VCC.   The LES may optionally set up a unidirectional point-to-point or point-to-multipoint control VCC to the LEC for distributing control traffic. This VCC may be set up by the LES as part of the initialization phase. If set up, the LEC is required to accept the control distribute VCC regardless of type. The LEC and LES must maintain this VCC while participating in the Emulated LAN.

Data Connections.   Data VCCs connect the LECs to each other and to the Broadcast and Unknown server. These carry Ethernet/IEEE 802.3 or IEEE 802.5 data frames as well as flush messages. Apart from flush messages, data VCCs never carry control traffic.

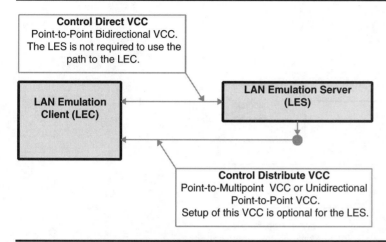

Figure 14.29   Configuration direct VCC

Data Direct VCC.   Bidirectional point-to-point VCCs are established between LECs that want to exchange unicast data traffic. When an LE client has a packet to send and the ATM address for that destination is unknown, the LE client shall generate an LE_ARP request to ascertain the ATM address for that destination. After the LEC receives a reply to the LE_ARP, it shall set up a point-to-point VCC, if not already established, over which to send all subsequent data to that LAN destination.

The LAN Emulation client that issues an LE_ARP request and receives an LE_ARP response is responsible for initiating the signaling to establish this bidirectional Data Direct VCC with the responding client named in the LE_ARP response. If the client has insufficient resources to set up a Data Direct VCC, it must not continue to send frames to the Broadcast and Unknown server that it should have sent on the Data Direct VCC. In this case, it should tear down an existing Data Direct VCC to another client in order to free up resources to allow the new Data Direct VCC to be set up (see Figure 14.30).

Multicast Send VCC.   An LEC sets up a bidirectional point-to-point Multicast Send VCC to the BUS. This VCC is set up using the same process as for Data Direct VCCs. The LEC first sends an LE_ARP and, when it receives the LE_ARP response, initiates signaling to establish this bidirectional VCC (the Multicast Send VCC) to the BUS. This VCC is used for sending multicast data to the BUS and for sending initial unicast data. The BUS may use the return path on this VCC to send data to the LEC, so this requires the LEC to accept traffic from this VCC.

The LEC must maintain this VCC while participating in the Emulated LAN.

Multicast Forward VCC.   After the LEC has set up the Multicast Send VCC, the BUS initiates the signaling for the Multicast Forward VCC to the LEC. This VCC is used for distributing data from the BUS. It can be either a point-to-multipoint VCC or a unidirectional point-to-point VCC. The LEC is required to accept the Multicast Forward VCC regardless of type. A Multicast Forward VCC from the BUS must be established before a LEC participates in the Emulated LAN. The LEC must attempt to maintain this VCC while participating in

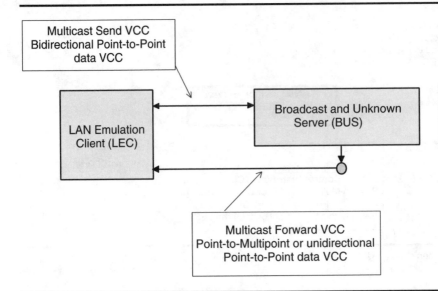

Figure 14.30 Data Direct VCC

the Emulated LAN. The BUS may forward frames to a LEC on either the Multicast Send VCC or the Multicast Forward VCC. A LEC will not receive duplicate frames forwarded from the BUS on both the Multicast Send and the Multicast Forward VCC, but must be able to accept frames on either VCC.

Emulated LAN Functions

Initialization The Initial state refers to the parameters that are configured at the "beginning of time." The initialization is completed after the Join and Initial Registration processes have completed and the connections to the LES and BUS have been established. At this point, the LE client becomes operational.

Initial State

In the Initial state there are parameters (such as addresses, Emulated LAN name, max frame size, and so on) that are known to the LE server and LE clients, respectively, about themselves, before participating in the Configuration and Join phase functions.

LECS Connect Phase

In the LECS Connect phase, the LE client establishes a Configuration Direct VCC to the LE Configuration server.

Configuration Phase

This is the phase in which the LE client discovers the LE service in preparation for the Join phase. In its simplest form, the LE client may use preconfigured parameters. If the LEC supports the optional LE Configuration protocol, it can use this to discover the LE service.

Join Phase

In the Join phase of ATM LAN Emulation initialization, the LE client establishes its control connections to the LE server. The Join procedure may have two outcomes: success or failure. After the Join phase has successfully completed, the LE client has been assigned a unique *LE client identifier* (LECID), knows the emulated LAN's maximum frame size and its LAN type (Ethernet/IEEE 802.3 or IEEE 802.5), and has established the Control VCC(s) with the LE server.

Initial Registration

After joining, an LE client may register any number of MAC addresses or route descriptors. This is in addition to the single MAC address that can be registered as part of the Join phase. Initial registration allows an LE client to verify the uniqueness of its local addresses before completing initialization and becoming operational.

Connecting to the BUS

To establish a connection to the BUS, the LE client LE_ARPs broadcasts all 1s for the MAC address and proceeds to set up the connection. The BUS then establishes the Multicast Forward VCC to the LE client.

Initialization Phases, Recovery, and Termination

Figure 14.31 shows the steps in initialization and paths for termination and recovery from various phases. The conditions for termination and recovery are discussed in sections that follow.

Registration

The address registration function is the mechanism by which Clients provide address information to the LAN Emulation server. An intelligent LE server may respond to address resolution requests if LECs register their LAN destinations (defined as MAC addresses or, for source-routing IEEE 802.5 LANs only, route descriptors) with the LE server. The LAN destinations may also be unregistered as the state of the client changes. A client must either register all LAN destinations for which it is responsible or join as a proxy.

Address Resolution

Address resolution is the procedure by which a client associates a LAN destination with the ATM address of another client or the BUS. Address resolution allows clients to set up data direct VCCs to carry frames.

When a LAN Emulation client is presented with a frame for transmission whose LAN destination is unknown to that client, it must issue a *LAN Emulation address resolution protocol* (LE_ARP) request frame to the LES over its control point-to-point VCC.

The LES may do one of the following:

- Forward this LE_ARP frame to the appropriate client(s) using the control distribute VCC or one or more Control Direct VCCs. Different LES implementations may use

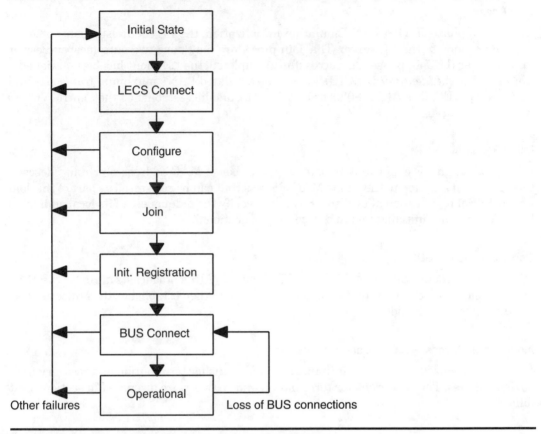

Figure 14.31 Initialization, recovery, and terminating the ELAN

different distribution algorithms. If a client responds to a forwarded LE_ARP request with an LE_ARP reply, that reply is also sent and relayed over the control VCCs to the original requester.

- Issue an LE_ARP reply on behalf of a client that has registered the requested LAN destination with the LES. A LAN Emulation client must respond to an LE_ARP request that it receives asking for a LAN destination it has registered with the LES, or for which it is a proxy.

Each LE client maintains a cache of LE_ARP replies and uses a two-period time-out mechanism to age entries in this cache. The aging time period is used for all entries learned from LE_ARP responses whose FLAGS field's Remote Address flag was zero. Responses for registered LAN destinations are always timed out with the Aging Time. For aging entries learned from LE_ARP replies with the Remote Address flags bit set to one and for entries learned by observing source addresses on Data VCCs, which time-out to use is determined by the state of the LE client's Topology Change flag. When this flag is set, such entries are aged using the forward delay time. When this flag is clear, such entries are aged using the

Aging Time parameter. The state of this flag may be altered either by local management action or by reception of LE_TOPOLOGY_REQUEST messages.

LANE Connection Management

In *switched virtual connection* (SVC) environments, the LAN Emulation entities (for example, LEC, LES, and BUS) set up connections between each other using UNI signaling. The connections at a minimum use best effort quality of service. The method of connection setup is summarized in the following sections.

Call Establishment

So that the called party can initiate data transfer on a Data Direct VCC, the ATM layer call establishment procedures are augmented by additional protocol.

In Figure 14.32, the SETUP, CONNECT, and CONNECT_ACK messages are the SVC call setup messages. When a call is being set up, the called party must not send its CONNECT message until it is ready to receive frames on the new VCC. Thus, the calling party should be able to assume that it can transmit frames after it has received the CONNECT message. Because the CONNECT_ACK message that is received by the called party may be generated by its local switch and is not an end-to-end indication from the calling party, it may be received by the called party before the calling party has received its CONNECT message. The calling party can only set itself up to receive frames on the VCC after it receives a CONNECT message that indicates the allocation of VPI/VCI numbers. Thus, there is no guarantee for the called party that its initial data will be received by the calling party until it receives some end-to-end indication from the far end.

The calling party must send a READY_IND message as soon as it is ready to receive frames on the newly-established VCC. At that point, the calling party considers call establishment

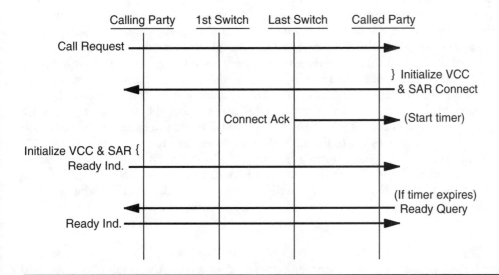

Figure 14.32 Call establishment: Ready Indicate/Query

to be complete. The calling party may also send data as soon as it is ready to receive frames on the newly-established VCC. Data may be sent before or after the sending of the READY_IND.

Unicast Frames

When a LAN Emulation client has established via the address resolution mechanism that a certain LAN destination corresponds to a certain ATM address, and when that client knows it has a Data Direct VCC to that ATM address, a frame addressed to that LAN destination must be forwarded via that Data Direct VCC. If a LAN Emulation client does not know which Data Direct VCC to use for a given unicast LAN destination, or if that Data Direct VCC has not yet been established, it may elect to transmit the frame over the Multicast Send VCC to the Broadcast and Unknown server. The Broadcast and Unknown server, in turn, forwards the frame to at least the client for which it is destined. If the LAN destination is unregistered, the frame must be forwarded to at least all proxy clients and may be forwarded to all clients.

On an emulated LAN, the case can arise where a frame can only reach its destination through an IEEE 802.1D transparent bridge, and that bridge does not know the whereabouts of that destination. The only way such a frame can be assured of reaching its destination is for the frame to be transmitted to all of the IEEE 802.1D transparent bridges via the Broadcast and Unknown server so they, in turn, can flood that frame to all of their other bridge ports, or at least the ones enabled by the spanning tree protocol. An LE client that chooses not to forward frames to the Broadcast and Unknown Server, therefore, may not be able to reach destinations via transparent bridges (or perhaps other proxy agents.)

Multicast Frames.   LAN Emulation clients may want to send frames to a multicast MAC address, or they may wish to receive frames addressed to a given multicast MAC address. To send frames to a multicast MAC address, an LE client MUST send the frames to the BUS. The address resolution mechanism is used during the initialization process to provide the ATM address of the BUS for multicast and broadcast traffic, and connection management will provide a point-to-point Multicast Send VCC over which to send such frames.

All that is required for the LEC to receive frames addressed to a given multicast MAC address is for the LE client to connect to the BUS, after which the BUS tries to set up a return path for all broadcast and multicast traffic. When a client connects to the BUS, the BUS will try to establish a Multicast Forward VCC to that client. It is expected that Multicast Forward VCCs will be unidirectional point-to-multipoint VCCs, but they may be implemented as point-to-point VCCs. This decision is left to the LAN Emulation service, not to the client.

An LE client receives all flooded unicast frames and all broadcast and multicast frames over either its Multicast Send VCC or its Multicast Forward VCC. Which VCC the BUS uses to forward frames to the LE client is at the discretion of the BUS. An LE client will not, however, receive duplicate frames.

Frame Ordering

There may be two paths for unicast frames between a sending LAN Emulation client and a receiving client: one via the Broadcast and Unknown Server and one via a data direct VCC between them. For a given LAN destination, a sending client is expected to use only one path at a time, but the choice of paths may change over time. Switching between those paths introduces the possibility that frames may be delivered to the receiving client out of order. Out-of-order delivery of frames between two LAN endpoints is uncharacteristic of LANs and undesirable in an ATM emulated LAN. The flush protocol is provided to ensure the correct order of delivery of unicast data frames. Sending clients may choose to use the flush message protocol or not. In particular, if a sending client waits for some period of time for address resolution to work before utilizing the Broadcast and Unknown server, out-of-order frames can be minimized at the cost of some delay. Any client receiving a flush request message must respond by sending a flush response message to the original sender.

Source Routing Considerations

Source-route bridging is the predominant bridging technology used within IEEE 802.5 token ring networks. The use of source routing does not preclude transparent bridging in these networks. A token ring end station will typically use a combination of source-routed and non-source-routed frames. The process described in this chapter allows an LEC to operate with both source routing and transparent bridging.

In addition to the *Destination Address* (DA) field and *Source Address* (SA) field, a source-routed frame contains a *Routing Information* (RI) field. The RI field contains a control field and a list of *route descriptors* (RD) that indicate the frame's path through the network. Therefore the information in the RI field determines which SR bridges will forward the frame. The LE client determines if the frame is to be forwarded by a SR bridge or if the LAN destination is a station on the ELAN.

The LE client determines whether the frame is to be forwarded by an SR bridge or if the LAN destination is a station on the local emulated LAN by examining the RI field. If the LAN destination is accessible through an SR bridge, the LAN destination is the Next Route Descriptor; otherwise, the LAN destination is the frame's Destination Address.

Frames with specifically routed source-routing information (an SRF frame) and unicast destination MAC addresses are sent down Data Direct VCCs following the usual LE_ARP and VCC setup process. Other source routing frames are sent to the BUS.

LAN Emulation Frame Formats

Data Frame.   Two data packet formats are used by this specification. One of the two formats must be used by an LE client that conforms to this specification. The first is based on ISO 8802.3/CSMA-CD (IEEE 802.3) and has the format shown in Table 14.3. The minimum LAN Emulation AAL5 SDU length for IEEE 802.3/Ethernet format data frames is 62 octets.

The length of the LAN Emulation header is two octets, and it also contains either the LECID value of the sending LE client or X0000. The LAN *frame check sequence*, FCS, must not be included. The second packet format is based on ISO 8802.5 (IEEE 802.5, or token ring) and has the format shown in Table 14.4. The minimum LAN Emulation AAL5 SDU length for IEEE 802.5 format data frames is 16 octets.

The length of the LAN Emulation header is two octets, and it also contains either the LECID value of the sending LE client or x0000. The LAN frame check sequence, FCS, MUST NOT be included. The AC PAD octet is not used in LAN Emulation. This may be set to any value on transmit and SHOULD be ignored on receipt. LAN Emulation only allows LLC frames to be sent.

Table 14.3   LAN Emulation data frame format for IEEE 802.3/Ethernet frames

0	LE HEADER	DESTINATION ADDR
4		DESTINATION ADDRESS
8		SOURCE ADDRESS
12	SOURCE ADDR	TYPE/LENGTH
16 and on		INFO

Table 14.4   LAN Emulation data frame format for IEEE 802.5 frames

0	LE HEADER	AC PAD FC
4		DESTINATION ADDRESS
8	DESTINATION ADDR	SOURCE ADDRESS
12		SOURCE ADDR
16 up to 46	ROUTING INFORMATION FIELD	
		INFO

Encoding of Ethernet/IEEE 802.3 Type/Length Fields

ATM LAN Emulation supports both IEEE 802.2 (LLC) data frames and DIX EtherType frames. Because ATM Emulated LANs allows data frames larger than those allowed on legacy LANs, an LE client must use the following rules to encode the Type/Length fields of data frames:

1. DIX Ethernet EtherType frames MUST be encoded by placing the EtherType field in the TYPE/LENGTH field. Data following the EtherType field follows this field immediately.

2. LLC data frames whose total length, including the LLC field and data, but not including padding required to meet the minimum data frame length (and not including the Frame Check Sequence, which is not used in ATM LAN Emulation), is less than 1536 must be encoded by placing that length in the TYPE/LENGTH field. The LLC field follows the TYPE/LENGTH field immediately.

3. LLC data frames longer than this maximum must be encoded by placing the value 0 in the TYPE/LENGTH field. The LLC data frame follows the TYPE/LENGTH field immediately.

When decoding data frames, the following rules may be used by an LE client:

1. If the TYPE/LENGTH field is 1536 or greater, the frame is DIX Ethernet encoded. The TYPE/LENGTH field is the EtherType, and the data follows. The length of the data may be obtained from the AAL-5 trailer by subtracting the length of the frame through the TYPE/LENGTH field (16). On short frames, this length has a minimum

value (46), so padding octets added to meet the minimum frame size cannot be identified at this level of decoding.

2. If the TYPE/LENGTH field is less than 1536, the frame is an IEEE 802.2 LLC frame. The LLC field immediately follows the TYPE/LENGTH field.

   a. If the TYPE/LENGTH field is non-zero, it indicates the length of the data, starting with the LLC octets. Because this length does not include padding to meet the minimum data frame length requirement, such padding can be identified.

   b. If the TYPE/LENGTH field is zero, the length of the LLC data field may be obtained from the AAL-5 trailer by subtracting the length of the frame through the TYPE/LENGTH field (16).

LE Control Frames

All LAN Emulation control frames, except for READY_IND and READY_QUERY, use the format described in Table 14.5.

The fields common to all frame formats are described in Table 14.6.

In the two fields in a control frame where a LAN Destination is specified, the 8-octet format described in Table 14.6 must be used. The tag value not present must only be used where explicitly allowed for individual frame formats and protocols. MAC addresses and Route Designators are in their natural bit/octet order (LSB for Ethernet/IEEE 802.3 or MSB for IEEE 802.5) according to the emulated LAN type. Where the emulated LAN type is undetermined, Ethernet/IEEE 802.3 bit ordering must be used. There are only three cases where the LAN type may be undetermined:

- LE_CONFIGURE_REQUEST, LAN-TYPE=0

- LE_CONFIGURE_RESPONSE, LAN-TYPE=0

- LE_JOIN_REQUEST, LAN-TYPE=0

Table 14.5 Control frame

0	MARKER = XFF00	PROTOCOL = X01		VERSION = X01	
4	OP-CODE	STATUS			
8		TRANSACTION-ID			
12	REQUESTER-LECID			FLAGS	
16		SOURCE-LAN-DESTINATION			
24		TARGET-LAN-DESTINATION			
32		SOURCE-ATM-ADDRESS			
52	LAN-TYPE	MAXIMUM-FRAME		NUMBER-TLVS	ELAN-SIZE NAME-SIZE
56	TARGET-ATM-ADDRESS				
76	ELAN-NAME				
108	TLVs BEGIN				

Table 14.6   Control frame header format

Size	Name	Function
2	MARKER	Control Frame=XFF00
1	PROTOCOL	ATM LAN Emulation protocol=X01
1	VERSION	ATM LAN Emulation protocol version=X01
2	OP-CODE	Controls frame type
2	STATUS	Always X0000 in requests
4	TRANSACTION-ID	Arbitrary value supplied by the requester and returned by the responder to allow the receiver to discriminate between different responses
2	REQUESTER-LECID	LECID of LE client sending the request (X0000 if unknown)
2	FLAGS	Bit flags
92	Meaning of remainder of fields depends on OP-CODE	

Table 14.7   LAN destination field format

Size	Name	Function
2	TAG	X0000=not present, X0001=MAC address, X0002=Route descriptor
6	MAC Address	6-octet MAC address if MAC address specified.
4	RESERVED	0, if route descriptor specified.
2	Route Descriptor	If route descriptor specified.

Table 14.8   Control frame FLAGS values

Name	Use
Remote address	LE_ARP_RESPONSE
Proxy flag	LE_JOIN_REQUEST
Topology change	LE_TOPOLOGY_REQUEST

LANE Initialization Protocol, Procedures, and Frame Formats

The initialization of an LE client is divided into an Initial state and five phases: LECS Connect phase, Configuration phase, Join phase, Initial Registration phase, and BUS Connect phase. These five phases must be performed in sequence, starting with the LECS Connect phase. Following the completion of the BUS Connect phase, the initialization procedure is complete, and the LE client is operational. If the initialization phase or the operational state terminates abnormally, the LE client must return to the Initial state and inform layer management.

All five phases of the initialization procedure are required for an LE client to expect to achieve full interoperability.

Initial State—LE Client View

The state of the variables defined in this section after the orderly termination of an LE client, or its abnormal termination from any initialization or operational phase, is an implementation issue not addressed in this specification.

Certain parameters contain minimum, maximum, or default values. A variable must not be set to a value smaller than its minimum value or larger than its maximum value. Most ATM Emulated LANs, if composed entirely of LAN Emulation components compliant with this specification, and whose components variable values are set to the default values, should operate correctly. The behavior of specific configurations may be optimized by altering the values away from the defaults.

The following parameters apply to each LE client:

C1   *LE Client ATM Addresses.*   The LE client owns ATM addresses. The primary ATM address used to connect to the LES and the BUS must be known before the Configuration and Join phases can start, and must not change without restarting the Configuration and Join phases. The Primary ATM address must be used to establish the LE Client Control Direct and Multicast VCCs and MUST be specified as the SOURCE-ATM-ADDRESS in the client LE_JOIN_REQUESTs. An LE client may have additional ATM addresses for use with Data Direct VCCs.

C2   *LAN Type.*   The type of LAN of which the LE client is, or wants to become, a member. This must be one of Ethernet/IEEE 802.3, IEEE 802.5, or Unspecified. It must not be Unspecified after a successful Join. This parameter must not be changed without terminating the LE client and returning to the Initial state.

C3   *Maximum Data Frame Size.*   The maximum AAL-5 SDU size of a data frame that the LE client wishes to send on the Multicast Send VCC or to receive on the Multicast Send VCC or Multicast Forward VCC. This parameter also specifies the maximum AAL-5 SDU of all of an LE client Data Direct VCCs. This must be either 1516, 4544, 9234, or 18190 octets, or Unspecified. Must not be Unspecified after a successful Join. It must not be changed without terminating the LE client and returning it to the Initial state.

C4   *Proxy.*   This indicates whether the LE client may have remote unicast MAC addresses in C27. For example, an IEEE 802.1D transparent bridge must not register with the LE server the MAC addresses of the endstations on its other LAN segments. This must be known before the Join phase can start.

C5   *ELAN Name.*   The identity of the emulated LAN the LE client wishes to join, or to which the LE client last joined. May be unspecified before Join. Never unspecified after a successful Join. The ELAN Name client parameter and ELAN_NAME field in the Join protocol provide a way to configure clients with human-readable strings for network management purposes.

C6   *Local unicast MAC Address(es).*   Each LE client has zero or more local unicast MAC addresses. In an operational LE client, every address in this variable MUST have been registered with the LE server. Two LE clients joined to the same emulated LAN must not have the same alocal unicast MAC address. An LE client MAC addresses may change during normal operations. When answering an LE_ARP_REQUEST for any address in this list, the "Remote Address" bit in the flags field of the LE_ARP_RESPONSE must be clear.

C7   *Control Time-out.*   It is the time-out period used for timing out most request/response control frame interactions, as specified elsewhere.

C8   Route Descriptor(s). Route descriptors exist only for source-routed IEEE 802.5 LE clients that are source-route bridges. All route descriptors in any given emulated LAN MUST be unique. An LE client may have zero or more route descriptors, and these route descriptors may change during normal operation. In an operational LE client, every local route descriptor in C8 must have been registered with the LE server. When answering an LE_ARP_REQUEST for any address in this list, the Remote Address bit in the FLAGS field of the LE_ARP_RESPONSE must be clear.

C9   *LE Server ATM Address.*   The ATM address of the LAN Emulation Server is used to establish thea Control Direct VCC. This is obtained in the Configuration phase. This address must be known before the Join phase can start.

C10   *Maximum Unknown Frame Count.*   Value: Minimum=1, Default=1, Maximum=10. (See parameter C11.)

C11   *Maximum Unknown Frame Time.*   Within the period of time defined by the Maximum Unknown Frame Time, an LE client will send no more than Maximum Unknown Frame Count frames to the BUS for a given unicast LAN destination, and it must also initiate the address resolution protocol to resolve that LAN Destination. Value: Minimum=1 second, Default=1 second, Maximum=60 seconds.

C12   *VCC Time-out Period.*   An LE client should release any Data Direct VCC that it has not been used to transmita or receive any data frames for the length of the VCC Time-out Period. This parameter is only meaningful for SVC Data Direct VCCs. Value: Minimum=None specified, Default=20 minutes, Maximum=Unlimited.

C13   *Maximum Retry Count.*   An LE client must not retry an LE_ARP_REQUEST for a given frame LAN destination more than the number of times specified by the Maximum Retry Count after the first LE_ARP_REQUEST for that same frame LAN destination. Value: Minimum=0, Default=1, Maximum=2.

C14   *LE Client Identifier.*   Each LE client requires a *LE client Identifier* (LECID) assigned by the LE server during the Join phase. The LECID is placed in control requests by the LE client and may be used for echo suppression on multicast data frames sent by that LE client. This value must not change without terminating the LE client and returning to the Initial state. A valid LECID must be in the range X0001 through XFEFF.

C15   *LE Client Multicast MAC Address(es).*   Each LE client may have a list of multicast MAC addresses that it wishes to receive and pass up to the higher layers. The broadcast address should be included in this list.

C16   *LE_ARP Cache.*   A table of entries, each of which establishes a relationship between a LAN destination external to the LE client and the ATM address to which data frames for that LAN destination will be sent.

C17   *Aging Time.*   The maximum time that an LE client will maintain an entry in its LE_ARP cache in the absence of a verification of that relationship. Value: Minimum=10 seconds, Default=300 seconds, Maximum=300 seconds.

C18   *Forward Delay Time.*   The maximum time that an LE client will maintain an entry for a non-local MAC address in its LE_ARP cache in the absence of a verification of that relationship, as long as the Topology Change flag C19 is true. Value: Minimum=4 seconds, Default=15 seconds, Maximum=30 seconds.

C19   *Topology Change.*   Boolean indication that the LE client is using the Forward Delay Time C18, instead of the Aging Time C17, to age non-local entries in its LE_ARP cache C16.

C20   *Expected LE_ARP Response Time.*   The maximum time that the LEC expects an LE_ARP_REQUEST/LE_ARP_RESPONSE cycle to take. Used for retries and verifies. Value: Minimum=1 second, Default=1 second, Maximum=30 seconds.

C21   *Flush Time-out.*   Time limit to wait to receive an LE_FLUSH_RESPONSE after the LE_FLUSH_REQUEST has been sent before taking recovery action. Value: Minimum=1 second, Default=4 seconds, Maximum=4 seconds.

C22   *Path Switching Delay.*   The time since sending a frame to the BUS after which the LE client may assume that the frame has been either discarded or delivered to the recipient. May be used to bypass the Flush protocol. Value: Minimum=1 second, Default=6 seconds, Maximum=8 seconds.

C23   *Local Segment ID.*   The segment ID of the emulated LAN. This is only required for IEEE 802.5 LE clients that are source routing bridges. This is the source routing segment ID for the emulated LAN.

C24   *Multicast Send VCC Type.*   Signaling parameter that should be used by the LE client when establishing the Multicast Send VCC. This is the method to be used by the LE client when specifying traffic parameters when it sets up the Multicast Send VCC for this emulated LAN.

C25   *Multicast Send VCC AvgRate.*   Signaling parameter that should be used by the LE client when establishing the Multicast Send VCC. Forward and backward sustained cell rate to be requested by LE client when setting up Multicast Send VCC, if using Variable bit rate codings.

C26   *Multicast Send VCC PeakRate.*   Signaling parameter that should be used by the LE client when establishing the Multicast Send VCC. Forward and backward peak cell rate to be requested by LE client when setting up the Multicast Send VCC when using either Variable or Constant bit rate codings.

C27   *Remote Unicast MAC Address(es).*   The MAC addresses for which this LE client will answer LE_ARP_REQUESTs, but that are not registered with the LE server. This list must be empty in any operational LE client that did not join the emulated LAN as a proxy agent (C4). When answering an LE_ARP_REQUEST for any address in this list, the Remote Address bit in the FLAGS word of the LE_ARP_RESPONSE MUST be set.

C28   *Connection Completion Timer (Optional).*   In Connection Establishment, this is the time period in which data or a READY_IND message is expected from a Calling Party. Value: Minimum=1 second, Default=4 seconds, Maximum=10 seconds.

Initial State—LANE Service Architecture

The following parameters apply per emulated LAN served by an LES service:

S1   *LE Server ATM Addresses.*   The LE server must know its own ATM addresses for LE clients to be able to establish a connection to it. An ATM address cannot be removed from this set as long as any LE client is connected to the LE server through it.

S2   *LAN Type.*   The type of this ATM Emulated LAN, either Ethernet/IEEE 802.3 or IEEE 802.5.

S3   *Maximum Data Frame Size.*   The maximum AAL-5 SDU size of a data frame that the LE service can guarantee not to drop because it is too large. Also the minimum AAL-5 SDU size that every LE client must be able to receive. It must be either 1516, 4544, 9234, or 18190 octets.

S4   *Control Time-out.* Time-out period used for timing out most request/response control frame interactions, as specified elsewhere. After an LE client establishes a Control Direct VCC to the LE server, the Join phase must complete within the Join Time-out time. If not, the LE service should release any Control VCCs to that LE client, terminating the Join phase. Value: Minimum=10 seconds, Default=120 seconds, Maximum=300 seconds.

S5   *Maximum Frame Age.* The BUS must discard a frame if it has not transmitted the frame to all relevant Multicast Send VCCs or Multicast Forward VCCs within the Maximum Frame Age following the BUS receipt of the frame over a Multicast Send VCC. Value: Minimum=1 second, Default=1 second, Maximum=4 seconds.

S6   *Broadcast and Unknown Server's ATM Address(es).* A Broadcast and Unknown Server must know at least one of its own ATM addresses for LE clients to be able to establish connections to it. A Broadcast and Unknown server may have several ATM addresses. Addresses may be added while the BUS is operational, but may not be removed as long as any LE client is connected to the BUS through them.

LECS Connect Phase

During the LECS Connect phase, the LE client establishes its connection with the LE Configuration server. If use of the LECS is not required, an LE client may execute a null LECS Connect phase by using a preconfigured SVC or PVC to the LES. This VCC is established by some means outside of this specification.

LECS Connect—LE Client View

The mechanisms used to locate the configuration service are as follows, in the order in which an LE client must attempt them:

1. Get the LECS Address via ILMI.

   The LE client must issue an ILMI Get or GetNext to obtain the ATM address of the LECS for that UNI. If the UNI connection to the obtained address fails, the LE client may issue an ILMI Get or GetNext request to determine if an additional LE Configuration server ATM address is available and attempt to establish the Configuration Direct VCC to that ATM address.

2. Use the well-known LECS address.

   If the LECS ATM address cannot be obtained from ILMI or if the LE client is unable to establish a Configuration Direct VCC to that address, the well-known address X47007900000000000000000000-00A03E000001-00 must be used to open a configuration VCC to the configuration service. 00 A0 3E is the ATM Forum-assigned OUI and 000001 has been allocated by the ATM Forum.

3. Use the well known VPI/VCI to connect to the LECS using VPI=0, VCI=17 decimal.

   If the LE client cannot establish a VCC to the well-known ATM address of the LECS, the well-known PVC of VPI=0, VCI=17 (decimal) must be used for the Configuration Direct VCC.

   Manual configuration for the LECS address is not recommended.

A description of each of these follow.

The LE client must attempt to establish a Configuration Direct VCC using the call parameters for LE Configuration Direct VCCs. The called party address must be the ATM addresses. The calling party address may be any valid ATM address belonging to the end station.

Finding at Least One LECS.   The provider of the LAN Emulation service must ensure that an LE client follow the rules to connect to an LE Configuration server.

Configuration Phase.   During the Configuration phase, the LE client (or other entity) obtains the ATM Address of the LE server, and may obtain additional configuration parameters. Configuration control frames are of two types:

- LE_CONFIGURE_REQUEST—Sent by the LE client or other interested party to the LECS to obtain configuration information

- LE_CONFIGURE_RESPONSE—Sent by the LE Configuration server in response to an LE_CONFIGURE_REQUEST

The configuration phase prepares an LE client for the Join phase by providing the necessary operating parameters for the emulated LAN that the client will later join. The Configuration phase may be performed either by using the LE configuration protocol or by static parameters in each LEC. The LE Configuration protocol allows the assignment of individual LE clients to different emulated LANs and provides information about the operating parameters of that LAN. Based on its own policies, configuration databases, and information provided by clients, an LE Configuration server assigns any client that requests configuration information to a particular LE service entity by giving it the LE server's ATM address and other parameters.

The LAN Emulation Configuration protocol will be used for more purposes than that of a non-bridge LE client discovering which ELAN it should join. A typical use for this protocol could include, for example:

A bridge, LAN switch, or concentrator supporting multiple LE clients and representing multiple legacy LAN endstations may determine which of its LE clients (ELANs) should be bound to which of its legacy endstations based on the endstations MAC addresses.

Configure Request

The request must issue an LE_CONFIGURE_REQUEST to the LE Configuration server containing at least the primary ATM address of the prospective LE client in the SOURCE-ATM-ADDRESS field. Other information may be included in the remaining fields of the LE_CONFIGURE_REQUEST.

Unsuccessful Configure Response

If the LE_CONFIGURE_RESPONSE does not contain 0 (Success) in the STATUS field, the Configuration phase has failed for the prospective LE client. If this answer is not satisfactory, for example, in the case of an LE client configuring itself, the LE client must return to the beginning of the Initialization procedure if it wishes to reattempt to configure itself.

Successful Configure Response

If the LE_CONFIGURE_RESPONSE does contain 0 (Success) in the STATUS field, the Configuration phase has succeeded for the prospective LE client. In this case, the LAN-TYPE, MAXIMUM-FRAME-SIZE, TARGET-ATM-ADDRESS, and ELAN-NAME parameters must be copied to the prospective LE client C2, C3, C9, and C5 variables, respectively.

Configuration—LE Service View

The LE Configuration server uses the information provided in the LE_CONFIGURE_ REQUEST to generate an LE_CONFIGURE_RESPONSE. This response may indicate success or failure, depending on whether the prospective LE client is to be allowed to attempt to join an LE server.

Requesters ATM Address

The calling party ATM address used in signaling the Configuration Direct VCC must not be considered by the LECS in determining to which ELAN to direct the requester, but may be used in deciding whether to respond or release the connection for security reasons.

LAN-TYPE Configure Response

If the LAN-TYPE in the LE_CONFIGURE_REQUEST is not Unspecified, the LAN-TYPE in the LE_CONFIGURE_RESPONSE must have the same value as the LE_CONFIGURE_ REQUEST. If the LAN-TYPE in the LE_CONFIGURE_REQUEST is Unspecified, the LAN-TYPE in the LE_CONFIGURE_RESPONSE MAY have any value.

MAXIMUM-FRAME-SIZE Configure Response

If the MAXIMUM-FRAME-SIZE in the LE_CONFIGURE_REQUEST is not Unspecified, the MAXIMUM-FRAME-SIZE in the LE_CONFIGURE_RESPONSE must have the same value as or a lower value than that in the LE_CONFIGURE_REQUEST, but must not be Unspecified. If the MAXIMUM-FRAME-SIZE in the LE_CONFIGURE_REQUEST is Unspecified, the MAXIMUM-FRAME-SIZE in the LE_CONFIGURE_RESPONSE may have any value.

Configure Response Ordering

The LECS may issue LE_CONFIGURE_RESPONSEs in a different order than that in which the corresponding LE_CONFIGURE_REQUESTs were received, even for LE_CONFIGURE_ REQUESTs received on the same Configure Direct VCC.

Configuration Response Frame—Parameter Encodings

Table 14.10 describes the T-L-V encodings of further optional operational parameters supplied by a LECS in answer to a configuration request by a LE client. An LE client must update its operational parameter set with these values if it can parse them. An LE client must

Table 14.9 **Configuration Frame Format**

Size	Name	Function
2	MARKER	Control Frame=XFF00
1	PROTOCOL	ATM LAN Emulation protocol=X01
1	VERSION	ATM LAN Emulation protocol version=X01
2	OP-CODE	Type of request: X0001 LE_CONFIGURE_REQUEST, X0101 LE_CONFIGURE_RESPONSE
2	STATUS	Always X0000 in requests
4	TRANSACTION-ID	Arbitrary value supplied by the requester and returned by the responder
2	REQUESTER-LEC-ID	Always X"0000" in requests, ignored on response
2	FLAGS	Always X0000 when sent, ignored on receipt
8	SOURCE-LAN-DESTINATION	MAC address or route descriptor ofprospective LE client. May be encoded as not present
8	TARGET-LAN-DESTINATION	Always X0000 when sent, ignored on receipt
20	SOURCE-ATM-ADDRESS	Primary ATM address of prospective LE client for which information is requested
1	LAN-TYPE	X00 Unspecified X01 Ethernet/IEEE 802.3 X02 IEEE 802.5
1	MAXIMUM-FRAME-SIZE	X00 Unspecified X01 1516 X02 4544 X03 9234 X04 18190
1	NUMBER-TLVS	Number of Type/Length/Value elements encoded in Request/Response
1	ELAN-NAME-SIZE	Number of octets in ELAN-NAME (may be 0)
20	TARGET-ATM-ADDRESS	ATM address of the LE server to be used for the LE client described in the request if Configure Response and STATUS="Success," else X'00'
32	ELAN-NAME	Name of emulated LAN
4	ITEM_1-TYPE	Three octets of OUI, one octet identifier
1	ITEM_1-LENGTH	Length in octets of VALUE field. Minimum=0
Variable	ITEM_1-VALUE	

And so on

Table 14.10 Configuration response frame—parameter encodings

Item	Type	Length	Reference/Value/Units
Control Time-out	00-A0-3E-01	2	C7/in seconds
Maximum Unknown	00-A0-3E-02	2	C10Frame Count
Maximum Unknown	00-A0-3E-03	2	C11/in secondsFrame Time
VCC Time-out Period	00-A0-3E-04	4	C12/in seconds
Maximum Retry Count	00-A0-3E-05	2	C13
Aging Time	00-A0-3E-06	4	C17/in seconds
Forward Delay Time	00-A0-3E-07	2	C18/in seconds
Expected LE_ARP	00-A0-3E-08	2	C20/in secondsResponse Time
Flush Time-out	00-A0-3E-09	2	C21/in seconds
Path Switching Delay	00-A0-3E-0A	2	C22/in seconds
Local Segment ID	00-A0-3E-0B	2	C23
Mcast Send VCC Type	00-A0-3E-0C	2	C24: X'0000' Best Effort: LE client should set the BE flag. Peak Cell Rates should be line rate. X'0001' Variable: LE client should provide a Sustained Cell Rate. X'0002' Constant: LE client should provide a Peak and a Sustained Cell Rate.
Mcast Send VCC	00-A0-3E-0D	4	C25/in cells perAvgRate second
Mcast Send	00-A0-3E-0E	4	C26/in cells per VCC PeakRate second
Connection CompletionTimer	00-A0-3E-0F	2	C28/in seconds where 00-A0-3E is the ATM Forum OUI.

ignore any encoded 'Type' values that it does not understand. The Value provided for any parameter is in the same units and the References are to that same section where appropriate.

Configuration Frames

The format of each AAL5 SDU for LE Configuration Request and LE Configuration Response packet is shown in Table 14.11.

Configuration Response Frame—Parameter Encodings

Table 14.12 describes the T-L-V encodings of further optional operational parameters supplied by a LECS in answer to a configuration request by a LE client. An LE client must update its operational parameter set with these values if it can parse them. An LE client must ignore any encoded 'Type' values it does not understand. The value provided for any parameter is in the same units.

Table 14.11   Configuration frame format

Size	Name	Function
2	MARKER	Control Frame=XFF00
1	PROTOCOL	ATM LAN Emulation protocol=X01
1	VERSION	ATM LAN Emulation protocol version=X01
2	OP-CODE	Type of request: X0001 LE_CONFIGURE_REQUEST X0101 LE_CONFIGURE_RESPONSE
2	STATUS	Always X0000 in requests
4	TRANSACTION-ID	Arbitrary value supplied by the requester and returned by the responder
2	REQUESTER-LEC-ID	Always X"0000" in requests, ignored on response
2	FLAGS	Always X0000 when sent, ignored on receipt
8	SOURCE-LAN-DESTINATION	MAC address or route descriptor of prospective LE client. MAY be encoded as not present.
8	TARGET-LAN-DESTINATION	Always X0000 when sent, ignored on receipt
20	SOURCE-ATM-ADDRESS	Primary ATM address of prospective LE client for which information is requested
1	LAN-TYPE	X00 Unspecified X01 Ethernet/IEEE 802.3 X02 IEEE 802.5
1	MAXIMUM-FRAME-SIZE	X00 Unspecified X01 1516 X02 4544 X03 9234 X04 18190
1	NUMBER-TLVS	Number of Type/Length/Value elements encoded in Request/Response
1	ELAN-NAME-SIZE	Number of octets in ELAN-NAME (may be 0)
20	TARGET-ATM-ADDRESS	ATM address of the LE server to be used for the LE client described in the request if Configure Response and STATUS="Success," else X'00'
32	ELAN-NAME	Name of emulated LAN
4	ITEM_1-TYPE	Three octets of OUI, one octet identifier
1	ITEM_1-LENGTH	Length in octets of VALUE field. Minimum=0
Variable	ITEM_1-VALUE	

Join Phase

During the Join phase, the LE client establishes its connection(s) with the LE server and determines the operating parameters of the emulated LAN. The LE client also may implicitly register one MAC address with the LE server as a result of joining the emulated LAN. Join protocol frames are of two types:

Table 14.12   Configuration Response Frame—Parameter Encodings

Item	Type	Length	Reference/Value/Units
Control Time-out	00-A0-3E-01	2	C7/in seconds
Maximum Unknown	00-A0-3E-02	2	C10Frame Count
Maximum Unknown	00-A0-3E-03	2	C11/in secondsFrame Time
VCC Time-out Period	00-A0-3E-04	4	C12/in seconds
Maximum Retry Count	00-A0-3E-05	2	C13
Aging Time	00-A0-3E-06	4	C17/in seconds
Forward Delay Time	00-A0-3E-07	2	C18/in seconds
Expected LE_ARP	00-A0-3E-08	2	C20/in secondsResponse Time
Flush Time-out	00-A0-3E-09	2	C21/in seconds
Path Switching Delay	00-A0-3E-0A	2	C22/in seconds
Local Segment ID	00-A0-3E-0B	2	C23
Mcast Send VCC	00-A0-3E-0C	2	C24:Type X'0000' Best Effort: LE client should set the BE flag. Peak Cell Rates should be line rate. X'0001' Variable: LE client should provide a Sustained Cell Rate. X'0002' Constant: LE client should provide a Peak and a Sustained Cell Rate.
Mcast Send VCC	00-A0-3E-0D	4	C25/in cells per secondAvgRate
Mcast Send VCC	00-A0-3E-0E	4	C26/in cells per secondPeakRate
Connection	00-A0-3E-0F	2	C28/in secondsCompletionTimer where 00-A0-3E is the ATM Forum OUI

- LE_JOIN_REQUEST—Sent by the LE client to the LE server. It requests that the LE client be allowed to join an ATM Emulated LAN.

- LE_JOIN_RESPONSE—Sent by the LE server to the LE client in response to an LE_JOIN_REQUEST frame. It confirms or denies the join request.

Join Phase—LE Client View

Control Direct VCC

The LE client *must* either initiate and complete UNI signaling procedures to establish a point-to-point bidirectional Control Direct VCC between its LE client ATM address C1 and the LE server ATM address C9, or identify the appropriate Control Direct PVC. If the LE client cannot establish this connection, it must terminate the Join procedure. SETUP request for this VCC must be signaled using the call parameters for LE Control Direct VCCs. The calling party ATM address used by the LE client when setting up the Control Direct VCC *must* be the client primary ATM address.

An LE server may accept a UNI signaling request to establish a Control Direct VCC to its own ATM address S1. An LE server must not accept a Control Direct VCC establishment unless the signaling SETUP indication contains the call parameters for LE Control Direct VCCs.

Control Distribute VCC

When the LE server receives an LE_JOIN_REQUEST, it must decide whether the Join request is to succeed or fail. If and only if the request is to succeed, the LE server may attempt to establish a Control Distribute VCC to the LE client using the call parameters for LE Control Distribute VCCs. This VCC must be established before the LE server can proceed with the Join phase. The LE server must not attempt to establish a Control Distribute VCC to an LE client after sending that LE client an LE_JOIN_RESPONSE.

REQUESTER-LECID

If the LE server returns an LE_JOIN_RESPONSE indicating a successful join, the response must include a REQUESTER-LECID for the LE client that is unique among all LE clients joined to that same emulated LAN. The REQUESTER-LECID must be in the range allowed for LE client LECIDs.

Completion of Join Phase

If the LE_JOIN_RESPONSE indicates a successful join, the LE client and LE server have completed the Join phase of initialization.

Control Distribute VCC and LE_JOIN_RESPONSE

The LE server must not send an LE_JOIN_RESPONSE with any status other than success if it has established a Control Distribute VCC.

Join Frames

The Join frames are used in the Join phase of LAN Emulation initialization and are described in Table 14.13.

Connecting to the BUS Protocol and Procedures.   The protocol and procedures for an LE client connecting to the BUS follow:

- *Determining BUS ATM Address.*   A client *must* connect to the BUS. The address of the BUS is determined by using the address resolution procedure (LE_ARP_REQUEST) to resolve the all 1's broadcast MAC address.

- *Multicast Send VCC.*   The LE service will respond to the LE_ARP_REQUEST with an LE_ARP_RESPONSE containing an ATM address of the BUS (S6), which the LE client *must* use as the called party in establishing a bidirectional Multicast Send VCC. The calling party ATM address used by the LE client must be the LE client's primary ATM

Table 14.13   Join frame format

Size	Name	Function
2	MARKER	Control Frame = XFF00
1	PROTOCOL	ATM LAN Emulation protocol = X01
1	VERSION	ATM LAN Emulation protocol version=X01
2	OP-CODE	Type of request:
		X0002 LE_JOIN_REQUEST
		X0102 LE_JOIN_RESPONSE
2	STATUS	Always X0000 in requests.
4	TRANSACTION-ID	Arbitrary value supplied by the requester and returned by the responder
2	REQUESTER-LECID	Assigned LECID of joining client if join response and STATUS=Success, else X0000.
2	FLAGS	Each bit of the FLAGS field has a separate meaning if set: X0080 Proxy Flag: LE client serves non-registered MAC addresses and therefore wishes to receive LE_ARP requests for non-registered LAN destinations.
8	SOURCE-LAN-DESTINATION	Optional MAC address to register as a pair with the SOURCE_ATM_ADDRESS
8	TARGET-LAN-DESTINATION	Always X00 when sent, ignored on receipt
20	SOURCE-ATM-ADDRESS	Primary ATM address of LE client issuing join request
1	LAN-TYPE	X00 Unspecified X01 Ethernet/IEEE 802.3 X02 IEEE 802.5
1	MAXIMUM-FRAME-SIZE	X00 Unspecified X01 1516 X02 4544 X03 9234 X04 18190
1	NUMBER-TLVS	Always X00 when sent, ignored on receipt
1	ELAN-NAME-SIZE	Number of octets in ELAN-NAME.X00 indicates empty ELAN-NAME
20	TARGET-ATM-ADDRESS	Always X00 when sent, ignored on receipt
32	ELAN-NAME	Name of emulated LAN. Expresses LE client preference in LE_JOIN_REQUEST, specifies name of LAN joined in successful LE_JOIN_RESPONSE, else not used. Format is SNMPv2 DisplayString.

address. This VCC is signaled using the call parameters for the LE Ethernet/IEEE 802.3 Multicast Send VCC or the LE IEEE 802.5 Multicast Send VCC. All multicast destination packets *must* be transmitted to the BUS over this VCC.

LE Client Accepts Multicast Forward VCC

In order to receive traffic sent to a multicast address on an emulated LAN, a client must first have a connection from the BUS. The act of opening the Multicast Send VCC described previously will automatically cause the BUS to connect back to the client to establish a Multicast Forward VCC. This connection will come either in the form of a point-to-point or point-to-multipoint connection indication, at the discretion of the BUS. The client must accept any such connection indications if it wishes to receive all of the broadcast and multicast frames (and potentially, unknown unicast frames) on the emulated LAN. The calling party identifier of the connection setup may or may not contain the ATM address that was returned to the client when it got the LE_ARP_RESPONSE described earlier. The called party identifier will contain the ATM address that the client used as the calling party identifier when it opened the Multicast Send VCC. The call parameters signaled by the BUS are those defined for LE Multicast Forward VCCs. An LE client should refuse any attempt to establish a second or subsequent Multicast Forward VCC.

BUS Opens Multicast Forward VCC

When an LE client successfully joins an emulated LAN and after the client successfully establishes a bidirectional Multicast Send VCC to the BUS (see previous text), the BUS must attempt to open a Multicast Forward VCC back to the client. This may be performed by opening a new point-to-point VCC to the client or by adding the client as a leaf to a point-to-multipoint call at the choice of the BUS implementation.

LANE Registration Process

Registration is the procedure whereby the LE client establishes with the LE server any additional (LAN destination, ATM address) pairs not registered in the Join procedure. Registration and Unregistration of LAN destinations may occur at any time after successfully joining an emulated LAN.

Registration protocol frames are of four types:

- LE_REGISTER_REQUEST—Sent by the LE client to the LE server. It requests that the LE server register one LAN destination—ATM address pair for the LE client.
- LE_REGISTER_RESPONSE—Sent by the LE server to the LE client in response to an LE_REGISTER_REQUEST frame. It confirms or denies the registration request.
- LE_UNREGISTER_REQUEST—Sent by the LE client to the LE server. It requests that the LE server remove the registration of one LAN destination—ATM address pair for the LE client.
- LE_UNREGISTER_RESPONSE—Sent by the LE server to the LE client in response to an LE_UNREGISTER_REQUEST frame. It confirms or denies the unregistration request.

LANE Address Resolution Protocol

The basic flow of the address resolution protocol and Data Direct VCC management. There are four types of frames associated with address resolution protocol:

Table 14.14   Registration frame format

Name	Function
MARKER	Control Frame=XFF00
PROTOCOL	ATM LAN Emulation protocol=X01
VERSION	ATM LAN Emulation protocol version=X"01"
OP-CODE	Type of request: X0004 LE_REGISTER_REQUEST X0104 LE_REGISTER_RESPONSE X"0005" LE_UNREGISTER_REQUEST X"0105" LE_UNREGISTER_RESPONSE
STATUS	Always X0000 in requests
TRANSACTION-ID	Arbitrary value supplied by the requester and returned by the responder
REQUESTER-LECID	LECID of LE client issuing the register or unregister request and returned by the responder
FLAGS	Always X"00" when sent, ignored on receipt
SOURCE-LAN-DESTINATION	Unicast MAC address or route descriptor LE client is attempting to register
TARGET-LAN-DESTINATION	Always X00 when sent, ignored on receipt
SOURCE-ATM-ADDRESS	An ATM address of LE client issuing the register or unregister request
RESERVED	Always X00 when sent, ignored on receipt

- LE_ARP_REQUEST—Sent by an LE client to determine the ATM address associated with a given MAC address or route descriptor
- LE_ARP_RESPONSE—Sent by the LE server or an LE client in response to an LE_ARP_REQUEST to provide the information requested
- LE_NARP_REQUEST—Sent by an LE client to advertise changes in Remote address bindings
- LE_TOPOLOGY_REQUEST—Sent by LE client or LE server to indicate whether network topology change is in progress

Obtaining BUS ATM Address

An LE client must obtain the address of the Broadcast and Unknown Server by sending an LE_ARP_REQUEST for the broadcast group address.

Generation of LE_TOPOLOGY_REQUESTs

An LE client that is acting as an IEEE 802.1D transparent bridge *must* send one LE_TOPOLOGY_REQUEST to its LE server for every Configuration BPDU it sends to the BUS. The Topology Change bit in the FLAGS field in the LE_TOPOLOGY_REQUEST must be set to the same value as the Topology Change bit in the Configuration BPDU.

Local Management Directives

A LE client MAY send LE_TOPOLOGY_REQUESTs to its LE server in response to local management or network management directives. However, such LE_TOPOLOGY_RE-QUESTs may be sent while bridge clients are still active and may have either value for the Topology Change bit. Note that adverse operation may result in all LE clients when more than one LE client generates LE_TOPOLOGY_REQUESTs and the topology change status values do not agree.

Spanning Tree Configuration BPDUs

An LE client that is acting as an IEEE 802.1D bridge may choose to base its LAN Emulation Topology Change state on Spanning Tree configuration BPDUs, rather than on received LE_TOPOLOGY_REQUESTs.

Unresolved LE_ARP_REQUESTs

An LE client must not retry an LE_ARP_REQUEST for a given frame LAN destination more than C13 times after the first LE_ARP_REQUEST for that same frame LAN destination. By the time the last-allowed LE_ARP_REQUEST has timed out, the LE client should have transmitted the frame to the BUS. This does not preclude sending that frame to the BUS before the failure of the address resolution protocol.

Address Resolution Frames

The LE_ARP frames used to resolve LAN destinations to ATM addresses, and thus VCCs, are described in Table 14.15.

Topology Change frames are used for notifying all LE clients that their cached LE_ARP information for remote LAN destinations may be incorrect. They are described in Table 14.17.

Flush Message Protocol, Procedures and Frame Formats

A LAN Emulation client may send unicast frames to the same destination LAN address via the Broadcast and Unknown Server and via a data direct VCC at different times. The flush message protocol allows the sender to avoid the possibility of delivering frames out of order caused by having two paths. When switching from the old path to the new path, the sender first transmits a flush message down the old path, and then sets appropriate table entries so any further frames for the given LAN destination will be held (or discarded) at the sender and not transmitted. The flush message is a special frame distinguishable from a data frame by having a reserved value (XFF00, marker for control frame) in the LAN Emulation data frame header in place of the LECID of the sender. The flush message must be returned to the sender by the receiving client via control VCCs. After the sender receives the returned flush message, it knows that the old path is clear of data for that LAN destination, and it can start using the new path.

> **NOTE:** *Flush messages may be exchanged between LE clients, but are never forwarded by a bridge to a legacy LAN.*

Table 14.15   LE_ARP frame format

Size	Name	Function
2	MARKER	Control Frame=XFF00
1	PROTOCOL	ATM LAN Emulation protocol=X01
1	VERSION	ATM LAN Emulation protocol version=X01
2	OP-CODE	Type of request:
		X0006 LE_ARP_REQUEST
		X0106 LE_ARP_RESPONSE
2	STATUS	Always X0000 in requests
4	TRANSACTION-ID	Arbitrary value supplied by the requester
2	REQUESTER-LECID	LECID of LE client issuing the LE_ARP request
2	FLAGS	Each bit of the FLAGS field has a separate meaning if set: X0001 Remote Address. The TARGET-LAN-DESTINATION is not registered with the LE server.
8	SOURCE-LAN-DESTINATION	Source MAC address from data frame that triggered this LE_ARP sequence. It may be encoded with not present LAN Destination tag.
8	TARGET-LAN-DESTINATION	Destination Unicast MAC address or next route descriptor for which an ATM address is being sought
20	SOURCE-ATM-ADDRESS	ATM address of originator of LE_ARP request
4	RESERVED	Always X00 when sent, ignored on receipt
20	TARGET-ATM-ADDRESS	X00 in LE_ARP request. ATM address of LE client that is responsible for target LAN destination in LE_ARP response.
32	RESERVED	Always X00 when sent, ignored on receipt

Flush Message Protocol and Procedures

The Flush Message Protocol ensures that data frames are delivered in the same order that they were transmitted. Flush Protocol messages are of two types:

- LE_FLUSH_REQUEST—Flush requests are sent by an LE client down a Data Direct VCC or Multicast Send VCC to ensure that all data frames in transit on that path have reached their destination LE client.

- LE_FLUSH_RESPONSE—Flush responses are returned by LE clients via Control Direct VCCs and Control Distribute VCCs in response to received LE_FLUSH_REQUESTs.

The following requirements apply to any LE client or LE service Component, whether or not the LE client chooses to implement the flush message protocol for ensuring the order of delivery for data frames.

Table 14.16   LE_NARP frame format

Size	Name	Function
2	MARKER	Control Frame=XFF00
1	PROTOCOL	ATM LAN Emulation protocol=X01
1	VERSION	ATM LAN Emulation protocol version=X01
2	OP-CODE	Type of request: X0008 LE_NARP_REQUEST
2	STATUS	Always X0000
4	TRANSACTION-ID	Arbitrary value supplied by the requester
2	REQUESTER-LECID	LECID of LE client issuing the LE_NARP request
2	FLAGS	Always X00""
8	SOURCE-LAN-DESTINATION	Not used. Encoded as X00.
8	TARGET-LAN-DESTINATION	Destination unicast MAC address or next route descriptor for which the target ATM address no longer applies
20	SOURCE-ATM-ADDRESS	ATM address of originator of LE_NARP request
4	RESERVED	Always X00 when sent, ignored on receipt
20	TARGET-ATM-ADDRESS	ATM address of LE client that was previously representing the target LAN destination
32	RESERVED	Always X00 when sent, ignored on receipt

Table 14.17   Topology change frame format

Size	Name	Function
2	MARKER	Control Frame=X"FF00"
1	PROTOCOL	ATM LAN Emulation protocol=X"01"
1	VERSION	ATM LAN Emulation protocol version=X"01"
2	OP-CODE	Type of request: X0009 LE_TOPOLOGY_REQUEST
2	STATUS	Always X0000
4	TRANSACTION-ID	Arbitrary value supplied by the requester
2	REQUESTER-LECID	LECID of LE client issuing the Topology Change request
2	FLAGS	Each bit of the FLAGS field has a separate meaning if set: X"0100" Topology Change Flag. A network topology change is in progress
92	RESERVED	Always X00 when sent, ignored on receipt

LE_FLUSH_REQUEST VCC

An LE client may send an LE_FLUSH_REQUEST over any Data Direct VCC or Multicast Send VCC.

Forwarding LE_FLUSH_REQUESTs

The BUS must distribute any LE_FLUSH_REQUEST received via its Multicast Send VCC to at least the LE client specified in that frame's target ATM address via its Multicast Send VCC or its Multicast Forward VCC(s), if that LE_FLUSH_REQUEST does not specify the BUS ATM address as its target. The BUS may distribute requests targeted to its own ATM addresses, as well.

Responding to LE_FLUSH_REQUEST on Control Direct VCC

An LE Service Component may respond to an LE_FLUSH_REQUEST directed to that LE Service component. If it does respond, it must respond to an LE_FLUSH_REQUEST specifying its own ATM address as the target in such a manner that the LE_FLUSH_RESPONSE will be returned to the requester on a Control VCC.

Responding to LE_FLUSH_REQUEST

An LE client must respond to an LE_FLUSH_REQUEST it receives on any VCC (if that LE_FLUSH_REQUEST specifies that LE client ATM address as its target) by returning an LE_FLUSH_RESPONSE to the sender of the LE_FLUSH_REQUEST. The responding LE client must use its Control Direct VCC to send the response.

Forwarding LE_FLUSH_RESPONSE

The LE server must relay LE_FLUSH_RESPONSEs whose SOURCE-ATM-ADDRESS field matches the information in the REQUESTER-LECID field to at least the LE client specified in the REQUESTER-LECID field.

Optional Protocol

An LE client may have two paths available to reach any given LAN destination: a Data Direct VCC, or the Multicast Send VCC to the Broadcast and Unknown Server. In order to ensure that data frames sent to a given LAN destination are delivered in the same order sent, an LE client should perform the following flush message protocol whenever it switches data paths to reach that LAN destination.

Transaction ID in LE_FLUSH_REQUEST

The LE client must send an LE_FLUSH_REQUEST on the old data VCC (either a Data Direct VCC or a Multicast Send VCC). This request must contain a Transaction ID not currently in use by the LE client. (The Transaction ID MAY, for example, be a counter that is incremented each time a new Transaction ID is needed.) It must also contain the requesters ATM address and the ATM address of the target LE client to which the path is being switched.

Changing Data Paths

Until the LE client originating the LE_FLUSH_REQUEST receives the LE_FLUSH_RESPONSE with a matching Transaction ID, or until it times out (time C21) waiting for that response, it must not send any data frames over the old data path destined for the same LAN destination that prompted sending the LE_FLUSH_REQUEST.

Discarding or Holding Data Frames

Data frames destined for a LAN destination that is awaiting an LE_FLUSH_RESPONSE may be discarded, or held by the LE client until the LE_FLUSH_RESPONSE is received or timed out.

Data Frame Handling

If an LE client times out an LE_FLUSH_REQUEST, and it is holding data frames awaiting the requests LE_FLUSH_RESPONSE, those held frames must either be discarded or sent down the old data path. The LE client MAY then send another LE_FLUSH_REQUEST with a new Transaction ID. If it does so, it must ignore any LE_FLUSH_RESPONSE received with the old Transaction ID. Note that limitations on the frequency of sending unicast frames to the BUS may require some held frames to be discarded.

Transmitting Held Frames

After the LE_FLUSH_RESPONSE is received, the LE client must transmit any held data frames on the new data path before transmitting any further frames on the new path.

Switching over Paths without Flush

When switching from the old path to a new path, if an LE client has not transmitted a data frame to a particular LAN destination via the old path for a period of time greater than or equal to the Path Switching Delay C22, it may start using the new path without employing the Flush protocol.

Flush Frames

Flush messages are used for ensuring the in-order delivery of data frames. They are described in Table 14.18.

Usage of ATM Addresses

In order to support SVC-only and mixed PVC/SVC environments, ATM LAN Emulation components must be able to reliably associate incoming LAN Emulation SVCs with particular emulated LANs and functions within each emulated LAN.

Primary ATM Address

An operational LE client must have a primary ATM address, and may have other ATM addresses.

Unique ATM Address

An operational LE client must have unique ATM addresses. None of an operational client's ATM addresses may be shared with any other LAN Emulation component, even if two LAN Emulation components are colocated and share the use of a UNI. ATM hosts can therefore associate an incoming LAN Emulation SVC with the proper LE client on the basis of the Called Party Number.

Table 14.18   **Flush frame format**

Size	Name	Function
2	MARKER	Control Frame=X"FF00"
1	PROTOCOL	ATM LAN Emulation protocol=X"01"
1	VERSION	ATM LAN Emulation protocol version=X"01"
2	OP-CODE	Type of request: X0007 LE_FLUSH_REQUEST X0107 LE_FLUSH_RESPONSE
2	STATUS	Always X0000 in requests
4	TRANSACTION-ID	Arbitrary value supplied by the requester and returned by the responder
2	REQUESTER-LECID	LECID of LE client issuing the flush request
2	FLAGS	Always 0 sending, ignored on receipt
16	SOURCE-LAN-DESTINATION	Always X00 when sent, ignored on receipt
20	SOURCE-ATM-ADDRESS	ATM address of originator of flush request
4	RESERVED	Always X00 when sent, ignored on receipt
20	TARGET-ATM-ADDRESS	ATM address of LE client to which flush request is directed
32	RESERVED	Always X00 when sent, ignored on receipt

LE Server ATM Addresses

An operational LE server must have at least one ATM address and may have more.

Sharing ATM Address

An LE server may share an ATM address with a Broadcast and Unknown Server on the same emulated LAN.

When Sharing ATM Addresses Is Not Valid

An operational LE server must not share an ATM address with any LAN Emulation component other than a BUS, even if two LAN Emulation components are colocated and share the use of a UNI. In particular, two LE servers for different emulated LANs must not share an ATM address.

BUS ATM Address Required

An operational Broadcast and Unknown Server must have at least one ATM address and may have more.

Sharing an ATM Address

A Broadcast and Unknown Server *may* share an ATM address with a LE server on the same emulated LAN.

When Sharing ATM Addresses Is Not Valid

An operational Broadcast and Unknown Server must not share an ATM address with any LAN Emulation component other than a LES, even if two LAN Emulation components are colocated and share the use of a UNI. In particular, two Broadcast and Unknown Servers for different emulated LANs must not share an ATM address.

LE Configuration Server ATM Addresses

ATM Address Required

An operational LE Configuration server must have at least one ATM address and may have more.

Sharing an ATM Address

Several operational LE Configuration servers may share a well-known ATM address, but any one LE client is only aware of a single instance: This is ensured by the assumed definition of a "well-known" address. Note that it is highly desirable for the LE Configuration server to be set up in such a way that clients who tear down and reestablish Configuration

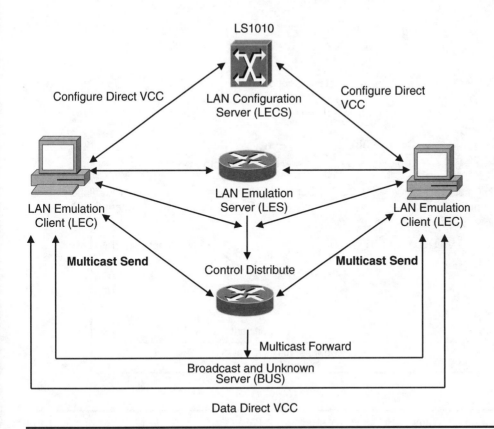

FIGURE 14.33 ATM LAN emulation connections

Direct SVCs see consistent information. How this is accomplished is beyond the scope of the LUNI.

When Sharing ATM Addresses Is Not Valid

An operational LE Configuration server must not share an ATM address with a LE client, LE server, or Broadcast and Unknown Server.

The following will summarize the functions required for a LANE client to connect to the various LANE server services. The ATM LAN emulation connections are shown in Figure 14.34.

Finding the LECS

When a LEC first powers up, it must obtain configuration information from the LECS in order to join an emulated LAN. The LANE specification offers several options for locating the LECS:

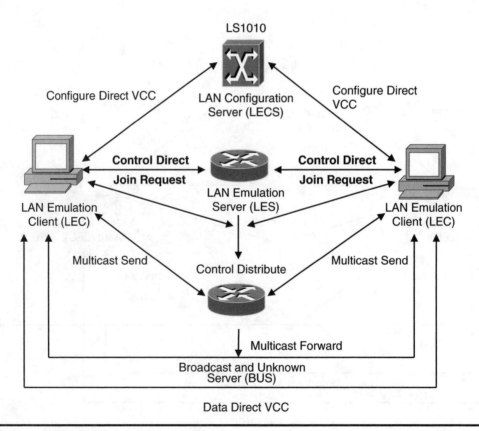

Figure 14.34 ATM LAN Emulation Connections

The LEC can use a "well-known address," conceptually an address such as

`47.00.79.00.00.00.00.00.00.00.00.00.00.00.a0.3e.00.00.01.00.`

This method provides an elegant, easy-to-implement solution for configuring multiple LECs.

The LEC can use the Interim *Local Management Interface* (ILMI) messages to its ATM switch via VPI=0, VCI=16 while obtaining its ATM Prefix using Cisco's implementation of LANE. This alternative requires the network manager to configure the address of the LECS in each ATM switch in the network. When the LEC powers up, it would send ILMI messages across the UNI requesting a LECS address; the attached switch would then respond. Currently this is the most convenient method for discovering the LECS because it requires the configuration of only ATM switches, not the hosts, bridges, routers, and other LEC devices on the network.

The LEC could use a predefined VPI=0, VCI=17 VCC. This alternative requires a preconfigured VCC to the LECS from every ATM interface on the network—every port with a UNI. This approach requires a large number of VCCs, the majority of which will be idle most of the time.

Finally, the LECS can be bypassed completely by configuring the ATM address of a LES in the LEC. This is called manual labor.

After the LEC locates the LECS, it sets up a connection and forwards some useful information, such as its ATM address, its MAC address, its LAN type, and its maximum frame size. The LECS responds with the actual LAN type, the actual maximum frame size, and the ATM address of a LES. By providing an LES address, the LECS implicitly assigns the LEC to an emulated LAN. The LANE specification currently does not define how devices with multiple ATM addresses, such as a LAN switch, organize their addresses. Similarly, it does not specify how the LECS maintains its database. These decisions are left to the individual LANE implementations and the network manager.

Joining an Emulated LAN

After an LEC knows the ATM address of the LES, it sets up a control direct point-to-point VCC connection to the LES (called Control Direct). When the LES receives the connection setup message from the client, it learns the LEC's ATM address from the calling party field in the message. Typically, it responds by adding the LEC as a leaf node on a point-to-multipoint connection.

The LEC then registers its MAC address and associated ATM address with the LES, and the LES assigns the client an LEC ID. The specification allows the LES to either discard the address or store it for future reference. At this point, the LEC now can resolve MAC addresses to ATM addresses. The first address it needs is that of the BUS.

The LEC issues a LE-ARP request message to the LES requesting the ATM address associated with the All-1s MAC address—the broadcast address. The format of this request looks like any *LAN Emulation Address Resolution Protocol* (LE-ARP) message. The LES responds with the ATM address of the BUS using a LE-ARP Response.

Questions

1. Identify the different AAL services.
   A. AAL1, AAL2, AAL3/4, and AAL5
   B. AAL2, AAL3/4, and ALL6
   C. AAL1 and AAL5
   D. None of the above

2. Which AAL layers require end-to-end timing for real time voice and video?
   A. AAL1
   B. AAL2
   C. AAL5
   D. AAL3/4

3. What AAL layer is used primarily for data?
   A. AAL5
   B. AAL2 and AAL5
   C. AAL3/4
   D. All of the above

4. What is the payload available for AAL1?
   A. 48 bytes
   B. 47 bytes
   C. 53 bytes
   D. 46 bytes

5. What is the payload available for AAL5?
   A. 48 bytes
   B. 47 bytes
   C. 53 bytes
   D. 46 bytes

6. What is the payload available for AAL3/4?
   A. 44 bytes
   B. 48 bytes
   C. 53 bytes
   D. 46 bytes

7. What is the function of the SAR layer?
   A. Providing timing
   B. Segmentation and reassembly
   C. Error detection and encapsulation

8. What is the purpose of the common part of the Convergence sublayer?
   A. Providing timing
   B. Segmentation and reassembly
   C. Error detection and encapsulation

9. What is the AAL5 end-of-message bit pattern?
   A. 000
   B. 001
   C. 010
   D. 111

10. Which field in the ATM cell header contains the EOM bit?
    A. VPI
    B. VCI
    C. Cell loss
    D. Payload type
    E. None of the above

11. What is the well-known VPI/VCI used for UNI 3.x signaling?
    A. 0,5
    B. 0,16
    C. 0,18
    D. 0,21
    E. None of the above

12. ILMI uses which well-known VPI/VCI?
    A. 0,5   **C.** 0,17
    B. 0,16   **D.** 0,18

13. ATM Dynamic Routing protocol is called _____.
    A. IISP   **C.** Enhanced IISP
    B. Integrated PNNI   **D.** PNNI Phase 1

14. Which of the following Physical layer cabling types do Cisco LANE modules support?
    A. STP   **D.** SMF
    B. UTP   **E.** All of the above
    C. MMF

15. ATM is broken up into how many layers?
    A. 2   **C.** 4
    B. 7   **D.** None of the above

16. The three types of ATM interfaces are _____.
    A. UNI, NNI, and B-ICI
    B. UNI, NIN, and B-ICI
    C. NUI, NNI, and B-ICI

17. ATM layers are made up of _____.
    A. Physical layer, ATM layer, ATM Adaptation layer, and ATM Higher layer
    B. Physical layer, ATM layer, ATM Network layer, and ATM Upper layer
    C. Physical layer, Transmission Convergence layer, ATM layer, and ATM Adaptation layer

18. Single mode fiber uses _____.
    A. LEDs   **C.** Copper
    B. Lasers   **D.** None of the above

19. DS3 runs at a speed of _____.
    A. 155-Mbps   **C.** 44.7-Mbps
    B. 100-Mbps   **D.** 622-Mbps

20. OC as in OC-3 is an abbreviation for:
    A. Optical circuit   **C.** Open connection
    B. Optical carrier   **D.** None of the above

21. OC-12 runs at a speed of _____.
    A. 155-Mbps   **C.** 45-Mbps
    B. 100-Mbps   **D.** 622-Mbps

22. What are SONET's three levels of overhead?
    A. Path, Line, and Section
    B. Path, Line, and Selection
    C. Line, Section, and Direction

23. STS-1 is an abbreviation for:
    A. Synchronous Transport Signal level 1
    B. Serial Transport Signal level 1
    C. Serial Sync Transport

24. STS-1 runs at a speed of _____.
    A. 100Mbps   **C.** 622Mbps
    B. 155Mbps   **D.** 51.84Mbps

25. Which service class gives you guaranteed service?
    A. VBR   **C.** UBR
    B. CBR   **D.** ABR

26. ATM signaling protocol was derived from _____.
    A. ISDN   **C.** X.25
    B. Frame Relay   **D.** Broadband ISDN

27. What type of signal is generated between an edge device and an ATM switch?
    A. UNI   **C.** INN
    B. NNI   **D.** All of the above

28. What is another name for a virtual LAN?
    A. Broadcast domain   **C.** Routing domain
    B. Collision domain   **D.** All of the above

29. Virtual LANs allow users to be represented _____.
    A. logically   **C.** structurally
    B. physically   **D.** as hybrid

30. Cisco high-speed serial interface can run at speeds up to _____.
    A. 45Mbps   **C.** 100Mbps
    B. 52Mbps   **D.** 155Mbps

31. ATM cards cannot be placed into which type of router?
    A. 2500   **C.** 7500
    B. 4700   **D.** 2600

32. When the Rx Carrier LED on the AIP card is lit, it indicates _____.
    A. receiving cells   **C.** module operational
    B. light source detected   **D.** sending cells

33. Multimode fiber sends signals using _____.
    A. laser   **C.** radio waves
    B. LED   **D.** light

34. How many virtual circuits would it take to be fully meshed, if you had four ATM routers?
    A. 4   **C.** 16
    B. 6   **D.** 24

35. What speed is the interface running at:
    A. 45Mbps   **C.** 155Mbps
    B. 100Mbps   **D.** 622Mbps

36. By default, what will the interface do to cells that do not conform to its QoS contract?
    A. Drop them   **B.** Switch them

```
ATM#sh lane database
LANE Config Server database table 'lecs_db' bound to interfaces/s: ATM0 no default
elan
elan 'elan1': un-restricted
server 47.00918100000001011B8C501.00E0F72C9041.01 (prio 0) active
elan 'elan2': un-restricted
server 47.00918100000000E01E42DB01.00E0FE594441.02 (prio 0) active
```

Answers

1. A
2. A
3. A
4. A
5. A
6. B
7. B
8. C
9. B
10. D
11. B
12. B
13. D
14. E
15. C
16. A
17. C
18. B
19. C
20. B
21. D
22. A
23. A
24. D
25. B
26. A
27. A
28. A
29. A
30. B
31. A
32. A
33. B
34. B
35. C
36. A

15

Wide Area Networking

This chapter provides an overview of three popular wide area networking technologies used in intranets around the world. As shown in Figure 15.1, these three WAN technologies are frame relay, X.25, and *Integrated Services Digital Network* (ISDN). This chapter provides architectural overviews of each with functional descriptions of how these technologies work within each environment. Frame relay is discussed followed by X.25 and ISDN. Each of these WAN technologies addresses a specific segment of the market, with frame relay and ISDN being the most popular due to Voice over Frame, Internet over Frame, and Internet services using ISDN.

Frame Relay Architecture

This chapter provides a discussion on the major functions of frame relay networks. The initial part describes how frame relay manages connections and user data. Issues such

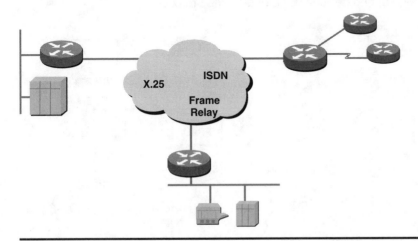

FIGURE 15.1 Wide area networking protocols

as congestion control and congestion notification are discussed. The chapter discusses connection identifiers and explains how frame relay users are identified to the network through logical connections called *data link connection identifiers* (DLCIs).

Frame relay, shown in Figure 15.2, describes an interface standard optimized for the transport of protocol-oriented data in discrete units of information (generic packets). Much like X.25, frame relay statistically multiplexes data that provides bandwidth sharing and efficiency. However, frame relay is efficient and X.25 is not. Traditional time division multiplexing and circuit switching dedicate bandwidth to each path (circuit) through the network on a static basis, and that bandwidth is dedicated for the duration of a call. For example, traditional voice calls use the same amount of bandwidth to transmit sounds as it does to transmit silence.

Virtually all data types have a similar "silence" between transmissions. In fact, LAN data transmissions are typically more "bursty" than voice conversations. Thus, bandwidth allocated to a circuit is essentially unused for a large percentage of the time (as are the carrier's facilities). Statistical multiplexing actually defines paths (virtual circuits) through the network. However, bandwidth is not allocated to a path until data actually needs to be transmitted. When transmission becomes necessary, the network dynamically allocates bandwidth.

If, for a short period of time, more data needs to be transmitted than the transmission facilities can accommodate, switches within the network buffer (store) the data for later transmission. In the event that oversubscription persists, frame relay invokes its congestion control mechanisms.

WHAT IS FRAME RELAY?

- Standards-based (ITU-T, ANSI)
- User-network interface, not a transport specification
- Most error-checking done at end devices using end-to-end protocols
- Relay function only
  - No error correction by network
  - Error frames discarded (without notification)
- High-speed network interface

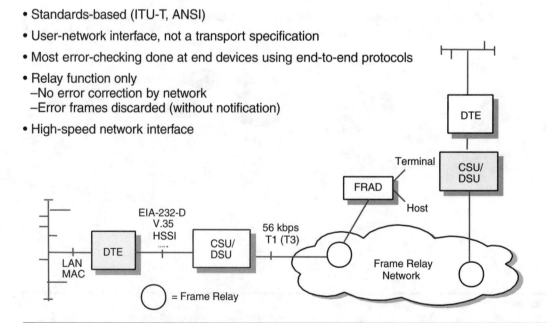

FIGURE 15.2 Frame relay defined

Frame relay also eliminates much of the protocol processing performed by the network and thereby reduces transmission latency—a concept that fits in well with LAN switching. It does this by eliminating error recovery functions within the network. Instead of the network carrying out these functions, endpoint devices guarantee error-free, end-to-end transfer of frames. This way protocol processing, which is still necessary to guarantee the accurate delivery of data, is carried out by higher layers. The network is left to do what it does best—transport data.

Frame relay's interface specification provides signaling and data transfer mechanisms between endpoints and frame relay networks. This interface allows bandwidth to be shared among multiple users and bandwidth to be allocated on demand. Each frame (or packet) contains the header information used to determine the routing. Header information allows endpoints to communicate with multiple destinations through a single access link. Instead of constantly allocating bandwidth to each link, frame relay allocates full bandwidth for the duration of short transaction bursts of data.

It is important to understand that frame relay defines an interface between user equipment and a WAN. It does not define the interfaces or protocols used within the WAN itself. That is, frame relay does not define how the nodes within the network interact with one another. Internally, the WAN may make use of protocols that do not appear to be related to frame relay. For example, a WAN supporting a frame relay interface may use *Asynchronous Transfer Mode* (ATM), which is based on fixed-length units of information called *cells*. As you will see, the differences in the internal implementation of a carrier's frame relay service play an important role in the overall performance, cost, and reliability of the network.

The *frame relay* (FR) protocol is a method of transmitting internetworking packets by combining the packet switching and port sharing of X.25 with the high speed and low delay of *time division multiplexing* (TDM) circuit switching. FR allows you to connect multiple LANs to a single, high-speed (1.544 Mbp/s) or higher WAN link with multiple point-to-point *permanent virtual circuits* (PVCs) or *switched virtual circuits* (SVCs) (see Figure 15.3).

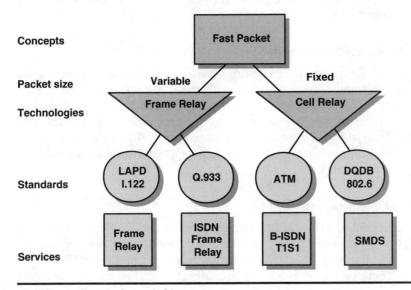

FIGURE 15.3 Fast packet switching

Frame relay networks consist of user devices and network devices that implement standard frame relay interfaces. User devices are responsible for delivering frames to the network in the format prescribed under frame relay specifications. The network is responsible for switching frames to the proper destination device. Both end devices are responsible for ensuring error-free transmission.

Frame relay offers the following features:

- Reduced internetworking cost
- Increased performance with reduced network complexity
- Increased interoperability via international standards
- Bandwidth on demand
- Less overhead than X.25
- High throughput and low delay
- Congestion detection
- Multiplexing protocols
- Network management option

Reduced Internetworking Costs

Statistically multiplexed traffic, running over a private frame relay backbone, reduces the total number of circuits and costs associated with wide-area high bandwidth. Public frame relay services generally save money when compared with equivalent services offered by dedicated leased lines.

Because frame relay provides multiple logical connections within a single physical connection, access costs are also reduced. Frame relay requires fewer physical links to a carrier network so equipment costs are reduced. Fewer physical circuits are needed to reach the network so remote access devices have lower access line charges.

Increased Performance with Reduced Network Complexity

Frame relay improves the performance and response time of applications by reducing the amount of network processing and efficiently using high-speed digital lines. Frame relay reduces network complexity without disrupting high-level network functions. In fact, it actually uses existing higher layer protocols to its advantage by providing a common network transport for multiple traffic types, which maintains transparency to higher level protocols. Each frame contains the addressing information that enables the network to route it to its proper destination.

Increased Interoperability via International Standards

Frame relay is a widely accepted interface standard that vendors and service providers are increasingly adhering to and implementing. The vast majority of frame relay standards have been well defined and approved by ANSI, the frame relay Forum, the IETF, and the ITU-T (formerly CCITT). Therefore, there is an exceptionally good agreement between each standard. Furthermore, equipment vendors and service providers have pledged their support for future frame relay development and standards. The simplicity of frame relay accommodates quick and easy interoperability testing between different vendors' devices. In fact, interoperability testing is always in progress among vendors as are certification processes for carriers providing frame relay services.

Frame relay is a high-speed, packet switching WAN protocol that connects geographically dispersed LANs. Frame relay is usually offered by a public network provider; however, private organizations can acquire and manage their own frame relay networks as well. Frame relay is a connection-oriented protocol, which means that it relies on existing end-to-end paths between devices connected across the network. It implements these connections using *permanent virtual circuits* (PVCs).

A PVC is a logical path the network provides to connect two devices. This path between the source and destination point is a dedicated connection, so the PVC is always available to the connected devices. Because many PVCs can coexist, devices can share the bandwidth of the transmission line.

Frame relay assumes that networks use transmission lines with low error rates, such as digital transmission media. Consequently, frame relay provides only basic error detection with no error recovery. This minimizes the processing required for each packet, allowing frame relay networks to operate at higher speeds with fewer network delays. Because frame relay performs only basic error checking, end stations running upper layer protocols such as *Internet Protocol* (IP) are responsible for resending packets that did not transmit correctly the first time.

How Frame Relay Works

Instead of requiring separate physical links for each frame relay conversation, each frame contains a *Data Link Connection Identifier* (DLCI), which denotes which conversation "owns" the information within the frame as depicted in Figure 15.4.

Each frame sent into the network contains addressing information the network uses to determine its destination. Devices within the network read this information and route each frame to its proper destination.

Note that frame relay is only an interface specification and doesn't specify how data will be routed. Instead, the network routes frames using whatever means network builders and providers choose during its creation. In some cases, frames are kept intact as they traverse the network. This is known as *frame switching*.

Virtual circuits are the mechanisms that address actual frames. Just as typical telephone cables contain multiple pairs of wires (one for each individual conversation) a single physical frame relay interface may contain many individual conversations. However, in frame relay, unlike conventional analog lines, each frame contains a circuit number (DLCI) that denotes which conversation "owns" each frame of information.

If this analogy is taken one step further, network telephone switches cross-connect physical circuits to other physical circuits until a complete connection is made throughout the entire network. Similarly, frame relay frames are routed by the network to their destination based on the DLCI within each frame. Frame relay uses LAPD frame format because it contains user data and address information, which can then be used to route frames.

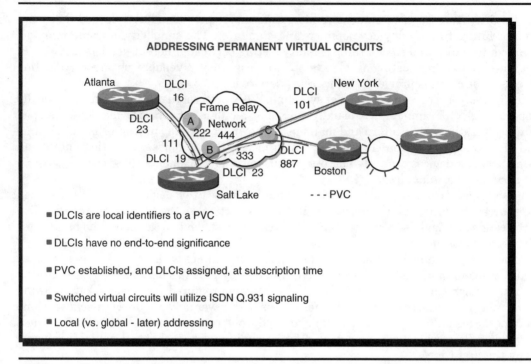

FIGURE 15.4 Frame relay addressing

The frame relay standards specify the use of either *switched virtual circuits* (SVCs) or PVCs. It is important to note that the protocol to establish SVCs is still undefined. PVCs are defined when the user initially subscribes to the frame relay service. Subscribers establish PVCs between access devices linking LANs across the frame relay network. When PVCs are used, the network operator—whether a private network or a services provider—assigns the end-point of each circuit. While the actual path taken through the network may vary from time to time (such as when automatic alternate routing is taking place), the beginning and end of a circuit does not change unless the administrator changes it. These circuits behave like dedicated point-to-point circuits. A PVC does not require a call-establishment procedure and may exist for weeks, months, or even years. All traffic for a PVC uses the same path through the frame relay network. A frame relay network can automatically reroute around failures within the network.

SVCs also comply with frame relay standards. When SVCs are used for frame relay, the actual user of the circuit (the caller) specifies the destination. Like a typical telephone call, there is a call set-up procedure (dialing) that takes place to establish a connection. A virtual circuit—using virtual circuit numbers (DLCI)—is then established for the duration of the call. Although there are standards defined to support SVCs and most frame relay switch vendors support them, SVCs are not generally available from public frame relay networks that still offer only PVCs as a subscription service.

Unlike a typical telephone call, multiple logical channels exist within a single physical circuit. Both PVCs and SVCs can share a single physical circuit. Also, no network resources are used when there is "silence" on the line; therein lies the real power of frame relay.

Inverse Address Resolution Protocol

Inverse ARP, described in RFC 1293, was created for frame relay networks. This protocol defines a method for routers on a frame relay network to learn the protocol addresses of other routers in a way that very efficiently reduces traffic by eliminating the need to use broadcast ARP packets for address resolution. Inverse ARP discovers a protocol address by sending Inverse ARP request packets to the hardware address as soon as the circuit becomes active. (For frame relay circuits the circuit identifier is the frame relay equivalent of a hardware address; for ATM, an ATM address is exchanged.) The remote router responds with its protocol address and the resulting mapping is stored in the ARP cache as shown in Figure 15.5.

The protocol address-to-hardware address entries learned by Inverse ARP do not time out when the ARP refresh timer expires. The mappings do not age at all except when the frame relay circuit goes down. This means that the router does not need to transmit any ARP broadcasts to update the ARP cache. However, the router permits updates to an entry when the other (remote) router changes its protocol address.

Support for both ARP and Inverse ARP greatly enhances the router's interoperability with other vendors' routers over frame relay for dynamic mapping of protocol and hardware addresses. If other frame relay-attached routers support Inverse ARP, then the mappings are dynamically learned as described. If the attached routers do not support Inverse ARP but support "traditional" ARP on frame relay, then the mappings still could be learned dynamically using ARP exchanges.

Cisco IOS frame-relay implementation uses the *Inverse Address Resolution Protocol* (InARP) to determine dynamically the network protocol address associated with a given DLCI in a frame-relay network. As described in *Local Management Interface* (LMI), the local management interface advertises the DLCIs that are active for a DTE. It does not report the physical addresses associated with the destination DTE. See Figures 15.5 and 15.6.

InARP is automatically enabled for serial adapters that are enabled for frame relay. However, like all other protocols, InARP requires that a peer device also implements InARP in order for them to communicate. If the Cisco router must communicate with a non-Cisco router on a frame relay network and that router does not implement InARP, the Cisco

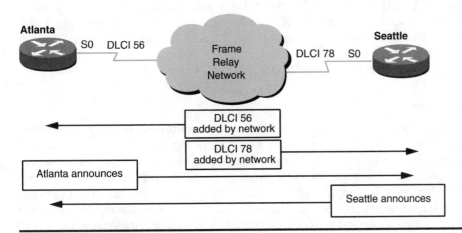

FIGURE 15.5 Inverse ARP

```
SUMMARY   Delta T     Destination   Source        Summary
    5    36.8393    DCE.DLCI.560  DTE.DLCI.560     DLC DTE->DCE Length=22
                                                   FRELAY DLCI=560
                                                   ETHER Type=8035, size=20
bytes
                                                   ARP C PA= PRO=Unknown


DLC:  --- DLC Header ---
DLC:
DLC:  Frame 5 arrived at  09:07:51.2338; frame size is 22 (0016 hex) bytes.
DLC:  Destination = DCE
DLC:  Source = DTE
FRELAY: --- Frame Relay ---
FRELAY:
FRELAY: Address word = 8F00
FRELAY:  1000 11..  0000 .... = DLCI 560
FRELAY:  .... ...1  .... ...0 = *** Invalid extended address: should be 0..1
FRELAY:  .... ..1.  .... .... = Command
FRELAY:  .... ....  .... 0... = No forward congestion
FRELAY:  .... ....  .... .0.. = No backward congestion
FRELAY:  .... ....  .... ..0. = Not eligible for discard
FRELAY:  .... ....  .... ...0 = Extended address
FRELAY:
ETYPE: Ethertype  = 8035 (ARP)
ETYPE:
ARP:  --- ARP/RARP frame ---
ARP:  Hardware type = 0 *** UNKNOWN TYPE ***
ARP:  Protocol type = 0002 (Unknown)
ARP:  Length of hardware address = 0 bytes
ARP:  Length of protocol address = 0 bytes
ARP:  Opcode 1 (ARP request)
ARP:  Sender's hardware address =
ARP:  Sender's protocol address =
ARP:  Target hardware address =
ARP:  Target protocol address =
```

FIGURE 15.6   Frame relay Inverse ARP header

router cannot use its InARP to learn the network-layer address associated with the other router. However, Cisco routers can receive ARP and learn the address. In the case of IP, IPX, and ARP, these can be transmitted over frame relay. In such instances, the network layer address associated with a given DLCI must be configured. Destination address DLCI pairs are configured on a per protocol basis for IP, IPX, XNS, DECnet, and VINES.

Elements of Frame Relay

Frame relay networks are made up of frame relay access equipment, frame relay switching equipment, and public frame relay services as shown in Figure 15.7.

Public service providers (carriers) offer frame relay services using the frame relay switching equipment deployed within their networks. An organization's frame relay access equipment and private frame relay switching equipment is generally connected to services provided by a carrier. Service providers maintain access to their frame relay networks via standard frame relay interfaces and charge customers to use their service. Access to a frame

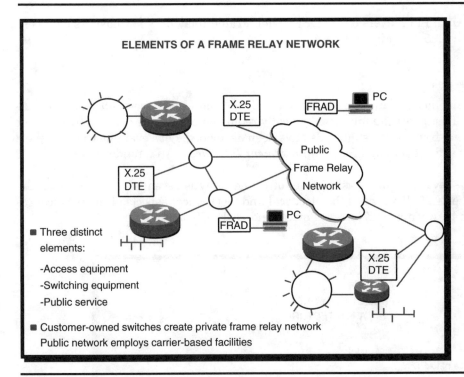

ELEMENTS OF A FRAME RELAY NETWORK

X.25 DTE
FRAD
PC
Public Frame Relay Network
X.25 DTE
X.25 DTE
FRAD
PC

- Three distinct elements:
  -Access equipment
  -Switching equipment
  -Public service
- Customer-owned switches create private frame relay network
  Public network employs carrier-based facilities

FIGURE 15.7   Elements of Frame Relay

relay service requires three elements: *Customer Premises Equipment* (CPE), a transmission facility, and the actual frame relay network. CPE may consist of any of the equipment named in the previous table as well as some others.

Access facilities must be appropriate for the customer's speed subscription, which is generally a 56/64 Kbps or T1/E1 link. When a customer desires fractional T1/E1 services, a full T1/E1 link is generally used; however, depending on the carrier's offering, the unused portion of the T1/E1 can be used to transport other traffic (such as voice). At the network interface, carriers are responsible for terminating the circuit and transporting information to the transmission facility at the receiving end of the virtual circuit. However, transmission facilities at the two ends of the circuit may operate at different speeds. This allows customers to mix and match equipment so that the virtual circuit's speed matches the actual aggregate traffic needs at each site. In this situation, the higher speed CPE slows down to accommodate the slower equipment.

Carriers generally offer several options for buying services. One option is to buy a given service as a dedicated facility. This option has the advantage of fixed pricing (no surprises), and the cost benefits can be easily compared with dedicated bandwidth alternatives.

Frame Relay and the OSI Model

Frame relay defines an interface between user equipment and a network. Unlike X.25, which operates at the lower three layers of the OSI model, frame relay defines only the

Physical and Data Link layers of the OSI model. Frame relay does not have its own Network layer like X.25. See Figure 15.8.

Levels of Frame Relay

Frame relay combines the functions of the Network and Data Link layers into a simple link-level protocol. To support the functions typically requiring the services of a Network layer protocol, optional frame relay standards have been developed. Let's examine the two levels of frame relay and the optional *Local Management Interface* (LMI) standard.

Physical Level—Level 1. The Physical level of frame relay is essentially the same as the Physical level of X.25. It specifies the electrical and mechanical aspects of the physical cable connection between a DTE (access device) and DCE (CSU/DSU).

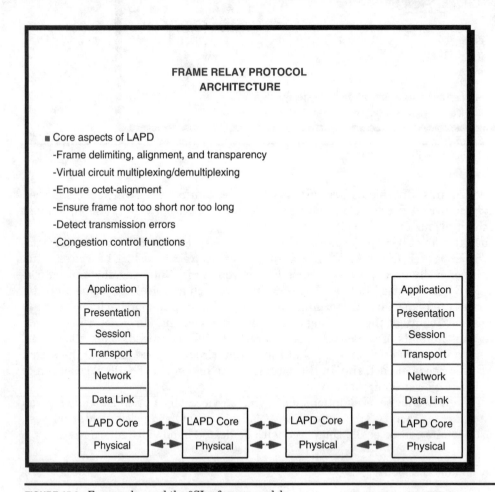

FIGURE 15.8 Frame relay and the OSI reference model

DTE to DCE Interface.   Like X.25, frame relay defines an interface between *Data Terminal Equipment* (DTE) and *Data Circuit Terminating Equipment* (DCE). A frame relay access device (DTE) connects non-frame relay equipment to the frame relay network. Because frame relay was designed for WAN interconnection, the most common access device is a router.

Link Level—Level 2.   At the link level, frame relay uses a subset of the *Integrated Services Digital Network* (ISDN) specification known as *Link Access Protocol-D* (LAPD). LAPD is a link-level standard that carries signaling information on the ISDN channel. The frames used for LAPD conform to ITU-T Recommendation Q.922 as depicted in Figure 15.9.

Framing Details.   A two-byte field within the LAPD frame is used for header information. The header information includes the 10 bits used for the *Data Link Connection Identifier* (DLCI). The DLCI's 10 bits permit more than a thousand virtual circuit addresses on each physical interface. The remaining bits are used for congestion information and other control functions.

At the end of each frame, the access device submits a *Frame Check Sequence* (FCS) to ensure bit integrity. Frames with errors are discarded.

LAPD's *Information field* (I-field) is variable in length. While, theoretically, the maximum integrity of the FCS is 4,096 bytes, the actual maximum is vendor specific. Frame relay standards ensure that the "minimum maximum" value supported by all networks is 1,600 bytes. The I-field contains data passed between devices over a frame relay network. User data may contain various types of protocols or *Protocol Data Units* (PDUs) used by access devices. According to IETF RFC-1490, the I-field may also include "multiprotocol encapsulation." With or without multiprotocol encapsulation, the protocol information sent in the information field is transparent to a frame relay network.

As mentioned previously, frame relay uses bits in the header to indicate network congestion. The network may send congestion condition notifiers to access devices through *Forward Explicit Congestion Notification* (FECN) and *Backward Explicit Congestion Notification* (BECN) bits. Access devices are responsible for restricting data flow under such congested conditions. In order to manage congestion and fairness, frames may be tagged for discard with a *Discard Eligibility* bit (DE bit). Frame relay specifications provide a

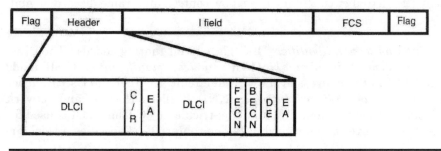

FIGURE 15.9   LAPD frame

method for flow control, but do not guarantee implementation of those standards on devices. This is a vendor-specific issue that is often an important difference in the performance of vendors' products, but it does not generally interfere with basic frame relay interoperability.

Network and access devices may pass special management frames with unique DLCI addresses. These frames monitor the status link and reflect whether it is active or inactive. Management frames also pass information regarding the current status of PVCs as well as any DLCI changes within the network. *Local Management Interface* (LMI) is the protocol used to provide information about PVC status. Frame relay's original specification did not provide for this kind of status. Since then, ANSI and ITU-T specifications developed and incorporated a method for LMI, now known "officially" as *Data Link Control Management Interface* (DLCMI).

The important protocol functions of frame relay are assigned to Level 2. The fact that frame relay is primarily a Level 2 protocol sets it apart from X.25 where the important packet-switching functions are handled at Level 3. Frame relay achieves its high performance by eliminating the use of not only the X.25 Packet layer (Level 3) protocols, but also many of the error handling and flow control procedures used at Level 2. In their place, frame relay requires the use of advanced technology that includes an error-free transmission facility and intelligent higher layer protocols in end user devices.

However, not all Level 3 functions can just be eliminated. The addressing and route selection functions performed at Level 3 have been moved down to Level 2. Also, the capability to support multiple virtual circuits over a single physical circuit has been moved down to Level 2. Frame relay makes use of variable length frames. The frames can range from only a few octets to over 8000 octets. However, the maximum frame size varies from switch vendor to switch vendor. This feature allows frame relay to work well with variable-length, bursty LAN traffic because it reduces the need for excessive fragmentation and reassembly by user equipment. However, the use of variable length frames means that the delays encountered during transmission are also variable.

Figure 15.10 shows the format of a Frame Relay frame.

The *High-level Data Link Control* (HDLC) flags are the first and last octet, and indicate the beginning and end of the frame. If there is only one flag between two consecutive frames, the closing flag of the first frame serves as the opening flag of the next frame.

Address Field.   The Address field consists of the frame relay control and management fields. These fields specify the virtual circuit numbering, flow control, and frame discard eligibility.

DLCI.   The *Data Link Connection Identifier* (DLCI) is a 10-bit routing address. The DLCI consists of noncontiguous *most significant bit* (MSB) and *least significant bit* (LSB) fields in the header. The DLCI is the address of the virtual circuit at either the *User-Network Interface* (UNI) or the *Network-Network Interface* (NNI). It allows the user and network management to identify the frame as being from a particular PVC. The DLCI is used for multiplexing several PVCs over one physical link. The router DLCI specifies a local virtual circuit.

For both ANSI T1.618 and the LMI standards, the DLCI addressing space allows 1,024 values at each local interface. Because some DLCIs are used for signaling, management,

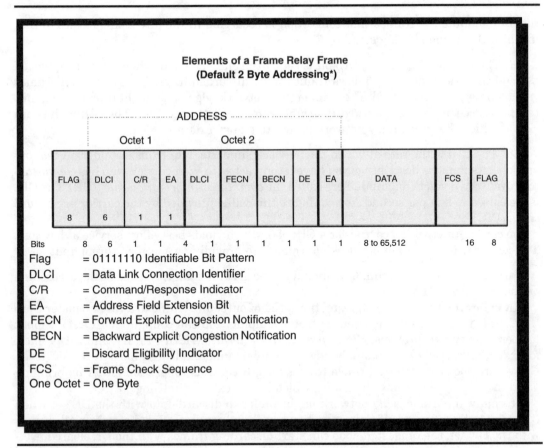

**Elements of a Frame Relay Frame
(Default 2 Byte Addressing*)**

Flag = 01111110 Identifiable Bit Pattern
DLCI = Data Link Connection Identifier
C/R = Command/Response Indicator
EA = Address Field Extension Bit
FECN = Forward Explicit Congestion Notification
BECN = Backward Explicit Congestion Notification
DE = Discard Eligibility Indicator
FCS = Frame Check Sequence
One Octet = One Byte

FIGURE 15.10 Elements of Frame Relay

and future specification, 992 of 1,024 DLCIs (16 through 1007) are available to address frame relay virtual circuits at each local interface.

C/R. The *Command/Response* (C/R) is not used in this industry-standard implementation. It is always set to 0.

EA. By enabling the frame relay header to extend to either 3 or 4 octets, the *Extended Address* (EA) allows for a DLCI longer than 10 bits and greatly expands the number of possible addresses.

FECN. *Forward Explicit Congestion Notification* (FECN) is set by the frame relay network to indicate that it has experienced congestion in the packet forwarding direction of the frame. When this bit is set to 1, the frame relay network notifies the user receiving the frames that congestion is occurring in the direction in which the frame is being sent.

BECN. *Backward Explicit Congestion Notification* (BECN) is set by the frame relay network to indicate that the network has experienced congestion in the reversed packet forwarding direction of the frame. When this bit is set to 1, the frame relay network notifies the user sending the frames that congestion is occurring in the direction opposite to that in which the frame is being sent.

DE. The *Discard Eligibility* (DE) bit is set by the end node and, when set and supported by the frame relay network, allows frames to be discarded in preference to other frames when a network is congested. The frame relay network edge node might discard transmitted data exceeding the *Committed Information Rate* (CIR) on a PVC. (The CIR is the data rate at which the frame relay network agrees to transfer data.)

CIR. The CIR is the rate at which the network supports data transfer under normal operations. Its name is descriptive: you have a contract with your carrier, who has *committed* to providing a given throughput, here called the *committed information rate* (CIR). The CIR is measured in bits per second. You configure this value provided by the carrier per *virtual circuit* (VC).

You can contract with a carrier for a CIR of 0, which yields best-effort service at low cost. The carrier transmits data but does not commit to providing a specified throughput.

Maximum CIR. The maximum CIR should not be greater than the speed of the access line on the slower end of a VC.

CIR enforcement means restricting the speed of outbound traffic to a rate no faster than the CIR. It is the major component of traffic shaping. You can configure CIR enforcement to operate over Synchronous, *High-Speed Serial Interface* (HSSI), T1, E1, and ISDN lines, for frame relay backup, demand, bandwidth-on-demand, and leased lines at the VC level. CIR enforcement operates on whole frames only. It controls congestion either by bringing down the VC, or by queuing the traffic, which is also called throttling.

Internally, the frame relay network might prefer to discard data with the DE set when it encounters congestion. If the congestion condition persists after discarding all frames with the DE set, the congested node can start discarding frames with the DE cleared. Network edge nodes can also set DE bits in response to user data that exceeds the committed burst size during a fixed measured interval.

Information Field. The Information field (also called the Data field) contains the protocol data packet being transmitted. The field can contain a maximum of 4,520 octets; however, the 16-bit *Frame Check Sequence* (FCS) is more effective with frames smaller than 4K. You should ensure that the network can handle the maximum frame size sent by the router.

Different network and frame relay switches are expected to support varying sizes. However, the maximum size of 4,520 octets should accommodate most LAN traffic and frame relay network variations. The maximum information field size is configurable on a per-port basis. To avoid or minimize segmentation and reassembly of higher level PDUs, choose an optimal frame size.

Cisco supports the multiprotocol encapsulation scheme described in RFC 1490 to multiplex multiprotocol LAN traffic over a single frame relay link. This means that higher level PDUs must be encapsulated so that receiving nodes can interpret and demultiplex them properly.

FCS. The FCS is the standard 16-bit *cyclic redundancy check* (CRC) used by HDLC. This field detects bit errors occurring in the frame bits between the opening flag and the FCS.

Frame Relay Network

Private line networks permanently allocate dedicated transmission resources between communication end points, regardless of the traffic conditions. Because the frame relay network uses statistical multiplexing, the transmission resources are not allocated until there are active communications. Network resources are shared dynamically among participating end points. However, the resources are still available and dedicated.

Frame relay networks provide the best features of *time-division multiplexing* (TDM) high-speed, low-delay circuit switching and the statistical multiplexing and port sharing of X.25 packet-switching technologies. These features guarantee bandwidth according to the set CIR, and allow bandwidth-on-demand bursts when available.

The frame relay network consists of frame relay switches, which usually are owned and administered by the carriers. The access connection to the frame relay network is typically provided by a *Local Exchange Carrier* (LEC); it can also be bundled into the frame relay provider's service. The network provider can be an LEC; a metropolitan frame relay service; an *Interexchange Carrier* (IXC); or an interstate, national, or global frame relay service.

Cisco frame relay encapsulates data frames and routes them through the frame relay network based on the DLCI, which identifies the router's local PVC end point. DLCIs are configured through the configuration process or learned through the Cisco frame relay link management protocol.

A frame relay network has the following characteristics:

- Transports frames transparently. The network modifies only the DLCI, congestion bits, and FCS.

- Detects transmission, format, and operational errors.

- Preserves the order of the frame transfer on individual PVCs.

- Does not acknowledge or retransmit frames.

With Cisco frame relay, you can have a logical end-to-end link (a virtual private line) between communication end points. Although Cisco frame relay appears as a dedicated private network to the user, the use of *virtual circuits* (VCs) and high-speed internode trunking make Cisco frame relay service more cost-effective than a dedicated line service, with similar performance. Cisco frame relay is intended primarily for high-speed, bursty data communications applications, such as LAN to WAN interconnections.

The *User Network Interface* (UNI) and *Network Node Interface* (NNI) standards define the interoperability between end points on the LAN and the end points of the frame relay network, and between frame relay networks.

Interoperability Standards.   UNI describes how a router connects and accesses frame relay network services.

NNI describes how frame relay networks interconnect. With NNI, users subscribing to different frame relay network providers can communicate. Note that the standards for NNI have been defined only recently, and few network providers and equipment manufacturers currently support NNI.

Local Management Interface (LMI)

LMI is used to monitor the status and add DLCIs to the list of active DLCIs. When a DTE connected to a frame relay network becomes active, its LMI determines which of the DLCIs available to the DTE are active. The DTE periodically polls the network to confirm that a DLCI is still active. LMI reports when a PVC becomes inactive or a new PVC is activated. Omitting the Network layer increases speed without significantly affecting reliability due to the technological advances that were discussed previously. It also means that basic frame relay does not offer a full range of services such as flow control to avoid network congestion and switched virtual circuit support. These services traditionally require Network layer functionality.

Vendors may compensate for the lack of these types of services by implementing optional features defined in auxiliary frame relay standards. The LMI is a proposed specification for the exchange of status information between frame relay access devices (bridge/routers) and the network. The LMI also provides facilities supporting multicasting, global addressing, and flow control. Although not yet fully standardized, the LMI is included in virtually every frame relay implementation.

The LMI standards define a method of managing congestion in a frame relay network. Fields within the frame-relay header are used to indicate whether there is congestion on a path that a frame just crossed or the path for which a frame is bound. Cisco Routers implement these functions, known as *forward explicit congestion notification* (FECN) and *backward explicit congestion notification* (BECN).

Bandwidth on Demand

Frame relay was designed to be used with networks that provide bandwidth on demand. Bandwidth is the information carrying capacity of a transmission system. For example, a standard T-1 line provides a bandwidth of 1.544 Mbps. Fair utilization of network bandwidth is an important issue because the cost of bandwidth represents a large part of the ongoing expense of operating a network.

Bandwidth on demand means that the capacity (bandwidth) of the communications facilities are provided to each user dynamically as the user needs (demands) them. This is the opposite of preallocating a fixed amount of bandwidth to each user and dedicating this bandwidth to that user regardless of whether there is data to transmit. This type of dedicated bandwidth is typically found in a circuit-switching network. When a circuit-switched connection is established between a pair of users, a dedicated circuit with a fixed amount of bandwidth is provided for the duration of the connection. The bandwidth is reserved and is not made available to other users even when the circuit is not actually transmitting data.

Dynamic allocation of bandwidth allows more efficient sharing of the network among its users. This is particularly important when the network traffic is bursty in nature. Dedicating fixed amounts of bandwidth to this type of intermittent traffic is inefficient because there are always periods when the network is not being utilized and the bandwidth is not available for other users.

Frame relay and other packet-switched technologies such as X.25 provide bandwidth on demand by using *statistical multiplexing*. Statistical multiplexing is based on the mathematical probability that not all users are transmitting at the same time. This means that the complete bandwidth of the access line is made available to a PVC if it has data to transmit. The frames from multiple PVCs are interleaved over the frame relay access line to the ingress switching node.

Cisco's Implementation of Frame Relay

With an initial product release in December 1990, Cisco was the first router-bridge vendor to support frame relay. Cisco's frame relay offering supports both public service and private backbone network configurations and complies with the consortium specification developed by Cisco, Stratacom (now owned by Cisco), Northern Telecom, and Digital. Various LMI extensions are included.

When the frame relay network to which a Cisco router is connected supports the LMI extensions, the Cisco router uses these to efficiently support dynamic address resolution and routing. However, when the frame relay network does not support the LMI extensions, the Cisco router can still utilize frame relay capacity. In this case, static maps are configured in the router to indicate how the internetwork level addresses correspond to DLCIs. Also, when the frame relay multicast feature is not available, the router can be configured to duplicate and send multiple copies of packets that would normally be broadcast.

Frame relay is available on all Cisco router chassis. Each frame relay access link requires a serial interface in the router that attaches to a DSU/CSU device, as appropriate. Frame relay is available from public and private frame relay networks at many different access speeds and with different physical interfaces. Users need to consult their frame relay network provider to ensure selection of the appropriate DSU/CSU devices.

Frame relay link speeds of up to four Mbps are supported by Cisco. Bridging, as well as the routing of the following protocols over frame relay is supported: IP, DECnet, IPX, Banyan VINES, XNS, OSI, and AppleTalk. In addition, protocols such as IBM's *Systems Network Architecture* (SNA) that are transported by Cisco using encapsulation in TCP/IP (such as serial tunneling and Source-Route bridging) are also supported over frame relay. Routing of additional protocols over frame relay is also planned.

Frame relay operations use a subset of the Data Link layer and the Network layer operations. DLCIs are used for user sessions identification. With few exceptions, DLCIs are premapped before data transmission occurs. Congestion notification is handled with the BECN and FECN bits, and discarding excessive traffic can be handled through the discard eligibility bit. Options are available to allow for global or local addressing with DLCIs, as well as multicasting capabilities.

X.25 Module

X.25 is a ITU-T recommendation describing the interface between *Data Terminal Equipment* (DTE) and *Data Circuit Terminating Equipment* (DCE) for packet-switched network services. A DTE is the source or destination of data flowing through a network. Terminals, controllers, and systems connected to an X.25 packet-switched network are referred to as DTEs. A DTE connects to a DCE that connects the user equipment to the X.25 network. DCEs are typically provided by the network supplier and are usually located on the customer's premises in close proximity to the DTEs.

Note that the X.25 recommendation deals only with the *interface* between a DTE and DCE and not with the packet-switched network itself, as shown in Figure 15.11. X.25 is based on packet-switching techniques with which data are assembled in the form of packets that are then routed through a network.

Packet Switching

Data flowing through a *packet-switched data network* (PSDN) does so in the form of *packets*—individual units or blocks of information. Packets contain both headers and data. Packet headers contain control information and information used to route the packet to the appropriate destination. The data portion of a packet contains either end-user data or control data. Interconnected packet-switching nodes form the backbone of a PSDN. These nodes are responsible for routing packets correctly between source and destination DTEs. To do this, they use information in the packet headers. In a PSDN, no dedicated connection exists between users as in a circuit-switched network. In a circuit-switched network such as a telephone network, for example, two users communicate over a point-to-point connection dedicated to them for the duration of their communication. During this time, other users are prevented from using this circuit.

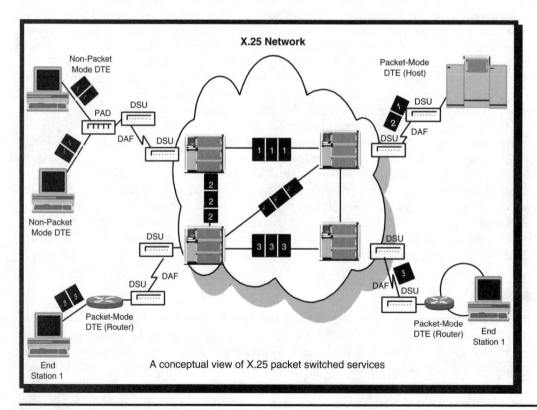

A conceptual view of X.25 packet switched services

FIGURE 15.11   X.25 packet switch services

With packet switching, physical circuits are shared by all network users. When two users are communicating, no physical circuit is dedicated to them. Instead, they are logically connected via a *virtual circuit* (VC). Their packets are dynamically routed along with packets from other users across the network. The packet-switching nodes dynamically determine the paths and physical circuits to use in routing packets. These networks support DTE interfaces conforming to X.25. Which protocols are actually used within a PSDN is not addressed by X.25; it deals only with the interface between DTE and DCE.

X.25 Levels

Three levels of functionality are addressed by X.25. These levels are shown in Figure 15.12. They are:

- Packet level
- Link level
- Physical level

These levels correspond to layers 3, 2, and 1 (Network, Data Link, and Physical, respectively) of the OSI Reference Model. In fact, X.25 is one accepted implementation standard for these OSI layers.

Physical Level

The physical level (level 1) of X.25, as with the Physical layers of OSI, defines the electrical and mechanical requirements for the physical interface between a DTE and DCE. X.21 is an *International Telecommunications Union* (ITU) Recommendation that defines just such a physical level interface and is the preferred physical level standard for X.25. X.21 was developed as a standard for interfacing to public circuit-switched networks. The X.21-bis standard was also established by ITU-T as a migration path to allow other existing physical standards to be used. X.21-bis is really a redefinition of a number of widely used modem interface standards, such as RS-232-C, V.24, and V.35. Support for these standards allowed them to be used in conjunction with X.25.

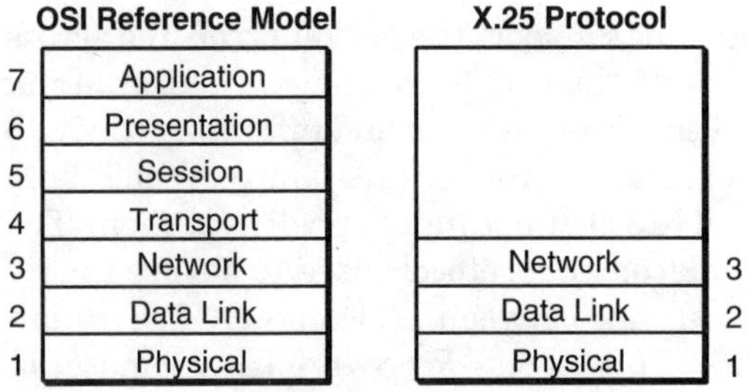

OSI Reference Model	X.25 Protocol
7 Application	
6 Presentation	
5 Session	
4 Transport	
3 Network	Network 3
2 Data Link	Data Link 2
1 Physical	Physical 1

FIGURE 15.12 X.25 OSI Model

- X.21 is a ITU-T recommendation for digital circuit operation. The X.21 interface operates over eight interchange circuits (i.e. signal ground, DTE common return, transmit, receive, control, indication, signal element timing, and byte timing). Their functions are defined in recommendation X.24 and their electrical characteristics in recommendation X.27.

- X.21-bis is a ITU-T recommendation that defines the analog interface to allow access to the digital circuit switched network using an analog circuit. X.21-bis provides procedures for sending and receiving addressing information that enables a DTE to establish switched circuits with other DTEs that have access to the digital network.

- V.24 is also a ITU-T recommendation. It provides procedures that enable the DTE to operate over a leased analog circuit connecting it to a packet switching node or concentrator.

X.21 Digital Interface

In 1976, ITU-T recommended a digital signaling interface called X.21. The recommendation specifies how the DTE can set up and clear calls by exchanging signals with the DCE.

The physical connector has 15 pins, but not all of them are used. The DTE uses the T and C circuits to transmit data and control information. The DCE uses the R and I circuits for data and control. The S circuit contains a signal stream emitted by the DCE to provide timing information so the DTE knows when each bit interval starts and stops. The B circuit may also provide the capability to group the bits into byte frames. If this option is not provided, the DCE and DTE must begin every control sequence with at least two SYN characters to enable each other to deduce the implied frame boundary.

It's important to remember what the Physical layer does not do. It assumes no responsibility for line transmission quality; its real task is to mask the nature of the physical media from the Data Link layer. The Physical layer's charter to transparently transmit the bit stream implies that it must be insensitive to data content. This implies that valid data and line errors receive the same treatment. They are both simply passed along the bit pipe. Any form of error control requires some method of "chopping" the data stream into individual blocks. Layer 2 performs the block creation done for error detection and correction.

X.25 Data Link Layer Operations

The primary purpose of the X.25 Data Link layer is to transport the packet error-free across the communications link between the user device and the packet exchange. The Data Link layer is also responsible for controlling the flow of traffic on the link and informing the X.25 network layer of unusual link problems such as excessive errors or link failure. While these services are limited, they are quite important, and X.25 cannot function without them. The X.25 link level (level 2) defines the logical data link control protocols used to ensure the reliable exchange of information across the physical link between DTE and DCE. Two different link-level procedures are included in X.25—*Link Access Procedure* (LAP) and *Link Access Procedure Balanced* (LAPB).

The functions performed by the link level include:

- Transfer of data in an efficient and timely fashion.
- Synchronization of the link to ensure that the receiver is in step with the transmitter.
- Detection of transmission errors and recovery from such errors.
- Identification and reporting to higher levels of procedural errors for recovery.

The link level uses data link control procedures that are compatible with the HDLC standardized by ISO, and with the *Advanced Data Communications Control Procedures* (ADCCP) standardized by ANSI.

There are several protocols that can be used in the link level.

- **Link Access Protocol, Balanced (LAPB)** is derived from HDLC and is the most commonly used. In addition to the other characteristics of HDLC, it enables a logical link connection to be formed.
- **Link Access Protocol (LAP)** is an earlier version of LAPB and is seldom used today.
- **Link Access Procedure, D Channel (LAPD)** is derived from LAPB and it is used for ISDN; that is, it enables data transmission between DTEs through the D channel, especially between a DTE and an ISDN node.
- **Logical Link Control (LLC)** is an IEEE 802 LAN protocol that enables X.25 packets to be transmitted through a LAN channel.

LAP defines separate primary and secondary link stations with a primary station being in control of the link. It is, therefore, an "unbalanced" set of procedures because primary stations have greater capability than secondary stations on a link. LAPB, on the other hand, describes "balanced" functionality, in which link stations have both primary and secondary capabilities. This combines the functions of primary and secondary in each station attached to the link. LAPB treats the DTE and DCE as equals. This means that either station may begin the transmission of frames without receiving permission from the other station. There is no permanent master (primary) or slave (secondary) relationship. If the DTE issues a command to which the DCE responds with an acknowledgment, the DTE is considered the primary station while the DCE is considered the secondary station. If the DCE issues a command to which the DTE responds, the DCE becomes the primary station and the DTE functions as the secondary station.

These X.25 link level procedures correspond to the ISO HDLC standard. All information flowing across an X.25 data link is in the frame format. Beginning and ending flags delimit the frame that also includes frame level control information, user data, and frame check sequencing information. Frame types supported include unnumbered, supervisory, and information.

High-Level Data Link Control

A substantial improvement over async and bisync is the ISO's *High Level Data Link Control* (HDLC). This protocol is largely based on the pioneering work done by IBM on its replacement for BSC, the *Synchronous Data Link Control* (SDLC) protocol. SDLC and HDLC represent a significant departure from their forerunners because they are bit-oriented rather than character-oriented. (Other contemporary bit-oriented protocols, such as ANSI's *Advanced Data Communications Control Procedure* (ADCCP) and Burrough's Data Link Control are closely related to HDLC.)

In a bit-oriented protocol, the frame length can be an arbitrary number of bits rather than a fixed multiple of any selected character size. A further advantage in using a bit-oriented protocol is a reduction in the number of framing and control characters needed because each bit in an 8-bit character may be used independently to achieve control significance.

All HDLC frames conform to the frame structure shown in Figure 15.13. Each begins and ends with a flag pattern: a bit sequence consisting of a binary 0, followed by six 1s and another 0. These 01111110 markers are used as reference points to provide frame synchronization. When a line is quiet or idle, these flags are sent continuously for interframe time fill and to maintain synchronization between sender and receiver. To be valid, a frame must have at least 32 bits between its flags. Invalid frames are disregarded. For the sake of economy, a single flag may be used to identify the end of one frame and the beginning of another.

When a receiver detects a flag, it examines the data stream for an 8-bit address field. The term "address" can be particularly misleading when discussing X.25. This is not the DTE's network address; it originates within HDLC (and SDLC). These protocols can be used on multipoint lines, supporting as many as 256 terminal control units or secondary stations per line. So in a multipoint circuit, this address field is used to poll control units.

X.25 uses HDLC only in point-to-point mode, so it puts this field to a different use. It is used to separate link commands from responses and can only have two values, 01 (a binary 00000001) or 03 (a binary 00000011). In X.25's newer version, *Link Access Procedure—Balanced* (LAPB), a 01 identifies frames containing commands from DTE to DCE and responses to these commands from DCE to DTE and responses from DTE to DCE.

X.25's Link Access Procedure—Balanced

Three distinct types of frames are used in LAPB: *Information* (I-frames), *Supervisory* (S-frames), and *Unnumbered* (U-frames) (Figure 15.14). Only I-frames transport data across the link and are the only frames requiring sequence numbers. This user data is contained in an information field that immediately follows the control field in an I-frame (Figure 15.15).

The header and other data contained within this information field combine to form a data packet, which is built under the direction of the Network Layer protocol.

I-frames are assigned pairs of sequence numbers that operate in both send and receive directions and ensure that no frames are lost or interpreted out of order. Each transmitted

HDLC Frame

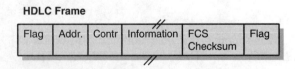

FIGURE 15.13 HDLC frame

HDLC Frame

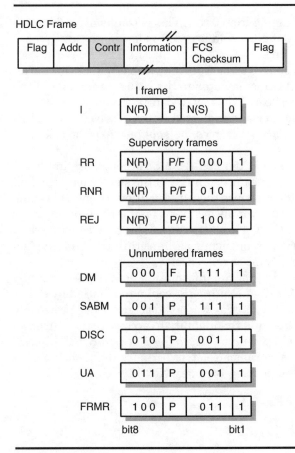

FIGURE 15.14 LAPB commands and responses

INFORMATION FRAMES AND PACKETS

I Frame

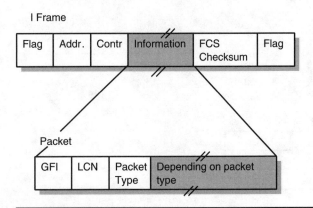

FIGURE 15.15 Information frames and packets

frame is given a frame sequence number ranging from 0 to 7. This is commonly referred to as a Modulo-8 frame-level window. A three-bit N(S) field is used to identify these sequence numbers and is advanced by 1 for each frame sent.

The receiver maintains as N(R) its own count of error-free frames received. Each time an error-free frame is received, the N(R) count is incremented to the sequence number of the next expected frame. Acknowledgements of correctly received frames flow back to the sender imbedded in frames sent by the receiver and indicated in the receiver's own N(R) count. As long as both sender and receiver pass I-frames, no separate explicit acknowledgement frames are required.

The single remaining bit used in an I-frame is the *Poll* (P) bit. Although originally intended to assert control of the line in a half-duplex node, in LAPB the sender uses the Poll bit to insist on an immediate response. In the response (non-Information) frame, this same bit becomes the receiver's *Final* (F) bit. The receiver always turns on the Final bit in its response to a command from the sender with the Poll bit set. The P/F bit may be used when either end becomes unsure about proper frame sequencing, perhaps through a missing acknowledgement, and wants to re-establish a point of reference.

Supervisory frames (Figure 15.16) are used to control information flow, request retransmissions, and acknowledge I-frames. The *Received Ready* (RR) command is used by either DTE or DCE to indicate readiness to receive I-frames as well as to acknowledge previously received I-frames. A temporary busy condition and the inability to accept further I-frames (as with buffer depletion), is communicated by sending *Receiving Not Ready* (RNR) commands. The *Reject* (REJ) command requests retransmission of I-frames commencing with N(R) and simultaneously acknowledges all preceding I-frames, N(R)-1.

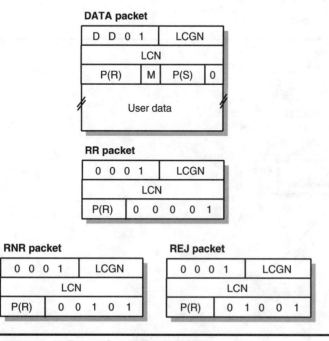

FIGURE 15.16   Data and supervisory packets

Unnumbered frames derive their name from the fact that they carry neither send nor receive sequence numbers. U-frames are intended to provide additional data link control functions, such as link initialization and disconnection, link reset after unrecoverable errors, and rejection of invalid frames. LAPB treats DTE and DCE as equals (no master/slave relation). Because this is a balanced link access procedure, either end can begin link initialization by sending out the *Set Asynchronous Balanced Mode* (SABM) command. The acceptance of the SABM is confirmed by the other (receiving) side when it issues an *Unnumbered Acknowledgement* (UA) response. At this point, I-frames may begin flowing. The N(S) and N(R) counters in these first I-frames are always reinitialized to 0.

Either DTE or DCE can suspend link operations by issuing a *Disconnect* (DISC) command. To acknowledge the receipt of this command, the receiver sends an *Unnumbered Acknowledgement* (UA) response. A disconnected phase is begun once the originator of the DISC gets this response. These disconnect procedures ensure a graceful link shutdown, as in the case when either DTE or DCE is taken out of service for maintenance.

Unrecoverable errors, such as those not corrected by the retransmission of identical frames, are indicated with *Frame Reject* (FRMR) response. Contained within this response are bit fields indicating the specific reason for a particular frame's rejection. Among the possible reasons are receipt of an undefined frame or invalid N(R) sequence numbers, or information fields exceeding maximum established sizes.

A critical function of the Data Link layer protocol is to ensure an error-free transmission. Most physical circuits are susceptible to errors induced by electromagnetic interference. This "noise" may come from radio frequency interference, AC power lines, lightning, or even from sunspots (in the case of satellite transmissions). However, digital circuits are stable.

Telephone lines are susceptible to noise from a variety of sources. It is often impossible or too costly to eliminate or shield against all sources of noise, so a mechanism must be employed to detect this noise and take corrective action.

HDLC uses a 16-bit *Frame Check Sequence* (FCS) to eliminate all single-error bursts up to 17 bits long, achieving an error rate of less than 1 in 10 bits. At framing time the address, control, and information fields of each HDLC frame are subjected to some additional processing in the transmitter's shift register. In this *Cyclic Redundancy Check* (CRC), the binary data stream is divided by the generator polynomial $X^{16} + X^{12} + X^5 + 1$ to produce a 16-bit remainder polynomial. This remainder is related to the length of each character (8 bits) and is appended to the preceding message as a two-octet (two-byte) FCS.

A trailing flag is added to complete the frame. For the receiver, this closing flag acts as a marker to indicate that the previous 16 bits should be interpreted as the FCS field.

The receiver processes the data stream in the same manner and computes its own FCS. It then compares the result with the FCS received in the frame. If they match, the data is good. If not, the frame is discarded and a retransmission request is issued.

Because flags are used for synchronization to identify the beginning and end of a frame, a problem arises when the data stream coincidentally contains the same 01111110 bit pattern as a flag. HDLC avoids this problem with bit stuffing or zero insertion:

"The DCE or DTE, when transmitting, shall examine the frame content between the two flag sequences, including the address, control, information, and FCS fields, and shall insert a 0 bit after all sequences of 5 contiguous 1 bits (including the last 5 bits of the FCS) to ensure that a flag sequence is not simulated. The DCE or DTE, when receiving, shall examine the frame content and shall discard any 0 bit which directly follows the 5 contiguous bits."

Automatic zero insertion and deletion are usually built-in features of retransmitter and receiver hardware.

Satellite Service and Modulo 128

Due to their long transit delays (about 250 milliseconds in one direction), satellite transmission links are not efficient for use in X.25 networks operating with frame windows of 7 (Modulo 8). In the case of frame acknowledgements, this delay becomes a round-trip of half a second. This is the same delay that makes voice communications over satellites somewhat unnerving, forcing long conversation pauses from speakers awaiting replies. In data communications, the net result of this delay is that the transmitter sits idle for relatively long periods of time, waiting for acknowledgements. Even though a satellite link may offer large amounts of bandwidth (typically in the megabit per second range), this bandwidth may be underutilized if not wisely managed.

As a solution to this problem, the ISO and ITU-T created an extended mode of operation within LAPB that supports a frame window up to 127 (Modulo 128). Up to 127 frames may be outstanding before an acknowledgement is required. The "pipe" stays fuller longer. This capability is only available from a PDN at the time of order (subscription time) and cannot be modified to toggle between Modulo 8 and 128 modes. This method of operation is specified at link setup time through the use of a *Set Asynchronous Balanced Mode Extended* (SABME), rather than SABM command. Extended frame formats, using longer 7-bit frame sequence numbers, are enabled once the SABME command is used.

Configurable Network Parameters

As insurance against events like lost or unacknowledged frames and link-deadlock conditions, several link-level timers and counters are utilized. The T1 timer establishes the amount of time the sender waits for an acknowledgement to be returned after transmitting a frame. Should this timer expire, frame retransmission occurs. The T1 timer is measured in milliseconds and is user-configurable within a range specified by the PDN. Typical values may be 100 to 10,000 milliseconds (0.1 to 10 seconds) and are dependent on link speed. The maximum number of attempts at retransmission is defined by the parameter N2, with common values in the 10 to 30 range.

Parameter N1 specifies the maximum number of bits in an I-frame (excluding flags and 0-bits inserted for transparency). This value, in turn, directly affects the maximum number of octets contained within the I-frame's information field and subsequently the maximum packet length. At a minimum, the ITU-T states that N1 should not be less than 1,080 bits; much larger values are commonplace.

Finally, the frame-window size, or maximum number of outstanding I-frames, is defined by parameter K. All networks are required to support a minimum K value of 7 (for Modulo 8), which may extend up to 127 for those networks or devices supporting the newer Modulo 128 operation.

Flag Field

A flag field is a special bit pattern consisting of a 0 bit followed by 6 consecutive 1 bits followed by a 0 bit (01111110). A frame is delimited by a beginning flag and an ending flag. Through special bit-handling techniques, it is guaranteed that this special flag bit pattern will never occur in the information carried between the beginning and ending flags unless an error has occurred.

Address Field

Follows the beginning flag of a frame. The address used in this field is either an A address (hexadecimal 03) to represent the DTE or a B address (hexadecimal 01) to represent the DCE. This field indicates whether the frame is a command frame or a response frame. Command frames always contain the address of the destination, while response frames always carry the address of the sending station.

Control Field

The control field dentifies the frame type and carries sequence numbers if applicable. There are three types of frames: Information, Supervisory, and Unnumbered. The bits in the Control field have a different meaning depending on the frame type.

Information Field

The content and size of the Information field is determined by the type of Level 3 frame it carries. An information frame may only carry one Level 3 packet at a time. Supervisory and Unnumbered frames (with the exception of a Frame Reject Response) do not contain an Information field.

FCS

FCS is the last field in the frame before the ending flag. As the frame is transmitted, the bits are passed through an algorithm to generate the 16-bit FCS field. When complete, the FCS is appended to the end of the frame. When the destination station receives the frame, it performs the same calculation on the bit stream. Based on the result, the receiving station can determine whether the frame was received with or without an error.

Packet Level

The X.25 packet level (level 3) defines the structuring of information into packets, flow control procedures, initiation and termination of logical connections, and other procedures. This level deals with the exchange of packets of information between DTE and DCE. A packet contains a header (which includes addressing information) and data (either user data or control data). The packet level describes how packets are structured for transmitting both end user and control information. It also describes the calls issued to set up, maintain, and clear the logical connections between DTEs.

A concept important to X.25 is *logical channels*. A logical channel represents a path between a DTE and DCE. Multiple logical channels can be mapped onto one physical channel (data link). Individual channels are identified by a logical channel identifier, which is kept in the packet header. The logical channel identifier associates the packet with a *virtual circuit* (VC). A VC is a logical end-to-end connection (channel) between a pair of DTEs. To DTEs, the VC appears to be a point-to-point circuit dedicated to the logical channel identifier in the packet header. The packet-switched network sets up the VC between DTEs and gives each DTE a logical channel ID to use to access that VC. The logical channel ID used by the DTEs can be different, but they both map to the same VC.

Virtual circuits (VCs) may be either switched or permanent. A switched VC functions somewhat like a switched telephone line. It is only temporary in nature, connecting a pair of DTEs only while communication is taking place. Setting up a switched VC requires the sending of a call request from the DTE attempting to initiate communications. A permanent VC is similar to a leased phone line; it is always there, whether or not any communications are taking place. Because *permanent virtual circuits* (PVCs) are always available, no call requests are required. This eliminates overhead both in call setup and call clearing.

Non-X.25 Devices

The discussion up to this point has assumed that each end system is performing all three levels of X.25 protocol processing. This allows intelligent devices to interact with the *Packet Switch Network* (PSN) across the DTE/DCE interface. But what about equipment that does not provide X.25 support?

One of the early forces behind the development of X.25 was to provide remote terminals access to host and mainframe computers. An asynchronous terminal (a nonintelligent character terminal) does not have its own processing capability and cannot implement X.25. Almost immediately after defining the host computer interface with X.25, ITU defined the interface for character mode terminals and the functions performed by the "gateway" that provides them access to the PSN.

Packet Assemblers/Disassemblers (PADS)

Non-X.25 devices connect to an X.25 network by using protocol converters called *packet assemblers/disassemblers* (PADs).

The PAD interacts with a device, such as an asynchronous terminal, using that terminal's native-mode asynchronous protocols. As characters are typed at the terminal, they are sent to the PAD. The PAD is responsible for assembling the characters into X.25 packets and forwarding them to the network. When the PAD receives packets from the network, it disassembles the packets and passes the user data one character at a time to the terminal with the appropriate start, stop, and parity bits set.

The PAD establishes and terminates VCs for its attached terminals. VCs are required for a terminal to communicate with other devices on the X.25 PSN. The PAD also performs other services related to the management of virtual circuits.

X.25 Protocols

ITU-T provides support for non-X.25 devices by extending X.25 with three related recommendations. These recommendations define the interface to, and the features of, the PAD.

- X.3
- X.28
- X.29

Recommendation X.3.   Recommendation X.3 defines the PAD parameters. The parameters make it possible to customize the PAD to allow communication with different types of asynchronous DTEs.

For example, some of the X.3 parameters define:

- The terminal data rate
- The terminal line length
- The PAD response when the user enters a break character
- The character that causes the PAD to transmit a partially full packet
- Whether the PAD echoes characters back to the terminal
- Whether the user can edit data that has been entered but not yet transmitted
- Whether XON/XOFF is used for PAD flow control
- Whether parity is checked and/or generated

X.3 Parameter Support.   X.3 defines the operation and function of the PAD in support of an asynchronous terminal. PAD operation is based on a set of X.3 PAD parameters set up during service establishment and can be modified by either the asynchronous terminal or the remote host during the call. Cisco's conformance to the ITU-T 1988 Blue Book specifications, which describes the functions performed by the PAD for the start-stop mode DTE, is given in Table 15.1.

Recommendation X.28.   Recommendation X.28 defines the terminal-to-PAD interface. The specification includes the procedures that control VCs, the exchange of user data, and the exchange of control information.

Some of the X.28 commands allow the asynchronous DTE to:

- Display the values of X.3 parameters that apply to the terminal
- Change the value of an X.3 parameter
- Set up a virtual circuit
- Check the status of a virtual circuit
- Terminate a virtual circuit

Some of the X.28 commands allow the PAD to inform the terminal that:

- The virtual circuit is established
- The called number is busy
- It has issued an invalid X.28 command

X.28 Commands Supported.   X.28 defines the procedures by which the asynchronous terminal can interact with the PAD. See Table 15.2.

Recommendation X.29.   Recommendation X.29 defines the protocol that runs between the PAD and an X.25 DTE (or remote PAD). It defines the PAD-to-remote DTE interface.

TABLE 15.1   Cisco's Conformance to ITU-T Specifications

X.3 Parameters	1988 ITU-T Description	Support
1	PAD Recall Defined Character	X
2	Local Echo	X
3	Data Forwarding Characters	X
4	Idle Timer or Data Forwarding Time out	X
5	Flow Control from the Network to the DTE	X
6	Control of PAD Service Signals	X
7	PAD action on Receipt of Break from Terminal	X
8	Discard Output	X
9	Padding after Carriage Return	X
10	Line Folding	—
11	Async Speed	X
12	Flow Control Terminal to PAD	X
13	Line Feed Insertion	X
14	Padding after Line Feed	X
15	Editing	X
16	Character Delete Defined Character	X
17	Line Delete Defined Character	X
18	Line Display Defined Character	X
19	Editing Service Signals-Not Valid if P6 = 0	—
20	Echo Mask	X

The remote X.25 DTE can read or set PAD parameters using X.29 procedures. It can also request that the PAD clear a virtual circuit. It does this by sending an "invitation to clear" message. In addition, the packet-mode DTE and the PAD can both send and receive indications of a break signal as well as error indications.

Dial X.25 (Recommendation X.32)

ITU-T Recommendation X.32 allows users to access an X.25 PSN over standard analog telephone lines rather than over a synchronous leased line. Many network providers, such as Telnet, Tymnet, and the Bell operating companies, offer Dial X.25.

Dial X.25 is designed for customers just beginning to use an X.25 PSN or those that do not need a full time connection to the PSN. Dial X.25 saves an organization the cost of leasing a dedicated access line, and allows users to access the PSN from unsupported locations.

For example, a customer service agent can access a host on the corporate PSN from any customer site with a laptop computer and modem. While the laptop is connected to the corporate network, it is a full member of the network with automatic error detection and correction.

TABLE 15.2   X.28 Command Support

Command	Function
clear or clr	Clears a virtual call
interrupt or int	Sends an interrupt packet
parameter or par	Shows current values of parameters
profile or prof	Loads a standard or named profile
reset	Resets the call
set	Changes parameters
setread	Changes and then reads parameters
status or stat	Requests connection status

Extended X.28 Command Support

Command	Function
break	Equivalent to an async BREAK per X.3 parameter 7
call	Calls a remote device
help	Invokes online help facility
iclear	Asks the remote device to clear the call
iclr	Asks the remote device to clear the call
read	Shows the current values of the parameters
rpar?	Shows the current values of the remote parameters
rread	Shows the values of the remote parameters
rset?	Sets and reads the remote parameter values
rsetread	Changes and then reads the remote parameters

X.25 Internetworking (Recommendation X.75)

X.25 was originally developed to allow communication between devices residing on a single PSN. However, as the number of PSNs has increased, it has become necessary to provide a facility that enables users residing on different PSNs to exchange data and share resources. X.75 was designed for this purpose. X.75 defines a procedure that allows PSNs to exchange packets in a manner transparent to the DTEs forming the virtual circuit. It enables a DTE attached to a PSN to communicate with a DTE attached to another PSN. In other words, X.75 allows X.25 internetworking. See Figure 15.17.

Virtual Circuits and Logical Channels

The Network Layer of X.25 offers two varieties of VCs. The temporary connection or association over the network of two DTEs is termed a virtual call or *switched virtual circuit* (SVC) by the ITU-T. As previously mentioned, SVCs are analogous to dial-up connections over the PSTN. SVCs require three separate phases: call setup, data transfer, and call

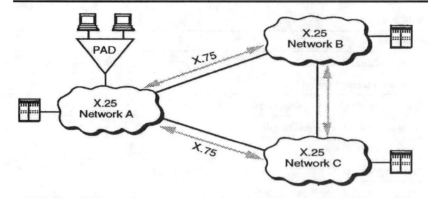

FIGURE 15.17

disconnection. If not activated, the logical resources for SVCs remain in a quiescent fourth (ready) state. For those applications requiring fixed point-to-point connections or leased lines, *permanent virtual circuits* (PVCs) are also supported by most networks. Recommendation X.2, which describes International User Services and Facilities in *Public Data Networks* (PDNs), classifies both SVCs and PVCs as "essential" services to be available internationally on all networks. Unlike SVCs, PVCs have only a single phase: data transfer. They cannot be established spontaneously as required, but rather must be requested in advance at the time of service subscription from the PDN. Also, some restrictions apply to the use of PVCs. Many PDNs do not support PVCs across X.75 or international gateways.

Both SVCs and PVCs are established via numbered logical channels. Typically, a public network assigns a block of logical channels, depending on line speed, with each X.25 leased line installed. (A handful of PDNs, like Argentina's ARPAC, charge for each logical channel required.) With only a couple of unusual packet types as exceptions, every packet flowing across the X.25 network interface contains the *logical-channel number* (LCN) used for the duration of the call. While SVCs and PVCs have end-to-end significance, logical channel numbers do not. LCNs are assigned only across the DTE/DCE interface at both the local and remote network connection. Therefore, the assigned logical channel numbers at the local and remote X.25 DTE/DCE interface are seldom the same.

X.25 has a well-structured technique for allocating LCNs efficiently. This is critical with SVCs, because each call gets a logical channel number assigned dynamically. Per X.25 link, there may be as many as 4,096 logical channel numbers divided into as many as five "variable-width zones." (That theoretical limit is far lower in practice. Based on the link access rate, most network operators publish recommendations on the maximum number of logical channels to be supported at a given bandwidth.) Not all configurations require the use of every zone; in most cases, only a single zone is necessary for full function. See Figure 15.18.

The lowest logical channel, LCN 0, is not available for normal calls. It is reserved for the overall Network Layer control of the link. The zone for PVCs begins at LCN 1 and increments upward to a predetermined number, LCN N. Again, with PVCs the LCN numbers

LOGICAL CHANNEL NUMBER ASSIGNMENTS

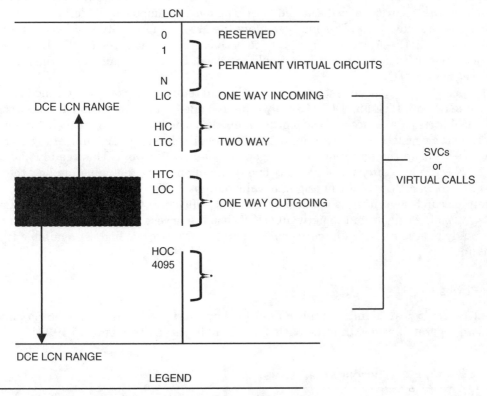

FIGURE 15.18   Logical channel number assignments

used by the DTE must match those assigned by the network supplier (who supplies the DCE). In practice, though PVCs are generally suited for fixed host-to-host connections, they are infrequently used. When a PVC is used, there is usually a fixed monthly charge in addition to the normal data traffic charges.

PVCs eliminate the call setups but limit flexibility. If a PAD port is connected to a PVC, the destination DTE is fixed, and that port cannot call any other remote DTEs. It is also important to note that PVCs don't operate like TDM time slots. If a PVC is idle (not carrying data) it uses no bandwidth on the link. After the highest logical channel number used by PVCs, all other LCNs are used for virtual calls or SVCs. If no PVCs are defined, then LCN 1 becomes available to the first grouping of SVCs. The reference of incoming and outgoing is always from the DTE's—not the DCE's—perspective.

Whether the connection is permanent or switched, incoming or outgoing data flow over a virtual circuit is always full-duplex. One-way incoming SVCs permit DTEs to receive calls from other DTEs but not originate them. This type of call restriction is one of many forms of network security to be discussed later. The most common way of defining virtual circuits is as two-way SVCs. This method offers the greatest flexibility and least administration by giving these circuits the ability to both originate and receive calls. If neither PVCs nor one-way incoming logical channels are used, LCN 1 is available as the *lowest two-way channel* (LTC).

For proper operation, the lowest or starting LCN and total number of LCNs defined must be the same for both DTE and DCE. Usually there is a one-for-one correspondence between the physical ports on a device and the logical channels needed. Therefore, with all ports active, a 16-port async PAD requires at least 16 logical channels on the X.25 link. Many DTEs also support remote configuration or management over the network. This requires additional LCNs. The last category of SVCs is one-way: outgoing. As the name implies, there are *virtual circuits* (VCs) that can originate calls but not receive them.

A simple search algorithm is used to dynamically allocate LCNs for switched virtual circuits. Incoming calls from the network (DCE) use the lowest available logical channel that is ready to accept a call. Outgoing calls from the DTE use the highest available logical channel.

Packet Formats

To identify the logical channel number used for any given packet among 4096 possible LCNs, two separate fields within the packet are actually used. See Figure 15.19.

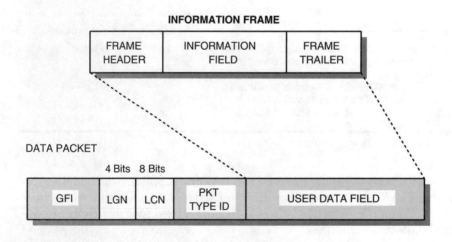

GFI = General Format Identifier
LCN = Logical Channel Number
LGN = Logical Channel Group Number

FIGURE 15.19 Packet format

The actual logical channel number specified is really the combination of two fields: the 4-bit *logical channel group number* (LGN) and 8-bit *logical channel number* (LCN). Because these fields are encoded in binary, combined they total 12 bits (2^{12}=4,096). Some networks treat these 12 bits as one continuous field, while others use LGNs to indicate "blocks" of logical channels. Certain LGNs may be designated for use by one-way SVCs only, for example. The first four high-order bits (bits 8, 7, 6, and 5) of every packet form the *general format identifier* (GFI). See Figure 15.20. The GFI is encoded in binary and indicates the layout of the remainder of the packed header.

The high-order bit, bit 8, is the Q or data qualifier bit, used to indicate two levels of user data or information within a packet. When set to 0, the Q bit denotes that the packet carries conventional user data. When set to 1, the Q bit indicates that the packet carries control information to be interpreted differently by the called DTE.

The only current ITU-T standardized use of the Q bit is to signify X.29 control packets used by asynchronous PADs. X.29 is one of three related ITU-T standards that specify how

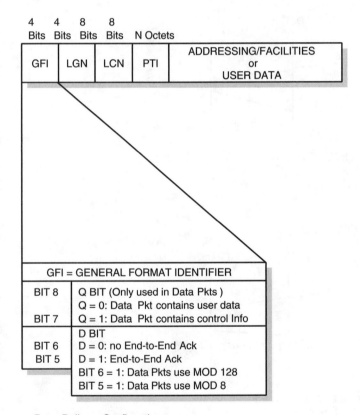

FIGURE 15.20   General format identifier

start-stop or asynchronous devices are supported on PDNs. Some vendors may use the Q bit to create their own "qualified" proprietary protocol within the packet.

Following the Q bit is bit 7, the delivery confirmation or D bit. The D bit is usually set to 0 and indicates that Packet Layer acknowledgments have only local significance between DTE and DCE. When set to 1 in a Call Setup or Data packet, the D bit indicates that acknowledgments have end-to-end significance between source and destination DTE. See Figure 15.21. (Some argue that this function is best handled by the Transport Layer and its inclusion in the Network Layer violates the rules of OSI.)

The D bit may be turned on and off selectively on a per packet basis. Use of the D bit is not universally supported on all networks and its use restricts throughput by imposing a round trip acknowledgment delay for every packet sent.

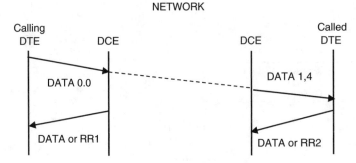

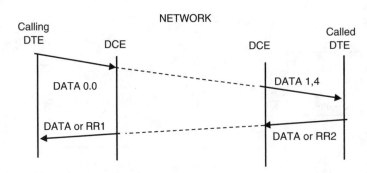

RR = Receive Ready
DATA 1,4 Means P(R) + P(S)

FIGURE 15.21   D bit acknowledgment options

Bit 5 and 6 are used in combination to indicate the modulus or sequence numbering of the packet. The Packet layer employs its own set of send and receive sequence number counters that operate independently of the Data Link layer counters, N(R) and N(S). The Packet layer counters are described as P(R) and P(S) and are used for Layer 3 window control. Only those packets that require or convey flow control information employ these counters. Data packets need both P(R) and P(S), while Receive Ready, Receive Not Ready, and Reject packets only use the P(R) or packet receive counter.

Within the GFI, the combination of bit 6 set to 1 and bit 5 set to 0 indicates Modulo 128 sequence numbering. Modulo 128 is also sometimes described as the *Extended Packet Sequence Numbering* facility.

In the reverse binary order, bit 6 set to 0 and 5 set to 1 convey that the more conventional Modulo 8 sequence numbering is used. Other patterns of these bits are not defined. Due to the considerable increase in buffer capacity needed to support Modulo 128 (127 outstanding packets) on every active virtual circuit at the Network layer, most manufacturers and PDNs don't yet support this option.

The packet sequence numbering scheme, either Modulo 8 or 128, must be the same at both sides of the DTE/DCE interface and is used for all logical channels.

Identifying Types of Packets

The third octet in the packet header is the *packet-type identification* field (PTI). (The ITU-T uses the term octet instead of byte to indicate 8 consecutive bits that are treated as an entity.) The PTI is used to differentiate among the 28 possible packet types, though in practice there are only 15 packet types because half of these packets are duplicates. Although the packet encoding is the same, the ITU-T descriptive name for a packet changes with its direction of travel between DTE and DCE. For example, the initial Call Setup packet travelling from DTE to DCE is a Call Request packet, while the same packet moving from DCE to DTE becomes an Incoming Call. Most other types of packets, such as the Clear Request/Clear Indication, have similar dual personalities. Usually the PTI contains a unique 8-bit binary identifier, except for those packets requiring send and receive sequence numbering.

Data packets are identified by merely setting the low order bit of the PTI to 0. In addition to containing both send and receive sequence numbers, a Data packet incorporates a unique fifth, or "M" bit. In an OSI environment, the M bit is set by the Transport Layer; otherwise, it may be set by some other layer above the Network Layer.

The M bit is set to 1 to tell the destination DTE that more data will follow in the next packet. Using the M bit, packets can be logically chained together to convey a large block of related information. Packets with the M bit on are always full. The last packet in the chain sets the M bit to 0, indicating that the series is completed.

Use of the M bit is a creative way to stuff long messages into small, 128-octet packets. This is a problem especially for a block mode terminal where an entire screen of data may amount to 2000 characters. File transfers of large blocks of data may also benefit from the use of the M bit.

The M bit can also be used to match unequal packet sizes at the DTE/DCE interface on either side of the network. For example, the source DTE may use a packet size of 512 octets, while the destination DTE only permits packets of 64 octets or fewer. In this case, using the

M bit, the DCE at the destination interface can split up the 512-octet packets into eight smaller 64-octet packets. The efficiency of D-bit use may also be improved with the M bit. As noted, normal D bit acknowledgments impart significant network delays and reduce effective throughput. Rather than incurring the delay caused by using D bit confirmation for every packet, the M bit can be set to 1 for the series of packets and the D bit set only in the last packet (with M = 0) in the series. The effect of this combination is that the single acknowledgment to the lone D bit can imply that all the preceding packets in the series (with M bit = 1) were also received correctly.

The Major Categories of X.25 Packets

There are five major categories of packets: Call Setup/Clearing, Data/Interrupt, Flow Control/Reset, Restart, and Diagnostic. *Switched virtual calls* (SVCs) must go through the three distinct phases of Call Setup, Data (transfer), and Call Clearing, while *permanent virtual circuits* (PVCs) require only the single phase of data transfer. In both cases, the vast majority of actual user data is carried by Data packets only. This section describes the role and characteristics of each of these packet types.

The Call Setup phase begins with the source creating a Call Request packet or calling DTE as shown in Figure 15.22. The Call Request packet is sent out by the DTE on its highest available logical channel number. In addition to the standard general format identifier, logical group/channel number, and packet type fields, the Call Request packet contains a number of other significant fields (see Figure 15.23).

The actual network address of the destination or called DTE is contained in the Call Request packet. In establishing a call, the called address serves the same purpose as a called party's telephone number. It allows the network to properly route the call to the destination. The called address is in Binary-Coded Decimal format and may range up to 14 digits long.

Octet 4 to the Call Request contains two 4-bit fields that specify the length of the calling and called address fields, respectively. These address fields contain the Public Data Network's DTE addresses, the format of which is described in the ITU-T X.121 Recommendation.

Private networks typically do not need 14 digits of addressing and can use much shorter address lengths. Following the called address field is the calling address, an optional field used by the destination to identify the originating DTE. If the original DTE does not provide a calling address, the PDN's own adjacent DCE may automatically insert this information.

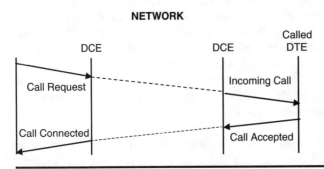

FIGURE 15.22 Call Setup

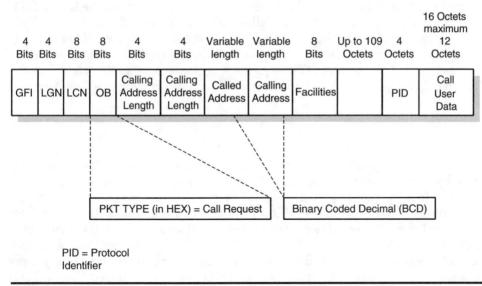

FIGURE 15.23   Call Request packet format

At each Call Setup time, users may request special network services beyond normal default offerings. These services span a wide range of possibilities and are classified as *optional user facilities*. Many networks require that users request these facilities at subscription or service establishment time and generally charge extra for their use. Some of these facilities, like reverse charging, take their inspiration from telephone network services—such as the collect call. Others provide enhanced security or network performance.

Following the calling address, an 8-bit field specifies the length of the facilities field, which may extend up to a maximum of 109 octets. The final field in the Call Request packet is the optional *call user data* field, which follows the facilities field. The call user data field enables users to transmit small amounts of actual data to the Called DTE at Call Setup time. Information in the call user data field is inserted by the Calling DTE and passed transparently by the network to the Called DTE.

In conventional Call Requests, this field can be up to 16 octets in length and can contain information like the user's identification, password, or even additional routing information for non-X.25-destination subnetworks. When the optional *fast select* facility is used, this special type of Call Request packet may support a call user data field up to 128 octets.

If present, the first four octets of the call user data field are called the *Protocol Identifier* (PID) and may be used to supply additional protocol information. For example, X.29 uses bits 8 and 7 in the first of these four octets to confirm its identify. Individual national networks may also use this to define their own network-specific protocols.

Assuming that the Call Request packet is acceptable to the destination, the called DTE returns a Call Accepted packet to the calling DTE. The Call Accepted packet appears to the calling DTE as a Call Connected packet; it uses the same format as the Call Request but for its lack of a call user data field.

If unable to deliver the options or facilities desired in the Call Request, the Called DTE may "negotiate" on some of these with the Calling DTE. Some negotiable items include packet window size, use of the D bit, and several of the optional facilities. Negotiation is always in a downward direction toward the default settings, with the lowest value always winning. For example, if the calling DTE requests a packet size of 1,024 octets, but the called DTE can only support up to 256, this lower value is returned in the Call Accepted packet.

Call Refusals

Not all calls are successful. Calls may be refused, either by the destination DTE or the network itself. In both cases, there may be a variety of reasons behind this refusal.

The called DTE may be busy and have no logical channels available. It may be out of service, or it may refuse the call because of a security authorization failure. The reasons for its rejection are included in either of two fields of the Clear Request/Clear Indication packet it returns. Octet 4 (the Clearing Cause field) contains the Clearing Cause Code, and octet 5 (the Diagnostic Code field) may contain an optional Diagnostic Code that gives more specific information about the cause. Over the years, the ITU-T has developed Clearing and Diagnostic Codes to cover most situations. Each PDN publishes its own directory containing both ITU-T and network-specific Clearing and Diagnostic Codes.

Packet-equipment vendors may also develop their own extensions to the basic set of ITU-T codes. Problems in identifying the actual source of the Clear Indication and then correctly interpreting this information may arise. This is frequently the case when crossing PDN boundaries, as with international calls, or when multiple vendors' equipment is in use.

Reasons for Call Refusal by the network (see Figure 15.24) are due to a variety of circumstances. Calls may be rejected due to improperly formed Call Request packets, incorrect addresses, invalid facility requests, or insufficient network access privileges. Other

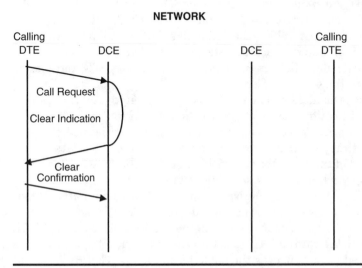

FIGURE 15.24   Call Refusal by the network

situations resulting in Call Refusals may be partial or complete network routing failures, such as network congestion or the loss of an X.75 gateway.

A Call Collision results when a DTE-placed Call Request and a DCE-placed Incoming Call land on the same logical channel at the same time. Despite the rarity of Call Collisions, X.25 has provided a means of resolving them. The local DCE processes its own DTE's Call Request normally and cancels the remote DTE's Incoming Call, which in turn gets disregarded by the local DTE (see Figure 15.25).

Data Transfers in Virtual Calls

The data transfer phase of a virtual call may begin once the Calling DTE receives its Call Connected packet. Data packets use a far more streamlined packet format structure than Call Requests and require only 3 octets of OSI Level 3 protocol overhead to carry 128 octets of user data (see Figure 15.26). The three octets of overhead contain the GFI, LGN/LCN, and P(R)/P(S) sequence numbers. If present, the Q, D, and M bits operate as previously described. When Modulo 128, extended packed sequence numbering, is specified in the GFI, two octets are needed to accommodate the send and receive sequence numbers.

Data packets require no network addresses. They rely only on their *Logical Channel Numbers* (LCNs), because the route to the destination through the network has already been established.

The ITU-T specifies the standard maximum user-data portion of a Data packet to be 128 octets. However, the specification allows network administrations to offer other optional lengths, including 16, 32, 64, 256, 512, 1,024, 2,048, and 4,096 octets. This is supported either by subscription or is negotiable on a per-call basis.

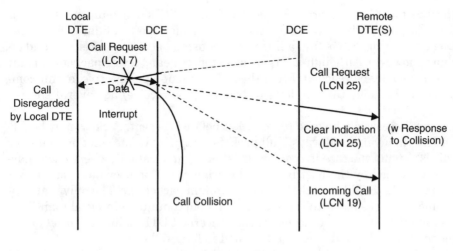

NETWORK

LCN = Logical Channel Number

FIGURE 15.25 Call Collision and Resolution

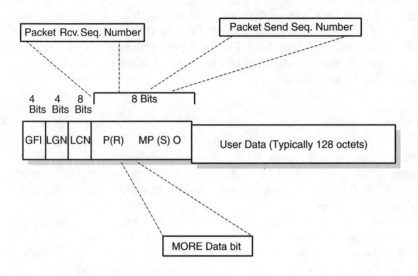

Typical Data Packet Format

GFI = General Format Identifier
LCN = Logical Channel Number
LGN = Logical Channel Group Number

FIGURE 15.26   Typical data packet format

Call Collision and Resolution

These PDN offerings must be tempered by the practical realities of attempting to buffer such large packets. Applications involving bulk data transfer are candidates for larger packet sizes. Don't expect to always find a linear relationship between packet size and effective throughput, however. Although a larger packet size means fewer packets, a point of diminishing returns may be reached. From the buffer queue's perspective, a unit composed of one large packet may take as long to transmit (or receive) as several shorter packets.

User data does not necessarily have to fill a packet before it is sent. Packets may be forwarded or "launched" in a variety of ways. Full packets contain only one octet or character of user data. This is usually the case in *echoplex* (host echo) applications, where each character transmitted is echoed by the host back to the originator. The user data field is not padded by null characters to fill the packet to the maximum packet size. The only real stipulation is that some networks insist that the user data field contain an integral number of whole octets. To comply with this requirement, the concerned DTE maintains *octet alignments in partial octets* by adding the extra bit needed to form full octets.

At first glance, it may seem redundant that this level requires its own set of packet send and receive sequence numbers, as a similar flow control mechanism is used by HDLC at OSI Level 2. While the sliding-window technique used at both layers is the same, Level 2 deals only with a single hop between DTE and DCE. The frame window at Level 2 affects all frames across that link. When the frame window is closed, the entire link is shut down until the window reopens.

At Level 3, a single link may carry dozens of simultaneous *virtual circuits* (VCs), with each of these VCs managed independently. The packet window supplies one way of accomplishing this. Also, depending on the state of the D bit, Level-3 acknowledgments operate either on a local or end-to-end basis.

For the sake of clarity, all Packet Layer activity shown is for a single logical channel: LCN 001. With other active calls, the same flow control process occurs for each VC. The P(R) or P(S) window for a single VC can be closed without affecting any other VCs or the overall Data Link Layer. As shown, because VCs operate in full duplex mode, to improve efficiency, P(R) and P(S) acknowledgments may be "piggybacked" within Data packets. This is in contrast to using explicit Flow Control packets like *Receive Ready* (RR) and *Receive Not Ready* (RNR) for the same purpose.

Interruption without Call Clearing

Situations infrequently arise when it is necessary to interrupt the normal host computer session from a terminal without clearing the active call. This function is usually performed by the Break key. In cases where the host has been flow controlled OFF, this function is not possible using the usual Data packets.

To circumvent this problem, Interrupt packets have been devised that do not contain packet sequence numbers and are not subject to normal flow procedures. The OSI Transport Layer procedure for expedited data uses these Layer 3 Interrupt packets. As a rule, they should be sparingly used; they are not intended to replace Data packets, but to carry a limited amount (up to 32 bits) or user data between local and remote DTEs at high speeds. Because they are unsequenced, they are placed at the top of each buffer queue. An Interrupt packet is acknowledged with an Interrupt Confirmation, with only one outstanding interrupt allowed at a time (Figure 15.27). The format of an Interrupt packet is shown in Figure 15.28.

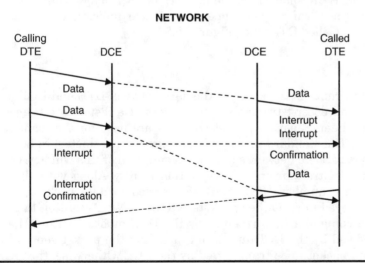

FIGURE 15.27   Interrupt procedure

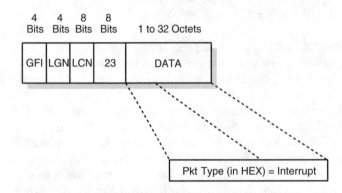

FIGURE 15.28 Interrupt Packet format

Terminating a Virtual Call

The orderly termination of a virtual call by the DTE is accomplished with the use of the *Clear Request*. This request is the equivalent of saying good-bye and hanging up the phone; it may be made at any time by the DTE. Keep in mind that a higher level protocol generates the original request to clear a call.

Specified within the Clear Request is the *Logical Channel Number* (LCN) to be cleared, along with a clearing-cause code and optional diagnostic code. This same packet may be used in the process of Call Refusal, as previously mentioned. When call termination is at the DTE's request, the clearing-cause field of this packet (octet 4) is set to a hex value of 00, indicating that the DTE originated the clearing action.

Once the Clear Request is acknowledged by a Clear Confirmation, the call is ended and the logical channel becomes available for future calls. Depending on specific network implementations, Clear Confirmations may have local or end-to-end significance as in Figure 15.29. If local, the confirmation is returned by the DCE. If end-to-end, the confirmation is returned by the Called DTE. In some cases, the network or DCE may terminate the call. From DCE to DTE, the same Clear Request appears as a Clear Indication simultaneously issued to both Calling and Called DTEs. See Figure 15.30.

Packet Layer Flow Control

Packet Layer flow control controls the speed of the data between DTE and DCE and ensures that the sending end doesn't transmit data packets at a faster rate than the receiving end can receive them. Separate packet windows are used for the transmit and receive sides of each VC. The standard packet window size (W parameter) in both direction for most networks is 2. Some networks support negotiation of this window, on a per-call basis, with the flow control parameter negotiation facility. Along with the packet receive and send sequence numbers P(R) and P(S) carried in data packets, P(R) acknowledgments are conveyed in two other packets, RR and RNR. According to the X.25 Recommendation, "The value of a P(R) received by the DCE must be within the range from the last P(R) received by the DCE up to and including the packet send sequence number of the next data packet to be transmitted by the DCE. Otherwise, the DCE will

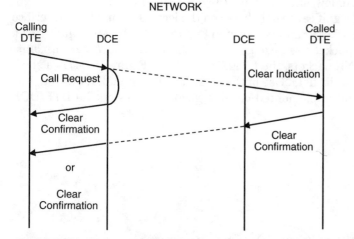

FIGURE 15.29 Call termination by DTE

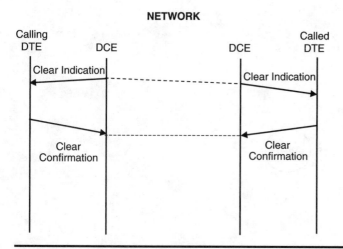

FIGURE 15.30 Call termination by the network

consider the receipt of this P(R) as a procedure error and will reset the virtual call or *permanent virtual circuit* (PVC). The DTE should follow the same procedure. The receive sequence number P(R) is less than or equal to the sequence number of the next expected data packet and implies that the DTE or DCE transmitting P(R) has accepted at least all data packets numbered up to and including P(R).

The use of RRs as acknowledgments is illustrated in Figure 15.31, RNRs and RRs operate at OSI Level 3 in the same manner as the Supervisory frames operating under the same names at Layer 2. RNRs tell the far end (DTE or DCE) to stop sending data packets and also acknowledge the receipt of all Data packets. RRs tell the opposite end to start sending data packets again within the window, starting with the designated P(R).

Again, acknowledgments have significance only between the local DTE and DCE interface unless the D-bit is used. The RR packet format is shown in Figure 15.32, RNR in Figure 15.33.

A third type of Flow Control packet used exclusively by the DTE is *packet retransmission*. Like the related RR and RNR packets, the DTE *Reject* (REJ) (Figure 15.34) is a short (three-octet) packet containing a P(R) field. Use of the DTE REJ is optional. If desired, it is specified at subscription time and implemented on all logical channels on the DTE/DCE

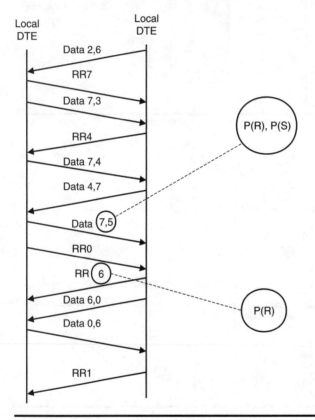

FIGURE 15.31 Packet-level flow control

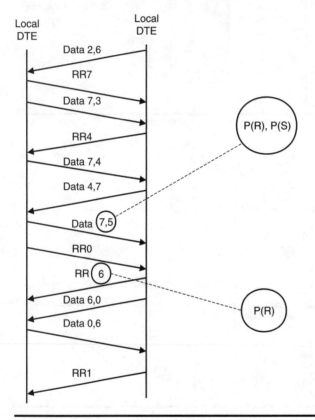

FIGURE 15.32 Receive-Ready packet format

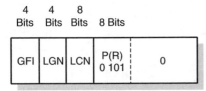

FIGURE 15.33   Receive-Not-Ready packet format

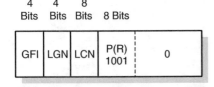

FIGURE 15.34   DTE Reject packet format

interface. As an optional facility, it is not necessarily available on all networks. The purpose of the DTE REJ is to request retransmission of one or more consecutive data packets from the DCE. The DCE retransmits data packets beginning with P(S) set equal to the P(R) value contained in the Reject packet. Normal data packets may be transmitted following these retransmitted packets.

Control Packets for Abnormal Conditions

Several other types of control packets are used to handle the abnormal conditions that may affect a virtual circuit. In cases in which the sequence numbers of data packets sent between DTE and DCE lose synchronization, more forceful measures are needed to re-establish normal data transfer.

The Reset procedure is used to reinitialize to 0 the P(R) and P(S) sequence counters of both the DTE and DCE on a single logical channel, whether it's SVC or PVC. Either DTE or DCE may initiate a Reset by issuing a Reset Request or Reset Indication, respectively. Any Data or Interrupt packets in transmit over the network are discarded in the process.

The ITU-T warns that "The maximum number of packets which may be discarded is a function of network end-to-end delay and throughput characteristics and, in general, has no relation to the local window size." A Reset Confirmation packet sent by either DTE or DCE acknowledges that the logical channel has been reset and allows data transfer to resume. See Figure 15.35.

For those situations in which all logical channels on a link are affected, a more extensive recovery method is needed. To initialize or reinitialize the entire Packet layer DTE/DCE interface and all SVCs and PVCs, the Restart procedure is used. Some networks also employ this procedure when the Packet layer is first brought up, to put the entire interface into a known state. Loss of the Physical—and consequently the Data Link—layers to events like power outages also involve this response.

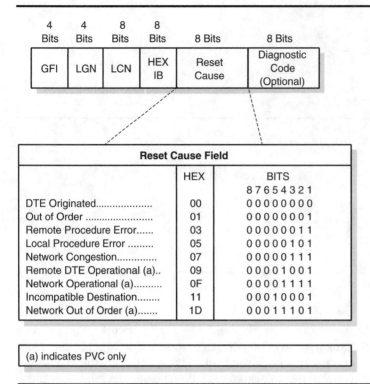

4 Bits	4 Bits	8 Bits	8 Bits	8 Bits	8 Bits
GFI	LGN	LCN	HEX IB	Reset Cause	Diagnostic Code (Optional)

Reset Cause Field

	HEX	BITS 8 7 6 5 4 3 2 1
DTE Originated....................	00	0 0 0 0 0 0 0 0
Out of Order	01	0 0 0 0 0 0 0 1
Remote Procedure Error......	03	0 0 0 0 0 0 1 1
Local Procedure Error	05	0 0 0 0 0 1 0 1
Network Congestion..............	07	0 0 0 0 0 1 1 1
Remote DTE Operational (a)..	09	0 0 0 0 1 0 0 1
Network Operational (a).........	0F	0 0 0 0 1 1 1 1
Incompatible Destination........	11	0 0 0 1 0 0 0 1
Network Out of Order (a).......	1D	0 0 0 1 1 1 0 1

(a) indicates PVC only

FIGURE 15.35   Reset Request/Indicator Packet

Should all SVCs or PVCs on a link be hung up, logical channel 0 is reserved as an escape mechanism to issue the Restart packet. Either the DTE or DCE may initiate the Restart procedure by sending either a Restart Request or Restart Indication, respectively, to their local DTE/DCE interface. While this is acknowledged locally by a restart confirmation, only active *virtual circuits* (SVC or PVC) at the remote interface need to be cleared. See Figure 15.36.

Diagnostic Packets and Unrecoverable Errors

The fifth and last major packet type is the Diagnostic packet. Such packets are used on some networks to carry diagnostic information under unusual circumstances, such as when the conventional Diagnostic packets (Reset, Clear, and Restart) are unsuitable. See Figure 15.37.

For unrecoverable errors, the diagnostic codes within these packets may be conveyed to higher levels for problem determination and analysis. Diagnostic packets require no confirmation and are sent on logical channel 0. Networks also may specify their own extensions to the normal set of ITU-T diagnostic codes.

Network Layer Timers

To ensure recovery form abnormal events at the Packet Layer, X.25 uses a variety of timers. In cases of missing or lost acknowledgments, for example, the use of timers appears to be

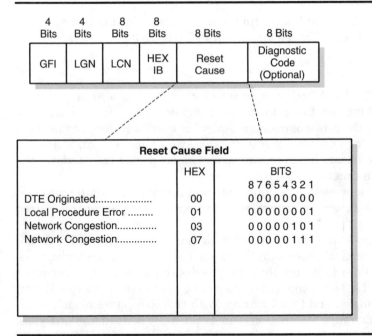

FIGURE 15.36   Restart Request Packet format

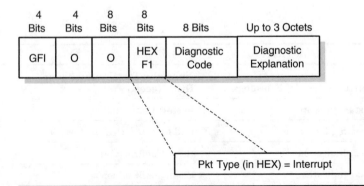

FIGURE 15.37   Diagnostic Packet format

the only way to ensure that errors are recognized and appropriate action taken. DTEs and DCEs have their own timers and are required to respond to certain packets from each other within a specified maximum time.

While the X.25 ITU-T Recommendation specifies default time-out values, many network suppliers choose to establish their own default values. These network-supplied default setting are fine in most cases.

Timers may also be tuned by users to accommodate network-specific characteristics such as transit delay. The ITU-T uses two digits in numbering the Network level timers to differentiate them from the Data Link level timers that use only a single digit. Some representative timers and their significance are shown in Table 15.3.

Packet Layer State Diagrams

Programmers describe the DTE/DCE Packet layer interface of X.25 as a *finite-state machine*. Although not of general interest to most network designers, the finite-state machine is a useful model for depicting the range of possible "states" or conditions for the interface. Each state defines a condition of either the overall Packet layer or, more often, of a single logical channel. States change phases based on two factors alone: packet transfer over the interface or the expiration of a timer.

In Figure 15.38, the ellipse represents a unique state and contains the state name and number. State transitions are shown by arrows, with the packet type being transferred shown alongside.

The entire set of Packet layer states can be shown with four state diagrams. These diagrams are arranged in a hierarchical order with the Restart state having the highest priority. An ellipse within an ellipse indicates that the process continues to a lower order diagram. The possible states of a logical channel correspond to four phases of a call: Ready, Call Establishment, Data Transfer, and Call Clearing. With this four-phase model, an interface's behavior under a wide range of situations can be precisely defined and analyzed. Such repeatable and verifiable responses form the basis of network conformance testing. Any reaction resulting in an incorrect or unknown state is considered an error and handled accordingly.

TABLE 15.3   Time-Out Table

DCE Time-Outs			
Time-Out Number	Time-Out Value	Started When DCE Issues:	Normally Terminated When DCE Receives
T10	60 sec.	Restart Indication	Restart Confirmation
T11	180 sec.	Incoming Call	Call accepted, clear request
T12	60 sec.	Reset Indication	Reset Confirmation
T13	60 sec.	Clear Indication	Clear Confirmation

DTE Time-Outs			
Time-Out Number	Time-Out Value	Started When DTE Issues:	Normally Terminated When DTE Receives
T20	180 sec.	Restart Request	Restart Confirmation
T21	200 sec.	Call Request	Call connected, clear indication
T22	180 sec.	Reset Request	Reset Confirmation
T23	180 sec.	Clear Request	Clear Confirmation
T28	300 sec.	Registration Request	Registration Confirmation

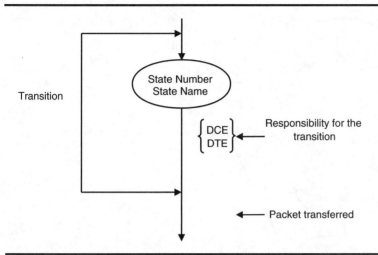

FIGURE 15.38 State Symbol definition

The example shown in Figure 15.39 shows the Call Setup process for a single logical channel across a single DTE/DCE interface. From the Ready state (p1), a Call Request packet changes the interface to DTE Waiting state (p2). The Ready state simply confirms that the logical channel is idle and ready to accept or place a call. After the receipt of a Call Connected acknowledgment from the DCE, the DTE enters the Data Transfer state (p4) and may begin passing data.

X.25 States, Error Handling, and the Frame Relay Approach

Because X.25 is a connection-oriented protocol, it must maintain considerable information about the ongoing connections. It must also maintain information about data transfer operations. It contains many rules on how connections are managed through the state tables, and actions that must be taken by the DCE or DTE upon receipt of specific packets while in certain states.

The point is that X.25 has extensive editing and diagnostic tools, all resulting in a very feature-rich service with resultant delay and overhead.

These operations create computational overhead. As you shall see, frame relay eliminates almost all of these operations.

The Frame Relay Approach to States and Errors. Frame relay also uses states, which are based on the ISDN Q.931 Recommendation. A number of vendors do not implement Q.931 with frame relay, however. Furthermore, frame relay has very few error checking and diagnostic features. Thus, the frame relay approach yields a relatively featureless service that is considerably faster than X.25.

X.25 Facilities and the Frame Relay Approach. X.25 has some very useful features called facilities. They are described in X.25 and in X.2. X.25 facilities published in the 1988 Blue Book are listed. As the reader might expect, frame relay networks do not offer facility services. The facility names for packet-switched service are as follows:

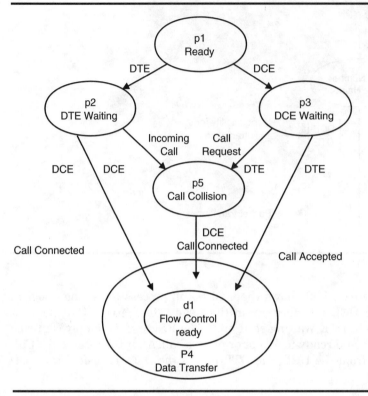

FIGURE 15.39   Call Setup State diagram

- Extended frame sequence numbering
- Multilink procedure
- Online facility registration
- Extended packet sequence numbering (Modulo 128)
- D-bit modification
- Packet retransmission
- Incoming calls barred
- Outgoing calls barred
- One-way logical channel outgoing
- One-way logical channel incoming
- Nonstandard default packet sizes 16, 32, 64, 256, 512, 1024, 2048
- Nonstandard default window sizes
- Default throughput classes assignment

- Flow Control parameter negotiation
- Throughput class negotiation
- Closed user group
- Closed user group with outgoing access
- Closed user group with incoming access
- Incoming calls barred within a closed user group
- Outgoing calls barred within a closed user group
- Bilateral closed user group
- Bilateral closed user group with outgoing access
- Fast select acceptance
- Reverse charging acceptance
- Local charging prevention
- Network user identification subscription
- NUI override
- Charging information
- RPOA subscription
- Hunt group
- Call redirection
- A bit (TOA/NPI)
- Direct call

Comparison of X.25 Operations to Frame Relay Operations.   This section provides a more detailed comparison of frame relay and X.25 operations at the Data Link and Network layers.

First a brief discourse is provided on the Physical layer. X.25 has been criticized because its Physical layer is slow. It stipulates slow-speed Physical interfaces such as V.28 and EIA-232-E. In contrast, frame relay typically employs a high-speed physical interface between the user device and the network switch, such as DS1, El, or subrates thereof. Nothing precludes using a faster physical-level operation on an X.25 interface. This approach would entail placing X.25's layer 2 (LAPBI) and layer 3 (packet layer procedures) on top of a technology such as DS1 and El. Therefore, the claim by some people that X.25 is inherently slow at the Physical layer is because many products are packaged with the X.25-compliant Physical layer, but higher speed interfaces can certainly be obtained.

Compression—X.25 Payload.   The Cisco IOS software supports X.25 payload compression of outgoing encapsulation traffic with an average compression ratio of 2:1. Compression reduces the size of an X.25 packet via lossless data compression. *Lossless compression* is the compression of data without loss of information, and the original data can be recovered exactly from the compressed data. This is different from *lossy compression*, which involves some loss of information, and data that has been compressed cannot be recovered exactly. The compression algorithm used by Cisco is *Stacker* (LZS), which is recommended when the bottleneck is the result of line bandwidth. Because X.25 payload compression is not standardized, you must implement a Cisco router on both sides of the network. Resources that must be taken into consideration when using compression are the use of memory as well as processor cycles to perform computations.

Compression—TCP Header.   Cisco supports the *Van Jacobson algorithm*, RFC 1144 for *TCP/IP header compression* (THC) on serial lines using HDLC and X.25 encapsulation. The implementation of compressed TCP over X.25 uses one Virtual Channel to pass the compressed packets. Noncompressed IP traffic (including standard TCP) is separate from THC traffic because it is carried over separate IP encapsulation Virtual Channels or identified separately in a multiprotocol Virtual Channel. Cisco can take a header of 40 bytes and compress it to 5 bytes, which represents an 8:1 ratio.

X.25 Virtual Interfaces

To enable more flexible network design, Cisco has implemented the concept of virtual interfaces. Virtual interfaces can be used to connect several networks to each other through a single physical interface. Routing protocols supported on Cisco routers using the split horizon principle may need help to determine which hosts need a routing update. In WAN environments using connection-oriented interfaces (such as X.25 and frame relay), other routers reached by the same physical interface might not have received the routing update. This feature enables you to provision subinterfaces that are treated as separate interfaces so that you can separate hosts into subinterfaces on a physical interface. The X.25 protocol is unaffected, and routing processes recognize each subinterface as a separate source of routing. Additionally, metrics can be assigned to each virtual interface to associate a cost to routes.

Connection—Mode Network Service

The *Connection—Mode Network Service* (CMNS) was previously known as the *International Organization for Standardization* (ISO) *Connection Oriented Network Service* (CONS). It provides a mechanism through which local X.25 switching can be extended to nonserial media through the use of *Open System Interconnection* (OSI) based *Network Service Access Point* (NSAP) addresses. This implementation runs packet-level X.25 over frame-level LLC2. Cisco's CMNS implementation allows LAN-based OSI resources such as a DTE host and a Sun workstation to be interconnected to each other via the router's LAN interfaces and to a remote OSI-based DTE through a WAN interface such as an X.25 *packet-switched network* (PSN).

Qualified Logical Link Control Support

Cisco's implementation of X.25 supports IBM's *Qualified Logical Link Control* (QLLC) protocol, which transports SNA terminal traffic over an X.25 network, which then communicates to an IBM NPSI host *front-end processor* (FEP). NPSI is IBM's X.25 *Network Control*

Program (NCP) packet-switching interface, which allows SNA traffic to be transmitted over an X.25 packet network.

ISDN Architecture

Integrated Services Digital Network (ISDN) is now one of the fastest growing telecommunications technologies in the world. ISDN is a digital version of switched-circuit analog telephone lines and is provided by local phone companies or PTTs. This technology supports networks capable of carrying voice, data, video, and other advanced services to homes and businesses

In data communications, a *channel* is a unidirectional conduit through which information flows. A channel can carry digital or analog signals comprising user data or network signaling information. In ISDN and other digital TDM environments, a channel is generally a time slot on a transmission facility and is full-duplex (bidirectional).

In today's telephone network, the local loop connection between the user and central office provides a single analog channel used for different types of information. First, the loop is used to carry signals between the user's equipment and the network. The telephone, for example, places a short circuit on the line to indicate that the handset has been taken off the hook. A dial tone from the network signals the user to enter the telephone number. Pulses or tones representing the dialed digits, busy signals, and ringing signals also appear over the local loop. Second, after the call is established, the loop carries user information, which may be voice, audio, video, or data, depending on the application. These two types of usage could be said to represent two logical channels, one for signaling and one for user services.

Organizations are interested in ISDN because of the types of services it provides (see Figure 15.40) and its potential for LAN-to-LAN, Internet, remote access, dial backup, and telecommuting applications.

Service Types

The standards that define ISDN provide for three types of services:

- Bearer services
- Teleservices
- Supplementary services

Bearer services provide the transport mechanisms required to transmit information across the user-network interface. The information is transparent to the bearer service and can be either voice, video, or data. The information exchanged through these services is not modified by the network. The bearer services map to the lower three layers of the OSI Reference Model.

Teleservices uses the bearer services to transport information across the user-network interface. They can be viewed as telecommunication applications that enable users to communicate using standard protocols. Teleservices operate at Layers 4 through 7 of the OSI Reference Model.

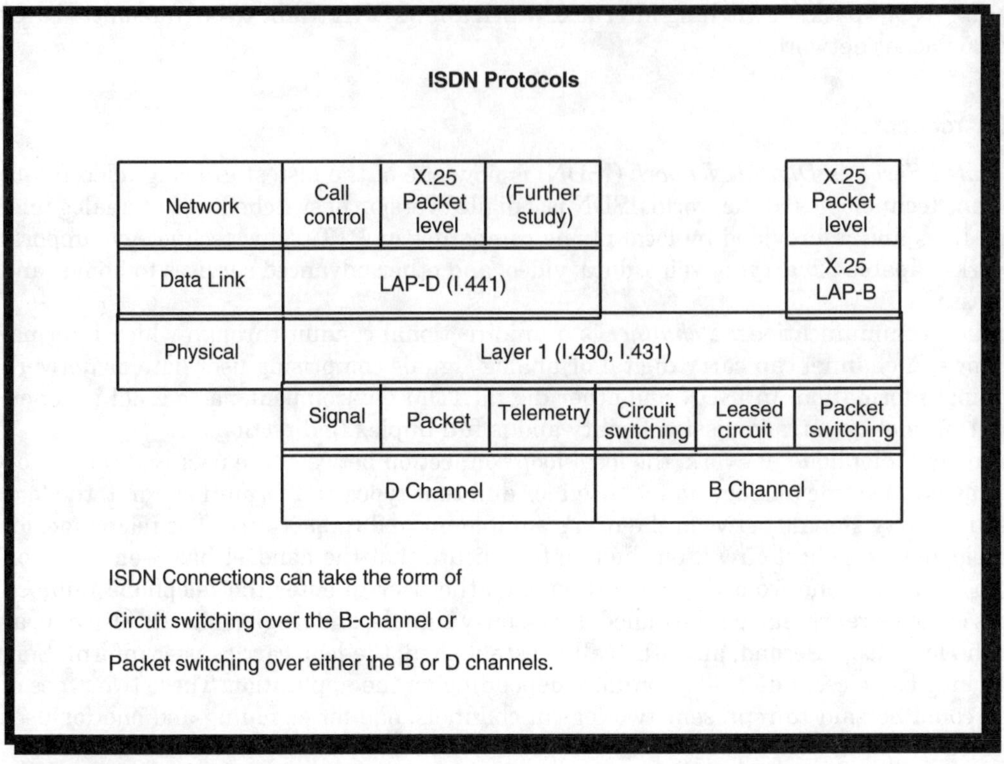

ISDN Protocols

Network	Call control	X.25 Packet level	(Further study)			X.25 Packet level
Data Link	LAP-D (I.441)					X.25 LAP-B
Physical	Layer 1 (I.430, I.431)					
	Signal	Packet	Telemetry	Circuit switching	Leased circuit	Packet switching
	D Channel			B Channel		

ISDN Connections can take the form of

Circuit switching over the B-channel or

Packet switching over either the B or D channels.

FIGURE 15.40   ISDN Services

Supplementary services may be used to enhance the bearer services or the teleservices. They provide additional features that are not usually provided by the basic bearer or teleservices. Supplementary services cannot be used alone but must be used in conjunction with another service or set of services.

ISDN and the OSI Reference Model

The protocols that provide user access to the ISDN operate at the lower three layers of the OSI Reference Model (see Figure 15.41). ISDN applications and teleservices operate at Layers 4 through 7.

The ISDN Physical-layer protocols, defined in 1.430 and 1.431, specify the procedures for both BRI and PRI access. At Layers 2 and 3, different protocols are defined depending on whether you are examining the D channel or the B channel.

The ISDN Physical-layer protocol provides support for both the BRI and the PRI accesses to the ISDN. The Physical layers of each interface are different.

The major functions performed by the ISDN Physical-layer protocol include:

- Transmitting data on the B channel

- Transmitting data on the D channel

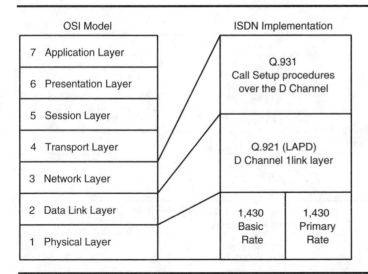

OSI Model

7	Application Layer
6	Presentation Layer
5	Session Layer
4	Transport Layer
3	Network Layer
2	Data Link Layer
1	Physical Layer

ISDN Implementation

Q.931
Call Setup procedures
over the D Channel

Q.921 (LAPD)
D Channel 1 link layer

| 1,430
Basic
Rate | 1,430
Primary
Rate |

FIGURE 15.41 ISDN OSI Model

- Multiplexing channels to create BRI or PRI access
- Timing and synchronization of Physical-layer frames
- Activating and deactivating *Terminal Equipment* (TE)

The Physical layer operates across the 5, T, or S/T Reference Points.

ISDN Physical Layer. In an ISDN network, the local loop carries only digital signals and comprises several channels used for signaling and user data. The different channels coexist on the local loop using TDM. There are three basic types of channels defined for ISDN user communications (see Table 15.4). They are differentiated by their function and bit rate.

- *D-channel.*   Carries signaling information between the user and the network; may also carry user data packets
- *B-channel.*   Carries information for user services including voice, audio, video, and digital data; operates at the DS-O rate (64 kbps)
- *H-channel.*   Same function as B-channel, but operates at bit rates above DS-O

The D-Channel. All ISDN devices attach to the network using a standard physical connector and exchange a standard set of messages with the network to request service. The contents of the service-request messages varies with the different services requested; an ISDN telephone, for example, requests different services from the network. All ISDN equipment, however, uses the same protocol and same set of messages. The network and user equipment exchange all service requests and other signaling messages over the ISDN

TABLE 15.4   ISDN Channel Types

Channel	Function	Bit rate
B	Bearer services	64 kbps
D	Signaling and packet-mode data	16 kbps (BRI 64 kbps (PRI)
S	Wideband bearer service	384 kbps
1	Wideband bearer services	1.472 Mbps
	$H^{10}(23B)*$ ~ (24B) $H^{12}(30B)$	1.536 Mbps 1.920 Mbps
N × 64	Variable bandwidth bearer services	64 kbps to 1.536 Mbps in 64-kbps increments
B-ISDN	Nonchannelized DS-3 Nonchannelized STM-1/OC-3 Nonchannelized STM-4/OC-12	44.736 Mbps 155.52 Mbps 622.08 Mbps

D-channel. Typically, a single D-channel provides the signaling services for a single ISDN interface (access point). It is possible for a single ISDN device (a PBX, for example) to be connected to the network with more than one ISDN interface. In this scenario, it is possible for the D-channel to provide signaling information for many ISDN interfaces. This capability saves channel and equipment resources by consolidating all signaling information on one channel; it is only available on the T-carrier ISDN interface, as discussed in the following text.

Although the D-channel's primary function is for user-network signaling, the exchange of these signaling messages is unlikely to use all the available bandwidth. Excess time on the D-channel is available for user's packet data, and, indeed, the transport of packet-mode data is the secondary function of the D-channel. The excess time is deemed to be great enough to allow service providers to offer user data services at rates up to 9.6 kbps on the D-channel. This is a bargain for users because the full 16 kbps of the D-channel is typically available. User network signaling messages always have priority over data packets.

The D-channel operates at either 16 or 64 kbps, depending on if it is a BRI or PRI.

The B-Channel.   Signals exchanged on the D-channel describe the characteristics of the service the user is requesting. For example, an ISDN telephone may request a circuit-mode connection operating at 64 kbps to support a speech application. This profile of characteristics describes what is called a *bearer service*. Bearer services are granted by the network, allocating a circuit-mode bearer channel between the requesting device and the destination. At the local loop, the B-channels are designated to provide this type of service.

The primary purpose of the B-channel, then, is to carry the user's voice, audio, image, data, and video signals. No service requests from the user are sent on the B-channel. B-channels always operate at 64 kbps, the bit rate required for digital voice applications.

The B-channel can be used for both circuit-switching and packet-switching applications. A circuit-mode connection provides a transparent user-to-user connection, allowing the connection to be specifically suited to one type of service (television or music for example). In the circuit mode, no protocols above the Physical layer (64 kbps) are defined for the B-channels; each user of a B-channel is responsible for defining the upper layer protocols to be used over the connection. It is also the users' responsibility to ensure compatibility between devices connected by B-channels. Packet-mode connections support packet switching equipment using protocols such as X.25 or frame relay. The ISDN can provide either an internal packet-mode service or access to an existing *Packet Switch Public Data Network* (PSPDN) for packet service. In the latter case the protocols and procedures of the PSPDN must be adhered to when requesting packet-mode service.

The most important point to remember with respect to the use of the B- and D-channels is that devices use the D-channel to exchange the signaling messages necessary to request services on the B-channel.

H-Channels. A user application requiring a bit rate higher than 64 kbps may be obtained by using wideband channels, or H-channels, which provide the bandwidth equivalent of a group of B-channels. Applications requiring bit rates above 64 kbps include LAN interconnection, high-speed data, high-quality audio, teleconferencing, and video services.

The first designated higher rate channel is an H-channel with a data rate of 384 kbps. This is equivalent to logically grouping six B-channels together.

An H1-channel comprises all available time slots at a single user interface employing a T1 or E1 carrier. An H_{12}-channel operates at 1.536 Mbps and is equivalent to 24 time slots (24 B-channels) for compatibility with the T1 carrier. An H_{12}-channel operates at 1.920 Mbps and is equivalent to 30 time slots (30 B-channels) for compatibility with the E1 carrier.

ANSI has designated an H_{10}-channel, operating at 1.472 Mbps and equivalent to 23 time slots on a T1 interface. This channel was defined by ANSI to support a single wideband channel and a D-channel on the same T1 access facility; with an H-channel, a D-channel and wideband channel cannot coexist on the same T1 interface.

H-Channel Summary. The H0 service provides 384 Kbps of bandwidth to a single connection. Up to three H0 (five in Europe) connections can be initiated on a single PRI interface.

- The H10 service provides 1,472 Kbps of bandwidth to a single connection.

- The H11 service provides 1,536 Kbps of bandwidth to a single connection.

- The H12 service provides 1,920 Kbps of bandwidth to a single connection.

A relatively new set of ISDN channels has been defined for variable bit rate applications, called an *N × 64 channel*. This channel is similar in structure to the H-channels except it offers a range of bandwidth options from 64 kbps to 1.536 Mbps in increments of 64 kbps. When a user requests an N × 64 channel for a given call, the service request contains the type of channel (N × 64) and the value of N (1 to 24). A benefit to users of an N × 64 channel is that they do not require inverse multiplexing equipment on the premises because the network maintains time slot sequence integrity between the N 64-kbps time slots. An advantage of the N × 64 channel is the capability to customize the bandwidth requirements to the application.

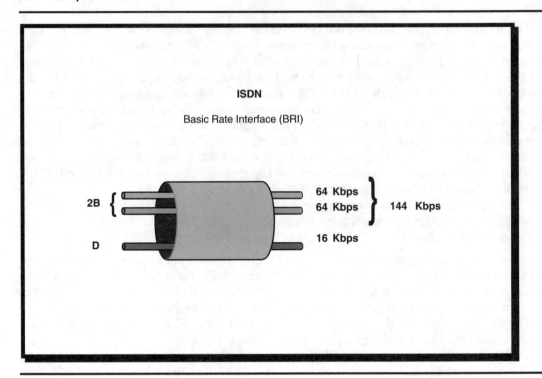

FIGURE 15.42   Basic Rate Interface

Basic Rate Interface.   The BRI comprises two B-channels and one D-channel as shown in Figure 15.42 and is designated *2B + D*. The BRI D-channel always operates at 16 Kbps. The BRI is typically used in one of two ways. First, it can provide ISDN access between a residential or business customer and the ISDN LE. Alternatively, it can provide ISDN access between user equipment and an ISDN-compatible PBX in a business environment. As a tariffed offering, the BRI can be ordered in configurations other than 2B + D, and other nomenclature may be encountered. If the BRI is to be used only for telephony and no data will be sent on the D-channel, the configuration is sometimes called *2B + S* (the D-channel is for signaling only). If only a single B-channel is required, a *1B + D* or *1B + S* arrangement may be ordered; packet data is allowed on the D-channel in the former and not in the latter. Finally, if only low speed (9.6-kbps) packet data is required, a *0B + D* configuration can be ordered. These configurations allow ISDN to be customized for customer applications and are priced differently based on the number of active channels. It should be noted that in all of these configurations, the interface's physical characteristics are the same; the only difference is in which channels have been activated by the LE and what type of traffic is allowed on the D-channel.

The user data rate on the BRI is 144 kbps (2 × 64 kbps + 16 kbps), although additional signaling for the physical connection requires that the BRI operate at a higher bit rate.

BRI Frame Structure. BRI transmissions are structured into fixed-length frames. Each frame is 48 bits long and contains 4 bits from the D channel and 16 bits (two groups of eight bits) from each of the B channels. The remaining 12 bits are used for framing, contention resolution, and DC balance. Transmission rate is 4000 frames per second.

The frames transmitted in the NT to TE direction are slightly different from the frames transmitted in the TB to NT direction. Figure 15.43 shows the BRI frame format. The top frame in the figure is transmitted from the NT to the TE. The bottom frame is transmitted from the TB to the NT. In the figure, there is a two-bit offset between the start of the two frames.

The NT is required to loop back the D channel information originating from TE. Data transmitted on the D channel in the direction from the TB to the NT is always retransmitted on the bus in the NT to TB direction. These bits in the NT to TB frame are referred to as the *D-Echo Channel*. The D-Echo channel bits are labeled E.

When the D-Echo Channel is idle, a TB determines that the D channel is idle if it receives all binary 1 bits in the D-echo channel. The 1 bits indicate an idle channel because pseudo-ternary line coding is used on the bus. A TB is allowed to access the D channel for signaling if it receives eight binary 1s in a row. The TB can access the D channel for packet-switched services if it receives ten 1s in a row.

Cisco's Implementation

The initial Cisco implementation of ISDN BRI treated the B and D channels as bundled together and were presented as a single interface or as a hunt group. With the new implementation, each channel is treated as a separate interface for configuring the parameters of X.25 over the D channel. The original BRI continues to represent the D, B1, and B2 channels. Numerous ISDN switch platforms such as the Nortel DMS-100 require that the end-user equipment use static *terminal endpoint identifiers* (TEIs) in order to access this service. Static TEIs are supported in the Cisco IOS ISDN software product. This design uses

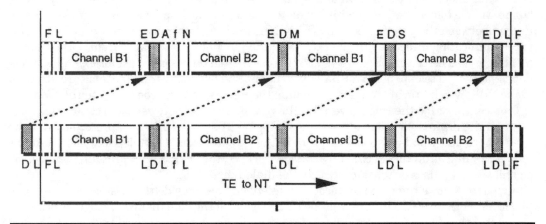

FIGURE 15.43 BRI transmission frames

the Layer 2 and Layer 3 as defined by the new X.25 modularization project. The D channel has a capacity of 16 kbps, of which a substantial part can be used for carrying the X.25 traffic; however, most ISDN services guarantee connectivity speeds of up to 9.6 kbps.

Primary Rate Interface (PRI).   The PRI also has a number of possible configurations. The most common configuration in North America and Japan is designated 23B + D, meaning that the interface comprises 23 B-channels plus a single D-channel operating at 64 kbps. Optionally, the D-channel on a given PRI may not be activated, allowing that time slot to be used as another B-channel; this configuration is designated 24B. This PRI description is based on the T1 digital carrier. It operates at a bit rate of 1.544 Mbps, of which 1.536 Mbps are user data.

Also defined is a A 30B + D PRI that comprises 30 B-channels and one D-channel. Based on the E1 digital carrier, it operates at 2.048 Mbps, of which 1.984 Mbps are user data. The PRI contains more channels than a typical end-user device will use. The PRI is, in fact, primarily intended to provide access to the network by some sort of customer premises switching equipment, such as a PBX, multiplexer, or host computer.

When a wide-band application requires more throughput than that provided by a B-channel, the PRI can be configured to provide H-channel access. When this configuration is used, the number of available B-channels decreases by the number of time slots used by the H-channel(s). An example would be a videoconferencing system needing 384 kbps (an H_0-channel) for a call. The supporting PRI would have extra bandwidth available for a D-channel and 17 B-channels. If the video system needed a channel, no B- or D-channel time slots would be available. This flexibility allows the PRI to act as a wideband access system and a narrowband access system, depending on the application active at any time. The same bandwidth (time slots) can be configured for different types of channels on demand.

Functional Devices and Reference Points

Several different devices may be present in the connection between CPE and the network to which the CPE is attached. Consider the relatively simple example of a customer's connection to the telephone network. All of the subscriber's telephones are connected to a junction box in the customer's building with inside wiring; the local loop provides the physical connection between the junction box and the LE. As far as the customer is concerned, the CPE is communicating directly with the exchange; the junction box is transparent. Other equipment may also be present. If a PC is attached to the telephone network, for example, a modem replaces the telephone. In a PBX environment, the telephones and modems are attached to the PBX, which provides on-site switching; the PBX is, in turn, connected to the LE.

Protocols describe the rules governing the communication between devices in a network. With all the devices mentioned here, questions might arise as to which protocols are to be used where and who is responsible for defining the protocols. The telephone, for example, uses a familiar protocol specified by the network; certain currents represent the off-hook signal; special pulses or tones represent the dialed digits, etc.

A modem follows the same protocol as a telephone on the side that connects to the telephone network. It uses a different protocol, however, on the side that connects to a PC; EIA-232-E and the Hayes AT-command set, for example, are commonly used between a PC and external modem. The modem acts as a signal converter so that digital signal output from the PC is suitable for the analog telephone network.

The presence of a PBX adds another layer of complexity. A telephone connected to a PBX follows protocols specified by the PBX manufacturer, which is why many PBX-specific telephones are not usable on the public telephone network. The PBX, in turn, must use network-specified protocols for the PBX-to-network communication. In today's communication environment it is often difficult to separate the devices from the functions they perform. The case of the PC communicating over the telephone network is an example. Three devices were described previously: a PC, a modem, and a network. Each has a specific function and is governed by a set of protocols. What would happen if the PC had an internal modem? The number of functional devices would remain the same, but the number of physical devices would be reduced to two, the PC and the network. In this example the number of functional devices and the number of actual physical devices differ due to the packaging of the devices.

These same ideas are extended to ISDN (see Figure 15.44). The ISDN standards define several different types of devices. Each device type has certain functions and responsibilities but may not represent an actual physical piece of equipment. For that reason, the standards call them *functional devices*.

Because the ISDN recommendations describe several functional device types, there are several device-to-device interfaces, each requiring a communications protocol. Each of these functional device interfaces is called a *reference point*.

ISDN Functional Devices

The network device providing ISDN services is the *LE*. ISDN protocols are implemented in the LE, which is also the network side of the ISDN local loop. Other LE responsibilities include maintenance, physical interface operation, timing, and providing requested user services.

Some ISDN exchange manufacturers further break down the functions of the LE into two subgroups called *local termination* (LT) and *exchange termination* (ET). The LT handles those functions associated with the termination of the local loop, while the ET handles switching functions. For simplicity and generality, this section refers only to the LE and avoids specific references to LT or ET except where necessary. Also included in the

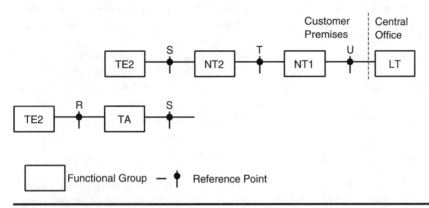

FIGURE 15.44   ISDN functional devices and reference points

LE is equipment specialized to support the ISDN services. Two of these have to do with the signaling used in ISDN and the incorporation of packet data in the ISDN list of services. The first is a *packet handler* (PH). This device is responsible for the decoding of all ISDN signaling packets passed between the LE and the ISDN subscriber. It is also used to distinguish user data from signaling data on the D-channel and routes the user data toward its destination. The second device (or devices) is the network signaling system employed for the ISDN. In today's environment this signaling system is *Signaling System No. 7* (SS7). The SS7 device is responsible for the creation and interpretation of the signaling messages used in the ISDN.

Network termination type 1 (NT1), or local loop terminator equipment, represents the termination of the physical connection between the customer site and the LE. The NT1's responsibilities include line performance monitoring, timing, physical signaling protocol conversion, electrical conversion, and power transfer.

Network termination type 2 (NT2) equipment includes those devices providing customer site switching, multiplexing, and/or concentration. This includes PBXs, multiplexers, host computers, terminal controllers, and other CPE for voice and data switching. An NT2 is absent in some ISDN environments, such as residential or Centrex ISDN service. NT2s distribute ISDN services to other devices attached to it. In this role, the NT2 might perform some protocol conversion functions as well as distribution functions. One of the primary distribution functions is the network signaling on behalf of the attached terminals. The NT2 is responsible for all signaling to the network. As an example, a PBX might terminate an analog telephone and allow access to an ISDN PRI for a connection to other subscribers. In this case the PBX is providing protocol conversion from the analog voice to the ISDN digital voice and is collecting the dialed digits from the telephone and creating a signaling message for the LE.

Terminal equipment (TE) refers to end-user devices such as an analog or digital telephone, X.25 data terminal equipment, ISDN workstation, or *integrated voice/data terminal* (IVDT). *Terminal equipment type 1* (TE1) are those devices utilizing the ISDN protocols and support ISDN services such as an ISDN telephone or workstation. *Terminal equipment type 2* (TE2) are non-ISDN compatible devices such as the analog telephones in use on today's telephone network.

A *terminal adapter* (TA) allows a non-ISDN device (TE2) to communicate with the network. TAs have particular importance in today's ISDN marketplace; nearly every device in use in today's data and telecommunications environment is TE2. TA's allow analog telephones, X.25 DTEs, PCs, and other non-ISDN devices to use the network by providing any necessary protocol conversion.

ISDN allows that a single physical piece of equipment can take on the responsibilities of two or more of the functional devices defined here. For example, a PBX might actually perform NT1 (local loop termination) and NT2 (customer site switching) functions; this combination is sometimes referred to as NT12. In the same vein, an ISDN router can be purchased with a TA and an NT1 built-in; this combination is referred to as a bargain.

ISDN Reference Points

The ISDN reference points define the communication protocols between the different ISDN functional devices. The importance of the different reference points is that different protocols may be used at each reference point. Four protocol reference points are commonly de-fined for ISDN, called R, 5, T, and U.

The R reference point is between non-ISDN terminal equipment (TE2) and a TA. The TA enables the TE2 to appear to the network as an ISDN device, just as a modem allows a ter-minal or PC to communicate over today's telephone network. There are no specific stan-dards for the R reference point; the TA manufacturer determines and specifies how the TE2 and TA communicate with each other. Examples of TA-to-TE2 communication include EIA-232-E, V.35, and the *Industry Standard Architecture* (ISA) bus.

The S reference point is between ISDN user equipment (that is, TEl or TA) and network termination equipment (NT2 or NT1). The T reference point is between customer site switching equipment (NT2) and the local loop termination (NT1). ISDN recommendations from the ITU-T, the primary international standards body for ISDN, specifically address protocols for the S and T reference points. In the absence of the NT2, the user-network in-terface is usually called the S/T reference point.

Layer 2 of ISDN

Link Access Procedure, D Channel, (LAPD) is the data link control protocol. LAPD enables devices to communicate with one another across the ISDN D Channel. It is specifically de-signed for the link across the ISDN user-to-network interface. LAPD is defined by ITU-T Rec-ommendation Q.921. Its primary use is for transporting signaling information. It can also be used for maintenance and general data transport due to the format of its addressing field.

LAPD has a frame format very similar to that of HDLC and LAPB (see Figure 15.45). LAPD provides for two octets for the address field. Each ISDN basic access can support up to eight stations.

The address field shown in Figure 15.46 is used to identify the specific terminal on the channel. The *service access point* (SAP) identifies a layer entity operating in the terminal above the LAPD layer. The address field contains the address field extension bits, a command/response indication bit, a *service access point identifier* (SAPI), and a *terminal endpoint identifier* (TEI).

The purpose of the address field extension is to provide more bits for an address. The pres-ence of a 1 in the first bit of an address field octet signifies that it is the final octet of the address field. Consequently, a two-octet address would have a field address extension value of 0 in the first octet and 1 in the second. The address field extension bit enables the use of both the SAPI in the first octet and the TE1 in the second octet.

Number of Octets

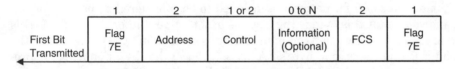

FIGURE 15.45 LAPD Packet header

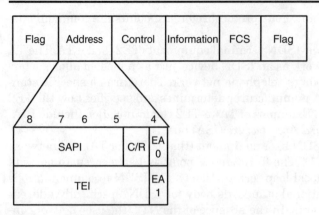

C/R - Command/response field bit

	FROM USER SIDE	FROM NETWORK SIDE
COMMAND	0	1
RESPONSE	1	0

EA   - Address field extension bit
    1 final octet
    0 additional octets follow
SAPI -Service access point identifier
    0   Call control procedures
    1 Packet mode using Q.931 Call procedures
    16 Packet communications conforming to X.25 Level 3 procedures
    63 Layer 2 Management procedures
All others reserved for future use
TEI   -Terminal endpoint identifier
    0-63 Non-automatic TEI assignment
    64-126 Automatic TEI assignment

FIGURE 15.46 Q.921 Address field

The *command/response* (C/R) field bit identifies the frame as either a command or a response. See Figure 15.47. The user side sends commands with the C/R hit set to 0. It responds with the C/R bit set to 1. The network does the opposite—it sends commands with C/R set to 1 and responses with C/R set to 0.

The EA bit allows for versatility in the address field length. A 0 in the EA field bit indicates that additional bytes of information are included to be considered as part of the address field. A 1 indicates that this byte is the last one of the current information field. This method is used in much more complex command streams such as in Q.931. For LAPD, the first byte's EA bit is 0, and the second byte's EA bit is 1. Use of the EA bit enables the protocol module to distinguish between LAPD and LAPB (X.25, layer 2).

The SAPI identifies the point at which the Data Link layer services are provided to the layer above LAPD.

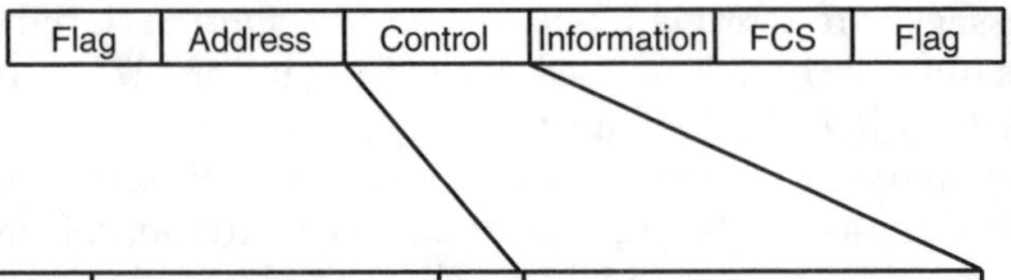

		Flag	Address	Control	Information	FCS	Flag

Application	Format	Message Type	C/R	87654321	Octet
Unacknowledged and Multiple Frame Acknowledged Information Transfer	Information Transfer	I (Information)	C	N(S)0 / N(R)P	4 / 5
	Supervisory	RR (Receive Ready)	C/R	00000001 / N(R) P/F	4 / 5
		RNR (Receive Not Ready)	C/R	00000101 / N(R) P/F	4 / 5
		REJ (Reject)	C/R	00001001 / N(R) P/F	4 / 5
	Un-numbered	SABME (Set Asynchronous Balanced Mode Extended)	C	011P1111	4
		DM (Disconnected Mode)	R	000F1111	4
		UI (Unnumbered Information)	C	000P0011	4
		DISC (Disconnect)	C	010P0011	4
		UA (Unnumbered Acknowledgement)	R	011F0011	4
		FRMR (Frame Reject)	R	100F0111	4
Connection Management		XID (Exchange Identification)	C/R	101 P/F 1111	4

FIGURE 15.47   Q.921 Control Field (Modulo 128)

Service access point identifier.   SAPI is used to determine the function of the data link. Two values are particularly important for LAPD. These are the values of 0 (for call control-signaling) and 63 (for layer 2 management procedures). The value of 16 enables use of the D-channel for X.25 level 3 data transport uses. Other values are still being defined, such as particular values for SVCs for frame relay.

Terminal endpoint identifier.   The TEI is a method of identifying the terminal (as opposed to the SAPI's use as determination of function). A TEI may be assigned either nonautomatically (or "fixed") or automatically by the switch. The range of values from 0 to 63 comprise the valid fixed TEI numbers. These are assigned by the terminal with subscription agreement by the network. Automatic TEI values lie in the range from 64 through 126 and are assigned by the network in response to a request from the terminal. These automatic TEI negotiation messages are sent via *Unnumbered Information* (UI) frames over the management SAPI link (63) as a broadcast message (TEI value of 127). Automatic TEI negotiation is covered more fully later in this appendix.

Generally, automatic TEIs are used with multipoint BRI terminals. Fixed TEIs are used in point-to-point terminal configurations and in FRI situations. It may be useful to use automatic TEI negotiation in cases in which cellular technologies are being used for physical layer connection to the network. This requiring prearranging the TEI between the terminal equipment and the network.

Network Level—Signal Protocol (Layer 3)

The ISDN Network layer defines the protocol that implements the signaling procedure between the subscriber and the network. The protocol runs on the D channel and specifies the procedures that manage the control of circuit-switched connections on the B and H channels. The standard is detailed in ITU-T Recommendations 1.450 (Q.930), 1.451 (Q.931), and 1.452 (Q.932).

Layer 3 of ISDN (Q.931)

The ISDN layer 3 specifications (ITU-T recommendations 1.450/1.451 and Q.930/Q.931) use many of the OSI concepts. They encompass circuit switch connections, packet switch connections, and user-to-user connections. They also specify the procedures to establish, manage, and clear a network connection at the ISDN user-to-network interface. The more widely used messages are summarized in Table 15.5 and a brief description of these messages fol-

TABLE 15.5   LAPD address values

SAPI	
Value	**Related Entity**
1	Call control procedures
16	Packet procedures
32-	Reserved for National use
47	Management procedures
63	Reserved
Others	

TEl	
Value	**User Type**
0-	Nonautomatic assignment
63	Automatic assignment
64-	
126	

lows. The table also shows which Q.931 messages are used with the frame relay Digital Signaling System Number 1 (DSS 1).

The SETUP message is sent to the establishment procedures by the user or network. The message contains several parameters defining the circuit connection, and it must contain the following three:

- **Protocol discriminator.** Distinguishes between user-to-network call control messages and others, such as other layer 3 protocols (frame relay and ATM, for example).

- **Call reference.** Identifies the ISDN call at the local user-to-network interface. It does not have end-to-end significance. All messages pertaining to one connection contain the same call reference number value.

- **Message type.** Identifies the message function; that is, the types.

Other parameters include the specific ISDN channel identification, origination, and destination addresses, an address for a redirected call, the designation for a transit network, etc.

The SETUP ACKNOWLEDGE message is sent by the user or the network to indicate that call establishment has been initiated. The parameters for the SETUP ACK message are similar to the SETUP message.

The CALL PROCEEDING message is sent by the network or the user to indicate the call is being processed. The message also indicates that the network has all the information it needs to process the call.

The CONNECT message and the CONNECT ACKNOWLEDGE messages are exchanged between the network and the network user to indicate that the call is accepted by either the network or the user. These messages contain parameters to identify the session, facilities, and services associated with the connection.

To clear a call, the user or the network can send a RELEASE or DISCONNECT message. Typically, the RELEASE COMPLETE is returned, but the network can maintain the call reference for later use, in which case the network sends a DETACH message to the user.

A call can be temporarily suspended. The SUSPEND message is used to create this action. The network can respond to this message with either a SUSPEND ACKNOWLEDGE or a SUSPEND REJECT.

During an ongoing ISDN connection, the user or network can issue CONGESTION CONTROL messages to control the flow of USER INFORMATION messages. The message simply indicates whether the receiver is ready to accept messages.

The USER INFORMATION message is sent by the user or the network to transmit information to a (another) user.

If a call is suspended, the RESUME message is sent by the user to request the call be resumed. This message can invoke a RESUME ACKNOWLEDGE or a RESUME REJECT.

The STATUS message is sent by the user or the network to report on the conditions of the call.

REGISTER ACKNOWLEDGE or REGISTER REJECT initiates the registration of a REGISTER facility (as well as confirmation and/or rejection).

FACILITY, FACILITY ACKNOWLEDGE, and FACILITY REJECT initiate access to a network facility (as well as confirmation or rejection).

CANCEL, CANCEL ACKNOWLEDGE, and CANCEL REJECT indicates a request to discontinue a facility (as well as confirmation or rejection).

ISDN supports numerous facilities that are managed with messages. Most of these facilities are self-explanatory. It is evident that the ISDN and X.25 connections have been given much thought by the standards groups (see Table 15.6).

TABLE 15.6   ISDN Layer 3 Messages

Call establishment messages	Call disestablishment messages
ALERTING*	DETACH
CALL PROCEEDING*	DETACH ACKNOWLEDGE
CONNECT*	DJSCONNECT*
CONNECT	RELEASE*
ACKNOWLEDGE*	
SETUP*	RELEASE COMPLETE*
SETUP ACKNOWLEDGE	
PROGRESS*	

Call information phase messages	Miscellaneous messages
RESUME	CANCEL
RESUME	CANCEL
ACKNOWLEDGE	ACKNOWLEDGE
RESUME REJECT	CANCEL REJECT
SUSPEND	CONGESTION CONTROL
SUSPEND	FACILITY
ACKNOWLEDGE	
SUSPEND REJECT	FACILITY
	ACKNOWLEDGE
USER INFORMATION	FACILITY REJECT
	INFORMATION
	REGISTER
	REGISTER ACKNOWLEDGE
	REGISTER REJECT
	STATUS*
	STATUS ENQUIRY*

Network Layer Message Format

The ISDN Network layer protocol uses messages to communicate between the user device and the network. Frame relay DSS 1 also uses this message for its operations. The message consists of the following fields (these fields were explained with the SETUP message):

- Protocol discriminator (required). See Figure 15.48.
- Call reference (required). See Figure 15.49.
- Message type (required). See Figure 15.50.
- Mandatory information elements (as required). See Figure 15.51.
- Additional information elements (as required).

8 7 6 54 3 2 1	Meaning
0000 0000 thru 0000 0000	Not available for use in the message protocol discriminator
0000 1000	Q.931/(I.451) user-network call control messages
0001 0000 thru 0011 1111	Reserved for other Network layer or layer 3 protocols, including Recommendation X.25
0100 0000 thru 0100 1111	National use
0101 0000 thru 1111 1110	Reserved for other Network layer or layer 3 protocols, including Recommendation X.25

FIGURE 15.48 Protocol discriminator values

8	7	6	5	4	3	2	1	Octet
0	0	0	0	Length of call reference value (octets)				1
flag	Call reference value							2

Call reference flag (Bit 8 of octet 2):
0 Message is sent from the side that originates the call reference
1 Message is sent to the side that originates the call reference

FIGURE 15.49 Call reference information element

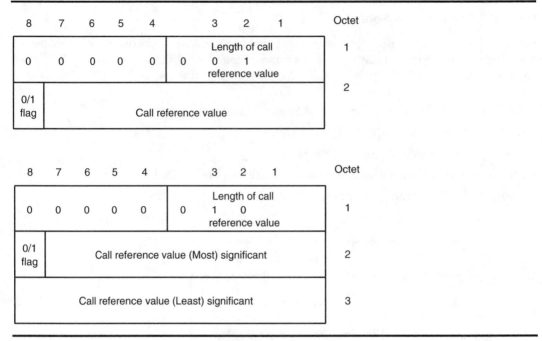

FIGURE 15.50 One octet call reference (Used for basic or primary rate)

The ISDN also enables other message formats to accommodate equipment needs and different information elements. This feature provides considerable flexibility in choosing other options and ISDN services.

Example of an ISDN Call

When the telephone is picked up (goes off-hook), the TE1 device issues a SETUP message to the ISDN network. As you learned earlier, this message initiates the call setup procedures. It contains a protocol discriminator, a call reference identifier, plus the message type and other optional identifiers that depend on the actual implementation. The ISDN node replies with a SETUP ACK, which is used by the TE1 to provide dial tone to the telephone. The user then enters the telephone number (the dialed digits), which are sent to the ISDN node.

- Delivery of origin address barred
- Connected address required
- Supply charging information after end of call
- Reverse charging requested
- Connect outgoing calls when free
- Reverse charging acceptance (allowed)
- Call redirection/diversion notification
- Call completion after busy request

87654321	MESSAGE
000....	Call Establishment
00001	Alerting
00010	Call Proceeding
00011	Progress
00101	Setup
00111	Connect
01101	Setup Acknowledge
01111	Connect Acknowledge
000....	Call Information Phase
00000	User Information
00001	Suspend Reject
00010	Resume Reject
00100	Hold
00101	Suspend
00110	Resume
01000	Hold Acknowledge
01101	Suspend Acknowledge
01110	Resume Acknowledge
10000	Hold Reject
10001	Retrieve
10011	Retrieve Acknowledge
10111	Retrieve Reject
010....	Call Cleaning
00101	Disconnect
00110	Restart
01101	Release
01110	Restart Acknowledge
11010	Release Complete
011....	Miscellaneous
00000	Segment
00010	Facility
00100	Register
01110	Notify
10101	Status Inquiry
11001	Congestion
11011	Information
11101	Status

FIGURE 15.51   Q.931/Q932 Message types

- Call completion after busy indication
- Origination address required on outgoing calls
- Origination address required on incoming calls
- Destination address required on incoming calls
- Connect incoming calls when free (waiting allowed)
- X.25 extended packet sequence numbering (Modulo 128)

- X.25 flow control parameter negotiation allowed
- X.25 throughput class negotiation allowed
- X.25 packet retransmission (allowed)
- X.25 fast select (outgoing) (allowed)
- X.25 fast select acceptance allowed
- X.25 local charging prevention
- X.25 extended frame sequence numbering

A call proceeding message is returned from the ISDN node to the originating device; it is used by the TE1 to transmit a ring-back to the user telephone. Once the connection is made, the network sends a connect message to the originating device, which removes the ring-back signal. Once these procedures have occurred on both sides of the ISDN interface, users are allowed to send traffic through the B or D channels. The session is disconnected with the RELEASE and RELEASE COMPLETE messages illustrated at the end of the table. These actions tear down an ISDN B channel.

ISDN Applications

The capability to dial up bandwidth on demand enables many different applications to be implemented using ISDN technology. Because you pay a small monthly charge plus a usage charge with ISDN, it provides an excellent way to augment your present data communications infrastructure without impacting your budget. Intelligent use of the ISDN network can increase network performance while minimizing communications costs.

Primary Line Backup

In this application, the bridge/router communicates with the central site via a dedicated primary link that could be a leased line, X.25, or frame relay link. When the primary link fails, the router is capable of dialing up the central site via the ISDN network to resume communications. When the primary link is restored, the ISDN connection is terminated.

Dial on Demand

In this application, the bridge or router has no dedicated connection to the central site. Rather, the bridge or router connects to the central site via ISDN only when there is data to be transmitted to or from the central site. Once a connection has been established, it is held open for other traffic. When there has been no traffic for a programmable amount of time, the bridge or router drops the call.

Telecommuting

In this application, the telecommuter has connected both a PC and an analog phone to the bridge or router. The data portion of the bridge or router uses both B channels unless there is an incoming or outgoing voice call. When a voice call is active, the bridge or router only uses a single B channel while the voice call uses the other one. This enables a telecommuter to have only a single incoming voice/data line.

ISDN Features

Because ISDN charges by connect time, it is important to not only minimize the connection times, but also to connect only when there is useful data to send. Today's LAN protocols were developed for the local environment where bandwidth is essentially free. (They are very "chatty" and if transported "as is" across an ISDN network would probably keep the link up most of the time resulting in large monthly charges.) Bridges or routers with ISDN interfaces must not only perform the connections to the ISDN network to route the data but must also optimize the usage of that network to minimize connection charges.

- **Access-list filters.** Although there may be many workstations and servers on a remote network, most stations do not need to connect with another location. Filters can be used to eliminate most of the traffic from generating an ISDN connection.

- **Data Compression.** Once a connection has been established, it is important that the application maximizes use of the available bandwidth. A bridge or router with Data Compression can transport up to four times more data across a 64 Kbps ISDN link than a regular ISDN terminal adapter. As well, end-to-end latency times are shortened.

- **SPX Spoofing.** Novell IPX/SPX are very "chatty" protocols. The file server sends a message to each remote client terminal SPX *keep-alives* every five minutes when there is no communication. In a network where the bridges or routers are use ISDN as the transport, these keepalive messages can increase the monthly connection charges significantly. Bridges or routers should implement a "spoofing" protocol whereby the bridge or router responds to the keepalive messages sent from the file servers without actually bringing up the link.

- **Demand RIP for IP/RIP and SAP for IPX.** The usual routing protocols cause bridges or routers to communicate with their neighbors to determine which paths are available for data transmission. They usually do this via periodic messages sent throughout the network. Most often, nothing has changed in the network, and the messages do not convey any new information. Bridge and routers should implement either static routing or demand RIP/SAP. Demand RIP/SAP sends routing and service updates only when the topology or status of a particular service changes. This minimizes ISDN connection charges because only changes are sent across the network.

- **Multilink PPP.** This feature allows a bridge or router to dial up additional B channels when there is a large amount of data traffic to be sent across the network. This additional bandwidth shortens the transfer time and improves interactive performance.

ISDN Security

Implementing ISDN access to the network opens the network to potential unauthorized access. To minimize this threat, there are several security procedures that can be implemented using the PPP link protocol.

The *Password Authentication Protocol* is used with PPP and provides a one-way authentication of the remote bridge or router calling into a central site. The remote bridge or router provides an unencoded user name and password that is validated by the central site bridge or router.

The *Challenge Handshake Authentication Protocol* (CHAP) security protocol utilizes a handshake for authentication. One side of the connection initiates the challenge with a key to a "secret." This secret is used to determine a response that is encoded and sent back to the initiator. The response is evaluated and either accepted or rejected. Additional challenges may be completed during the session to ensure that the caller is valid. The nature of the challenge is random to avoid response duplication.

Questions

1. The top speed for a frame relay connections is_____.

   A. 45Mbps   **C.** 56Kbps
   B. 10Mbps   **D.** 64Kbps

2. Frame relay networks are considered to be_____.
   A. Non-broadcast multi-access   **C.** Shared media
   B. Broadcast multi-access   **D.** Point-to-point

3. With frame relay, the encapsulation type should agree_____.
   A. between end devices
   B. between the end device and the switch
   C. between switches
   D. between the end devices and the switches

4. With frame relay, the LMI type should agree_____.
   A. between end devices
   B. between the end device and the switch
   C. between switches
   D. between the end devices and the switches

5. A frame relay switch makes decisions based on:
   A. Application layer addresses
   B. Network later addresses
   C. Data link layer address
   D. None of the above

6. ILMI provides the communications between a frame relay switch and a frame relay end device:
   A. Router   **D.** FRAD
   B. LAN switch   **E.** Frame relay end device
   C. Frame relay switch

7. CIR refers to____.
   A. the minimum bandwidth available on a frame relay link
   B. the maximum bandwidth available on a frame relay link
   C. the average bandwidth available on a frame relay link
   D. the guaranteed bandwidth available on a frame relay link

8. Which of the following are among the most commonly used frame relay configurations?
   A. Star
   B. Partial mesh
   C. Point-to-point
   D. Full mesh

9. In order to support a point-to-multi point configuration, a Cisco router interface must be configured manually with_____.
    A. sub-interfaces
    B. MAC addresses
    C. DLCIs
    D. none of the above

10. The end node addressing for frame relay is____.
    A. DLCN
    B. BECN
    C. ESI
    D. DLCI

11. The DLCI for frame relay is guaranteed to be unique:
    A. Across the frame relay cloud
    B. Across a provider's frame relay network
    C. Across the router's interfaces
    D. Across a frame relay switch's interfaces
    E. None of the above

12. When configuring a frame relay static route, you must specify____.
    A. the destination layer 3 address and local DLCI
    B. the destination layer 3 address and destination DLCI
    C. the local layer 3 address and local DLCI
    D. any of the above

13. The Frame Relay service address provided by the service provider is called a _____.
    A. X.121
    B. DLCI
    C. telephone number
    D. 164

14. LMI is the____.
    A. signaling interface between the router and the Frame Relay Switch
    B. X.25 signaling format
    C. ISDN signaling interface
    D. V.35 connection to DECNet
    E. none of the above

15. The primary difference between frame relay and X.25 are:
    A. Media types
    B. Error correction and flow control
    C. Service providers
    D. Routing protocols

16. Frame Relay, as a frame-based fast packet switching protocol, provides for all of the following except:
    A. Frame Relay is based on standards and is not a proprietary scheme.
    B. Frame Relay specifies only the interface between the network and the user.
    C. Frame Relay supports both PVCs and SVCs.
    D. Frame Relay provides an unreliable, connectionless-oriented mechanism to transfer data across the network.

17. On defining the network and user interface interaction in Frame Relay, which of the following is true?
  A. The standards were developed by ANSI, ITU-T, the FRF, and the IETF.
  B. Frame Relay defines the underlying transport for this interaction to occur.
  C. All error detection and recovery are performed by the user interface devices.
  D. Unlike X.25, Frame Relay only specifies the lower two layers of the OSI Reference Model.

18. The Frame Relay Data Link Layer provides for all of the following except:
  A. Addressing
  B. Sequencing and Acknowledgements
  C. Framing and transparency
  D. Byte alignment
  E. Bit error detection

19. *Link Access Procedures for Frame Mode Bearer Services* (LAPF) is similar to LAPD; ISDN's frame format. LAPF is responsible for all of the following except:
  A. Verify that frames meet the minimum and maximum size restrictions
  B. Packet alignment
  C. Perform virtual circuit multiplexing and demultiplexing
  D. Congestion notification and control functions

20. LAPF uses the ITU-T signaling specifications. Which one of the following is not true?
  A. Q.930 contains the general principles of all user and network interface signaling.
  B. Q.931 defines call-control messages used between user and network interfaces.
  C. Q.932 defines the specifications for the connection between the user and network interfaces and the physical medium.
  D. Q.933 details the signaling used for frame-mode based services, including SVCs.

21. Frame Relay supports Virtual Circuits. Which of the following is true?
  A. PVCs and SVCs are supported in half-duplex mode.
  B. PVCs and SVCs are supported in full-duplex mode.
  C. Only PVCs are supported.
  D. PVCs are supported in half-duplex and full-duplex mode, SVCs are supported only in half-duplex mode.

22. Which of the following is not true about Frame Relay standards?
  A. Frame Relay was first described by CCITT's Blue Book in 1988.
  B. Because of some functionality was missing from the first Frame Relay standards, DEC, Cisco, Stratacom, and Nortel wrote an extension to the ANSI standard.
  C. Initially, DEC, Cisco, Stratacom, and Nortel consortium were called the "Frame Relay Implement's Forum," and was also known as the Gang of Four.
  D. The Gang of Four became, as we know it today, the Frame Relay Forum, defining formal standards for the definition and implementation of Frame Relay.

23. Frame Relay is related to X.25 and ISDN. Which of the following is true about the ties Frame Relay has with these one or both of these protocols?
  A. Frame Relay and X.25 are connection-oriented, cut-through switching technologies.
  B. LAPF and LAPD have very similar frame formats: both have a flag field with a bit pattern of "00111100" that is used to delimit the beginning and end of a frame.
  C. ISDN and X.25 have a frame CRC, unlike Frame Relay.
  D. Frame Relay is usually a software upgrade for telephone companies' current X.25 switches.

24. A frame relay switch performs the following responsibilities:
   A. Verifies that the frame has no bit errors, byte-alignment errors, and that the frame itself is of legal size; if this is not true, the frame device corrects the frame error
   B. Verifies that the DLCI address is valid, otherwise the frame device will broadcast the frame to every end-node device
   C. Forwards the frame to the end-node device
   D. Sets up hard-SVCs through switched-fabric to the destination when the end-node it is connected to is using a PVC

25. Which of the following elements in a frame is not used for congestion control?
   A. Forward Explicit Congestion Notification
   B. DLCI/DL-CORE Indication
   C. Backward Explicit Congestion Notification
   D. Discard Eligibility

26. Which of the following is true about DLCIs?
   A. DLCI stands for Data Link Constraint Identifier.
   B. It uses an 11-bit value to specify up to a total of 1024 possible DLCI values.
   C. All DLCI values can be arbitrarily assigned by end-users to provide connectivity to remote destinations in the Frame Relay cloud.
   D. There is an Extended Address bit which allows for the creation of DLCI values larger than 1024.

27. Which is true about DLCI usage?
   A. DLCI values can be expanded from the default size of 1024 values up to 16, 17, 23, or 32 bits in length.
   B. DLCI 0 is reserved for ILMI.
   C. DLCI 16 is reserved for in-channel signaling no matter how large the DLCI value is (1-8,388,607).
   D. DLCI definitions are stated in CCITT's Q.922.

28. Which of the following is true about Frame Relay?
   A. Frame Relay service can be offered over the D-channel.
   B. DLCIs have global significance in the Frame Relay network.
   C. Frame Relay provides Quality of Service, similar to QOS in the ATM specification.
   D. Frame Relay only uses the D-channel for signaling, even with extended addressing.

29. What is true about CIR and Frame Relay?
   A. CIR uses the Discard Eligibility bit to help control congestion in a Frame Relay network.
   B. It stands for Committed Information Rate and is not a Frame Relay standard.
   C. The CIR can never be exceeded by an end-node device.
   D. CIR is an immediate, real-time measurement of a transmission.

30. CIR is derived from two values. Which is not true about the following?
   A. CIR uses Committed Rate Measurement Interval (Tc) which defines the time interval over which the transfer rate is measured.
   B. CIR uses Committed Burst Size (Bc) which defines the maximum throughput that the network provider will guarantee during the time interval.
   C. It is possible to have a Committed Burst Size of 112,000Kbps, yet only have a CIR of 56Kbps.
   D. The formula used for CIR is CIR = (Tc) / (Bc).

31. Given the following four examples, which would allow for more "burstiness" of traffic, i.e., which would provide better throughput?
   A. Bc = 64,000 and Tc = 1
   B. Bc = 128,000 and Tc = 2
   C. Bc = 256,000 and Tc = 4
   D. Bc = 640,000 and Tc = 10

32. CIR guarantees a certain amount of bandwidth over a specified period of time. What mechanism does Frame Relay not implement to allow the CIR to be exceeded?
   A. The Excess Burst Size (Be) defines the total number of bits above the CIR that will be tolerated by the network.
   B. The *Excess Information Rate* (EIR) is a formula used to determine discard eligibility. It defines the number of bits per second, in total (CIR + Be) that the network will attempt to deliver in the specified time interval.
   C. If the CIR is exceeded, the discard eligibility bit is set for a frame and the frame is forwarded if the Excess Burst Size has not been exceeded.
   D. Frames where the *Discard Eligibility* bit (DE) is set to "1" are eligible for discard if congestion occurs.

33. Which of the following is not true about CIR?
   A. The CIR may different in both directions (End-Node A→End-Node B having a CIR of 32Kbs for a 56Kbs circuit and End-Node B→End-Node A have a CIR of 16Kbps for its 56Kbps circuit).
   B. CIR can be different for every VC on the same physical connection.
   C. It is not allowable for the combined CIR rates of all of the VCs on a line to exceed the line speed.
   D. It is possible to have a CIR of "zero".

34. The congestion management techniques implemented in Frame Relay are:
   A. UDI information transfer capability
   B. Usage of the Explicit Congestion Notification bits
   C. Usage of the Implicit Congestion Notification bits
   D. The *Consolidate Link Layer Management* protocol (CLLM)
   E. ILMI source quenching
   F. A, B, & C
   G. B, C, & E
   H. B, C, & D

35. Which of the following are true about FECN and BECN?
   A. If congestion occurs as a frame is travelling to its destination, a frame relay switch will mark the FECN bits to note congestion.
   B. If congestion occurs as a frame is travelling to its destination, a frame relay switch will mark the BECN bits to note congestion.
   C. FECN and BECN are mutually exclusive, ie., they cannot be used simultaneously in a VC connection.
   D. Setting both FECN and BECN informs frame relay switches that this frame is eligible for discard.
   E. BECN is usually used with protocols like TCP/IP.

36. Implicit congestion notification refers to_____.
    A. PNNI information being shared between frame relay switches to share congestion information
    B. ILMI information being shared between the two end-node devices about congestion information
    C. Upper-layer protocols determining congestion by examining the round-trip time of a packet or the number of packets that had to be retransmitted.
    D. FECN and BECN bit marking by frame relay switches

37. Which is true about *Consolidate Link Layer Management* Protocol (CLLM)?
    A. Standardized by ANSI T1.618
    B. Standardized by ITU-T Q.922
    C. CLLM, on a frame relay switch, generates a message back to the source about congestion problems.
    D. The control field indicates the DLCIs affected, the cause of congestion, and the expected duration of the congestion.
    E. A, C, & D
    F. A, B, & C
    G. B & C

38. Which of the following is false about the DLCI LMI uses?
    A. The Gang of Four specify that LMI use DLCI 1023.
    B. Both ANSI and CCITT specify that LMI use DLCI 0.
    C. Both ANSI and the Gang of Four specify that LMI use DLCI 1023.
    D. CCITT specifies that LMI use DLCI 0.
    E. The Protocol Discriminator identifies the use of the LMI, ie., what information the LMI frame contains.

39. Which of the following is false about LMI?
    A. It is bi-directional; both users and the network can send queries and responses.
    B. A STATUS ENQUIRY message asks about the status of PVC connections.
    C. A STATUS message is returned by the device receiving the STATUS ENQUIRY message containing information about the PVCs.
    D. It is used to maintain the physical link between two frame relay devices.

40. Which of the following are true about Frame Relay switches and LMI?
    A. They use STATUS messages to determine whether an end-node device is still there.
    B. Theses messages are roughly exchanged every 10 seconds between the two devices.
    C. The Control Field is used to send back the status information to the end-node.
    D. By default, a Full Status Message is sent from the end-node client in every sixth status request which the switch responds back to.

41. Frame Relay is a non-broadcast, multi-access service. In order to implement multicasts, steps must be performed. Of these steps, which of the following is not true?
    A. A special DLCI, called a Multicast, or MDLCI, must be created, which can be any DLCI.
    B. There is a "root" device who is responsible for forwarding a multicast frame to every member in the multicast group.
    C. The Frame Relay Forum specifies the components and their interaction for multicasts.
    D. There are "leaves" who are members of the multicast group. They can initiate a multicast, sending their frame to the "root", or receive a multicast frame.

42. Which is not specified with Phase 2 of NNI for Frame Relay?
   A. Defines the implementation for Quality of Service
   B. Defines higher speed interfaces
   C. Defines link management and data transfer operations between two different frame relay networks
   D. Defines specifications for both PVCs and SVCs

43. To set up Frame Relay on a Cisco router to interoperate with other vendors equipment by meeting the requirements of RFC 1490, which of the following statements would one apply to a serial interface?
   A. Encapsulation frame-relay
   B. Frame-relay encapsulation
   C. Encapsulation frame-relay ietf
   D. Encapsulation frame-relay 1490

44. What is the `frame-relay intf-type` command used for on a serial interface on a Cisco router?
   A. Used to distinguish PVCs from SVCs and vice versa
   B. Determines the LMI type used
   C. Specifies multicast group information
   D. Determines the interface type: DTE, DCE, or switch-to-switch connection

45. What command is used to create static mappings on a frame relay switch to switch an incoming PVC connection to an outgoing port?
   A. `Frame-relay switch`
   B. `Frame-relay map`
   C. `Frame-relay route`
   D. `Frame-relay port`

46. The valid fields in a Frame Relay frame are:
   A. Flag, address, control, information, and FCS
   B. Flag, address, control, XID, information, and FCS
   C. Flag, address, message type, data, and CRC
   D. Flag, address, message type, XID, information, and FCS

47. All of the following are true about NNI except:
   A. Detects the removal of a PVC
   B. Detects a failure with a connecting UNI or NNI
   C. Detects the addition of a PVC
   D. Uses ILMI to share SVC routing information
   E. Verifies PVC segment accessibility

48. Which of the following is true about Frame Relay?
   A. It uses Time Division Multiplexing.
   B. It automatically provides network performance improvements.
   C. It deals with burstiness traffic better than cell-switching protocols.
   D. It provides all of the functionality of HDLC.
   E. It provides a real-time status of all PVCs.

49. LMI is responsible for all of the following except:
   A. Verifying link between a user and the network
   B. Notifying additions and deletions of PVCs
   C. Responding to status messages
   D. Moving frames between frame-relay devices

50. The Cisco Router command `frame-relay lmi-type` sets the LMI type for the specified interface. Which of the following is not a valid LMI type?
   A. CISCO
   B. ANSI
   C. Q933A
   D. ITUT-9

51. Frame Relay supports which of the following protocol parameters with the "frame relay map protocol" Cisco router configuration statement?
   A. IP, DECnet, Appletalk, IPX, XNS, and SNA
   B. IP, DECnet, Appletalk, IPX, Vines, CLNS, and XNS
   C. IP, DECnet, Appletalk, IPX, Vines, and XNS
   D. IP, Appletalk, IPX, Vines, CLNS, and XNS

52. Cisco's implementation of Frame Relay supports which of the following compression techniques?
   A. Payload compression
   B. All types of header compression
   C. Frame compression
   D. TCP/IP header compression
   E. A & B
   F. A & D
   G. A, C, & D

53. Which is true about assigning priorities to DLCIs on a Cisco router?
   A. It provides a way to define multiple parallel DLCIs for different types of traffic.
   B. DLCI priority levels assign priority queues within the router or access server; in fact, they are independent of the device's priority queues.
   C. If you enable queuing and use the same DLCIs for queuing, then high-priority DLCIs cannot be put into high-priority queues.
   D. The command to implement this is `frame-relay priority-group`.

54. What advantage does sub-interfaces provide in configuring Frame Relay on a Cisco Router?
   A. Allows the usage of SVCs
   B. Needed to implement multicasts
   C. Overcomes the problem of split horizon
   D. Provides multiple active paths for a connection using a routing protocol like OSPF

55. The Cisco Router `show frame-relay pvc` command reveals the following information:

```
DLCI = 300, DLCI USAGE = LOCAL, PVC STATUS = ACTIVE, INTERFACE = Serial0.103
      input pkts 10              output pkts 7              in bytes 6222
      out bytes 6034             dropped pkts 0             in FECN pkts 0
      in BECN pkts 0             out FECN pkts 0            out BECN pkts 0
      in DE pkts 0               out DE pkts 0
      pvc create time 0:13:11   last time pvc status changed 0:11:46
```

Which is true about the DLCI USAGE value listed above?
   A. Refers to a DCE device
   B. Refers to a DTE/DCE device
   C. Refers to only a DCE device
   D. Refers to a DCE or NNI device

56. What Cisco router command would you use to determine the LMI type and its corresponding DLCI # that is used on a connection?
   A. `Show frame-relay intf-type`
   B. `Show interface`
   C. `Show frame-relay interface`
   D. `Show frame-relay lmi`

57. What is the purpose of the following command: `frame-relay local-dlci 100`?
   A. DLCI of the remote Frame Relay device
   B. CIR for the local Frame switch
   C. Local DLCI assigned to the router
   D. None of the above

58. Which of the following ISDN service types is not available in the United States?
   A. Basic Rate
   B. T1 Primary Rate
   C. Tarrifed Rate
   D. E1 Primary Rate

59. ISDN signaling is handled _____.
   A. in-band
   B. out of band
   C. distributed
   D. none of the above

60. T1 primary rate ISDN has how many channels for data transport?
   A. 2
   B. 8
   C. 24
   D. 32

61. The "B" in B channel stands for:
   A. "Beta"
   B. "Bearer"
   C. "Basic"
   D. "Binary"

62. The ISDN U interface is:
   A. Digital
   B. Analog
   C. Digital or Analog
   D. All of the above

63. What type of traffic can be carried using the ISDN B channel?
   A. Voice
   B. Data
   C. Video
   D. Control Signaling
   E. None of the above

64. Which of the following is used to connect a serial router interface to an ISDN line?
   A. Modem
   B. Converter bow
   C. Terminal adapter
   D. EIA/TIA-232 Cable

65. Channelized T1 can not be configured on which of these router types?
   A. 7500
   B. 4000
   C. 2600
   D. 3600
   E. A,B & C
   F. All of the above

66. An ISDN BRI SPID is used to identify _____.
    A. the telephone number for the line
    B. the physical connection into the ISDN switch
    C. the number of users supported on the ISDN line
    D. whether the ISDN line may be used for voice or data

67. Primary Rate ISDN has ____ D channel(s).
    A. 1   C. 4
    B. 2   D. 6

68. ISDN is a _____ service.
    A. non-switched   C. analog
    B. dedicated   D. dialup

69. All ISDN lines must have a _____ associated with them.
    A. SPID   C. X.131 address
    B. router   D. Switch type

70. Which line encapsulation is valid for an ISDN connection?
    A. X.25   D. HDLC
    B. Frame Relay   E. All of the above
    C. PPP

71. A router uses which of the following to determine whether an ISDN session is voice or data?
    A. Sub-address field   C. CLID
    B. Device ID   D. Network layer address

72. How many SPIDs may be associated with a BRI line?
    A. 1   C. 4
    B. 2   D. 6

73. ISDN B channels provide bandwidth in units of _____.
    A. 16Kbps   C. 64Kbps
    B. 56Kbps   D. 128Kbps

74. "2B+D" refers to_____.
    A. The channel characteristics of a Channelized T1 link
    B. The channel characteristics of a PRI link
    C. The physical characteristics of a E1 link
    D. The channel characteristics of a *Basic Rate Interface* (BRI)

75. ISDN is designed to provide:
    A. Integrated voice and data
    B. Faster Internet dial-up access
    C. Simultaneous multi-protocol dial access
    D. Support for Remote Access VPN's
    E. Connecting two routers via dedicated a link

76. In order for ISDN to operate on a Cisco router, which of the following protocols must be enabled on the interface?
  A. PPP
  B. LAPB
  C. DDR
  D. HDLC
  E. Frame relay
  F. None of the above

77. Combing ISDN channels for more bandwidth is termed:
  A. Ether-channel
  B. Bonding
  C. Load Balancing
  D. Trunking
  E. None of the above

78. What is a *Service Profile Identifier* (SPID)?
  A. A BISDN ID
  B. A channel assignment ID found in the header of the ISDN packet
  C. A string of numbers identifying the type of central office switch in the local exchange
  D. The address of the subscriber's ISDN equipment
  E. None of the above

79. What is the maximum length of an ISDN address?
  A. 40 digits
  B. 55 digits
  C. 12 digits
  D. 15 digits

80. What is the bandwidth of a PRI in the United States?
  A. 1.544Mbps
  B. 64Kbps
  C. 192Mbps
  D. 2.048Mbps

81. What is the bandwidth of a PRI in Europe?
  A. 384Kbps
  B. 2.048Mbps
  C. 1.544Mbps
  D. 128Kbps

82. An NT1 can support how many devices?
  A. 10
  B. 12
  C. 8
  D. 2
  E. 1

83. What is the layer 2 protocol used over the D channel in ISDN?
  A. LAPD
  B. LAPB
  C. X.25
  D. LABF
  E. 931

84. Identify the line coding used over the U interface on a BRI.
  A. AMI
  B. 2B1Q
  C. HDB3
  D. ZBTSI

85. What does a *Service Access Point Identifier* (SAPI) identify?
  A. A service layer 3
  B. An ISDN device on a connection
  C. A connection endpoint within a service
  D. All of the above

86. What Q.931 message is sent over the D channel to request a connection?
    A. Setup
    B. SABME
    C. Connect
    D. Release

87. In LAPD, the sequence number can be any value from____ to____.
    A. 7, 127
    B. 7, 128
    C. 8, 127
    D. 8, 128

88. ISDN has a call set up time of ___.
    A. 1 minute
    B. 30 seconds
    C. less than 2 seconds
    D. seconds to establish call

89. A router with a U reference port has _____.
    A. an external NT1
    B. an internal NT1
    C. no NT1
    D. none of the above

90. What is the maximum number of decimal digits in ISDNs numbering plan?
    A. 24
    B. 55
    C. 12
    D. 64

91. The most common ISDN implementation in the United States is:
    A. 2b+d
    B. 23b+d
    C. 30B+d
    D. A & B

92. Identify the sequence of steps used in ISDN session setup.
    A. Setup
    B. Call Proceeding
    C. Connect
    D. Connect Ack

93. Identify ISDN B-channel protocols.
    A. PPP
    B. BONDING
    C. Multi-link PPP
    D. V.120
    E. All of the above

94. A NT1 performs:
    A. 2 wire to 4 wire conversion
    B. 2 wire to 8 wire conversion
    C. 2 wire only
    D. None of the above

95. The distance from the ISDN Switch to the user premise is:
    A. 2000 ft
    B. 18,000 ft
    C. 6000 ft
    D. 5280 ft

96. What three functions should you receive from an ISDN provisioned circuit?
    A. SPIDs
    B. Telephone Number
    C. Circuit Identification Code
    D. Channel Number

97. The ISDN Data Link layers protocol used:
    A. I.431
    B. 1.453
    C. Q.921
    D. Q.933

98. The ISDN Network Layer Signaling Protocol is:
   A. Q.931   C. Q.2931
   B. Q.922   D. None of the above

99. Identify the SAPI values reserved by the ITU-T.
   A. 16   C. 0
   B. 63   D. 17

100. LAP-D has __ different states.
   A. 2   C. 8
   B. 6   D. 10

101. The address size in bytes for LAP-D is:
   A. 2   C. 1
   B. 4   D. 6

102. The Default Timer for T202 is:
   A. 2 seconds   C. 6 seconds
   B. 4 seconds   D. 8 seconds

103. The maximum number of retransmits using N200 is:
   A. 3   C. 2
   B. 6   D. 1

104. What is the Default Timer for T200?
   A. 1 seconds   C. 6 seconds
   B. 3 seconds   D. 10 seconds

105. What is the Default Timer for T202?
   A. 2 seconds   C. 6 seconds
   B. 4 seconds   D. 8 seconds

106. What is the Default Timer for T203?
   A. 10 seconds   C. 4 seconds
   B. 8 seconds   D. 12 seconds

107. What is the Default Timer for T303?
   A. 5 seconds
   B. 7 seconds
   C. 8 seconds

108. What is the Default Timer for T308?
   A. 4 seconds   C. 19 seconds
   B. 8 seconds   D. 10 seconds

109. What is the Default Timer for T310?
   A. 60 seconds   C. 45 seconds
   B. 30 seconds   D. 15 seconds

110. What is the Default Timer for T313?
- **A.** 4 seconds
- **B.** 3 seconds
- **C.** 2 seconds
- **D.** 9 seconds

111. What is the Default Timer for T316?
- **A.** 120 seconds
- **B.** 60 seconds
- **C.** 30 seconds
- **D.** 15 seconds

112. What is the Default Timer for T318?
- **A.** 4 seconds
- **B.** 6 seconds
- **C.** 8 seconds
- **D.** 10 seconds

113. What is the Default Timer for T319?
- **A.** 4 seconds
- **B.** 10 seconds
- **C.** 12 seconds
- **D.** 20 seconds

114. The ISDN D channel uses Q.931 for signaling.
- **A.** True
- **B.** False

115. Identify the LAP-D frame format.

ISDN Show Commands

```
hostname Orlando
!
enable password san-fran
!
username Seattle password 7 104D000A0618
isdn switch-type basic-5ess
!
interface Ethernet0
 ip address 3.0.0.1 255.0.0.0

interface BRI0
 ip address 2.0.0.2 255.0.0.0
 encapsulation ppp
 dialer map ip 2.0.0.1 name Seattle 1001
 dialer-group 1
 ppp authentication chap
!
ip host Seattle 2.0.0.1
no ip classless
ip route 1.0.0.0 255.0.0.0 2.0.0.1
logging buffered
!
dialer-list 1 protocol ip permit
!
line con 0
 password cisco
 login
line aux 0
line vty 0 4
 password cisco
 login
!
end
```

116. What type of WAN data link layer protocol is being used over Bri 0?
- **A.** PPP
- **B.** ISDN
- **C.** HDLC
- **D.** Frame relay

117. What traffic type would cause the ISDN link to activate?
- **A.** IP
- **B.** IPX
- **C.** NetBIOS
- **D.** SNA

118. The switch type basic-5ess refers to:
- **A.** AT&T basic rate switch
- **B.** National ISDN
- **C.** NTT ISDN Switch
- **D.** None of the above

119. The destination network that you are trying to reach over ISDN is:
- **A.** 1.0.0.0
- **B.** 2.0.0.0
- **C.** 3.0.0.0
- **D.** 2.0.0.2

120. In the dialer-map statement, 1001 refers to:
- **A.** An ISDN telephone number
- **B.** An SPID number
- **C.** An application port number
- **D.** None of the above

121. The Europe PRI service provides for ____ B channels.
- **A.** 24
- **B.** 30
- **C.** 16
- **D.** 32

122. The D channel using 23+B ISDN services uses time slot ___.
- **A.** 23
- **B.** 24
- **C.** 1
- **D.** None of the above

Answers

1. A
2. A
3. A
4. B
5. D
6. C, E
7. D
8. B
9. A
10. D
11. E
12. A
13. B
14. A
15. B
16. D
17. D
18. B
19. B
20. C
21. B
22. D
23. D
24. C
25. B
26. D
27. D
28. A
29. A
30. D
31. D
32. B
33. C
34. H
35. A
36. C
37. F
38. C
39. A
40. B
41. A
42. A
43. C
44. D
45. C
46. A
47. D
48. C
49. D

50. D
51. B
52. F
53. A
54. C
55. A
56. B
57. C
58. D
59. B
60. C
61. B
62. D
63. A, B, C
64. C
65. F
66. A
67. A
68. D
69. A
70. C
71. A
72. A
73. C
74. D
75. A, B, C, D
76. A
77. B
78. D
79. D
80. A
81. B
82. D
83. A
84. B
85. D
86. A
87. B
88. C
89. B
90. B
91. D
92. A, B, C, D
93. E
94. A, B
95. B
96. A, B, C
97. C
98. A
99. A, B, C

100. C
101. A, B
102. A
103. A
104. A
105. A
106. A
107. A
108. A
109. A
110. A
111. A
112. A
113. A
114. A
115. Flag, address, control, information, FCS, flag
116. A
117. B
118. A
119. A
120. A
121. B
122. B

CCNA Exam Bonus Questions

OSI Reference Model

1. The OSI reference model is a seven-layer reference model that originated from the:
   - **A.** ISO standards committee
   - **B.** ITU standards committee
   - **C.** IEEE standards committee
   - **D.** ANSI standards committee

2. Identify the seven-layers of the OSI reference model.
   - **A.** Application, presentation, dialog, transport, network, datalink, bit
   - **B.** Application, data format, dialog, transport, network, datalink, bit
   - **C.** Application, data format, dialog, end-to-end connection, network, datalink, bit
   - **D.** Application, presentation, session, transport, network, data link, physical

3. What is the function of the Application Layer as described by the OSI reference model?
   - **A.** Provides network services to user applications
   - **B.** Provides desktop connectivity to the LAN
   - **C.** Provides desktop connectivity to the WAN
   - **D.** None of the above

4. Data is referred to as _____ at the Application Layer.
   - **A.** Data
   - **B.** Packets
   - **C.** Segments
   - **D.** Bits
   - **E.** Frames

5. What are some of the common standards that are implemented at the Application Layer?
   - **A.** SMTP, TELNET, FTP, CMIP, WWW
   - **B.** NetBIOS, LAT, DDP, SNA
   - **C.** IP, IPX, DDP
   - **D.** SDLC, LAT, NETBIOS

6. What is the function of the Presentation Layer, as described by the OSI reference model?
   - **A.** Provides data representation and format to the Application Layer
   - **B.** Provides presentation services to the Presentation Layer
   - **C.** Converts application data to binary
   - **D.** Converts application data to EBCDIC

7. What are some of the common standards that are implemented at the Presentation Layer?
   A. TFTP, SMTP, SNMP, TELNET
   B. NetBIOS, LAT, DDP, SNA
   C. JPEG, PIC, MPEG, QTIME, ASN.1, SMB, NCP
   D. SDLC, LAT, NETBIOS

8. What is the function of the Session Layer, as described by the OSI reference model?
   A. Conversation steering
   B. Conversation steering in half-duplex mode
   C. Establishes, maintains and manages sessions between applications
   D. Conversation negotiations

9. What are some of the common standards that are implemented at the Session Layer?
   A. TFTP, SMTP, SNMP, TELNET
   B. NetBIOS names, SNA Session, NFS, Xwindows, RPC, SQL
   C. JPEG, PIC, MPEG, QTIME, ASN.1, SMB, NCP
   D. SDLC, LAT, NETBIOS

10. What is the function of the Transport Layer, as described by the OSI reference model?
    A. Management of streaming data
    B. Segments and reassembles data into a data stream
    C. Always guarantees delivery
    D. Never guarantees delivery

11. Data is referred to as _____ at the Transport Layer.
    A. Data   D. Bits
    B. Packets   E. Frames
    C. Segments

12. What are some of the common standards that are implemented at the Transport Layer?
    A. TFTP, SMTP, SNMP, TELNET
    B. NetBIOS names, SNA Session, NFS, Xwindows, RPC, SQL
    C. JPEG, PIC, MPEG, QTIME, ASN.1, SMB, NCP
    D. TCP, UDP, SPP, SPX

13. What is the function of the Network Layer, as described by the OSI reference model?
    A. Manages device addressing and tracks location of devices on the network
    B. Manages the connectivity of all networks within an antonymous system
    C. Manages the availability of all networks within an antonymous system
    D. All of the above

14. What devices operate at the Network Layer?
    A. Layer 2 switch   D. Layer 3 Switch
    B. Bridges   E. Routers
    C. Hubs

15. Data is referred to as _____ at the Network Layer.
    A. Data   D. Bits
    B. Packets   E. Frames
    C. Segments

16. What are some of the common standards that are implemented at the Network Layer?
    A. LAT, NETBIOS, IP, DDP
    B. NetBIOS, LAT, DDP, SNA
    C. IP, IPX, DDP, VIP
    D. SDLC, LAT, NETBIOS

17. Identify the function of the Data Link Layer, as described by the OSI reference model.
    A. Provides access to the physical media
    B. Describes the framing standard
    C. Describes the error correction mechanism that will be used
    D. None of the above

18. What are some common standards that are implemented at the Data Link Layer?
    A. Ethernet
    B. IEEE 802.3
    C. IEEE 802.5
    D. Frame-Relay
    E. HDLC
    F. Token Ring
    G. FDDI
    H. None of the above
    I. All of the above, except H

19. Data is referred to as _____ at the Data Link Layer.
    A. Data
    B. Packets
    C. Segments
    D. Bits
    E. Frames

20. What devices operate at the Data Link Layer?
    A. Switches
    B. Bridges
    C. Hubs
    D. Routers

21. What is the primary difference between an Ethernet and IEEE 802.3 frame?
    A. Ethernet has a length field and the IEEE 802.3 frame has a type field.
    B. Ethernet has a type field and the IEEE 802.3 frame has a length field.
    C. The preamble field is larger in the Ethernet Frame.
    D. The preamble field is smaller in the Ethernet Frame.

22. IEEE committee subdivided the Data Link Layer into two sublayers. They are:
    A. SNAP and SAP sublayers
    B. LLC and SAP sublayers
    C. LLC and MAC sublayers
    D. LLC and SNAP sublayers

23. How does IEEE 802.3 reference what protocol type resides at layer three?
    A. Ethernet type field
    B. Length field
    C. LLC header
    D. None of the above

24. What is the function of the Physical Layer, as described by the OSI reference model?
    A. Provides the electrical, mechanical, procedural and functional means for activating and maintaining the physical link between systems
    B. Binary transmission
    C. Physical Layer encoding
    D. All of the above

25. Data is referred to as _____ at the Physical Layer.
    A. Data
    B. Packets
    C. Segments
    D. Bits
    E. Frames

26. What devices operate at the Physical Layer?
    A. Switches
    B. Bridges
    C. Hubs
    D. Routers

OSI Reference Model Answers

1. A
2. D
3. A
4. A
5. A
6. A
7. C
8. C
9. B
10. B
11. C
12. D
13. A
14. D, E
15. B
16. C
17. A
18. I
19. E
20. A, B
21. B
22. C
23. D
24. D
25. C
26. A

IP Routing

1. TCP is an acronym for _____.
   A. Transport Control Protocol
   B. Transport Control Point
   C. Transport Communication Protocol
   D. Transmission Control Protocol

2. IP is an acronym for _____.
   A. Information Protocol
   B. Internet Protocol
   C. Internal Program
   D. Interface Program

3. How many bits are in an octet?
   A. 4 bits
   B. 8 bits
   C. 1 bit
   D. 2 bits

4. What are the four commonly used classes of IP addresses?
   A. Class A
   B. Class B
   C. Class C
   D. Class D
   E. All of the above

5. What is the default net mask for Class A?
   A. 255.255.255.0
   B. 255.255.0.0
   C. 255.255.255.255
   D. 255.0.0.0

6. What is the default net mask for Class B?
   A. 255.255.255.0
   B. 255.255.0.0
   C. 255.255.255.255
   D. 255.0.0.0

7. What is the default net mask for Class C?
   A. 255.255.255.0
   B. 255.0.0.0
   C. 255.255.0.0
   D. 255.255.255.255

8. What is the beginning range for a layer three multicast address?
   A. 244.0.0.0
   B. 224.0.0.0
   C. 239.0.0.0
   D. 255.0.0.0

9. Given the IP address 198.176.174.202 with a 28 bit subnet mask. Select the subnet number and subnet broadcast address, respectively.
   A. 198.176.174.192–198.176.174.207
   B. 198.176.174.128–198.176.174.192
   C. 198.176.174.200–198.176.174.207
   D. None of the above

10. Using a Class B address with a mask of 255.255.255.128, how many networks and hosts are allowed, respectively?
    A. 126 networks and 512 hosts
    B. 512 networks and 128 hosts
    C. 128 networks and 512 hosts
    D. 510 networks and 126 hosts

11. Which is an illegal subnet mask?
    A. 255.255.255.254
    B. 255.128.0.0
    C. 255.255.255.242
    D. 255.255.255.192

12. What command defines an alias host name on a router?
    A. `ip domain-lookup`
    B. `ip alias`
    C. `ip host`
    D. None of the above

13. What command defines a DNS server for the router to use to resolve logical names?
    A. `ip domain-lookup`
    B. `ip host`
    C. `ip name-server`
    D. None of the above

14. PING and Traceroute test what layers of the OSI reference model?
    A. Physical
    B. DataLink
    C. Network
    D. Application
    E. All of the above

15. What routing protocols are distance vector?
    A. RIP
    B. IGRP
    C. RTMP
    D. IPX RIP
    E. None of the above
    F. A, B, C, D

16. What routing protocols are Link State?
    A. OSPF
    B. NLSP
    C. IS-IS
    D. PNNI
    E. None of the above
    F. A, B, C, D

17. What is the metric used by IP RIP?
    A. Hop count
    B. Hop count and tick
    C. Bandwidth, load, delay, reliability, and MTU
    D. Cost

18. What is the metric used by IPX RIP?
    A. Hop count
    B. Hop count and tick
    C. Bandwidth, load, delay, reliability, and MTU
    D. Cost

19. What is the metric used by IGRP?
    A. Hop count
    B. Hop count and tick
    C. Bandwidth, load, delay, reliability, and MTU
    D. Cost

20. What is the metric used by OSPF?
    A. Hop count
    B. Hop count and tick
    C. Bandwidth, load, delay, reliability and MTU
    D. Cost

21. What is the administrative distance for RIP?
   A. 90
   B. 100
   C. 110
   D. 120
   E. None of the above

22. What is the administrative distance for EIGRP?
   A. 90
   B. 100
   C. 110
   D. 120
   E. None of the above

23. What is the administrative distance for IGRP?
   A. 90
   B. 100
   C. 110
   D. 120
   E. None of the above

24. What is the administrative distance for OSPF?
   A. 90
   B. 100
   C. 110
   D. 120
   E. None of the above

25. Choose some examples of routed protocols.
   A. IPX, NETBUEI, IP VINES
   B. IPX, IP, VINES, LAT
   C. IPX , IP, VINES IP, DECnet
   D. IPX, IP VINES, SNA

26. Choose some examples of link state protocols
   A. OSPF, RIP2, ISIS
   B. OSPF, ISIS, NLSP
   C. OSPF, NLSP, IGRP
   D. None of the above

27. Choose some examples of routing protocols.
   A. IPX, RIP, OSPF
   B. OSPF, RIP, IGRP
   C. IP, IPX, IGRP, OSPF
   D. IP, OSPF, IGRP, ISIS

28. How many routing tables can a CISCO router support at any given time?
   A. 1
   B. 4
   C. 1 per routing protocol
   D. 1 per routed protocol

29. What is a routing protocol?
   A. A protocol that is used to carry user data between routers
   B. A protocol that is used to carry routing updates between routers
   C. A protocol that is used to maintain neighbors adjacencies
   D. None of the above

30. What is a routed protocol?
   A. A protocol that is used to carry user data between routers
   B. A protocol that is used to carry routing updates between routers
   C. A protocol that is used to maintain neighbors' adjacencies
   D. None of the above

31. What is similar about a static route and a default route?
  A. Both only require one entry for all networks.
  B. Both must be manually entered initially.
  C. Both increase overhead on the router.
  D. Both are dynamic.

32. Choose an example of a Hybrid Protocol.
  A. IGRP   **C.** OSPF
  B. EIGRP   **D.** RIP

33. If you had multiple routed protocols running all at once, what would be the most efficient routing protocol to run?
  A. IGRP   **C.** OSPF
  B. EIGRP   **D.** RIP

34. Select some of the characteristics of convergence.
  A. Convergence occurs when all routers use a consistent perspective of network topology.
  B. After a topology changes, routers must recompute routes, which disrupts routing.
  C. The process and time required for router reconvergence varies in routing protocols.
  D. Convergence time is the same on all routers running the same protocol.
  E. Convergence time can be disable.

35. If you were running the RIP protocol, how long should it take before a down network is removed from the routing table (assuming all of the defaults)?
  A. 180 seconds   **C.** 300 seconds
  B. 240 seconds   **D.** 90 seconds

36. How many possible subnets could you have in a class B Network?
  A. 16384   **C.** 14
  B. 16382   **D.** 12

37. How many possible subnets could you have is a class C network?
  A. 64   **C.** 6
  B. 62   **D.** 4

38. A class C address with a subnet mask of 255.255.255.248 allows how many host per network?
  A. 16   **C.** 30
  B. 14   **D.** 32

39. A class C address with a subnet of 255.255.255.224 allows how many networks?
  A. 16   **C.** 8
  B. 22   **D.** 6

40. What is the default time-out timer for RIP in a Cisco router?
  A. 90 seconds   **C.** 240 seconds
  B. 180 seconds   **D.** 30 seconds

41. A class A address with a subnet of 255.255.255.252 allows how many host per networks?

    A. 2
          C. 6

    B. 4
          D. 1024

42. When RIP 2 advertises, it uses a Layer 2 multicast address of:

    A. FF-FF-FF-FF-FF-FF
          D. 00-00-00-00-00-00

    B. 01-00-5E-00-00-09
          E. None of the above

    C. 01-00-5E-00-00-05

43. When RIP 2 advertises, it uses a Layer 3 address of:

    A. 224.255.255.255
          C. 224.9.0.0

    B. 224.0.0.9
          D. 255.255.255.255

44. When RIP 1 advertises, it will:

    A. Not advertise the subnet mask

    B. Advertise the subnet mask

    C. Add default mask to all interfaces

    D. Remove subnet mask from all interfaces

45. The command `no ip domain-lookup` will do the following:

    A. Disable DNS lookup

    B. Ignore NT NetBIOS name lookup

    C. Disable OSPF Area to Area routing

    D. Ignore IGRP autonomous system

46. What is the cause of the following ping response. [.!!!!]?

    A. Too much traffic on the network—ping probe died.

    B. ARP request

    C. Station not found

    D. Load sharing

47. What is the cause of the following ping response. [.!.!.]?

    A. Too much traffic on the network—ping probe died.

    B. ARP request

    C. Station not found

    D. Load sharing

48. Which of the following protocols will load balance by default?

    A. RIP 1
          C. OSPF

    B. IGRP
          D. ISIS

49. How many possible addressable hosts are there on the subnetwork 155.229.22.0?

    A. 240
          C. 12

    B. 255
          D. Cannot determine without a mask

50. How many IP routing tables are there on a Cisco router ?

    A. 1
          C. 1 per network

    B. 1 per port
          D. 1 per service provider (ISP)

IP Routing Answers

1. D
2. B
3. B
4. E
5. D
6. B
7. A
8. B
9. A
10. D
11. C
12. C
13. C
14. A, B, C
15. F
16. F
17. A
18. B
19. C
20. D
21. D
22. A
23. B
24. C
25. C
26. B
27. B
28. C
29. B
30. A
31. B
32. B
33. B
34. A, B, C
35. C
36. A
37. A
38. C
39. C
40. A
41. A
42. B
43. B
44. A
45. A
46. B
47. D
48. B
49. D
50. A

IPX Routing

1. What command activates IPX forwarding on the router?
    A. IPX routing   **C.** No IPX routing
    B. IPX forwarding   **D.** None of the above

2. Within the NetWare Protocol suite, which protocol provides connection-oriented services?
    A. IPX   **C.** SAP
    B. SPX   **D.** NCP

3. IPX address is _____ bits.
    A. 32
    B. 24
    C. 80

4. The IPX node address is _____ bits.
    A. 32   **C.** 48
    B. 24   **D.** 16

5. What is the default routing protocol for IPX?
    A. NLSP   **C.** IGRP
    B. RIP   **D.** EIGRP

6. Novell Services are advertised via _____.
    A. GNS   **C.** IPX
    B. SAP   **D.** ARP

7. What are the four types of Ethernet framing supported by Novell?
    A. Ethernet_IEEE 802.3; Ethernet_802.2; Ethernet II; Ethernet_SNAP
    B. Ethernet_DIX; Ethernet_LLC; Ethernet_IEEE; Ethernet_RAW
    C. Ethernet_802; Ethernet I; Ethernet_III; Ethernet_IEEE

8. What are the four types of Ethernet framing supported by the Cisco IOS?
    A. Novell_Ether; sap; arpa; snap
    B. Ethernet_IEEE 802.3; Ethernet_802.2; Ethernet II; Ethernet_SNAP
    C. Ethernet_802; Ethernet I; Ethernet_III; Ethernet_IEEE

9. Identify the Cisco equivalency to the following Novell encapsulation:
    Ethernet_IEEE802.3;Ethernet_802.2;Ethernet II; Ethernet_SNAP
    A. Novell_Ether,sap,arpa,Novell_cisco
    B. Novell_Ether,arpa,sap,Novell_cisco
    C. Novell_Ether,sap,arpa,snap
    D. None of the above

10. What is the default Ethernet encapsulation type for Novell?
    A. Arpa   **C.** Novell_Ether
    B. Sap   **D.** Snap

11. What is the default encapsulation type of Novell on a Token Ring interface?
    A. Novell_Ether   C. Snap
    B. Sap   D. Arpa

12. What is the default encapsulation type for Novell on a FDDI Ring interface?
    A. Snap   C. Arpa
    B. Sap   D. Novell_Ether

13. What is the default encapsulation type for serial interfaces?
    A. X.25   C. HDLC
    B. Frame-Relay   D. Arpa

14. What is the periodic broadcast timer for IPX RIP?
    A. 30 seconds   C. 90 seconds
    B. 45 seconds   D. 60 seconds

15. What is the periodic timer for SAP broadcasts?
    A. 30 seconds   C. 90 seconds
    B. 45 seconds   D. 60 seconds

16. If there is no local server on a segment, when a client sends a GNS request up, what action will the router perform?
    A. Forward to the nearest server
    B. Drop the packet
    C. Broadcast the request out of all interfaces
    D. Respond to the request

17. If there are multiple encapsulation types on an interface, what two methods may be used to define the encapsulation types?
    A. Sub-interfaces; specify secondary
    B. Multiple encapsulation types can not reside on a single interface
    C. Specify a primary and secondary

18. How many entries can a router SAP message contain?
    A. 25   C. 1
    B. 50   D. 7

19. How many entries can a RIP message from a router contain?
    A. 25   C. 1
    B. 50   D. 7

20. In a IPX network, a Tick count is measured in what increments?
    A. 30 seconds   C. 1 second
    B. 60 seconds   D. 1/18 second

21. How many Ethernet encapsulations does a Cisco router support?
    A. 16   C. 8
    B. 12   D. 4

22. What is the maximum hop count allowed for RIP 1?
    A. 127   C. 15
    B. 16   D. No limit

23. Cisco IPXWAN protocol is used for which of the following reasons?
    A. Interoperability across HDLC
    B. Interoperability across PPP
    C. Interoperability across Frame Relay
    D. Not supported

24. The GNS broadcast is known as what type of protocol?
    A. RIP   C. NLSP Update
    B. SAP   D. IPX Update

IPX Routing Answers

1. A
2. B
3. C
4. C
5. B
6. B
7. A
8. A
9. C
10. C
11. B
12. A
13. C
14. D
15. D
16. D
17. A
18. D
19. B
20. D
21. D
22. C
23. B, C
24. B

Access-List

1. What are the two types of IP access lists?
   - **A.** Regular and Standard
   - **B.** Standard and Extended
   - **C.** Even and Odd
   - **D.** None of the above

2. In a standard IP access list, what fields within the IP packet can be tested?
   - **A.** Source address, destination address
   - **B.** Source address, destination address, protocol, port
   - **C.** Destination address
   - **D.** Source address

3. What is the range of a Standard IP access list?
   - **A.** 0 to 99
   - **B.** 1 to 99
   - **C.** 100 to 199
   - **D.** 1 to 199

4. Every access list carries an implicit _____.
   - **A.** permit any
   - **B.** permit any any
   - **C.** deny all

5. What is the command to apply IP access list 101 to an interface?
   - **A.** `ip access-group 101 [in/out]`
   - **B.** `ip access-list 101`
   - **C.** `access-list 101`
   - **D.** `access-group 101`

6. What is the default direction of the access-list?
   - **A.** Inbound
   - **B.** Outbound
   - **C.** In and out
   - **D.** Out and in

7. What does the following access list command do?
   `Access-list 1 permit 172.16.36.0 0.0.0.255`

   - **A.** Permits traffic originating from the 172.16.36.0 subnet
   - **B.** Permits traffic destine for 172.16.36.0 subnet
   - **C.** Permits traffic to and from the 172.16.36.0 subnet
   - **D.** This is an invalid statement.

8. What is accomplished with this access list?
   ```
   Access-list 1 deny 172.16.36.236 0.0.0.0
   Access-list 1 permit 172.16.36.0 0.0.0.255
   Access-list 1 deny any

   Interface Ethernet 0
       Ip address 172.16.36.1 255.255.255.0
   Ip access-group 1 in
   ```

   - **A.** Blocks all traffic destined for the host 172.16.36.236 but allows all other traffic
   - **B.** Blocks all traffic destined for the host 172.16.36.236 and allows traffic for others only on the 172.16.36.0 subnet
   - **C.** Blocks all traffic originating from the host 172.16.36.236 but allows all other traffic
   - **D.** Blocks all ip traffic originating from the host 172.16.36.236 and allows traffic from others only on the 172.16.36.0 subnet

9. Which access list will block traffic from 192.168.33.8?
   A. `access-list 1 deny 192.168.33.8 0.0.0.0`
      `access-list 1 permit any`
      `access-list 1 deny any`
   B. `access-list 1 permit 192.168.33.0 0.0.0.255`
      `access-list 1 deny 192.168.33.8 0.0.0.0`
      `access-list 1 deny any`
   C. `access-list 1 deny 192.168.33.8 0.0.0.255`
      `access-list 1 permit 192.168.33.0 0.0.0.0`
      `access-list 1 deny any`

10. Where should a standard access-list be placed?
    A. Close to the source
    B. Close to the destination
    C. In the core
    D. At the distribution level

11. What is this access list function?
   `Access-list 1 deny 136.147.27.236 0.0.0.0`
   `          Access-list 1 permit any`

   `Int ethernet 0`
   `   Ip address 136.146.27.1 255.255.255.0`
   `   Ipx network 1f3c`
   `   Ip access-group 1 in`

   A. Keeps traffic originating from 136.146.27.236 from being received on ethernet 0
   B. Keeps traffic destined for 136.146.27.236 from being received on ethernet 0
   C. Keeps all traffic originating from the ethernet from transmitting through ethernet 0
   D. Keeps all IP traffic originating from the ethernet from transmitting through ethernet 0

12. Is the following access list valid?
   `Access-list 1 deny 136.146.27.236 0.0.0.0`

   A. Yes
   B. No, there is an implied deny any at the end

13. Name the three logical parts of the IPX Network Layer header.
    A. Network, host, port
    B. Network, host, socket
    C. Network, subnetwork, port
    D. Network, host, sublayer

14. Sap filters access-list numbers are _____.
    A. 500–599
    B. 600–699
    C. 100–199
    D. 1000–1099

15. IPX standard access-list numbers are _____.
    A. 800–899
    B. 900–999
    C. 1000–1099
    D. 100–199

16. IPX extended access-list numbers are _____.
    A. 800–899
    B. 700–799
    C. 600–699
    D. 900–999

17. What command applies an outbound sap filter to an interface?
- **A.** `ipx output-sap-filter`
- **B.** `sap-output-filter`
- **C.** `sap-outbound-filter`
- **D.** `outbound-sap-filter`

18. The acronym ACL is short for _____.
- **A.** Access Common List
- **B.** All Control Lines
- **C.** Access Control List
- **D.** None of the above

19. Novell SAP protocol uses _____ for router and server updates.
- **A.** Multicast
- **B.** Broadcast
- **C.** Anycast
- **D.** Unicast

20. In a Novell network, how does a client find the nearest server?
- **A.** ARP request
- **B.** SAP request
- **C.** GNS request
- **D.** Must be statically into the client

21. What affect do input sap filters have on router SAP tables?
- **A.** No affect l
- **B.** Little affect
- **C.** Increase the size
- **D.** Decrease the size

22. What affect do output sap filters have on routers SAP tables?
- **A.** No affect
- **B.** Little affect
- **C.** Increase the size
- **D.** Decrease the size

23. What would be some good reasons for using SAP filters?
- **A.** Because the capability is there
- **B.** To reduce the amount of unnecessary broadcast traffic
- **C.** To restrict access to certain IPX services
- **D.** To reduce bandwidth utilization

Access List Answers

1. B
2. D
3. B
4. C
5. A
6. B
7. A
8. D
9. A
10. B
11. A
12. A
13. B
14. D
15. A
16. D
17. A
18. C
19. B
20. C
21. D
22. A
23. B, C, D

Serial Connection

1. What are three basic types of WAN services that the CISCO router can use?
    A. Call setup services, TDM, Packet Data services (X.25, FR and ATM)
    B. Call setup services, TDM, FDM
    C. SS7, FDM, STDM
    D. None of above

2. TDM WAN services offers and are usually traditional _____ circuits?
    A. fixed time slots; lease line circuits point-to-point
    B. sets up and clears calls between hosts; SVCs
    C. non-dedicated path between source and destination, SVCs
    D. uses virtual circuits, PVCs

3. What are the two components on a WAN interface and which component is the router?
    A. DTE and DCE, router is DTE
    B. CPE and DTE, router is DTE
    C. CPE and DCE, router is DCE
    D. CPE and CO, router is CP

4. Is Cisco HDLC protocol interoperable with other vendors HDLC?
    A. Yes. HDLC is a standard.
    B. No. Cisco HDLC is a proprietary implementation.

5. What is a common standard found at the physical level standard for X.25?
    A. RS-232
    B. RS-449
    C. X.21 bis
    D. X.25

6. ISDN stands for _____?
    A. I still don't no and provides an integrated voice and data capability service to the customer
    B. Integrated Services Digital Network and provides an integrated voice and data capability service to the customer premise
    C. Integrated Switched Digital Network and provides voice grade service to the customer

7. The Bearer channel speed is _____ and the D-Channel speed is _____?
    A. 128K, 64K
    B. 64K, 16K
    C. 64K, 64K
    D. None of above

8. The ISDN standard is organized into three groups. What are the groups and what does each groups specify?
    A. E, I and Q Series. E-Addressing scheme; I-Concepts and Terminology; Q-Signalling standards
    B. S/T, U, and I Series. S/T – Interfaces specification; U-Users interface; I-Concepts and Terminology
    C. TA, S/T, and U Series. TA – Terminal interface; S/T – Interface specification; U-Users interface

9. What are the two types of access a customer may subscribe?

    A. BRI, PRI   **C.** DDR, PPP

    B. BRI, DDR   **D.** BRI, Q.931

10. If you are connecting an ISDN circuit to your router into a Series interface, what kind of device must you connect into the serial port?

    A. TA   **C.** S/T

    B. NT1   **D.** TE1

Serial Connection Answers

1. A
2. A
3. A
4. B
5. C
6. B
7. B
8. A
9. A
10. A

Frame Relay

1. Frame Relay is _____?
   - **A.** Connection-oriented
   - **B.** Connectionless
   - **C.** Connectionless acknowledged
   - **D.** Connectionless acknowledged

2. What protocol is the predecessor to FR?
   - **A.** SNA
   - **B.** HDLC
   - **C.** SDLC
   - **D.** X.25

3. What are the two FR encapsulation types supported within the CISCO IOS?
   - **A.** CISCO, IETF
   - **B.** CISCO, ANSI
   - **C.** ANSI, IETF
   - **D.** None of the above

4. What are the three LMI types that are supported within the CISCO IOS?
   - **A.** CISCO, ANSI, Q931
   - **B.** CISCO, ANSI, IETF
   - **C.** CISCO, ANSI, Q921
   - **D.** CISCO, ANSI, Q933a

5. What is the top speed for FR connections is _____?
   - **A.** 45Mbps
   - **B.** 10Mbps
   - **C.** 56Kbps
   - **D.** 64Kbps

6. Frame Relay networks are considered to be ____?
   - **A.** non-broadcast
   - **B.** broadcast
   - **C.** multicast
   - **D.** point-to-point

7. With Frame-relay, the encapsulation type should agree between _____?
   - **A.** end devices
   - **B.** the end device and the switch
   - **C.** switches
   - **D.** the end devices and the switches

8. With Frame-relay, the LMI type should agree between _____?
   - **A.** end devices
   - **B.** the end device and the switch
   - **C.** switches
   - **D.** the end devices and the switches

9. A frame relay switch makes decisions based on _____?
   - **A.** Application Layer addresses
   - **B.** Network Layer addresses
   - **C.** Data Link Layer address
   - **D.** none of the above

10. CIR refers to _____?
    - **A.** the minimum bandwidth available on a frame relay link
    - **B.** the maximum bandwidth available on a frame relay link
    - **C.** the average bandwidth available on a frame relay link
    - **D.** the guaranteed bandwidth available on a frame relay link

11. The end node addressing for frame-relay is _____?
    A. BECN
    B. FECN
    C. DLCI
    D. ESI

12. The DLCI for frame relay is guaranteed to be unique _____?
    A. across the frame relay cloud
    B. across a providers frame relay network
    C. across the router's interface
    D. across a frame relay switch's interfaces
    E. none of the above

13. The Frame relay service address provided by the service provider is called a _____?
    A. DLCI
    B. X.121
    C. SPID
    D. Telephone number

14. When configuring a frame relay static route, you must specify _____?
    A. the destination layer 3 address and local DLCI
    B. the destination layer 3 address and destination DLCI
    C. the local layer 3 address and local DLCI
    D. any of the above

15. LMI is the _____?
    A. signaling interface between the router and the Frame Relay Switch
    B. X.25 signaling format
    C. ISDN signaling interface
    D. V.35 connection to DECNet

16. In order to support a point-to-multipoint configuration, a Cisco router interface must be configured manually with _____?
    A. sub-interfaces
    B. MAC addresses
    C. DLCIs
    D. none of the above

17. Which of the following element in a frame is not used for congestion control?
    A. Forward Explicit Congestion Notification
    B. DLCI/DL-CORE Indication
    C. Backward Explicit Congestion Notification
    D. Discard Eligibility

Frame Relay Answers

1. A
2. D
3. A
4. D
5. A
6. A
7. B
8. B
9. C
10. D
11. C
12. E
13. A
14. A
15. A
16. A
17. B

PPP

1. PPP stands for _____?
   A. Point-to-Point Protocol
   B. Packet-to-Packet Protocol
   C. Point-to-Packet Protocol
   D. None of the above

2. PPP can be configured on which of the following types of interfaces?
   A. Asynchronous serial
   B. HSSI
   C. ISDN
   D. Synchronous serial
   E. All of the above

3. During LCP negotiations what parameters are negotiated?
   A. Authentication
   B. Compression
   C. Error Detection
   D. Multilink
   E. None of above
   F. All of the above

4. What is negotiated during the NCP negotiation phases?
   A. Window size
   B. Inverse ARP
   C. The layer 3 protocol
   D. Flow control mechanism

5. What are the two types of authentication methods commonly used with PPP?
   A. TACACS
   B. SecurID
   C. PAP and CHAP
   D. RADIUS

PPP Answers

1. A
2. E
3. F
4. C
5. C

Ethernet Switching

1. What are the three types of switching modes?
   A. Store-and-forward, real-time, Fragmentation
   B. Store-and-forward, real-time, Fragmented
   C. Store-and-forward, Cut-through, FragmentFree
   D. Store-and-forward, real-time, Fragment

2. Of the three types of switching modes, which one carries the most latency?
   A. Store-and-forward
   B. Real-time
   C. Cut-through
   D. Fragmentation

3. What is the minimum legal size of an Ethernet frame?
   A. 1518 bytes
   B. 48 bytes
   C. 24 bytes
   D. 64 byte

Ethernet Switching Answers

1. C
2. A
3. D

Basic Router Operations

1. What are various sources from which a router may be configured?
    A. Console Port
    B. Auxiliary Port
    C. Virtual Terminals
    D. TFTP
    E. All of the above

2. To configure a router from the console port, what type of application must you run on the desktop?
    A. Any asynchronous terminal emulation software
    B. ConfigMaker
    C. Windows Hyperterminal
    D. None of the above

3. What two internal router components does router configuration information reside?
    A. RAM
    B. NVRAM
    C. FLASH
    D. ROM

4. The Cisco IOS resides in _____. The _____ and _____ resides in ROM.
    A. FLASH; bootstrap program and IOS subnet
    B. FLASH; backup IOS and configuration file
    C. FLASH; configuration file and bootstrap program
    D. None of the above

5. What are the two user interface modes on a router and what symbols indicates the respective mode?
    A. User and Privilege; >,#
    B. User and Manager; >,#
    C. User and Root; >,#
    D. User and Super; >,#

6. To recall the last command entered, used the _____key? (Select all that apply)
    A. up arrow
    B. control P
    C. control H
    D. down key

7. To show all available command while in an EXEC mode, enter the _____ key?
    A. help
    B. help ?
    C. help all
    D. ?

8. What is the key stroke for command completion?
    A. Tab
    B. Up arrow
    C. Down arrow
    D. Shift tab

9. When you go pass the end of line, what key stroke must you enter to get to the beginning of the line?
    A. Control A
    B. Control E
    C. Control B
    D. ESC A

10. When you go pass the end of line and you have to enter the key stroke to get you to beginning of line, what key stroke must you enter to get to the end of the line.
    A. Control A
    B. Control E
    C. Control B
    D. ESC A

11. To display the contents of the current configuration file enter what command? (select all that apply.)
    A. Show run
    B. Show running
    C. Show running-config
    D. All of the above

12. To display the contents of the backup configuration file, enter what command? (Select all that apply.)
    A. Show start
    B. Show startup-configuration
    C. Show startup-config
    D. All of the above
    E. A, C

13. The right-most four bits of the _____ determines where the bootstrap program is to get the IOS to load.
    A. config-regist
    B. config-reg
    C. config-register
    D. configuration register

14. Multiple _____ commands create a boot fallback sequence.
    A. boot
    B. config-regist
    C. boot system
    D. none of the above

15. To see what protocols are configured on the router use the _____ command.
    A. Show protocols
    B. Show protocols*
    C. Show protocol all
    D. Show protocol detail

16. What command should be entered to get into the global configuration mode? (Select all that apply.)
    A. Config-regist
    B. Config terminal
    C. Configure terminal
    D. Config t

17. To assign a banner to the router, use the _____ command?
    A. Banner login
    B. Banner motd
    C. Banner welcom
    D. none of the above

18. What command is use to assign a clockrate to an interface?
    A. Clock rate 56K
    B. Clock rate 56000
    C. Clockrate 56K
    D. Clockrate 56000

19. What command is used to determine if an interface is cabled as a DCE?
    A. Show controllers <interface> <interface number>
    B. Show controllers DCE interface
    C. Show controllers all
    D. none of the above

20. What are the ISDN switch types that are supported on Cisco routers?
    A. 5ESS
    B. NI1
    C. DMS100
    D. Seimens
    E. All of the above

21. What ISDN Specification Series describes number system?
    A. I-Series
    B. E-Series
    C. Q-Series
    D. A-Series

22. What ISDN Specification Series describes Switching and Signaling?
    A. I-Series
    B. E-Series
    C. Q-Series
    D. A-Series

23. What ISDN Specification Series describes Concepts and Terminology?
    A. I-Series
    B. E-Series
    C. Q-Series
    D. A-Series

24. What kind of interfaces does TA have?
    A. S/T
    B. U
    C. DTE
    D. DCE

25. What kind of interface does a NT1 have?
    A. S/T
    B. U
    C. DTE
    D. DCE

Basic Router Operations Answers

1. E
2. A, C
3. A, B
4. A
5. A
6. A
7. D
8. A
9. A
10. B
11. D
12. A, C
13. D
14. C
15. A
16. B, C, D
17. B
18. B
19. A
20. E
21. B
22. C
23. A
24. A
25. B

Cisco Discovery Protocol

1. CDP default periodic timer is _____?
   - **A.** 60
   - **B.** 30
   - **C.** 90
   - **D.** 180

2. CDP default holdtime is _____?
   - **A.** 60
   - **B.** 30
   - **C.** 90
   - **D.** 180

3. CDP uses a _____ address and is a _____ protocol?
   - **A.** Multicast; Data Link Layer
   - **B.** IP; Network
   - **C.** IPX; Network
   - **D.** IP; HDLC

4. What commands show a local routers neighbors IOS version number? (Select all that apply.)
   - **A.** `Show cdp neighbors`
   - **B.** `Show cdp entry <neighbors name>`
   - **C.** `Show cdp neighbors detail`
   - **D.** `Show cdp entry` *

5. What CDP command shows an abbreviated form of the advertised CDP information? (Select all that apply.)
   - **A.** `Show cdp neighbors`
   - **B.** `Show cdp neighbors detail`
   - **C.** `Show cdp entry` *
   - **D.** None of the above

Cisco Discovery Protocol Answers

1. A
2. D
3. A
4. B, C, D
5. A

CCNP Exam Bonus Questions

BCRAN

1. What does the M suffix in the Cisco 700 series indicate?
   A. faster Motorola CPU
   B. routers with 1.5 MB of system RAM
   C. routers with S/T interface
   D. multiprotocol support

2. Cisco 700 series routers support which of the following?
   A. IP protocol
   B. IPX protocol
   C. transparent bridging
   D. Appletalk protocol

3. Cisco 700 series routers support which of the following?
   A. DHCP relay agent
   B. DHCP server
   C. PAT
   D. TFTP Server

4. Cisco 700 series support which of the following routing protocols?
   A. RIP v1
   B. RIP v2
   C. EIGRP
   D. OSPF

5. Cisco 700 series have which of the following physical media support?
   A. ethernet 10 Mbps
   B. BRI
   C. PRI
   D. token ring
   E. analog telephone service

6. Cisco 700 series support which of the following ISDN switch types in North America?
   A. AT&T 5ESS
   B. Northern Telecom DMS 100
   C. NI-1
   D. NET3

7. Cisco 700 series support which of the following international ISDN swicth types?
   A. I-CTR3/NET3
   B. INS HSD 64/128
   C. VN3
   D. ITR 6
   E. TPH

8. Cisco 700 series configures with which of the following permanent profiles?
   A. LAN   D. external
   B. internal   E. system
   C. standard

9. Cisco 700 series support a maximum of _____ profiles.
   A. 16   C. 20
   B. 3   D. 4

A Cisco 700 series router has been configured with a user profile called Atlanta and Seattle. Answer the following questions:

10. Call from remote router (named Atlanta) will be accepted via _____ profile.
    A. LAN   D. Atlanta
    B. internal   E. Seattle
    C. standard

11. Call from unknown router is accepted via _____ profile.
    A. LAN   D. Atlanta
    B. internal   E. Seattle
    C. standard

12. Path for routing call from Atlanta router (if routing is enabled):
    A. user profile->bridge profile-> internal profile->IP/IPX routing engine-> LAN profile-> out to ethernet connection
    B. standard profile->bridge profile-> internal profile->IP/IPX routing engine-> LAN profile-> out to ethernet connection
    C. user profile-> IP/IPX routing engine-> LAN profile-> out to ethernet connection
    D. standard profile-> IP/IPX routing engine-> LAN profile-> out to ethernet connection

13. Path for routing unknown call (if routing is enabled):
    A. user profile->bridge profile-> internal profile->IP/IPX routing engine-> LAN profile-> out to ethernet connection
    B. standard profile->bridge profile-> internal profile->IP/IPX routing engine-> LAN profile-> out to ethernet connection
    C. user profile-> IP/IPX routing engine-> LAN profile-> out to ethernet connection
    D. standard profile-> IP/IPX routing engine-> LAN profile-> out to ethernet connection

14. Which of the following is true regarding the Cisco 700 series router command SET?
    A. SET automatically saves into NVRAM.
    B. You need to issue save (`wr mem`) command to activate the SET command.
    C. You need to reload the router to activate the SET command.
    D. SET is not a valid command for Cisco 700 series routers.

15. Which of the following commands is used to view active configuration in Cisco 700 series routers?
    A. `download`   C. `write terminal`
    B. `show run`   D. `upload`

16. Which of the following commands is used to erase configuration in Cisco 700 series routers?
   A. `wr erase` followed by `reload`
   B. `set default` followed by `reload`
   C. `set default` followed by `reset`
   D. `wr erase` followed by `reset`

17. The command to specify the name of the Cisco 700 series router is:
   A. `Set name _____`
   B. `Set hostname _____`
   C. `Hostname _____`
   D. `Set systemname _____`
   E. `Set routername _____`

18. SPID is used for the following reason.
   A. to authenticate that a call request is within contract specified
   B. to set ISDN speed
   C. to indicate phone number to call
   D. to indicate ISDN channel the call will go through

19. SPID are used in the following ISDN switches.
   A. national ISDN–1
   B. DMS–100
   C. AT&T 5ESS
   D. NET3

20. Cisco 700 series routers support the following WAN encapsulations.
   A. PPP
   B. SLIP
   C. CPP
   D. HDLC

21. Which of the following commands is used to monitor routing in the Cisco 700 series routers?
   A. `sh ip configuration all`
   B. `sh ip route all`
   C. `sh lan route`
   D. `sh wan route`

22. Which of the following commands is used to authenticate the ISDN caller in 760 routers?
   A. `set SPID _____`
   B. `set callidreceive _____`
   C. `set caller _____`
   D. `set callerid _____`

23. Which of the following commands is used to authenticate the ISDN caller in IOS 2500 routers:
   A. `isdn caller _____`
   B. `isdn SPID _____`
   C. `isdn callid _____`
   D. `isdn phoneid _____`

24. True or False: PPP callback is supported in Cisco 700 series routers.
   A. True
   B. False

25. Which of the following is an equivalent IOS command of `IP helper _____` in a 700 series router?
   A. `set dhcp relay _____`
   B. `set dhcp server _____`
   C. `set ip helper _____`
   D. `set bootp server _____`

26. To view the DHCP configuration in 700 series router:
   A. `show dhcp relay server`
   B. `show dhcp server`
   C. `show dhcp config`
   D. `sh ip config`

27. The command `set ppp authentication outgoing chap` indicates:
    A. Set the 700 series router to authenticate outgoing WAN call.
    B. Set the 700 series router to authenticate incoming WAN call.
    C. This is the default in Cisco 700 series routers.
    D. Authentication is required for incoming chap.

28. Standard Profile in 700 series is used for
    A. routing traffic to ethernet interface
    B. determining how data is passed between the bridge engine and the IP/IPX router engine
    C. incoming ISDN connections that do not have a profile
    D. all calls before forwarding to user profile

29. The Data Link layer protocol in ISDN D-channel is
    A. LAPB   C. LAPD
    B. LABM   D. LABC

30. True or False: ISDN PRI require NT1.
    A. True   B. False

31. ISDN PRI generally is configured over
    A. T1   C. T3
    B. E1   D. E3

32. PPP encapsulation can be used with
    A. asynchronous serial   C. synchronous serial
    B. ISDN   D. ATM circuits

33. PPP LCP negotiate the following options:
    A. authentication   C. multilink
    B. compression   D. line quality

34. X.25 Data Link layer protocol:
    A. LAPD   C. PPP LCP
    B. LAPB   D. HDLC

35. The Ready LED in a Cisco 3600 router front panel indicates
    A. Router is forwarding data packets.
    B. 3600 router is active.
    C. Functional module has been installed.
    D. Network activity in the module is installed.

36. Enable (EN) LED in network modules indicates
    A. Router is forwarding data packets.
    B. Module has passed its self-test and is available to the router.
    C. Functional module has been installed.
    D. Network activity in the module is installed.

37. **Link** LED in Ethernet module indicates
    A. Functional module has been installed.
    B. Network activity in the module is installed.
    C. Ethernet port is receiving the link integrity signal from the hub.

38. Digital modem modules have 5 LEDs, which indicate
    A. It has 5 digital modems.
    B. It has 5 MICA module banks that passed diagnostics.
    C. It has 5 analog modems module banks.
    D. The state of the internal modems like DCD, Rx, TX, DTR and DSR.

39. Current FCC regulations limit modem speeds to _____ in the United States.
    A. 56 Kbps   C. 51 Kbps
    B. 53 Kbps   D. 33.6 Kbps

40. RS-232 standard defines the interface between
    A. DTE and DCE   C. DTE and DTE
    B. DCE and DCE   D. UNI and NNI

41. RTS signal indicates
    A. DCE has buffers available to receive from DTE.
    B. DTE has buffers available to receive from DCE.
    C. Modem is in online mode.
    D. Modem is in offline mode.

42. The common data compression protocol used in modems is
    A. predictor and stacker   C. MNP 2 and MNP 5
    B. MNP 5 and v.42 bis   D. MNP 4 and LAPM

43. The common error control protocol used in modems is
    A. MNP4 and LAPM   C. LAPM, LAPD, LABP
    B. MNP4 and MNP 5   D. CRC 16

44. Which compression algorithms will provide a 4:1 compression ratio?
    A. V.42 bis   C. MNP 5
    B. V.42   D. MNP 4

45. The newest modem standard for 56 Kbps is
    A. V.53   C. V.56
    B. V.90   D. xDSL

46. Which of the following are ways to terminate an existing modem connection?
    A. DTE Initiated : NAS drops DTR.
    B. DCE Initiated : NAS detects Carrier Detect (CD) low and terminates connection.
    C. DCE Initiated : MODEM drops DTR.
    D. DTE Initiated : MODEM detects DC low and terminates connection.

47. Which of the following represents null modem wiring with DB-25 connector: (Pin 2 = TxD, Pin 3 = RxD, Pin 4 = RTS, Pin 5 = CTS, Pin 6 = DSR, Pin 7 = GND, Pin20 = DTR)
    A. 3->3,2->2, 7->7, 4->4, 5->5, 6->6, 20->20
    B. 2->3,3->2, 20->7, 7->20, 5->6, 6->4, 4->5
    C. 2->3,3->2, 7->7, 4->5, 5->4, 20->6, 6->20
    D. 2->3,3->2, 7->7, 20->5, 5->4, 4->6, 6->20

48. TTY lines correspond to
    A. synchronous interface   C. incoming Telnet session
    B. asynchronous interface   D. virtual terminal

49. Which of the following is the command to suspend a session in IOS?
    A. Alt-Shift-6 followed by Z
    B. Alt-Shift-7 followed by Z
    C. Control-c
    D. Control-Shift-6 followed by X

50. Which of the following is the command to display current connections for the user?
    A. `show session`   C. `show line`
    B. `show users`   D. `show connection`

51. AccO and AccI fields in the show line output command indicates
    A. accumulated output/input noise
    B. accepted number of packets
    C. output and input access-list number configured for the line
    D. total input/output accounting information

52. A typical escape sequence in modems is
    A. - - -   C. ~ ~ ~
    B. +++   D. atdt

53. Which of the following is a modem command to load factory settings?
    A. AT   C. AT&T
    B. ATDT   D. AT&F

BCRAN Answers

1. B
2. A, B, C
3. A, B, C
4. A, B
5. A, B, E
6. A, B, C
7. A, B, C, D, E
8. A, B, C
9. C
10. D
11. C
12. A
13. B
14. A
15. D
16. A
17. C
18. A
19. A, B
20. A, C
21. A, B
22. B
23. A
24. A
25. A
26. C
27. B
28. C
29. C
30. A
31. A, B
32. A, B, C
33. A, B, C
34. B
35. C
36. B, C
37. C
38. B
39. B
40. A
41. B
42. B
43. A
44. A
45. B
46. A, B
47. C

48. B
49. D
50. A
51. C
52. B
53. D

VOIP Questions

1. Which of the following are the 4 components in an H.323 framework?
   A. terminal
   B. gateway
   C. gatekeeper
   D. MCU
   E. RAS
   F. PBX

2. Which component is the "brain" of the H.323 framework?
   A. terminal
   B. gateway
   C. gatekeeper
   D. MCU
   E. RAS
   F. PBX

3. Which of the following statements are true about H.323?
   A. H.323 is an umbrella recommendation from ITU.
   B. This standard is for multimedia communication over LANs and does not provide QoS.
   C. This standard specifies components, protocols, and procedures that provide multimedia communication service over packet networks.
   D. H.323 is another buzzword in the industry.
   E. H.323 is a sophisticated compression technique.

4. What is the default queue technique in Cisco router speeds less than T1/E1?
   A. FIFO
   B. WFQ
   C. PQ
   D. CQ

5. Select the following true statements:
   A. WFQ assigns a weight to each flow, which determines the transmit order for queued packets.
   B. Fair queue brings interactive traffic packets to the front of the queue to reduce response time.
   C. WFQ works with both of Cisco's primary QoS signaling techniques, IP Precedence and RSVP.
   D. WFQ schedules interactive traffic to the front of the queue to reduce response time, and it fairly shares the remaining bandwidth between high-bandwidth flows.

6. WFQ weights are affected by
   A. frame relay discard eligible (DE)
   B. frame relay FECN
   C. frame relay BECN
   D. CIR
   E. Bc
   F. Be

7. Which of the following can be done with VoIP to improve voice quality?
   A. `MTU bytes`
   B. `fair-queue [congestive-discard-threshold [dynamic-queues [reservable-queues]]]`
   C. `traffic-shape rate bit-rate [burst-size [excess-burst-size]]`
   D. `frame-relay ip rtp header-compression`
   E. `ppp multilink`
   F. `ppp mulitlink interleave`
   G. `req-qos {best-effort | controlled load| guaranteed-delay}`
   H. `ip precedence number`
   I. `ip rsvp bandwidth [interface-kbps] [single-flow-kbps]`
   J. `vad`

8. What is the propagation delay for heritage per km?
   A. 5 microseconds per kilometer
   B. 6 microseconds per kilometer
   C. 7 microseconds per kilometer
   D. 1 microseconds per kilometer

9. A remote phone is attached at port 1/0/0. The command to route voice call to IP 10.16.1.4 is
   A. `session target ip 10.16.1.4`   C. `session target ip:10.16.1.4`
   B. `session target ipv4:10.16.1.4`   D. `port 1/0/0`

10. A local phone is attached to port 1/0/1 in Cisco 2600. How do you specify the phone number for the attached phone?
    A. no need to hard code the phone number
    B. Configure in IOS CLI : dial-peer voice 1 pots
       Destination-pattern 100
       Port 1/0/1
    C. Configure in IOS CLI : dial-peer voice 1 pots
       Destination-pattern 100
       Session target 1/0/0
    D. Configure in IOS CLI : dial-peer voice 1 pots
       Session target 100 1/0/1

11. What protocol header needs to be in place for carrying voice across IP?
    A. RTP   C. PCM stream
    B. VoFr based on Frf.11   D. http

12. What is the total header involved in carrying voice across an IP network (exclude the layer two protocol header)?
    A. IP (30 bytes) + TCP (20 bytes) + RTCP (12 bytes) = 62 bytes
    B. IP (10 bytes) + RTP (12 bytes) = 22 bytes
    C. IP (2 byes) + UDP (8 bytes) + 10 byes = 20 bytes
    D. IP (20 bytes) + UDP (8 bytes) + RTP (12 bytes) = 40 bytes

13. What are the interfaces supported by frame relay configuration in Mc3810?
    A. serial 0   C. serial 0:X
    B. serial 4   D. serial 1:x

14. Select the following correct statements:
    A. Frame relay is a networking technology that allows multiple logical paths to be connected via a single access line to form virtual meshed networks.
    B. Frame relay and TDM based networks are the same.
    C. Frame relay and X.25 are the same with the only difference being in regional deployment.
    D. Mc3810 supports voice over X.25 networks.

15. True or False: For frame relay, both data and voice segments can be configured to use the same PVC.
    A. True   B. False

16. To improve voice quality in VoFr, which of the following needs to be done?
    A. frame fragmentation
    B. voice prioritization
    C. traffic shaping to ensure no discard of voice frames
    D. voice compression

17. What is the industry standard for fragmentation?
    A. FRF.9   C. FRF.12
    B. FRF.5   D. FRF.11

18. What is the bandwidth required for voice over frame relay per call for G.729 compression?
    A. 10 Kbps
    B. 8 Kbps
    C. 64 Kbps
    D. bandwidth largely varies, depends on how loud a talker speaks in the phone

19. Where are the precedence bits located in the IP header?
    A. RTP header   C. TTL
    B. Protocol   D. TOS

20. The H.322 gatekeeper is required to perform which of the following?
    A. address translation   D. zone management
    B. admission control   E. multipoint conference
    C. bandwidth management

21. Which of the following analog voice modules are supported in Cisco voice-capable devices?
    A. FXS
    B. FXO
    C. E&M
    D. software-configurable interface that supports FXS, FXO, and E&M

22. Which of the following are Cisco voice-capable devices?
    A. Cisco 2600   D. MC3810
    B. Cisco 3600   E. Cisco 2500
    C. Cisco 7200/7500

23. Which of the following are Cisco voice-capable devices that support VoIP?
    A. Cisco 2600   D. MC3810
    B. Cisco 3600   E. Cisco 2500
    C. Cisco 7200/7500

24. How many network modules can be installed in Cisco 2600?
    A. 1   C. 3
    B. 2   D. 4

25. How many network modules can be installed in Cisco 3620?
    A. 1   C. 3
    B. 2   D. 4

26. How many network modules can be installed in Cisco 3640?

    A. 1   **C.** 3

    B. 2   **D.** 4

27. How many analog voice ports can be installed in Cisco 3810?

    A. 2   **C.** 6

    B. 4   **D.** 8

VOIP Answers

1. A, B, C, D
2. C
3. A, B, C
4. B
5. A, B, C, D
6. A, B, C
7. A, B, C, D, E, F, G, H
8. B
9. A
10. B
11. A
12. D
13. A, B, C
14. A
15. A
16. A, B, C
17. C
18. A
19. D
20. A, B, C, D
21. A, B, C
22. A, B, C, D
23. A, B, C
24. A
25. B
26. D
27. C

PIX

1. What is the meaning of stateful firewall?
   A. secure method of analyzing data packets that places extensive information about a data packet into a table
   B. real-time embedded OS
   C. routers with access-list
   D. state of health of any firewall

2. Select the correct security level for a PIX firewall:
   A. security level 0—outside, security level 50—DMZ, security level 100—inside
   B. security level 100—outside, security level 50—DMZ, security level 0—inside
   C. security level 100—outside, security level 50—DMZ, security level 1—inside
   D. security level 50—outside, security level 100—DMZ, security level 0—inside

3. Which of the following does Cisco PIX firewall support?
   A. 10/100 Mbps ethernet NIC   C. 10 Mbps ethernet NIC
   B. 4/16 Mbps token ring NIC   D. 4 Mbps token ring NIC

4. PIX firewall runs on which of the following OS?
   A. NT   C. IOS
   B. UNIX   D. Cisco Embedded Operating System

5. The PIX processor is a _____ CPU.
   A. Motorola   C. AMD
   B. Intel Pentium   D. Cisco Secure Processor

6. Which of the following are recommended Pix firewall LAN configuration interfaces?
   I. 2 Ethernet NIC
   II. 3 Ethernet NIC
   III. 3 Token Ring NIC
   IV. 2 Ethernet NIC and 1 Token Ring NIC
   V. 2 Token Ring NIC
   VI. 1 Ethernet NIC and 1 Token Ring NIC
   A. I, II, III, IV, V, VI   C. I, II, III, IV, V
   B. I, II, IV, V, VI   D. I, II, III

7. A Pix firewall can authenticate which of the following traffic:
   I. Telnet
   II. FTP
   III. HTTP
   IV. SHTTP
   A. I, II, III, IV
   B. I, II, III
   C. I, II
   D. I

8. Which of the following are ways to access a PIX firewall:
   I. User Authentication (TACACS+ or RADIUS Database)
   II. Static conduit (tunnel) map
   III. Response to valid outbound user request form inside
   IV. Via Cisco authenticated license Key
   A. I, II, III, IV   C. I, II
   B. I, II, III   D. I

9. Choose the correct statement:
   A. Cisco PIX firewalls support load balancing between two PIX firewalls.
   B. Cisco PIX firewalls support Nat and PAT.
   C. Cisco IOS feature set runs in the PIX firewall.
   D. Cisco PIX firewall is able to run IGRP and EIGRP routing protocols.

PIX Answers

1. A
2. A
3. A, B, C
4. D
5. B
6. B
7. B
8. B
9. B

MC3810—Questions

1. MC3810 has which of the following physical interfaces?
   - **A.** UIO SO
   - **B.** UIO S1
   - **C.** 10/100 Mbs Ethernet
   - **D.** Chanalized T1/E1 Interface

2. The MC3810 default clock is internal Stratum level
   - **A.** 1
   - **B.** 2
   - **C.** 3
   - **D.** 4

3. The MC3810 default clock source is if both DVM and MFT are installed.
   - **A.** controller 1
   - **B.** controller 0
   - **C.** serial 0
   - **D.** SCB

4. In MC3810, clock conflicts are avoided by using which of the following IOS commands?
   - **A.** `network clock base rate`
   - **B.** `vlock rate network`
   - **C.** `network-clock-select`
   - **D.** `clock rate`

5. How much bandwidth needs to be allocated for a voice over a HDLC circuit for 5 simultaneous phone calls with G.729a?
   - **A.** 40 Kbps
   - **B.** 50 Kbps
   - **C.** 8 Kbps
   - **D.** 10 Kbps

6. How much bandwidth is needed to allocate for a voice over a HDLC circuit for 5 simultaneous phone calls with G.729?
   - **A.** 40 Kbps
   - **B.** 50 Kbps
   - **C.** 8 Kbps
   - **D.** 10 Kpbs

7. How much bandwidth is needed to allocate for a voice over a HDLC circuit for 5 simultaneous phone calls with G.726?
   - **A.** 40 Kbps
   - **B.** 50 Kbps
   - **C.** 175 Kbps
   - **D.** 160 Kbps

8. How much bandwidth is needed to allocated for a voice over a HDLC circuit for 5 simultaneous phone calls with G.711?
   - **A.** 70 Kbps
   - **B.** 350 Kbps
   - **C.** 87 Kbps
   - **D.** 160 Kbps

9. What is the default frame size for VOHDLC voice frames for G.729a?
   - **A.** 37 bytes
   - **B.** 30 bytes
   - **C.** 17 bytes
   - **D.** 10 bytes

10. What is the default frame size for VOHDLC voice frames for G.729?
   - **A.** 37 bytes
   - **B.** 30 bytes
   - **C.** 17 bytes
   - **D.** 10 bytes

11. What is the default frame size for VOHDLC voice frames for G.726?
   A. 80 bytes   C. 10 bytes
   B. 30 bytes   D. 87 bytes

12. What is the default frame size for VOHDLC voice frames for G.711?
   A. 87 bytes   C. 711 bytes
   B. 80 bytes   D. 100 bytes

13. What is the recommended data fragmentation size for a 128K leased circuit form Atlanta to NY?
   A. 160 bytes
   B. 128 bytes
   C. 1500 bytes
   D. depends on distance measured between Atlanta and NY
   E. depends on propagation delay experienced from Atlanta to NY

14. What is the IOS command to enable voice on an HDLC circuit?
   A. `Hold queue`
   B. `encapsulation hdlc voice`
   C. `voice encapsulation`

15. Is traffic shaping a must for a VOHDLC leased circuit?
   A. yes   C. may be
   B. no   D. depends on bandwidth usage

16. What is the global command to route voice traffic?
   A. `voice-port`   C. `router igrp 200`
   B. `dial-peer`   D. `voice-encap`

17. What are the commands to route a voice call to serial 1 for phone number 232?
   A. `dial-peer voice 1 vohdlc`
      `destination-pattern s1`
      `session target 232`
   B. `dial-peer voice 232 vohdlc`
      `session target s 1`
   C. `dial-peer voice 232 vohdlc`
      `destination-pattern 2`
      `session target s 1`
   D. `dial-peer voice 2. vohdlc`
      `destination-pattern 232`
      `session target s 1`

18. To hear a dial tone in a local phone attached to the MC3810 port 1/1, which of the following needs to be done by an administrator?
   A. `voice-port 1/1, no shut`
   B. `voice-port 1/1, enable dial-tone`
   C. No need to do anything; user should be able to listen dial tone by default (factory setting).
   D. `voice-port 1/1, dial-type dtmf`

19. What is the hold-queue size when voice is enabled in the serial lines?
- **A.** 1024 bytes
- **B.** 64 bytes
- **C.** 128 bytes
- **D.** depends on segmentation size

20. How do you verify whether an interface is connected to a DTE or DCE cable in the MC3810?
- **A.** `show controller`
- **B.** `sh clock rate`
- **C.** `sh ver`
- **D.** `sh network-clock`

21. Which of the following are the voice transport encapsulations for MC3810?
- **A.** ATM
- **B.** frame relay
- **C.** HDLC
- **D.** PPP

22. How many voice calls can be compressed in the MC3810 (maximum)?
- **A.** 12
- **B.** 24
- **C.** 30
- **D.** 6

23. What are the options available for the clock source command?
- **A.** loop
- **B.** internal
- **C.** external
- **D.** line

24. What is the command used to view all the voice ports in brief view:
- **A.** `Sh voice port summary`
- **B.** `Sh interface brief`
- **C.** `Sh voice port brief`
- **D.** `Sh vocie port all`

25. How much bandwidth is needed to allocate a voice over a frame relay circuit for 5 simultaneous phone calls with G.729a?
- **A.** 40 Kbps
- **B.** 50 Kbps
- **C.** 8 Kbps
- **D.** 10 Kbps

26. How much bandwidth is needed to allocate a voice over a frame relay circuit for 5 simultaneous phone calls with G.729?
- **A.** 40 Kbps
- **B.** 50 Kbps
- **C.** 8 Kbps
- **D.** 10 Kbps

27. How much bandwidth is needed to allocate for a voice over frame relay circuit for 5 simultaneous phone calls with G.726?
- **A.** 40 Kbps
- **B.** 50 Kbps
- **C.** 175 Kbps
- **D.** 160 Kbps

28. How much bandwidth is needed to allocate for a voice over frame relay circuit for 5 simultaneous phone calls with G.711?
- **A.** 70 Kbps
- **B.** 350 Kbps
- **C.** 87 Kbps
- **D.** 160 Kbps

29. What is the default frame size for VOFR voice frames for G.729a?
- **A.** 37 bytes
- **B.** 30 bytes
- **C.** 17 bytes
- **D.** 10 bytes

30. What is the default frame size for VOFR voice frames for G.729?
- **A.** 37 bytes
- **B.** 30 bytes
- **C.** 17 bytes
- **D.** 10 bytes

31. What is the default frame size for VOFR voice frames for G.726?
- **A.** 80 bytes
- **B.** 30 bytes
- **C.** 10 bytes
- **D.** 87 bytes

32. What is the default frame size for VOFR voice frames for G.711?
- **A.** 87 bytes
- **B.** 80 bytes
- **C.** 711 bytes
- **D.** 100 bytes

33. What is the recommended data fragmentation size for a fractional T1 (4 DSO) leased circuit from Atlanta to NY with 128K PVC? Note: NY has full T1 (with 24 DSO).
- **A.** 160 bytes
- **B.** 320 bytes
- **C.** 1500 bytes
- **D.** 128 bytes

34. What is the IOS command to enable voice on a Frame Relay circuit?
- **A.** `encapsulation frame-relay 80`
- **B.** `frame-relay interface-dlci 200 vocie-encap 80`
- **C.** `voice encapsualtion 80`
- **D.** `voice-encapsualtion 80`

35. Select the correct order of the clocking hierarchy.
- **A.** controller t1 1, controller t1 0, serial 0, SCB
- **B.** SCB, serial 0, controller t1 0, controller t1 1
- **C.** controller t1 0, controller t1 1, serial 0, SCB
- **D.** serial 0, SCB, Controller t1 0, controller t1 1

36. Which is the default setting for a frame relay configuration in the MC3810?
- **A.** no frag-pre-queuing
- **B.** frag-pre-queuing
- **C.** fifo
- **D.** custom queue

37. What are the commands to route a voice call to serial1, local dlci 100, remote dlci 200 for phone number 232?
- **A.** `dial-peer voice 1 vofr`
      `destination-pattern s1 dlci 100`
      `session target 232`
- **B.** `dial-peer voice 232 vofr`
      `Destination-pattern 232`
      `session target s 1 100 200`
- **C.** `dial-peer voice 2 vofr`
      `destination-pattern 2`
      `session target s 1 100`
- **D.** `dial-peer voice 232 vofr`
      `destination-pattern 232`
      `session target s 1 200`

38. What is the command used to limit bandwidth used by a voice call?
- **A.** `bandwidth`
- **B.** `voice-encap`
- **C.** `voice-cir`
- **D.** `traffic-shaping frame-relay`

39. Which of the following commands are used for frame-relay traffic shaping?
    A. `frame-relay cir`
    B. `frame-relay be`
    C. `frame-relay adaptive-shaping becn`

40. How many DSPs will be taken by a 4 fax call made through a remote bank branch?
    A. 4 dsp
    B. 1 dsp
    C. 2 dsp
    D. No dsp is required since fax call is digital.

41. MFT is available as
    A. RJ-48 connection
    B. BNC connection
    C. MMF—fiber Multimode
    D. SMF—fiber single mode

42. MFT and DVM are available with which of the following options?
    A. T1
    B. E1
    C. T3
    D. OC-3

43. MC3810 is available as
    A. AC power 100 to 240 VAC
    B. DC power: −40 to −70 VDC
    C. AC power 110 only with +/−5%
    D. DC power with +48 VDC

44. Analog Mc3810 has which of the following slots?
    A. MFT
    B. VCM
    C. DVM
    D. AVM

45. Digital Mc3810 has which of the following slots?
    A. MFT
    B. VCM
    C. DVM
    D. AVM

46. How much bandwidth is needed to allocate a voice over an ATM circuit for 4 simultaneous phone calls with G.729a?
    A. 40 Kbps
    B. 60 Kbps
    C. 15 Kbps
    D. 43 Kbps

47. How much bandwidth is needed to allocate a voice over an ATM circuit for 5 simultaneous phone calls with G.729?
    A. 40 Kbps
    B. 60 Kbps
    C. 15 Kbps
    D. 43 Kbps

48. How much bandwidth is needed to allocate a voice over an ATM circuit for 5 simultaneous phone calls with G.726?
    A. 43 Kbps
    B. 200 Kbps
    C. 172 Kbps
    D. 1544 Kbps

49. How much bandwidth is needed to allocate a voice over a frame relay circuit for 5 simultaneous phone calls with G.711?
    A. 300 Kbps
    B. 340 Kbps
    C. 87 Kbps
    D. 1544 Kbps

50. What is the default frame size for VOATM voice frames for G.729a?
    - **A.** 53 bytes
    - **B.** 47 bytes
    - **C.** 48 bytes
    - **D.** 30 bytes

51. What is the default frame size for VOATM voice frames for G.729?
    - **A.** 53 bytes
    - **B.** 47 bytes
    - **C.** 48 bytes
    - **D.** 30 bytes

52. What is the total default frame size for VOATM voice frames for G.726?
    - **A.** 53 bytes
    - **B.** 53 cells
    - **C.** 1500 bytes
    - **D.** 2 cells

53. What is the total default frame size for VOFR voice frames for G.711?
    - **A.** 2 ATM cells
    - **B.** 53 bytes
    - **C.** 106 cells
    - **D.** 100 bytes

54. What is the recommended data fragmentation size for a T1/ATM circuit from Atlanta to NY with a 128K PVC voice channel?
    - **A.** 160 bytes
    - **B.** 320 bytes
    - **C.** 1500 bytes
    - **D.** No need to define ATM segmentation size.

55. What is the IOS command to enable voice on an ATM pvc circuit?
    - **A.** `Aal1`
    - **B.** `Aa5voice`
    - **C.** `Aal5snap`
    - **D.** `voice-encapsualtion 80`

56. Which of the following parameters are needed to configure aa5voice?
    - **A.** Peak-rate
    - **B.** Average-rate
    - **C.** burst
    - **D.** clp

57. 768K video traffic that needs to be encapsulated into aal1 requires which of the following PVC circuits?
    - **A.** atm aal1 870 870
    - **B.** atm aa5snap 768 768
    - **C.** atm aal1 768 768
    - **D.** atm aal1 1536 768 30

58. What are the commands to route a voice call to serial1, local VCD 100, VPI 200, VCI 10, for phone number 232?
    - **A.** `dial-peer voice 1 voatm`
      `destination-pattern atm 0 dlci 100`
      `session target 232`
    - **B.** `dial-peer voice 232 voatm`
      `Destination-pattern 232`
      `session target atm 0 200`
    - **C.** `dial-peer voice 2 voatm`
      `destination-pattern 2`
      `session target atm 0 100`
    - **D.** `dial-peer voice 232 voatm`
      `destination-pattern 232`
      `session target atm 0 100 200 10`

59. How is the peak rate calculated for a voice call in an ATM PVC?
   A. average rate X 2
   B. bandwidth percall X 15kbps
   C. (# no calls possible) X 4
   D. (# of calls possible) X (bandwidth per call)

60. How is the average rate calculated for a voice call in an ATM PVC?
   A. average rate X 2
   B. bandwidth percall X 15kbps
   C. (# no calls possible) X 4
   D. (# of calls possible) X (bandwidth per call)

61. MC3810 supports which of the following RFC's?
   A. RFC 1483   **C.** RFC 3321
   B. RFC 2222   **D.** No RFC's will be supported.

62. MC3810 is fully compliant with the Frame Relay Forum's (FRF) definition of
   A. FRF-10   **C.** FRF-3
   B. FRF-5   **D.** FRF-8

63. True or False: Subinterfaces are supported on the MC3810 fr-atm interfaces.
   A. True   **B.** False

64. True or False: Traffic Shaping on the fr-atm interface should not be necessary because the frame traffic does not go to a frame-relay network.
   A. True   **B.** False

65. Select all the commands that are useful in a Frame Relay–ATM interworking environment:
   A. `show frame-relay pvc`   **D.** `show interface atm 0`
   B. `show interface fr-atm x`   **E.** `show controller T1/E1 0 or 1`
   C. `show atm pvc`   **F.** `show fr-atm pvc`

66. What is the command that connects an ATM circuit and an fr-atm circuit?
   A. `frame relay route 495 interface fr-atm 19 200`
   B. `fr-atm connect dlci 200 atm 0 pvc 5/50`
   C. `frame-relay interface-dlci 100 voice-encap 320`
   D. `encapsulation fr-atm`

67. The best practice for PCR calculation for aal5mux frame-relay is
   A. 1.1.3 x (FR CIR + Bc + Be)   **C.** 1.14 (FR CIR)
   B. 1.13 (FR CIR)   **D.** FR CIR

68. The best practice for PCR calculation for aal5mux frame-relay is
   A. 1.1.3 x (FR CIR + Bc + Be)   **C.** 1.14 (FR CIR)
   B. 1.13 (FR CIR)   **D.** FR CIR

69. Which of the following are the cards that are supported with the IGX for interworking?
   A. Frame Trunk Module (FTM)   **C.** Universal Voice Module (UVM)
   B. Frame Relay Module (FRM)   **D.** Channelized Voice Module (CVM)

70. Which of the following compressions are not supported by UVM?
- **A.** G.729
- **B.** G.711
- **C.** G.729a
- **D.** G.726

71. Select the level of interworking integration possible between the MC3810 and the IGX:
- **A.** overlay
- **B.** partial interworking
- **C.** Cisco's interworking
- **D.** full interworking

72. The max data frames exiting the FTM are no more than _____ bytes long.
- **A.** 77
- **B.** 70
- **C.** 1500
- **D.** 53

73. The max size of data payload exiting the FTM are no more than _____ bytes long.
- **A.** 77
- **B.** 70
- **C.** 1500
- **D.** 53

74. Select the different types of connections within the interworking functions:
- **A.** data connections
- **B.** management connections
- **C.** session connections
- **D.** voice connections
- **E.** frame connections
- **F.** cell connections

75. Directed voice connections must terminate on _____.
- **A.** UVM or CVM card
- **B.** another MC3810
- **C.** FTM cards elsewhere in the network
- **D.** FTM cards or another MC3810 (back to back)

76. Session voice connections must terminate on _____.
- **A.** UVM or CVM card
- **B.** another MC3810
- **C.** FTM cards elsewhere in the network
- **D.** FTM cards or another MC3810 (back to back)

77. Data connections must terminate on _____.
- **A.** UVM or CVM card
- **B.** another MC3810
- **C.** FTM cards elsewhere in the network
- **D.** FTM cards or another MC3810 (back to back)

78. Management connections must terminate on _____.
- **A.** UVM or CVM card
- **B.** another MC3810
- **C.** FTM cards elsewhere in the network
- **D.** FTM cards or another MC3810 (back to back)

MC3810 Answers

1. A, B, D
2. D
3. B
4. C
5. B
6. B
7. C
8. B
9. A
10. A
11. D
12. A
13. A
14. C
15. B
16. B
17. C
18. C
19. A
20. A
21. A, B, C, D
22. B
23. A, B, D
24. A
25. B
26. B
27. C
28. B
29. A
30. A
31. D
32. A
33. B
34. B, D
35. A
36. B
37. C
38. C
39. A, B, C
40. A
41. A, B
42. A, B
43. A, B
44. A, B, D
45. A, B, C
46. B
47. B
48. C

49. B
50. A
51. A
52. D
53. A
54. D
55. B
56. A, B
57. A
58. C
59. A
60. D
61. A
62. B
63. B
64. A
65. A, B, C, D, E
66. B
67. A
68. B
69. A, B, C, D
70. B
71. A, B, D
72. A
73. B
74. A, B, C
75. A
76. B
77. C
78. D

References

ATM Forum, ATM *User Network Interface* (UNI) Specification Version 3.0

ATM Forum, ATM *User Network Interface* (UNI) Specification Version 3.1

ATM Forum, ATM *User Network Interface* (UNI) Specification Version 4.0

ATM Forum, ATM *Interim Interswitch Signaling Protocol* (IISP) Specification

ATM Forum, *Private Network-Network Interface* Specification Version 1.0 (PNNI 1.0)

ATM Forum, LAN Emulation Over ATM 1.0

Banyan Vines Protocol Architecture Reference

Digital Equipment Corporation, DECnet Digital Network Architecture Phase IV General Description

`http://www.cisco.com/univercd/home/home.htm` (A special thanks to Cisco for providing outstanding resources)

Novell IPX Protocol Definition

RFC1795 Data Link Switching

RFC1001/1002 NetBios of TCP/IP

RFC1541 Dynamic Host Configuration Protocol

RFC1577 Classical IP and ARP over ATM

RFC1771 A Border Gateway Protocol 4(BGP-4)

Works Cited

IBM Token Ring Network Architecture Reference, 3rd ed. Order number SC30-3374-02.

Naugle, Matthew. *Network Protocol Handbook*, McGraw-Hill, Inc. 1994, ISBN 0-07-046461-8.

Kapoor, Atul. *SNA Architecture, Protocols, and Implementation*, McGraw-Hill, Inc. 1992, ISBN 0-07-033727-6.

Taylor, D Edgar. *The McGraw-Hill Internetworking Handbook*, McGraw-Hill, Inc. 1994, ISBN 0-07-063263-4.

Kessler, Gary C. and Peter Southwick. *ISDN Concepts, Facilities, and Services*, McGraw-Hill, Inc. 1996, ISBN 0-07-034249-0.

McDysan, David and Darren L. Spohn. *Hands-On ATM*, McGraw-Hill, Inc. 1998, ISBN 0-07-045047-1.

Schlar, Sherman K. *Inside X.25 A Managers Guide*, McGraw-Hill, Inc., ISBN 0-07-607007-7.

Apple Computer, Inc.'s Inside MACINTOSH Networking, Addison Wesley 1994.

Index

Symbols

link-access protocols, AppleTalk, 267
100BASE-T Ethernet, 46
100BASE-TX Ethernet, 45
802.3_RAW frames, 313

A

AAL (ATM Adaptation layer), ATM, 708, 715–717
AAL1, CBR Services (Constant Bit Rate), 718
AAL2, VBR Timing-Sensitive Services (Variable Bit Rate), 719
AAL3/4, 719
AAL5, SEAL (Simple and Efficient Adaptation Layer), 721
AARP addresses (AppleTalk Address Resolution Protocol), 267
  assigning, 268
  mapping, 269
ABM (asynchronous balanced mode), LLC2, 151

abnormal conditions, X.25 flow control, 847
ABR (Available Bit Rate), ATM, 739, 742
ABRs (Area Border Routers), OSPF, 525
AC field (Access Control), Token Ring frames, 54
access list filters, ISDN, 875
access restrictions, TCP/IP, 453
ACK packets, SPX, 351
acknowledge numbers, SPX, 352
active loops, 169
active monitors, Token Ring, 72–74
Active state, BGP, 589
Adaptation layer, ATM, 705
ADCCP (Advanced Data Communications Control Procedures), 821
Address field, Frame Relay, 812
Address Mask Reply messages, ICMP, 425
Address Mask Request messages, ICMP, 425

C

I

M

Q

R

Z

About the CD

The enclosed CD offers you additional tools to help you prepare for certification: actual configurations you can study and an interactive certification exam from FastTrak Express™. Note that all questions on the CD are sample questions that may not reflect the official Cisco® CCIE™ R/S # 350-001 exam.

Configurations

To help augment your understanding of real-world Cisco® networking, industry expert Roosevelt Giles has provided actual router configurations for you to review. These configurations provide you with in-depth debugging and troubleshooting examples to help you better understand the world of router configuration.

The configurations appear in PDF format. To read PDF format, you need Adobe Acrobat. If you do not have Adobe Acrobat, it is provided for you on the CD.

To launch Adobe Acrobat

1. Insert the CD-ROM in your CD-ROM drive.
2. Open the directory named "Acrobat."
3. Double-click on the file named RS40ENG.EXE and follow the instructions.

After you have Acrobat installed on your computer, you can view the configurations. To view,

1. Click on the PDF_TOC.PDF file to view a list of all the available configurations.
2. Click on the configuration you wish to view. You will automatically link to that configuration.

Additional information is included in a file named README.TXT.

FastTrak Express™

FastTrak Express provides interactive certification exams to help you prepare for certification. With the enclosed CD, you can test your knowledge of the topics covered in this book with more than 200 multiple choice questions.

To Install FastTrak Express

1. Insert the CD-ROM in your CD-ROM drive.
2. FastTrak Express Setup will launch automatically. Follow the instructions to complete the Setup.
3. When the Setup is finished, you may immediately begin using FastTrak Express.
4. FastTrak Express will ask you to insert a license key number before you begin. That number is 974313132303.

FastTrak Express offers two testing options: the Adaptive exam and the Standard exam.

The Adaptive Exam

The Adaptive exam style does not simulate all of the exam environments that are found on certification exams. You cannot choose specific subcategories for the adaptive exam, and after a question has been answered you cannot go back to a previous question.

You have a time limit in which to complete the adaptive exam. This time varies from subject to subject, although it is usually 15 to 25 questions in 30 minutes. When the time limit has been reached, your exam automatically ends.

To Take the Adaptive Exam

1. Click the Adaptive Exam button from the Main window. The Adaptive Exam window will appear.
2. Click the circle or square to the left of the correct answer.

   Note: There may be more than one correct answer. The text in the bottom left corner of the window instructs you to Choose the Best Answer (if there is only one answer) or Mark All Correct Answers (if there is more than one correct answer).
3. Click the Next button to continue.
4. To quit the test at any time, click the Finish button. After about 30 minutes, the exam exits to review mode.

After you have completed the Adaptive exam, FastTrak Express displays your score and the passing score required for the test.

- Click Details to display a chapter-by-chapter review of your exam results.
- Click on Report to get a full analysis of your score.

To Review the Adaptive Exam

After you have taken an Adaptive exam, you can review the questions, your answers, and the correct answers. You may review your questions only immediately after an Adaptive exam. To review your questions

1. Click the Correct Answer button.
2. To see your answer, click the Your Answer button.

The Standard Exam

After you have learned about your subject using the Adaptive sessions, you can take a Standard exam. This mode simulates the environment that might be found on an actual certification exam.

You cannot choose subcategories for a Standard exam. You have a time limit (this time varies from subject to subject, although it is usually 75 minutes) to complete the Standard exam. When this time limit has been reached, your exam automatically ends.

To Take the Standard Exam

1. Click the Standard Exam button from the Main window. The Standard Exam window will appear.
2. Click the circle or square to the left of the correct answer.

   Note: There may be more than one correct answer. The text in the bottom left corner of the window instructs you to Choose the Best Answer (if there is only one answer) or Mark All Correct Answers (if there is more than one correct answer).

3. If you are unsure of the answer and wish to mark the question so you can return to it later, check the Mark box in the upper lefthand corner.
4. To review which questions you have marked, which you have answered, and which you have not answered, click the Review button.
5. Click the Next button to continue.
6. To quit the test at any time, click the Finish button. After about 75 minutes, the exam exits to review mode.

After you have completed the Standard Exam, FastTrak Express displays your score and the passing score required for the test.

- Click Details to display a chapter-by-chapter review of your exam results.
- Click on Report to get a full analysis of your score.

To Review a Standard Exam

After you have taken a Standard exam, you can review the questions, your answers, and the correct answers.

You may review your questions only immediately after a Standard exam.

To review your questions

1. Click the Correct Answer button.
2. To see your answer, click the Your Answer button.

Changing Exams

FastTrakExpress provides several practice exams to test your knowledge. To change exams, select the exam for the test you want to run from the Select Exam window.

If you experience technical difficulties, please call (888) 992-3131. Outside the United States call (281) 992-3131. Or, you may e-mail `brucem@bfq.com`. For more information, visit the `BeachFrontQuizzer` site at `www.bfq.com`.

SOFTWARE AND INFORMATION LICENSE

The software and information on this diskette (collectively referred to as the "Product") are the property of The McGraw-Hill Companies, Inc. ("McGraw-Hill") and are protected by both United States copyright law and international copyright treaty provision. You must treat this Product just like a book, except that you may copy it into a computer to be used and you may make archival copies of the Products for the sole purpose of backing up our software and protecting your investment from loss.

By saying "just like a book," McGraw-Hill means, for example, that the Product may be used by any number of people and may be freely moved from one computer location to another, so long as there is no possibility of the Product (or any part of the Product) being used at one location or on one computer while it is being used at another. Just a book cannot be read by two different people in two different places at the same time, neither can the Product be used by two different people in two different places at the same time (unless, of course, McGraw-Hill's rights are being violated).

McGraw-Hill reserves the right to alter or modify the contents of the Product at any time.

This agreement is effective until terminated. The Agreement will terminate automatically without notice if you fail to comply with any provisions of this Agreement. In the event of termination by reason of your breach, you will destroy or erase all copies of the Product installed on any computer system or made for backup purposes and shall expunge the Product from your data storage facilities.

LIMITED WARRANTY

McGraw-Hill warrants the physical diskette(s) enclosed herein to be free of defects in materials and workmanship for a period of sixty days from the purchase date. If McGraw-Hill receives written notification within the warranty period of defects in materials or workmanship, and such notification is determined by McGraw-Hill to be correct, McGraw-Hill will replace the defective diskette(s). Send request to:

Customer Service
McGraw-Hill
Gahanna Industrial Park
860 Taylor Station Road
Blacklick, OH 43004-9615

The entire and exclusive liability and remedy for breach of this Limited Warranty shall be limited to replacement of defective diskette(s) and shall not include or extend any claim for or right to cover any other damages, including but not limited to, loss of profit, data, or use of the software, or special, incidental, or consequential damages or other similar claims, even if McGraw-Hill has been specifically advised as to the possibility of such damages. In no event will McGraw-Hill's liability for any damages to you or any other person ever exceed the lower of suggested list price or actual price paid for the license to use the Product, regardless of any form of the claim.

THE McGRAW-HILL COMPANIES, INC. SPECIFICALLY DISCLAIMS ALL OTHER WARRANTIES, EXPRESS OR IMPLIED, INCLUDING BUT NOT LIMITED TO, ANY IMPLIED WARRANTY OF MERCHANTABILITY OR FITNESS FOR A PARTICULAR PURPOSE. Specifically, McGraw-Hill makes no representation or warranty that the Product is fit for any particular purpose and any implied warranty of merchantability is limited to the sixty day duration of the Limited Warranty covering the physical diskette(s) only (and not the software or information) and is otherwise expressly and specifically disclaimed.

This Limited Warranty gives you specific legal rights; you may have others which may vary from state to state. Some states do not allow the exclusion of incidental or consequential damages, or the limitation on how long an implied warranty lasts, so some of the above may not apply to you.

This Agreement constitutes the entire agreement between the parties relating to use of the Product. The terms of any purchase order shall have no effect on the terms of this Agreement. Failure of McGraw-Hill to insist at any time on strict compliance with this Agreement shall not constitute a waiver of any rights under this Agreement. This Agreement shall be construed and governed in accordance with the laws of New York. If any provision of this Agreement is held to be contrary to law, that provision will be enforced to the maximum extent permissible and the remaining provisions will remain in force and effect.